T
EQUI
• SCHOOLS BOOK •
1997

IN ASSOCIATION WITH

THE SUNDAY TIMES

THE INDEPENDENT GUIDE
TO INDEPENDENT SECONDARY SCHOOLS

Editors
KLAUS BOEHM
JENNY LEES-SPALDING

This edition has been sponsored by
THE EQUITABLE LIFE ASSURANCE SOCIETY

BLOOMSBURY

This edition published in 1996 by Bloomsbury Publishing Plc,
2 Soho Square, London W1V 6HB

This edition was sponsored by
THE EQUITABLE LIFE ASSURANCE SOCIETY

About the Equitable Life Assurance Society
The Equitable Life Assurance Society was founded in 1762, making it the oldest mutual life assurance society in the world, and the first to develop the sound actuarial principles on which all modern life companies are based. Throughout its long history The Equitable has steadfastly refused to pay commission to third parties for the introduction of new business; a policy that has helped to achieve the Society's consistently low level of expenses. The Equitable Life is listed as a school fee specialist by ISIS. The Equitable School Fee Trust was developed specifically to meet the requirements of those wishing to arrange school fees in a flexible and cost-effective manner.

Publisher's note
The information in this book was correct to the best of the Editors' and Publisher's belief at the time of going to press. While no responsibility can be accepted for errors and omissions, the Editors and Publisher would welcome corrections and suggestions for material to include in subsequent editions of this book.

A copy of the CIP entry for this book is available
upon request from the British Library

ISBN 0 7475 2762 8

10 9 8 7 6 5 4 3 2 1

Typeset by Hewer Text Composition Services, Edinburgh
Printed in England by Cox & Wyman Ltd, Reading

• Contents •

• About the book •

This is a consumer book. To be precise, it is a book for parents looking for an indepedent secondary school for their child. Its premise is that a child will flourish in some schools and flop in others, because no school can do equally well for all types of children.

The book aims to help you shortlist schools. It is no substitute for your own enquiries, your own scrutiny of school propectuses, your own school visits and the exercise of your own judgement on behalf of your child.

The book contains over 520 *School Reports* on individual secondary schools, arranged alphabetically. To help you identify possible schools, there is a geographical search index, *What's Where*, at the back of the book. At the front, *What's What* explains some of the more common terms, structures and financial considerations – streaming, SHMIS, sex education, scholarships and so on.

Money matters. Significant sums are involved with school fees. Look up our *School Reports* for current levels of fees and, if you cannot cope with the fees, what help is available (about 25% parents obtain help of some kind). *What's What* explains the different sources of help – assisted places, bursaries etc.

• About the editors •

Klaus Boehm specialises in reference books, particularly sponsored titles. **Jenny Lees-Spalding** left what is now called London Guildhall University (where she was an academic registrar) to develop reference books. Their joint titles are often concerned with education and include *The Student Book*, the leading guide for sixth formers planning to go on to university. Most contain a European dimension (Klaus Boehm Publications was one of two commended publishers in the 1991 European Information Association's Awards for European Sources).

All their work shares a common non-prescriptive philosophy: readers are intelligent people who make their own choices; reference books make a good starting point for many preliminary investigations but are no substitute for primary sources.

• Foreword •

Smoke Screens and Shortcuts

Schools are in the news. The education pages are awash with information, data, statistics, and TV and radio cannot leave it alone. It is hard to get away from it all and harder still to know how to interpret it when choosing a school.

Heads of schools are becoming adept at finding the nugget of information that shows their school in a glowing light – pass rates are a favourite. But, increasingly, presentation is the task of the newest recruit to the traditional school staff, the Marketing Officer. Many of them set up such a smoke screen that it is hard to find out what really happens in the school.

Educational information is always complex because the three key variables are the quality of the pupil intake (selection), the quality of the teaching and the ethos of the school – all inherently difficult to nail down. And so develops the temptation to rank schools in tidy, simplistic league tables – as one Head of a successful school described them, 'about as charming as mosquitoes'. The precise position of a school in a league table tells you almost nothing about it. For example, one first division school with over 100 in the upper sixth, reports that two revised results, if notified earlier, would have moved the school up 12 places in one league table. And the basis for ranking can leave it wide open to manipulation (would *you* encourage a marginal candidate to take an extra A-level if the league tables are based on percentage A and B grades?). No use as a shortcut.

So, it comes down to parents having to work out what they need to know for themselves. We offer no simple shortcuts, but instead a three-pronged approach.

1. How Academic is the School?

Not all schools are as academic as they claim. And the exam results they achieve will, of course, reflect the pupils they select as well as the standard of teaching they deliver. UCAS points seem the best measure of achievement at A-level (they reflect both the number taken and the grades achieved); the UCAS points for the average sixth former are given in the *School Profiles* in England and Wales. Only 8% of these schools have an average score over 25 (that is, the average sixth former passes three A-levels probably with grades A and B); these are for the brightest children. A further 34% of these schools have an average score of 20–24 (that is in a range from one grade B and two Cs, to two grade As and B); these are strong academic schools with bright children. Most schools with average UCAS points 15–20 will often have, and be equally helpful to, a wider a range of academic ability; if your child is academically able, you should think twice about a school with UCAS points of 10 or below.

2. What the Pupils go on to Do

Almost all independent school sixth-formers now go on to higher education. The *School Profiles* give information on where and what they study. At the top academic schools, about a third go on to Oxbridge and large numbers go to medical and veterinary schools – no room here for future hotel managers. At others, no-one goes on to Oxbridge or medical schools but large numbers go on to vocational subjects such as physiotherapy, education and leisure management and many pupils going on to art college; not necessarily the place for a boffin but may suit less academic pupils who are practical and have a clear idea of their future.

3. What Else Goes on in the School?
First find schools which are the right academic level, then decide on other grounds. You are looking for somewhere you child will flourish as a teenager so it is the ethos and activities that will matter in the end. What is it that is important? The possibility of white-water rafting, social networks, strong discipline, music for the talented, music for all, teaching for dyslexia, the creative arts, soccer, Young Enterprise, vegetarianism, religion, prefects, independence for the sixth form, rowing, family connections. No two lists will be the same.

Acknowledgements

We are very grateful for the tremendous help we have had from Heads of schools in preparing our schools reports. We are especially grateful to Patricia Metham, Tristram Jones-Parry, Colin Niven and Ian Small for briefing us on general, current developments.

We would also wish to record our appreciation of J A Cuddon, consultant editor on the first eight editions of the book. Always a continuous source of information, wisdom and erudition, he was enormously valuable in shaping the book.

Klaus Boehm
Jenny-Lees-Spalding

June 1996

Abbreviations

The world of education is peppered with abbreviations and acronyms, some of which are worth knowing. Here are some of the more useful ones, all referred to in this book:

AAA Amateur Athletic Association
ABRSM Associated Board of the Royal Schools of Music
ACE Advisory Centre for Education
ACSC Association of Catholic Schools and Colleges
ADT Art, design and technology
AHIS Association of Heads of Independent Schools
AICE Advanced International Certificate of Education
A-level Advanced level examination
Alumni Latin term for old boys/girls of a school
AoT Association of Tutors
APS Assisted Places Scheme
APT Advanced Placement Test (North America)
ARCM Associate of the Royal College of Music
ARCO Associate of the Royal College of Organists
ARCS Accreditation, Review & Consulting Service (of ISJC)
ARELS Association of Recognised English Language Schools
ASA Amateur Swimming Association
AS-level Advanced Supplementary level
ATC Air Training Corps
ATI Association of Tutors Incorporated
BA Bachelor of Arts degree
BAC British Accreditation Council
BAGA British Amateur Gymnastics Association
BAYS British Association of Young Scientists
BBC British Broadcasting Corporation
BCU British Canoe Union
BDA British Dyslexia Association
BEd Bachelor of Education
BHS British Horse Society
BSA Boarding Schools Association
BSc Bachelor of Science
BSES British Schools Exploring Society
BTEC Business and Technician Education Council
BTF British Trampolining Federation
c./c/ca circa (Latin for approximate)
CAD Computer-aided design
Cantab abbreviated Latin term for Cambridge University
CCF Combined Cadet Force
CCPR Central Council for Physical Recreation
CCSC Conference of Catholic Schools and Colleges
CDET Council for Dance Education and Training
CDT Craft Design Technology
CE Common Entrance exam
CEE Certificate of Extended Education; can also mean Common entrance exam
CERN Conseil Européen de Recherches Nucléaires (European Organization for Nuclear Research)
Cert Ed Certificate of Education
CGLI City & Guilds of London Institute
CHE College of Higher Education
CIFE Conference for Independent Further Education
CLAC Commercial Language Assistant Certificate
CLAIT Computer literacy and information technology
COBISEC Council of British Independent Schools in the European Communities
C of E Church of England
CPVE Certificate of Pre-vocational Education
CREST Creativity in Science and Technology
CSA Choir Schools Association
CSCo / **CSCL** } Church Schools Company Ltd
CSV Community Service Volunteers

CSYS Certificate of Sixth-Year Studies Examination
CTF Catholic Teachers Federation
CV Curriculum vitae
DFEE Department for Education and Employment
DipED Diploma of Education
D of E Duke of Edinburgh's Award Scheme
DPVE Diploma in Pre-vocational Education
DT Design technology
EC European Community
ECIS European Council of International Schools
EEAC European Executive Assistant Certificate
EFL English as a Foreign Language
ERASMUS European Community Action Scheme for the Mobility of University Students
ESAA English Schools Athletic Association
ESB English Speaking Board
ESF English Schools Foundation Hong Kong
ESHA European Secondary Heads Association
ESL English as a Second Language
ESSA English Schools Swimming Association
ESU English Speaking Union
EU European Union
EYE English for Young Europeans
FCA Fellow of the Institute of Chartered Accountants
FEFC Further Education Funding Council
FGA Fellow of the Geographical Society
FRSA Fellow of the Royal Society of Arts
FLAW Foreign Languages at Work
FLIC Foreign Languages for Industry & Commerce
FT/PT Full Time/Part Time
GAP Gap Activity Projects (or Government Assisted Places)
GBA Governing Bodies Association
GBGSA Governing Bodies of Girls' Schools Association
GCSE General Certificate of Secondary Education
GNSM Graduate of Northern School of Music
GNVQs General National Vocational Qualifications
GPDST Girls' Public Day School Trust
GSA Girls' Schools Association
GSVQ General Scottish Vocational Qualifications
HAS Headteachers Association in Scotland
HM Headmaster/Headmistress
HMC Headmasters' Conference
HMI Her Majesty's Inspectorate/Inspector(s)
Hons Honours degree
HRF Health-related fitness
IAPS Incorporated Association of Preparatory Schools
IB International Baccalaureate
i/c In charge
IGCSE International GCSE
IQ Intelligence quotient
ISAI Independent Schools Association Incorporated
ISBA Independent Schools Bursars' Association
ISCO Independent Schools Careers Organisation
ISIB Independent Schools Examinatio Board
ISIS Independent Schools Information Service
ISJC Independent Schools Joint Council
ISSF International Schools Sports Federation
ISTD Imperial Society of Teachers of Dancing
JMB Joint Matriculation Board
LAMDA London Academy of Music and Dramatic Art
LATE Looking at the Environment
LCC(I) London Chamber of Commerce (and Industry)
LEA Local Education Authority
LINGUA Community Action Programme to Promote Foreign Language Conferences in the European Community
LRAM Licentiate of the Royal Academy of Music
LSE London School of Economics
MA Master of Arts
N/A Not applicable
NABSS National Association of British Schools in Spain

NACCW National Advisory Centre on Careers for Women
NADFAS National Association of Decorative & Fine Arts Societies
NAHT National Association of Head Teachers
NC National Curriculum
NFER National Foundation for Educational Research in England and Wales
NNEB National Nursery Examination Board
NVQs National Vocational Qualifications
OB Old Boys
OC Officer Commanding
OFSTED Office for Standards in Education
OG Old Girls
OU Open University
Oxbridge Oxford and Cambridge Universities
Oxon Abbreviated Latin term for Oxford University
pa per annum
PE Physical Education
PGCE Postgraduate Certificate of Education
PHAB Physically Handicapped and Able Bodied
PHSE Personal Health and Social Education
PRISM Peace and Reconciliation Inter-Schools Movement
PSD Personal and social development
PSE Personal and social education
PT Physical Training
PTA Parent-Teacher Association
PTFA Parent, Teachers and Friends Association
RAD Royal Academy of Dance
RADA Royal Academy of Dramatic Art
RC Roman Catholic
RE/RI/RS Religious Education/Instruction/Studies
RLSS Royal Life Saving Society
RNIB Royal National Institute for the Blind
RSA Royal Society of Arts
RYA Royal Yachting Association
SAT Standard Assessment Tasks. (UK) / Stanford Achievement Tests (US)
SCE Scottish Certificate of Education
SCIS Scottish Council for Independent Schools
Scotvec Scottish Vocational Education Council
SEN Special Educational Needs
S-grade Standard grade examination
SHA Secondary Heads' Association
SHMIS Society of Headmasters and Headmistresses of Independent Schools
SLD or SPLD Specific Learning Difficulties
SRN State Registered Nurse
STABIS State Boarding Information Service
Steiner schools Schools founded by Rudolf Steiner
STEP Sixth Term Exam Paper (entrance exam for Cambridge University)
SVQs Scottish Vocational Qualifications
TEC Training Enterprise Council
TEFL Teaching English as a foreign language
UCAS Universities and Colleges Admissions Service
U16 under 16
U18 under 18
URC United Reform Church
V, VI Roman numerals five and six (sometimes used to mean fifth and sixth forms)
VDU Visual Display Unit
VSO Voluntary Service Overseas
wef with effect from

• What's what •

Contents

Accreditation and inspection

There is no longer any government certificate of efficiency for independent schools. New schools have to register with the government, which involves a Registration Inspection – a one or two day visit from HMI to ensure that the school meets eg fire regulations – and subsequent visits every three years or so; no report is published. Boarding schools are subject to inspection by their local social services departments to check that welfare arrangements are adequate.

HMI conducts Reporting Inspections to provide OFSTED with information about standards in independent education; alternatively, inspections are specially commissioned by the DFEE – sometimes in response to complaints by parents or the public, in connection with a school's registration. These are team inspections taking up to a week and a report is usually published.

But none of this adds up to the sort of guarantee consumers expect when buying other professional services – eye surgery, legal advice or a trans-Atlantic flight. So independent schools have set up their own system of accreditation and inspection.

HMC membership, which is rightly thought to be a guarantee of a school's general educational standards, involves schools in a regular inspection by HMC in tandem with OFSTED. Inspection reports are always published, with copies to the school (Head and the Chairman of Governors), HMC and OFSTED. Parents may or may not be shown all or a part of the report.

All the other main independent school associations (GSA, IAPS, ISAI, SHMIS: see List of Abbreviations) use the Accreditation, Review & Consultancy Service (ARCS) of the ISJC. ARCS works closely with OFSTED and accreditation always involves inspection. Accreditation is a pre-requisite of membership of all ISJC organizations.

Each school's affiliation (eg to HMC or GSA) is given in our *School Reports* and in our search index, *What's Where*.

Aegrotat

Latin term for 'is sick'. In schools this means permission, usually in writing, for a pupil to be excused from a class or sporting activity on grounds of illness or injury.

Affiliation

Nearly all of the schools (and all the tutorial colleges) in our *School Reports*, even those located overseas, are affiliated to some sort of association. It isn't always clear exactly what such affiliation entails but a school or head will probably have been vetted before being accepted, indicating a degree of quality control and uniformity of aims. In some cases affiliation is through the Head (eg HMC); in others (eg Steiner) it indicates a particular educational philosophy. We do not itemise the junior school affiliations or those that relate to eg the bursar or the governing body.

Age at joining

Our *School Reports* cover only secondary schools. Many of them have their own junior or prep departments, and maybe nursery schools as well, so the school can educate your child from the age of 3 to 18. However, 15 years in the same school is a very long time and it is worth reviewing your choice at say, 8, 11, 13 and 16 to make sure the school is still the best for your child. You need to consider:

- How many years of school fees do you want to pay?
- When does the school have intakes (usually at 5, 7–8, 11–13 and into the sixth)? It's easier not to be the only new kid in the class.
- Moves during GCSE or A-level courses should be avoided if at all possible.
- Whether you want to keep your child in a state primary school and move at 11 (12 in Scotland).

AICE – Advanced International Certificate of Education

This is a new pre-university qualification, offered by some international schools and leading on from the IGCSE. Together they constitute a fully integrated curriculum for pupils in their last four years of school.

Aided Pupils Scheme

This is a government-funded scheme, under which a proportion of the fees are paid for pupils at specialist music and ballet schools. As with assisted places, the proportion is linked to family income; it differs both in the size of the contribution and by covering boarding fees as well as tuition fees, travel etc. The aided pupils scheme is open to pupils at six schools in this book – Arts Educational School in Tring, Chetham's, Purcell, Royal Ballet, St Mary's Music, Wells Cathedral and Yehudi Menuhin. Apply direct to each school.

AIDED PLACES: ROUGH GUIDE FOR THE YEAR 1996/7

	Parents' contribution to			
	DAY FEES		BOARDING FEES	
Parents' 1995/96 income	One aided day pupil	For each of two aided day pupils	One aided boarding pupil	For each of two aided boarding pupils
£8,490	£0	£0	£0	£0
£12,000	£141	£105	£507	£378
£20,000	£942	£705	£1716	£1191
£30,000	£1941	£1455	£2967	£1941
£50,000	£3942	£2955	£5469	£3441
£84,000	£7341	£5505	£9717	£5991

A-levels

A-levels matter. Three, with good grades, are needed to get into the top university courses; 2 for others and for direct entry into professions like accountancy and the army. The A-level course is designed to take 2 years to complete – usually between the ages of 16 and 18. Some schools may allow their more academic pupils to take one (or maybe an AS-level) after one year in the sixth form. Most schools help match A-level choices with what your child wants to do after school. Some A-levels (eg general studies and art) are not always acceptable for entrance to degree courses. Find out which subjects and – most important – which combinations of subjects are available; some schools have an arts or science bias. Ask to look at results for the past few years (ask for results by subject and by pupil; be suspicious of pass rates).

A-levels are still designed for a minority of students; vocational qualifications (GNVQs) may be worth considering as an alternative and are accepted by many universities for admission to degree courses.

Allied schools

This is a group of 6 Church of England schools established during the 1920s.

Alumni

Latin for 'foster children', this means former pupils of a school. Some girls' schools use the feminine form – alumnae.

Most schools have associations of former pupils who keep in touch with each other and the school. They can be useful to the school when it needs to raise cash for new facilities; they also use them to talk to pupils about careers or life at university.

Art

There are no independent secondary schools specialising in art but art is offered throughout almost the entire independent sector, usually up to A-level. Unlike music and dance pupils, secondary school pupils wanting to specialise in art cannot get financial support from the government's aided places scheme. Schools have relatively few art scholarships and bursaries but it is worth checking our School Reports to see what's on offer.

Broadly speaking, schools approach art in three different ways: teach it to the obviously talented only and exclude the rest from the studio; provide it as a recreational activity to all interested pupils; or try providing a mixture of the two.

From our School Reports, you can get an idea of a school's approach to art – whether the facilities are open to non-examination pupils, the numbers going on to art college (usually more than go to music or drama college), a note of exhibitions of work, pupils winning competitions (design of bank notes, town mural competition, T-shirts etc). Also look at the number of GCSE and A-level candidates – a school may excel with the talented but show less enthusiasm for others.

AS-levels

Advanced Supplementary level exams, AS-levels, were designed to broaden the sixth-form syllabus but have not been taken up to the extent that was hoped. Two AS-levels are equivalent to 1 A-level and pupils can opt to replace 1 or more A-levels with AS-levels, either to complement their specialisation (eg a language with sciences) or to broaden it (eg maths for biologists). AS-levels are mainly accepted by university admissions tutors as an extra to A-levels so pupils take 2 or 3 A-levels and 1 AS-level.

Assisted Places Scheme

Under this scheme the government pays a proportion of the school fees of children whose parents can't afford them. It also helps with transport, uniform etc. Parents make a contribution to the fees according to a means test for the first three children. A fourth or subsequent child is free. You apply directly to a school which is in the scheme.

There have been over 36,000 assisted places at over 350 schools in England, Scotland and Wales, accounting for over 8% of the total independent school population. But the numbers are rising sharply (7,400 new places this year).

What you pay this year depends on your family income last year. Check the small print but you will be able to get a pretty good idea of where you stand by using our Rough Guide below.

ASSISTED PLACES: ROUGH GUIDE FOR THE YEAR 1996/7

1995/6 INCOME (income after allowances for dependants)	PARENTS' CONTRIBUTION TO DAY FEES		
	One assisted place holder	For each of two assisted place holders	For each of three assisted place holders
£9870	£0	£0	£0
£10,000	£21	£15	£12
£12,000	£264	£195	£150
£14,000	£615	£459	£357
£16,000	£1044	£780	£606
£18,000	£1524	£1140	£885
£20,000	£2076	£1554	£1209
£23,000	£3066	£2298	£1785
£25,000	£3726	£2793	£2172
£30,000	£5376	£4029	£3132
£35,000	£7026	£5268	£4095

The scheme operates in different ways north and south of the border. In England and Wales each school in the scheme has a limited number of assisted places which it fills using its own method of selection. In Scotland, schools are given a sum of money which they distribute as they think fit.

Government assisted places do not include boarding fees but some participating schools run their own boarding fees bursaries to complement the assisted places scheme. Ask the schools which interest you how they select and whether your child is likely to meet their selection criteria. As a rule of thumb you can assume that schools with a substantial proportion of assisted places have a relatively wider social mix than those that have not. The Conservatives aim to double the numbers (recently the age limit has been lowered, while there are new schools in the scheme and most schools have more assisted places available). However the Labour Party and the Liberal Democrats are committed to phasing out the scheme. Further information and lists of participating schools from:

- England: Assisted Places Scheme, Department for Education and Employment, Mowden Hall, Darlington, Co Durham DL3 9BG (tel 01325 392154).
- Wales: Welsh Office Education Department, Cathays Park, Cardiff CF1 3NQ (tel 01222 825111, ext 6080/6082).
- Scotland: Scottish Education Department, Area 2a North, Victoria Quay, Edinburgh EH6 6QQ (tel 0131 244 0952).

BAYS

BAYS is the Youth Section of the British Association for the Advancement of Science and provides a network of science and technology clubs for anyone under 18. There are individual members and group members and many independent schools participate. Enquiries to BAYS, British Association for the Advancement of Science, 23 Savile Row, London W1X 1AB (tel 0171 973 3061).

Boarding schools

Boarding schools range from day schools with perhaps the odd boarder to boarding schools with the occasional day pupil. A large number now offer weekly boarding as a half-way house or flexi-boarding which enables pupils to stay on at school when participating in extra-curricular activities eg sport and clubs.

What is on offer varies considerably. Quite obviously there is very much more time to present a full educational programme, including outdoor, sporting, cultural and community activities, than there is at a day school. Good boarding schools capitalise on this and, if they take day pupils as well, may expect them to be there late in the day and at weekends; inefficient ones, or those with few boarders, may ignore the weekends and evenings.

Most boarding schools are independent but there are 37 maintained secondary boarding schools in England too, at which you only pay for the boarding, not the tuition. (You can find out about them from STABIS.) There has been a trend away from boarding, doubtless exacerbated by the recession. You should also feel confident that the school is not winding down boarding if you want your child to avoid rattling around in half-empty accommodation.

Boarding makes especially good sense to parents if there are no suitable day schools within reach, if you are likely to move during critical periods of your child's school career or if your work makes it difficult to manage children at day schools. From the child's stand-point, you need to make sure your child is happy with the idea, particularly if there are problems at home. Some independent children will flourish in a boarding school; others may be homesick, feel rejected and become demotivated. It's worth thinking about:

- Distance: most parents choose a boarding school that's within about 1½ hours' travelling time of home (you can support the school's team and easily stay in touch). If that's impossible, is there one close to grandparents, friends or relations?
- Schedule and extra-curricular activities: what's available, especially at weekends; how much of the day is scheduled and organised? Is it geared to boarders or day pupils? Are children free to pursue their own interests as well as those that the school regards as appropriate? What sort of contact is there with the local community or other schools? Are they allowed into the local town – accompanied or unaccompanied?
- Food: more important for boarders who can't rely on daily supplements from home. What other food can they buy or keep?

- Meet the house staff and find out about the routine in the boarding houses, eg are children expected to help with table-laying? What are dormitories and other rooms like? How much privacy do pupils have? Are they allowed into dormitories/bedrooms during the day? Are bed-times sensible?
- Exeats: how many and for how long? Are they fixed or flexible? What if you want to take your child out of school at short notice, or before the end of term? Is weekly boarding available and how widespread is it?
- What provision is there for ill children? Is there a nurse on the premises and a nearby doctor on call?

Boys' schools

Some boys' secondary schools take boys from 11, some from 13. The traditional public schools start at 13, although a few have small junior departments for boys of 11 and 12, and many have associated prep schools taking boys from 8 (or 5) to 13. Many boys' schools take girls into the sixth; an increasing number have subsequently become co-ed throughout.

British schools overseas

This book includes some 20 British schools in Europe and Hong Kong. Some are affiliated to British organisations such as HMC (Headmasters' Conference) or international organisations such as ECIS (European Council of International Schools); many in Europe belong to COBISEC (Council of British Independent Schools in the European Communities).

They generally have an atmosphere very different to equivalent schools in the UK. They are almost all co-educational, with no prior history of being single-sex; there is rarely a uniform or formal structures such as houses and almost never prefects; there are usually a large number of nationalities represented among the pupils (especially in the main business communities); and leavers may be just as likely to go on to universities in Europe and the US as to UK universities. Some of the markers which may be used to identify levels of activity in UK schools – such as pupils representing their county/country in a sport or taking drama and music exams – may be irrelevant.

Because these schools cater for a transient population, parents can often be more involved with them than in the UK and the schools are necessarily flexible about the stage at which pupils join the school.

BTEC

The Business and Technician Education Council (BTEC) runs vocational qualifications, including GNVQs, which are taught in some schools and in colleges of further education. Enquiries to BTEC, Central House, Upper Woburn Place, London WC1H 0HH (tel 0171 413 8400)

Bullying

It happens. It is inherent in institutional life – never believe the contrary. There are many causes but good schools try hard to eradicate it; poor schools pretend it does not exist. You may find Heads' attitudes illuminating.

Remember your child can either be the bully or the one who is bullied. If you think your child is being bullied, tell the Head or housemaster/mistress. The problem may not be soluble immediately but a good Head will find out what's going on and can advise you and your child on how to deal with it. If you get no help, or if your child continues to be unhappy at school, investigate further: you might have chosen the wrong school.

Burning out

It doesn't happen often but it does happen. Everyone wants their children to work hard and do the best they can but children who push themselves, or who are pushed too hard, can burn out. And then you have problems.

Bursaries

These are means-tested awards made by some schools to the children of parents who can't afford to pay full fees. They are frequently only available to existing pupils or are ear-marked for eg children of clergymen, service personnel or alumni. Our School Reports note where they are available.

Careers

Most independent schools concentrate on getting their pupils into higher education, leaving most decisions about occupational choice for the future. But there will usually be advice available during GCSE and A-level choices, to ensure as far as possible that students do not close off avenues which might be needed for a future career.

Most sixth formers now go on to degree courses so careers advice has become more or less synonymous with advice about higher education. It can include:

- A careers library, with university and college prospectuses.
- At least one adviser to point pupils towards the next step if they know what they want to do, and towards some books if they don't.
- Attendance at higher education and careers fairs arranged for several schools.
- Psychological aptitude tests.
- Films and talks about careers options: the services; industry; or, depending on the Head's friends, careers in falconry or bookmaking. Parents are often used for careers talks as well.
- Membership of ISCO.

Some schools do not send the bulk of their pupils on to higher education. Here occupational information and advice is more important; check what is provided, especially if your child is not very academic.

Valuable work experience can be gained in some schools – pupils sent on short-term job placements with local industry during the holidays or after exams; running miniature companies selling tuck or stationery; or running a school bank; writing; designing, editing and producing their own magazine.

CCF

The modern Combined Cadet Force was formed in 1948, from the OTC (Officers' Training Corps) and ATC (Air Training Corps) to provide military training units in schools and universities. A large number of schools run a CCF (boys and girls), often only one section (Army, Navy, RAF or Royal Marines), sometimes 2 or even 3. In a few schools it may be compulsory for a period. Many CCFs have a band (drums, brass; in Scotland, bagpipes).

Basic training will include foot drill, arms drill, tactics, weapons training, shooting (with rifles), aircraft recognition, map-reading, camping, first aid, radio communications, signals, assault courses, survival techniques and so on. Some schools have commando and SAS-type exercises (including yomping). Most CCFs have an annual camp which is based on some form of military installation. There are also manoeuvres (sometimes in conjunction with other schools) and there is usually an annual inspection by somebody suitably distinguished in the services.

Membership of the CCF appeals to those who enjoy teamwork, team spirit, discipline and self-discipline, physical and mental challenge and an element of adventure accompanied by some hazard. There are agreeable perks, too, such as visits to naval bases (perhaps a guided tour of a warship), to RAF bases where you may get a flight, and to army depots where you may sample the full hardware of modern warfare.

Child abuse

Schools, and boarding schools in particular, are not immune from the predatory sexual proclivities of evil adults placed in a position of authority over vulnerable children. While child abuse is rare, there have been convictions and the Department for Education and the Independent Schools Joint Council therefore funded a short-term helpline to establish needs. It is now operated by the child abuse charity, ChildLine; pupils can get advice from an experienced counsellor by telephoning ChildLine direct on 0800 1111.

Child psychologist

If your child has an emotional, social or learning difficulty, he or she may be helped by a child psychologist. The school may be able to refer you to one; otherwise you'll have to find one yourself. The best first step is consult the Register of Chartered Psychologists in your public library published annually by the British Psychological Society. If that fails try the BPS direct at St Andrew's House, 48 Princess Road East, Leicester LE1 7DR (tel 0116 254 9568).

Choir schools

There are 39 choir schools in the UK attached to and providing choristers for churches, cathedrals and college chapels. Of these 14 teach up to A-level, the rest are prep schools only. While choir schools are usually thought of as boys' schools, they increasingly accept girls and a growing number have a separate girls' choir. Only one (in Edinburgh) has a mixed choir. If your children are good at singing and enjoy it enough to spend a lot of their time singing in church services and concerts they may be able to get all (or a part) of their fees paid as a chorister. This usually means passing a voice trial some time between the ages of 7 and 10.

Further information – including a list of choir schools, details such as their voice trial dates and the precise age at which children can take them – is available from the Administrator, Choir Schools Association, The Minster School, Deangate, York YO1 2JA (tel 01904 625217; fax 01904 632418).

CIFE

The Conference for Independent Further Education (CIFE) is the professional body for independent sixth form and tutorial colleges. Full members must achieve and retain recognition by BAC (British Accredition Council) which involves five-yearly and interim inspection. Candidate members have three years to attain BAC recognition. CIFE insists that all its members' published exam results are subject to audit – so you can rely on their accuracy before choosing a college – and has introduced a binding code of practice governing the use of exam results in members' publicity. Details of full and candidate members and their courses from CIFE, Buckhall Farm, Bull Lane, Bethersden, Nr Ashford, Kent TN26 3HB (tel 01233 820797).

City and Guilds

The City and Guilds operates GNVQs as alternatives to GCSE and A-levels. Contact Vocational Education Unit, 1 Giltspur Street, London EC1A 9DD (tel 0171 294 2468, fax 0171 294 2400).

Class size

Does the size of the classes in which your children are taught matter? The government insists that no educational research demonstrates that class size affects children's academic performance. But intuitively, many think differently. Some children only flourish in classes of up to 10; others are bored by very small classes.

To the surprise of many parents, class sizes in some academically excellent schools may not be significantly smaller than those in state schools. This will depend on the children (their age and ability), the subject and the level at which it is being taught. It is easier to imagine a successful class of 25 where geography is being taught to 11-year olds of comparable ability than, say, remedial reading to 7-year olds or an A-level music class.

COBISEC

The Council of British Independent Schools in the European Communities is a non-profit foundation of schools in Europe following the British curriculum. It provides a forum in which Heads, senior teachers, governors and trustees can exchange ideas and discuss matters of common interest. Membership of COBISEC is by invitation only.

All member schools can be inspected by arrangements with the Office for Standards in Education, using OFSTED Inspectors. COBISEC is lobbying the British government to persuade it to bear some degree of responsibility for the education of British expatriates in continental EU countries (eg perhaps an educational grant scheme, on the lines of the Assisted Places Scheme). More information and a list of member schools from COBISEC Secretariat c/o St Julian's School, 2777 Carcavelos, Codex, Portugal (tel 35 11 4570140)

Co-ed schools

Co-educational schools admit girls and boys. More and more schools are becoming co-educational as single-sex schools admit the opposite sex or merge with a brother/sister school. Much of this is in response to market demand but some schools believe there is no longer any justification for educating the sexes separately in a world where they will work together.

Some heads opt for a specific male:female ratio, others let one evolve. In schools that have always been co-ed, this tends to be about 50:50. Schools that used to be single-sex may still be dominated by that sex and its ethos for some years. If you are looking at a school that has recently become co-ed, you may like to check the following:

- the prospectus, for reading between the lines. If girls have not been integrated into a boys' school's prospectus, they're unlikely to be integrated into the school (eg schools with a strong house structure where girls board with staff).
- how many boys, how many girls are in positions of authority, eg prefects?
- how many men and women are in the staff common room?
- the house system – if the school has competitive houses, how has it integrated co-education eg mixed houses or twinned single-sex houses?

Co-ed schools often have a wider range of activities because they are less affected by generalised beliefs such as boys don't sew and girls don't like electronics. Conversely, some research (much quoted by Heads of girls' schools) suggests that girls do better academically in girls' schools, particularly in science. As with so many issues, it will depend on the child: for some co-ed is the obvious answer; others will prefer a single-sex school. If you are not sure, you can consider brother/sister schools where they are taught separately but join for eg extra-curricular activities and some sixth-form teaching. Several schools are now linked so that pupils are taught separately from 11 to 16 but the sixth form is co-educational.

Common Entrance

Many independent secondary schools use the same entrance exam, called Common Entrance (CE). The papers are set by the Independent Schools Examinations Board (ISEB) and the answers marked by the senior school for which the child is entered. The exam is taken at age 11, 12 or 13, depending on the senior school; the 13+ exam may be taken in any school term; the 11+ and 12+ only in the autumn or spring terms. The exam is usually (but not always) taken in your child's current school. The subjects covered will depend on the age at which the exam is taken. At 13 they include English, maths and a modern language, science, history, geography and RE.

Prep schools traditionally prepare pupils for CE. If your child is at a school that does not normally enter candidates for CE, either contact the senior school you are interested in, or apply direct to the ISEB for an entry form. Contact the Administrator, Independent Schools Examinations Board, Jordan House, Christchurch Road, New Milton, Hampshire BH25 6QJ (tel 01425 621111, fax 01425 620044). You should do this at least 10 weeks before the exam, and ideally a lot earlier to allow time to prepare. The ISEB can provide past papers.

Each school sets its own pass mark which reflects the demand for places; thus the pass mark for one school may be 70%, for another 45%. If you have registered at a second school and you fail to gain entry to your first choice, the scripts are forwarded to the second choice. If you haven't already registered at a second school, it is up to you to ask the first school to send the scripts on to another.

CE isn't always necessary. Schools that use Common Entrance often have an alternative exam for applicants of non-standard age and sometimes for those from state schools as well. Our School Reports highlight each school's entrance procedure under Entrance.

Community service

Some schools organise their pupils to help in the community outside the school. This is often offered as an alternative to sport, CCF, etc for senior pupils – very occasionally it is compulsory. In practice, school community service usually means visiting old people (talking to them, entertaining them and doing odd jobs like decorating and gardening), it may involve work with children or the mentally handicapped. A handful of schools take it much further and organise local services such as mountain rescue and fire-fighting.

Computing

All schools have some computing facilities, some extremely sophisticated. Many integrate the use of computers with the teaching of a wide range of other subjects such as sciences, geography and maths, as well as offering it as a subject in its own right. We note computing facilities in our School Reports.

Corporal punishment

Still a delicate matter. It has long been banished from the maintained sector. It only exists (at any rate officially) in a handful of independent secondary schools and some are very coy about it. The vast majority of Heads stress emphatically that it is never used. Nowadays it is more likely that teachers will suffer corporal punishment in the form of assault (with or without weapons) by a pupil or pupils. Not so long ago, a London Headmaster told his staff: 'You must not hit the boys.' Then he added: 'And the boys must not hit you.'

Within the other EU member states there is a divergence of law and practice (Italy prohibits it by law; in Spain it seems to be in use). Parents looking for British schools overseas need to look at the position in each school.

CSV

Community Service Volunteers (CSV) will arrange community work in the UK for anybody aged 16–35. This is full-time, somewhere in the UK but away from home, and is for periods of 4–12 months. This makes it an option for students after A-levels. Volunteers get food, accommodation and pocket money of £23 a week. Details from CSV, 237 Pentonville Road, London N1 9NJ (tel 0171 278 6601).

CSYS

Certificates of Sixth Year Studies (CSYS) are Scottish exams which some pupils sit the year after Highers. They are very roughly comparable with A-levels but are often not recognised as such, especially south of the border.

Curriculum

For the first few years at secondary school, most pupils follow roughly the same curriculum: English, maths, at least one modern language (usually French), history, geography, some science, Latin (sometimes), religious studies (usually), art/craft, music and physical education. Most Heads of independent schools believe they cover the National Curriculum and more.

At 14, they choose the subjects they will do at GCSE (S-grade in Scotland) within the constraints imposed by the school (English, maths and a language but some may insist on eg French or the three separate sciences). Usually they take between 7 and 10 subjects and sit the exams when they are 16.

By the time they come to the sixth form (16–18), they'll have to limit themselves to taking 2 to 4 subjects seriously (5 or 6 if they're doing Highers). A-level courses (and GNVQ advanced level courses) last 2 years, the exams normally taken at age 18.

Dance

Most people with a future as professional dancers start very young. Ballet dancers have to begin intensive training at the age of 11. Some schools are specialist ballet schools such as the Royal Ballet School, Elmhurst, Hammond and Micklefield Wadhurst; others such as the Arts Educational Schools and Italia Conti concentrate on dance with drama. Only pupils at the Royal Ballet School and the Arts Educational School in Tring qualify for assistance under the government's Aided Pupils Scheme; and unlike music, non-specialist schools have virtually no dance scholarships or bursaries. Check out each of the schools in our School Reports to see what financial help is available.

Otherwise dance tends to be part of physical education. Some, especially boys' schools, don't bother with it at all while others offer a wide range including folk, modern, ballet, ballroom – and reels in Scotland. Some emphasise free movement while others still regard dancing as a social accomplishment. Some offer Royal Academy of Dance (RAD) or ISTD qualifications; a few schools note successes in dancing in local productions or on TV. You can learn a little about a school's approach to dance from our School Reports.

Day schools

Day schools are becoming more popular, and entry more competitive. There are a number of special factors you'll need to consider as well as finding a school that suits your child academically and socially. Your choice of day school is limited by the time it takes to travel to school and back home again. Make sure that you calculate this time in terms of the transport your child will actually use to get to school; it is no good assuming that, because you can drive to a school in 20 minutes, your child can do the same if it involves walking to the station, changing buses, etc. Find out what time pupils leave school at the end of the day and whether they are expected to be there at weekends. Some schools that are predominantly boarding schools have a very extended day and expect day pupils to play a full part (some have a separate category of 'day-boarders').

Distance

Choose a day school that's close enough to home to allow your child to take part in after-school activities, and accessible by public transport: you may not mind driving a 7-year-old to school every day but what about a 16-year old? More means worse: if you have four children at four different day schools you can be on a perpetual school run.

Boarders now tend to live within 1½ hours' travelling distance from home. This makes it easier for you to get to each other and also increases the likelihood of your child having at least a few school friends within reach for holidays and weekends.

Children who live abroad have special problems of access from airports and motorways. Many schools prospectuses estimate travelling time to eg Heathrow, M25. All will tell you if you ask and some schools will drop and collect children from airports.

Divorce and separation

Divorce and separation is becoming a real problem to schools. Heads report that this is by far the largest cause of pupils' behavioural problems. Let the school know what's going on. This is probably not the time to change your child's school unless absolutely unavoidable. If your child is already at boarding school this can be an advantage as it can provide valuable continuity – but make sure that you keep in closer touch than usual. Don't expect your children to do anything to make life easier for you. If they have any sympathy with, or understanding of, what's going on they may do their best to hide it. Divorce and separation often make it more difficult to keep paying school fees; if this looks likely, make sure you keep in touch with the school's bursar.

Drama

There are schools which specialise in drama (many of which also supply young actors for TV, West End and local theatre). We profile four of them in our School Reports: Arts Educational Schools in London and Tring, Italia Conti and Sylvia Young. Their pupils do not qualify for government assistance though they may get help from their local education authority (don't bank on it). But professional actors emerge from many non-specialist schools, even though drama often isn't taught as a curriculum subject. Many schools have theatres equipped to professional standards; most schools put on dramatic productions every year. Non-specialist schools rarely have drama scholarships or bursaries.

Broadly speaking there are three different approaches to drama: to teach it to the obviously talented only; to teach it as an adjunct to the academic curriculum; or to provide it as a recreational activity to anyone interested. You can learn quite a lot about an individual school's approach from our School Reports where schools have often noted how many pupils go to drama schools (normally far fewer than go on to art college), successes in local drama festivals, debating and public speaking competitions. A few have pupils in the National Youth Music or National Youth Theatre groups. You can often find out what a school puts on by way of pupil productions – The Sound of Music, Shakespeare, Pinter, Greek tragedies, French plays in French, house drama competitions. See how many pupils are involved in productions – is everyone involved in some way or another (scene builders, wardrobe, publicity) or only a few enthusiasts? Is there a drama club?

Drinking

While buying alcohol in pubs or shops is illegal for under-18s, most children have the occasional drink long before this. Day schools don't allow drinking. Neither do many boarding schools, which leaves young people to find out about drinking in the holidays or after they leave school. A number of boarding schools allow limited (supervised) drinking of beer and wine in sixth-form clubs/bars (spirits are almost always prohibited). This may stop alcohol from having quite the illicit appeal that drugs and cigarettes enjoy but it may not stop teenagers experimenting with cheap wine and strange spirits. Habitual heavy drinking is far worse for adolescents than for adults. Their bodies are less able to cope with quantities of alcohol and there is an increased likelihood of dependence. If teenagers are drinking heavily and regularly (especially if they're drinking alone) it could be a symptom of other problems. You should speak to your GP or consult Alcoholics Anonymous (local address in the telephone directory).

Drugs

All schools take drugs very seriously and most include the issues of drug abuse in their teaching of personal and social education. An increasing number of prestigious boarding schools conduct random drugs tests, usually with the overwhelming support of parents. The few that refuse to accept drugs as a feature of modern life might be viewed with a little scepticism. You can help by not making drugs an unmentionable horror; make sure that your children are aware of the legal and health risks involved; and remain approachable. You ought to know as soon as possible if your child is in difficulty because of drugs – either legal (such as alcohol and tobacco) or illegal (such as cannabis, Ecstasy, heroin).

If you are worried that your children are taking drugs, speak to a sympathetic doctor; or contact Families Anonymous, which is a support group and holds meetings all over the country for parents and relations of drug addicts (Families Anonymous, The Doddington and Rollo Community Association, Charlotte Despard Avenue, London SW11 5JE, tel 0171 498 4680).

Duke of Edinburgh's Award Scheme

'Designed as an introduction to leisure-time activities, a challenge to the individual to personal achievement, and as a guide to those people and organisations who are concerned about the development of our future citizens' (HRH the Duke of Edinburgh). Duke of Edinburgh's Awards can be taken outside school or as an extra-curricular activity within the school. There are 3 levels: bronze (taken from the age of 14), silver (15) and gold (16). Awards are made on successful completion of a programme of community service, physical recreation, adventure training and practical skills. Courses must be finished by the age of 24. Further information from the Duke of Edinburgh's Award Scheme headquarters at: Gulliver House, Madeira Walk, Windsor, Berks SL4 1EU (tel 01753 810753, fax 01753 810666).

Dyslexia

Dyslexia (Specific Learning Difficulty or SPLD) is a congenital condition in which you have difficulty organising letters, words, ideas and sometimes numbers. Short-term memory may also be impaired. All this leads to problems with reading, writing and learning and holds sufferers back. If you suspect that your child may be a sufferer you can arrange for an assessment through your school, GP, or one of the network of Dyslexia Institutes. Eileen Simpson has described her experience of dyslexia in Reversals (Gollancz, 1980).

You can contact a support group, the British Dyslexia Association, 98 London Road, Reading, Berkshire RG1 5AU (tel 01734 668271, fax 01734 351927) which has some 90 local organisations so there should be one in easy reach of you. Or contact the Dyslexia Institute which specialises in testing and assessment at 133 Gresham Road, Staines, Middlesex TW18 2AJ (tel 01784 463851, fax 01784

460747). You may also find a child psychologist helpful. A number of the schools in this book give extra help to dyslexic children. Make sure the dyslexia provision is suitable for your child's needs as it varies a lot in frequency and intensity (check our search index *What's Where*).

ECIS

The European Council of International Schools Inc (ECIS) is a membership organisation of international schools, the largest component of which are US or British schools. It publishes an annual directory, The International Schools Directory, which is available from ECIS Publishing Services, 23 Leckhampstead Road, Wicken MK19 5BY (tel 01908 571307, fax 01908 571407).

EFL

English as a Foreign Language (or English as a Second Language, ESL) is taught at some boarding and a few day schools (check our search index, *What's Where*).

Entrance exams

Many schools set their own entrance exams; even those that use Common Entrance have their own exams for state school applicants or pupils entering at non-standard ages. Some have their own preliminary exams some years before CE. Exams are often held early in the academic year prior to entry, so approach the school well in advance. You may be able to get hold of some past papers – each school's will be different.

Taking too many entrance exams is not a good idea. In London, where competition is fierce, some schools have formed consortia, each setting a single paper. Try not to enter your child for more than 2 or 3 exams; that means applying only to schools that really are right and, perhaps, choosing one that's less competitive than the others.

Don't throw your child into an entrance exam without adequate preparation. Many of the more hairy anecdotes of childhood examination failure are rooted in the parents' failure to ensure proper preparation, particularly when transfer from a maintained primary school is being attempted and the exam syllabus is unfamiliar.

Equipment

Depending on the school and the child, you'll have to buy a variety of equipment from pencils to bagpipes. You can expect to have to provide things like a calculator, a dictionary (even if you aren't expected to buy other books), various bits and pieces for sport and any optional extras. Boarders will need more – their own clothes, suitcases, towels, duvet, clock, games and hobbies equipment etc.

Europe

Make sure your children pick up European language skills at school. As always, the range is enormous. Some schools offer French only, some offer as many as eight European languages (often now including Russian). Some schools have interesting language arrangements in the sixth form – eg accelerated courses to GCSE and A-level, commercial language, continuation languages for all. Most run regular exchanges to the countries whose languages they offer; many run educational or cultural visits to one or more countries. A few are involved in the European Youth Parliament, run special European events, teach European languages to parents, send pupils to work experience places or have regular sporting fixtures with schools in Europe or even take a whole class to France to be taught all their GCSE subjects in French.

Exam results

Results matter. And this is what most parents assume they are buying when they send their children to independent schools. Raw educational statistics suggest they are right. Independent schools score outstandingly well in DFEE statistics.

To go on to a degree course, two or three A-levels are needed (or, maybe, an equivalent GNVQ), as well as a respectable clutch of GCSE at grade C or above. But achieving this is not of itself a good gauge of a good education. Some schools emphasise their academic results at the expense of all else – apparently a reflection of parents' concerns and certainly in response to league tables. Many schools are keen to advertise their percentage pass rates. This of course allows a school to show a 100% pass rate having put one successful candidate in for one exam. In this book we give the number of passes per pupil, usually GCSE in upper fifth, A-levels in upper sixth (this will be higher where general studies is taken). We also give the average UCAS points achieved by the upper sixth, without general studies (look these up separately – 20 points means 3 good passes at A-level, at least a grade B and 2 Cs; over 25 is a very strong academic school). We hope the discerning parent will not look only at those figures in the school profiles. A school may have done a better job getting a marginal candidate through any exams at all, than a bright pupil through 4 A-levels at grade A.

It's worth keeping academic results in perspective and remember the aptitudes of your child. Some children will thrive in academic hothouses where the principal aim is to get the maximum number of pupils through 3 or 4 A-levels; many will not and do better with, say, 2 modest A-levels or a GNVQ in a less academic school. If a child feels seriously pressurised the results can be frightening – anorexia, depression and, in rare cases, even suicide.

Exeat

Exeat is a Latin word meaning 'let him escape'. At school (especially boarding school) it is used to mean permitted time spent away from school during term. Most schools have a policy of allowing a certain number of overnight or weekend exeats a term – this can vary from any weekend to only one break at half-term. You'll have to decide which is the most appropriate for your family; if you live abroad, your child may be happier at a school that doesn't empty at weekends, whereas if you live within easy travelling distance of the school, weekly boarding may be possible.

Expulsion

The ultimate deterrent at most schools. Expulsion need not be the end of the world: it lurks in the background of many of the great and the good. It goes on to your child's academic record and may be picked up in the future. The immediate problem will be finding another school; the present school might be prepared to help with this (depending on the reason for expelling your child in the first place).

Some schools expel more readily than others and it's worth finding out something of the school's policy from the Head when you visit.

If your child is heading for expulsion or has actually been expelled it may be worth consulting a child psychologist to help overcome any personal problems that may have contributed to the predicament. At least one school, Allington Manor, specialises in taking children that other schools have decided they cannot educate (you can look it up in the School Reports).

Extra-curricular activities

A vital part of education, giving children the opportunity to try out a range of activities, outside the formal curriculum. They allow a child who is not very academic to pick up a range of skills and interests while at school; they provide a necessary diversion from exam obsession for all children. Many schools offer a wide range of indoor and outdoor pursuits to a high standard eg Highland Cattle Society, Young Enterprise groups, BAYS, bedsit cookery, computer clubs, fencing, curling, Duke of Edinburgh's Award Scheme, CCF. Check the *School Reports*.

Extras

As well as fees, most schools charge extras, often some £500 pa, possibly much, much more. Parents are usually charged extra for eg instrumental tuition, sports coaching and excursions, including those that are compulsory; less often for eg team transport to away matches, lunch for day pupils, laundry for boarders, and exam fees. Ask what's included in school fees and what you should expect to pay on top of that.

Fee levels

Most schools quote fees by the term (though some international schools have an annual fee). Annual figures can look horrific and many boarding schools have long since broken the £12,000 pa barrier.

Fees now range from about £1,000–£3,000+ per term for day pupils and about £2,500–£4,500 for boarding – and then there are extras. Specialists schools (whether say music schools or for pupils who are blind or dyslexic) cost much more but there is usually extra help eg in the form of Aided Places or LEA support. Fees usually go up each year. The heavily-endowed schools still tend to charge very high fees but pay their staff well, have good facilities and a lot of scholarships. Schools charging very low fees may be constrained by low income.

Some schools offer a monthly payment structure. Others accept a capital sum to commute future fees – you buy, say, £1000 per term of fees over five years at a discount (the discount depending on market conditions and how long in advance you buy them). Schools don't like non-payers. At least one threatens to exclude children after half term if the accounts are not fully paid up. Another Head set aside 20% of the entire fee income as bursaries to help parents in trouble through being made redundant etc. Nearly 30% pupils now receive some sort of financial help – about 17% scholarships and bursaries and 9% assisted places.

Fees – paying them

There are ways of alleviating the burden of fees, even if you are not eligible for any financial assistance eg government assisted places. Here are some.

If you are lucky enough to be able to pay fees out of capital, you can greatly reduce the costs by paying into an educational trust. These offer considerable advantages by utilising their charitable status. Many independent schools offer them together with a reduction in fees for parents paying in this way. Typically, you can save up to 15% of fees if you pay a lump sum when your child starts school.

The most popular way of saving for school fees used to be to take out a series of life assurance endowment policies. Since the removal of tax relief on life assurance premiums in 1984, this method has lost some of its appeal but is still regarded by many parents as one of the cheapest and least risky ways of saving for school fees. It involves parents taking out a policy a year over, say, seven years. As each matures, the lump sum it pays out will provide that year's school fees. The ideal time to start is before your child's first birthday, so that the endowments can run a full ten years before you need to pay secondary school fees, thus maintaining the qualifying status of the policy.

There are drawbacks. Once started, it may be difficult to alter, if for example you need fees earlier than anticipated. Also, although in the first year you pay a reasonably affordable sum into only one policy, by the time your savings plan is in full swing you can be pretty stretched to fund the lot. Say you commit yourself to £40.00 per month in the first year, by year seven you will be paying £280.00 per month if you are putting the same amount into each policy.

Other forms of savings, with greater growth potential, for school fees – eg unit trust savings schemes, PEPs, or, if you are of an age where you may be eligible to take early retirement, personal pension plans – are growing in popularity.

As with all savings, there is a lot on offer and it's up to you to choose where you want to place your money, taking into account the level of risk you want to take between, say, the safer with-profits type endowment policies, their unit-linked counterparts, various forms of direct equity investment or speculating on the commodity markets.

A straightforward loan or overdraft is a very expensive way of funding school fees. If you are a homeowner, you may be able to use a home equity release scheme (sometimes called a capital drawdown plan). These schemes allow you to borrow usually 60–80% of the current value of your house, less any outstanding mortgage.

You may be eligible for a grant from the Ministry of Defence, the Foreign Office or your firm. Finally, some schools give reductions in fees for second and subsequent children or the children of, for example, the clergy or old pupils.

You should not expect your children to move schools if you fall ill, on hard times or – heaven forbid – you die. You can insure against your inability to pay through death, illness or redundancy. Some school fees remission schemes may also reimburse you if your child is absent from school through illness for a long time. Ask your insurance broker, ISIS or BIBA, 14 Bevis Marks, London EC3A 7NT (tel 0171 623 9043). Some schools have their own support schemes for parents who fall on hard times. Investigate these in advance.

Payment of fees is, for most people, a heavy financial burden and mistakes are expensive. Consult ISIS.

Food

Although children are unlikely to starve, many schools continue to serve up overcooked vegetables and stodgy puddings although there is usually a choice these days. Dynamic Heads are unlikely to throw their energy into dietary improvements while they've got things like exam results and discipline to sort out. But several schools have food committees. When you visit a school try to find out about the food and what choice there is. This is especially important for boarders who cannot top up the school's diet at home. Find out what other food is available (tuck shops, etc). Some day schools allow packed lunches; and senior boarders may have some cooking facilities. Most schools will cater for children who are vegetarian or those with special diets.

Former pupils

The School Reports include pupils who have made their mark, as listed by the schools. The range of former pupils shows something of the ethos of the school even if it doesn't necessarily imply that it'll turn your child into a great rugby player, writer or spy.

Friends' schools

These are schools run by Quakers (Society of Friends). They hold regular Quaker religious meetings which pupils may or may not have to attend and emphasise the importance of tolerance of other people and of responsibility to the community. Friends' schools accept non-Quaker pupils from all creeds and faiths and from a variety of backgrounds and nationalities. Further information on Quaker education from the Heads of any of the nine Friends' schools: Ackworth, Ayton, Bootham, Friends (Lisburn), Friends (Saffron Walden), Leighton Park, The Mount, Sibford and Sidcot or from the Friends' Schools Joint Council, Friends House, 173–177 Euston Road, London NW1 2BJ (tel 0171 387 3601).

Gap year

The gap year is the year after leaving school, before taking up a degree course or a career. This is a good opportunity to do something completely different, either on the person's own initiative or through one of the established organizations; your child's school may have links with one or look in the Gap Year Book (Cavendish Educational Consultants, Cambridge). They can provide about 6 months' overseas voluntary work in schools, farms, hospitals and businesses for young people in part of their gap year.

Schools have very different attitudes to gap years: in some schools, no one takes a gap year; in others 60%–75% of pupils do. See the School Reports.

GBA

The Governing Bodies Association is a co-ordinating organisation for representatives from the governing boards of independent boys' or co-ed schools. Many of them are HMC or SHMIS schools.

GBGSA

The Governing Bodies of Girls' Schools Association is a co-ordinating organisation for representatives from the governing bodies of independent girls' schools – many of them are GSA schools.

GCSE

GCSE (the General Certificate of Secondary Education) is taken at 16, following a two-year course in Years 10 and 11. It is designed to provide a single system of examination across the whole ability range and to enable candidates at all levels to demonstrate their knowledge, abilities and achievements; it includes in-course assessment as well as exams. It aims to test the ability to apply what is learned to practical situations rather than merely the ability to remember and re-present factual knowledge which has been acquired in the classroom. GCSEs may be taken in a variety of subjects including physical education and arts options.

GCSE passes at grades A–C are required by university admissions tutors – so they matter, and it is worth keeping your eye on what subjects a school offers, and in what combination your children would be allowed to take them. Our School Reports show that the range on offer in any one school is between 10 and 25 subjects and that most schools let pupils take up to nine or ten GCSEs. Beyond that, generalisation is more difficult; it will depend on the school timetable, the ability of individual pupils and the school's policy. English, maths, a modern language and a science will be the core but the school may insist on all pupils taking eg French, the three separate sciences or two arts subjects. This can reduce the choice if the maximum is of 9 or 10 and force your children to drop subjects: art or music, German or Latin, all by the time they are fourteen – ludicrously early. Languages can sometimes be picked up later – an increasing number of schools encourage sixth formers to take extra languages.

Gifted children

Gifted children may be held back and frustrated by their less able contemporaries. If your child is gifted in one or more areas – music, maths, painting, etc – contact the National Association for Gifted Children, NNGC, Park Campus, Boughton Green Road, Northampton NN2 7AL (tel 01604 792300).

Girls' schools

Girls' secondary schools usually take pupils from the age of 11; remember this if your daughter is at a prep school that goes on to 13. Many have their own prep or junior schools, which may be co-ed and some are now taking boys throughout.

There is some evidence that girls do better in the more protected environment of a single-sex school where, for example, there is no gender-typing pressure to steer away from hard sciences, and exam results are better. This evidence is hotly disputed by Heads of co-ed schools and the truth is that some girls doubtless flourish in girls' schools and others in co-ed.

The market for girls' schools has toughened as many boys' schools have become co-ed. Some have expanding and flourishing sixth forms. Find out which way your shortlisted schools are moving, starting with our School Reports.

Some girls' schools are particularly good at providing the non-academic pupils with a good grounding for moving straight into a career. There are some lively one-year courses (including languages, financial skills etc) for pupils who want to stay on after GCSE but who are not interested in/advised to take A-levels; and two-year GNVQs. Such courses are not always easy to find – girls' schools are regrettably inclined to hide these lights under bushels, preferring to advertise their A-level pass rates.

Many girls' schools have brother schools; most share activities, events and sometimes classes with local boys' schools; a few remain socially isolated.

GNVQs

General National Vocational Qualifications (GNVQs) are new vocational qualifications developed as an alternative to the traditional academic curriculum. They are taught in schools or colleges and examined by one of the three organisations involved – BTEC, City & Guilds or RSA. (They are different to NVQs, which are specific job-related qualifications developed by the industry concerned.)

GNVQs may be taught in schools at three levels (and a fourth for 14-year olds planned): the Foundation and Intermediate levels, which are broadly equivalent to GCSEs; and Advanced level, sometimes called vocational A-levels. The Advanced level is equivalent to two GCE A-levels and may be accepted for admission to universities. They are in broad occupational areas such as leisure and tourism, business studies, health and social care and built environment.

Governors

The Governors are responsible for the school's success as a business. Their main job is to ensure that there's enough money to run the school – a large, well-endowed boarding school has an annual turnover of some £10 million. They usually appoint the Head.

GPDST

Founded in 1872. Until 1975 the schools in the Girls' Public Day School Trust were direct grant grammar schools. Currently there are 26 member schools providing education for day girls of 5–18. Further information from GPDST, 26 Queen Anne's Gate, London SW1H 9AN (tel 0171 222 9595).

Grant-maintained schools

Grant-maintained schools are a part of the maintained system but are not under the control of the local education authority. Instead they are self-governing and receive funding direct from the Department for Education and Employment. They do not charge fees.

Grants

There are a few educational grants, funded by trusts and charities for purposes which they themselves define. If you have difficulties with fees, and you cannot get help from the school, you can consult the Directory of Grant Making Trusts and the Education Grants Directory in a library; don't bank on getting anything.

Grapevines

Schools change: Heads move every 5–10 years and there's a complete change of pupils every 6 years or so. And schools are now in a period of particularly rapid change: single-sex schools are becoming co-educational; day schools become more popular than boarding; schools subtly alter their historical emphasis on religion as they adjust to an increasingly secular society. So, gossip about schools dates quickly. Reputations, however, live longer: 'that's the school where the first eleven burnt down the cricket pavilion after losing a home match.'

A parent with a child already at the school will be able to give you the lowdown but their view of a school will be coloured by the very personal experience of their child, which may or may not be relevant. The information that prep school Heads have should be up-to-date and objective, if you are interested in the schools they feed.

GSA

The Girls' School Association is a club for the Heads of some 240 girls' secondary schools. It is roughly the female equivalent of the HMC, regarding itself as representing the élite. It meets to discuss educational issues affecting its schools; and keeps information flowing between them. Its address is GSA, 130 Regent Road, Leicester LE1 7PG (tel 0116 2541619).

Guardians

Guardians step in for half-terms, at school events or in emergencies if you can't yourself. Your child will need a guardian if you live overseas or a long way from school. You can get help with finding a guardian through the school or ISIS, but it's better to find someone your child knows and likes.

Head Boy/Girl

This is a responsible position – sometimes for the year, sometimes the term. The method of selection varies from school to school. Some are chosen by the staff and Head, sometimes after consultation with pupils; others are elected. It can provide useful experience and it looks good on a CV.

Heads

Choosing a school means choosing a Head. Heads have their own careers to follow and last (on average) only 8 years at each school. They have a terrific influence while they're there, so find out as much as you can about the Head's policies, principles and obsessions. Heads have very varied backgrounds: some have never taught in school before their appointment; some were pupils at the school of which they are Head, having left only to spend a few years at university; many have already been Head, or Housemaster, at another school before; and some have experience of a wide range of schools, in this country and abroad, in the state and independent system.

A lot of the business of choosing a Head falls back on instinct, but while you're visiting schools and talking to Heads consider:

- how well would you trust their judgement?
- how approachable are they?
- how compatible are their special interests and concerns with your child's interests and needs?
- do they seem willing to admit to problems and to be capable of doing something about them?

Although Heads usually know about children and teaching, they are not infallible. Don't hesitate to let your child's Head know if you honestly think that they are wrong. Cultivating an aura of authority is part of the job. Don't be put off. But remember that the Head is running an enterprise of maybe 1000+ people with an annual turnover of up to £10 million.

Letters from School by John Rae (Collins, 1987) and Road to Winchester by John Thorn (Weidenfeld and Nicolson, 1989) will remind you that Heads are human.

Highers

These are exams taken in Scotland at the age of 16 or 17. Four or five good Higher grades are needed for a place at university in Scotland. Highers are sat the year after S-grades, so Scottish students traditionally go to university a year earlier than they do in England (although this practice is decreasing in popularity). Many Scottish schools also offer A-levels or CSYS, which are taken a year later. Universities and colleges south of the border still find Highers confusing, so these are possibly a better bet for sixth-formers who want to go south. Highers are being revised, under a programme called Higher Still, and this will affect all pupils now starting secondary school.

HMC

The Headmasters' Conference (HMC) started in 1869 as a club for Headmasters. Recently it has elected a handful of Headmistresses and now has some 240 UK members (plus 20 associate members) and regards itself as representing the élite of the independent secondary boys' schools and co-educational schools. The Heads of some schools become members automatically; others have to apply. HMC also has 75 overseas members; the schools profiled in this book are listed under Europe and Hong Kong in What's Where. HMC is now a professional organisation which assesses the schools and keeps its members informed and generates discussion on educational issues affecting their schools. You can contact HMC at 130 Regent Road, Leicester LE1 7PG (tel 0116 285 4810).

Homosexuality

Not as prevalent in schools as it is supposed to have been in the past. This is probably mainly due to the less monastic or nunnish existence of most schoolchildren nowadays and to a more open attitude towards sexuality in general. Children in single-sex schools are far more likely to fear the possibility of being homosexual than to feel encouraged to be so. Nowadays, if somebody is homosexual, it is unlikely to be because that is the norm at school.

Housemasters/mistresses

Usually a member of the teaching staff. This is a prestigious position in boarding schools; the housemaster or housemistress is in loco parentis. Make sure you trust them and that they'll get on well with your child. While the Head has a massive influence on the school, houses within a school can vary a lot according to the personality of the housemaster/mistress in charge. This is usually the first person you should contact if you're worried about your child's happiness or health.

Houses

A lot of schools separate their pupils into different houses for competitive and/or pastoral purposes. Sometimes houses represent all age groups and are competitive (sometimes described as vertical or parallel). Here, they usually have roughly equal numbers from each year and, depending on how seriously the school takes the house system, they may have a senior pupil as head of house, distinguishing ties or badges, etc. In other schools, membership of houses is according to age group (sometimes described as horizontal).

Pupils at most boarding schools sleep in separate houses – which may be the same as the competitive houses. There is often a separate sixth form (or upper sixth) house. The boarding house is in the charge of a housemaster or mistress (usually a member of the teaching staff) and some assistants. The pupils may eat in the house or in a central dining room shared with the rest of the school.

In co-ed schools, the boarding houses are sometimes mixed and sometimes single-sex. Where houses are also competitive, it is not always clear how eg a single girls' house fits into the system. In some cases, boys' and girls' houses may be twinned for competitive purposes. In a few single-sex schools, houses in a boys' school are twinned with houses in a neighbouring girls' school.

IGCSE

The International General Certificate of Secondary Education (IGCSE) has been developed by Cambridge University Local Examinations Syndicate. It parallels the British GCSE but has been tailored to international needs and has international credibility. It is offered by a number of overseas schools described in the School Reports.

Independent schools

These are schools that are not maintained by local or national government and are financed by fees and endowments. They include so-called public schools and private schools and decide their own policies and priorities. They are not required to follow the National Curriculum.

Under 10% of schoolchildren in the UK are educated at independent schools. There are staggering regional variations: 4% in Scotland and 11% in London and the South East. A fifth of all sixth formers are in independent schools. About half of the parents did not themselves attend independent schools.

Insurance

Check what your school offers. Many are involved in group insurance schemes with very favourable terms. If your school cannot help you, you can of course insure yourself individually but this is likely to cost you more. You may want to consider the following:

- school fees insurance;
- life insurance – yours and your child's;
- redundancy;
- health insurance (yours and your child's – you'll still pay a term's fees if your child can't attend);
- accident disability insurance – eg for riding/rugby injuries;
- your child's personal property insurance.

International Baccalaureate Diploma

This is taken in the sixth form and is accepted as an entrance qualification for degree courses throughout the world. It is offered at some 650 schools and colleges worldwide but at only 30 in the UK. It is sometimes offered alongside A-levels so pupils can choose to take one or the other. In the UK, teaching for the IB is always in English.

6 subjects are studied (3 at higher level and 3 at subsidiary or standard level), including maths, 1 human science, 1 experimental science, mother tongue and a second modern language and 1 subject of the candidate's choice. Each examined subject is graded on a scale from 1–7 (where 7 is maximum). To get a Diploma the student must meet defined standards and conditions including a minimum total of 24 points and the satisfactory completion of the extended essay, TOK (theory of knowledge) course and CAS (creativity, action, service) activities. The maximum score of 45 points includes 3 bonus points for an exceptional essay and work in TOK.

For further information, including a list of UK schools in the IB Diploma Programme, contact the International Baccalaureate Organisation, 15 route des Morillons, CH-1218 Grand-Saconnex, Geneva, Switzerland (tel 41 22 791 02 74, fax 41 22 791 02 77, e-mail ibhg@ibo.org).

International schools

International schools are schools in one country that teach the curriculum of another. American schools are usually prefixed with 'International' and British schools by 'British'. There are over 20 international schools in the book (see the School Reports); many offer the International Baccalaureate.

ISAI

The Independent Schools Association Incorporated (ISAI), founded in 1895, is a club of about 300 Heads of a variety of schools (co-ed, single-sex, day, boarding), both secondary and preparatory. Contact ISAI at Boys' British School, East Street, Saffron Waldon, Essex CB10 1LS (tel 01799 523619).

ISCO

The Independent Schools Careers Organisation (ISCO) provides training, advice and resources for careers advisers and pupils at its 400+ member schools. Their regional directors administer psychological vocational tests used at schools. Contact ISCO, 12a–18a Princess Way, Camberley, Surrey GU15 3SP (tel 01276 21188) for further information.

ISEB

The Independent Schools Examinations Board is the new name (1996) for the Common Entrance Board; see Common Entrance.

ISIS

The Independent Schools Information Service acts as a useful intermediary between parents who are trying to find a school and its 1300 prep and secondary school members. It provides advice on financing school fees, and how to choose a school; ISIS itself doesn't recommend individual schools but it does provide consultancy and placement services. There are 8 regional offices; details from the central office at 56 Buckingham Gate, London SW1E 6AG (tel 0171 630 8793). ISIS International provides a service for overseas parents considering a British independent school; the address is the same but a different telephone number (0171 630 8790). ISIS is an extremely useful enquiry point if you need information on any aspect of independent education.

ISJC

The Independent Schools Joint Council (ISJC) is an umbrella organisation that represents nine other independent school associations: HMC, SHMIS, GBA, GBGSA, GSA, IAPS, ISAI, ISIS and ISBA. The ISJC set up the Accreditation, Review & Consultancy Service (ARCS) which inspects schools before granting them accreditation.

Junior schools

There is a growing trend for independent secondary schools to set up their own junior schools. These may take children from 5 onwards, or sometimes from as young as 2½. Some are on a separate site, so that there is a real feeling of new horizons for the children when they move up to the senior school; in others, the junior department is physically integrated in the main school, so pupils remain in the same environment throughout their school careers. The junior school may benefit from the senior school's sports grounds and specialist facilities even when it is housed separately.

Some parents assume they can buy their way into the senior school by entering their child to the junior school. Transfer is not normally guaranteed although the junior school pupils will undoubtedly be well prepared for the senior school's entrance exam and interview.

Parents should choose a junior school to suit their children, rather than because it is a feeder school to a favoured secondary school. Junior schools are often very different from their senior school – for instance a junior school may be small, cosy and supportive while its senior school is large, boisterous and competitive. And it is worth reviewing your choice periodically in your children's development, particularly at ages 9 and 11.

Language skills

As an academic discipline the study of modern European languages has a distinguished tradition in British schools but the needs of non-specialists have been less adequately met. New language courses have been introduced into many schools to develop spoken and written (rather than literary) skills. Some schools require all sixth formers to continue with a modern language (examined or non-examined) irrespective of their A-levels. Russian, Japanese and Arabic are beginning to feature in some schools, as well as the standard western European languages.

Schools offer a number of practical language qualifications eg FLIC (Foreign Languages for Industry and Commerce), FLAW (Foreign Languages at Work), and the qualifications of the Institute of Linguists. Both FLIC and some of the Institute of Linguists exams are oral only; none covers the literature of the language and all are highly practical and applied.

Late developers

Children develop at different rates and education systems don't always cater for this. If your child seems to be having problems keeping up with the rest of the class, investigate the possibility of learning difficulties. You may do better finding a school that caters for a wide range of ability: children often do better once they're out of an environment where they're always at the bottom of the class. Some slow starters have turned out to be high-fliers (Einstein, for example).

Latin

Still taught in many schools despite pressure to replace it with a modern European language. Latin is widely regarded as a useful training and intellectual discipline, especially in the learning of logical and precise expression, in sound grammatical usage, and also in the development of vocabulary. Much scientific nomenclature is Latin. Tens of thousands of words in the English language derive from Latin; children with a sound knowledge of the language have a richer vocabulary. The teaching of Latin has been revolutionised to make the language more accessible and entertaining. However, it remains a bugbear for many children who find it difficult, and therefore that it involves hard work. In actuality it is no more difficult than modern languages such as Serbian and very much easier than, say, Hungarian.

League tables

While the publication of academic results is a good thing, ranking schools by public examination results alone tell you very little: you would expect a highly selective school to achieve better academic results than a school with a comprehensive intake. But there is no significance in a school moving 5 places up or down a league table one year – a handful of successful appeals may move it a score of places.

Although the rankings in themselves are not very revealing, it is essential to know about academic achievement when finding the right educational environment for your child. In our School Reports, we give the number of A-level passes achieved by the upper sixth in the school and the average UCAS points gained. In our search index, What's Where, we identify those schools where average UCAS points are 20 or more; that is where pupils typically pass three A-levels with results between, say, 2 As and a B through to a B and 2 Cs. We hope that is more useful than knowing the school is 68th in a table, whatever that means. See also the Foreword.

Learning difficulties

Intelligent parents often find it difficult to admit that their children have learning problems. However, some children do. Reading problems are often the first to be noticed. Poor eyesight could be the reason, so get your child's eyes tested. If your child still seems to be having problems, speak to the school or to an educational or child psychologist. You can arrange testing and assessment at the Dyslexia Institute, 133 Gresham Road, Staines, Middlesex TW18 2AJ (tel 01784 463851, fax 01784 460747). Look at What's Where for schools with special provision for children with learning difficulties. Many academic failures from strongly academic schools flourish in other schools where they are more fully exposed to practical or creative subjects (gardening, mechanics, music, sports, drama). Find something that your child enjoys doing and is reasonably good at.

Mixed Sixths

A mixed sixth is a co-educational sixth form in a secondary school which is otherwise single-sex. They have often been a transitory phase in the development of a school from single-sex to fully co-educational. A number of boys' schools and a few girls' schools now have them. For boys and girls it can make a sensible stepping stone from single-sex education to the hurly-burly of life on a degree course. Some brother/sister schools run joint sixth forms.

However, most girls entering a boys' school need to be mature for their age and have both a sense of humour and a robust character as the first few weeks can be difficult. Both sexes are defensive as they survey the new set-up, and the boys can be unkind until they get used to their new colleagues. Once the dust settles, it can be a positive experience in a well-run school. Check that your child will be properly integrated in the school. Start with the prospectus; one included the following: 'The word boys refers also to sixth form girls unless obviously inappropriate.' The balance is worth looking at too: your daughter could be one of only 2 girls in a large sixth form which may or may not suit her.

Music

Broadly speaking, schools approach music in three different ways – they teach it to the obviously talented only; they treat it as a recreational activity open to all comers; or they provide a mixture of both. A handful of schools have virtually no music; others have a massive commitment which involves some two-thirds of the pupils learning an instrument; and there are specialist music schools.

A surprising number of independent schools are very strong in music and our School Reports reflect some stunningly rich musical experience and exceptionally high standards. Schools of all sorts have pupils in county orchestras, possibly in the National Youth Orchestra or the National Youth Music Theatre group. They compete in local festivals and in national competitions (the Young Musician of the Year and the Choir Boy/Girl of the Year among many others). Unless your children are exceptionally talented, you are likely to learn more from looking at more general local successes.

And it is not just mainstream music. Lively schools often have pupils in local brass bands and success in, for instance, jazz competitions or the Panasonic Rock Competition. There is also a huge range of musical groups: some schools have just an orchestra, choir and recorder group; others have dozens of groups including eg different orchestras, choirs, chamber groups, jazz groups, madrigals, flute choir, barber shop and R & B.

Specialist music schools cater specifically for the needs of musically gifted children who have a future as professional musicians and the vast majority of them go on to music college. Children at music schools tend to spend most of their free time in musical activities and may have a limit (often 2) on the number of A-levels they can take (although they often do extremely well in those they do take and may get good university places).

Government financial assistance, in the form of the aided pupil scheme, is available to pupils at five specialist music schools: Chetham's, Purcell, St Mary's Music, Wells Cathedral and Yehudi Menuhin. Unlike art, dance and drama there are many scholarships and bursaries for music scattered throughout a very great range of schools and these are listed in our School Reports.

National Curriculum

Independent schools are excluded from the requirement to implement the National Curriculum (NC) and have complete freedom to teach what they like. But life is not that simple. Most Heads believe their schools are broadly in line with the NC. What the NC means is that all pupils cover three core subjects (English, maths, science) and seven other foundation subjects (technology, history, geography, music, art, physical education and a modern language). Because the NC dictates broadly what is covered at what stage, it has made changing schools easier without the danger of, for example, studying the Romans three years running – in particular it has made it easier to transfer between state and independent schools.

Objectives

Like any business, schools spell out their aims, objectives and mission statements. A neatly stated objective should be treated with caution. Prospectuses often wax lyrical about realising pupils' potential and achieving academic excellence. But what does that mean to individual children, especially those who don't fit the mould eg a highly creative child at a highly academic school?

Open days

Most schools have open days. A bit like a living prospectus, open days give you the opportunity to see the facilities for science, sports, art, music, eating, sleeping, etc and to look at classrooms (at their best) and noticeboards. Probably more important, you should be able to talk to staff and pupils and so get a real feel for the school (you could try showing pupils the prospectus and see what comments it provokes). Try to go to at least three to make some real comparisons.

Outward Bound

Many schools offer Outward Bound opportunities. The Outward Bound Trust is an outdoor personal development organisation which runs a variety of programmes (not only for young people) in its own centres. Its philosophy is based on two simple beliefs – that everyone is capable of achieving more than they might realise and that few people have a real appreciation of what can be achieved by teamwork. Financial aid to young people is available. Discuss with your school or contact: Outward Bound Trust, Watermillock, Near Penrith, Cumbria CA11 0JL (tel 0990 134227).

Overseas parents

If you live overseas and are sending your child to school in Britain, you will need to think about the following.

You'll have to appoint a guardian. This can be a friend or relation with whom the child can stay at half-terms and for exeats; who is on call for emergencies and who can help to arrange travel home for holidays. Choose someone your child knows and likes, who is responsible and fun, and who lives within easy travelling distance of school. If you can't come up with anyone yourself, some schools help with lists of suitable guardians or contact ISIS.

If English isn't your child's first language, arrange for some initial coaching. Survival at school requires very fluent English although many school-age children can pick it up quickly once they're there. Schools with their own EFL provisions may be better able to deal with non-native English speakers (see What's Where).

Choose a school where there are other pupils with parents overseas. What provisions are made at weekends and over half-term for those who can't go home? What transport to the airport does the school arrange? Will it arrange any necessary immunisation?

You can get advice from ISIS International, which specialises in helping overseas parents looking for a British school. Contact them at 56 Buckingham Gate, London SW1E 6AG (tel 0171 630 8790).

Parent participation

Attitudes to parent participation in the educational process are changing. Most independent schools now see it as a bonus. Many parents seek an active role and few now take the old approach that as they are paying for education, the school can take care of all that. All of what, precisely?

The borderline between positive participation and negative interference is elusive. Parents inevitably delegate more and more responsibility to teachers as their children progress from nursery education to the sixth form although they may still exert a great deal of influence right up to the choice of A-levels and first degrees. But the last educational decision they can take completely on behalf of their children is the choice of secondary school.

Schools now try and involve parents actively, providing a great deal more frequent and detailed feedback, by way of reports and tutorial accessibility so that educational and personal progress can be monitored.

Beyond that there are formal parent participation structures. These come in many different forms, one of the most brutal of which is fundraising, whereby parents' energies are harnessed to school fundraising efforts creating in effect, not only a reserve force that can be called to the colours when new projects demand new cash, but also an almost inexhaustible source of the cash itself. At a different level, these may draw on parents' specific skills with the aim of teaching them in class, or on work shadowing or job placement.

At a curricular level, and in terms of a child's personal and social development, the process is rather more subtle. Education is usually seen in one of two ways: as a simple bilateral relationship between pupil and teacher or as a three-way relationship – between pupil, teacher and parent – an altogether more complex affair.

Parental aspirations

It is difficult to be entirely objective about your children's abilities, whether sporting, academic, musical etc. Parents' success or failure can be a handicap to their children. One head told us 'untold damage is done to children by their parents' aspirations'. Another told us that daughters particularly suffered from the weight of parental aspirations placed on them where there were no brothers. There are hairy tales of children being packed off to psychologists because they are not achieving the 'correct' academic level at the right time and sometimes of children suffering from stress and depression from as early an age as eight.

Parents' associations

Increasingly important, the role of parents' associations varies. A lot depends on how much parental involvement the Head can cope with but, on the whole, there is a move towards allowing and encouraging more of them. School parents' associations may:

- have representatives on the board of governors;
- act as a sounding board for the Head; presenting complaints or suggestions; giving reactions to proposed changes;
- help with fund-raising, selling second-hand uniforms, books, etc;
- provide a useful source of careers information and work placements.

They're more likely to be effective if the Head and parents get on with one another.

Parents' meetings

Most schools arrange for you to meet your child's teachers for a progress report at least once a year. At boarding schools this is often at the end of term or fixed exeat when you are likely to be at the school anyway. This provides a chance for you to raise any minor questions or concerns. For anything pressing, don't wait; make an appointment immediately to speak to the teacher, housemaster/mistress or the Head.

Pass rates

These are impressive-looking statistics often presented by schools but we do not publish them. Good pass rates tell you very little, other than that the school is good at judging pupils' chances of success before entering them for exams. (Put one successful pupil in for one exam and, bingo! – 100% pass rate.) If your child is marginal, you may prefer a school which will simply let them have a go – in which case the school will not sport well-polished pass rates.

To find out what really goes on, find out the number of GCSEs and A-levels passed by real pupils (start with the School Reports in this book). Looking at a school's passes in individual subjects may also be revealing although you should judge these against the national spread of grades in the subjects (eg most pupils taking GCSE Greek get grade A; only reasonably bright children take Greek).

Personal and social education

Personal and social education is handled differently within each independent school. In educational jargon, it is often described as PSE, PSHE (personal, social and health education) etc. It usually consists of both a taught component of the school curriculum and the traditional activities reaching well beyond the standard academic curriculum – plays, concerts, sport, CCF, Duke of Edinburgh's Award or community service. The taught component is essentially cross-curricular. It deals with the physical, sexual, spiritual, cultural, moral, social and vocational aspects of education. For instance, human reproduction, the destruction of the Brazilian rainforest, or the disposal of radioactive waste can be taught either in biology, geography or physics classes or they can be presented by teachers or external experts within PHSE lectures, discussions or tutor groups.

Prefects

These are senior pupils whose responsibilities and method of selection vary from school to school. Some are chosen by the staff and Head, sometimes after consultation with pupils; others are elected. It can provide useful experience and look good on a CV.

Prep schools

Preparatory (or prep) schools traditionally prepare pupils for Common Entrance. They take pupils (day or boarding) from the age of 7 or 8 until they start at secondary school at 11, 12 or 13. Some junior schools which do not prepare pupils for CE now call themselves prep schools.

If you want to send your child to a secondary school that starts at 11 then you'll need to make sure the prep school knows what you are aiming at, especially if most of its pupils plan to stay till 13. Some of the senior schools recruiting at 11 will be very competitive and use entrance examinations for which the main stream of your prep school may not be prepared.

Prep schools are the right starting point if you want your child prepared for the Common Entrance exam; heads of good prep schools will act as useful guides and are usually very experienced at matching their pupils to the secondary schools in their area which use Common Entrance. Some have links with, or are prep departments of, specific secondary schools. An increasing number have pre-prep departments, taking pupils from age 5 or even 2½. ISIS will help you find one that suits your child.

Private schools

Strictly, these are privately-owned schools; there are very few of them. The term is often used to describe independent schools generally.

Progressive schools

Many of the practices and theories initiated by progressive schools from the end of the last century onwards have been adopted by others, so do not expect anything too revolutionary or liberal. Progressive schools tended to put the emphasis on community atmosphere and were less affected than many others by the hangovers of Victorian public school values (such as unquestioning deference to authority and the status quo). Now most of them are co-ed and many offer a wide range of non-academic activities including farming, gardening, adventure training and community service. Schools that have been regarded as progressive include Abbotsholme, Bedales and St Christopher's (Letchworth), as well as all the Friends' schools and those belonging to the Round Square Conference.

Prospectuses

Essential reading. They vary enormously, from being totally inadequate 4-page leaflets which look as if they've been cobbled together by the school's media research officer, to 60-page brochures, with elegant text and beautiful photographs, created by highly professional PR firms and first-class printers; there may be an accompanying video or CD-Rom. There is often a correspondence between the quality of a prospectus and the quality/reputation of a school. Crummy schools that nobody's ever heard of provide crummy prospectuses with little information while most good schools provide high-gloss, detailed brochures; a handful of the most distinguished provide an exception, making no attempt to sell themselves at all.

Prospectuses should be perused thoroughly and with caution. Not infrequently they are out-of-date. In any case, their aim is to present all or most of the best features of a school. They are advertisements and do not, therefore, dwell on emetic food, pederastic staff, the nymphomaniac matron, cannabis behind the cricket pavilion – or indeed any of the other shortcomings which, from time to time, surface even in the best-run establishments.

An original prospectus is rare for the very good reason that it is extremely difficult to produce a truthful and persuasive portrait of so complex a microcosm as a school. Too often they contain standard and cliché-ridden waffle about developing potential and producing well-rounded individuals in a caring environment. Nevertheless, a close study of a prospectus (including the essential reading between the lines) can be rewarding and provide a lot of information. Be suspicious, for example, of the school which dismisses the curriculum in one paragraph but requires a whole page of the prospectus to deal with fees in lieu of notice. The prospectus has to be considered in conjunction with the obligatory visit to the school.

Public schools

The exact definition of a public school is unclear. Usually it is used to refer to independent schools with Heads who are members of the HMC or GSA. Some boys' public schools are enormously well endowed and can afford outstanding facilities. Public schools can be sub-divided into major and minor, depending on the viewpoint and the alma mater of those using the expression.

Punishments

Although some of the archaic, petty, time-wasting punishments such as writing lines have been dropped at most schools, nearly all have some sort of penal code for dealing with non-conforming and unruly pupils. Some have an explicit tariff of punishments; others treat each case individually. A few still regard beating children as defensible as a last resort if it is done by a Head or housemaster. Many punishments involve deprivation of free time in detention, manual work (sweeping leaves, picking up litter) or, at boarding schools, a system of gating. For repeated or more serious offences many schools suspend pupils for a period. For dire offences, most will resort to expulsion, in which case you start the whole process of finding a school all over again.

Pupils

Our School Reports give the age range of pupils and the mix of day/boarders and boys/girls. This should be enough to give you a feel for whether the school is likely to be what you want for your child. Is there a strong boarding community? Is the school fully co-educational?

When you visit a school observe the relationship between the pupils with one another and with you. Do they reflect the impression you have of the school? Are they overwhelmed with homework? Are they interested in all those extracurricular activities or is high attendance at clubs and societies a result of coercion? No matter how impressed you may be by their impressive manners and smart appearance, how well would your child get on with them? Pupils can also be a valuable source of information about the school. Find out what they like or don't like about the school. What would they change if they could?

Pupil/staff relations

Education is essentially about people – in the first place the pupils in the school and those who teach them. The inter-personal relationships – between the pupils themselves, between pupils and teachers and between teacher and teacher largely determine the character and success of a school. Much can be learned by watching pupils and teachers as they move about the school. You may be able to see some classes in action when you visit. What's the atmosphere like? Better still, how do pupils and staff treat each other at school sports days and plays, when they're out of the formal setting of school? Do they seem to like each other? Do the staff treat the senior pupils as adults and is there any forum (eg staff/sixth form bar) in which they can meet as equal adults?

Range of schools

Investigate a range of schools to test your assumptions; you might find that a school of 1,000 provides more individual attention than one of 200, or that the nearest girls' school has the best science facilities in the area. Go to as many open days as possible (at least 4 or 5) and get a good background on which to base decisions about what's right for your child. Investigate:

- co-ed and single-sex schools;
- town, suburban, country schools;
- long-established and new schools;
- big and small schools.

Reception

Joining a secondary school can be traumatic. Find out the school's approach – does it encourage pupils to come into the school and familiarise themselves with the place before they join? Does it start term for the new intake early?

Registration

Once you've found the right school you'll have to register your child for entrance tests and interviews. The school's prospectus will tell you how. Usually it means filling in a form with details of your child's name, age, address and current school. You may have to pay a non-returnable registration fee.

Some schools accept all applications just a year before entry; for others you are recommended to register your child several years beforehand (for a tiny handful, you must do this before they are out of nappies); investigate well in advance. Many schools (particularly boarding schools) are technically fully booked ten years ahead but always have places available for next year because parents make multiple applications. It's difficult to match a secondary school to a new-born baby and the child will still have to pass through the school's entry procedure; early registration is no guarantee of acceptance. So have back-up choices up your sleeve and make absolutely sure that it is the right school before automatically embarking on the selection procedure.

Religion

The majority of independent schools have a declared religious persuasion and are often a religious, usually a Christian, foundation. During the last 25 years the ecumenical movement has had considerable and beneficial effects, as has racial integration. There is much less bigotry, much more tolerance. Nowadays most schools are ecumenically disposed towards a miscellany of faiths or those of no particular persuasion.

Provisions for religious instruction and worship vary greatly. Schools with a clearly prescribed policy make it clear if they are willing to accept pupils of any persuasion or none; and Muslims, Hindus, Jews et al are often allowed to opt out from any arrangements for Christians and are able to follow their own religious practices.

With the exception of sixth-form and tutorial colleges, nearly all UK independent schools have religious education of some kind on the curriculum. This often includes a study of world religions so children develop an idea of what inspires people of different faiths, and learn their practices, customs, laws, conventions and traditions.

A large number of schools are Church of England foundations and follow, to varying degrees, Protestant/Anglican practice. Some make a token subscription in the form of a prayer and perhaps a hymn at assembly, and occasional attendance at chapel; others make a certain amount of worship compulsory. Candidates are often prepared for Confirmation.

Methodist, Quaker, Presbyterian and Jewish schools tend to have a clearly defined policy and give considerable attention to religious worship and instruction.

The Roman Catholic schools, administered by the Benedictines, the Christian Brothers and other Orders, and by various teaching Orders of nuns, have very clear and comprehensive policies to educate and nurture children in the Faith so that they become devout and mature Catholics. There is considerable stress on religious instruction and on worship according to the liturgy of the Church, regular attendance at high and low Mass on Sundays and Holidays of Obligation, the taking of the sacraments, attendance at prayers, benediction, vespers, saying the Angelus, and so on. For a list of Catholic schools contact the Catholic Education Service, 39 Eccleston Square, London SW1V 1BX (tel 0171 828 7604).

In an overwhelmingly secular adult society in which religious observance plays a very small part, many people still think that it is not a bad thing for their children to be brought up according to some religious doctrine and set of beliefs. If it does matter to you that your child receives definite religious instruction and has the opportunity of worship and cultivating a spiritual life, you will find that very many independent schools agree with you.

Reports

Reports come in a wide variety of formats; virtually every school has its own. They are usually sent 2 or 3 times a year. Basically a report comprises a grade mark on each taught subject – increasingly separate grades for effort and attainment. In addition, there will probably be a comment from any or all of the following: Headteacher, housemaster/mistress, tutor, form teacher, deputy head, games teacher. Some schools provide commodious reports in which there is much detail. Quite often there is so little space allotted to each subject that only 10–15 words of comment are possible. Reports which bear subject comments such as 'satis.', 'more effort needed', 'a good term's work', 'could work harder' and nothing else are the product of inefficiency, ignorance or laziness (or, conceivably, mere weariness). Whatever the reason, they should not be accepted. Remember that you are paying a large sum of money for your child's education and you are entitled, at the very least, to a thorough report. In other words – complain. Make sure you get your money's worth with a detailed report which goes into your child's merits and shortcomings. Teaching staff should always be prepared to answer any questions and discuss any problems you may have.

Revision courses

Tutorial colleges and some boarding schools now offer revision courses for GCSE and A-level candidates from other schools, often in the Easter holiday,

Round Square Conference

Named after the Round Square, one of the buildings at Gordonstoun where this association started. There are some 15 member schools all over the world which follow the educational theories and methods of Kurt Hahn, the founder of Gordonstoun, who placed much importance on the value of Outward Bound and community service activities.

Routine

Anybody who is trying to co-ordinate the movements of hundreds of children and teenagers, with the demands of a curriculum that requires their attendance at classes, has to work to a rigid schedule. School days are timetabled to the minute. In an attempt to make this less stultifying, some schools operate a timetable over a 6- or 7-day cycle so that Monday doesn't always start with double maths. Senior pupils may be granted some autonomy in private study periods.

At boarding schools routine can stretch throughout the day, ending with set supper and bed-times and baths according to a rota – and even into the weekend with organised trips to the local town on Saturday afternoons after playing sport for the school in the morning. This sort of routine is far more restricting than any they will encounter in adult life; it won't necessarily foster self-motivation or the ability to use time properly when they leave school and find that timetables are not externally enforced. Many children need to have some time to themselves, for reading, talking to friends, playing tennis, painting, catching up on homework – or doing nothing. Your child may be better off at a school with a range of truly optional extras than at one where every hour is filled from a list of permissible options.

RSA

The Royal Society of Arts (RSA) has a long tradition of leadership in vocational education. Many schools teach for its secretarial qualifications and, increasingly, GNVQs. Enquiries to Royal Society of Arts, Progress House, Westwood Way, Coventry CV4 8HS (tel 01203 470033, fax 01203 468080).

Rules

There will be a set of rules for you and a set for the pupils. Yours may look like a particularly repressive contract of employment, with strict instructions to inform the school of the least departure from your child's normal routine, and so on. But ask to see a copy of the pupils' school rules. These indicate how much restriction the school places on its pupils and the importance of traditions such as only sixth-formers may walk on the grass. How much control does the school try to exert over its pupils when they aren't in school? Is it a bossy set of rules with no obvious rationale, or a reasonable code of conduct for an orderly community? A lot of schools don't publicise their policies on issues like smoking, drinking, sex and drugs because they believe parents will assume that by mentioning them there is a real smoking/drinking/sex/drugs problem in the school. That may suit the school but it is probably a lot more use to your child to have explicit prohibitions of (say) drinking and sexual misconduct and explicit penalties for flouting them.

Some children flourish in a fairly regimented environment, others find it a strain to be constantly bumping up against authority. Your child is likely to find it easier if the school's insistence on conforming to rules matches your child's instinct and family experience.

Scholarships and exhibitions

Nearly one in every six independent school pupils can have all or a proportion of their fees paid by a scholarship or bursary. The well-endowed schools often have scores of scholarships; most have at least a handful. They are awarded by the school, on the strength of the pupil's potential, usually judged by exam or test. Depending on the school, scholarships may be given to pupils of various ages, for academic ability, art, music, prowess at sport and, indeed, for all-rounders. They are sometimes awarded irrespective of parental income, increasingly means tested. Our School Reports note where they are available.

A few well-endowed schools which recruit at 13 offer prep school scholarships to state primary school children at 11; this allows them to spend two years at a feeder prep school before joining the school at 13.

School consultants

These are people who give advice on suitable schools for your child. They may be worth considering if you really don't know where to begin in matching school and child. Consultants are sometimes paid a retainer by schools who want to be recommended. Get advice about reputable consultants from ISIS.

School councils

This is a forum in which pupil representatives from every form, or perhaps just senior forms, meet the staff to discuss issues such as food, discipline, school outings, and to air grievances. Some Heads and staff at independent schools do not warm to this democratisation.

School leaving age

The minimum age at which children can lawfully leave school is 16, that is usually at the end of Year 11. Do not even think about the possibility of your children leaving until the end of their sixth-form course – Year 13. If you can't fund the extra two years' fees, then move them into a state sixth-form college.

Why? About one third of the entire 18+ age group now goes on to higher education. Do you want to encourage your children to join the (educationally) lower two thirds, with all that that will imply in terms of qualifications for jobs? Letting children leave at 16 will do them no favours at all. Encourage them to stay the course.

Science

Biology, chemistry and physics may be taught as separate subjects leading to separate GCSEs. The alternative is to teach integrated science (biology, physics and chemistry, plus possibly some geology and astronomy); depending how much pupils do, they can take one or two GCSE's worth. Plainly the two different systems suit different children and both are found in independent schools.

Scotland

The educational system in Scotland is different to the English in a number of respects. Some Scottish independent schools follow the Scottish system, others stick to the English one, and others are a hybrid of the two.

Secondary schooling in Scotland starts at 12, rather than 11 or 13; and the secondary year numbers are from S1 to S6. While English and Welsh pupils are doing GCSEs, Scots are doing S-grades (standard grade) in S4; these are followed a year later by Higher-grade (Highers) in S5; and maybe Certificate of Sixth Year Studies (CSYS) a year after that. The post-16 courses are currently being revised under a programme called Higher Still, which will affect all pupils now starting secondary school. For further information, contact the Scottish Examination Board, Ironmills Road, Dalkeith, Midlothian EH22 1LE (tel 0131 663 6601). Vocational qualifications in Scotland are being developed by Scotvec.

Scottish pupils often sit S-grades only in those subjects that they aren't going to continue to Higher or A-level, so that some of the ablest pupils will have only 3 or 4 S-grades. (However, they must pass the Higher in a subject to take it on to CSYS). Many independent schools take Highers and A-levels together so the upper sixth take a mixture of Highers, CSYS and A-levels. All of which is much more flexible for the pupils but much harder to assess the achievements of a particular cohort because they are not all sitting the same exams at the same time. You need to bear this in mind when reading the School Reports.

Traditionally, Scottish students went on to degree courses after taking Highers in S5 when they were 17; some still do if they are going to a Scottish university. But increasingly they stay on in the sixth form, particularly if they want to move south of the border. There is a strong tradition for students in Scottish schools to stay in Scotland and not to head for Oxbridge; indeed Glasgow schools (for example) often lead pupils to Glasgow universities.

Scotvec

The Scottish Vocational Education Council (Scotvec) is the national body responsible for developing a comprehensive system of vocational qualifications in Scotland, some of which are widely available in Scottish schools. As with its English counterpart, Scotvec runs Scottish Vocational Qualifications (SVQs), designed for the needs of an industry, and General SVQs, which are broadly-based qualifications available in schools and colleges for 16–19 year olds. It differs from the English system in having over 3,000 modules, which can be taken independently and which are widely available in Scottish schools. You can either add these modules to eg Highers or A-levels, or you may take clusters of modules, which you can then build up to General SVQs. For more information, contact Scotvec, Hanover House, 24 Douglas Street, Glasgow G2 7NQ (tel 0141 248 7900).

Service children

The Ministry of Defence may give grants towards fees for the children of armed service personnel. You can find out more from your local Service Education Unit or from MoD, Service Children's Education Agency, Building 31, Worthy Down, Winchester, Hampshire SA21 2RG (tel 01962 887945).

Setting

Some schools split children into teaching groups for particular subjects according to ability judged on performance in exams and class. Setting is distinct from streaming, where a pupil is assigned to a class for all subjects on the basis of ability, age etc. The advantage of setting is that groups of similar ability in a subject are easier to teach, thus preventing quick learners from being held back and allowing slower ones to move at a less pressured pace. It is used particularly for maths and languages. The disadvantage is that children can be held back by being wrongly setted, particularly if movement between sets is difficult.

Sex

Most school children don't have the opportunity to indulge in active sex lives, but they do think and talk about sex a lot. This book doesn't attempt to assess the sex education provision of individual schools since a straightforward account of human copulation and reproduction, as provided in many sex education classes, isn't necessarily the most relevant way of finding out about sex – it can confuse rather than clarify. It is also difficult to measure sex education as it crops up in other subjects and classroom discussions.

Many parents find it difficult to think of their children as being sexually active (and vice versa) while adolescents sometimes resent what they see as parental interference in their personal lives. However, it's worth braving the mutual embarrassment: while the repercussions of an unplanned pregnancy are as traumatic and lasting as ever, AIDS has made ignorance an even greater danger than it was before. There are lots of books about sex around. You can start basic with Clare Rayner's Body Book (Deutsch, 1982) and Where Did I Come From? and What's Happening to Me? (both Macmillan). Women's Experience of Sex (Penguin) and Love Talk (Channel 4 Books) are the recommendations of Dr John Collee in the Observer.

S-grades

Broadly speaking, the Scottish equivalent of GCSE – designed to test the whole ability range. Subjects are broken down into different elements such as application and understanding, and assessment is based on exams and set classwork during the course.

Scottish pupils often sit S-grades only in those subjects that they aren't going to continue to Higher or A-level. This means that some of the ablest Scottish pupils will have only 3 or 4 S-grades. Bear that in mind when you read our School Reports on Scottish schools.

SHA

The Secondary Heads Association (SHA) is a club for the majority of Heads and deputies of secondary schools, some 8,500 members. It provides a rare forum for Heads of state and independent schools to discuss educational matters common to both sectors. Its address is 130 Regent Road, Leicester LE1 7PG (tel 0116 247 1797).

SHMIS

The Society of Headmasters and Headmistresses of Independent Schools (SHMIS) is a club for Heads – mostly of smaller independent senior schools, with a tradition of boarding. It was established in 1961 to provide a forum for the exchange of ideas, because membership of the HMC was full. Some Headmasters are members of both HMC and SHMIS. The address is The Coach House, 34a Heath Road, Upton, Chester CH2 1HX (01244 379649)

Siblings

Very often siblings are automatically sent to the same school. This has advantages: younger siblings have a familiar face around from day one, it's convenient for them to have roughly the same daily and holiday routine, and some schools reduce the fees for second and subsequent children. However, siblings can have very different educational needs and may flourish in very different schools. Where children scrape into a school attended by an elder sibling, especially under family pressure, there is a strong risk of future disaster.

Sickness

Schools like to be informed if your child needs to be kept at home/hospital, especially if an infectious disease is involved or the child's activity will be curtailed after going back to school. When they like to be informed varies – some only want to know when the child returns to school, others want to know as soon as possible. Check with the school.

School itself isn't necessarily any more dangerous than home but sickness can strike and accidents happen there, as anywhere. You should leave home and office telephone numbers with the school and be very specific about when and where you can be contacted; this can save much anxiety for frantic teachers. If for any reason you can't be contacted, arrange to have a friend standing by to step in if your child is ill or has an accident at school.

You can insure school fees against long absences from school due to illness; speak to an insurance broker about this or contact ISIS.

Single-sex schools

Although it may be an artificial environment, some children are happier in all girls' or all boys' schools. Many of the heavyweight schools (academically and socially) have remained single-sex, particularly girls' schools. Academically, pupils from single-sex schools appear to get better exam results than those from co-ed schools. Much statistical data is produced to back single-sex schools' claims but the question facing parents is the future of their own children – will they flourish in a single-sex school?

Most schools make some attempt to introduce pupils to the opposite sex at some stage. Many team up with other schools (particularly if there is a brother/sister school) and share activities, productions and outings. Some may also have joint facilities, join forces for A-levels or in the prep/junior department. A few, however, appear to remain completely socially isolated.

Sixth form

The lower and upper sixth forms are usually described simply as the sixth form (Years 12 and 13 in the national numbering system). The sixth form lasts for two years but some pupils stay for only one year, normally studying for additional GCSEs or a GNVQ. Most stay for two years on A-level courses (or GNVQ Advanced Level).

It is now not unusual to move after GCSEs – to the sixth form of another school or to a sixth-form college. In some cases, it is the right thing to do to give a 16-year-old somewhere new and challenging. But some Heads see this move as reducing the effective A-level course to 4 terms by the time the pupil has settled in during the first term and sat the exams at the start of the sixth term. Good schools will take the trouble to assess how easily a child will settle into their school, as well as looking at academic ability.

Size of school

Independent secondary schools range in size from about 120 pupils to over 2,000. Just as some people are happier in the bustle of large cities than they are in small towns, some children prefer a certain size of school. Consider the facilities and subjects offered; there may be more going on at a large school and possibly better, newer facilities, but there isn't always a bigger range. Large schools can often give pupils some of the advantages of small schools by breaking down the whole school into houses with a life of their own. It does not necessarily follow that small schools can provide a more caring environment, although it is obvious some do.

Smoking

Smoking is still prevalent in schools in spite of massive anti-smoking campaigns from Heads and the government. Most schools prohibit smoking, many expel those caught. In general, if children get through school without smoking they'll probably never start but peer pressure and the need to flout authority makes this difficult. Many of those who don't smoke have parents who do. Girls appear more inclined to smoke than boys.

Making children aware of the dangers doesn't seem to stop them: teenagers regard themselves as immortal and don't appreciate how difficult giving up can be. One Head recommends massive parental bribes for not smoking before they are 21 (at least £1,000 to be worth considering). Schools with an 'expulsion for smoking' policy have been known to have to climb down when the entire sixth form is caught.

Special Needs

A mildly handicapped child, especially an intelligent one, may do better at a mainstream school than a special one. Many schools make provision for children with special needs due to, for example, mild handicap, learning or language difficulties. Some of these are listed in What's Where.

If your child has special educational needs because of learning difficulties or more serious handicaps, the Parents Charter spells out their rights to a proper education. Arrangements in England, Scotland, Wales and Northern Ireland are not identical although they are converging. You can get parents' publications and direct information as follows.

England: Department for Education and Employment, Schools Branch 2 Division B (Special Education), Sanctuary Buildings, Great Smith Street, London SW1P 3BT (tel 0171 925 5000).

Wales: Welsh Office Education Department, Schools Administration Branch 3, Crown Buildings, Cathays Park, Cardiff CF1 3NQ (tel 01222 826078).

Scotland: Scottish Office Education Department, SPO4, Victoria Quay, Edinburgh EH6 6QQ (tel 0131 244 0946).

Northern Ireland: Department of Education for Northern Ireland, Special Education Branch, Rathgael House, Balloo Road, Bangor, Northern Ireland BT19 7PR (tel 01247 279000).

Sports and games

There is still much emphasis on sports and games in independent schools and still pressure to play the team sport of the term in traditional schools eg rugby (autumn), hockey (spring) and cricket (summer). In some, 5 or 6 afternoons a week (plus other times) are devoted to them and most schools have excellent facilities on-site or nearby (including an increasing number of sports halls). Even so, performances at national and international level remain poor and the facilities provided in schools (particularly maintained schools) are inferior to those available in many other countries. Many schools run sports and games on a voluntary basis and nowadays it is comparatively rare to find a school which insists on everyone taking part in official sports and games regardless of ability, physique and inclination.

The principal and most popular field games are: rugby union, cricket, hockey, soccer, lacrosse, handball, softball, rounders and forms of baseball. Some Irish schools provide hurling and Gaelic football. The main court games are: lawn tennis, hard-court tennis, badminton, basketball, squash, rackets, volleyball, and croquet; plus Eton fives and Rugby fives. A few schools provide real tennis.

Of the course games, golf is easily the most popular. Quite a lot of schools have 9-hole courses on their estates, or have access to courses nearby.

Athletics is very popular and most schools can provide a full range of field and track events (quite a few schools have all-weather running tracks). Cross-country running is very popular. Some martial arts are available including judo, karate, kendo and kung-fu. Fencing is popular, but school boxing is a thing of the past.

Target sports (eg archery, clay-pigeon shooting, rifle-shooting – small and fullbore – and pistol-shooting) are available in quite a lot of schools and are linked with activities in the CCF.

Water sports (especially swimming, water polo, surfing, canoeing, sailing, rowing and diving) are always popular. Schools situated near the sea, a river or lake tend to make good use of water. Many schools have their own swimming pool (some indoors).

Gymnastic sports are extremely popular and most schools have good facilities for these.

Some schools (particularly an increasing number of girls' schools) can provide riding and some show-jumping.

Outdoor pursuits are often closely associated with sport (or are sports in their own right), and include sailing, canoeing, skiing, rock-climbing, fell-walking, cliff-scaling, gliding and parachuting. A few schools even manage to have their own packs of beagles. Country schools (especially those in Scotland and the North of England) have a very full range of outdoor pursuits/sports including outdoor pursuit centres which pupils can visit for a few days at a time. Such activities have links with various enterprises in the Duke of Edinburgh's Award Scheme. The *mens sana in corpore sano* philosophy – no doubt a continuation of the Victorian cult of athletic prowess and muscular Christianity – is still widespread and many schools see team and individual sports and games as valuable character-building influences. Most schools have a hard core of dedicated sports/games enthusiasts on the staff (some Heads are fanatics) who are qualified to coach, referee and umpire and who are prepared to devote an enormous amount of time and effort to their chosen activity. The majority of schools run sports and games on a competitive basis, with inter-house competitions and numerous fixtures with other schools.

STABIS

The State Boarding Information Service (STABIS) provides information on 37 maintained schools which provide boarding – full boarding, mixed day/boarding etc. Parents who are UK nationals pay only for the cost of boarding, not for tuition, so that typically, they pay between £850 – £1,450 per term – a lot less than the equivalent cost at an independent boarding school. Many of these schools perform well in academic league tables. STABIS publishes the Directory of Maintained Boarding Schools in conjunction with the BSA (free). Enquiries to Mr Michael Kirk, Secretary, STABIS, Ysgol Nant, Valley Road, Llanfairfechan, Gwynedd, LL33 0ES (tel and fax 01248 680542).

Staff

You'll probably get a list of staff and their credentials with the prospectus. You can investigate them further when you visit. What is the male:female ratio? Which departments have the largest teaching staff? How old are they (or do they seem)? The average pupil:staff ratio is about 11:1 or 12:1, but this varies a lot and you're probably more interested in the teaching groups. What do you think your child will make of the staff, and how interesting would you find them? Can you find out how long they've served? Most School Reports in this book give the annual staff turnover – usually about 5% which gives a reasonable influx of new blood to the staff. When turnover is low, is this because the staff are good, happy teachers or because they are inert?

Starting out

Before your child's first day at a new school, check:

- whether there are other new pupils in the class;
- what time the new pupils are expected to get there;
- what time the day ends; or, at a boarding school, when the first exeat is; and
- that you've got all the necessary equipment and uniform.

Try to introduce your child to some of the other pupils in the class so that there'll be someone familiar on the first day.

State schools

More than 90% of schoolchildren in the UK go to state schools; mostly at day schools but a handful at boarding schools. These schools don't charge tuition fees because the school is fully funded by the local education authority or by central government (grant maintained status); the few that take boarders charge a boarding fee. Children can transfer from state schools to independent schools. It is easiest at age 11 (12 in Scotland) or at 16 after GCSE.

Stealing

Theft is inherent and pretty well inevitable in all institutional life. In any school, at any given moment, there is likely to be a thief or two about. Petty pilfering (of pens, watches, calculators, cash and items of clothing) is especially frequent in day schools (the swag can be got away easily). Life is often easy for the petty thief because pupils are so careless about their belongings, especially on games days; changing-rooms are easy targets. In many schools, easily portable valuables are collected before games, but many pupils forget to hand them in. Naming children's property can help schools reduce the scale of the problem; mark everything that can be marked. Don't send your child to school with large amounts of cash or other valuables; if this can't be avoided, make sure it is handed to a member of staff for safe keeping (and that your child knows which one).

Steiner schools

Schools whose teaching follows the philosophy of Rudolf Steiner who placed great emphasis on the development of the individual and who believed that spiritual truth was human rather than in some way divine. The first Steiner school opened in Germany in 1914; they were closed by the Nazis in 1938. Currently there are about 200 worldwide. Many of them are prep only but a few teach up to A-level. Further details from the Secretary, Steiner Schools Fellowship, Kidbrooke Park, Forest Row, East Sussex RH18 5JA (tel 01342 822115, fax 01342 826004).

Streaming

A form of internal organisation in which pupils are grouped across the curriculum by such criteria as age, intelligence, ability and aptitude (or a combination of two or more of these). It is largely based on achievement in the three Rs. Depending on the size and intake of the school, there may be two or more streams for each year group, perhaps with several classes in each stream. Streaming is to be distinguished from setting, a system by which pupils are grouped for particular subjects (usually maths, modern languages) according to ability.

Subjects offered

The range of GCSE and A-level subjects schools offer is enormous – between 10 and 25. But if you are impressed by 25, remember there will be at least 15 subjects that your child will not be able to take.

The curriculum narrows at age 14 first by the selection of some 9–10 GCSEs and then down to 3 or 4 A-levels. Some pupils may be forced into an exclusively arts or science bias at 16, though increasingly they take a mixture; our School Reports give the number of pupils combining arts and sciences at A-level. Some schools don't encourage pupils to combine the two or don't have the facilities to teach both.

Transfer from state schools

Nearly half the pupils in independent secondary schools have not attended an independent junior school but there are huge variations in the proportion of children each independent school recruits from the state sector – from under 1% to over 80%. There is a growing trend for popular day schools, which have long had a high intake from state primary schools, to start their own junior schools. This can be expected to reduce their intake from the maintained sector.

For parents the good news is that the majority of secondary Heads see no problem in transferring from a state school. Many are more positive ('... they should try it'; 'they take to us like ducks to water'; 'tends to be a very stimulating move'). And the bad news? Very little, but you'll need to concentrate on:

- the age you want to make the transfer
- the entrance examination
- settling in.

Transfer age You should assume, broadly, that transfer at 11 or into the sixth form works well; at other ages it's more tricky. Schools that recruit at 13 are the main difficulty and have few state entrants; usually boys' schools using the Common Entrance. Schools that recruit at 11 (or 12 in Scotland) take many more; some actually expect their pupils to come from local primary schools (mainly former direct grant grammar schools).

Entrance examination Almost all independent secondary schools have one; many use the Common Entrance, most have their own. You may find it necessary to get a private tutor to help your child through, particularly if it is highly selective school. Most entrance exams are quite suited to state pupils but the Common Entrance examination is not – at least at present, although its curriculum is being tailored to the requirements of the National Curriculum so there could be some convergence in the future.

Settling in At 11, Heads report few problems apart from the fact that state primary schools do not teach languages, in contrast to independent schools where pupils will certainly have studied at least one. The most frequently mentioned problems are discipline (academic and personal); hard work, homework and commitment ('inability to hide poor homework'; 'adjustment to small classes and consequent need to concentrate through the whole lesson'; 'six day week'; 'different attitude to out of work activities eg games').

At 16, after GCSE, there can be problems for science pupils transferring into an independent sixth form – they may have to switch from integrated science to individual sciences; they may also find that they are not ready for an A-level maths course. Neither is a real barrier to those prepared to work hard.

Problems of social integration at either 11 or 16 are reported to be very rare. What may disconcert a child might seem trivial to an adult – classroom silence after the hubbub of their primary school classroom; weekly tests in different subjects; standing up when the teacher comes into the room; remembering on no account to call her 'Miss'. The problems children encounter are those common to any school transfer, not normally to any incompatibility between the state and independent systems.

Tutorial colleges

These can be day or boarding, are nearly always co-ed and, much like sixth-form colleges, they usually take students from the age of 16 for A-levels or additional GCSEs. Some also offer other courses – the IB or GNVQs. Fees are often charged according to the number of subjects studied and are not cheap.

Tutorial colleges tend to have fewer rules than schools, and a lot less community spirit and extra-curricular activity. This could make them a good option for sixth formers who have had enough of school discipline and tradition. They are not simply crammers. You may want to consider them seriously if your child has rejected school but wants to continue with education, or needs to re-sit A-levels and cannot face the prospect of spending a year with erstwhile juniors.

We include some tutorial colleges in our School Reports because we recognise their special place in the spectrum of independent secondary education. Some children are a lot happier studying away from school. You can get a complete list of accredited tutorial colleges from CIFE, Buckhall Farm, Bull Lane, Bettersden, Ashford, Kent TN26 3HB (tel and fax 01233 820797) or from the Association of Tutors (Sunnycroft, 63 King Edward Road, Northampton NN1 5LY (tel 01604 24171, fax 01604 24718).

Tutors

Tutors, working as individuals (not as members of a tutorial college), can provide one-to-one teaching to help children overcome their learning difficulties or prepare for an examination. They are often useful when children are about to transfer from a state primary school to an independent secondary school or need help with a particular subject eg languages or maths.

To check up on tutors' bona fides, try asking whether they are members of their professional body, the Association of Tutors (AoT contact: Dr D J Cornelius, Sunnycroft, 63 King Edward Road, Northampton NN1 5LY, tel 01604 24171, fax 01604 24718). Not all good tutors are AoT members. However all its members carry professional indemnity and public liability insurance and the AoT certifies individual members every year. Prospective members' credentials are checked (more stringently since parents have become concerned about child abuse) and has the list of persons no longer permitted to hold a teaching post (DFEE List 99)

UCAS Points

University and college conditional offers of places are given by UCAS (Universities and Colleges Admissions Service) in terms of specified A-level grades or UCAS points – the total of each AS and A-level grade achieved according to the following table.

UCAS POINTS	
AS-Level	A-level
A = 5	A = 10
B = 4	B = 8
C = 3	C = 6
D = 2	D = 4
E = 1	E = 2

Neither the International Baccalaureate (IB) nor GNVQs yet rate in the UCAS points system and the position in Scotland is confused.

For schools in England and Wales, our School Reports give the average UCAS points gained by the upper sixth, excluding A-level general studies (which is usually taken as an extra). This ranges from under 10 to over 30 – ie from 2 A-level passes at grade C and D, through to 3 or 4 straight As.

Uniform

Most independent schools have a uniform. Often it won't have changed for a long time. This usually means buying a special tie and blazer; skirts/trousers, shirts, shoes, jumpers, even knickers, in the right colour. In addition you may need to buy special sports equipment and clothes, school colours for sports teams, summer clothes, formal dress (maybe a kilt for a Scottish school), coats, macs, smocks for art, etc. Schools will let you know where to buy the uniform, including any second-hand sources, before your child joins. Some are more demanding than others about what will or will not do.

Many boarding schools allow pupils to wear clothes of their own choice in the evenings and at weekends. In the sixth form, uniform is quite often waived completely or replaced by a dress code; where the sixth is mixed this sometimes applies to the girls, but not the boys. This is indicated in the School Reports.

University and college entrance

About a third of all 18 year olds now go on to degree courses and almost all sixth formers go on to university or college. Our School Reports show you the sort of subjects they go on to study and whether they take a gap year first.

There are some common indicators of strong academic schools and we show the proportion going to Oxbridge, to medical school and to read science. One rule of thumb of a strong academic school is said to be 10% going to Oxbridge (a few schools send over a third, some none); but this clearly does not apply to eg Scotland where there is no tradition of going to Oxbridge.

Some schools have a large proportion of pupils going on to degrees in vocational subjects such as physiotherapy, primary education, hotel and catering management; others have small numbers, reading say architecture or pharmacy. In small schools, there may be huge variations between the years.

Vocational qualifications

Some schools offer very specific vocational qualifications – commercial French, Leith's cookery courses, typing and word processing, BHS instructor qualifications. Increasingly the new GNVQs are offered in schools, usually the Advanced GNVQ as an alternative to A-level in the sixth form.

Voluntary-aided schools

These are voluntary in so far as they have been founded by a voluntary religious body (eg the Church of England or the Roman Catholic Church) and aided in that they are supported by public funds. The voluntary body has the right to choose staff and decide on what religious education may be given. There are not many voluntary-aided schools today and most of them are Church schools.

Woodard Schools

Nathaniel Woodard founded 7 schools starting with Lancing in 1848. The Woodard Corporation now maintains 23 schools throughout the country and a further 10 are associated with it, some from overseas. All have an Anglican foundation and together form the largest group of Church schools in England and Wales.

Work experience and work shadowing

Pupils aged 15, 16 and 17, who are studying academic courses, may be offered the opportunity of working for a week or more in a real work situation; some schools call this work shadowing, perhaps more accurately. Each school has its own approach to work experience; in some schools it is optional, in others compulsory. Many schools involve parents in finding placements. Our School Reports note where it is offered. On vocational courses, pupils may be required to engage in extended periods of work experience as an integral part of the course.

Year numbers

Schools use all kinds of year numbering systems; most often GCSE is taken in the upper fifth; A-levels in the upper sixth. Some use words such as Shell or Remove instead of numbers. All very confusing.
A growing number of schools has replaced these numbers with the national year numbering system, brought in with the National Curriculum, so that GCSEs are taken in Year 11, A-levels in Year 13. For secondary schools, the numbering works like this:

SCHOOL YEAR NUMBERS		
Year numbers	Normal age of pupils	Public exams
Year 7	11–12	CE (girls)
Year 8	12–13	CE (girls)
Year 9	13–14	CE (boys and girls)
Year 10	14–15	
Year 11	15–16	GCSE
Year 12	16–17	
Year 13	17–18	A-levels

In Scotland, the primary numbers (eg P3) are usually numbered separately from the secondary (eg S3). Scottish secondary education starts at age 12, so instead of Years 8–13, they have S1 to S6, with S-grades taken in S4, Highers in S5 and CSYS in S6.

Young Enterprise

Young Enterprise is a business/education partnership. It is best known for helping young people (aged 15–19) who are still at school or college form and run their own companies. This offers them a way of developing their enterprise skills and smoothing the difficult transition from school to work. Business consultants advise each company. There is a one-term course devised to meet many of the requirements of the National Curriculum for economic and environmental awareness and an examination (run by the Oxford board). Many schools participate in the scheme. It also runs Profit Business (UK) which introduces 14-16 year olds to the world of business and economics and provides a working context for A-level and GNVQ students. You can find out more from Young Enterprise, Ewert Place, Summertown, Oxford OX2 7BZ (tel 01865 311180, fax 01865 310979).

520 SCHOOL REPORTS

• How to read the school reports •

We present over 520 reports on independent secondary schools, arranged alphabetically. Some of these have associated junior, prep, pre-prep and/or nursery schools or departments, although it is not always clear whether these are departments of the same school, or separate entities where pupils pass through a real threshold to the senior department.

All our schools are secondary schools, taking pupils through to 18. They have sixth forms or offer specialist teaching. Most reports are based on a questionnaire, with specific questions, completed by the school and returned to Heads for checking. Where a school has a junior department, this is indicated in the age range; there is no further attempt to cover the junior department: boarding may not be available for younger children and IAPS affiliation has not been given.

Fees are those charged in the summer term 1996 (except where indicated otherwise eg some international schools charge by the year rather than the term).

At the top, all school reports summarise key facts – the overall size: boys/girls, day/boarding; fees (summer 1996) for day, boarding and weekly boarding; size of the upper sixth (ie the A-level year); and affiliations, either the Head's (eg HMC) or the school's (eg Woodard); those of eg the governing body, bursars etc are not included. Other sections are:

What it's like Our view of what the school is like.

School Profile Hard facts about the school. These are intended to be indicative not definitive. Some figures are presented as percentages, some as actual numbers; some are for a specific year, some are an average over three years; many are approximations. But the numbers should give you a fair picture of the school.

Pupils Total numbers of pupils, also broken down into day/boarding and boys/girls. Where the school takes pupils below secondary school age, the size and age range of the senior department is also given, as are any established feeder schools. The proportion of the intake which has come from state schools (sometimes the proportion to the sixth is very high but the total intake at that stage may be very small).

Entrance How the school selects and what financial assistance is available; you can look up eg scholarships, assisted places in the *What's What* section.

Parents Where they live and what they do.

Head and staff Name and background of the Head. Staff numbers and turnover.

Exam results Size of the GCSE and A-level groups (or equivalents); and passes per pupil – not pass rates. So you can see, for example, if all pupils pass 2 A-levels or some pass 4 and some 1. Average UCAS points gained (exclusive of general studies). You can look UCAS points up in *What's What* to understand its significance.

University and college entrance What sixth-form leavers go on to do; a breakdown of subjects they study; the proportion going on to Oxbridge and first taking a gap year.

Curriculum Public exams taken; the number of subjects offered (including whether or not A-level general studies is offered, which is sometimes taken as an extra A-level); any subjects that are unusual; any vocational qualifications offered and whether work experience is available; European languages offered and at what level; regular exchanges run and any other relevant initiatives.

If you are interested in Scottish schools, but are not familiar with the Scottish exam system look up Scotland in *What's What* before looking up the individual Scottish schools. The exams are different to those in England and are not necessarily taken by a whole cohort.

The arts The proportion of pupils involved in music, drama and art; the number of musical groups and the exams that can be taken; and notable recent achievements. Remember that some schools nurture only the very talented; others try and involve the maximum number of pupils to the best of their ability; some manage to look after both. The information given here should give you some idea.

Sports, community service and clubs The range of sports and games offered; compulsory and optional sports; and notable recent achievements, either by teams or individuals. Whether the Duke of Edinburgh's Award Scheme, CCF and community service are available; and the number and range of clubs and societies. Lively schools have a lot going on – obviously larger schools can support more of a range than smaller ones. But some schools appear to be surprisingly inactive.

Uniform/Houses/Prefects/Religion/Social To help you judge the flavour of the school.

Discipline A very sensitive area. We felt it was important to know what a school's attitude was to discipline. Whilst it is obvious that each case must be judged individually, we asked schools what they would expect by way of punishment in two cases – a relatively minor incident (failure to produce homework on a single occasion) and an obviously serious offence (smoking cannabis). We must emphasise that, in this latter case, we asked for punishment other than any police involvement and that schools answered the question hypothetically. It is not safe to assume that a school has a drugs problem simply because it has a policy. Some general information on discipline may also be included. Very few schools now allow corporal punishment but if it is still permitted, we say so.

Boarding The way boarding is organised and when pupils are allowed out.

Alumni Association How to get in touch with the person who runs the old boys'/girls' association.

Former pupils Names selected by the school.

A

• ABBOTSHOLME

Abbotsholme School, Rocester, Uttoxeter, Staffordshire ST14 5BS. Tel 01889 590217, Fax 01889 591001

• Pupils 235 • Boys 11–18 (Day/Board/Weekly) • Girls 11–18 (Day/Board/Weekly) • Upper sixth 23 • Termly fees £2538 (Day) £3797 (Board/Weekly) • HMC, SHMIS, Round Square • Enquiries/application to the Headmaster

What it's like

Founded in 1889 by Dr Cecil Reddie, it was the first of a series of new schools which had considerable influence both in Britain and throughout Europe. He was the originator of a movement which embraced the Lietz Schule in Germany and led to the foundation of Bedales, Gordonstoun and many others. The methods pioneered by Abbotsholme have since been adopted in many schools. It was one of the first boys' schools to become fully co-educational, in 1969. Its handsome and well-equipped buildings lie in 140 acres of splendid private grounds in some of the most beautiful countryside in England, at the edge of the Peak District National Park. The main buildings include a fine chapel, music and art blocks and engineering workshops; there is a huge and well-equipped sports centre. It has the advantages of a small school; the emphasis is on informality, a friendly and relaxed atmosphere and the creation of a strong community spirit. Parental involvement is encouraged to an unusual degree. Careful attention is given to religious education and all pupils attend a chapel service each day. A very favourable staff:pupil ratio of about 1:9 permits small sets and classes and much individual attention. Results are good and the majority of sixth form leavers goes on to degree courses each year. But the academically less able are also well catered for. Music, drama and art are all vigorously supported. Its Arts Society (open to the public by subscription) has a wide reputation, with many recitals/concerts given by musicians of international renown. 20 acres of excellent playing fields provide for a standard range of sports and games. A large number of clubs and societies cater for a wide range of extra-curricular activity. There is much emphasis on open-air pursuits and outdoor education is an integral part of the school's programme (these include skiing, caving, canoeing, camping, mountaineering and rock-climbing). Many pupils take part successfully in the Duke of Edinburgh's Award Scheme and a big commitment to highly-organised local community services. A 70-acre farm is an integral part of school life with pupils responsible for feeding, lambing, harvesting etc.

School profile

Pupils Age range 11–18; 235 pupils, 82 day (48 boys, 34 girls), 153 boarding (101 boys, 52 girls). Main entry ages, 11, 12, 13 and into sixth. 5% are children of former pupils. *State school entry:* 25% main intake, plus 50% to sixth.

Entrance Common Entrance and own exam used. No special skills or religious requirements. Parents not expected to buy text books. No compulsory extras – charges vary. Up to 8 scholarships/bursaries pa, 33–50% fees.

Parents 15+% from industry/commerce. 10–30% live within 30 miles, 10–30% live overseas.

Head and staff *Headmaster:* Darrell J Farrant, in post for 12 years. Educated at King George V School, Southport, and Oxford University (law). Previously Housemaster and Head of English at Merchiston Castle and Headmaster at Shawnigan Lake School. Also Schoolmaster Fellow, Jesus College, Cambridge; President, British Columbia Independent Schools Association; Chairman of SHMIS. *Staff:* 26 full time, 4 part time. Annual turnover 2%. Average age 39.

Exam results In 1996, 50 pupils in fifth, 23 in upper sixth. *GCSE:* in 1995, 43% of fifth gained at least grade C in 8+ subjects; 24% in 5–7 subjects. *A-levels:* 45% upper sixth passed in 4+ subjects; 38% in 3; 7% in 2; and 10% in 1 subject. Average UCAS points 16.1 (including general studies 19.9).

University and college entrance 87% of 1995 sixth-form leavers went on to a degree course (13% after a gap year); others typically go on to further education or training, retake A-levels or into employment. Of those going on to university, 6% went to Oxbridge; 26% took courses in science and engineering, 3% in law, 26% in humanities and social sciences, 6% in art and design, 10% in vocational subjects eg nursing, animal care.
Curriculum GCSE and A-levels. 22 subjects at GCSE; 16 at A-level, including history of art and general studies. 20% take science A-levels; 25% arts/humanities; 55% both. *Vocational:* Work experience available; also RSA business spell test. *Computing facilities:* Econet system running Archimedes 3000s, and stand-alone machines in most departments. *Special provision:* Specialist teachers for both dyslexia and EFL. *Europe:* French and German offered at GCSE, AS and A-level. Regular exchanges to France and Germany. Number of students from European countries for short periods. Regularly participates in joint ventures with European schools for community service overseas.
The arts *Music:* Over 40% of pupils learn a musical instrument; instrumental exams can be taken. 7 musical groups including orchestra, choir, wind band. Some pupils achieve grade 8 distinction. *Drama and dance:* Drama offered. LAMDA exams may be taken. Many pupils involved in major school productions. *Art:* On average, 18 take GCSE, 13 A-level. Design, pottery also offered.
Sport, community service and clubs *Sport and physical activities:* Compulsory sports: rugby, soccer, cricket, tennis, swimming, athletics, netball, hockey, rounders, badminton, squash, volleyball; all optional to some extent in fifth and sixth form. County representatives at cricket, hockey, netball and riding. *Community service:* Pupils take bronze, silver and gold Duke of Edinburgh's Award. Community service compulsory for 1 term age 14, optional for other pupils. Conservation has a high profile (recently won a national Queen's Anniversary Award). *Clubs and societies:* Up to 15 clubs, eg film-making, table tennis, art, go-kart building, typing, clay-pigeon shooting, riding, electronics.
Uniform School uniform worn throughout.
Houses/prefects Competitive houses. Head boy/girl, prefects, head of house and house prefects, appointed by the Head and elected by the school.
Religion Attendance at religious worship compulsory.
Social Academic lectures, university visits, general knowledge competitions, outdoor expeditions joint with other schools. Annual French trip (forms 1–3), Round Square exchange students (Germany, Canada, America, South Africa and India) and international service projects. Pupils allowed to bring own bike/horse. Meals self-service. School shop. No tobacco/alcohol allowed.
Discipline Pupils failing to produce homework once could expect work to be re-done under supervision on a half-holiday; those caught smoking cannabis on the premises could expect expulsion.
Boarding 20% have own study bedrooms; 70% share with 1–3 others; 10% in dormitories of 6+. Single sex houses of 13–35, same as competitive houses. Resident qualified nurse. Pupils can provide and cook own food. 3 weekend exeats a term plus 2 days. Visits to the local town allowed twice a week for all ages – younger ones only in a group.
Alumni association is run by Mr M Roberts, Flat B, 4 Parkhills Road, Bury, Lancashire.

• ABINGDON

Abingdon School, Abingdon, Oxfordshire OX14 1DE. Tel 01235 521563, Fax 01235 536449
• Pupils 760 • Boys 11–18 (Day/Board/Weekly) • Girls None • Upper sixth 112 • Termly fees £1754 (Day) £3283 (Board/Weekly) • HMC • Enquiries/application to the Admissions Secretary

What it's like

Founded in 1256, re-endowed in 1563, it was rebuilt on its present site in 1870. This is a most agreeable estate of some 35 acres of grounds and handsome buildings, which is a few hundred yards from the centre of the attractive market town of Abingdon and six miles from Oxford. Over the past 50 years there has been steady expansion, most recently adding a new sixth form and teaching centre. Facilites are now good and boarding accommodation comfortable (weekly boarding is a deliberate policy). The school is

Anglican by tradition and the chapel is a focus of its life. It has the reputation of being a versatile school which provides a successful all-round education. A staff:pupil ratio of 1:11 ensures high academic standards and results are excellent. Nearly all leavers proceed to degree courses, including many to Oxbridge. Music is particularly strong. A very large number of pupils learn a musical instrument; orchestras and choirs have vigorous support, as do other musical groups. Drama is also pretty strong. Facilities for sports and games are first rate. High standards are attained, with a fair number of representatives at county level and rowing at a national standard. Numerous clubs and societies exist. An enterprising variety of overseas trips is organised annually. The Young Enterprise Scheme is well supported; the CCF works in conjunction with community services and the Duke of Edinburgh's Award Scheme. There are close connections with the local community and with The Mercers' Company.

School profile

Pupils Age range 11–18; 760 boys (630 day, 130 boarding). Main entry ages 11, 13 and into sixth. 4% are children of former pupils. Pupils from a variety of prep schools including the Dragon School, Moulsford, Josca's, New College School, Christ Church, Brockhurst, St Hugh's, Pinewood. *State school entry:* 65% main intake, 5 pa to sixth form.

Entrance Common Entrance and own exam used. No special skills or religious requirements. Lunches and text books are included in the fees; extras £10 average. 20 pa assisted places. 15 pa means-tested scholarships, including music and technology, values vary up to full fees.

Parents 30+% are doctors, lawyers etc; 35+% in industry/commerce; 17% academics. 80% live within 30 miles, under 10% live overseas.

Head and staff *Headmaster:* Michael St John Parker, in post for 21 years. Educated at Stamford and Cambridge (history). Previously Head of History at Winchester and Schoolmaster Student at Christ Church, Oxford. Also Council Member Hansard Society. *Publications:* The British Revolution – Social and Economic History 1750–1970 (1972). *Staff:* 63 full time, 11 part time plus 28 music. Annual turnover 8%. Average age 40.

Exam results In 1995, 141 pupils in fifth, 117 in upper sixth. *GCSE:* In 1995, 132 upper fifth gained at least grade C in 8+ subjects; 9 in 6–7 subjects. *A-levels:* 26 upper sixth passed in 4+ subjects; 83 in 3; 6 in 2; and 1 in 1 subject. Average UCAS points 25.3.

University and college entrance 99% of sixth-form leavers go on to a degree course (10% after a gap year), 22% to Oxbridge; 50% took courses in medicine, science and engineering, 45% in humanities, social sciences and art, 5% in vocational subjects.

Curriculum GCSE, AS and A-levels. 27 subjects offered, including Greek but no A-level general studies; 7 to AS-level. 34% take science A-levels; 30% arts/humanities; 46% both. *Vocational:* Work experience available. *Computing facilities:* Apple Macintoshes and laser printers in IT centre and classrooms. Use of computers across curriculum in music, technology, modern languages etc. *Special provision:* Ad hoc arrangements for dyslexics. Additional English for non-native English speakers. *Europe:* French, German and Russian offered to GCSE, AS and A-level; also GCSE Spanish. 30% take French GCSE early; Russian is offered one year, German the next. Regular exchanges to France, Russia and Germany. Satellite link for French and German TV programmes and computer link with French schools.

The arts *Music:* 60% of pupils learn a musical instrument; instrumental exams can be taken. Some 20+ musical groups including 3 orchestras, 5 bands, 2 choirs, choral society, flute, cello, clarinet, brass ensembles, jazz, various chamber groups. Winners of Daily Telegraph Jazz Competition; regional finalists in National Chamber Music Competition; finalist in National Choirboy of the Year Competition; member of National Jazz Youth Orchestra; 25 boys in regional youth orchestra. *Drama and dance:* Drama offered. GCSE and A-level drama may be taken. Some pupils in school and house/other productions. *Art:* On average, 28 take GCSE, 3 AS-level, 8 A-level. Design, pottery also offered. On average, 4 pupils a year accepted for art school; 1 pupil commissioned to do 6ft ceramic sculpture for local art centre.

Sport, community service and clubs *Sport and physical activities:* Compulsory sports: rugby, hockey, cricket (11–13). *Optional:* rowing, tennis, cross-country, athletics, badminton, table tennis, fencing, swimming, sailing, golf, rugby fives, squash, shoot-

ing. Rugby, 6 county U16 representatives, 4 U19, 1 regional U16; hockey, 1 county U14, 2 county U18, 1 regional U18; cricket, several county players at various age groups, 1 regional U15; tennis, 4 county U15 reps, winners Clark Cup 1995, runners-up Thames Bowl; rowing, 1st VIII in national top ten, 9 internationals last year, 8 Great Britain trialists 1994. *Community service:* Pupils take bronze, silver and gold Duke of Edinburgh's Award. CCF and community service optional. *Clubs and societies:* Up to 30 clubs, eg chess, debating, electronics, brewing, politics, bridge, literary, Young Enterprise Scheme.
Uniform Simple school uniform worn throughout.
Houses/prefects Moderately competitive houses. Head boy, prefects, head of house and house prefects.
Religion Attendance at religious worship compulsory (unless dispensation granted before entry).
Social Joint activities with other schools include debates, drama productions (local girls' schools), careers evenings, choral work, joint Young Enterprise Companies; Abingdon inter-sixth form society; some joint sixth form teaching with neighbouring girls' school. Annual cultural visits to eg Turkey, Egypt, Italy; ski trips; language exchanges to Russia, Germany and France. Pupils allowed to bring own bike, sometimes car/motorbike. Meals occasionally formal, usually self-service. School shop. No tobacco/alcohol allowed.
Discipline Response to misdemeanours depends on age and past record but poor work is penalised, separately, in a special work detention. Major, ie law-breaking, offences (drugs, theft) punished by expulsion.
Boarding 5% have own study bedrooms; 75% share with 1–3 others. 20% in dormitories of 6+. Houses of 10–50, same as competitive houses. Resident qualified nurse; doctor attends frequently. Pupils can provide and cook own food. Weekly boarders can stay at weekends. Visits to the local town allowed at housemaster's discretion.
Alumni association is run by The Secretary, The Old Abingdonian Club, c/o the school.
Former pupils Robert Hayward, Francis Maude, Sir George Sinclair (former MPs); Ben Macintyre (Times journalist); Tom Kempinski (playwright); Robin Kermode, Tom Hollander (actors); Radiohead (pop group); Tim Parker (Kenwood); Matthew Harding (Benfield Assurance).

• ACKWORTH

Ackworth School, Ackworth, Pontefract, West Yorkshire WF7 7LT. Tel 01977 611401, Fax 01977 616225

• Pupils 435 • Boys 7–18 (Day/Board) • Girls 7–18 (Day/Board) • Upper sixth 46 • Termly fees £1772 (Day) £3111. (Board) • HMC, SHMIS, Quaker • Enquiries/application to the Head

What it's like

Founded in 1779 in the village of Ackworth (4 miles from Pontefract). It has an estate of some 300 acres, including a magnificent Grade I listed Georgian block, spacious gardens and playing fields. There are many modern facilities and new buildings including a sports hall, music centre and computer centre. Through a school council, the pupils can make their views felt and there are strong bonds with the local community. It is a Quaker foundation and the Quaker Christian ethos, with its emphasis on quiet reflection and the search for God within oneself and within others, lies at the heart of the school. It was founded as a co-educational school; a family atmosphere prevails and this is much encouraged. Academic standards are high and results good; the majority of sixth-form leavers go on to degree courses. A good range of activities and sports (particularly strong in hockey). Music is a particular strength. Very active involvement in the Duke of Edinburgh Award Scheme.

School profile

Pupils Total age range 7–18; 435 pupils, 315 day (143 boys, 172 girls), 120 boarding (61 boys, 59 girls). Senior department 11–18, 380 pupils (181 boys, 199 girls). Main entry ages, 7, 11, 13 and into sixth. Approx 10% are children of former pupils. *State school entry:* 60% senior intake, plus 10% to sixth.

Entrance Own entrance exam and Common Entrance used. Keen on musical entrants. Parents are expected to buy some textbooks in the sixth form; few other extras. Assisted places available. Several scholarships/bursaries available (including music and art), up to 50% of full fees.
Parents 30% in professions; 30% in industry/commerce. 10+% live overseas.
Head and staff *Head:* Martin Dickinson, in post since 1995. Educated in York and at Cambridge University (history). Previously Acting Head of Hinchingbrooke School, Huntingdon. *Staff:* 37 full time, 11 part time, 18 music staff. Annual turnover 5%. Average age 40.
Exam results In 1995, 79 pupils in upper fifth, 30 in upper sixth. *GCSE:* on average, 59% upper fifth gain at least grade C in 8+ subjects; 34% in 5–7 subjects. *A-levels:* 9 upper sixth pass in 4+ subjects; 14 in 3; 3 in 2; and 3 in 1 subject. Average UCAS points 15.9.
University and college entrance 95% of 1995 sixth-form leavers went on to a degree course (15% after a gap year); others typically go on to employment, either overseas or in family businesses. Of those going on to university, 8% went to Oxbridge; 10% took courses in medicine, dentistry and veterinary science, 50% in science and engineering, 10% in law, 15% in humanities and social sciences, 10% in art and design, 5% in vocational subjects eg physiotherapy, architecture.
Curriculum GCSE and A-levels. 17 subjects offered, including A-level business studies, general studies and economics. 34% take science A-levels; 59% arts/humanities; 7% both. *Vocational:* Work experience available for all fifth year. *Computing facilities:* 24 RM Nimbus computers. *Special provision:* Individual help (1 hour/week) available from specialist EFL teachers. *Europe:* French and German offered to GCSE and A-level; GCSE Spanish and Italian for keen linguists in the sixth. Regular visits to France and Germany. Each year, German 16-year olds in the school.
The arts (Pupils aged 11 and over) *Music:* Up to 50% of pupils learn a musical instrument; instrumental exams can be taken. Some 8 musical groups including orchestra, choir, chamber choir, brass and concert bands, jazz and pop groups. *Drama and dance:* Drama offered. Some pupils are involved in school productions and house/other productions. *Art:* On average, 30 take GCSE, 6 A-level. Design, pottery, textiles, fabric printing, photography also offered.
Sport, community service and clubs (Pupils aged 11 and over) *Sport and physical activities:* Compulsory sports: football, hockey, netball, cricket, cross-country, rounders, swimming. Optional sports: badminton, squash, basketball etc. 1 England hockey player, 2 county players. *Community service:* Pupils take bronze, silver and gold Duke of Edinburgh's Award – includes community service. D of E is very strong with an average of 15–20 gold each year, over 40 doing bronze. *Clubs and societies:* Over 30 clubs, eg aeromodelling, aerobics, Amnesty, gymnastics, canoeing, beekeeping, squash, tae-kwan-do, riding for the disabled etc.
Uniform School uniform worn, adapted for sixth formers.
Houses/prefects Competitive houses for sport, music and drama. No prefects, all sixth formers share duties. Head and deputy boy and girl, heads of houses, appointed by the Head and house staff after consultation with sixth formers. School Council.
Religion Religious worship is encouraged. All boarders attend Meeting for Worship in the manner of the Society of Friends but the school accepts and welcomes staff and pupils of other denominations and faiths and seeks to support their commitment.
Social Membership of Riding for Disabled Association, Mencap swimming and of local Music Society; involved in recycling and local crime prevention. Skiing and trips to cultural centres abroad. Travel scholarships are awarded to 15 sixth formers per year. Pupils encouraged to bring bike to school; day pupils bring cars with special permission. School shop.
Discipline Each case looked at on its own merits. Slack work or no homework would result in detention; misbehaviour at mealtime would result in clearing up afterwards. Alcohol and tobacco are not tolerated; anyone using drugs could expect to be expelled. The aim is to encourage self-discipline, and to 'talk through' a problem with a pupil and concerned adults.
Boarding Sixth formers in small bedrooms and also have single or double studies. Fifth formers can study in houses or the extensive library. Single-sex houses, divided by age group. Resident qualified medical staff. Central dining rooms. Pupils can provide and

cook own snacks. Weekend leave by arrangement with house staff. Visits to the local town allowed.
Alumni association is run by Keith Daniel, The General Secretary, Ackworth Old Scholars Association, Daleswater Cottage, 4 Derwent Court, Silsden, Keighley, W. Yorks.
Former pupils John Bright, Richard Denby (former President, The Law Society); Prime Minister of Nepal; Basil Bunting (poet); numerous academics.

• ADCOTE

Adcote School for Girls, Little Ness, Near Shrewsbury, Shropshire SY4 2JY. Tel 01939 260202, Fax 01939 261300

• Pupils 120 • Boys None • Girls 5–18 (Day/Board/Weekly) • Upper sixth 9 • Termly fees £950–£1700 (Day) £2420–£3065 (Board) £2135–£2780 (Weekly) • GSA • Enquiries/application to the Headmistress

What it's like

Founded in 1907, it occupies a neo-Tudor Grade I listed building (1879) in a glorious landscaped parkland with a view to the Briedden and south Shropshire hills; a comfortable and well-equipped establishment. A proportion of pupils' parents are on overseas contracts or serving abroad and full travel arrangements are made for such pupils. It also welcomes a few foreign girls. A very small school and a friendly and family atmosphere prevails. It gives a sound academic education and results are good. A wide range of extra-curricular activities are offered in a disciplined and caring community.

School profile

Pupils Total age range 5–18; 120 girls, 70 day, 50 boarding. Senior department 11–18, 94 girls. Main entry ages 5–14 and into sixth.
Entrance Admission by school's own day of assessment. No special skills or religious requirements although school is Anglican. Parents expected to buy textbooks for A-level pupils; other extras vary. Scholarships/bursaries available for sixth form and children from service families.
Head and staff *Headmistress:* Mrs Susan B Cecchet, in post for 16 years. Educated at Kings Norton Grammar, Birmingham, and at Birmingham University (physics) and Cambridge (education). Previously taught physics at Malvern (Girls), Greenmore College, St Agnes Grammar and Sir James Henderson (Milan). Lecturer at Portsmouth College of Education; Research assistant at Nuclear Physics Department, Oxford. *Staff:* 9 full time, 13 part time.
Exam results On average, 15 pupils in upper fifth, 9 in upper sixth. *GCSE:* On average, 46% upper fifth gain at least grade C in 8 subjects; 23% in 5–8; 31% in 1–4 subjects. *A-levels:* all upper sixth usually pass in 3 subjects. Average UCAS points 18.0
University and college entrance 90% of 1995 sixth form leavers went on to a degree course; others typically go on to non-degree courses or straight on to careeers.
Curriculum GCSE and A-levels. 16 subjects offered to GCSE; 12 to A-level. *Vocational:* Work experience available; also RSA qualifications in IT. *Computing facilities:* Curriculum subject and IT club. *Special provision:* Extra specialist teaching available for dyslexics and EFL. *Europe:* French (compulsory age 11-13) and German offered to GCSE, AS and A-level. Regular exchanges to France and Germany. Several European pupils enrolled in school.
The arts (Pupils aged 11 and over) *Music:* Up to 50% of pupils learn a musical instrument; instrumental exams can be taken. Musical groups include school choir; girls also sing with Shrewsbury School Choir and play with their big band and orchestra. *Drama and dance:* Drama and dance offered. GCSE dance, ESB exams etc may be taken. Some pupils are involved in school productions. *Art:* On average, 50% take GCSE. Design, pottery, photography, screen printing also offered.
Sport, community service and clubs (Pupils aged 11 and over) *Sport and physical activities:* Compulsory sports: netball, lacrosse, tennis, rounders, athletics, gym, dance, cross country. BAGA, RLSS exams may be taken. *Community service:* Pupils take bronze and silver Duke of Edinburgh's Award. *Clubs and societies:* Up to 10 clubs, eg several sporting clubs, drama, motor vehicle, art, IT.

Uniform School uniform worn except in the sixth form.
Houses/prefects Competitive houses. Prefects, heads of house and head girl appointed by staff.
Religion School assembly compulsory. Boarders attend local C of E or RC church.
Social Music, drama, lectures (both careers and other) and discos with local HMC schools. Organised trips abroad (skiing and cultural); exchange systems with schools abroad. Pupils allowed to bring own car/bike to school. Some meals formal, others self service. School shop sells stationery, tuck.
Discipline Pupils failing to produce homework could expect to have to do it. School publishes its school rules, of behaviour/expectations and sanctions.
Boarding Sixth formers have single or twin study bedrooms, others in rooms of 3–6. School doctor attends. Central dining room. Weekly boarding available. Unaccompanied visits to the local town allowed for seniors. Sixth-form centre.

• AIGLON

Aiglon College, 1885 Chesières-Villars, Switzerland. Tel 41 25 35 27 21, Fax 41 25 35 28 11 • Pupils 285 • Boys 11–18 (Day/Board) • Girls 11–18 (Day/Board) • Upper sixth 45 • Termly fees SFr 9115–SFr 12,325 (Day) SFr 14,754–SFr 17,619 (Board) • HMC, Round Square, COBISEC, ECIS • Enquiries/application to the Head of Admissions

What it's like

Founded in 1949 by John Corlette, it occupies a spectacular position on a sheltered plateau at 4000 ft in the Swiss Alps in the French-speaking village of Chesières-Villars. From here it looks across the Rhône Valley towards the Dents du Midi and Mont Blanc. It is an HMC school and a member of the Round Square. Much of the daily life revolves around the houses which are designed as family units of staff and pupils within the larger community. Recent building has a provided new science laboratories, a computer centre and a music department with a recording studio. In adddition there are language labs, an extended art school and three libraries. Aiglon is a multi-faith community, but acknowledges its allegiance to Christianity. All Christians are required to attend services in the local Anglican or Catholic churches. Unusually, a school day begins with meditation (the equivalent of assembly) and an address of spiritual import. It has a strong pastoral care system. A large staff permits a staff:pupil ratio of about 1:6. The students are from international backgrounds, representing over 45 nationalities. They study for GCSEs and A-levels as well as US American College Board exams. Academic results are very good and a very high proportion of leavers goes on to university. Music, drama and art are vigorously supported and there is a wide range of extra-curricular activities (some 20+ societies, clubs, options). Sports and games are well catered for, with a variety of sporting surfaces and a gym and access to swimming pools, skating rink, a sports centre and extensive skislopes. Cultural excursions are arranged. There is a considerable commitment to the Duke of Edinburgh's Award scheme and the whole school is concerned with community services, within the school, the community and with international service projects on all continents.

School profile

Pupils Age range 11–18; 285 pupils, 10 day (8 boys, 2 girls), 275 boarding (157 boys, 118 girls). Main entry is 11, 14 and a few into the sixth.
Entrance Common Entrance and own entrance exam used. No special skills or religious requirements. Termly fixed charge SFr 1935–SFr 2900 (textbooks, ski passes, laundry etc) included in fees. Some scholarships available, including for music, up to £12,000.
Parents 15+% in industry/commerce. More than 60% live overseas.
Head and staff *Headmaster:* Richard McDonald, 3 years in post. Educated at Christ's Hospital and Oxford (French and German). Previously Senior Housemaster at Christ's Hospital. *Staff:* 51 full time, 15 part time. Annual turnover, 5%.
Exam results *GCSE:* In 1995, 52 in upper fifth, of whom 14 gained at least grade C in 8+ subjects; 24 in 5–7 subjects. *A-levels:* 45 in upper sixth, of whom 9 passed in 4 subjects; 22 in 3; 8 in 2 subjects. Average UCAS points 24.7.
University and college entrance Almost all 1995 sixth-form leavers went on to degree courses, mostly to universities in North America or Europe; these include Oxford, St

Andrew's, Bristol, Exeter, Kent, Boston, Brown, Pennsylvania and Georgetown.
Curriculum GCSE and A-levels offered; also IB French and geography, SAT and EFL. A-Level subjects include further maths, economics, and theatre studies. School policy is for all GCSE and most A-level candidates to take a mixture of science, language and arts/humanities subjects. *Computing facilities:* Network of Pentium multi-media PCs in computer centre and classrooms, including Internet access and e-mail; other machines in classrooms and boarding houses; pupils encouraged to use own portables. Desktop publishing in English department, Macintosh graphics in art. Use of IT encouraged in all subjects. Specialist computer courses taught age 11–15. *Specialist provision:* Full-time LD specialist for diagnosis and support work. Special English school for intensive EFL teaching; 'Bridge' programme for EFL support in main school. *Europe:* French (compulsory from age 11–16), German and Spanish offered to GCSE and A-level; also French IB. Over 75% pupils take GCSE in more than one language.
The arts *Music:* Up to 25% pupils learn a musical instrument; instrumental exams can be taken. 6+ musical groups – choirs, string ensemble, jazz/rock band, folk group and recorder consort. *Drama and dance:* Drama and dance offered; pupils may take GCSE drama. Some pupils involved in school and house/other productions. Most recent production was On Ne Badine Pas Avec l'Amour. *Art:* On average, 30 take GCSE, 8 A-level. A number of pupils each year go on to art schools in the UK or US.
Sport, community service and clubs *Sport and physical activities:* Compulsory: skiing, athletics, swimming, basketball, tennis; *Optional:* skating, dance, squash, rock climbing, volleyball, football. Teams successful in competition with other private schools; achievement in skiing outstanding. *Community service:* Pupils take bronze, silver and gold Duke of Edinburgh's Award. Community service compulsory for all ages within the school; optional within the community and overseas projects (India, Africa, Hungary etc.). School is heavily involved in international service projects. Every year at least 35 pupils participate in Round Square Conference Schemes and the school has its own projects involving aid to Somalia, Eastern Europe and other charities; a summer course for disadvantaged English children in care. *Clubs and societies:* Up to 30 clubs and all pupils take part in an Options programme of 20+ activities eg choir, cooking, film club, crafts, recycling, yoga, ballet.
Uniform School uniform worn for first 4 years; after that, only for special occasions.
Houses/prefects Competitive houses. Head boy and girl (School Guardians), house prefects and house captains – appointed by Headmaster and Housemasters. School Council.
Religion Religious worship compulsory unless there are good reasons.
Social Cultural expeditions each autumn to places of interest in Europe; Round Square Conference projects abroad and exchanges with other RSC schools. Meals formal. School shop. No alcohol/tobacco allowed.
Discipline Pupils failing to produce homework once might expect a short detention with written work to complete; any pupil caught taking drugs will be expelled immediately.
Boarding 7% have own study bedrooms; others share with 1–4. Single-sex houses of approx 45. Resident qualified nurse; doctors in village. Pupils allowed to provide own snacks. Two exeats (1½ days) termly. Visits to the village allowed at any age twice a week.

• ALBYN

Albyn School for Girls, 17/23 Queens Road, Aberdeen AB9 2PA. Tel 01224 322408, Fax 01224 209173

• Pupils 432 • Boys 2½–5 only (Day) • Girls 2½–18 (Day) • Upper sixth 30 • Termly fees £1308 (Day) • HAS • Enquiries/application to the Head Mistress

What it's like

Founded in 1867, it was privately owned until 1949 when it passed to the company which now controls it. It comprises four large, handsome, granite houses in the residential west end of Aberdeen which lie in pleasant grounds. It combines nursery and preparatory departments. There have been substantial additions to the main buildings in recent years and it is now a well-equipped establishment. Academic standards are high and results are good. Most sixth formers proceed to degree courses each year. There is plentiful musical activity; drama and arts are well supported. A standard range of sports and games is available and good standards are achieved (several representatives at county level). Clubs and societies are well catered for and the school participates in the Duke of Edinburgh's Award Scheme.

School profile

Pupils Total age range 2½–18; 432 day pupils (23 boys, 409 girls). Senior department 12–18, 250 girls. Main entry ages 5, 10, 12 and into fifth.
Entrance Own entrance exam used. No special skills or religious requirements. Parents expected to buy textbooks; other extras variable. 22 pa assisted places. Some scholarships available.
Head and staff *Headmistress:* Miss Norma Smith, in post for 14 years. Educated at George Watson's Ladies College, and Edinburgh University (chemistry). Previously Assistant Head Teacher (guidance) at Berwickshire High School, Head of Chemistry and Assistant Housemistress at Gordonstoun, Head of Chemistry at St Christopher's (Letchworth) and Assistant Teacher at St Leonard's (St Andrews). Also JP; Outdoors Activities Adviser, Berwickshire Girl Guides; Walking Consultant, Scottish Girl Guides; currently Young Leader Adviser, Aberdeen City Guides. *Staff:* 31 full time, 10 part time. Annual turnover 2–4%.
Exam results In 1995, 43 in S-grade year (SIV); 44 in Higher year (UV); 30 in CSYS year (SVI). *S-grade:* In 1995, 93% SIV pupils passed with grade 3 or above in 5-8 subjects (school policy to take 8 subjects maximum). *Highers:* 14 passed in 5 subjects; 22 in 3; 6 in 1 subject.
University and college entrance 91% of 1995 sixth-form leavers went on to a degree course (6% after a gap year); others typically go on to HND courses or nursing. Of those going on to university, 40% took courses in science, engineering and medicine, 30% in humanities and social sciences, 10% in art and architecture, 13% in business studies, 7% in dance.
Curriculum S-grade, Highers, CSYS. *Computing facilities:* New computer lab. Scotvec modules available. *Special provision:* Some special arrangements for dyslexic pupils. *Europe:* French (taught from age 8) and German offered at S-grade, Higher and CSYS. Often European pupils whose parents are working in Aberdeen.
The arts (Pupils aged 11 and over) *Music:* Instrumental exams can be taken. Some 7 musical groups including orchestra, choir, wind band, recorder groups. *Drama and dance:* Majority of pupils are involved in school productions. Major school production eg The Boyfriend; pupils frequently participate in productions coming to Aberdeen. *Art:* On average, 23 take S-grade, 18 Higher, 4 CSYS.
Sport, community service and clubs (Pupils aged 11 and over) *Sport and physical activities:* Compulsory (at certain ages): gymnastics, dance, swimming, hockey, basketball, netball, tennis, athletics, volleyball, badminton, fitness. *Optional:* aerobics, trampolining, lacrosse, dance, dry skiing. S-grade and RLSS exams may be taken. National representative at hockey and badminton; district/county, 2 hockey representatives, 1 tennis, 1 swimming, 2 athletics, 2 badminton. *Community service:* Pupils take bronze, silver and gold Duke of Edinburgh's Award. Community service optional. *Clubs and societies:* Clubs include debating, musical and sports.
Uniform School uniform worn throughout.
Houses/prefects Competitive houses. Prefects, head girl, head of house and house prefects – elected by the school. School Council.
Social Debates with other local schools. Some organised trips abroad. Meals self service. No tobacco/alcohol allowed.
Alumni association is run by Mrs F Clark, c/o the School.

• ALDENHAM

Aldenham School, Elstree, Hertfordshire WD6 3AJ. Tel 01923 858122, Fax 01923 854410
• Pupils 370 • Boys 11–18 (Day/Board/Weekly) • Girls 16–18 (Day/Board/Weekly) • Upper sixth 56 • Termly fees £1665–£2620 (Day) £2665–£3820 (Board) £3110 (Dayboarders) • HMC
• Enquiries/application to the Headmaster

What it's like

The school was founded in 1597 by Richard Platt, a brewer. It occupies its original site, which has since been extended to 135 acres of grounds and farm land, in the Hertfordshire green belt 15 miles from London. The school has firm ties with the Worshipful Company of Brewers. The Elizabethan School was demolished in 1825 and the buildings that replaced it have been upgraded and added to constantly so as to maintain up-to-date, fully-equipped facilities in an historic framework. It is a Christian foundation and Christian ideals are evident in its structure and life but all denominations are welcome. A small school with a strong house structure for both boarders and day pupils, it enjoys a family atmosphere and has a reputation as a close-knit and supportive community. The school seeks the all-round development of its pupils and sets high standards of achievement and mutual responsibility and participation in an extensive games and activities programme. The staff:pupil ratio is about 1:9, with no classes bigger than 20.

School profile

Pupils Age range 11–18; 370 pupils; 267 day (253 boys, 14 girls), 100 boarding (90 boys, 10 girls). Senior department 13–18, 300 pupils (286 boys, 14 girls). Main entry ages 11 and 13 (boys) and into sixth (boys and girls). Approx 5% are children of former pupils. *State school entry:* 50% intake at 11.

Entrance Common Entrance (at 13) and own entrance test used (at 11 and 16) plus interview and school reports. 5 pa assisted places. 9 pa scholarships (for art, music, sport, technology and academic).

Parents 15+% are doctors, lawyers, etc; 35+% in industry or commerce. 80+% live within 30 miles; 10+% live overseas.

Head and staff *Headmaster:* Stephen Borthwick, in post since 1994. Educated at universities of Bangor and Cambridge. Previously Deputy Head at Bishop's Stortford College, Head of Physics and Technology at Marlborough College and teacher at Rugby and Bloxham. *Staff:* 40 full time, 2 part time. Annual turnover 10%. Average age 39.

Exam results In 1995, 66 pupils in fifth, 56 in upper sixth. *GCSE:* In 1995, 60% in fifth gained at least grade C in 8+ subjects; 27% in 5–7; and 13% in 1–4 subjects. *A-levels:* 7% upper sixth passed in 4+ subjects, 52% in 3; 27% in 2; and 8% in 1 subject. Average UCAS points 13.0.

University and college entrance 85% of 1995 sixth-form leavers went on to a degree course (25% after a gap year); others typically go on to art, drama or music colleges, or into careers eg retailing, small businesses. Of those going on to university, 5% went to Oxbridge; 5% took courses in medicine, dentistry and veterinary science, 15% in science and engineering, 5% in law, 65% in humanities and social sciences, 5% in art and design.

Curriculum GCSE and A-levels. 19 GCSE subjects offered; 21 at A-level, including sports science. 20% take science A-levels; 40% arts/humanities; 40% both. *Vocational:* European UK or work experience compulsory. *Computing facilities:* Lab with desktop facilities. *Special provision:* Extra help available, often one-to-one; dyslexic and EFL tuition available. *Europe:* French (compulsory), German and Spanish offered to GCSE and A-level. Regular exchanges to France and Germany and work experience arranged for lower sixth in France, Germany and Spain.

The arts *Music:* Over 30% of pupils learn a musical instrument. Some 6 musical groups including orchestra, choir, brass, wind, string quartet. *Drama and dance:* all pupils are involved in school and house/other productions. *Art:* On average, 21 take GCSE, 10 A-level. Design, pottery, textiles, photography, sculpture also offered. Regular successes to foundation courses and art school.

Sport, community service and clubs *Sport and physical activities:* Compulsory sports: soccer, hockey, cricket, athletics. Optional: fives, squash, cross-country, badminton, basketball, swimming, fencing, judo, sailing, tennis, netball, lacrosse, rounders. County and regional representatives in all main sports; England representatives at cricket and football, 3 in past 4 years. *Community service:* Pupils take bronze, silver and gold Duke of Edinburgh's Award; 3–4 golds on average each year. Community service optional at age 16. *Clubs and societies:* Up to 15 clubs, eg art, computing, motor, chess, bridge, history, law, philosophy, debating.

Uniform School uniform (unobtrusive) worn throughout.

Houses/prefects Houses form pastoral and social structure (3 boarding, 3 day and junior house for 11–12 year olds). School prefects appointed by the Headmaster; house prefects within the house.

Religion Compulsory framework of religious worship and teaching supplemented by a strong programme of voluntary worship. Non-Christians encouraged in their own religion outside the compulsory framework.
Social Involvement in local competitions, joint events etc with local schools. Organised trips abroad and exchange systems eg skiing, mountaineering, sailing, geography, language (recent expedition to Himalayas). Upper sixth day pupils allowed to bring own car. Meals self-service. School shop. No tobacco allowed; sixth-form bar for over 17s.
Discipline Pupils failing to produce homework once might expect to be placed in detention and reported to tutor/housemaster; any involvement in illegal drugs is likely to lead to expulsion.
Boarding Pupils in fifth and sixth have studies, some have study bedrooms. Resident qualified nurse. Central dining room. Pupils can provide and cook some food. Very flexible boarding/weekly boarding arrangements and pupils can return home every weekend. Dayboarders are members of boarding houses and leave for home at 9 pm each evening.
Alumni association is run by Secretary, R C Wood, c/o the school.
Former pupils Bishops of Winchester and Exeter; Lord Justice Kerr; Field Marshal Sir Richard Vincent; N Durden-Smith; Sir Denys Roberts.

• ALICE OTTLEY

The Alice Ottley School, Britannia House, Upper Tything, Worcester WR1 1HW. Tel 01905 27061
• Pupils 719 • Boys None • Girls 3–18 (Day) • Upper sixth 69 • Termly fees £1595 (Day) • GSA
• Enquiries/application to Admissions Secretary

What it's like

Founded in 1883 as the Worcester High School for Girls and renamed in 1914 after its first Headmistress. It has a fine site in the middle of the cathedral city. The main building is a splendid Georgian mansion, in delightful grounds. New buildings have been added steadily over the last hundred years, and the school is now well equipped with two libraries, a technology suite, performing arts studio and a sixth form centre. It adheres to Church of England traditions, but is ecumenical in spirit and practice. The junior school is nearby. Academic standards are high and results are very good. Almost all sixth formers go on to degree courses, including Oxbridge. Music and drama are strongly supported and half the senior girls have individual tuition in instruments. There are two orchestras, smaller instrumental groups and three choirs. A wide range of drama is presented each year, often in conjunction with the neighbouring boys' school. There are good facilities for a standard range of sports and games; levels of performance are high, especially in lacrosse (a lot of representatives at county and national level) and athletics. There is a plentiful variety of extra-curricular activities (including archery and judo). Many girls take part successfully in the Duke of Edinburgh's Award Scheme. There are regular theatre visits to Stratford, Birmingham and London and much use is made of the cultural facilities of Worcester (particularly in connection with festivals and other events at the cathedral).

School profile

Pupils Total age range 3–18, 719 day girls. Senior department 10–18, 575 girls. Main entry ages 11 and into sixth. *State school entry:* 29% at 11, 1% to sixth.
Entrance Own entrance exam used. Assisted places and some scholarships available.
Head and staff *Headmistress:* Miss Christine Sibbit, in post for 10 years. Educated at Milham Ford School, Oxford, at Leicester University (geography, history and archaeology); Research Scholar at Leicester University. Previously Deputy Head at Tunbridge Wells Girls Grammar School, Head of Geography at Ashford Girls Grammar School (now Highworth School) and Assistant Geography Teacher at St Felix School. Also Field Officer at the Oxford City and County Museum; member of GSA membership and education committees. *Staff:* 56 full time, 20 part time.
Exam results In 1995, 92 pupils in upper fifth, 66 in upper sixth. *GCSE:* In 1995, 90 upper fifth gained at least grade C in 8+ subjects; 2 in 5–7 subjects. *A-levels:* 47 upper sixth passed in 4+ subjects; 12 in 3; and 6 in 2; 1 in 1 subject. Average UCAS points 22.7 (including general studies 28.0).

University and college entrance 95% of 1995 sixth-form leavers went on to a degree course (20% after a gap year); others typically go on to art and design foundation, nursing or other diploma courses. Of those going on to university, 10% went to Oxbridge; 17% took courses in medicine, dentistry and veterinary science, 7% in science and engineering, 12% in law, 57% in humanities and social sciences, 3% in art and design, 4% in vocational subjects eg agriculture.
Curriculum GCSE and A-levels. 22 subjects offered, including A-level general studies. 17% take science A-levels; 59% arts/humanities; 24% both. *Vocational:* Work experience available; also RSA stages 1 and 2 IT. *Computing facilities:* Archimedes in computer room, technology suite, science laboratories, home economics area, sixth-form centre, lecture theatre; Amstrad in careers room. *Special provision:* Extra coaching is available. *Europe:* French, German and Spanish offered at GCSE and A-level; also AS-level French and Spanish and French for all non-linguists in the sixth-form. Regular exchanges to France.
The arts (Pupils aged 11 and over) *Music:* Over 40% of pupils learn a musical instrument; instrumental exams can be taken. Some 15 musical groups including 3 orchestras, 5 choirs, 2 recorder groups, 2 string groups. School string quartet regional semi-finalist in Schools' Chamber Music Competition; all choirs have gained first place in local music festivals. *Drama and dance:* Drama offered. GCSE drama, ESB, LAMDA exams may be taken. Some pupils are involved in school and house/other productions. 4 girls gained distinction in ESB certificate of language arts. *Art:* On average, 35 take GCSE, 3 AS-level, 10 A-level. Textiles also offered.
Sport, community service and clubs (Pupils aged 11 and over) *Sport and physical activities:* Compulsory sports (at different ages): dance, gymnastics, swimming, rounders, lacrosse, netball, tennis, athletics, badminton. Optional: cross-country, volleyball, basketball, hockey, trampolining, cricket. Sixth form only: weights, keep fit/aerobics. BAGA, RLSS exams, trampolining awards may be taken. County, regional and national representatives in cross-country, lacrosse, tennis and athletics; county representatives in netball. *Community service:* Pupils take bronze, silver and gold Duke of Edinburgh's Award; expedition to Mauritius as part of gold award. Community service optional; includes visiting and helping at primary schools, nurseries, nursing homes and homes for elderly, mentally and physically handicapped. *Clubs and societies:* Up to 30 clubs, eg archery, gym, computing, drama, music, Young Enterprise, judo, quiz, BAYS, photography, sports.
Uniform School uniform worn except in the sixth.
Houses/prefects Competitive houses. Prefects, head girl, head of house and house prefects elected by sixth-form and staff.
Religion Attendance at religious worship not compulsory.
Social Joint drama productions, concerts, debates with Worcester Royal Grammar School. Exchange with school in Provence, French exchange to Nantes. Pupils allowed to bring own car/bike to school but not on the premises. Meals formal. No tobacco/alcohol allowed.
Discipline Pupils failing to produce homework once might expect to report after assembly to the Deputy Headmistress; those caught smoking cannabis on the premises might expect immediate suspension followed by expulsion.

• ALLEYN'S

Alleyn's School, Townley Road, Dulwich, London SE22 8SU. Tel 0181 693 3422
• Pupils 928 • Boys 11–18 (Day) • Girls 11–18 (Day) • Upper sixth 125 • Termly fees £1880 (Day) • HMC • Enquiries/application to the Headmaster

What it's like

Founded in 1619, endowed by Edward Alleyn the Elizabethan actor-manager. It stands in 26 acres of fine grounds and playing fields in Dulwich. The main buildings date from 1887 and recent additions include a sports hall, swimming pool and a well-equipped music school. The facilities are being systematically upgraded with immediate plans for a new IT centre, astroturf all-weather pitch and a theatre. The junior school is on the same site. The spacious grounds allow a full range of sporting activities within the school boundaries. Academically and intellectually, it is one of the foremost in southern

England; a friendly and purposeful school providing a first-rate traditional education. Results are very good and almost all pupils go on to degree courses, including Oxbridge. Originally a boys' school, it has twenty years' experience of admitting girls and a strong commitment to co-education. It is a C of E foundation but assemblies are ecumenical in character. Particular attention is given to pupils with individual needs, including those with slight physical handicaps. A very strong and active music school; it is also good in drama (the National Youth Theatre was developed at the school) and in art. It is highly regarded in the locality where it enjoys vigorous support.

School profile

Pupils Age range 11–18; 928 day pupils, 463 boys, 465 girls. Main entry ages 11, 13 and into sixth. Approx 10% are children of former pupils. Own junior school (tel 0181 693 3457). *State school entry:* 80% main intake, plus 20% to sixth.
Entrance Own entrance exam used. No special skills or religious requirements. Parents not expected to buy textbooks. 25 pa assisted places at 11; 5 at 13; and 5 at 16. 12 scholarships pa, up to half fees.
Head and staff *Headmaster:* Dr Colin H R Niven, appointed in 1992. Educated at Dulwich and Cambridge (modern languages). Previously Principal at St George's English School, Rome, and the Island School, Hong Kong, Head of Languages at Sherborne, and Housemaster at Fettes. Also member of Children's Panel, Edinburgh, and of the Chinese Heads Association and English Schools Foundation, Hong Kong; formerly Chairman European Division, HMC. *Staff:* 82 full time, 12 part time. Annual turnover 5–6%. Average age 38.
Exam results On average, 134 pupils in Year 11, 125 in Year 13. *GCSE:* On average, 92% of Year 11 gain at least grade C in 8+ subjects; 8% in 5-7 subjects. *A-level:* 17% of Year 13 pass in 4+ subjects; 65% in 3; 9% in 2 and 6% in 1 subject. Average UCAS points 23.6.
University and college entrance 94% of 1995 sixth-form leavers went on to a degree course (16% after a gap year); others typically go on to employment or retaking A-levels. Of those going on to university, 10% went to Oxbridge; 7% took courses in medicine, dentistry and veterinary science, 15% in science and engineering, 3% in law, 62% in humanities and social sciences, 8% in art and design, 8% in vocational subjects eg education, journalism, accountancy.
Curriculum GCSE and A-levels. 21 subjects offered at GCSE; 24 at A-level (all undertake an extension study in addition to A-levels). 40% take science A-levels; 56% arts/humanities; 25% both. *Vocational:* Work experience available. *Computing facilities:* Apple Macintosh in IT department, PCs in maths. *Europe:* French (compulsory for 3 years), German and Spanish offered at GCSE and A-level. Regular exchanges to France, Germany and Spain. European studies offered to sixth-form. Satellite TV for linguists.
The arts *Music:* Over 25% pupils learn a musical instrument; instrumental exams can be taken. Some 50 musical groups, including orchestras, choirs, wind bands, large number of chamber ensembles. Choirboy of the Year 1992–94; 1 pupil in National Youth Orchestra; pupils regularly accepted for music colleges. *Drama and dance:* A-level theatre studies available. 5 main productions a year; sixth-formers direct Bear Pit plays. Regular entrants to drama college and university drama courses. Pupils members of National Youth Theatre and National Youth Music Theatre. (National Youth Theatre developed here.) *Art:* On average, 60 take GCSE, 20 A-level. Design, pottery and photography also offered. Some 12 pa accepted to art college and art-related courses.
Sport, community service and clubs *Sport and physical activities:* Compulsory: football, hockey, cricket, athletics, tennis, swimming, trampolining, netball, gymnastics, rounders, cross-country. Options include: judo, fencing, keep fit, fives, aerobics, badminton, dance, fitness and weight training, water polo, basketball, table tennis, volleyball, squash, golf, horse riding. Regular county and regional representation (gym, swimming, hockey, cricket, badminton, fencing, basketball, fives, judo, netball, football, athletics, cross country). *Community service:* Pupils take bronze, silver and gold Duke of Edinburgh's Award. All pupils take D of E, CCF or community service for 1 year. *Clubs and societies:* Include printing, choral, bridge, railway, Amnesty, Christian Union, ceramics, debating.
Uniform School uniform worn, except in Years 12 and 13.

Houses/prefects Competitive houses. Prefects, school captain and house captains appointed by the Headmaster in consultation with housemasters. School council.
Religion Assemblies broad Anglican; Jewish and Muslim parents may withdraw pupils.
Social Occasional joint careers conferences and debates with local schools. Regular organised holiday visits; exchanges with French, German and Spanish schools. Weekly visiting speakers for Upper School (sixth-form). Upper School allowed to bring own car/ bike/motorbike to school. Meals self service. No tobacco/alcohol allowed.
Discipline Detentions are given for bad work and bad behaviour; those caught in possession of illegal drugs on the premises can expect expulsion.
Alumni association, the Edward Alleyn Club, run by Dr Michael Sneary, c/o the school.
Former pupils Julian Glover; Simon Ward, John Stride, Ray Cooney (actors); Stuart Blanch, former Archbishop of York; C S Forester, V S Pritchett; (authors) Micky Stewart; Prof R V Jones.

• ALLINGTON MANOR

Allington Manor School, Allington Lane, Fair Oak, Eastleigh, Hampshire S05 7DE. Tel 01703 692621

• Pupils 10 • Boys 6–18 (Day/Board/Weekly) • Girls 6–18 (Day/Board/Weekly) • Termly fees Variable • Enquiries/application to the Director

What it's like

Established in 1978, this highly original school is located just outside Fair Oak in Hampshire, a few miles from Winchester. The accommodation is a handsome manor house in beautiful grounds and gardens of 7½ acres which contain a lake, open-air swimming pool, tennis court and playing field. A small farm has been developed as part of the school. It caters for up to 12 children (of both sexes), on a day, boarding or weekly boarding basis, who have 'failed' or who are having difficulties at home or at the school where they are residing. It operates on three main declared principles: firstly, to provide an education for children from 6 onwards who find it difficult to fit into an ordinary school. Secondly once a child has been accepted by the school, to avoid rejecting or dismissing the child whatever the difficulties in learning or behaviour (no child has ever been excluded; should a child be dismissed for any reason whatsoever, the school guarantees to refund the fee for the relevant term). And thirdly, to try to develop to the maximum in every child who is accepted, the willingness to succeed educationally, socially and emotionally; and to develop with co-operation the self-realisation and potential of each child.

The main purpose is to heal, repair or motivate children so that they may gain self-esteem which they frequently have lost as a result of experiences elsewhere. Many of the children have not been diagnosed for their problems. All are initially given intelligence tests. Academic work is assessed through standardised testing of reading, spelling and mathematics. There are also tests for dyslexia and dysgraphia, and for emotional and personality development. 23 therapeutic approaches to helping children placed with the centre have been developed. The ratio of teachers to pupils is very high and every effort is made to have one member of staff for every 5–6 children. Pupils work in groups of four or five. The curriculum covers standard primary and secondary education subjects including art and craft, cookery, carpentry and other practical courses to cater for individual interests and abilities; both City and Guilds and RSA courses are offered.

The school aims to provide a secure, non-competitive environment and a family atmosphere of love, affection and care to encourage learning and responsibility to self and others. Children are encouraged to discuss their problems and to learn to accept guidance and to help one another through individual and group therapy sessions. Also there is milieu therapy, behaviour modification techniques, therapeutic recreation and family counselling. There is no corporal punishment; children are restrained if they become aggressive, violent or self-destructive in their behaviour or hurt others. The emphasis is on rewarding good behaviour rather than punishing infringement of rules.

Leisure and sporting activities include swimming, football, cricket, rounders, volleyball, canoeing, riding. There are frequent educational outings. The small farm introduces children to animal husbandry and animals in general, and this is a form of therapy. It particularly benefits those from city areas. Pupils may go to the cinema and attend discos and functions in the local community.

Head Director: Dr Ludwig Lowenstein. In post since he founded the school in 1978. Educated at University of Western Australia and London University (Birkbeck and Institute of Psychiatry). Chartered Psychologist (BPS). Previously Chief Educational Psychologist at Hampshire County Council. Also Principal Psychologist, Southern England Psychological Services; Former Chairman, National Association of Gifted Children. European Council of International Schools (Associate Member).

• AMPLEFORTH

Ampleforth College, York YO6 4ER. Tel 01439 766000, Fax 01439 788330

• Pupils 538 • Boys 13–18 (Day/Board) • Girls None • Upper sixth 112 • Termly fees £2065–£3245 (Day) £4005 (Board) • HMC • Enquiries/application to the Admissions Office.

What it's like

Established at Ampleforth in 1802, the school adjoins the Benedictine monastery and abbey of St Laurence in a stretch of magnificent Yorkshire countryside a mile from the local village. The monastic community descended from the monks who, in 1608, founded a monastery at Dieulouard in Lorraine. The Headmaster and some of the teaching staff are monks. The main purpose is to educate Catholics in their faith and in all branches of learning. The boarding houses are scattered over a big site and provide comfortable accommodation. Many first-rate modern facilities. The staff:pupil ratio is very favourable – about 1:9. A very good education is given and academic results are very good. The great majority of boys go on to degree courses, many to Oxbridge. An unusually strong music staff; musical activities play a major role in the life of the school. Games and outdoor pursuits are very popular and standards are high. As a Catholic school, discipline is somewhat tighter than elsewhere, but is exercised in the context of a strongly supportive community. The junior school is at Gilling Castle, two miles from the college.

School profile

Pupils Age range 13–18, 538 boys, (24 day, 514 boarding). Main entry ages 13 and into sixth. About 35% of intake from own junior school, Ampleforth College Junior School (tel 01439 788238). Approx 25 + % are children of former pupils.

Entrance Common Entrance and own entrance exam used. No special skills required. Boys are normally Roman Catholic. 12–14 pa scholarships, including academic and music scholarships, up to half fees, also a number of bursaries.

Parents 15 + % are doctors, lawyers etc; 15 + % in industry and commerce. Up to 10% live within 30 miles; up to 25% live overseas.

Head and staff *Headmaster:* The Reverend G F L Chamberlain OSB, 3 years in post. Educated at Ampleforth and Oxford (modern history). Previously Housemaster and Senior History Master at Ampleforth. Also Member of the Council of Management of Keston College and of the Catholic Bishops' Advisory Committee on Europe. *Staff:* 62 full time, 15 part time.

Exam results Average size of upper fifth 113; upper sixth 116. *GCSE:* On average 93% upper fifth gain grade A–C in at least 5 subjects. *A-levels:* 47% upper sixth pass in 4 subjects; 38% in 3; and 15% in 1 or 2 subjects. Average UCAS points 23.7.

University and college entrance 90% of 1995 sixth-form leavers went on to a degree course (60% after a gap year); others typically go on to other courses or into employment. Of those going on to university, 10% went to Oxbridge; 5% took courses in medicine, dentistry and veterinary science, 25% in science and engineering, 5% in law, 45% in humanities and social sciences, 5% in art and design, 20% in other subjects.

Curriculum GCSE, AS and A-levels. 22% take science or maths A-levels; 58% take arts/humanities; 20% a mixture. *Vocational:* Holiday work experience programme. *Computing facilities:* A college-wide Novell network running 486 PC work stations plus several free-standing PCs in the sciences and CDT departments. *Special provision:* for eg mild handicap, learning difficulties and EFL. *Europe:* French, German and Spanish to GCSE, AS and A-level; also GCSE Italian. Regular exchanges to France, Germany and Spain, including term-time exchanges for sixth-form linguists. Pupils from elsewhere in Europe on temporary or permanent basis. Initiatives underway with schools in Russia and Eastern Europe.

The arts *Music:* Over 30% of pupils learn a musical instrument; instrumental exams can be taken. Numerous musical groups including orchestra, Schola Cantorum, singers, string, brass, wind ensembles. NYO trumpeter, NYO violinist; organ and choral scholars to Oxbridge. *Drama and dance:* No dance; drama not offered as exam subject. Many pupils are involved in school productions. 3 former pupils in National Youth Theatre, 1 in Bristol Old Vic School, 1 to Central School. *Art:* On average, 30% take GCSE, 12% A-level. Design, pottery, photography, CDT.

Sport, community service and clubs *Sport and physical activities:* Sport compulsory; choice from – rugby, cricket, squash, swimming, tennis, badminton, fencing, athletics, soccer, hockey, cross-country. BAGA, RLSS, RYA, Red Cross, First Aid exams may be taken. Rugby, county representatives and England trialist. *Community service:* Pupils take bronze, silver and gold Duke of Edinburgh's Award. CCF and community service optional. D of E community care programme; strong Cheshire Homes and hospital links; official group working under Forestry Agencies. *Clubs and societies:* Over 35 clubs, eg natural history, karate, bridge, public speaking, sub-aqua, Red Cross, photography, golf, Westminster.

Uniform None but dress regulations (jacket and tie, suit on Sundays).

Houses/prefects House competition on some levels. Prefects and head boy, appointed by the Headmaster; head of house and house prefects, by housemasters.

Religion Roman Catholic worship compulsory.

Social Theatrical and choral productions and debates with other schools. Regular exchanges with schools in France and Germany. Schola tours; skiing, climbing etc abroad. Pupils allowed to bring own bike to school. Some meals formal. School shop. No alcohol/tobacco allowed.

Discipline All punishments are dependent on circumstances.

Boarding 20% have own study bedroom, 20% share with 2–3; 60% are in dormitories of 6+. Houses of 55+. Local doctor and resident nursing staff. No central dining room at present. Sixth form can provide and cook some own food. 1 weekend exeat in the autumn term and half-term in the autumn and Lent term. Visits to local towns allowed.

Alumni association is run by The Secretary, The Ampleforth Society, Ampleforth Abbey, York YO6 4ER.

• ARDINGLY

Ardingly College, Ardingly, Haywards Heath, West Sussex RH17 6SQ. Tel 01444 892577, Fax 01444 892266

• Pupils 630 • Boys 2½–18 (Day/Board) • Girls 2½–18 (Day/Board) • Upper sixth 85 • Termly fees £360–£3065 (Day) £2400–£3880 (Board) • HMC, Woodard • Enquiries/application to the Registrar

What it's like

Founded in 1858, it lies in one of the most beautiful parts of Sussex on a big estate. At the heart of its handsome buildings is the chapel. As a Woodard school it caters for and appeals to those seeking a C of E education. A boys' school until 1981, it is now fully co-educational and with its own junior school and a mix of boarding and day co-ed, the aim is very much to be a family school. One of its prides is the fine pastoral system based on individual tutors for each pupil. It offers a good all-round education and results are good; most pupils go on to degree courses. The staff:pupil ratio is very favourable, about 1:9. There is music, art and drama, the CCF and a very well-organised house system; plus a lot of emphasis on outdoor activities. Practical skills are much encouraged.

School profile

Pupils Total age range 2½-18; 630 pupils, 260 day (150 boys, 110 girls), 370 boarding (222 boys, 148 girls). Senior department 13–18, 458 pupils (272 boys, 186 girls). Main entry ages 3, 7, 11, 13 and into sixth. Approx 5% are children of former pupils. Approx 40% senior intake from own junior school. *State school entry:* 50% intake at 11, 10% at 13 and 25% intake to sixth.

Entrance Common Entrance and own entrance exam used. No special skills except for scholarship candidates. Pupils expected to be in sympathy with aims and ethos of C of E. 5 pa assisted places at 11. Approx 25 pa scholarships/bursaries including for children of clergy and for instrumental tuition; maximum value, full fees.
Parents 50+% live within 30 miles; 15+% live overseas.
Head and staff *Headmaster:* James W Flecker, in post for 16 years. Educated at Marlborough and Oxford (Lit Hum). Previously Assistant Master at Marlborough, at Latymer and at Sydney Grammar, NSW. Also HMC Representative of the Hockey Association; Executive Committee, BSA (special responsibility for National Conference on Boarding Schools at National Boarding Week); writer and producer of six children's operas; orchestral flute player. *Staff:* 70 full time, 25 part time. Annual turnover 10%. Average age 35.
Exam results On average, 94 pupils in upper fifth, 85 in upper sixth. *GCSE:* on average, 48% upper fifth gain at least grade C in 8+ subjects; 41% in 5–7 subjects. *A-level:* 6% upper sixth pass in 4+ subjects; 52% in 3; 22% in 2; and 10% in 1 subject. Average UCAS points 17.0.
University and college entrance 75% of 1995 sixth-form leavers went on to a degree course (33% after a gap year); others typically go on to employment, vocational or other courses (eg secretarial) or to the military. Of those going on to university, 6% went to Oxbridge; 8% took courses in medicine, dentistry and veterinary science, 14% in science and engineering, 4% in law, 40% in humanities and social sciences, 18% in art, design and music, 22% in business and management, and 14% in other vocational subjects.
Curriculum GCSE and A-levels. 23 subjects offered including theatre studies and archaeology (no A-level general studies). 20% take science A-levels; 40% arts/humanities; 40% both. *Vocational:* Work experience available. *Computing facilities:* 2 specialist rooms - 60 IBM compatible 486 machines. Specialist facilities such as image scanning, CD ROMs, laser printing and satellite machine systems are widely used. *Special provision:* Limited specialist remedial teaching; some EFL from own qualified staff. *Europe:* French, German, Italian and Spanish offered to GCSE and A-level; also AS-level French. Regular exchanges to France, Germany and Spain. EYE (English for Young Europeans) programme, 3 week to 1 year visits for European pupils aged 11–18. Increasing number of British bi- or tri-lingual pupils.
The arts (Pupils aged 11 and over) *Music:* Up to 75% of pupils learn a musical instrument; instrumental exams can be taken. Some 3 musical groups including Ardingly Singers, choir, big band. *Drama and dance:* Drama and dance offered. All pupils are involved in school productions and majority in house/other productions. Recent productions of musicals Gypsy, Pacific Overtures and Chess. *Art:* Design, pottery, textiles, photography, fine art, history of art also offered. Recent winner of Young Craftsman of the Year award.
Sport, community service and clubs (Pupils aged 11 and over) *Sport and physical activities:* Compulsory sports: hockey, football, cricket, tennis, volleyball, netball, swimming. Optional: basketball, sailing, riding, fencing, yoga, karate, squash, table tennis etc. A-level sports studies may be taken. Recent South American football tour; area team representatives. *Community service:* Pupils take bronze Duke of Edinburgh's Award. CCF and community service optional. School has raised £17,000 for charity in a year. *Clubs and societies:* Up to 30 clubs, eg computer, Les fauves, debating, international, various sporting and music, literature and poetry groups etc.
Uniform School uniform worn except in the sixth-form.
Houses/prefects Competitive houses. Prefects, head boy/girl, head of house and house prefects – appointed after consultation.
Religion Compulsory religious studies and chapel attendance.
Social Continuous contact with local schools. Exchange with schools in Paris, Baden-Baden and Pamplona; many other organised trips abroad. Day pupils allowed to bring own car/bike to school. Meals self service. School shop. No tobacco allowed; alcohol in supervised bar for upper sixth only.
Discipline Pupils failing to produce homework once might expect to be asked the reason; those caught smoking cannabis on the premises expect instant expulsion.
Boarding 40% have own study bedroom or share with 1 other; 60% in dormitories of 6+. Houses of 40+, single-sex, except for upper sixth house. 3 resident qualified nurses.

Central dining room. Pupils can provide and cook some own food. 2–5 exeats termly (24 hours) plus half term (4–8 days). Visits to the local town allowed when free, to 6.30 pm (4.30 in winter).
Alumni association R C Munyard, FCA, c/o Touche Ross & Co, Hill House, 1 Little New Street, London EC4A 3TR.
Former pupils Terry-Thomas; Dr Hayes (Director of National Portrait Gallery); Cdr Longhurst (potential astronaut); Ian Hislop (Private Eye); Stephen Oliver (composer); Andrew Bowden and T Gorst (MPs).

• ARNOLD

Arnold School, Lytham Road, Blackpool, Lancashire FY4 1JG. Tel 01253 346391, Fax 01253 407245

• Pupils 1150 • Boys 4–18 (Day) • Girls 4–18 (Day) • Upper sixth 96 • Termly fees £1183 (Day) • HMC • Enquiries/application to the Headmaster

What it's like

Founded in 1896, it is situated in Blackpool half a mile from the sea. It has adequate buildings and nearby playing fields. Considerable expansion in recent years has provided good up-to-date facilities. Originally a boys' school, it first admitted girls in 1977. The aim is to inculcate lasting values of service, loyalty and self-discipline. Religious worship is encouraged and religious assemblies are compulsory. It has a reputation for sound traditional academic training and results are good. Vocational qualifications are offered. Almost all sixth-formers go on to degree courses, including Oxbridge. Strong back-up from old Arnoldians. There is a good range of sport and games. A bonus is the outdoor pursuits centre at Glenridding, described as a classroom in the Lake District; there is also a new all-weather pitch. A very large CCF and the Duke of Edinburgh Award Scheme is actively pursued.

School profile

Pupils Total age range 4–18, 1150 day pupils, (637 boys, 513 girls). Senior department 11–18, 810 pupils (445 boys, 365 girls). Main entry ages 5, 7, 11 and into sixth. Approx 5% are children of former pupils. 30+% senior intake from own junior school. *State school entry:* 60% senior intake plus 10% to sixth.
Entrance Common Entrance and own entrance exam used. No special skills or religious requirements. Parents not expected to buy text books; maximum extras, £95 including lunch for day pupils. 10 pa assisted places plus 5 in sixth. 10 pa scholarships/bursaries, £500–£1700.
Parents 25% professionals, consultants, solicitors etc; 15% in hotel/tourism.
Head and staff *Headmaster:* W T Gillem, in post since 1994. Educated at Royal Belfast Academical Institution, and Queen's University, Belfast, and Cambridge University (English). Previously Headmaster, King's School, Tynemouth, and Deputy Headmaster, Royal Grammar, Guildford. *Staff:* 72 full time, 4 part time. Annual turnover 2%. Average age 38.
Exam results In 1995, 130 pupils in upper fifth, 96 in upper sixth. *GCSE:* In 1995, 95% upper fifth gained at least grade C in 8+ subjects; 5% in 5–7 subjects. *A-levels/GNVQs:* 74 upper sixth passed in 4+ A-level subjects; 11 in 3; 3 in 2; and 3 in 1 subject. Average UCAS points 19.7.
University and college entrance 99% of 1995 sixth-form leavers went on to a degree course (under 1% after a gap year); others typically go directly on to employment. Of those going on to university, 10% went to Oxbridge; 10% took courses in medicine, dentistry and veterinary science, 35% in science and engineering, 15% in law, 30% in humanities and social sciences, 5% in art and design, 5% in vocational subjects eg physiotherapy.
Curriculum GCSE, A-levels and GNVQs. A-level subjects include law and general studies. 60% take science A-levels. *Vocational:* RSA qualifications in secretarial skills. *Computing facilities:* 2 laboratories with 44 PCs including 22 new IBM personals, one Weatherstat Satellite Dish. *Special provision:* Special teacher to help with learning difficulties, especially dyslexia. *Europe:* French and German offered to GCSE, AS and A-level. Regular exchanges to France and Germany. Number of European pupils in school.

The arts (Pupils aged 11 and over) *Music:* 20% of pupils learn a musical instrument; instrumental exams can be taken. Some 5 musical groups including choir, orchestra, wind group, brass ensemble. *Drama and dance:* Both offered. Some pupils are involved in school productions and a few in house/other productions. *Art:* On average, 15 take GCSE, 12 A-level. Design, pottery, textiles, photography also offered.
Sport, community service and clubs (Pupils aged 11 and over) *Sport and physical activities:* Compulsory sports: rugby, cricket, athletics (boys); hockey, netball, athletics, tennis (girls). *Optional:* swimming, squash, badminton, golf, rounders. International rugby U18 representative; national karate champion. *Community service:* Pupils take bronze, silver and gold Duke of Edinburgh's Award. CCF compulsory for 2 years at age 13 (largest CCF in the country). Community service optional. *Clubs and societies:* Up to 30 clubs, eg chess, IT, drama, philately, golf, debating, science, French.
Uniform School uniform worn throughout.
Houses/prefects Competitive houses. Prefects, head boy/girl, head of house and house prefects – appointed by the Headmaster and school.
Religion Encouraged (religious assemblies are compulsory).
Social Debates, concerts, visits etc with local schools. Organised trips abroad for French, German, geology, geography; hockey tour of Holland, rugby tour of Canada and Australia. Pupils allowed to bring own car/motorbike/bike to school. Meals self service. School shop. No tobacco/alcohol allowed.
Discipline Pupils failing to produce homework once might expect a homework detention. Those caught smoking cannabis on the premises would be expelled.
Alumni association is run by P B Warhurst, 26 Edwinstowe Road, Ansdell FY8 4BG.
Former pupils David Ball (Soft Cell); Chris Lowe (Pet Shop Boys); J Armfield; G Eastham; Sir Walter Clegg MP; Peter Boydell QC; T Graveney; Stanley Matthews (junior tennis); Sir William Lyons (Jaguar Cars); Keith Oats (Marks & Spencer).

• ARTS EDUCATIONAL (London)

The Arts Educational London School, Cone Ripman House, 14 Bath Road, London W4 1LY. Tel 0181 994 9366, Fax 0181 994 9274

• Pupils 140 • Boys 8–16+ (Day) • Girls 8–16+ (Day) • Termly fees £1250-£1854 (Day) • ISAI
• Enquiries/application to the Registrar

What it's like

Founded in 1919, it occupies a single site in a pleasant residential area of West London, with well-designed buildings and good facilities. Its aim is to deliver an academic curriculum whilst training boys and girls in the performing arts. It also offers post-16 courses, a foundation drama course offering A-levels in English, art, drama and dance; 3-year accredited courses in dance, musical theatre, and adult drama and a 1-year postgraduate acting course for mature students. Naturally, everyone is involved in dance, music and drama. Extra-curricular activities and frequent participation in national events concerned with the performing arts. No sport is offered, because of the danger of developing the wrong muscles for dance.

School profile

Pupils Age range 8–16+; 140 day pupils (35 boys, 105 girls). Senior department, 11–16; 118 pupils (32 boys, 86 girls). Main entry ages 8 and 11. Approx 10% are children of former pupils. *State school entry:* 20% main intake.
Entrance Own entrance exam used based on national tests. Skills in dance and drama optional; no religious requirements. Maximum £100 extras; lunch included in fees.
Head and staff *Principal:* Peter Fowler, in post for 10 years. Educated at Royal Academy of Music (singing and piano), London University (Masters) and St Luke's College Exeter (education). Previously Inspector of Schools (music) to Metropolitan Borough of Solihull and in Hertfordshire; Director of Music at Queen Elizabeth's Hospital and at Bristol Grammar School; Head of Music at St Mary Redcliffe's and Temple School, Bristol, and Master of Choristers at St Mary Redcliffe Church. Also his choirs and orchestras have made television appearances, performing in many European cities, Canada, the USA and given many concerts in the UK. *Staff:* 32 full time, 120 part time. Annual turnover (part time) 10%. Average age 40.

Exam results On average 30 pupils in upper fifth. *GCSE:* 13% gained grade C or above in 8+ subjects; 45% in 5-7 subjects.
University and college entrance 50% of sixth-form leavers go on to degree courses, 50% into careers in dance, drama and musical theatre.
Curriculum GCSE offered, 8 subjects including drama and dance. *Computing facilities:* New computer laboratory. IT taught as part of syllabus. *Special provision:* Private lessons within timetable for dyslexic children. *Europe:* French (compulsory) offered to GCSE. Regular exchanges to France.
The arts *Music:* Up to 50% of pupils learn a musical instrument; instrumental exams can be taken. 2 musical groups, junior and senior choir. *Drama and dance:* Drama and dance offered; GCSE in both, LAMDA, RAD, ISTD (ballet, modern) exams may be taken. Performances with Royal Opera House, English National Ballet and English National Opera; BBC TV drama. *Art:* On average, 18 take GCSE. Pottery also offered.
Sport, community service and clubs No sports or community service offered. Up to 5 clubs, eg Christian Union.
Uniform School uniform worn throughout.
Houses/prefects No competitive houses. Prefects, head boy and girl, selected by staff; class captains elected. Elected School Council.
Religion No compulsory worship. School assembly thrice weekly.
Social Local events organised occasionally. Meals self service. No tobacco/alcohol allowed for pupils to age 16.
Discipline Pupils failing to produce homework or committing other infringement might expect a detention. In extreme cases a suspension.
Former pupils Julie Andrews; Claire Bloom; Leslie Crowther; Nigel Havers; Glynis Johns; Margaret Lockwood; Sarah Miles; Jane Seymour; Antoinette Sibley; Teresa Jarvis; Seth Gilber; Catherine Becque; Finola Hughes; Sarah Brightman; Josephine Campbell.

• ARTS EDUCATIONAL (Tring)

The Arts Educational School, Tring Park, Tring, Hertfordshire HP23 5LX. Tel 01442 824255, Fax 01442 891069

• Pupils 220 • Boys 8–18 (Day/Board) • Girls 8–18 (Day/Board) • Upper sixth 25 • Termly fees £1590–£2226 (Day) £2756–£3604 (Board) • SHA, BSA Enquiries/application to the Registrar

What it's like

Set in 17 acres of attractive and secluded grounds, the school is principally housed in a superb mansion, formerly the home of the Rothschild family. Originally a girls' school, boys were first admitted in 1993 and the school is now co-educational throughout. A large staff permits an unusually good staff:pupil ratio. All pupils are prepared for GCSE and most stay to take A-levels. The vocational courses in dance, drama and music are a very important part of the curriculum. Older pupils specialise in one particular artistic subject but participation in the general application of the other two disciplines may be required. The courses prepare pupils to a high standard in dance, drama or music while providing a thorough academic education and provide the foundation for entry to dance, drama or music colleges or degree courses for the arts. The purpose above all is to create first-class communicators. Naturally standards of achievement in music, drama and dance are distinguished and there is a large number of events each year. The school is closely involved with local churches and also with various charities. Religious worship is compulsory. Some basic sports and games are provided and there is a range of extra-curricular activities. Financial help is now available through the government Aided Places Scheme.

School profile

Pupils Total age range 8–18, boys and girls. Senior department 11–18; 220 pupils, 65 day (2 boys, 63 girls) 155 boarding (13 boys, 142 girls). Main entry ages 8–10, 11–14 and 16. 5% are children of former pupils. *State school entry:* 50% main intake, plus 25% to sixth.
Entrance Audition and academic test. Special skills required in music, dance and drama, varying according to course applied for; no religious requirements. Aided places available. Discretionary grants may be available from local authorities. Some scholarships.

Parents Up to 30% live within 30 miles; up to 5% live overseas.
Head and staff *Principal:* Mrs Jane Billing, 5 years in post. Educated at Uttoxeter Girls' High School, Guildhall School of Music and London University (music). Previously Deputy Head of St Hilary's, Sevenoaks. Also FRSA and Governor of Milton Keynes Prep School. *Staff:* 40 full time, 35 part time. Annual turnover 2%. Average age 40.
Exam results In 1995, 32 in fifth, 22 in upper sixth. *GCSE:* In 1995, 78% of fifth formers gained grade C or above in 5+ subjects. *A-levels:* 90% of sixth-formers gained A-level passes. Average UCAS points 13.2.
University and college entrance Most pupils go on to further training in the performing arts or to degrees in the arts and humanities, followed by careers in the theatre or media. A few pupils go on to degree courses unrelated to the arts.
Curriculum GCSE and A-levels. 15 GCSE subjects offered; 12 A-level, including theatre studies, dance and music; no general studies. *Vocational:* RSA word processing qualifications offered; also RAD and ISTD dance up to teaching qualifications; Guildhall drama (acting and solo speech) to grade 8. *Computing facilities:* 10 computers in computer room with individual study carrels. *Special provision:* Specialist member of staff gives help in English, individually or in small groups.
The arts (Pupils aged 11 and over) *Music:* Almost all pupils learn a musical instrument; instrumental exams can be taken. Some 7 musical groups including choirs, saxophone group, orchestras. Chamber choir runners-up and previous winners of Sainsbury's choir of the year competition. *Drama and dance:* GCSE drama, A-level in both theatre studies and dance, Guildhall, ISTD, RAD exams may be taken. All pupils are involved in school productions and majority in house/other productions. *Art:* On average, 35 take GCSE, 15 A-level in art and design.
Sport, community service and clubs (Pupils aged 11 and over) *Sport and physical activities:* Compulsory sports: swimming (up to fifth form). Optional: riding, tennis.
Uniform School uniform except in the sixth.
Houses/prefects Competitive houses. Prefects, head pupil, head of house and house prefects appointed by the Principal in consultation with staff.
Religion Compulsory worship.
Social Meals self service. No tobacco/alcohol allowed.
Discipline Any students caught taking drugs on the premises would be expelled.
Boarding All pupils in shared rooms in three houses, divided by age group. Two qualified nursing sisters. Central dining room. Half terms (one week) and two weekend exeats per term. Visits to local town allowed (accompanied at weekends to age 13, relaxed to sixth-formers can go out at weekends if classes and duties allow).
Former pupils Jane Seymour, Stephanie Lawrence, Anna Carteret, Gillian Lynn, Thandie Newton, Lia Williams.

• ASHFORD

Ashford School, East Hill, Ashford, Kent TN24 8PB. Tel 01233 625171, Fax 01233 647185
• Pupils 517 • Boys None • Girls 3–18 (Day/Board/Weekly) • Upper sixth 59 • Termly fees £318–£1950 (Day) £3007–£3493 (Board) £2972–£3448 (Weekly) • GSA • Enquiries/application to the Headmistress

What it's like

Founded in 1898, it occupies 23 acres of very pleasant grounds in the town, together with land bordering the Stour. The oldest building is the 17th-century Alfred House. Expansion has incorporated neighbouring houses and much accommodation is now purpose-built with many excellent modern facilities. A sound education is given and and results are very good. The great majority of sixth-formers go on to degree courses, including many to Oxbridge. It is strong on music and drama and has a well-organised house system. Being an urban school it has plentiful local ties and is well supported by the community. There is a pronounced sense of service to the town (helping the handicapped, elderly et al).

School profile

Pupils Total age range 3–18; 517 girls, 447 day, 70 boarding. Senior department 11–18, 378 girls. Main entry ages 3, 5, 7, 11, 13 and into sixth. Approx 5% are children of former

pupils. Own junior department provides approx 50% of senior intake. *State school entry:* 40% main senior intakes, plus a handful to the sixth.
Entrance Own entrance exam used. No special skills or religious requirements. Parents expected to buy GCSE and A-level textbooks only; other extras vary. 8 pa assisted places. 4–6 pa scholarships/bursaries (including 1 music), usually 50% tuition fees.
Parents 15+% are doctors, lawyers, farmers, etc; 15+% in industry or commerce. 30+% live within 30 miles; 10+% live overseas.
Head and staff *Headmistress:* Mrs Patricia Metham, 5 years in post. Educated at Upper Chine and Bristol University (English and drama). Previously Headmistress at Farlington, Head of English and drama at Francis Holland and taught at Wimbledon High. Also JP; School Teacher Fellowship at Merton College, Oxford; associate editor for Methuen; published commentary and textual notes for number of plays in Methuen Student Edition series. *Staff:* 53 full time, 6 part time (plus music). Annual turnover 4%. Average age 44.
Exam results In 1995, 58 pupils in upper fifth, 52 in upper sixth. *GCSE:* On average, 86% upper fifth gain at least grade C in 8+ subjects; 12% in 5–7 subjects. *A-levels:* 8% upper sixth pass in 4+ subjects; 73% in 3; 14% in 2; and 2% in 1 subject. Average UCAS points 20.5.
University and college entrance 92% of sixth-form leavers go on to a degree course (11% after a gap year); others typically go on to business management or secretarial courses. Of those going on to university, 15% went to Oxbridge; 13% took courses in medicine, dentistry and veterinary science, 26% in science and engineering, 6% in law, 34% in humanities and social sciences, 6% in art and design, 15% in vocational subjects eg nursing, pharmacy, education.
Curriculum GCSE and A-levels. 22 subjects offered, including ancient Greek, theatre studies, economics, technology, business studies and history of art; A-level business studies but not general studies. 21% take science A-levels; 33% arts/humanities; 47% both. *Computing facilities:* 24 Archimedes, also Acorn 5000s; computers also in many departments and each boarding house. Access to the Internet available. *Special provision:* Ad hoc extra help, with guidance from experts. *Europe:* French, German and Spanish offered at GCSE, AS-level and A-level. Regular exchanges to France, Germany and Spain. Some European girls in school for 1–2 years. Work experience links being forged in Germany.
The arts (Pupils aged 11 and over) *Music:* Over 50% of pupils learn a musical instrument; instrumental exams can be taken. Some 10+ musical groups including orchestras, band, choirs, jazz, recorder, string quartets, various chamber groups. 4 members of county youth orchestra; member of National Youth Orchestra. *Drama and dance:* Both offered. GCSE drama, A-level theatre studies and Guildhall exams may be taken. Some pupils are involved in school productions and majority in house/other productions. Several girls reading drama/English, media studies etc at university; honours gained at grade 7 (Guildhall) in public speaking and acting. *Art:* On average, 23 take GCSE, 2 AS-level, 8 A-level. Textiles and history of art A-level also offered. Pupils regularly go on to art foundation courses.
Sport, community service and clubs (Pupils aged 11 and over) *Sport and physical activities:* Compulsory sports: hockey, netball, gym, athletics, tennis, swimming. Optional: judo, fencing, aerobics, trampolining. GCSE, BAGA, RLSS exams may be taken. 2 county netball representatives; 3 county hockey; 1 national swimmer; 2 county and 1 national fencer. *Community service:* Pupils take bronze, silver and gold Duke of Edinburgh's Award; 35–40 pa enrol for bronze. Community service optional for 3 years at age 14.
Uniform School uniform worn except in the sixth-form.
Houses/prefects Competitive houses. Prefects, 2 head girls (one day, one boarding), head of house and house prefects elected by girls, staff and Headmistress.
Religion Compulsory, non-denominational Christian-based assembly. Boarders attend Parish Church or in-house services on Sundays. Confirmation classes available. Religious Studies in the curriculum is academically based, but with the major emphasis on Christianity.
Social Many joint events with local schools, eg productions and debates, local guitar orchestra, host discos, formal sixth-form supper dance etc. Annual ski trip; other recent trips include Mediterranean cruise, Egypt, Greece, Russia, China, Italy and America. Pupils with need allowed to bring own car/motorbike to school. Meals self service. No tobacco/alcohol allowed.

Discipline Pupils failing to produce homework once might expect a reprimand, thereafter detention; those caught smoking cannabis on the premises can expect to be expelled. Other infringements of school rules would bring progressive loss of privileges, communication with parents, suspension and, eventually, expulsion.
Boarding 25% have own study bedroom, 20% share, 55% are in dormitories. Qualified nurse; weekly doctor's surgery. Central dining room. Sixth formers can provide and cook own food at weekends. Flexible weekend exeats. Visits to the local town allowed (accompanied and occasional to 13; unmonitored in sixth).
Alumni association is run by Mrs M Stevens, c/o the school.

• ASHVILLE

Ashville College, Harrogate, North Yorkshire HG2 9JR. Tel 01423 566358, Fax 01423 505142
• Pupils 720 • Boys 4½–18 (Day/Board) • Girls 4½–18 (Day/Board) • Upper sixth 65 • Termly fees £1300–£1560 (Day) • £2594–£2918 (Board) • HMC • Enquiries/application to the Headmaster

What it's like

Founded in 1877 by the United Methodist Free Church, it has incorporated two other non-Conformist schools: Emfield College and New College. It first accepted girls in 1983 and is now fully co-educational. It owns a fine estate of 45 acres on the south side of the spa town. During the 1980s extensive additions were made and it now possesses many excellent facilities. It is kept fairly small deliberately to preserve the benefits of life in a family community. Religious services are compulsory but the religious ethos is ecumenical. Its academic record is very sound and results are good; most sixth-formers go on to degree courses. Culturally, there is close rapport with the town; and there is a good deal of emphasis on outdoor activities (eg fishing, fell walking and rock climbing).

School profile

Pupils Total age range 4½–18; 720 pupils, 564 day (338 boys, 226 girls), 156 boarding (100 boys, 56 girls). Senior department 11–18, 495 pupils (318 boys, 177 girls). Main entry ages 7, 8, 11, 13 and into sixth. Approx 3% are children of former pupils.
Entrance Common Entrance and own entrance exam used. No special skills or religious requirements but school is Methodist. Parents not expected to buy text books; music tuition and some incidentals extra. Assisted places available. 12 pa scholarships/ bursaries.
Parents 15+% in industry or commerce. 60+% live within 30 miles; up to 10% live overseas.
Head and staff *Headmaster:* M H Crosby, in post for 9 years. Educated at Kingswood and Cambridge (history). Previously Housemaster, Head of History and Head of Sixth at Stamford and Assistant Master at Loughborough Grammar. *Staff:* 45 full time, 8 part time. Annual turnover 5%. Average age about 40.
Exam results In 1995, 91 in fifth; 57 in upper sixth. *GCSE:* In 1995, 60 in fifth gained at least grade C in 8+ subjects, 20 in 5–7; 5 in 1–4 subjects. *A-levels:* 44% upper sixth pass in 4 subjects; 22% in 3; 18% in 2 and 16% in 1 subject. Average UCAS points 21.2.
University and college entrance 98% of 1995 sixth-form leavers went on to a degree course (15% after a gap year); others typically go on to employment or retake A-levels. Of those going on to university, 2%% went to Oxbridge; 4% took courses in medicine, dentistry and veterinary science, 10% in science and engineering, 2% in law, 60% in humanities and social sciences, 4% in art and design, 20% in vocational subjects.
Curriculum GCSE and A-levels. 24% take science/engineering A-levels; 49% take arts and humanities; 27% a mixture. *Vocational:* Work experience available; also Advanced GNVQ business and finance; CLAIT. *Computing facilities:* Computer room with 12 BBC computers and some in other departments. *Special provision:* Links with the Dyslexia Institute in Harrogate; qualified EFL staff. *Europe:* French and German offered at GCSE and A-level. Regular exchanges to France and Germany.
The arts (Pupils aged 11 and over) *Music:* 30% of pupils learn a musical instrument; instrumental exams can be taken. Some 8 musical groups including string ensembles, bands, 3 choirs. *Drama and dance:* Drama offered; GCSE and LAMDA exams may be

taken. Some pupils are involved in school and house/other productions. *Art:* On average, 25 take GCSE, 2 AS-level, 17 A-level.
Sport, community service and clubs (Pupils aged 11 and over) *Sport and physical activities:* Compulsory sports (to 14): rugby, cricket, netball. Optional: hockey, badminton, squash, tennis, cross-country, swimming. *Community service:* Pupils take bronze, silver and gold Duke of Edinburgh's Award. Community service optional at age 15. *Clubs and societies:* Up to 10 clubs, eg chess, debating, Christian Union.
Uniform School uniform worn throughout; different uniform in sixth-form.
Houses/prefects Competitive houses. Prefects, head boy and girl, head of houses – appointed by the Headmaster.
Religion Compulsory attendance at worship.
Social Joint sixth-form society with Harrogate Ladies' College. Organised trips abroad. Pupils allowed to bring own car with school approval. Meals self service. School shops for tuck and clothing. No tobacco/alcohol allowed.
Discipline Pupils failing to produce homework more than once might expect a prep detention; those caught smoking cannabis on the premises would be suspended, probably expelled.
Boarding Sixth form have own study bedroom or share with 2 or 3. Single sex houses of approximately 45. Resident qualified nurses. Central dining room. 3 exeats each term (2 nights) plus half-term. Visits to the local town allowed on Saturday mornings.
Alumni association is run by Mr B Bonser, 159 Forest Lane, Harrogate.
Former pupils Sir Alastair Burnett.

• ATHERLEY

The Atherley School, Hill Lane, Southampton, Hampshire SO15 5RG. Tel 01703 772898
• Pupils 449 • Boys 3-11 only • Girls 3–18 (Day) • Upper sixth 15 • Termly fees £1424 • GSA, SHA, CSCL • Enquiries/application to the Head Mistress

What it's like

Opened in 1926 and governed by the Church Schools Company. At present it is located on a 5-acre site on the edge of Southampton Common. The junior school is magnificently located in 30 acres at Grove Place, between Southampton and Romsey. Planning permission has been granted to build an entirely new senior school in the Grove Place grounds. A sound education is provided and results are good. Nearly all sixth-formers go on to degree courses.

School profile

Pupils Total age range 3–18; 449 day pupils. Senior department 11–18, 270 girls. Main entry ages 3+ (boys and girls), 11 and into sixth (girls). Approx 1% are children of former pupils. Large senior intake from own junior, Atherley Junior School (tel 01703 732406). *State school entry:* 30% main senior intake.
Entrance By interview, tests and junior school report. Reasonable ability required; no religious allegiance necessary but school is C of E. Parents not expected to buy textbooks. Assisted places at age 5, 11 and into sixth. 5–6 pa scholarships/bursaries at 11 and 16.
Head and staff *Headmistress:* Mrs Catherine Madina, in post since 1994. Educated at Croydon High and at Leeds University (English). Previously Deputy Head at Skinners' Company's Girls' School. *Staff:* 35 full time, 12 part time. Annual turnover 3%.
Exam results In 1995, 47 pupils in Year 11, 8 in upper sixth. *GCSE:* In 1995, 32 in Year 11 gained at least grade C in 8+ subjects; 8 in 5-7 subjects. *A-levels:* Average UCAS points 19.1.
University and college entrance 75% of 1995 sixth-form leavers go on to a degree course (10% after a gap year); others typically go on to work or to art foundation courses.
Curriculum GCSE and A-levels. 16 subjects offered (no A-level general studies). 63% arts/humanities A-levels; 38% both arts and sciences. *Vocational:* Work experience available; also City and Guilds cookery and NVQ business and CLAIT. *Computing facilities:* Nimbus network in senior school and 12 Archimedes in junior school. *Europe:* French (from age 6), German and Spanish offered to GCSE, AS and A-level. Regular exchanges to France, Germany and Spain.

The arts (Pupils aged 11 and over) *Music:* Over 30% of pupils learn a musical instrument; instrumental exams can be taken. Some 9 musical groups including choir, orchestra, wind band, recorder group, jazz, string quartet. *Drama and dance:* Some pupils are involved in school productions and all in house/other productions. *Art:* On average, 40 take GCSE, 6 A-level. Design, pottery, photography also offered. Art facilities open to non-examination pupils.
Sport, community service and clubs (Pupils aged 11 and over) *Sport and physical activities:* Compulsory sports: lacrosse, netball, rounders, athletics, tennis. Optional: volleyball, badminton, table tennis. Sixth form only: squash, swimming. National athletics representative. *Community service:* Pupils take bronze Duke of Edinburgh's Award. Community service optional. *Clubs and societies:* Clubs, eg electronics, drama, art, computers, Christian Union, public speaking.
Uniform School uniform worn throughout.
Houses/prefects Competitive houses. Prefects, head girl and head of house – elected by the staff and senior pupils.
Religion C of E but pupils of all faiths and none are welcomed.
Social Public speaking, games, BAYS with local schools. Organised trips abroad. Pupils allowed to bring own car/bike to school. Meals cafeteria-style (including optional breakfast). School shops (tuck and uniform). No tobacco/alcohol allowed.
Discipline Those caught smoking on the premises or on the way to or from school could expect to be suspended, pending further action. Detentions are used and minus house points, according to seriousness of offence. Bullying and drugs policies in place.
Alumni association is run by Mrs A M Dawood, c/o the school.

• ATLANTIC COLLEGE

United World College of the Atlantic, St Donat's Castle, Llantwit Major, South Glamorgan CF6 9WF. Tel 01446 792530

• Pupils 350 • Boys 16–19 (Board)) • Girls 16–19 (Board) • Upper sixth 175 • Termly fees (only two terms) £4760 (Board) • United World Colleges • Enquiries/application to the Principal

What it's like

A sixth-form college, founded in 1962 (the co-founder was Kurt Hahn), it is one of eight United World Colleges – the others being in British Columbia, Singapore, Mbabane (Swaziland), Trieste, Montezuma (New Mexico), Hong Kong and western Norway. It has an unusually fine single-campus site of 150 acres, rural and coastal. The heart of the college is the historic St Donat's Castle, a magnificent, intact 12th-century stronghold whose curtain walls surround an Elizabethan courtyard. Next to it, in delightful gardens, are modern and very well-equipped buildings. Like its sister colleges, it offers students of all races and creeds the opportunity to develop international understanding through a programme which combines high-quality academic studies with activities which encourage a sense of adventure and social responsibility. United World Colleges have two main aims: to promote international understanding through education; and to provide a pattern of education to meet the special needs of our time. It was the first school in the world to abandon national examinations in favour of an international diploma – the International Baccalaureate – in 1971. There are two terms: early September to early December; mid-January to end of May. A well-qualified staff (who represent many different countries and cultures) provide an excellent all-round pre-university education and there is a very favourable staff:pupil ratio of about 1:9. Standards are high and results consistently very good. Almost all leavers proceed to degree courses, many to Oxbridge. Music and drama are very well supported. Sports and games are not stressed but there is a range of outdoor activities, including sailing, canoeing, swimming and orienteering. Clubs and societies (over 50) cater for a phenomenal number of enterprises and these play an important part in the life of the college. All students give college service: maintenance, simple building, cleaning, estate improvement. Estate service involves running the 50-acre college farm; some students choose to receive instruction in livestock management, crop-rotation, grassland management and market gardening. An environmental monitoring group is trained in scientific sampling and survey techniques. Cultural and aesthetic pursuits and training include music of all kinds, pottery, sculpture, typography, silk-screen printing, film-making and drama. All students are engaged in local community services of which there are a wide range. In 1962 the college initiated the first co-ordinated cliff, beach and inshore rescue service in Britain and it is an official station of the RNLI and HM Coastguards.

School profile

Pupils Age range 16–19; 350 boarding pupils (175 boys, 175 girls). Entry age 16. 1% are children of former pupils. *State school entry:* 95%.

Entrance By competition for scholarships which are awarded on merit, by interview and school report. No special skills but must be academically suited to pre-university education; no religious requirements. Parents not expected to buy textbooks. Average extras £400 per annum. 160–170 pa scholarships/bursaries available, value up to £11,200 (aim is to provide full scholarship for vast majority, although these may be means tested).

Parents 70+% live overseas.

Head and staff *Principal:* Colin Jenkins, in post for 6 years. Educated at Fishguard County Secondary and Aberystwyth University (zoology). Previously Head of Biology at Teignmouth Grammar, and special responsibility for biology at Douglas High, Isle of Man. Also Deputy Director General and Director of Examinations, International Baccalaureate Organisation; Chairman of Intergovernmental (UNESCO) Marine Education Conference. *Staff:* 40 full time, 2 part time. Annual turnover 2–3%. Average age 36.

Exam results In 1995, 175 pupils in upper sixth; 95% awarded IB Diploma with an average of 34 IB points.

University and college entrance 98% of 1995 sixth-form leavers went on to a degree course; others typically go on to art, drama or music colleges or other non-degree courses. Of those going on to university, 10% went to Oxbridge; 20% took courses in medicine, dentistry and veterinary science, 30% in science and engineering, 45% in humanities and social sciences, 3% in art and design, 2% in drama and music.

Curriculum International Baccalaureate. 35 subjects offered (including Arabic, design technology, environmental systems, peace studies, theatre studies). 30% took science IB higher levels; 30% arts/humanities; 40% both. *Computing facilities:* Nimbus network system in open access computing room; departmental machines throughout. *Special provision:* Pupils with visual, hearing, slight physical handicaps accepted, although narrow spiral stone stairs can present insuperable problems to the severely physically handicapped. *Europe:* Danish, Dutch, French, German, Spanish offered to IB. Regular exchanges to France and Spain. School has pupils from all European countries, east and west.

The arts *Music:* Up to 50% of pupils learn a musical instrument; instrumental exams can be taken. Some 8 musical groups including choirs, orchestra, jazz, pop groups. *Drama and dance:* Drama offered. Majority of pupils are involved in school productions and house/other productions. *Art:* On average, 10 take IB subsidiary, 12 higher. Design, pottery, textiles, photography, sculpture also offered.

Sport, community service and clubs *Sport and physical activities:* No compulsory sports. Optional: rugby, soccer, basketball, hockey, volleyball, sailing, surfing, canoeing, climbing. RLSS exams may be taken. *Community service:* Community service compulsory. Part of National Coastal Rescue Service, HM Coastguard, RNLI lifeboat; college provides emergency call-out services with student manpower. *Clubs and societies:* Over 30 clubs, eg Amnesty, Africa society, world affairs, environment, photography, video, community arts centre, sub-aqua, orienteering, chess.

Uniform No school uniform.

Houses/prefects No competitive houses, head of school or prefects. House representatives, elected by the house. School Council.

Religion Arrangements made for attendance at religious worship if desired; not compulsory.

Social School visits to enable the international students to provide an input to local schools. A number of language-orientated trips organised. Pupils not allowed to bring own transport. Meals self-service. School shop. Tobacco/alcohol allowed (under certain constraints of place and time).

Discipline Pupils failing to produce homework once could expect warning; those involved with illegal drugs on the premises could expect expulsion. Atlantic College operates on a set of guidelines agreed by staff and students.

Boarding All share study bedrooms with 3 others. Pupils divided into houses of approx 48. Resident qualified nurse. Pupils can provide and cook own food. 2 exeats per term and more informally. Visits to the local town allowed at any time convenient.

• AUSTIN FRIARS

Austin Friars School, Carlisle, Cumbria CA3 9PB. Tel 01228 28042, Fax 01228 810327
• Pupils 319 • Boys 11–18 (Day/Board) • Girls 11–18 (Day) • Upper sixth 30 • Termly fees £1518 (Day) £2652 (Board) • SHMIS • Enquiries/application to the School Secretary

What it's like

Founded in 1951, it is situated in spacious grounds overlooking the historic city of Carlisle. Originally a boys' school, it first accepted girls in 1986. It is an Augustinian school but open to all denominations. It aims to foster its pupils spiritually, academically, socially and physically and all pupils are encouraged to develop their potential. A sound education is provided and results are good. Almost all sixth-formers go on to degree courses. There is a good range of sports and activities and a number of county representatives. A fair commitment to local community schemes and the Duke of Edinburgh's Award Scheme. Good use is made of the cultural and physical attributes of the Borders and Lake District.

School profile

Pupils Age range 11–18; 319 pupils, 295 day (168 boys, 127 girls), 24 boarding boys. Main entry ages 11, 13 and into sixth.

Entrance Common Entrance and own entrance exam used. No special skills required; a Catholic school but all denominations welcomed. Parents not expected to buy books; average extras, £50. Assisted places available. 8 pa scholarships, £482-£964.

Parents 15+% are doctors, lawyers, etc; 15+% in industry or commerce. 60+% live within 30 miles; up to 10% overseas.

Head and staff *Headmaster:* Michael Taylor, in post since 1994. Educated at Glasgow University (history). Previously at St Joseph's College, Dumfries. *Staff:* 27 full time, 5 part time. Annual turnover 5%. Average age 45.

Exam results Average size of fifth form 55; upper sixth 42. *GCSE:* Fifth formers gain at least grade C in 8.6 subjects. *A-levels:* 65% upper sixth pass in 4 subjects; 17% in 3; 9% in 2; and 8% in 1 subject. Average UCAS points 19.2.

University and college entrance 95% of 1995 sixth-form leavers went on to a degree course (5% after a gap year); others typically go on to straight into careers. Of those going on to university, 5% went to Oxbridge; 16% took courses in medicine, dentistry and veterinary science, 16% in science and engineering, 10% in law, 37% in humanities and social sciences, 5% in art and design, 16% in vocational subjects.

Curriculum GCSE and A-levels, including A-level general studies. 40% take science/engineering A-levels; 45% take arts/humanities; 15% both. *Computing facilities:* SJ Nexus network with 3 file servers. 20 Archimedes micros. *Special provision:* English lessons for non-native speakers. Help for dyslexic pupils. *Europe:* French and German offered at GCSE and A-level. Pupils in school from France, Spain and occasionally Italy.

The arts *Music:* 30% of pupils learn a musical instrument; instrumental exams can be taken. Some 6 musical groups: band, chamber music groups, choirs, brass ensemble. Members of city, county and regional youth orchestras. *Drama and dance:* Both offered. LAMDA exams may be taken. Some pupils are involved in school and house/other productions. *Art:* On average, 25 take GCSE, 5 A-level. Photography, graphics, batik, 3D also offered.

Sport, community service and clubs *Sport and physical activities:* Compulsory sports: rugby, hockey, cricket, athletics, basketball, tennis, netball, dance, gymnastics, volleyball, cross-country, swimming. Optional: orienteering, soccer, badminton, windsurfing, canoeing, golf. County representatives at rugby and hockey; national tennis finalists; county honours in wide range of sports. *Community service:* Pupils take bronze, silver and gold Duke of Edinburgh's Award. Community service optional at age 14. Regular mountaineering expeditions to French and Austrian Alps; climbing/walking trips to Scotland and Lakes; adventure course to North-West Highlands. *Clubs and societies:* Up to 15 clubs, eg computer, debating, chess, bridge, judo, indoor cricket.

Uniform School uniform worn, except in the sixth-form when suits are an alternative.

Houses/prefects 3 competitive houses. Prefects, school captain, head of house and house prefects – appointed by the Headmaster and housemasters/mistresses.
Religion Assembly compulsory four days a week. All encouraged to attend Mass during the week; Sunday Mass for boarders.
Social Public speaking competitions, choral works, careers conventions with other local schools. Organised trips abroad to eg France. Sixth formers allowed to bring own car/bike/motorbike to school. Lunch self-service; other meals formal. School tuck shop and clothing shop. No tobacco allowed; alcohol on supervised social occasions.
Discipline Pupils failing to produce homework once might expect to receive extra work; those caught smoking cannabis on the premises could expect expulsion.
Boarding 30% have own study bedroom; 10% share doubles; 60% are in dormitories of up to 4, divided by age. Resident qualified nurse, weekly visit by local GP. Central dining room. 1-week exeat each term plus 2 days in autumn term. Visits to the local town allowed on Saturday afternoons.

• AYTON

Ayton School, High Green, Great Ayton, North Yorkshire TS9 6BN. Tel 01642 722141, Fax 01642 724044

• Pupils 207 • Boys 4–18 (Day/Board/Weekly) • Girls 4–18 (Day/Board/Weekly) • Upper sixth 12 • Termly fees £1475 (Day) £3165 (Board) £2785 (Weekly) • Quaker • BSA • Enquiries/application to the Head

What it's like

Founded in 1841 as a co-educational Quaker school, originally for children of Friends who had 'married out of the Society'. It has a fine site of 30 acres of beautiful grounds in the shadow of the North Yorkshire moors, 9 miles south of Middlesbrough. The attractive buildings are very well equipped with modern facilities. The Quaker foundations of the school still underpin its ethos (although most of the pupils are not Quakers) and it lays stress on the need for self-discipline and the creation of a calm, well-ordered community. A lively and purposeful establishment, it is interested in academic success and gets good results. Strong in music, drama and art. There is an excellent range of sports and games and these are pursued with enthusiasm and in a spirit of vigorous competition. A wide variety of extra-curricular activities is provided. Considerable commitment to local community schemes and national charities.

School profile

Pupils Total age range 4–18; 207 pupils, 193 day (102 boys, 91 girls), 14 boarding (10 boys, 4 girls). Senior department 11–18; 124 pupils (67 boys, 57 girls). Main entry ages 4, 7, 11, 13 and into sixth. Approx 12% are children of former pupils. *State school entry:* 50% main senior intake, plus 10% to sixth.
Entrance Own exam used. No special skills or religious requirements; 10% come from Quaker backgrounds. Parents expected to buy only very few specialist sixth-form textbooks; other extras vary. Various bursaries.
Parents 15+% in industry or commerce; 15+% are doctors, lawyers, etc. 60+% live within 30 miles; up to 10% live overseas.
Head and staff *Head:* Alice Meager appointed in 1995. Educated at Keele and Durham universities and Institute of Education (London). Previously Assessment Co-ordinator County Durham and Head of Science at Greenfield School, Newton Aycliffe. *Staff:* 20 full time, 7 part time. Annual turnover 10%. Average age 40.
Exam results In 1995, 35 pupils in upper fifth, 12 in upper sixth. *GCSE:* In 1995, 12 pupils gained grade C or above in 8+ subjects; and 10 in 5-7 subjects. *A-levels:* 8 passed in 4+ subjects; 2 in 3; 1 in 1 subject. Average UCAS points 17.0.
University and college entrance 92% of 1995 sixth-form leavers went on to a degree course (8% after a gap year); others typically go on to employment.
Curriculum GCSE and A-levels. 20 subjects offered, including A-level general studies. *Computing facilities:* new computer area. *Special provision:* Qualified teacher of EFL and for dyslexic pupils. *Europe:* French (from age 9) and German offered to GCSE and A-level; also GCSE Spanish. Small number of European pupils in school.
The arts (Pupils aged 11 and over) *Music:* Up to 25% of pupils learn a musical

instrument; instrumental exams can be taken. Musical groups include choir, orchestra, various ensembles. Various members of county orchestras; numerous winners of Middlesbrough Music Festival; school orchestra won Saltburn Festival 1995. *Drama and dance:* Drama offered. Majority of pupils are involved in regular school productions and house/other productions. *Art:* On average, 15–30% take GCSE. Design, pottery, textiles, photography also offered.

Sport, community service and clubs (Pupils aged 11 and over) *Sport and physical activities:* Compulsory sports: major sports include football, hockey, cricket, tennis, athletics, cross-country, netball, swimming, rounders. Optional: badminton. Regular regional and county representatives. *Community service:* Pupils take bronze, silver and gold Duke of Edinburgh's Award. Ongoing charitable work. *Clubs and societies:* Up to 15 clubs, eg badminton, art, various musical, chess, computer, drama, mountain biking, hiking.

Uniform School uniform worn except in the sixth.

Houses/prefects 3 competitive houses. No prefects; all sixth-form share responsibilities. Head boy/girl appointed by the Head after consultation; heads of houses appointed by houses.

Religion Daily assemblies compulsory. Meeting for worship after the manner of the Religious Society of Friends.

Social Support village events, local (and distant) charities and take part in competitions eg public speaking. Trip abroad annually. Pupils allowed to bring own car/bike/motorbike to school. Meals informal. School shops (food and second-hand uniform). No tobacco/alcohol allowed.

Discipline Pupils failing to produce homework once will produce it next morning.

Boarding Most are in rooms of 2, 3 or 4; not divided into houses. Central dining room. Pupils can provide and cook some food. School closes for 1 week at half term; 2 further weekends for leave-out with parents and according to individual circumstances. Visits to local town allowed for pupils of 14 and above.

Former pupils Ian Gilmour (actor); David Holden (reporter).

B

• BABLAKE

Bablake School, Coundon Road, Coventry CV1 4AU. Tel 01203 228388 Fax 01203 631947

• Pupils 1050 • Boys 7–18 (Day) • Girls 7–18 (Day) • Upper sixth 102 • Termly fees £925–£1250 (Day) • HMC • Enquiries/application to the Headmaster

What it's like

Founded 1344 and refounded in 1563 (after the dissolution of the monasteries), it moved to its present urban site in 1890. The school is now set in 11 acres approximately a mile from the city centre. During the last 30 years, the facilities have been thoroughly modernised, including new science labs, a sports hall and astroturf hockey pitches and tennis courts. Recent additions include the new junior school and a study centre in Normandy. The school is Christian but non-denominational and pupils from all faiths are welcome. It prides itself on being a 'very welcoming, caring school'. Academically strong, its results are very good. Almost all sixth-formers go on to university. Drama is strong, with productions at the Edinburgh Festival for the last 10 years; pupils take leading parts in local amateur dramatics and youth operetta. It is particularly strong in debating and regularly competes in national competitions. The school has its own weather centre, recognised by the Met Office, and Bablake Weather is a regular feature in the local newspaper. Sport is strong with much success at county and regional level in cricket, hockey, netball and rugby. It participates in the Duke of Edinburgh's Award Scheme.

School profile

Pupils Total age range 7–18; 1050 pupils, 580 boys, 470 girls. Senior department 11–18. Main entry ages 7, 11 and into sixth. Approx 15% are children of former pupils. 37% senior pupils from own junior school (Bablake Junior School, tel 01203 634052). *State school entry:* 60% of senior intake, 70% to sixth.

Entrance Own entrance exam used. No special skills or religious requirements. Parents not expected to buy textbooks. 34 pa assisted places. 14 pa scholarships, £900–full fees.

Parents 15+% are doctors, lawyers, etc; 15+% in industry or commerce.

Head and staff *Headmaster:* Dr S Nuttall appointed 1991. Educated at Blackpool Grammar School and universities of Salford and Bristol (chemistry). Previously Deputy Head of Royal Grammar School, Guildford, and Head of Chemistry at Stonyhurst. Also Chairman Central ISIS; HMC representative on RSA Steering Group; member of Coventry EBP Steering Group and Industry 96 Working Group. *Staff:* 67 full time staff, 11 part time. Annual turnover 4%. Average age 40.

Exam results In 1995, 121 pupils in upper fifth, 102 in upper sixth. *GCSE:* In 1995, 117 upper fifth gained at least grade C in 8+ subjects; 4 in 5–7 subjects. *A-levels:* 90 upper sixth passed in 4+ subjects; 7 in 3; 2 in 2; and 3 in 1 subject. Average UCAS points 24.0 (including general studies, 30.7).

University and college entrance 97% of 1995 sixth-form leavers went on to a degree course (12% after a gap year); others typically go straight in to employment. Of those going on to university, 10% went to Oxbridge; 6% took courses in medicine, dentistry and veterinary science, 40% in science and engineering, 3% in law, 12% in humanities and social sciences, 1% in art and design, 2% in other vocational subjects eg nursing, pharmacy, 15% in other subjects eg business, computing, languages.

Curriculum GCSE, AS and A-levels. 15 subjects offered, including A-level general studies. 45% take science A-levels; 35% arts/humanities; 20% both. *Vocational:* Work experience available. *Computing facilities:* 3 rooms with Acorns, plus PCs in science. New whole-school network of PCs in 1996. *Special provision:* Some help for dyslexic pupils. *Europe:* French and German offered to GCSE and A-level (both compulsory for 3 years); also Italian and Spanish GCSE. Regular exchanges (to France and Germany). School owns a manoir in Normandy; all Year 8 pupils spend one week there.

The arts (Pupils aged 11 and over) *Music:* Over 25% of pupils learn a musical instrument; instrumental exams can be taken. Some 10 musical groups including

orchestras, string and wind bands, choirs, madrigal group. 1 member of National Youth Orchestra (to 1993); winner of Leamington Festival small choir competition (1994). *Drama and dance:* Drama and dance offered. GCSE drama may be taken. Some pupils are involved in school productions, the majority in house/other productions. School production in Edinburgh Festival for last 10 years; pupils take leading parts in local amateur dramatics and in Coventry Youth Operetta. *Art:* On average, 40 take GCSE, 6 A-level. Design, textiles also offered.
Sport, community service and clubs (Pupils aged 11 and over) *Sport and physical activities:* Compulsory sports: rugby and cricket for boys, hockey and netball for girls. Optional: hockey, cross-country, athletics, tennis, rounders. Sixth form only: golf, squash, basketball. RLSS, ASA and National Pool Life-guard exams may be taken. U19 cricket team regularly Warwickshire champions; U15 rugby team in semi-finals of Daily Mail national competition 1996; girls U15 and U18 hockey teams Warwickshire champions 1996; U16 and U18 netball, regional finalists 1996; 1 pupil national schools senior javelin champion 1995. *Community service:* Pupils take bronze, silver and gold Duke of Edinburgh's Award. Community service optional. Pupils give parties for local pensioners twice a year. *Clubs and societies:* Up to 30 clubs, eg ballroom dancing, canoeing, archery, science.
Uniform School uniform worn except in the sixth-form, when suits are worn.
Houses/prefects Competitive houses. Prefects, school captain and vice captain – both Head and pupils involved in appointment. School Council.
Religion Attendance at religious worship compulsory.
Social Joint events with other schools include debating competitions (eg Observer Mace, Midland Debating Competition). Organised exchanges to schools in France (Chambery) and Germany (Hemer); annual ski trip (eg USA); annual rugby tour (eg Ireland, Zimbabwe). Pupils allowed to bring own car/bike/motorbike to school. Meals self-service. School shop. No tobacco/alcohol allowed.
Discipline Pupils failing to produce homework once might expect a warning that punishment would be given the next time; any pupil caught smoking cannabis on the premises could expect immediate suspension for a period of days, followed by lengths of community service and counselling.
Alumni association is run by J B Vent, c/o the school.
Former pupils Nick Skelton (show jumper), Robert Clift (Olympic hockey referee).

• BADMINTON

Badminton School, Westbury on Trym, Bristol BS9 3BA. Tel 0117 962 3141 Fax 0117 962 8963 • Pupils 365 • Boys None • Girls 4–18 (Day/Board) • Upper sixth 45 • Termly fees £2075 (Day) £3750 (Board) • GSA, ECIS • Enquiries/application to the Headmaster

What it's like

Founded in 1858, agreeably sited on the outskirts of Bristol near the Downs and in spacious grounds. The style of the school is a combination of discipline and warmth. Staff-pupil relationships are mature and friendly, based on principles of courtesy and mutual respect. All pupils are encouraged to work hard and play hard; the all-rounder is encouraged. There is an emphasis on 'thinking people' and opportunity for exceptional talent. It has a reputation for good teaching and a distinguished academic record. Results are very good and almost all sixth-formers go on to degree courses, including Oxbridge. It is very good on music (which is particularly strong) and the creative arts. There is a lot of emphasis on Europe and the wider world with participation, for example, in the Model United Nations and European Youth Parliament. Full advantage is taken of the facilities of the city and its university. Good range of clubs and societies and it participates in the Duke of Edinburgh's Award Scheme. A good range of sports and extra-curricular activities.

School profile

Pupils Total age range 4–18; 365 girls, 150 day, 215 boarding. Senior department 11–18, 300 girls. Main entry ages 7, 11, 12, 13 and into sixth. Approx 5% are children of former pupils. *State school entry:* 10% of senior intake.
Entrance Common Entrance and own entrance exam used. Special skills in music,

science, sport, languages, art looked for; no religious requirements. Parents expected to buy some textbooks; average extras £30 per term. 20 pa scholarships/bursaries, £800–£4000.

Parents 45+% are doctors, lawyers, etc; 25+% in industry or commerce. 30+% live within 30 miles, 20+% English overseas, 7% foreign.

Head and staff *Headmaster:* Clifford Gould, in post for 15 years. Educated at Haileybury and Trinity College, Dublin (English), and King's College, London (education). Previously Deputy Headmaster, Housemaster and Head of English at Frensham Heights. Also FRSA and member of Court of Bristol University. *Staff:* 36 full time staff, 16 part time. Annual turnover 5%. Average age 40.

Exam results In 1995, 53 pupils in upper fifth, 46 in upper sixth. *GCSE:* In 1995, all upper fifth gained at least grade C in 8+ subjects. *A-levels:* 6 upper sixth passed in 4+ subjects; 40 in 3 subjects. Average UCAS points 23.5.

University and college entrance 95% of 1995 sixth-form leavers went on to a degree course (20% after a gap year); others typically go on to art or music college. Of those going on to university, 10% went to Oxbridge; 15% took courses in medicine, dentistry and veterinary science, 20% in science and engineering, 33% in humanities and social sciences, 5% in art and design, 12% in eg music, drama.

Curriculum GCSE and A-levels. 18 subjects offered (no A-level general studies). 40% take science A-levels; 50% arts/humanities; 10% both. *Vocational:* Work experience available; also RSA stages 1 and 2 in word processing and languages; Pitmans 1, 2 and 3 touchtyping and keyboard skills. *Computing facilities:* Separate rooms with 6 BBCs for juniors; 14 BBCs for middle school; 14 IBMs for seniors. *Special provision:* Very little. *Europe:* French, German and Spanish offered to GCSE, AS and A-level; also non-examined Italian and RSA language courses. Regular exchanges to France, Germany and Spain. Take part in European Youth Parliament; Model United Nations. Bilinguals in school.

The arts (Pupils aged 11 and over) *Music:* Over 85% of pupils learn a musical instrument; instrumental exams can be taken. Some 47 musical groups including orchestras, string groups, wind groups, 4 choirs, jazz groups, 35 small ensembles. 2 members of National Youth Orchestra; 6 in county orchestra; tours of Russia, Italy; performances in cathedrals in Bath, Bristol etc. *Drama and dance:* Drama and dance offered. A-level theatre studies, ESB, Poetry Society, LAMDA, RAD exams may be taken. Some pupils are involved in school productions and all in house/other productions. Parts taken in professional theatre. *Art:* On average, 90% take GCSE, 30% A-level. Design, pottery, textiles, photography, jewellery, screenprinting, wood/metal work, engraving etc also offered. Recent winners of art exhibition at Bristol Cathedral and photography exhibition at Royal Photographic Society, Bath.

Sport, community service and clubs (Pupils aged 11 and over) *Sport and physical activities:* Compulsory sports: hockey, netball, swimming, athletics, tennis, rounders, gym. Optional: fencing, squash, golf, judo, aerobics, badminton, riding, volleyball, dance. Sixth form only: self defence. BAGA, BHS, RLSS, RYA exams may be taken. National level swimmer; ISODE teams. *Community service:* Pupils take bronze, silver and gold Duke of Edinburgh's Award. Community service optional. *Clubs and societies:* Up to 30 clubs, eg Young Engineers, Young Enterprise, Model United Nations, languages, public speaking, magazine, science.

Uniform School uniform worn except in sixth-form.

Houses/prefects Competitive houses; head girl and head of house elected. School Council.

Religion Worship encouraged but not compulsory.

Social Joint events including Bristol Schools Debating; choral/orchestral with Clifton and Queen Elizabeth Hospital; Science Society with Clifton; debates, socials, sports. Organised exchanges to France, Spain, Germany. Skiing trips abroad and expeditions to Italy, Jordan, Paris, Madrid, Russia. Day pupils allowed to bring own car/bike to school. Lunch formal with grace; other meals self service. Second-hand uniform shop. No tobacco/alcohol allowed.

Discipline Firm approach to discipline. Pupils failing to produce homework once might expect report/detention; those caught with drugs would expect instant expulsion.

Boarding 20% have own study bedroom, 30% share; 10% in dormitories of 6+. Houses of 35–50, divided by age. Qualified medical staff available. Central dining room.

Sixth form can provide own breakfasts. 2 termly exeats (1 night) plus half-term. Weekend visits to the local town allowed but never alone nor after dark; reporting back in person.
Alumni association is run by Miss Christabel Thomas, 12 Tormead, Hythe, Southampton, Hants SO4 5AW.
Former pupils Dame Iris Murdoch; Indira Gandhi; Polly Toynbee; Dame Margaret Miles; Claire Bloom.

• BALEARES INTERNATIONAL

Baleares International School, c/Cabo Mateu Coch 17, San Agustin, 07015 Palma, Mallorca, Spain. Tel (34 71) 403161/401812, Fax (34 71) 700319, e-mail bispmi@ibm.net

• Pupils 225 • Boys 3–19 (Day/Board/Weekly) • Girls 3–19 (Day/Board/Weekly) • Upper sixth 10 • Termly fees £500–£1335 (Day) £2860 (Board) £2775 (Weekly) • COBISEC, ECIS, NABSS • Applications/enquiries to the Headmaster

What it's like

Founded in 1957, it has a 4 acre semi-urban site in a residential district near the sea on the western edge of Palma de Mallorca. Three rather handsome Majorcan-type buildings have been converted to create good modern accommodation and facilities. There is a staff:pupil ratio of about 1:14. A British curriculum is provided. There is a strong emphasis on language teaching to a high level. All pupils take GCSE English and Spanish. The school works closely with German education authorities to facilitate the placing of students at universities and all students who complete the lower sixth-form course receive an American credit option to study in the USA. About 25 nationalities are represented. Some music and drama, sport and games. Extra-curricular activities include sailing, pottery, journalism and film-making. Flourishing Scout, Girl Guide and Ranger groups.

School profile

Pupils Total age range 3–19; 225 pupils, 210 day (111 boys, 99 girls), 15 boarding (10 boys, 5 girls). Senior department 11–19, 116 pupils (61 boys, 55 girls). Main entry ages 3 and into sixth. *State school entry:* 80% at 11, plus 50% to sixth.
Entrance No entrance exam. No special skills or religious requirements. Average extras £150; parents not expected to buy textbooks. 4 scholarships pa, £1000–£1750.
Parents 15+% are in industry. 60+% live within 30 miles, 10% overseas.
Head and staff *Headmaster:* John Barrie Wiggins, 10 years in post. Educated at Bedford School and Kings College, London (botany and zoology). Previously Head of Science at Frankfurt International School, Senior School Director at Munich International and Assistant Housemaster at St Albans College, South Africa. *Staff:* 16 full time, 5 part time. Annual turnover 5%. Average age 35.
Exam results In 1995, 18 pupils in Year 11, 10 in Year 13. *GCSE:* In 1995, 2 pupils in Year 11 gained at least grade C in 8 subjects; 13 in 5–7 subjects. *A-levels:* 3 in Year 13 passed in 3 subjects; 4 in 2 and 1 in 1 subject.
University and college entrance 75% of 1995 sixth-form leavers went on to a degree course (5% after a gap year); others typically go on to tourism or hotel management. Of those going on to university, 10% took courses in science and engineering, 50% in humanities and social sciences, 25% in art and design, 10% in eg business.
Curriculum GCSE and A-levels. 8 subjects offered (no A-level general studies). 20% take maths/science A-levels; 40% arts/humanities; 40% a mixture of both. *Computing facilities:* 20 machines (1 in each senior class). Word-processing expected of older students: plenty of printers, scanners etc. *Special provision:* Additional help for dyslexic pupils. Special lighting and help for visually impaired. ESL programme. *Europe:* Spanish, French and German offered to GCSE and A-level; Spanish compulsory from age 6 to GCSE; German taught for native speakers (from 6) and as a foreign language (from 13). European studies taught.
The arts (Pupils aged 11 and over) *Music:* Up to 15% of pupils learn a musical instrument; instrumental exams can be taken. 2 musical groups, choir and popular music. Choir sings in local churches, concert in old people's home etc; pupil built several Renaissance instruments, accepted at Goldsmith's; 13-year-old pianist gained grade 7 distinction. *Drama and dance:* Drama and dance offered. RAD exams may be taken. Some pupils are involved in school productions. 5 pupils involved with local amateur

dramatics. *Art:* On average, 16 take GCSE, 5 A-level. Journalism design and layout, pottery, textiles, photography also offered. Pupils regularly accepted for art school and go on to be professional artists and designers.
Sport, community service and clubs (Pupils aged 10 and over) *Sport and physical activities:* 3 Compulsory sports: soccer, basketball, athletics, swimming. Optional: volleyball, hockey, tennis, sailing. Athletics team winners of inter-schools competition. *Community service:* Scouts, Guides and Rangers groups with community service involvement.
Uniform No school uniform.
Houses/prefects Competitive houses in junior school only. No prefects. School Council.
Religion Attendance at religious worship not compulsory.
Social Sports, occasional dramatic productions and charity walks with other schools. Organised trips to Germany, England, France or mainland Spain; school ski trip. Pupils allowed to bring own car/bike/motorbike to school. Meals self service. School shop. No tobacco/alcohol allowed.
Discipline Pupils failing to produce homework once might expect to receive a warning, with possible mark-down of work; those caught smoking cannabis on the premises could expect to be expelled.
Boarding 25% have own rooms, 75% share with one other; single-sex sections. Resident nurse; doctor on call. Variable number of 4-day exeats each term. Pupils 14+ allowed to visit town at weekends.

• BANCROFT'S

Bancroft's School, Woodford Green, Essex IG8 0RF. Tel 0181 505 4821, Fax 0181 559 0032
• Pupils 952 • Boys 7–18 (Day) • Girls 7–18 (Day) • Upper sixth 114 • Termly fees £1436–£1898 (Day) • HMC, SHA • Enquiries/application to the Head Master

What it's like

Founded in 1737, it occupied its present premises in Woodford about 100 years ago. There are long-standing links with the Company of Drapers. The main buildings are handsome Victorian architecture and most of the later structures blend in sympathetically. The school is well equipped with excellent modern facilities; the playing fields are nearby. There is some religious worship in the Anglican tradition. Founded as a boys' school, it is now fully co-educational having first admitted girls in 1973. A well-run school with vigorous local support, it provides good teaching and the academic results are very good. The majority of leavers proceed to degree courses each year, including Oxbridge. A wide range of sports and games is played with considerable success (a large number of county representatives and some internationals). Good range of clubs and societies. A certain amount of commitment to local community schemes and an impressive record in the Duke of Edinburgh's Award Scheme.

School profile

Pupils Total age range 7–18, 952 day pupils. Senior department 11–18, 746 pupils (347 boys, 399 girls). Main entry ages 7, 11, 13 and into sixth. Approx 5% are children of former pupils. *State school entry:* 50% senior intake and 80% to sixth.
Entrance Own entrance exam used. No special skills or religious requirements. Parents not expected to buy textbooks; £50 maximum extras. 25 pa assisted places (5 at age 7, 10 at 11 and 10 in sixth). Approx 10 pa scholarships, 5 pa bursaries (including music scholarship), £4011–£5298 pa.
Head and staff *Head Master*: Dr Peter Scott, appointed in 1996. Educated at Nottingham High and Oxford (chemistry). Previously Deputy Head at Royal Grammar, Guildford, and taught at Charterhouse. *Staff:* 58 full time, 4 part time. Annual turnover 5%. Average age 33.
Exam results In 1995, 104 pupils in upper fifth, 114 in upper sixth. *GCSE:* In 1995, 100 upper fifth gained at least grade C in 8+ subjects; 4 in 5–7 subjects. *A-levels:* 17 upper sixth passed in 4+ subjects; 73 in 3; 7 in 2; and 3 in 1 subject. Average UCAS points 23.1.
University and college entrance 98% of 1995 sixth-form leavers went on to a degree course; others typically go on to careers or art/drama college. Of those going on to

university, 12% went to Oxbridge; 10% took courses in medicine, dentistry and veterinary science, 35% in science and engineering, 40% in humanities and social sciences, 10% in art and design, 5% in eg drama and music.
Curriculum GCSE and A-levels. 21 GCSE subjects offered; 22 at A-level. 22% take science A-levels; 43% arts/humanities; 35% both. *Vocational:* Work experience available. *Computing facilities:* 2 specialised rooms and about 45 machines in classrooms. *Europe:* French (compulsory 11–16), German and Spanish offered to GCSE and A-level; French AS-level. Regular exchanges to France and Germany. Biennial tour to European centres.
The arts (Pupils aged 11 and over) *Music:* Up to 50% of pupils learn a musical instrument; instrumental exams can be taken. Some 12 musical groups including Bancroft's Singers, 3 orchestras, 2 pop bands. Bancroft's Singers recent tours to China and Egypt. *Drama and dance:* Majority of pupils are involved in school productions and house/other productions. National ESU public speaking champions 1990. *Art:* On average, 30 take GCSE, 15 A-level. Design, pottery, photography also offered. On average 6 pupils to art college each year.
Sport, community service and clubs (Pupils aged 11 and over) *Sport and physical activities:* Compulsory sports: hockey, netball, tennis (girls); rugby, hockey, cricket (boys). Optional: badminton, squash, volleyball, basketball, orienteering, aerobics, golf, swimming, athletics etc. BAGA, RLSS exams may be taken. Many county players at various sports. *Community service:* Pupils take bronze, silver and gold Duke of Edinburgh's Award. CCF optional for 5 years at age 13; CCF camp Munden Trophy winners. Community service optional for 3 years at age 15. *Clubs and societies:* Over 30 clubs, eg poetry, drama, Amnesty, green, chess (Times semi-finalists), electronics (YEDA national finalists), history, singers workshop.
Uniform School uniform worn throughout.
Houses/prefects Competitive houses. Prefects, head boy/girl, head of house – appointed by the Head Master. School Council.
Religion Chapel/assemblies. Special Catholic and Jewish assemblies, Muslim prayers.
Social Lectures organised by departments. French and German exchanges plus other trips abroad. Pupils allowed to bring own car/bike to school. Meals self-service. School shop. No tobacco/alcohol allowed.
Discipline Pupils failing to produce homework once might expect detention; those caught smoking cannabis on the premises might expect expulsion.
Alumni association run by The Secretary, P J Denhard Esq, Lower Flat, 20 Kendall Road, Beckenham, Kent BR3 4PZ.
Former pupils Denis Quilley; Sir Neil Macfarlane; Prof Sir Frederick Warner; Fred Emery; David Pannick QC.

• BARNARD CASTLE

Barnard Castle School, Barnard Castle, Durham DL12 8UN. Tel 01833 690222, Fax 01833 638985

• Pupils 610 • Boys 4–18 (Day/Board) • Girls 4–18 (Day/Board) • Upper sixth 75 • Termly fees £1649 (Day) £2786 (Board) • HMC • Enquiries/application to the Headmaster

What it's like

The present foundation dates from 1883 derived, partially, from St John's Hospital (founded in the 13th century by John Baliol, whose widow founded the Oxford College). It is on a fine site in the Teesdale countryside on the outskirts of Barnard Castle. The main Victorian building is used for administration and accommodation; all the teaching is done in purpose-built classrooms. In the last 25 years there has been much modernisation and development and facilities are now excellent. Originally a boys' school, it first admitted girls in 1984 and became fully co-educational in 1993. A good academic record with many pupils going on to degree courses. Chapel assembly on all weekdays; compulsory Sunday chapel for boarders. The design technology is outstanding, strong on music, drama and sport. Vigorous local support and commitment to the community. Altogether a well-run and flourishing establishment.

School profile

Pupils Total age range 4–18; 610 pupils, 392 day (342 boys, 50 girls), 218 boarding (189 boys, 29 girls). Senior department 11–18; 528 pupils (462 boys, 66 girls). Main entry ages 4, 7, 11, 13 and into sixth. Approx 5% are children of former pupils. 30+% intake from own prep school. *State school entry:* 50% senior intake, plus 50% to sixth.

Entrance Common Entrance and own entrance exam used. No special skills or religious requirements. Parents not expected to buy textbooks; no other compulsory extras. Assisted places. Scholarships/bursaries available, variable value.

Head and staff *Headmaster:* F S McNamara, 16 years in post. Educated at Bishop's Stortford and at King's College, Newcastle, Durham University (geography, economics). Previously Vice Principal at King William's (Isle of Man); Housemaster and Head of Geography at Strathallan. Also Chairman of HMC NE Division. HMC committee member; NEAB committee member. *Staff:* 56 full time, 6 part time, plus music staff. Small annual turnover.

Exam results In 1995, 94 pupils in Year 11, 75 in upper sixth. *GCSE:* In 1995, 60% in Year 11 gained at least grade C in 8 + subjects; 21% in 5–7 subjects. *A-levels:* 57% upper sixth passed in 4+ subjects; 23% in 3; 12% in 2; and 8% in 1 subject. Average UCAS points 19.1.

University and college entrance 85% of 1995 sixth-form leavers went on to a degree course (5% after a gap year); others typically go on to HND or art foundation course. Of those going on to university, 5% went to Oxbridge; 8% took courses in medicine, dentistry and veterinary science, 40% in science and engineering, 12% in law, 36% in humanities and social sciences, 2% in art and design, 2% in eg optometry, education.

Curriculum GCSE and A-levels. 20 subjects offered, including A-level general studies; 9 subjects at AS-level. 41% take science A-levels; 46% arts/humanities; 14% both. *Vocational:* Work experience available. *Computing facilities:* Well-equipped computer room, plus computer club. *Special provision:* Specialist dyslexic teaching; EFL teaching. *Europe:* French and German offered to GCSE, AS and A-level; also GCSE Spanish in the sixth. Regular exchanges to France (inter-school student exchange).

The arts (Pupils aged 11 and over) *Music:* Up to 50% of pupils learn a musical instrument; instrumental exams can be taken. Musical groups include orchestras, jazz band, brass, ensemble, various choirs. 2 members county orchestra; Daily Telegraph jazz competition winners; Teesdale music competition winners. *Drama and dance:* Drama and dance offered. Many pupils are involved in school productions and majority in house/other productions. Several pupils have obtained places with National Youth Theatre; very high standards in school plays and musicals. *Art:* On average, 25 take GCSE, 12 A-level. Design, pottery, textiles, photography, screenprinting also offered. Pupil (aged 13) won Quaker Foods national design a T-shirt competition.

Sport, community service and clubs (Pupils aged 11 and over) *Sport and physical activities:* Compulsory sports: rugby, hockey, cross-country, athletics, swimming, squash, netball, volleyball. Optional: golf, badminton, fencing, canoeing, soccer. RLSS, BCU exams may be taken. 3 rugby internationals, 2 county representatives. *Community service:* Pupils take silver and gold Duke of Edinburgh's Award; 24 silver and 8 gold awards a year. CCF and community service optional for 3 years at age 14. *Clubs and societies:* Up to 40 clubs, eg music, drama, sporting, service and academic.

Uniform School uniform worn throughout.

Houses/prefects Competitive houses. Prefects, head boy/girl, head of house and house prefects appointed by the Head and house staff.

Religion Compulsory Sunday chapel for boarders; chapel assembly each weekday.

Social Organised trips abroad. Pupils allowed to bring own bike to school; cars as privilege. Meals self-service, few formal. School tuck and stationery shops. No tobacco allowed; alcohol allowed in sixth-form club.

Discipline Pupils failing to produce homework once would be dealt with according to circumstances; those caught smoking or possessing cannabis on the premises could expect to be expelled.

Boarding 10% have own study bedroom, 70% share; 15% in dormitories of 6+. Houses of 50–60. Resident qualified medical staff. Central dining room. Pupils can provide and cook some own food. 2 exeats a term (1.5 days), plus half-term. Visits to the local town allowed at housemaster's discretion.

Alumni association is run by Mrs C Rushsbrook, OB Secretary, Barnard Castle School.

Former pupils Lord Mills (Minister of Power); Geoffrey Smith (TV gardening expert); Craig Raine (poet); Kevin Whately (actor); Bentley Beetham (climber – Everest Expedition 1924); Sir Edward Mellanby, FRS (MRC); Rory Underwood, Tony Underwood, Robert Andrew and Tom Danby (rugby internationals); Brian Patterson, Ian Nuttall, Peter Verow (squash internationals); Geoff Turner (international athlete); Kim Hamilton (international modern pentathlete); George Macaulay (test cricketer).

• BASTON

Baston School, Hayes, Bromley, Kent BR2 7AB. Tel 0181 462 1010, Fax 0181 462 0438
• Pupils 220 • Boys None • Girls 3–18 (Day/Board/Weekly) • Upper sixth 15 • Termly fees £1485 (Day) £2900 (Board) £2850 (Weekly) • ISAI • Enquiries/application to the Headmaster

What it's like

Founded in 1933, it has a very pleasant 14-acre site of playing fields, gardens and orchards, on the edge of broad common land in the green belt on the southern outskirts of Bromley. Many of its facilities are purpose built and of a high order (providing comfortable accommodation for the boarders). Well equipped for games and outdoor activities. It gives a sound traditional education and many sixth-formers go on to degree courses. Strong in music, drama, arts and crafts. Plentiful use is made of the amenities of London. A congenial school with a friendly, informal atmosphere. The preparatory department is on the same site.

School profile

Pupils Total age range 3–18; 220 girls, 195 day, 25 boarding. Senior department 11–18, 120 girls. Main entry ages 3, 4, 5, 7, 11, 14 and into sixth. Approx 8% are children of former pupils.
Entrance Own entrance exam used. No special skills or religious requirements. Parents expected to buy sixth-form textbooks only; no other compulsory extras. Up to 3 pa scholarships/bursaries at 11, £150–£450 per term.
Parents 80+% live within 30 miles; up to 10% live overseas.
Head and staff *Headmaster:* Charles Wimble, 13 years in post. Educated at Marlborough and Cambridge (mathematics). Previously Housemaster of sixth-form house at Lancing. Also Treasurer of Kent Women's Lacrosse Association. *Staff:* 20 full time, 11 part time. Annual turnover 3%.
Exam results In 1995, 28 pupils in Year 11; 15 in Year 13. *GCSE:* In 1995, 14 pupils in Year 11 passed in 8+ subjects; 8 in 5–7; 6 in 1–4. *A-levels:* 5 in Year 13 passed in 3 subjects; 4 in 2 subjects. Average UCAS points 13.3.
University and college entrance 50% of 1995 sixth-form leavers went on to a degree course; others typically go on to non-degree courses or straight into careers. Of those going on to university, 15% took courses in science and engineering, 85% in humanities and social sciences.
Curriculum GCSE and A-levels. Business studies offered to GCSE/A-level. 13% take science/engineering A-levels; 53% arts/humanities; 33% a mixture. *Vocational:* Work experience available. *Computing facilities:* 5 BBC B/Master, 14 Acorn A3000, 1 Amstrad 2386 + 17 IBM compatibles. *Special provision:* for EFL and dyslexic pupils. *Europe:* French and German offered to GCSE and A-level; also GCSE Spanish. Regular exchanges to France.
The arts (Pupils aged 11 and over) *Music:* Up to 40% of pupils learn a musical instrument; instrumental exams can be taken. Some 10+ musical groups including 2 orchestras, 3 choirs, percussion groups, instrumental ensembles. Pupils regularly win classes at Beckenham and Bromley festivals. *Drama and dance:* Drama and dance offered. ESB exams may be taken. Majority of pupils are involved in school productions and house/other productions. 30–40 take and pass ESB exams a year. *Art:* On average, 12 take GCSE, 3 A-level. Pottery, textiles also offered. 2–3 pupils go on to art school each year.
Sport, community service and clubs (Pupils aged 11 and over) *Sport and physical activities:* Compulsory sports: athletics, gymnastics, lacrosse, netball, swimming, tennis. Optional: aerobics, football, table tennis, volleyball. Sixth form only: squash. GCSE may be taken. Recent successes include: Tennis, county senior and U16 champions, Greater London U15 champions, Aberdare Cup senior finalists, national Midland Bank U15 runners-up; Lacrosse, county champions U13; Netball, county runners-up U12. *Com-*

munity service: Pupils take bronze and silver Duke of Edinburgh's Award. Community service optional. *Clubs and societies:* Up to 15 clubs, eg pottery, drama, music, computer, country dancing, environment, etc.
Uniform School uniform worn, except in the sixth-form.
Houses/prefects Competitive houses. Prefects, head girl, head of house and house prefects – appointed by staff.
Religion Assemblies compulsory.
Social Organised trips abroad; ski trips, exchange visits to France and Germany, Russian trips, educational cruises, visit to Oberammergau for Passion play. Trips to Orlando and Germany. Upper sixth allowed to bring own car to school. Meals self-service. No tobacco/alcohol allowed.
Discipline Pupils failing to produce homework once might expect admonishment; those caught smoking cannabis on the premises could expect expulsion.
Boarding 5% own study bedroom, 95% share with 2–5. No resident medical staff. Central dining room. Pupils can provide and cook own food. 3 weekend exeats each term. Weekend visits to local town allowed.
Alumni association is run by Mrs Jill C Wimble, c/o the School.
Former pupils Carol Thatcher; Gillian Lynn.

• BATH HIGH

Bath High School, Hope House, Lansdown, Bath, Avon BA1 5ES. Tel 01225 422931, Fax 01225 484378

• Pupils 670 • Boys None • Girls 4–18 (Day) • Upper sixth 53 • Termly fees £978–£1328 • GSA, GPDST • Enquiries/application to the Headmistress

What it's like

Founded in 1875 and a member of the Girls' Public Day School Trust, it occupies beautiful Georgian buildings at Lansdown. There is a large terraced garden and fine views over the city. Games facilities are nearby. There have been extensive modern additions in the last 25 years, most recently a new sixth-form centre and music, art and drama centre. The junior school and senior school are combined. A good general education is provided and academic standards are high. Results are very good and most sixth-formers go on to degree courses, including to Oxbridge. Music, drama and art are all strong. Full use is made of Bath's cultural amenities. Much time and care is devoted to careers advice. A good range of sports and games is provided and standards are very creditable (a lot of representatives at county level). There is a wide variety of clubs and societies and considerable commitment to local community services.

School profile

Pupils Total age 4–18, 670 day girls. Senior department 11–18, 435 girls. Main entry age 11 and into sixth. Significant senior intake from own junior, Bath High Junior School (tel 01225 314458). *State school entry:* 33% at 11, plus 10% to sixth.
Entrance Own entrance exam used. Assisted places and scholarships available.
Head and staff *Headmistress:* Miss Margaret Winfield, in post for 11 years. Educated at Wolverhampton High, Kings Norton Girls' Grammar and Leicester University (history). Previously Headmistress at Hulme Girls' Grammar and Head of History and Second Mistress at Bolton Girls School. Also member of GSA Council; Chairman GSA Membership Committee. *Staff:* 26 full time (senior school), 18 part time. Annual turnover 5%. Average age 40.
Exam results In 1995, 57 pupils in Year 11, 46 in upper sixth. *GCSE:* In 1995, 92% of Year 11 girls gained at least grade C in 8+ subjects; 8% in 5–7 subjects. *A-levels:* 4 upper sixth passed in 4+ subjects; 39 in 3; and 3 in 2 subjects. Average UCAS points 23.8 (including general studies 27.4).
University and college entrance 90% of 1995 sixth-form leavers went on to a degree course (30% after a gap year); others typically go on to physiotherapy, art foundation courses. Of those going on to university, 10% went to Oxbridge; 13% took courses in medicine, dentistry and veterinary science, 13% in science and engineering, 3% in law, 60% in humanities and social sciences, 3% in art and design, 8% in eg occupational therapy, education, accountancy, management.

Curriculum GCSE, AS and A-levels. 22 subjects offered (including A-level general studies). 32% take science A-levels, 46% arts/humanities, 22% both. *Vocational:* Work experience available. *Computing facilities:* IBM compatible machines, some networked; IT centre and computers in most departments; CD-Rom in library, careers and several departments; access to internet. *Europe:* French and German offered to GCSE, AS and A-level; also Spanish GCSE and A-level. Regular exchanges to France (Aix-en-Provence) and Germany (Berlin and Hanover).
The arts (Pupils aged 11 and over) *Music:* Over 30% of pupils learn a musical instrument; instrumental exams can be taken. Some 8 musical groups including orchestra, wind band, jazz group, choirs. *Drama and dance:* Speech and drama offered. LAMDA, Guildhall exams may be taken. Majority of pupils are involved in school and house/other productions. Regular success in Mid-Somerset Festival competition in music and speech/drama. *Art:* On average, 20 take GCSE, 2 AS-level, 10 A-level. Design, pottery, textiles also offered.
Sport, community service and clubs (Pupils aged 11 and over) *Sport and physical activities:* Compulsory sports: hockey, netball, gym, athletics, swimming, tennis, basketball, dance, rounders. Optional: judo, badminton, squash. Sixth form only: aerobics, golf. GCSE, A-level, BAGA exams may be taken. Netball, U14 team represents county; county representatives in athletics, swimming and cross-country; badminton, international U18 representative, national runner-up. *Community service:* Pupils take bronze, silver and gold Duke of Edinburgh's Award. Community service optional at age 14+. *Clubs and societies:* Up to 15 clubs, eg judo, computing, cookery, art, Young Enterprise, drama, crafts, environment.
Uniform School uniform worn except in the sixth.
Houses/prefects House system. 'Leaders', head girl and deputy, elected jointly by staff and sixth-form.
Religion Attendance at religious worship compulsory.
Social Bath Society of Young Musicians, mini-United Nations events, film society joint with other local schools. Links with schools in Prague and St Petersburg. Regular school trips and ski trips annually. Sixth formers allowed to bring own cars. Meals self-service. Sixth form run tuck shop. No tobacco/alcohol allowed.
Discipline Sanctions policy (debits, detentions, on report, suspension, expulsion); credits also given. Pupils failing to produce homework once might expect a warning of a debit next time; those caught smoking cannabis on the premises would be asked to leave the school (strong drugs policy).
Former pupils Helen Rollason (sports commentator); Hilary Williams (Chief Executive, Girl Guides Association); Lady Howe (Equal Opportunities Commission); Dr Elizabeth Hallam-Smith (Public Records Office); Dame Josephine Barnes; Dr Elizabeth Howe (writer and lecturer).

• BATLEY

Batley Grammar School, Carlinghow Hill, Batley, West Yorkshire WF17 0AD. Tel 01924 474980, Fax 01924 420513

• Pupils 550 • Boys 11–19 (Day) • Girls 11–19 (Day) • Upper sixth 76 • Termly fees £1209 (Day) • HMC • Enquiries/application to the Headmaster

What it's like

Founded in 1612, it lies on the outskirts of Batley, near the countryside. The playing fields adjoin it. The buildings are of Yorkshire stone and brick. They are well appointed and all the modern facilities are first class. Recent developments include spacious labs, a sixth-form centre, sports hall and a technology centre. It has remained very much a grammar school in the old tradition of such establishments and provides a sound education which produces consistently good results. Originally a boys' school, it has admitted girls into the sixth-form since 1988. It is now set to become fully co-educational, taking girls at 11 in 1996. Many sixth-formers go on to degree courses. Strong in music (particularly brass bands), sport and outdoor pursuits. Vigorous local support and commitment to the community.

School profile

Pupils Age range 11–19; 550 day pupils (500 boys, 50 girls). Main entry ages 11, 12, 13 and into sixth (girls admitted at 11 from 1996). Approx 5% are children of former pupils. *State school entry:* 92% main intake, plus 85% to sixth.

Entrance Own entrance exam used. No special skills or religious requirements. Parents not expected to buy textbooks; holiday trips etc extra. 68 pa assisted places (44 at age 11 and 8 each at 12, 13 and 16). 5–10 pa scholarships and bursaries, 25%–50% fees.

Head and staff *Headmaster:* William Duggan, in post since 1995. Educated at King's School, Canterbury, and Cambridge (classics). Previously Deputy Head at Warwick School and Head of Classics at Manchester Grammar School. *Staff:* 43 full time, 10 part time. Annual turnover less than 5%. Average age 43.

Exam results In 1996, 94 pupils in upper fifth, 88 in upper sixth. *GCSE:* in 1995, 87% upper fifth gained at least grade C in 8+ subjects; 12% in 5–7; and 1% in 1–4 subjects. *A-levels:* 79% upper sixth passed in 4+ subjects; 14% in 3; 4% in 2; and 3% in 1 subject. Average UCAS points 17.0 (including general studies 25.8).

University and college entrance 80% of 1995 sixth-form leavers went on to a degree course (8% after a gap year); others typically go on to eg banking, armed services, technical apprenticeships, retake A-levels. Of those going on to university, 5% went to Oxbridge; 10% took courses in medicine, dentistry and veterinary science, 35% in science and engineering, 5% in law, 40% in humanities and social sciences, 5% in art and design.

Curriculum GCSE and A-levels. 19 GCSE subjects offered; 2 AS; 19 A-level (including general studies, ancient history and literature, English language). 33% take science A-levels; 45% arts/humanities; 32% both. *Computing facilities:* 16 newly-equipped stations, Archimedes A3000 computing room; 10-station senior computing room; 26 departmentally-based. *Europe:* French (compulsory from age 11) and German offered at GCSE and A-level; also French AS-level. Regular exchanges to France and Germany. Trips to Britanny (second year), Paris (sixth-form) and Rhineland. Satellite TV links.

The arts *Music:* Up to 50% of pupils learn a musical instrument; instrumental exams can be taken. Some 9 musical groups including choir, brass, concert, swing bands, orchestra, recorder, chamber groups, electronic music group. First school band invited by FA to play at Wembley (1991); 3rd in the National Brass Bands Competition, 1994. *Drama and dance:* Some pupils are involved in school productions and house/other productions. *Art:* On average, 25 take GCSE, 5 A-level. Design also offered.

Sport, community service and clubs *Sport and physical activities:* Compulsory sports: football, cross-country, athletics, cricket. Optional: basketball and many other gym sports. Sixth form only: aerobics, squash, water sports eg sailing, canoeing, windsurfing. Recent pupil England rugby captain 16, 18, 21, English Students; 2 Cambridge Blues each in cricket and soccer and one in golf, England U18 player (1992); county soccer champions 1992–3 and semi-finalists of Independent Schools Soccer Cup 1994. *Community service:* Pupils take bronze, silver and gold Duke of Edinburgh's Award. CCF optional from age 14, community service from age 16. *Clubs and societies:* Up to 10 clubs, eg chess, photographic, environment.

Uniform School uniform worn throughout.

Houses/prefects Competitive houses. Prefects, head boy and head girl appointed by Headmaster. Head of house and house prefects appointed by Housemasters.

Religion Morning assembly compulsory unless parents request exclusion.

Social Local road safety quiz organised by seniors; BAYS meetings. Language trips to France and Germany; 2 organised ski trips; classical trip to Greece/Italy; outward bound trips. Pupils allowed to bring own car/bike to school with Headmaster's permission. Meals self-service. No tobacco/alcohol allowed.

Discipline Pupils failing to produce homework once might initially expect extra work; Saturday detention for repeated offences.

Alumni association is run by Mr B Battye, 72 Greenacres Drive, Birstall, Batley WF17 9RA.

Former pupils Sir Willie Morris (Ambassador); Professor Norman Franklin (UKAEA); Joseph Priestley (discovered oxygen in 1774).

• BATTLE ABBEY

Battle Abbey School, Battle, East Sussex TN33 0AD. Tel 01424 772385, Fax 01424 773573 • Pupils 250 • Boys 2½–18 (Day/Board/Weekly) • Girls 2½–18 (Day/Board/Weekly) • Upper sixth 15 • Termly fees: £1030–£1875 (Day); £2430–£3030 (Board/Weekly) • GSA • Enquiries/application to the Headmaster's Secretary

What it's like

Battle Abbey moved to its present site in 1922 and thus enjoys the privilege of being housed in one of the most remarkable buildings in Britain (set in 52 acres of fine parkland). As a part of a valuable ancient monument it is maintained to the highest standards by English Heritage. In 1995 the school merged with Charters-Ancaster and its buildings in Bexhill now house the prep department. Battle Abbey is very comfortable and civilised and has excellent modern facilities. It offers a good all-round education in a family atmosphere and has all the advantages of a small school. Many pupils learn a musical instrument, all take art and take part in sport (astro-turf pitch); everyone, if at all possible, is involved in dramatic productions. Its major strength lies with pupils who lack self-confidence and who might sink without trace in a larger establishment. At Battle Abbey they can be big fish in a small pond; there are no 'also-rans'. It can produce confident young adults from sometimes the most unlikely of pupils. The house system is competitive in work, conduct, manners and sport. High standards of conduct and manners are expected and achieved.

School profile

Pupils Total age range 2½–18; 250 pupils, 200 day (100 boys, 100 girls), 50 boarding (25 boys, 25 girls). Senior department 11–18, 150 pupils (75 boys, 75 girls). Main entry ages 3–5, 7, 11, 13 and into sixth. Approx 5% are children of former pupils. *State school entry:* 10% senior intake plus 10% to sixth.

Entrance Common Entrance and own entrance exam used. No special skills or religious requirements, although school is Christian. Parents expected to buy A-level textbooks only; no other compulsory extras. Automatic bursary for serving members HM forces, 12% of fees.

Parents 15+% in armed services.

Head and staff *Headmaster:* David Teall, in post for 14 years. Educated at Stamford School and Newcastle University (applied science). Previously Deputy Head at St James's, Grimsby, and Head of Biology at King's, Peterborough. Also Secretary, Battle Rotary Club. *Staff:* 16 full time, 7 part time. Low annual turnover. Average age 45.

Exam results On average, 25 pupils in Year 11, 12 in upper sixth. *GCSE:* In 1995, 60% of Year 11 gained at least grade C in 7+ subjects; 10% in 5–6; and 30% in 1–4 subjects. *A-levels:* 75% upper sixth passed in 3 subjects; 25% in 2 subjects. Average UCAS points 19.0.

University and college entrance Some sixth-form leavers go on to degree courses, some to art colleges and others to further eduction colleges. Curriculum GCSE and A-levels. 12 GCSE subjects offered; 11 at A-level (no A-level general studies). 40% take science A-levels; 40% arts/humanities; 20% both. *Vocational:* Work experience available. *Computing facilities:* Large computer room with IBM compatibles, BBC computers in many classrooms. *Special provision:* Special additional lessons can be arranged. *Europe:* French and German offered to GCSE and A-level. Regular exchanges to France and Germany. Week-long trip to France or Germany annually. 4–6 European pupils for all or part of each summer term.

The arts (Pupils aged 11 and over) *Music:* 30% of pupils learn a musical instrument; instrumental exams can be taken. Some 5 musical groups including choirs, madrigal group, orchestra, recorder group. Madrigal group recently won Open Ladies Choir at Hastings Festival. *Drama and dance:* Both offered. RAD exams may be taken. All pupils are involved in school productions, on or off stage. *Art:* On average, 12 take GCSE art and graphics, 12 art and design, 5 A-level. Design and textiles also offered. GCSE design group work exhibited at the Design Centre, London – the Timber Federation sponsoring building of one of designs (children's playground).

Sport, community service and clubs (Pupils aged 11 and over) *Sport and physical activities:* Compulsory sports (choice from): rugby, soccer, hockey, cricket, basketball (boys); netball, hockey, rounders (girls). Optional: badminton, swimming, athletics, tennis, volleyball, cross-country. Sixth form only: squash, weight training. BAGA, RYA exams, tennis, badminton, hockey, swimming, athletics awards may be taken. *Community service:* Pupils take bronze, silver and gold Duke of Edinburgh's Award. Community service optional. A group of pupils regularly attend the local ATC (Air Training Corps) *Clubs and societies:* Up to 30 clubs, eg music, riding, outdoor pursuits – canoeing, rock climbing, abseiling, sailing, dance, computers, driving, judo, photography, bell ringing, Scouts, Guides, golf.

Uniform School uniform worn except in sixth-form.

Houses/prefects Competitive houses. Prefects, head of house and house prefects appointed by the Headmaster or housemaster/mistress. School council.

Religion Christian morning assembly compulsory. Boarders attend Sunday Church (non-Christians excused).

Social Discos once or twice a term. Organised trips to France and Germany, skiing. Meals formal. Sixth formers may have wine for 18th birthdays.

Discipline Pupils failing to produce homework once might expect extra work and an order mark (counting against their house); those caught smoking cannabis on the premises could expect to be expelled without hesitation.

Boarding Sixth have study bedrooms; others in dormitories of 5. Central dining room. Seniors can provide and cook own food. 3 or 4 weekend exeats per term, half-term and 4 Sundays. Visits to the local town allowed.

Alumni association is run by Mrs M Steward, c/o the school.

• BEARWOOD

Bearwood College, Wokingham, Berkshire RG41 5BG. Tel 01734 786915, Fax 01734 773186

• Pupils 216 • Boys 11–18 (Day/Board/Weekly) • Girls 11–18 (Day/Board/Weekly) • Upper sixth 31 • Termly fees £1755–£1950 (Day) £3150–£3500 (Board/Weekly) • SHMIS • Enquiries/application to the Headmaster

What it's like

The present school grew out of the Royal Merchant Navy School, founded in 1827 for orphans of merchant seamen. It has now reverted to co-education, admitting girls from 1995, who live in a refurbished accommodation with their own resident tutor, and now offers education to pupils from any background. A handsome neo-Renaissance mansion forms the central part of the college, set in a splendid country estate. Recent improvements to facilities include a re-equipped computer centre, sixth-form centre, a theatre, music school and photography unit. A relatively small school with a generous staff:pupil ratio of about 1:8. It offers a complete family education, with individual care and development for pupils with a broad range of abilities and backgrounds, from the UK and overseas. A special learning unit is available for those with dyslexia.

School profile

Pupils Age range 11–18; 216 pupils, 211 boys (101 day, 110 boarding); 5 girls (3 day, 2 boarding – girls admitted from 1995). Main entry ages 11, 13 and into sixth but any entry age considered. Transfer from the junior to senior house is automatic.

Entrance Common Entrance at 13, own entrance test at 11. Pupils accepted with a broad range of abilities; all religious denominations welcome. Parents expected to pay £25 per term for books and stationery; extras include music, golf, riding, etc. Open and closed (HM services and British Merchant Navy) scholarships for academic ability, sport, art, drama, music; also bursaries.

Parents 55% live within 30 miles, 21% live overseas.

Head and staff *Headmaster:* Dr R J Belcher, in post for 4 years. Educated at Tonbridge and the universities of East Anglia and London. Previously Deputy Warden at Kingham Hill and head of science at Bloxham. *Staff:* 25 full time, 6 part time. Annual turnover under 8%. Average age 38.

Exam results In 1995, 35 pupils in fifth, 26 in upper sixth. *GCSE:* In 1995, 12 fifth gained at least grade C in 8 + subjects; 11 in 5–7 subjects. *A-levels:* 6 upper sixth passed in 3 subjects; 3 in 2; and 2 in 1 subject. Average UCAS points 7.6.

University and college entrance 50% of 1995 sixth-form leavers went on to a degree course (15% after a gap year); others typically go on to HND or other non-degre courses.

Of those going on to university, 8% took courses in medicine, dentistry and veterinary science, 42% in science and engineering, 42% in humanities and social sciences, 8% in art and design.
Curriculum GCSE and A-level. 17 A-level subjects offered (including general studies). 23% take science A-levels; 15% arts/humanities; 62% both. *Computing facilities:* 20 IBM PS2 including server network. *Special provision:* Language support unit for dyslexic pupils; Specialist EFL teachers. *Europe:* French and German offered at GCSE, AS and A-level.
The arts *Music:* Up to 50% of pupils learn a musical instrument. Music offered at A-level. Musical groups include string orchestra, jazz, choir. Choir sings annually at St Pauls Cathedral (Seafarers Service). *Drama and dance:* Drama offered at GCSE and A-level. Many pupils are involved in school productions. (eg. Bonnie and Clyde and The Odd Couple). *Art:* Art and photography offered at A-level.
Sport, community service and clubs *Sport and physical activities:* Main games: rugby, football, cricket, athletics. Other sport available: tennis, squash, cross-country, basketball, canoeing, sailing, archery, swimming, golf and riding. *Community service:* CCF (army) and Duke of Edinburgh's Award available. *Clubs and societies:* Up to 12 clubs, eg debating, computing, chess, music and outdoor activities (expeditions to eg Alaska, New Zealand and South America).
Uniform School uniform worn; variation allowed in the sixth-form.
Houses/prefects Competitive houses. Prefects appointed by the Headmaster.
Religion Daily chapel (C of E), but all denominations welcomed.
Social Social programme with other local schools. Activity Club travel; ski and sailing trips. Pupils allowed to bring own bike to school. Central cafeteria. School sports shops. No tobacco allowed; limited alcohol (beer/lager) for 17+ in sixth-form club.
Discipline Pupils failing to produce homework once might expect a verbal warning, twice would result in detention; those caught smoking cannabis could expect instant dismissal.
Boarding 20% have own study bedroom, 73% share (2–4), 7% are in dormitories of 4+. Resident staff in medical centre. Weekly boarding available.
Alumni association is run by P J Christian, c/o the College.
Former pupils Francis Scarfe (poet/novelist); Philip Jacobs (textile designer); Lt Cdr R B Stannard VC; Tim Hatley (costume/stage designer).

• BEDALES

Bedales School, Petersfield, Hampshire GU32 2DG. Tel 01730 263286

• Pupils 397 • Boys 13–18 (Day/Board) • Girls 13–18 (Day/Board) • Upper sixth 78 • Termly fees £2980 (Day) £4126 (Board) • HMC, SHMIS, SHA • Enquiries/application to the Registrar for Admissions

What it's like

One of the first co-ed schools in Britain, it opened in 1893. It has a splendid site of 120 acres in East Hampshire, 16 miles from the sea, on a hill overlooking the Rother valley. Civilised and comfortable buildings in beautiful grounds. The Memorial Library is one of the best school libraries in Britain. It was founded as a pioneer school by J H Badley who developed it as a reformed version of the contemporary public schools. His reforms involved a serious commitment to the arts and crafts, rural skills and work out of doors as well as to academic study. Always progressive in the best sense, it is a product of its dissenting origins and idealistic drives; a school within a supporting community, believing strongly in itself and what it has to offer and resistant to orthodoxies and bureaucracies. It is a one-off school with a unique character. Very strong on art, crafts, drama and dance – and music, which has a central position in the life of the school. A feature is the outdoor work department where pupils maintain a large tree nursery, grow fruit, keep livestock, and have rebuilt two barns. It is run as a self-financing concern. Sport is taken seriously and sometimes played at county level. Very much a family atmosphere, relaxed and friendly; informal personal relationships between pupils and staff. Very good academic results, with most leavers going on to degree courses.

School profile

Pupils Age range 13-18; 397 pupils, 99 day (55 boys, 44 girls), 298 boarding (131 boys, 167 girls). Main entry ages 13 and into sixth. 50% of intake from own junior school, Dunhurst (tel 01730 262984). *State school entry:* 3% main intake plus 40% to sixth.
Entrance Own entrance exam used. School looks for pupils with a broad base including academic, art, music, design, drama etc with potential for 8+ GCSEs and 3 A-levels. Parents expected to buy a few textbooks. Assisted places. Scholarships/bursaries available (including academic, music, sixth-form).
Parents Up to 10% live within 30 miles; 15% live overseas; 50% in London and south.
Head and staff *Head:* Alison Willcocks, in post since 1995. Educated at universities of Cambridge (history) and Birmingham (music). Previously Deputy Head and Housemistress at Bedales and taught at Portsmouth High School. *Staff:* 45 full time, 7 part time plus 30+ visiting music teachers.
Exam results In 1995, 87 pupils in fifth year, 66 in upper sixth. *GCSE:* In 1995, 76 upper fifth gained at least grade C in 8+ subjects; 8 in 5 subjects. *A-levels:* 4 upper sixth passed in 4+ subjects; 46 in 3; 12 in 2; and 2 in 1 subject. Average UCAS points 20.5.
University and college entrance 82% of 1995 sixth-form leavers went on to a degree course; others typically go on to art, drama and music colleges. Of those going on to university, 9% went to Oxbridge; 7% took courses in medicine, dentistry and veterinary science, 18% in science and engineering, 3% in law, 56% in humanities and social sciences, 20% in art and design, 3% in drama.
Curriculum GCSE and A-levels. 19 subjects offered (no A-level general studies). 14% take science A-levels; 58% arts/humanities; 29% both. *Vocational:* Work experience available. *Computing facilities:* Industry-standard network of IBM compatible PCs made by RM. *Special provision:* Extra English in year 3 (2 or 3 lessons/week) and year 4 (1 or 2 lessons/week); remedial English lessons on a private basis. *Europe:* French, German and Spanish offered to GCSE, AS and A-level; also Italian GCSE. All lower sixth may study a language in addition to A-level studies. Regular exchanges to France, Germany and Spain. Most sixth-form linguists find summer jobs abroad and some attend language courses. Always has a few European pupils in school. European Committee to promote more interchange.
The arts *Music:* Up to 75% of pupils learn a musical instrument; instrumental exams can be taken. Some 16 musical groups including chamber and symphony orchestras, choirs, instrumental ensembles. Member of National Youth Orchestra; member of county youth orchestra and junior chamber ensembles. *Drama and dance:* Drama and dance offered. GCSE drama and A-level theatre studies, LAMDA exams may be taken. Majority of pupils are involved in school and house productions. Dance troupe to international festival in Dubai; drama group to Edinburgh Fringe. *Art:* On average, 45 take GCSE, 20+ A-level. Design, pottery, textiles, photography, printmaking, etching, screenprinting also offered. Many teach art in developing countries during gap year.
Sport, community service and clubs *Sport and physical activities:* Large choice including gymnastics, dance, swimming, life saving, water polo, canoeing, volleyball, basketball, athletics, badminton, tennis, judo, karate, squash, fencing, hockey, all forms of outdoor pursuits available, plus football and cricket (boys) and netball (girls) and ODW (outdoor work). RLSS exams may be taken. County level cricket, hockey, football, tennis. *Community service:* Pupils take bronze, silver and gold Duke of Edinburgh's Award. Community service optional eg building of sports facilities and wildlife area for local primary school. *Clubs and societies:* Up to 15 clubs, eg cinema, drama, chess, photography.
Uniform School uniform not worn.
Houses/prefects No competitive houses. Head boy/girl but no prefects. Sixth-form committee; boarding house committees and central committee; School Council elected by pupils. Advisory and management skills learnt through committee system.
Religion No compulsory worship but pupils made welcome at adjacent, lively Parish Church where a number are confirmed each year. PRSE in small groups in the curriculum.
Social Organised trips abroad include visits to Spain, ski trips etc. Meals self-service. School shop. Café.
Discipline Anyone caught buying, bringing in or consuming drugs must expect to be expelled. Pupils punished for smoking and drinking.

Boarding Small, mixed age dormitories in single sex houses. Upper sixth-formers in rooms for 1–3 in new co-ed house (preparation for student life). Resident medical staff. Central dining room. Pupils can provide and cook own snacks. Exeats allowed on all but 1–2 weekends a term.
Alumni association is run by RA Wake, c/o the School.

• BEDFORD

Bedford School, Burnaby Road, Bedford MK40 2TU. Tel 01234 340444, Fax 01234 340050
• Pupils 1110 • Boys 7–18 (Day/Board) • Girls None • Upper sixth 127 • Termly fees £1595–£2335 (Day) £2495–£3715 (Board) • HMC • Enquiries/application to the Registrar

What it's like

Founded in 1552, it lies in 50 acres of peaceful and extensive grounds in the centre of Bedford. All but two boarding houses are on site; two within 5 minutes' walk. The interior of the main school building was gutted by fire in 1979. All has been rebuilt and, over the last 30 years, there have been many modern additions. Its facilities are now excellent. It provides continuous education for boys from 7–18 with a mix of local day and international boarders. Strong in all academic disciplines with very good exam results. Almost all leavers go on to degree courses, including at Oxbridge. Also very good at athletics, games and rowing. It has a fine range of extra-curricular activities, plus CCF, Duke of Edinburgh's Award Scheme, community service unit and outdoor pursuits. Vigorous local support and good back-up from alumni.

School profile

Pupils Total age range 7–18; 1110 boys, 860 day, 250 boarding. Senior department 13–18, 713 boys. Main entry ages 7, 8, 11, 13 and into sixth-form. Approx 10% are children of former pupils.
Entrance Common Entrance and own entrance exams used. No special skills or religious requirements. Parents not expected to buy textbooks. 14 pa assisted places. 32 pa scholarships £500 to full fee remission; plus means tested bursaries for boys resident in Bedfordshire.
Parents 15+% are doctors, lawyers, etc; 15+% in industry or commerce. 30+% live within 30 miles; 10+% live overseas.
Head and staff Head Master: Dr I Philip Evans, 6 years in post. Educated at Ruabon Grammar School; and at Cambridge (natural sciences), Imperial College (PhD) and Australian National University, Canberra (post-doctoral fellowship). Also member SCAA Authority and various scientific committees, former Chief Examiner A-level Chemistry (ULEAC). *Staff:* 114 full time, 7 part time. Annual turnover 7%. Average age 35.
Exam results In 1995, 155 in fifth form, 127 in upper sixth. *GCSE:* In 1995, 133 fifth formers gained at least grade C in 8+ subjects; 17 in 5–7 subjects. *A-levels:* 10 upper sixth passed in 4 subjects; 104 in 3; 11 in 2; and 2 in 1 subject. Average UCAS points 22.9.
University and college entrance 93% of 1995 sixth-form leavers went on to a degree course (3% after a gap year); others typically go straight into careers or to eg art college. Of those going on to university, 10% went to Oxbridge; 15% took courses in medicine, dentistry and veterinary science, 20% in science and engineering, 15% in business and administration, 25% in humanities and social sciences, 5% in arts and education, 20% in other subjects.
Curriculum GCSE, AS and A-levels. 27% take science/engineering A-levels; 46% take arts and humanities; 28% a mixture. *Computing facilities:* 100+ Archimedes BBC computers networked into central hard disk facility. *Europe:* French and German offered at GCSE, AS and A-level; Spanish to GCSE and A-level. Regular exchanges to France, Germany and Spain. German pupils (especially from Mülheim) regularly attend lower sixth and some French pupils.
The arts (Pupils aged 11 and over) *Music:* Over 50% of pupils learn a musical instrument; instrumental exams can be taken. Some 6+ musical groups including 3 orchestras, dance, school bands, chamber groups. Wind players have reached finalists' concert of Chamber Music For Schools Trust competition at St John's Smith Square. *Drama and dance:* Drama offered and GCSE, AS and A-level drama may be taken. Many

pupils are involved in school productions and majority in house/other productions. *Art:* On average, 40 take GCSE, 10 A-level. Design, pottery, photography also offered.
Sport, community service and clubs (Pupils aged 11 and over) *Sport and physical activities:* Compulsory sports (for juniors): rugby, hockey. Optional: cricket, hockey and indoor hockey, rowing, rugby, athletics, badminton, basketball, boxing, canoeing, clay-pigeon shooting, croquet, cross-country, fives, fencing, jujitsu, shooting, soccer, squash, swimming, table tennis, tennis, sub-aqua, water polo, weight training, golf, mountaineering. Indoor hockey, regional and occasionally national champions U16 and U18; national and county representatives at various sports. *Community service:* Pupils take bronze, silver and gold Duke of Edinburgh's Award. CCF and community service both optional for 4 years at age 14. Wide range of alternative activities for boys aged 16+. *Clubs and societies:* Over 30 clubs, eg all sports, computing, charities, bridge, all academic activities, mountaineering, wine, music, photography, printing, public speaking, Young Enterprise.
Uniform School uniform worn throughout.
Houses/prefects Competitive houses. Prefects, head boy, head of house and house prefects – appointed by the Head. Various advisory committees.
Religion Compulsory assembly and chapel on Sunday for boarders (unless parents object on valid religious grounds).
Social Joint debates, choral productions, theatrical productions, dances with sister schools. Numerous organised trips abroad. Pupils allowed to bring own car/bike/motorbike to school with permission. Canteen system for meals. School shop. No tobacco allowed. Limited beer for over 18s at weekends.
Discipline Any pupil failing to produce homework once might expect detention; mild anti-social behaviour would lead to half-hour litter collection. Pupils caught smoking cannabis would expect suspension or expulsion. The school aims to inculcate self-discipline by fostering a sense of judgement and personal accountability, combined with respect and responsibility for others, within a framework of clear guidelines governing essential matters of routine; minimal need for, and minimal resort to, punishment.
Boarding Upper sixth have own study bedroom. Senior pupils divided into 6 houses of 35–45, parallel to day houses. Resident qualified nurse. Central dining room. Pupils can provide and cook some own food. Flexible weekend leave, including 2 formal exeats per term plus half term (up to 2 weeks). Visits to local town allowed.
Alumni association is run by John Sylvester, OB Club Office, 10 Glebe Road, Bedford MK40 2PL. Tel 01234 359201.

• BEDFORD HIGH

The High School, Bromham Road, Bedford, Bedfordshire MK40 2BS. Tel 01234 360221, Fax 01234 353552

• Pupils 920 • Boys None • Girls 7–18 (Day/Board from age 8) • Upper sixth 85 • Termly fees £1583 (Day) £3014 (Board) £2980 (Weekly) • GSA, BSA • Enquiries/application to the Headmistress

What it's like

Opened in 1882 as a sister school to Bedford School. It is sited in the centre of Bedford with 21 acres of excellent playing fields. Academic standards are high and results very good; most sixth-formers go on to degree courses. Music, art and drama are all strong. Sports and games are well catered for and include golf, judo and show jumping as well as the standard range. Many county and regional representatives. Numerous clubs and societies cater for most needs and there is keen participation in the Duke of Edinburgh's Award Scheme.

School profile

Pupils Total age range 7–18; 920 girls, 848 day, 72 boarding (from age 8). Senior department 11–18, 740 girls. Main entry ages 7, 8, 9, 11, 13 and into sixth. *State school entry:* 75% senior intake, plus 6% to sixth.
Entrance Own exam used. 22 pa assisted places. 6 pa scholarships and means-tested bursaries.
Head and staff *Headmistress:* Mrs Barbara Stanley, in post since 1995. Educated at

Glenlola Collegiate School, Northern Ireland, and Queen's University, Belfast (geography). Previously Deputy Head at Channing, Head of Department at St Bernard's Convent, Slough, and Head of House at Forest School. Also, formerly member of Amma Northern Ireland Executive; Northern Ireland Council for Educational Research; PCC; Girls' Brigade Captain. *Staff:* 85 full time, 20 part time.

Exam results In 1995, 124 pupils in upper fifth, 85 in upper sixth. *GCSE:* In 1995, 109 upper fifth gained at least grade C in 8+ subjects; 11 in 5–7 subjects. *A-levels:* 13% upper sixth passed in 4+ subjects; 73% in 3; 8% in 2; and 7% in 1 subject. Average UCAS points 20.8.

University and college entrance 84% of 1995 sixth-form leavers went on to a degree course (13% after a gap year); others typically go on to non-degree courses eg HND, art foundation. Of those going on to university, 9% went to Oxbridge; 5% took courses in medicine, dentistry and veterinary science, 30% in science and engineering, 5% in law, 52% in humanities and social sciences, 9% in vocational subjects eg architecture, education, orthoptics.

Curriculum GCSE, AS and A-levels. 23 GCSE subjects offered; 12 at AS-level; 26 at A-level (including general studies). 20% take science A-levels; 55% arts/humanities; 25% both. *Vocational:* Work experience available. *Computing facilities:* Large computer rooms, many departmental computers; computer studies lessons; special art/design computers. *Europe:* French, German and Spanish offered at GCSE, AS and A-level (French compulsory from age 10; either German or Spanish from 13); also GCSE Russian. Regular exchanges to Belgium, Germany and Spain.

The arts (Pupils aged 11 and over) *Music:* Over 50% of pupils learn a musical instrument; instrumental exams can be taken. Some 15 musical groups including choirs, orchestras, woodwind, wind, big bands, madrigal group, brass, strings, flute ensembles. Exchange visits with Germany – performances in Berlin; girls regularly record BBC school music programmes. *Drama and dance:* Both offered and available to GCSE. A-level theatre studies, LAMDA, RAD, ISTD exams may be taken. Many pupils are involved in school productions. *Art:* On average, 45–50 take GCSE, 9 AS-level, 12 A-level. Design, pottery, textiles, photography, CAD also offered.

Sport, community service and clubs (Pupils aged 11 and over) *Sport and physical activities:* Compulsory sports (at different ages): gymnastics, swimming, hockey, lacrosse, netball, rowing. Optional: basketball, volleyball, aerobics, trampolining, table tennis, jogging, show jumping, judo, diving, self defence, fitness. Sixth form only: windsurfing, sailing, golf. BAGA, RLSS, RYA exams may be taken. County hockey champions U16, U18; regional lacrosse champions U12; tennis, national finalists Aberdare Cup, 6 regional representatives; national pentathlete; national level ice skating. *Community service:* Pupils take bronze, silver and gold Duke of Edinburgh's Award. Community service optional from age 15. Inner city play scheme; local youth newspaper; drama scheme with elderly. *Clubs and societies:* Over 30 clubs, eg computer, swimming, Christian Union, German, design and technology, photography, art, chess, junior writers, public speaking, judo, fencing, beekeeping, Italian, classics, chemistry.

Uniform School uniform worn throughout.

Houses/prefects Competitive houses. Prefects, head girl – elected by sixth-form. School Council.

Religion Attendance at religious worship compulsory unless written permission obtained.

Social Skiing holidays; lacrosse, hockey tours to Canada, Barbados. Pupils may bring own bike; car/motorbike with permission but no parking facilities. Meals self-service. School shop. No tobacco/alcohol allowed.

Discipline Pupils failing to produce homework once might expect an order mark. 3 order marks or a more serious offence leads to detention; any pupil caught smoking may expect suspension or expulsion.

• BEDFORD MODERN

Bedford Modern School, Manton Lane, Bedford MK41 7NT. Tel 01234 364331, Fax 01234 270951

• Pupils 1140 • Boys 7–19 (Day/Board) • Girls None • Upper sixth 122 • Termly fees £1033–£1477 (Day) £2113–£2860 (Board) • HMC • Enquiries to the Headmaster • Application to the Admissions Secretary

What it's like

One of the Harpur Trust schools of Bedford, sharing in the endowment made to Bedford by Sir William Harpur in 1566. In 1974 the school moved to entirely new buildings on the northern outskirts of the town. It is a 45-acre wooded hill site with spacious playing fields. The new school is extremely well equipped in every respect and includes sophisticated facilities for sport, a new technology block and a new sixth-form centre. Academic standards are high and results very good; a large number go on to degree courses each year, including to Oxbridge. A number of pupils go into agriculture and industry. Strong in music and sport and a wide variety of clubs and societies. A flourishing school with strong local support.

School profile

Pupils Total age range 7–19; 1140 boys, (1095 day, 45 boarding). Senior department 11–19, 934 boys. Main entry ages 7, 8, 9, 11, 13 and into sixth. *State school entry:* 70% intake 11+, plus some to sixth.

Entrance Common Entrance and own entrance exam used. No special skills or religious requirements. Parents not expected to buy textbooks; lunch for day boys and music tuition extra. 25 pa assisted places. Bursaries (for inhabitants of Bedfordshire), remission according to income.

Parents 80+% live within 30 miles; up to 5% live overseas.

Head and staff *Headmaster:* Stephen Smith, appointed 1996. Educated at Loughborough Grammar and Oxford (history and education). Previously Deputy Head of Birkenhead School and Deputy Head and Head of History at Loughborough Grammar. *Staff:* 84 full time, 2 part time. Annual turnover 5–10%. Average age 38.

Exam results In 1996, 153 pupils in upper fifth, 122 in upper sixth. *GCSE:* in 1995, 84% upper fifth gained at least grade C in 8 subjects; 13% in 5–7; and 2% in 1–4 subjects. *A-levels:* 10% upper sixth passed in 4+ subjects; 72% in 3; 12% in 2; and 4% in 1 subject. Average UCAS points 20.6.

University and college entrance 84% of 1995 sixth-form leavers went on to a degree course; others typically go on to non-degree courses or into careeers eg banking, estate agency. Of those going on to university, 12% went to Oxbridge; 10% took courses in medicine, dentistry and veterinary science, 42% in science and engineering, 48% in humanities and social sciences.

Curriculum GCSE and A-levels. 22 subjects offered (including AS-level general studies). 40% take science A-levels; 40% arts/humanities; 20% both. *Special provision:* Some provision for non-native English speakers. *Europe:* French and German offered to GCSE and A-level; also French AS-level. Regular exchanges to France and Germany. Close links with schools in Bamberg, Germany.

The arts (Pupils aged 11 and over) *Music:* Up to 40% of pupils learn a musical instrument; instrumental exams can be taken. Some 27 musical groups including orchestras, school band, wind, dance bands, woodwind, brass quintets, jazz etc. *Drama and dance:* Drama offered. GCSE expressive arts and A-level theatre studies may be taken. Many pupils are involved in school productions. Community drama group. *Art:* On average, 30 take GCSE, 10 A-level. Design, pottery, printing, photography also offered.

Sport, community service and clubs (Pupils aged 11 and over) *Sport and physical activities:* Compulsory sports: rugby, cricket (up to age 13+), athletics. Optional: rowing, hockey, football, cross-country, fives. Sixth form only: golf, croquet, sailing, shooting, water polo. GCSE, RLSS, RYA exams may be taken. Rugby, county and regional representatives at U16, U18; table tennis, national champions U19, 1995. *Community service:* Pupils take bronze, silver and gold Duke of Edinburgh's Award. CCF and community service optional. Wide range of activities with services programme includes music, drama, stage design, lighting, publications, audio-visual, computer services, school bank, archives. *Clubs and societies:* Up to 30 clubs, eg badminton, fencing, squash, water polo.

Uniform School uniform worn throughout.

Houses/prefects Competitive houses. Prefects, head boy – appointed by the Headmaster after consultation with staff and sixth-form. Sixth form council.

Religion C of E assemblies (compulsory for those not specifically withdrawn). Optional communion services.

Social Debates, concerts, plays with other local schools. About 15 organised trips abroad each year, including French and German exchanges. Sixth form allowed to bring own car/bike/motorbike to school. Meals cafeteria style. School shop. No tobacco/ alcohol allowed.
Discipline Pupils failing to produce homework once might expect a warning or imposition; those caught smoking cannabis on the premises could expect to be suspended.
Boarding One house only. Central dining room. Exeats at half-term and weekends as necessary. Visits to the local town allowed, as requested.
Alumni association is run by A G Underwood, c/o the School.
Former pupils Keith Speed MP; R E G Jeeps (rugby); Vice Admiral Sir Ted Horlick; Major General Keith Burch; Richard Janko (Professor of Classics, University of Los Angeles); Sir Nicholas Lloyd (former Editor Daily Express); Christopher Fry.

• BEDGEBURY

Bedgebury School, Goudhurst, Kent TN17 2SH. Tel 01580 211221/954, Fax 01580 212252
• Pupils 363 • Boys 3–8 only • Girls 3–18 (Day/Board) • Upper sixth 41 • Termly fees £2226 (Day) £3596 (Board/Weekly) • GSA, BSA • Enquiries/application to the Headmistress or Registrar

What it's like

Founded in 1860, it lies in the Kentish Weald and consists of two establishments 6 miles apart. The Lower School at Hawkhurst is accommodated in the fine Victorian and Georgian houses of Lillesden and Collingwood which have delightful grounds. The Upper School occupies a fine 17th century country house in Bedgebury Park – a superb estate of 250 acres. Excellent modern accommodation and facilities are available, including a new arts and technology centre and purpose-built sixth-form boarding house. A pleasant friendly atmosphere prevails. Staff:pupil ratio of about 1:10. The main aim is to achieve the all-round development of each girl and bring out her best by building confidence across a range of achievements. A sound general education is provided and results are creditable; most go on to degree courses. A wide range of vocational qualifications is offered. Very strong art and design, with highly specialised facilities, and good music and drama departments. An excellent range of sports, games and outdoor pursuits – water sports on school's lake, 15-stage assault course, abseiling tower and climbing wall. Activities are plentiful and include riding for many pupils. There are big stables (BHS grade 5) teaching to full instructor standard and over 50 horses and ponies (girls may bring their own). Some local community service work and a good record in the Duke of Edinburgh's Award Scheme.

School profile

Pupils Total age range 3–18; 363 pupils, 350 girls (145 day, 205 boarding), 13 day boys. Senior department 13–18, 222 girls. Main entry ages 3–16. *State school entry:* 10% intake at 11–13, plus 15% to sixth.
Entrance Common Entrance or own entrance exam. A variety of skills (academic and extra-curricular) looked for; personality regarded as important. A C of E school but other religions accepted. Parents not expected to buy text books. Approx 10 pa scholarships (including for music, art, drama, sport), up to 33% day fees; may be augmented to 66% in case of need. Also bursaries and fee inclusion scheme.
Parents 25+% live within 30 miles, 25+% live overseas.
Head and staff *Headmistress:* Mrs Lindsey Griffin, appointed 1995. Educated at Swanshurst Girls' Grammar School and King Edward VI High School, Birmingham, and at the universities of Cardiff (English) and York (medieval studies). Previously Headmistress of St Michael's Burton Park, and Head of Sixth Form and English at Scarborough College. Also Governor of Arundale School, Pulborough. *Staff:* 37 full time, 20 part time. Annual turnover 7%.
Exam results In 1995, 44 pupils in Year 11, 41 in upper sixth. *GCSE:* In 1995, 52% of Year 11 gained at least grade C in 8+ subjects; 17% in 5–7 subjects. *A-levels:* Average UCAS points 13.3.
University and college entrance 92% of 1995 sixth-form leavers went on to a degree

course; others typically go on to careers eg stable work. Of those going on to university, 26% took courses in science and engineering, 57% in humanities and social sciences, 17% in art and design.

Curriculum GCSE, AS and A-levels. 21 GCSE subjects offered; 7 at AS and 25 at A-level (including computing, theatre studies, communication studies, Latin, business studies and further maths). *Vocational:* Work experience available; also BTEC National Diploma in business and finance (equestrian studies). City and Guilds qualifications in fashion, dressmaking and cookery; RSA stages 1, 2 and 3 in shorthand, typewriting skills and wordprocessing; BHS qualifications in riding, horsemanship and teaching. *Computing facilities:* 25 computers in 2 computer rooms, plus 15 computers in business studies; others in a variety of other departments. *Special provision:* Dyslexic units with 6 trained staff. *Europe:* French, German and Spanish offered at GCSE and A-level; Italian as an extra. Exchanges or visits for older pupils to France, Germany and Spain; and work experience arranged. French club.

The arts (Pupils aged 11 and over) *Music:* Over 50% of pupils learn a musical instrument or take singing lessons; instrumental exams can be taken. GCSE, AS and A-level offered. Musical groups include choirs, orchestra and wind band. Involvement in local youth orchestra, choral concerts, musical productions, local music festivals and scratch performances. Pupils regularly go on to conservatoires and university music courses. *Drama and dance:* Drama offered. A-level theatre studies and LAMDA exams may be taken. Majority of pupils are involved in school and house/other productions. recently 2nd place in youth entry of Kent One Act Play Festival; national finalists in Rose Theatre national Shakespeare challenge. *Art:* On average, 30 take GCSE, 15 A-level. Design, pottery, textiles, photography, jewellery also offered. Girls regularly gain entry to art colleges.

Sport, community service and clubs (Pupils aged 11 and over) *Sport and physical activities:* Compulsory sports: netball, tennis, rounders, hockey, athletics, swimming, diving, trampolining, volleyball, basketball, gymnastics, dance, lacrosse. Optional: gymnastics, riding, squash, golf, badminton, tabletennis, aerobics, cross-country, weight training. Other activities include abseiling, climbing, assault course, canoeing, sailing, windsurfing (scuba diving, ice skating, dry slope skiing, paintballing, parascending can also be arranged). Representatives in: lacrosse, 1 in county senior, 1 in county U15; netball, 1 in district; athletics 8 in district; cross country, 2 intercounties. *Community service:* Pupils take bronze and gold Duke of Edinburgh's Award. *Clubs and societies:* Up to 30 clubs, eg Christian Union, drama, photography, pets, computing, screenprinting, various sports and music. Young drivers course, self-defence for sixth-form. All girls in year 9 and lower sixth-forms have 2 days compulsory personal development course.

Uniform School uniform worn except in the sixth.

Houses/prefects Competitive houses. Prefects, head girl and heads of houses – appointed by the Headmistress after consultations. School council and food committee.

Religion Compulsory daily chapel or assembly; Sunday church or school chapel (Catholics go to own church; Muslims may have own instruction).

Social Joint musical and drama activities, debates and drama workshops, discos with other schools. Summer expeditions to eg Ecuador or Himalayas. Exchanges with France, Germany and Australia. Pupils allowed to bring own car/horse to school. Meals mostly self service. School shop. No tobacco/alcohol allowed.

Discipline Regular failure to produce work would lead to a week 'on report' for lessons. Aims for a firm and consistent framwork of discipline but few petty rules. Good standard of appearance expected.

Boarding 30% have own study bedroom, 70% share. Houses divided by age. 2 qualified nurses. Central dining rooms on each site. Sixth formers can provide and cook some meals. 2 weekend exeats each term, more for older girls by special arrangement. Visits to local town allowed; sixth may go to London for weekends. Weekly boarding available.

Former pupils Duchess of Somerset (née Jane Thomas); Virginia Elliot (née Holgate), Kristina Gifford (3-day eventers).

• BEECHWOOD SACRED HEART

Beechwood Sacred Heart, Pembury Road, Tunbridge Wells, Kent TN2 3QD. Tel 01892 532747, Fax 01892 536164

• Pupils 220 • Boys 2–11 only • Girls 2–18 (Day/Board/Weekly) • Upper sixth 30 • Termly fees £850-£2110 (Day) £3535(Board/Weekly) • GSA • Enquiries/application to the Headmaster

What it's like

Founded in 1915, it is single-site on the outskirts of Tunbridge Wells in 22 acres of beautiful grounds. Handsome buildings and very good modern facilities. A friendly family school which has all the advantages of being small. It is a Roman Catholic foundation which welcomes all denominations. A favourable staff:pupil ratio of about 1:10. A good, broad general education is provided and results are good. Most leavers proceed to university. Music is strong; drama and art flourish. A good range of sport, games, societies and clubs. Strong commitment to the Duke of Edinburgh's Award Scheme. Full use is made of the cultural amenities of the town.

School profile

Pupils Total age range 2–18; 220 pupils, 147 day, 73 boarding. Senior department 11–18, 150 girls. Main entry ages 2 and 5 (boys and girls), 11, 14 and into sixth (girls). Approx 3% are children of former pupils. A significant proportion of senior pupils from its own junior department (Beechwood Preparatory School) and from other local prep and primary schools. *State school entry:* 30% main senior intakes, 5% to sixth.

Entrance Own examination for scholarships, or interview and school reports. No special skills required. Roman Catholic foundation but any denomination welcome. Parents not expected to buy textbooks; other extras vary. 10 pa major and minor scholarships; bursaries available to girls already in school in financial need.

Parents 40+% live within 30 miles; 40+% live overseas.

Head and staff *Headmaster:* Trevor Hodkinson, in post since 1994. *Staff:* 22 full time, 11 part time. Annual turnover 5%. Average age 37.

Exam results On average, 22 pupils in Year 11, 30 in Year 13. *GCSE:* On average, 71% of Year 11 gain at least grade C in 8+ subjects; 29% in 5–7 subjects. *A-levels:* 35% of Year 13 pass in 4+ subjects; 32% in 3; 18% in 2; and 14% in 1 subject. Average UCAS points 24.0.

University and college entrance 95% of 1995 sixth-form leavers went on to a degree course (20% after a gap year); others typically go on to further training eg business course, pilot training. Of those going on to university, 5% went to Oxbridge; 2% took courses in medicine, dentistry and veterinary science, 30% in science and engineering, 10% in law, 25% in humanities and social sciences, 10% in art and design, 2% in eg equine studies.

Curriculum GCSE, AS and A-levels. 16 subjects offered, including law and business studies; no A-level general studies but Diploma of Achievement. 18% take science A-levels; 27% arts/humanities; 55% both. *Vocational:* Work experience available. *Special provision:* Extra EFL classes for foreign students. *Europe:* French (compulsory) and Spanish offered to GCSE and A-level; other languages by arrangement. Number of European pupils.

The arts (Pupils aged 11 and over) *Music:* Over 50% of pupils learn a musical instrument; instrumental exams can be taken. Musical groups include choirs, Baroque recorder ensemble, flute choir, chamber orchestra. Joint concerts with Tonbridge School; own 2-day music festival; international artistes give masterclasses and concerts (Thea King, 1996). One recently pupil now at Julliard School, New York. *Drama & dance:* Drama offered. GCSE, AS and A-level drama may be taken. Majority of pupils are involved in school and house/other productions. *Art:* On average, 10 take GCSE, 3 AS-level, 3 A-level. Design, textiles, photography also offered.

Sport, community service and clubs (Pupils aged 11 and over) *Sport and physical activities:* Sports: swimming, tennis, netball, hockey, rounders, basketball, volleyball, badminton, table tennis, gymnastics, dance. Optional: riding, aerobics, ballet, tap. Recent achievements include Junior and Ladies England volleyball player; representatives at county level in hockey, netball, volleyballl, basketball and swimming. *Community service:* Pupils take bronze, silver and gold Duke of Edinburgh's Award. St Vincent de Paul Society. Community service optional. *Clubs and societies:* Up to 15 clubs, eg

chess, bridge, debating, drama, gymnastics, art, Amnesty.
Uniform School uniform worn, modified in the sixth (own clothes in certain colours).
Houses/prefects Competitive houses. Head girl, heads of houses and prefects nominated by the school and academic staff.
Religion Compulsory weekly worship; Sunday mass for boarders.
Social Dances, discos, debates with other schools; occasonal joint theatrical productions. Annual ball for parents and seniors. Frequent fixtures in all sports and activities. Organised trips. Pupils allowed to bring own car/bike to school. Meals self service. School shop. No tobacco allowed; wine only at formal functions.
Discipline Order marks and merit marks. Detention (rarely used). Suspension or expulsion in extreme cases (not used in recent years.)
Boarding 70 have own study bedroom, 30 share with 1 other; 12 are in dormitories of 4–6. Qualified nurse on call. Central dining room. Exeats at parents'/guardians' discretion. Visits to local town allowed.
Former pupils Libby Purves (journalist); Baroness Cumberledge, Pauline Gower.

• BELFAST ROYAL ACADEMY

Belfast Royal Academy, Belfast BT14 6JL. Tel 01232 740423, Fax 01232 352737
• Pupils 1664 • Boys 4–18 (Day) • Girls 4–18 (Day) • Upper sixth 165 • Annual fees £80 (Day) plus £40 per term • HMC • Enquiries/application to the Headmaster

What it's like

Founded in 1785 (the oldest school in the city), its new premises were opened in 1880 in north Belfast. The neo-Gothic buildings of that period have received extensive additions and modernisation now providing excellent facilities. It is non-denominational and has been co-educational since 1891 (it was originally a boys' school). All fees are paid by the local authority. A very high standard of teaching and consistently good results; many go on to degree courses. Very strong in music, drama and sport (many Ulster and Ireland representatives). A large number of extra-curricular activities. Substantial commitment to local community schemes and Duke of Edinburgh's Award Scheme.

School profile

Pupils Total age range 4–18; 1664 day pupils (829 boys, 835 girls). Senior department 11–18, 1368 pupils (604 boys, 704 girls). Main entry ages 4, 11 and into sixth. Approx 15% are children of former pupils. Over 20% of senior intake from own prep.
Entrance Admission by test set by the Department of Education. Academic competence required; no religious requirements. Parents not expected to buy textbooks. No scholarships/bursaries available; all pupils have fees paid by LEA.
Parents 6% engineering; 10% science and technology; 20% business and finance; 15+% doctors, lawyers, teachers.
Head and staff *Headmaster:* W M Sillery, in post for 16 years. Educated at Methodist College and Cambridge University (modern and medieval languages). Previously Deputy Headmaster, Vice-Principal and Head of Modern Languages at Belfast Royal Academy. Also NI Committee, UFC; Educational Adviser, Ulster Television. *Staff:* 81 full time, 13 part time. Annual turnover 5%. Average age 40.
Exam results In 1995, 211 pupils in upper fifth, 191 in upper sixth. *GCSE:* in 1995, 146 upper fifth gained at least grade C in 8+ subjects; 48 in 5–7; and 17 in 1–4 subjects. *A-levels:* 16 upper sixth passed in 4+ subjects; 138 in 3; 23 in 2; and 11 in 1 subject. Average UCAS points 19.0.
University and college entrance 90% of 1995 sixth-form leavers went on to a degree course (3% after a gap year); others typically go on to employment, armed forces or retake A-levels. Of those going on to university, 5% went to Oxbridge; 10% took courses in medicine, dentistry and veterinary science, 28% in science and engineering, 6% in law, 25% in humanities and social sciences, 4% in art and design, 24% in vocational subjects eg accountancy, podiatry, sport and leisure.
Curriculum GCSE and A-levels. 19 GCSE subjects offered; 3 at AS level; 21 at A-level (no A-level general studies); Russian and Japanese taught in sixth-form. 34% take science A-levels; 30% arts/humanities; 36% both. *Vocational:* Work experience available; also RSA stage 3 in typewriting skills and wordprocessing. *Computing facilities:* BBC and

Nimbus networks. *Europe:* French, German and Spanish offered to GCSE and A-level; also French AS-level. Contacts with schools in France and Germany.

The arts (Pupils aged 11 and over) *Music:* Up to 10% of pupils learn a musical instrument in school; instrumental exams can be taken. Some 6 musical groups including orchestra, band, choirs, string quartet, jazz band. 2 members of Ulster Youth Orchestra and Irish Youth Orchestra. *Drama and dance:* Drama offered and GCSE may be taken. Many pupils are involved in school productions and house/other productions (some 150 pupils involved in senior play; up to 200 in the junior play). *Art:* On average, 39 take GCSE, 15 A-level. Design, pottery, textiles, photography also offered. 2 pupils selected for exhibition of best GCSE and A-level work in Northern Ireland in 1995.

Sport, community service and clubs (Pupils aged 11 and over) *Sport and physical activities:* PE compulsory through curriculum. Options include: rugby, hockey, cricket, badminton, tennis, football, volleyball, netball, cross-country, athletics, swimming, sailing, golf, squash, basketball. A significant number of pupils represent Ulster and Ireland in a variety of sports each year. *Community service:* Pupils take bronze, silver and gold Duke of Edinburgh's Award. ATC and community service optional. Pupils run youth club for mentally handicapped, visit the elderly, sign-language courses, Christmas parties for elderly and handicapped. *Clubs and societies:* Over 30 clubs, eg community service, Christian Union, variety of sports and musical groups, debating, lifesaving, chess, computers, electronics, drama etc.

Uniform School uniform worn throughout.

Houses/prefects Competitive houses. Prefects, head boy and girl, house captains, junior house leaders, elected by pupils.

Religion Non-denominational morning assembly compulsory, unless exemption requested by a parent.

Social Youth club for handicapped children organised with community service group of neighbouring grammar school. Annual ski trip; three trips to France and at least one other trip abroad; English trip to Stratford and choir to Edinburgh. Close contacts with Belvedere College, Dublin. Pupils allowed to bring own car/bike/motorbike to school. Meals self-service. School tuck shop. Sixth-form centre. No tobacco/alcohol allowed.

Discipline Pupils failing to produce homework once might expect a scolding or extra work. Smoking cannabis would entail permanent exclusion.

Alumni association Hon Secretaries: Mr M McGuiggan, 28 The Village, Templepatrick BT39 OAA (boys); and Mrs S Swanton, 139 Ballymena Road, Doagh, Ballyclare (girls).

Former pupils Sir Francis Evans (soldier and diplomat); Viscount Garmoyle, Earl Cairns (Lord Chancellor); Archbishop John Armstrong; Archbishop Robin Eames; Major-General Eric Girdwood; Rear Admiral Dudley Gurd; John Cole, Douglas Gageby (journalists); Jack Kyle (sportsman); Colin Middleton (artist); Kate Hoey (MP); Rt Hon Sir Donald Murray (Justice of Appeal).

• BELLVER INTERNATIONAL

Bellver International College, Jose Costa Ferrer 5, Marivent, Palma, Spain. Tel 34 71 401679/ 404263, Fax 34 71 401762

• Pupils 270 • Boys 3–18 (Day) • Girls 3–18 (Day) • Upper sixth 14 • Termly fees £1350 (Day) • COBISEC, ECIS, NABSS • Enquiries/application to the Registrar

What it's like

Founded in 1950 as a co-educational school and, over the years, has gradually expanded from 55 to 270 pupils who come from at least 25 different countries. It is the avowed aim to remain a small school (maximum 300) so that all teachers and management staff know each pupil personally. It occupies agreeable urban, purpose-built premises in Palma, overlooking the bay and is opposite the King of Spain's summer residence. On site it features a range of facilities including a library, gymnasium, 2 laboratories, art room and computer lab. A staff:pupil ratio of about 1:11 permits a good deal of individual attention. It is a pioneer of the new AICE, offered by the Cambridge Exam Board and academic results are good; almost all leavers go on to a degree course. A special programme is available for those with a low level of English. Art is strong; there is drama and some music. Sports and games include football, basketball, volleyball, tennis and karate on local playing fields. About 20% of senior pupils are involved in local community schemes.

School profile

Pupils Total age range 3–18; 270 day pupils (155 boys, 115 girls). Senior department 11–18, 109 pupils (69 boys, 40 girls). Main entry ages 3–4 and into sixth-form but all ages accepted. 4% are children of former pupils.
Entrance Interview; English language and maths test can be required. Second language skills looked for; no religious requirements. Average extras (optional) £150 per term; parents rent rather than buy textbooks. 2 pa bursaries (£1000-£1500).
Parents 15+% are doctors, lawyers, etc. 35% in industry; 10% pilots; 15% in education.
Head and staff Director of Administration: Mark Muirhead, 14 years in post. *Staff:* 26 full time, 3 part time. Annual turnover 8%. Average age 40.
Exam results In 1996, 18 in upper fifth, 6 in upper sixth. *GCSE:* On average, 74% upper fifth gain at least grade C in 8+ subjects; 26% in 5–7 subjects. AICE: 80% upper sixth pass in 6 subjects; 15% in 5 subjects. Average UCAS points 22.0.
University and college entrance 90% of 1995 sixth-form leavers went on to a degree course (10% after a gap year); others typically go in to family business. Of those going on to university, 10% took courses in medicine, dentistry and veterinary science, 20% in science and engineering, 20% in law, 30% in humanities and social sciences, 20% in art and design.
Curriculum GCSE, AICE and Spanish Baccalaureate; pupils are also prepared for the Spanish university entrance exam (Selectividad). 16 subjects offered to GCSE, 15 to AICE (not including general studies); a teacher will be sought for any subject in which 5 or more pupils are interested. 40% take arts/humanities AICE; 60% a mixture of science and arts. *Vocational:* RSA stage 1, 2 and 3 word processing offered. *Computing facilities:* Computing/IT room with 24 486/386DX IBM compatibles (for use also by the prep department). Special provisions: Extra classes can be arranged. *Europe:* French and Spanish offered at GCSE and AICE (Spanish compulsory from age 6, French and Catalan from age 11); German as extra. Trips within Europe eg to France, Portugal, Italy, UK.
The arts (Pupils aged 11 and over) *Music:* 5% of pupils learn a musical instrument. *Drama and dance:* Drama and dance offered as an extra-curricular subject. Majority of pupils are involved in school productions and house/other productions. *Art:* On average, 15 take GCSE, 9 AICE. Design, pottery also offered.
Sport, community service and clubs (Pupils aged 11 and over) *Sport and physical activities:* Compulsory sports: football or volleyball. Optional: tennis, karate, gymnastics. *Community service:* optional for sixth-form. *Clubs and societies:* Some 5 clubs, eg Scottish dancing, gym, computer, drama.
Uniform School uniform worn throughout.
Houses/prefects Competitive houses. Head boy/girl and head of house appointed by the Headteachers.
Religion No religious worship on campus (school is non-denominational).
Social Joint functions with other schools include annual sports day and musical band visit. Pupils allowed to bring own car/bike/motorbike to school. School or packed lunches. No alcohol/tobacco allowed.
Discipline Pupils failing to produce homework once might expect a verbal warning (after three warnings a detention); possession of non-prescribed drugs or alcohol on the school premises will result in immediate expulsion.
Alumni association Mrs Stephanie Muirhead, c/o the School.

• BELMONT HOUSE

Belmont House School, Sandringham Avenue, Newton Mearns, Glasgow G77 5DU. Tel 0141 639 2922, Fax 0141 639 9860

• Pupils 364 • Boys 3–18 (Day) • Girls None • Higher year 58 • Termly fees £1270 (Day) • HAS, SHA • Enquiries/application to the Headmaster

What it's like

Founded in 1929, it is suburban single-site, 7 miles from the centre of Glasgow. The main building is a mansion on the Broom estate. Playing fields are nearby and the surroundings are pleasant. Good facilities are available. The school stresses the fact that it fosters an intimate caring attitude in the classroom with maximum individual attention so that a pupil can reach his academic potential in preparation for adult life. Academic standards are good and most pupils go on to degree courses. Vocational qualifications are offered. The school prides itself on its tutorial service: all members of staff stay on for an extra hour one day per week to give extra help for those who may need it. Adequate range of sports, games and activities. Community services and Duke of Edinburgh's Award Scheme.

School profile

Pupils Total age range 3–18; 364 day boys. Senior department 12–18, 250 boys. Main entry ages 3, 5 and 12. *State school entry:* 80% main senior intake.

Entrance Own entrance exam used. No special skills or religious requirements (number of ethnic minority pupils). Parents not expected to buy textbooks (book rental scheme); maximum extras, £52. Assisted places 23 pa. 50% fee reduction for 3rd child (joint scheme with Craigholme).

Parents 15+% are doctors, lawyers, etc; 15+% in industry or commerce.

Head and staff *Headmaster:* John Mercer, in post for 24 years. Educated at Eastwood Senior Secondary and Glasgow University (history). Previously Principal English Teacher at Belmont House and Assistant Teacher English/history at Mossvale Secondary. Also former President, Eastwood Rotary Club; former Session Clerk, Mearns Kirk. *Staff:* 31 full time, 2 part time. Annual turnover 5%. Average age 44.

Exam results In 1995, 58 pupils in S-grade year, 35 in Higher year. S-Grade: 100% pupils gained 5–7 subjects (7 subjects maximum). *Highers:* 37% passed in 4+ subjects; 9% in 3; 20% in 2; and 20% in 1 subject.

University and college entrance 88% of 1995 sixth-form leavers went on to a degree course; others typically go straight into employment. Of those going on to university, 5% took courses in medicine, dentistry and veterinary science, 30% in science and engineering, 20% in law, 35% in humanities and social sciences, 10% in art and design.

Curriculum S-grades, Highers, CSYS, Scotvec National Certificate. 15 subjects offered. *Vocational:* Work experience available; also Scotvec modules offered in eg electronics, computing, ceramics. *Computing facilities:* Network of 10 Apple Macs; computers in most classrooms; multi-media package. *Special provision:* Specialist tuition 3 days per week for dyslexic pupils. *Europe:* French (from age 6), German (from age 12) offered at S-grade; also Scotvec module in Spanish. Exchange visits with schools in Leipzig and Caen. European dimension introduced to all subjects.

The arts (Pupils aged 11 and over) *Music:* Up to 25% of pupils learn a musical instrument; instrumental exams can be taken. 2 musical groups – choral and chamber groups. Members of regional independent schools orchestra. *Drama and dance:* Drama offered. Majority of pupils are involved in school productions and house/other productions. *Art:* On average, 15 take S-grade, 12 Higher. Design, pottery, photography also offered. Regular prizewinners in area art competitions; silver and bronze medallists in Glasgow Art Galleries annual competition.

Sport, community service and clubs (Pupils aged 11 and over) *Sport and physical activities:* Compulsory sports: cricket, rugby, cross-country, athletics, swimming, gymnastics. Optional: tennis, squash, skiing, canoeing, orienteering, soccer, hillwalking. BACA, AAA exams may be taken. Regularly county champions at skiing; county rugby school sevens champions. *Community service:* Pupils take bronze, silver and gold Duke of Edinburgh's Award Community service optional for 2 years at age 14+. *Clubs and societies:* Up to 10 clubs, eg chess, hillwalking, scripture union, football.

Uniform School uniform worn throughout.

Houses/prefects Competitive houses. Prefects, head boy – appointed by Headmaster and staff; head of house and house prefects – elected by pupils.

Religion School prayers held each morning; Rabbi visits daily for Jewish pupils.

Social Debates, dances, socials with local girls' schools. Participation in national competitions – public speaking, debating. Inter-school Trivial Pursuits competition hosted and organised by Belmont. Local schools top of the form (winners 1991–93). Continental ski trip and 1 sightseeing trip annually. Pupils allowed to bring own car/bike/motorbike to school. Cafeteria system (or packed lunch). No tobacco/alcohol allowed.

Discipline Punishment exercises, chores, after school detention. Pupils failing to produce homework once might expect to rewrite it with additional work. Those caught smoking cannabis on the premises might expect expulsion.
Former pupils Lord Goold (former Chairman of Scottish Conservative Party); Sandy Carmichael (most-capped Scottish rugby forward).

• BELVEDERE

The Belvedere School, 17 Belvidere Road, Prince's Park, Liverpool L8 3TF. Tel 0151 727 1284, Fax 0151 727 0602

• Pupils 651 • Boys None • Girls 3–18 (Day) • Upper sixth 57 • Termly fees £944–£1380 (Day)
• GSA, GPDST • Enquiries/application to the Headmistress

What it's like

Opened in 1880 under the name of Liverpool High School, it has long been a part of Liverpool life and there are currently girls in the school representing at least two generations of their family to be educated there. It aims at a wide social spread. The senior school occupies four large Victorian houses (three of which are scheduled buildings) overlooking Prince's Park. It has agreeable gardens and lawns and some sports facilities on site; others are nearby. There have been extensive additions, including an assembly hall/gymnasium, craftwork, art and music rooms, a science block. The junior school, including a new nursery, is in a separate building nearby. A pleasant friendly atmosphere prevails and the aim of the school is to educate the whole person. A general education is provided and results are good. Each year most sixth-formers proceed to degree courses. There is a good variety of sports and games and a plentiful range of extra-curricular activities. The school also has a creditable record in the Duke of Edinburgh's Award Scheme.

School profile

Pupils Total age range 3–18; 651 day girls. Senior department 11–18, 477 girls. Main entry ages 3, 4, 7, 11 and into sixth. Approx 10% are children of former pupils. *State school entry:* 75% senior intake.
Entrance Own entrance exam used. Parents not expected to buy textbooks; no other extras. 25 pa assisted places plus 5 in sixth-form. Number of bursaries; at least 1 entrance + 5 pa sixth-form scholarships (including 2 for daughters of chemists, grocers and travelling salesmen), value varies.
Head and staff *Headmistress:* Mrs Carole Evans, 5 years in post. Educated at Maghull Grammar and Bangor University (economics and mathematics). Previously Head of Mathematics and Director of Studies at Merchant Taylors' Girls, Crosby. *Staff:* 43 full time, 10 part time. Annual turnover almost nil.
Exam results In 1995, 71 pupils in upper fifth, 45 in upper sixth. *GCSE:* In 1995, 88% upper fifth gained at least grade C in 8+ subjects; 12% in 5–7 subjects. *A-levels:* 60% upper sixth passed in 4+ subjects; 31% in 3; 4% in 2; and 5% in 1 subject. Average UCAS points 18.0 (including general studies 22.0).
University and college entrance 95% of 1995 sixth-form leavers went on to a degree course (4% after a gap year); others typically go on to vocational courses or work. Of those going on to university, 7% went to Oxbridge; 19% took courses in medicine, dentistry and veterinary science, 23% in science and engineering, 7% in law, 37% in humanities and social sciences, 3% in art and design, 11% in eg speech pathology, music.
Curriculum GCSE and A-levels. 22 subjects offered (including A-level general studies). 35% take science A-levels; 35% arts/humanities; 31% both. *Vocational:* Work experience available. *Computing facilities:* 2 computer suites, fully networked. *Europe:* French, German and Spanish offered to GCSE and A-level (German and Spanish are alternatives). French exchange visits (organised by Amitié Internationale des Jeunes); also to Austria, Germany and Spain. Travel scholarship for sixth-former to visit and study European Parliament.
The arts (Pupils aged 11 and over) *Music:* Over 50% of pupils learn a musical instrument; instrumental exams can be taken. Some 7 musical groups including orchestra, choirs, woodwind, string, recorder groups, keyboard club. Recorder group 1st in Liverpool Festival; members of county youth orchestra; pupils in high scorers'

concert of ABRSM. *Drama and dance:* Drama offered and GCSE, A-level and LAMDA exams may be taken. Some pupils are involved in school and other productions. *Art:* On average, 8–12 take GCSE. Design, pottery, textiles also offered.

Sport, community service and clubs (Pupils aged 11 and over) *Sport and physical activities:* Compulsory sports: lacrosse, netball, swimming, tennis, rounders, volleyball, basketball, badminton, unihoc. 7 in county lacrosse junior squad, 3 recent leavers international U21 squads (2 Wales, 1 England goalkeeper); 1 regional water polo team, 1 national U20. *Community service:* Pupils take bronze, silver and gold Duke of Edinburgh's Award. *Clubs and societies:* Up to 30 clubs, eg chess, classics, various academic and music clubs, aerobics, debating, drama, table tennis, trampolining.

Uniform School uniform worn except in the sixth.

Houses/prefects No houses or prefects; head girl and deputies elected by school and staff.

Religion All attend non-denominational assembly.

Social Debates and occasional musical events with local schools. Trips abroad arranged each year. Pupils allowed to bring own car/bike. Meals self service. No tobacco/alcohol allowed.

Discipline Punishment appropriate to offence. Detention is given for continuous unsatisfactory work.

Alumni association is run by Miss Eirlys Owen.

Former pupils Dame Rose Heilbron (High Court Judge); Alyson Bailes (Diplomatic Service); Muriel St Clare Byrne (writer); Anita Samuels (High Sheriff of Liverpool).

• BENENDEN

Benenden School, Cranbrook, Kent TN17 4AA. Tel 01580 240592

• Pupils 440 • Boys None • Girls 11–18 (Board) • Upper sixth 63 • Termly fees £4210 (Board) • GSA • Enquiries/application to the Admissions Secretary

What it's like

Founded in 1923, the main building is a neo-Elizabethan mansion (built in 1862) in enormous gardens designed in the 19th century, set in 240 acres of parkland and woods in one of the loveliest regions of Kent. Numerous recent developments and excellent facilities. Exceptionally well equipped for sports, games and recreations. Predominantly a middle/upper-class school, it is a fully boarding community of high academic achievement. Its results are excellent and nearly all leavers go on to degree courses, including many to Oxbridge. A large staff allows a very favourable staff:pupil ratio of about 1:7. It is strong in art, music and drama and has a good range of sports and games; lacrosse is a particularly strength. The school follows Christian principles and its worship is based on Anglican practice (the Archbishop of Canterbury is the Visitor). It enjoys flourishing links with the local community. Senior girls help and visit the elderly in the neighbourhood and all girls are encouraged to make friends in the local community, particularly within the parish. Local voluntary organisations call on the school's support. There is liaison with local boys' schools for debates, dances and musical entertainment, as well as established house links.

School profile

Pupils Age range 11–18; 440 boarding girls. Main entry ages 11, 12, 13 and into sixth. Approx 11% are children of former pupils.

Entrance Common Entrance and own exam used. No special skills or religious requirements. Parents expected to buy textbooks; extras £72 per term for squash, £132 for music. Substantial academic, music and art scholarships.

Parents 65% live within 1½ hours of the school; 20% live overseas, of which 11% are foreign passport holders from 26 different countries.

Head and staff *Headmistress:* Mrs Gillian du Charme, in post for 11 years. Educated at Beckenham Grammar for Girls and Cambridge University (modern languages). Previously Headmistress at The Town School (New York), Director of Admissions at Concord Academy (Mass) and Head of Upper School at Park School (Brookline, Mass). *Staff:* 58 full time, 39 part time. Annual turnover 5%. Average age 42.

Exam results In 1995, 62 pupils in upper fifth, 63 in upper sixth. *GCSE:* In 1995, 97%

upper fifth gained at least grade C in 8+ subjects; 3% in 6–7 subjects. *A-levels:* 65% of upper sixth passed in 4+ subjects; 30% in 3; and 5% in 2 subjects. Average UCAS points 25.9.

University and college entrance All sixth-form leavers go on to a degree course (often after a gap year), 15% to Oxbridge.

Curriculum GCSE and A-levels. 17 GCSE subjects; 28 at A-level (including Latin and Greek; and AS-level general studies). 20% take science A-levels; 50% arts/humanities; 30% both. *Computing facilities:* Computer centre equipped with Acorn. Network extends across the whole campus. IT taught extensively. *Special provision:* Short-term assistance for learning difficulties and EFL. *Europe:* French, German and Spanish offered to GCSE and A-level. 80% take GCSE in more than 1 language. Short stay students (1–3 terms) regularly from Germany and other parts of Europe. Cross-curricular and exhange trips to France, Austria and Spain

The arts *Music:* Over 50% of pupils learn a musical instrument; GCSE, AS and A-level and instrumental exams can be taken. Musical groups include choirs, wind band, full symphony orchestra, brass, string, vocal groups. Pupil in National Youth Brass Band; pupils in county youth orchestras; winners of various categories in local music festivals. Music festival hosted by the school. Choir in annual combined choirs concert at Canterbury Cathedral. *Drama and dance:* GCSE and A-level drama, ESB, LAMDA exams may be taken. Ballet, modern dance and tap. Majority of pupils are involved in school productions and all in house/other productions. Two debating societies; compete at Oxford and Cambridge Union debating competitions. Sixth formers encouraged to run drama and debating clubs. *Art:* On average, 30 take GCSE, 5 A-level; 14 take history of art A-level. Design, sculpture, pottery, painting, drawing and textiles offered. On average 2 a year into leading London art schools.

Sport, community service and clubs *Sport and physical activities:* Compulsory sports: lacrosse, netball, tennis, swimming, gym, athletics, rounders, volleyball. Optional: riding, fencing, judo, self defence, trampolining, squash, clay pigeon shooting. BAGA, RLSS exams may be taken. Majority of lacrosse 1st team in county and regional teams. *Community service:* Pupils take bronze, silver and gold Duke of Edinburgh's Award. Community service optional. *Clubs and societies:* Over 30 clubs, including literary, Young Enterprise (2 companies), debating society, cookery skills, textiles, clay-pigeon shooting.

Uniform School uniform worn throughout.

Houses/prefects Prefects elected by staff and students. Student Union with elected officials.

Religion Morning prayers, Sunday church service, weekday Communion.

Social Ad hoc joint functions with other schools, eg debating, drama and music; house links with Tonbridge School. Organised trips abroad eg skiing or recently to Russia, China. Senior students allowed to bring own bike to school. All meals self-service. School shop. No smoking allowed; sixth-form allowed glass of wine in supervised weekly social club.

Discipline Students failing to produce homework once might expect work to be marked down or supervised to get it done; set penalties for smoking; possession of drugs would result in expulsion.

Boarding Sixth formers have own study bedrooms; 250 are in rooms of 2–4 or dormitories of 4–8. Two resident qualified nurses, doctor on call. Central dining room. 2–3 weekend (1½ days) exeats a term plus half term (4+ days). Visits to the local towns allowed in small groups.

Alumni association is run by the Seniors' Secretary, c/o the School.

Former students The Princess Royal, Baroness Ryder of Warsaw, Lady Medawar, Joanna Foster; Mrs Ellen Winser, Liz Forgan, Penny Junor, Major Vanessa Lloyd-Davies, Rev Angela Berners-Wilson.

• BERKHAMSTED

Berkhamsted School, Castle Street, Berkhamsted, Hertfordshire HP4 2BB. Tel 01442 863236, Fax 01442 877657

Pupils 750 • Boys 7–18 (Day/Board/Weekly) • Girls 16–18 (Day) • Upper sixth 100 • Termly fees £2368 (Day) £3888 (Board/Weekly) • HMC • Enquiries/application to the Deputy Principal's Secretary

What it's like

Founded in 1541 by John Incent, Dean of St Paul's in the historic centre of Berkhamsted, a prosperous town surrounded by Chiltern countryside. The original school building, the Old Hall, is still used; the rest comprises pleasant 19th-century buildings, and many modern additions. All-round facilities are excellent. Links with Berkhamsted School for Girls, which were already close, have been strengthened. From 1996, they share not only a common board of governors but a single Principal (there is a Deputy Principal in charge of each school; there are no plans to merge the senior schools). The school provides a strong all-round education for boys plus a co-educational sixth-form. Exam results are very good and almost all sixth-formers go on to universities, including Oxbridge. Strong in sports (frequent representation at county, regional and national level), CCF, community service and Duke of Edinburgh's Award Scheme. Music, art and drama flourish. There is flexibility between day, boarding and weekly boarding. The boarding section has an international element (some being expats, 25% foreign). The school is committed to the concept of all-roundness and encourages pupils to develop their particular strengths. The aim is to turn out intelligent, considerate young people who can think for themselves.

School profile

Pupils Total age range 5–18; 750 pupils, 680 day, 70 boarding. Senior department 13–18, 480 pupils (450 boys, 30 girls). Main entry ages 5, 10 and 13 (boys) and into sixth (boys and girls). Approx 15% are children of former pupils. Own prep and junior departments provide 60+% senior intake. *State school entry:* 4% senior intake, plus 4% to sixth.

Entrance Common Entrance exam or own entrance assessment, or if appropriate, interview and reports. No religious requirements (although school itself is Christian). Maximum extras £150 per term; fees include lunches and books. 5 pa assisted places. 10–12 pa scholarships up to half fees (plus bursaries in case of need).

Parents 45+% in industry or commerce. 60+% live within 30 miles; up to 5% live overseas.

Head and staff *Principal:* Dr Priscilla Chadwick, appointed 1996. Educated at Oxford High and at the universities of Cambridge (theology) and London. Previously Dean of Educational Development at South Bank University and Head of Bishop Ramsey School, Acton. *Staff:* 66 full time, 10 part time. Annual turnover 5%. Average age 37.

Exam results In 1996, 100 pupils in upper fifth, 100 in upper sixth. *GCSE:* In 1995, 98 upper fifth gained at least grade C in 8+ subjects; 2 in 5–7 subjects. *A-levels:* 10 upper sixth passed in 4+ subjects; 68 in 3 subjects. Average UCAS points 23.0.

University and college entrance 98% of 1995 sixth-form leavers went on to a degree course (3% after a gap year); others typically go on to eg armed services.

Curriculum GCSE, AS- and A-levels, 24 subjects offered including Japanese language and culture and general studies. 34% take maths/science A-levels; 32% arts/humanities; 34% both. *Vocational:* Work experience available. *Computing facilities:* new computer suite – 25 machines; CD Roms; BBC Masters in prep school. *Special provision:* Extra tuition from study skills department. *Europe:* French, German, Russian and Spanish offered to GCSE and A-level. Regular exchanges to France. Sixth form attending Paris conference on business and job opportunities in EU. Several pupils from Europe attending school.

The arts (Pupils aged 11 and over) *Music:* Up to 35% of pupils learn a musical instrument; instrumental exams can be taken. Some 12 musical groups including orchestra, choirs, cathedral choristers, bands, jazz, ensembles. *Drama and dance:* Some pupils are involved in school productions and majority in house/other productions. Recent school productions of Twelfth Night, As You Like It, Toad of Toad Hall, A Picture of Dorian Gray. *Art:* On average, 30 take GCSE, 8 A-level. History of Art A-level, ceramics, photography also offered. Several go to art college or to study fine art or architecture.

Sport, community service and clubs (Pupils aged 11 and over) *Sport and physical activities:* football, rugby, hockey compulsory for certain age groups. Optional sports:

cricket, tennis, squash, swimming, cross-country, rowing, shooting, golf, Eton fives, athletics, canoeing, sailing, badminton, lifesaving, judo, karate, fencing, weight-training. Swimming, 30 at county level, 5 district trophies, 2 area; athletics, 5 county champions; squash, 2 county representatives; golf, 2 county reps, 2 national; hockey, 1 county rep; rugby, 6 county/area reps, 1 national; shooting, 1st Ashburton cadet pairs, Staniforth Trophy; Eton fives, national quarter-finalists U16; judo, county championship 2 silver, 2 bronze. *Community service:* Pupils take bronze, silver and gold Duke of Edinburgh's Award; CCF (army, navy and airforce sections) and community service both optional for 3 years at age 14. *Clubs and societies:* Up to 15 clubs, eg IT, bridge, CDT, sports, chess, history, biology, economics.

Uniform School uniform worn throughout.

Houses/prefects House system (academic and pastoral). Head of school, school prefects, heads of houses and house prefects – appointed by the Principal, after consulting housemasters, masters and senior pupils.

Religion Chapel attendance expected once a week (and Sundays for boarders), but parents' conscience clause.

Social Co-operation with Berkhamsted (Girls), especially in music, Duke of Edinburgh Award Scheme, drama, Chapel, CCF and social activities. Organised trips abroad for modern languages, skiing, classics, CCF, history. Day pupils allowed to bring own car/bike/motorbike to school. Meals self service. School shops for sports clothes, second-hand clothing, stationery. No tobacco/alcohol allowed.

Discipline Pupils failing to produce homework once might expect a ticking-off; those caught smoking cannabis on or off the premises would be expelled. Bullying regarded as a very serious offence. The principal aim is to encourage self-discipline.

Boarding Some study bedrooms, 60% share 2–4 per room; 25% are in dormitories of 6+. Houses of 45–55. Qualified nurses available; visiting school medical officer. Central dining room. Pupils can sometimes provide and cook own food. Flexible leave-outs – two weekends in three, plus half-term; other optional exeats. Visits to local town allowed as requested.

Alumni association is run by John Flashman, The Secretary, Old Berkhamstedian Association, c/o The Bursary, Berkhamsted School.

Former pupils Antony Hopkins (musician); Mr Justice Michael Coombe; Alexander Goehr (composer); Richard Mabey (writer and naturalist); Sir Kenneth Cork (former Lord Mayor of London); Tarn Hodder (chairman, Hockey Association); Alan Grimsdell (President RFU); Michael Meacher MP (Labour); Keith Mans MP (Conservative); John Bly (antique dealer and broadcaster); Michael van Straten (naturopath and broadcaster); Robin Knox-Johnston (explorer); Graham Greene (novelist); Sir Bryan Carsberg (Ombudsman); Sir Anthony Cleaver (UKAEA).

• BETHANY

Bethany School, Goudhurst, Cranbrook, Kent TN17 1LB. Tel 01580 211273, Fax 01580 211273 • Pupils 275 • Boys 11–18 (Day/Board/Weekly) • Girls 11–18 (Day/Board/Weekly) • Upper sixth 23 • Termly fees £2013 (Day) £3147 (Board/Weekly) • SHMIS • Enquiries/application to the Headmaster

What it's like

Founded on its present site in 1866 by the Rev J J Kendon, a Baptist minister. Thereafter it was run as a small family school until 1948 by members of the minister's family. It remains a small school with a family atmosphere and the chapel is at the centre of its life. Services are in the evangelical tradition and every effort is made to relate religious teaching to daily modern life. The school has a delightful rural setting and its buildings comprise houses round the village green of Curtisden Green, near Goudhurst. It was a boys' school until 1991 when girls were first admitted. A large staff allows a favourable staff:pupil ratio of about 1:10. Most sixth-formers go on to degree courses each year. There is considerable commitment to music, drama and art. A large variety of sports and games is provided and there are the usual extra-curricular activities. A big commitment to the Duke of Edinburgh Award Scheme.

School profile

Pupils Age range 11–18; 275 pupils, 102 day (94 boys, 8 girls) 173 boarding (168 boys, 5

girls). Main entry ages 11, 12, 13 and into sixth. Approx 3% are children of former pupils. *State school entry:* 50% main intake, plus most into sixth.
Entrance Common Entrance and own exam used. No special skills or religious requirements. Parents not expected to buy text books; maximum extras £200. 10 pa scholarships/bursaries, 10%–50% of fees.
Parents 30+% live within 30 miles; up to 15% live overseas.
Head and staff *Headmaster:* William Harvey, in post 7 years. Educated at Trinity (Croydon) and Oxford University (geography). Previously Deputy Headmaster at Scarborough, Housemaster/Director of Studies at Kingham Hill, Head of Geography at Emerson Park Comprehensive (Havering) and Assistant Master at Bedford. Also member SHMIS Professional Development Committee. *Staff:* 28 full time, 4 part time. Annual turnover 10%. Average age 39.
Exam results In 1995, 57 pupils in upper fifth, 23 in upper sixth. *GCSE:* In 1995, 21 upper fifth gain at least grade C in 8+ subjects; 23 in 5–7 subjects. *A-levels:* 2 upper sixth passed in 4+ subjects; 16 in 3; 3 in 2; and 2 in 1 subject. Average UCAS points 13.8.
University and college entrance 90% of 1995 sixth-form leavers went on to a degree course (35% after a gap year); others typically go on to non-degree courses or into employment. Of those going on to university, 5% went to Oxbridge; 5% took courses in medicine, dentistry and veterinary science, 50% in science and engineering, 5% in law, 20% in humanities and social sciences, 5% in art and design, 15% in eg business.
Curriculum GCSE and A-levels; also GNVQ. 15 subjects offered (no A-level general studies). 55% take science A-levels; 30% arts/humanities; 15% both. *Vocational:* Work experience available; Advanced GNVQ in business; City and Guilds basic level in IT and photography. *Computing facilities:* Specialist computer rooms with Nimbus computers; computers in all departments and boarding houses. *Special provision:* Long-established dyslexic unit for pupils with above-average IQ. *Europe:* French and German offered to GCSE, AS and A-level. Regular exchanges to France. European pupils study in school at any time.
The arts *Music:* Up to 50% of pupils learn a musical instrument; instrumental exams can be taken. Some 6 musical groups including orchestra, choir, choral society, brass, wind, string. *Drama and dance:* Drama and dance offered. Some pupils are involved in school productions and house/other productions. *Art:* On average, 50% take GCSE, 12% AS-level, 30% A-level. Design, pottery, textiles, photography also offered. Several pupils have obtained places at art colleges.
Sport, community service and clubs *Sport and physical activities:* A wide range of sports (some compulsory in junior years) including rugby, cricket, cross-country, netball, hockey, swimming, rounders, aerobics, badminton, basketball, football, dance, squash, volleyball, weight training. GCSE and A-level PE may be taken. Member of England rugby U19 squad. *Community service:* Pupils take bronze, silver and gold Duke of Edinburgh's Award; 75% of pupils are involved voluntarily. Community service optional (part of D of E). *Clubs and societies:* Up to 30 clubs, eg archery, art, car mechanics, chess, Christian Union, computing, cookery, model railway, sailing, shooting, windsurfing.
Uniform School uniform worn except in the sixth where there are dress regulations.
Houses/prefects Competitive houses. Prefects, head of school, head of house and house prefects – appointed by Head and Housemasters/Housemistresses. School Council.
Religion Compulsory religious worship.
Social Discos, lectures, drama and choral events. Rugby, skiing, cycling, natural history camping trips abroad. Pupils allowed to bring own bike to school. Meals self-service. School tuck shop. No tobacco allowed, some alcohol in presence of staff (sixth-form only).
Discipline Pupils failing to produce homework once might expect to be detained to complete it. A pupil caught smoking cannabis on the premises would be expelled and the incident referred to the police.
Boarding 15 have own study bedroom; 35 share with 1 other; remainder in dormitories mostly of 4. Single-sex houses of 15–60, divided by age. Resident qualified nurses, doctor in village. Central dining room. 2 overnight exeats per term plus each Sunday, weekly boarding available. Weekend visits to village allowed.
Alumni association run by P S Holmes Esq, Secretary, c/o the School.
Former pupils Lord Stamp.

• BIRKDALE

Birkdale School, Oakholme Road, Sheffield S10 3DH. Tel 0114 266 8408, Fax 0114 267 1947
Pupils 780 • Boys 4–18 (Day) • Girls 16–18 (Day) • Upper sixth 70+ • Termly fees £1533 (Day) • SHA, SHMIS • Enquiries/applications to the Head Master

What it's like

Founded at the turn of the century, it moved in 1915 to its present agreeable site in a Victorian residential suburb near the university and 1½ miles from the city centre. The pre-preparatory and preparatory schools are nearby. A sixth-form was established in 1988 and girls were first admitted to it in 1995. Since the mid-sixties there has been steady development which includes excellent laboratories, an art and design building, a sixth-form centre, music school and sports hall. There has been vigorous supporting response from the local community and wide interest outside the city. It is a Christian school; there is some emphasis on religious education and all pupils are expected to attend morning prayers. Academic standards and results are good; virtually all sixth-form leavers go on to degree courses. Music is quite strong and includes successful jazz and swing bands. Some drama (joint productions with girls' school) and art. A standard range of sports and games, including soccer, is provided and there are good facilities for these on 9½ acres of fields nearby. Outdoor pursuits (eg hill walking, climbing) are an integral part of the curriculum; there are regular expeditions arranged for all pupils from 12+. Some community service is undertaken and the Duke of Edinburgh's Award Scheme is well supported.

School profile

Pupils Total age range 4–18; 780 day pupils (760 boys, 20 girls). Senior department 11–18, 470 pupils (450 boys, 20 girls). Main entry ages, 4, 7 and 11 (boys) and into sixth (boys and girls). 10% are children of former pupils. Own junior department, Birkdale Preparatory School provides 66% senior intake. *State school entry:* 30% main intake, plus 85% to sixth.

Entrance Common Entrance and own exam used. No special skills or religious requirements. Parents not expected to buy textbooks. Average £10 extras. Some assisted places. 10pa scholarships/bursaries, £100–£600 per term.

Parents 15+% are doctors, lawyers, etc; 15+% from industry/commerce.

Head and staff Head Master: Rev Michael D A Hepworth, in post for 13 years. Educated at Monkton Combe and Cambridge (theology). Previously Senior House-master, Senior Chaplain and Head of RE at Bedford and Assistant Master at Eastbourne and Windsor Grammar. Also Chairman of Trustees, Carnoch Outdoor Centre, Glencoe (1986). *Staff:* 57 full time, 10 part time. Annual turnover 4%. Average age 37.

Exam results In 1995, 66 pupils in fifth, 45 in upper sixth. *GCSE:* In 1995, 55 fifth gained at least grade C in 8+ subjects; 7 in 5–7; and 4 in 1–4 subjects. *A-levels:* 31 upper sixth passed in 4+ subjects; 9 in 3; 4 in 2 subjects. Average UCAS points 19.0.

University and college entrance 95% of 1995 sixth-form leavers went on to a degree course (15% after a gap year), up to 10% to Oxbridge; 10% take courses in medicine, dentistry and veterinary science, 25% in science and engineering, 20% in law, 30% in humanities and social sciences, 5% in art and design, 10% in vocational subjects.

Curriculum GCSE and A-levels. 20 A-level subjects offered (including general studies). 27% take science A-levels; 43% arts/humanities; 30% both. *Vocational:* Work experience (1 week) for all lower sixth; some placements in France and Germany. *Computing facilities:* New IT centre with Nimbus machines. 20 other machines in subject areas throughout senior school. CAD in design department. *Special provision:* Specialist teachers for dyslexic pupils. *Europe:* French and German offered to GCSE, AS and A-level. Regular exchanges to France and Germany and work placements as part of A-level coursework. Link schools with Kepler Gymnasium, Tübingen; annual study trip to France. Lectures from MEPs; French and German assistants; satellite TV.

The arts (Pupils aged 11 and over) *Music:* Up to 25% of pupils learn a musical instrument; instrumental exams can be taken. Some 7 musical groups including jazz, swing bands, quartet, 2 orchestras, choir, early music group. Jazz band area runners-up in Daily Telegraph Young Jazz 1992. *Drama and dance:* Some pupils are involved in school productions and house/other productions. 2 boys in National Youth Theatre; junior boys in Granada TV's Children's Ward and in productions at Lyceum Theatre,

Sheffield. Produced Royal Hunt of the Sun at Crucible Theatre in 1995, Shaffer's Black Comedy, 1996. *Art:* On average, 20 take GCSE, 5 A-level. Design, photography also offered.

Sport, community service and clubs (Pupils aged 11 and over) *Sport and physical activities:* Compulsory sports: rugby, soccer, cricket, athletics. Optional: tennis, swimming, basketball, golf. GCSE PE may be taken. Boys represent Yorkshire and South Yorkshire at rugby. Winners, South Yorkshire Sevens (1994). *Community service:* Pupils take bronze, silver and gold Duke of Edinburgh's Award. *Clubs and societies:* Up to 30 clubs, eg debating, chess, war games, music, drama, Christian Union.

Uniform School uniform worn throughout.

Houses/prefects Competitive houses. Head of school, prefects, head of house and house prefects, appointed by the Head.

Religion Attendance at religious worship compulsory.

Social Trips to Germany/France. Pupils allowed to bring own cars. Meals self-service. School shop. No tobacco/alcohol allowed.

Discipline Corporal punishment allowed in theory but never used. Pupils failing to produce homework once could expect, at most, supervision; detention if unsatisfactory. Those caught smoking cannabis on the premises likely to be suspended; expulsion for pushers.

Alumni association is run by M R Eckersley, Chairman OBA, 9 Harewood Way, Whirlowdale Park, Sheffield S11 9QR.

Former pupils Antony Favell MP; Mr Justice Paul Kennedy (High Court judge); Lord Riverdale; Colonel John Boddy (High Sheriff); Michael Palin; Rex Harrison, Mark Roe.

• BIRKENHEAD

Birkenhead School, 58 Beresford Road, Birkenhead, Wirral, Merseyside L43 2JD. Tel 0151 652 4014

Pupils 1065 • Boys 3–18 (Day) • Girls None • Upper sixth 98 • Termly fees £1221 (Day) • HMC • Enquiries/application to the Headmaster

What it's like

Founded in 1860 and soon established as the leading boys' school in the locality, it has pleasant late Victorian and modern buildings on an estate of some 50 acres on an open site in the village of Oxton, a suburb of Birkenhead. All the main buildings are on the same campus. The principal playing fields are central and others are two minutes' walk away. There have been many additions and improvements to facilities in the last 20 years. The school is organised in 3 departments: the prep for pupils aged 3–11; the junior school, aged 11–13; and the senior school aged 13–18. There is a favourable staff:pupil ratio, especially in the sixth-form. A good general education is given and academic results are very good. Almost all pupils go on to degree courses each year, including a number to Oxbridge. The school has a strong Christian tradition and prayers are held each morning in the chapel. The Chapel choir is well known to be outstanding and performs at the level of a cathedral choir. The music, drama and art departments are very active. A good range of sports and games in which high standards are attained. There is also a wide variety of extra-curricular activities and a flourishing CCF contingent. The Duke of Edinburgh's Award Scheme is well supported and pupils have had many successes.

School profile

Pupils Total age range 3–18; 1065 day boys. Senior department 11–18, 681 boys. Main entry ages 3, 4, 11, 13 and into sixth. Approximately 15% are children of former pupils. Large proportion of senior intake from own prep department (tel 0151 652 4114) *State school entry:* 55% main senior intake, plus 5% to sixth.

Entrance Common Entrance and own exam used. Academic excellence and breadth of interests looked for; no religious requirements. Parents not expected to buy textbooks. 36 pa assisted places. 20 pa scholarships/bursaries dependent on parental need, £100–£1,000.

Parents 15+% doctors, lawyers etc; 15+% in industry and commerce; 15+% university staff.

Head and staff *Headmaster:* Stuart Haggett, in post for 8 years. Educated at Dauntsey's,

Cambridge University (French, German) and College of St Mark and St John (education). Previously taught at King's (Rochester) and Canford. *Staff:* 82 full time, 3 part time. Annual turnover 5%. Average age 42.

Exam results In 1995, 112 pupils in upper fifth, 94 in upper sixth. *GCSE:* In 1995, 106 upper fifth gained at least grade C in 8+ subjects; 6 in 5–7 subjects. *A-levels:* 78 upper sixth passed in 4+ subjects; 10 in 3; 4 in 2 subjects. Average UCAS points 21.2 (including general studies 28.9).

University and college entrance 98% of 1995 sixth-form leavers went on to a degree course (9% after a gap year); others typically go straight into employment. Of those going on to university, 10% went to Oxbridge; 6% took courses in medicine, dentistry and veterinary science, 25% in science and engineering, 4% in law, 40% in humanities and social sciences, 6% in vocational subjects eg psychology, computing.

Curriculum GCSE and A-levels. 19 subjects offered (including A-level general studies). 30% take science A-levels; 31% arts/humanities; 39% both. *Vocational:* Work experience available. *Computing facilities:* Two fully equipped laboratories with Acorn, BBC and Archimedes. *Europe:* French (compulsory age 11-14), German and Spanish offered at GCSE, AS and A-level. Regular exchanges to France and Germany.

The arts (Pupils aged 11 and over) *Music:* Over 30% of pupils learn a musical instrument; instrumental exams can be taken. Some 8 musical groups including choir, choral society, 2 orchestras, bands. Brass ensemble winners Bromborough Festival; chapel choir on Radio 4, Radio Merseyside etc. *Drama and dance:* Some pupils are involved in school productions and majority in house/other productions. *Art:* On average, 22 take GCSE, 4 A-level.

Sport, community service and clubs (Pupils aged 11 and over) *Sport and physical activities:* Optional sports: rugby, cricket, hockey, athletics, tennis, swimming, cross-country etc. Some pupils play cricket for England; many in county teams. *Community service:* CCF, community service and Young Enterprise both optional for 3 years at age 15. *Clubs and societies:* Up to 15 clubs.

Uniform School uniform worn throughout; prefects and monitors wear gowns.

Houses/prefects Competitive houses. Prefects, head boy, head of house and house prefects – appointed by the Headmaster in consultation with staff and outgoing prefects.

Religion Daily service in the school chapel.

Social Joint debates, concerts, plays with Birkenhead High. 2 French exchange schemes, numerous other individual visits, ski trips, classical trips etc. Pupils allowed to bring own car/bike to school. Meals self-service. School shop. No tobacco/alcohol allowed.

Discipline Pupils failing to produce homework once would be given extra work and expected to produce the original work; those caught smoking cannabis on the premises could expect automatic expulsion.

Alumni association is run by I W Bakewell, Rollestone, Oldfield Drive, Heswall L60 6SS.

Former pupils Rt Hon Sir Donald Nicholls, Alan Rouse, Earl of Birkenhead, Canon Graham Routledge, Sir Gordon Willmer, Professor Neville Willmer, Lord Evans of Claughton, Rt Hon H Graham White.

• BIRKENHEAD HIGH

Birkenhead High School, 86 Devonshire Place, Birkenhead, Merseyside L43 1TY. Tel 0151 652 5777

• Pupils 1000 • Boys None • Girls 3–18 (Day) • Upper sixth 92 • Termly fees £1200 (Day)
• GSA, GPDST • Enquiries/application to the Headmistress

What it's like

Founded in 1901, it is single-site in a quiet, pleasant, residential district. The junior school is on the same campus. There have been many modern developments and additions to its late Victorian buildings. A high standard of teaching to a traditional curriculum and results are very good. The vast majority of girls go on to degree courses, including Oxbridge (not a few go into medicine and the law). A distinguished school with vigorous local support, it is fundamentally Christian in ethos. A friendly, informal atmosphere in which plenty of freedom is given to sixth-formers who play a considerable part in running the school. A wide range of sport and games, numerous societies and clubs. Very strong indeed in music and drama. Substantial commitment to local community schemes and much success in the Duke of Edinburgh's Award Scheme.

School profile

Pupils Total age range 3–18; 1000 day girls. Senior department 11–18, 700 girls. Main entry ages 11 and into sixth. Approx 5% are children of former pupils. Over 20% of senior intake from own junior dept. *State school entry:* 50% intake at 11+, 75% intake at 16+.

Entrance Own entrance exam used. No special skills or religious requirements. Parents not expected to buy textbooks; no other extras. 40 pa assisted places. Some scholarships/ bursaries available.

Parents 15+% in industry or commerce; 15+% are doctors, lawyers etc.

Head and staff *Headmistress:* Mrs Kathleen Irving, in post for 10 years. Educated at Birkenhead High and Liverpool University (zoology). Previously Deputy Headteacher at Joseph Leckie Comprehensive and Brownhills Comprehensive, Sixth Form Tutor/Head of Biology at Codsall Comprehensive, and Head of Biology at Ockbrook Moravian. *Staff:* 57 full time, 19 part time.

Exam results In 1995, 121 pupils in upper fifth, 92 in upper sixth. *GCSE:* In 1995, 93% upper fifth gained at least grade C in 8 + subjects. *A-levels:* 44% upper sixth passed in 4 + subjects; 47% in 3; 5% in 2; and 3% in 1 subject. Average UCAS points 21.3 (including general studies 25.2).

University and college entrance 94% of 1995 sixth-form leavers went on to a degree course (6% after a gap year); others typically go on to art foundation courses, employment or the armed forces. Of those going on to university, 8% went to Oxbridge; 15% took courses in medicine, dentistry and veterinary science, 27% in science and engineering, 7% in law, 40% in humanities and social sciences, 3% in art and design, 7% in vocational subjects.

Curriculum GCSE and A-levels. 20 GCSE subjects offered; 22 at A-level, including general studies and Russian. 40% take science A-levels; 40% arts/humanities; 20% both. *Vocational:* Work experience available. *Computing facilities:* 30 station network 486 machines. (Archimedes in junior department.) *Europe:* French (compulsory from year 7), German, Spanish and Russian offered at GCSE, AS and A-level. Regular exchanges to France.

The arts (Pupils aged 11 and over) *Music:* Up to 50% of pupils learn a musical instrument; instrumental exams can be taken. Some 8 musical groups including 2 orchestras, 3 choirs. School holds own music festival with 300 individual and group entries. *Drama and dance:* Drama offered. GCSE and A-level drama and Poetry Society exams may be taken. Majority of pupils are involved in school productions and house/ other productions. *Art:* On average, 20 take GCSE, 5 A-level. Design, photography also offered.

Sport, community service and clubs (Pupils aged 11 and over) *Sport and physical activities:* Compulsory sports: swimming, squash, volleyball, trampolining. GCSE PE may be taken. Netball teams regularly in national finals. *Community service:* Pupils take bronze, silver and gold Duke of Edinburgh's Award. Community service optional. *Clubs and societies:* Over 30 clubs, eg Christian Union, politics, French, drama, all sports, history, debating.

Uniform School uniform worn except in sixth.

Houses/prefects Competitive houses. No prefects. Head girl and 3 deputies – elected by the school.

Religion Christian morning assembly.

Social Debates and joint theatrical productions with local boys' independent school. Organised trips abroad. Pupils allowed to bring own car/bike/motorbike to school. Meals self service. No tobacco/alcohol allowed.

Discipline Pupils failing to produce homework once might expect a reprimand or lunchtime detention.

Former pupils Patricia Routledge (actress and singer); Ann Bell (actress); Judith Collins (first woman Curator of the Tate Gallery); Janet McNeill (novelist, especially of children's books); Doreen Sloane (actress); Dr Vivienne Nathanson (BMA); Penny Hughes (Coca-Cola).

• BISHOP CHALLONER

Bishop Challoner School, 228 Bromley Road, Shortlands, Kent BR2 0BS. Tel 0181 460 3546, Fax 0181 466 8885

• Pupils 392 • Boys 2½–18 (Day) • Girls 2½–18 (Day) • Upper sixth 19 • Termly fees £820–£1285 (Day) • ISAI • Enquiries/application to the Headmaster

What it's like

Founded in 1946 by two local parish priests, it is single-site and semi-rural on 4½ acres and combines nursery, junior and senior schools. In 30 years there have been numerous extensions to the original house to provide good modern facilities. A sound education is given. About 50% of pupils are Roman Catholic. Assemblies are religious, Mass is said regularly and the curriculum incorporates religious education to A-level. Fencing is especially strong.

School profile

Pupils Total age range 2½–18; 392 day pupils (324 boys, 68 girls). Senior department 11–18, 186 pupils. Main entry ages 4, 11 and into the sixth. Own junior school provides approximately 50% of senior intake.

Entrance Own entrance exam used. No special skills or religious requirements but majority are Roman Catholic. Parents not expected to buy textbooks. Scholarships/bursaries available in senior school including sixth-form.

Parents 15+% in industry or commerce; 15+% are doctors, lawyers etc.

Head and staff *Headmaster:* Terence Robinson, in post for 11 years. Educated at Ushaw College, Durham, and universities of Newcastle and Oxford (botany and zoology; educational management). Previously Head of Science at St Edmund Campion, Oxford, and Head of Lower School at Ushaw College, Durham. Also Oxfordshire Education Department Science Advisory Group. *Staff:* 27 full time, 9 part time. Annual turnover 1%. Average age 40.

Exam results In 1995, 30 pupils in fifth form, 17 in upper sixth. *GCSE:* In 1995, 9 pupils in fifth form passed at least grade C in 8+ subjects; 11 in 5–7 subjects. *A-levels:* 9 upper sixth passed in 3 subjects; 4 in 2; 1 in 1 subject. Average UCAS points 13.5.

University and college entrance 90% of 1995 sixth-form leavers went on to a degree course; others typically go straight into careers eg aircraft engineering. Of those going on to university, 80% took courses in science and engineering, 20% in humanities and social sciences.

Curriculum GCSE and A-levels. *Vocational:* Work experience available (1 week in fourth year). *Computing facilities:* Computer room with 8 486Xs (2 with CD-Rom), 4 printers; facilities for GCSE and A-level computer studies. *Special provision:* dyslexic pupils given special help. *Europe:* French (from age 8) and Spanish offered at GCSE and A-level.

The arts (Pupils aged 11 and over) *Music:* Up to 15% of pupils learn a musical instrument; instrumental exams can be taken. 2 musical groups, both choirs. *Drama and dance:* Majority of pupils are involved in school productions and house/other productions. Recent productions of Orton's Erpingham Camp and of Wind in the Willows. *Art:* On average, 8 take GCSE, 2 A-level. Design also offered.

Sport, community service and clubs (Pupils aged 11 and over) *Sport and physical activities:* Compulsory sports: PE, soccer, cricket, athletics. Optional: fencing, rugby, basketball, tennis. GCSE may be taken. Tennis and rugby, county representatives; fencing, county cup winners; awards in national finals. *Clubs and societies:* Up to 15 clubs, eg chess, art, computers, golf, fishing.

Uniform School uniform worn except in the sixth.

Houses/prefects No competitive houses. Prefects and head boy – appointed by the Headmaster after consulting school. School Council.

Religion All attend religious assemblies. Regular Mass for Catholics.

Social Organised trips abroad for skiing, classics, adventure etc. Pupils allowed to bring own car/bike/motorbike to school. Meals formal. No tobacco/alcohol allowed.

Discipline Pupils failing to produce homework once might expect loss of free time to do the work and/or be put on report; those caught smoking cannabis on the premises could expect expulsion.

• BISHOP'S STORTFORD

Bishop's Stortford College, Maze Green Road, Bishop's Stortford, Hertfordshire CM23 2QZ.
Tel 01279 758575, Fax 01279 755865

• Pupils 317 • Boys 13–18 (Day/Board) • Girls 13–18 (Day/Board) • Upper sixth 65 • Termly fees £2580 (Day) £3580 (Board) • HMC • Enquiries/application to the Headmaster

What it's like

The college was founded in 1868 in East Anglia, and was then primarily intended for the education of Nonconformists. It was reconstituted in 1904 and now accepts members of all Christian denominations; religious instruction and worship are non-denominational. It has a fine site on high ground on the edge of the pleasant town, next to open countryside, with gardens and grounds covering 100 acres. The buildings are agreeable and well equipped. At their centre stands an impressive Memorial Hall (erected in 1921). Recent improvements include a new centre for physics, design technology and information technology, and an artificial grass pitch for hockey and tennis in 1997. Originally a boys' school, it first admitted girl in the sixth-form in 1977 and at all ages in 1995. Overall there is a favourable staff:pupil ratio of about 1:10. Academic standards are high and results are very good. Virtually all sixth-formers go on to degree courses. Music is very strong throughout the school, and so is drama with good collaboration between the two departments. There is a good range of sports and team games in particular are pursued to a high level. A plentiful variety of extra-curricular activities is available including projects related to the community and the environment.

School profile

Pupils Age range 13–18, 317 pupils, 192 day (164 boys, 28 girls), 125 boarding (111 boys, 14 girls) – girls admitted throughout the age range in 1995. Main entry ages 13 and into sixth. 70% intake from own prep. *State school entry:* a small number at 13+ but over 50% at sixth-form.

Entrance Common Entrance or own entry testing as applicable. 10 pa assisted places (4 at 11, 2 at 13, 4 at 16). Also scholarships, awards for sons of Free Church ministers and bursaries for those showing financial need.

Head and staff *Headmaster:* Stephen G G Benson, 12 years in post. Educated at The Leys and Cambridge (history). Previously Housemaster and Head of History at Gresham's. Also Chairman HMC Eastern Division (1994).

Exam results In 1995, 80 pupils in upper fifth, 65 in upper sixth. *GCSE:* In 1995, 73 upper fifth gained at least grade C in 8+ subjects; 4 in 5–7 subjects. *A-levels:* 3% upper sixth pass in 4 subjects; 89% in 3; 8% in 2 subjects. Average UCAS points 20.9.

University and college entrance 87% of 1995 sixth-form leavers went on to a degree course (26% after a gap year); others typically go on to art foundation courses or direct to employment. Of those going on to university, 10% went to Oxbridge; 5% took courses in medicine, dentistry and veterinary science, 10% in science and engineering, 5% in law, 65% in humanities and social sciences, 5% in art and design, 10% in vocational subjects eg speech therapy, education.

Curriculum GCSE and A-levels (no A-level general studies; Japanese offered as a non-examined subject). 17% take science A-levels; 48% arts/humanities; 35% both. *Vocational:* Work experience available for all upper fifth and for sixth-form on request. *Computing facilities:* Apple Macintosh – classroom of 24. Many others in departments and library. No formal exam in computer studies/science but IT for all. *Special provision:* Learning support department. *Europe:* French and German offered to GCSE and A-level; also GCSE Spanish. Regular exchanges to Germany. European pupils regularly in lower sixth.

The arts *Music:* Up to 50% of pupils learn a musical instrument; instrumental exams can be taken. Some 12+ musical groups including orchestra, wind, dance bands, guitar, string quartets, brass group, choirs, choral society, various ensembles and pop groups. Own recording studio. *Drama and dance:* Drama offered. Many pupils are involved in school productions and majority in house/other productions. *Art:* On average, 12 take GCSE, 7 A-level. Design, pottery, photography, print-making, glass engraving also offered. 3 consecutive prize winners in Bowater design competition; winner town mural competition.

Sport, community service and clubs *Sport and physical activities:* Sports compulsory 3

afternoons/week: main sports – (boys) rugby, hockey, cricket, swimming, cross-country, tennis, water polo, netball; also – badminton, soccer, athletics; (girls) hockey, netball, rounders, tennis, swimming etc. *Community service:* Pupils take bronze, silver and gold Duke of Edinburgh's Award. Community service optional; strong links with old people's homes and centres for those with physical or mental handicaps; Saturday meals on wheels service. Environmental projects. *Clubs and societies:* Up to 15 clubs, eg science, natural history, local history, literary, expeditions, chess, debating, Schools Challenge (general knowledge), choral, poetry, numerous activities.
Discipline Range of sanctions applied including detentions, loss of privileges and house duties; suspension and even expulsion are ultimate punishments. Pupils failing to produce homework once might expect an extension to be granted; those caught smoking cannabis on the premises could expect almost certain expulsion.
Former pupils Ben Clarke (rugby player international), Stephen Lander (Head of MI5).

• BLACKHEATH HIGH

Blackheath High School, Vanbrugh Park, Blackheath, London SE3 7AG. Tel 0181 853 2929, Fax 0181 853 3663

• Pupils 600 • Boys None • Girls 4–18 (Day) • Upper sixth 31 • Termly fees £1140–£1548 (Day) • GSA, GPDST • Enquiries/application to the Headmistress

What it's like

Opened in 1880, it was the first purpose-built school in the Girls' Public Day School Trust. Its agreeable, well-equipped buildings lie close to Greenwich Park and the Heath itself and pupils are drawn from a wide catchment area. The senior school moved in 1994 to new premises, comprised of purpose-built and historic buildings with many excellent new facilities. The junior department occupies the refurbished buildings once occupied by the senior school. A broad general education is provided and results are very good. A feature of the overall programme is the stimulating cross-curricular work in Years 7 and 8. The majority of sixth-form leavers proceed to university. Music is strong: many pupils learn an instrument and are involved with school orchestras and school choirs and with chamber music groups. Concerts are often given. Art is also strong, and drama is well supported, with school plays and drama competitions. Sports and games are very well catered for and include netball (representation at county level), volleyball, gymnastics, badminton, rowing, athletics, tennis, softball and cricket. There is a plentiful variety of clubs and societies and the whole school is very active in charity work and local community schemes. Ample use is made of London's cultural amenities.

School profile

Pupils Age range 4–18; 600 day girls. Senior department 11–18, 365 girls. Main entry ages 4, 7, 11 and into sixth. Under 1% are children of former pupils. Own junior school provides more than 20% intake. *State school entry:* 45% at 11, plus 50% to sixth.
Entrance Own entrance exam. No special skills or religious requirements. Parents not expected to buy textbooks; average extras £85 per term (music lessons). 14 pa assisted places at 11, 6 pa in sixth-form. 3 pa scholarships and bursaries (including music award), £50 to half fees.
Parents 15+% are doctors, lawyers, etc. 15+% in industry.
Head and staff *Headmistress:* Miss R K Musgrave, 7 years in post. Educated at Cheltenham Ladies' College, and at universities of Oxford, Reading and London (English language and linguistic science). Previously Head of English at Channing, Head of Sixth at Haberdashers' Aske's (Girls), taught English at Latymer Grammar and Camden School for Girls. Also Chairman of London Region of SHA and Chairman of Professional Development Committee of GSA. *Staff:* 32 full time, 14 part time. Annual turnover 5%. Average age 44.
Exam results In 1995, 55 pupils in upper fifth, 31 in upper sixth. *GCSE:* In 1995, 38 upper fifth gained at least grade C in 8+ subjects; 15 in 5–7 subjects. *A-levels:* 6 upper sixth passed in 4+ subjects; 18 in 3; 3 in 2 subjects. Average UCAS points 21.0.
University and college entrance 90% of 1995 sixth-form leavers went on to a degree course, 7% went to Oxbridge; 5% took courses in medicine, dentistry and veterinary science, 18% in science and engineering, 72% in humanities and social sciences, 5% in music.

Curriculum GCSE and A-levels. 18 subjects offered (including GCSE Latin; no A-level general studies). 5% take science A-levels; 36% arts/humanities; 59% a mixture of both. *Vocational:* Work experience available. *Computing facilities:* Fitted computer room including Apple Macs. *Special provision:* Visiting teacher for dyslexic pupils. *Europe:* French and German offered to GCSE and A-level; also GCSE Spanish. Regular exchanges to France and Germany.
The arts (Pupils aged 11 and over) *Music:* 35% of pupils learn a musical instrument; instrumental exams can be taken. Some 7 musical groups including 3 orchestras, choirs, wind band, recorder, chamber groups. *Drama and dance:* Both offered. GCSE drama may be taken. Majority of pupils are involved in school and other productions. *Art:* On average, 15 take GCSE, 6 A-level. Photography also offered.
Sport, community service and clubs (Pupils aged 11 and over) *Sport and physical activities:* Compulsory sports: hockey, netball, tennis, volleyball, badminton. Sixth form only: rowing. 1 county netball representative. *Community service:* Community service optional at age 14. *Clubs and societies:* Up to 10 clubs, eg science, history/current affairs, dance, sports.
Uniform School uniform worn except in the sixth.
Houses/prefects Competitive houses, for sport. Prefects, head girl, elected by the school. School Council.
Religion Attendance at school assembly compulsory.
Social Exchanges with schools in St Raphael (France) and Berlin. Pupils allowed to bring own car/bike to school. Meals self- service. No tobacco/alcohol allowed.
Discipline Pupils failing to produce homework once might expect a detention and support/help from a member of staff; those caught smoking cannabis on the premises could expect expulsion.
Alumni association Mrs Barbara Moyce, 12 Kingswood Avenue, Bromley BR2 0NY.
Former pupils Sophie Aldred, Mary Quant, Katie Stewart, Margaret Jay.

• BLOXHAM

Bloxham School, Bloxham, Near Banbury, Oxfordshire OX15 4PE. Tel 01295 720222, Fax 01295 721714

Pupils 356 • Boys 11–18 (Day; Board from age 13) • Girls 16–18 (Day/Board) • Upper sixth 88 • Termly fees £2095–£3085 (Day) £3950 (Board) • HMC, Woodard • Enquiries/application to the Registrar

What it's like

Founded in 1860 by the Rev Philip Egerton on the site of a former grammar school and given to the Woodard Corporation in 1896. It has a very agreeable setting on the edge of the village of Bloxham, between Banbury and Oxford and close to M40. Its handsome buildings of local stone lie in 60 acres of gardens and playing fields. There is comfortable modern accommodation and facilities are good. It is an Anglican foundation but welcomes pupils of other faiths and special arrangements can be made for them to attend their own churches. All are expected to attend some school chapel services. Girls have been admitted to the sixth-form since the early eighties. A sound general education is provided and academic results are good. Most pupils go on to degree courses. Drama, music and art are well catered for. A wide range of sports and games is available and there are numerous extra-curricular activities. Each pupil has the option of training with the CCF. Small groups of pupils are also involved in local public works, and there is a highly organised community service programme in the neighbourhood (over a hundred visits to the elderly, handicapped etc are made each week).

School profile

Pupils Age range, 11–18. Senior department 13–18. 356 pupils, 104 day (90 boys, 14 girls), 252 boarders (225 boys, 27 girls); boarding from age 13. Main entry ages 11, 13 (boys) and into sixth (boys and girls). *State school entry:* 5–10% main intake, plus 15% to sixth.
Entrance 14 pa assisted places at 11, 13 and 16. Scholarships/bursaries available.
Head and staff *Headmaster:* D K Exham, 6 years in post. Educated at Radley and at universities of Cambridge (mathematics) and Nottingham (education). Previously

Second Master at Repton and Head of Mathematics and Housemaster at King's, Taunton.

Exam results On average, 59 pupils in fifth, 85 in upper sixth. *GCSE:* 71% fifth gain at least grade C in 8+ subjects; 20% in 5–7; and 9% in 1–4 subjects. *A-levels:* 43% upper sixth pass in 4+ subjects; 34% in 3; 19% in 2; and 4% in 1 subject. Average UCAS points 17.5.

University and college entrance 90% of 1995 sixth-form leavers went on to a degree course (18% after a gap year); others typically go on to work or resit A-levels. Of those going on to university, 8% went to Oxbridge; 4% took courses in medicine, dentistry and veterinary science, 30% in science and engineering, 5% in law, 45% in humanities and social sciences (including 65% in business related subjects), 16% in art and design.

Curriculum GCSE and A-levels. 20 subjects offered (including A-level general studies). 18% take science A-levels; 55% arts/humanities; 27% both. *Vocational:* Work experience available. *Computing facilities:* Computer laboratory (Apple Macs); computers in departments. *Special provision:* Dyslexia unit (5 pupils per year, IQ greater than 120); EFL. *Europe:* French, German and Spanish offered to GCSE, AS and A-level. Regular exchanges to Germany. Several European pupils in school.

The arts *Music:* Up to 25% of pupils learn a musical instrument; instrumental exams can be taken. Several musical groups including woodwind ensembles, brass groups, guitar groups, string ensembles and vocal groups. Periodic concerts. Some pupils play in youth and other orchestras outside school. *Drama and dance:* Drama offered. Some pupils are involved in school productions and majority in house/other productions. Considerable success with pupils directing their own plays. *Art:* On average, 28 take GCSE, 14 A-level. Design, pottery, photography also offered.

Sport, community service and clubs (Pupils aged 11 and over) *Sport and physical activities:* Compulsory sports (for third form): rugby, hockey, cricket. Additional options (fourth form up): cross-country, squash, fives, athletic, swimming, tennis, fencing. Sixth-form girls – hockey, netball, rounders. County representatives in rugby, hockey, cross-country, girls' hockey and netball. *Community service:* Pupils take bronze, silver and gold Duke of Edinburgh's Award. CCF and community service optional for 4–6 years. *Clubs and societies:* Up to 15 clubs, eg art, electronics, chess, bell-ringing, debating, photography, computer, science, play-reading.

Houses/prefects Prefects, head of house and house prefects.

Religion Some services compulsory; school is Anglican foundation.

Social Orchestral and choral concerts with Tudor Hall. Skiing trip, sports tours etc. Wine and beer for 17+ in JCR with parents' permission.

Discipline Pupils failing to produce homework once could expect counselling; those caught smoking cannabis on the premises could expect expulsion.

Boarding All fifth and sixth-formers have own study bedroom. 6 boys' houses; girls in two separate houses. Central dining room. Pupils can provide and cook snacks.

• BLUNDELL'S

Blundell's School, Tiverton, Devon EX16 4DN. Tel 01884 252543

• Pupils 372 • Boys 11–18 (Day/Board) • Girls 11–18 (Day/Board) • Upper sixth 100 • Termly fees £1880–£2350 (Day) £2265–£3850 (Board) • HMC, BSA • Enquiries/application to the Registrar

What it's like

Founded and endowed in 1604 at the sole charge of the estate of Peter Blundell, clothier of Tiverton, by Sir John Popham. In 1882 it moved to the outskirts of Tiverton, on a fine estate of 100 acres of beautiful gardens, playing fields and other grounds. Its pleasant and well-equipped buildings provide good facilities and comfortable accommodation. The school maintains a Christian tradition and Anglican practice; all pupils are expected to attend weekday morning chapel and the school service on Sundays. Exclusively a boys' school until 1976, when it first accepted girls to the sixth-form, it became fully co-educational in 1993. There is an unusually large sixth-form and a staff:pupil ratio of about 1:9. Academic standards are high and results good. Most pupils go on to degree courses. The school has always been strong in music and a good music centre provides excellent facilities. Drama is also very strong and there is much dramatic activity (and two theatres). Art, crafts and technology are also flourishing fields of work and study. A wide variety of sports and games is available and standards are high. Many clubs and societies cater for most conceivable interests. There is a large CCF (Army and Navy sections) and other activities include climbing, canoeing, abseiling, flying, sailing and expeditions on Dartmoor and Exmoor. There is an unusually big commitment to local community service.

School profile

Pupils Age range 11–18, 372 pupils, 142 day (114 boys, 28 girls) 230 boarding (186 boys, 44 girls). Main entry ages: 11 (from 1996), 13 and into the sixth (fully co-educational since 1993). 10–15% are children of former pupils. *State school entry:* 5–10% main intake, plus 20–25% to sixth.

Entrance Common Entrance and own exam used. All special skills are welcome; so is the all-rounder. No religious requirements. Over 50 pa scholarships/bursaries available up to 100% fees. Parents not expected to buy text books.

Parents 30+% live within 30 miles; 10+% live overseas.

Head and staff *Headmaster:* Jonathan Leigh, 5 years in post. Educated at Eton and Cambridge (history). Previously Second Master, Head of History and Housemaster at Cranleigh. *Staff:* 40 full time, 20 part time. Annual turnover 5%.

Exam results On average 70 pupils in upper fifth, 100 in upper sixth. *GCSE:* 55% upper fifth gain at least grade C in 8+ subjects; 40% in 5–7; and 5% in 1–4 subjects. *A-levels:* 5% upper sixth pass in 4+ subjects; 90% in 3; 5% in 2; and 1% in 1 subject. Average UCAS points 19.5.

University and college entrance 90% of 1995 sixth-form leavers went on to a degree course (25% after a gap year); others typically go on to commerce or military. Of those going on to university, 5% went to Oxbridge; 5% took courses in medicine, dentistry and veterinary science, 25% in science and engineering, 5% in law, 25% in humanities and social sciences, 5% in art and design, 30% in business-related subjects.

Curriculum GCSE and A-levels. Wide range of general studies courses but no A-level. 30% take science A-levels; 45% arts/humanities; 25% both. *Vocational:* Work experience available. *Computing facilities:* Computing centre plus computers in departments. *Special provision:* Tuition for dyslexics and EFL available. *Europe:* French, Spanish and German offered to GCSE, AS and A-level. Regular trips to France, Holland, Germany and Czech Republic; links with schools and exchanges arranged. Travel bursaries available for development of international understanding. European students regularly in sixth-form.

The arts *Music:* Up to 50% of pupils learn a musical instrument; instrumental exams can be taken. Some 12 musical groups including 2 orchestras, 3 choirs, big band, chamber music groups, pop groups. *Drama and dance:* Drama offered and GCSE and A-level may be taken. Some pupils are involved in school productions and majority in house/other productions. *Art:* On average, 35 take GCSE, 2 AS-level, 15 A-level. Design, pottery, photography, history of art, sculpture also offered. Recent pupil now photographer for National Trust, another promo editor for Carlton TV.

Sport, community service and clubs *Sport and physical activities:* Compulsory sports: rugby, cricket (boys); hockey (girls). Optional: fives, squash, hockey, football, fencing, judo, athletics, cross-country, tennis, swimming, basketball, shooting, netball, sailing, canoeing, golf, badminton, archery. GCSE, A-level, RLSS exams may be taken. Current national squash champion; 2 Test cricketers in recent years; many county rugby players. Present pupils represent county at rugby, cricket, squash, hockey, athletics; region at athletics, basketball, fives, judo, fencing. *Community service:* CCF and community service optional. *Clubs and societies:* Up to 30 clubs, eg astronomy, music, Blundell's Action (to help the community), ferreting, sailing, debating, literary, Young Farmers, French, history etc.

Uniform School uniform worn throughout, except in houses.

Houses/prefects Competitive houses – 1 junior (11–13 year olds), 4 boarding boy, 1 day boy, 2 girl. Monitors, head boy/girl (2 girls as head of school so far), head of house and house monitors – appointed by Headmaster after consultation with monitors, Housemasters etc.

Religion Daily service for whole school; 6 Sunday services per term.

Social Debates, general knowledge competitions, musical events etc with local schools.

Exchanges, links with schools in Canada, Australia, Berlin, South Africa, Czech and Slovak Republic and Russia; plus trips to Germany, Russia etc. Pupils allowed to bring own bike to school. Meals self-service (staff always present). School tuck and tailor's shop. No tobacco allowed.
Discipline Pupils failing to produce homework once can expect appropriate admonition; those connected with cannabis would expect to leave; repeated smoking and illegal drinking also lead to expulsion.
Boarding 30% have own study bedroom, 50% share (with 1–3); 20% are in dormitories of 6+. Houses of approx 50. 2 resident qualified nurses; doctor visits daily. Central dining room. Pupils can provide and cook own food. Exeats at half-term plus 2 weekends (Sat 4pm – Sun 9pm). Visits to local town allowed at all ages at Housemaster's discretion.
Alumni association is run by E R Crowe, c/o the School.
Former pupils Lord Stokes; Michael Mates MP; Sir John Gray; Richard Sharp; Clem Thomas; Vic Marks; Hugh Morris; Peter Hurford; Paul Levi; General Sir John Hackett; Christopher Ondaatje.

• BOLTON (Boys)

Bolton School Boys' Division, Chorley New Road, Bolton, Lancashire BL1 4PA. Tel 01204 840201, Fax 01204 849477

• Pupils 1027 • Boys 8–18 (Day) • Girls None • Upper sixth 118 • Termly fees £1492 (Day) • HMC • Enquiries/application to the Headmaster

What it's like

Originally founded in 1524, endowed by Robert Lever in 1641 and re-endowed in 1913 by Sir W H Lever (later Viscount Leverhulme). It comprises impressive and very large buildings with a great hall, plus recent additions. It is on an estate of 32 acres, in an urban residential area, a mile north west of the town centre. The prep and junior departments are nearby. The boys' and girls' divisions are in the same building and though the organisation of the two divisions provides basically single-sex schools there are many opportunities for boys and girls to meet and co-operate in the running of societies etc. A broad traditional education is given and it has a high reputation far beyond Bolton. Academic standards are high and results very good; most pupils go on to degree courses, many to Oxbridge. There is a large number of pupils on assisted place. Though non-denominational, Christian beliefs are encouraged. Music strong; scouting strong. A good deal of emphasis on health, fitness and outdoor pursuits courses (based on its own hostel by Ullswater, in the Lake District).

School profile

Pupils Total age range 8–18; 1027 day boys. Senior department 11–18, 850 boys. Main entry ages 8,11 and into sixth. Approx 5% are children of former pupils. 30% of senior intake from own junior school. *State school entry:* 60% intake at 11, plus 95% to sixth.
Entrance Own entrance exam used. No special skills or religious requirements. Parents not expected to buy text books. 38 pa assisted places.
Head and staff *Headmaster:* Alan Wright, in post for 13 years. Educated at Manchester Grammar and Birmingham University (chemistry). Previously Head of Chemistry and Sixth Form Supervisor at Royal Grammar (Newcastle) and Assistant Chemistry Master at King Edward's (Birmingham). *Staff:* 76 full time, 5 part time. Annual turnover 3%. Average age 38.
Exam results In 1995, 108 pupils in fifth, 101 in upper sixth. *GCSE:* in 1995, 107 fifth gained at least grade C in 8+ subjects; and 1 in 5–7 subjects. *A-levels:* 97 upper sixth passed in 4+ subjects; 3 in 3; 1 in 2 subjects. Average UCAS points 24.4 (including general studies 32.0).
University and college entrance 95% of 1995 sixth-form leavers went on to a degree course; others typically go on to non-degree courses. Of those going on to university, 14% went to Oxbridge; 10% took courses in medicine, dentistry and veterinary science, 40% in science and engineering, 50% in humanities and social sciences.
Curriculum GCSE, AS and A-levels. 24 subjects offered, including A-level general studies taken by all sixth-formers. 42% took science A-levels; 38% arts/humanities; 21% both. *Vocational*: Work experience available. *Computing facilities:* Networked

computer studies room, CAD facilities in technology dept; senior school central PC facilities and others in departments. *Special provision:* Lift, giving access to all floors, available for physically handicapped. *Europe:* French, German and Russian offered at GCSE, AS and A-level; all pupils take French and one other language at GCSE. Regular exchanges to France and Germany. French and Dutch pupils (parents on short-term contracts locally).

The arts (Pupils aged 11 and over) *Music:* Up to 40% of pupils learn a musical instrument; instrumental exams can be taken. Some 6+ musical groups including orchestras, choirs, wind band, concert band. 1 pupil in National Youth Orchestra; many members of city and county youth orchestras; pupils regularly perform in town hall, major works for charitable enterprises. *Drama and dance:* Drama offered and GCSE may be taken. Some pupils are involved in school and other productions. Major opera/musical annually (over 100 involved), joint production with girls' division of the foundation. *Art:* On average, 20 take GCSE, 6 A-level. Design, pottery, photography, plastics, CDT also offered.

Sport, community service and clubs (Pupils aged 11 and over) *Sport and physical activities:* Compulsory sports (at different ages): soccer, cricket, rugby, badminton, hockey. Additional options (from fourth year) include cross-country, athletics, swimming, basketball, volleyball, tennis. Compulsory outdoor pursuits for first 3 years (school has own centre in Cumbria). RLSS exams may be taken. Water polo, recent national squad representation; soccer, selection for Independent Schools XI; cricket, team awarded Henry Grierson Trophy by XL Club 1993. *Community service:* Pupils take bronze, silver and gold Duke of Edinburgh's Award. Community service optional for 3 years at age 15+. Large, flourishing Scout group. *Clubs and societies:* Up to 10 clubs, eg debating, computer, art, craft, Christian Union, geographical, scientific.

Uniform School uniform worn except in the sixth-form.

Houses/prefects Competitive houses. Monitors, school captain (appointed by Head), head of house and house captains of sports (elected by staff and school).

Religion Compulsory broadly Christian assembly.

Social Joint drama, music, opera, debating society, Christian Union, swimming team with adjacent girls' division of same foundation. Organised German and French exchanges each year; Russian visit every other year; school trips to Rhineland, classical sites in Europe; 4 weeks in central southern Europe or Asia each summer (trek camp); 3 ski trips each winter. Pupils allowed to bring own car/bike/motorbike to school. Meals formal. School shop. No tobacco/alcohol allowed.

Discipline Pupils failing to produce homework once might expect evening detention; those caught smoking cannabis on the premises could expect immediate and indefinite suspension.

Alumni association is run by N Slater, Hon Sec, Old Boltonians Association, c/o the School.

Former pupils Lord Haslam (former Chairman of National Coal Board); Nigel Short (chess champion); the late Sir Geoffrey Jackson (British Ambassador to Uruguay); Sir Ian McKellen (actor); Peter Jarvis (Chairman, Whitbread), Judge Michael Lever, QC.

• BOLTON (Girls)

Bolton School Girls' Division, Chorley New Road, Bolton, Lancashire BL1 4PB. Tel 01204 840201, Fax 01204 498910

• Pupils 1150 • Boys 4–8 only (Day) • Girls 4–18 (Day) • Upper sixth 107 • Termly fees £1075–£1492 (Day) • GSA • Enquiries/application to the Headmistress

What it's like

Founded in 1877, it moved to its present site in 1928. The boys' and girls' divisions are a single foundation, provided for by the first Viscount Leverhulme on an excellent site of 32 acres on the western side of Bolton and a mile from the centre. The handsome sandstone buildings are set among lawns, playing fields and woodland. They are extremely well equipped with a fine library and spacious hall and a traditional theatre. Recent additions include an arts and conference centre and an indoor sports complex. The school also has an outdoor pursuits centre, Patterdale Hall, in Cumbria. The school has a notable reputation in the locality and further afield. Results are consistently very good and each year most go on to take degree courses, including Oxbridge. Music and drama are very strong and involve a large number of pupils, who reach high levels of achievement. A wide range of sports and games is available and the school has had many representatives at county, regional and national level. Numerous clubs and societies cater for extra-curricular needs. The school organises regular expeditions at home and abroad. Pupils also have a commitment to the school's local community service and Duke of Edinburgh's Award Scheme.

School profile

Pupils Total age range 4–18, 1150 day pupils (100 boys, 1050 girls). Senior department 11–18, 805 girls. Main entry ages 4 (boys and girls), 8, 11 and into sixth (girls). Own junior department provides 40% senior intake. *State school entry:* 60% senior intake, plus about 10% to sixth.

Entrance Own entrance exam used. No religious requirements. Parents not expected to buy text books; lunch included in the fees. 48 pa assisted places (5 in junior school, 38 at 11 and 5 pa to sixth). 1 pa music bursary.

Head and staff *Headmistress:* Miss E J Panton, 3 years in post. Educated at state grammar school and upper sixth at Merchant Taylors' (girls); Oxford University (history), the Courtauld Institute (Renaissance Studies) and West Midland College of Education, Walsall (education). Previously Headmistress at Merchant Taylors' (Girls), Head of Sixth Form at Clifton High, Senior Mistress at Shrewsbury High and taught at Moreton Hall. Also FRSA; member of Liverpool University Council, of FHSA, Professional Committee GSA, HMC/GSA Assisted Places Working Party and of ISIS North; Oxford hockey and tennis blues. *Staff:* 80 full time, 14 part time.

Exam results On average, 120 pupils in Year 11, 101 in upper sixth. *GCSE:* 98% in Year 11 gain at least grade C in 8 + subjects. *A-levels:* In 1995, 87% passed in 4+ subjects; 10% in 3; 3% in 2 subjects. Average UCAS points 21.8.

University and college entrance 95% of 1995 sixth-form leavers went on to a degree course, 12% to Oxbridge; 22% took courses in science and engineering, 17% in humanities and social sciences, 31% in arts, 15% in vocational subjects and 10% in combined courses.

Curriculum GCSE and A-levels. 27 subjects offered at A-level, including Greek and general studies. 16% take science A-levels; 53% arts/humanities, 31% both. *Vocational:* Work experience and workshadowing available. *Computing facilities:* Two fully-equipped computer rooms; most departments have their own computer facilities. *Special provision:* Lift for wheelchairs. *Europe:* French (compulsory 11–14), German and Spanish offered at GCSE, AS-level and A-level; also GCSE Italian in sixth. Regular exchanges to France, Germany and Spain. Interactive multi-media programs for individual language study.

The arts (Pupils aged 11 and over) *Music:* Majority of pupils learn a musical instrument or take singing lessons; instrumental exams can be taken. Several musical groups including 4 choirs, orchestra, string orchestra, training band, flute and clarinet choirs, recorder consort. Pupils in National Children's Orchestra; leaders of 3 youth orchestras; 2 pupils in Cappricio (string ensemble working for RNCM with William Byrd Singers). Much joint musical activity with the Boys' Division. *Drama and dance:* Both offered. GCSE drama may be taken. Many pupils are involved in joint and school productions. *Art:* On average, 36% take GCSE, 10% A-level. Design, pottery textiles also offered.

Sport, community service and clubs (Pupils aged 11 and over) *Sport and physical activities:* Compulsory sports (at different ages): lacrosse, netball, gymnastics, rounders, dance, cross-country, swimming, life-saving, tennis, athletics, badminton, basketball, volleyball, aerobics and health-related fitness. Sixth form only: climbing, self defence, football, golf, canoeing, aquafit, trampolining, aerobics, table tennis. GCSE PE, BAGA, RLSS, BTF, ASA exams may be taken. Lacrosse, national finalists, North Representative players, county players; netball, Bolton Town Championship winners, U12, U13, U14, U15 and U16; swimming, senior international representative, county swimmers, national schools finalists, senior medley and free-style teams, Bolton Town Championships, juniors and seniors; tennis, U13 winners of Midland Bank trophies; athletics, winners of U12 and U13 town championships. *Community service:* Pupils take Duke of Edinburgh's bronze awards. Community service optional. *Clubs and societies:* Many clubs including, for example, computing, literary and debating, life-saving and gemmology.

Uniform School uniform worn except in the sixth.
Houses/prefects Prefects, head girl – elected by sixth-form.
Religion Attendance at morning assembly compulsory but withdrawal by parents possible.
Social Number of joint activities with Boys' Division eg literary and debating society, drama productions, instrumental groups, field trips to Berlin and skiing holidays. Annual exchanges to France, Spain and Germany. Meals self-service. School shop. No tobacco/alcohol allowed.
Alumni association run by Mrs K Morley, c/o the School.
Former pupils Dame Janet Smith QC, Ann Taylor MP.

• BOOTHAM

Bootham School, York Y03 7BU. Tel 01904 623636, Fax 01904 652106

• Pupils 340 • Boys 11–18 (Day/Board) • Girls 11–18 (Day/Board) • Upper sixth 40 • Termly fees £2198 (Day) £3387 (Board/Weekly) .HMC • Enquiries/application to the Headmaster

What it's like

Founded in 1823, a Quaker Foundation (The Religious Society of Friends), it has an agreeable site of 10 acres just outside York's medieval walls and a few minutes' walk from the city centre. Playing fields adjoin it. A number of Georgian houses constitute the core; there are numerous modern extensions and facilities. Full use is made of the city's amenities (several excellent museums, the theatre and art gallery). Quaker beliefs underlie the daily life of pupils and staff and those of other persuasions are welcome. Now fully co-educational, it was a boys' school until 1985 when it first accepted girls into the sixth-form. A sound education is provided and results are good. Almost all sixth-formers go on to degree courses including Oxbridge. Strong in music, art and drama. A good range of sports and games and high standards (county and national representatives). Good range of clubs and societies. Most seniors take part in a variety of local community schemes and there is vigorous local support. The Duke of Edinburgh's Award Scheme is well supported.

School profile

Pupils Age range 11–18; 340 pupils, 245 day (145 boys, 100 girls), 95 boarders (70 boys, 25 girls). Main entry ages, 11, 13 and into sixth. *State school entry:* 55% main intake, plus 80% to sixth.
Entrance Common Entrance and own exam used. No special skills or religious requirements. Parents not expected to buy textbooks; music tuition etc extra. Assisted places at 11. 12 pa scholarship entrance awards and bursaries according to need as far as possible, value 12%–50% fees; art and music scholarships to 50% fees. Bursary help adds to scholarships where there is need.
Parents 25+% in industry or commerce, 15+% are doctors and lawyers etc. 40+% live within 30 miles; up to 10% live overseas.
Head and staff *Headmaster:* Ian Small, in post for 8 years. Educated at Brentwood School, Harvard School (California), Sussex University (English and American studies) and Oxford University (education). Previously Housemaster and Head of Drama at Stowe, Housemaster and Head of English at Abbotsholme. Also former Chairman BSA; member of HMC Academic Policy Committee. *Publications:* Norwich Tapes – Four Shakespeare Commentaries (1983). *Staff:* 32 full time, 8 part time. Annual turnover 3%. Average age 40.
Exam results In 1995, 59 pupils in upper fifth, 40 in upper sixth. *GCSE:* In 1995, 47 upper fifth gained at least grade C in 8+ subjects; 9 in 5–7 subjects. *A-levels:* 31 upper sixth passed in 4+ subjects; 3 in 3, 3 in 2; and 3 in 1 subject. Average UCAS points 19.1 (including general studies 23.1).
University and college entrance 98% of 1995 sixth-form leavers went on to a degree course (6% after a gap year); others typically go on to eg HND courses. Of those going on to university, 10% went to Oxbridge; 15% took courses in medicine, dentistry and veterinary science, 27% in science and engineering, 3% in law, 46% in humanities and social sciences, 3% in art and design, 6% in vocational subjects eg sports science, hotel and catering.

Curriculum GCSE and A-level, including A-level general studies. 43% take science A-levels; 35% arts/humanities; 23% both. *Vocational:* Work experience expected in Year 11. *Computing facilities:* 2 computer education rooms (30 work stations, PCs, BBC and Archimedes); computers (including CD-Rom) in 6 departments. *Special provision:* Dyslexic teaching in school or at local branch of Dyslexia Institute; EFL tuition. *Europe:* French and German offered at GCSE, AS and A-level; also GCSE Spanish in sixth. Regular exchanges to Germany and France. European Studies taught. European Society (started 1991) German resident graduates on 1-year exchanges.

The arts *Music:* Up to 50% of pupils learn a musical instrument; instrumental exams can be taken. Some 10+ musical groups including orchestra, choir, choral society, string, brass ensembles, wind band, rock group. Pupils have toured with York Schools Symphony Orchestra, played in Guildhall Orchestra, York Symphony Orchestra etc. *Drama and dance:* Drama offered. LAMDA exams may be taken. Majority of pupils are involved in school productions and some in house/other productions. Pupil in National Youth Theatre; players in York Mystery Plays; recent school productions include Ruddigore, Tom and Huckleberry, A Midsummer Night's Dream, The Vackees, Billy. *Art:* On average, 20 take GCSE, 3 AS-level, 6 A-level. Pottery, photography also offered. Several go on to art foundation courses.

Sport, community service and clubs *Sport and physical activities:* Compulsory sports: soccer, cricket, athletics, swimming, hockey (boys); hockey, netball, swimming, rounders (girls). Optional: tennis, squash, rowing, badminton, riding, fencing, softball, water polo etc. County representatives at athletics, netball, hockey, riding; national riding. *Community service:* Pupils take bronze, silver and gold Duke of Edinburgh's Award. Community service optional. *Clubs and societies:* Up to 30 clubs, eg natural history, debating, geographical, drama, electronics, computing, bridge, chess, candle-making, cookery, art, music etc. Printing (off-set litho) department set up by Stationer's Company.

Uniform School uniform worn in first three years; guidelines thereafter.

Houses/prefects Competitive houses for sport, music and speech-making. Prefects (Reeves), head boy/girl, head of house and house prefects – elected by the school.

Religion Quakerism (The Religious Society of Friends).

Social Joint drama productions with sister school, The Mount. Organised exchanges with schools in Germany and France; skiing trips and language trips abroad (including Russia). Pupils allowed to bring own car/bike/motorbike to school. Meals usually self-service, few special meals formal. No tobacco/alcohol allowed.

Discipline Pupils failing to produce homework once might expect 'columns' (writing out words from a dictionary) or gating (staying within the school campus) for more serious misdemeanors; those caught smoking cannabis on the premises should expect expulsion.

Boarding 40% of sixth-formers have own study bedroom, 60% share (with 1); very few pupils are in dormitories of 6 +. Houses divided by age. Resident qualified nurse/doctor. Central dining room. Pupils can provide and cook own food. 2 weekend exeats each term. Visits to the local town allowed as required.

Alumni association is run by The Secretary, BOSA, c/o the School.

Former pupils A J P Taylor (historian); Philip Noel-Baker (Nobel Peace Prize); Nicolas Kent (BAFTA winner).

• BOSWORTH

Bosworth Tutorial College, 9–12 St George's Avenue, Northampton NN2 6JA. Tel 01604 719988, Fax 01604 791418

• Pupils 88 • Boys 14–20 (Day/Board) • Girls 14–20 (Day/Board) • Upper sixth 40 • Termly fees £1947 (Day) £3567 (Board) • BAC, CIFE • Enquiries/application to the Principal

What it's like

A co-educational tutorial college, founded in 1977, it has an agreeable site overlooking parkland ten minutes' walk from the town centre. The full-time staff of ten is assisted by 29 part-timers, providing a very favourable staff:pupil ratio. Average class size is six and there is much flexibility in subject combinations. Students get very individual attention.

Academic results are good and some 80% of leavers proceed to degree courses. Social arrangements are informal. Sport and games are optional.

School profile

Pupils Age range 14–20; 88 pupils, 43 day (24 boys, 19 girls), 45 boarding (29 boys, 16 girls). Main entry age 14. *State school entry:* 20%.
Entrance No entrance exam; no special skills or religious requirements. Parents are expected to buy textbooks. 1 pa scholarship and bursaries for under-16s.
Parents 15+% are in industry/commerce. Up to 60% live within 30 miles of the school; up to 60% overseas.
Head and staff *Principal:* Mark A V Broadway, in post for 6 years. Educated at Henbury School, Bristol, and Bangor University (marine physics). *Staff:* 10 full time, 29 part time. Annual turnover 15%. Average age 37.
Exam results In 1995, 20 pupils in upper fifth, 33 in upper sixth. *GCSE:* On average 5% upper fifth gain at least grade C in 8+ subjects; 65% in 5–7; and 30% in 1–4 subjects; (very few sit 8 subjects). *A-levels:* In 1995, 28 pupils passed in 3 subjects; 5 in 2 subjects. Average UCAS points 17.5.
University and college entrance 80% of sixth-form leavers go on to a degree course (5% after a gap year); others typically go on to higher education, art colleges, family business or other work. Of those going on to university, 2% go to Oxbridge; 20% take courses in medicine, dentistry and veterinary science, 30% in science and engineering, 5% in law, 20% in humanities and social sciences, 10% in art and design, 15% in vocational subjects.
Curriculum GCSE and A-levels offered. 25 examination subjects offered, including law, accounts, psychology; no A-level general studies. 40% take science A-levels; 50% arts/humanities; 10% both. *Vocational:* RSA level 1 and 2 available in word processing/typing. *Computing facilities:* Computer room with 7 terminals. *Special provision:* Diagnostic tests, individual tuition and extra classes for dyslexic pupils; several EFL classes. *Europe:* French, German and Spanish offered to GCSE and A-level. Private tuition in other languages can be arranged. Usually 1–2 European students at college.
The arts *Music:* Up to 15% pupils learn a musical instrument; instrumental exams can be taken. Pop music groups occasionally. *Art:* on average, 10 take GCSE, 2 A-level.
Sport, community service and clubs *Sport and physical activities:* No compulsory sports. *Clubs and societies:* Up to 5 clubs – generally informal.
Uniform None.
Houses/prefects No competitive houses or prefects. School Council.
Religion No compulsory worship.
Social Sports and social events with other local schools. Students may bring own car/bike/motorbike to school. Meals self-service; drinks/sweet machines on site. Tobacco allowed; alcohol at organised functions only.
Discipline Pupils failing to produce homework might expect to be kept in that night to do it.
Boarding 40% have own study bedrooms; others share 2–3 per room. New independent accommodation for those over 18. Houses are single sex. Students are allowed to provide food and cook to a limited extent. Exeats allowed at weekends plus 1 week at half-term. Visits to the local town allowed (having signed out if under 18).

• BOX HILL

Box Hill School, Mickleham, Dorking, Surrey RH5 6EA. Tel 01372 373382, Fax 01372 363942
• Pupils 244 • Boys 11–18 (Day/Board) • Girls 11–18 (Day/Board) • Upper sixth 22 • Termly fees £2050 (Day) £3400 (Board) £3280 (Weekly) • SHMIS, Round Square • Enquiries/application to the Registrar

What it's like

Founded in 1959, it is in the village of Mickleham in whose life the school plays an active part. The main building is a handsome Victorian mansion (plus purpose-built modern facilities) situated in 40 acres of delightful grounds, with big playing fields. It belongs to The Round Square and is run on the principles of Kurt Hahn, founder of Salem and Gordonstoun, setting academic work at the centre of a broad education. It thus has close international links with schools in Europe, USA, Canada, India, Australia and Kenya and there is an efficient system of exchanges and post-A-level attachments with them. There is a strong tutorial system and pupils meet their tutors twice daily. A wide range of activities and expeditions is operated in the belief that all pupils may excel at something, will develop through challenging experiences, and should emerge as well-rounded citizens. Drama, music and art are regarded as particularly important. It was founded as a co-educational school. The staff includes two dyslexia specialists and two specialists in teaching English as a second language. A sound education is given and nearly all sixth-form leavers go on to universities. Expeditions to York, Canterbury and the Lake District form part of the junior curriculum.

School profile

Pupils Age range 11–18; 244 pupils, 102 day (67 boys, 35 girls), 142 boarding (94 boys, 48 girls). Main entry ages 11, 12, 13 and into sixth. Very few are children of former pupils (because of age and initial size of school). *State school entry:* Approx 20% of intake.

Entrance Common Entrance and own exam used. Good music or art and an ability to contribute to school life looked for; no religious requirements. Parents expected to buy some A-level text books; other extras vary. 2 pa scholarships up to half fees; 8–10 pa sixth-form scholarships, £300-£500 per term; scholarships and bursaries lower down the school for all-round qualities.

Parents 15+% in industry or commerce. 65+% live within 30 miles; 25% live overseas.

Head and staff *Headmaster:* Dr Rodney Atwood, in post for 9 years. Educated at Canadian High School, and at universities of McMaster (Ontario) and Cambridge (history). Previously History/Careers Master and Tutor in Girls' House at Repton and History Master at King's (Wimbledon) and at Hampton. *Staff:* 22 full time, 16 part time. Annual turnover 5%.

Exam results In 1995, 61 pupils in Year 11, 22 in Year 13. *GCSE:* In 1995, 17 in Year 11 gained at least grade C in 8+ subjects; 22 in 5–7 subjects. *A-levels:* 2 in Year 13 passed in 4+ subjects; 11 in 3; 5 in 2; and 2 in 1 subject. Average UCAS points 12.4.

University and college entrance 85% of 1995 sixth-form leavers went on to a degree course (15% after a gap year); others typically go on to non-degree courses or into employment. Of those going on to university, 5% took courses in medicine, dentistry and veterinary science, 25% in science and engineering, 10% in law, 35% in humanities and social sciences, 5% in art and design, 20% vocational subjects eg journalism, accountancy, tourism.

Curriculum GCSE and A-levels. 17 GCSE subjects offered; 15 at A-level. 14% take science A-levels; 50% arts/humanities; 36% both. *Vocational:* RSA qualifications available in IT and core text processing. *Computing facilities:* One room of Apple Macintosh computers; others, including Amstrads, held in departments. *Special provision:* Two qualified dyslexia specialists and two qualified teachers of English as a second language. *Europe:* French and German offered to GCSE and A-level. Regular exchanges to France and Germany.

The arts *Music:* Over 30% of pupils learn a musical instrument; instrumental exams can be taken. Some 4 musical groups including orchestra, choirs, pop. *Drama and dance:* Drama offered. GCSE drama may be taken. Some pupils are involved in school productions and all in house/other productions. *Art:* On average, 25 take GCSE, 3 A-level. Design, photography also offered.

Sport, community service and clubs *Sport and physical activities:* No compulsory sports though all take part in some sport. Optional: wide range including soccer, rugby, cricket, tennis, athletics, swimming, netball, hockey, volleyball, riding, squash, badminton, karate, judo, fencing, table tennis, climbing (expeditions and indoor climbing wall). GCSE PE and A-level sport studies may be taken. District, county & national representatives an athletics; county representatives in tennis and swimming. *Community service:* Pupils take bronze, silver and gold Duke of Edinburgh's Award. *Clubs and societies:* Up to 10 clubs, eg Box Hill Society, economics and politics, electronics, school magazine, debating.

Uniform School uniform worn; smart formal wear in the sixth-form.

Houses/prefects Competitive houses. Prefects, head boy and girl, head of house and house prefects. School council.

Religion Non-denominational service every Sunday from which parents may request exemption.

Social Sixth-form conference and careers conference. Organised trips to Germany; mountaineering trips to Alps; well developed exchanges. Sixth-form and society/club dinners formal; self-service at other times. School shop sells books. No tobacco/alcohol allowed.
Discipline Pupils failing to produce homework would be kept in on one afternoon; those caught smoking cannabis on the premises could expect expulsion.
Boarding 4% have own study bedroom, 76% share (1–4); 20% are in dormitories of 6+. Single sex houses, of approximately 35–50, divided by age. Weekly boarding allowed. 1 SRN, 2 school doctors (non-resident). Central dining room. 2 weekend exeats each term for full boarders plus half-term. Visits to the local town allowed.
Alumni association is run by Mr Jeremy Taylor, Box Hill School Association Chairman, c/o the school.

• BRADFIELD

Bradfield College, Reading, Berkshire RG7 6AR. Tel 01734 744203, Fax 01734 744195
• Pupils 580 • Boys 13–18 (Day/Board) • Girls 16–18 (Day/Board) • Upper sixth 130 • Termly fees £3058 (Day) £4075 (Board) • HMC • Enquiries/application to the Head Master's Secretary

What it's like

Founded in 1850, it became well-known by 1900 as one of the leading independent schools in southern England. In effect the school is the village of Bradfield and vice versa; a very attractive village of brick-and-half-timber and brick-and-flint houses in one of the prettiest regions of Berkshire. The total grounds cover about 200 acres. Its accommodation is excellent and it has outstandingly good facilities (including a design centre, electronics centre, TV studio and satellite tracking equipment). It is a C of E foundation and Christian values are embodied in the life of the school, but those of other denominations are very welcome. Girls were first accepted into the sixth-form in 1989. Results are very good and the vast majority of sixth-formers go on to degree courses, including to Oxbridge. Strong in sport and games, with numerous representatives at county and regional level. Also very strong in music and drama; it is unusual in having an open-air Greek theatre where plays in Greek are performed every three years. There is a large CCF unit (much emphasis on adventure training and leadership skills), plentiful outdoor activities plus recreations such as fly-fishing on the Pang and sailing on the gravel pits at Theale. A point is made of keeping close contacts with industry, with attachments for all lower sixth pupils.

School profile

Pupils Age range 13–18; 580 pupils, 30 day (25 boys, 5 girls), 550 boarding (475 boys, 75 girls). Main entry ages boys 13; boys and girls into sixth. Approx 15% are children of former pupils. *State school entry:* 3% main intake, plus 25% to sixth.
Entrance Common Entrance exam plus own scholarship examination used. No special skills required, but any are taken into account. No religious requirements. Parents expected to buy textbooks at sixth-form level. 6 pa assisted places in sixth-form only. 18 pa scholarships bursaries, 10%–50% of fees.
Parents 15+% are in industry or commerce, 15+% are doctors, lawyers etc. 10+% live within 30 miles; up to 10% live overseas.
Head and staff Head Master: Peter Smith, in post for 11 years. Educated at Magdalen College School and Oxford University (history). Previously Housemaster and Head of History at Rugby. Also Captain, Oxfordshire County Cricket Club (1977); Committee Member, Joint Educational Trust; HMC Committee and ISIS National Committee. *Staff:* 56 full time, 21 part time. Annual turnover 4%. Average age 33.
Exam results In 1995, 100 pupils in upper fifth, 133 in upper sixth. *GCSE:* In 1995, 82 upper fifth gained at least grade C in 8+ subjects; 10 in 5–7 subjects. *A-levels:* 6 upper sixth passed in 4+ subjects; 121 in 3; 4 in 2; and 1 in 1 subject. Average UCAS points 20.4.
University and college entrance 80% of 1995 sixth-form leavers went on to a degree course; others typically go on to non-degree courses, art colleges or straight into careers eg army. Of those going on to university, 15% went to Oxbridge; 5% took courses in medicine, dentistry and veterinary science, 46% in science and engineering, 42% in humanities and social sciences, 5% in art and design, 2% in eg drama and music.

Curriculum GCSE and A-levels. 18 GCSE subjects offered including Japanese; 25 at A-level (no A-level general studies). 33% take science A-levels; 33% arts/humanities; 33% both. *Vocational:* Work experience available. *Computing facilities:* Central information technology room, plus computers in all departments and all houses. *Europe:* French, Spanish and German offered at GCSE and A-level; also AS-level French and non-examined courses in all three languages and Italian. Regular exchanges to France and Spain. A number of European pupils (Dutch, German, Spanish, Russian) in school.
The arts *Music:* Up to 75% of pupils learn a musical instrument; instrumental exams can be taken. Some 10 musical groups including orchestra, band, jazz, swing bands, choirs, barbershop, brass, wind, string ensembles. Regular winners in Oxford Music Festival. *Drama and dance:* Drama offered. GCSE drama and LAMDA exams may be taken. Majority of pupils are involved in school productions and all in house/other productions; Greek play every third year. *Art:* On average, 20 take GCSE, 10 A-level. Design, pottery, also offered. Around 6 enter art colleges annually.
Sport, community service and clubs *Sport and physical activities:* Sports (mainly optional): football, hockey, cricket, athletics, swimming, golf, sailing, karate, fives, squash, cross-country, basketball, shooting, tennis, badminton, netball, lacrosse, rugby. Numerous county and regional representatives at various sports. *Community service:* Pupils take bronze, silver and gold Duke of Edinburgh's Award. CCF and community service both optional for 3 years at age 13. Adventure training a compulsory element for all pupils. *Clubs and societies:* Over 30 clubs, eg classic cars, wine tasting, classical and literary, photography, clay-pigeon shooting, Shakespeare.
Uniform School uniform worn throughout.
Houses/prefects Prefects, head boy, head of house and house prefects appointed by the Head in consultation with staff and pupils.
Religion Attendance at school Chapel, once on Sunday, twice per week for morning prayers.
Social Many joint theatrical and choral productions with local girls' schools. Several organised holiday expeditions each year. French school exchange. Pupils allowed to bring own bike to school. Meals self-service. School shop. No tobacco allowed; school bar for 17 year olds.
Discipline Pupils failing to produce homework once would be asked to do it; those caught smoking cannabis on the premises could expect to be expelled.
Boarding 60% have own study bedroom, 30% share 1–3; 10% are in dormitories of 6+. Houses of approximately 60. Resident qualified medical staff. Central dining room. Pupils can provide and cook own food. Up to 4 weekend exeats per term. Visits to the local town allowed for sixth-form.
Alumni association is run by E B Williams, c/o the College.
Former pupils Richard Adams (author); Lord Owen; Martin Ryle (astronomer).

• BRADFORD GRAMMAR

Bradford Grammar School, Keighley Road, Bradford, West Yorkshire BD9 4JP. Tel 01274 542492, Fax 01274 548129

• Pupils 1097 • Boys 8–18 (Day) • Girls 16–18 (Day) • Upper sixth 133 • Termly fees £1411 (Day) • HMC • Enquiries/application to the Headmaster

What it's like

It has existed since about 1548 and was incorporated by royal charter in 1662. A mile from the centre of Bradford, it comprises five main buildings on a 20-acre site. These include the Clock House, a 17th-century manor house for the juniors and the handsome senior school (opened in 1949). More modern buildings house the library and IT centre, a sports hall and the Hockney Theatre. Its overall amenities are first-rate. The two principles of discipline laid down are: firstly, that pupils are expected to know what is and what is not good conduct and to do nothing likely to bring themselves and their school into disrepute; secondly, that study is a discipline in itself. It provides a sound, traditional education in many branches of learning, including not only classics and information technology but also economics and electronics and sets very high all-round standards. Girls were first admitted to the sixth-form in 1984. It enjoys strong local loyalties and support and in fact has long been one of the most distinguished schools in

Britain with very good results. Almost all pupils go on to degree courses including a high proportion to Oxbridge. Sports and games are played to very high standards; successful regional and national representation (eg rugby, cross-country, tennis, rowing etc). Wide range of clubs and societies.

School profile

Pupils Total age range 8–18; 1097 day pupils (1066 boys, 31 girls). Senior department 11–18, 918 pupils (887 boys, 31 girls). Main entry ages: 8, 9, 10, 11, 12, 13 (boys) and into sixth (boys and girls). Approx 10% are children of former pupils. *State school entry:* 50% intake 11+, plus 20% to sixth.

Entrance Own entrance exam used. No special skills or religious requirements. Parents not expected to buy textbooks. 45 pa assisted places.

Parents 15+% in industry or commerce; 15+% are doctors, lawyers etc.

Head and staff *Headmaster:* David Smith, in post for 22 years. Educated at City of Bath Boys' School and Oxford University (history). Previously Headmaster at King's, Peterborough, Head of History at Rossall and Assistant Master at Manchester Grammar. Also JP; Chairman, Assisted Places Committee; Chairman of HMC (1988). *Publications:* A History of England (1961); Left and Right in Twentieth Century Europe (1970); Russia of the Tsars (1971). *Staff:* 80 full time, 8 part time. Annual turnover 4%. Average age 42.

Exam results In 1995, 134 pupils in upper fifth, 133 in upper sixth. *GCSE:* in 1995, 87% upper fifth gained at least grade C in 8+ subjects; 12% in 5–7; and 1% in 1–4 subjects. *A-levels:* 12% upper sixth passed in 4+ subjects; 83% in 3; 5% in 1 or 2 subjects. Average UCAS points 24.3.

University and college entrance 97% of 1995 sixth-form leavers went on to a degree course; others typically go straight on to careers eg banking. Of those going on to university, 18% went to Oxbridge; 6% took courses in medicine, dentistry and veterinary science, 30% in science and engineering, 64% in humanities and social sciences.

Curriculum GCSE, AS and A-levels. 22 GCSE subjects offered; 9 at AS; 22 at A-level, including general studies. 23% take science A-levels; 46% arts/humanities; 31% both. *Vocational:* Work experience available. *Computing facilities:* Purpose-built information technology centre with 50+ PCs. *Europe:* French and German offered at GCSE, AS and A-level; also GCSE Spanish. Regular exchanges to France and Germany.

The arts (Pupils aged 11 and over) *Music:* Up to 25% of pupils learn a musical instrument; instrumental exams can be taken. Some 14 musical groups including orchestras, choir, jazz group. 3 choral awards to Oxbridge; 6 pupils passed at grade 8, 2 with distinction. *Drama and dance:* Drama offered and GCSE may be taken. Some pupils are involved in school productions. Recent production of operetta La Vie Parisienne. *Art:* Design and technology also offered. Pupil involved with an animation project with company near Bristol.

Sport, community service and clubs (Pupils aged 11 and over) *Sport and physical activities:* Compulsory sports: rugby, cross-country, swimming, athletics, cricket, tennis. Optional: badminton, table tennis, basketball, hockey, rowing, netball, outdoor pursuits, water polo, squash. GCSE may be taken. Rugby, 2 England representatives, 3 regional, 17 county; cross-country, 1 regional and 19 city representatives; tennis, 5 county and Northern Schools champions (U12 and U16), runners-up at national level; athletics, 1 regional rep, 10 district; cricket, 1 county and 8 city reps; cycling, 3 national reps; hockey, 1 regional. *Community service:* Pupils take bronze and gold Duke of Edinburgh's Award. CCF and community service optional. *Clubs and societies:* Over 30 clubs, eg debating, chess, fly fishing, drama, theatre, philosophy, history, classics.

Uniform School uniform worn except in fifth and sixth.

Houses/prefects No competitive houses. Prefects and head boy/girl appointed by the Head.

Religion School prayers.

Social No organised local events; some trips abroad. Meals self-service. School shop. No tobacco/alcohol allowed.

Discipline Pupils failing to produce homework once might expect a detention; those caught smoking cannabis on the premises could expect expulsion.

Alumni association is run by President: BGS Old Boys' Association, c/o the School.

Former pupils Dennis Healey; David Hockney; Sir Maurice Hodgson.

• BRADFORD (Girls)

Bradford Girls' Grammar School, Squire Lane, Bradford, West Yorkshire BD9 6RB. Tel 01274 545395

• Pupils 925 • Boys None • Girls 4–18 (Day) • Upper sixth 85 • Termly fees £1332 (Day) • GSA • Enquiries to the Headmistress • Applications to the Registrations Secretary

What it's like

Founded in 1876, it comprises fine, solid, well-equipped buildings and excellent up-to-date facilities on 17 acres of pleasant grounds, playing fields and woodland, in an urban residential area near the city centre. It has its own sixth-form college on site. Its reputation is high and its pupils motivated. Results are very good and many pupils go on to degree courses, including Oxbridge. It is especially strong in music and drama and sports and games are played to very high standards (many regional and national representatives). It enjoys vigorous local community support as well as support from alumni.

School profile

Pupils Total age range 4–18; 925 day girls. Senior department 11–18, 690 girls. Main entry ages 4, 9, 11 and into sixth. Approx 10–15% are children of former pupils. *State school entry:* 50% main intake at 11, plus 5% to sixth.

Entrance Own entrance exam used. No special skills or religious requirements. Parents not expected to buy textbooks; music, dancing etc charged extra. 60 pa assisted places. Bursaries available according to need.

Parents 15+% in industry or commerce; 15+% are doctors, lawyers etc.

Head and staff *Headmistress:* Mrs L J Warrington, in post for 9 years. Educated at Kesteven & Sleaford High and Leeds University (physics and education). Previously Deputy Head at Bradford (Girls). Also JP. *Staff:* 45 full time, 16 part time. Annual turnover 5–10%. Average age 35–40.

Exam results On average 110 pupils in upper fifth, 85 in upper sixth. *GCSE:* on average, 95% upper fifth gain at least grade C in 8+ subjects; 5% in 5–7 subjects. *A-levels:* 20% upper sixth pass in 4+ subjects; 78% in 3; 1% in 2; and 1% in 1 subject. Average UCAS points 23.3 (including general studies 30.0).

University and college entrance 84% of 1995 sixth-form leavers went on to a degree course; others typically go on to HND courses, art colleges, or straight into careers eg building societies, management. Of those going on to university, 10% went to Oxbridge; 15% took courses in medicine, dentistry and veterinary science, 25% in science and engineering, 57% in humanities and social sciences, 3% in art and design.

Curriculum GCSE and A-levels. 18 GCSE subjects offered; 26 at A-level (including general studies). 50% take science A-levels; 50% arts/humanities. *Vocational:* Work experience available; also RSA to stage 3 in audiotyping, wordprocessing, CLAIT and typewriting. *Computing facilities:* 3 IT centres with Nimbus network and stand-alone computers in various departments. *Europe:* French, German, Russian and Spanish offered at GCSE, AS and A-level and for Institute of Linguists. Regular exchanges to France, Germany and Spain.

The arts (Pupils aged 11 and over) *Music:* Up to 50% of pupils learn a musical instrument; instrumental exams can be taken. Some 5 musical groups including 3 choirs, orchestra, brass ensemble plus ad hoc chamber groups etc. *Drama and dance:* Drama offered. Performing arts at AS level and ABRSM speech and drama exams may be taken. Majority of pupils are involved in school productions and some in other productions. Pupils participate in public speaking competitions eg Shakespeare on the Platform, Business and Professional Women's Public Speaking. *Art:* On average, 15–26 take GCSE, 1–2 AS-level, 5–10 A-level. Design, textiles also offered. 1 pupil direct entry into Glasgow School of Art, won poster competition 1992.

Sport, community service and clubs (Pupils aged 11 and over) *Sport and physical activities:* Compulsory sports: dance, gymnastics, swimming, hockey, netball, badminton, squash, table tennis, volleyball, basketball, tennis, rounders, athletics, HRF. Optional: aerobics, martial arts, sailing. Sixth form only: dry skiing, canoeing, yoga. A-level PE, BAGA, exams, community sports leaderships and various coaching awards may be taken. Hockey, 1 national, 5 regional, 18 county representatives, national champions U16, U13, runners-up U18; athletics, national and county reps; squash and netball, county reps. *Community service:* Pupils take bronze, silver and gold Duke of Edinburgh's Award. Community service optional for 2 years at age 16. BBC Children in Need appeal; link-up with special school for visually impaired, school for hearing impaired; club sailing; outward bound-style activities; competitions eg BP, Boat Show. *Clubs and societies:* Up to 10 clubs, eg modern languages, Christian Union, riding, debating.

Uniform School uniform worn except in the sixth.

Houses/prefects No competitive houses. Prefects, President of Junior Common Room – elected by school and staff. School Council.

Religion Daily act of worship compulsory except in sixth-form or unless withdrawn by parents.

Social Occasional careers conventions and debating society joint with other schools. Organised trips including 1st year to outdoor pursuits centre and exchanges with France, Germany and Spain. Pupils allowed to bring own car/bike/motorbike to school in sixth-form only. Meals self-service. School shop. No tobacco/alcohol allowed.

Discipline Pupils failing to produce homework once might expect a detention if there was no good reason; those caught smoking cannabis on the premises could expect expulsion.

• BRENTWOOD

Brentwood School, Ingrave Road, Brentwood, Essex CM15 8AS. Tel 01277 214580, Fax 01277 260218

• Pupils 1043 • Boys 11–18 (Day/Board) • Girls 11–18 (Day/Board) • Upper sixth 131 • Termly fees £1929 (Day) £3370 (Board) • HMC • Enquiries/application to the Headmaster

What it's like

Founded in 1557, it occupies a single site in the small town of Brentwood with extensive gardens and nearly 70 acres of playing fields. It is architecturally pleasing (the old 'Big School' built in 1568 is still in use). There have been many modern developments including a new building for the girls' school and a new technology block; facilities are now first rate. Originally a boys' school it first accepted girls into the sixth-form in 1974. From 1988, girls were admitted at 11 but are educated separately to GCSE; the sixth-form remains fully co-educational. Results are very good and almost all sixth-form leavers proceed to degree courses, including to Oxbridge. Some of its main strengths lie in music, drama and art. Notable successes in some sports and games, particularly fencing, tennis and girls' hockey. There is a flourishing CCF. It enjoys good local support.

School profile

Pupils Age range 11–18; 1043 pupils, 976 day (643 boys, 333 girls), 67 boarding (boys and girls from 1994). Main entry ages, 11, 13 and into sixth. Approx 5% are children of former pupils. Own prep school (boys) provides 40% of intake. *State school entry:* 33% at 11, 60% to sixth.

Entrance Own exam at 11, Common Entrance at 13. No religious requirements but Anglican tradition. Parents not expected to buy textbooks; fencing, music, CCF etc extra. 18 pa assisted places at 11 and 5 pa for sixth-form. 16 pa scholarships, bursaries available.

Parents 15+% in industry or commerce; 15+% are doctors, lawyers etc. 60+% live within 30 miles.

Head and staff *Headmaster:* John Kelsall, 4 years in post. Educated at the Royal Grammar School, Lancaster, and at Cambridge University (economics). Previously Headmaster at Arnold and at Bournemouth. *Staff:* 94 full time, 8 part time. Annual turnover approx 10%. Average age 36.

Exam results In 1995, 147 pupils in upper fifth, 116 in upper sixth. *GCSE:* In 1995, 95 fifth gained at least grade C in 8+ subjects; 48 in 5–7 subjects. *A-levels:* 20 upper sixth passed in 4 subjects; 78 in 3; 12 in 2; and 6 in 1 subject. Average UCAS points 21.5.

University and college entrance 92% of 1995 sixth-form leavers went on to a degree course (10% after a gap year); others typically go on to the City, armed services. Of those going on to university, 10% went to Oxbridge; 5% took courses in medicine, dentistry and veterinary science, 38% in science and engineering, 6% in law, 42% in humanities and social sciences, 3% in art and design, 6% in vocational subjects eg hotel management, education, agriculture.

Curriculum GCSE and A-level. Electronic systems and ancient history offered to GCSE/A-level. 33% take science/engineering A-levels; 50% take arts and humanities; 17% a mixture. *Vocational:* Work experience available; also BTEC qualifications. *Computing facilities:* Computer lab with 16 BBCs, 3 Amstrads, 2 Apples (Sinclair Spectrums in reserve), 16 Archimedes. *Special provision:* Subsidiary EFL classes offered. *Europe:* French, German and Spanish offered at GCSE and A-level; also AS-level French, GCSE Italian and Russian and Institute of Linguists exams in Spanish. Regular to France, Germany and Spain. Close contacts, especially musical, with twin town in Bavaria. Visits to First World War battlefields, and classical sites; developing links with Zaragoza.

The arts *Music:* Some 30% of pupils learn a musical instrument; instrumental exams can be taken. Some 13 musical groups including orchestras, big band, concert band choirs, brass ensemble etc. County schools musician of the year 1992; big band, 4 CDs released, frequent foreign tours; choirs, cathedral visits; many members of county youth orchestra, town orchestra etc. *Drama and dance:* Drama offered, GCSE may be taken. Some pupils are involved in school and house/other productions. Recent school productions of The Crucible, Much Ado About Nothing, Hamlet; ESU Shakespeare on the Platform regularly entered, successes at local level. *Art:* On average, 40 take GCSE, 2 AS-level, 16 A-level. Design, pottery, textiles, photography, art history also offered. Former pupils have gone on to courses in fine art, industrial, graphic and textiles design, animation, also graduates and post-graduates in art history.

Sport, community service and clubs *Sport and physical activities:* Compulsory sports: soccer, cricket. Optional: badminton, basketball, HRF, rugby, cross-country, volleyball, short tennis, athletics, swimming, tennis, PE. Sixth form only: indoor soccer, squash, table tennis, racketball, trampolining, weight training, circuit training, indoor hockey. GCSE and A-level may be taken. Soccer, 2 independent schools U19, 1 regional, 3 national U16; athletics, 3 county champions; cricket, captain signed to Essex, plays for 2nd XI, 4 county U13; basketball, county champions; volleyball, area champions U19, U16; fencing, public schools champions last 3 years, 3 British team, 2 national champions; tennis, 1st 6 unbeaten in last 2 years; hockey (girls) 2 county U16. *Community service:* Pupils take bronze, silver and gold Duke of Edinburgh's Award. CCF or community service compulsory for 3–5 years at age 13+. *Clubs and societies:* Over 30 clubs, eg archery, athletics, music, Christian Union, film, fencing, golf, science and technology, geography, debating, theatre.

Uniform School uniform worn throughout.

Houses/prefects Competitive houses. Prefects, head boy/girl, head of house and house prefects – appointed by the Headmaster.

Religion Regular chapel (C of E) services.

Social Debates, historical society, drama, foreign exchange visits, county sports of various kinds. Organised trips to Germany, France, USA and ESU scholars both ways. Pupils allowed to bring own car/cycle to school with permission. Self-service meals. School shop. No tobacco/ alcohol allowed.

Discipline Punishment by admonishment, detention and suspension.

Boarding 40% have own study bedroom, 60% share. Single-sex houses, of up to 18 (girls), 50 (boys). Resident qualified medical staff. Central dining room. Visits to local town allowed with housemaster's permission.

Alumni association run by Mr I R West, Secretary, 11 Regent Square, London E3 3HQ.

Former pupils Sir Hardy Amies; Sir Robin Day; H Whittaker (Almanack); Jack Straw MP; Bishop Griggs of Ludlow; Bishop Adams late of Barking; Air Marshal Sir John Rogers; Douglas Adams (author); George Cansdale (TV); Griff Rhys-Jones (TV); Prof Roger Cowley (Prof of Experimental Philosophy, Oxford University); Dr Stephen Fleet (Registrar Cambridge Univ. & Vice Master of Downing College); Peter Stothard (Editor of The Times).

• BRIGHTON COLLEGE

Brighton College, Eastern Road, Brighton, East Sussex BN2 2AL. Tel 01273 697131
• Pupils 464 • Boys 13–18 (Day/Board/Weekly) • Girls 13–18 (Day/Board/Weekly) • Upper sixth 85 • Termly fees £2618 (Day) £3980 (Board) £3560 (Weekly) • HMC • Enquiries/application to the Headmaster

What it's like

Founded in 1845, it stands on high ground in the Kemp Town district of Brighton. It enjoys handsome buildings (the school chapel, which is in regular use, is especially striking) in attractive surroundings with ample playing fields. Originally a boys' school, girls were admitted to the sixth-form in 1973 and it became fully co-educational in 1988. The teaching is of a high standard and academic results are very good. The staff:pupil ratio is about 1:10. Most go on to degree courses, including a number to Oxbridge. It is a good all-round school, with plenty of regard for the less talented, and a dyslexic support unit for highly intelligent children. Strong in music, art and drama; also in sports and games. It offers a wide range of activities and there is considerable involvement in local community schemes. Full use is made of the cultural amenities of Brighton.

School profile

Pupils Age range 13–18; 464 pupils, 372 day (281 boys, 91 girls), 91 boarding (59 boys, 32 girls). Main entry ages 13 and into sixth. Own prep school provides 60% of intake. Approx 15% are children of former pupils.

Entrance Common Entrance exam used. Pupils who have a positive contribution to make in any sphere are welcomed. No religious requirements but the college is a C of E foundation. Parents expected to buy textbooks. 15 pa assisted places at 11. 30 pa scholarships/bursaries, 10%–50% of fees.

Parents 15+ % in industry or commerce; 15+% are doctors and lawyers etc. 60+% live within 30 miles; up to 10% live overseas.

Head and staff *Headmaster:* John Leach, in post for 9 years. Educated at St Edward's (Oxford) and Oxford University (classics). Previously Housemaster, Director of Studies and Head of Classics at St Edward's (Oxford) and Assistant Master at Sherborne. *Staff:* 49 full time, 5 part time. Annual turnover 4%. Average age 35.

Exam results In 1995, 97 pupils in upper fifth, 85 in upper sixth. *GCSE:* In 1995, 65% upper fifth gained at least grade C in 10+ subjects; 25% in 5–7 subjects. *A-levels:* 74 upper sixth passed in 3+ subjects; 11 in 2 subjects. Average UCAS points 22.1.

University and college entrance 95% of 1995 sixth-form leavers went on to a degree course; others typically go straight on to careers or other courses. Of those going on to university, 14% went to Oxbridge; 5% took courses in medicine, dentistry and veterinary science, 50% in science and engineering, 35% in humanities and social sciences, 10% in art, drama and music.

Curriculum GCSE and A-levels (subjects include geology A-level). Over one-third take science/engineering A-levels; one-third arts/humanities; under one-third a mixture. *Vocational:* Work experience available: also some vocational qualifications. *Computing facilities:* Computer laboratories; 16-work station network, with separate stations in departments. Laser printers, computer graphics. *Special provision:* Dyslexic support unit for children assessed as dyslexic but with high intelligence, to take a suitably adjusted GCSE course within the normal curriculum, with the opportunity to proceed to A-levels. *Europe:* French and German offered to GCSE, AS and A-level. Regular exchanges to France.

The arts *Music:* some 30% of pupils learn a musical instrument; instrumental exams taken. Some 9 musical groups including orchestra, choirs, concert band, wind, brass, string ensembles. Members of Brighton and East Sussex youth orchestras; semi-finalists in Chamber Music for Schools competition. *Drama and dance:* Drama offered. ESU public speaking competitions. Many pupils are involved in school productions. Recent productions of My Fair Lady and As You Like It. *Art:* On average, 25 take GCSE, 10 A-level. Design, pottery, textiles, photography also offered. 4–5 per year go on to art school.

Sport, community service and clubs *Sport and physical activities:* Compulsory sports: rugby, hockey, cricket, netball. Optional: badminton, football, squash, water polo, swimming, basketball, tennis, sailing, athletics, judo, golf, fencing, cross-country, table-tennis. Regular county representation (hockey, cricket, rugby, athletics, swimming). *Community service:* Pupils take bronze, silver and gold Duke of Edinburgh's Award.

CCF compulsory for 2 years at age 14. Community service optional. *Clubs and societies:* Up to 30 activities, eg aerobics, bridge, choral, computing, cookery, drama, electronics, public speaking, satellite.
Uniform School uniform worn including in the sixth.
Houses/prefects Competitive houses. Prefects, head boy/girl, head of house and house prefects – appointed by the Headmaster and housemaster/mistress.
Religion Religious worship compulsory, in College Chapel or own place of worship for those of non C of E persuasion.
Social Public speaking competitions, concerts, participation in Brighton Festival, Challenge of Industry Conference. Organised trips abroad. Day pupils allowed to bring own car/bike/motorbike to school (with permission from the Headmaster). Meals self-service. School shop. No tobacco allowed; limited bar in sixth-form club.
Discipline Pupils failing to produce homework once might expect a 'Yellow Paper' signed by the housemaster; those caught smoking cannabis on the premises could expect expulsion.
Boarding 40% have own study bedroom, 40% share; 20% are in dormitories of 4–8. Houses of about 50. Resident matron, doctor visits daily. Central dining room. Pupils can provide and cook own snacks. Weekend exeats, by arrangement. Visits to the local town allowed.
Alumni association run by Mrs H Williamson, c/o the College.
Former pupils George Sanders (actor); Prof Noel Odell (mountaineer and Cambridge Professor); John Worsley (artist); Rt Rev T J Bavin (former Bishop of Portsmouth); Rear Admiral P G V Dingemans (Falklands); Sir Michael Hordern (actor); Sir Vivien Fuchs (explorer); Sir Humphrey Edwardes-Jones (Air Commodore); Lord Alexander QC (Chairman of NatWest); Jonathan Palmer (doctor and Formula 1 racing driver); Professor Lord Skidelsky (economist).

• BRISTOL CATHEDRAL

Bristol Cathedral School, College Square, Bristol BS1 5TS. Tel 0117 929 1872
• Pupils 470 • Boys 10–18 (Day) • Girls 16–18 (Day) • Upper sixth 60 • Termly fees £1398 (Day)
• CSA • Enquiries/application to the Head Master

What it's like

The origins of the School are in the Grammar School of St Augustine's Abbey founded in 1140. It was refounded by Henry VIII in 1542 and is Bristol's only royal foundation. It stands in the cathedral precinct and the buildings span 800 years of architectural history. The main classrooms are on the original site of the Abbey School. There have been many modern developments and facilities are very good. A sound, liberal education is provided and results are very good. Most sixth-formers go on to degree courses. Because of the close links with the cathedral (which is the school's chapel), there is considerable emphasis on pastoral care and religious education. The staff:pupil ratio is about 1:13. The art, drama and music departments are extremely strong and the school is well known for its range of musical activities. A wide range of sports and games is available and there is a fair variety of extra-curricular activities, clubs, societies, etc. Work experience is undertaken by all members of the fifth form and the school has close links with a wide range of commercial and industrial concerns in and about the city. Full use is made of the city's cultural amenities.

School profile

Pupils Age range 10–18, 470 day pupils (445 boys, 25 girls). Main entry ages 10 (choristers) 11 (boys) and 16 (boys and girls).
Entrance Own entrance exam used. 35+ pa assisted places; music, academic and instrumental scholarships.
Head and staff Head Master: K J Riley, 3 years in post. Educated at Norwich School and at Aberystwyth and Bristol universities. Previously Deputy Headmaster, Head of English at Wolverhampton Grammar, and Master at Pocklington.
Exam results On average, 75 pupils in fifth, 60 in upper sixth. *GCSE:* On average, 91% gain at least grade C in 5+ subjects. *A-level:* 4 in upper sixth pass in 4 subjects; 35 in 3; 14 in 2; and 6 in 1 subject. Average UCAS points 21.8.
University and college entrance 90% of 1995 sixth-form leavers went on to a degree course (10% after a gap year); others typically go on to other schools or colleges or

straight into employment. Of those going on to university, 10% went to Oxbridge; 40% took courses in medicine, science and engineering, 27% in social sciences, 33% in arts.
Curriculum 21 GCSE subjects, 9 AS subjects and 17 A-levels. *Computing facilities:* IT laboratory plus departmental facilities. *Europe:* French and German offered at GCSE, AS and A-level; also GCSE Italian in sixth. Use made of satellite television, video camera and language assistants. Regular exchanges to France and Germany. Europe and EU modules in current affairs and general studies.
The arts *Music:* Over 50% of pupils learn a musical instrument; instrumental exams can be taken. Up to 10 musical groups including two orchestras, brass group, choir, chamber choir, various ensembles. First orchestra chosen for National Festival of Music for Youth, 1994. *Drama and dance:* Drama offered. Majority of pupils involved in school and house/other productions. Recent large scale production of West Side Story. *Art:* On average, 15 take GCSE, 5 A-level.
Sport, community service and clubs *Sport and physical activities:* Compulsory sports: rugby, football or hockey, cricket. Wider range for fifth and sixth-forms including badminton, weight-training, squash, swimming, tennis, athletics, sailing and aerobics. *Community service:* optional for 2 years at age 15. Pupils take bronze and silver Duke of Edinburgh's Award. *Clubs and societies:* Up to 15 clubs, eg bell ringing, judo, photography, technology.
Uniform School uniform worn except in the sixth where dress regulations apply.
Houses/prefects Competitive houses for sport. All upper sixth are prefects; two head prefects elected by peers. School Council.
Religion No compulsory attendance at religious worship.
Social Occasional concerts, plays etc with other schools. Exchanges with schools in Germany and Uganda. Pupils allowed to bring own car/bike/motorbike to school. Meals self-service. No alcohol/tobacco allowed.

• BRISTOL GRAMMAR

Bristol Grammar School, University Road, Bristol BS8 1SR. Tel 0117 973 6006

• Pupils 1210 • Boys 7–18 (Day) • Girls 7–18 (Day) • Upper sixth 138 • Termly fees £1296 (Day) • HMC • Enquiries/application to the Headmaster

What it's like

Founded in 1532, it lies in Tyndall's Park, to the north-west side of Bristol next to the university. Its core consists of handsome Victorian buildings (especially the Great Hall) and there have been many developments in the last 15 years. It now has one of the best school libraries in England as well as a magnificent sports hall, art school and technology centre. Originally a boys' school, it first accepted girls in 1980 and is now fully co-educational. It enjoys a high reputation academically. Results are very good and almost all pupils go on to degree courses, including Oxbridge. It has played a major part in the educational life of the city. Flourishing local ties and back-up from the community and from Old Bristolians. An exceptional number of activities on offer each week. A very friendly atmosphere and much is done to maintain high standards of pastoral care through the house system and year head/form tutor organisation. The Duke of Edinburgh's Award Scheme is well supported.

School profile

Pupils Total age range 7–18; 1210 day pupils (870 boys, 340 girls). Senior department 11–18, 1000 pupils (690 boys, 310 girls). Main entry ages 7, 11, 13 and into sixth. Approx 20% are children of former pupils. *State school entry:* 70% intake at 11 and 13, plus 10% to sixth.
Entrance Own entrance exam at 11 used. No special skills or religious requirements. Parents not expected to buy textbooks; no other extras. 50 pa assisted places (government and Governors). 7 pa scholarships/bursaries, 20%–50% fees.
Parents 15+% in industry or commerce; 15+% are doctors, lawyers etc.
Head and staff *Headmaster:* Charles Martin, in post for 10 years. Educated at Lancing, and at the universities of Cambridge (English) and Bristol (education). Previously Headmaster at King Edward VI Camp Hill, Birmingham, Deputy Head and Head of English at Pocklington, Head of Sixth Form at Sevenoaks and Assistant

Master at Leighton Park. *Staff:* 70 full time, 9 part time. Annual turnover 5%. Average age 38.

Exam results In 1995, 148 pupils in Year 11, 138 in upper sixth. *GCSE:* In 1995, 96% gained at least grade C in 8+ subjects; 4% in 5–7 subjects. *A-levels:* 129 upper sixth passed in 3+ subjects; 7 in 2; 2 in 1 subject. Average UCAS points 22.0.

University and college entrance 98% of 1995 sixth-form leavers went on to a degree course (15% after a gap year); others typically go on to careers eg the services. Of those going on to university, 10% went to Oxbridge; 15% took courses in medicine, dentistry and veterinary science, 25% in science and engineering, 5% in law, 35% in humanities and social sciences (including 15% in languages), 5% in art and design, 15% in vocational subjects eg physiotherapy, journalism, business, education, leisure.

Curriculum GCSE and A-levels. 20 subjects offered, including Greek, Russian; wide-ranging non-examined general studies programme. 25% take straight science A-levels; 40% arts/humanities; 35% a mixture. *Vocational:* Work experience available. *Computing facilities:* Over 70 PCs for academic use. *Europe:* French (compulsory from 11–16), German and Russian offered at GCSE and A-level.

The arts (Pupils aged 11 and over) *Music:* Up to 50% of pupils learn a musical instrument; instrumental exams can be taken. Some 6 musical groups including orchestras, choirs. 4 members of National Youth Orchestra. *Drama and dance:* Drama and dance offered. Some pupils are involved in school productions and house/other productions. Recent productions include Joseph And His Amazing Technicolour Dreamcoat and The Lady's Not For Burning. *Art:* On average, 30 take GCSE, 10 A-level. Textiles, photography also offered. Pupils regularly proceed to art/design courses.

Sport, community service and clubs (Pupils aged 11 and over) *Sport and physical activities:* Compulsory sports (early years, increasing choice further up school): rugby, hockey, cricket, netball. Optional: cross-country, golf, squash, badminton. Pupils regularly compete at county, regional and national level; netball team current county representatives; rugby, Daily Mail national runners-up in 1995, U15. *Community service:* Pupils take bronze, silver and gold Duke of Edinburgh's Award (very large scheme). Community service optional. *Clubs and societies:* Over 30 clubs, from cookery and glass engraving to iceskating and windsurfing.

Uniform School uniform worn but with greater flexibility in the sixth.

Houses/prefects 6 competitive houses. Prefects, head boy/girl, head of house and house prefects – appointed by the Head in consultation with staff. School Council.

Religion No compulsory religious worship.

Social Regular local, area and national debating competitions and joint competitions with neighbouring schools. Regular exchanges to St Petersburg, Bordeaux and Darmstadt; trips to France, Russia, Italy and Greece; sports tours Zimbabwe and Barbados, expedition to Borneo (1996). Pupils allowed to bring own bike/motorbikes to school. Meals self-service. Second-hand uniform shop. No tobacco/alcohol allowed.

Discipline Punishment for pupils failing to produce homework would depend on circumstances; those caught smoking cannabis on the premises could expect expulsion.

Alumni association run by Dr Philip Golding, c/o the school.

Former pupils Lord Franks (Ambassador to USA plus Oxford University), Tom Graveney (cricketer); Robert Lacey (author); Brian Barron (BBC); Clive Ponting (ex-Civil Servant); Fred Wedlock (entertainer); General Tunku Osman (Malaysian Army); Geoffrey Cutter (hockey); Rt Rev Peter Nott (Bishop of Norwich); John Currie (rugby); Canon G A Ffrench-Beytagh (anti-apartheid); Basil Greenhill (Maritime Museum, Greenwich); G H Heath-Grace (organist); Dave Prowse (film star); Prof Keith Robbins (historian); Sir Richard Sheppard (architect); David Drew (ballet).

• BRITISH HIGH (Bonn)

British High School Bonn e V, Friesdorfer Strasse 57, 53173 Bonn, Germany. Tel 49 228 31 12 57, Fax 49 228 31 92 69

• Pupils 116 • Boys 11–19 (Day) • Girls 11–19 (Day) • Upper sixth 17 • Termly fees £2000–£2200 (Day) • COBISEC, ECIS • Enquiries/application to the Headmaster .

What it's like

Founded in 1983, it is an urban, purpose-built and single-site school in the district of Bonn-Bad Godesberg. It was founded as a co-educational school; some 60% of pupils have parents in the diplomatic corps. A most favourable staff:pupil ratio of 1:8 allows much individual attention. Languages are particularly strong and many pupils speak two, three or even four. Most sixth-form leavers go on to degree courses. Music is well supported. The sports and games offered can depend on demand. There is close contact with the French Lycée and German Gymnasien. Many pupils belong to local German clubs for the purpose of sporting and cultural activities and quite a high proportion are involved in local community schemes.

School profile

Pupils Age range 11–19; 116 day pupils, (66 boys, 50 girls). Main entry ages 11, 13 and into sixth. British Embassy Prep School provides some 20% of intake.

Entrance EFL tests for non-English speakers; previous exam records for sixth-form entry. Knowledge of English as a first or second language required; no religious requirements. Extras for exam fees only; parents not expected to buy textbooks.

Parents 57% in diplomatic service; 43+% in industry etc. 70+% live within 30 miles; less than 10% overseas.

Head and staff *Headmaster:* Stephen Wilkerson, 2 years in post. Educated at Whitchurch Grammar, Cardiff, and the universities of Nottingham (physics), Southampton (cyrogenics) and Essex (research). Previously Head of Science and Housemaster at Copford College, Essex, and physics teacher at Sir Charles Lucas Comprehensive, Colchester, and at Colne High School, Essex. Also member of LEAG exam board Colchester and North East Essex subject panel. *Staff:* 12 full time, 3 part time. Annual turnover under 10%. Average age 36.

Exam results In 1995, 19 in upper fifth, 10 in upper sixth. *GCSE:* In 1995, 63% upper fifth gained at least grade C in 8+ subjects; 24% in 5–7 subjects. *A-levels:* In 1995, 50% upper sixth passed in 3 subjects; 30% in 2; and 20% in 1 subject. Average UCAS points 11.0.

University and college entrance 70% of sixth-form leavers go on to a degree course (20% after a gap year); others typically go on to other courses, apprenticeships, or national service. Of those going on to university, 10% take courses in medicine, dentistry and veterinary science, 35% in science and engineering, 5% in law, 40% in humanities and social sciences, 5% in art and design, 5% in eg music.

Curriculum GCSE and A-levels. 12 subjects offered (no A-level general studies). 30% take science A-levels, 30% arts/humanities; 40% a mixture of both. *Vocational:* Work experience occasionally possible (difficult to arrange in Germany); also RSA qualifications in IT, keyboard skills etc. *Computing facilities:* Computer lab with 9 IBM compatibles (plus 6 elsewhere in school). *Special provision:* Remedial and EFL and ESL teaching available. *Europe:* French and German offered at GCSE and A-level. Regular visits to other European countries. Pupils represent 34 nationalities, all following a British curriculum in a European setting. Languages are particularly strong.

The arts *Music:* Up to 50% of pupils learn a musical instrument; instrumental exams can be taken. Some 3 musical groups including orchestral, choir, pop. *Drama and dance:* Dance available as a club; majority of pupils involved in school productions. *Art:* On average, 5 take GCSE.

Sport, community service and clubs *Sport and physical activities:* Compulsory sports (up to fifth form): hockey, volleyball, basketball, soccer. Optional: badminton, table tennis, rugby, cricket (depending on demand). *Clubs and societies:* Up to 12 clubs, eg computers, crafts, musical, sport, magazine, photography, electronics, role-play games, self defence, cookery, outdoor activities.

Uniform No school uniform.

Houses/prefects Competitive houses. 2 house captains (1 boy, 1 girl), elected by house. Year representatives elected to attend PTA meetings.

Religion There is no religious worship.

Social Close contact and frequent exchange days with French Lycée, German Gymnasien. Major annual trip (eg Russia, Hungary); skiing trip and many other short trips to Paris, Luxembourg, Vienna, London. Year 13 allowed to bring own car/bike/motorbike to school. No meals at school. No tobacco/alcohol allowed.

Discipline Failure to produce homework can result in work done in detention; those caught smoking cannabis on the premises would be expelled (never happened).

• BRITISH SCHOOL (Brussels)

The British School of Brussels asbl, Leuvensesteenweg 19, 3080 Tervuren, Belgium. Tel 32 2 767 47 00, Fax 32 2 767 80 70

• Pupils 956 • Boys 3–18 (Day) • Girls 3–18 (Day) • Upper sixth 68 • Termly fees BF 181.000 (Day) • HMC, COBISEC, ECIS • Enquiries/application to the Admissions Office

What it's like

Founded in 1969, it lies in the commune of Tervuren, 20 minutes from the centre of Brussels. Its purpose-built premises occupy a very attractive site in wooded surroundings near to the Royal Museum of Central Africa with its park and lakes. Although it is a day school, it offers a number of places with host families. The programme is predominantly British but within a European context, taking advantage of the location to arrange visits, school journeys and fieldwork throughout the continent. It was founded as a co-educational school; 75% of the students are British but over 50 nationalities are represented. Academic standards are high and results good. Vocational qualifications are also offered. A large staff permits a staff:student ratio of about 1:11. Music plays a major part in the life of the school. Drama, art and dance are also well-supported and public performances are held in the purpose-built theatre including many by visiting companies. There are good sports facilities, including gymnasia, a sports hall, an outdoor, all-purpose activity area and large playing fields, all of which are available out-of-school hours to families and friends. There are numerous extra-curricular activities and the school publishes its own newspaper three times a year. Local involvement with the school is vigorous and the campus is a focal point for community activities including adult studies and a summer school. Widespread use is made of the facilities of the capital and students also take part in events such as Model United Nations in The Hague.

School profile

Pupils Total age range 3–18; 956 day pupils, 510 boys, 446 girls. Senior section 11–18. School runs a host family scheme for children whose families live too far away for daily travel to school; hosting can be on a weekly, monthly or termly basis.

Entrance Comprehensive, all aptitudes welcomed. Some assisted places available.

Parents Very international – some 50 nationalities.

Head and staff *Principal:* Jennifer M Bray, 4 years in post. Educated at Leeds High and at the universities of Oxford, Ibadan and Leicester (geography, law). Previously Principal of Shatin College, Hong Kong. *Publications:* author, editor or translator of seven books. *Staff:* 78 full time, 27 part time and 20+ visiting instrumental music teachers.

University and college entrance 85% of 1995 sixth-form leavers went on to a degree course (4% after a gap year); others typically go on to HND or art foundation courses, followed by a degree. Of those going on to university, 7% went to Oxbridge; 5% took courses in medicine, dentistry and veterinary science, 14% in science and engineering, 5% in law, 14% in humanities and social sciences, 7% in art and design, 44% in vocational subjects eg architecture, business, hotel management.

Curriculum GCSE and A-level, also Advanced GNVQ in business. Broadly follows the British National Curriculum to age 16 but with special emphasis on languages and creative arts. 19 A-level subjects offered. *Vocational:* Advanced GNVQ in business. Work experience available. *Special provision:* Learning support department with ESL specialists, an educational psychologist and a counsellor. *Europe:* French (compulsory from age 5) and German taught.

The arts *Music:* Up to 50% of pupils learn a musical instrument; instrumental exams can be taken. Some 19 musical groups – 3 wind bands, 2 orchestras, big band, choirs, rock bands. *Drama and dance:* Drama offered to A-level. Many pupils are involved in a variety of productions. *Art:* On average, 45 take GCSE, 16 A-level. Graphic design, ceramics, textiles, history of art, sculpture, printmaking also offered. Several students each year accepted at colleges of art and design in UK, US and continental Europe.

Sport, community service and clubs *Sport and physical activities:* Sports: broad range of team games, activities and sports compulsory to 15; choice of activities thereafter. BAGA exams may be taken. Successful in the International Schools circuit, with 1st places in many ISST championships over many years. *Community service:* Community service compulsory for 1–2 years at age 16+, senior pupils help in primary school, also

serve on charity committee and organise school plays and school's termly newspaper.
Uniform No uniform worn.
Religion No religious affiliation.

• BRITISH SCHOOL (Netherlands)

The British School in the Netherlands, Boerderij Rosenburgh, Rosenburgherlaan 2, 2252 BA Voorschoten, Netherlands. Tel 31 71 5616966

• Pupils 1300 • Boys 3–18 (Day) • Girls 3–18 (Day) • Upper sixth 57 • Termly fees FL1955–FL6510 (Day) • HMC, COBISEC, ECIS • Enquiries/application to the Principal

What it's like

Founded in The Hague in 1935, it has grown steadily from 20 pupils and 4 staff to 1300 pupils and 105 full-time staff. It has three sites not far apart, on the northern side of the city. The infant and junior departments have urban premises; the senior school has an agreeable semi-rural position in the suburb of Voorschoten. All are extremely well equipped and the senior establishment enjoys ample playing fields on site, plus cricket wicket and floodlit all-weather tennis courts etc. The school offers a British education following the National Curriculum, with an international dimension. Some 60% of pupils are British; the rest come from 50 other nations. A core stays for their complete education; the remainder spend 3–4 years before being relocated. Non-British pupils are given intensive tuition in English as necessary. A favourable staff:pupil ratio of roughly 1:10 allows a good deal of individual attention. The staff all have UK qualifications. Academic standards are high and AS and A-level results very good; almost all leavers go on to degree courses. Music is strong and drama well supported and there is some emphasis on public speaking and oratory. A standard range of sports and games is available, including hockey and rugby (teams are members of Dutch clubs and take part in the national leagues and there have been representatives at national level in these games). Large numbers of pupils take exams in swimming and gymnastics. Extra-curricular activities including Young Enterprise scheme; and many cultural, language and sports trips to other countries. Extensive use is made of the cultural facilities of The Hague.

School profile

Pupils Total age range 3–18; 1300 day pupils (650 boys, 650 girls). Senior department, 12–18, 530 pupils (265 boys, 265 girls). Entry at all ages and into sixth; worldwide intake.
Entrance Own assessment tests. No special skills or religious requirements. Average extras: week-long field courses, about FL500; parents not expected to buy textbooks. 10 pa places assisted by school. 2 pa bursaries, 50%–90% fees.
Parents 15+% are doctors, lawyers, etc; 70+% in industry; 15+% in diplomatic service. Many different nationalities represented.
Head and staff *Principal:* Michael J Cooper, 6 years in post; educated at Sutton High School, Plymouth, and York University (biology and education). Previously Headteacher at Hillcrest, Hastings; Deputy Head at Valley, Worksop and taught at Chassa School (Zambia), Mill Hill and Moulsham High. *Staff:* 105 full time, 25 part time. Annual turnover 5%. Average age 33.
Exam results On average, 85 in Year 11, 57 in Year 13. *GCSE:* on average, 80% year 11 gain at least grade C in 8+ subjects; 15% in 5–7 subjects. *A-levels:* 25% Year 13 pass in 4 subjects; 67% in 3; 6% in 2 and 2% in 1 subject.
University and college entrance 94% of 1995 sixth-form leavers went on to a degree course; others typically go on to art/drama colleges or to other courses. Of those going on to university, 3% went to Oxbridge; 2% took courses in medicine, dentistry and veterinary science, 36% in science and engineering, 29% in humanities and social sciences, 11% in art and design, 2% in drama and acting.
Curriculum GCSE, AS-level, A-levels; also Dutch exams. 21 subjects offered (no A-level general studies). 27% take science A-levels; 19% arts/humanities; 54% a mixture of both. *Vocational:* Work experience available; also Young Enterprise Scheme. *Computing facilities:* Extensive – Nimbus network, Acorns, IBMs and BBC Archimedes. *Special provision:* Special needs and ESL department. *Europe:* Dutch, Spanish, French and German offered at GCSE, AS and A-level. Majority of students study 4 languages from

age 12; many take GCSE in more than one. European studies taught; summer school for non-English children; annual field courses to Germany, UK, Switzerland.
The arts (Pupils aged 11 and over) *Music:* Up to 50% of pupils learn a musical instrument; instrumental exams can be taken. Some 4 musical groups: percussion, string, brass, rock. Edith Stein Competition success. *Drama and dance:* Drama, theatre studies and dance offered. GCSE drama and A-level theatre studies may be taken. Majority of pupils are involved in school productions and house/other productions. Recent winners ECIS speech and debate team award; annual musical or dramatic production. *Art:* On average, 40 take GCSE, 15 A-level. Design, sculpture, textiles, photography also offered. Half of art and design students go on to art courses.
Sport, community service and clubs (Pupils aged 11 and over) *Sport and physical activities:* Compulsory sports: soccer, rugby, hockey, gymnastics, cricket, basketball, netball, swimming, cross-country, volleyball, tennis, athletics. Optional: judo, ice skating. Sixth form only: riding, weight training, fencing, self defence. *Clubs and societies:* Up to 15 clubs, eg photography, theatre, various musical, Scouts, Guides, chess.
Uniform School uniform worn, except in the sixth.
Houses/prefects Competitive houses. Head of house elected by the school. School council with representatives from each year group.
Religion Attendance at religious worship not compulsory.
Social Netherlands/England public speaking, international schools tournaments, debating and oratory, sporting competitions, hockey and rugby in Dutch league. Many cultural, language and sports trips to other countries. Pupils allowed to bring own car/bike/motorbike to school. No school meals (packed lunches only). Tuck shop and uniform shop. No tobacco/alcohol allowed.
Discipline Pupils failing to produce homework once would be expected to complete it the following day; those caught smoking cannabis on the premises would be expelled.
Former pupils Antoinette V Bellen (actress); Conrad Bartelski (ski champion). Anna Walker, (TV presenter).

• BROMLEY HIGH

Bromley High School, Blackbrook Lane, Bickley, Bromley, Kent BR1 2TW. Tel 0181 468 7981, Fax 0181 295 1062

• Pupils 828 • Boys None • Girls 4–18 (Day) • Upper sixth 60 • Termly fees £1548 (Day) • GSA, GPDST • Enquiries/application to the Headmistress

What it's like

Founded in 1883 by the Girls' Public Day School Trust in the centre of Bromley. In 1981 it moved to Bickley to occupy new buildings, set in 24 acres of beautiful grounds. Modern facilities, include specialist rooms for art, technology, ceramics and drama and a music wing. Sports facilities include a gymnasium, athletics tracks and six-lane swimming pool. The junior department is on the same site. Entrants come from well beyond Bromley. Academic studies are of paramount importance but enthusiastic involvement in music, drama, art, sport and community activities is expected. Academic standards are high and results very good: most of the upper sixth go on to degree courses. The school is strong in the performing arts. High standards in sports and games are maintained with members appearing in regional and national squads and the school holds championship titles in several sports. Extra-curricular activities flourish; the Duke of Edinburgh's Award Scheme, Young Enterprise, work experienceand voluntary service all enjoy enthusiastic support.

School profile

Pupils Total age range 4–18; 828 day girls. Senior department 11–18, 546 girls. Main entry ages 4, 11 and into sixth. Significant proportion of senior pupils from own junior department and from St David's College (tel 0181 777 5852); also St Olave's (0181 850 9175), Eden Park (0181 650 0365), West Lodge (0181 300 2489) and many junior and primary schools.
Entrance Own entrance exam used. No special skills or religious requirements. Parents not expected to buy textbooks. 30 pa assisted places; various scholarships/bursaries, including music scholarship.

Head and staff *Headmistress:* Mrs Joy Hancock, in post 7 years. Educated at Queen's College, Harley Street, and the universities of Nottingham (history) and Sussex (education). Previously Deputy Head at Brighton and Hove High. *Publications:* Teaching History (1970). *Staff:* 42 full time, 29 part time (plus 24 music and speech/drama).
Exam results Average size of upper fifth 84; upper sixth 60+. *GCSE:* In 1995, 98% upper fifth gained at least grade C in 8+ subjects; 2% in 6–7 subjects. *A-levels:* 66 upper sixth passed in 3+ subjects; 3 in 2 subjects. Average UCAS points gained 22.6.
University and college entrance 98% of 1995 sixth-form leavers went on to a degree course; others typically go straight into careers eg advertising. Of those going on to university, 7%% went to Oxbridge; 12% took courses in medicine, dentistry and veterinary science, 12% in science and engineering, 64% in humanities and social sciences, 6% in art and design.
Curriculum GCSE and A-levels. Japanese and Russian taught in the sixth-form. 33% take science A-levels; 33% arts/humanities; 33% take both. *Vocational:* Work experience available. *Computing facilities:* Nimbus networks. Stand-alones also in departments and junior school. *Europe:* French, German and Spanish offered to GCSE and A-level; also courses in FLAW. 95% take GCSE in more than 1 language. Regular exchanges to France, Germany and Spain. Talks from MEPs; work experience in Dieppe, study conferences (France).
The arts (Pupils aged 11 and over) *Music:* Up to 75% of pupils learn a musical instrument; instrumental exams can be taken. Some 10+ musical groups including jazz band, recorders, chamber choir, orchestras, bands, various ensembles. *Drama and dance:* GCSE drama and Guildhall exams may be taken. Annual dance production. Some pupils are involved in school productions and majority in other productions. *Art:* On average, 30 take GCSE, 6 A-level. Design, pottery, textiles, photography also offered.
Sport, community service and clubs (Pupils aged 11 and over) *Sport and physical activities:* Compulsory sports: tennis, hockey, athletics, netball, gym, dance. Optional: archery, fencing, rowing. Sixth form only: squash, riding etc. GCSE PE and BAGA exams may be taken. Successes include regional netball U16/U18 champions. *Community service:* Pupils take bronze, silver and gold Duke of Edinburgh's Award. Community service optional. Also Young Enterprise, Neighbourhood Engineer scheme. *Clubs and societies:* Over 30 clubs, eg computing, chess, pets, literary, Greek, Christian Union etc.
Uniform School uniform worn except in the sixth-form.
Houses/prefects No competitive houses. Prefects, 2 head girls and 4 deputies, elected by girls and staff. School Council.
Religion Christian tradition, non-denominational; assembly daily.
Social Regular exchanges to France, Germany and Spain; field courses include Alternative Energy Centre (North Wales); other holidays trips abroad (Italy, Russia, Egypt, safari to Kenya), skiing biannually. Pupils allowed to bring own car/bike to school. Meals self-service. No tobacco/alcohol/personal stereos allowed.
Discipline Girls expected to behave with consideration for others and work to best of their abilities. Detention system but school values frequent consultation with parents. Serious offences, such as smoking or stealing would warrant suspension. School insists on punctuality and commitment to homework.
Former pupils Mrs Marion Roe, MP; Dr Janet Sondheimer; Professor Marilyn Strathern; Dame Dorothy Brock; Professor Joan Walsh; Dr Lucy Campion.

• BROMSGROVE

Bromsgrove School, Bromsgrove, Worcestershire B61 7DU. Tel 01527 579679, Fax 01527 576177

• Pupils 1090 • Boys 7–18 (Day/Board) • Girls 7–18 (Day/Board) • Upper sixth 100 • Termly fees £1430–£2050 (Day) £2515–£3275 (Board) • HMC • Enquiries/application to the Headmaster

What it's like

Founded in 1548, a development of a medieval charity school and one of the original fourteen schools at the foundation of the HMC in 1869. Its site comprises 100 acres of beautiful grounds and very attractive buildings, near the centre of Bromsgrove and half an hour from both Birmingham and Stratford-on-Avon. It has strong links with Worcester College, Oxford, through endowment by Sir Thomas Cookes, founder of

Worcester in 1693. Its modern facilities are excellent and there have been many major developments in the last five years. A sense of family (in the Christian tradition) is regarded as of prime importance. The Chapel is in regular use. Originally a boys' school, girls were first accepted in 1976 and it is now fully co-educational. The school provides a wide range of opportunities for its pupils and its well-organised pastoral system encourages pupils to identify and develop their talents to the full. It enjoys a high degree of academic success (results are good) and sends almost all sixth-form pupils on to degree courses each year, including Oxbridge. Music, drama and art are all strong and well supported. There is considerable strength, too, in sports and games (a large number of representatives at county, regional and national level). Thirty or more clubs and societies cater for most extra-curricular activities. There is great emphasis on outdoor pursuits linked with a vigorous CCF contingent. Local community services are an important feature of the school life and there is a substantial commitment to the Duke of Edinburgh's Award Scheme with an impressive record of success.

School profile

Pupils Total age range 7–18; 1090 pupils, 718 day (443 boys, 275 girls), 372 boarding (219 boys, 153 girls). Upper school 13–18, 670 pupils (399 boys, 271 girls). Main entry ages 7, 8, 11, 13 and into sixth. 70% of upper school from own lower school. *State school entry:* 15% of senior intakes, plus 40% of sixth-form intake.

Entrance Common Entrance and own exam used. School looks for a wide range of pupils (good all-rounders, talented pupils, good citizens, honest triers). No religious requirements although school is an Anglican foundation. Parents not expected to buy text books; few extras. 29 pa assisted places. Large number of scholarships, exhibitions, including music scholarships, all-rounder and forces bursaries, 10%–80% fees.

Parents 15+% in industry or commerce. 60+% live within 30 miles; 10+% live overseas.

Head and staff *Headmaster:* T M Taylor, in post for 10 years. Educated at Crewkerne Grammar School and Oxford University (biology). Previously Headmaster of Millfield Junior School (Edgarley Hall) and Housemaster and Senior Tutor at Millfield. Also Director of West Midlands Examination Board and of Central England TEC, Member of HMC Professional Development Sub-Committee and of SHA Hereford and Worcester Branch, and Governor of Hallfield School, Edgbaston; formerly President Oxford University Athletics Club, Chairman of Independent School (Midland Area) Training Board and of Midland Division of HMC. *Staff:* 85 full time, 10 part time. Annual turnover 5%. Average age approx 38.

Exam results In 1995, 141 pupils in fifth, 100 in upper sixth. *GCSE:* In 1995, 71% fifth gained at least grade C in 8+ subjects; 23% in 5–7 subjects. *A-levels:* 67% upper sixth passed in 4+ subjects; 15% in 3; 13% in 2; and 3% in 1 subject. Average UCAS points 24.5.

University and college entrance 95% of 1995 sixth-form leavers went on to a degree course (some after a gap year); others typically go on to art foundation courses or straight into careers. Of those going on to university, 9% went to Oxbridge; 8% took courses in medicine, dentistry and veterinary science, 30% in science and engineering, 50% in humanities and social sciences, 5% in art and design, 7% in drama and music.

Curriculum GCSE and A-levels and GNVQ. Subjects include A-level general studies. 20% took science A-levels; 30% arts/humanities; 50% both. *Vocational:* Work experience available. GNVQ in business offered *Computing facilities:* 65 Acorn Risc PCs in computer centre; 30 Archimedes, 30 BBCs and 20 PCs in other departments. *Special provision:* A small amount of extra tuition available, also back-up support from teachers and encouragement and understanding. *Europe:* French, German and Spanish offered to GCSE, AS and A-level; also Institute of Linguists courses in sixth, so a language can be studied from scratch. Usually up to 20 European pupils in sixth-form.

The arts (Pupils aged 11 and over) *Music:* 30% of pupils learn a musical instrument; instrumental exams can be taken. Some 20 musical groups including orchestra, wind bands, jazz bands, close harmony, instrumental ensembles, chapel choir, choral society. *Drama and dance:* Both offered. GCSE drama (30 pupils) and AS-level performing arts (18 pupils) may be taken. Majority of pupils are involved in school and house/other productions. *Art:* On average, 50 take GCSE, 16 A-level.

Sport, community service and clubs (Pupils aged 11 and over) *Sport and physical*

activities: Compulsory: rugby, hockey, netball. Optional: cricket, tennis, swimming, soccer, athletics, squash, basketball, riding, badminton, archery and many others. GCSE, RLSS exams may be taken. Many outdoor activities including camping, canoeing, climbing, sub-aqua, expeditions. *Community service:* Pupils take bronze, silver and gold Duke of Edinburgh's Award. CCF (RAF) compulsory for 1 year at age 14. Community service optional. *Clubs and societies:* Up to 30 clubs, eg debating, history, astronomy, computing, aero-modelling, expeditions.
Uniform School uniform worn except in the sixth.
Houses/prefects Pastoral and competitive houses. Prefects, head boy/girl, head of house and house prefects – appointed by the Headmaster and houseparents.
Religion Compulsory worship.
Social Some trips abroad. Day pupils may drive to and from school. Meals self-service. School shop. No tobacco allowed; alcohol under supervision for sixth-form only.
Discipline Pupils failing to produce homework once might expect to repeat it, if necessary in detention; those caught smoking cannabis on the premises would be asked to leave.
Boarding 33% have own study bedroom, 33% share (with 1–4 others); 33% in dormitories of 6–12. Single-sex houses of 50–70, same as competitive houses. Resident nurse, visiting doctor. Central dining room. Pupils can provide and cook snacks. 6–8 weekend exeats per term. Visits to local town allowed, frequency depending on age.
Alumni association is run by the Registrar, c/o the school.

• BRUTON (Sunny Hill)

Bruton School for Girls, Sunny Hill, Bruton, Somerset BA10 0NT. Tel 01749 812277
• Pupils 520 • Boys None • Girls 8–18 (Day/Board/Weekly) • Upper sixth 40 • Termly fees £1262 (Day) £2330 (Board/Weekly) • GSA, BSA • Enquiries/application to the School Registrar

What it's like

Founded in 1900, it has a fine 40-acre rural site on the edge of the small town of Bruton in a beautiful part of Somerset with views of the Quantocks and the Mendips. Bath, Bristol and Salisbury are easily accessible and full use is made of their cultural facilities. The school is known locally as Sunny Hill. Its buildings are pleasant and very well-equipped and facilities are good. It serves the local community (which gives good support) and represents all sections of society. Boarders come from all over the British Isles and overseas. Its declared aims are to provide a full, well-balanced education, while at the same time developing musical, artistic and dramatic talents. Results are very good and many sixth-form leavers go on to degree courses. A good range of sport and games (many county and national representatives). There is a strong commitment to local community schemes and to the Duke of Edinburgh's Award Scheme.

School profile

Pupils Total age range 8–18; 520 girls, 320 day, 200 boarding. Senior department 11–18, 450 girls. Main entry ages 8, 11, 13 and into sixth. *State school entry:* 60% intake at 11, plus 20% to sixth.
Entrance Own entrance exam used. No special skills or religious requirements. Parents not expected to buy text books; no other compulsory extras. 25 pa assisted places (20 at 11); 7 pa scholarships, 15%–50% tuition; also music scholarships.
Parents 15+% in the armed services. 60+% live within 30 miles; up to 10% live overseas.
Head and staff *Headmistress:* Mrs Judith Wade, in post 9 years. Educated at King Edward VI High (Birmingham), Altrincham County Grammar (Girls) and at London and York universities (physics). Previously Deputy Head and Head of Physics at Bruton, Physics/Maths teacher at Nonsuch (Sutton) and Howard of Effingham (Surrey), and Lecturer at Rachel McMillan College of Education and Norwood Technical College. *Staff:* 42 full time, 10 part time. Annual turnover 5%. Average age 42.
Exam results In 1995, 84 pupils in Year 11, 44 in upper sixth. *GCSE:* In 1995, 70 in Year 11 gained at least grade C in 8+ subjects; 12 in 5–7 subjects. *A-levels:* 3 upper sixth passed in 4 subjects; 30 in 3; 10 in 2; and 1 in 1 subject. Average UCAS points 20.2.
University and college entrance 92% of sixth-form leavers go on to a degree course

(10% after a gap year); others typically go on to art/drama college and other non-degree courses. Of those going on to university, 5% go to Oxbridge; 5% take courses in medicine, dentistry and veterinary science, 20% in science and engineering, 2% in law, 50% in humanities and social sciences, 10% in art and design.

Curriculum GCSE and A-levels. 21 GCSE subjects offered, 23 at A-level. 30% take science A-levels; 45% arts/humanities; 25% both. *Vocational:* Work experience available. *Computing facilities:* 2 computer rooms, plus computers in subject areas. *Special provision:* Specialist teaching for dyslexia; ESL support programme. *Europe:* French, German and Spanish offered to GCSE and A-level. Regular exchanges to France, Germany and Spain.

The arts (Pupils aged 11 and over) *Music:* Up to 75% of pupils learn a musical instrument; instrumental exams can be taken. *Drama and dance:* Drama and dance offered. GCSE and A-level drama, LAMDA exams may be taken. All pupils are involved in school productions. *Art:* On average, 30 take GCSE, 4 A-level. Design, pottery, textiles, photography also offered.

Sport, community service and clubs (Pupils aged 11 and over) *Sport and physical activities:* Compulsory sports: hockey, netball, tennis, swimming, rounders, athletics, gymnastics. Optional: dance, aerobics, badminton, volleyball, basketball, lacrosse, cricket. County representatives at athletics, cross-country, hockey, netball, tennis; national reps at athletics, cross country. *Community service:* Up to 15 clubs, eg public speaking, debating, technology and electronics, bridge, sports, cookery, art.

Uniform School uniform worn except in the sixth.

Houses/prefects Competitive houses. Head girl and prefects, appointed. Heads of house elected.

Religion Daily assembly. Sunday service (conducted by school chaplain) for boarders.

Social Some brothers attend King's School, Bruton; joint social events are arranged with local schools. Organised trips abroad. Senior pupils allowed to bring own bikes to school. Meals self-service. School shop. No tobacco/alcohol allowed.

Discipline Pupils failing to produce homework once might expect to do a repeat; those caught smoking cannabis on the premises would expect instant expulsion.

Boarding Single/double study bedrooms in upper sixth house; 3 senior houses of approx 50; lower sixth study cubicles, plus own sitting room and kitchen; fifth study cubicles; years 2–4 dormitories of 4+. Study rooms in each house. Junior house (8–10) dormitories of 6. Resident qualified medical staff. Central dining room. Sixth formers may provide and cook their own food. At least one fixed exeat each half term, others optional. Visits to the local town allowed.

Alumni association run by Mrs Jane Bennett, c/o the School.

• BRYANSTON

Bryanston School, Blandford, Dorset DT11 0PX. Tel 01258 452411

Pupils 630 • Boys 13–18 (Board) • Girls 13–18 (Board) • Upper sixth 130 • Termly fees £4410 (Board) • HMC • Enquiries/application to the Admissions Secretary

What it's like

Founded in 1928, it lies in a magnificent 400-acre estate just outside Blandford Forum, bordering a 2½-mile stretch of the Stour in one of the most beautiful parts of England. The main building is a palatial country house in red brick banded with Portland stone, designed by Shaw and completed in 1897: an example of monumental classicism, its main corridor is 100 yards long and it is the heart of the school. Some of the satellite buildings are, by comparison, somewhat plain and functional but they are well-designed and exceptionally well-equipped. There is also an open-air Greek theatre (built by the pupils), an observatory and the Coade Hall with a theatre seating 600. Originally a boys' school, it has been fully co-educational since the mid-seventies. Academic standards are high and results very good. Nearly all pupils go to degree courses each year, including to Oxbridge. There is much emphasis on creativity, on the development of individual talents; also on self-discipline, self-motivation, self-organisation and finding out how to find out on your own. It has long been outstanding for its commitment to music; the majority of pupils learn a musical instrument and there are many musical events. The drama and art departments are also very strong. At least 15 plays a year are produced, and the Arts

Centre brings in some 20 professional musical and dramatic productions each year (eg Welsh National Opera). Sport is compulsory for virtually everyone although there is an old-fashioned amateur approach which in no way affects the high standards that are attained. There is a substantial commitment to local community activities and the Duke of Edinburgh's Award Scheme.

School profile

Pupils Age range 13–18; 630 boarding pupils (360 boys, 270 girls). Main entry ages 13 and into sixth. Approx 15% are children of former pupils. *State school entry:* 3% main intake, plus 10% to sixth.

Entrance Common Entrance and own exam used. No special skills or religious requirements. Parents expected to buy text books. 20 pa scholarships/bursaries, 15%–50% of fees.

Parents 15+% in industry or commerce; 15+% are doctors, lawyers etc; 15+% in the armed services; 15+% in theatre, media and music. Up to 10% live within 30 miles; 10+% live overseas.

Head and staff *Headmaster:* Tom Wheare, in post for 13 years. Educated at Magdalen College School (Oxford), and the universities of Cambridge (history) and Oxford (education). Previously Housemaster at Shrewsbury and Assistant Master at Eton. Also Treasurer of HMC. *Staff:* 67 full time, 36 part time. Annual turnover 6%. Average age 40.

Exam results In 1995, 128 pupils in upper fifth, 125 in upper sixth. *GCSE:* In 1995, 108 upper fifth gained at least grade C in 8+ subjects; 17 in 5–7 subjects. *A-levels:* 40 passed in 4+ subjects; 70 in 3; 10 in 2; 4 in 1 subject. Average UCAS points 21.6.

University and college entrance 94% of 1995 sixth-form leavers went on to a degree course; others typically go on to non-degree courses, art/music colleges or straight into careers. Of those going on to university, 12% went to Oxbridge; 7% took courses in medicine, dentistry and veterinary science, 35% in science and engineering, 51% in humanities and social sciences, 5% in art and design, 3% in drama and music.

Curriculum GCSE, AS and A-levels. 23 GCSE subjects; 14 AS-levels; 23 A-levels (not including general studies). 9% take science A-levels; 53% arts/humanities; 38% both. *Computing facilities:* Apple Macintoshes, Archimedes, BBC Bs and PC Emulators. *Special provision:* Tutorial provision. *Europe:* French, German and Spanish offered to GCSE, AS and A-level; also non-examined Italian. Regular exchanges to France and Germany.

The arts *Music:* Over 60% of pupils learn a musical instrument; instrumental exams can be taken. Some 20 musical groups including orchestras, 6 choirs, various pop groups, concert band, instrumental groups. Several pupils in county youth orchestra. *Drama and dance:* Drama offered. LAMDA exams may be taken. Majority of pupils are involved in school productions and house/other productions. *Art:* On average, 43 take GCSE, 9 A-level. Design, pottery, textiles also offered. Pupils regularly accepted at art colleges.

Sport, community service and clubs *Sport and physical activities:* Compulsory sports: pupils must play some games but can choose from a range including rugby, hockey, cricket, tennis, rowing, athletics, netball, swimming, canoeing, lacrosse, cross-country, archery, squash, badminton, fencing. A-level sport studies may be taken. Pupils regularly represent county in eg rugby, hockey, athletics. *Community service:* Pupils take bronze, silver and gold Duke of Edinburgh's Award. Community service compulsory for 2 years at age 14. *Clubs and societies:* Up to 30 clubs eg chess, film, bell ringing, astronomy, reptiles, jazz, clay-pigeon shooting.

Uniform None.

Houses/prefects Prefects, head boy and girl, head of house and house prefects – elected by the school and appointed by the Head.

Religion Religious worship encouraged but not compulsory.

Social Very few organised local events. Regular exchanges with a German school, visits to France and Italy and skiing trips. Pupils allowed to bring own bike to school. Meals self-service. School shop. Alcohol allowed for the upper sixth.

Discipline Overseen centrally by the Headmaster, punishments are administered by pastoral and tutorial staff and can rise as high as suspension or expulsion (eg for drugs).

Boarding Upper sixth have own study bedroom, lower sixth share in 2s; remainder are in dormitories of up to 6. Single-sex houses of 55, divided by age group. Resident

qualified nurse. Central dining room. Pupils can provide and cook some own food. Visits to local town allowed – any age, twice a week on average.
Alumni association run by W E Potter, c/o the School.
Former pupils Sir Terence Conran; Jasper Conran; Lucien Freud; Fred Sanger OM; John Eliot Gardner; Mark Elder; Howard Hodgkin; Philip de Glanville; Mark Wigglesworth.

• BURY GRAMMAR (Boys)

Bury Grammar School for Boys, Tenterden Street, Bury, Lancashire BL9 0HN. Tel 0161 797 2700

• Pupils 865 • Boys 7–18 (Day) • Girls None • Upper sixth 90 • Termly fees £1234 (Day) • HMC
• Enquiries/application to the Headmaster

What it's like

Founded early in the 17th century, re-endowed in 1726. After World War II a new boys' school was erected near the original buildings in the town. It is purpose-built with every desirable amenity, enhanced by a recent building programme. There are spacious playing fields. The school has many active Christians among masters and boys, but is non-denominational and welcomes pupils of many faiths. It has a well-established tradition of good teaching and good results. Almost all pupils go on to degree courses, including Oxbridge. Very well-equipped workshops and technology department (many pupils go on to become professional engineers). Flourishing ties with local community and good mutual support. Strong in sport and games (a number of representatives at national and county level); also outdoor pursuits in the Lake District.

School profile

Pupils Total age range 7–18; 865 day boys. Senior department 11–18, 700 boys. Main entry ages 7, 8, 9, 10, 11 and 16. Own junior school provides 40% of senior intake. *State school entry:* 60% intake at 11; plus 5% to sixth.
Entrance Own entrance exam used. No special skills or religious requirements. Parents not expected to buy textbooks; lunch (£60 per term) and school trips extra. 45 pa assisted places (5 at age 8, 35 at 11, 5 in the sixth). 5 pa scholarships.
Head and staff *Headmaster:* Keith Richards, 6 years in post. Educated at Bristol Grammar and Cambridge University (classics). Previously Head of Classics at Repton and King's (Chester) and Assistant Master at Manchester Grammar. *Staff:* 62 full time, 3 part time. Annual turnover 3%. Average age 42.
Exam results In 1995, 102 pupils in upper fifth, 90 in upper sixth. *GCSE:* In 1995, 79% upper fifth gained at least grade C in 8+ subjects; 16% in 5–7 subjects. *A-levels:* 79% upper sixth passed in 4+ subjects; 10% in 3; 10% in 2; and 1% in 1 subject. Average UCAS points 19.2 (including general studies 25.0).
University and college entrance 91% of 1995 sixth-form leavers went on to a degree course; others typically go on to non-degree courses, re-take A-levels. Of those going on to university, 4% went to Oxbridge; 5% took courses in medicine, dentistry and veterinary science, 36% in science and engineering, 59% in humanities and social sciences.
Curriculum GCSE and A-levels. 21 subjects offered, including A-level general studies. 29% take science A-levels; 37% arts/humanities; 34% both. *Vocational:* Work experience available for fifth formers and others. *Computing facilities:* Computer suite; computers for teaching and learning other subjects spreading through the school. *Europe:* French and German offered to GCSE and A-level (French compulsory to GCSE, German for 1 year); also GCSE Spanish. Regular exchanges to Germany and France.
The arts (Pupils aged 11 and over) *Music:* Over 15% of pupils learn a musical instrument; instrumental exams can be taken. Some 10 musical groups including choral society, orchestra, dance band, wind group. A number of boys play in town youth orchestra. *Drama and dance:* Drama offered. Some pupils are involved in school productions. *Art:* On average, 12 take GCSE, 5 A-level. Design, pottery, sculpture also offered. Recent pupil became head of design on The Face magazine.
Sport, community service and clubs (Pupils aged 11 and over) *Sport and physical*

activities: Compulsory sports (to end of third year): rugby, hockey, soccer, cross-country, swimming, basketball, badminton, cricket, tennis, athletics. Optional: all the above from fourth year on. Sixth form only: walking. County representatives at rugby, soccer, swimming, tennis, gymnastics, squash; international canoeing. *Community service:* CCF and community service optional. *Clubs and societies:* Up to 15 clubs eg Young Enterprise, chess, bird-watching, hiking.
Uniform School uniform worn to the fifth year.
Houses/prefects Competitive houses. Prefects, head boy, head of house – appointed.
Religion Morning assembly compulsory.
Social Joint productions with Bury Grammar (Girls). French, German and ski trips, exchanges with schools in Tulle, Cologne and Lilienthal. Pupils allowed to bring own bikes to school. Meals self-service. No tobacco/alcohol allowed.
Discipline Great care is taken to suit the punishment of offenders to the character and age of each individual. Very strict line taken on drugs; pupils who introduced drugs to school would be expelled.
Alumni association run by Mr I K G Hyde, 29 St Joseph's Avenue, Whitefield, Manchester M48 6NT.
Former pupils David Trippier MP; Alistair Burt MP.

• BURY GRAMMAR (Girls)

Bury Grammar School (Girls), Bridge Road, Bury, Lancashire BL9 0HH. Tel 0161 797 2808, Fax 0161 763 4658

• Pupils 1100 • Boys 4–7 only (Day) • Girls 4–18 (Day) • Upper sixth 100 • Termly fees £1234 (Day) • GSA • Enquiries/application to the Headmistress

What it's like

Founded in 1884, it lies a few minutes from the town centre and close to the rail and bus stations. The main school is housed in a handsome Edwardian building (to which there have been many fine modern additions), surrounded by ample playing fields. A Christian foundation, it has connections with Bury parish church but is ecumenical in spirit. All pupils follow a course of religious education and philosophy throughout the school. Results are very good and almost all sixth-formers go on to degree courses, including Oxbridge. There are good facilities for art, design and technology, music and drama. There is a strong tradition of achievement in sport and games, particularly swimming; plus many clubs and societies. Vigorous local support. Extensive work is done on behalf of national charities.

School profile

Pupils Total age range 4–18; 1100 day pupils (70 boys, 1030 girls). Senior department 11–18, 800 girls. Main entry ages 4, 11 and into sixth.
Entrance Own entrance exam used. No special skills or religious requirements. Parents not expected to buy textbooks; dinners extra. 35 pa assisted places. 5 pa scholarships, partial remission of fees.
Parents 15+% in industry or commerce; 15+% are doctors, lawyers etc.
Head and staff *Headmistress:* Miss Janet Lawley in post for 10 years. Educated at The Friary School, Lichfield, and universities of Bristol (geography) and Oxford (education). Previously Vice Principal at King George V Sixth Form College, Southport, and Senior Mistress at Merchant Taylors' (Crosby). Also Council Member, Geographical Association (1986); GSA Education Committee Member and representative on SCAA Teacher's Advisory Panel. *Staff:* 76 full time, 31 part time.
Exam results In 1995, 128 pupils in upper fifth, 105 in upper sixth. *GCSE:* In 1995, 125 upper fifth gained at least grade C in 8+ subjects; 3 in 5–7 subjects. *A-levels:* 84 upper sixth passed in 4+ subjects; 16 in 3; 4 in 2; 1 in 1 subject. Average UCAS points 20.6 (including general studies 26.9).
University and college entrance 91% of 1995 sixth-form leavers went on to a degree course (7% after a gap year); others typically go on to art or drama training or straight into carers (eg banking). Of those going on to university, 7% went to Oxbridge; 6% took courses in medicine, dentistry and veterinary science, 30% in science and engineering, 6% in law, 49% in humanities and social sciences, 3% in art and design, 6% in vocational

subjects eg diagnostic radiology, equine business, hospitality management.
Curriculum GCSE, AS and A-levels. 30 subjects, including A-level general studies. *Vocational:* Work experience available. *Computing facilities:* Two computer rooms and library resource area; computers within departments (BBC and Acorn Archimedes and PCs); computing used across the curriculum. *Special provision:* Good relations with local authority special sources. *Europe:* French (taught from age 11) and German offered to GCSE, AS and A-level; GCSE Italian and Spanish. Regular exchanges to France. Represented England in International Youth Conference in Belgium.
The arts (Pupils aged 11 and over) *Music:* Up to 50% of pupils learn a musical instrument; instrumental exams can be taken. Some 10 musical groups including orchestras, chamber quartet, brass, wind bands, oboe trio, choirs. Semi-finalists in Sainsbury's Choir of the Year; chamber group 2nd place in regional competition. *Drama and dance:* Drama offered. Some pupils are involved in school productions. *Art:* On average, 25 take art and design GCSE, 9 A-level. Design, pottery, textiles also offered. Recent pupil top student at Rochdale art foundation course.
Sport, community service and clubs (Pupils aged 11 and over) *Sport and physical activities:* Compulsory sports: hockey, netball, swimming, gymnastics, dance, tennis, rounders, basketball, volleyball, badminton, health-related fitness. Optional: lifesaving. Sixth-form only: squash, canoeing, golf, tenpin bowling. RLSS exams may be taken. Swimming, regular county, occasional national representatives; netball, England rep; badminton, 1 county senior, 2 county junior reps. *Community service:* Community service optional at age 16–18. *Clubs and societies:* Up to 30 clubs, eg science, European, badminton, debating, environment.
Uniform School uniform worn except in the sixth.
Houses/prefects No competitive houses or prefects. Head girl – elected. School Council.
Religion Compulsory religious study and philosophy throughout the school.
Social Many concerts, plays and societies are joint with Bury Grammar (Boys). Both schools share sixth-form common room facilities. Meals self-service. No tobacco/alcohol allowed.
Discipline Pupils failing to produce homework would be expected to hand it in the next day; those involved in drugs or smoking could expect immediate suspension. Anyone with drugs on the premises could expect expulsion.
Former pupils Victoria Wood.

C

• CAMBRIDGE CENTRE

Cambridge Centre for Sixth Form Studies, 1 Salisbury Villas, Station Road, Cambridge CB1 2JF. Tel 01223 316890, Fax 01223 358441

• Pupils 183 • Boys 14–19 (Day/Board) • Girls 14–19 (Day/Board) • Upper sixth 80 • Termly fees £1660–£2627 (Day) £3118–£4085 (Board) • CIFE • Enquiries/application to the Director of Studies

What it's like

Founded in 1981 as a co-eduational sixth-form college, it has three main teaching sites in the city centre. Comfortable school houses, with individual study bedrooms, communal facilities and supervision by resident staff, are located within easy reach of the college. All A-level students receive individual tuition alongside classroom teaching in small groups. All students complete a general studies programme and take foundation course options in the lower sixth. Exam results are very creditable and 85% of leavers proceed to university. There is a standard range of optional games and sports. Regular trips abroad are organised in relation to subjects studied.

School profile

Pupils Age range 14–19; 183 pupils, 75 day (35 boys, 40 girls), 108 boarding (63 boys, 45 girls). Main entry is into the sixth. *State school entry:* 15%.

Entrance No entrance exam; no special skills or religious requirements. Parents not expected to buy textbooks; average £100–£150 pa extras. 5 pa scholarships available, value £2500–£7500.

Parents 15+% are in industry/commerce. Up to 30% live within 30 miles of the school; 35% overseas.

Head and staff Co-Principals: Dr A M Dawson and Mr P C Redhead, both in post for 15 years. Dr Dawson educated at Magdalen College School, Oxford, and at Cambridge University (history and Latin American studies). Previously taught at St Andrews Tutorial College, Cambridge. Also member of CIFE and recent Chairman of its Public Relations Committee. Mr Redhead educated at Sevenoaks and Cambridge (applied biology). Previously taught at St Andrews Tutorial College, Cambridge. Recent Chairman of CIFE Membership Committee. *Staff:* 24 full time, 29 part time. Annual turnover, 10%. Average age, 40.

Exam results In 1995, 23 pupils in upper fifth, 80 in upper sixth. *GCSE:* In 1995, 15% upper fifth gained at least grade C in 8+ subjects; 38% in 5–7; and 38% in 1–4 subjects. *A-levels:* 60% upper sixth passed in 3+ subjects; 29% in 2; and 8% in 1 subject.

University and college entrance 85% of 1995 sixth-form leavers went on to a degree course (30% after a gap year); others typically go straight in to work or to secretarial courses. Of those going on to university, 2% went to Oxbridge; 4% took courses in medicine, dentistry and veterinary science, 26% in science and engineering, 4% in law, 64% in humanities and social sciences, 2% in art and design.

Curriculum GCSE and A-levels offered. 29 examination subjects offered, including photography, fashion and textiles, media studies, psychology and Japanese; no A-level general studies. 10% take science A-levels; 68% arts/humanities; 23% both. *Computing facilities:* Open access PC room with IBM compatibles running Microsoft Works. *Europe:* French, German and Spanish offered to GCSE, AS and A-level; also modern Greek at A-level and Italian and Russian to GCSE and A-level. Some European studies taught as part of the general studies programme.

The arts *Music:* Few pupils learn a musical instrument; no musical groups. Drama & dance: GCSE and A-level theatre studies offered. A few take part in school productions. *Art:* On average, 6 take GCSE, 12 A-level. Textiles and photography also offered. 2–5 go to art schools each year.

Sport, community service and clubs *Sport and physical activities:* Some compulsory sports for fifth year; squash, badminton, hockey, tennis, volleyball, basketball, soccer, swimming, shooting, rowing, cricket, rugby, trampolining, aerobics, weight training are optional. *Community service:* Pupils can take bronze, silver and gold Duke of Edinburgh's Award. Community service optional. Clubs & societies: Up to 5 clubs eg politics society, Christian Union.

Uniform None.

Houses/prefects No competitive houses or prefects. School Council.

Religion No compulsory worship.

Social Regular trips related to subjects eg Italy (history of art), Europe (languages), Russia/America (politics and history). Students may bring own bike to school. School shop. No alcohol allowed.

Discipline Pupils failing to produce homework once might expect a discussion with their subject teacher; students caught smoking cannabis on the premises should expect expulsion.

Boarding 90% have own study bedrooms; 10% share with 1 other. Supervised houses of 5–28, divided by age group – some single sex, some mixed. Resident qualified nurse. Unlimited exeats allowed at weekends, so long as students are up to date with their work. Unlimited visits to the local town (day/early evening).

• CAMPBELL COLLEGE

Campbell College, Belfast BT4 2ND. Tel 01232 763076

• Pupils 705 • Boys 11–18 (Day/Board/Weekly) • Girls None • Upper sixth 76 • Termly fees £331 (Day) £1765 (Board/Weekly) • HMC • Enquiries/application to the Headmaster

What it's like

Founded in 1894 to give a liberal education similar to that in English and Scottish public schools. The college (and its prep department, Cabin Hill) lies on the eastern outskirts of Belfast, five miles from the city centre, on a splendid 100-acre estate with fine trees, an ornamental lake and superb playing fields; a tranquil and beautiful setting. An excellent all-round education is provided and results are very good. Many go on to degree courses, including Oxbridge. Strong in music and drama and outstanding in sport and games (many national and provincial representatives). A flourishing and large CCF with a pipe band. Social services are extensive. Though basically a Protestant foundation it is ecumenical.

School profile

Pupils Age range 11–18; 705 boys (640 day, 65 boarding). Main entry ages 11, 13 and into sixth. Approx 20% are children of former pupils. Own prep schoo, Cabin Hill, provides 35+% of intake. *State school entry:* 65% main intake, plus 10% to sixth.

Entrance Satisfactory report from present school. No special skills or religious requirements. Books supplied by LEA. 4 pa scholarships/bursaries, £100–£1000. Maximum extras, £50.

Parents 15+% are doctors, lawyers, etc; 15+% in industry or commerce. 80+% live within 30 miles; up to 10% live overseas.

Head and staff *Headmaster:* Dr Ivan Pollock, in post for 9 years. Educated at Royal School (Dungannon) and Belfast University (chemistry). Previously Housemaster and Head of Chemistry at Campbell College. Also Vice-President, Ulster Heads' Association. *Staff:* 49 full time, 14 part time. Annual turnover 1%. Average age 42.

Exam results In 1995, 132 pupils in fifth, 81 in upper sixth. *GCSE:* In 1995, 86 fifth gained at least grade C in 8+ subjects; 30 in 5–7; and 16 in 1–4 subjects. *A-levels:* 9 upper sixth passed in 4+ subjects; 48 in 3; 12 in 2; and 6 in 1 subject.

University and college entrance 82% of 1995 sixth-form leavers went on to a degree course; others typically go straight on to careers, eg estate agency, business. Of those going on to university, 6% went to Oxbridge; 14% took courses in medicine, dentistry and veterinary science, 39% in science and engineering, 46% in humanities and social sciences.

Curriculum GCSE and A-levels. 20 subjects offered (no A-level general studies). 45% take science A-levels; 35% arts/humanities; 20% both. *Vocational:* Work experience available; City and Guilds level 3 in computing. *Computing facilities:* 40 Apple Macs and 11 Nimbus; 11 science lab BBC systems. *Europe:* French, German and Spanish offered to GCSE and A-level.

The arts *Music:* Up to 25% of pupils learn a musical instrument; instrumental exams can be taken. Some 7 musical groups including orchestra, choir, jazz orchestra, various ensembles, pipe band etc. 3 in National Youth Orchestra. Drama & dance: Drama offered. Some pupils are involved in school productions and majority in house/other productions. *Art:* On average, 40 take GCSE, 10 A-level. Design, pottery, photography also offered

Sport, community service and clubs *Sport and physical activities:* Compulsory sports: choice from rugby, football, hockey, cross-country, cricket, athletics, tennis, sailing, squash, swimming, shooting. Optional: badminton. International and provincial representatives at rugby, hockey, cross-country, cricket, athletics, sailing, swimming, shooting. Team successes at shooting, Bisley; athletics, English public schools championships; swimming, Irish championships; rugby, Irish Rugby School of the Year, in 1993; cricket, provincial champions. *Community service:* CCF/community service compulsory for 3 years at age 13. *Clubs and societies:* Up to 30 clubs, eg archery, computers, bridge, chess, croquet, debating, history, mountaineering, photography.

Uniform School uniform worn throughout.

Houses/prefects Competitive houses for sport, drama, music etc. Prefects, head prefect, head of house and house prefects – appointed by the Headmaster. Sixth Form Committee.

Religion Morning prayers. Family and parish services for boarders.

Social Dramatic productions, carol service, senior citizens' Christmas party run by social services group. Organised trips to France, Germany and skiing parties to Austria etc. Pupils allowed to bring own car/bike to school. Meals self-service. School shop. No tobacco/alcohol allowed.

Discipline Pupils failing to produce homework once might expect to have homework extended; those caught smoking cannabis on the premises could expect immediate expulsion.

Boarding All sixth-form have own study bedroom. Others in dormitories of 6+. Houses of approximately 65, same as competitive houses. Resident matron. Central dining room. Half-term and 2 weekend exeats each term. Visits to local town allowed in sixth-form, usually once a week.

Alumni association is run by C F Gailey, c/o the College.

Former pupils Michael Gibson (rugby, captained Ireland, British Lions); Iain Johnstone (BBC interviewer and producer); Mark Lambert (Royal Shakespeare actor and film star); Air Marshal A H W Ball; Air Vice Marshal F D Hughes; Air Vice Marshal C J Thomson.

• CANFORD

Canford School, Wimborne, Dorset BH21 3AD. Tel 01202 841254

• Pupils 505 • Boys 13–18 (Day/Board) • Girls 13–18 (Day/Board) • Upper sixth 100 • Termly fees £3050 (Day) £4070 (Board) • HMC, SHA, BSA • Enquiries/application to the Registrar

What it's like

Founded in 1923, it stands in a magnificent 300-acre park, on the edge of Canford Heath, 2 miles from Wimborne Minster and 6 from Bournemouth. The northern boundary is formed by the river Stour; there are beautiful formal gardens and splendid playing fields. The oldest part of the buildings is a fine medieval hall (known as John of Gaunt's Kitchen), all that survives of the medieval Canford. Part of the present building is Georgian, the rest was designed by Sir Charles Barry in 1847. There have been many modern additions to the buildings to provide excellent facilities, including an art and design centre, a music school, an open-air theatre, rifle range and a sports centre. The school became fully co-educational in 1995, having taken girls in the sixth-form since the sixties. A very favourable staff:pupil ratio of about 1:9. Academic results are good and almost all leavers go on to university, including many to Oxbridge. Religious education is an important part of the curriculum. Services (C of E) are held in the Norman church of Canford Magna in the school grounds. Music and art are particularly strong; drama is well supported. Games and sports are very strong (many representatives at county and regional level and some at national level); facilities include a 9-hole golf course in the grounds and one of the few real tennis (or royal tennis) courts in the country. An unusually wide variety of extra-curricular activities including a flourishing CCF contingent (Army, Navy and Marine sections) and pupils are encouraged to take part in local community services. Considerable enterprise has been shown in overseas expeditions to many parts of the globe. a large number of scholarships, many funded by the £7m sale of an Assyrian frieze in 1994.

School profile

Pupils Age range 13–18; 505 pupils, 157 day (128 boys, 29 girls), 348 boarding (283 boys, 65 girls). Main entry is at 13 and into the sixth. Some 5% are children of former pupils. *State school entry:* usually about 10 in main intake, same in sixth.

Entrance Common Entrance and own entrance/scholarship exam used. No special skills or religious requirements; school is C of E but pupils accepted from other denominations and faiths. Parents expected to buy sixth-form textbooks; extras £175 average. 10 pa assisted places plus 10 to sixth. Large number of scholarships at 13 and 16 (academic, music, art, all-rounder and Royal Naval).

Parents 15+% in armed services. Up to 40% live within 30 miles.

Head and staff *Headmaster:* John D Lever, 4 years in post. Educated at Westminster and the universities of Cambridge (geography) and Oxford (education). Previously Housemaster at Winchester. *Staff:* 56 full time, 4 part time. Annual turnover, 5%.

Exam results In 1995, 94 pupils in upper fifth, 99 in upper sixth. *GCSE:* In 1995, all upper fifth gained at least grade C in 7+ subjects. *A-levels:* 5 passed in 4 subjects; 88 in 3; 4 in 2; and 1 in 1 subject. Average UCAS points 22.1.

University and college entrance 91% of 1995 sixth-form leavers went on to a degree course; others typically go on to art colleges. Of those going on to university, 14% went to Oxbridge; 14% took courses in medicine, dentistry and veterinary science, 30% in science and engineering, 52% in humanities and social sciences, 1% in art and design, 3% in eg music and drama.

Curriculum GCSE and A-levels offered. 17 examination subjects offered (no A-level general studies). 30% take science A-levels; 35% arts/humanities; 35% both. *Vocational:* Work experience available. *Computing facilities:* Computer room with 25 Macintoshes; other computers in departments and library. *Special provision:* Special teacher for dyslexic pupils. *Europe:* French, German and Italian offered to GCSE and A-level (French compulsory from 13–16); also GCSE Spanish. Regular exchanges (France and Germany). Few German pupils in sixth, usually for 1 year.

The arts *Music:* 50% pupils learn a musical instrument; instrumental exams can be taken. 15 musical groups – orchestras, bands, choirs, string quarters, jazz bands, rock groups. Regular finalists in National Schools Chamber Music Competition; leaders of Dorset Youth Orchestra; evensong in Westminster Abbey and Salisbury Cathedral. Drama & dance: Drama offered; pupils may take LAMDA exams. Majority of pupils involved in house/other productions. Consistently winners in Dorset Drama Festival; individual winners in Ivy Owen Drama Award. *Art:* On average, 23 take GCSE, 12 A-level. Design, pottery, photography also offered. Some 5 pa go on to art colleges.

Sport, community service and clubs *Sport and physical activities:* Major sports: rugby, hockey, rowing, cricket, lawn tennis, netball. Minor sports: squash, cross-country running, real tennis, athletics, swimming, golf, sailing, shooting. Regular members of county and area teams in rugby, hockey, cricket, cross-country running, squash; several selected for regional/divisional sides, some for national teams. *Community service:* pupils take bronze, silver and gold Duke of Edinburgh's Award. CCF optional at age 14, community service optional at 16. Links with several local schools including Langside Spastic School; regular participation in Kielder Challenge (for mixed teams of able/disabled young people). Clubs & societies: Up to 30 clubs including debating, orchestra, table tennis, juggling, literary, fishing, chess, canoeing, bridge, bell ringing, beekeeping, art, choral.

Uniform School uniform worn throughout.

Houses/prefects Competitive houses. Head boy/girl prefects, house prefects and house captains appointed by the Head. School Prefects Committee.

Religion Attendance at services compulsory.

Social Joint orchestral concert with local school annually. Trips abroad: trekking (Ecuador, Nepal); rugby (Australia, South Africa, Hong Kong); cricket (Kenya, Barbados); biology (Costa Rica, Red Sea); cultural (Russia, Jordan, Eastern Europe); skiing (France); geography (France); history (France). Pupils may bring own bike to school; day

pupils may bring own car. Meals self-service. School shop. No tobacco allowed; beer and cider available in Junior Club Bar for over 17s.
Discipline Pupils failing to produce homework once might expect to do it again in detention; any pupil caught smoking cannabis might expect expulsion.
Boarding 20% have own study bedrooms; 60% share with 2–4; 20% in dormitories of 6+. Single-sex boarding houses of 65–70, mixed ages (day houses are mixed). Qualified nurse on duty 24 hours/day. Pupils allowed to provide and cook their own food. Regular exeats (1½ days). Visits to Wimborne allowed by all pupils; sixth-form allowed to Bournemouth.
Alumni association run by A Wadsworth, 58 Floral Farm, Canford Magna, Wimborne, Dorset BH21 3AU.
Former pupils Simon Preston (ex-organist, Westminster Abbey); Sir Ronnie Hampel (Chairman ICI); Henry Cecil (race horse trainer); General Sir Brian Kenny; Air Chief-Marshal Sir Roger Palin; Sir Hector Monro (MP); John Drummond (Director BBC Proms); Sir Anthony Bramall (former MP and ILEA Chairman); Sir Derek Bradbeer; Sir Derek Hornby; Lord Maclean.

• CARMEL COLLEGE

Carmel College, Mongewell Park, Wallingford, Oxfordshire OX10 8BT. Tel 01491 837505
• Pupils 200 • Boys 11–18 (Day/Board) • Girls 11–18 (Day/Board) .Upper sixth 36 • Termly fees £2460 (Day) £3000–£4355 (Board) £5880 (Overseas boarders) • SHMIS • Enquiries/application to the Headmaster

What it's like

Founded in 1948 by Rabbi Kopul Rosen, it opened at Greenham Common and in 1953 moved to Mongewell Park near Wallingford on the Thames. The mansion house is the focal point of a large and beautiful estate and it has excellent modern facilities and accommodation. It is a Jewish public school committed to cultivating a love and appreciation of Jewish practice, learning and culture. It offers a 'total Jewish environment' within which Judaism is of prime importance. All pupils attend morning services and they are required to have Tefillin and Siddurim. Attendance at Shabbat service is compulsory for all. Everyone is encouraged to take part in the Synagogue ritual by taking service and reading from the weekly Parashah. It has been co-educational since 1969. Academic standards are high and results are good. Most sixth-formers go on to degree courses each year. Hebrew and Jewish studies are an important part of the curriculum. Strong music, art and drama (there is an amphitheatre). A good range of sport and games; rowing is quite strong. A plentiful range of extra-curricular activities.

School profile

Pupils Age range 11–18; 200 pupils, 8 day (6 boys, 2 girls), 192 boarding (128 boys, 64 girls). Main entry ages 11 and into sixth. Approx 10% are children of former pupils. *State school entry:* 40% main intake, plus 5% to sixth.
Entrance Own entrance exam used. No special skills but required to be Jewish. Deposit for extras, £200 per term. 13 pa assisted places. Approx 20 pa scholarships/bursaries, £2800–£5100 pa.
Parents 15+% are doctors, lawyers, etc; 20+% in industry or commerce. Up to 10% live within 30 miles; 25+% live overseas.
Head and staff *Headmaster:* Philip Skelker, in post for 12 years. Educated at Colfe's and the universities of Oxford and Cambridge (English literature). Previously Headmaster at King David High School and Head of English at Watford Grammar and at Hasmoneon. *Staff:* 30 full time, 6 part time. Annual turnover 5%. Average age 40.
Exam results In 1995, 37 pupils in fifth, 35 in upper sixth. *GCSE:* In 1995, 19 upper fifth gained at least grade C in 8+ subjects; 12 in 5–7 subjects. *A-levels:* 5 upper sixth pass in 4 subjects; 21 in 3; 6 in 2 subjects. Average UCAS points 18.5.
University and college entrance 95% of 1995 sixth-form leavers went on to a degree course (10% after a gap year); others typically go on to Israeli Defence Forces or employment. Of those going on to university, 4% went to Oxbridge; 9% took courses in medicine, dentistry and veterinary science, 14% in science and engineering, 29% in law, 30% in humanities and social sciences, 17% in art and design.

Curriculum GCSE and A-levels. 18 subjects offered, including Hebrew; no A-level general studies. 12% take science A-levels; 41% arts/humanities; 47% both. *Vocational:* Work experience available. *Computing facilities:* Two network systems (BBC Bs and research machine Nimbuses). *Special provision:* Study skills and EFL departments. *Europe:* French, German, Russian and Spanish offered to GCSE and A-level. Visits to France. Possible links with Jewish schools in Europe. The school has EU grant to develop curriculum material for Jewish studies.
The arts *Music:* Up to 50% of pupils learn a musical instrument; instrumental exams can be taken. Some 4 musical groups: choral, jazz, wind band, guitar group. Drama & dance: Drama and dance offered to GCSE and A-level. Majority of pupils are involved in school productions and house/other productions. *Art:* On average, 24 take GCSE, 10 A-level. Pottery, photography, sculpture, printmaking also offered. All art college applicants accepted by first choice.
Sport, community service and clubs *Sport and physical activities:* Compulsory sports: soccer, tennis, hockey, rowing, cricket. Optional: basketball, squash, swimming, badminton, karate. *Community service:* Pupils take bronze, silver and gold Duke of Edinburgh's Award. Community service optional. School has close links with Ravenswood Village for Jewish handicapped. *Clubs and societies:* Up to 30 clubs, eg table tennis, geography, riding, canoeing, German film.
Uniform School uniform worn except in the sixth.
Houses/prefects Competitive houses. Prefects, head boy and girl, head of house and house prefects – appointed by the Head after consultation with pupils and the staff. School Council.
Religion Compulsory attendance at religious service daily.
Social Many visits from local groups who wish to find out about Judaism. Organised trips abroad. Meals self-service, formal on Sabbath. School shop. No tobacco/alcohol allowed (apart from wine on Sabbath).
Discipline Pupils failing to produce homework once might expect detention; those caught smoking cannabis on or off the premises will be expelled.
Boarding 5% have own study bedroom, 75% share with 1 other; 15% are in dormitories of 6 +. Single-sex houses, of 26–80, divided by age group. Resident qualified medical staff. Central dining room. 2 weekend exeats each term (additional 2 for sixth-form). Visits to local town allowed.
Alumni association c/o the College.
Former pupils Roland Joffe; Gary Davis; Prof Edward Lutwak; Professor Raymond Dwek; Rabbi Dr Abraham Levy; Stephen Frankel.

• CASTERTON

Casterton School, Kirkby Lonsdale, Carnforth, Cumbria LA6 2SG. Tel 015242 71202, Fax 015242 71146

• Pupils 351 • Boys 4–7 only • Girls 4–18 (Day/Board from age 8) • Upper sixth 41 • Termly fees £2010 (Day) £3206 (Board) • GSA • Enquiries/application to the Headmaster

What it's like

Founded in 1823 (the Brontë sisters attended the school in 1824), it was established at Casterton in 1833 It stands in its own grounds of 50 acres on the outskirts of the village. The surroundings are very beautiful. Handsome solid buildings, excellent modern facilities, comfortable boarding accommodation. A sound traditional education is provided and results are very good. The majority of sixth-formers go on to degree courses, including to Oxbridge. Its religious life is based on Anglican practice and the village parish church is used regularly for worship. A happy, friendly place with a family atmosphere, it is strong in music and drama and the Duke of Edinburgh's Award Scheme. Plentiful use is made of the superb Cumbrian countryside for outdoor pursuits (riding, fell walking, canoeing, camping, sailing, climbing). The junior school is adjacent.

School profile

Pupils Total age range 4–18; 351 pupils, 83 day, 268 boarding (boarding from age 8). Senior department 11–18, 301 girls. Main entry ages 11 and into sixth. Approx 3% are children of former pupils. *State school entry:* 50% intake at 11+ and into sixth.

Entrance Own entrance exam used. No special skills required; school is Anglican though all denominations are accepted. Parents not expected to buy textbooks. 9 pa assisted places. 7 pa scholarships/bursaries, £300–£2000.
Parents 15+% in industry or commerce. 10+% live within 30 miles; 10+% live overseas.
Head and staff *Headmaster:* A F Thomas, 7 years in post. Educated at William Hulme's Grammar School and Cambridge University (mathematics). Previously Housemaster and Head of Mathematics at Sedbergh. Also Assistant Chief Examiner in GCSE Mathematics. *Publications:* Co-author of SMP Additional Mathematics. England Lacrosse International (tour of USA/Canada and World Cup, 1967). *Staff:* 37 full time, 14 part time. Annual turnover 3%. Average age 43.
Exam results In 1995, 45 pupils in upper fifth, 41 in upper sixth. *GCSE:* In 1995, 40 upper fifth gained at least grade C in 8+ subjects. *A-levels:* 41 upper sixth pass in 3+ subjects. Average UCAS points 21.2.
University and college entrance 93% of 1995 sixth-form leavers went on to a degree course (25% after a gap year); others typically go on to nursing or art foundation courses. Of those going on to university, 2% went to Oxbridge; 10% took courses in medicine, dentistry and veterinary science, 7% in science and engineering, 5% in law, 44% in humanities and social sciences, 5% in art and design, 1% education.
Curriculum GCSE and A-levels. 25 subjects offered (including A-level general studies). 27% take science A-levels; 73% arts/humanities. *Vocational:* Work experience available; also RSA course in typing, word processing, etc. *Computing facilities:* 28 terminal RM Nimbus Network in 2 rooms. Separate BBC micros in science dept. *Special provision:* Caters for mild dyslexia. *Europe:* French, German and Spanish offered to GCSE and A-level. Regular exchanges.
The arts (Pupils aged 11 and over) *Music:* Over 50% of pupils learn a musical instrument; instrumental exams can be taken. Some 14 musical groups including orchestras, wind band, string orchestra, chamber group, choirs, close harmony. 7 pupils in county youth orchestra. *Drama & dance*: Both offered. Associated Board exams may be taken. Some pupils are involved in school productions and majority in house/other productions. Main school productions in 1995, My Fair Lady, The Crucible. *Art:* On average, 16 take GCSE, 6 A-level. History of art A-level, ceramics, textiles, photography also offered.
Sport, community service and clubs (Pupils aged 11 and over) *Sport and physical activities:* Compulsory sports: hockey, netball, rounders, swimming. Optional: lacrosse, tennis, badminton, golf, sailing. 2–3 players regularly in county hockey, netball and lacrosse teams. *Community service:* Pupils take bronze, silver and gold Duke of Edinburgh's Award. Community service optional. *Clubs and societies:* Up to 15 clubs, eg photography, art, golf, wine-making, sailing.
Uniform School uniform worn throughout. Home clothes at off-duty times.
Houses/prefects Competitive houses. Prefects, head girl, head of house and house prefects – appointed by the Headmaster.
Religion Anglican, but girls of other denominations are accepted.
Social Theatre performances, Young Enterprise, debates and many social events with other schools. Cultural trips organised in UK and Europe; skiing trips. Senior pupils allowed to bring own bike. Meals formal. School shop. No tobacco/alcohol allowed.
Discipline Honesty, self-discipline and consideration for others expected. Disciplinary offences are dealt with sympathetically but firmly. Serious misdemeanours are rare. involvement with drugs would lead to expulsion.
Boarding 10% have own study bedroom, 35% share (1–3). Houses of 20–45 (separate sixth-form houses). Resident SRN. Central dining room. Sixth form can cook own food at weekends. 3 weekend exeats each term. Visits to the local town allowed at weekends.
Alumni association run by Mrs M Crisp, c/o the school.

• CATERHAM

Caterham School, Harestone Valley, Caterham, Surrey CR3 6YA. Tel 01883 343028, Fax 01883 347795.

• Pupils 910 • Boys 3–18 (Day/Board) • Girls 3–18 (Day/Board) • Upper sixth 112 • Termly fees £1932 (Day) £3532 (Board) • HMC, SHA • Enquiries/application to the Headmaster

What it's like

Founded in 1811 in Lewisham, the school moved to Caterham in 1884. It stands in 80 acres of delightful grounds in a wooded valley of the North Downs. In 1995 the school became fully co-educational throughout the age range, having first taken girls into the sixth-form in 1981. The prep school has its own buildings and staff. The senior school has very pleasant modern buildings and excellent facilities with more planned. It has strong links with the United Reformed Church. The aim is to provide a broad education based on Christian principles and practice. Academic standards are high and results excellent. Most sixth-formers go on to degree courses, including Oxbridge. The drama, music and creative arts departments are strong. A wide variety of sports and games is available and standards are high in the major games, rugby, netball, cricket and hockey (many county representatives). There are numerous clubs and societies for extra-curricular activities.

School profile

Pupils Total age range 3–18; 910 pupils, 760 day (545 boys, 215 girls), 150 boarding (125 boys, 25 girls). Senior department 11–18; 720 pupils (510 boys, 210 girls). Main entry ages 3, 4, 7, 10, 11, 13 and into the sixth. 10% are children of former pupils. *State school entry:* 30% intake, plus 10% to sixth.

Entrance Common Entrance and own exam used. No special skills or religious requirements; school has URC affiliation but pupils of many faiths within school. Parents not expected to buy textbooks; extras £100 maximum. 20 pa assisted places. 15 pa scholarships, 25%–50% fees, plus bursaries for children of clergy, services and foreign office.

Parents Wide mix of professions. 60+% live within 30 miles.

Head and staff *Headmaster:* Robert Davey, in post since 1995. Educated at Royal Academy Belfast, and at Trinity College Dublin (modern languages) and Oxford University (education). Previously Deputy Head at Wells Cathedral School, Head of Modern Languages and Boarding Housemaster at Rydal and Assistant Master (modern languages) at Mill Hill. Also played rugby for Oxford University. Member of HMC and Secondary Heads' Association. *Staff:* 60 full time, 7 part time (senior school). Annual turnover approx 10%. Average age approx 38.

Exam results In 1995, 94 pupils in fifth, 84 in upper sixth (112 in 1996). *GCSE:* In 1995, 73% of fifth gained at least grade C in 8+ subjects; 23% in 5–7 subjects. *A-levels:* 21% upper sixth passed in 4+ subjects; 75% in 3; 4% in 2 subjects. Average UCAS points 25.1.

University and college entrance 98% of 1995 sixth-form leavers went on to a degree course (10% after a gap year); others typically go straight on to employment. Of those going on to university, 10% went to Oxbridge; 5% took courses in medicine, dentistry and veterinary science, 40% in science and engineering, 54% in humanities and social sciences, 1% in music.

Curriculum GCSE and A-levels. 18 subjects offered, no A-level general studies. 30% take science A-levels; 30% arts/humanities; 40% both. *Vocational:* Work experience available. *Computing facilities:* 2 specialist networked IT rooms, plus IT room for design & technology. *Special provision:* Specialist dyslexic teacher available if required for small number. *Europe:* French, German and Spanish offered to GCSE and A-level. Some short sixth-form language courses in general studies. Regular exchanges (France, Spain and Germany). Assistants from German, Spanish and French universities.

The arts *Music:* Up to 25% of pupils learn a musical instrument; instrumental exams can be taken. Some 8 musical groups including orchestras, choirs, jazz group, chamber music ensembles. *Drama & dance*: Drama offered. Some pupils are involved in school productions and house/other productions. *Art:* Design, pottery also offered.

Sport, community service and clubs (Pupils aged 11 and over) *Sport and physical activities:* Compulsory sports (up to 16): rugby, hockey, cricket (boys); netball, hockey, lacrosse, dance (girls). Optional: tennis, swimming, athletics, squash, badminton, golf.

England cricket U15 representative; recent Rosslyn Park rugby sevens winners; many pupils in county cricket and rugby teams. *Community service:* Pupils take bronze, silver and gold Duke of Edinburgh's Award. CCF and community service optional. *Clubs and societies:* Up to 15 clubs, eg chess, science, debating, Christian Fellowship, current affairs, history, geography, opera, computer, bridge, English, Young Enterprise.
Uniform School uniform worn, option of suits in sixth.
Houses/prefects Competitive houses. Prefects, head boy/girl, heads of house. Head of school elected by year group, ratified by Headmaster. Regular prefects' meeting.
Religion Attendance at religious worship in school assemblies compulsory (exemption on Sundays for Hindu/Muslim etc).
Social Regular debates, music courses with other local schools. Exchange with German, Spanish and French schools. Upper sixth allowed to bring own car/bike/motorbike to school. Meals self-service and compulsory. School sports/uniform shop. No tobacco/alcohol allowed.
Discipline Pupils failing to produce homework once might expect to re-do with extra work, possibly academic detention. Pupils caught smoking cannabis on school premises could expect expulsion.
Boarding 25% have own study bedroom, 50% share (with 1 or 2); 10% in dormitories of 6+. Houses of approx 50. Resident qualified nurse. All weekends are flexi-weekends; other days out at weekends, depending on seniority. Visits to the local village permitted, on request.

• CENTRAL NEWCASTLE HIGH

Central Newcastle High School, Eskdale Terrace, Newcastle upon Tyne NE2 4DS. Tel 0191 281 1768, Fax 0191 281 6192

• Pupils 902 • Boys None • Girls 4–18 (Day) • Upper sixth 85 • Termly fees £976–£1328 (Day) • GSA, GPDST • Enquiries/application to the Headmistress

What it's like

Opened in 1895, a member of The Girls' Public Day School Trust, it has occupied the same premises in Eskdale Terrace since 1900. Numerous additions over the last twenty years include a science wing, art department with CDT laboratory; a fully equipped music school and indoor tennis court have recently been completed. It serves a wide catchment area and draws its pupils from many different backgrounds; a varied social mix is a feature of its philosophy. It enjoys a high reputation in the region and gets very good results. The vast majority of sixth-formers go on to degree courses, including Oxbridge. Good in music and an impressive range of extra-curricular activities. Strong local support. The junior school is in Gosforth, 3 miles away.

School profile

Pupils Total age range 4–18; 902 day girls. Senior department 11–18, 609 girls. Main entry ages 4, 7, 9, 11 and into sixth. *State school entry:* 40% senior intake, plus 15% to sixth.
Entrance Own entrance exam used. No special skills or religious requirements. Parents not expected to buy textbooks; music tuition extra. 18 pa assisted places and 5 at sixth-form. Approx 4 pa scholarships; bursaries.
Parents 20+% in industry or commerce; 20+% are doctors, lawyers, etc.
Head and staff *Headmistress:* Mrs Angela Chapman, in post for 12 years. Educated at Queen Victoria High School, Stockton-on-Tees, at Bristol University and the Sorbonne (French and Spanish). Previously Deputy Head at Newcastle Church High. Also FRSA. *Staff:* 44 full time, 28 part time.
Exam results In 1995, 86 pupils in upper fifth, 70 in upper sixth. *GCSE:* In 1995, all upper fifth gained at least grade C in 7+ subjects. *A-levels:* 95% upper sixth passed in 3+ subjects. Average UCAS points 22.3 (including general studies 25.4).
University and college entrance 90% of 1995 sixth-form leavers went on to a degree course, 10% to Oxbridge; 33% took courses in medicine and science. Curriculum GCSE and A-levels (including A-level general studies); and certificated courses in Arabic and Japanese. 40% take science A-levels; 50% arts/humanities; 10% both. *Vocational:* Work experience available. *Computing facilities:* 2 computer rooms equipped with 2 computer

networks with a total of 32 micros; plus various departmental computers. *Special provision:* some available for dyslexic pupils. *Europe:* French, German and Spanish offered at GCSE, AS and A-level (one is compulsory); Russian and Spanish to GCSE and certificated courses. Pupils taking GCSE early are expected to take a rapid GCSE course in another language. Regular exchanges (France and Germany), including European work experience for lower sixth. Talks from people involved in Europe.

The arts (Pupils aged 11 and over) *Music:* Up to 75% of pupils learn a musical instrument; instrumental exams can be taken. Some 9 musical groups including chamber choirs, orchestras, wind bands. Several members of National Youth Orchestra and National Children's Orchestra; regular successes in local music festivals. *Drama & dance*: Drama and dance offered. GCSE drama, Royal Society exams may be taken. Productions in school and in local theatre; majority of pupils are involved in school productions and house/other productions. Numerous successes in public speaking and debating. *Art:* On average, 28 take GCSE, 5 AS-level, 6 A-level. Design, photography, paper engineering and textiles also offered.

Sport, community service and clubs (Pupils age 11 and over) *Sport and physical activities:* Compulsory sports: netball, dance, swimming, tennis, athletics, hockey, cross-country. Optional: keep fit, fencing, cricket, rounders, real tennis, badminton, squash, golf. Sixth form only: yoga. GCSE, BAGA, RLSS, Milk Cup exams may be taken. National: TSB cross-country; tennis Midland Bank U11 champions and U13 runners-up; trampolining. County: tennis, hockey, cross-country, athletics, badminton, netball, swimming, squash. *Community service:* Pupils take bronze, silver and gold Duke of Edinburgh's Award. CCF optional (good and rising attendance at neighbouring Royal Newcastle Grammar School). Community service optional. *Clubs and societies:* Up to 30 clubs, eg gymnastics, computers, Christian Union, debating, poetry, pony trekking.

Uniform School uniform worn except in the sixth.

Houses/prefects 4 houses compete in sport, music and drama. Prefects, head girl and heads of house – elected by the girls. School Council.

Religion Non-denominational assembly, non-Christians can opt out. Regular Jewish assembly.

Social Senior debates, sixth-form drama and musical productions with Royal Grammar School for boys. Organised exchange to France, Germany; ski trips, trips to Greece. Pupils allowed to bring own car/bike to school. Meals self-service. School shop sells uniform; also tuckshop. Sixth form coffee shop with Royal Newcastle Grammar. No tobacco/alcohol allowed.

Alumni association is run by Mrs Helen Turnbull, 86 Polwarth Road, Brunton Park, Gosforth, Newcastle upon Tyne NE3 5NE.

Former pupils Miriam Stoppard, Pamela Denham.

• CHANNING

Channing School, Highgate, London N6 5HF. Tel 0181 340 2328, Fax 0181 341 5698

• Pupils 470 • Boys None • Girls 5–18 (Day) • Upper sixth 34 • Termly fees £1785–£1960 (Day)
• GSA • Enquiries/application to the Headmistress

What it's like

Founded in 1885 for 'the daughters of Unitarian ministers and others', the school occupies the large 19th-century building now known as Channing, on Highgate Hill. The present school is a combination of old and modern buildings which have been adapted and improved over the years. The senior school occupies a 3½ acre site with fine views over London; the junior school is nearby. There are pleasant gardens and playing fields. A broad, general education is provided and results are very good; almost all sixth-form leavers go on to higher education. The music and drama departments are very active. Sports and games are well catered for; there is a variety of extra-curricular activities and a substantial commitment to local community services.

School profile

Pupils Total age range 5–18; 470 day girls. Senior department 11–18, 321 girls. Main entry ages 5, 11 and into sixth. Approx 4% are children of former pupils. Over 40%

senior school from own junior. *State school entry:* 25% main senior intake plus 5% to sixth.

Entrance North London Consortium entrance exam used. No special skills or religious requirements. Parents not expected to buy textbooks until GCSE and A-level. Some assisted places. Scholarships at 11 and 16, 33%–66% fees; internal bursaries for music and cases of financial need.

Parents 25% are doctors, lawyers etc; 60+% in industry or commerce.

Head and staff *Headmistress:* Mrs Isabel Raphael, in post for 12 years. Educated at Cheltenham Ladies College and Cambridge (classics and English). Previously Head of Classics at City of London (Girls') and classics teacher at Putney High, Brearley School (New York) and Channing. Also Committee Member, National Campaign for Nursery Education 1974; GSA Education Committee; Council member, Classical Association 1991; President London Branch of Classical Association 1992; Trustee Whipple Trust, and Highgate Literary & Scientific Institution. Director of the Maria Montessori Training Organisation. *Staff:* 31 full time, 13 part time.

Exam results In 1995, 53 pupils in Year 11, 40 in upper sixth. *GCSE:* In 1995, 47 in Year 11 gained grade C or above in 8+ subjects, 6 in 5–7 subjects. *A-levels:* 2 upper sixth passed in 4 subjects; 36 in 3 (or 3½); 2 in 2 subjects. Average UCAS points 23.9.

University and college entrance 95% of 1995 sixth-form leavers went on to a degree course (20% after a gap year); others typically go straight on to employment. Of those going on to university, 10% went to Oxbridge; 10% took courses in medicine, dentistry and veterinary science, 12% in science and engineering, 4% in law, 55% in humanities and social sciences, 4% in art and design, 9% in vocational subjects eg pharmacy, music, banking, hotel management.

Curriculum GCSE and A-levels. 15 subjects offered (no A-level general studies). 15% take science A-levels; 48% arts/humanities; 38% both. *Vocational:* Work experience compulsory. RSA CLAIT exams and copytyping speed test available. *Europe:* French, German and Spanish offered to GCSE and A-level (French compulsory from 11–14); also AS-level German. Regular exchanges (France, Germany and Spain).

The arts (Pupils aged 11 and over) *Music:* Over 50% of pupils learn a musical instrument; instrumental exams can be taken. Musical groups include choirs, orchestras, flute band, clarinet band, swing band, string ensembles, and recorder consorts. *Drama & dance*: Drama and dance offered. Majority of pupils are involved in school and other productions. All pupils given opportunity to perform work produced in dance class; annual school and form drama and musical productions. *Art:* On average, 22 take GCSE, 6 A-level. Design, pottery, textiles, photography, life class also offered.

Sport, community service and clubs (Pupils aged 11 and over) *Sport and physical activities:* Compulsory sports: hockey, gym, dance, rounders, tennis, HRF, aerobics, swimming. Optional: badminton, volleyball, basketball, football, stoolball, athletics, fencing, trampolining, self-defence. Sixth form only: ice skating, riding and extra tennis coaching. BAGA exams may be taken. *Community service:* Pupils take bronze and gold Duke of Edinburgh's Award. Community service compulsory for 1 term at 14 and a year at age 16; work with handicapped, senior citizens, children and charity shops. *Clubs and societies:* Over 20 clubs, eg life drawing, drama, Young Enterprise, dance, trampolining, chamber choir, photography, book group.

Uniform School uniform worn except in the sixth-form.

Houses/prefects No competitive houses or prefects. Head girl and school officers. School Council.

Religion Compulsory school assembly and RE classes.

Social Many organised local events and trips abroad including exchanges to Europe and USA. Pupils allowed to bring own bike to school. Meals self-service. No tobacco/alcohol allowed.

Discipline After-school detentions are given if work is not done satisfactorily. Girls found chewing gum are given practical chores to do, eg weeding or picking up litter. Anyone found smoking or drinking would be suspended from school. Involvement with drugs would mean compulsory counselling or expulsion.

Alumnae association run by Mrs C Elworthy, 27 Cholmeley Crescent, London N6 5EX.

• CHARTERHOUSE

Charterhouse, Godalming, Surrey GU7 2DN. Tel 01483 291501, Fax 01483 291507

• Pupils 700 • Boys 13–18 (Day/Board) • Girls 16–18 (Day/Board) • Upper sixth 144 • Termly fees £3516 (Day) £4255 (Board) • HMC • Enquiries to the Admissions Registrar

What it's like

Founded in 1611, on the site of a Carthusian monastery in London, it moved in 1872 to Godalming. It stands in a superb estate of 200 acres on a plateau above the River Wey with fine views south and south-west. With its towers and spires and its blend of neo-Gothic and neo-Tudor buildings in stone and brick, it presents an almost emblematic image of the traditional English public school. Over the years a large number of modern buildings have been added and the whole place is superbly equipped with virtually every facility that one might expect and hope for. A first-rate education is provided and results are very good. Virtually all Carthusians proceed to degree courses, including a large entry to Oxbridge. Very strong in music, drama and art. It has the advantages of exceptionally good libraries, a museum, an art studio, a design and technology centre, a music school and a theatre which would be the envy of many professional companies. A new sports centre opened in 1995. Outdoor pursuits are various and popular. There is an impressive range of extra-curricular activities. The CCF, scouts and social services (locally and in London) are vigorously supported. There is a strong sporting tradition and wide range of sports and games, played successfully at school, county and national levels.

School profile

Pupils Age range 13–18; 700 pupils, 25 day (19 boys, 6 girls), 675 boarding (601 boys, 74 girls). Main entry ages 13 (boys) and into sixth (boys and girls). Approx 12% are children of former pupils. *State school entry:* None at 13; 15% to sixth.
Entrance Common Entrance and own scholarship exam. Academic ability and sound character looked for; no religious requirements. Parents not expected to buy text books in the Under School. 5 pa assisted places (sixth-form only). Scholarships at 13 and 16 (21 academic, 7 music, 4 art), £500 to full fees (in cases of financial hardship). Also an award for sons of lawyers: awards may be supplemented by bursaries in case of financial need.
Parents 15+% in industry/commerce. 30+% live within 30 miles; 10+% live overseas.
Head and staff *Headmaster:* The Revd John Witheridge appointed 1996. Educated at St Alban's and universities of Kent (English and theology) and Cambridge. Previously Conduct of Eton. *Staff:* 84 full time (plus music staff). Annual turnover 3%. Average age 40.
Exam results In 1995, 126 pupils in upper fifth, 144 in upper sixth. *GCSE:* In 1995, 99% of upper fifth gained grade C or above in 8+ subjects. *A-levels:* 9 upper sixth passed in 4+ subjects; 128 in 3; 4 in 2; and 3 in 1 subject. Average UCAS points 24.5.
University and college entrance 98% of 1995 sixth-form leavers went on to a degree course (75% after a gap year); others typically go on to art foundation courses, HNDs or straight into employment. Of those going on to university, 22% went to Oxbridge; 5% took courses in medicine, dentistry and veterinary science, 23% in science and engineering, 5% in law, 52% in humanities and social sciences, 8% in art, design and architecture, 7% in vocational subjects eg business management, hotel and catering, educaion.
Curriculum GCSE and A-levels. 18 GCSE subjects; 20 at A-level (no general studies). Approx 21% take science A-levels; 59% arts/humanities; 21% both. *Vocational:* Work experience available. *Computing facilities:* Network of Archimedes machines. *Europe:* French, German and Spanish offered to GCSE, and A-level; also AS-level French and German and 1-year language courses in post-GCSE French. German pupils regularly in school.
The arts *Music:* Up to 75% of pupils learn a musical instrument; instrumental exams can be taken. Some 20 musical groups including 2 symphony orchestras, 3 string orchestras, 2 bands, 4 choirs, wind, brass and string ensembles, various chamber music combinations. *Drama & dance*: Strong tradition of drama. GCSE drama may be taken. Some pupils are involved in school productions and majority in house/other productions. *Art:* On average, 25 take GCSE, 12 A-level. Design, pottery, textiles, photography, history of art and printmaking also offered. Many places obtained at art school.
Sport, community service and clubs *Sport and physical activities:* Major sports: soccer, hockey, cricket, netball, lacrosse. Minor: cross-country, Eton fives, swimming, rugby, squash, shooting, tennis, athletics, golf, fencing, sub-aqua, sailing, climbing, karate. RLSS exams may be taken. Family golf and tennis tournaments. *Community*

service: Silver and gold Duke of Edinburgh's Award. CCF or scouts compulsory for all to 15, after which community service optional. Adventurous activities throughout UK, trekking in Himalayas and Africa. *Clubs and societies:* Over 30 clubs, eg astronomy, bridge, debating, magical, opera, poetry, recording, Spanish, Thackeray.
Uniform School uniform worn throughout.
Houses/prefects Competitive houses. Prefects (monitors), Head of school, head of house and house monitors – appointed.
Religion Charterhouse is a Christian foundation: regular religious worship compulsory.
Social Organised trips abroad annually. Meals formal. Four shops. Club for senior pupils; no tobacco.
Boarding 81% have own study bedroom, 11% share with 1 other. Houses, of approximately 65. Resident qualified nurses. Dining by houses. Pupils can provide and cook own food. Half-term and leave weekends. Visits to local town allowed.
Alumni association is run by The Recorder, c/o the School.
Former pupils include Lord Dacre, David Hicks, Daisy Bates, Helena Drysdale, Frederick Raphael, Simon Raven, Sir Greville Spratt, The Rt Rev Michael Whinney, Sir John Banham, Kenneth McAlpine, Peter de Savary, Lord Donaldson, Lord Griffiths, David Dimbleby, Jonathan Dimbleby, Max Hastings, Sir William Rees-Mogg, Lord Richardson, Lord Wakeham, Air Chief Marshal Sir Brian Burnett, Charles Swallow, Stephen Venables.

• CHEADLE HULME

Cheadle Hulme School, Claremont Road, Cheadle Hulme, Cheadle, Cheshire SK8 6EF. Tel 0161 485 4142

• Pupils 1145 • Boys 7–18 (Day) • Girls 7–18 (Day) • Upper sixth 120 • Termly fees £1091–£1362 (Day) • HMC • Enquiries/application to the Headmaster

What it's like

Founded in 1855, formerly the Manchester Warehousemen and Clerks' Orphan Schools. A single site in urban surroundings near Manchester and set in 80 acres of grounds. The original Victorian building has been modernised and there have been extensive additions over the years. The junior school is nearby. An excellent academic education is given and results are good; the majority of sixth-formers go on to higher education, including a number to Oxbridge. Strong in music, art and drama.

School profile

Pupils Total age range 7–18; 1145 day pupils, (571 boys, 574 girls). Senior department 11–18, 970 pupils (481 boys, 489 girls). Main entry ages 7, 8, 9, 11 and into sixth.
Entrance Own entrance exam used. No special skills or religious requirements. Parents not expected to buy textbooks. 20 pa assisted places. 4 pa scholarships/bursaries for excellence in music or drama at sixth-form level.
Parents 15+% in industry or commerce; 15+% are doctors, lawyers etc.
Head and staff *Headmaster:* Donald J Wilkinson, 6 years in post. Educated at Royal Grammar School, Lancaster, and Oxford University (history). Previously Head of Sixth Form at Newcastle-under-Lyme, Head of History at Oakham and Assistant Master at Manchester Grammar. *Staff:* 71 full time, 9 part time. Annual turnover 5%. Average age 45.
Exam results In 1995, 134 pupils in upper fifth, 116 in upper sixth. *GCSE:* In 1995, 93% of upper fifth gained at least grade C in 8 + subjects; 6% in 5–7 subjects. *A-levels:* 82% upper sixth passed in 4+ subjects; 14% in 3; 3% in 2; and 1% in 1 subject. Average UCAS points 19.9.
University and college entrance 95% of 1995 sixth-form leavers went on to a degree course; others typically go on to art colleges. Of those going on to university, 10% went to Oxbridge; 8% took courses in medicine, dentistry and veterinary science, 46% in science and engineering, 40% in humanities and social sciences, 4% in art and design.
Curriculum GCSE and A-levels. Over 20 subjects offered, including Greek and A-level general studies. 42% take science A-levels; 35% arts/humanities; 23% both. *Vocational:* Work experience available. *Computing facilities:* Numerous hands-on facilities for pupils. *Europe:* French and German offered to GCSE and A-level. Regular exchanges (France and Germany).

The arts (Pupils aged 11 and over) *Music:* Up to 50% of pupils learn a musical instrument; instrumental exams can be taken. Some 12 musical groups including 3 orchestras, choirs, 2 wind bands, various string groups. Pupils regularly accepted by music colleges or to read music at university. *Drama & dance*: Drama offered and GCSE may be taken. Some pupils are involved in school productions. *Art:* On average, 30 take GCSE, 8 A-level. Design, pottery, textiles, photography also offered.
Sport, community service and clubs (Pupils aged 11 and over) *Sport and physical activities:* All pupils encouraged to take part in school's wide-ranging games programme including rugby, hockey, soccer, cross-country, netball, swimming, tennis, cricket, athletics, badminton. BAGA, RLSS exams may be taken. National teams occasional representatives; regular representatives at county level in a number of sports. *Community service:* Pupils take bronze Duke of Edinburgh's Award. Community service optional. *Clubs and societies:* Clubs include computer, electronics, beekeeping, chess and others.
Uniform School uniform worn throughout.
Houses/prefects No competitive houses. Prefects, head boy/girl – appointed by the Head on advice. School Council.
Religion No compulsory religious worship.
Social No organised events with other schools. Many organised trips to France, Germany, Italy/Greece, skiing each year. Pupils allowed to bring own car/bike/motorbike to school. Meals self service. No tobacco/alcohol allowed.
Discipline Pupils failing to produce homework once might expect a verbal reprimand and to do the homework; those caught smoking cannabis on the premises would be expelled.
Alumni association Run by Mrs V Moore, 24 Hill Top Avenue, Cheadle Hulme, Cheadle, Cheshire SK8 7HY.

• CHELTENHAM COLLEGE

Cheltenham College, Bath Road, Cheltenham, Gloucestershire GL53 7LD. Tel 01242 513540, Fax 01242 577746

• Pupils 565 • Boys 13–18 (Day/Board) • Girls 16–18 (Day/Board) • Upper sixth 145 • Termly fees £3075 (Day) £4070 (Board) • HMC • Enquiries/application to the Registrar

What it's like

Founded in 1841, it has a fine site on the edge of the town. Handsome Victorian buildings in beautiful gardens and playing fields. Recent developments and modernisations have produced excellent facilities. It is a C of E foundation and chapel services and some Sunday services are compulsory. However, it is fully ecumenical. Originally a boys' school, it has taken girls into the sixth-form since 1982 and will be fully co-educational in 1998. Academic standards are high and results very good; the vast majority of sixth-formers go on to degree courses, many to Oxbridge. Technology is strong; the college has frequently won the Young Engineer for Britain and Young Inventor of the Year competitions. Music thrives and plays a large part in the lives of many pupils and there are joint musical activities with the Ladies' College. Drama and art are also strong. There are fine facilities for sports and games and the college achieves a high standard; many national and county representatives. A plentiful range of extra-curricular activities, clubs, societies and so on. A very energetic community scheme serves the town. Wherever possible all college facilities are made available to the town and other schools. One of the school's aims is to maintain a tradition of service to a modern industrial society.

School profile

Pupils Age range 13–18; 565 pupils, 180 day (165 boys, 15 girls), 385 boarding (305 boys, 80 girls). Main entry ages 13 (boys), and into sixth (boys and girls). Own junior school provides more than 40% of intake. Approx 10% are children of former pupils.
Entrance Common Entrance and own sixth-form scholarship or entry tests used. Motivation looked for; C of E foundation. Parents expected to buy sixth-form tex-books; extras £100 approx. 20 pa scholarships/bursaries (at 13 and 16), 10%–50% of fees.
Parents 15+% in industry or commerce. 50+% live within 30 miles; up to 14% live overseas.

Head and staff *Headmaster:* P D V Wilkes, 6 years in post. Educated at Radley and Oxford (Lit Hum). Previously Headmaster at Ryde, Housemaster at Rugby and taught at Charterhouse. Also worked in Zimbabwe and Iran for a number of years. *Staff:* 61 full time, 7 part time. Annual turnover 8%. Average age 34.
Exam results In 1995, 88 pupils in upper fifth, 132 in upper sixth. *GCSE:* In 1995, 88% upper fifth gained at least grade C in 8+ subjects; 10% in 5–7 subjects. *A-levels:* 30 passed in 4+ subjects; 85 in 3; 9 in 2; and 7 in 1 subject. Average UCAS points 22.0.
University and college entrance 95% of 1995 sixth-form leavers went on to a degree course (20% after a gap year); others typically go on to employment. Of those going on to university, 15% went to Oxbridge; 6% took courses in medicine, dentistry and veterinary science, 15% in science and engineering, 7% in law, 43% in humanities and social sciences, 10% in art and design, 10% in vocational subjects eg accountancy, land management.
Curriculum GCSE and A-levels. 18 GCSE subjects offered; 23 at A-level (no general studies). 22% take science A-levels; 58% arts/humanities; 20% both. *Vocational:* Work experience available. *Computing facilities:* 3 IT centres with networked Apple Macintosh computers; Nimbus computers in maths department computer centre. Computers in classrooms for inter-active learning. *Europe:* French, German and Spanish offered at GCSE and A-level (French compulsory from 13-16); Russian also available. Regular exchanges (France, Germany and Spain). 8% of sixth-form are European.
The arts *Music:* Over 50% of pupils learn a musical instrument; instrumental exams can be taken. Some 10 musical groups including big band, wind band, jazz improvisation, chamber choir, orchestra, close harmony group. Pupils in county youth orchestra. *Drama & Dance*: Drama offered. Majority of pupils are involved in school and house/other productions. *Art:* On average, 37 take GCSE, 18 A-level. Design, pottery, photography also offered.
Sport, community service and clubs *Sport and physical activities:* Compulsory major sports: rugby, cricket, hockey, rowing. Optional minor sports: swimming, athletics, rackets, squash, tennis, shooting, cross-county, sailing, badminton, netball, golf, polo. Numerous county representatives at rugby, hockey, cross-country, athletics, squash, tennis. *Community service:* CCF compulsory for 1 year at age 14, optional thereafter. Community service optional for 2 years at age 16. *Clubs and societies:* Up to 30 clubs, eg astronomy, drama, falconry, mountaineering, opera.
Uniform School uniform worn throughout.
Houses/prefects Competitive houses. Prefects, senior prefect (head boy), head girl, head of house and house prefects – appointed by Headmaster.
Religion Compulsory daily chapel.
Social Musical links with Cheltenham Ladies' College. Pupils allowed to bring own bike to school. Meals self service. School shop. No tobacco; limited beer for sixth only in licensed club.
Discipline Taking or handling drugs leads to automatic expulsion.
Boarding Fifth and sixth-form have own study bedroom; juniors in dormitories of 6+. Single-sex houses of approximately 65, same as competitive houses. Resident matron in each house. Central dining room. Pupils can provide and cook snacks in houses. 2 termly exeats. Visits to town allowed by arrangement with housemaster.
Former pupils Nigel Davenport; Lindsay Anderson; Patrick White; Major General Sir Jeremy Moore; General Sir Michael Rose; Peter Brownley; Lord Richard.

• CHELTENHAM LADIES

The Cheltenham Ladies' College, Bayshill Road, Cheltenham, Gloucestershire GL50 3EP. Tel 01242 520691, Fax 01242 227882

• Pupils 841 • Boys None • Girls 11–18 (Day/Board) • Upper sixth 140 • Termly fees £2600 (Day) £4095 (Board) • GSA, SHA, BSA • Enquiries to the Principal • Application to the Registrar

What it's like

Founded in 1853, it flourished for most of its first 50 years under Miss Dorothea Beale, a pioneer of the belief that the education of girls is every bit as important as that of boys. In 1873 it moved into fine new buildings at Bayshill, a pleasant area of Regency Cheltenham. There have been many additions since to provide a well-equipped school – recently a sports hall, swimming pool, drama studio and editing suite; an art and technology block is planned. The boarding houses are scattered within 10 minutes' walk of the main teaching block. Girls are expected to attend Prayers (in the Anglican tradition) which are held every morning and a Sunday service at a local parish churche. A civilised, friendly atmosphere prevails. The College has a strong academic tradition with a large, well-qualified staff, which permits a staff:pupil ratio of about 1:7. Academic standards are high and results are consistently very good. Almost all girls go on to degree courses, including many to Oxbridge. Music, drama and art are strong and good standards are continuously achieved. Facilities for sports are first-rate and a wide variety of sports is available; again, high standards are attained and the College has produced many representatives at county, regional and national level (especially in hockey, lacrosse, squash and gymnastics). The College is also closely associated with local community services and many girls participate successfully in the Duke of Edinburgh's Award Scheme.

School profile

Pupils Age range 11–18; 841 girls (201 day, 640 boarding). Main entry ages, 11, 12, 13 and into sixth. *State school entry:* 10% main intake, plus 5% to sixth-form.

Entrance Common Entrance and own scholarship and sixth-form exams. No special skills or religious requirements although the school is run on Christian lines. Parents not expected to buy textbooks. Average £150 per term extras. 10 pa assisted places at 11 years old. 12 pa scholarships/bursaries available, 25%–50% fees.

Parents 15+% doctors, lawyers. etc; 15% from industry/commerce. 25% live within 30 miles; 15% live overseas.

Head and staff *Principal:* Mrs Anne V Tuck appointed 1996. Masters degree in applied European studies. Previously Deputy Head at City of London School, Head of Modern Languages at Bromley High and French and Italian Teacher at Putney High. Also worked as PGCE Course Director at Institute of Education; Member of the Institute of Linguists. *Staff:* 98 full time, 50 part time. Annual turnover 5%. Average age 40.

Exam results In 1995, 126 pupils in fifth year, 140 in upper sixth. *GCSE:* In 1995, 99% fifth year gained at least grade C in 8+ subjects. *A-levels:* 23% upper sixth passed in 4+ subjects; 76% in 3 subjects. Average UCAS points 24.6.

University and college entrance 90% of 1995 sixth-form leavers went on to a degree course; others typically go on to non-degree eg secretarial, art foundation courses. Of those going on to university, 14% went to Oxbridge; 13% took courses in medicine, dentistry and veterinary science, 13% in science and engineering, 71% in humanities and social sciences, 3% in music.

Curriculum GCSE and A-levels. 24 subjects offered, including Greek and Latin available; no A-level general studies. 29% take science A-levels, 43% arts/humanities; 28% both. *Vocational:* Work experience available; also RSA computing course. *Computing facilities:* 4 well-equipped networked computer rooms. *Special provision:* for those with mild dyslexia. Pupils should be fluent in English before being accepted. *Europe:* French, German, Spanish, Italian and Russian offered to GCSE and A-level.

The arts *Music:* 65% of pupils learn a musical instrument; instrumental exams can be taken. Musical groups include 12 chamber groups, 5 choirs including madrigal group, 2 large orchestras, 2 chamber orchestras, 3 flute choirs, jazz band, string, piano, wind ensembles. Several groups in finals concerts of National Schools Chamber Music Competition; runner-up in county Young Musician of the Year. *Drama & dance:* Drama offered. GCSE and A-level drama, LAMDA, Guildhall exams may be taken. Majority of pupils are involved in school and house/other productions. Performed at Edinburgh Richard de Marco Gallery, 1995. *Art:* 50% take GCSE, 20% A-level. Ceramics, sculpture, silk screen-printing also offered. Many girls gain entry to top schools of art and architecture.

Sport, community service and clubs *Sport and physical activities:* Compulsory sports: hockey, lacrosse, netball, gymnastics, dance, tennis, swimming, athletics, rounders, HRF, multi-gym. Optional: riding, fencing, sailing, judo, special tennis, self-defence, squash, aerobics, badminton, basketball, volleyball, cricket. Sixth form only: dry slope skiing, rowing, windsurfing, golf. National hockey champions 1994; national lacrosse finals; win majority of local hockey tournaments and some county netball tournaments. County

representation in most major sports. *Community service:* Pupils take bronze, silver and gold Duke of Edinburgh's Award. Community service optional; much charitable work, biennial fête raising money for local charities, support for Tower Hamlets community centre. *Clubs and societies:* Over 30 clubs, eg history of art, debating, computer, Green, Christian Union, classical, photography, numerous games, art and music clubs.
Uniform School uniform worn throughout.
Houses/prefects Senior prefect, prefects elected by the school; head of house and house prefects. School Council.
Religion Attendance at religious worship compulsory.
Social Joint choral events, drama productions, debates, dances, etc. with other schools. French exchange to Annecy annually; other trips to Russia, Paris (art trip), hockey trips, cruises, cultural holidays. Meals formal; self-service in sixth-form houses. No tobacco/ alcohol allowed.
Discipline Pupils failing to produce homework once could expect a mild reprimand; anyone caught smoking cannabis on the premises would be dismissed.
Boarding All sixth-formers have own study bedrooms. 25% in dormitories of 6+. Pupils divided into different houses of approx 65. Resident qualified nurse. Pupils can provide and cook own food. Exeats at half-term, two weekends, plus Sundays after Church. Visits to the local town allowed by all year groups weekly, senior girls daily.
Alumni association is run by Mrs B Morane-Griffiths, c/o the school.
Former pupils Bridget Riley (artist); Katherine Hamnet; Mary Archer; Penelope Walker (singer), Sue Lloyd-Roberts (broadcaster); Cheryl Gillan MP; Rachel Lomax (Vice Chairman, World Bank).

• CHERWELL TUTORS

Cherwell Tutors, Greyfriars, Paradise Street, Oxford OX1 1LD. Tel 01865 242670, Fax 01865 791761

• Pupils 150 • Boys 16–18 (Day/Board) • Girls 16–18 (Day/Board) • Upper sixth 70 • Termly fees £2800 (Day) £3750 (Board/Weekly) • BAC, CIFE • Enquiries/application to the Principal

What it's like

Founded in 1973, as a co-educational tutorial establishment, which enjoys an historic site, Greyfriars, almost right in the middle of the city. Greyfriars (originally a Franciscan foundation) comprises two main buildings: the Master's Lodgings and the Cloisters, separated by an open courtyard. The Cloisters area houses classrooms, laboratories, library and common room for the students. There are four halls of residence which lie in north central Oxford; all handsome and comfortable houses within ten minutes' cycle ride of Greyfriars and each supervised by a house-mother with a domestic staff. Mature students may be allowed to take other lodgings in the city. There is no prescribed curriculum; tutorial arrangments are designed to suit each pupil's individual needs. Both the full time and part time staff are very numerous and this means that virtually all the tutorial work is done on a one-to-one basis. Individual instruction is supplemented by study in small groups in weekly seminars. There are also weekly 'trials' (written tests). The teaching is highly organised and concentrated for A-level, AS-level and university entrance. Exam results are very good and a high proportion of students go on to pursue degree courses. All pupils have a counsellor for pastoral care, to oversee academic work and in general to act *in loco parentis*. Organised social functions occur 3–4 times a term. Sport and games are optional but there are facilities for quite a few standard games; also for riding, fencing and swimming.

School profile

Pupils Age range 16–19; 150 students, 20 day (10 boys, 10 girls), 130 boarding (65 boys, 65 girls). *State school entry:* 5%.
Entrance No entrance exam. Boarding places oversubscribed. No special skills required although students must reflect high level of commitment and motivation; no religious requirements, college multi-denominational. Some 5 pa scholarships, £500–£3000.
Parents 15+% are in theatre/media/music; 20+% doctors/lawyers; 45+% industry/ commerce. Under 10% live within 30 miles of the school; under 10% overseas.

Head and staff *Principal:* Paul J Gordon, in post for 23 years. Educated at Littlemore Grammar and Oxford (earth sciences). Previously taught at Aylesbury Grammar School and tutored geography and geology in Oxford. *Staff:* 54 full time, 42 part time. Annual turnover, 1–2%. Average age, 40.
Exam results On average, 10 pupils in upper fifth, 75 in upper sixth. *GCSE:* In 1995, 98% of pupils gained at least grade C in 5-7 subjects. *A-levels:* In 1995, 2 pupils passed in 4+ subjects; 46 in 3; 18 in 2; and 9 in 1 subject (college policy to stagger the timing of examinations). On average UCAS points 24.0.
University and college entrance 84% of 1995 sixth-form leavers went on to a degree course (1% after a gap year – not encouraged); others typically go on to art or agricultural college or to work in Sotheby's or Christies. Of those going on to university, 3% went to Oxbridge; 5% took courses in medicine, dentistry and veterinary science, 5% in science and engineering, 17% in law, 60% in humanities and social sciences, 5% in art and design, 7% in vocational subjects eg physiotherapy.
Curriculum Some GCSE, mainly A-levels, AS-levels offered; also all EFL exams. All subjects offered, including Chinese, Russian and A-level communication and media studies. 10% take science A-levels; 85% arts/humanities; 5% both. *Computing facilities:* Computer room with RM Nimbus facility, for A-level computer science students. *Europe:* All European languages offered to GCSE, AS-level and A-level.
The arts *Music:* Up to 15% pupils play a musical instrument; instrumental exams can be taken. *Art:* On average, 10 take A-level. Design, pottery and photography also offered.
Sport, community service and clubs *Sport and physical activities:* All sport is optional. A number of pupils of national and international ranking. *Community service:* Pupils can take bronze, silver and gold Duke of Edinburgh's Award. CCF and community service optional. *Clubs and societies:* Many pupils are members of clubs/societies associated with the university.
Uniform None.
Houses/prefects No competitive houses or prefects.
Religion No compulsory worship.
Social Trips abroad organised, particulary by departments of art and earth sciences. Students may bring own car/bike/motorbike to school. No alcohol/tobacco allowed in college, smoking allowed in halls.
Discipline Students expect to be embarrassed if work is not completed for their tutor; students caught smoking cannabis on the premises might expect immediate expulsion.
Boarding 20% have own study bedrooms; 80% share with 1 other. Mixed houses of 17–20, divided by age group; some self-catering accommodation. Students treated as adults, so exeats not limited.

• CHETHAM'S

Chetham's School of Music, Long Millgate, Manchester M3 1SB. Tel 0161 834 9644, Fax 0161 839 3609

• Pupils 288 • Boys 8–18 (Day/Board) • Girls 8–18 (Day/Board) • Upper sixth 50 • Termly fees £4025 (Day) £5200 (Board) • HMC • Enquiries/application to the Headmaster or Headmaster's Secretary

What it's like

Founded in 1653, it lies in the centre of Manchester in its own grounds. The buildings are well-designed and well-equipped. The boarding accommodation is comfortable with two new boarding houses. It has been a specialist music school since 1969 when it also first admitted girls. It is possible to study any musical instrument, keyboard, guitar or voice. All entrants who have been resident in this country for at least two years prior to admission qualify automatically for the government Aided Pupil Scheme. Whilst specialist music tuition forms the core of the curriculum, the school follows the National Curriculum as far as possible. About one-third of the time-tabled time is devoted to music. Pupils normally study one first-study instrument (or voice or composition) and one second study. They are also prepared for GCSE and A-levels and results are outstanding, given the time devoted to musical studies. Most leavers go on to study music, some at a music college, some at university and a very high proportion to

Oxbridge. The range of facilities for sport and games and other recreations is limited by the city centre site, but includes swimming pool, squash court, gymnasium and multi-gym.

School profile

Pupils Total age range 8–18; 288 pupils, 58 day (37 boys, 21 girls), 230 boarding (90 boys, 140 girls). Senior department 11–18, 266 pupils (116 boys, 150 girls). Entry at any age (mainly 11 and 16). *State school entry:* 90% main entry at 11, plus 80% to sixth.
Entrance Admission only by audition. Musical potential looked for; no religious requirements. Parents not expected to buy text books. Aided Pupil Scheme for all entrants resident in UK for at least 2 years prior to entry, value up to £15,600 pa (means tested) plus travel and uniform grants.
Parents 10+% live within 30 miles; up to 10% live overseas.
Head and staff *Headmaster:* The Rev Peter Hullah, 4 years in post. Educated at Bradford Grammar School and at London and Makerere universities (theology). Previously Head of International House at Sevenoaks and Senior Chaplain at King's, Canterbury. *Staff:* 41 full time, 80 part-time. Annual turnover 8%. Average age 43.
Exam results On average, 36 pupils in upper fifth, 50 in upper sixth. *GCSE:* On average, 32 upper fifth gain at least grade C in 5–7 subjects; and 4 in 1–4 subjects. *A-levels:* 20% upper sixth pass in 4+ subjects, 20% in 3; 50% in 2; and 10% in 1 subject. Average UCAS points 18.9.
University and college entrance 35% of sixth-form leavers go on to a degree course (6% after a gap year); the majority go on to music colleges. Of those going on to university, 20% go to Oxbridge; 2% take courses in medicine, dentistry and veterinary science, 6% in science and engineering, 2% in law, 10% in humanities and social sciences, 2% in art and design, 80% in music.
Curriculum GCSE and A-levels. 16 subjects offered. including A-level music technology and general studies. 76% take A-levels in arts/humanities; 24% both arts and sciences. *Computing facilities:* 30 computers (mainly Archimedes in new lab). *Special provision:* Limited tuition for ESL/dyslexic pupils. *Europe:* French and German offered to GCSE, AS and A-level.
The arts (Pupils aged 11 and over) *Music:* All pupils learn a musical instrument; instrumental exams can be taken. Some 60 musical groups including duets, trios, quartets, quintets, wind band, percussion ensemble, chamber choir, chamber orchestra, symphony orchestra. 10 members of the National Youth Orchestra. *Drama & dance:* Drama offered and GCSE may be taken. Some pupils are involved in school productions. *Art:* On average, 4 take GCSE and A-level. Pottery, photography also offered.
Sport, community service and clubs (Pupils aged 11 and over) *Sport and physical activities:* Optional sports: aerobics, running, trampolining, fitness training, swimming, squash, badminton, weight training, table tennis, rounders.
Uniform School uniform worn with choice in the sixth-form.
Houses/prefects No competitive houses. Prefects, head boy/girl, head of house and house prefects – appointed by the Headmaster/heads of houses.
Religion Weekly (non-denominational) service in Manchester Cathedral except for those who specifically opt out. Sunday service is encouraged. RCs have own weekly instruction or service.
Social Regular weekend outings for boarders. Organised choral/orchestral tours (about 2 per year); skiing. Meals self service. School tuckshop. No tobacco/alcohol allowed.
Discipline Pupils failing to produce homework once might expect a reprimand, extra work; policy of involving families early in serious pastoral/moral/disciplinary matters. Headmaster has power of suspension, Governors have power of expulsion.
Boarding 39% share (2 to a room); 9% in rooms of 6. Single sex houses, of approximately 50. Resident and day-time nurses, 3 visiting doctors. Central dining room. Pupils can provide and cook own food in houses. Any number of weekend exeats. Visits to the local town allowed.
Alumni association is run by The Chairman, Chetham's Association, c/o the school.
Former pupils Peter Donohoe, Stephen Hough and Anna Markland (all pianists); Grant Llewellyn, Daniel Harding (conductors); Mike Lindup (pop group – Level 42); John Mundy (BBC TV announcer); Omar (Hammer) (pop singer).

• CHIGWELL

Chigwell School, Chigwell, Essex IG7 6QF. Tel 0181 500 1396/2570, Fax 0181 500 6232
• Pupils 662 • Boys 7–18 (Day/Board/Weekly) • Girls 16–18 (Day/Board/Weekly) • Upper sixth 75 • Termly fees £1351–£2077 (Day) £2120–£3157 (Board) £2004–£2989 (Weekly) • HMC
• Enquiries/application to Admissions Secretary

What it's like

Founded in 1629, and set in fine open countryside in Chigwell village on a delightful 70-acre estate, only 10 miles from central London. Architecturally, it makes a most satisfying unit and the original 17th-century building is still in use. It has many excellent modern facilities. The junior school is combined. Originally a boys' school, it is about to become fully co-educational after nearly 25 years' experience of a mixed sixth-form: girls will be admitted at age 7 in 1997 and 11 in 1998. A sound general education is provided and results are very good. Almost all leavers go on to degree courses, including Oxbridge. It is Christian in its ideals and inspiration. There is a wide variety of music-making. Drama and art are strongly supported. A good range of sports and games and considerable all-round success (numerous representatives at regional and national level). Plus plentiful extra-curricular activities, including commitment to the Duke of Edinburgh's Award Scheme.

School profile

Pupils Total age range 7–18; 662 pupils, 605 day (581 boys, 24 girls), 57 boarding (51 boys, 6 girls). Senior department 13–18, 372 pupils (348 boys, 24 girls). Main entry ages 7, 11, 13 (boys) and into sixth (boys and girls); girls also admitted at 7 in 1997 and 11 in 1998. Approx 10% are children of former pupils. *State school entry:* 40% intake at 11, plus 75% to sixth.
Entrance Own entrance exam used; few by Common Entrance. Pupils with skills in music and art given special consideration; no religious requirements. Parents expected to buy some textbooks; £50 pa maximum extras. 15 pa assisted places. 6 pa scholarships/bursaries up to 100% of tuition fees.
Parents 15+% in industry or commerce. Over 60% live within 30 miles; up to 10% live overseas.
Head and staff *Headmaster:* David Gibbs, appointed in 1995. Educated at Ardingly and Durham University (economics). Previously Boarding House Master at Haileybury and Head of Economics and Politics at Charterhouse. *Staff:* 53 full time, 18 part time (music). Annual turnover 5%. Average age 38.
Exam results In 1995, 84 pupils in upper fifth, 66 in upper sixth. *GCSE:* In 1995, 87% upper fifth gained at least grade C in 8+ subjects; 10% in 5–7 subjects. *A-levels:* 6% upper sixth passed in 4 subjects; 85% in 3; and 9% in 2 subjects; in addition lower sixth pupils take A-levels if considered able. Average UCAS points 22.7.
University and college entrance 93% of 1995 sixth-form leavers went on to a degree course (20% after a gap year); others typically go on to employment in eg the City. Of those going on to university, 12% went to Oxbridge; 15% took courses in medicine, dentistry and veterinary science, 25% in science and engineering, 5% in law, 45% in humanities and social sciences, 5% in art and design, 5% in vocational subjects.
Curriculum GCSE and A-levels. 24 subjects offered (no A-level general studies but GCSE taken by all sixth-form; Japanese available). *Vocational:* Work experience available; also City & Guilds course in basic competence in IT. *Computing facilities:* 2 computer teaching rooms (40 Acorn Risc PC) plus network with computers available in all senior classrooms. 110 computers around the school. *Special provision:* EFL specialist: assessment and teaching programme in place. *Europe:* French and German offered at GCSE and A-level; also courses in Dutch and London Chamber of Commerce courses (elementary, beginners and advanced) in French, German and Spanish. Regular exchanges (France and Germany). Some French and German pupils in sixth-form.
The arts (Pupils aged 11 and over) *Music:* Over 30% of pupils learn a musical instrument; instrumental exams can be taken. Some 15 musical groups including orchestras, swing band, chapel choir, symphonic wind band, rock groups. National Chamber Music for Schools finals; 1 member of National Youth Orchestra; 1 LRSM diploma in recorder; Havering Young Musician of the Year. *Drama & dance*: Drama offered and GCSE and A-level may be taken. Majority of pupils are involved in school

productions and house/other productions. Pupils recently cast in TV and film (Jeeves and Wooster, Young Indiana Jones). *Art:* On average, 25 take GCSE, 10 A-level. Design, pottery, photography also offered.

Sport, community service and clubs (Pupils aged 11 and over) *Sport and physical activities:* Compulsory sports: soccer, cricket, cross-country, athletics, swimming, basketball, tennis, gymnastics. Optional: hockey, rugby, badminton, shooting, archery, netball. BAGA exams may be taken. Successes in all sports, many at national level. *Community service:* Pupils take bronze, silver and gold Duke of Edinburgh's Award. Community service optional. Large Scout troop (boys and girls); county records for Queen's Scouts awards. *Clubs and societies:* Up to 30 clubs, eg chess, philately, astronomy, arts appreciation, model, drama, computer.

Uniform School uniform worn to 16; suits in the sixth-form.

Houses/prefects Competitive houses. Prefects, head boy, head of house and house prefects – appointed.

Religion All pupils attend Chapel but opting out possible on conscientious grounds.

Social Occasional joint musical functions with other schools. 8+ organised trips abroad or exchanges each year. Pupils allowed to bring own car/bike/motorbike to school. Meals self-service. School shop. No tobacco/alcohol allowed.

Discipline Pupils failing to produce homework once might expect a warning or additional work; those caught smoking cannabis on the premises could expect expulsion.

Boarding 40% share (2 or 3); 60% are in dormitories of 4–6. Houses, same as competitive houses. Resident qualified nurse. Central dining room. Pupils can provide and cook own food. Exeats every weekend. Visits to the local town allowed.

Former pupils Professor Bernard Williams; Michael Thomas CMG, QC (former Attorney General of Hong Kong); Ian Holm (actor).

• CHRIST COLLEGE (Brecon)

Christ College, Brecon, Powys LD3 8AG. Tel 01874 623359, Fax 01874 611478

• Pupils 341 • Boys 11–18 (Day/Board) • Girls 11–18 (Day/Board) • Upper sixth 70 • Termly fees £2430 (Day) £3135 (Board) • HMC • Enquiries to the Headmaster's Secretary, applications to the Headmaster

What it's like

Founded by Henry VIII in 1541, it has a magnificent site on the River Usk just to the north of the Brecon Beacons and a couple of minutes walk from the pleasant market town of Brecon. The college chapel is part of the original Dominican friary, as are the two dining halls. The school enjoys handsome and well-equipped modern buildings in beautiful grounds: all lie within a designated national park. During the last ten years, major developments and extensions have included a CDT centre, new teaching blocks and new boarding houses. Originally a boys' school, it is now becoming fully co-educational after many years' experience of a mixed sixth. Pupils of all faiths are accepted: the Anglican liturgy is used in services. Importance is attached to spiritual education. Academically sound with a reputation for good teaching; a small school with a large staff, the very favourable staff:pupil ratio is about 1:9. Academic results are good and almost all leavers go on to degree courses. Music is very strong, as are drama and art. Numerous societies and clubs cater for an extremely wide range of needs. Sports and games are very well organised and the college has a distinguished record in many, particularly rugby and cricket; many pupils have been selected for county and national representation. There is a large and vigorous CCF contingent and much emphasis is put on outdoor pursuits, leadership and self-reliance. A number of pupils take part in local community schemes and the college has had an impressive record in the Duke of Edinburgh's Award Scheme.

School profile

Pupils Age range 11–18; 341 pupils, 81 days (68 boys, 13 girls), 260 boarders (227 boys, 33 girls). Main entry ages 11, 13 and into the sixth. Some 3% are children of former pupils. *State school entry:* Most of intake at 11, 10% at 13.

Entrance Common Entrance and own exam used. Skill in sport, music, drama, chess, general knowledge an advantage. No religious requirements, but school is Anglican. 26 pa assisted places. 20 pa scholarships/bursaries (academic, music, all-rounder, sport), up

to 50%. Parents not expected to buy textbooks.
Parents 15+% in industry or commerce; 15+% doctors, lawyers etc. Up to 15% live within 30 miles; up to 15% live overseas.
Head and staff *Headmaster:* D P Jones, appointed in 1996. Educated at Midsomer Norton Grammar School and Cambridge (geography). Previously Head of Geography and 1st XV rugby coach at Downside and Head of Geography and Master i/c Rugby at Sherborne. Also A-level examiner in geography; played rugby for Bath. *Publications:* Hydrology (an A-level text-book). *Staff:* 35 full time, 3 part time. Annual turnover 8%. Average age 39.
Exam results In 1995, 53 pupils in fifth, 70 in upper sixth. *GCSE:* In 1995, 64% fifth gained at least grade C in 8+ subjects; 25% in 5–7; and 11% in 1–4 subjects. *A-levels:* 3% upper sixth passed in 4+ subjects; 75% in 3; 16% in 2; and 6% in 1 subject. Average UCAS points 18.4.
University and college entrance 95% of 1995 sixth-form leavers went on to a degree course (11% after a gap year); others typically go on to careers eg retailing or to art college. Of those going on to university, 4% went to Oxbridge; 4% took courses in medicine, dentistry and veterinary science, 40% in science and engineering, 51% in humanities and social sciences, 3% in art and design, 2% in music.
Curriculum GCSE and A-levels. 22 A-level subjects offered (including CDT, business studies, archaeology and AS-level general studies). 25% take science A-levels; 33% arts/humanities; 42% both. *Computing facilities:* Computer room (10 networked IBM compatibles); CAD in CDT, multi-media in careers. *Special provision:* EFL available; specialist tutor for mild dyslexia. *Europe:* French, German and Spanish at GCSE, AS and A-level; also Welsh GCSE and A-level. Regular exchanges (France). Number of European pupils in school.
The arts *Music:* Over 50% of pupils learn a musical instrument, and exams are taken. Some 10 musical groups including strings, choirs, orchestras, brass groups, wind group. 3 pupils recently represented the UK in a UNICEF CBS recording made in Poland;1 girl recently won vocal scholarship to RCM. *Drama & dance*: Both offered. Some pupils are involved in school productions and house/other productions. Recent production of A Comedy of Errors. *Art:* On average, 7 take GCSE, 1 AS-level, 5 A-level. Design, pottery, photography, silkscreen, sculpture, printmaking also offered.
Sport, community service and clubs *Sport and physical activities:* Compulsory sports (to 14): basketball, cricket, netball, tennis, volleyball, gymnastics, athletics, rugby, hockey, soccer, squash, badminton. Optional: swimming, canoeing, aerobics, sailing, climbing, golf, fencing, triathlon, horse-riding. GCSE and A-level PE may be taken. Several Welsh schoolboy caps in rugby and cricket. *Community service:* Pupils take bronze, silver and gold Duke of Edinburgh's Award. CCF compulsory for 2 years at age 13; community service for 1 year at age 16 and optional otherwise. *Clubs and societies:* Over 30 clubs, eg stage management, ornithology, science olympiad, calligraphy, railway modelling, Crusaders, shooting.
Uniform School uniform worn; some variations allowed in sixth.
Houses/prefects Competitive houses. Prefects, head boy/girl, head of house and house prefects – appointed by Head.
Religion Compulsory attendance at religious worship.
Social Joint music society with town; large choral society. CCF linked with local Army. Organised ski trips and exchange systems. Pupils allowed to bring own bike to school. Meals self-service. School shop and tuck shop. Sixth-form bar, no private drink or tobacco allowed.
Discipline Pupils failing to produce homework once would be expected to get it done by a deadline with extra work; any caught smoking cannabis on the premises might well be expelled.
Boarding 20%–25% have own study bedroom, 20%–25% share (with 1 other); 45%–50% are in dormitories of 6+. Houses, of approximately 60, same as for competitive purposes plus one junior house (11–13 years) and two girls' houses. Resident medical staff. Central dining room; tuck shop gives café-type service. Pupils can provide and cook snacks. 2 termly exeats plus half-term. Limited visits to local town allowed (number increasing with age).
Alumni association is run by R Whiting, Secretary, Charles, Crookes & Jones, 51 The Parade, Cardiff CF2 3AB.

Former pupils E P Silk (Clerk to the Energy Committee of the House of Commons); P R Watkins (film producer The War Game, Privilege); Wg Cdr R M Thomas (former leader of the Red Arrows); Rev Professor D P Davies (Deputy Principal, Lampeter); Roscoe Howells (author); Judge W L N Davies; His Honour Judge Robin David; Simon Hughes MP; Robert Ackerman and Andrew Lewis (rugby footballers); Clive Dytor (MC, Falklands); His Honour Judge D A Thomas; Jamie Owen (BBC newsreader); Barrie Stephens (chairman, Siebe plc).

• CHRIST'S HOSPITAL

Christ's Hospital, Horsham, West Sussex RH13 7LS. Tel 01403 252547, Fax 01403 255283
• Pupils 821 • Boys 11–18 (Board) • Girls 11–18 (Board) • Upper sixth 102 • Termly fees £0–£3433 per term means tested • HMC, SHA • Enquiries/application to the Admissions Officer, Tel 01403 211297

What it's like

Founded in 1552 by King Edward VI for children in need. In 1985 the boys' school at Horsham and the girls' at Hertford joined to form one co-educational boarding school. Originally the boys' school had moved out of London in 1902 and a complete new school was built on an estate of 1200 acres. The buildings and campus are splendid and facilities are first-rate, including a fine library and a purpose-built theatre. A new sports and social centre offers not only the finest facilities for the school, but also a chance to integrate with a wider community. It has been described as 'an extraordinary school for the children of ordinary people' and it is an apt description. Worship in the Anglican tradition is compulsory (within the 1944 Act) and the Chapel is central to the school life. The school is a well-run establishment with high standards of teaching and very good results. The staff:pupil ratio is about 1:9. Most pupils go on to degree courses each year, including Oxbridge. There is great strength in the music and drama departments. The school is famous for its marching and concert bands. Numerous dramatic entertainments are staged each year. Also very strong in games and sport. A wide variety of activities is available. The CCF has a big contingent and the scout group is very active.

School profile

Pupils Age range 11–18; 821 boarding pupils (504 boys, 317 girls). Main entry ages 11–12. Approx 5% are children of former pupils. (Most former pupils are prevented from entering their children because of income bar.)
Entrance Own entrance exam used. Oversubscribed. Music and drama skills looked at; no special religious requirements. Parents not expected to buy textbooks, uniform etc; extras means tested if not free. 80% of all costs are currently funded from the Hospital's endowments according to parental income which, in most cases, must not exceed £40,887 gross at date of entry. Many families pay nothing at all; only one in 48 pays full fee. The original charitable intention is still very strongly maintained. Children are assessed on grounds of need as well as ability.
Parents 30% live within 30 miles; very few live overseas.
Head and staff Head Master: Dr Peter Southern, appointed in 1996. Educated at Magdalen College School and at the universities of Oxford and Edinburgh (history). Previously Head Master of Bancroft's, Head of History at Westminster and taught at Dulwich and Malosa School, Malawi. Also Oxford and Cambridge Board A-level Awarder (1988), Reviser (1990). *Staff:* 86 full time, 40 part time. Annual turnover 6%. Average age 41.
Exam results Average size of upper fifth 120; upper sixth 100. *GCSE:* on average, 101 gain at least grade C in upper fifth in 8+ subjects; 13 in 5–7; 6 in 1–4 subjects. *A-levels:* 5 in upper sixth pass in 4 subjects; 73 in 3; 17 in 2; and 5 in 1 subject. Average UCAS points 21.4.
University and college entrance 96% of 1995 sixth-form leavers went on to a degree course (40% after a gap year); others typically go on to retake A-levels. Of those going on to university, 9% went to Oxbridge; 8% took courses in medicine, dentistry and veterinary science, 25% in science and engineering, 8% in law, 35% in humanities and social sciences, 10% in art and design, 6% vocational subjects eg physiotherapy, architecture.

Curriculum GCSE and A-levels (including GCSE drama and A-level archaeology and business studies). 15% take science/engineering A-levels; 50% take arts and humanities; 35% take a mixture. *Vocational:* Work experience available in England, France and Germany. *Computing facilities:* Micros and PCs in computer centre, all laboratories, departments and boarding houses. *Special provision:* for mild dyslexia. *Europe:* French, German and Russian offered to GCSE and A-level (French compulsory to GCSE, another language for one year); also non-examined continuation languages in sixth-form; Italian and Spanish offered occasionally. Regular exchanges (France and Germany). Many European visits (drama, history, archaeology, classics, music, sport).

The arts *Music:* Over 50% of pupils learn a musical instrument; instrumental exams can be taken. Some 25 musical groups including 3 orchestras, 6 choirs, choral society, marching, concert, symphonic, wind, show, jazz and other bands. Recently, saxophone quartet finalists in National Chamber Music for Schools competition; boy lead role in National Youth Music Theatre tour of America; marching band plays at international and Test matches, Twickenham and Lords; choir in broadcast with BBC Symphony Orchestra of Honegger's Joan of Arc; several CDs in preparation; national and European choir tours. *Drama & dance*: Both offered. GCSE drama may be taken. Majority of pupils are involved in school and house/other productions. Regular drama tours to Germany; former pupil actor in lead role in TV series; 6 student productions in 10 weeks including Romeo and Juliet and The Physicists; school theatre combines professional and student work in full programme accessible to general public. *Art:* On average, 25+ take GCSE, 13+ A-level. Pottery, textiles, printmaking, history of art (12 per year) also offered. 100% successful entry for art college.

Sport, community service and clubs *Sport and physical activities:* Compulsory sports: rugby, soccer, cricket, hockey (boys); netball, tennis, rounders (girls). Optional: tennis, swimming, squash, fencing, badminton, fives, judo, karate, aerobics, volleyball. RLSS exams may be taken. County rugby, hockey (boys and girls), netball and cricket representatives at several age groups. *Community service:* Pupils take bronze, silver and gold Duke of Edinburgh's Award. CCF and community service both optional for 4 years at age 14+; 50–100 actively involved: disabled sports club and day centre; Romanian community service project; work at primary and special schools locally and old people's home centre. Mixed Scout and Venture Scout units. *Clubs and societies:* Up to 15 clubs, eg chess, ecology, philately, golf, debating, natural history, photography, model railway, astronomy.

Uniform Distinctive school uniform worn throughout, provided by the school.

Houses/prefects Competitive houses. Prefects, head boy/girl, head of house and house prefects – appointed by Headmaster and/or housemaster/mistress.

Religion Chapel (C of E) compulsory.

Social Strong community service element. Organised trips abroad and exchange systems, heavily subsidised. Senior pupils allowed to bring own bike to school. Formal lunch (march in with school band), cafeteria system. School shop. No tobacco allowed; pupils over 17 may join sixth-form club and buy beer and wine.

Discipline Pupils failing to produce homework once might expect a warning. System of disciplinary or academic detentions and 'drills' (practical work) for less serious matters.

Boarding Senior houses; 25% have own study bedroom, 35% share, 40% in larger groups; juniors tend to be in groups/dormitories. Single-sex houses average 52, same as competitive houses. Resident qualified nurses; visiting doctors (male and female). Central dining room. Pupils can provide and cook own food. Regular leave weekends. Visits to local town allowed for over 14s.

Alumni association CH Club, c/o Hospital (President R C Poulton).

Former pupils John Snow; Stuart Holland; Lord Stewart; Keith Douglas; Air Cmdr E M Donaldson; Bryan Magee; Bernard Levin; Colin Davis; Barnes Wallis; Edmund Blunden; Michael Marland; Ruth Deech; Elizabeth Llewellyn-Smith.

• CHRISTIAN BROTHERS'

Christian Brothers' Grammar School, Glen Road, Belfast BT11 8NR. Tel 01232 615321, Fax 01232 600299

• Pupils 1200 • Boys 11–18 (Day) • Girls None • Upper sixth 165 • Termly fees None
• Enquiries/application to the Headmaster

What it's like

Founded in 1866, it has two sites: one in the centre of Belfast, the other in the suburbs. It is a Roman Catholic foundation but pupils of all faiths are admitted. Religious worship is encouraged. There is strong emphasis on hard work and academic excellence. Many go on to degree courses. Strong in art, music and drama. Vigorous participation in local community schemes. Irish or Ulster champions in several sports.

School profile

Pupils Age range 11–18; 1200 day boys. Main entry ages, 11 and into the sixth. 40% are children of former pupils. *State school entry:* 3% main intake, plus 10% to sixth.
Entrance Own selection procedure used. No special skills or religious requirements but school is a Catholic foundation. Parents not expected to buy text books.
Head and staff *Headmaster:* Rev Br Denis Gleeson, 8 years in post. Educated at St Mary's, Swords, Dublin, and Maynooth University (theology). Previously Head of Religious Education at Christian Brothers'. Also Chairman of Governors, Christian Brothers' Secondary School (Belfast). *Staff:* 71 full time, 2 part time. Annual turnover 4%. Average age 36.
Exam results On average, 176 pupils in upper fifth, 165 in upper sixth. *GCSE:* on average, the vast majority of upper fifth pupils gain at least grade C in 8+ subjects. *A-levels:* 7% upper sixth pass in 4+ subjects; 60% in 3; 20% in 2; and 13% in 1 subject.
University and college entrance 63% of sixth-form leavers go on to a degree course; others typically go on to non-degree courses or straight into careers. Of those going on to university, 5% took courses in medicine, dentistry and veterinary science, 30% in science and engineering, 61% in humanities and social sciences, 4% in art and design.
Curriculum GCSE and A-levels. 25 subjects offered. 40% take science A-levels; 38% arts/humanities; 23% both. *Vocational:* Work experience available. *Computing facilities:* 2 RM Nimbus networks, 2 Apple Macintosh networks, 4 stand alone Apple Macintosh, 9 stand-alone BBC micros. *Europe:* French, Irish, Italian and Spanish offered to GCSE, AS and A-level; also GCSE German. Language assistants in all 5 languages.
The arts *Music:* 15% of pupils learn a musical instrument; instrumental exams can be taken. 2 musical groups including orchestra. National finals of Traditional Music Competition. *Drama & dance*: Both offered. GCSE and A-level drama may be taken. Majority of pupils are involved in school productions and some in house/other productions. Pupils selected for BBC TV film. *Art:* On average, 30 take GCSE, 8 AS-level, 13 A-level. Design, pottery, textiles, photography, printing, computer graphics also offered.
Sport, community service and clubs *Sport and physical activities:* Compulsory sports: PE. Optional: football, hurling, water polo, athletics, skiing, basketball, swimming, weight training, badminton, handball, athletics, cross-country. GCSE may be taken. Irish champions at water polo; Ulster champions at football, hurling, skiing, cross-country. *Clubs and societies:* Up to 30 clubs, eg chess, debate, quiz, art, traditional music, computer, golf, Third World, PRISM, RAY, fishing.
Uniform School uniform worn except in the sixth.
Houses/prefects Prefects, head boy – elected. School council.
Religion Religious worship encouraged.
Social Peace and Reconciliation Inter Schools Movement (PRISM). Strong debating society – All-Ireland Champions many times. Organised trips to Western and Eastern Europe, USA and Canada. Pupils allowed to bring own car/bike/motorbike to school. Meals self-service. Senior pupils allowed tobacco, no alcohol.
Alumni association run by Mr P Cochrane, President, 287 Antrim Road, Belfast.
Former pupils The late Cardinal Conway; The Most Rev Dr P Walsh (Bishop of Down and Connor); Bernard Davey (BBC TV); Professor Vincent McBriarty (Trinity College Dublin); Professor John Larkin (Trinity College Dublin); Patrick Carville (Permanent Sec NI Department of Education); Professor Daniel McCaughan.

• CHURCHER'S

Churcher's College, Petersfield, Hampshire GU31 4AS. Tel 01730 263033, Fax 01730 231437

• Pupils 708 • Boys 4–18 (Day) • Girls 4–18 (Day) • Upper sixth 62 • Termly fees £870–£1665 (Day) • HMC • Enquiries/application to the Headmaster

What it's like

Founded in 1722 by Richard Churcher, an East India Company merchant, it opened in Petersfield and in 1881 moved to new buildings on the present site on the edge of the very pleasant market town. To the agreeable Victorian buildings have been added a number of modern extensions, and facilities are good. The school overlooks spacious grounds and gardens. It embraces a Christian ethos and religious studies is a compulsory part of the curriculum. A boys' school originally, it first accepted girls in 1980. A traditional, sound academic education is provided and results are good. Most leavers go on to degree courses. Music and drama are very strongly supported. A wide variety of sports and games is available and facilities for these are excellent. High standards are achieved and there have been many representatives at county level. Extra-curricular activities are well catered for and there is much emphasis on outdoor pursuits, including adventure training, canoeing, sailing and shooting. The school has a large CCF unit and a number of pupils take part in local community schemes.

School profile

Pupils Total age range 4–18; 708 day pupils (449 boys, 259 girls). Senior department 11–18, 574 pupils (371 boys, 203 girls). Main entry ages 11, 12, 13 and into sixth. *State school entry:* 40% main intake, plus 5% to sixth.

Entrance Common Entrance and own exam used. No special skills or religious requirements. Parents not expected to buy textbooks; other extras £80 maximum. 24 pa assisted places. Variable number of scholarships/bursaries up to half fees.

Head and staff *Headmaster:* G W Buttle, 8 years in post. *Staff:* 51 full time, 21 part time. Annual turnover 5%. Average age 36.

Exam results In 1995, 92 pupils in upper fifth, 62 in upper sixth. *GCSE:* In 1995, 82 upper fifth gained at least grade C in 8+ subjects; 10 in 5–7 subjects. *A-levels:* 2 upper sixth passed in 4+ subjects; 56 in 3; 4 in 2 subjects. Average UCAS points 19.7.

University and college entrance 90% of 1995 sixth-form leavers went on to a degree course (20% after a gap year); others typically go on to HND and vocational courses. Of those going on to university, 4% went to Oxbridge; 5% took courses in medicine, dentistry and veterinary science, 40% in science and engineering, 5% in law, 40% in humanities and social sciences, 3% in art and design, 8% in vocational subjects eg nursing, music, equine studies, food marketing.

Curriculum GCSE and A-levels (no A-level general studies). 16% take science A-levels; 39% arts/humanities; 45% both. *Vocational:* Work experience available; also RSA qualification in CLAIT. *Computing facilities:* Archimedes Econet System, Amstrad PCs. *Europe:* French, German and Spanish offered to GCSE and A-level (French compulsory from age 11); also a business language course in sixth. Regular exchanges and visits (France, Germany and Spain). German nationals as pupils in sixth-form. French and German language assistants.

The arts *Music:* About 50% of pupils learn a musical instrument; instrumental and singing exams can be taken. Musical groups include orchestra, string orchestra, wind, training, jazz bands, clarinet groups, recorder consort, choirs etc. 3 members of Hampshire Youth Orchestra/Training Orchestra. *Drama & dance*: Drama GCSE is offered. Some pupils are involved in school productions and majority in house/other productions. *Art:* On average, 35 take GCSE, 1 AS-level, 6 A-level. Design, pottery, photography also offered. 3 commended and 2 highly commended certificates at Petersfield arts and crafts exhibition.

Sport, community service and clubs *Sport and physical activities:* Compulsory sports: rugby, hockey, cricket, rounders, netball. Optional: football, badminton, table tennis, tennis, swimming, basketball, cross-country. Sixth form only: squash. A-level may be taken. County representatives at netball, rugby, cricket, hockey and swimming. *Community service:* Pupils take either Duke of Edinburgh's Award (bronze, silver, gold), CCF or community service for 2 years at age 14+. *Clubs and societies:* Up to 15 clubs, eg chess, bridge, desk-top publishing, electronics, computers, karate, photography, debat-

ing, drama, model cars, war games, karate, debating, bookworms, adventure clubs (expeditions, walking and cycling).
Uniform School uniform worn, modified in sixth.
Houses/prefects Competitive houses. Prefects, head boy/girl, head of house and house prefects – appointed by the Headmaster.
Religion Religious worship encouraged.
Social Exchanges and visits to France, Germany, Spain and Austria, plus ski trips and cultural tours. Sixth-form pupils allowed to bring own car/bike to school. Meals self-service. School shop. No tobacco/alcohol allowed.
Discipline Pupils failing to produce homework once might expect a detention; those involved with drugs could expect immediate expulsion.
Alumni association is run by Old Churcherians Society President, Mr G W Buttle, c/o the school.

• CITY OF LONDON (Boys)

City of London School, Queen Victoria Street, London EC4V 3AL. Tel 0171 489 0291
• Pupils 850 • Boys 10–18 (Day) • Girls None • Upper sixth 125 • Termly fees £1944 (Day)
• HMC • Application to the Admissions Secretary

What it's like

The original foundation dates from 1442. The first school building opened in 1837 and the school moved to its present brand-new and very fine buildings in 1986. These occupy a superb riverside site, near Blackfriars with St Paul's vista as the eastern boundary. The new buildings are outstandingly well equipped and comfortable in every respect. The playing fields are at Grove Park. A very high standard of academic excellence is aimed at and achieved. Almost all leavers go on to degree courses, very large numbers to Oxbridge (also to medical schools: the study of medicine is a vigorous tradition). There is also a strong tradition of musical excellence (the choristers of the Temple Church and the Chapel Royal, St James's, are all pupils). Drama and art also flourish. Sport and games are compulsory and standards are high. A substantial commitment to local community schemes.

School profile

Pupils Age range 10–18; 850 day boys. Main entry ages 10, 11, 13 and into sixth. *State school entry:* 70% main intake, plus 80% to sixth.
Entrance Own entrance exam used. No special skills or religious requirements. Parents not expected to buy textbooks. 25 pa assisted places. 25 pa scholarships (academic, music) up to 50% fees. Choral bursaries, two-thirds fees.
Head and staff *Headmaster:* Roger Dancey, appointed 1995. Educated at Lancing and Exeter University (economic history and government). Previously Headmaster at King Edward VI Camp Hill School for Boys. *Staff:* 80 full time, 5 part time. Annual turnover 3%.
Exam results In 1995, 133 pupils in upper fifth, 119 in upper sixth. *GCSE:* In 1995, 128 upper fifth gained grade C or above in 8+ subjects; 4 in 5–7 subjects. *A-levels:* 17 upper sixth passed in 4+ subjects; 98 in 3; 2 in 2; and 1 in 1 subject. Average UCAS points 25.3.
University and college entrance 98% of 1995 sixth-form leavers went on to a degree course (25% after a gap year); others typically go on to employment. Of those going on to university, 20% went to Oxbridge; 13% took courses in medicine, dentistry and veterinary science, 11% in science and engineering, 7% in law, 39% in humanities and social sciences, 3% in art and design, 19% in other subjects eg accountancy, architecture, computer science.
Curriculum GCSE and A-levels. 20 subjects offered, including Japanese; no A-level general studies. *Vocational:* Work experience available. *Computing facilities:* Some 80 machines either in computer centre or spread around the departments. *Special provision:* Facility for wheelchair pupils. *Europe:* French, German, Russian and Spanish offered to GCSE and A-level. Regular exchanges (Germany and France).
The arts *Music:* Up to 50% of pupils learn a musical instrument; instrumental exams can be taken. Some 10 musical groups including orchestra, wind band, string ensemble, choirs. Recent organ scholarship to Cambridge, piano scholarship to RAM. *Drama &*

dance: Drama offered and GCSE may be taken. Some pupils are involved in school and house/other productions. *Art:* On average, 20 take GCSE, 5 A-level. Pottery, history of art, printmaking, sculpture also offered.
Sport, community service and clubs *Sport and physical activities:* Compulsory sports: rugby, soccer, cricket, athletics, swimming. Optional: fencing, squash, karate, badminton, table tennis, sailing, real tennis, hockey, cross-country, water polo, basketball, golf, tennis. RLSS exams may be taken. National representatives at badminton, fencing; regional, water polo; county, water polo, hockey, fencing, badminton, cross-country. *Community service:* Pupils take bronze, silver and gold Duke of Edinburgh's Award. CCF and community service both optional for 1 year at age 14. Fund-raising for charity: £30,000 raised in 1995. *Clubs and societies:* Over 30 clubs, eg BAYS, bridge, Christian, Dr Who, Interact, Jewish, law, economics, politics, railways, science.
Uniform School uniform worn except in the sixth, when suits are worn.
Houses/prefects Competitive houses. Prefects, head boy, head of house and house prefects – elected. School Council.
Religion No compulsory worship.
Social Several joint functions with City of London (Girls). Organised trips and an exchange with a school in Hamburg. Pupils allowed to bring own bike to school. Meals self-service. No tobacco/alcohol allowed.
Discipline Inclining to the traditional; pupils failing to produce homework might expect detention; use of drugs could lead to expulsion.
Alumni association is run by G A Coulson, 11 Mapleton Close, Bromley, Kent.
Former pupils H H Asquith; Kingsley Amis; Denis Norden; Mike Brearley.

• CITY OF LONDON (Girls)

City of London School for Girls, Barbican, London EC2Y 8BB. Tel 0171 628 0841, Fax 0171 638 3212
• Pupils 660 • Boys None • Girls 7–18 (Day) • Upper sixth 80 • Termly fees £1698 (Day) • GSA
• Enquiries/application to the Admissions Secretary

What it's like

Founded in the City in 1894, it is on a single-site with some open spaces. A very well-equipped establishment in the attractive and stimulating Barbican. Strong academically, results are very good. Almost all leavers go on to degree courses, including a high percentage to Oxbridge. The music and art departments are especially strong. The majority of the school is involved in music and drama and there are many opportunities for pupils to perform to national audiences. There is a good range of clubs and societies. Being in the Barbican there are numerous opportunities for trips to the theatre, art galleries and museums. The Corporation of London provides further opportunities for girls to participate in a variety of civic functions.

School profile

Pupils Total age range 7–18; 660 day girls. Senior department 11–18, 550 girls. Main entry ages 7, 11 and into sixth. Less than 1% are children of former pupils. *State school entry:* 40% main senior intake, 20% to sixth.
Entrance Own entrance exam used. No special skills or religious requirements. Parents not expected to buy textbooks. 20 pa assisted places. Scholarships up to full fees, at least 4 pa at 11+ and 1 pa at 16; 1 scholarship joint with Guildhall School of Music and Drama; one leaving scholarship; bursaries available to older pupils in financial need.
Head and staff *Headmistress:* Dr Yvonne Burne, appointed 1995. Educated at Redland High and Westfield College, London (French and German). Previously Headmistress at St Helens, Northwood, Head of Modern Languages and Careers at Northwood College, Head of German and Careers at Lowlands Sixth Form College (mixed) and teacher of French and German at Harrow County School for Girls. Also FRSA; member of Hillington Family Health Service Authority. *Publications:* Children's stories and articles for children's magazines. Has been sponsoring editor for UK and US educational publishing houses. *Staff:* 64 full time, 9 part time.
Exam results In 1995, 78 pupils in upper fifth, 79 in upper sixth. *GCSE:* in 1995, 77 upper fifth gained at least grade C in 8+ subjects. *A-levels:* 13 upper sixth passed in 4+ subjects; 63 in 3; and 2 in 2 subjects. Average UCAS points 24.2.
University and college entrance Over 99% of 1995 sixth-form leavers went on to a

degree course (40% after a gap year), 18% to Oxbridge; 10% took courses in medicine, dentistry and veterinary science, 12% in science and engineering, 6% in law, 40% in humanities and social sciences, 6% in art and design, 9% in vocational subjects eg osteopathy, business studies

Curriculum GCSE and A-levels. 22 subjects offered, including history of art; no A-level general studies. 21% take science A-levels; 35% arts/humanities; 45% both. *Vocational:* Work experience available; also RSA Stage 1 in CLAIT. *Computing facilities:* 2 computer rooms with Archimedes network. Whole school networked with PCs, access to CD-Rom and to the Internet. *Special provision:* No special teaching but cooperation with extra-mural specialists. *Europe:* French and German offered at GCSE, AS and A-level; also Russian and Spanish GCSE and A-level, and Italian in sixth-form. Over 25% take GCSE in more than 1 language. Exchanges: Regular exchanges for pupils to France and Germany.

The arts *Music:* Up to 50% of pupils learn a musical instrument; instrumental exams can be taken. Some 12 musical groups including 3 orchestras, 3 choirs, chamber choir, chamber ensembles etc. Recording with LSO under Richard Hickox; BBC Ascension Day Broadcast; Barbican Concert. *Drama & dance*: Drama offered; A-level, LAMDA, and Guildhall exams may be taken. Many of pupils are involved in school productions and some in other productions. Girls occasionally take part in RSC productions and TV series. *Art:* On average 27 take GCSE, 8 A-level. 3D design, pottery, textiles, sculpture also offered. Many students go on to leading art schools or related university courses, some going on to become successful artists and designers.

Sport, community service and clubs *Sport and physical activities:* Compulsory sports: netball, gym, swimming (years 1–3); volleyball, basketball, badminton (year 3–5). *ptional:* hockey, multi-gym, aerobics, aqua-aerobics. BAGA, RLSS exams may be taken. 1 member of national volleyball squad; regional gym medallists; regional fencing team champions. *Community service:* Pupils take bronze, silver and gold Duke of Edinburgh's Award. Community service compulsory for 1 year at age 16+. *Clubs and societies:* Up to 15 clubs, eg sports, design and technology, debating, maths, theatre, computer, textiles.

Uniform School uniform worn except in the sixth.

Houses/prefects No competitive houses or prefects. Head girl – nominated and elected by staff and sixth-form. School Council.

Religion Daily act of worship for all.

Social Joint concerts, theatrical productions, and occasional social activities with City of London (Boys). Organised exchanges to France/Germany, trips to eg, Italy and Greece. Meals self-service. No tobacco/alcohol allowed.

Discipline Pupils failing to produce homework once might expect a warning and firm deadline; those caught smoking cannabis on the premises could expect expulsion.

Alumni association CLOGA, c/o the school.

Former pupils Anne Farrell (actress); Claire Rayner (author); Katharine Dyson (D'Oyly Carte); Elizabeth Emmanuel (dress designer).

• CITY OF LONDON FREEMEN'S

City of London Freemen's School, Ashtead Park, Ashtead, Surrey KT21 1ET. Tel 01372 277933, Fax 01372 276165

• Pupils 725 • Boys 7–18 (Day/Board/Weekly) • Girls 7–18 (Day/Board/Weekly) • Upper sixth 60 • Termly fees £2046 (Day) £3189 (Board) £3092 (Weekly) • HMC, SHMIS • Enquiries/application to the Headmaster

What it's like

Founded in 1854, it moved to Ashtead Park in 1926 where it stands in 57 acres of splendid parkland, playing fields and woodlands, between Epsom and Leatherhead. The main building is a magnificent 18th-century house; conversion and modernisation have provided good facilities, including a sports hall complex. A major redevelopment of the senior school is underway. About 5% of parents have taken out Freedom of the City and about 40% of the pupils have siblings at the school (it was founded as a co-educational school). Thus, with its Foundation, Corporation patronage and City connections the school has a flourishing family and community element. The declared aims are to promote the spiritual, academic and social development of all to the fullest extent in an atmosphere of hard work, self-criticism, loyalty and enthusiasm. A sound general education is provided and results are very good. Most sixth-form leavers go on to degree courses, including Oxbridge. The school is strong in music and drama. The art department is also flourishing. A good range of sports and games is available and high standards are achieved (many county and national representatives). There are many clubs and societies for extra-curricular activities, of which one of the most popular is the Duke of Edinburgh's Award Scheme in which the school has a remarkable record of successes. There is also active commitment to local community services in the parish among the senior pupils.

School profile

Pupils Total age range 7–18; 725 pupils, 685 day (307 boys, 378 girls), 40 boarders (20 boys, 20 girls). Senior department, age range 13–18, 408 pupils (216 boys, 192 girls). Main entry ages 7, 13 and into sixth. 2% are children of former pupils. *State school entry:* 30% of intake at 7, 10% main intake at 13, plus 10% to sixth.
Entrance Common Entrance and own entrance exam used. Any and all special skills looked for at entry. No religious requirements; school is inter-denominational with C of E affiliation. 5 pa assisted places at 11. Scholarships, 25+ pa (funded by Corporation of London) up to half tuition fees. Approx 25 bursaries, £200–£3000 pa.
Parents 60+% live within 10 miles; up to 10% live overseas.
Head and staff *Headmaster:* D C Haywood, in post for 9 years. Educated at Nottingham High (Boys) and Cambridge (geography). Previously Second Master at Dauntsey's, Head of Geography at King Edward's (Birmingham) and Assistant Geography Teacher at Brentwood. *Staff:* 70 full time, 25 part time (incl music). Annual turnover 4–5%. Average age 37.
Exam results On average, 90 pupils in upper fifth, 60 in upper sixth. *GCSE:* 80 upper fifth gain at least grade C in 8+ subjects; 9 in 5–7; and 1 in 1–4 subjects. *A-levels:* 39 upper sixth pass in 4+ subjects; 13 in 3; 5 in 2; and 3 in 1 subject. Average UCAS points 20.4 (including general studies, 26.3).
University and college entrance 90% of 1995 sixth-form leavers went on to a degree course (12% after a gap year); others typically go on to foundation courses or into careers. Of those going on to university, 7% went to Oxbridge; 15% took courses in medicine, dentistry and veterinary science, 25% in science and engineering, 50% in humanities and social sciences, 5% in art and design, 2% in music.
Curriculum GCSE, AS and A-levels. 21 GCSE subjects offered; 8 at AS-level; 20 at A-level (including general studies). 45% take science A-levels; 24% arts/humanities; 31% both. *Vocational:* Work experience available. *Computing facilities:* Computing laboratories (junior and 2 senior) plus computers in various departments, boarding houses etc. *Special provision:* Limited individual support for young dyslexic pupils; mildly visually handicapped supported. *Europe:* French and German (taught from age 9) and Spanish offered to GCSE, AS and A-level. Regular exchanges (France and Germany). European pupils often boarders in lower sixth.
The arts *Music:* Over 30% of pupils learn a musical instrument; instrumental exams can be taken. Some 20+ musical groups including orchestras, choirs, wind, jazz bands, saxophone quartet, chamber music groups. About 10 exhibitioners annually for London colleges Saturday teaching; regular winners Chamber Music for Schools competition different classes; senior orchestra and choir Prague concert tour 1995; chamber music group concert tour Germany 1992; wind band to Denmark 1994. *Drama & dance*: Drama offered. GCSE drama and A-level theatre studies, Poetry Society exams may be taken. Majority of pupils are involved in school and house/other productions. Senior production 1995 Kafka's The Trial; musical (every 2 years), Jesus Christ Superstar. Many pupils in outside theatrical/music productions locally, some regularly in TV series. *Art:* On average, 26 take GCSE, 11 A-level. Design, pottery, textiles, photography also offered. Regular successes in local competitions.
Sport, community service and clubs *Sport and physical activities:* Compulsory sports: rugby, cricket, athletics, swimming (boys); hockey, tennis, athletics, swimming (girls). Fifth and sixth-form only: squash, badminton, golf, basketballl, netball. Numerous county, some national honours including: hockey, 15 girls in county squads, county champions U18, U16; rugby, England Schools U16 and U18 international, boys in county squads; cricket, boys in county squads; county swimming and athletics honours, etc. *Community service:* Pupils take bronze, silver and gold Duke of Edinburgh's Award.

Community service optional, all ages. *Clubs and societies:* Up to 30 clubs, eg debating, engineering, Christian Union, karate, fencing, computer, art, drama, Young Investigators, chess, other sports.
Uniform School uniform worn throughout.
Houses/prefects Competitive houses. Prefects, head boy/girl, head of house and house prefects – appointed by Head after consultation with staff and pupils. School Council.
Religion Morning assembly daily.
Social Organised trips abroad and exchange systems. Pupils allowed to bring own car/bike/motorbike to school. Meals self service. No tobacco/alcohol allowed.
Discipline Pupils failing to produce homework once might expect a detention; those caught smoking or bringing cannabis on the premises could expect expulsion.
Boarding 15% have own study bedroom. Single-sex houses, of up to 30, whole age range. Resident qualified nurse, GP local. Central dining room. Flexible weekend exeats. Visits to local town allowed, mainly in the sixth.
Alumni association is run by Mr Alastair Law, c/o the school.

• CLAIRES COURT

Claires Court School, Ray Mill Road East, Maidenhead, Berkshire SL6 8TE. Tel 01628 411470, Fax 01628 411466

• Pupils 805 • Boys 2½–18 (Day) • Girls 2½–18 (Day) • Upper sixth 35 • Termly fees £1700 (Day) • ISAI • Enquiries/application to the Registrar

What it's like

Founded in 1960 as a prep school. A secondary department (13–16) was added in 1977 and a sixth-form in 1994. It now comprises 3 establishments: the senior boys' school is sited in the middle of Maidenhead not far from Boulter's Lock, the junior boys are at Ridgeway on an open site to the west of the town, while the girls' school is at Maidenhead College, also in the town. Academic standards are good and GCSE results credible. Music, drama and art are well supported. A fair range of sports and games (including sailing and rowing on the Thames, and judo). Community work and the Duke of Edinburgh's Award Scheme are popular.

School profile

Pupils Total age range 2½–18; 805 day pupils, 550 boys, 255 girls. Senior department 11–18, 370 pupils, 280 boys, 90 girls. Main entry ages 2½, 11 and into sixth. *State school entry:* 30% of intake at 11, plus 10% to sixth.
Entrance Common Entrance and interview used. All skills appreciated (particularly sport, music,drama); no religious requirements (25% pupils Catholic but all denominations represented). Parents expected to buy textbooks from Year 9. Scholarships, 10 pa at age 11, 12, 13 and sixth-form, £400–£1600 pa.
Head and staff *Headmaster:* James Wilding, 15 years in post. Educated at Douai and Leicester University (biology and psychology). Previously Second Master and Science Master at Claires Court. Also Member of Executive Council and Area Co-ordinator London West of ISAI. *Staff:* 51 full time, 34 part time. Annual turnover 5%. Average age 42.
Exam results In 1995, 50 pupils in Year 11; upper sixth expected to be 35 (new sixth-form). *GCSE:* In 1995, 59% of Year 11 gained at least grade C in 8+ subjects; 20% in 5–7 subjects.
Curriculum GCSE, AS and A-levels. 20 GCSE subjects offered, 18 at A-level (including general studies A-level). 30% upper sixth taking science A-levels; 30% arts/humanities; 40% both. *Vocational:* Work experience available. *Computing facilities:* RM network throughout 3 school sites. Research machines in IT room. CD-Rom in library and 2 internet PCs. *Special provision:* Qualified teachers give individual help to dyslexics. ESL help. *Europe:* French (compulsory from age 7), German, Italian and Spanish offered to GCSE; also French, German and Spanish AS-level and French A-level. Regular exchanges (France, Germany and Belgium). Twinned with Belgian and French schools. European studies taught in Year 9.
The arts (Pupils aged 11 and over) *Music:* Over 15% of pupils learn a musical instrument; instrumental exams can be taken. Some 5 musical groups including

orchestra, choir, jazz band and rock group. Pupils involved in Maidenhead secondary school music festival and East Berks Music Centre. *Drama & dance*: Drama offered and GCSE and A-level may be taken; dance offered for girls. All pupils may be involved in school productions. National ISAI best actor and best senior play, 1993 and 1994. *Art:* On average, 30% take GCSE; 20% expected to take A-level. Design also offered.
Sport, community service and clubs (Pupils aged 11 and over) *Sport and physical activities:* Compulsory sports (to age 13): rugby, soccer, cricket, athletics, swimming (boys); netball, hockey, swimming (girls). Additional options: rowing, sailing, tennis, badminton, basketball, judo, archery. Sixth formers are members of local health and fitness facilities. GCSE and A-level sports studies and RYA may be taken. Competes nationally in rowing and sailing, finalists in ARA National Championships every year; county representatives in cricket, rugby, athletics, tennis, hockey and netball. *Community service:* Pupils take bronze, silver and gold Duke of Edinburgh's Award. *Clubs and societies:* 20 clubs eg public speaking, electronics, photography, hovercraft.
Uniform School uniform worn except in sixth.
Houses/prefects Competitive houses. Prefects, head boy/girl – appointed by Head after consultation with staff and pupils. Year group councils.
Religion Morning assembly compulsory.
Social Boys' and girls' schools combine for public speaking, drama and music. Exchanges with Belgium, France and Germany; annual ski and canoeing trips. Pupils allowed to bring own car/bike/motorbike to school. Meals self-service. No tobacco/alcohol allowed.
Discipline Pupils failing to produce homework once might expect to complete it by the next lesson; those caught smoking on the premises could expect expulsion.
Alumni association is run by Mrs Rosemary Barker, c/o the school.

• CLAYESMORE

Clayesmore School, Iwerne Minster, Blandford Forum, Dorset DT11 8LL. Tel 01747 812122, Fax 01747 811343

• Pupils 283 • Boys 13–18 (Day/Board) • Girls 13–18 (Day/Board) • Upper sixth 39 • Termly fees £2610 (Day) £3730 (Board) • SHMIS • Enquiries/application to the Headmaster

What it's like

Founded in 1896, Clayesmore was formerly in London, Pangbourne and near Winchester. In 1933 it moved to its present site, the former seat of Lord Wolverton on the edge of the picturesque village of Iwerne Minster. The impressive house has large gardens and a 62-acre estate, surrounded by beautiful Dorset countryside. Extensive modern additions, including a new floodlit synthetic grass pitch, provide first-rate facilities. The playing fields are on the estate. Chapel services are in the Anglican tradition. A boys' school originally, girls were first admitted in 1970. A staff:pupil ratio of about 1:10. Many sixth-form leavers go on to degree courses. Very active music, art and drama departments. A good reputation for sports and games (many representatives at county level). A lively CCF and considerable emphasis on outdoor pursuits for which the environment is ideal. Great commitment to local community services and an impressive record in the Duke of Edinburgh's Award Scheme.

School profile

Pupils Age range 13–18; 283 pupils, 70 day (40 boys, 30 girls), 213 boarding (132 boys, 81 girls). Main entry ages 13 and into sixth. Approx 3% are children of former pupils. About 40% of intake from own prep. *State school entry:* 10% main intake, plus 10% to sixth.
Entrance Common Entrance and own tests used. No special skills or religious requirements. Services are C of E but all denominations and faiths are welcome. Textbooks supplied, maximum extras £200. Up to 20 pa scholarships/bursaries including music and art, 5%–50% fees.
Parents 15+% in the armed services. 40+% live within 30 miles; 10+% live overseas.
Head and staff *Headmaster:* David Beeby, in post for 10 years. Educated at Tonbridge and Cambridge (history). Previously Housemaster and Head of History at Gresham's

and Assistant Master at Mill Hill and St Lawrence, Ramsgate. *Staff:* 26 full time, 6 part time. Annual turnover 15%. Average age 39.

Exam results In 1995, 64 pupils in fifth, 39 in upper sixth. *GCSE:* In 1995, 24 fifth gained at least grade C in 8+ subjects; 17 in 5–7; and 19 in 1–4 subjects. *A-levels:* 2 upper sixth passed in 4+ subjects; 27 in 3; 5 in 2; and 4 in 1 subject. Average UCAS points 14.9.

University and college entrance 85% of 1995 sixth-form leavers went on to a degree course (30% after a gap year); others typically go on to non-degree courses. 10% took courses in medicine, dentistry and veterinary science, 20% in science and engineering, 10% in law, 30% in humanities and social sciences, 5% in art and design, 25% in other subjects eg sport and leisure, music.

Curriculum GCSE and A-levels. 19 subjects offered, including ceramics, food and nutrition. 14% take science A-levels; 58% arts/humanities; 28% both. *Vocational:* Work experience available. *Computing facilities:* 24 IBM compatible PCs in computer teaching room. Computers in most departments. *Special provision:* Learning Support Centre catering for EFL and those with learning difficulties. *Europe:* French and German offered at GCSE, AS and A-level. Regular exchanges to France and Germany. Some 8 European pupils in school.

The arts *Music:* Up to 50% of pupils learn a musical instrument; instrumental exams can be taken. Some 8 musical groups including orchestras, choir, concert band, wind ensemble, Europa pops orchestra, barbershop etc. *Drama & dance*: Dance offered. LAMDA exams may be taken. Many pupils are involved in school and other productions. *Art:* On average, 20 take GCSE, 5 A-level. Design, pottery, textiles, photography also offered.

Sport, community service and clubs *Sport and physical activities:* Compulsory sports (initially): rugby, hockey, cricket; hockey, netball, tennis. Optional: soccer, squash, swimming, cross-country, badminton, judo, lacrosse, athletics, golf, sailing. RLSS exams may be taken. GB representatives at junior gymnastics and show-jumping; county representatives at rugby (U18), hockey (U16, U14), cricket (U15, U14, U13) and cross country. *Community service:* Pupils take bronze, silver and gold Duke of Edinburgh's Award. CCF compulsory for 2 years at age 14+. Community service optional. *Clubs and societies:* Up to 10 clubs, eg radio, basketball, fencing, debating etc.

Uniform School uniform worn except the sixth.

Houses/prefects Competitive houses. Prefects, head boy and girl, heads of house appointed by the Head.

Religion Church of England. Compulsory daily assembly service in chapel; longer service on Sunday.

Social Regularly and successfully involved in debating, public speaking and general knowledge competitions. Regular exchanges organised by modern languages department; visits abroad by games teams, choirs etc. Pupils allowed to bring own bike to school. Meals self-service. School shop. No tobacco allowed. Sixth-form bar twice a week.

Discipline Pupils failing to produce homework once should expect to repeat it or do additional work; those caught smoking cannabis on the premises will be expelled.

Boarding Most upper sixth have own study bedroom, lower sixth share. Single-sex houses of approx 55, same as competitive houses. Resident nurse. Central dining room. Pupils can provide and cook own food. Two regular weekend exeats each term, more can be requested. Visits to local town allowed once a week.

Alumni association Ms Jane Salkeld, Chairman of Old Clayesmorian Society, c/o the school.

• CLIFTON

Clifton College, 32 College Road, Clifton, Bristol BS8 3JH. Tel 0117 973 9187, Fax 0117 946 6826

• Pupils 630 • Boys 13–18 (Day/Board) • Girls 13–18 (Day/Board) • Upper sixth 135 • Termly fees £2810 (Day) £4050 (Board) • HMC • Enquiries/application to the Director of Admissions

What it's like

Founded in 1862, it became a prominent public school very quickly. It first accepted girls in 1987 and was the first of the great Victorian foundations to adopt co-education at all levels. It is fortunate in its situation above the city, on the edge of Clifton Downs and near open country. Its handsome buildings are neo-Tudor and neo-Gothic and stand in beautiful grounds. Much money has been spent and its facilities are exceptionally good; these include a large leisure development with three artificial pitches, a modern theatre and two superb libraries (as well as house libraries). An unusual feature is that one of the boarding houses is reserved for boys of Jewish faith. Religious worship is compulsory for Jews at their synagogue. Some Christian services are compulsory for others. It provides a thoroughly good and liberal education and results are very good. Of the leavers who go on to degree courses, a high proportion go to Oxbridge. Very strong indeed in music and the arts. A very high standard in games and sports (many national representatives). Unique in having a research scientist in residence. Numerous extra-curricular activities and a strong CCF. A big commitment to local community schemes and the Duke of Edinburgh's Award Scheme. Much use is made of Bristol's cultural amenities.

School profile

Pupils Age range 13–18; 630 pupils, 250 day (190 boys, 60 girls), 380 boarding (260 boys, 120 girls). Main entry ages 13 and into sixth. Approx 5% are children of former pupils. Clifton College Prep provides about 65% of intake. *State school entry:* 1% main intake plus 2% to sixth.

Entrance Common Entrance and own entrance exam used. No special skills or religious requirements. Parents expected to buy textbooks; £500 maximum extras. Assisted places available (awarded at age 8 and 11 in prep school, and at 16). 24 pa scholarships, bursaries, for academic, artistic, musical and all-round excellence, up to half-fees.

Parents 15+% are doctors, lawyers, etc; 15+% in industry or commerce. 30+% live within 30 miles; 15+% live overseas.

Head and staff *Headmaster:* Hugh Monro, in post for 5 years. Educated at Rugby and Cambridge (history and economics). Previously Headmaster at Worksop, Head of History and Housemaster at Loretto and Assistant History Master at Noble and Greenwich (USA) and Haileybury. Also Governor of three prep schools; member of Court of Bristol University. *Staff:* 70 full time, 8 part time. Annual turnover 4%. Average age 37.

Exam results In 1995, 122 pupils in fifth, 125 in upper sixth. *GCSE:* In 1995, 100 fifth gained at least grade C in 8+ subjects; 17 in 5–7 subjects. *A-levels:* 15% upper sixth passed in 4+ subjects; 68% in 3; 17% in 2 subjects. Average UCAS points 20.0.

University and college entrance 90% of 1995 sixth-form leavers went on to a degree course (20% after a gap year); others typically go on to non-degree courses (sports management, marketing), art or music colleges or into careers (eg family business, sevices). Of those going on to university, 20% went to Oxbridge; 5% took courses in medicine, dentistry and veterinary science, 35% in science and engineering, 45% in humanities and social sciences, 12% in art and design, 3% in music.

Curriculum GCSE and A-levels. 25 subjects offered (including A-level general studies; Italian, Chinese and other less used languages by request). 24% take science A-levels; 44% arts/humanities; 32% both. *Vocational:* Work experience for all lower sixth. *Computing facilities:* 2 rooms of 20 IBM compatibles plus many departmental computers, and one in each boarding house. *Europe:* French, German and Spanish offered at GCSE and A-level; also GCSE Italian. Extra language tuition on request. Exchanges: Regular exchanges to France, Germany, Spain, Argentina and Mexico. Some European students in sixth.

The arts *Music:* Up to 50% of pupils learn a musical instrument; instrumental exams can be taken. Some 10 musical groups including orchestra, wind, jazz bands, choirs, madrigal group. Members of National Youth Orchestra, local youth orchestras etc. *Drama & dance*: Drama offered; GCSE drama and A-level theatre studies may be taken. Some pupils are involved in school productions and majority in house/other productions. 14 pupil-directed plays a year. *Art:* On average, 20 take GCSE, 12 A-level. Design, pottery, textiles also offered. Exhibitions locally.

Sport, community service and clubs *Sport and physical activities:* A major sport compulsory for first year. Options: netball, hockey, soccer, cricket, rugby, rackets, fives, squash, tennis, rowing, swimming, fencing, athletics. National teams at cricket, rugby, rowing etc; British rackets champion. *Community service:* Pupils take bronze, silver and gold Duke of Edinburgh's Award. CCF voluntary; Community service is alaternative. *Clubs and societies:* Up to 30 clubs, eg chess, science, politics, green, Amnesty International, debating (Oxford Union finalists last 3 years).

Uniform School uniform worn throughout.
Houses/prefects Head of school, Prefects, head of house and house prefects – appointed by the Headmaster, after consultation.
Religion For Jewish pupils attendance at Synagogue is compulsory. For Christians some Chapel services are compulsory, others voluntary.
Social School debates, co-productions of plays, including modern language play, subject conferences with other local schools. Strong connection with, and organised trips to, earthquake-damaged school in Mexico City. Exchanges with France, Germany, Spain, Mexico, India, Pakistan and Japan. Meals self service. School stationery shop. No tobacco allowed; bar for over-17s.
Discipline Pupils failing to produce homework once might expect detention. Those caught smoking cannabis on the premises would have specific circumstances considered before disciplinary action taken, but should expect expulsion.
Boarding 25% have own study bedroom, 45% share with others; 30% are in study-bedrooms of 3–6. Single-sex houses of approximately 60. School doctor visits daily, two qualified nurses in sanatorium. Central dining room. Pupils can provide and cook own snacks. 2 Saturday night exeats plus half-term each term. Visits to the local town allowed with permission.
Alumni association is run by T C W Gover, Old Clifton Society, c/o the college.
Former pupils Clive Thomson (Rentokil): Peter Job (Reuters); Julian Richer (Richer Sounds); Lord (Clyde) Hewlett and Lord (Patrick) Jenkin (politicians); Sir Michael Redgrave; Trevor Howard; John Cleese; John Houseman and Simon Russell Beale (the stage); Sir David Willcocks and Joseph Cooper (music); Mark Tully, David Bonavia and Stephen Pile (the media).

• CLIFTON HIGH

Clifton High School, College Road, Clifton, Bristol, BS8 3JD. Tel 0117 973 0201, Fax 0117 923 8962, e-mail clifton@rmplc.co.uk

• Pupils 767 • Boys 3–11 only (Day) • Girls 3–18 (Day; Board/Weekly from age 16) • Upper sixth 60 • Termly fees £1425 (Day) £2720 (Board) £2585 (Weekly) • GSA • Enquiries/applications to the Headmistress

What it's like

Founded in 1877, it occupies a splendid site in the middle of the Georgian village of Clifton, near the Downs and the Suspension Bridge. The facilities and accommodation are first-class. Religious worship is non-denominational, and religious studies are taught until the age of 16. The school has a long-standing reputation for providing an excellent education and results are very good. Each year the majority of sixth-formers go on to degree courses, including Oxbridge. There are strong music, drama and creative arts departments involving a large number of pupils. There is also a good choice of games and sports (with representatives at county and national level). There is a great commitment to social services and the school has a good record in the Duke of Edinburgh's Award Scheme. Full use is made of Bristol's cultural amenities.

School profile

Pupils Total age range 3–18; 767 pupils, 744 day (91 boys, 653 girls), 23 boarding girls (boarding age 16 upwards only). Senior department 11–18, 415 girls. Main entry ages, 3, 7 (boys and girls), 10, 11 and into sixth (girls). Approx 10% are children of former pupils. *State school entry:* 35% intake at 11, plus 5% to sixth.
Entrance Own entrance exam used. Skills in sport, music and art welcomed; no religious requirements. Parents not expected to buy textbooks; extras include eg music tuition £111 per term. 23 pa assisted places; 10 pa scholarships available at 11, plus 10 pa for entry to sixth.
Parents 40+% are professional; 40+% in industry or commerce. Most live within 30 miles; up to 5% live overseas.
Head and staff *Headmistress:* Mrs Yvonne Graham, appointed 1996. Educated at Alex-Hegiusgymnasium, Holland, and the universities of Amsterdam and London (English and linguistics). Previously Headmistress of Lavant House School, and taught German and English at Loretto High, Dutch at Bedford College, linguistics at Queen's University,

and English at Ceciliengymnasium and at Prior's Field. *Staff:* 59 full time, 17 part time. Annual turnover 5%. Average age 35.
Exam results In 1995, 87 pupils in upper fifth, 52 in upper sixth. *GCSE:* In 1995, 81 upper fifth gained at least grade C in 8+ subjects; 5 in 5–7 subjects. *A-levels:* 6 upper sixth passed in 4+ subjects; 34 in 3; and 7 in 2 subjects. Average UCAS points 21.6.
University and college entrance 90% of 1995 sixth-form leavers went on to a degree course (10% after a gap year); others typically go on to FE colleges or take further A-levels. Of those going on to university, 10% went to Oxbridge; 7% took courses in medicine, dentistry and veterinary science, 20% in science and engineering, 7% in law, 25% in humanities and social sciences, 7% in art and design, 34% in eg business, drama, education, sports studies .
Curriculum GCSE and A-levels. 21 subjects offered, including Greek; no A-level general studies. 20% take science A-levels; 50% arts/humanities; 30% took both. *Vocational:* Work experience available. *Computing facilities:* 2 computer rooms (plus one in junior school), with multi-media and Internet link. *Europe:* French, German and Spanish offered to GCSE, AS and A-level (French compulsory from 7 to GCSE); also Italian to RSA. Regular exchanges to France, Germany and Spain.
The arts *Music:* Up to 50% of pupils learn a musical instrument; instrumental exams taken, also GCSE and A-level. Many musical groups including orchestra, wind bands, choirs, chamber groups. Variety of performances, choir tours. Drama & dance: Drama and dance offered. GCSE drama, A-level theatre studies. LAMDA exams may be taken. Many pupils are involved in school productions and house/other productions. *Art:* On average, 20+ take GCSE, 19 A-level. Pottery, textiles also offered.
Sport, community service and clubs *Sport and physical activities:* Compulsory sports: hockey, netball, tennis, swimming, athletics, rounders. Optional: basketball, volleyball, aerobics, fencing, squash, badminton. County representatives at athletics, cross-country, swimming, fencing, hockey, netball, tennis. *Community service:* Pupils take silver and gold Duke of Edinburgh's Award. Regular visits to elderly and Mencap; fund-raising through house activities. *Clubs and societies:* Up to 15 clubs, eg art, computer, debating, electronics, technology, gym, French, Christian Union.
Uniform School uniform worn except in the sixth.
Houses/prefects Competitive houses. Prefects, head girl, head of house and house prefects – appointed by staff and school. School Council.
Religion Non-denominational religious worship.
Social Debates, plays, choral performances with other local schools. Organised trips to France, Ireland, Mediterranean, Iceland, Switzerland, Germany. Meals self-service. Second-hand clothes shop. No tobacco/alcohol allowed.
Discipline Aims to encourage self-discipline by being firm and fair; those caught using drugs on the premises would be expelled.
Boarding for sixth-form only, who share bedrooms or have individual studies. Exeats most weekends. Visits to village allowed daily; Bristol centre at weekends.
Alumni association is run by Mrs J Anstee, 16 Bramble Drive, Sneyd Park, Bristol, BS9 3PE.
Former pupils Jo Durie; Mary Renault, Stephanie Cole.

• COBHAM HALL

Cobham Hall, Cobham, Kent DA12 3BL. Tel 01474 824319/823371, Fax 01474 822995

• Pupils 180 • Boys None • Girls 11–18 (Day/Board/Weekly) • Upper sixth 30 • Termly fees £2200–£2750 (Day) £4285 (Board/Weekly) • GSA, BSA, Round Square • Enquiries/application to the Registrar

What it's like

It opened as an independent public school for girls in 1962. It is a member of the Round Square and thus its aims are based on the pioneering ideals of Kurt Hahn. The main building was once the home of the Earls of Darnley, a very fine example of an Elizabethan country mansion which contains some work by Inigo Jones. It lies in a superb site of 150 acres of landscaped gardens and parkland in the countryside. There are modern extensions including a purpose-built activities centre. The house system operates and there is an efficient tutorial system. The school is international and interdenominational.

The staff:student ratio is a very favourable 1:5 and results are good. Most sixth-formers go on to degree courses. Music, drama and art play an important part in the life of the school. Sport and games are well catered for and standards are high. There is a plentiful range of extra-curricular activities. Many of the senior girls are involved in voluntary community services locally and help local organisations in their spare time; many participate in the Duke of Edinburgh's Award Scheme.

School profile

Pupils Age range 11–18; 180 girls, 20 day, 160 boarding. Main entry ages 11, 12, 13 and into sixth. *State school entry:* 1% intake.

Entrance Own entrance exam used. All-rounders looked for; no religious requirements. Parents not expected to buy textbooks; maximum extras £100. Assisted places at 11, 13 and sixth-form. 10 pa scholarships (including junior and sixth-form), 33%–100% fees.

Parents 15+% in industry or commerce. 10+% live within 30 miles; 10+% live overseas.

Head and staff *Headmistress:* Mrs Rosalind McCarthy, in post 7 years. Educated at Folkestone Girls' Grammar School and Leeds University (theology). Previously Head of Religious Studies and Head of House at Ashford and Head of Humanities at Brockhill and St Leonard's School (Hythe). Also member of GSA Council and its Boarding Committee, BSA Executive Committee and its Training Committee, Leney Trust Committee, ISIS Committee (SE Region). *Staff:* 36 full time, 15 part time. Average age 40.

Exam results In 1995, 39 pupils in upper fifth, 30 in upper sixth. *GCSE:* On average, 25% upper fifth gain at least grade C in 8+ subjects; 73% in 5–7 subjects. *A-levels:* 60% upper sixth pass in 3 subjects; 30% in 2 subjects. Average UCAS points 19.4.

University and college entrance 90% of 1995 sixth-form leavers went on to a degree course (20% after a gap year); others typically go on to at college. Of those going on to university, 10% went to Oxbridge; 5% took courses in medicine, dentistry and veterinary science, 9% in science and engineering, 5% in law, 59% in humanities and social sciences, 10% in art and design, 12% in other subects eg osteopathy, hotel management.

Curriculum GCSE and A-levels (no A-level general studies). 41% take science A-levels; 59% arts/humanities. *Computing facilities:* New computer department. *Special provision:* Dyslexic unit; EFL. *Europe:* French, German, Russian and Spanish offered at GCSE and A-level. Regular exchanges to France, Germany, Russia and Spain. Lectures, cultural festivals, foreign film club. 25 pupils from Europe in school.

The arts *Music:* Over 50% of pupils learn a musical instrument; instrumental exams can be taken. Musical groups include orchestra, choir, wind band. Regular concerts and music festivals. *Drama & dance*: Drama offered; also ballet and tap dancing as extras. GCSE theatre studies, A-level drama, RSA exams may be taken. Many pupils are involved in school productions. *Art:* On average, 22 take GCSE, 10 A-level. Design, photography also offered. Typically, 8 pa pupils accepted for art school.

Sport, community service and clubs *Sport and physical activities:* Sports (some compulsory): swimming, tennis, netball, hockey, volleyball, table tennis, cross-country, rounders, athletics, golf, dance, trampolining, gymnastics, yoga, aerobics, self defence, badminton, lifesaving, riding, weight training, skiing, judo. *Community service:* Pupils take bronze, silver and gold Duke of Edinburgh's Award. Community service optional; many take part in local community schemes. *Clubs and societies:* Clubs include computer, driving, cookery, pottery, toymaking, craft, languages, psychology, textiles, gymnastics.

Uniform School uniform worn except in sixth.

Houses/prefects Competitive houses. Head girl and deputy elected by school; head of house and house prefects. School council.

Religion All religions welcomed.

Social General knowledge quizzes, debates, joint musical productions, sixth-form dances and discos with other schools. Organised weekend activities. Dungeon Cafe run by girls. Trips to Russia, America, France, Spain, Italy, Egypt; exchanges with America, Switzerland, Germany, France, Spain, India. Senior pupils allowed to bring own bike to school. Meals self-service. School shop. No tobacco/alcohol allowed.

Discipline Firm discipline but not repressive. Pupils failing to produce prep might expect detention and work re-done at weekend under Headmistress's supervision (at discretion of staff concerned).

Boarding Sixth form have own study bedroom in separate houses. Other houses, of approx 30, mixed ages. Resident qualified nurse. Central dining room (seniors can provide and cook own food). 2–3 termly exeats. Visits to local town allowed at weekends.
Alumni association Cobham Hall Elders – Chairman: Mrs S Buchanan, Victoria Cottage, Wrotham Road, Meopham, Kent DA13 OAN.
Former pupils Jane How; Taryn Power; Ramina Power; Princess Mutawakkilah of Brunei; Mary-Ann Sieghart.

• COLERAINE

Coleraine Academical Institution, Castlerock Road, Coleraine, Londonderry BT51 3LA. Tel 01265 44331, Fax 01265 52632

• Pupils 850 • Boys 11–19 (Day/Board) • Girls None • Upper sixth 103 • Termly fees £905 (Day) £1200 (Board/Weekly EU residents) £2133 (Board/Weekly non-EU residents) • HMC • Enquiries/application to the Headmaster

What it's like

Founded in 1859, it is semi-rural and single-site in 70 acres of playing fields and grounds on the outskirts of Coleraine with a view over beautiful landscapes and the lower reaches of the River Bann. A well-run school with high academic standards, it aims to provide a full and thorough instruction in all branches of a liberal education. Results are good and many leavers go on to degree courses. Music and drama are strong departments. There is a good range of sports and games (many Ulster and Ireland representatives). A fair commitment to local community schemes and the Duke of Edinburgh's Award Scheme.

School profile

Pupils Age range 11–19; 850 boys, 790 day, 60 boarding. Main entry ages 11 and into sixth. Approx 25% are children of former pupils. *State school entry:* 95% main intake, plus 75% to sixth.
Entrance Very few admitted by Common Entrance. Above average IQ expected; no religious requirements. Parents not expected to buy textbooks; maximum other extras £25. Sons of clergymen given 10% reduction of fees.
Parents Up to 10% of boarders' parents live within 30 miles; 40+% live overseas.
Head and staff *Headmaster:* Robert Stanley Forsythe, in post for 12 years. Educated at Belfast High and Belfast University (chemistry). Previously Headmaster at Dungannon Royal and Head of Department at Portadown College and Armagh Royal School. *Staff:* 56 full time, 6 part time. Annual turnover 2%. Average age 45.
Exam results In 1995, 144 pupils in upper fifth, 103 in upper sixth. *GCSE:* In 1995, 85 upper fifth gained at least grade C in 8+ subjects; 42 in 5–7 subjects. *A-levels:* 10 upper sixth passed in 4+ subjects; 67 in 3; 12 in 2; and 11 in 1 subject. Average UCAS points 17.6.
University and college entrance 93% of 1995 sixth-form leavers went on to a degree course (1% after a gap year); others typically go on to HND courses or into the forces. Of those going on to university, 3% went to Oxbridge; 12% took courses in medicine, dentistry and veterinary science, 48% in science and engineering, 5% in law, 29% in humanities and social sciences, 5% in art and design, 1% in vocational subjects eg physiotherapy.
Curriculum GCSE and A-levels. 23 subjects offered (no A-level general studies). 47% take science A-levels; 21% arts/humanities; 32% both. *Vocational:* Work experience available. *Computing facilities:* Three networks. *Special provision:* EFL assistance. *Europe:* French, German and Spanish offered at GCSE and A-level; also non-examined French. Regular exchanges to France. European studies offered in sixth. Participation in talks/lectures presented in Northern Ireland.
The arts *Music:* Up to 25% of pupils learn a musical instrument; instrumental exams can be taken. 3 musical groups, orchestra, choir, popular. *Drama & dance*: Some pupils are involved in school productions and house/other productions. *Art:* On average 40 take GCSE, 15 A-level. Design, pottery, textiles, photography also offered.
Sport, community service and clubs *Sport and physical activities:* Compulsory sports: rugby in first year. Optional: cricket, athletics, swimming, cross-country, tennis, squash,

badminton, rowing, sailing, angling, canoeing. GCSE may be taken. Ulster and Irish successes in badminton, rugby, swimming, golf, cross-country, athletics, tennis, bridge. *Community service:* Pupils take silver and gold Duke of Edinburgh's Award. Community service optional. *Clubs and societies:* Up to 15 clubs, eg archery, rowing, bridge, chess.
Uniform School uniform worn throughout.
Houses/prefects Competitive houses. Prefects, head boy, head of house and house prefects – elected by staff and sixth-form.
Religion Religious worship is encouraged.
Social Joint schools' community service group, debating society with other local schools and girls assist in drama. Ski trip, modern language trip and rugby tour each year. Pupils allowed to bring own car to school. Meals self-service. School shop. No tobacco/alcohol allowed.
Discipline Pupils failing to produce homework once might expect to do it by the following day; those caught smoking cannabis could expect expulsion.
Boarding 70% have own study bedroom, 30% are in dormitories of 6+. Houses of 15–20, divided by age group. Resident qualified nurse. Central dining room. Pupils can provide and cook own food. 2 day exeats 3–5 times a term depending on term length. Visits to local town allowed.
Former pupils Air Marshal Sir George Beamish.

• COLFE'S

Colfe's School, Horn Park Lane, London SE12 8AW. Tel 0181 852 2283/4

• Pupils 970 • Boys 3–18 (Day) • Girls 3–6; 16–18 (Day) • Upper sixth 109 • Termly fees up to £1558 (Day) • HMC • Enquiries/application to the Registrar

What it's like

Founded in 1652 on a site below Blackheath. In 1964 it moved to Lee, in south-east London, to new purpose-built premises on a single urban site with 18 acres of pleasant grounds and playing fields. It retains strong links with the Leathersellers' Company and its official visitor is Prince Michael of Kent who takes a close interest in the school. Worship and religious instruction are encouraged (C of E foundation). A very good general and academic education is provided and results are very good. There is a tremendously strong music department involving a great many people, also much strength in drama and art. An excellent range of sports and games is available and high standards are attained. A good range of extra-curricular activities.

School profile

Pupils Total age range 3–18; 970 day pupils (920 boys, 50 girls). Senior department 11–18, 722 pupils (672 boys, 50 girls). Main entry ages 3–6 (boys and girls), 7–13 (boys) and into sixth (boys and girls). Approx 1% are children of former pupils. *State school entry:* 55% main intake at 11, plus 10% to sixth.
Entrance Common Entrance and own entrance exam used. Candidates who are strong academically and in sports and music looked for; no religious requirements. Parents not expected to buy textbooks; maximum £125 extras. 36 pa assisted places. 30 pa scholarships/bursaries, £750-half fees.
Head and staff *Headmaster:* Dr David J Richardson, 6 years in post. Educated at Reigate Grammar School and universities of Nottingham and Kent (economics). Previously Headmaster of Laxton and Housemaster at Rugby. *Staff:* 69 full time, 9 part time. Annual turnover minimal. Average age 36.
Exam results In 1995, 97 pupils in upper fifth, 109 in upper sixth. *GCSE:* In 1995, 73 upper fifth gained at least grade C in 8+ subjects; 20 in 5–7 subjects. *A-levels:* 22 upper sixth passed in 4+ subjects; 76 in 3; 9 in 2; and 2 in 1 subject. Average UCAS points 21.0.
University and college entrance 75% of 1995 sixth-form leavers went on to a degree course (1% after a gap year); others typically go on to non-degree courses or straight into careers. Of those going on to university, 10% went to Oxbridge; 2% took courses in medicine, dentistry and veterinary science, 28% in science and engineering, 2% in law, 66% in humanities and social sciences, 2% in art and design.
Curriculum GCSE, AS and A-levels. 18 subjects offered plus 6 AS-level. Pupils taking 2 or 3 A-levels also take AS-levels or extra GCSEs. 25% take science A-levels; 25% arts/

humanities; 50% both. *Computing facilities:* A network of 15 micro computers. *Special provision:* for mild dyslexia. *Europe:* French (compulsory for 3 years), German and Spanish offered to GCSE and A-level; also French and German AS-level. All pupils must study at least one foreign language for GCSE. Regular exchanges to Germany. Regular trips to France, including a stay with a French family.
The arts (Pupils age 11 and over) *Music:* Up to 25% pupils learn a musical instrument; instrumental exams can be taken. Musical groups including orchestra, choir, pop group, band, wind ensemble. Pupils in local youth orchestras. Some accepted to music colleges. *Drama & dance*: GCSE and A-level drama may be taken. Many pupils involved in school productions. *Art:* On average, 40 take GCSE, 20 A-level. Regular entrants to art college.
Sport, community service and clubs (Pupils age 11 and over) *Sport and physical activities:* Sports available: cricket, tennis, golf, swimming, football, rugby, squash, athletics, judo, sailing, hockey, netball, basketball, badminton, table tennis, windsurfing, cross-country, climbing, abseiling, canoeing, orienteering, and fell-walking. County representatives in rugby. *Community service:* Pupils take bronze, silver and gold Duke of Edinburgh's Award. ATC and community service optional. Also Barnardo's awards. *Clubs and societies:* Clubs include computer, technology, chess, crafts, badminton, comics, photography, art, Christian Union, modelling, war games and ski-training.
Uniform School uniform worn throughout.
Houses/prefects Competitive houses. Prefects and head boy/girl – appointed by the Head and staff .
Religion Attendance at worship encouraged.
Social Occasional large-scale choral productions with other schools. Organised trips to France, Germany, USA, Russia, Egypt, Romania, Switzerland. Some meals formal, some self-service. School shop. No tobacco/alcohol allowed.
Discipline Pupils failing to produce homework once might expect rebuke; those caught smoking cannabis on the premises might expect expulsion.
Former pupils Eric Ambler; Henry Williamson; sundry ambassadors.

• COLSTON'S COLLEGIATE

Colston's Collegiate School, Stapleton, Bristol BS16 1BJ. Tel 0117 965 5207, Fax 0117 965 5207
• Pupils 570 • Boys 3–18 (Day/Board/Weekly) • Girls 3–18 (Day/Board/Weekly) • Upper sixth 51 • Termly fees £1100–£1915 (Day) £2970–£3530 (Board) £2870–£3380 (Weekly) • HMC, SHMIS
• Enquiries/application to the Headmaster's Secretary

What it's like

Founded in 1710, it is single-site at Stapleton in the northern outskirts of Bristol, having merged with The Collegiate School, Winterbourne in 1991. The present school has 30 acres of good grounds and playing fields and the main building is the former palace of the Bishop of Bristol. There have been numerous modern developments and facilities are of a high standard. The junior department is nearby. A sound education is provided and many sixth-formers go on to degree courses. Being a C of E school, chapel is quite an important part of school life; all denominations are welcome. There are flourishing music, art and drama departments. Sport is strong. There is a substantial commitment (nearly 50% of pupils) to their own local community schemes. Full use is made of the cultural and other amenities of Bristol.

School profile

Pupils Total age range 3–18; 570 pupils, 536 day (472 boys, 64 girls), 34 boarding (27 boys, 7 girls). Senior department 11–18. Main entry ages 4, 7, 11, 13 and into the sixth. Approx 5% are children of former pupils. *State school entry:* 50% main senior intake, plus 50% to sixth.
Entrance Common Entrance and own exam used. Any special ability is taken into account; no religious requirements. Parents not expected to buy textbooks; extras vary £3–£100. 15 pa assisted places. 8 pa scholarships/bursaries, £300 per term to full fees.
Parents 15+% in industry or commerce; 15+% are doctors, lawyers, etc. 30+% live within 30 miles; 11–30% live overseas.
Head and staff *Headmaster:* D G Crawford, 2 years in post. Educated at The Perse School and Loughborough University. Previously Headmaster of Cokethorpe School,

Head of Department at Abingdon School and Assistant Teacher at Bryanston. *Staff:* 49 full time, 6 part time. Annual turnover 5%. Average age 40.

Exam results On average, 75 pupils in fifth form, 50 in upper sixth. *GCSE:* 28 gain at least grade C in 8+ subjects; 22 in 5–7; and 23 in 1–4 subjects. *A-levels:* 3 upper sixth pass in 4+ subjects; 26 in 3; 9 in 2 subjects. Average UCAS points 13.6.

University and college entrance 58% of 1995 sixth-form leavers went on to a degree course; others typically go on to non-degree courses, or straight into employment. Of those going on to university, 44% took courses in science and engineering, 36% in humanities and social sciences, 20% in the arts.

Curriculum GCSE and A-levels. 17 subjects offered (including AS-level general studies). 16% take science A-levels; 52% arts/humanities; 32% both. *Vocational:* Work experience available. *Computing facilities:* 12 IBM-compatible, 10 Amstrad, 2 Apple, 6 BBC model B. *Special provision:* Dyslexia for limited numbers. *Europe:* French and German offered to GCSE and A-level. Regular exchanges to France.

The arts (Pupils aged 11 and over) *Music:* Up to 50% of pupils learn a musical instrument; instrumental exams can be taken. Some 7 musical groups including orchestras, 3 choirs, pop group, wind band. *Drama & dance*: Drama and dance offered. GCSE and A-level drama may be taken. Some pupils are involved in school productions and majority in house/other productions. *Art:* On average, 40 take GCSE, 12 A-level. Textiles also offered.

Sport, community service and clubs (Pupils aged 11 and over) *Sport and physical activities:* Compulsory sports (to 13): rugby, hockey, cricket (boys); netball, hockey, rounders (girls). Optional: badminton, squash, athletics, tennis, cross-country, swimming. Many county and regional representatives (rugby, hockey, cricket, cross-country, tennis, squash, badminton). *Community service:* Pupils take silver Duke of Edinburgh's Award. CCF and community service optional. *Clubs and societies:* Up to 30 clubs, eg debating, chess, computing, gym, calligraphy, origami, table tennis, music appreciation.

Uniform School uniform worn throughout (some relaxation in the sixth).

Houses/prefects Competitive houses. Prefects, head prefect, head of house and house prefects – appointed by the Headmaster.

Religion Attendance at religious worship compulsory.

Social Choir, choral society and plays often with other schools. Organised French and German exchanges. Pupils allowed to bring own bike to school; day pupils only may bring cars. Meals self-service. School shop. No tobacco/alcohol allowed.

Discipline Pupils failing to produce homework once might expect to do it by the following day; those caught smoking cannabis on the premises could expect expulsion.

Boarding 15% have own study bedroom, 20% share (with 1 other); 50% are in dormitories of 6+. Houses, of 30–40, same as competitive houses. Resident qualified nurse. Central dining room. Kitchens are provided; pupils can prepare hot drinks and snacks. Flexible weekend arrangement. Visits to the local town allowed by arrangement with housemaster.

Alumni association run by J J Cook, Dean Lodge, Iron Acton, Bristol.

Former pupils Professor Peter Mathias (Master of Downing College, Cambridge); Chris Broad (England cricketer); Alan Morley and Austin Sheppard (England rugby players); John Mason (Daily Telegraph rugby correspondent); Simon Mugglestone (international athlete).

• COLSTON'S GIRLS

Colston's Girls' School, Cheltenham Road, Bristol BS6 5RD. Tel 0117 942 4328, Fax 0117 942 6933

• Pupils 500 • Boys None • Girls 10–18 (Day) • Upper sixth 60 • Termly fees £1195 (Day) • GSA • Enquiries/application to the Head Mistress's Secretary

What it's like

Founded in 1891, it is an urban, inner city school with a single-site. The original buildings form the nucleus of the modern school and have been extensively augmented to provide very good facilities. Every girl is treated as an individual and encouraged to discover her own strengths and gifts so that she can further them. The teaching is good, as are the results. Most sixth-formers go on to degree courses. Religious education is Christian but non-denominational. A fair range of standard sports, games and activities. There is a big commitment to music, with a fine string ensemble, and to drama.

School profile

Pupils Age range 10–18; 500 day girls. Main entry age 10 and into sixth. Approx 5% are children of former pupils. State school entries: 90% main intake, plus 5% to sixth.
Entrance Own entrance exam used. No special skills required. C of E foundation, but all denominations welcome. Parents not expected to buy textbooks; lunch is optional extra. 24 pa assisted places. 8 pa scholarships/exhibitions (music and sixth-form) and school assisted places, value variable.
Parents 50+% in industry or commerce; 25+% are professionals.
Head and staff *Headmistress:* Mrs Judith P Franklin, in post 7 years. Educated at Howell's School (Llandaff) and Cardiff University (English). Previously Deputy Head at Evesham High and Head of Sixth Form at South Bromsgrove High School. Also member of ISJC Assisted Places Committee. *Staff:* 39 full time, 11 part time. Annual turnover 4%. Average age 36.
Exam results In 1995, 69 pupils in fifth, 64 in upper sixth. *GCSE:* In 1995, upper fifth gained at least grade C in 8.5 subjects. *A-levels:* 41 upper sixth passed in 4+ subjects; 10 in 3; 8 in 2; and 5 in 1 subject.
University and college entrance 90% of 1995 sixth-form leavers went on to a degree course; others typically go on to art college. Of those going on to university, 4% went to Oxbridge; 4% took courses in medicine, dentistry and veterinary science, 15% in science and engineering, 68% in humanities and social sciences, 10% in art and design, 4% in music.
Curriculum GCSE and A-levels. 23 subjects offered, including Russian. 20% take science A-levels; 66% arts/humanities; 14% both. *Vocational:* Work shadowing available. *Computing facilities:* Apple Macintosh network. IT is taught throughout the school; computing facilities in most departments. *Europe:* French, German, Russian and Spanish offered to GCSE and A-level. Regular exchanges to France and Germany.
The arts *Music:* Up to 25% of pupils learn a musical instrument; instrumental exams can be taken. Some 15 musical groups including orchestras, chamber orchestra, chamber groups, choir, chamber choir, Buskers. Regional prize National Chamber Music Competition; 5 members of county schools orchestra; 2 pupils recently made a record. *Drama & dance*: Drama and dance offered. A-level theatre studies may be taken. Majority of pupils are involved in school and other productions. *Art:* On average, 50 take GCSE, 15 A-level. Design, textiles also offered.
Sport, community service and clubs *Sport and physical activities:* Compulsory sports: swimming, hockey, netball, athletics, tennis. Optional: aerobics, body tone, squash, badminton, volleyball. GCSE PE may be taken. England team representatives at cross-country, gymnastics and trampolining. *Community service:* Pupils take bronze, silver and gold Duke of Edinburgh's Award. Community service optional for sixth-form. *Clubs and societies:* Up to 15 clubs, eg debating, chess, computing, design, Christian Union, drama, Young Enterprise.
Uniform School uniform worn except in the sixth.
Prefects Senior prefect management team selected by sixth-form and staff.
Religion Religious worship encouraged. Religious services in church once a term, with major Commemoration at Bristol Cathedral.
Social Debates, choir, drama productions, dance with other schools. Organised trips to Russia, Germany, Austria, France, Spain, Italy, Greece. A few pupils allowed to bring own car/bike/motorbike to school. Meals self-service. Small tuckshop. No tobacco/alcohol allowed.
Discipline A co-operative approach between home and school. Pupils failing to produce homework once might expect a discussion with staff member; those caught smoking cannabis on the premises could expect expulsion.

• COMBE BANK

Combe Bank School Educational Trust Ltd, Sundridge, Sevenoaks Kent TN14 6AE. Tel 01959 563720, Fax 01959 561997

• Pupils 410 • Boys (3–5 only) • Girls 3–18 (Day) • Upper sixth 25 • Termly fees £1720 (Day) • GSA SHA • Enquiries/application to the Secretary

What it's like

Founded in 1924, it passed to the Educational Trust in 1972. Housed in a superb Palladian country mansion built in 1720 and set in 27 acres of beautiful parkland. The prep school is on the same site. It is of Roman Catholic foundation but accepts all denominations. Christian doctrine is central to the curriculum; the syllabus is ecumenical. It caters for a wide range of abilities and talents and some vocational qualifications are offered. Second years are offered a cuisine and culture tour to France. It is strong in music and drama. There is a range of sports, games and activities and the standard in games is high. Vigorous participation in local community schemes.

School profile

Pupils Total age range 3–18; 410 day pupils (17 boys, 393 girls). Senior department 11–18, 211 girls. Main entry ages 3, 11, 12, 13 and into sixth. *State school entry:* 25% senior intakes, plus 40% to sixth.

Entrance Common Entrance and own exam used. No special skills or religious requirements; any special skills (eg music) an advantage. School is Roman Catholic foundation although only 20% pupils are RC. Parents expected to buy some textbooks. Up to 6 pa scholarships available, 50% fees plus small number at 13 and to sixth.

Head and staff *Headmistress:* Miss Nina Spurr, 4 years in post. Maths graduate. Previously Deputy Head at King Edward VI High, Stafford. Member GSA Council. *Staff:* 35 full time, 20 part time. Annual turnover under 10%. Average age about 40.

Exam results In 1995, 31 pupils in fifth, 24 in upper sixth. *GCSE:* In 1995, 23 pupils gained at least grade C in 8+ subjects; 4 in 5–7 subjects. *A-levels:* In 1995, 13 pupils passed in 3 subjects; 6 in 2; and 4 in 1 subject. Average UCAS points 12.9.

University and college entrance 67% of 1995 sixth-form leavers went on to a degree course (25% after a gap year); others typically go on to art college, employment or vocational training. Of those going on to university, 10% took courses in medicine, dentistry and veterinary science, 5% in science and engineering, 5% in law, 50% in humanities and social sciences, 10% in art and design, 20% vocational subjects or combined courses.

Curriculum GCSE and A-levels (no general studies). *Vocational:* Work experience available; also RSA stages 1–3 typing, word processing, commercial French, and GNVQ levels 2 and 3 in leisure and tourism and in health and social care. *Computing facilities:* Archimedes network. *Special provision:* Extra teaching for mild dyslexia. *Europe:* French, German and Spanish offered at GCSE and A-level; also AS-level French and German, and French or Spanish for business offered. Regular exchanges to France, Germany and Spain. Second year tour to France, French cuisine and culture.

The arts *Music:* Up to 50% of pupils learn a musical instrument; instrumental exams can be taken. Musical groups include choirs, chamber groups, orchestra, etc. Specially commissioned musical entered for national competition. *Drama & dance*: Speech and drama offered. GCSE theatre studies may be taken. Some pupils are involved in school productions and house/other productions. Performed with local choir in premiere of Hellfire Corner at St. John's Smith Square. *Art:* On average, 14 take GCSE, 4 A-level. Pottery also offered.

Sport, community service and clubs *Sport and physical activities:* Compulsory sports: hockey, netball, tennis, athletics, swimming, self defence. Optional: badminton, cross-country, volleyball, unihoc, basketball. Sixth form only: aerobics, fitness training. GCSE, BAGA exams may be taken. Occasional county players; regular finalists in country tournaments, occasionally winners. *Community service:* Pupils take bronze, silver and gold Duke of Edinburgh's Award. Community service optional from age 13. *Clubs and societies:* Up to 10 clubs, eg pottery, computer, swimming.

Uniform School uniform worn except in the sixth.

Houses/prefects Competitive houses for sport. Head girl (appointed after discussion by staff), prefects, head of house and house prefects. School Council.

Religion Religious worship encouraged; occasional services compulsory.

Social Young Enterprise, voluntary service (with all Sevenoaks schools), choir with schools and local choirs, Ernest Reed concerts. Ski trip, French, German and Spanish exchange, Russian trip, hockey tour to Zimbabwe. Sixth form allowed to bring own car/bike to school. Meals self-service. School shop sells second-hand uniform. No tobacco/alcohol allowed.
Discipline Pupils failing to produce homework once might expect to have to repeat in detention. Those caught smoking cannabis on the premises could expect immediate suspension, almost certain expulsion.
Alumni association run by Mrs D Mills, c/o the School.

• COMMONWEAL LODGE

Commonweal Lodge, Woodcote Lane, Purley, Surrey CR8 3HB. Tel 0181 660 3179, Fax 0181 660 1385

• Pupils 250 • Boys None • Girls 3–18 (Day) • Upper sixth 5 • Termly fees £1505 (Day) • GSA
• Enquiries/application to the Headmistress

What it's like

Founded in 1916, it lies on the west side of Purley in an agreeable residential area with four acres of private grounds. The buildings are purpose-designed and have good facilities. The junior school is on the same site. Its general aim is to educate girls to use their individual abilities – mentally, physically, spiritually. Sound standards and values based on Christian principles are fostered. Assembly and religious education are an integral part of the life. Sport, games and extra-curricular activities are an important part of the school day.

School profile

Pupils Total age range 3–18; 250 day girls. Senior department 11–18, 135 girls. Main entry ages 3, 5, 8, 11. Approx 1% are children of former pupils. *State school entry:* 25% intake at 11+.
Entrance Own entrance exam used. No special skills or religious requirements. Parents not expected to buy textbooks; maximum extras £75 plus music tuition. 3 pa scholarships/bursaries, including 1 for music.
Head and staff *Headmistress:* Mrs Sheila Law, appointed in 1995. Educated at St Peter's, Coulsdon, and London University (drama and English). Previously Principal of Waterside School, Hertfordshire, Deputy Head of Bexley-Erith Technical High School and Head of English at Charles Edward Brooke School. Also worked in theatre administration and local government; local councillor in Tandridge. *Staff:* 17 full time, 14 part time. Annual turnover 6–10%. Average age 40.
Exam results In 1995, 22 pupils in Year 11, 5 in upper sixth. *GCSE:* In 1995, 12 in Year 11 gained at least grade C in 8+ subjects; 9 in 5–7 subjects. *A-levels:* 1 in upper sixth passed in 3 subjects; 3 in 2; and 1 in 1 subject.
University and college entrance All 1995 sixth-form leavers went on to a degree course (none took a gap year).
Curriculum GCSE and A-levels (no A-level general studies). *Vocational:* Work experience integral; RSA stage 2 in typewriting and English. *Computing facilities:* 10 IBM PCs (3 with CD-Rom) and 9 BBCs. *Special provision:* EFL specialist teacher. Visiting teacher for the dyslexic. *Europe:* French and German offered at GCSE, AS and A-level; also foundation Spanish, and business French for sixth-form. Regular exchanges to France.
The arts *Music:* Up to 75% of pupils learn a musical instrument; instrumental exams can be taken. Some 3 musical groups including orchestra (plays wide variety of music from jazz to classical). *Drama & dance*: Drama offered and GCSE may be taken. Many pupils are involved in school productions and house/other productions. 2 pupils in recent production of Hansel and Gretel at Fairfield Hall. *Art:* On average, 10 take GCSE, 2 A-level. Textiles also offered.
Sport, community service and clubs *Sport and physical activities:* Compulsory sports (to age 14); swimming, rounders, tennis, netball, lacrosse. Optional from 14, badminton. Sixth form only, squash. BAGA exams may be taken. *Clubs and societies:* Up to 15 clubs, eg chess, bridge, art, sports, musical, drama, needlecraft, languages.
Uniform School uniform worn except in the sixth.

Houses/prefects Competitive houses. Prefects, head girl, head of house and house prefects – appointed by the Head and the school.
Religion Religious worship is encouraged. Daily assemblies.
Social No regular events with local schools. Trips to France and Germany, ski parties and Mediterranean cruises. Pupils allowed to bring own car/bike/motorbike to school. Meals self-service. No tobacco/alcohol allowed.
Discipline Pupils failing to produce homework once might expect a warning; detention for three misdemeanours. No incidents of drugs.
Alumni association run by The Old Knots Secretary, Miss W J King, 28 Fairways, Wells, Somerset BA5 2DF.
Former pupils Jacqueline du Pré (cellist); Alex Hildred (archaeologist); Angharad Rees (actress); Yvonne Sintes (first woman airline pilot).

• CONCORD

Concord College, Acton Burnell Hall, Shrewsbury, Shropshire SY5 7PF. Tel 01694 731631, Fax 01694 731389

• Pupils 280 • Boys 12–20 (Day/Board) • Girls 12–20 (Day/Board) • Upper sixth 100 • Termly fees £1450 (Day) £3950 (Board) • CIFE, BAC • Enquiries/application to the Principal

What it's like

Founded in 1949 by Paul Oertel and Monica Carr-Taylor, it is a tutorial college specialising in university entrance. From 1995 pupils have been accepted from age 12. It is unusually fortunate in its site and buildings. These are part of a large rural estate, next to the pretty village of Acton Burnell in a particularly beautiful part of Shropshire. The principal building is a very elegant regency (1811) mansion. Other very attractive buildings are within a couple of minutes walk; all lie amidst lawns and gardens. The college's name is claimed to symbolise its life and ethos; it is multi-national with representatives from some 50 countries. There are many excellent modern facilities (art studio, workshops, laboratories, library). New student blocks provide very comfortable accommodation in single or twin-study bedrooms (boys and girls in separate residential blocks). There is a very favourable staff:pupil ratio of 1:8. Academic results are very good and a high proportion of leavers go on to degree courses. Music and drama appear to be well supported. A standard range of sports and games. Regular excursions to the continent (eg Paris, Amsterdam).

School profile

Pupils Age range 12–20; 280 pupils, 10 day (5 boys, 5 girls), 270 boarding (165 boys, 115 girls). Main entry at 12, 14 and into the sixth. 20% are children of former pupils. *State school entry:* 5% intake into sixth.
Entrance No entrance exam. No special skills except general competence in secondary school subjects; no religious requirements. Parents are expected to buy textbooks; average extras £200 pa. College remains open during half-terms and holidays (except summer); no additional charge for holiday accommodation. Scholarships available, £330–£1500 per term
Parents 15+% are in industry/commerce; 15+% doctors/lawyers etc. Up to 10% live within 30 miles of the school; over 60% overseas.
Head and staff *Principal:* Anthony Morris, in post for 21 years. Educated at Wales University (economics and history). Previously Vice-Principal and Economics Master at Concord College. Also Rotarian, Chairman of CIFE. *Staff:* 36 full time, 5 part time. Annual turnover under 5%. Average age 44.
Exam results In 1995, 20 pupils in upper fifth, 100 in upper sixth. *GCSE:* In 1995, 12 upper fifth gained at least grade C in 5–7 subjects. *A-levels:* 10 passed in 4+ subjects; 76 in 3; 12 in 2; and 2 in 1 subject. Average UCAS points 23.9.
University and college entrance 94% of 1995 sixth-form leavers went on to a degree course; others typically go on to art college. Of those going on to university, 6% went to Oxbridge; 8% took courses in medicine, dentistry and veterinary science, 42% in science and engineering, 50% in humanities and social sciences.
Curriculum GCSE and A-levels offered. 12 exam subjects offered, including Japanese and Mandarin Chinese (no A-level general studies). 60% take science A-levels; 40% arts/humanities; maths common to both groups. *Computing facilities:* 16 computers in

computer room, others in library and laboratories. *Special provision:* EFL department. *Europe:* French, German and Italian offered to GCSE, AS-level and A-level.
The arts *Music:* Up to 15% pupils learn a musical instrument; instrumental exams can be taken. 3 musical groups, orchestra and choir. *Drama & dance*: Drama and dance offered. Majority of pupils in school or other productions. *Art:* On average, 15 take GCSE, 20 A-level; design, pottery, textiles and photography also offered. Art facilities open to non-examination pupils.
Sport, community service and clubs *Sport and physical activities:* No compulsory sports; soccer, rugby, basketball, badminton, tennis, karate, archery, swimming and riding all optional. *Clubs and societies:* Up to 15 clubs.
Uniform None.
Houses/prefects Competitive houses. Head boy/girl, prefects and head of house and house prefects – elected by the school.
Religion No compulsory worship.
Social Regular excursions to Paris, Amsterdam; art tours, ski trips. Students may bring own bike to school. Meals self-service. Smoking allowed only in a student's single study-bedroom.
Discipline Pupils failing to produce homework once might expect a reprimand; students caught smoking cannabis on the premises would face expulsion.
Boarding 90% have own study bedrooms; 10% share with 1 other. Single-sex houses of about 8, divided by age group. Resident qualified nurse. Students allowed to provide and cook own food in recreation time. Full dining room meals provided. Exeats allowed each weekend. Visits to the local town allowed, restricted hours, transport provided by college.

• CRAIGHOLME

Craigholme School, 72 St Andrew's Drive, Glasgow G41 4HS. Tel 0141 427 0375
• Pupils 470 • Boys 3–8 only • Girls 3–18 (Day) • Higher year 54 • Sixth year 34 • Termly fees £400–£1265 (Day) • SHA, HAS • Enquiries/application to the Secretary or Headmistress

What it's like

Founded in 1894, it has handsome well-equipped premises in a pleasant residential suburb of Glasgow. The playing fields are on the Pollok estate a few minutes away. Primary and secondary departments are combined, the infant department on a separate site. Excellent facilities are provided. Religious worship is compulsory. Academic standards are high and results good. Vocational qualifications are offered. Many pupils proceed to degree courses each year. There is a tremendously strong music department and much strength in drama (a third of the school being engaged in productions each year). Sports and games are also of a high standard and quite a lot of pupils represent the school at regional level. A plentiful range of extra-curricular activities. Many enterprising trips and expeditions at home and abroad are organised. The school's record in the Duke of Edinburgh's Award Scheme is outstanding. The sixth-form operates a Young Enterprise Company.

School profile

Pupils Total age range 3–18; 470 day pupils. Senior department 12–18, 280 girls. Main entry ages 3, 5 and 11–12. Approx 30% are children of former pupils. *State school entry:* 10% main intake at 11.
Entrance Own entrance exam used. No special skills or religious requirements. Parents expected to buy textbooks/music lessons/lunch. 5 pa assisted places. 2–4 pa bursaries, means-tested assistance with fees; 2 bursaries for European work experience.
Head and staff *Headmistress:* Mrs Gillian Burt, 6 years in post. Educated at Mary Erskine and Edinburgh University (geography). Previously Head of Careers at St Margaret's (Edinburgh) and Head of Geography at St Hilary's School, Edinburgh. Also in charge of industry/business liaison in St Margaret's, Edinburgh. *Staff:* 42 full time, 7 part time. Annual turnover 2 or 3. Average age 40.
Exam results In 1995, 59 pupils in S-grade year, 45 in Higher. *S-grade:* In 1995, all pupils passed in 5+ subjects (maximum of 7 subjects sat). *Highers:* 62% passed in 4+ subjects; 15% in 3; 18% in 2; and 2% in 1 subject. *CSYS*: On average, 5 pass in 3 subjects; 3 in 2; 10 in 1 subject.

University and college entrance 92% of 1995 sixth-form leavers went on to a degree course (8% after a gap year); 11% took courses in medicine, dentistry and veterinary science, 26% in science and engineering, 3% in law, 38% in humanities and social sciences, 3% in art and design, 11% in eg accountancy, nursing, music, sport.
Curriculum S-grades, Highers, CSYS and Scotvec National Certificate. 18 subjects offered. 50% take science; 20% arts/humanities; 30% both. *Vocational:* Work experience available; also Scotvec National Certificate in computing studies, secretarial studies, IT, food and fabric, European studies and media studies. *Computing facilities:* Computer room with 10–12 computers (BBCs and Amstrads) plus 40 networked 486 PCs recently installed throughout school. *Special provision:* Remedial help by staff and one part-time specialist dyslexic teacher. *Europe:* French, Spanish and German offered to S-grade, Higher, CSYS and Scotvec (French compulsory from age 5 to S-grade). Regular exchanges and visits to France and Germany, including Paris European Seminar. Work experience placements in German industry.
The arts (Pupils aged 11 and over) *Music:* Up to 50% of pupils learn a musical instrument; instrumental exams may be taken. Some 8 musical groups including orchestra, choir, showtime group, flute, recorder groups. 8 in regional independent schools orchestra. *Drama & dance*: Drama offered. Majority of pupils are involved in school productions and house/other productions; also many in public speaking. Annual school show/play/musical. *Art:* On average, 20 take S-grade, 10–15 Higher. Pottery, photography and jewellery also offered. Public Art Galleries competition 2 gold medals including Honeyman Award.
Sport, community service and clubs (Pupils aged 11 and over) *Sport and physical activities:* Compulsory sports; hockey, tennis, cross-country. Optional: badminton, volleyball, swimming, skiing, self-defence. Scotland U16 winners of Midland Bank tennis; 3 girls in regional hockey teams U18, U16. *Community service:* Pupils take bronze, silver and gold Duke of Edinburgh's Award. Community service optional for 1 year at age 16+. *Clubs and societies:* Up to 10 clubs, eg country dancing, public speaking, literary and debating, technology.
Uniform School uniform worn throughout.
Houses/prefects Competitive houses. Head girl and deputes appointed by peers. Head of house and house prefects (elected). School Forum.
Religion Assembly compulsory three mornings a week; separate Jewish assembly weekly.
Social Joint discos for charity with local schools. Frequent organised trips abroad (at least one annually) including skiing and to France, Germany, Russia, China and Egypt. Pupils allowed to bring own bike to school. Meals self-service. No tobacco/alcohol allowed.
Discipline After-school detentions – S1 to S6. Pupils failing to produce homework once might expect extra homework.
Alumni association run by Miss Ruth Campbell, 3 Herries Road, Glasgow G41.
Former pupils Susan Wighton (nurse) Scotswoman of the Year 1987; Lesley Bale (MD Aberdeen Airport); Jacqueline Morrison (actress).

• CRANLEIGH

Cranleigh School, Cranleigh, Surrey GU6 8QQ. Tel 01483 273997, Fax 01483 267398
• Pupils 513 • Boys 13–18 (Day/Board) • Girls 16–18 (Day/Board) • Upper sixth 129 • Termly fees £3110 (Day) £4140 (Board) • HMC • Enquiries/application to the Headmaster

What it's like

Founded in 1865 as a boys' boarding school it has included girls in the sixth-form since 1971. It has a splendid site in over 200 acres of Surrey farmland near the small town of Cranleigh. The buildings are striking and well-appointed. During the last 15 years there has been considerable expansion and the school is now extremely well-equipped; most recent developments include a new studio theatre, second astro-turf and refurbishment of the computing facilites. The prep school adjoins the main campus. The chapel was built as the central point of the school and the policy is to maintain Christian values as a way of life. There is an emphasis on worship and instruction in the Anglican tradition. It is a well-run, energetic and purposeful school which displays considerable enterprise in many fields. A large staff allows a staff:pupil ratio of about 1:9. Academic standards are high and results very good. Almost all pupils go on to degree courses each year, including a number to Oxbridge. It has a high reputation for art, music and drama; there are three theatres (one open-air) and some 12 productions each year, including plays in French, Spanish and German. First-rate facilities are available for art, ceramics, sculpture and printing. The school also has a long-standing reputation for its achievements in games and sports, of which there is a wide range available including sailing and golf (there is a 9-hole course on the estate). Numerous clubs and societies cater for most needs. A large and active voluntary CCF; there is a fire brigade section (with its own engine). Field trips and expeditions overseas are frequent and varied. Travel grants are available to allow pupils to carry out their own projects. The school has a substantial commitment to local community services; especially through the physically handicapped/able bodied course, a residential event at the school. There has been considerable success in the Duke of Edinburgh's Award Scheme.

School profile

Pupils Age range 13–18, 513 pupils, 91 day (89 boys, 2 girls) 422 boarding (357 boys, 71 girls). Main entry age 13 (boys) and into the sixth (boys and girls). 20% intake from own prep.

Entrance Common Entrance exam used. Assisted places. Exhibitions, closed awards and many scholarships available.

Head and staff *Headmaster:* Anthony Hart, in post for 12 years. Educated at City of Bath School and Oxford University (PPE). Previously Assistant Secretary at HM Treasury, seconded to Government of Malawi as Transport Adviser and Principal at Ministry of Transport. Also formerly President of Oxford Union. *Staff:* 53 full time, 6 part time. Annual turnover 5%. Average age 40.

Exam results In 1995, 92 pupils in upper fifth, 116 in upper sixth. *GCSE:* In 1995, 75 upper fifth gained at least grade C in 8+ subjects; and 13 in 5–7 subjects. *A-levels:* 18 upper sixth passed in 4+ subjects; 77 in 3; 15 in 2; and 5 in 1 subject. Average UCAS points 19.0.

University and college entrance 95+% of sixth-form leavers go on to a degree course (40% after a gap year); others typically go straight into business. Of those going on to university, 13% go to Oxbridge; 5% take courses in medicine, dentistry and veterinary science, 20% in science and engineering, 5% in law, 60% in humanities and social sciences, 5% in art and design, 5% in vocational subjects eg physiotherapy, susrveying.

Curriculum GCSE and A-levels. 22 subjects offered (no A-level general studies). 12% take science A-levels; 65% arts/humanities; 23% both. *Vocational:* Work experience available; also compulsory RSA in CLAIT. *Computing facilities:* 2 computing laboratories with Archimedes and Risc PCs, networked around school; laser, colour printing and image scanners. *Special provision:* Occasional EFL lessons and dyslexia tuition. *Europe:* French, German and Spanish offered at GCSE, AS and A-level; 8 languages taught over last 5 years. Regular exchanges to France, Germany and Spain. Parental involvement in exchange/training schemes and conferences on European issues.

The arts *Music:* Up to 40% of pupils learn a musical instrument; instrumental exams can be taken. Some 9 musical groups including orchestra, wind band, big band, strings, trios, quartets, choir. Some 30 pa concerts, some with professionals. *Drama & dance*: A-level theatre studies may be taken. Majority of pupils are involved in school productions and house/other productions. 10+ productions a year; drama tour to Kenya (1995). *Art:* On average, 64 take GCSE, 40 A-level. All art masters are practising artists.

Sport, community service and clubs *Sport and physical activities:* Compulsory participation in a choice of sport or physical activity; 16 team sports and many individual sports – rugby, hockey, cricket, tennis, athletics, swimming, golf; also clay-pigeon shooting, cross-country, fencing, fives, karate, riding (stables on estate), sailing, shooting, soccer, squash, water polo, netball, lacrosse. Pupils regularly represent county at athletics, hockey, water polo, cricket and rugby. *Community service:* Pupils take bronze, silver and gold Duke of Edinburgh's Award. CCF and community service optional; PHAB; sponsorship for education of Third World children. *Clubs and societies:* 42 clubs, eg bridge, chess, debating, science, Schools Challenge, photography, karate, wine tasting, astronomy, angling.

Uniform School uniform worn throughout by boys (working day); no uniform but dress code for girls.
Houses/prefects Competitive houses. Prefects, head girl/boy (appointed by Head); head of house and house prefects (appointed by housemasters).
Religion Attendance at religious worship compulsory three times a week.
Social Annual choral concert and social service jointly with other schools. Regular field trips and expeditions to Italy, Hebrides, Iceland, France. Pupils allowed to bring own bike/horse to school; no cars. Meals self-service. School book and tuck shops. No tobacco allowed. Alcohol permitted in upper sixth buttery at restricted times under supervision.
Discipline Close relationship between staff and pupils (drawn from boarding structure) where discipline is maintained through mutual respect. Pupils caught with drugs on the premises will be expelled.
Former pupils Dr Derek Bourgeois (composer), Christian Roberts (actor), Andrew Roberts (historian), David Westcott (GB hockey captain), Julia Ormond (actress), E W Swanton (cricket and rugby correspondent, commentator and author), Alan Rusbridger, (Guardian Editor).

• CROFT HOUSE

Croft House School, Shillingstone, Blandford, Dorset DT11 OQS. Tel 01258 860295, Fax 01258 860552

• Pupils 120 • Boys None • Girls 11–18 (Day/Boarding /Weekly) • Upper sixth 15 • Termly fees £2295 (Day) £3250 (Board/Weekly) • GSA • Enquiries to the Headmaster

What it's like

Started in 1941 by Colonel and Mrs Torkington in their own house to provide education for their daughter and the daughters of friends. Thus began the tradition of a small family school which has been preserved. It has a very pleasant environment and there have been considerable extensions over the years. It is C of E by foundation but other persuasions are welcomed. A sound education is provided. There is a large staff for such a small school and individual tuition is available. The music, art and drama departments are active and there is a good range of sports, games and other activities, including a flourishing riding school.

School profile

Pupils Age range 11–18; 120 girls, 20 day, 100 boarding. Main entry ages 11, 12, 13 and into the sixth. *State school entry:* 10% main intake, few to sixth.
Entrance Own entrance exam used. Parents expected to buy sixth-form textbooks. 6 pa major scholarships and some bursaries (riding, academic, art, music, drama, sixth-form), up to 40% of fees.
Parents 10% in the armed services. 30% live within 30 miles; 15% live overseas.
Head and staff *Headmaster:* M P Hawkins, 3 years in post. Educated at Allhallows and Melbourne University (philosophy). Previously Head of St Anne's, Windermere, of the International School, Algarve, and of Clayesmore, Director of Activities at Dover College and Head of Economics at Bedales. *Staff:* 14 full time, 12 part time. Annual turnover 5%. Average age 42.
Exam results In 1995, 17 pupils in fifth, 20 in upper sixth. *GCSE:* In 1995, 6 pupils in fifth gained at least grade C in 8+ subjects; 5 in 5–7; 6 in 1–4 subjects. *A-levels:* 1 upper sixth passed in 4 subjects; 6 in 3; 7 in 2; and 3 in 1 subject. Average UCAS points 11.7.
University and college entrance 80% of sixth-form leavers go on to a degree course (50% after a gap year); others typically go on to non-degree courses. Of those going on to university, 10% took courses in science and engineering, 10% in law, 40% in humanities and social sciences, 30% in art and design, 10% in vocational subjects eg equine studies.
Curriculum GCSE and A-levels. 20 subjects offered, including drama and keyboard applications. 15% take science A-levels, 70% arts/humanities; 15% both. *Vocational:* Work experience available; also some vocational qualifications. *Computing facilities:* 2 computer rooms, mainly Apple Macs/Archimedes. *Special provision:* Some EFL tuition; pupils with mild dyslexia and minor physical handicaps accepted. *Europe:* French and Spanish offered at GCSE, AS and A-level; also French for business as a non-examined subject. Girls from Europe frequently stay in school.

The arts *Music:* Many pupils learn a musical instrument. *Drama & dance:* Drama and theatre studies offered at GCSE and A-level. Many pupils are involved in school productions. Some girls go on to careers in the theatre. *Art:* Pottery, screen printing and photography also offered. Girls often accepted for art college.
Sport, community service and clubs *Sport and physical activities:* Sports: hockey, netball, tennis, swimming, athletics, basketball, gymnastics, volleyball, badminton, rounders and riding available. Everyone takes sport. *Community service:* Community service in sixth. *Clubs and societies:* Clubs include computer, riding, modern dance, ballet.
Uniform School uniform worn except in the sixth.
Houses/prefects Competitive houses (halls). Prefects, head girl, head of house and house prefects – appointed by staff discussion.
Religion Anglican religious worship encouraged.
Social Choral society; debating; dances etc with local schools. Organised trips abroad. Senior pupils allowed to bring own bike to school. School tuck shop and stationery shop. No tobacco/alcohol allowed.
Discipline A high standard of behaviour is expected and encouraged.
Boarding Most sixth-form have own study bedroom, others share with one other. Houses 40–50 pupils. Central dining room. Qualified medical staff. 2 termly exeats.

• CROHAM HURST

Croham Hurst School, 79 Croham Road, Croydon, Surrey CR2 7YN. Tel 0181 680 3064, Fax 0181 688 1142

• Pupils 500 • Boys None • Girls 4–18 (Day) • Upper sixth 31 • Termly fees £740–£1530 (Day) • GSA • Enquiries to the Headmistress's Secretary. Application to the Headmistress

What it's like

Founded in 1899, it is single-site in an attractive open area of south Croydon. Altogether it is a pleasant environment with gardens and playing fields, and well served by public transport. The junior school is nearby. The extensive facilities include a modern science block, computer and technology rooms, a fine music suite and on-site playing fields and swimming pool. Academic results are good.

School profile

Pupils Total age range 4–18; 500 day girls. Senior department 11–18, 310 girls. Main entry ages 4, 7, 11. 5% are children of former pupils. *State school entry:* Up to 40% senior intakes.
Entrance Own exam used. No special skills or religious requirements. Parents not expected to buy textbooks; music, drama etc extra, £80 each per term. Assisted places. 5 pa scholarships/bursaries at 11 and 16, 25%–100% fees.
Head and staff *Headmistress:* Miss Susan Budgen, 2 year in post. Educated at Godolphin and Latymer and at universities of Exeter (English) and Oxford (education). Previously Deputy Headmistress at Surbiton High. *Staff:* 36 full time, 18 part time. Annual turnover less than 10%. Average age 38.
Exam results In 1995, 65 pupils in upper fifth, 31 in upper sixth. *GCSE:* In 1995, 82% upper fifth gained at least grade C in 8+ subjects; 12% in 5–7 subjects. *A-levels:* 71% upper sixth passed in 3 subjects; 19% in 2; and 10% in 1 subject. Average UCAS points 19.9.
University and college entrance 80% of 1995 sixth-form leavers went on to a degree course; others typically go on to non-degree courses (eg occupational therapy) or into careers. Of those going on to university; 10% took courses in medicine, dentistry and veterinary science, 10% in science and engineering, 50% in humanities and social sciences, 20% in art and design.
Curriculum GCSE and A-levels. 20 GCSE subjects offered; 19 at A-level (no general studies). 25% take science A-levels; 52% arts/humanities; 23% both. *Vocational:* Year 11 undertake work experience. *Computing facilities:* Computer room in senior school and several departmental computers. *Special provision:* Outside tuition (linked with school) recommended for learning difficulties. *Europe:* French and German offered to GCSE and A-level; also GCSE Spanish. Regular exchanges to France and Germany.

The arts (Pupils aged 11 and over) *Music:* Over 30% of pupils learn a musical instrument. Musical groups include orchestras, wind bands, choir. *Drama & dance:* Drama and theatre studies offered. *Art:* On average, 15 take GCSE, 6 A-level. Art, design and textiles offered. Pupils regularly accepted for art college.
Sport, community service and clubs (Pupils aged 11 and over) Sports available: lacrosse, netball, tennis, rounders, athletics, basketball, swimming. *Clubs and societies:* Include computer, debating and drama clubs.
Uniform School uniform worn except in the sixth.
Houses/prefects Competitive houses. No prefects. Head girl and head of house – elected by the school. School Council.
Religion Christian assembly compulsory.
Social Debates with other schools; joint theatre productions with Whitgift School. Exchange trips to Germany and France; ski trips; foreign tours. Pupils allowed to bring own car/bike to school. Meals self-service.
Discipline Consideration for and co-operation with others insisted on.
Alumni association run by Secretary, Mrs M Willifer, c/o the school.

• CROYDON HIGH

Croydon High School for Girls, Old Farleigh Road, Selsdon, South Croydon, Surrey CR2 8YB. Tel 0181 651 5020, Fax 0181 657 5413

• Pupils 1050 • Boys None • Girls 4–18 (Day) • Upper sixth 90 • Termly fees £1192–£1548 (Day)
• GSA, GPDST • Enquiries/application to the Headmistress

What it's like

Founded in 1874, it moved to its present site on the outskirts of Croydon in 1966. This comprises a purpose-built and extremely well-equipped and comfortable establishment in beautiful landscaped grounds. The teaching is known to be very good and standards are high. Academic results are very good and almost all sixth-formers go on to degree courses, including Oxbridge. It is particularly strong in music and in drama. Sport and games are played to high standards (many county and national representatives). Big commitment to local community schemes and the Duke of Edinburgh's Award Scheme.

School profile

Pupils Total age range 4–18; 1050 day girls. Senior department 11–18, 700+ girls. Main entry ages 4, 5, 7, 11 and into sixth. Approx 10% are children of former pupils. *State school entry:* 50% intake from other schools at 11. (National Curriculum followed in junior department, so girls from maintained sector can merge easily.)
Entrance Own entrance exam used. Good academic ability required; no religious requirements. Parents not expected to buy textbooks. 25 pa assisted places plus 5 in sixth and others in junior department. 4 pa scholarships (11+ and sixth-form), up to 50% fees.
Head and staff *Headmistress:* Mrs Pauline Davies, 6 years in post. Educated at Guildford County School for Girls and Manchester University (botany and zoology). Previously Deputy Head at King Edward VI School, Chelmsford, and Head of Biology at Urmston Girls' Grammar School. *Staff:* 62 full time teaching staff, 23 part time. Annual turnover less than 10%.
Exam results In 1995, 110 pupils in the fifth year, 75 in upper sixth. *GCSE:* In 1995, all of fifth obtained grade C or above in 8+ subjects. *A-levels:* (excluding general studies) 15 upper sixth passed in 4+ subjects; 60 in 3. Average UCAS points 23.9.
University and college entrance 95% of 1995 sixth-form leavers went on to a degree course; others typically go on to art or drama colleges or straight into careers. Of those going on to university, 9% went to Oxbridge; 10% took courses in medicine, dentistry and veterinary science, 19% in science and engineering, 59% in humanities and social sciences, 3% in art and design, 4% in eg drama and music.
Curriculum GCSE, AS and A-levels. 22 A-level subjects offered, 10 at AS level. 42% take science/maths A-levels; 32% arts/humanities; 25% both. *Vocational:* Work experience available; also City & Guilds preliminary computer competence. *Computing facilities:* 2 networks, both Apple Macintosh. *Europe:* French, German and Spanish offered to GCSE and A-level and for Institute of Linguists exams. Regular exchanges to France, Germany and Spain.

The arts *Music:* Up to 50% of pupils learn a musical instrument; instrumental exams can be taken. Some 10+ musical groups including 4 orchestras, wind band, 4 choirs, ad hoc choirs, chamber groups, popular groups etc – most weekly groups have 30+ members. *Drama & dance*: Drama and dance offered. GCSE drama, Poetry Society, LAMDA, Guildhall exams may be taken. All pupils are involved in school productions and majority in other productions. Successful Theatre in Education group. *Art:* On average, 35 take GCSE, 8 A-level; pottery, textiles, photography also offered. Regular entrants to foundation courses.
Sport, community service and clubs *Sport and physical activities:* Compulsory sports: netball, hockey, dance, gym, tennis, athletics, swimming. Optional: rounders, volleyball, basketball, badminton, cricket, table tennis. Sixth form only: aerobics, lifesaving, outdoor education, squash. Netball umpiring exams may be taken. Netball, a number of county representatives U18, U16, national finalists U18, U14; national table tennis representatives, national finalists U19; county representatives at hockey, tennis, squash, trampolining, table tennis, cross-country, athletics. *Community service:* Pupils take bronze, silver and gold Duke of Edinburgh's Award. Community service compulsory for 1 term at age 16+, optional otherwise. *Clubs and societies:* Up to 15 clubs, eg video production, computer, design and technology, chess, debating, drama, sports, UN.
Uniform School uniform worn except in the sixth.
Houses/prefects No competitive houses. Prefects, 5 senior prefects and 2 head girls – elected by staff and senior girls. School Council.
Religion All pupils attend daily assembly.
Social Joint sixth-form society with Trinity Boys' School. Exchange trips, educational courses, study trips, and ski trips abroad. Meals self-service. Second-hand uniform shop. No tobacco/alcohol allowed.
Discipline In any disciplinary actions parents are always closely involved. For example, pupils failing to produce homework would expect a letter home at the third instance.
Alumni association run by Mrs M Knight, c/o the School.
Former pupils Baroness Seear; Marion Roe; Jill Tweedie; Jane Drew; Wendy Savage; Jacqueline du Pré.

• CULFORD

Culford School, Bury St Edmunds, Suffolk IP28 6TX. Tel 01284 728615, Fax 01284 728631
• Pupils 630 • Boys 2–18 (Day/Board from 8) • Girls 2–18 (Day/Board from 8) • Upper sixth 75 • Termly fees £1758–£2257 (Day) £2737–£3467 (Board/Weekly) • HMC • Enquiries/application to the Headmaster

What it's like

Founded in 1881, it has a splendid site 4 miles north of Bury St Edmunds. The main building is Culford Hall, a fine and palatial 18th-century mansion (formerly the seat of the Earl of Cadogan) in 450 acres of beautiful gardens and parkland. Numerous modern extensions, including boarding houses (including a sixth-form house with its own study centre), a sports complex and design and arts block. It is a Methodist foundation but all denominations are welcome. The school has a deep-rooted respect for tradition in teaching methods, manners and behaviour and sees education as something that goes on outside as well as in the classroom. It seeks to establish a partnership with parents and expects pupils to work hard and make the most of their abilities whether they are outstanding academically or not. Originally a boys' school, it first accepted girls in 1972 and is now fully co-educational. Results are good and most sixth-form leavers go on to degree courses, including Oxbridge. Strong emphasis on sense of community and extra-curricular activites. The music and drama departments are very vigorous and there are many outdoor pursuits (including sailing, D of E and world-wide expeditions). Sport and games are played to high standards (many county and regional representatives). There are close community service ties with Bury. The prep school is also in the park.

School profile

Pupils Total age range 2–18; 630 pupils, 400 day (230 boys, 170 girls), 230 boarding (135 boys, 95 girls) – boarding from age 8. Senior department 13–18, 380 pupils (210 boys, 170 girls). Main entry ages 8, 11, 13 and into sixth. Approx 5% are children of former pupils.

Entrance Common Entrance and own exam used. No special skills or religious requirements. Parents not expected to buy textbooks; few extras. 10 pa assisted places. 8 pa scholarships (including 1 music) up to 50% fees; forces bursaries.
Parents 15+% in industry or commerce; 15+% in the armed services. 70+% live within 30 miles; 10+% live overseas.
Head and staff *Headmaster:* John Richardson, 5 years in post. Educated at Rossall and Cambridge (engineering and PGCE mathematics). Previously Mathematics Teacher, Housemaster Designate, Master i/c U16 rowing and CO CCF (RAF Section) at Eton; and Mathematics Teacher and House Master at Dean Close. Also (1973) Pre-University Officer Cadetship (RAF); Scripture Union Scotland summer camp organiser for Scottish secondary schoolchildren (1992); Member of Mathematical Association and of the London Institute for Contemporary Christianity. *Staff:* 76 full time, 6 part time. Annual turnover 5%. Average age 39.
Exam results In 1995, 95 pupils in upper fifth, 46 in upper sixth. *GCSE:* In 1995, 56% of upper fifth gained grade C or above in 8+ subjects; 27% in 5–7 subjects. *A-level:* 20% passed in 4+ subjects; 50% in 3; 14% in 2; and 14% in 1 subject. Average UCAS points 18.5 (including general studies 21.5).
University and college entrance 92% of 1995 sixth-form leavers went on to a degree course (7% after a gap year); others typically go on to eg financial, estate agency work. Of those going on to university, 10% went to Oxbridge; 3% took courses in medicine, dentistry and veterinary science, 20% in science and engineering, 15% in law, 45% in humanities and social sciences, 12% in art and design, 5% in vocational subjects eg physiotherapy, psychology.
Curriculum GCSE and A-levels. *Vocational:* Work experience available; also RSA stages 1 and 2 CLAIT. *Computing facilities:* Econet terminal in each classroom of main teaching block. Computer room with 15 terminals. Computers in other departments. *Special provision:* for dyslexia, EFL. *Europe:* French, German and Spanish offered to GCSE and A-level (French compulsory from age 10 to GCSE). Exchanges to France and Germany.
The arts *Music:* Up to 50% of pupils learn a musical instrument; instrumental exams can be taken. Some 12 musical groups including orchestras, choirs, choral society, wind band etc. 2 pupils within last 4 years in National Youth Orchestra; choral scholarship to Cambridge, violin scholarship to Royal Northern College of Music. *Drama & dance:* Drama and dance offered. GCSE drama, LAMDA, MIDDA exams may be taken. Majority of junior, some senior pupils are involved in school productions and house/other productions. *Art:* On average, 24 take GCSE, 8 A-level. Design, pottery, textiles, photography, printmaking, scenery/props making, history of art also offered.
Sport, community service and clubs *Sport and physical activities:* Compulsory sports: swimming and PE (wide range of mainly indoors activities). Optional: rugby, hockey, cricket, tennis, athletics, swimming, rounders, badminton, squash, volleyball, basketball, water polo, aerobics, gymnastics etc. GCSE may be taken. British triple jump champion U17; England hockey (boys) U16 member; England hockey captain (girls) U16; regular county and regional successes for teams and individuals, boys and girls, at hockey, rugby, cricket, netball. *Community service:* Pupils take bronze, silver and gold Duke of Edinburgh's Award; over 60 pupils registered. CCF and community service optional. *Clubs and societies:* Over 60 clubs, eg chess, aviation, arts, aerobics, badminton, recorder, science, expedition (trips to eg Borneo, Himalayas).
Uniform School uniform worn throughout.
Houses/prefects Competitive houses. Prefects, head boy and girl, head of house and house prefects – nominated by staff and pupils, appointed by the Headmaster.
Religion Religious worship compulsory; a Methodist foundation.
Social Some organised local events and trips abroad. Upper sixth allowed to bring own car/bike/motorbike to school. Meals self-service. School shop. No tobacco/alcohol allowed.
Discipline Punishments include: detentions (offences related to academic work); work units, withdrawal of privileges (other offences); fines (smoking); gating (breaking bounds); suspension/expulsion, both rare (drug offences, gross bullying, cheating, stealing). School sees discipline primarily as a pastoral concern and this attitude affects the reaction to breaches of discipline.
Boarding Most share study bedrooms; none in large dormitories. Single-sex houses,

divided by age group in senior school. Resident qualified medical staff. Central dining room. Pupils can provide and cook own food. 2 exeats each term. Visits to the local town allowed.

Alumni association run by Robert Dellow, Messrs Barlow Dellow Harker, 30a & 30b High Street, Newmarket, Suffolk.

Former pupils Sir David Plastow (Vickers); Admiral Sir Derek Reffell; John Motson (sports commentator); Judy Aslett (foreign correspondent ITN); Gary Newbon (Head of Sport, Central TV).

D

• DAME ALICE HARPUR

Dame Alice Harpur School, Cardington Road, Bedford MK42 0BX. Tel 01234 340871, Fax 01234 344125

• Pupils 935 • Boys None • Girls 7–18 (Day) • Upper sixth 100 • Termly fees £1446 (Day) • GSA • Enquiries to Headmistress's PA • Appliction to the Headmistress

What it's like

Opened in 1882, it is one of the four schools of the Bedford Charity, the Harpur Trust. They share equally in the benefaction of Sir William Harpur and Dame Alice, his wife, who originally endowed the foundation with land in Holborn (London) and Bedford. It has a Christian ethos but, while upholding traditional values and standards, is fundamentally ecumenical. The main school has modern buildings, plus agreeable gardens and playing fields, on a riverside site. It has good facilities including a new library, design technology and drama facilities and two listed Georgian houses have been adapted to provide a sixth-form centre and music centre. The junior school is opposite. The school offers a broad general education and results are good. Most sixth-form leavers go on to degree courses, including Oxbridge. Drama is strong and the music department is especially flourishing (with four choirs, four orchestras, string quartets, a string orchestra, wind band, and other ensembles). A wide range of sports and games is provided; many teams compete at county and regional level, and some regularly at national level. Extra-curricular activities include the Duke of Edinburgh's Award Scheme, debating, chess, juggling, archaeology, field courses and a wide range of outdoor activities and visits.

School profile

Pupils Total age range 7–18; 935 day girls. Senior school 11–18, 738 girls. Main entry ages 7, 9, 11, 13 and into the sixth. *State school entry:* 70% of senior intake plus 10% those joining in sixth.

Entrance Own entrance exam, heads' reports and interviews. Assisted places from age 7. Bursaries from age 11.

Head and staff *Headmistress:* Mrs Rosanne Randle, 6 years in post. Educated at Holme Valley Grammar School, Southampton University (history and music) and Hull University (educational management and administration). Previously Headmistress of Avonbourne School. Also former Secretary, Dorset Association of Secondary Heads; current Chairman GSA Education Committee. *Staff:* 68 full time, 17 part time. Annual turnover 5%.

Exam results In 1995, 115 pupils in Year 11, 88 in upper sixth. *GCSE:* In 1995, 109 Year 11 gained grade C or more in 8+ subjects; 6 in 5–7 subjects. *A-levels:* 25 upper sixth passed in 4+ subjects; 52 in 3; 7 in 2; and 3 in 1 subject. Average UCAS points 19.6 (including general studies 22.0).

University and college entrance 90% of sixth-form leavers go on to a degree course; others typically go on to careers eg banking, nursing or non-degree courses. Of those going on to university, several go to Oxbridge; 8% take courses in medicine, dentistry and veterinary science, 30% in science and engineering, 40% in humanities and social sciences, 10% in art and design, 12% in music and drama.

Curriculum GCSE and A-levels. On average 20% take science A-levels; 50% arts/humanities; 30% both. *Vocational:* Range of work experience opportunities; RSA stages 1–3 in typewriting and word processing; GNVQ level 3 secretarial link course with Bedford College. *Computing facilities:* Computer room with 14 workstations; other workstations for individual use; computers in some departmental areas; design and communications computer room. *Europe:* French and German offered at GCSE, AS and A-level; also Greek and Spanish to GCSE. Regular exchanges (France and Germany.

The arts (Pupils aged 11 and over) *Music:* Over 50% of pupils learn a musical instrument; instrumental exams can be taken. Some 12 regular musical groups and numerous ad hoc orchestras, jazz group, flute choir, wind band, choirs etc. *Drama & dance*: Drama and dance offered. GCSE and A-level drama may be taken; thriving Saturday drama school. Several girls selected each year for county youth theatre; occasionally national honours. *Art:* On average, 20 take GCSE, 14 A-level. Design, computer-aided design, pottery, textiles, photography also offered.

Sport, community service and clubs *Sport and physical activities:* Compulsory sports: hockey, netball, tennis, swimming, athletics etc. Optional: wide range including golf, squash, badminton, trampolining, self defence, yoga. GCSE, BAGA, RLSS exams may be taken. County and regional success in several sports each year, many representatives at national levels including youngest ever member of full England squad (hockey); indoor hockey national runners-up U19, national champions U18 outdoor hockey. *Community service:* Pupils take bronze, silver and gold Duke of Edinburgh's Award. Community service available. Very active charity fund-raising; close links with local residences for the elderly and local special schools. *Clubs and societies:* debating, mathematics, physics, chess, juggling, lace, art, drama, photography, plus numerous sports and music clubs.

Uniform School uniform worn throughout.

Houses/prefects Competitive houses. Head girl and team elected by senior girls and staff. No prefects (sixth-formers share responsibilities).

Religion Attendance at religious worship expected.

Social Performances, concerts, plays jointly with Bedford and Bedford Modern linked boys' schools. Many visits and exchanges. Pupils allowed to bring own bike to school; sixth-form may bring cars/motorbikes but no parking on campus. Meals self-service. School shop. No tobacco/alcohol allowed.

Discipline Everyday misdemeanours are dealt with routinely by the teacher involved at the time, or the form tutor. The very rare occurrences of more serious disciplinary matters are dealt with by senior staff in liaison with parents.

• DANIEL STEWART'S AND MELVILLE

Daniel Stewart's and Melville College, Queensferry Road, Edinburgh EH4 3EZ Tel 0131 332 7925, Fax 0131 343 2432

• Pupils 780 • Boys 12–18 (Day/Board) • Girls None • Higher year 130 • Termly fees £1470 (Day) £2760 (Board) • HMC • Enquiries/application to the Principal

What it's like

Founded in 1972 through the amalgamation of Daniel Stewart's Hospital (founded in 1855 and transformed into a day school in 1870) with Melville College (formerly Edinburgh Institution, founded in 1832). There is a particularly close association with the Mary Erskine girls' school and a joint junior school. All three schools are administered by a single governing body and the senior schools share a common Principal. Joint activities are intended to ensure that senior pupils receive the advantages of both single-sex and combined education. The college has a fine site near the centre of Edinburgh. The main building (the original college) is a kind of Victorian extravaganza resembling a mixture of private mansion/palace and hotel de ville, with towers, turrets and pinnacles, plus neo-classical and pseudo-Tudor features. It stands in superb gardens and grounds and its rooms are very fine. Overall the school is well equipped, including a state-of-the-art technology centre. Morning assemblies take the form of non-denominational religious services. Academic standards are high and results consistently creditable. Many pupils go on to degree courses although in the Scottish tradition, not large numbers to Oxbridge. Music is very strong indeed and most of the orchestral activity is combined with Mary Erskine, including orchestras, choirs, concert bands and a jazz band. Drama and debating are also very strong. There is much strength and depth in sports and games especially rugby, cricket, hockey, squash and rowing. Many pupils have won individual national honours. The large voluntary CCF contingent has Army, Navy and Air Force sections (which also involve girls from the Mary Erskine School) and its Pipe Band is famous. There is much emphasis on outdoor education, with numerous activities in the Highlands. The Duke of Edinburgh's Award Scheme is encouraged and a wide variety of clubs and societies provides for most conceivable needs.

School profile

Pupils Age range 12–18, 780 boys (740 day, 40 boarding). Main entry age 12. Own junior school with Mary Erskine. *State school entry:* 20% main intake.
Entrance Own entrance exam used. Assisted places and 6 pa scholarships.
Head and staff *Principal:* Patrick Tobin, 7 years in post. Educated at St Benedict's, Ealing, and Oxford University (history). Previously Headmaster at Prior Park, Head of History at Tonbridge and at Christ (Brecon) and Head of Economics at St Benedict's. Also Chairman, HMC Professional Development Sub-committee; member of Scottish Consultative Council on the Curriculum and Results; Committee Member, Scottish Council of Independent Schools. *Staff:* 70 full time, 2 part time. Annual turnover 4%. Average age 40.
Exam results In 1995, 141 pupils in main S-grade year (Form IV), 122 in Higher year (Form V), 101 in CSYS year (Form VI). *S-grade:* In 1995, 77% Form IV gained passes in 8+ subjects; 20% in 5–7 subjects. *Highers:* 5–7 of Form V passed in 5+ subjects; 39 passed 3–4 subjects. CSYS: 21 in Form VI passed in 3+ subjects; 48 in 1–2 subjects; also 149 Higher passes in form VI.
University and college entrance 90% of 1995 sixth-form leavers went on to a degree course (4% after a gap year); others typically go on to vocational courses. Of those going on to university, 3% went to Oxbridge; 9% took courses in medicine, dentistry and veterinary science, 36% in science and engineering, 5% in law, 48% in humanities and social sciences, 2% in art and design.
Curriculum S-grade, Highers and CSYS. 18 subjects offered. *Computing facilities:* 2 computer rooms, networked and many other computers. New technology centre. *Europe:* French and German offered to S-grade, Higher and CSYS; also Spanish Higher (French or German compulsory to S-grade). Regular exchanges (France and Germany). Visits to Europe, including to European Parliament and skiing; cultural tours eg pipe band.
The arts *Music:* Many pupils learn one (or more) musical instruments. Most orchestral activity joint with Mary Erskine. Music groups include 3 orchestras, 2 concert bands, jazz band, numerous chamber groups, large choirs, specialised groups eg madrigal, close harmony, active parents' choir.
Sport, community service and clubs *Sport and physical activities:* Rugby, cricket, hockey, tennis, athletics, curling, golf, swimming, squash, sailing and shooting available. Pupils are frequently members of national teams in many sports. *Community service:* CCF (all three service sections). Duke of Edinburgh's Award Scheme. *Clubs and societies:* include pipe band, drumming, hill walking and other outdoor activities.
Uniform School uniform worn throughout.
Houses/prefects Competitive houses. Prefects, head boy, head of house and house prefects – appointed by the Principal. School Council.
Religion Attendance at religious worship compulsory.
Social Twinned with Mary Erskine School with which many extra-curricular activities shared; sports fixtures, debates, tours etc with other local schools. Language trips to France and Germany; skiing and holiday tours; trips to USA; orchestral visit to Prague. Pupils allowed to bring own car/bike/motorbike to school. Meals self-service. No tobacco/alcohol allowed.
Boarding All in a single house, sharing dining and recreational facilities with boarders of Mary Erskine School.
Alumni association is run by Dr E J Wilkins, c/o the school.

• DAUNTSEY'S

Dauntsey's School, West Lavington, Devizes, Wiltshire SN10 4HE. Tel 01380 812446, Fax 01380 813620

• Pupils 620 • Boys 11–18 (Day/Board) • Girls 11–18 (Day/Board) • Upper sixth 90 • Termly fees £2164 (Day) £3514 (Board) • HMC • Enquiries/application to the Headmaster or Academic Registrar

What it's like

Founded in 1542, it lies on 100 acres of fine estate in West Lavington, a pleasant village in the Vale of Pewsey, five miles south of Devizes. The junior school is in an attractive manor house nearby, with its own estate. It is a Christian foundation, ecumenical in spirit and practice, and aims to provide a sound education avoiding undue specialisation. Standards of teaching are high and academic results are very good. Virtually all sixth-form leavers go on to degree courses. A very strong tradition in music and good in drama and art. It enjoys a good reputation for sport and games (a new astro-turf pitch). There are many other activities, including outdoor pursuits and ocean sailing.

School profile

Pupils Age range 11–18; 620 pupils, 320 day (170 boys, 150 girls), 300 boarding (160 boys, 140 girls). Main entry ages 11, 13 and into the sixth. 3–5% are children of former pupils. *State school entry:* 50% intake at 11, plus 20% to sixth.

Entrance Common Entrance and own exam used. No special skills or religious requirements. Parents not expected to buy textbooks; maximum extras £30 plus music lessons. 15 pa assisted places (10 at age 11, 5 in sixth). Flexible number of scholarships/bursaries, £150–£1600 per term.

Parents 15+% in industry or commerce; 15+% in the armed services; 15+% are doctors, lawyers, etc. 50+% live within 30 miles; up to 10% live overseas.

Head and staff *Headmaster:* C R Evans, in post for 11 years. Previously Second Master at Taunton School. *Staff:* 64 full time, 18 part time. Annual turnover 8%. Average age 38.

Exam results In 1995, 101 pupils in fifth, 90 in upper sixth. *GCSE:* In 1995, 25% of fifth gained at least grade C in 8+ subjects; 74% in 6 subjects. *A-levels:* 60% upper sixth passed in 4+ subjects; 24% in 3; 15% in 2; and 1% in 1 subject. Average UCAS points 22.0.

University and college entrance 95% of 1995 sixth-form leavers went on to a degree course; others typically go on to art, drama and music colleges. Of those going on to university, 10% went to Oxbridge; 50% took courses in science and engineering, 40% in humanities and social sciences, 6% in art and design, 45% in drama and acting.

Curriculum GCSE, AS and A-levels. 22 subjects offered. 45% took science A-levels; 25% arts/humanities; 30% both. *Vocational:* Work experience available. *Computing facilities:* 25 Archimedes machines. *Special provision:* Some help for pupils with special learning difficulties (dyslexia), mild cases only. Some classes for foreign pupils, JMB test in English (for university entrance). *Europe:* French and German offered at GCSE, AS and A-level; also Russian and Italian GCSE. Regular exchanges (France). Exchange/work experience organised by Wiltshire County Council with Niart in France and a school in Germany.

The arts *Music:* Over 50% of pupils learn a musical instrument; instrumental exams can be taken. Some 12–15 musical groups including orchestras, choirs, dance band, wind band, pop group. *Drama & dance*: Both offered. Majority of pupils are involved in school productions and some in house/other productions, local Eisteddfod. *Art:* On average, 35 take GCSE, 15 A-level. Design, pottery, textiles, photography also offered.

Sport, community service and clubs *Sport and physical activities:* Sports available: rugby, hockey, squash, tennis, cricket, athletics, netball, swimming, fencing, riding, badminton, cross-country, golf, gymnastics, ocean-sailing, canoeing, water polo, volleyball, basketball, squash. BAGA exams may be taken. Number of county and regional representatives (rugby, hockey, netball, athletics, tennis, swimming). *Community service:* Pupils take bronze, silver and gold Duke of Edinburgh's Award. Community service optional. *Clubs and societies:* Up to 15 clubs, eg beekeeping, debating, bird-watching, sailing, model railway, electronics, wine appreciation.

Uniform School uniform worn; guided choice of own clothes in sixth.

Houses/prefects Prefects, head boy and girl, head of house and house prefects – appointed by the Headmaster and house staff.

Religion Christian non-denominational assembly compulsory except for those embracing non-Christian faith.

Social Regular visits abroad, ski trips, climbing/adventure club expeditions, ocean sailing, French and German exchange. Sports tours recently to Holland and Canada. Day pupils allowed to bring own car/bike/motorbike to school. Meals self-service. School shop. No tobacco allowed; alcohol only in sixth-form club.

Discipline Pupils failing to produce homework once might expect to have to do it; those caught smoking cannabis on the premises will be excluded.

Boarding 40% have own study bedroom, 60% share with one other. Single-sex houses

of approx 55. Resident qualified sister. Central dining room. Pupils can provide and cook own food. Exeats on request. Visits to local towns allowed.
Alumni association run by H J Hodges, c/o the School.
Former pupils Desmond Morris; Revd W Awdry (Thomas the Tank Engine); Simon May; Jeremy James Taylor; Andrew Gardner.

• DAVIES LAING & DICK (DLD)

Davies Laing & Dick, 10 Pembridge Square, London W2 4ED. Tel 0171 727 2797, Fax 0171 792 0730

• Pupils 287 • Boys 16–19 (Day) • Girls 16–19 (Day) • Upper sixth 155 • Termly fees £2730 (Day) • CIFE, BAC • Enquiries/application to the Principal

What it's like

Founded in 1931 as a co-educational sixth-form college, it has handsome premises in a very agreeable quiet garden square, in the Notting Hill area of west London. The buildings are large mid-19th century town houses. The college is well served by bus routes and is within a few minutes walk of three tube stations. It is a well-equipped establishment with over twenty classrooms and four laboratories, plus an art studio and a more than adequate library. The staff (most of whom come from Oxbridge or London University) is predominantly young; the staff:pupil ratio is roughly 1:11; the average set size 5.6. The curriculum caters for 2-year and 1-year A-level courses, retake A-levels, GCSE retakes and preparation for university entrance. In fact the vast majority of leavers go on to pursue degree courses and the results are very good. There is a lot of emphasis on examination techniques. Each student has a personal tutor and the college sets some store by the tutorial arrangements and the monitoring of an individual's work and progress. The staff expect high standards from their pupils and there is emphasis on the need for proper attendance, punctuality in submitting work and so forth. Sports and games are optional at the Kensington Centre where there are facilities for basketball, swimming and squash.

School profile

Pupils Age range 16–19; 287 day pupils (151 boys, 136 girls). Main entry is into the sixth. 10% are children of former pupils. *State school entry:* 20%.
Entrance No entrance exam; no special skills or religious requirements. Oversubscribed in some subjects. Fee is charged per subject (£470 for GCSE, £867 for A-level). Parents are not expected to buy textbooks; no other extras. 10 pa bursaries for financial need and scholarships, 10%–100% fees for academic excellence.
Parents 15+% are in industry/commerce; 15+% doctors/lawyers. Over 60% live within 30% miles; 5% live overseas.
Head and staff *Principal:* Peter W Boorman, in post for 9 years. Educated at King's School, Ely, and Cambridge University (mathematics and mechanical sciences). Previously Headmaster at Aldenham and Housemaster at King's School, Canterbury. *Staff:* 25 full time, 15 part time. Annual turnover 20%. Average age 31.
Exam results In 1995, 14 pupils in upper fifth, 155 in upper sixth. *GCSE:* In 1995, 70% upper fifth gained at least grade C in 5–7 subjects. *A-levels:* 80% passed in 3 subjects. Average UCAS points 22.0.
University and college entrance 92% of 1995 sixth-form leavers went on to a degree course; others typically go on to employment or other courses eg drama. Of those going on to university, 1% went to Oxbridge; 11% took courses in medicine, dentistry and veterinary science, 20% in science and engineering, 1% in law, 56% in humanities and social sciences, 5% in art and design, 1% in vocational subjects eg physiotherapy.
Curriculum A-levels and some GCSE offered. 37 examination subjects offered, including photography and media studies; no A-level general studies. 31% take science A-levels; 44% arts/humanities; 25% both. *Vocational:* Work experience available. *Computing facilities:* Fully-equipped computer room. *Special provision:* None; good skills in English expected. *Europe:* French, German, modern Greek, Italian and Spanish offered to A-level; all but Greek to GCSE.
The arts *Music:* Under 15% pupils learn a musical instrument; no musical groups in college. *Drama & dance*: A-level theatre studies offered. *Art:* On average, 5 take GCSE,

10 A-level. Textiles, photography, life classes and graphics also offered.
Sport, community service and clubs *Sport and physical activities:* No compulsory sports; sports centre nearby may be used by students. National representatives in eg tennis, polo, rowing.
Uniform None.
Houses/prefects No competitive houses or prefects.
Religion No compulsory worship.
Social No sports or social events organised. Students may bring own car/bike/motorbike to school. Meals self-service. No alcohol allowed; smoking only in specially designed smoking room.
Discipline Pupils failing to produce homework once would expect a reprimand; students caught smoking cannabis on the premises would expect instant dismissal.

• DEAN CLOSE

Dean Close School, Cheltenham, Gloucestershire GL51 6HE. Tel 01242 522640, Fax 01242 244758

• Pupils 443 • Boys 12–18 (Day/Board) • Girls 12–18 (Day/Board) • Upper sixth 81 • Termly fees £2845 (Day) £4075 (Board) • HMC • Enquiries/application to the Headmaster

What it's like

Founded in 1886 and named after Francis Close, Dean of Carlisle and erstwhile Rector of Cheltenham. It enjoys an agreeable 50-acre site, five minutes from the centre of the town. The compact core of its central building is characteristic of late Victorian school architecture. There has been steady expansion since 1945 and there are a number of modern buildings – including a fine purpose-built theatre. It is an evangelical C of E foundation (though members of other denominations are welcome) and the principles and aims of the founders are still regarded as fundamental. Attendance at chapel is compulsory and there are also voluntary meetings. Originally a boys' school, it has been fully co-educational since 1972. The staff:pupil ratio is about 1:9 and there is a large part-time staff. Academic standards and results are consistently very good. The vast majority of sixth-form leavers go on to degree courses including to Oxbridge. Music is very strong: there is a variety of musical groups and the fine chapel choir often sings for the BBC. There is much dramatic activity (some in the open-air). Ample playing fields on-site provide first-class facilities for sport and games (those on offer include golf, riding, archery, sailing, shooting and clay-pigeon shooting) and there are many county, regional and national representatiaves. There is a remarkable number of clubs and societies and a thriving CCF (army, navy and airforce sections). A substantial commitment to the Duke of Edinburgh's Award Scheme and to local community services.

School profile

Pupils Age range 12–18, 443 pupils; 160 day (84 boys, 76 girls), 273 boarding (158 boys, 115 girls). Main entry ages 12, 13 and into the sixth. 6% are children of former pupils. 66% senior intake is from own junior school. *State school entry:* 3% main intake, 11% to sixth.
Entrance Common Entrance and own entrance exam used. Any skills welcome; school is C of E but other pupils welcome. Parents not required to buy textbooks (except Bible, atlas and dictionary); average extras £50 per term. Around 12 pa scholarships, 10%–50% of fees; also some bursaries.
Parents 15+% in industry/commerce; 15+% in armed services and 15+% in church. Over 30% live within 30 miles, less than 10% overseas.
Head and staff *Headmaster:* Christopher J Bacon, 18 years in post. Educated at Cranbrook and Oxford (chemistry). Previously Head of Science and Housemaster at Oakham and Assistant Chemist at Canford. Previously Chairman of HMC Co-education Committee, co-opted member of HMC Committee and member of HMC CCF Committee. *Staff:* 50 full time, 20 part time. Annual turnover 6%. Average age 33.
Exam results In 1995, 85 pupils in upper fifth, 81 in upper sixth. *GCSE:* In 1995, 83% of upper fifth gained at least grade C in 8+ subjects; 13% in 5–7 subjects. *A-levels:* 8% passed in 4 subjects; 79% in 3; 12% in 2; and 1% in 1 subject. Average UCAS points 24.8.
University and college entrance 93% of 1995 sixth-form leavers went on to a degree course (8% after a gap year); others typically go on to further education or training. Of

those going on to university, 9% went to Oxbridge; 9% took courses in medicine, dentistry and veterinary science, 12% in science and engineering, 24% in humanities and social sciences, 6% in art and design, 19% in vocational subjects eg accountancy, agriculture, journalism and 17% in other subjects eg drama, languages.

Curriculum GCSE and A-levels offered. 16 subjects offered, including occasional Chinese and Japanese; no A-level general studies. 40% take science A-levels; 50% arts/humanities; 10% both. *Computing facilities:* Computer room with 25 PCs; CD-Rom; whole school networked. Computers in departments, houses and library. *Special provision:* Dyslexia unit for bright children. EFL. *Europe:* French (compulsory), German and Spanish offered at GCSE and A-level; occasionally Italian and Russian. Regular exchanges to France and Germany for pupils age 14–18. European pupils accepted for a term/year.

The arts *Music:* About 50% pupils learn a musical instrument; instrumental exams can be taken. Many musical groups, including orchestra, chamber orchestra, string group, choirs, wind band, jazz group. Recent pupil won Gloucestershire Musician of the year; regular organ and choral scholarships to Oxbridge; several musicians participate in junior RAM and RCM; many members of Gloucestershire Youth Orchestra; recent choir and orchestra trip to Europe; choir at St Paul's Cathedral, on BBC and recent CD. *Drama & dance*: Drama and dance offered; pupils may take GCSE drama, LAMDA, RAD and Guildhall exams. Some pupils involved in school productions, majority in house/other productions. *Art:* On average, 30 take GCSE, 10 A-level. Design, pottery, textiles, photography and printmaking also offered.

Sport, community service and clubs *Sport and physical activities:* Compulsory sports: Rugby, hockey, cross-country, cricket (boys). Netball, hockey, tennis (girls). Optional: sailing, athletics, swimming, golf, volleyball, basketball, squash, badminton, archery, lacrosse, soccer, shooting (including clay-pigeon shooting) and riding. Pupils may take A-level PE. Many county hockey players; national finalists Barclays Bank U16 girls hockey; national schools, county and regional representatives in athletics; county school boys cricket. *Community service:* Pupils take bronze, silver and gold Duke of Edinburgh's Award. CCF compulsory for 3 years at 13 (but conscientious objectors' clause), optional thereafter; community service optional for 2 years at 16+. 3 ex-pupils recently spent gap year at an orphanage in Kenya. *Clubs and societies:* Over 30 clubs including photography, natural history, electronics, chess, archery, drama technicals, dancing and astronomy.

Uniform School uniform worn except in the sixth (where there is a dress code).

Houses/prefects Competitive houses. Head boy/girl, school and house prefects and heads of houses, appointed by Head after consulting housemasters. School Council.

Religion Chapel attendance compulsory.

Social Many joint events with schools in Cheltenham and Gloucester. Cultural/educational visits to France, Russia and Italy. Pupils may bring own car/bike/horse to school. Meals self-service. School shop. No tobacco allowed; alcohol allowed in authorised circumstances but no bar.

Discipline Pupils failing to produce prep/homework once might expect extra work/mild reprimand; those caught smoking or procuring cannabis on the premises will be expelled (but help given in finding another school).

Boarding 15% have own study bedroom; 25% share with 1–3 others. 30% in dormitories of 6+. Single-sex houses of 30–60, same as competitive houses. Resident qualified nurse; doctor visits daily. Pupils can provide and cook own food. 2 exeats each term: half term plus 1 weekend. Visits allowed to local town (not more than 3 a fortnight and always accompanied).

Alumni association run by R C Padfield c/o the school.

• DENSTONE

Denstone College, Uttoxeter, Staffordshire ST14 5HN. Tel 01889 590484, Fax 01889 590091

• Pupils 300 • Boys 11–18 (Day/Board/Weekly) • Girls 11–18 (Day/Board/Weekly) • Upper sixth 50 • Termly fees £2590 (Day) £3630 (Board) • HMC, Woodard • Enquiries to the Registrar • Application to the Headmaster

What it's like

Founded in 1868, a Woodard school, it stands five miles north of Uttoxeter in open hilly countryside on 70 acres of very pleasant grounds. The main building is Victorian. Numerous modern buildings provide excellent up-to-date facilities of all kinds, including IT and CDT centres and a 9-hole golf course. Results are good and the majority of sixth-formers go on to degree courses, including to Oxbridge. It is particularly strong in music and drama and has a very impressive range of clubs and societies. Major sports played to high standard (county, regional, national successes). Vigorous participation in the Duke of Edinburgh's Award Scheme (20 gold awards in one year). The declared aim is to encourage pupils to develop their individual talents – to the extent of awarding scholarships to any outstanding talent which contributes to the life of the school. A friendly hard-working school where high standards of manners are maintained without rigid formality or oppression.

School profile

Pupils Age range 11–18; 300 pupils, 130 day (90 boys, 40 girls), 170 boarding (122 boys, 48 girls). Main entry ages 11, 13 and into sixth. *State school entry:* 20% main intake, plus 12% to sixth.
Entrance Common Entrance and own exam used. Special skills required for scholarships only. No religious requirements but pupils expected to attend C of E services. Parents expected to buy sixth-form textbooks (but a buy-back scheme operates). Assisted places. Scholarships (academic, instrumental, choral, sporting, art and other talents, eg drama) and bursaries (for children of clergy, servicemen) – up to 50% fees.
Parents 15+% in industry or commerce; 15+% in farming. 30+% live within 30 miles; up to 10% live overseas.
Head and staff *Headmaster:* Hugh Carson, in post for 6 years. Educated at Tonbridge and the universities of London and Reading (modern history, history of economics, politics). Previously Housemaster (of boys' boarding house) at Epsom. Also 11 years in the Royal Tank Regiment. *Staff:* 29 full time, 7 part time. Annual turnover 8%. Average age 36.
Exam results In 1995, 45 pupils in upper fifth, 47 in upper sixth. *GCSE:* In 1995, 52% upper fifth gained at least grade C in 8+ subjects; 19% in 5–7 subjects. *A-levels:* 14 upper sixth passed in 4+ subjects; 18 in 3; 8 in 2; and 7 in 1 subject. Average UCAS points 15.9.
University and college entrance 88% of 1995 sixth-form leavers went on to a degree course; others typically go on to non-degree courses eg agriculture, secretarial or art. Of those going on to university, 4% went to Oxbridge; 2% took courses in medicine, dentistry and veterinary science, 27% in science and engineering, 46% in humanities and social sciences, 16% in art and design, 9% in music and drama.
Curriculum GCSE and A-levels. 18 subjects offered, including A-level general studies. 20% take science and technology A-levels; 37% arts/humanities; 21% both. *Vocational:* Work experience available. *Computing facilities:* IT centre. *Special provision:* Specialist teaching for dyslexic pupils and for EFL. *Europe:* French and German offered to GCSE and A-level; also French AS-level and AO French for business studies; Spanish GCSE and A-level for native speakers. Regular exchanges (Germany and France). German pupils regularly attend sixth-form (EFL courses available).
The arts *Music:* 30% of pupils learn a musical instrument; instrumental exams can be taken. Some 6 musical groups including choirs, orchestra, wind band. *Drama & dance*: Drama offered. Majority of pupils are involved in school and house/other productions. *Art:* On average, 20 take GCSE, 10 A-level, including design, pottery. Numerous pupils go on to art colleges.
Sport, community service and clubs *Sport and physical activities:* Compulsory sports: rugby, cricket, cross-country, swimming, hockey, netball, rounders, athletics. Optional: squash, fives, badminton, keep fit, shooting, golf. Country champions in rugby and hockey; national and local honours in cricket and rugby. *Community service:* Pupils take silver and gold Duke of Edinburgh's Award. CCF optional. *Clubs and societies:* Up to 15 clubs, eg debating, drama, Christian Union, cantata choir, golf, swimming, photography.
Uniform School uniform worn throughout (sensible home clothes after school day).
Houses/prefects Competitive houses. Prefects, head boy/girl, head of house and house prefects – appointed by Headmaster in consultation with staff.
Religion Attendance at Chapel compulsory (simple service Tue–Fri; full scale communion service weekly; Sunday worship for full boarders).
Social Foreign tours by Schola Cantorum; study tours to USA, Russia, Czech Republic;

expeditions abroad for climbing/hill-walking; annual ski holiday; CCF camp abroad; rugby and cricket tours (eg South Africa); school exchanges. Pupils allowed to bring own bike to school. Meals self service. School tuck, general equipment, paperback book, and uniform shops. No tobacco allowed; alcohol allowed only in sixth-form bar.
Discipline Withdrawal of privileges and community help used.
Boarding 10% have own study bedroom, 55% share; 35% in dormitories of 6+. Single-sex houses of approx 50, same as competitive houses (boys), divided by age (girls). Girls are members of main school houses for social/tutorial/competitive purposes. Resident qualified nurses. Central dining room. Pupils can provide and cook own food. 28-hour exeats twice termly and half-term. Visits to local town allowed. Weekly boarding available.
Former pupils T A Kemp (physician/rugby international/President RFU); Geoffrey Smith (political columnist); Alistair Hignell (rugby international); John Makepeace (furniture designer); Ian Platt (operatic singer); Sir Christopher French (High Court Judge); Rear Admiral P G Hammersley; P D Kelly (Walker Cup captain); Professor A K Mant (pathologist); Professor M L H Green (chemist); W P C Davies (rugby international); T Marlow, M Liggins (broadcasters).

• DIXIE GRAMMAR

Dixie Grammar School, Market Bosworth, Nuneaton, Leicestershire CV13 0LE. Tel 01455 292244, Fax 01455 292151

• Pupils 265 • Boys 10–18 (Day) • Girls 10–18 (Day) • Upper sixth 14 • Termly fees £1250 (Day) • ISAI • Enquiries/application to the Headmaster's Secretary

What it's like

Reputed to be the oldest grammar school in the county (although there are no records before 1320), the Dixie was refounded in 1987 as a co-educational school. It has a very agreeable site in the middle of the attractive and historic market town. The principal and handsome surviving old buildings (dating from 1828) have their frontage on to the main town square. In recent years there have been a number of additions and the school is well equipped. Its pretty gardens and grounds occupy 4 acres and the rear of the school overlooks open countryside. It has recently acquired 38 acres of playing fields half a mile away. With its own prep school continuous education is possible from age 4. The long-term policy is to keep the school relatively small. It is non-denominational, but religious education is an integral part of the curriculum and all pupils are expected to attend assembly and prayers. The staff:pupil ratio is about 1:9. Academic standards and results are good and most sixth-form leavers go on to degree courses. Music and drama are well supported. A standard variety of sports and games is available, including hockey, squash, rugby and tennis. There is a wide range of clubs and societies for extra-curricular activities and strong participation in the Duke of Edinburgh's Award scheme.

School profile

Pupils Age range 10–18; 265 day pupils (136 boys, 129 girls). Main entry ages 10, 11, 13, 14 and into sixth. 70% intake from own prep school, Wolstan Preparatory School (tel 01455 292244). *State school entry:* 30% at 11.
Entrance Common Entrance and own exam used. No special skills or religious requirements. Parents not expected to buy textbooks; no other extras. 7 pa scholarships/bursaries, £312–£417 per term.
Head and staff *Headmaster:* R S Willmott, appointed in 1993. Educated at King's College School, Wimbledon and at universities of Cambridge and East Anglia. Previously Deputy Headmaster at Brighton College, English Master at Manchester Grammar School and Norwich School. *Staff:* 29 full time, 11 part time. Annual turnover 3%. Average age 37.
Exam results In 1995, 52 pupils in upper fifth, 14 in upper sixth. *GCSE:* In 1995, 60% upper fifth gained at least grade C in 8+ subjects; 29% in 5–7; and 9% in 1–4 subjects. *A-levels:* 79% upper sixth passed in 3 subjects; and 14% in 2 subjects. Average UCAS points 18.3 (including general studies 21.3).
University and college entrance 70% of 1995 sixth-form leavers went on to a degree course (10% after a gap year); others typically go on to HND, employment in local

business or family firm. Of those going on to university, average of 4% go to Oxbridge; 10% took courses in medicine, dentistry and veterinary science, 15% in science and engineering, 5% in law, 25% in humanities and social sciences, 25% in art and design, 20% in other subjects eg physiotherapy.

Curriculum GCSE and A-levels. 17 subjects offered (including A-level general studies). 14% take science A-levels; 50% arts/humanities; 36% both. *Vocational:* Work experience available. *Computing facilities:* Research Nimbus network of 186/386 PCs. CD-Rom in library, plus CAD and various computers in departments. *Europe:* French and German offered at GCSE, AS and A-level (both compulsory to age 14). German and French exchanges.

The arts *Music:* Over 15% of pupils learn a musical instrument; instrumental exams can be taken. Some 7 musical groups including orchestra, choirs, wind band, recorder group, modern music. *Drama & dance*: Drama offered. LAMDA exams may be taken. Some pupils are involved in school productions. *Art:* On average, 20 take GCSE, 6 A-level.

Sport, community service and clubs *Sport and physical activities:* Compulsory sports: rugby/hockey, swimming, cross-country, netball, cricket/rounders. Optional: soccer, tennis. Sixth form only: squash. RLSS exams may be taken. *Community service:* Pupils take bronze, silver and gold Duke of Edinburgh's Award. Community service compulsory for 1 year at age 17. *Clubs and societies:* Up to 15 clubs, eg Young Enterprise, chess, drama, music groups.

Uniform School uniform worn throughout (separate uniform for sixth-form).

Houses/prefects Competitive houses. Prefects, head boy/girl, heads of house – appointed by the Headmaster (after consultation).

Religion Attendance at religious worship expected but not compulsory.

Social Regular ski trips to French Alps or Canada. Pupils allowed to bring own car/bike to school. Meals self-service. School shop. No tobacco/alcohol allowed.

Discipline Pupils failing to produce homework once might expect to do it at lunchtime under supervision; those caught smoking cannabis on the premises could expect expulsion.

Alumni association run by Mrs J Godby, 5 The Drive, Masons Farm, Kibworth Beauchamp, Leicester LE8 0JW.

• DOUAI

Douai School, Upper Woolhampton, Reading, Berkshire RG7 5TH. Tel 01734 715200, Fax 01734 715241

• Pupils 220 • Boys 10–18 (Day/Board/Weekly) • Girls 10–18 (Day/Board/Weekly) • Upper sixth 35 • Termly fees £2175 (Day) £3375 (Board) £3275 (Weekly) • HMC • Enquiries/application to the Headmaster

What it's like

Founded in 1615 in Paris, the school and the Benedictine community moved to the present site in 1903. Its handsome buildings lie in a setting of considerable beauty and comprise 200 acres, bordered by fields and woodlands on the southern edge of the Berkshire Downs, overlooking the Kennet valley. The school adjoins the Benedictine monastery and its abbey church. It is run by monks (the Head is a monk) as well as lay staff and the pupils are brought up in the Benedictine tradition of learning and service to God and the community in which they live. Girls were accepted for the first time in 1993 and have integrated successfully at every level. It is very well-equipped with modern facilities (including comfortable boarding accommodation) and has particularly fine playing fields. The teaching is of a high standard and results are good. Most sixth-form leavers go on to degree courses. There is much emphasis on physical fitness and games and sports are important. Music, drama and art are flourishing. Very good facilities for such activities as light engineering, electronics and woodwork. There is a strong tradition of participation in community service and an impressive record in the Duke of Edinburgh's Award Scheme.

School profile

Pupils Age range 10–18; 210 pupils; 170 boys (65 day, 106 boarding), 33 girls; girls first accepted in 1993. Main entry ages 10, 11, 13 and into sixth. Approx 4% are children of former pupils. *State school entry:* 33% main intake, plus 5% to sixth.

Entrance Common Entrance and own exam used. No special skills required; most pupils are Roman Catholics, other Christians welcome. Parents not expected to buy textbooks; extras £200 maximum. 5 pa assisted places. 10 pa scholarships/bursaries.

Parents 7+% in the armed services; 13+% are doctors, lawyers, etc. 50% live within 30 miles; 25% live overseas.

Head and staff *Headmaster:* Rev Edmund Power OSB, 3 years in post. Educated at Exeter and London universities (philosophy and theology). Previously lecturer of theology at Collegio Sant'Anselm in Rome and Housemaster and Head of RS at Douai. *Staff:* 21 full time, 9 part time. Annual turnover 5%. Average age 45.

Exam results In 1995, 41 pupils in upper fifth, 20 in upper sixth. *GCSE:* In 1995, 22 upper fifth gained at least grade C in 8+ subjects; 10 in 5–7 subjects. *A-levels:* 1 upper sixth passed in 4+ subjects; 10 in 3; 5 in 2; and 4 in 1 subject. Average UCAS points 16.6.

University and college entrance 66% of 1995 sixth-form leavers went on to a degree course (5% after a gap year); others typically go on to employment or other higher education course. Of those going on to university, 3% went to Oxbridge; 10% took courses in medicine, dentistry and veterinary science, 20% in science and engineering, 5% in law, 50% in humanities and social sciences, 5% in art and design, 10% in other subjects eg hospitality management, product design.

Curriculum GCSE and A-levels. 19 subjects offered, including theology, philosophy, photography GCSE and A-level; and A-level general studies. 20% take science A-levels; 65% arts/humanities; 15% both. *Vocational:* Work experience available. *Computing facilities:* Network of PCs, plus scanners and CD ROM. Other computers in departments. *Special provision:* Dyslexic and EFL teachers attend each week. *Europe:* French, German and Spanish offered at GCSE and A-level. Regular exchanges (France and Germany). European students (especially German, Italian, Spanish) join the school.

The arts *Music:* Over 30% of pupils learn a musical instrument; instrumental exams can be taken. Some 9 musical groups including orchestral, choral, brass ensemble, wind band, string trio, concert band, music drama group. *Drama & dance:* Drama offered and AS-level may be taken. Pupils are involved in school and house/other productions. *Art:* On average, 25 take GCSE, 10 A-level. Design, pottery, photography also offered.

Sport, community service and clubs *Sport and physical activities:* Compulsory sports (to different ages): PE, soccer, rugby, cricket. Optional: fencing, badminton, squash, sailing, cross-country, multi-gym, swimming, athletics, tennis, basketball, netball, table tennis, handball, trampolining, gymnastics. *Community service:* Pupils take bronze, silver and gold Duke of Edinburgh's Award. Community service optional. *Clubs and societies:* Up to 30 clubs, eg bridge, cookery, international politics, graphics, various sports and musical clubs.

Uniform School uniform worn, relaxed for sixth-form.

Houses/prefects Competitive houses. Prefects, head of school, head of house and house prefects – appointed after consultation with staff and pupils.

Religion Compulsory Sunday Mass; other religious events available during week. Daily assembly.

Social Debates with other schools, dances and other social functions. Regular ski trips, art trips, sporting tours; exchanges with Germany and France. Meals self-service. School shop. No tobacco/alcohol allowed, except in monitored sixth-form bar.

Discipline For breaches in academic discipline, a system of detentions and report sheets is used. For breaches of school rules, a system involving community service, gating and suspensions operates.

Boarding Fifth and sixth-forms have own study bedroom; others in dormitories of 6+. Houses are administrative (60 in each), not residential. 3 SRNs in rotation; doctor visits daily. Central dining room. 2 weekend exeats each term and half-term. Visits to local town allowed for fifth form and above.

• DOVER COLLEGE

Dover College, Dover, Kent CT17 9RH. Tel 01304 215079

• Pupils 265 • Boys 11–18 (Day/Board/Weekly) • Girls 11–18 (Day/Board/Weekly) • Upper sixth 50 • Termly fees £1235–£2050 (Day) £2600–£3840 (Board) £2235–£3625 (Weekly) • HMC • Enquiries to the Registrar • Application to the Headmaster

What it's like

Founded in 1871 and granted a royal charter by George V in 1923, it has a fine site in Dover on the grounds formerly occupied by the medieval Priory of St Martin, some of whose monastic buildings survive and are occupied by the school: the Refectory (c.1130) is the school dining hall and the Gatehouse contains the sixth-form study centre and careers suite. The College Close is surrounded by the ancient buildings. There have been numerous improvements and extensions in recent years and the school is now very well equipped. Now co-educational, it was a boys' school until 1978 when girls were first admitted. The college aims to increase children's capacity for a satisfying adult life through industry and self-discipline. A sound general education is provided and results are consistently creditable. Most leavers go on to degree courses. Music plays an important part in the school's life. There is an orchestra, a choir and various ensembles and bands. Drama is also strong and there are several productions each year, plus a house drama festival. Art and information technology are well provided for. A wide range of sports and games is available (many county regional representatives).

School profile

Pupils Age range 11–18; 265 pupils, 98 day (63 boys, 35 girls), 167 boarders (105 boys, 62 girls). Main entry ages 11, 13 and into sixth. 5% are children of former pupils. *State school entry:* 15% main intake, plus 5% to sixth.

Entrance Common Entrance and some own tests used. General range of skills looked for; no religious requirements. 5 pa assisted places. 12 pa scholarships/bursaries £200 to full fees.

Parents 15+% in industry. Up to 50% live within 30 miles; 25+% live overseas.

Head and staff *Headmaster:* Martin Wright, 5 years in post. Educated at Taunton's School, Southampton, and the universities of Bristol, London and Cambridge (economics, statistics, history and economics of social history). Previously Senior Master at Clifton; Housemaster and Head of Department at Highgate; and Economics Master at Queenswood and Taunton's School, Southampton. Also JP Inner London (1983), Bristol (1991) and Dover; Vice Chairman, London Economics Association; member Court of Bristol and Kent universities. *Staff:* 25 full time, 8 part time. Annual turnover 10%. Average age 36.

Exam results In 1995, 50 pupils in upper fifth, 40 in upper sixth. *GCSE:* In 1995, 78% upper fifth gained at least grade C in 5+ subjects. *A-levels:* 3 upper sixth passed in 4+ subjects; 14 in 3; 12 in 2; and 8 in 1 subject. Average UCAS points 14.1.

University and college entrance All 1995 sixth-form leavers went on to a degree course (14% after a gap year), 3% to Oxbridge; 3% took courses in medicine, dentistry and veterinary science, 20% in science and engineering, 20% in humanities and social sciences, 9% in art and design, 45% in vocational subjects eg hotel management, PE, media studies.

Curriculum GCSE and A-levels. 17 GCSE subjects offered; 16 at A-level (no A-level general studies). 20% take science A-levels; 40% arts/humanities; 40% both. *Vocational:* Work experience available. *Computing facilities:* Acorn computers in many departments. Computer lab equipped with DAN 486 multi-media computers. *Special provision:* Good EFL provision. Special needs provision (dyslexia). *Europe:* French, German and Spanish offered at GCSE, AS and A-level. Regular exchanges (France, Germany and Spain) plus individual visits and exchanges. European pupils (particularly German) for 1–3 terms.

The arts *Music:* Up to 50% of pupils learn a musical instrument; instrumental exams can be taken. Some 4 musical groups including jazz, orchestra, choirs. Musical groups perform in Canterbury Festival; European choir tours. *Drama & dance*: Drama is offered at various levels; GCSE may be taken. Many pupils are involved in school productions and majority in house/other productions. *Art:* On average, 15–20 take GCSE, 5 A-level. Design, pottery, textiles, photography also offered.

Sport, community service and clubs *Sport and physical activities:* Compulsory sports:

rugby, hockey, netball, cricket. Optional: cross-country, tennis, squash, athletics, swimming. GCSE, AS-level, BAGA, RLSS, RYA exams may be taken. Regional and county hockey representatives; county cricketers. *Community service:* Pupils take bronze, silver and gold Duke of Edinburgh's Award. Community service compulsory for 3 years at age 15. *Clubs and societies:* Up to 15 clubs, eg chess, bridge, debating, photography, library, boat maintenance, conservation.
Uniform School uniform worn, modified in the sixth-form.
Houses/prefects Competitive houses. Prefects, head boy/girl, head of house and house prefects – appointed by the Headmaster.
Religion Compulsory worship, with specific exceptions.
Social Occasional joint functions with other local schools. Some organised trips abroad. Pupils allowed to bring own bike to school, cars only with specific permission. Meals self-service. No tobacco allowed; sixth-form common room is licensed.
Discipline Pupils failing to produce homework once might expect rebuke and a new deadline; those caught smoking cannabis would be dismissed instantly.
Boarding 70% have own study bedroom, 20% share (with 2 or 3). Single-sex houses, of 30–65, same as for competitive purposes. Resident qualified nurse. Central dining room. Pupils can provide and cook snacks in houses. Unlimited termly exeats subject to Sunday Chapel attendance. Visits to local town allowed daily for an hour or so.
Alumni association is run by Mrs J Glyn Thomas, Endfield, 6 Lookers Lane, Saltwood, Hythe, Kent.
Former pupils Sir Frederic Ashton, Lord Maugham (Lord Chancellor), General Sir Gerald Duke, Sir Michael Weston, Richard Aldington.

• D'OVERBROECK'S

d'Overbroeck's, Beechlawn House, Park Town, Oxford OX2 6SN. Tel 01865 310000, Fax 01865 52296

• Pupils 240 • Boys 14–19 (Day/Board) • Girls 14–19 (Day/Board) • Upper sixth 108 • Termly fees £1950–£3055 (Day) £3150–£4255 (Board) • ISAI • Enquiries/application to the Principal

What it's like

Founded in 1989 by the merger of Beechlawn and d'Overbroeck's, it is a progressive, co-educational tutorial college for students preparing for GCSE and A-levels. It provides a real alternative to a traditional independent school whilst placing a good deal of emphasis on academic achievement. The aim is to create an atmosphere in which learning is an interesting and exciting experience. The staff:pupil ratio is 1:4 and the staff are very approachable. Teaching takes place either in small groups or on an individual basis, the choice between the two methods being largely up to the pupil or parents. The academic programme is highly flexible: almost all A-level and GCSE subjects may be studied in any combination. It is geared equally for high fliers of Oxbridge standard and those who are less academically ambitious. Supervision is close and personal. Considerable guidance from experienced staff is given to higher education and applications and the number gaining entry to university are high. Good modern facilities include new science laboratories and IT centre. A varied sporting programme and the cultural and social benefits of being in the centre of Oxford.

School profile

Pupils Age range 14–19; 240 pupils (boys and girls) 110 day, 130 boarding. Approx 25–30 join at 14, the remainder at 16; also courses for 18 year olds needing a third year in the sixth-form.
Parents Varied in background; 85% British; 42% live within commuting distance.
Head and staff Principals: R Knowles (4 years in post) and S Cohen (1 year). *Staff:* 30 full time, 25 part-time. Average age 35.
University and college entrance The majority of leavers proceed to a degree course.
Curriculum GCSE and A-levels. Wide range of GCSEs and almost all A-levels offered. Each student has a Director of Studies to provide guidance and advice.
Europe French, Spanish, German, Italian and other European languages offered. Overseas courses organised as required.
The arts Extra-mural activities are various and include theatre trips, field work and gallery visits.

Sport, community service and clubs Sports include rugby, hockey, football, rowing, squash, tabletennis and basketball. Skiing trips organised.
Uniform None.
Houses/prefects None.
Religion Non-denominational.
Social Trips organised for theatres, museums, galleries, field work and sporting fixtures. Student social events organised every term.
Discipline Emphasis on internally imposed discipline, pupils learning to organise their own time and taking responsibility for their own academic progress.
Boarding Either in college halls of residence or with carefully chosen families; older students may stay in shared housing. All arrangements handled by college's accommodation staff.

• DOWNE HOUSE

Downe House, Cold Ash, Newbury, Berkshire RG18 9JJ. Tel 01635 200286, Fax 01635 202026
• Pupils 618 • Boys None • Girls 11–18 (Day/Board) • Upper sixth 71 • Termly fees £3000 (Day) £4140 (Board) • GSA, BSA • Enquires/application to the Registrar

What it's like

Founded by Miss Olive Willis in 1907 in Darwin's home, Downe House in Kent, it moved to its present site in 1921. This is a very beautiful site of 110 acres in the village of Cold Ash, on a wooded ridge 5 miles north of Newbury. Extensive modernisation and building has taken place over the years and facilities are now first-rate. The accommodation is very civilised. Life in the sixth-form is planned to give girls a greater degree of independence to provide a transition between school and higher education. The school has its own chapel which is central to school life. The teaching is good and results are excellent. All sixth-formers go on to degree courses, a number to Oxbridge. The school is very strong indeed in music; the art and drama departments are very active. There are excellent sports facilities and a wide range of extra-curricular activities.

School profile

Pupils Age range 11–18, 618 girls (33 day, 585 boarding). Main entry ages 11, 12 and 13. *State school entry:* 3% main intake.
Entrance Common Entrance exam and own assessment used. Assisted places and scholarships (academic and music) available.
Head and staff *Headmistress:* Miss S Cameron, appointed 1989. Educated at Wycombe Abbey and London University (history). Previously Headmistress at Cobham Hall and House Mistress at Sherborne. Also Governor of Repton and a school inspector
Exam results In 1995, 87 pupils in upper fifth, 71 in upper sixth. *GCSE:* In 1995, all upper fifth gained grade C or above in 9+ subjects. *A-levels:* 96% upper sixth passed in 4+ subjects; 4% in 3 subjects. Average UCAS points 26.3.
University and college entrance All 1995 sixth-form leavers went on to a degree course (65% after a gap year), 15% to Oxbridge; 10% took courses in medicine, dentistry and veterinary science, 10% in science and engineering, 10% in law, 55% in humanities and social sciences (including languages), 5% in art and design, 10% in vocational subjects eg sports science, physiotherapy, education.
Curriculum GCSE and A-levels. 25 subjects offered, including A-level general studies. 16% take science A-levels; 41% arts/humanities; 43% both. *Vocational:* RSA Stage 1 word processing taken by all lower sixth. *Europe:* French (compulsory), German, Russian and Spanish offered at GCSE and A-level; also Italian GCSE and French and German AS-level. All 12-year-olds spend a term in France; regular exchanges (aged 14–16 to France).
The arts *Music:* Almost all pupils learn a musical instrument; instrumental exams can be taken. Some 10 musical groups including 2 orchestras, 4 choirs, wind, brass bands. National Chamber Music Competition finalists and semi-finalists. *Drama & dance*: Both offered. GCSE drama and Poetry Society exams may be taken. Majority of pupils are involved in school and house/other productions. *Art:* On average, 30 take GCSE, 4 A-level; 25 take GCSE photography in sixth. Pottery, textiles also offered. All A-level art students accepted to foundation courses.
Sport, community service and clubs *Sport and physical activities:* Compulsory sports: tennis, squash, lacrosse, swimming, athletics, aerobics, gymnastics, trampolining, cross-

country, running, dance. Sixth form only: golf. National, county and territory lacrosse representatives. *Community service:* Pupils take bronze, silver and gold Duke of Edinburgh's Award. CCF and community service optional. Summer holiday camp for deprived children; entertainment for elderly. *Clubs and societies:* Up to 30 clubs, eg clay-pigeon shooting, debating, fencing, art appreciation.
Discipline Pupils failing to produce homework once might expect detention; those caught smoking cannabis on the premises, expulsion.

• DOWNSIDE

Downside School, Stratton-on-the-Fosse, Bath, BA3 4RJ. Tel 01761 232206, Fax 01761 233575, e-mail, downside@rmplc.co.uk

• Pupils 350 • Boys 10–18 (Day/Board) • Girls None • Upper sixth 60 • Termly fees £1980 (Day) £3710 (Board) • HMC • Enquiries/application to the Head Master

What it's like

Founded in 1606 at Douai for English Catholics in exile because of the penal laws. At the time of the French Revolution the monks fled to England and in 1814 the school moved to Downside, where the English Benedictine community of St Gregory became established. It lies at the foot of the Mendip Hills in splendid Somerset country, 12 miles from Bath. Handsome buildings and excellent modern facilities make a compact campus of which the monastery and its Abbey Church are a part. Superb playing fields, gardens and grounds surround it. The aim of the school is to help each pupil to become fully Catholic and adult. The monastic influence is strong. The Head Master and some housemasters are monks, as are some 7 members of the teaching staff. The staff:pupil ratio is 1:6. A good general education is provided and results are good. Almost all sixth-formers go on to degree courses, including Oxbridge. The music and art departments are active, and much use is made of the purpose-built theatre for a wide range of dramatic productions. The school is strong in sports and games (about 20 are available). A very large number of societies and clubs (about 30) cater for extra-curricular activities.

School profile

Pupils Age range 10–18; 350 boys, almost all boarders. Senior department 13–18, 301 boys. Main entry ages 10, 13 and into sixth. Approx 20% are children of former pupils. Significant intake from own junior house (Plunkett House) and a number of Catholic and non-Catholic prep schools.
Entrance Common Entrance and own exam used. No special skills required; Roman Catholicism desirable, though other Christian denominations considered. Parents not expected to buy textbooks but are charged a hiring fee. Scholarships (academic, art, music and maths) at 13+; also sixth-form entrance scholarships. Bursaries available at discretion of Head Master.
Parents Up to 10% live within 30 miles; 20+% live overseas.
Head and staff Head Master: Dom Antony Sutch, appointed in 1996. Educated at Downside and Exeter University. Previously Housemaster and Teacher at Downside. *Staff:* 55 full time, 17 part time.
Exam results In 1995, 60 pupils in upper fifth, 68 in upper sixth. *GCSE:* 90% of upper fifth gained grade C or above in 5+ subjects. *A-levels:* 22% passed in 4+ subjects; 59% in 3; 12% in 2; and 5% in 1 subject. Average UCAS points 19.5.
University and college entrance 90% of 1995 sixth-form leavers went on to a degree course; others typically go on to non-degree course eg land management, into the services or to art college. Of those going on to university, 10% went to Oxbridge; 3% took courses in medicine, dentistry and veterinary science, 18% in science and engineering, 75% in humanities and social sciences, 3% in art and design.
Curriculum GCSE and A-levels. 20% take science/engineering A-levels; 50% take arts/humanities; 30% take a mixture. *Vocational:* Work experience available. *Special provision:* for EFL, dyslexia, mild visual, aural or physical handicap and special dietary needs. *Europe:* French, German, Italian and Spanish offered to GCSE and A-level; also French and Spanish AS-level and Russian A-level (French taught in first year, other languages from second). Regular exchanges (France, Austria, Hungary, Russia and Spain). European library; special committee fosters European links. Several members of staff (beside linguists) have family links and/or have studied at European universities.

The arts *Music:* Over 50% of pupils learn a musical instrument; instrumental exams can be taken. Many musical groups including 3 orchestras, 4 choral, 5 bands, various small ensembles, groups, concert band, 4 jazz bands. Recent pupils include a former Vienna Choir Boy, now international soloist, and a violin player, now international recitalist; jazz trio runner-up in Daily Telegraph National Jazz Competition; flautist in Young Musician of the Year. *Drama & dance*: Drama offered. Majority of pupils are involved in house/other productions. First amateur production of Shadowlands by William Nicholson (old boy). *Art:* On average, 24 take GCSE, 12 A-level. 3D design, pottery and ceramics also offered.
Sport, community service and clubs *Sport and physical activities:* Major sports: rugby (Michaelmas), hockey (Lent) and cricket (summer term); all pupils encouraged to play. Optional sports: soccer, cross-country, orienteering, tennis, swimming, fencing, athletics, archery, squash, golf, basketball (all with school matches arranged); also badminton, volleyball, table tennis, short tennis, and indoor hockey. Number of county and regional representatives; national representatives at eg rugby, squash, croquet, sabre. *Community service:* Pupils take bronze, silver and gold Duke of Edinburgh's Award. CCF optional. Charity links and exchanges with Belgium, Germany, Romania and Kenya. *Clubs and societies:* Over 30 clubs, eg debating, jazz, various music, judo, golf, fencing, orienteering, Hispanic, Russian, chess, Young Enterprise, amateur radio, drama.
Uniform School uniform worn.
Houses/prefects Houses. Prefects, head boy, head of house and house prefects – appointed by the Headmaster.
Religion Mass on Sunday; house service once a week; morning and evening prayers, all compulsory.
Social School dances and choral society production with local girls' schools. Occasional theatrical productions and debates with local comprehensive schools. Organised trips abroad for skiing, various sports tours, exchanges with schools in Europe. Pupils allowed to bring own bike to school. Meals self-service. School shop. No pupils allowed tobacco.
Discipline Pupils failing to produce homework once might expect to be kept from the Sunday film; those caught with drugs will be expelled; rustication for bringing alcohol into the school; 3 weeks gating for being found in a pub.
Boarding Fifth and sixth-form have own study bedroom, others in dormitories. Houses of approximately 60. Resident qualified nursing staff on site 24 hrs a day, local doctor visits daily. Central dining rooms. 2 voluntary weekend exeats each term. Weekend visits to the local town allowed for sixth-form.
Alumni association (St Gregory's Society) is run by Dom Daniel Rees, c/o the School.
Former pupils Richard Stokes (Privy Seal); Lord Rawlinson (former Attorney General); Simon Halliday (rugby international); Maurice Couve-de-Murville (Archbishop of Birmingham); Auberon Waugh; Lord Hunt (former cabinet secretary); William Nicholson (playwright); Sir Rocco Forte.

• DUCHY GRAMMAR

The Duchy Grammar School, Tregye, Truro, Cornwall TR3 6JH. Tel 01872 862289
• Pupils 103 • Boys 3–18 (Day/Board/Weekly) • Girls 3–18 (Day/Board/Weekly) • Upper sixth 4 • Termly fees £1625 (Day) £2788 (Board) £2694 (Weekly) • ISAI • Enquiries/application to the Headmaster

What it's like

Founded in 1982 as a co-educational school, it lies on a single site of eight acres in pleasant countryside 4 miles from Truro. The central building is Tregye, a small 19th-century country house. A sound general education is provided and its ethos is intended to reflect the values of the former Cathedral School from which it derives. There are good modern facilities and comfortable boarding accommodation. A more than adequate range of sport and games (some individual county honours).

School profile

Pupils Total age range 3–18; 103 pupils, 72 day (47 boys, 25 girls), 27 boarding (17 boys, 10 girls). Senior department 11–18, 80 pupils (53 boys, 27 girls). Main entry ages 11 and into sixth. *State school entry:* 75% intake at 11, plus 30% to sixth.

Entrance No special skills or religious requirements. Parents not expected to buy textbooks; extras approx £20 per term (music, extra-curricular activities etc). 6 pa scholarships/bursaries, 33%-75% tuition fees.
Parents 60+% live within 30 miles; up to 10% live overseas.
Head and staff *Headmaster:* Michael Fuller, in post for 10 years. Educated at Finchley Grammar School and London and Exeter universities (geography and education). Previously Master of the Preparatory School and Head of Geography at Truro Cathedral School and Thetford Fulmerston School. Also Chairman, School Governors and PCC. *Staff:* 11 full time, 7 part time. Annual turnover 5%. Average age 32.
Exam results In 1995, 18 pupils in upper fifth, 5 in upper sixth. *GCSE:* In 1995, 10 upper fifth gained at least grade C in 8+ subjects; 7 in 5–7 subjects. *A-levels:* 1 upper sixth passed in 4 subjects; 4 in 3 subjects. Average UCAS points 12.7.
University and college entrance 90% of 1995 sixth-form leavers went on to a degree course (none takes a gap year); others typically go on to the armed forces. Of those going on to university, 10% took courses in medicine, dentistry and veterinary science, 50% in science and engineering, 40% in humanities and social sciences.
Curriculum GCSE and A-levels. 20 subjects offered (including GCSE drama and PE; no A-level general studies). 70% take science A-levels; 30% take both science and arts/humanities. *Vocational:* Work experience available. *Computing facilities:* 6 micros in a computing base, 4 in graphics department. *Special provision:* Individual tuition with dyslexic specialist. EFL course. *Europe:* French (compulsory from Year 6) and German offered to GCSE, AS and A-level. Regular exchanges to France and Germany.
The arts (Pupils aged 11 and over) *Music:* Up to 15% of pupils learn a musical instrument; instrumental exams can be taken. Some 3 musical groups including choirs, recorder groups. *Drama & dance*: Drama offered and GCSE may be taken. Some pupils are involved in school productions and all in house/other productions. *Art:* On average, 6 take GCSE, 1 A-level. Design, pottery, photography also offered. Regional winner National Calendar Competition.
Sport, community service and clubs (Pupils aged 11 and over) *Sport and physical activities:* Compulsory sports: soccer, rugby, hockey, athletics, cricket, netball, basketball, cross-country. Optional: badminton, tennis, volleyball, swimming, table tennis. GCSE exams may be taken. County honours in rugby; regional honours, swimming. *Community service:* Pupils take bronze, silver and gold Duke of Edinburgh's Award. Community service optional for 2 years at age 16+. Outdoor education course compulsory for Years 7–10: hiking, first aid, canoeing, sailing, sailboarding, riding, campcraft. *Clubs and societies:* Up to 10 clubs, eg pottery, chess, 5-a-side soccer.
Uniform School uniform worn throughout.
Houses/prefects Competitive houses. Prefects, head boy/girl, head of house and house prefects – appointed by the Headmaster. School Council.
Religion Daily assembly.
Social 5-day French visit. 7-day skiing trip. Exchange visits with pupils in Germany. Pupils allowed to bring own car/bike/motorbike to school. Meals formal. School shop. No tobacco/alcohol allowed.
Discipline Pupils failing to produce homework once might expect immediate after-school detention; those caught smoking cigarettes on the premises could expect talk in presence of parents and suspension; expulsion for subsequent offences.
Boarding 20% have own study bedroom, 60% share (in 3s); 20% are in dormitories of 4+. Central dining room. Senior pupils allowed to provide and cook food and drink. 2 weekend exeats each term. Visits to local town allowed at weekends.

• DUKE OF YORK'S

Duke of York's Royal Military School, Dover, Kent CT15 5EQ. Tel 01304 245029, Fax 01304 245019, e-mail duke@easynet.co.uk

• Pupils 500 • Boys 11–18 (Board) • Girls 11–18 (Board) • Upper sixth 34 • Termly fees £265 (Board) • SHMIS, BSA • Enquiries/applications to the Headmaster

What it's like

Founded in 1803, the modern establishment is purpose-built, in about 150 acres of pleasant parkland 2 miles from Dover. Its president is the Duke of Kent and the governing body consists of 15 commissioners some of whom are appointed by the monarch. Though largely financed by the Ministry of Defence it is a school not a military unit. The aim is to offer a broad, traditional grammar boarding school education for children of service personnel, whose different postings can otherwise disrupt education. It was founded as a co-educational school. Standards are high and academic results are good. In religious terms it is in the main stream of Anglican practice. Sports and games are well supported; high standards are expected and attained. There is a range of extra-curricular activities, including a large and active CCF.

School profile

Pupils Age range 11–18; 500 boarders (348 boys, 152 girls). Main entry ages 11 and 13; exceptionally into sixth.
Entrance Own entrance exams used (English and maths). Ability to benefit from a grammar boarding education looked for. Only children of service personnel of at least 4 years' service (serving or retired) admitted; must accept the Christian ethos of the school.
Head and staff *Headmaster:* Colonel G H Wilson, 4 years in post. *Staff:*pupil ratio 1:10.
Exam results In 1995, 64 in upper fifth, 34 in upper sixth. *GCSE:* In 1995, 56% upper fifth gained grade C or above in 8+ subjects; 23% in 5–7 subjects. *A-levels:* 38% upper sixth passed in 4+ subjects; 41% in 3; 18% in 2 subjects. Average UCAS points 19.7.
University and college entrance 88% of 1995 sixth-form leavers went on to a degree course (13% after a gap year); others typically go on to further education, training courses or into the services. Of those going on to university, 3% went to Oxbridge; 2% took courses in medicine, dentistry and veterinary science, 33% in science and engineering, 22% in humanities and social sciences, 2% in art and design, 41% in vocational subjects eg business studies, radiography, sports science.
Curriculum GCSE and A level and GNVQs. Some 35% sixth-form take vocational qualifications instead of A-levels; all of these undertake work experience in the UK or abroad. *Europe:* All sixth-form study a European language.

• DULWICH

Dulwich College, Dulwich, London SE21 7LD. Tel 0181 693 3601

• Pupils 1400 • Boys 7–18 (Day/Board/Weekly) • Girls None • Upper sixth 186 • Termly fees £2045 (Day) £4090 (Board) £3925 (Weekly) • HMC, BSA, SHA • Enquiries to the Master • Application to the Admissions Secretary

What it's like

Founded in 1619 by Edward Alleyn, the Elizabethan actor-manager as his College of God's Gift at Dulwich. In 1857 Alleyn's College was reconstituted by Parliament – the upper part was known as Dulwich College and moved in 1870 to its present site. It has very handsome, patrician buildings (designed by Charles Barry the younger) on a big expanse of playing fields; extensive building programmes have provided excellent facilities. Religious instruction is part of the curriculum for all pupils up to the fifth form; sixth-formers do further work in the philosophy of religion. There are daily assemblies and regular celebrations of Eucharist for Anglicans and of Mass for Roman Catholics; visiting Hindu, Jewish and Moslem ministers assist in frequent denominational services. Academic studies are extremely well run by a large and well qualified staff who consistently produce very good results. Most leavers go on to degree courses (including many to Oxbridge). Music plays an important part in the life of the school. A 250-strong choir undertakes major works and there are several orchestras and smaller groups. Drama involves a large number of pupils in numerous productions and the art school produces work of a high order. The design and technology centre has workshops for engineering, boatbuilding and cabinet making. A wide variety of sports and games is available; standards are high and there have been many representatives at county, regional and national level. There are 3 scout troops, a venture scout unit, an active and enterprising CCF contingent and a voluntary service unit. About 50 clubs and societies form the College Union.

School profile

Pupils Total age range 7–18; 1400 boys (1300 day, 100 boarding). Senior department 11–

18, 1250 boys. Main entry ages 7, 10, 11, 13 and into the sixth. Approx 10% are children of former pupils. *State school entry:* 70% intake at 11, 5% at 13, plus 60% to sixth-form.

Entrance Common Entrance and own exam used. No special skills required other than the potential to gain from what the school offers; no religious requirements (wide religious and ethnic mix). Parents not expected to buy textbooks; extras vary widely – often zero. 57 pa assisted places. 30 pa scholarships/bursaries, including music and art – £450 to 50% school fees (more if genuine financial need).

Parents 65+% in industry or commerce. 85+% live within 30 miles; up to 10% live overseas.

Head and staff Master: Graham G Able, in post from 1997. Educated at Worksop and Cambridge (natural sciences). Previously Headmaster of Hampton, Second Master of Barnard Castle and Housemaster at Sutton Valence. Also member of HMC Committee and its Academic Policy Sub-Committee, former member of ISJC Assisted Places Committee. *Staff:* 120 full time, 6 part time. Annual turnover approx 5%. Average age approx 40.

Exam results In 1995, 198 pupils in upper fifth, 170 in upper sixth. *GCSE:* In 1995, 182 upper fifth gained at least grade C in 9+ subjects; 16 in 5–8 subjects. *A-levels:* 29 upper sixth passed in 4+ subjects; 117 in 3; 19 in 2; and 5 in 1 subject. Average UCAS points 23.2.

University and college entrance 95% of 1995 sixth-form leavers went on to a degree course; others typically go on to at college or straight into careers (City, armed services, family business). Of those going on to university, 15% went to Oxbridge; 9% took courses in medicine, dentistry and veterinary science, 33% in science and engineering, 56% in humanities and social sciences, 2% in art and design.

Curriculum GCSE and A-levels. 17 GCSE subjects offered, 19 at A-level; general studies an extensive non-examined subject, no A-level. 33% take science A-levels; 45% arts/humanities; 22% both. *Vocational:* Work experience available. *Computing facilities:* Networks of Archimedes and Apple Macintosh, each for class-size groups. Other machines are available in smaller numbers. *Europe:* French, German, Italian and Spanish offered to GCSE and A-level. Regular exchanges (France, Germany, Italy and Spain).

The arts *Music:* Over 20% of pupils learn a musical instrument; instrumental exams can be taken. Some 17 musical groups including 2 full orchestras, 2 brass groups, 2 wind bands, 3 choirs, chamber orchestra, big band. *Drama & dance*: Drama offered. Some pupils are involved in school productions and majority in house/other productions. House production of Arctic Willy (written by pupil) featured in Lloyds Bank Theatre Challenge at Royal National Theatre. *Art:* On average, 70 take GCSE, 10 A-level; AS-level history of art also offered. Art facilities open to non-examination pupils.

Sport, community service and clubs *Sport and physical activities:* Curriculum sports: rugby, hockey, cricket, swimming. Optional: athletics, tennis, badminton, squash, cross-country, soccer, basketball, fencing, riding, rowing, shooting, golf, weight training, martial arts, lifesaving. RLSS exams may be taken. Rugby, 4 national, 6 regional and 11 county players; Hockey, 4 county U18 representatives; Athletics, TSB Milk Cup Schools Champions and National Club discus champion. *Community service:* Pupils take bronze, silver and gold Duke of Edinburgh's Award. CCF and community service optional. Scout group (3 troops and venture unit), 15 Queen's Scouts in past 3 years. *Clubs and societies:* Up to 30 clubs, eg computers, debating, mathematics, political (prominent politicians often invited to speak), rocketry (twice termly firings).

Uniform School uniform worn throughout.

Houses/prefects Competitive houses. Prefects, school captain, heads of house – appointed by the Master with advice from pupils and staff.

Religion Parents may opt pupils out of attendance at religious worship.

Social Drama, music, joint society meetings, lectures, shared classes in certain minority subjects with sister school (JAGS). Regular holiday visits abroad (educational and recreational) and language exchanges; rugby, hockey, cricket tours. Pupils allowed to bring own car/bike/motorbike to school. Meals self-service. School shop. No tobacco/alcohol allowed.

Discipline Pupils failing to produce homework secure lunchtime detentions. Aim is for discipline that is firm and fair.

Boarding All boarders over 14 have own study bedroom; younger boarders in

dormitories of 6+. Junior house (10–14) feeds two senior houses of 30–36 pupils. Resident nurse; local GP on call. Limited cooking facilities for senior pupils for supplementary foods. Half-term (2 weeks in October, 3 days in other terms) plus 2 weekend exeats each term; weekly boarding is popular. Visits to the local shops and to London allowed, with permission and at the discretion of house master.
Alumni association is run by T J Walsh, Secretary of the Alleyn Club, c/o Dulwich College.
Former pupils P G Wodehouse, A E W Mason, Trevor Bailey, Raymond Chandler, Graham Swift, Sir Ernest Shackleton, Sir Harold Hartley, Gordon Jacob, 5 First World War VCs, 3 Second World War VCs.

• DUNDEE HIGH

High School of Dundee, Euclid Crescent, Dundee DD1 1HU. Tel 01382 202921, Fax 01382 229822
• Pupils 1140 • Boys 5–18 (Day) • Girls 5–18 (Day) • Higher year 128 • Termly fees £1303 (Day)
• HMC, SCIS • Enquiries/application to the Rector

What it's like

Founded in 1239 by the Abbot of Lindores as a boys' school, it has been co-educational since the middle of the 18th century. The main buildings are very striking: neo-classical/ Georgian erected in 1832–4. Excellent modern facilities are provided. The playing fields are about a mile away. The school enjoys a very strong corporate life and spirit and has a high reputation, with vigorous local support. Academically strong, it produces results that are consistently very good. Very many pupils go on to degree courses each year in the Scottish universities and a few to Oxbridge. It is notably strong in music, drama and art. There is a very large number of extra-curricular activities and many of these are carried to high levels of achievement. Sports and games are also of a high standard and the school produces many representatives at county level. The record in the Duke of Edinburgh's Award Scheme is impressive.

School profile

Pupils Total age range 5–18; 1140 day pupils (570 boys, 570 girls). Senior department 12–18, 780 pupils (390 boys, 390 girls). Main entry ages 5, 9, 10, 11, 12 and a few into sixth. Approx 35% are children of former pupils.
Entrance Own entrance exam used. Good average ability looked for; no religious requirements. Parents expected to buy textbooks; other extras mostly optional. 25 pa assisted places. 30 pa scholarships/bursaries £200 – half fees.
Head and staff Rector: Robert Nimmo, in post for 19 years. Educated at universities of Edinburgh, Caen, Freiburg and Heidelberg (modern languages; French, German, Russian). Previously Depute Headmaster, Head of Modern Languages at George Heriot's. Also Vice-Chairman, Scottish Examination Board; member, Howie Committee (Curriculum and Assessment in fifth and sixth-forms) and Higher Still Development. *Staff:* 85 full time, 7 part time. Annual turnover 5%. Average age 40.
Exam results On average, 120 pupils in S-grade year, 128 in Higher year, 105 in CSYS year. *S-grade:* On average 110 pupils gain at least grade C in 8+ subjects; 8 in 5–7; and 2 in 1–4 subjects. *Highers:* 81 pass in 5+ subjects; 13 in 4; 12 in 3; 11 in 2; and 3 in 1 subject.
University and college entrance 94% of 1995 sixth-form leavers went on to a degree course (2% after a gap year); others typically go on to employment or further education. Of those going on to university, 5% went to Oxbridge; 12% took courses in medicine, dentistry and veterinary science, 35% in science and engineering, 8% in law, 27% in humanities and social sciences, 2% in art and design, 16% in vocational subjects eg physiotherapy, accountancy, physical education, hospitality management.
Curriculum S-grade, Highers and CSYS. 30 subjects offered. Most take a combination of arts and science Highers. *Vocational:* Scotvec word processing modules offered. *Computing facilities:* 2 computer laboratories; computers in most departments. *Special provision:* Learning skills centre. *Europe:* French, German and Spanish offered to S-grade, Higher and CSYS (1 language compulsory to S-grade). Regular exchanges (France, Germany and Spain).
The arts (Pupils aged 11 and over) *Music:* Over 30% of pupils learn a musical instrument; instrumental exams can be taken. Some 20 musical groups including

orchestral, choral, chamber, wind bands, recorder, guitar. National Youth Orchestra and National Wind Band members; regional and national competition successes. *Drama & dance*: Both offered. Trinity College exams may be taken. Some pupils are involved in school and house/other productions. Recent productions of Jane Eyre, Daisy Pulls It Off, A Murder is Announced. 3 in Trinity College exhibition. *Art:* On average, 28 take S-grade, 14 Higher. Art facilities open to non-examination pupils.
Sport, community service and clubs (Pupils aged 11 and over) *Sport and physical activities:* Compulsory sports: choice of rugby, hockey, athletics, cricket, tennis. Hockey, girls runners-up in Scottish Schools Championships; skiing, boys won Scottish Schools Championships; swimming, 3 winners in Scottish Schools Championships. *Community service:* Pupils take bronze, silver and gold Duke of Edinburgh's Award. CCF optional for 6 years at age 12, community service for 2 years at 16. School has Interact Club (junior Rotary) with membership of 100+, largest in the country. *Clubs and societies:* Over 30 clubs, eg chess, china painting, fly-tying, photography, weight training.
Uniform School uniform worn throughout.
Houses/prefects Competitive houses. Prefects, head boy and girl – elected by staff and pupils. School Council.
Religion Weekly school assembly and end-of-term services.
Social Debates, ESU, United Nations, Press and Journal with other local schools. Organised exchanges; trips to Italy, Belgium; ski trips; rugby/hockey tours to Canada. Meals self-service. School tuck and thrift shops. No tobacco/alcohol allowed.
Discipline Pupils failing to produce homework once might expect to write it out twice for next day; anyone caught smoking cannabis on the premises could expect expulsion.
Alumni association run by Harvie Findlay, 8 Abercrombie Street, Barnhill, Dundee.
Former pupils Sir Robert Lickley (designer of the Harrier jet); Lord Perry (Open University); Sir David Anderson (designer of Forth Road Bridge); Sir Alan Peacock (economist); Lord Fulton (Sussex University); Lord Ross (Lord Justice Clerk); Chris Rae (sports commentator); Bill Hamilton (BBC newscaster); Lord Cullen (High Court Judge).

• DUNOTTAR

Dunottar School, High Trees Road, Reigate, Surrey RH2 7EL. Tel 01737 761945, Fax 01737 779450

• Pupils 440 • Boys None • Girls 4–18 (Day) • Upper sixth 23 • Termly fees £920–£1510 (Day)
• GSA, SHA, AHIS • Enquiries/application to the Headmistress

What it's like

Founded in 1926, it lies high on the North Downs on the south side of Reigate. The site includes some Grade 2 listed buildings in very pleasant surroundings with beautiful gardens and playing fields. Teaching facilities are very good. A non-denominational school, but with the Christian ethos; religious studies are included in the curriculum and there is a daily assembly. A happy and efficient working atmosphere is maintained by the encouragement of common sense, an insistence on self-discipline and good behaviour. Academic standards and results are good and all sixth-formers go on to degree courses. Music is a strong tradition, as are sports and games and high standards are achieved (many county, regional and national events). A number of extra-curricular activities is provided for all ages and the school participates successfully in the Duke of Edinburgh's Award Scheme, at bronze, silver and gold levels.

School profile

Pupils Total age range 4–18, 440 day girls. Senior department 11–18. Main entry ages 4, 5, 7, 8, 11, 12, 13 and into sixth. *State school entry:* 50% intake at 11, plus 65% to sixth.
Entrance Common Entrance and interview. No special skills or religious requirements. 4 scholarships at age 11 and for sixth-form, and 2 music scholarships (at 11 and 14).
Head and staff *Headmistress:* Miss Jane Burnell, in post for 12 years. Educated at Wolverton Grammar, Bucks, and at Royal Holloway College and King's College, London (zoology, botany, chemistry, education). Previously Head of Science at Guildford High and Senior Biologist at Putney High. Also FRSA. Committee member of AHIS; member of ISJC Accreditation and Review Inspection Panel; Member of Army Scholarship Selection Board. *Staff:* 33 full time, 12 part time. Annual turnover 4%. Average age 35.

Exam results In 1995, 35 pupils in Year 11, 16 in upper sixth. *GCSE:* On average, 94% Year 11 gain at least grade C in 8+ subjects; 6% in 5–7 subjects. *A-levels:* 88% upper sixth pass in 3 subjects; 6% in 2 subjects. Average UCAS points 17.0.
University and college entrance All 1995 sixth-form leavers went on to a degree course (25% after a gap year), usually 1 or 2 to Oxbridge. 6% took courses in medicine, dentistry and veterinary science, 6% in science and engineering, 62% in humanities and social sciences, 13% in art and design, 13% in other subjects eg occupational therapy, media, tourism.
Curriculum GCSE and A-levels. 18 subjects offered to GCSE, 23 to A-level (including sociology, theatre studies, business and economics). 30% take science A-levels; 70% arts/humanities. *Vocational:* Work experience available; also RSA word processing. *Computing facilities:* Fully-equipped computer rooms containing Archimedes machines, laser printer, and desk-top publishing system. *Special provision:* Some help for dyslexic pupils. *Europe:* French (taught from age 8), German and Spanish offered to GCSE and A-level. Regular exchanges or visits (France, Germany and Spain); trip to France for juniors.
The arts (Pupils aged 11 and over) *Music:* Over 15% of pupils learn a musical instrument; instrumental exams are taken. Some 12 musical groups including string group, choirs, orchestra, ensemble groups. Choral scholarship to Oxford; members of National Youth Choir and National Youth Orchestra. *Drama & dance*: Both offered. LAMDA, modern, tap, ballet exams may be taken. Majority of pupils are involved in school productions and all in house/other productions. Local speech and drama festivals; 1 pupil attends Guildhall for drama tuition. *Art:* On average, 25 take GCSE, 4 A-level. Design, pottery, textiles, photography also offered. Pupil commended in open art competition; pupil commended in Fairfield Design a T-shirt competition.
Sport, community service and clubs (Pupils aged 11 and over) *Sport and physical activities:* Compulsory sports: tennis, swimming, gym, dance, lacrosse, netball, rounders, athletics. Optional: aerobics, volleyball, basketball, football, unihoc, stoolball, softball, badminton, cricket, weights, table tennis, croquet. Sixth form only: trampolining, squash, body conditioning. GCSE, BAGA, RLSS, Coca Cola tennis/swimming, ASA exams may be taken. National lacrosse honours; regional swimming; county hockey, lacrosse, swimming, tennis, netball, squash. *Community service:* Pupils take bronze, silver and gold Duke of Edinburgh's Award. Charity fund-raising; visits to elderly, with gifts etc. *Clubs and societies:* Over 40 clubs, eg electronics, science (CREST award success), all sports, photography, gardening, Christian Fellowship, modern languages, sports, current affairs.
Uniform School uniform worn except in the sixth.
Houses/prefects Competitive houses. Head girl and heads of houses democratically elected by pupils in Year 9 and above, and by staff.
Religion Attendance at daily religious worship compulsory.
Social Sports and games fixtures with other local schools; Rotary public speaking competition; Royal Institute of Chemistry competition; Great Egg Race physics competition. Annual exchange and visits to France, Germany and Spain. Pupils allowed to bring own car/bike/motorbike to school. Meals self-service. School shop organised by sixth-form. No tobacco/alcohol allowed.

• DURHAM

Durham School, Durham City DH1 4SZ. Tel 0191 384 7977, Fax 0191 383 1025
• Pupils 325 • Boys 11–18 (Day/Board) • Girls 16–18 (Day/Board) • Upper sixth 70 • Termly fees £2473 (Day) £3802 (Board) • HMC • Enquiries/application to the Headmaster's Secretary

What it's like

One of the oldest schools in England, it has been closely associated with the Dean and Chapter of Durham Cathedral for 450 years. As the Bishop's School it was reorganised and re-endowed by Cardinal Langley in 1414 and refounded in 1541 by Henry VIII. It has occupied its present site since 1844 and enjoys a magnificent position below the west towers of the cathedral. First-class facilities have been added over the years, including most recently, a new science laboratory and a centre for art, craft, design and technology. It is physically compact with playing fields nearby and makes full use of the advantages of an ancient cathedral and university city. A strong Anglican tradition prevails and religious worship is compulsory with a daily service in the school chapel. A high standard of education is provided (staff:pupil ratio of about 1:9). Results are good and most sixth-form leavers proceed to degree courses. Strong in music, drama and art and local community services. Very strong in sport, particularly rugby and cricket, with players at county and national level.

School profile

Pupils Age range 11–18; 325 pupils, 200 day (184 boys, 16 girls), 125 boarding (104 boys, 21 girls). Main entry ages 11 and 13 (boys) and into sixth (boys and girls). Approx 20% are children of former pupils. Many pupils from: Bow School and The Chorister School, both in Durham, and Newlands Preparatory School, Gosforth. *State school entry:* 34% main intake, plus 38% to sixth.
Entrance Common Entrance and own exam used. No special skills or religious requirements but school is C of E foundation. Maximum £150 extras. 8 pa assisted places (6 at age 11, 2 at 13). 9 pa scholarships, including 2 sixth-form.
Parents 60+% live within 30 miles; up to 10% live overseas.
Head and staff *Headmaster:* M A Lang, in post for 15 years. Educated at Bristol Grammar and Oxford (mathematics). Previously Deputy Headmaster at Dauntsey's and Housemaster and Head of Mathematics at The Leys. Also HMC Committee Member; Chairman, NE Division of HMC. *Staff:* 31 full time, 9 part time. Annual turnover 10%.
Exam results In 1995, 50 pupils in upper fifth, 65 in upper sixth. *GCSE:* In 1995, 30 upper fifth gained at least grade C in 8+ subjects; 11 in 5–7; and 8 in 1–4 subjects. *A-levels:* 34 upper sixth passed in 4+ subjects; 13 in 3; 7 in 2; and 6 in 1 subject. Average UCAS points 17.1 (including general studies 20.3).
University and college entrance 90% of 1995 sixth-form leavers went on to a degree course; others typically go straight on to careers eg marketing. Of those going on to university, 5% went to Oxbridge; 33% took courses in science and engineering, 67% in humanities and social sciences.
Curriculum GCSE, AS and A-levels. Subjects offered include Japanese and Chinese and A-level general studies. 20% take science A-levels; 67% arts/humanities; 13% both. *Vocational:* Work experience available. *Computing facilities:* 20 research machines and 2 Archimedes; desk-top publishing facility. *Special provision:* Dyslexia and EFL teaching available. *Europe:* French offered to GCSE, AS and A-level; also GCSE German. Annual visits to France. Talks to sixth-form by MEPs. Pupils from France, Germany and Spain in school regularly.
The arts *Music:* Over 30% of pupils learn a musical instrument; instrumental exams can be taken. Some 8 musical groups including orchestra, choral society, chapel choir, jazz group, concert band. National Chamber Music Competition regional semi-finalists; 2 in National Youth Choir; CD of chapel choir on sale nationally. *Drama & dance*: Drama offered. Some pupils are involved in school productions and majority in house/other productions. 6 productions annually ranging from Shakespeare to The King and I. *Art:* On average, 18 take GCSE, 6 A-level. Design, photography also offered.
Sport, community service and clubs *Sport and physical activities:* All pupils do games at least 3 times a week with a choice from: rugby, cricket, athletics, swimming, tennis, rowing, hockey, shooting, squash, cross-country, badminton, fives. GCSE may be taken. Rugby, 1st XV Rugby World team of the year 1992, 3 unbeaten seasons in last 5 years, 1 England representative, 3 U18 reps, 1 U16; cricket, 1 England U18 representative; rowing, 1 England representative; other England reps in chess, equestrian etc. *Community service:* Pupils take bronze, silver and gold Duke of Edinburgh's Award. CCF compulsory for 2 years at age 14, optional thereafter; community service compulsory for 1 year at age 16. *Clubs and societies:* Up to 10 clubs, eg debating, chess, drama, design & technology, computing, fitness, bridge.
Uniform School uniform worn throughout.
Houses/prefects Competitive houses. Prefects, head boy/girl, head of house and school prefects – appointed by the Headmaster.
Religion Religious worship compulsory.
Social Many organised trips abroad. Meals self-service. School shop. No tobacco/alcohol allowed.
Discipline Pupils failing to produce homework once might expect repeat work; those caught smoking cannabis could expect expulsion.

Boarding All sixth-formers share study bedroom with one other; middle and lower schools are in dormitories of 4+. Single-sex houses of approx 70, same as competitive houses. Resident qualified nurse. Central dining room. Pupils can provide and cook own food. Flexible weekend boarding arrangement. Visits to local town allowed.
Alumni association run by N G E Gedye, c/o the school.

• DURHAM HIGH

Durham High School for Girls, Farewell Hall, Durham DH1 3TB. Tel 0191 384 3226
• Pupils 427 • Boys 4–7 only (Day) • Girls 4–18 (Day) • Upper sixth 34 • Termly fees £864 – £1459 (Day) • GSA • Enquiries/application to the Headmistress

What it's like

Founded in 1884 by the Church Schools Company, and transferred to a local governing body in 1910. In 1968 it moved to new purpose-built premises at Farewell Hall – a semi-rural site on the southern edge of Durham. The campus is compact; there are playing fields and a nature reserve within the grounds. The junior school is combined. Its aim is to give a sound general education within a Christian framework but all faiths are accepted. Academic results are good and the majority of sixth-form leavers go on to degree courses, including Oxbridge. The school enjoys a good local reputation. Music is very strong; drama and art well supported. A fair range of extra-curricular activities, sports and games available (county and regional representation in hockey). Good record in Duke of Edinburgh's Award Scheme (100th Gold in 1994).

School profile

Pupils Total age range 4–18; 427 day girls. Senior department 11–18, 273 girls. Main entry at 4½ 10, 11 and into the sixth. 75% senior intake is from own junior school. *State school entry:* 20% at 11, 5% to sixth.
Entrance Own entrance exam used. No special skills or religious requirements. Parents expected to buy few textbooks (eg sixth-form books); average extras £150 including lunch. 5 pa scholarships (including sixth-form) and 3–4 bursaries, value £120–£3400.
Parents 15+% in industry/commerce; 15+% doctors/lawyers; 5+% school/university teachers.
Head and staff *Headmistress:* Miss Margaret L Walters, 4 years in post. Educated at Brownshills High School, Stoke on Trent, and at Leicester and Nottingham universities (classics and education). Previously Deputy Head and Head of Classics at Queen's School, Chester, and Head of Classics at Sydenham High School. *Staff:* 36 full time, 16 part time. Annual turnover 5%.
Exam results In 1995, 45 pupils in upper fifth, 19 in upper sixth. *GCSE:* In 1995, 42 upper fifth gained at least grade C in 8+ subjects. *A-levels:* 1 upper sixth passed in 4 subjects; 12 in 3; and 4 in 2 subjects. Average UCAS points 18.1.
University and college entrance 94% of sixth-form leavers go on to a degree course (3% after a gap year); others typically go on to art foundation courses. Of those going on to university, 6% go to Oxbridge; 9% take courses in medicine, dentistry and veterinary science, 9% in science and engineering, 6% in law, 50% in humanities and social sciences, 6% in art and design, 20% in vocational subjects eg physiotherapy, optometry.
Curriculum GCSE and A-levels offered. 19 GCSE subjects offered; 20 A-level (including general studies). 20% take science A-levels; 47% arts/humanities; 38% both. *Vocational:* Work experience available. Fujitsu Adopt-A-School scheme. *Computing facilities:* Specialist computer rooms and computers in other departments; mainly Acorn and IBM compatibles, also DTP and CD-Rom; control equipment eg robot arm, lego, buggy. *Europe:* French (from age 6) and German (from 11) offered at GCSE, AS and A-level; also GCSE Italian and non-examined courses in all 3 languages and Spanish. Regular exchanges (France and Germany). French chateau study holiday for 10-year olds, 12-year olds to Paris.
The arts (Pupils aged 11 and over) *Music:* 50% pupils learn a musical instrument; instrumental exams can be taken. Musical groups – orchestra, choir, chamber choir, wind band, recorder consort, various chamber groups. 3 in National Youth Choir (1993); 1 in National Children's Orchestra. *Drama & dance*: Drama and dance offered; pupils may take LAMDA exams. Majority of pupils involved in annual school productions,

some in house/other productions. *Art:* On average, 14 take GCSE, 4 A-level. Design, textiles and photography also offered. Art facilities open to non-examination pupils.

Sport, community service and clubs (Pupils aged 11 and over) *Sport and physical activities:* Compulsory sports: athletics, tennis, rounders, hockey, netball, dance, gym, swimming, badminton. Optional: football, aerobics, table tennis, volleyball and karate. Sixth form only: squash, rowing. Pupils may take Carlton badminton awards, ASA and BAGA exams. NE regional hockey players, county hockey and netball players. 3 gold rowing medals (1 pupil rowed for GB in 1993). *Community service:* Pupils take bronze, silver and gold Duke of Edinburgh's Award. Community service optional for 4 years at 14. School actively involved in, and raises money for, Durham Mencap play scheme. *Clubs & societies*: Up to 10 clubs including photography, dance, gym, hockey, badminton, netball, karate, tennis, Amnesty International, computing, Young Enterprise, economics.

Uniform School uniform worn except in sixth.

Houses/prefects Competitive houses. Head girl and house captains; no prefects as all sixth-form take school responsibilities.

Religion Religious worship compulsory.

Social Trips to France at age 10 and 12; regular exchanges to France and Germany for 14–18; annual ski trips; occasional trips to eg Rome, China. Sixth form may bring own car/bike/motorbike to school. Meals self-service. No alcohol/tobacco allowed.

Discipline Disciplinary procedures decided as situation arises.

Former pupils Wendy Gibson (BBC North News); Wendy Craig (actress); Charmian Welsh.

• EALING COLLEGE

Ealing College Upper School, 83 The Avenue, London W13 8JS. Tel 0181 997 4346

• Pupils 140 • Boys 11–18 (Day) • Girls 16–18 (Day) • Upper sixth 25 • Termly fees £1360 (Day) • ISAI • Enquiries/application to the Headmaster or Secretary

What it's like

Founded in 1820, it is single-site in a residential area with good public transport facilities. It comprises pleasant and well-equipped buildings with recent extensions. Its declared philosophy is to maximise the potential of each individual whatever their innate ability. A sound general education is provided. Girls have been accepted to the sixth-form since 1982. There are some sport and games, for which local grounds are used; and there is some art.

School profile

Pupils Age range 11–18; 140 day pupils (134 boys, 6 girls). Main entry ages 11, 12 and 13 (boys) and into sixth (boys and girls). Approx 1% are children of former pupils.
Entrance Own informal tests set in English and maths. No special skills or religious requirements. Parents expected to buy textbooks beyond Form 3, maximum approx £40. Annual scholarships/bursaries for sixth-form entrants.
Head and staff *Headmaster:* Barrington Webb, in post for 12 years. Educated at Bristol Cathedral School and at universities of Exeter, Leicester and London (history of art, education). Previously Head of Department at Ealing College and Assistant Master at Saltash (Cornwall). Also member ISAI Academic Policy Committee. *Publications:* Art in Education (1983). *Staff:* 17 full time, 2 part time. Annual turnover 4%. Average age 35–40.
Exam results On average, 35 pupils in upper fifth, 25 in upper sixth. *GCSE:* 5 upper fifth gain at least grade C in 8+ subjects; 21 in 5–7; and 9 in 1–4 subjects. *A-levels:* 1 upper sixth passes in 4+ subjects; 9 in 3; 7 in 2; and 8 in 1 subject. Average UCAS points 14.5.
University and college entrance 95% of 1995 sixth-form leavers went on to a degree course (2% after a gap year); others typically go on to HND or foundation courses. Of those going on to university, 3% went to Oxbridge; 5% took courses in medicine, dentistry and veterinary science, 65% in science and engineering, 5% in law, 20% in humanities and social sciences, 2% in art and design, 3% in vocational subjects eg chiropody.
Curriculum GCSE and A-levels. 32% take science A-levels; 20% arts/humanities; 48% both. *Computing facilities:* Amstrad PCs in computer room; computers used by other departments. *Special provision:* Extra English language tuition available for overseas students; help for dyslexics. *Europe:* French offered to GCSE and A-level.
The arts *Art:* On average, 6 take GCSE, 2 A-level. Pottery also offered.
Sport, community service and clubs *Sport and physical activities:* Optional sports: football, cricket, tennis, badminton, table tennis, squash. *Community service:* Charity fund-raising optional. *Clubs and societies:* Up to 5 clubs, eg sixth-form sports.
Uniform School uniform worn except in the sixth.
Houses/prefects Competitive houses. Prefects, head boy/girl – appointed by the Headmaster.
Religion No compulsory worship; religious studies is part of the curriculum.
Social Special activities week (end of summer term). Annual ski trip, outward bound activities and trips to France. Meals self-service. School canteen. No tobacco/alcohol allowed.

• EASTBOURNE

Eastbourne College, Old Wish Road, Eastbourne, East Sussex BN21 4JX. Tel 01323 737655, Fax 01323 416137

• Pupils 476 • Boys 13–18 (Day/Board) • Girls 13–18 (Day/Board) • Upper sixth 123 • Termly fees £2673 (Day) £3621 (Board) • HMC • Enquiries/application to the Headmaster

What it's like

Founded in 1867 by the 8th Duke of Devonshire, it has an excellent site in the residential area of Eastbourne. Elegant buildings with fine grounds and gardens are 400 yards from the sea front and within easy reach of the South Downs. The school became fully co-educational in 1996, after more than 25 years' experience of girls in the sixth-form. It is a Christian school and all pupils have religious instruction and attend chapel services. There is considerable involvement in the local community; pupils assist elderly residents and entertain them with plays and concerts; others help in primary schools and with local conservation. The academic standards are high and results are very good; 90% of leavers go on to degree courses, including Oxbridge. The music, drama and art departments are all strong and work closely together, forming an integral part of the academic and cultural life of the school. There is a strong liaison with the Eastbourne Symphony Orchestra and the College has its own professional music series. There is a variety of quality drama, including visits by theatre groups, in the purpose-built theatre. The technology, electronics and computer departments have excellent facilities. It has a reputation for excellence in team games as well as a considerable variety of individual pursuits including golf and sailing. Many pupils have played at county, regional and national levels. The CCF and Duke of Edinburgh's Award Scheme allow for considerable emphasis on adventure training and expedition. Numerous clubs and societies foster intellectual and esoteric pursuits.

School profile

Pupils Age range 13–18, 476 pupils, 185 day (149 boys, 36 girls), 291 boarders (243 boys, 48 girls). Main entry ages 13 and into sixth; girls accepted age 13 from 1996. 20% are children of former pupils. 26% of pupils from St Andrew's School, Eastbourne. *State school entry:* 3% main intake, plus 6% to sixth.

Entrance Common Entrance exam used. Skills in sport, music and drama an asset; no religious requirements. Parents not expected to buy textbooks; extras £10–£100 per term, eg exam fees, outings, insurance premium (voluntary). Scholarships, 10 pa academic and up to 8 pa music and art, 50% fees max. Bursaries also available dependent on parental need.

Parents 15+% in industry; 15+% doctors, lawyers etc. 30+% live within 30 miles; up to 10% live overseas.

Head and staff *Headmaster:* Charles M P Bush, 4 years in post. Educated at Melbourne Church of England Grammar School and Oxford University (mathematics). Previously Housemaster and Head of Mathematics at Marlborough, Head of Mathematics at Abingdon, Head of Pure Mathematics at Aylesbury Grammar School and teacher at the Dragon School. Also Hockey Association Coach. *Staff:* 49 full time, 5 part time. Annual turnover 5%. Average age 35.

Exam results In 1995, 90 pupils in fifth, 106 in upper sixth. *GCSE:* In 1995, 96% fifth gained at least grade C in 8+ subjects. *A-levels:* 88% upper sixth passed in 3 subjects. Average UCAS points 20.8.

University and college entrance 95% of 1995 sixth-form leavers went on to a degree course (5% after a gap year); others typically go on to art or music colleges or straight into careers. Of those going on to university, 12% went to Oxbridge; 8% took courses in medicine, dentistry and veterinary science, 15% in science and engineering, 36% in humanities and social sciences, 3% in art and design, 5% in other subjects eg drama, music.

Curriculum GCSE and A levels. 22 GCSE subjects offered, 21 at A-level (no A-level general studies). 27% take science A-levels; 49% arts/humanities; 24% both. *Computing facilities:* Extensive facilities: purpose-built computer centre. *Europe:* French, German and Spanish offered to GCSE and A-level. Regular exchanges and trips to France, Germany and Spain.

The arts *Music:* Over 30% of pupils learn a musical instrument; instrumental exams can be taken. Many musical groups including orchestras, choirs, swing, military bands, chamber music groups, pop groups. Regular organ and choral scholarships to Oxbridge. *Drama and dance:* Drama offered and GCSE, and A-level may be taken. All pupils act in a play in their first year. Many pupils are involved in school productions and majority in house/other productions. *Art:* On average, 40 take GCSE, 20 A-level. Photography,

printing also offered. Some 60% of A-level students accepted for tertiary art/design studies.
Sport, community service and clubs *Sport and physical activities:* No compulsory sports, except in first year. Optional: rugby, soccer, cricket, hockey, volleyball, lacrosse, tennis, squash, badminton, swimming, water polo, fives, athletics, basketball, judo, fencing, rowing, sailing. GCSE exams may be taken in PE; 2 international and 50 county representatives at various sports. *Community service:* Pupils take bronze, silver and gold Duke of Edinburgh's Award. CCF compulsory for 1 year at 14 or community service for 2 years at 15 (helping with homeless at St Botolph's, London). *Clubs and societies:* Up to 30 clubs, eg Victorian Society, charity, history, wine, classics.
Uniform School uniform worn throughout.
Houses/prefects Competitive houses. Prefects, head boy/girl, head of house and house prefects – appointed by the Headmaster.
Religion Compulsory worship
Social Debates with other local schools. Organised trips abroad and exchange systems. Day pupils may bring own car to school. Meals self-service. School shop.
Discipline Pupils failing to produce homework once would have their Housemaster informed and be made to do it at some time inconvenient to the pupil (eg when he/she should have had some free time); anyone involved in drugs would be expelled.
Boarding Majority of sixth-form have own study bedroom; forms 3–5 in rooms of about 4; very few in dormitories of 6+. Single-sex houses of approx 60. Resident qualfied medical staff. Central dining room. Cooking areas provided for students. 1 weekend exeat in Lent term; 2 in other terms.
Alumni association is run by Robin Harrison, The Bursary, Old Wish Road, Eastbourne, East Sussex BN21 4JY.
Former pupils Gwilym Lloyd George; Sir Hugh Casson; Sir Woodrow Wyatt; Professor Soddy; John Wells; Sir Christopher Leaver; Sir Derek Empson; Michael Fish; Michael Praed.

• EDGBASTON HIGH

Edgbaston High School for Girls, Westbourne Road, Edgbaston, Birmingham B15 3TS. Tel 0121 454 5831

• Pupils 964 • Boys None • Girls 2¼–18 (Day) • Upper sixth 62 • Termly fees £1405 (Day)
• GSA • Enquiries/application to the Admissions Secretary

What it's like

Founded in 1876 it is the longest established girls' independent school in Birmingham. It comprises pre-prep and prep departments and a senior school on an attractive 4-acre site (plus 8 acres of playing fields) next to the Botanical Gardens and 2 miles from the city centre. The school moved to its present site in 1962 and is very well equipped with an indoor swimming pool and new facilities for IT, home economics and textiles, as well as new laboratories. Academic standards are high and results are good. Nearly all the sixth-form proceed to higher education, including to Oxbridge. Parents are very supportive in time and energy and the staff place emphasis on the importance of good relationships with their pupils and do much to create a friendly atmosphere. There is a good variety of cultural activities. Music is particularly strong; drama is well supported. There is a wide range of sports (including canoeing, fencing, aikido and sailing) and standards are high particularly in tennis and hockey – an impressive number of teams and individual representations at county, regional and national level. Notable success in the Duke of Edinburgh's Award Scheme. The girls have opportunities for community service, work experience and an excellent careers programme which aims to help each girl develop as an individual.

School profile

Pupils Total age range 2¼–18. 964 day girls. Senior department 11–18, 495 day girls. Main entry ages 11 and into sixth.
Entrance Own entrance exam and interview. Assisted places on admission at 5, 11, 13 and into sixth. Scholarships at age 11 (including one music), means tested and up to 50% fees; 6 in sixth-form, including for music and sport.

Head and staff *Headmistress:* Mrs S J Horsman, in post for 9 years. Educated at St Leonard's School, and Cambridge University (classics). Previously Head at Barr's Hill Girls' Grammar and Barr's Hill School and Community College (Coventry) and Head at Lugulu Girls' High, Kenya. Also past president NAHT, Coventry; past chairman Comprehensive Heads Group, Coventry. *Staff:* 66 full time, 27 part time. Annual turnover 10%. Average age 43.

Exam results In 1995, 80 pupils in Year 11, 58 in upper sixth. *GCSE:* In 1995, 94% Year 11 gained at least grade C in 8+ subjects; 5% in 5–7 subjects. *A-levels:* 66% upper sixth passed in 4+ subject; 19% in 3; 12% in 2 and 3% in 1 subject. Average UCAS points 18.6.

University and college entrance 85% of 1995 sixth-form leavers went on to a degree course; others typically go on to art or drama colleges. Of those going on to university, 13% went to Oxbridge; 10% took courses in medicine, dentistry and veterinary science, 20% in science and engineering, 66% in humanities and social sciences, 4% in other subjects eg music.

Curriculum GCSE, AS and A-levels. Subjects offered include Latin and Greek. 17% take science A-levels; 41% arts/humanities; 41% both. *Vocational:* Work experience available; also RSA CLAIT and word processing Stage 1. *Computing facilities:* 24 networked BBCs, 23 Archimedes, 6 PCs, 1 AppleMac, 4 CD-Rom and satellite TV. *Europe:* French (from age 9), German and Spanish offered to GCSE and A-level; also French AS-level. Regular exchanges (France, Germany and Spain).

The arts (Pupils aged 11 and over) *Music:* About 50% of pupils play a musical instrument; instrumental exams taken each term. Several musical ensembles: choirs, orchestra, windband, recorders, strings, flutes, brass and guitar. Pupils also involved in local and county orchestras and competitive festivals. *Drama and dance:* Both offered. GCSE theatre studies may be taken (in the sixth-form). At least one major production per year eg The Boyfriend, The Tailor of Gloucester, involving some 80 girls (acting, production etc). Variety of dance offered: ballet, contemporary dance, jazz tap etc. Dance show involving girls of all ages and professional companies invited to give workshops. *Art:* On average 45 take GCSE, 2 AS level, 10 A-level. Computer graphics, ceramics, textiles, photography, metal and woodwork also offered. Regular visits to exhibitions and galleries throughout the country; trips abroad; annual art exhibition.

Sport, community service and clubs (pupils aged 11 and over) *Sport and physical activities:* Compulsory sports: hockey, netball, tennis, swimming, gymnastics, athletics. Optional: volleyball, table tennis, basketball, aerobics, dance, diving, aikido, fencing, canoeing, cricket, running, badminton and synchronised swimming. Sixth form only: dry skiing, squash, sailing, sub-aqua, bowling, ballroom dancing, fitness training, windsurfing, yoga. BAGA, RLSS exams may be taken. 1 British U16 tennis player, 4 regional (U18) and 8 county (U18) players; 3 county netball (U16 and 18) players, 4 county athletes, 12 county hockey players (various ages); tennis teams 3rd in national Aberdare Cup, 2nd in Senior Students National, 4th Midland Bank (U13) and county schools winners (U14); netball U18 team Birmingham Schools winners; county life saving winners; hockey teams Barclays Bank U18 West Midlands South champions, runners-up in U16, semi-finalists Midlands U18. *Community service:* Pupils take bronze, silver and gold Duke of Edinburgh's Award. Sixth form option – Community Sports Leaders Award CCPR. Community service optional for 2 years at 16: over half sixth-form involved in visiting the elderly, helping at hospitals, special needs schools etc; major charity support and fundraising for various national and international appeals, including Children in Need. *Clubs and societies:* Up to 30 clubs, eg aikido, aerobics, ceramics, Christian Union, cookery, drama, lifesaving, technology, science.

Uniform School uniform worn except in sixth.

Houses/prefects Competitive houses. Sixth-form committee, head girl and deputies, and head of house – elected by the school. School council equivalent.

Religion Non-denominational. Regular school assemblies. Attendance at religious worship encouraged but not compulsory.

Social Young Enterprise, debates and careers functions with other local schools. School exchanges with France, Denmark and Russia (St Petersburg); visits and exchanges with France, Germany and Spain. Sports links with USA, Australia and Malawi. Strong links with local business community. Pupils discouraged from bringing own car/bike/

motorbike to school because of parking difficulties. Meals self-service. No tobacco/alcohol allowed.
Discipline Pupils failing to produce homework once would be asked to bring it on the following day; those caught smoking cannabis on the premises might expect expulsion.

• EDGEHILL

Edgehill College, Bideford, Devon EX39 3LY. Tel 01237 471701
• Pupils 450 • Boys 3–18 (Day/Board/Weekly) • Girls 3–18 (Day/Board/Weekly) • Upper sixth 43 • Termly fees £845–£1755 (Day) £2290–£3190 (Board) £2070–£2885 (Weekly) • GSA
• Enquiries/application to the Admissions Secretary

What it's like

Founded in 1884, this Methodist foundation is single-site in the splendid North Devon countryside, overlooking Bideford and the Torridge estuary. Its five elegant houses and other buildings form part of an estate of 50 acres in a peaceful and delightful situation. Comfortable accommodation and excellent modern facilities. The co-educational junior and kindergarten departments are attached. The senior school was a girls' school until it became co-educational in 1993. A Christian school, it worships in Bideford Methodist church. A sound education is provided and a most sixth-form leavers go on to degree courses. The music and drama departments are flourishing and there is a good range of sport (some county representation) and extra-curricular activities.

School profile

Pupils Total age range 3–18; 450 pupils, 360 day (116 boys, 244 girls), 90 boarding (30 boys, 60 girls). Senior department 11–18, 330 pupils (18 boys, 312 girls). Main entry ages 3–5, 11, 13 and into sixth. Approx 10% are children of former pupils. *State school entry:* 50% main senior intake, plus 10% to sixth.
Entrance Common Entrance and own exam used. No special skills or religious requirements. Parents not expected to buy textbooks. 20 pa assisted places at 11; 2 at 16. Scholarships/bursaries, up to full fees.
Parents 30+% live within 30 miles; up to 10% live overseas.
Head and staff *Headmistress:* Mrs Elizabeth Burton, in post for 9 years. Educated at Bede Girls Grammar and King's College London, (physics). Previously Deputy Head at Putney High and Rickmansworth Masonic. *Staff:* 43 full time, 6 part time. Annual turnover 3%.
Exam results In 1995, 59 pupils in upper fifth, 43 in upper sixth. *GCSE:* In 1995, 29 upper fifth gained at least grade C in 8+ subjects; 19 in 5–7 subjects. *A-levels:* In 1995, 15 upper sixth pupils passed in 3+ subjects; 9 in 2; and 14 in 1 subject. Average UCAS points 14.4.
University and college entrance 93% of 1995 sixth-form leavers went on to a degree course (15% after a gap year); others typically go on to work. Of those going on to university, 4% took courses in medicine, dentistry and veterinary science, 20% in science and engineering, 2% in law, 20% in humanities and social sciences, 8% in art and design, 24% in vocational subjects eg physiotherapy, business management, drama, hotel and catering.
Curriculum GCSE and A-levels. 19 GCSE subjects offered; 20 at A-level (no A-level general studies). 20% take science A-levels; 70% arts/humanities; 10% both. *Vocational:* Work experience available; also RSA stage 2 in IT. *Computing facilities:* 4 computer studies rooms; computers in many departments. *Special provision:* Specialist teachers for dyslexic children and for EFL. *Europe:* French and German offered to GCSE, AS and A-level; also GCSE Italian and Spanish. Regular exchanges (France and Germany). European studies offered. French and German pupils.
The arts (Pupils aged 11 and over) *Music:* Over 50% of pupils learn a musical instrument; instrumental exams can be taken. Some musical groups including strings, wind band. Choir regularly wins local music festivals. *Drama & dance*: Both offered. GCSE, AS and A-level drama and LAMDA exams may be taken. Majority of pupils are involved in school productions and all in house/other productions. *Art:* On average, 12 take GCSE, 4 AS-level, 6 A-level. Design, pottery, textiles, photography, life drawing also offered.

Sport, community service and clubs *Sport and physical activities:* Compulsory sports: hockey, netball, football, rugby, athletics, rounders, gym, cricket. Optional: archery, swimming, trampolining, badminton, volleyball, tennis, riding, outdoor pursuits, judo, lifesaving. Sixth form only: squash, golf. GCSE exams may be taken. Hockey, county champions U16, regional 2nd; county tennis champion U14. *Community service:* Pupils take bronze, silver and gold Duke of Edinburgh's Award. Community service optional. *Clubs and societies:* Up to 30 clubs, eg CREST, typing, archery, public speaking, calligraphy, Chinese cookery, Weatherwatch, Young Investigators, music.
Uniform School uniform worn except in the sixth.
Houses/prefects Competitive houses. Prefects, head pupil, head of house and house prefects – elected by the school. School Council.
Religion Sunday morning worship. Morning assembly. Christian Union.
Social Dancing lessons, dances/socials, joint choir, theatrical productions and film society with nearby schools. Organised trips abroad. Meals self-service. School shop. No tobacco/alcohol allowed.
Boarding Houses, of 40–50, same as competitive houses; separate sixth-form house. Resident qualified nurse. Central dining room. Pupils can provide and cook own food. Two weekend exeats each term. Visits to local town allowed.
Former pupils Debbie Thrower; Lorraine Pascale (model).

• EDINBURGH ACADEMY

The Edinburgh Academy, 42 Henderson Row, Edinburgh EH3 5BL. Tel 0131 556 4603, Fax 0131 556 9353

Pupils 835 • Boys 3–18 (Day/Board/Weekly) • Girls 3–4 and 16–18 (Day/Board/Weekly) • Upper sixth 70 • Termly fees £1761 (Day) £3755 (Board) Check for weekly/flexi-boarding • HMC • Enquiries/application to the Rector

What it's like

Founded in 1824 (Sir Walter Scott was one of the founding spirits). The upper school buildings include the handsome original hall, and the playing fields are a short walk from the school. The Academy is well known as a civilised establishment which provides an extremely thorough, broad education. It is non-denominational within the Christian tradition; there are monthly school services and boarders attend the local church. The Academy has a tradition of academic excellence – it achieves high standards of scholarship and excellent results while providing for the whole person. Most leavers go on to degree courses, including Oxbridge. The creative subjects – drama, art and music are particularly strong – performances and exhibitions being held regularly for the general public in the city. High standards are also attained in sport and games of which there is a wide range including fives, fencing and curling. There is a wide variety of extra-curricular activities and considerable emphasis on outdoor pursuits (it has its own field centre in the Highlands). The CCF contingent is strong and the Pipe Band are recent Scottish champions. It has a good record in the Duke of Edinburgh's Award Scheme. Much use is made of Edinburgh's cultural amenities and there is an interesting programme of visiting lecturers.

School profile

Pupils Total age range 3–18; 835 pupils, 790 day (750 boys, 40 girls), 45 boarding (35 boys, 10 girls). Upper school 10–18, 470 pupils (440 boys, 30 girls). Main entry ages 5, 10 and 12 (boys) and into sixth (boys and girls). Approx 10% are children of former pupils. *State school entry:* Some at age 11 and 12; 20% to sixth.
Entrance Own entrance exam or Common Entrance used. No special religious requirements; overseas pupils should immediately be able to receive all teaching in English. Parents billed for textbooks; maximum extras usually £150 per term. 7 pa assisted places. 9 pa scholarships (including 2 sixth-form and 1 for a state primary school entrant), up to 50% day fees, plus 25% boarding fee if required.
Parents 15+% are doctors, lawyers; some in media or creative arts; 15+% in industry or commerce. 60+% live within 30 miles; up to 10% live overseas.
Head and staff Rector: John Light, in post since 1995. Educated at Sedbergh and at Cambridge (modern languages) and Manchester Business School. Previously Headmaster

at Oswestry, Housemaster at Sedbergh and Assistant Master at Haileybury, Uppingham and Glenalmond. Also six years in industry, mainly in Germany. *Staff:* 54 full time, 5 part time plus 11 part time music staff. Annual turnover 5%. Average age 43.

Exam results In 1995, 78 pupils in GCSE year, 70 in Higher, 70 in A-level year. *GCSE:* On average, 56 upper fifth gained at least grade C in 8+ subjects; 16 in 5–7; and 6 in 1–4 subjects. *Highers and A-level:* 78 leavers in 1995; 20 with 30+ UCAS points, 11 with 24–29; 21 with 18–23 points; 14 with 12–17; 7 with 6–11 pts and 5 with 0–5 pts.

University and college entrance 90% of 1995 sixth-form leavers went on to a degree course (35% after a gap year); others typically go on to FE or tutorial colleges. Of those going on to university, 8% went to Oxbridge; 6% took courses in medicine, dentistry and veterinary science, 35% in science and engineering, 3% in law, 29% in humanities and social sciences, 11% in art and design, 8% in vocational subjects eg physiotherapy, hotel management, 11% in other subjects eg drama.

Curriculum GCSE, Highers, A-levels. 20 subjects offered (including classical civilisation and business studies; no A-level general studies). 29% take science subjects, 39% arts/humanities and 33% both. *Vocational:* Work experience available; also Scotvec modules in personal finance, car user, computing. *Computing facilities:* 80 computers (mostly PCs for pupil use), new Pentium network. *Special provision:* Learning support services for pupils with specific learning difficulties who are otherwise able to cope with the curriculum. *Europe:* French, German and Russian offered at GCSE, Higher and A-level; French or German compulsory from age 11 to GCSE. Regular exchanges (some for up to 1 year) and visits to France and Germany. Usually 3–5 French boys in the school at any time.

The arts (Pupils aged 11 and over) *Music:* 30% of pupils learn a musical instrument; instrumental exams can be taken. Musical groups including orchestras, choirs, dance, concert, wind bands, chamber music groups. Member of National Youth Orchestra of Scotland; member of Edinburgh Youth Orchestra. *Drama & dance*: Drama offered. Some pupils are involved in school and house/other productions. *Art:* On average, 35 take GCSE, 20 Higher, 14 A-level. Design, pottery also offered.

Sport, community service and clubs (Pupils aged 11 and over) *Sport and physical activities:* Compulsory sports: rugby (for 4 years), cricket (for 2 years). Optional: football, cross-country, squash, swimming, fives, hockey, athletics, shooting, curling, sailing, tennis, skiing, judo, golf, fencing, badminton. Scottish Schools or National age group honours recently: 5 in athletics; 1 cricket; 2 squash; 2 fencing; 3 rugby; 2 hockey; 2 skiing; 1 basketball. *Community service:* Pupils take bronze, silver and gold Duke of Edinburgh's Award. CCF compulsory for 1½ years at age 14. Community service optional in sixth. 70 pupils took part in Water of Leith clear up. Major drive in 1994 to raise funds for Health Unlimited. *Clubs and societies:* Up to 15 clubs, eg science, literary, art, politics, Scripture Union, Scottish country dance, chess.

Uniform School uniform worn throughout.

Houses/prefects Competitive houses (Divisions). Prefects (Ephors), head boy and girl, head of house and house prefects – Ephors appointed by Rector after nomination by pupils and staff.

Religion Non-denominational morning prayers for whole school; school services once a month; compulsory local church attendance or monthly services for boarders; weekly RE teaching period for all.

Social Regular joint drama productions, debates, Burns Suppers, reel club with St George's Girls School. Organised trips and exchange systems with schools abroad. Pupils allowed to bring own bike to school (car may be parked nearby with permission). Meals self-service. School shop (books and stationery). No tobacco/alcohol allowed.

Discipline Graded punishments. Parents of pupils failing to produce homework more than once might expect notification; pupils caught smoking cannabis on the premises may expect automatic expulsion.

Boarding 18 have own study bedroom; 5 share; 2 dormitories of 6+ per senior house. Houses of up to 35, two for boys over 13, one for boys under 13 and senior girls. 1 resident qualified nurse, plus 2 matrons. Central dining room. Pupils can provide and cook own food. 2 weekend exeats and half-term each term. Visits to city allowed. Weekly and flexi-boarding available; prices on application.

Alumni association Run by Mr J J Burnet, Secretary, Edinburgh Academical Club, c/o the Academy.

Former pupils Magnus Magnusson (TV presenter, Mastermind); Gordon Honeycombe (author, former TV newsreader); Paul Jones (radio presenter, formerly singer with Manfred Mann); Lord Cameron of Lochbroom; Giles Gordon; David Caute; Admiral Jock Slater; Sir Iain Vallance; Iain Glen; Nicky Campbell (radio DJ).

• EGERTON-ROTHESAY

Egerton-Rothesay School, Durrants Lane, Berkhamsted, Hertfordshire HP4 3UJ. Tel 01442 865275, Fax 01442 864977

Pupils 497 • Boys 2–18 (Day) • Girls 2–18 (Day) • Upper sixth 4 • Termly fees £1120–£1830 (Day) • ISAI • Enquiries/application to Admissions Secretary (01442 877060)

What it's like

Founded in 1922, it developed from a small prep school to having a flourishing secondary department. It has always been co-educational. The lower school (2–7 years) is in the centre of Berkhamsted and the middle school (8–10) and secondary department (11–18) are sited together on the rural periphery. The sixth-form opened in 1994. The purpose-built premises are in their own grounds. Attendance at Christian worship is compulsory. There is a learning enhancement department and the staff has a full-time chartered educational psychologist. A feature of the school is close cooperation between parents and staff. Music and art are very well supported. Drama is especially strong: every class has at least one drama session each week; many do GCSE drama and there are particularly good LAMDA results. A fair range of standard sports and games, some of which are compulsory, with some representation at district and county level. GCSE sport is a popular option. There is a wide variety of clubs and societies, plus the Duke of Edinburgh's Award Scheme and local community services.

School profile

Pupils Total age range 2–18; 497 day pupils, 294 boys, 203 girls. Senior department 11–18, 240 pupils (141 boys, 99 girls). Main entry age 2–3 and 11. Some 6% are children of former pupils. Large senior intake from own junior school (tel 01442 866305).

Entrance Common Entrance and own entrance tests used. No special skills or religious requirements. Parents expected to buy textbooks from Year 6 upwards; average £35 extras. 15 pa bursaries available, value £140–£1595.

Head and staff *Headmaster:* John R Adkins, 15 years in post. Educated at Trinity (Croydon) and London University (physics). Previously Deputy Head at Rokeby School (Newham) and Head of Physics at John Ruskin Grammar (Croydon). Also President and founder of a youth activities organisation; founder member of governing committee for young men's rehabilitation hostel in East London. *Staff:* 42 full time, 21 part time. Annual turnover 3%. Average age 38.

Exam results In 1995, 28 pupils in upper fifth, 1 in upper sixth (new sixth-form). *GCSE:* In 1995, 29% upper fifth gained at least grade C in 8+ subjects; 25% in 5-7; 46% in 1–4 subjects.

University and college entrance 35% of leavers go on to art, drama, music colleges, 35% to non-degree courses eg NNEB, catering, training courses, 20% to sixth-forms elsewhere, 10% entered school's own new sixth-form.

Curriculum GCSE and A-levels offered. 21 subjects offered; including A-level general studies. *Vocational:* Work experience available. Special provisions: Special needs unit, supervised by a full time chartered educational psychologist, caters for those arriving with no English, those with specific learning difficulties and gifted pupils. *Europe:* French (compulsory from age 6), German, Spanish and Turkish offered to GCSE. Regular exchanges to France.

The arts (Pupils aged 11 and over): *Music:* 30% of pupils learn a musical instrument; instrumental exams are taken. Some 4 musical groups: choral, choirs, recorders and orchestra. Junior choir York Shield for 2 consecutive years at Chesham Arts Festival. *Drama & dance*: Drama offered; GCSE and LAMDA exams may be taken (90% of LAMDA candidates gained distinction). Majority of pupils involved in school and house/other productions. *Art:* On average, 45% take GCSE. Design, pottery, graphics, drawing and painting also offered. Usually win art cups and trophies at Chesham Arts Festival.

Sport, community service and clubs *Sport and physical activities:* Compulsory sports for all: cross-country, athletics, tennis, swimming, gymnastics; for boys, football, cricket;

for girls: netball, rounders. Optional: hockey. GCSE sport, BAGA, AAA 5 star and ASA awards may be taken. Badminton, pupil in U14 England team; football, district; trampolining, pupil represented GB in World Age Group Games 1992; U16 UK synchro champion, girls gymnastics squad has several individual medals and team cups in Independent Schools' Gymnastic Competition. *Community service:* Pupils take bronze and silver Duke of Edinburgh's Award. Community service optional. *Clubs and societies:* Up to 30 clubs including pottery, cookery, gym squad, swimming, drama workshop, country dancing, computer, gardening.
Uniform School uniform worn throughout.
Houses/prefects Competitive houses. Head boy/girl prefects, house prefects and house captains – appointed by the Headmaster and School Council.
Religion Attendance at Christian worship compulsory.
Social No joint functions with local schools. Exchanges with French students; 30 Russian children to school in 1993. Meals self-service. No alcohol/tobacco allowed.
Discipline Pupils failing to produce homework once might expect a warning and a check on their homework diary.

• ELIZABETH COLLEGE

Elizabeth College, Guernsey, Channel Islands. Tel 01481 726544
• Pupils 677 • Boys 4–18 (Day/Board) • Girls 16–18 (Day) • Upper sixth 66 • Termly fees £820 (Day) £2045 (Board) £1830 (Weekly) • HMC • Enquiries to the Principal's Secretary • Application to the Bursar

What it's like

Founded in 1563 by royal charter of Queen Elizabeth, it is one of the original HMC schools. It comprises an upper school, a lower school and a pre-prep school. The former lies in a hill overlooking the town and harbour of St Peter Port. The playing fields are on 2 sites of about 20 acres. A well-equipped establishment with plentiful modern resources. Religious worship is compulsory. A sound basic education is given and results are good. Most sixth-formers go on to degree courses. A good range of games, sports and activities is provided. It is strong in music and drama. It has an active community service unit, a voluntary CCF and takes part in the Duke of Edinburgh's Award Scheme.

School profile

Pupils Total age range 4–18; 677 pupils, 672 boys (642 day, 30 boarding), 5 day girls. Senior department 11–18, 536 pupils (531 boys, 5 girls). Main entry ages 7, 11 and 13 (boys), into sixth (boys and girls). Approx 25% are children of former pupils. *State school entry:* 55% senior intakes.
Entrance Common Entrance and own exam used. No special skills or religious requirements. Parents not expected to buy textbooks; maximum extras £100 although most charged none. Gibson Fleming scholarships.
Parents 50+% in industry or commerce. 90% live within 10 miles; up to 10% live overseas.
Head and staff *Principal:* J H F Doulton, in post 7 years. Educated at Rugby and Oxford (Greats). Previously Housemaster at Radley. *Staff:* 54 full time. 2 part time. Annual turnover less than 4%. Average age 40.
Exam results In 1995, 74 pupils in fifth, 78 in upper sixth. *GCSE:* In 1995, 60 fifth gained at least grade C in 8+ subjects; 8 in 5–7 subjects. *A-levels:* 2 upper sixth passed in 4+ subjects; 61 in 3; 8 in 2; and 4 in 1 subject. Average UCAS points 17.6.
University and college entrance 74% of 1995 sixth-form leavers went on to a degree course; others typically go straight into careers, eg civil service, finance, or to art colleges. Of those going on to university, 5% went to Oxbridge; 2% took courses in medicine, dentistry and veterinary science, 19% in science and engineering, 67% in humanities and social sciences, 7% in art and design.
Curriculum GCSE and A-levels. 14 subjects offered (no A-level general studies). 14% take science A-levels; 35% arts/humanities; 51% both. *Vocational:* Work experience available. *Computing facilities:* Computing centre equipped with 30 BBC Archimedes linked by Econet. *Europe:* French, German and Spanish offered at GCSE and A-level; also as non-examined subjects. Regular exchanges (France, Germany and Spain).

The arts (Pupils aged 11 and over) *Music:* 40% of pupils learn a musical instrument; instrumental exams can be taken. Some 7 musical groups including orchestra, band, chamber, jazz, choir. *Drama & dance*: Drama offered. Some pupils are involved in school productions and in house/other productions. *Art:* On average, 25 take GCSE, 10 A-level. Design, pottery, textiles, photography also offered.
Sport, community service and clubs (Pupils aged 11 and over) *Sport and physical activities:* Compulsory sports: soccer, hockey, cricket, cross-country, athletics. Optional: tennis, squash, basketball, swimming, shooting, sailing, badminton, volleyball. Sixth form only: rugby, outdoor pursuits, fencing, golf. *Community service:* Pupils take bronze, silver and gold Duke of Edinburgh's Award. CCF and community service optional. *Clubs and societies:* Up to 30 clubs, eg photography, debating, model railway, war games, canoeing.
Uniform School uniform worn throughout.
Houses/prefects Competitive houses. Prefects, head boy, head of house and house prefects – appointed by Principal.
Religion Christian worship compulsory.
Social Debates, joint theatre, ski trips, music occasions with local schools. Exchanges and trips to France, Germany, Spain. Pupils allowed to bring own car/bike/motorbike to school. School tuck and book shops. No tobacco/alcohol allowed.
Boarding 15% share with 1 or 2 others; 85% in dormitories of 6+. Resident qualified nurse. Central dining room. Pupils can provide and cook own food. 2 overnight exeats per term plus half-term; other leave as required. Visits to local town allowed at housemaster's discretion.
Alumni association run by R C N Roussel, Cobo Farm, Castel, Guernsey.
Former pupils Air Chief Marshal Sir Peter Le Cheminant (Lt Governor of the Bailiwick of Guernsey); 4 Victoria Crosses.

• ELMHURST

Elmhurst Ballet School, Heathcote Road, Camberley, Surrey GU15 2EU. Tel 01276 65301, Fax 01276 670320

• Pupils 250 • Boys 8–19 (Day/Board) • Girls 8–19 (Day/Board) • Second year sixth 30 • Termly fees £2340 (Day) £3190 (Board) • SHMIS • Enquiries/application to the Principal

What it's like

Founded early in the 20th century as a girls' school, Elmhurst gradually evolved to its present position as a leading centre for training in dance and drama and has an international reputation. It is now co-eduational, first accepting boys in 1972. It has very pleasant premises (many new buildings) and gardens in Camberley and excellent modern facilities, including a purpose-built 230-seat theatre. The school is basically C of E but other denominations are welcome. Services are held in the chapel. A full academic programme for GCSE and A-levels, as well as business studies, is provided. The main vocational emphasis, of course, is on dance and drama. A highly-qualified staff give instruction on all aspects of dance. The school has a number of large modern studios. Classical ballet, modern and contemporary dance, jazz, tap as well as Spanish and national dance are taught. Naturally, music and singing are a very strong part of the school life. The three-year sixth-form senior dance course is accredited by the Council for Dance Education and Training. Basic cookery, word processing and vocational qualifications for occupations other than dance are also offered.

School profile

Pupils Total age range 8–19; 250 pupils; 33 day (4 boys, 29 girls), 217 boarding (31 boys, 186 girls).
Entrance By dancing audition.
Head and staff *Principal:* John McNamara, in post for 2 years. Educated at the universities of Birmingham (drama) and Nottingham (English). Previously Director of Drama at Marlborough, Chief Examiner for A-level Drama and Theatre Arts and Senior Lecturer at Chester College. *Artistic Director*: Alfreda Thorogood, former prima ballerina of the Royal Ballet
University and college entrance 30% of 1995 sixth-form leavers went on to a degree

course (none take a gap year); others go on to professional careers in the theatre and media – as dancers, actors, choreographers and performers in musical theatre. Of those going on to university, 70% took courses in humanities and social sciences, 10% in art and design, 20% in vocational subjects eg hotel management, theatre arts, teaching of ballet.

Curriculum Range of GCSE subjects and selected A-level subjects. *Vocational:* Work experience available. All pupils take vocational qualifications: vocational dance training, accredited by the Council for Dance Education and Training; City and Guilds basic cookery; RSA Stages 1 and 2 in typing, in word processing and in core text skills.

The arts *Music:* Over 30% of pupils learn a musical instruments; instrumental exams can be taken. Musical groups include 2 choirs, orchestras. *Drama & dance*: Both offered. GCSE drama and A-level theatre studies, RAD, ISTD exams may be taken. All pupils are involved in school productions. *Art:* On average, 30 take GCSE, 10 A-level

Sport, community service and clubs *Sport and physical activities:* No organised games; physical development through vocational dance training. *Community service:* Some pupils take Duke of Edinburgh's Award during school holidays.

Discipline A supportive pastoral system is used to address most disciplinary problems. Parental involvement is encouraged in resolving such problems.

Former pupils Fiona Fullerton, Jenny Agutter, Fiona Lumanis, Hayley and Juliet Mills, Dame Merle Park, Jennifer Jackson, Tracy Childs, Sarah Brightman and Helen Baxendale.

• ELTHAM COLLEGE

Eltham College, Grove Park Road, London SE9 4QF. Tel 0181 857 1455

• Pupils 765 • Boys 7–18 (Day/Board/Weekly) • Girls 16–18 (Day) • Upper sixth 1055. Termly fees £1817 (Day) £3835 (Board) £3716 (Weekly) • HMC • Enquiries/application to the Headmaster

What it's like

Founded in 1842, originally for the sons of missionaries, it occupies a single suburban site of 25 acres, in handsome buildings (originally the mansion of Lord Bathurst). It remains loyal to its Christian foundation. It has admitted girls into the sixth-form since 1978; its sister school, Walthamstow Hall, is in Sevenoaks. The junior school is attached and 90% of its pupils move on to the senior school. Results are very good and almost all sixth-formers go on to degree courses, a high proportion to Oxbridge. Very strong indeed in musical activities, travel and in drama (fine performing arts centre). Excellent all-round facilities are provided. Standards in sports and games are high and there is a fine new sports centre. There is a substantial commitment to local community service and a wide range of clubs and societies.

School profile

Pupils Total age range 7–18; 765 pupils, 755 day (704 boys, 61 girls), 10 boarding boys. Senior department 11–18, 590 pupils (540 boys, 61 girls). Main entry ages 7, 8 and 11 (boys) and into sixth (boys and girls). Approx 8% are children of former pupils. *State school entry:* 50% main intake at 11, plus 35% to sixth.

Entrance Own entrance exam used. All special skills welcome. No religious requirements but Christian (non-denominational) foundation emphasised. Parents not expected to buy textbooks; maximum £140 extras. 25 pa assisted places. 30 pa scholarships/bursaries, 33%–66% fees.

Parents 20+ % in industry or commerce; 15+ % in theatre, media, music, etc; 20+ % are doctors, lawyers, etc. 90+ % within 30 miles; up to 5% live overseas.

Head and staff *Headmaster:* Malcolm Green, 6 years in post. Educated at Bryanston and Cambridge (English). Previously Headmaster at Warminster, Housemaster at Bryanston, English teacher at Canford and Michaelhouse, South Africa, and librarian at Glenalmond. Also Schoolmaster Fellow, Oriel College, Oxford; Academic Committee SHMIS; Director, West Wilts Enterprise Agency; Governor, Lavant House School; Member, Admiralty Interview Board; Committee and Council, Southern Examining Group; HMC Community Service Committee; Captain, Cambridge University Modern

Pentathlon Club; Winchester Cathedral chorister. *Staff:* 60 full time, 6 part time. Annual turnover 5%. Average age 34.

Exam results In 1995, 77 pupils in upper fifth, 91 in upper sixth. *GCSE:* In 1995, 96% upper fifth gained grade C or above in 5+ subjects. *A-levels:* 32% upper sixth passed in 4 subjects; 60% in 3; 8% in 2 subjects. Average UCAS points 24.0.

University and college entrance 97% of 1995 sixth-form leavers went on to a degree course (30% after a gap year); others typically go on to employment. Of those going on to university, 15% went to Oxbridge; 12% took courses in medicine, dentistry and veterinary science, 30% in science and engineering, 4% in law, 20% in humanities and social sciences, 4% in art and design, 30% in other subjects eg pharmacology, architecture, education, business and management.

Curriculum GCSE and A-levels. 20 subjects offered, including A-level geology, design and technology, computer science; no A-level general studies. 30% take science A-levels; 30% arts/humanities; 40% both. *Vocational:* Work experience available. *Computing facilities:* 2 networks of 24. Stand alone PC-AT machines; various departmental IBM machines; networked CD-Rom resource. *Europe:* French and German offered at GCSE, AS and A-level; also GCSE Russian. Regular exchanges (France, Germany, Estonia and Russia).

The arts (Pupils aged 11 and over) *Music:* Over 30% of pupils learn a musical instrument; instrumental exams can be taken. Some 12 musical groups including community orchestra, 2 string orchestras, saxophone ensemble, brass, jazz bands, choirs, rock. Several winners in Beckenham Festival; many members of district youth orchestras and ensembles; Oxford choral awards; singer with English National Opera. *Drama & dance*: Drama offered, and GCSE and LAMDA exams may be taken. Majority of pupils are involved in school and house/other productions. Productions of Shaffer's Amadeus, Orff's Carmina Burana, Maxwell Davies's Cinderella. Ex-pupil now lighting director National Youth Theatre. *Art:* On average, 20 take GCSE, 15 A-level. Design, pottery, printing, photography also offered. Many admissions to art foundation courses.

Sport, community service and clubs (Pupils aged 11 and over) *Sport and physical activities:* Compulsory sports: rugby, cricket, athletics, swimming. Optional: football, tennis, golf, squash, netball. Sixth form only: hockey, lacrosse, aerobics, rowing. International representatives at biathlon, rugby, swimming; regional representatives at atheltics, tennis, golf, cricket, rugby. *Community service:* Pupils take bronze, silver and gold Duke of Edinburgh's Award (120 in scheme). 5 Chief Scout's Award. Community service compulsory for 1 year at age 16: old people's homes, schools, hospitals etc. *Clubs and societies:* Up to 30 clubs, eg technology, computing, chess, astronomy, debating, maths, drama, printing, photography, Christian Union.

Uniform School uniform worn throughout.

Houses/prefects Competitive houses. Prefects, head boy/girl, head of house and house prefects – elected by the school, appointed by the Headmaster. School council.

Religion Daily chapel compulsory.

Social Debates, conferences, dances, discos regularly shared with other local schools. 6 partner schools in France, Germany, Russia and Estonia; approximately 120 exchanges annually. Pupils allowed to bring own car/bike/motorbike to school. Meals formal. No tobacco/alcohol allowed.

Discipline Pupils failing to produce homework once might expect either a 40-minute detention or a double homework; those engaged in any drug-connected activities could expect expulsion. Constant contact between school and home actively encouraged and practised.

Boarding Small boarding unit for long-term boarders and pastoral support of day school pupils where problems arise at home. All boys in single study bedrooms. Emphasis is on the freedoms and disciplines of a normal family household.

• EMANUEL

Emanuel School, Battersea Rise, Wandsworth, London SW11 1SH. Tel 0181 870 4171, Fax 0181 875 0267

• Pupils 750 • Boys 10–19 (Day) • Girls 10–19 (Day) • Upper sixth 90 • Termly fees £1529 (Day) • HMC • Enquiries/application to the Headmaster

What it's like

Founded in Westminster in 1594 by Lady Dacre, it moved to Wandsworth in 1883 where it occupies a 10-acre site next to Wandsworth Common, just off the south circular and a few minutes' from Clapham Junction. There are many fine trees, lawns and big playing fields with other playing fields at Raynes Park and a boat house at Barnes Bridge. The main building is a handsome example of mid-Victorian architecture and recent developments include new labs, computer centre and a sixth-form centre. Facilities are good. The school is interdenominational and ecumenical; worship in the Anglican tradition is encouraged. Orignally a boys' school, it first admitted girls into the sixth-form in 1995 and is now going fully co-educational. Academic standards are high and results good; nearly all sixth-formers go on to degree courses. The music department is particularly strong and there is considerable strength in drama and art. The CDT centre is a very active and successful part of school life. A good range of sports and games is available and standards are high, especially in rowing – it has produced 5 Olympic oarsmen and over 50 international 'vests'. There is an Army-based CCF and a fair range of extra-curricular activities; and much use is made of London's cultural amenities.

School profile

Pupils Total age range 10–19; 750 day pupils; girls admitted to the sixth-form in 1995 and fully co-educational from September 1996. Main entry ages 10, 11, 13 and into sixth. Approx 1% are children of former pupils. *State school entry:* 75% main intake, plus 50% to sixth.

Entrance Common Entrance and own exam used. Music, art and sport skills looked for; no religious requirements. Parents not expected to buy textbooks; £110 maximum extras, 46 pa assisted places. 12 pa scholarships/bursaries, £100 to 50% fees.

Head and staff *Headmaster:* Tristram Jones-Parry, in post since 1994. Educated at Oxford University (maths). Previously Under Master at Westminster. *Staff:* 70 full time, 5 part time. Annual turnover 8%. Average age 35–40.

Exam results On average, 122 pupils in upper fifth, 63 in upper sixth. *GCSE:* On average, 82% upper fifth gain at least grade C in 8 + subjects. *A-levels:* 5 upper sixth pass in 4+ subjects; 44 in 3; 6 in 2; and 5 in 1 subject. Average UCAS points 17.9.

University and college entrance 90% of sixth-form leavers go on to a degree course, 8% to Oxbridge; 10% take courses in medicine, dentistry and veterinary science, 50% in science and engineering, 35% in humanities and social sciences, 5% in art and design.

Curriculum GCSE and A-levels. 26 GCSE subjects offered (including Greek); 23 at A-level. 52% take science A-levels; 36% arts/humanities; 12% both. *Vocational:* Work experience available. *Computing facilities:* 25 Apple Macs in main centre plus facilities in CDT and science departments. *Special provision:* Sympathetic approach to dyslexia with some individual help. *Europe:* French, German and Russian offered to GCSE and A-level (French compulsory to GCSE); also French AS-level. Regular exchanges (France and Germany).

The arts *Music:* Some 6–7 musical groups including orchestral, choral, chamber, jazz, pop. Regular concerts outside school – hospitals, V&A and Royal Institution. *Drama & dance*: Theatre studies offered. Many of pupils are involved in junior school productions, some in senior. *Art:* On average, 20 take GCSE, 6 AS-level, 14 A-level. Design, pottery, photography also offered. Regional art prize; involvement with borough projects.

Sport, community service and clubs *Sport and physical activities:* Compulsory sports: choice from rugby, soccer, rowing, swimming, tennis, athletics, netball or cricket. Optional: gymnastics, water polo, table tennis, badminton, basketball. Sixth form only: golf. GCSE may be taken. International oarsman each year; county cricket and rugby each year; Great Britain junior fencing champion. *Community service:* Pupils take bronze, silver and gold Duke of Edinburgh's Award. CCF optional; Royal Navy Scholarship to South Africa for senior Sea Cadet 1992. Community service optional.

Clubs and societies: Up to 15 clubs, eg Christian Union, chess, computers, electronics, French, art, pottery, scrabble, travel groups.
Uniform School uniform worn, with some relaxation in the sixth-form.
Houses/prefects Competitive houses. Prefects, head boy, head of house and house prefects – appointed by Headmaster after consultation with staff.
Religion Pupils attend assembly/chapel (can be exempt if parents wish); communion services.
Social 3–4 trips abroad pa; exchange with French schools. Pupils allowed to bring own bike/motorbike to school. Meals self-service. No tobacco/alcohol allowed.
Discipline Pupils failing to produce homework once might expect reprimand or detention; other offences might involve detention on Saturday morning, suspension or expulsion.
Former pupils Stuart Surridge (cricketer); Michael Aspel (TV presenter); Leslie Henson (actor); Sir Denis Noble FRS; N F Simpson (dramatist); Peter Goddard FRS; Colin Chambers (literacy adviser to the RSC); Clive Wilmer (poet); Steve Gooch (playwright); Kevin Jackson (writer, broaadcaster), Naveen Andrews (film actor).

• EMBLEY PARK

Embley Park School, Romsey, Hampshire SO51 6ZE. Tel 01794 512206, Fax 01794 518737 • Pupils 380 • Boys 3–18 (Day/Board/Weekly) • Girls 3–18 (Day/Board/Weekly) • Upper sixth 25 • Termly fees £445–£2020 (Day) £3315 (Board/Weekly) • SHMIS, SHA, BSA • Enquiries/application to the Headmaster's Secretary

What it's like

Founded in 1946, it is housed in a Gothic mansion (formerly the family home of Florence Nightingale). It is in 100 acres of private park, including wild gardens, woodland and a lake, surrounded by splendid countryside bordering the New Forest. Altogether a delightful and healthy environment. It has all the advantages of a small school and takes pupils of a wide ability range, with remedial provision for a few with sound IQs. Originally a boys' school, it is now fully co-educational, having first accepted girls in 1988. A co-educational junior school opened in 1995 close by. Its ethos and regime is basically that of a boarding school although the majority are now day pupils. Most sixth-formers go on to degree courses. Very good, modernised facilities, including a new sports hall. Drama, art and design are quite strong, and there is strong emphasis on games and activities – which form part of every afternoon's curriculum. For a small school it has an impressive record of success in the Duke of Edinburgh's Award Scheme.

School profile

Pupils Age range 3–18; 380 pupils, 283 day (163 boys, 120 girls), 97 boarding (77 boys, 20 girls). Senior department, 11–18; 230 pupils (210 boys, 20 girls). Main entry ages 3, 7, 11, 13 and into sixth. Approx 5% are children of former pupils. Own junior school (tel 01794 515737). *State school entry:* 20% main intake, plus 20% to sixth.
Entrance Common Entrance and own exam used. Wide ability range accepted (100+ IQ); no special skills or religious requirements. Average extras, £30. Academic/sporting scholarships and bursaries, up to half termly fee; bursaries for the children of services, clergy and teachers.
Parents 60% in industry or commerce; 15+% in the armed services. 30+% live within 30 miles; 12+% live overseas.
Head and staff *Headmaster:* David Chapman, 9 years in post. Educated at Churcher's and Durham University (English language and medieval literature). Previously Housemaster at Churcher's and Assistant Master at St John's and Maidwell Hall. Also former member of the Full England Committee, Rugby Football (Schools' Union); chairman Hampshire Schools RFU; member of SHMIS Education Sub-Committee. *Staff:* 33 full time, 10 part time. Annual turnover 10%. Average age 35.
Exam results In 1995, 38 pupils in upper fifth, 18 in upper sixth. *GCSE:* In 1995, 70% upper fifth gained at least grade C in 8+ subjects; 20% in 5–7; and 10% in 1–4 subjects. *A-levels:* 9 upper sixth passed in 3 subjects; 7 in 2; and 2 in 1 subject. Average UCAS points 12.5.
University and college entrance 80% of 1995 sixth-form leavers went on to a degree

course (10% after a gap year); others typically go on to employment. Of those going on to university, 10% went to Oxbridge; 5% took courses in medicine, dentistry and veterinary science, 30% in science and engineering, 5% in law, 55% in humanities and social sciences, 5% in art and design.

Curriculum GCSE, AS and A-levels. 20+ subjects offered, including PE, environmental science, government & politics and A-level general studies. 25% take science A-levels; 50% arts/humanities; 25% both. *Vocational:* Work experience available. *Computing facilities:* 12 IBM compatibles, 3 Archimedes in computer centre; 20 computers in other departments. *Special provision:* for dyslexia; EFL expert on staff. *Europe:* French and German offered to GCSE, AS and A-level. Regular language trips for to France. Small numbers of European pupils visit, particularly from France/Spain, some join the sixth-form. MEP visits school occasionally. Extra language tuition available.

The arts *Music:* 30% of pupils learn a musical instrument; instrumental exams can be taken. 3 musical groups, choir, orchestra. *Drama & dance*: Drama offered. GCSE drama and New Era Academy speech and drama exams may be taken. Majority of pupils are involved in school productions and all in house/other productions. *Art:* On average, 25 take GCSE, 6 A-level. Design, pottery, photography also offered.

Sport, community service and clubs *Sport and physical activities:* Compulsory sports: rugby, hockey and cricket to age 15. Optional: athletics, netball, swimming, cross-country, basketball, volleyball, football, squash, canoeing. A-level sport studies may be taken. 2–3 members of each age group in county rugby and cricket sides, 1–2 in area, divisional sides; 1 England rugby player U16. *Community service:* Pupils take bronze, silver and gold Duke of Edinburgh's Award; 4–6 gold each year. *Clubs and societies:* Up to 20 clubs, eg drama, computing, dungeons and dragons (Southern area champions).

Uniform School uniform worn throughout, except in sixth-form.

Houses/prefects Competitive houses. Prefects, head pupil, senior girl, head of house and house prefects – appointed by housemaster and Headmaster.

Religion Ecumenical chaplain (C of E, RC in junior school). Some compulsory religious worship; more encouraged.

Social Ski trips (France), cultural exchanges (France and Germany), canoeing, geography field trip (S France) and sports studies trip. Pupils allowed to bring own car/bike to school. Meals cafeteria. School shop. No tobacco/alcohol allowed.

Discipline Pupils failing to produce homework once might expect to re-do work, be detained, gated or put on housemaster's report; those caught smoking cannabis on the premises could expect expulsion. Saturday afternoon detention and fines for misdemeanours.

Boarding 10% have own study bedroom (but all sixth have studies), 50% are in dormitories of 6+. Resident matron and assistant (RGN). Central dining room. Pupils can provide and cook own food. 3 weekend exeats each term. Visits to local town allowed occasionally and where necessary (15+).

Alumni association (Old Embleians) run by R Bell, Hon Secretary, 3 Windbrook Meadow, Stratton St Margaret, Swindon, Wiltshire.

• EPSOM COLLEGE

Epsom College, Epsom, Surrey KT17 4JQ. Tel 01372 723621, Fax 01372 726277

• Pupils 650 • Boys 13–18 (Day/Board/Weekly) • Girls 13–18 (Day/Board/Weekly) • Upper sixth 157 • Termly fees £2872 (Day) £3865 (Board) £3812 (Weekly) • HMC • Enquiries/application to the Headmaster

What it's like

Founded in 1855, the college is on a fine 80-acre site, close to open countryside on Epsom Downs and 15 miles south of central London. The main buildings are of handsome Victorian architecture; the modern buildings fit in well. There has been considerable modernisation and extension in recent years, and the college is now very well equipped. Originally a boys' school, it is becoming fully co-educational after 20 years' experience of a mixed sixth-form; girls were first accepted at 13 in 1996. It is a school which expects pupils to aim for high academic standards and at the same time to be fully involved in the general life of an active community. Academic results are very good and all leavers go on to degree courses, including many to Oxbridge. Art is a particularly strength. A wide range of sport and games (very many county representatives), plus a large number of clubs and societies. Very strong in music and drama. A substantial commitment to local community schemes. As a C of E school, religious worship is encouraged.

School profile

Pupils Age range 13–18; 650 pupils, 313 day (295 boys, 18 girls), 337 boarding (291 boys, 46 girls). Main entry ages 13 and into sixth (girls accepted throughout the school from 1996). Approx 10% are children of former pupils. *State school entry:* 7% main intake plus 15% to sixth.

Entrance Common Entrance and own entrance exam used. No special skills or religious requirements. Parents not expected to buy textbooks; music tuition only major extra. 10 pa assisted places. 30 pa scholarships/bursaries for academic, all-rounder, sport, music and art, 5%–50% fees.

Parents 20+% in industry or commerce; 20+% are doctors, lawyers, etc. 70+% live within 30 miles; up to 10% live overseas.

Head and staff *Headmaster:* A H Beadles, 4 years in post. Educated at Epsom College and Oxford. Previously Headmaster at King's School, Bruton, and Head of History and Housemaster at Harrow. Chairman HMC (SW) in 1982 and Chairman of the Independent Schools Examination Board. *Staff:* 65 full time, 20 part time (mostly music). Annual turnover 5%. Average age 38.

Exam results In 1995, 125 pupils in upper fifth, 151 in upper sixth. *GCSE:* in 1995, 117 upper fifth gained at least grade C in 8+ subjects; and 8 in 5–7 subjects. *A-levels:* 36 upper sixth passed in 4+ subjects; 107 in 3; 5 in 2; and 3 in 1 subject. Average UCAS points 23.9.

University and college entrance All 1995 sixth-form leavers went on to a degree course, 15% to Oxbridge; 18% took courses in medicine, dentistry and veterinary science, 27% in science and engineering, 5% in law, 32% in humanities and social sciences, 4% in art and design, 15% in other subjects eg drama, music, agriculture, stage management.

Curriculum GCSE and A-levels. 17 subjects offered (no A-level general studies). 45% take science A-levels; 35% arts/humanities; 20% both. *Vocational:* Work experience available. *Computing facilities:* Well-equipped computer studies department; most other departments have own computers. *Special provision:* A small learning support department. *Europe:* French, German and Spanish offered to GCSE and A-level and as non-examined courses in sixth-form. Regular exchanges (France and Germany).

The arts *Music:* Over 30% of pupils learn a musical instrument; instrumental exams can be taken. Musical groups including orchestra, chapel choir, choral society, concert band, madrigals, various ensembles. *Drama & dance*: Drama offered. Some pupils are involved in school productions and majority in house/other productions. Major recent productions include Guys and Dolls and A Midsummer Night's Dream. *Art:* On average, 35 take GCSE, 20 A-level. Pottery also offered. Pupils regularly go on to art college.

Sport, community service and clubs *Sport and physical activities:* Compulsory sports: rugby, hockey, athletics, swimming (for 2 years). Optional: badminton, cricket, tennis, netball, lacrosse, basketball, fencing, squash, golf, sailing, cross-country. Sixth form only: soccer. Strong county representation in all age groups at rugby, hockey, cricket, squash, athletics, cross-country. *Community service:* Pupils take bronze, silver and gold Duke of Edinburgh's Award. CCF compulsory for 2 years at age 14. Strong emphasis on leadership training in CCF; outstanding shooting record, many hold first aid qualifications, numerous outdoor pursuits. Community service optional for 2 years at age 16. *Clubs and societies:* Up to 30 clubs, eg bridge, car maintenance, chess, computing, photography, pottery, woodwork.

Uniform School uniform worn throughout.

Houses/prefects Competitive houses. Prefects, head boy/girl and head of house appointed by the Headmaster or housemaster. Leadership and management courses for all prefects.

Religion Worship compulsory except for practising members of non-Christian religions. 2 chaplains.

Social Debates, intellectual and sporting competitions. Average of 5 trips abroad a year. Pupils allowed to bring own car/bike/motorbike to school. Meals self-service. School

shop. Upper sixth allowed beer on supervised occasions. No tobacco allowed.
Discipline All breaches of discipline dealt with according to the circumstances.
Boarding 15% have own study bedroom, 65% share; 20% are in dormitories of 6+. Single-sex houses, of about 60. Two resident qualified nurses. Central dining room. Pupils can provide and cook own food. Exeats each weekend or each 3 weeks. Visits to the local town allowed.
Alumni association is run by Mrs H Hartley, c/o the college.
Former pupils Graham Sutherland; John Piper.

• ETON

Eton College, Eton, Windsor, Berkshire SL4 6DW. Tel 01753 671000
• Pupils 1270 • Boys 13–18 (Board) • Girls None • Upper sixth 240 • Termly fees £4296 • HMC
• Enquiries/application to the Registrar

What it's like

Founded in 1440 by Henry VI for the worship of God, and for the training of young men to the service of Church and State. His aim was to have 70 so trained, first at Eton then at King's College, Cambridge. These were his Scholars. He also provided for other boys to be taught at Eton, paying for their own maintenance. In Henry's time, or shortly afterwards, most of the school's ancient buildings were completed. These include the chapel, the cloisters, the lower school, College Hall and part of College. Building and rebuilding have gone on ever since. The whole architectural complex constitutes an urbane and civilised enclave. The numerous premises are scattered in the town of Eton and thus there is a close 'town and gown' relationship. There are beautiful gardens and playing fields and the school is one of the best-equipped. There are several excellent libraries: both College and School Libraries have remarkable collections of rare books and manuscripts. Worship is designed to meet a boy's spiritual needs at each stage of his development. Academically, Eton is very high-powered indeed. A large and very well-qualified staff permits a staff:pupil ratio of 1:9. Academic results are outstanding. Each year most sixth-formers go on to university, including very large numbers to Oxbridge. Under its general studies arrangements senior boys are offered an exceptional range of linguistic options – Arabic, African, Oriental and European. It is immensely strong in music (600 boys learn an instrument) and in drama. The purpose-built Farrer Theatre is in constant use and the English department has two drama studios in the Caccia Schools. In the course of a year there may be 20 main productions and house plays. The art department is also extremely strong. There is a very wide range of sports and games (including the Eton Wall Game and the Eton Field Game, both peculiar to the College) in which very high standards are achieved, especially in rowing, cricket and rackets. Some 40 or more clubs and societies are active and cater for every conceivable need. The school has its own newspaper (The Eton College Chronicle) which has been published regularly each term since 1863. There is a substantial commitment to local community services, plus the Eton-Dorney Project for conferences, discussion and social work involving disadvantaged children from elsewhere, and the Eton Action fund-raising organisation. The CCF is very well supported.

School profile

Pupils Age range 13–18; 1270 boarding boys. Main entry ages 13 and exceptionally into sixth. Approx 40% are children of former pupils. *State school entry:* 1% main intake, plus 35% to sixth.
Entrance Common Entrance used, following preliminary entrance exam at age 10. No special skills or religious requirements, although school is C of E. Parents expected to buy a few senior textbooks; private tuition (eg music) extra. 31 pa scholarships (academic, music, junior and sixth-form for boys from maintained schools), £250 per term to full fees. 120 bursaries.
Parents 15+% are doctors, lawyers etc; 15+% in industry or commerce. 30+% live within 30 miles; up to 10% live overseas.
Head and staff Head Master: John Lewis, 3 years in post. Educated in Auckland and at Cambridge University (classics). Previously Master-in-College at Eton and Headmaster of Geelong Grammar School, Australia. *Staff:* 146 full time, 10 part time. Annual turnover 6%. Average age mid-30s.

Exam results In 1995, 254 pupils in upper fifth, 240 in upper sixth. *GCSE:* In 1995, 253 upper fifth gained at least grade C in 8+ subjects. *A-levels:* 78 upper sixth passed in 4+ subjects; 149 in 3; 11 in 2; and 2 in 1 subject. Average UCAS points 29.5.

University and college entrance 86% of 1995 sixth-form leavers went on to a degree course; others typically go on to careers in eg City, armed services or to art and music colleges. Of those going on to university, 32% went to Oxbridge; 6% took courses in medicine, dentistry and veterinary science, 21% in science and engineering, 68% in humanities and social sciences, 4% in art and design, 1% in drama and music.

Curriculum GCSE and A-levels. 30 subjects offered (including A-level general studies and Arabic, Chinese and Japanese at certificate level). 20% took science A-levels; 64% arts/humanities; 16% both. *Vocational:* Work experience available. *Computing facilities:* Two computer rooms and one or more computers in most departments. *Europe:* French, German, Russian and Spanish offered to GCSE and A-level; Italian and Portuguese offered to seniors. all boys take French in their first batch of GCSEs, subsequently may choose another language or take additional French. Regular exchanges (France, Germany and Spain).

The arts *Music:* Over 40% of pupils learn a musical instrument; instrumental exams can be taken. Some 20 musical groups including 3 orchestras, 4 choirs, 2 bands, 5 chamber groups, 2 jazz bands etc. 5 pupils in National Youth Orchestra; 6 Oxbridge organ scholarships; runners-up in Panasonic rock band competition. *Drama & dance*: Both offered. A-level drama may be taken. Some pupils are involved in school productions and majority in house/other productions. Some 12 boys at major drama schools; 1 recently left Guildhall, now at Birmingham Rep; president of OUDS; Double Edged Drama, highly successful Edinburgh Fringe company composed of current and former pupils. *Art:* On average, 45 take GCSE, 25 A-level. Sculpture, printmaking also offered. Several accepted for art college foundation courses.

Sport, community service and clubs *Sport and physical activities:* Compulsory sports (for new boys): rugby or soccer; cricket, rowing, tennis or athletics; field game or hockey. Optional: rackets, fives, swimming, polo, water polo, fencing, judo, squash, karate, golf, badminton, shooting, basketball, the Wall Game. Rowing, several Great Britain representatives most years (World Junior Championships); rugby and athletics, county representatives each year; cricket, occasional national rep, eg 1 current U15 player; rackets, occasional public schools winner, currently U15. *Community service:* CCF and community service both optional for 2 years at age 16+. Regular assistance at local primary schools, local physically and mentally handicapped facilities; fund-raising through Eton Action events, annual charity fair and sponsored events; holidays for disadvantaged children project. *Clubs and societies:* Up to 40 clubs, eg Amnesty, Caledonian, Green, Mind and Brain, photography, political, Keynes (economics), Wotton (philosophy), film.

Uniform School uniform worn throughout.

Houses/prefects Competitive houses. Prefects, head boy, head of house and house prefects.

Religion Compulsory religious assembly unless parents request otherwise.

Social 3-day exchanges with certain comprehensive schools. French, Spanish, German and Russian exchanges; 1- or 2-person exchanges with India, USA, Japan; occasional trips to Kenya, Malawi, Australia etc. Meals formal in some houses, self-service in the remainder. Some alcohol allowed for senior boys; no tobacco.

Discipline Pupils failing to produce homework once might expect extra work; those caught smoking cannabis on the premises might expect rustication or expulsion.

Boarding All have own study bedroom. Houses, of approximately 50, same as competitive houses. Resident qualified nurses and doctors. Central dining room (for half houses). Pupils can provide and cook own food within limits. 1 major exeat per term (week in autumn term, weekend in other 2 terms). Visits to local town allowed.

Alumni association run by N J T Jaques Esq, c/o the College.

Former pupils 19 Prime Ministers including Lord Home of the Hirsel and Harold Macmillan; Douglas Hurd; Lord Hailsham; Lord Armstrong; William Waldegrave; Anthony Powell; Lord Carrington; Robin Leigh-Pemberton; Archbishop of York.

• EWELL CASTLE

Ewell Castle, Church Street, Ewell, Surrey KT17 2AW. Tel 0181 393 1413

• Pupils 420 • Boys 3–18 (Day) • Girls 3–11 and 16–18 (Day) • Upper sixth 27 • Termly fees £1475 (Day) • SHMIS • Enquiries/application to the Headmaster

What it's like

Founded in 1926, the main building is a castellated mansion in 15 acres of gardens and playing fields which were once part of Nonsuch Park (the grounds of Henry VIII's Nonsuch Palace). Altogether a pleasant environment in the Surrey green belt. There have been extensive modern additions and facilities are good. The co-educational junior school has a separate site close by. An interdenominational school, it is not narrowly academic but most sixth-form leavers go on to degree courses. Its sporting record is good particularly in soccer, golf and squash, and there are regularly county representatives in a variety of sports and games. It has a well-organised pastoral system. High standards of discipline are expected.

School profile

Pupils Total age range 3–18; 420 day pupils (400 boys, 20 girls). Senior department 11–18, 300 pupils (all boys). Main entry ages 3 (boys and girls); 11 and 13 (boys); and into sixth (boys and girls). Approx 5% are children of former pupils. *State school entry:* 50% intake at 11 and 13.

Entrance Common Entrance and own exam used. No special skills or religious requirements. Parents not expected to buy textbooks. Some scholarships/bursaries available, up to 100% fees.

Head and staff *Headmaster:* R A Fewtrell, in post for 13 years. Educated at Royal Grammar, High Wycombe, and Leeds University (economics and history). Previously Head of Sixth Form at Bablake School, Coventry. Also JP. *Staff:* 35 full time. Annual turnover 5%.

Exam results In 1995, 44 pupils in Year 11, 27 in upper sixth. *GCSE:* In 1995, 14 Year 11 gained at least grade C in 8+ subjects; 21 in 5–7 subjects. *A-levels:* 1 upper sixth passed in 4+ subjects; 18 in 3; 3 in 2; and 4 in 1 subject. Average UCAS points 13.0.

University and college entrance 85% of 1995 sixth-form leavers went on to a degree course (5% after a gap year); others typically go on to employment or vocational training.

Curriculum GCSE, AS and A-levels. 17 GCSE subjects offered; 20 at AS/A-level (including A-level general studies). On average, 50% take science A-levels; 25% take arts and humanities; 25% both. *Vocational:* Work experience available. *Computing facilities:* 40 Apple Macintosh in subject areas. *Special provision:* Setting in English and maths; individual help for dyslexic pupils; also ESL. *Europe:* French and German offered to GCSE and A-level; also French AS-level. Regular exchanges (France, Germany).

The arts (Pupils aged 11 and over) *Music:* Up to 25% of pupils learn a musical instrument; instrumental exams can be taken. Professional recording of school choir; school used by Fitznell's School of Music. *Drama & dance*: Drama offered. Majority of pupils are involved in school productions. *Art:* On average, 15 take GCSE, 5 A-level. 1–2 art school acceptances each year.

Sport, community service and clubs (Pupils aged 11 and over) *Sport and physical activities:* Compulsory sports: soccer, rugby, cricket, athletics. Optional: squash, badminton, volleyball, fencing, shooting. Sixth form only: golf, weight training. GCSE and A-level sport studies may be taken. Squash, U19 team have been county champions and national finalists; golf, county schools champions; county and national representation in various sports. *Community service:* Pupils take bronze, silver and gold Duke of Edinburgh's Award. Community service optional from age 16. *Clubs and societies:* Over 10 clubs, eg aikido, history, film, fencing, IT, design, badminton, chess, Italian, art, science, air-rifle shooting, drama.

Uniform School uniform worn throughout.

Houses/prefects Competitive houses. Prefects and head boy – appointed by Headmaster.

Religion Religious worship is compulsory unless exempted by parental request.

Social Annual dramatic and music productions within local community. Regular exchanges; European field trips; overseas sports tours. Pupils allowed to bring own car/bike/motorbike to school. Meals self-service. No tobacco/alcohol allowed.

• EXETER

Exeter School, Exeter, Devon EX2 4NS. Tel 01392 73679

• Pupils 710 • Boys 11–18 (Day/Board/Weekly) • Girls 11–18 (Day) • Upper sixth 126 • Termly fees £1400 (Day) £2650 (Board/Weekly) • HMC • Enquiries to the Headmaster • Application to the Headmaster's Secretary

What it's like

Founded in 1633, it stands in 26 acres of pleasant grounds within a mile of the city centre. It has occupied its present site since 1880 and most of its well-designed buildings date from that time. There have been many recent additions and it now enjoys first-rate facilities. Originally a boys' school, it is about to become fully co-educational; girls have been accepted in the sixth-form since 1981 and will be accepted at 11 from 1997. A C of E school, its moral and spiritual life depends on a general acceptance of Christian values. There is emphasis on encouragement of the individual, on self-discipline and self-motivation. A well-run school with high all-round standards and very good academic results. Most go on to degree courses, including a high proportion to Oxbridge. There is a massive involvement in music and drama. A very good range of games and sports (high standards attained, especially in hockey; very many county representatives) and outdoor activities (eg Ten Tors adventure training on Dartmoor); very large voluntary CCF. The school has always been closely involved with the life of the city and its university and it has a substantial commitment to local community schemes.

School profile

Pupils Age range 11–18; 710 pupils, 665 day (640 boys, 35 girls), 45 boarding boys. Main entry ages 11, 12 and 13 and into sixth (girls accepted at 11 from 1997). Approx 20% are children of former pupils. 25% of intake from Exeter Prep School. *State school entry:* 40% main intake, plus 50% to sixth.

Entrance Common Entrance and own entrance exam used. No special skills required but sport and the arts help. No particular religious persuasion required, but Christians fit most easily. Parents not expected to buy textbooks; extras unlikely to exceed £20 (CCF, sixth-form common room sub etc). 30 pa assisted places. 4+ pa scholarships/bursaries, 10%–50% fees.

Parents 70+% live within 30 miles; up to 1% live overseas.

Head and staff *Headmaster:* N W Gamble, 4 years in post. Educated at Stockport Grammar School and at Manchester, Nottingham and Oxford universities (economics). Previously Head of King Edward VI Aston School, Head of Economics and Politics at Repton. Also: Oxford Cricket Blue and minor county player. *Staff:* 56 full time, 8 part time. Average age 40.

Exam results In 1995, 110 pupils in upper fifth, 127 in upper sixth. *GCSE:* In 1995, 90% upper fifth gained at least grade C in 8+ subjects; 8% in 5–7 subjects. *A-levels:* 78 upper sixth passed in 4+ subjects; 37 in 3; 10 in 2; and 2 in 1 subject. Average UCAS points 20.4 (including general studies 24.6).

University and college entrance 95% of 1995 sixth-form leavers went on to a degree course (30% after a gap year); others typically go on to employment. Of those going on to university, 11% went to Oxbridge; 11% took courses in medicine, dentistry and veterinary science, 28% in science and engineering, 8% in law, 23% in humanities and social sciences, 4% in art and design, 7% in vocational subjects eg architecture, land management, 18% others.

Curriculum GCSE and A-levels. 20 GCSE subjects offered; 28 at A-level (including electronics; voluntary A-level general studies entries plus non-examined sixth-form course). 45% take science A-levels; 40% arts/humanities; 15% both. *Vocational:* Work experience available; active participation in Young Enterprise (individual national prize 1994). *Computing facilities:* 64 computers in total: 15 in main and 8 in smaller lab, plus one or more in each main department. *Special provision:* Mild handicaps accepted. *Europe:* French and German offered at GCSE, AS and A-level and as non-examined subjects; also Spanish AS and A-level and Italian GCSE in sixth. Regular exchanges (France and Germany). Talks from MEPs. Some pupils go on to become language assistants in France.

The arts *Music:* Over 35% of pupils learn a musical instrument; instrumental exams can be taken. Some 12 musical groups including 3 full orchestras with total of 250 pupils, choir (200 pupils), 2 jazz bands; all joint major ensembles with St Margaret's. Orchestra has performed in School Proms at Royal Albert Hall 3 times in past 4 years; orchestra, jazz band and chamber choir perform annually in National Festival of Youth Music at Royal Festival Hall. *Drama & dance*: Drama offered, and GCSE and A-level may be taken. Large number of pupils are involved in school productions and some in house/other productions. Pupils accepted at drama school. *Art:* On average, 40 take GCSE, 5 AS-level, 18 A-level. Design, pottery also offered. Art facilities open to non-examination pupils and parents.

Sport, community service and clubs *Sport and physical activities:* Compulsory sports (to certain age): rugby, hockey, cricket, cross-country, swimming, athletics. Optional: tennis, squash, badminton, basketball, canoeing, golf, volleyball, shooting. National indoor U16 hockey champions 1994, U18 runners-up 1996. Over 60 pupils represent county at cricket, squash, golf, tennis, rugby, badminton, athletics, hockey, basketball, athletics; U19 sailing world champion; schoolboy internationals at hockey, archery and cross-country skiing. Ten Tors endurance challenges, first team home 15 years running. 10 pupils accepted for British School Exploring Society expeditions in last 2 years. *Community service:* Pupils take bronze, silver and gold Duke of Edinburgh's Award. CCF optional at age 14–18; 360 participate, winner of Tremlett Trophy (national CCF simulated artillery fire championships) for 2 years junior and senior. Community service optional age 16–18, over 100 pupils involved. *Clubs and societies:* Up to 20 clubs, eg computing, chess, classics, debating.

Uniform School uniform worn except in the sixth-form.

Houses/prefects Competitive houses. Prefects, head boy, head of house and house prefects – appointed by the Head, staff and upper sixth.

Religion Some morning assemblies in chapel, 11–16 year olds.

Social Joint sixth-form lessons and theatrical productions with local girls' schools. Annual trips abroad. Exchanges to Rennes and Hildesheim, Russia and USA. Australian exchange student for a year (reciprocal arrangement). Pupils allowed to bring own car/bike/motorbike to school. Meals self-service. School shop. No tobacco/alcohol allowed.

Discipline Pupils failing to produce homework once might expect detention; if caught smoking cannabis on the premises, punishment would be permanent exclusion.

Boarding Sixth formers have own study bedroom, others share with 1 or 2; all in single boarding house. Qualified resident matron; school doctor visits. Central dining room. Pupils can provide and cook own food. Visits to the local town allowed.

Alumni association is run by D Mullins, c/o the school.

Former pupils MPs, bishop, TV commentators, actors, conductors, generals, explorers, scientists and so on. Former CinC NATO NW Europe and Commandant of the Parachute Regiment.

F

• FARLINGTON

Farlington School, Strood Park, Horsham, West Sussex RH12 3PN. Tel 01403 254967

• Pupils 353 • Boys None • Girls 4–18 (Day/Board) • Upper sixth 24 • Termly fees £1930 (Day) £3120 (Boarding) • GSA, BSA • Enquiries/application to the Headmistress

What it's like

Founded in 1896, it lies in delightful grounds and gardens in a large park. The main building, formerly a country house, is part Jacobean and part Georgian. Other handsome buildings are nearby. In recent years there have been a number of additions and facilities are now good, including a purpose-built science building. A sound all-round education is provided and results are good. Most upper sixth leavers go to degree courses each year. The music, PE and art departments are very active. A large staff permits a staff:pupil ratio of about 1:10. A good range of sport and games with notable success in riding and county representation in hockey. A school farm is run by sixth-formers. Excellent record in the Duke of Edinburgh's Award Scheme.

School profile

Pupils Total age range 4–18; 353 girls (314 day, 39 boarding). Senior department 11–18, 250 girls. Main entry ages 11, 12, 13 and into sixth. Approx 1% are children of former pupils. *State school entry:* 30% intake over 11, plus 2% to sixth.

Entrance Own entrance exam used. No special religious requirements; favours girls with active extra-curricular interests (music, sport). Parents not expected to buy textbooks. 16 pa scholarships/bursaries, 33%-50% fees.

Head and staff *Headmistress:* Mrs Petrina Mawer, 4 years in post. Previously Assistant Rector at Dollar Academy and Deputy Head at Friends' (Saffron Walden). *Staff:* 31 full time, 27 part time. Annual turnover 7%. Average age 43.

Exam results In 1995, 46 pupils in Year 11, 24 in upper sixth. *GCSE:* In 1995, 90% Year 11 gained at least grade C in 8+ subjects. *A-levels:* 66% upper sixth passed in 3 subjects; 16% in 2; and 10% in 1 subject. Average UCAS points 17.2.

University and college entrance 95% of 1995 sixth-form leavers went on to a degree course (20% after a gap year); others typically go on to work. Of those going on to university, 5% usually go to Oxbridge; 13% took courses in medicine, dentistry and veterinary science, 13% in science and engineering, 7% in law, 47% in humanities and social sciences, 20% in vocational subjects eg speech therapy, education.

Curriculum GCSE, AS and A-levels. 18 examination subjects offered. 21% take science A-levels; 58% arts/humanities; 21% both. *Vocational:* Work experience available; also RSA Stages 1–3 in IT. *Computing facilities:* Word processors and 14 Archimedes computers plus graphic design facilities in an IT room, in classrooms 7 BBC computers, and 3 IBM PCs and 1 Nimbus in the science department. *Special provision:* Some individual help can be arranged. *Europe:* French, German and Spanish offered to GCSE and A-level; also GCSE Russian in sixth. French compulsory from age 8, a further language from 12; all sixth-form study a language. Regular exchanges (France, Germany and Spain). Regularly host girls from France, Germany and Spain.

The arts (Pupils aged 11 and over) *Music:* Over 60% of pupils learn a musical instrument; instrumental exams can be taken. Some 8 musical groups including orchestra, wind band, choirs, madrigal, jazz band, recorder ensemble. Several girls a year take grade 8 in individual instruments. Pupils prepared for conservatoires. *Drama & dance*: Both offered. GCSE and A-level drama and LAMDA exams may be taken. Majority of pupils are involved in school productions and all in house/other productions. Frequent dramatic productions to local community. *Art:* On average, 20 take GCSE, 4 A-level. Painting, stained glass, textiles, printing, graphics, sculpture, ceramics offered, also figure drawing at local college. Students regularly accepted for art college. Sport, community service and clubs (Pupils aged 11 and over) *Sport and physical activities:* Compulsory sports: hockey, netball, tennis, swimming, volleyball, basketball, gymnas-

tics, rounders, athletics. Optional: trampolining, judo, jazz, keepfit, riding, badminton. Sixth form only: squash, shooting, HRF etc. A-level may be taken. National schools riding champions; regional volleyball champions; county and regional hockey players. *Community service:* Pupils take bronze, silver and gold Duke of Edinburgh's Award. Community service optional for 2 years at age 16+. School farm run by sixth-form with help of younger pupils. *Clubs and societies:* Clubs include debating, chess, trampolining, choirs, Young Enterprise, history.
Uniform School uniform worn except in the sixth.
Houses/prefects Competitive houses. Prefects, head girl, head of house and house prefects – elected by staff and pupils. School Council.
Religion Church of England school: short religious assembly each day.
Social Joint concerts, mainly choral, with neighbouring schools eg Cranleigh, Hurstpierpoint. Annual ball and discos. Organised trips to France, art trips to Italy, ski holidays in Alps, water sports trip to Spain. Upper sixth allowed to bring own car/bike to school. Some meals self-service. School tuck shop. No tobacco/alcohol allowed.
Discipline Pupils failing to produce homework once might expect discussion with the subject teacher; those caught smoking on the premises should expect a warning, then parental involvement, suspension and, finally, expulsion; drug abuse would incur immediate expulsion.
Boarding 5% have own study bedroom, 12% share with others; 70% in dormitories of 6. Qualified nurse on site. Central dining room. Visits to the local town allowed arranged for all age groups.
Alumni association is run by Mrs D Heath, c/o the School.

• FARNBOROUGH HILL

Farnborough Hill, Farnborough, Hampshire GU14 8AT. Tel 01252 545197
• Pupils 525 • Boys None • Girls 11–18 (Day) • Upper sixth 56 • Termly fees £1476 (Day)
• GSA, SHA • Enquiries to the Headmistress

What it's like

Founded in 1889 by the Religious of Christian Education, the school is now an educational trust. It is housed in the former home of the Empress Eugenie of France. A purpose-built school has been added which includes science laboratories, a chapel, indoor heated swimming pool, gymnasium etc. It is Roman Catholic but girls of other Christian denominations and religious faiths are welcomed provided that they participate in the religious activities of the school and respect its Christian ideals. The school is committed to the education of the whole person within an environment based on gospel values. Each pupil is valued for herself and helped to develop her gifts in a friendly and stable atmosphere. Results are very good and the vast majority of sixth-formers go on to degree courses. There are also considerable achievements which are prized, in creative arts and sports.

School profile

Pupils Age range 11–18; 525 day girls. Main entry ages 11 and into sixth. *State school entry:* 60% main intake, plus 2% to sixth.
Entrance Own entrance examination, report and interview. No special skills required. Preference given to Roman Catholics, but girls from all Christian denominations are welcomed. Parents not expected to buy text-books. 30 pa assisted places. 20 pa bursaries; 9 pa scholarships (3 at age 11, 6 for sixth-form).
Head and staff *Headmistress:* Ms Rita McGeoch, appointed 1996. Educated at Elmwood, Lanarkshire, and the universities of Glasgow and Bristol (English, drama and education). Previously Deputy Headmistress at St Leonards Mayfield and Head of English at St Bernard's Convent, Berkshire. *Staff:* 41 full time, 10 part time. 8% annual turnover.
Exam results In 1995, 85 pupils in fifth year, 54 in upper sixth. *GCSE:* In 1995, 94% fifth gained at least grade C in 8+ subjects; 5% in 5–7 subjects. *A-levels:* 4% upper sixth passed in 4+ subjects; 85% in 3; 7% in 2; and 2% in 1. Average UCAS points 20.3.
University and college entrance 91% of 1995 sixth-form leavers went on to a degree course (7% after a gap year); others typically retake A-levels. Of those going on to

university, 4% went to Oxbridge; 8% took courses in medicine, dentistry and veterinary science, 24% in science and engineering, 7% in law, 58% in humanities and social sciences, 1% in art and design, 1% in vocational subjects eg nursing.
Curriculum GCSE, AS and A-levels. 20 GCSE subjects offered, 10 at AS-level and 25 at A-level (no general studies). 19% take science A-levels; 56% arts/humanities; 26% both. *Vocational:* Work experience available for all fifth-year pupils. RSA exams available for sixth-form in word processing, spreadsheet, desktop publishing, CLAIT, business communication and commercial French. *Computing facilities:* 18 networked BBC Masters, 30 Apple Macintosh. Word processing and computing lessons for all. *Special provision:* Remedial help in English. *Europe:* French, German and Spanish offered at GCSE and A-level. Regular exchanges (France, Germany and Spain).
The arts *Music:* Up to 20% of pupils learn a musical instrument; music exams can be taken. Musical groups include orchestra, woodwind band, chamber groups, Just a Note instrumental and choral group, 2 choirs. GCSE and A-level music offered. *Drama & dance*: GCSE drama and A-level theatre studies offered. Up to 40% of pupils take extra drama and may do Guildhall exams. Jazz dance option available. Regular school drama productions and strong tradition in public speaking; national finalists for last four years in Knights of St Columba Competition. *Art:* GCSE, AS-level and A-level art offered. Painting, drawing, sculpture, printmaking, pottery, textiles and photography offered.
Sport, community service and clubs Sports and physical activities: Compulsory sports: hockey, netball, basketball, volleyball, tennis, badminton, table tennis, athletics, swimming, gymnastics, keep fit. Optional: football, cross-country. Sixth form options: archery, squash, riding, golf, skating. BAGA, RLSS, ASA, CTA, 5 star athletics awards may be taken. School teams compete at district and regional level particularly netball, hockey, gymnastics, athletics. County representatives at hockey, netball, athletics, tennis, swimming. *Community service:* Community service optional. *Clubs and societies:* Up to 30 clubs, including art, choir, orchestra, drama, debating, IT, public speaking, various sports and music with the handicapped.
Uniform School uniform worn except in the sixth-form.
Houses/prefects Houses competitive for sports and interhouse challenges. Prefects, head girl, head of house (house captain) – appointed by the Headmistress after consultation with staff and senior pupils.
Religion School Mass compulsory on holy days of obligation and pupils attend assembly. The school aims to build a Christian community of faith. There are regular opportunities to attend Mass and receive the Sacrament of Reconciliation.
Social Debates with other schools; oratoria with other schools and parents. Regular visits abroad; exchanges with France, Spain, Germany. Pupils allowed to bring own car/bike to school. School meals or sandwiches. School shop. No tobacco/alcohol allowed.
Discipline Various sanctions imposed according to misdemeanour. Detentions may be given outside school hours. Suspension reserved for serious offences.
Alumni association Run by Mrs A Berry (Secretary), FHOGA.

• FARRINGTONS & STRATFORD HOUSE

Farringtons & Stratford House, Chislehurst, Kent BR7 6LR. Tel 0181 467 0256/5586, Fax 0181 467 5442

• Pupils 575 • Boys None • Girls 2½–18 (Day/Board/Weekly) • Upper sixth 38 • Termly fees £1215–£1735 (Day) £3028–£3343 (Board) £2900–£3221 (Weekly) • GSA • Enquiries to the Registrar

What it's like

Formed in 1994 from the merger of two local girls' schools, both dating from the turn of the century. It is situated in 25 acres of fine wooded parkland in Chislehurst, 12 miles south-east of central London on the borders of Kent. The buildings are well designed and the facilities good, including a full-size sports hall with dance studio and weights room and an outdoor, heated swimming pool. The boarding accommodation is comfortable. The nursery and junior school share the combined site and facilities, so education may be continuous from 2½–18. A Christian atmosphere is fostered; the chapel is central both physically and spiritually. Girls come from a broad spectrum of ability; exam results overall are good and almost all sixth-formers go on to degree courses. The music and drama departments are flourishing and the choir sings regularly at the Royal Festival Hall and Westminster Abbey. A good range of sports and games is offered (several county and national representatives). Girls participate in the Duke of Edinburgh Award Scheme and the Young Enterprise Scheme is flourishing. There are numerous clubs from computers to fencing.

School profile

Pupils Total age range 2½–18; 575 girls, 347 day, 228 boarding. Senior department 11–18, 350 girls. Main entry ages 2½ 5, 11 and into sixth. *State school entry:* 10% main secondary intake, plus 5% to sixth.
Entrance Own entrance exam used. No special skills or religious requirements. Organ scholarship; 4 pa bursaries, up to full fees.
Parents Many in industry, commerce, HMSO, diplomatic service (both British and others). 60% live within 30 miles; 30+% live overseas.
Head and staff *Headmistress:* Mrs Barbara Stock, in post for 10 years. Educated at Chesterfield Saint Helena Girls' High and Leeds University (German and French). Previously Head of German at Crown Woods and Head of Modern Languages at Rock Hills. *Staff:* 42 full time teaching/house staff. Annual turnover 2%. Average age 35.
Exam results On average, 60 pupils in Year 11, 40 in upper sixth. *GCSE:* In 1995, 91% of Year 11 gained at least grade C in 5+ subjects. *A-levels:* 6% upper sixth pupils passed in 4+ subjects; 42% in 3; 31% in 2; and 17% in 1 subject. Average UCAS points 15.5 (including general studies 16.8).
University and college entrance 98% of 1995 sixth-form leavers went on to a degree course (6% after a gap year); others typically go on to work or vocational training. Of those going on to university, 8% went to Oxbridge; 8% took courses in medicine, dentistry and veterinary science, 21% in science and engineering, 3% in law, 60% in humanities and social sciences, 8% in art and design.
Curriculum GCSE and A-level. 21 GCSE subjects offered; 22 at A-level. *Vocational:* Work experience compulsory for Year 11; also LCCI, Pitmans and RSA courses in typing and CLAIT; commercial French (FLAW). *Computing facilities:* 2 computer rooms, each with 16 terminals; also computers in departments, CD-Rom in library. GCSE, AS and A-level computer studies. *Special provision:* Extra coaching, extra English lessons, EFL. *Europe:* French (from age 7), German and Spanish offered at GCSE, AS and A-level; also commercial French (FLAW). Regular exchanges (France and Germany). Pupils from France, Germany and Spain boarding in school.
The arts (Pupils aged 11 and over) *Music:* Up to 25% of pupils learn a musical instrument; instrumental exams can be taken. Many musical groups including choirs, woodwind group, string ensembles. Choir sings at Westminster Abbey; instrumentalists and singers in concert at Central Hall Westminster. *Drama & dance*: Both offered. GCSE drama, A-level performing arts, LAMDA exams may be taken. Majority of pupils are involved in school productions and some in house/other productions. International festival bi-annually. *Art:* On average, 30 take GCSE, 8 A-level. Ceramics also offered.
Sport, community service and clubs *Sport and physical activities:* Compulsory sports: netball, lacrosse, tennis, athletics, swimming, gym, dance. Optional: badminton, table tennis, basketball, volleyball, cricket, rounders, weight training, fencing. GCSE, BAGA, RLSS, 5 star athletics, ASA exams may be taken. Several county lacrosse players, U18, U15; county athletics representatives at all age groups. *Community service:* Pupils take bronze, silver and gold Duke of Edinburgh's Award. Community service compulsory over 2 years at age 16+. *Clubs and societies:* Clubs include drama, debating, computing, dance, all sports, music, jazz dance, aerobic, chess.
Uniform School uniform worn except in the sixth-form (best uniform on special occasions).
Houses/prefects 3 competitive houses. Prefects, head girl and head of house elected by the upper sixth and appointed by the Headmistress. School Council.
Religion Religious attendance compulsory.
Social Organised trips abroad; outings to theatres, exhibitions, galleries, etc in London. Pupils allowed to bring own car/bike to school. Meals self-service. School tuck and second-hand uniform shops. No tobacco/alcohol allowed.
Discipline Pupils failing to produce homework once might expect to repeat it twice; those caught smoking/drinking on the premises could expect expulsion.

Boarding Houses divided by age group. Qualified nurse. Central dining room. 2-day exeats twice a term. Visits to the local town allowed on Saturday afternoons and, in senior school, after 4pm; sixth-form have greater weekend freedom.
Alumni association is run by Mrs Melanie O'Neill, c/o the school.

• FELSTED

Felsted School, Dunmow, Essex CM6 3LL. Tel 01371 820258, Fax 01371 821232
• Pupils 360 • Boys 13–18 (Day/Board) • Girls 13–18 (Day/Board) • Upper sixth 82 • Termly fees £3010 (Day) £4120 (Board) • HMC • Enquiries/application to the Headmaster

What it's like

Founded in 1564, it lies in the village of Felsted in beautiful countryside. A number of the original 16th-century buildings are still in use. Many modern developments. Architecturally the whole school is extremely pleasing and it has splendid grounds covering some 70 acres. Virtually every conceivable modern facility is provided, including comfortable boarding accommodation. It is a C of E school and all pupils attend the various services in chapel. The school (and the prep school) have been fully co-educational since 1993, having first accepted girls to the sixth-form in 1970. An excellent all-round education is provided and results are very good. The vast majority of sixth-formers proceed to degree courses, including Oxbridge. The music, drama and art departments are strong and there is a very good range of sports and games in which high standards are achieved (many international, regional and county representatives). Good range of extra-curricular activities. Substantial commitment to local community services and participation in the Duke of Edinburgh's Award Scheme.

School profile

Pupils Age range 13–18; 360 pupils, 60 day pupils (40 boys, 20 girls), 300 boarding (252 boys, 48 girls). Main entry ages 13 and into sixth. Approx 12% are children of former pupils. More than 20% intake from own prep, Felsted Prep School (tel 01371 820252). *State school entry:* 5% main intake, plus 15% to sixth.
Entrance Common Entrance and own exam used. No special skills or religious requirements. Parents expected to buy books in sixth-form only; £150 average extras. 13 pa assisted places. 16 pa scholarships/bursaries, 10%–50% of fees with extra bursary funding available in cases of proven need.
Parents 10+% live within 30 miles; up to 10% live overseas.
Head and staff *Headmaster:* Stephen Roberts, 4 years in post. Educated at Mill Hill and Oxford (physics). Previously Housemaster and Head of Physics at Oundle and physics/electronics teacher at Christ's Hospital. *Staff:* 50 full time, 2 part time. Annual turnover 6%. Average age 40.
Exam results In 1995, 63 pupils in upper fifth, 82 in upper sixth. *GCSE:* In 1995, 95% upper fifth gained grade C or above in 8+ subjects; 5% in 5-7 subjects. *A-levels:* 12 passed in 4+ subjects; 55 in 3; 11 in 2; and 3 in 1 subject. Average UCAS points 21.7.
University and college entrance 95% of 1995 sixth-form leavers went on to a degree course (45% after a gap year); others typically go in to the City. Of those going on to university, 5% went to Oxbridge; 8% took courses in medicine, dentistry and veterinary science, 13% in science and engineering, 5% in law, 45% in humanities and social sciences, 5% in art and design, 10% in vocational subjects eg land management, physiotherapy, 10% in other subjects.
Curriculum GCSE and A-levels. 25 subjects offered (no A-level general studies). Slightly more took arts/humanities than science. *Vocational:* Work experience available. *Computing facilities:* Extensive network around both residential and teaching areas. *Special provision:* Certificate of competence in English taken. *Europe:* French, German and Spanish (and occasionally modern Greek) offered to GCSE and A-level; German, Portuguese, Russian and Spanish offered at RSA and as non-examined subjects. All pupils study 2 modern foreign languages during the first year. Regular exchanges on demand to France, Germany and Spain. Some European pupils in school.
The arts *Music:* Up to 75% of pupils learn a musical instrument; instrumental exams can be taken. Some 15+ musical groups including 2 orchestras, 4 choirs, bands (including jazz), chamber groups, rock bands. Places won at music college including 1

scholarship; several members of county youth orchestra; CD recording released 1993. *Drama & dance*: Drama offered. A-level theatre studies may be taken. Majority of pupils are involved in school and house/other productions. Group performed successfully for 2 weeks on the Edinburgh Fringe. *Art:* On average, 18 take GCSE, 15 A-level, Design, pottery, textiles, photography also offered. Places gained at the Slade and l'Ecole des Beaux Arts. Annual arts festival.

Sport, community service and clubs *Sport and physical activities:* Compulsory sports (initially): hockey, rugby, cricket. Optional: badminton, basketball, squash, fives, table tennis, athletics, swimming, tennis, netball, rounders, water polo, climbing, sub-aqua, cross-country, cycling, shooting, riding. International representatives at rugby, hockey, cricket; many county and regional representatives; continued success against other schools in a number of sports. *Community service:* Pupils take bronze, silver and gold Duke of Edinburgh's Award. CCF optional for 5 years at age 14; community service for 2 years at 16. *Clubs and societies:* Up to 30 clubs, eg classical, fine arts, hill walking and mountaineering, photography, public speaking, debating.

Uniform School uniform worn.

Houses/prefects Prefects who support house masters/mistresses.

Religion Chapel (C of E) 4 times per week (pupils of other religions may be exempted at parents' request). Voluntary Holy Communion services weekly.

Social Meals self-service. School shop sells clothing, sports equipment and tuck. No tobacco allowed; sixth-form bar at weekends (wine and beer).

Boarding 66% in studies of 1 or 2. Single-sex houses, same as competitive houses, up to 60 pupils. Resident SRNs; daily doctor's surgery. Central dining room. Half-term plus 2 weekend exeats (one in spring term).

• FERNHILL

Fernhill School, Fembrae Avenue, Femhill, Rutherglen, Glasgow G73 4SG. Tel 0141 634 2674
• Pupils 165 • Boys None • Girls 12–18 (Day) • Higher year 32 • Termly fees £950–£1020
• Enquiries/application to the Headmistress

What it's like

Founded in 1972, it is a single site of 9 acres in the southern outskirts of Rutherglen, high above Glasgow and overlooking the Cathkin Braes and a golf course; an altogether pleasant and healthy environment. It has good accommodation. A Roman Catholic school but other denominations are welcome. Attendance at religious services in school is compulsory. Its declared priorities are the training of the intellect and will according to Christian principles, the development of habits of hard work, the fostering of good social relationships and success in study. A sound education is given and results are good. Many pupils go on to degree courses. Strong in music, art, drama and chess. Hockey is strong.

School profile

Pupils Age range 12–18; 165 day girls. Main entry age 12. Own primary department provides over 50%. *State school entry:* 45% main intake, plus 8% to sixth.

Entrance Own entrance exam used. No special skills; school is Roman Catholic but other denominations accepted. Parents not expected to buy textbooks. 6 pa assisted places.

Parents 15+% are doctors, lawyers etc; 15+% in industry or commerce.

Head and staff *Headmistress:* Mrs Louisa M McLay, 4 years in post. Previously Deputy Headmistress. *Staff:* 12 full time, 7 part time. Annual turnover low. Average age 43.

Exam results On average, 28 pupils in S grade year, 32 in Highers, 4 in A-level year. *S-grade:* On average, 22 pupils pass in 7 subjects; 5 in 5, and 1 in 1–4 subjects. *Highers:* 16 pupils pass in 5+ subjects; 8 in 4; 5 in 3; 2 in 2; and 1 in 1 subject. *A-levels:* On average 1 pupil passes in 3 subjects; 2 in 2; and 1 in 1 subject.

University and college entrance 90% of sixth-form leavers go on to a degree course (none took a gap year); others typically go on to further education colleges. Of those going on to university, 1% go to Oxbridge; 12% take courses in medicine, dentistry and veterinary science, 13% in science and engineering, 60% in law, humanities and social sciences, 5% in art and design, 5% in vocational subjects.

Curriculum S-grades, Highers and A-levels. 15 subjects offered (no A-level general studies). 15% take science Highers; 15% arts/humanities; 70% both. *Vocational:* Work experience available. *Computing facilities:* One computer room and facilities in the science lab. *Europe:* French (compulsory) and German offered from age 11 and at S-grade and Higher; also Spanish.

The arts *Music:* Over 20% of pupils learn a musical instrument; instrumental exams can be taken. Some 3 musical groups including chamber ensemble, wind group, choirs. Girls won classes in city festivals; 5 pupils in Scottish Independent Schools Orchestra summer school; 1 in National Youth Orchestra; 5 pupils in regional schools orchestra/wind band; finalist in Audi Young Musician; recital at Glasgow University. *Drama & dance:* Majority of pupils are involved in school/house productions. *Art:* Printmaking, jewellery, fabric crafts, soft sculpture, graphics etc also offered. 3 commended in art galleries competition; Scottish Independent Schools Art exhibition, 9 chosen for display; Edinburgh Fringe 3 posters displayed.

Sport, community service and clubs *Sport and physical activities:* Compulsory sports: hockey, netball, volleyball, swimming. Hockey, representatives in national U16 and regional U18, U16 teams; golf, 1 pupil gained golf scholarship to US university. *Community service:* Great deal of work for charity and close links with local schools for handicapped. *Clubs and societies:* 5 clubs; debating, chess, choir, Pro-life, music.

Uniform School uniform worn, modified in sixth.

Houses/prefects Competitive houses. Prefects, head girl, head of house and house prefects elected by staff and school.

Religion Attendance at services compulsory; participation not.

Social Chess, debates, hockey, swimming competitions with local schools; regular ski trips in Scotland and abroad, occasional educational trips abroad. Pupils allowed to bring own car/bike/motorbike to school. Meals self-service. No tobacco/alcohol allowed.

Discipline Pupils failing to produce homework once might expect a warning; any pupils caught smoking cannabis on the premises would be expelled.

Alumni association run by Headmistress.

• FETTES

Fettes College, Carrington Road, Edinburgh EH4 1QX. Tel 0131 332 2281, Fax 0131 332 3081 • Pupils 485 • Boys 10–18 (Day/Board) • Girls 10–18 (Day/Board) • Higher year 80 • Termly fees £2745 (Day) £4085 (Board) • HMC, SHA • Enquiries/application to the Headmaster

What it's like

Founded in 1870 under the will of Sir William Fettes, twice Lord Provost of Edinburgh, it occupies a splendid estate of 85 acres, 1½ miles from the centre of the city. The main building is Victorian Gothic and over the past 50 years, there have been extensive additions including a new technology and computing centre. The Junior House is in the college grounds. The college has a Christian approach but is inter-denominational; there are Anglican and Presbyterian chaplains and there is emphasis on religious instruction and worship. Now fully co-educational, it was originally a boys' school and first accepted girls in 1970. It is a distinguished school with a friendly atmosphere, in which great attention is given to individual needs. Its declared aim is to provide a balanced and challenging education. Pupils are encouraged to aim at and to achieve the very highest standard of which they are capable. Academic standards are high and results are very good. The vast majority of pupils go on to degree courses, including many to Oxbridge. Very strong indeed in music, art and drama. Excellent range of sports and games (very high standards) and an all-weather games pitch; equally good range of extra-curricular activities. The CCF (founded 1908) is a large and particularly active contingent. Much emphasis on specialist skills and adventure training. The college has a big commitment to community service and a strong record in the Duke of Edinburgh's Award Scheme. Copious use is made of Edinburgh's extensive cultural amenities.

School profile

Pupils Age range 10–18; 485 pupils, 109 day (48 boys, 61 girls), 377 boarding (217 boys, 160 girls). Main entry ages, 10, 11, 12, 13 and into the sixth. 17% are children of former pupils. Own Junior House provides over 20% of intake. *State school entry:* 20% main intake, plus 30% to sixth.

Entrance Common Entrance and own exam used. Special skills taken into account; no religious requirements. Parents buy textbooks on a sale or return basis; branch of university bookshop on campus. Assisted places available. 8 pa scholarships (academic and music), up to 50% fees; foundation awards, bursaries and assisted places up to the full value of the fees; bursaries for clergy and Old Fettesians; 12½% fee reduction for children of HM forces.

Parents 26% in professions, 15+% in industry or commerce. 55% live in Scotland; 15% elsewhere in the UK; 30% overseas.

Head and staff *Headmaster:* Malcolm Thyne, 8 years in post. Educated at The Leys and Cambridge University. Previously Headmaster at St Bees, Assistant Master at Edinburgh Academy and Housemaster at Oundle. *Staff:* 64 full time, 3 part time. Annual turnover 5%. Average age 40.

Exam results In 1995, 76 pupils in main GCSE year, 78 in A-level/Higher year (46 of whom took A-level, 32 Highers). *GCSE:* In 1995, 56 pupils passed in 8+ subjects; 13 in 5–7 subjects. *A-levels:* 3 passed in 4+ subjects; 41 in 3; 2 in 2 subjects. Average UCAS points 21.4.

University and college entrance 95% of 1995 sixth-form leavers went on to a degree course (8% after a gap year); others typically go on to further study. Of those going on to university, 9% went to Oxbridge; 12% took courses in medicine, dentistry and veterinary science, 24% in science and engineering, 3% in law, 53% in humanities and social sciences, 8% in other subjects eg ophthalmics, building, marketing.

Curriculum GCSE (20 subjects), Highers (17 subjects), A-levels (19 subjects, no general studies). 59% of the year take A-levels, the rest take Highers. Usually an equal number of pupils study science and arts/humanities. *Vocational:* Work experience available; also City and Guilds basic certificate in competence in IT. *Computing facilities:* Compaq system; network links 3 teaching rooms. *Special provision:* Extra tuition in English and maths. *Europe:* French (taught from age 10), German and Spanish offered to GCSE, Higher and A-level. Regular exchanges to France. European Society arranges lectures from international lawyers, civil servants, academics, MEPs.

The arts *Music:* Up to 50% of pupils learn a musical instrument; instrumental exams can be taken. Some 20 musical groups including 6 choirs, 3 orchestras, brass ensemble, jazz band, flute band, rock group, 6 chamber groups, chamber orchestra. Chapel choir tour to Canada (1995). *Drama & dance*: Drama and dance offered. GCSE drama, ESB, Central, Guildhall, LAMDA exams may be taken. Majority of pupils are involved in school productions and all in house/other productions. Production of Oedipus Rex at 1992 Edinburgh Fringe won Edinburgh Evening News Capital award. Productions of Agamemnon and The Prime of Miss Jean Brodie in 1994 Fringe, Equus in 1995. *Art:* On average, 25 take GCSE, 7 A-level. Design, pottery, photography also offered. Regular prizewinners for art work in Scotsman school magazine competition.

Sport, community service and clubs *Sport and physical activities:* Compulsory sports: rugby, cricket, hockey (boys); lacrosse, hockey (girls). Optional: athletics, tennis, squash, fives, swimming, badminton, fencing, netball, basketball, fencing, volleyball. RLSS exams may be taken. 2 Scottish Schools lacrosse A side representative, 3 B side; 1 district girl hockey rep; 1 Scottish Schools rugby international representative; 2 nationally ranked squash players. *Community service:* Pupils take bronze, silver and gold Duke of Edinburgh's Award. CCF compulsory for 2 years at age 14; CCF and community service optional for sixth-form. *Clubs and societies:* Up to 10 clubs, eg political, history, debating, Europe , Christian Fellowship, bridge, skiing.

Uniform School uniform worn including the sixth.

Houses/prefects Competitive houses. Prefects, head boy and girl, head of each house and house prefects.

Religion Daily interdenominational chapel services.

Social Joint careers talks and society meetings with other local schools. Organised expeditions to eg Norway, Kashmir, Ecuador, Kenya, Siberia, Nepal and New Zealand; exchanges with Canadian, American, German and Australian schools. Meals self-service. No tobacco allowed; alcohol on specified occasions for sixth-formers.

Discipline Strong emphasis on discipline and good manners. Pupils failing to produce homework may get detention or extra work. Anyone involved in drugs would be expelled.

Boarding All sixth-form in study bedrooms; most others in dormitories of 4–6. Single-sex houses, of approx 60. Resident qualified medical staff. Central dining room. Pupils can provide and cook own food to a limited extent. 4 Sunday exeats or 2 weekends each term. Visits to the local town allowed at specified times.
Alumni association is run by J W Hills c/o the College.
Former pupils Iain Macleod; Selwyn Lloyd; Lord Fraser of Kilmorack; Lord Drumalbyn; Tilda Swinton; General Sir John Learmont; Tony Blair MP; Lord Justice Woolf; General AGD de Chastelain; Vice Admiral Sir Robert Walmsley.

• FOREST

Forest School, College Place, Near Snaresbrook, London E17 3PY. Tel 0181 520 1744
• Pupils 1230 • Boys 7–18 (Day/Board/Weekly) • Girls 7–18 (Day) • Upper sixth 130 • Termly fees £1828 (Day) £2870 (Board/Weekly) • HMC • Enquiries/application to the Warden

What it's like

Founded in 1834 as The Forest Proprietary School, it became Forest School in 1847 and has a big campus in an open part of Epping Forest. Although they share the same campus, boys and girls are taught seperately between the ages of 11 and 16; the prep school and the sixth-form are both co-educational. The original Georgian building is used for dormitories, libraries, recreation rooms and offices. There have been many additions, including a theatre, a sports hall and a large computer centre. Excellent playing fields cover the 27 acres. Religious worship is in accordance with Anglican faith and practice and all pupils are required to attend services in chapel. A broad general education is provided and results are good. The music, drama and art departments are strong. A good range of sports and games is available and all pupils are expected to take part in these. There are many regional and county representatives and standards in hockey, cricket, soccer and rowing are high. Extra-curricular activities are numerous. There is a big commitment to local community services. Full use is made of the cultural amenities of London.

School profile

Pupils Total age range 7–18; 1230 pupils (800 boys, 430 girls); small number of boarding boys. Senior department 11–18, 835 pupils (475 boys, 360 girls). Main entry ages 7, 11 and into sixth. *State school entry:* 47% senior intake, plus 85% to sixth.
Entrance Common Entrance and own exam used. Assisted places. Substantial number of scholarships and bursaries, including music.
Head and staff *Warden*: A G Boggis, 4 years in post. Educated at Marlborough and at Oxford (modern languages) and Cambridge (education). Previously Master-in-College (Housemaster to Kings' Scholars) at Eton; Assistant master at Hitchin Boys' School. *Staff:* 103 full time, 5 part time. Annual turnover 5%.
Exam results In 1995, 159 pupils in upper fifth, 123 in upper sixth. *GCSE:* In 1995, 81% upper fifth gained at least grade C in 8+ subjects; 14% in 5–7 subjects. *A-levels:* 75% upper sixth passed in 4+ subjects; 13% in 3, 7% in 2; and 3% in 1 subject. Average UCAS points 19.5 (including general studies 24.0).
University and college entrance 90% of 1995 sixth-form leavers went on to a degree course (10% after a gap year); others typically go direct in to employment (often in City). Of those going on to university, 10% went to Oxbridge; 10% took courses in medicine, dentistry and veterinary science, 35% in science and engineering, 10% in law, 30% in humanities and social sciences, 5% in art and design, 10% in vocational subjects.
Curriculum GCSE, AS and A-levels. 21 GCSE subjects offered, 13 AS-level and 21 at A-level (including computer studies at AS/A-level and general studies at A-level). 21% take science A-levels; 47% arts/humanities; 32% both. *Vocational:* Work experience available; also RSA Stage 1 word processing and Stages 1 and 2 computer literacy. *Computing facilities:* 3 fully-equipped labs with Acorn Risc PCs and 6 km of networking to every department of school. *Europe:* French, German and Spanish offered to GCSE and A-level; also French and German AS-level. Regular exchanges (France, Germany, Hungary, Russia and Sweden, Austria).
The arts (Pupils aged 11 and over) *Music:* Up to 50% of pupils learn a musical instrument; instrumental exams can be taken. Some 20 musical groups including

orchestras, choirs, jazz bands, chamber groups etc. Chapel choir tour of Czech Republic; organ scholarship to Cambridge. *Drama & dance*: Drama and dance offered. Some pupils are involved in school productions and house/other productions. *Art:* On average, 25 take GCSE, 8 A-level. Design, pottery, textiles, photography also offered. All A-level students attain first choice places on art and design courses.

Sport, community service and clubs (Pupils aged 11 and over) *Sport and physical activities:* Compulsory sports: wide range of sports under the PE programme. Optional: more than 20 different sports and activities. A number of regional, county and district representatives at hockey, netball, football, athletics, cross-country, fencing, judo. *Community service:* Pupils take bronze, silver and gold Duke of Edinburgh's Award. CCF and community service optional. *Clubs and societies:* Up to 15 clubs, eg chess, choral, debating, film, music, natural history, photography, science, voluntary service, bridge, shooting.

Uniform School uniform worn throughout.

Houses/prefects Competitive houses. Prefects, monitors head boy/girl, head of house and house prefects and monitors – appointed by the Warden. School Council.

Religion Attendance at religious worship compulsory.

Social ESU speaking competitions held jointly with other local schools. Exchanges to Australia, France, Germany, Hungary, Russia, Sweden and USA. Pupils allowed to bring own car to school. Meals formal. School shop. No tobacco/alcohol allowed.

Discipline Pupils failing to produce homework once might expect no punishment, possibly detention; those caught smoking cannabis on the premises might expect expulsion.

Former pupils Nicholas Grace, Adam Woodyatt, Anthony Venditti (actors); Mark Petchey, David Felgate (tennis); Nasser Hussain (cricket); Jangu Banatrolo (medicine); Richard Dunn (TV); Michael Swash (neurology).

• FRAMLINGHAM

Framlingham College, Framlingham, Woodbridge, Suffolk IP13 9EY. Tel 01728 723 789, Fax 01728 724546

• Pupils 440 • Boys 13–18 (Day/Board) • Girls 13–18 (Day/Board) • Upper sixth 75 • Termly fees £2072 (Day) £3229 (Board) • HMC • Enquiries/application to the Head's Secretary.

What it's like

Founded in 1864, it has a splendid rural site on a hill overlooking the ruins of Framlingham Castle and the town below. There are 50 acres of gardens and playing fields. The well-designed buildings are excellently equipped and provide comfortable boarding accommodation. It has a particularly fine technology and activities centre, a large science school and a floodlit, artificial grass hockey/tennis surface. Now fully co-educational, it was originally a boys' school which first accepted girls in 1976. Religious worship in the Anglican tradition is encouraged. Strong in music, drama and art. The academic expectations are high; exam results are consistently good. Nearly all sixth-formers go on to degree courses. there is an excellent range of sports and games in which high standards are achieved.

School profile

Pupils Age range 13–18; 440 pupils, 140 day (80 boys, 60 girls), 300 boarding (200 boys, 100 girls). Main entry ages 13 and into sixth. Approx 20% are children of former pupils. Own junior school, Brandeston Hall, provides 30+% of intake. *State school entry:* 4% main intake, plus 4% to sixth.

Entrance Common Entrance and own exam used. No special skills or religous requirements but school is C of E. Parents not expected to buy text books; other extras minimal. Assisted places. Scholarships (academic, music, art, drama and science), 10%–100% tuition fees.

Parents 50+% live within 50 miles; 10+% live overseas.

Head and staff *Head:* Mrs Gwendolen Randall, in post from 1994. Educated at Mary Datchelor School, London, and Bristol University (French). Previously Deputy Head at Dauntsey's and Head of Drama and of Modern Languages at St Mary's (Calne). Also actively involved in local politics. *Staff:* 50 full time, 3 part time, plus music staff. Annual turnover 10%. Average age 37.

Exam results In 1995, 104 pupils in Year 11, 75 in upper sixth. *GCSE:* In 1995, 60% in Year 11 gained at least grade C in 8+ subjects; 30% in 5–7 subjects. *A-levels:* 6% upper sixth passed in 4+ subjects; 70% in 3; 10% in 2; and 8% in 1 subject. Average UCAS points 18.0.

University and college entrance 87% of 1995 sixth-form leavers went on to a degree course (26% after a gap year); others typically go on to farming, family business. Of those going on to university, 7% went to Oxbridge; 8% took courses in medicine, dentistry and veterinary science, 30% in science and engineering, 3% in law, 48% in humanities and social sciences, 2% in art and design, 9% in vocational subjects eg agriculture, management, drama.

Curriculum GCSE, AS and A-levels. 20 GCSE subjects offered, 35 at A-level; also AS-level subjects and some vocational qualifications. 20% take science A-levels; 60% arts/humanities; 20% both. *Vocational:* Work experience available; GNVQ leisure and tourism; also RSA in IT and typing. *Computing facilities:* 2 fully-equipped computer centres, computers in sixth-form centres and in main teaching areas; word processors in all houses and desktop publishing facilities. *Special provision:* Special classes with specialist teachers for EFL with additional tutorial support; also help for dyslexia. *Europe:* French, German and Spanish offered to GCSE, AS and A-level, also as vocational language courses and as non-examined subjects. European pupils in school (particularly Danes, Germans and Spanish). Links being developed with Eastern Europe. European affairs taught as part of general studies.

The arts *Music:* Over 50% of pupils learn a musical instrument; instrumental exams can be taken. Musical groups include choirs, barbershop, orchestra, wind band, pop groups, recorder consort, variety of ensembles. *Drama & dance*: Drama offered. GCSE and A-level theatre studies may be taken. Majority of pupils are involved in school and house/other productions. *Art:* On average, 45 take GCSE, 25 A-level. Design, pottery, textiles, photography, jewellery making also offered.

Sport, community service and clubs *Sport and physical activities:* Games/sports compulsory 2 afternoons per week. Options: hockey, rugby, netball, cricket, cross-country, athletics, sailing, shooting (.303, .22, clay pigeon), squash, swimming, badminton, football, archery, gymnastics, multiple indoor games, tennis, sailing, golf, rounders. Regular county representation at rugby, hockey and cricket U18, U16; cricket, winners of Lord's Taverners county competition U14; hockey, girls county champions U18, U16; squash, divisional champions U14. *Community service:* Pupils take bronze, silver and gold Duke of Edinburgh's Award: CCF and community service both optional from age 13+. Charity events for local and national charities eg East Anglian coastal walk. *Clubs and societies:* Over 30 clubs, eg electronics, chess, bridge, karate, cookery, printing, pottery, drama, photography, debating, clay-pigeon shooting, gymnastics.

Uniform School uniform, modified in the sixth, worn throughout formal part of the day.

Houses/prefects Competitive houses. Prefects, head boy/girl, head of house and house prefects – appointed by Head and housemasters/mistress.

Religion Religious worship (C of E) encouraged.

Social Debates, choral productions, dances. Organised trips abroad. Day pupils allowed to travel to school in own car. Meals self-service. School shop. Sixth-form centre, fifth form centre. No tobacco allowed; limited alcohol allowed for upper sixth.

Discipline Pupils failing to produce homework once would have to do it as soon as possible and may be put into detention. A pupil caught smoking cannabis on the premises must expect to have his or her right to remain at the College removed.

Boarding Approx 25% have own study bedroom, 55% share with 1–3, 10% in dormitories of 6+. Single-sex houses, of 50–55, same as competitive houses. Resident qualified nurse. Central dining room. Pupils can provide and cook own food. Sunday exeats, except when there are other commitments, and overnight. Visits to the local town allowed.

Alumni association is run by V Bromage, 51 Park Road, Aldeburgh, Suffolk IP15 5EN.

Former pupils Gen Sir Patrick Howard Dobson (former ADC to the Queen); Capt G M Flowerdew VC; Capt A W S Agar VC DSO; N F Borrett (former world squash champion); J F Larter (cricket international); A Hancock (rugby international); J Paice MP (minister for employment and educaton); Sir Alfred Munnings (artist).

• FRANCIS HOLLAND (Regent's Park)

Francis Holland School, Clarence Gate, London NW1 6XR. Tel 0171 723 0176, Fax 0171 706 1522
• Pupils 370 • Boys None • Girls 11–18 (Day) • Upper sixth 49 • Termly fees £1765 (Day) • GSA
• Enquiries/application to the Headmistress

What it's like

The Francis Holland (C of E) schools were founded by Canon Francis Holland. The first was opened in 1878 in Baker Street, London, and transferred in 1915 to its present building near Regent's Park. There has been a continuous programme of modernisation, most recently new classrooms and an indoor swimming pool; the facilities in its fine buildings are excellent. A sophisticated school with high academic standards, it produces very good results. Nearly every student goes on to a degree courses each year. Religious teaching is based on the principles of the Church of England. There is much emphasis on music throughout the school and the drama and art departments are very strong and active. Regent's Park provides good facilities for sports and games, in which standards are also high. There is a good range of extra-curricular activities. Full use is made of the cultural amenities of the capital.

School profile

Pupils Age range 11–18; 370 day girls. Main entry ages 11 and into sixth. 5%–10% are children of former pupils. *State school entry:* 30% main intake, plus 7% to sixth.
Entrance Own entrance exam used. No special skills or religious requirements. Parents expected to buy text books. 10 pa assisted places (5 at age 11, 5 to sixth). 1 music and 2 pa sixth-form scholarships, £380–£2265.
Parents 15+% are doctors, lawyers etc; 15+% from theatre, media, music; 15+% from industry/commerce.
Head and staff *Headmistress:* Mrs Pamela Parsonson, in post for 8 years. Educated at Casterton and Oxford (mathematics). Previously Head of Mathematics and Director of Studies at North London Collegiate and Mathematics Teacher at Harrow County Girls and Christ's Hospital, Hertford. *Staff:* 27 full time, 19 part time.
Exam results In 1995, 55 pupils in upper fifth, 49 in upper sixth. *GCSE:* In 1995, 99% upper fifth gained at least grade C in 8+ subjects. *A-levels:* 9 upper sixth passed in 4+ subjects; 38 in 3; and 2 in 2 subjects. Average UCAS points 23.0.
University and college entrance All 1995 sixth-form leavers went on to a degree course (40% after a gap year). Of those recently going on to degree courses, 5–10% went to Oxbridge; 10% took courses in medicine, dentistry and veterinary science, 30% in science and engineering, 60% in humanities and social sciences.
Curriculum GCSE, AS and A-levels. 20 subjects offered (no A-level general studies). 16% take science A-levels; 39% arts/humanities; 45% both. *Vocational:* Work experience available; also City and Guilds course and RSA Stages 1 and 2 in computing. *Computing facilities:* Network of 15, mainly Apple Macs, plus 20 others in school. *Europe:* French (from 11), German and Italian (from 13) offered to GCSE and A-level; also French and German AS-level and Spanish GCSE in sixth-form. Regular exchanges to France.
The arts *Music:* Up to 50% of pupils learn a musical instrument; instrumental exams can be taken. Some 12 musical groups including orchestras, flute band, 3 choirs, chamber trios, quartets. *Drama & dance*: Drama offered. GCSE drama, LAMDA exams may be taken. Some pupils are involved in school productions and majority in form/other productions. *Art:* On average, 25 take GCSE, 10 A-level. Design, pottery, textiles, photography also offered.
Sport, community service and clubs *Sport and physical activities:* Compulsory sports: hockey, tennis, netball, rounders, swimming, volleyball. Optional: badminton, table tennis. Member of county netball team. *Community service:* Pupils take part in the Duke of Edinburgh's Award. Community service optional for 1 year at age 16; girls help in hospitals, schools and old people's homes. *Clubs and societies:* Up to 15 clubs, eg art, drama, debating, philosophy, sports, cookery, maths, photography.
Uniform School uniform worn except in the sixth.
Houses/prefects No competitive houses or prefects. Head girl, elected by the school and staff. School Council.
Religion Attendance at religious worship compulsory.

Social Occasional debates with other schools. Trips abroad by sixth-form historians (Paris); history of art group (Italy); school trip (eg Russia, Italy, Greece); skiing and activity holidays, French exchange and individual exchanges encouraged. Pupils allowed to bring own bike. Meals self-service. No tobacco/alcohol allowed.
Discipline Pupils failing to produce homework once would be spoken to; if consistently failing then parents would be contacted (a rare problem). Those caught smoking cannabis on the premises would be suspended, probably expelled.
Alumni association is run by Mrs Carol Michaelson, 66 Marlborough Place, St John's Wood, London NW8.

• FRANCIS HOLLAND (Sloane Square)

Francis Holland School, 39 Graham Terrace, London SW1W 8JF. Tel 0171 730 2971

• Pupils 350 • Boys None • Girls 4–18 (Day) • Upper sixth 18 • Termly fees £1460-£1980 • GSA • Enquiries/application to the Headmistress

What it's like

The Francis Holland (Church of England) Schools Trust was founded in 1878. This school opened in 1881 in Eaton Terrace and transferred in 1884 to its present site, near Sloane Square in central London. It has close links with its sister school in Regent's Park. The junior school shares the main site. It has handsome buildings which have been well adapted to modern needs. A strong local and family tradition prevails. Its position makes possible a wide use of London's amenities for outings of all kinds. The teaching and academic results are good. A high proportion of leavers go on to degree courses, including Oxbridge. There is a strong music department and drama is popular. Some sport and games take place on the school site, otherwise local sports centres and Battersea Park are used.

School profile

Pupils Total age range 4–18; 350 day girls. Senior department 11–18, 180 girls. Main entry ages 4, 5, 11 and into the sixth. Own junior school provides about 50% senior intake. *State school entry:* Minimal.
Entrance Own entrance exam used. No special skills; C of E school but all denominations accepted. Parents expected to buy textbooks. Bursaries available; 3 pa scholarships of one-twelfth fees; 2 pa sixth-form scholarships, half fees.
Parents Drawn from a wide range of professions: medicine, law, banking, the Church, the academic world, the theatre etc.
Head and staff *Headmistress:* Mrs Jennifer Anderson, in post for 15 years. Educated at St Paul's and at Cambridge (modern and medieval languages) and King's College London (French). Previously Assistant Mistress at Francis Holland (Regents Park) and also part time at Sloane Square, part time tutoring at Westminster Tutors (and other colleges), civil servant at Ministry of Education and Assistant Mistress at Malvern (Girls). Also active member of GSA. *Staff:* 32 full time, 13 part time.
Exam results In 1995, 27 pupils in upper fifth, 18 in upper sixth. *GCSE:* In 1995, 98% upper fifth gained at least grade C in 8+ subjects. *A-levels:* 14 upper sixth passed in 3 subjects; and 4 in 2 subjects. Average UCAS points 18.0.
University and college entrance 80% of 1995 sixth-form leavers went on to a degree course (66% after a gap year); others typically go on to art college, travel or retake A-levels. Of those going on to university, 15% went to Oxbridge; 5% took courses in science and engineering, 5% in law, 70% in humanities and social sciences, 10% in art and design, 10% in vocational subjects eg physiotherapy.
Curriculum GCSE and A-levels. 22 subjects offered, including history of art; AS-level general studies, not A-level. *Vocational:* Work experience available for 2 weeks following GCSE; RSA stage 1 course in IT. *Computing facilities:* Apple Macintoshes in special room and some elsewhere. *Special provision:* Time concessions requested for dyslexic girls in public exams. *Europe:* French, German and Spanish offered to GCSE and A-level; Italian as a non-examined subject. Pupils arrange personal exchanges and go on language courses.
The arts (Pupils aged 11 and over) *Music:* Over 50% of pupils learn a musical instrument; instrumental exams can be taken. Some 9 musical groups including

orchestra, choirs, wind, string groups etc. GCSE and A-level taken. *Drama & dance:*: Both offered. LAMDA and ballet exams may be taken. Majority of pupils are involved in school productions and all in house/other productions. *Art:* On average, 12 take GCSE, 4 A-level. Pottery, textiles, photography also offered.
Sport, community service and clubs (Pupils aged 11 and over) *Sport and physical activities:* Compulsory sports: netball, hockey, tennis, swimming, gymnastics. Sixth form only: squash, canoeing, riding, rowing, karate. BAGA exams may be taken. *Community service:* Pupils take bronze, silver and gold Duke of Edinburgh's Award. Community service optional (but most participate) for 3–5 years at age 14; visiting local old people widespread long-term commitment, including Harvest Festival and Christmas party. *Clubs and societies:* 5 clubs, pottery, photography, drama, debating, gymnastics.
Uniform School uniform worn except in sixth.
Houses/prefects Competitive houses. Head girl, head of house and house prefects – elected by school and staff. School Council.
Social Organised trips abroad including skiing and history of art to Italy, language visits to France and Spain. Meals self-service. No tobacco/alcohol allowed.
Discipline Conduct marks for minor offences, detention for more serious ones. Suspension or expulsion in extreme cases.

• FRENSHAM HEIGHTS

Frensham Heights School, Rowledge, Farnham, Surrey GU10 4EA. Tel 01252 792134, Fax 01252 794335

• Pupils 296 • Boys 11–18 (Day/Board/Weekly) • Girls 11–18 (Day/Board/Weekly) • Upper sixth 41 • Termly fees £2490 (Day) £3890 (Board/Weekly) • HMC, BSA

What it's like

Founded in 1925 as part of a progressive movement to promote co-education and less formal relationships between teachers and pupils. It has always been a genuinely co-educational school, and believes in the equality of the sexes. It has no religious affiliation but sees the pursuit of enlightenment and liberal values as a fundamental aim. It opposes all forms of bigotry, racial, religious or social, and every effort is made to deepen understanding of human nature and behaviour and develop self-esteem. The site comprises 100 acres of beautiful woodland and parkland. Boarding accommodation is comfortable. The school is spacious, well-equipped and deliberately small enough for everyone to be known as a person. The average class size is 16 and academic results are very good. All pupils must choose two GCSEs from the creative and performing arts, for which the school is both well-known and very strong (there is a new, well-equipped art and design centre). Wide range of clubs and societies. It has a sports hall, outdoor education centre and new sixth-form and IT centres.

School profile

Pupils Age range 11–18; 296 pupils, 167 day (89 boys, 78 girls), 129 boarding (58 boys, 71 girls). Main entry age 11, 12, 13 and into sixth. Significant intake from own junior school, St George's (and Little Dragons' Nursery). *State school entry:* 40% main intake, plus 15% to sixth.
Entrance Common Entrance and own exam used; sixth-form entry, 5 GCSE at grade C or above, plus interview and reference. Assisted places. Some scholarships available.
Head and staff *Headmaster:* Peter M de Voil, 4 years in post. Educated at Northampton Grammar School and at Cambridge (classics and English) and Oxford (education). Previously Housemaster at Uppingham. Also FRSA. *Staff:* 37 full time, 7 part time. Annual turnover 5%. Average age 41.
Exam results In 1995, 58 pupils in upper fifth, 41 in upper sixth. *GCSE:* In 1995, 59% gained grade C or above in 8+ subjects; 19% in 5–7 subjects. *A-levels:* 11% passed in 4 subjects; 86% in 3 subjects; and 1% in 2 subjects. Average UCAS points 21.0.
University and college entrance 98% of 1995 sixth-form leavers went on to a degree course (15% after a gap year); others typically go on to art foundation courses. Of those going on to university, 5% went to Oxbridge; 5% took courses in medicine, dentistry and veterinary science, 15% in science and engineering, 10% in law, 40% in humanities and social sciences, 15% in art and design, 5% in vocational subjects eg nursing, 10% other

subjects eg drama, media.

Curriculum GCSE and A-level. 19 GCSE subjects offered, 16 at A-level (no A-level general studies). Pupils whose native tongue is other than English are encouraged to take GCSE and A-level in their language. *Vocational:* Work experience available and Young Enterprise Scheme. *Computing facilities:* IT centre with Acorn computers. *Special provision:* For dyslexics, only if able to follow curriculum without remedial help. Also ESL. *Europe:* French and German offered to GCSE and A-level; also GCSE Spanish. *Other*: Annual visits to France. Special provision for pupils from Europe, including ESL lessons. 2 free places for Bosnian refugees.

The arts All pupils take two arts subjects to GCSE out of art, ceramics, drama, music, dance, design technology. *Music:* Over 50% of pupils learn a musical instrument; vocal and instrumental exams can be taken. Some 8 musical groups: 2 orchestras, 4 choirs, chamber group, brass ensemble. Several pupils play for county and national youth orchestras. Annual choir and orchestra tour to Europe. Links with National Youth Music Theatre. *Drama & dance*: Both offered at GCSE; A-level theatre studies may be taken. Majority of pupils are involved in school productions. *Art:* Photography also offered to GCSE.

Sport, community service and clubs *Sport and physical activities:* Compulsory sports: tennis, netball, swimming, soccer, basketball, athletics, cricket, hockey, rugby. Optional: volleyball, rounders, cross-country running, badminton, softball, outdoor education and adventure challenge programme. *Community service:* Many pupils take bronze, silver and gold Duke of Edinburgh's Award. Community service optional; recycling programme in conjunction with local council. *Clubs and societies:* Over 30 activities eg karate, batik, ceramics, photography, canoeing, riding, weight training, Amnesty International.

Uniform No school uniform.

Houses/prefects Competitive sports houses. Counsellors (prefects), sixth-form committee. School council.

Religion Non-denominational.

Social Joint sports meetings with other schools. Ski and snow-boarding trips annually; choir tours abroad; foreign visits. Pupils allowed to bring own bike to school in spring and summer; cars in special cases. Meals self-service; special diets catered for. No tobacco/alcohol allowed below the sixth-form.

Discipline Pupils failing to produce homework once might expect to do it during their lunch break or after school; those caught smoking cannabis on the premises might expect immediate expulsion.

Former pupils Sir Claus Moser (Warden, Wadham College, Oxford); Tom Legg QC (Lord Chancellor's office); Nick Mason (drummer, Pink Floyd); Jon Pertwee (actor); Richard Hough (author); Larry Adler (harmonica player).

• FRIENDS' (Lisburn)

The Friends' School, 6 Magheralave Road, Lisburn, Antrim, Northern Ireland, BT28 3BH. Tel 01846 662156, Fax 01846 672134.

• Pupils 1133 • Boys 4–19 (Day/Board/Weekly) • Girls 4–19 (Day/Board/Weekly) • Upper sixth 108 • Termly fees Nil (Day) £1085 (Board) £1043 (Weekly) • Enquiries/application to the Headmaster.

What it's like

A Quaker school, founded in 1774, its site is on Prospect Hill near the centre of the town. The grounds are spacious and provide ample playing areas. Since 1960 there has been extensive development and modernisation, including a sixth-form centre, library, art and technology building and lecture theatre. Excellent boarding accommodation and good up-to-date facilities of all kinds. It was founded as a co-educational school. Pupils are taken from a wide range of religious backgrounds and a general form of Christian worship is practised. Academic attainments are high and results are good. Very strong musically. A good range of games and sports. A remarkable record in the Duke of Edinburgh's Award Scheme.

School profile

Pupils Total age range 4–19; 1133 pupils, 1083 day (520 boys, 563 girls), 50 boarding (26 boys, 24 girls). Senior department 11–19, 951 pupils (454 boys, 497 girls). Main entry ages 4, 11 and into sixth. Approx 28% are children of former pupils. *State school entry:* 88% main senior intake, plus 15% to sixth.

Entrance Good academic ability required; no religious requirements. Tuition fees paid by Education Department for all pupils admitted who are resident in Northern Ireland.

Parents 60+% live within 30 miles; up to 3% live overseas.

Head and staff *Headmaster:* Trevor Green, 7 years in post. Educated at Friends' (Lisburn), and at Trinity College Dublin, Queen's Belfast and Ulster universities (modern history and political science). Previously Head of History at Woodford, Headmaster at Friends' School, Cumbria, Head of History at Sullivan Upper (Co Down) and Assistant History Master at Mountjoy (Dublin). *Staff:* 64 full time, 5 part time. Annual turnover 3%–4%. Average age 40.

Exam results In 1995, 138 pupils in fifth, 108 in upper sixth. *GCSE:* In 1995, 109 fifth gained at least grade C in 8+ subjects; 22 in 5–7; and 6 in 1–4 subjects. *A-levels:* 4 upper sixth passed in 4+ subjects; 73 in 3; 24 in 2; and 4 in 1 subject.

University and college entrance 85% of 1995 sixth-form leavers went on to a degree course (2% after a gap year); others typically go on to teacher training, nursing or other employment. Of those going on to university, 2% went to Oxbridge; 7% took courses in medicine, dentistry and veterinary science, 30% in science and engineering, 3% in law, 43% in humanities and social sciences, 2% in art and design, 15% in vocational subjects eg business and accounting.

Curriculum GCSE, AS and A-levels. 19 GCSE subjects offered; 2 at AS; 17 at A-level (no A-level general studies). 19% take science A-levels; 37% arts/humanities; 44% both. *Vocational:* Work experience available; also City and Guilds basic course in IT. *Computing facilities:* 2 Nimbus networks, 25 stations; 20 other computers in departments. IT courses forms 1–4 and lower sixth. *Special provision:* Extra tuition is available (but not included in fees). *Europe:* French, German and Spanish offered at GCSE and A-level. Regular exchanges (France and Germany).

The arts (Pupils aged 11 and over). *Music:* 20% of pupils learn a musical instrument; instrumental exams can be taken. Some 4 musical groups including chamber orchestra, concert group, Friends' Singers. *Drama & dance*: Both offered. Some pupils are involved in school productions. *Art:* On average 30 take GCSE, 12 A-level.

Sport, community service and clubs (Pupils aged 11 and over) *Sport and physical activities:* Compulsory sports: hockey, rugby, netball, athletics, swimming cricket, tennis. Optional: soccer, watersports, skiing, badminton, squash, dance. Hockey, 2 Irish representatives, 3 Ulster; cricket, 1 Ulster; athletics, 2 Irish and Ulster; skiing, 2 Ulster schools representatives; badminton, 1 Irish and 1 Ulster representative. *Community service:* Pupils take bronze, silver and gold Duke of Edinburgh's Award. Community service optional at age 17+. School bank run by fifth and sixth-form. *Clubs and societies:* Up to 15 clubs, eg debating, literary, politics, chess, photography, Scripture Union, and drama.

Uniform School uniform worn throughout.

Houses/prefects Competitive houses. Prefects (non-selective), head boy/girl and deputies (appointed) and heads of house (elected). School forum.

Religion General Christian worship with Bible teaching, prayer and praise.

Social Joint visit to Corrymeela Reconcilation Centre with local grammar school. Frequent ski trips and cultural visits to Europe. Pupils allowed to bring own bike to school. Lunch self-service; meals for boarders cafeteria system. School shop. No tobacco/alcohol allowed.

Discipline Pupils failing to produce homework etc placed in detention; suspension and expulsion reserved for very serious offences.

Boarding 10% share a study bedroom with 1 other. 2 single-sex boarding wings. Resident qualified nurse, doctor on call. Central dining room. Pupils can provide and cook own food at weekends. Saturday and Sunday afternoon exeats. Visits to local town allowed.

Alumni association is run by Mrs F Macleod, Friends' School OS Association, c/o the school.

• FRIENDS' (Saffron Walden)

Friends' School, Mount Pleasant Road, Saffron Walden, Essex CB11 3EB. Tel 01799 525351, Fax 01799 523808

• Pupils 272 • Boys 3-18 (Day/Board/Weekly) • Girls 3-18 (Day/Board/Weekly) • Upper sixth 20 • Termly fees £1175–£2123 (Day) £2654–£3538 (Board/Weekly) • SHMIS • Enquiries/application to the Head

What it's like

Founded in 1702, it is single-site and on the edge of the countryside. It has handsome well-equipped buildings in delightful grounds; facilities are very good. Saffron Walden itself is a most attractive country town in a beautiful part of Essex. Christian worship in the Quaker tradition is compulsory. A good all-round education is provided and results are good. A large proportion of sixth-form leavers go on to degree courses. Strong in art and drama. Hockey strong (many county representatives). A good range of games, sports and activities.

School profile

Pupils Total age range 3–18; 272 pupils, 177 day (91 boys, 86 girls), 95 boarding (39 boys, 56 girls). Senior department 11–18. Main entry age 5, 7, 11, also 12, 13, 14 and into sixth. Approx 2% are children of former pupils. *State school entry:* 40% main senior intake, plus 5% to sixth.

Entrance Own entrance exam used. No special skills or religious requirements. Parents not expected to buy textbooks; extras voluntary, £50 average. 15 pa assisted places. Sixth-form awards and Quaker bursaries, means tested.

Parents 50% live within 30 miles; up to 10% live overseas.

Head and staff *Head:* Jane Laing, appointed in 1996. Educated at St Helen's, Northwood, and at the universities of Reading (philosophy) and London (social studies). Previously Head of St Martin's Lower School, Brentwood. *Staff:* 28 full time, 6 part time. Annual turnover 10%. Average age 40.

Exam results On average, 45 pupils in upper fifth, 20 in upper sixth. *GCSE:* On average, 10 upper fifth gain at least grade C in 8+ subjects; 30 in 5–7; 5 in 1–4 subjects. *A-levels:* On average, 12% upper sixth pass in 4 subjects; 48% in 3; 32% in 2 and 8% in 1 subject. Average UCAS points 15.1.

University and college entrance 95% of 1995 sixth-form leavers went on to a degree course; others typically go straight on to careers. Of those going on to university, 15% took courses in medicine, dentistry and veterinary science, 25% in science and engineering, 35% in humanities and social sciences, 15% in art and design, 10% in drama and music.

Curriculum GCSE, AS and A-levels, 15 subjects offered (including A-level general studies). 40% take science A-levels; 40% arts/humanities; 20% both. *Vocational:* Work experience compulsory. *Computing facilities:* Adequate. *Special provision:* Dyslexic unit and EFL support. *Europe:* French and German offered to GCSE, AS and A-level. Regular exchanges (Germany and France).

The arts (Pupils aged 11 and over) *Music:* Over 50% of pupils learn a musical instrument; instrumental exams can be taken. Musical groups including choir, instrumental group, orchestra, pop groups. Members of county youth orchestras. *Drama & dance*: Drama offered. A-level theatre studies, LAMDA exams may be taken. Many pupils are involved in school productions. Musical by head of music and head of drama selected for second round of Lloyds Bank Theatre Challenge. *Art:* On average, 25 take GCSE, 2 AS-level, 8 A-level. Pottery, textiles, photography also offered. School art gallery displays works by pupils and professional artists.

Sport, community service and clubs (Pupils aged 11 and over) *Sport and physical activities:* Compulsory sports: cricket, athletics, swimming, football, hockey, cross-country, tennis. Optional: basketball, rugby, badminton, volleyball. County hockey players at all ages. *Community service:* optional for all ages; Community Action Group tackling matters of concern; sixth-form organises collection of unwanted furniture and distribution to those in need. *Clubs and societies:* Up to 15 clubs, eg photography, beekeeping, hiking, judo, portrait, drama, Scouts.

Uniform School uniform worn except in the sixth.

Houses/prefects Competitive houses. No prefects. Head boy/girl – elected by the

school and staff. School Council.
Religion Religious worship compulsory.
Social Organised local events and trips abroad. Pupils allowed to bring own bike to school. Meals self-service. No tobacco/alcohol allowed.
Discipline Pupils failing to produce homework once might expect detention. Detentions, gating, work around the school all used. Attempts made to ensure the punishment fits the crime. Suspension and expulsion for serious offences.
Boarding Accommodation divided by age; sixth-form in separate co-educational house. Qualified nurse (non-resident). Central dining room. Exeats, any weekend. Visits to local town allowed daily.
Former pupils Tom Robinson; Ralph Erskine; Eric Beale; Deborah Norton; Matthew Evans.

• FULNECK

Fulneck School, Pudsey, West Yorkshire LS28 8DS. Tel 0113 257 0235, Fax 0113 255 7316
• Pupils 510 • Boys 3–18 (Day/Board/Weekly) • Girls 3–18 (Day/Board/Weekly) • Upper sixth 38 • Termly fees £580–£1540 (Day) £2440–£2885 (Board) £2270–£2570 (Weekly) • SHMIS, GSA
• Enquiries/application to the Admissions Secretary

What it's like

Established in 1994 by the amalgamation of Fulneck Boys' School and Fulneck Girls' School. Both were originally founded in 1753 by the Moravian Church (Unitas Fratrum) to educate and care for the sons and daughters of the Church's ministers and missionaries. Essentially a Christian establishment, religious education is quite an important part of the curriculum although children of all faiths are welcome. It aims to provide a broad education both through the formal curriculum and a wide range of extra-curricular activities which will prepare a pupil to lead a fulfilling life. The Grade I listed buildings stand in a semi-rural site on the side of a valley in the green belt between Leeds and Bradford. It has modern facilities with extensive grounds and playing fields. A sound traditional education is given and many sixth-formers go to degree courses. Boys and girls are taught separately between the ages of 11 and 16, but have joint classes in the sixth-form. The boarding department has separate boys' and girls' houses, but most meals are shared and facilities and social activities are available to both.

School profile

Pupils Total age range 3–18; 510 pupils, 460 day, 50 boarding. Senior school 11–18. Main entry at 3, 5, 7, 11 and 13. Own junior school provides the majority of senior intake. *State school entry:* approximately 20%.
Entrance Own entrance exam used. No special skills or religious requirements. Parents not expected to buy textbooks. 13 pa scholarships (4 at age 7, 4 at 11, 5 at 16), value £300–25% day fees.
Parents 15% in industry/commerce. Most live within 30 miles; up to 7% overseas.
Head and staff *Principal:* Mrs Honorée Gordon, appointed in 1996. Educated at James Gillespie's High School, Edinburgh, and the universities of Bradford and Leeds (Russian and French). Previously Deputy Head at Crossley Heath Grammar School, Halifax, and Head of Languages at Pudsey Grangefield School. *Staff:* 41 full time, 11 part time. Annual turnover, 4%. Average age, 43.
Exam results In 1995, 76 in Year 11, 44 in upper sixth. *GCSE:* In 1995, 43 Year 11 gained at least grade C in 8+ subjects; 20 in 5–7 subjects. *A-levels:* 17 upper sixth passed in 4+ subjects; 6 in 3; 10 in 2; and 10 in 1 subject. Average UCAS points 11.0.
University and college entrance 65% of 1995 sixth-form leavers went on to a degree course (5% after a gap year); others typically go on to HND or art foundation courses and (5%) direct to employment. Of those going on to university, 20% took courses in science and engineering, 3% in law, 15% in humanities and social sciences, 12% in art and design, 50% in vocational subjects eg management, occupational therapy, nursing, education.
Curriculum GCSE and A-levels offered. 17 examination subjects offered (including A-level general studies). 40% take science A-levels; 40% arts/humanities; 20% both. *Vocational:* Work experience available. *Computing facilities:* Specialised IT room.

Special provision: Small classes. Language support unit, staffed by 2 specialists in EFL and dyslexia. *Europe:* French and German offered at GCSE and A-level; also GCSE Spanish in sixth-form. French compulsory from 10, German from 11. Regular exchanges to Germany. Regular study tours to France; boarding bursaries for 2 Czech students for a term.

The arts *Music:* Over 50% of pupils learn a musical instrument; instrumental exams can be taken. Musical groups include choirs, wind bands, recorder, flute choir and orchestral group. Choir invited annually to sing choral evensong in York Minster. *Drama & dance:* Drama offered; theatre workshop with at least two productions annually. GCSE drama may be taken and Poetry Society exams. Some pupils are involved in school productions and majority in house/other productions. Successes in Wharfedale Festival 1995; regional silver medal finalists and finalist in national Thomas Cranmer Awards in speech and drama. *Art:* On average 15 take GCSE, 3 A-level. Design, photography also offered.

Sport, community service and clubs *Sport and physical activities:* Compulsory sports: athletics, cricket, hockey, netball, rounders, rugby, tennis. Optional: aerobics, badminton, canoeing, cross-country, golf, sailing, squash, soccer, swimming, table tennis, volleyball. Pupils may take CFS sports studies. Netball, U13 and U16 teams Leeds City Champions 1994/5, 7 members of Leeds City teams; athletics, 5 in Leeds City teams, 2 West Yorkshire champions; rugby, 5 pupils played for Leeds Schools teams; cricket, 2 play for Yorkshire schools; table tennis, 1 pupil England ranking. *Community service:* Community service optional for two years at age 16. Pupils take bronze, silver and gold Duke of Edinburgh's Award. *Clubs and societies:* Clubs include aeromodelling, art, chess, computer, design and technology, drama, netball, hockey, model railway, Scrabble, summer sports, table tennis, video film making and young ornithologist, school newspaper (produced by in-house team).

Uniform School uniform worn except in the sixth.

Houses/prefects Competitive houses. Prefects, head girl, head boy, house captains elected by staff and sixth-form.

Religion Religious worship compulsory.

Social Trips abroad eg France, Germany, Eastern Europe. Pupils allowed to bring own car/bike/motorbike to school. Meals self-service. No alcohol/tobacco allowed.

Discipline Pupils failing to produce homework might expect a lunchtime detention. Should it ever occur, a pupil smoking cannabis on the premises would expect immediate suspension and consultation with the Chairman of Governors; permanent exclusion would occur.

Boarding Under 10% have own study bedrooms; 65% share with 1–3; 25% in dormitories of 6+. Qualified resident matrons. Pupils allowed to provide and cook own food (toaster, cooker and microwave available). Some weekend exeats. Visits to local town allowed at weekends; unsupervised for older pupils; supervised for others.

Alumni association OGA run by Mrs E Dawson; OBA Secretary, Mr L Fairclough; both c/o the school.

Former pupils Diana Rigg; Sir Frank Cooper (former Permanent secretary, MOD).

G

• GEORGE HERIOT'S

George Heriot's School, Lauriston Place, Edinburgh EH3 9EQ. Tel 0131 229 7263, Fax 0131 229 6363

• Pupils 1492 • Boys 5–18 (Day) • Girls 5–18 (Day) • Higher year 170 • Termly fees £715-£1250 • HMC • Enquiries/application to the Headmaster

What it's like

Founded in 1628 by George Heriot, an Edinburgh jeweller and banker and goldsmith to James VI and I, for the fatherless sons of burgesses. It has very elegant buildings and fine grounds in the centre of Edinburgh. The original building has been preserved and comprises the chapel, council room, common room, classrooms and school offices. In the last 100 years a succession of developments has produced excellent facilities; recent additions include junior and nursery school buildings and a new library and music suite. Non-denominational, Heriot's is deeply rooted in the Scottish tradition and its pupils come from far afield and from a wide variety of social backgrounds. The playing fields are at Goldenacre. It consistently produces very good results and the majority of pupils go on to degree courses each year, including Oxbridge. Music and drama flourish. Virtually all sports and games are available and high standards are achieved (regular representatives at regional and national level). There is a CCF contingent, plus a Scout troop and Guides. Some 50 clubs and societies cater for an unusually wide range of extra-curricular activities. There is much emphasis on outdoor pursuits and a fine record in the Duke of Edinburgh's Award.

School profile

Pupils Total age range 5–18; 1492 day pupils (860 boys, 632 girls). Senior department 12–18, 986 pupils (580 boys, 406 girls). Main entry ages 5, 10, 12 and into sixth. Approx 15% are children of former pupils. *State school entry:* 95% main senior intake, plus 5% to sixth.

Entrance Own entrance exam used. No special skills or religious requirements. Parents expected to buy senior school text books. 37 pa assisted places. 4 pa scholarships and 10 pa foundationers.

Parents 15+% in education; 15+% are doctors, lawyers etc; 15+% in industry or commerce.

Head and staff *Headmaster:* Keith Pearson, in post for 13 years. Educated at Preston Grammar School, and universities of Cambridge and Madrid (French and Spanish). Previously Deputy Principal and Head of Languages at George Watson's and Head of Languages at Rossall. Fellow of the Royal Society of Edinburgh; Council Member, Headteachers' Association of Scotland and Scottish Council for Independent Schools; Secretary of HMC Scottish Division; former member, Scottish Central Committee on Modern Languages and Scottish Central Council on the Curriculum. *Staff:* 96 full time, 8 part time. Annual turnover 4%. Average age 40.

Exam results On average, 170 pupils in S-grade year; 170 in Higher; 130 in CSYS year. *Highers:* On average, 104 pupils pass in 5+ subjects; 20 in 4; 12 in 3; 16 in 2; and 10 in 1 subject.

University and college entrance 86% of 1995 sixth-form leavers went on to a degree course; others typically go on to non-degree courses or art/drama colleges. Of those going on to university, 4% went to Oxbridge; 4% took courses in medicine, dentistry and veterinary science, 39% in science and engineering, 55% in humanities and social sciences, 1% in art and design, 1% in drama and music.

Curriculum S-grade, Highers and CSYS. Approx 25 subjects offered. 60% take science/engineering Highers; 30% take arts and humanities; 10% both. *Vocational:* Work experience available; also Scotvec modules. *Computing facilities:* 30 Apple Macs with an Image writer and laser printer in computing department; 25 Apple Macs with Inkjet printer in business studies; facilities in most departments; BBC micros in all junior rooms.

Special provision: for dyslexia. *Europe:* French, German and Spanish offered at S-grade, Higher and CSYS; also S-grade Italian. Regular exchanges (France and Germany). School attracts families of foreign diplomats, encourages exchanges etc. Strong International Club invites speakers, including MEP. Orchestra tours abroad. Pupils encouraged to undertake work experience abroad.

The arts (Pupils aged 11 and over) *Music:* Over 20% of pupils learn a musical instrument; instrumental exams can be taken. Some 12+ musical groups including orchestras, concert band, junior band, swing band, saxophone group, several choirs. Music exchange with Munich. *Drama & dance*: Drama offered. Some pupils are involved in school/house productions. Hamlet performed on Edinburgh Festival Fringe. *Art:* Design, pottery, textiles, photography also offered. Scottish Independent Schools Art Exhibition, pupil highly commended.

Sport, community service and clubs (Pupils aged 11 and over) *Sport and physical activities:* Compulsory sports: rugby, cricket (boys); hockey (girls); athletics. Optional cross-country, badminton, curling, swimming, table tennis, tennis, squash, fencing, rowing. Regular representation at national and regional level in a variety of sports. *Community service:* Pupils take bronze, silver and gold Duke of Edinburgh's Award. CCF and community service optional. Several pupils have participated in Operation Raleigh and BSES expeditions. *Clubs and societies:* Over 50 clubs, eg Christian Union, fencing, mountain biking, debating (representation in World Schools Debating).

Uniform School uniform worn throughout.

Houses/prefects Competitive houses. Prefects, head boy and girl and house captains – elected by upper school.

Religion Compulsory morning assembly with broad Christian element.

Social Music, inter-school and ESU debating with other schools; own school theatrical production. Many organised trips abroad including to Canada, Greece, Majorca, Zimbabwe; music and sporting trips abroad; art tour to Paris and school French exchange. Pupils allowed to bring own bike to school. Meals self-service; tuck shop. No tobacco/alcohol allowed.

Discipline Pupils failing to produce homework once might expect a written exercise or detention.

Former pupils Lord Mackay (Lord Chancellor); several ex-Lord Provosts of Edinburgh; former Chief Constable of Lothian and Borders Police; Robert Urquhart and Paul Young (actors); Sir William Ryrie (World Bank); Professor Norman Dott; many well-known sporting figures including Kenneth Scotland, Andrew Irvine, Iain and Kenneth Milne and George Goddard.

• GEORGE WATSON'S

George Watson's College, Colinton Road, Edinburgh EH10 5EG. Tel 0131 447 7931, Fax 0131 452 8594

• Pupils 2100 • Boys 3–18 (Day/Board) • Girls 3–18 (Day/Board) • Higher year 212 • Termly fees £1380 (Day) £2760 (Board) • HMC • Enquiries/application to the Principal

What it's like

Founded in 1741, it moved to its present site in 1932. The George Watson's Ladies' College and the Boys' College were amalgamated in 1974. The site is on the outskirts of the city and playing fields on the campus. The impressive buildings are very well equipped with modern facilities. It is a school with a distinguished record of achievement where excellent teaching is provided and academic standards are high. Most of the pupils are local. Its declared objectives are to enable pupils to live their lives to the full, to understand the world they live in, to be active in serving other people and to commit themselves to causes with open-eyed and critical awareness. It caters for individualists. Most pupils go on to degree courses, 70% to Scottish universities, others to English universities including Oxbridge. Immensely strong music, drama, art and technology depts involving a very large number of pupils. A wide variety of sports and games are available (including curling) and high standards are achieved. (A very large number of county and international representatives.) About 50 clubs and societies cater for most extra-curricular activities. There is a big commitment to local community schemes and an active Scout group. Considerable emphasis on outdoor pursuits and much use is made of the fine outdoor centre at Glen Isla. The college's record in the Duke of Edinburgh's Award is outstanding.

School profile

Pupils Total age range 3–18; 2100 pupils, 2070 day (1140 boys, 930 girls), 30 boarding. Senior department 12–18, 1260 pupils (690 boys, 570 girls). Main entry ages 3, 5, 10, 11, 12 and into sixth.

Entrance Own entrance exam used. No special skills or religious requirements. Parents expected to buy textbooks. 35 pa assisted places. 11 pa scholarships/bursaries, 25%–50% of day fees.

Parents 25+% are doctors, lawyers, etc, 15+% in industry or commerce. 85+% live within 30 miles; up to 5% live overseas.

Head and staff *Principal:* Frank Gerstenberg, in post for 11 years. Educated at Glenalmond, and universities of Cambridge (history) and London (education). Previously Headmaster at Oswestry, Housemaster and Head of History at Millfield and Assistant History Teacher at Kelly College. Also Member of Scottish Consultative Council on the Curricululm; Education Committee member of Scottish Conservative and Unionist Association. *Staff:* 128 full time, 12 part time. Annual turnover 4%. Average age 44.

Exam results On average, 212 in S-grade year, 212 in Higher, 200 in CSYS year. *Highers:* On average, 96 pass in 5+ subjects; 43 in 4; 61 in 3; 66 in 2; and 69 in 1 subject. *CSYS*: 14 pass in 4+ subjects; 17 in 3; 34 in 2; and 43 in 1 subject.

University and college entrance 83% of 1995 sixth-form leavers went on to a degree course (70% to Scottish universities); others typically go on to non-degree courses (eg secretarial), into careers (eg printing, hotels) or to art/drama colleges. Of those going on to university, 4% went to Oxbridge; 6% took courses in medicine, dentistry and veterinary science, 32% in science and engineering, 59% in humanities and social sciences, 2% in art and design, 1% in drama and acting.

Curriculum S-grade, Highers and CSYS. Most highers are taken in the fifth year; however some are taken in sixth year in addition to, or instead of, CSYS. 43% take science CSYS, 37% arts/humanities; 20% both. *Vocational:* Work experience available; also Scotvec modules. *Computing facilities:* 3 computer labs and numerous computers in departments. *Special provision:* Highly specialised learning support department for dyslexic pupils; EFL teaching. *Europe:* French, German and Spanish offered to S-grade, Higher and CSYS; Italian and Russian to S-grade and Higher; Portuguese to Higher and CSYS. Regular exchanges (France, Germany, Italy and Spain). Attendance at Youth Parliament in Strasbourg.

The arts (Pupils aged 11 and over) *Music:* Over 30% of pupils learn a musical instrument; instrumental exams can be taken. Some 10+ musical groups including 4 orchestras, choirs, jazz band, string quartets. *Drama & dance*: Both offered. S-grade drama may be taken. Some pupils are involved in school productions and majority in house/other productions. Some pupils accepted for drama school. *Art:* On average, 50 pupils take S-grade and 20 Higher. Pupils occasionally accepted for art college.

Sport, community service and clubs (Pupils aged 11 and over) *Sport and physical activities:* Compulsory sports: Angling, athletics, badminton, basketball, cricket, cross-country, curling, fencing, golf, gymnastics, hockey, orienteering, rowing, rugby, sailing, skiing, squash, table tennis, tennis and volleyball. S-grade exams may be taken. Regional and national representatives at a variety of sports. *Community service:* Pupils take bronze, silver and gold Duke of Edinburgh's Award. Community service optional. Scout and guide groups. *Clubs and societies:* Over 30 clubs.

Uniform School uniform worn throughout.

Houses/prefects Competitive houses. Prefects, head boy and girl, head of house and house prefects – elected by pupils, confirmed by Head. School Council.

Religion Morning assembly compulsory.

Social Some co-operation with other Merchant Company schools (Daniel Stewart's, Mary Erskine). Exchanges with France, Germany, Spain, Italy, United States, Russia and many other organised trips abroad. Day pupils allowed to bring own car/bike/motorbike to school. Meals self-service. School shop sells second-hand clothing. No tobacco/alcohol allowed.

Discipline Pupils failing to produce homework once expected to do it within 24 hours.

Parents of those caught smoking cannabis or taking other drugs on the premises would be asked to withdraw the pupil; if parents refused, pupil would be expelled.
Boarding Half share with 1 or 2 others; others in dormitories of 6+. Resident qualified nurse. Central dining room. Pupils can provide and cook some own food. Exeats any weekend. Visits to local town allowed.
Alumni association run by Alastair Davie, Myreside Pavilion, Myreside Road, Edinburgh.
Former pupils Malcolm Rifkind MP; Sir David Steele MP; Gavin Hastings (rugby); Scott Hastings (rugby); Alison Kinnaird (clarsach); David Johnstone (rugby); Eric Anderson (Master of Lincoln College, Oxford); Martin Bell (ski); Magda Sweetland (novelist); Sir Ian MacGregor.

• GIGGLESWICK

Giggleswick School, Giggleswick, Settle, North Yorkshire BD24 0DE. Tel 01729 823545, Fax 01729 824187

• Pupils 318 • Boys 13–18 (Day/Board) • Girls 13–18 (Day/Board) • Upper sixth 58 • Termly fees £2552 (Day) £3848 (Board) • HMC • Enquiries/application to the Headmaster

What it's like

Founded in 1512, it moved to its present site on the edge of the village in 1869 where it is in a beautiful position overlooking the Ribble Valley in the Yorkshire Dales and within convenient distance of Manchester, Leeds, Bradford and the Lakes. It has handsome buildings and the boys' accommodation has been completely refurbished. A recent development programme includes new boarding accommodation for girls, a sixth-form centre and a design centre. The preparatory school, Catteral Hall, is on an adjacent site and continuous education is available from 3–18. Originally a boys' school, it first accepted girls in 1977 and became fully co-educational in 1983. The school prides itself on its happy atmosphere and offers an excellent all-round education. Academic results are good and most sixth-form leavers go on to degree courses. Much importance is attached to personal courtesy and the school aims to develop the whole person whilst having proper regard for the importance of helping all pupils to achieve their best personal academic potential. There is a strong careers service and a flourishing industrial links scheme. Drama and art are strong departments and there is a considerable strength in a variety of sports and games, with fixtures against most other major northern independent schools. An extensive range of outdoor pursuits includes fell-walking, orienteering, rock-climbing, canoeing, mountaineering and potholing and a good deal of success in the Duke of Edinburgh's Award Scheme.

School profile

Pupils Age range 13–18; 318 pupils, 62 day (26 boys, 36 girls), 256 boarding (174 boys, 82 girls). Main entry ages 13 and into sixth. Approx 10% are children of former pupils. *State school entry:* 12% main intake, plus 10% to sixth.
Entrance Common Entrance, interviews and other methods used. Anglican foundation but other faiths and convictions welcomed. Fees include textbooks, stationery, art, CDT and home economics materials, compulsory GCSE visits etc. Assisted places. Scholarships/exhibitions available (academic, music, sport, drama, design, general distinction and continuation), up to full fees; also means-tested forces bursaries.
Parents 15+% in industry or commerce. Most from Lancashire, Yorkshire and Cumbria; up to 18% live overseas.
Head and staff *Headmaster:* Anthony Millard, 4 years in post. Educated at Solihull School, at the LSE (economics) and Oxford University (education). Previously Headmaster at Wycliffe, Deputy Headmaster and Housemaster at Wells Cathedral School and teacher at Zambian Institute of Technology and Kulushi Secondary School. Also experience in industry and European Commission; FRSA; Governor St John's School, Porthcawl. *Staff:* 36 full time, 6 part time. Annual turnover 5%. Average age 40.
Exam results On average, 59 pupils in upper fifth, 58 in upper sixth. *GCSE:* On average, 46% upper fifth gain at least grade C in 8+ subjects; 44% in 5–7; and 10% in 1–4 subjects. *A-levels:* 47% upper sixth pass in 4+ subjects; 21% in 3; 21% in 2; 6% in 1 subject. Average UCAS points 18.1 (including general studies 25.0).

University and college entrance 90% of 1995 sixth-form leavers went on to a degree course (14% after a gap year); others typically go in to parents' business. Of those going on to university, 8% went to Oxbridge; 3% took courses in medicine, dentistry and veterinary science, 30% in science and engineering, 23% in law-based course, 22% in humanities and social sciences, 12% in art and design, 10% in vocational subjects eg management.

Curriculum GCSE and A-levels. 21 subjects offered, including A-level general studies. 17% take science A-levels; 46% arts/humanities; 37% both. *Vocational:* Work experience available; also RSA qualifications in IT and drama. *Computing facilities:* Computing department with 20 computers; other departments have their own computers. *Special provision:* Some special coaching for dyslexics. *Europe:* French and German offered at GCSE, AS and A-level; also Spanish in sixth-form. Regular exchanges (Bordeaux, Frankfurt and Oslo). European pupils spend some time in the school.

The arts *Music:* 33% of pupils learn a musical instrument; instrumental exams can be taken. *Drama & dance:* Drama and dance offered. A-level theatre studies may be taken. Some pupils are involved in school productions and all in house/other productions. Pupils run Young Friends of Shakespeare's Globe, performed Hamlet at Elsinore, A Midsummer Night's Dream, and The Boyfriend in Australia. *Art:* On average, 20 take GCSE, 12 A-level. Design, pottery, textiles, photography also offered. 1 pupil accepted direct to Ruskin College.

Sport, community service and clubs *Sport and physical activities:* Compulsory sports: hockey, netball, rugby, athletics, rounders, tennis, cricket. Optional: soccer, golf, badminton, basketball, fencing, shooting, squash, volleyball, fives, swimming. A-level PE offered. County representation in rugby, athletics, hockey; international representation in canoeing. *Community service:* Pupils take bronze, silver and gold Duke of Edinburgh's Award. CCF compulsory for 2 years at age 14 (Army and RAF sections). Community service optional. *Clubs and societies:* Up to 30 clubs, eg mountain rescue unit, debating society.

Uniform School uniform worn except in the sixth.

Houses/prefects Pastoral/competitive houses. Prefects (praepostors) and head of school appointed by Head; head of house and house prefects, appointed by senior house staff.

Religion House prayers, morning services and chapel services on Sunday are compulsory.

Social Rugby, hockey, music, drama and ski trips abroad; foreign language visits to stay with families; rugby trip to eg Canada, concert band trip to Austria. Sixth-form centre has facilities for debates, balls, discos, reading rooms and a bar where strictly limited amounts of beer and wine are served with parents' permission and under staff supervision; no tobacco allowed.

Discipline Pupils failing to produce prep once might expect extra work; anyone found in possession of drugs would be expelled.

Boarding 50% have own study bedroom, others in doubles or small study dormitories of 3 or 4. Single-sex houses of 50–60. Resident SRN matron with a qualified assistant; doctor visits 4–5 times a week. Central dining room. Pupils can provide and cook own snacks. 2 weekend exeats each term and half-term. Visits to local market town of Settle allowed at set times.

Alumni association is run by Secretary OG Club, c/o the school.

Former pupils Judges Christopher Oddie and Roger Hunt; Sir Douglas Glover; Sir Anthony Wilson; Richard Whiteley; Keith Duckworth.

• GLASGOW ACADEMY

The Glasgow Academy, Colebrooke Street, Glasgow G12 8HE. Tel 0141 334 8558, Fax 0141 337 3473

• Pupils 1025 • Boys 4–18 (Day) • Girls 4–18 (Day) • Higher year 100 • Termly fees £1430
• HMC • Enquiries/application to the Rector

What it's like

Founded in 1846, it is the oldest independent school in the West of Scotland. It is single-site (with its own nursery/kindergarten/junior departments) in the west end of the city. In

1991 it amalgamated with the Westbourne School for Girls (founded in 1877). It enjoys a compact campus with handsome buildings in the classical Victorian manner. The excellent modern facilities include IT labs, a fine new library and a new music school opened in 1995. The Academy has a high reputation academically and produces consistently very good results; some 90% of leavers go on to degree courses. Music, drama and art are all strongly supported. There is a range of sports and games in which high standards are attained. (The Scottish Rugby Union was founded in The Academy Common Room.) First-rate games and sports facilities are at Anniesland in the western end of the city. There is a very active CCF with army, navy and airforce sections and a pipe band. Considerable emphasis on outdoor activities; notably sailing, climbing, canoeing and orienteering. A good range of clubs and societies, and strong participation in the Duke of Edinburgh's Award Scheme.

School profile

Pupils Total age range 4–18; 1025 day pupils, 699 boys, 326 girls. Senior department 11–18, 585 pupils, 418 boys, 167 girls. Main entry ages 4, 8, 11 and into sixth. Approx 20% are children of former pupils. *State school entry:* 15% main senior intake, plus 2% to sixth.

Entrance Own entrance exam used. No special skills or religious requirements. Maximum extras £200. 10 pa assisted places. Various scholarships/bursaries, up to 50% of fees.

Parents 15+% are doctors, lawyers etc; 15+% in industry or commerce.

Head and staff Rector: David Comins, in post since 1994. Educated at Scarborough High School and Cambridge University (mathematics). Previously Deputy Head at Queen's College, Taunton, and Head of Maths and Director of Studies at Glenalmond. *Staff:* 85 full time, 7 part time. Annual turnover 2%. Average age 40.

Exam results On average, 100 pupils in S-grade year, 100 in Higher, 40 in A-level year. *Highers:* On average, 45 pupils pass in 5+ subjects; 20 in 4; 12 in 3; (many Highers taken as an extra, with A-levels). *A-levels:* 12 pupils pass in 3 subjects; 11 in 2 subjects.

University and college entrance 86% of 1995 sixth-form leavers went on to a degree course (2% after a gap year); others typically go on to other courses (most leading to degree courses). Of those going on to university, 3% went to Oxbridge; 12% took courses in medicine, dentistry and veterinary science, 37% in science and engineering, 6% in law, 20% in humanities and social sciences, 9% in art and design, 16% in other subjects.

Curriculum S-grade, Highers and A-levels. 50% take science A-levels; 40% arts/humanities; 10% both. *Vocational:* Work experience available; also Scotvec modules in computing, photography, etc. *Computing facilities:* Computer laboratories. *Europe:* French and German offered at S-grade, Higher and A-level; also Spanish S-grade and Scotvec module in S5. Regular exchanges to France.

The arts (Pupils aged 11 and over) *Music:* Up to 25% of pupils learn a musical instrument; instrumental exams can be taken. Some 6 musical groups including choirs, wind band, orchestra, chamber group. Pupils in West of Scotland Independent Schools Musical Concert. *Drama & dance*: Drama offered. Many pupils are involved in school productions. *Art:* On average, 20 take S-grade, 15 Higher, 5 A-level. Pottery, photography also offered.

Sport, community service and clubs (Pupils aged 11 and over) *Sport and physical activities:* Compulsory sports: rugby, cricket, hockey, tennis, athletics. Optional: squash, badminton, shooting, sailing, canoeing. S-grade may be taken. *Community service:* Pupils take bronze, silver and gold Duke of Edinburgh's Award. CCF compulsory in S4 only. *Clubs and societies:* Up to 30 clubs, eg debating, chess, electronics, natural history, sub-aqua.

Uniform School uniform worn throughout.

Houses/prefects Competitive houses. Prefects, head boy and girl, head of house and house prefects – appointed by the Rector, after consulting pupils and staff.

Religion Compulsory morning assembly for all.

Social Debates, Young Enterprise Scheme, drama, some games (eg hockey), dances with other local schools. Organised trips to France, Greece, Crete; skiing at Christmas and Easter. Pupils allowed to bring own car/bike to school. Meals self service but formal seating. School shops (tuck, uniform and stationery). No tobacco/alcohol allowed.

Discipline Pupils failing to produce homework once might expect to do it or detention; those caught taking drugs on the premises can expect expulsion.
Alumni association run by The President, Glasgow Academical Club, New Anniesland, Helensburgh Drive, Glasgow.
Former pupils Lord Reith (BBC Governor General); Jeremy Isaacs (Royal Opera House); Iain Vallance (Chairman, BT); Robert MacLennan, MP; Lord Goold; Donald Dewar, MP; John Beattie (Scotland, British Lions); Sir Norman Stone (Regius Professor of Modern History, Oxford, author and journalist).

• GLASGOW HIGH

The High School of Glasgow, 637 Crow Road, Glasgow G13 1PL. Tel 0141 954 9628, Fax 0141 954 9628

• Pupils 989 • Boys 3–18 (Day) • Girls 3–18 (Day) • Higher year 91 • Termly fees £498-£1422
• HMC • Enquiries/application to the Rector

What it's like

Founded in 1124 and closely associated with the cathedral. It was closed in 1976 but the new, co-educational High School came into being the same year as a result of a merger involving the Former Pupil Club of the old High School and Drewsteignton School in Bearsden. The senior school has modern purpose-built premises at Anniesland on the western outskirts of the city next to 23 acres of playing fields. The junior school is in the former Drewsteignton School buildings about 3 miles away which have been modernised and extended. The school is non-denominational. Its academic standards are high, results are very good and relationship between teachers and pupils excellent. Almost all pupils go on to university, most to Scottish ones but a number to Oxbridge and other English universities. Music and drama are strong and achievements in debating and public speaking exceptional. It has a good record in games and sports (many representatives at county level) and an excellent range of activities. An impressive list of awards in the Duke of Edinburgh's Award Scheme. Full use is made of the city's cultural amenities.

School profile

Pupils Total age range 3–18; 989 day pupils (497 boys, 492 girls). Senior department 11–18, 623 pupils (328 boys, 295 girls). Main entry ages 4, 10 and 11. Approx 5–10% are children of former pupils. Majority of senior intake is from own junior school, The High School of Glasgow Junior School (tel 0141 942 0158). State shool entry: 95% main senior intake.
Entrance Own entrance exam used. Academic potential is looked for and ability to contribute to life of school; no religious requirements but school has a Christian background. Parents not expected to buy textbooks in the senior school; maximum £20 extras. 6 pa assisted places. 2 pa scholarships, 5 pa bursaries, £900 to 50% fees.
Parents 15+% in industry or commerce, 15+% are doctors, lawyers etc.
Head and staff Rector: Robin Easton, in post for 13 years. Educated at Kelvinside and Sedbergh and at the universities of Cambridge (French and German) and Oxford (education). Previously Head of Modern Languages at George Watson's, Housemaster and Deputy Head of French at Daniel Stewart's and Melville and teacher of French and German at Melville College. Also former Chairman, HMC Scottish Division. *Staff:* 46 full time in senior school, 16 part time. Annual turnover up to 5%. Average age 39.
Exam results In 1995, 91 pupils in S-grade year, 87 in Higher. *S-grade:* In 1995, 90 pupils gained at least grade 3 in 5–8 subjects; and 1 in 1–4 subjects. *Highers:* 65 pupils passed in 5+ subjects; 12 in 4; 6 in 3 subjects.
University and college entrance 93% of 1995 sixth-form leavers went on to a degree course (5% after a gap year); others typically go on to further education. Of those going on to university, 7% went to Oxbridge; 20% took courses in medicine, dentistry and veterinary science, 25% in science and engineering, 14% in law, 25% in humanities and social sciences, 3% in art and design, 13% in vocational subjects eg business studies, accounting, architecture.
Curriculum S-grade, Highers and CSYS: 19 subjects offered. *Vocational:* Work experience available; also Scotvec modules in PE, keyboarding, accounting, maths, media studies, fitness training and football. *Computing facilities:* 2 computer laboratories with

BBC B Econet network (10 BBC Masters), 24 Apple Macs, 17 IBM compatibles. *Europe:* French (compulsory from age 8) and German offered to S-grade, Higher and CSYS; also Spanish S-grade and Higher.

The arts (Pupils aged 11 and over) *Music:* Over 30% of pupils learn a musical instrument; instrumental exams can be taken. Some 12 musical groups including chamber orchestra, other orchestras, wind band, jazz band, brass ensemble, choirs. UK National Chamber Music Competition winners. *Drama & dance*: Drama offered. Many pupils are involved in school, year-group and other productions. Recent productions of Juno and the Paycock, A Midsummer Night's Dream, Godspell. Debating: ESU Scottish Schools champions 1995 and 1996; Cambridge Union Society Debating champions 1996, Durham University Union champions 1996; 1 pupil in Scottish team for World Schools Debating championship 1996. *Art:* On average, 15 take S-grade, 16 Higher. Design, pottery, textiles, photography, printing, sculpture also offered. Highly commended in Independent Schools Art Exhibition.

Sport, community service and clubs (Pupils aged 11 and over) *Sport and physical activities:* Rugby, hockey, athletics, cricket, swimming, tennis, cross-country, basketball, netball, volleyball, badminton, golf, sailing, orienteering, skiing, table tennis, hill walking. BAGA, RLSS exams may be taken. 2 swimming internationals, 2 badminton, 1 skiing, 2 athletics, 2 national rugby trialists, 1 girl in U16 Scottish hockey team, 3 boys in Scottish cricket XIs; pupils in district hockey and cricket teams; 5 in Glasgow Schools rugbyXV; recently champions in Scottish hockey outdoor and indoor, Glasgow cross-country, Scottish relay (boys and girls, various ages); 68 medals Glasgow athletics championships, 18 in Glasgow Schools swimming championships. *Community service:* Pupils take bronze, silver and gold Duke of Edinburgh's Award. Community service optional and encouraged for all ages; pupils raise around £6,000 each year for various charities; each house supports a charity through school year. *Clubs and societies:* Up to 40 clubs, eg literary and debating, historical, zoological, philosophy, computing, Scripture Union, chess, model railway, radio satellite tracking, various sport and music activities.

Uniform School uniform worn throughout.

Houses/prefects Competitive houses. Prefects, head boy and girl (school captains), head of house and house prefects – voting by senior pupils and staff used by Head in making appointments.

Religion Morning assembly (non-denominational).

Social Debating and public-speaking competitions. Scripture Union meetings. Usually 2–3 organised trips abroad per annum. Pupils allowed to bring own car/bike/motorbike to school. Meals self-service. No school shop but some items of uniform are sold. No tobacco/alcohol allowed.

Discipline Pupils failing to produce homework once might expect additional work. Those caught in possession of cannabis will be expelled (hypothetical).

Alumni association run by N M Alexander, Secretary, Messrs Bird, Semple, Fyfe, Ireland, 249 West George Street, Glasgow G2 4RB.

Former pupils Sir Henry Campbell-Bannerman, Andrew Bonar Law (prime ministers); Viscount James Bryce (diplomat); Sir Teddy Taylor MP; Lord Macfarlane of Bearsden.

• GLENALMOND

Glenalmond College, Perthshire PH1 3RY. Tel 01738 880205, Fax 01738 880410

• Pupils 300 • Boys 12–18 (Day/Board) • Girls 12–18 (Day/Board) • Upper sixth 65 • Termly fees £2550 (Day) £3850 (Board) • HMC • Enquiries/application to the Registrar

What it's like

Founded in 1841 as Trinity College by Mr W E Gladstone and others, it stands in magnificent countryside, 10 miles west of Perth, beside the River Almond on the edge of the Highlands. It has an estate of about 300 acres, with beautiful gardens and playing fields. A very healthy environment. The main buildings are grouped round two quadrangles and belong to the Victorian collegiate style, with neo-Gothic features, towers and turrets. There have been many modern developments, including a girls' house, built in 1991. The chapel, built by the Episcopalian founders, is one of the finest in the country. Originally a boys' school, it admitted girls to the sixth-form in 1990 and then, in 1995, right through the age range. Religious education forms part of the curriculum and all denominations attend chapel. Academic standards are high and results consistently good. Very many pupils go on to degree courses each year, including Oxbridge. Music is very strong and plays a central part in school life. The theatre is in regular use. Art is also strong. There is a wide range of sports and games and the college has long had a reputation for excellence in these (a large number of representatives at county and national level). A very wide range of clubs and societies cater for most needs. Unique features are the College's own professionally designed golf course, salmon fishing in the River Almond, ice-climbing, sailing, windsurfing, canoeing and hill walking (Munro Club). There is a large CCF with its own pipe band. A substantial commitment to local community services and a promising record in the Duke of Edinburgh's Award Scheme.

School profile

Pupils Age range 12–18; 300 pupils, 30 day (20 boys, 10 girls), 270 boarding (240 boys, 30 girls). Main entry ages 12, 13 and into sixth (became fully co-educational in 1995). 15%–20% are children of former pupils. *State school entry:* 20% main intakes, plus occasional pupil in sixth.

Entrance Common Entrance and own entrance tests used. No special skills or religious requirements. Maximum extras £100. Assisted places. Scholarships (academic and musical) up to 50% of fees.

Parents 5+% in the armed services; 25+% are doctors, lawyers etc; 30+% in industry or commerce. 10+% live within 30 miles; up to 10% live overseas.

Head and staff *Warden*: Ian Templeton, 4 years in post. Educated at Gordonstoun and at Edinburgh and London universities (mathematics and philosophy). Previously Headmaster at Oswestry, Assistant Headmaster at Robert Gordon's and Housemaster at Daniel Stewart's and Melville College. *Staff:* 36 full time, 7 part time. Annual turnover up to 5%.

Exam results In 1995, 45 pupils in fifth, 62 in upper sixth. *GCSE:* In 1995, 30 fifth gained at least grade C in 8+ subjects; 8 in 5–7 subjects. *A-levels:* 4 upper sixth passed in 4+ subjects; 36 in 3; 3 in 2 subjects.

University and college entrance 90% of 1995 sixth-form leavers went on to a degree course (30% after a gap year); others typically go on to non-degree courses eg HND. Of those going on to university, 6% went to Oxbridge; 2% took courses in medicine, dentistry and veterinary science, 20% in science and engineering, 10% in law, 45% in humanities and social sciences, 10% in art and design, 13% in vocational subjects eg education, agriculture, music.

Curriculum GCSE, Highers, A-levels. 20 subjects offered (AS-level general studies). Sixth-form courses in A-levels or in Scottish Highers. Strong tradition of classics supported by travel bursaries for study in Greece and Italy. 22% take science A-levels; 54% arts/humanities; 24% both. *Vocational:* Work experience available. *Computing facilities:* Large computing laboratory in new CDT centre networked to other departments. *Europe:* French, German and Spanish offered at GCSE, Higher and A-level. Regular exchanges to France. Frequent holiday trips to Europe (eg Paris, Berlin, Rome). Up to 3 scholarships available to Nordic countries. Several European pupils completing British exams for entry to European universities.

The arts *Music:* Over 50% of pupils learn a musical instrument; instrumental exams can be taken. Some 10 musical groups including orchestra, wind, brass, pipe bands, chamber group, string quartet, choirs, rock bands. 4 performance standard organists; several pupils in Scottish Youth Orchestra; several in Perth Symphony Orchestra. *Drama & dance*: Drama offered. Scotvec drama exams may be taken. Majority of pupils are involved in school productions and house/other productions. *Art:* On average, 10 take GCSE, 8 A-level. Design, pottery, photography, screen printing, glass engraving. 3-month artist in residence programme for special interests; places at art colleges in Edinburgh and North of England; many family connections with art world.

Sport, community service and clubs *Sport and physical activities:* Main sports: rugby, cricket, hockey. Others: tennis, golf, squash, badminton, volleyball, basketball, sailing, windsurfing, climbing, sub-aqua, shooting, and many more. RLSS exams may be taken. National, 3 Scottish rugby trialists; county representatives in rugby (U18, U16), hockey (U18, U16, boys & girls), cricket. *Community service:* Pupils take bronze, silver and gold

Duke of Edinburgh's Award. CCF compulsory for 2 years at age 14, optional in sixth-form; Army and RAF sections. Community service optional; plays, Christmas party etc for local elderly and disabled. *Clubs and societies:* Up to 30 clubs, eg debating/public speaking, sporting, drama, flying, skiing, Scripture Union, musical, art & design, historical, photography.

Uniform School dress is a relaxed uniform worn by all; kilt is worn on Sundays and on formal occasions.

Houses/prefects Competitive houses (5 boys, 1 girls). Prefects, head boy, heads of houses and house prefects appointed by the Warden and housemasters.

Religion Attendance at Chapel services is compulsory for pupils of all Christian denominations; exceptions made for those of other religions.

Social Public speaking competitions, theatrical productions, and some dances with local schools. Skiing trips abroad; trips to Paris, Moscow, Rome; hockey tour to Holland, rugby to South Africa. Pupils allowed to bring own bike to school. Meals informal. School shops (tuck and sports equipment). No tobacco allowed. Upper sixth-form bar opens once each week.

Discipline Pupils failing to produce homework once might expect extra work or detention; any involvement with drugs would result in immediate expulsion.

Boarding 20% have own study bedroom, 30% share with 1 or 2; 2% are in dormitories of 6+; remainder in cubicles. 6 houses of 45–50, including a girls' house. 2 resident qualified nurses. Central dining room for 5 houses (1 house eats separately). Pupils can provide and cook own food. 2 weekend exeats each term plus half-term. Visits to local town allowed.

Alumni association run by A R Muir, Springkell, Callum's Hill, Crieff, Perthshire P47 3LS.

Former pupils Sandy Gall (TV newscaster); Sir David Wilson (former Governor, Hong Kong); David Leslie, David Sole and Rob Wainwright (Captains of Scottish Rugby XV); Lord Sanderson of Bowden (politician); Allan Massie (novelist).

• GODOLPHIN

The Godolphin School, Milford Hill, Salisbury, Wiltshire SP1 2RA. Tel 01722 333059, Fax 01722 411700

• Pupils 446 • Boys None • Girls 7–18 (Day/Board) • Upper sixth 49 • Termly fees £1733–£2152 (Day) £3593 (Board) • GSA, BSA • Enquiries/application to the Headmistress

What it's like

The original foundation is based on the will of Elizabeth Godolphin made in 1726 and moved to its present site under the pioneering headship of Mary Alice Douglas in 1891. The main school building is Victorian and the remainder reflect the full range of 20th-century architectural styles, as the school has steadily developed, all surrounded by gardens and playing fields overlooking open countryside. A performing arts centre opens in 1996. It is a C of E foundation; morning prayers and some religious services are compulsory and there are regular services in Salisbury Cathedral. A broad general education is provided and results are good. There is considerable emphasis placed on careers and higher education advice and the majority of girls go on to degree courses. There are very active music, drama and art departments and the school is well equipped with sporting facilities, including a modern sports hall. There is a fair range of extra-curricular and weekend activities, open to day girls and boarders.

School profile

Pupils Total age range 7–18; 446 girls, 243 day, 203 boarding (age 11 upwards only). Senior department 11–18, 399 girls. Main entry ages 11, 12, 13 and into sixth. Significant intake from own prep department (tel 01722 421698). *State school entry:* 30% main intakes, some to sixth.

Entrance Common Entrance used. 10 pa assisted places (5 at age 8, 5 at 11). Scholarships and bursaries.

Head and staff *Headmistress:* Miss Jill Horsburgh, appointed in 1996. Educated at the universities of Oxford (history) and Leicester and the Sheffield Business School. Previously Assistant Head, Head of History and Housemistress at Benenden and taught

at Downe House. *Staff:* 43 full time, 3 part time. Annual turnover 4%. Average age, 40.
Exam results In 1995, 56 pupils in upper fifth, 41 in upper sixth. *GCSE:* In 1995, all upper fifth gained at least grade C in 7+ subjects. *A-levels:* 20 upper sixth passed in 4+ subjects; 18 in 3; 2 in 2; and 1 in 1 subject. Average UCAS points 20.0.
University and college entrance 78% of 1995 sixth-form leavers went on to a degree course (40% after a gap year); others typically go on to art, fashion, secretarial courses, engineering apprenticeship. Of those going on to university, 5% went to Oxbridge; 10% took courses in medicine, dentistry and veterinary science, 20% in science and engineering, 5% in law, 25% in humanities and social sciences, 15% in art and design, 25% in vocational subjects eg education, physiotherapy, hotel management, sports studies, agriculture.
Curriculum GCSE and A-levels. 18 subjects offered (including GCSE theatre studies and A-level general studies). 28% take science A-levels; remainder arts/humanities. *Vocational:* Work shadowing in lower sixth; also RSA Stages 1 and 2 CLAIT and word processing. *Computing facilities:* 3 PC-based networks with 50+ stations, CD-Rom based PCs, including multi-media machines; further PCs in each department. *Special provision:* For dyslexic pupils, some support lessons. *Europe:* French and German offered to GCSE, AS and A-level; also GCSE Spanish; also Italian, Japanese and Greek for fun. French GCSE compulsory; all sixth-form may continue with languages regardless of A-level subjects. Cable TV access to European networks. Regular visits, exchanges and work shadowing (France and Germany). Visits by MEP.
The arts (Pupils aged 11 and over) *Music:* 75% of pupils learn a musical instrument; instrumental exams taken. Some 20 musical groups including choirs, bands, orchestras, string orchestras, ensembles. Pupils are members of county youth orchestra, National Children's Orchestra, county youth choirs. Pupils regularly go on to conservatoires. *Drama & dance*: Drama offered and GCSE and A-level may be taken. Majority of pupils are involved in school and house/other productions. *Art:* On average, 50+% take GCSE, 25% A-level. 3D design, pottery, textiles, photography, wood/metal work, sculpture, printing, art history, life class also offered. Artist-in-residence. Regular external art commissions (eg Salisbury District Hospital and South West Trains).
Sport, community service and clubs (Pupils aged 11 and over) *Sport and physical activities:* Compulsory sports: netball, lacrosse, gym, athletics, tennis, swimming. Optional: choice of 24 others. RLSS exams may be taken. 1 pupil in national fencing team, 1 in cross-country, 2 in eventing teams; 26 county players (in various sports). *Community service:* Pupils take bronze, silver and gold Duke of Edinburgh's Award. *Clubs and societies:* Up to 30 clubs, eg debating. lifesaving, pets, biotechnology, astronomy, conservation, lacemaking, silversmithing, cordon bleu.
Uniform School uniform worn except in sixth.
Houses/prefects Competitive houses. Prefects, head girl, head of house and house prefects – appointed by the Headmistress after school election.
Religion Attendance at religious worship compulsory.
Social Combined concerts and plays with local boys' schools; charities fair; sixth-form insight into management course. French trips; safari trip to Africa; ski trip; regular music tours to Europe. Upper sixth allowed to bring own car to school. Meals self-service. School shop. No tobacco/alcohol allowed.
Discipline Personal tutors impose penalties for poor performance and encourage and support achievements, both academic and other, through a commendation/order mark system. School rules establish that serious offences (eg use of tobacco or bullying) are dealt with firmly and immediately: expulsions for possession of illegal drugs and suspension for repeated smoking.
Boarding Separate sixth-form house.

• GODOLPHIN AND LATYMER

Godolphin and Latymer, Iffley Road, Hammersmith, London W6 OPG. Tel 0181 741 1936, Fax 0181 746 3352

• Pupils 700 • Boys None • Girls 11–18 (Day) • Upper sixth 84 • Termly fees £1975 (Day) • GSA • Enquiries/application to the Head Mistress

What it's like

Founded in 1905 (formerly the Godolphin School for Boys, built in 1861). It is single-site and urban on 4 acres of grounds with playing fields attached. Extensive additions, including a new art, science and technology building, have been made to the original Victorian buildings and facilities are first rate. A well-run and academically high-powered school which gets excellent results. Nearly all pupils go on to degree courses each year, including many to Oxbridge. Very strong indeed in music, drama and art; there is a massive commitment among the pupils. An excellent record in games and sports, of which a wide variety is offered. There is also an impressive number of clubs and societies.

School profile

Pupils Age range 11–18; 700 day girls. Main entry ages 11 and into sixth. Approx 4% are children of former pupils. *State school entry:* 40% main intake, plus 7% to sixth.

Entrance Own entrance exam used. No special skills or religious requirements. Fees include textbooks, stationery and public examination fees. 25 pa assisted places available at 11, 3 pa at 16. Music scholarship worth half fees available. School bursaries awarded in cases of need.

Parents 15+% are doctors, lawyers, etc; 15+% in industry or commerce; 15+% in theatre, media, music, etc.

Head and staff *Headmistress:* Miss Margaret Rudland, in post for 11 years. Educated at Sweyne School, Rayleigh, and Bedford College, London (mathematics and physics). Previously Deputy Head Mistress at Norwich High, and Second Mistress and Head of Mathematics at St Paul's Girls'. Also 1996 President of GSA. *Staff:* 45 full time, 28 part time.

Exam results In 1995, 100 girls in upper fifth; 84 in upper sixth. *GCSE:* In 1995, 96% gained at least grade C in 8+ subjects; 4% in 5–7 subjects. *A-levels:* 9 upper sixth passed in 4+ subjects; 73 in 3; 2 in 2 subjects. Average UCAS points 26.2.

University and college entrance 98% of 1995 sixth-form leavers went on to a degree course (30% after a gap year); others typically go on to art foundation courses or into employment. Of those going on to university, 15% went to Oxbridge; 12% took courses in medicine, dentistry and veterinary science, 20% in science and engineering, 58% in humanities and social sciences, 5% in art and design, 2% in vocational subjects eg physiotherapy, hotel management.

Curriculum GCSE and A-levels. 19 GCSE subjects offered; 23 at A-level (no A-level general studies). 17% take science A-level; 40% arts/humanities; 43% both. *Vocational:* Work experience available to all after their GCSE exams and again in the sixth-form (including in France and Germany). *Computing facilities:* A specialist computer room with network of BBC computers. *Special provision:* Some pupils for whom English is not native tongue, but no special provision is made. *Europe:* French, German and Spanish offered at GCSE and A-level; also GCSE Italian and A-level Russian. Regular exchanges (France, Germany, Russia and Italy).

The arts *Music:* Over 50% of pupils learn a musical instrument; instrumental exams can be taken. Some 12+ musical groups including orchestra, various choirs, jazz group, wind band, brass group. Pupil recent leader of National Youth Orchestra; 8 pupils attend Royal Academy and Royal College of Music junior depts. *Drama & dance*: Both offered. LAMDA exams may be taken. Some pupils are involved in school productions and all in house/other productions. *Art:* On average, 40 take GCSE, 15 A-level. Design, pottery, textiles, photography also offered.

Sport, community service and clubs *Sport and physical activities:* Compulsory sports: gymnastics, hockey, basketball, tennis, rounders, fitness training. Optional: jazz dance, yoga, fencing, squash, rowing, swimming, Scottish country dance. Hockey, county champions U18 and U15, 6 county players; many club hockey and tennis players. *Community service:* Pupils take silver and gold Duke of Edinburgh's Award. Commu-

nity service optional. *Clubs and societies:* Up to 30 clubs, eg chess, debating, BAYS, computing, junior club.
Uniform School uniform worn except the sixth.
Houses/prefects No competitive houses or prefects. Head girl and team of deputies – elected by the school. School Council.
Religion Morning assembly for whole school.
Social Joint orchestra with Latymer Upper School. Exchange visits to France, Germany, Italy, Russia and USA. Senior pupils allowed to bring own bike to school. Meals self-service. School shop. No tobacco/alcohol allowed.
Discipline Discipline matters are looked after on an individual basis. High standards of honesty and courtesy are expected. Pupils failing to produce homework are followed up and extra help given when required.

• GORDONSTOUN

Gordonstoun School, Elgin, Morayshire IV30 2RF. Tel 01343 830445, Fax 01343 830241
• Pupils 428 • Boys 13–18 (Day/Board) • Girls 13–18 (Day/Board) • Upper sixth 100 • Termly fees £2685 (Day) £4160 (Board) • HMC, Round Square • Enquires/application to the Headmaster

What it's like

Founded in 1934 by Kurt Hahn, it began in two historic houses: Gordonstoun House and the famous 17th-century Round Square. There has been much expansion and development and it is now one of the best-equipped schools in the country. The complex lies on a 150-acre estate in magnificent countryside which includes a mile of the Moray Firth foreshore. The prep school is at Aberlour House, 20 miles away. There are beautiful gardens and playing fields at both. The school's motto is, appropriately, *Plus est en vous* (There is more in you than you think). Hahn's celebrated Platonic view of education has been made a basis for a philosophy of education which is exemplified in Gordonstoun life. Originally a boys' school, it admitted girls throughout the school in 1972. It aims to harness all the attributes of every boy and girl, thus preparing them as complete people for life. It strives for all-round development and lays emphasis on skill, enterprise, a sense of adventure and compassion, as well as self-reliance and responsibility to oneself and to others. Hahn's vision of a school as a place where international understanding should be fostered has also become part of the Gordonstoun way of life. About 25% of the school come from overseas and exchanges are made regularly with schools around the world. All pupils attend non-denominational Chapel services and assemblies. A large staff allows a staff:pupil ratio of 1:7. The teaching is very good and academic standards are high; most pupils go on to degree courses. Music and drama are very strong indeed and there are frequent music and drama tours including overseas. A wide range of sports and team games is offered with a high level of attainment and plenty of fixtures. Outdoor pursuits include skiing, gliding, game shooting, fishing, canoeing and rock-climbing and all pupils do a course in seamanship and expeditions. Not surprisingly the school has a remarkable record in the Duke of Edinburgh's Award Scheme. All pupils are involved in service to the community including a fire service, a coastguard unit plus mountain rescue and inshore rescue units. There is an Air Training Corps and a large community service unit.

School profile

Pupils Age range 13–18; 428 pupils, 23 day (13 boys, 10 girls), 405 boarding (249 boys, 156 girls). Main entry ages 13 and into sixth. Approx 10% are children of former pupils. Own prep school, Aberlour House, provides approx 20% of intake. *State school entry:* 15% main intake, plus 40% to sixth.
Entrance Common Entrance and own scholarship exams used. No special skills or religious requirements but abilities in different areas will always be helpful. Parents not expected to buy textbooks. 26 pa assisted places. 30 pa scholarships/bursaries, many approx 50% of fees; music scholarships; art bursary; bursaries for sons of armed forces personnel.
Parents 15% live within 100 miles; 20% live overseas.
Head and staff *Headmaster:* Mark Pyper, 6 years in post. Educated at Winchester and

London University (history). Previously Deputy Head at Sevenoaks and Assistant Headmaster at St Wilfrid's Preparatory School, Seaford. Also Director Sevenoaks Summer Festival (1979-90). *Staff:* 55 full time, 32 part time. Annual turnover 2–3%. Average age 38.

Exam results On average, 80 pupils in upper fifth, 100 in upper sixth. *GCSE:* On average, 75% fifth gain at least grade C in 8+ subjects; 23% in 5–7; and 2% in 1–4 subjects. *A-levels:* 15% upper sixth pass in 4+ subjects; 72% in 3; 12% in 2; and 1% in 1 subject.

University and college entrance 93% of 1995 sixth-form leavers went on to a degree course; others typically go on to art colleges or vocational courses. Of those going on to university, 7% went to Oxbridge; 9% took courses in medicine, dentistry and veterinary science, 35% in science and engineering, 44% in arts, social sciences and education, % 12% in professional and vocational subjects.

Curriculum GCSE and A-levels. 19 GCSE subjects offered, 21 at A-level. No A-level general studies although all sixth-form take a general studies course, including Russian. 45% take science A-levels; 36% arts/humanities; 19% both. *Vocational:* Work experience available. *Computing facilities:* Campus-wide network, linking library, teaching departments and boarding houses; multi-media facilities and access to Internet. Some GCSE and certificate courses in IT; aim also to develop IT skills through other subjects. *Special provision:* Full learning support department for EFL, ESL and specific learning difficulties. *Europe:* French, German and Spanish offered at GCSE, AS and A-level; also GCSE Italian. Regular exchanges (France, Germany and Spain). School runs an International Summer School for 250 students aged 11–16 from 27 countries.

The arts *Music:* Over 40% of pupils learn a musical instrument; instrumental exams can be taken. Some 7 musical groups including orchestra, choirs, swing band, Scottish ensemble, woodwind. 4 pupils in regional orchestra, 2 National Children's Orchestra, 2 NYO of Scotland, 1 quarter-finalist BBC Young Musician. *Drama & dance:* Both offered. GCSE, AS and A-level drama may be taken. Majority of pupils are involved in school and house/other productions. *Art:* On average, 18 take GCSE, 20 A-level. Design, pottery, photography, history of art also offered. Semi-finalist Toshiba Year of Invention Award.

Sport, community service and clubs *Sport and physical activities:* Compulsory sports: 3 from athletics, cricket, cross-country, golf, hockey, netball, rugby, soccer, tennis. Optional: badminton, basketball, orienteering, skiing, squash, swimming, sailing, canoeing, rock climbing, karate, aerobics, dance, clay-pigeon shooting. GCSE, RLSS, RYA, First Aid exams may be taken. British national skiing, national cricket, regional cross-country, swimming, hockey, netball. *Community service:* Pupils take bronze, silver and gold Duke of Edinburgh's Award. Community service compulsory for 3 years at age 15: fire service, HM Coastguard, mountain rescue, corps of canoe lifeguards, surf lifesaving, community service volunteers, nature conservation service, air training corps. *Clubs and societies:* Include cooking, debating, folk music, photography, pottery, electronics, wine tasting, philosophy.

Uniform Relaxed school uniform worn throughout the formal day.

Houses/prefects Prefects (Colour Bearers), head boy/girl, head of house and house prefects. School Councils at different age levels.

Religion Services are non-denominational and pupils are expected to attend.

Social Many games fixtures and debates with other schools. Exchanges with schools in USA, Canada, Australia, New Zealand, India as well as European countries; trips abroad for skiing and with rugby, squash teams and orchestra. Pupils allowed to bring own bike to school. Meals self-service. School shop. No tobacco allowed; beer and wine allowed on specified occasions for sixth-form.

Boarding Single-sex houses of 55–60. Resident qualified medical staff. Central dining room. Pupils can on occasion provide and cook their own food. Weekend exeats and visits to local town allowed.

Alumni association run by G Neil (Chairman), The Gordonstoun Association, c/o the school.

• GRANGE

The Grange School, Bradburns Lane, Hartford, Northwich, Cheshire CW8 1LU. Tel 01606 74007, Fax 01606 784581

• Pupils 1090 • Boys 4–18 (Day) • Girls 4–18 (Day) • Upper sixth 66 • Termly fees £875–£1225 (Day) • HMC • Enquiries/application to the Admissions Secretary

What it's like

Founded in 1933 as a kindergarten and prep school. In 1978, as a result of parental concern about comprehensivisation, a senior school was built. The school has pleasant modern buildings with 22 acres of sports grounds. Facilities are good and a new classroom block and a junior school opened in 1996. A busy, purposeful school with an expanding sixth-form where academic results are very good. Most sixth-formers go on to university. There are active music, drama and art departments. A good range of games and sports, plus extra-curricular activities. A large number involved in the Duke of Edinburgh's Award Scheme.

School profile

Pupils Total age range 4–18; 1090 day pupils (536 boys, 554 girls). Senior department 11–18, 595 pupils (287 boys, 308 girls). Main entry ages 4, 11 and into sixth. *State school entry:* 35% main senior intake, plus 15% to sixth.

Entrance Own entrance exam used. No special skills or religious requirements. Assisted places. Scholarships (music, sport, drama and academic) at 11, plus several academic sixth-form scholarships.

Parents 75+% in industry or commerce.

Head and staff *Headmaster:* Scott Marshall, in post for 19 years. Educated at Coleraine and Foyle College (Northern Ireland) and Manchester University (English). Previously Headmaster at Foyle College Preparatory School. Also Member of HMC, Executive Council of Independent Schools Association, and of Guild of Drama Adjudicators LGSM. *Staff:* 57 full time, 14 part time (excluding peripatetics).

Exam results In 1995, 64 pupils in upper fifth, 57 in upper sixth. *GCSE:* In 1993, 62 upper fifth gained at least grade C in 8+ subjects; 2 in 5–7 subjects. *A-levels:* 47 upper sixth passed in 4+ subjects; 7 in 3; and 3 in 2 subjects. Average UCAS points 20.4 (including general studies 28.0).

University and college entrance 96% of 1995 sixth-form leavers went on to a degree course, 12% to Oxbridge.

Curriculum GCSE and A-levels. 24 subjects offered (including Latin and A-level general studies). 45% take science A-levels; 45% arts/humanities; 10% both. *Vocational:* Work experience available. *Computing facilities:* 3 BBC, 25 Amstrad 2000 computers in a specialist room and 31 in classrooms. *Europe:* French, German and Spanish offered to GCSE and A-level. Regular visits (France, Germany and Spain). Talks from MEPs. Sixth formers attend Spanish university for 2 week course.

The arts (Pupils age 11 and over) *Music:* Over 75% pupils learn a musical instrument; instrumental exams can be taken. Some 10 musical groups including choirs, orchestra, brass, woodwind, string, guitar, recorder groups, theory class etc. Pupils attend Royal Northern College of Music Saturday school; play in various youth orchestras/choirs; participate in ISAI Music Festival. *Drama & dance*: Drama offered. GCSE and A-level drama, ESB and Guildhall exams may be taken. Some pupils are involved in school and house/other productions. Annual Gilbert & Sullivan production; pupils successfully participate in drama festivals. *Art:* On average, 15 take GCSE, 7 A-level. Design, textiles, 3D also offered.

Sport, community service and clubs (Pupils age 11 and over) *Sport and physical activities:* Compulsory sports: football, rugby, athletics, cricket, tennis, rounders, volleyball, basketball, gymnastics (until sixth-form then all optional). Sixth form only: squash, golf, swimming. Athletics, county representatives; hockey, county representatives (girls). *Community service:* Pupils take bronze, silver and gold Duke of Edinburgh's Award. Community service optional; visits to old people's homes, assistance to the elderly, fund-raising for charitable institutions. *Clubs and societies:* Up to 30 clubs, eg pottery, photography, chess, debating, sports, literary, art, computing.

Uniform School uniform worn except in the sixth.

Houses/prefects Competitive houses. Student council, head boy/girl, head of house

and house prefects – appointed by Headmaster and staff.
Religion Regular religious worship.
Social Organised trips abroad. Sixth-form students allowed to bring own car/motorbike to school. Meals self-service. Clothing shop. No tobacco/alcohol allowed.

• GREENACRE

Greenacre School for Girls, Sutton Lane, Banstead, Surrey SM7 3RA. Tel 01737 352114
• Pupils 420 • Boys None • Girls 3–18 (Day) • Upper sixth 24 • Termly fees £420–£1660 (Day)
• GSA • Enquiries/application to the Headmistress

What it's like

Founded in 1933, it is single-site on the edge of the green belt in pleasant surroundings. The buildings are varied and attractive and are mainly purpose-built. Facilities are good. A sound general education is provided and results are creditable. A high proportion of the girls are involved in music, drama and art. A range of games and sports and other activities and a new sports hall. Duke of Edinburgh's Award Scheme offered.

School profile

Pupils Total age range 3–18, 420 day girls. Senior department 11–18. Main entry ages 3, 4, 11 and into sixth. 5% are children of former pupils. *State school entry:* 20% senior intake.
Entrance Own entrance exam used. No special skills or religious requirements. Parents not expected to buy textbooks. 1 pa scholarship at 11+ (half fees); several sixth-form scholarships and bursaries; 10% reduction for service children, 5% for siblings.
Parents 15+% are doctors, lawyers, etc; 15+% in industry or commerce.
Head and staff *Headmistress:* Mrs Patricia Wood, 6 years in post. Educated at the Convent of the Ladies of Mary (Scarborough) and Hull University (geography). Previously Head of Geography, House Tutor and Examinations Officer at Queenswood, member of Humanities Department, i/c library at Shelley High (Huddersfield) and Geography teacher and Head of House at Stocksbridge School (Sheffield). Also Examiner and Team Leader for MEG Geography. *Staff:* Annual turnover 5%.
Exam results In 1995, 37 pupils in Year 11, 20 in upper sixth. *GCSE:* In 1995, 65% Year 11 gained grade C or above in 5+ subjects; 32% in 5–7 subjects. *A-levels:* 60% upper sixth passed in 4+ subjects; 35% in 3; 5% in 2 subjects. Average UCAS points 13.6.
University and college entrance 65% of 1995 sixth-form leavers went on to a degree course; others typically go on to art, drama or music colleges. Of those going on to university, 12% took courses in medicine, dentistry and veterinary science, 28% in science and engineering, 40% in humanities and social sciences, 20% in art and design.
Curriculum GCSE and A-levels. 17–20 subjects offered, including photography and A-level general studies. 20% take science A-levels; 60% arts/humanities; 20% both. *Vocational:* Work experience available; also RSA Stage 1 CLAIT and Stage 2 IT. *Computing facilities:* PCs in 2 computer labs (1 junior, 1 senior). *Special provision:* EFL lessons. Remedial teaching can be arranged for slight cases. Teacher responsible for dyslexic girls' exam entries. *Europe:* French (compulsory), German and Spanish offered at GCSE, AS and A-level and Institute of Linguists. Regular exchanges (France, Germany and Spain). Often have European pupils in school, particularly French.
The arts (Pupils aged 11 and over) *Music:* Over 15% of pupils learn a musical instrument; instrumental exams can be taken. Some 7 musical groups including choirs, guitar, orchestral, recorder. Recent Cambridge choral scholarship. *Drama & dance*: Drama offered. GCSE, AS and A-level drama, Poetry Society and LAMDA exams may be taken. Majority of pupils are involved in school and house/other productions. Recent successes in creative writing competitions. *Art:* On average, 15 take GCSE, 7 A-level. Design, textiles, photography, 3D also offered. De Beers commendation in jewellery design.
Sport, community service and clubs (Pupils aged 11 and over) *Sport and physical activities:* Compulsory sports: netball, tennis, rounders, swimming, badminton, athletics, gymnastics, volleyball, basketball, dance. Choice of sports from Year 11; sixth-form only: golf, badminton, riding, aerobics. ASA, AAA, Esso 5-star awards, IBM 10 step awards, TSB athletics awards may be taken. 2 in county lacrosse team U15. *Community*

service: Pupils take bronze, silver and gold Duke of Edinburgh's Award. *Clubs and societies:* Up to 15 clubs, eg drama, computers, RS.
Uniform School uniform worn except in sixth.
Houses/prefects Competitive houses. Prefects, head girl, head of house and house prefects – elected by the school. School Council.
Religion Non-denominational.
Social Local community involvement. Many organised trips abroad. Pupils allowed to bring own car/bike to school. Meals formal for younger pupils; self-service for upper school. Sixth form have facilities to provide own lunch or may go out. No tobacco/ alcohol allowed.
Discipline Discipline system through form or subject staff according to offence. Deputy Headteacher, Headteacher or parents involved if necessary.

• GRESHAM'S

Gresham's School, Holt, Norfolk NR25 6EA. Tel 01263 713271

• Pupils 520 • Boys 13-19 (Day/Board/Weekly) • Girls 13–19 (Day/Board/Weekly) • Upper sixth 106 • Termly fees £2750 (Day) £3930 (Board) £3535 (Weekly) • HMC • Enquiries/application to the Registrar

What it's like

Founded in 1555 by Sir John Gresham, the endowments were placed under the management of the Fishmongers' Company with which the school retains close associations. It enjoys a fine position in one of the most beautiful parts of England, a few miles from the sea near Sheringham. There are delightful grounds of about 50 acres as well as some 90 acres of woodland. All the buildings except the Old School House (1870) are 20th century. Since 1964 there have been extensive developments and accommodation and facilities are now excellent. It is a C of E foundation and a good deal of attention is given to religious instruction. However, all denominations are accepted. Originally a boys' school, it first admitted girls in 1976 and is now fully co-educational. The staff:pupil ratio is about 1:9. Academic standards are high and results very good; the vast majority of leavers go on to university each year, especially to Cambridge. A wide variety of sports and games is available and the facilities for these are first-rate including two astro-turf hockey and tennis surfaces. Music and drama are an important part of the school's life and there is considerable strength in these fields. A very good range of extra-curricular activities. The CCF contingent is strong and there is a good deal of emphasis on outdoor pursuits and 20 gold Duke of Edinburgh's Awards a year. The prep school and pre-prep school are affiliated.

School profile

Pupils Age range 13–19; 520 pupils, 183 day (109 boys, 74 girls), 337 boarding (202 boys, 135 girls). Main entry ages, 13 and into sixth. 10% are children of former pupils. 30% of intake from own prep, Gresham's Prep School (tel 01263 712227). *State school entry:* 5% main intake, plus 10+% to sixth.
Entrance Common Entrance and own scholarship exam used. All special skills are encouraged; no special religious requirements. Parents not expected to buy textbooks. Average charge for extras £200 per term. 12 pa assisted places (5 at 13, 7 at 16). 34 pa scholarships (including music), £600 to 50% fees.
Parents 15+% farmers. 10+% live within 30 miles, up to 10% live overseas.
Head and staff *Headmaster:* John Arkell, 6 years in post. Educated at Stowe and Cambridge (English). Previously Headmaster at Wrekin, Founder Head of Fettes Junior and Housemaster at Fettes Senior, and Head of Sixth Form English at Framlingham. Also Chairman, ISIS Central Committee (1991); Secretary, HMC Midland Division (1991). *Staff:* 55 full time, 20 part time. Annual turnover low. Average age 35.
Exam results In 1995, 97 pupils in fifth, 86 in upper sixth. *GCSE:* In 1995, 86 fifth gained at least grade C in 8+ subjects; 10 in 5–7 subjects. *A-levels:* 10% upper sixth passed in 4+ subjects; 74% in 3; 16% in 2 subjects. Average UCAS points 21.3.
University and college entrance 95% of 1995 sixth-form leavers went on to a degree course (15% after a gap year); others typically go on to art foundation courses. Of those going on to university, 7% went to Oxbridge; 9% took courses in medicine, dentistry and

veterinary science, 25% in science and engineering, 8% in law, 25% in humanities and social sciences, 10% in art and design, 1% in vocational subjects.
Curriculum GCSE and A-levels. 19 subjects offered; introduction to Arabic, Russian, Italian and Japanese in sixth. 20% take science A-levels; 30% arts/humanities; 50% both. *Vocational:* Work experience available. *Computing facilities:* Computing room with network of machines; CDT department with CAD machines. *Special provision:* Help available from specialist member of staff. *Europe:* French and German offered to GCSE and A-level; also GCSE Italian and Spanish in sixth. Regular exchanges (France and Germany). German pupils each year.
The arts *Music:* Over 30% of pupils learn a musical instrument; instrumental exams can be taken. Some 16 musical groups including 3 choirs, 2 orchestras, 3 chamber, brass, guitar, recorder, jazz, popular. School choir in finals of National Choral Competition at Royal Festival Hall, 3 of past 5 years; concerts in United States, Budapest, Odessa and Sweden. *Drama & dance*: Both offered. GCSE and A-level drama may be taken. Some pupils are involved in school productions and majority in house/other productions. *Art:* On average, 25 take GCSE, 12 A-level. Design also offered.
Sport, community service and clubs *Sport and physical activities:* Compulsory sports: for 2 years rugby, hockey (boys). Optional: all sports. Extensive representation at national and county level in a number of sports. *Community service:* Pupils take bronze, silver and gold Duke of Edinburgh's Award; 20 gold a year on average. CCF and community service optional. *Clubs and societies:* Up to 30 clubs, eg fishing, shooting, debating etc.
Uniform School uniform except in sixth.
Houses/prefects Competitive houses. Head boy/girl, prefects, head of house and house prefects, appointed by the Headmaster. No formal School Council but regular meetings with prefects and Deputy Head.
Religion Attendance at religious worship compulsory.
Social Many joint events with other schools, mostly sport. Day pupils allowed to bring own car/bike/motorbike. Meals self-service. School shop. Alcohol allowed in sixth-form club; no tobacco.
Discipline Pupils failing to produce homework once could expect extra work period; those caught smoking cannabis on the premises could expect expulsion.
Boarding 45% have single study bedrooms; 22% share with 1–3 others. 33% in dormitories of 6+. Single-sex houses 38–69, same as competitive houses. Resident qualified nurse and sanatorium. 2 exeats per term (1–2 nights). Visits to the local town allowed for all (2 hours Mon–Sat and on Sunday afternoons). Own school counsellor.
Alumni association is run by Bursar's Secretary, c/o the School.
Former pupils Stephen Spender; W H Auden; Lennox Berkeley; John Reith; Benjamin Britten; Sir Christopher Cockerell (inventor hovercraft); Leslie Everett Barnes (swing wing aircraft inventor); James Dyson (inventor ball barrow).

• GUILDFORD HIGH

Guildford High School, London Road, Guildford, Surrey GU1 1SJ. Tel 01483 561440, Fax 01483 306516

• Pupils 783 • Boys None • Girls 4-18 (Day) • Upper sixth 62 • Termly fees £1008–£1700 (Day) • GSA • Enquiries/application to the Admissions Secretary .

What it's like

Founded in 1888, it is one of seven independent schools governed by the Church Schools Company Ltd. Urban, single-site, with spacious grounds and pleasant buildings (all, at different times, purpose-built), it is very accessible by public transport. Numerous recent additions make it a well-equipped establishment. The junior school is housed in its own new building on the same site. There are 2 large libraries, modern labs and a fine design and technology centre. A Church of England school, there is some emphasis on religious education and attendance at worship is compulsory. The staff:pupil ratio is roughly 1:12 plus a large part-time staff. Academic standards are high and results are excellent. Virtually all leavers proceed to degree courses (about 10% to Oxbridge). Very strong in music; drama is well supported. There is good representation in sport and games at district and county level. An adequate range of clubs and societies (including Christian Fellowship and Christian Discovery Groups). The Duke of Edinburgh Award Scheme is popular and plentiful use is made of the cultural resources of Guildford.

School profile

Pupils Total age range 4–18, 783 day girls. Senior department 11–18, 497 girls. Main entry ages 4, 7, 11 and into sixth. *State school entry:* 40% senior intake, plus 25% to sixth.

Entrance Own exam used. No special skills or religious requirements. Parents not expected to buy textbooks: extras are £110 (lunch) and school trips. 5 pa assisted places at 11, others at age 5 and 16. Scholarships at age 7, 11 and to sixth, including music; up to 33% fees.

Parents 15% + are doctors, lawyers etc, 15% + in industry or commerce.

Head and staff *Headmistress:* Mrs Susan Singer, 6 years in post. Educated at St Mary's, Calne, and at the Open University (mathematics) and London University (education). Previously Head of Middle School and Head of Mathematics at St Paul's Girls School. *Staff:* 57 full time, 20 part time, plus 25 visiting music and drama staff.

Exam results In 1995, 72 pupils in Year 11, 57 in upper sixth. *GCSE:* In 1995, all in Year 11 passed in 8+ subjects. *A-levels:* 7 upper sixth passed in 4+ subjects; 48 in 3; 2 in 2 subjects. Average UCAS points 25.9.

University and college entrance All 1995 sixth-form leavers went on to a degree course, 10% to Oxbridge. 10% took courses in medicine, dentistry and veterinary science, 10% in science and engineering, 72% in humanities and social sciences, 4% in para-medical subjects, 4% in music.

Curriculum GCSE, A-levels (no A-level general studies). 18% take science A-levels; 44% arts/humanities; 38% both. *Vocational:* Work experience available; also RSA level 1 CLAIT. *Computing facilities:* Nimbus networks in sixth-form block, science department, and junior school. AppleMacs in computer room. Mathematics and other departments have PCs. *Europe:* French, German and Spanish offered to GCSE and A-level and non-examined subjects; also GCSE Italian and Russian. German compulsory from age 5, French from 9. Exchanges for all senior age groups (France and Germany). European Sixth Form conference in St Etienne; European Awareness Day for Year 11.

The arts *Music:* 47% of pupils learn a musical instrument; exams can be taken. 14 musical groups including orchestras, concert band, chamber choir, wind band, recorder consort and numerous chamber groups. 2 pupils in National Youth Choir, 1 in National Youth Orchestra, 12 in county youth orchestra. 4 groups in Chamber Music Competition for Schools 1996 semi-finals. *Drama & dance*: Drama offered; Guildhall and LAMDA exams may be taken. Some pupils are involved in school productions. *Art:* On average 20 pupils take GCSE art, 6 A-level. History of art also offered.

Sport, community service and clubs *Sport and physical activities:* Compulsory sports: lacrosse, netball, rounders, tennis, swimming, gymnastics, athletics. Optional: aerobics, volleyball, basketball, cross-country, hockey, health-related fitness. Sixth form only: fencing, squash, trampolining, ice-skating, weight-training, badminton, bowling. BAGA exams offered. 1 pupil in junior England tennis squad; 2 junior regional lacrosse players; 8 district athletes; 13 county lacrosse players, 1 netball, 2 cross-country; 1st lacrosse team in National Finals Day, U14 and U15 teams are Surrey champions; U15 netball team runners-up in district tournament; tennis team Branston shield winners, finalists in Surrey league; swimming, 1 pupil achieved national gold in every stroke; badminton, finalists in Surrey Knockout Competition. *Community Service*: Pupils take bronze, silver and gold Duke of Edinburgh's Award. 6 pupils selected for British Schools Exploring Society expeditions, 1996. *Clubs and societies:* Up to 10 clubs, eg science, film, debating, Christian Union.

Uniform School uniform worn except in the sixth.

Houses/prefects Competitive houses only in junior school. Prefects and head girl – elected by school. School Council.

Religion Compulsory attendance at religious worship.

Social Drama productions and sixth-form general studies with other local schools. Trips abroad to eg Italy, Russia, Israel and Switzerland 2 ski trips. Pupils allowed to bring their own car/bike/motorbike to school. Meals self-service. No tobacco/alcohol allowed.

Discipline Any pupil involved with drugs would be instantly suspended, followed by investigation and expulsion.

Alumni association run by Miss M Sale, c/o of the school.

Former pupils Celia Imrie and Julia Ormond (actresses).

H

• HABERDASHERS' ASKE'S (Boys) 

The Haberdashers' Aske's School, Butterfly Lane, Elstree, Borehamwood, Hertfordshire WD6 3AF. Tel 0181 207 4323, Fax 0181 207 4439

• Pupils 1300 • Boys 7–18 (Day) • Girls None • Upper sixth 152 • Termly fees £1877 (Day) • HMC • Enquiries/applications to the Headmaster's Secretary

What it's like

Founded in 1690 by the Worshipful Company of Haberdashers; the original buildings were opened at Hoxton in 1692. The school moved to Elstree in 1961 and, thirteen years later, the Haberdashers' Aske's School for Girls moved to the adjoining site. The two now occupy fine grounds and playing fields in green-belt country covering about 104 acres. With the exception of the original building (Aldenham House) all were purpose-built. The result is a fine modern school with spendid facilities. Academic standards are high and results are excellent. Almost all sixth-formers go on to degree courses, including a high proportion to Oxbridge. Very strong in music, drama and art. Also has much strength in sports and games. There are no fewer than 48 clubs and societies. Extra-curricular activities are shared with the girls' school. Excellent results in the Duke of Edinburgh's Award Scheme.

School profile

Pupils Total age range 7–18; 1300 day boys. Senior department 11–18, 1100 boys. Main entry ages 7, 11 and smaller numbers at 13 and 16. Approx 5% are children of former pupils. *State school entry:* 70% intake at 11.

Entrance Own entrance exam used; Common Entrance sometimes. No special skills or religious requirements. Parents not expected to buy textbooks; maximum extras £360 (music, lunches, coaches etc). 35 pa assisted places. 12 bursaries (including at least one for music), £900–£1500. Small number of scholarships.

Parents 15+% in industry or commerce; 15+% are doctors, lawyers, etc.

Head and staff *Headmaster:* Keith Dawson, in post for 9 years. Educated at Nunthorpe Grammar School, York, and Oxford University (modern history). Previously Principal at King James's College of Henley and at Scarborough Sixth Form College; Headmaster at John Mason (Abingdon) and Head of History at Haberdashers' Aske's. *Staff:* 100 full time, 26 part time. Annual turnover 8%. Average age 39.

Exam results In 1995, 160 pupils in upper fifth, 152 in upper sixth. *GCSE:* In 1995, 153 upper fifth gained at least grade C in 8+ subjects; 7 in 5–7 subjects. *A-levels:* 34 upper sixth passed in 4+ subjects; 114 in 3; 3 in 2; and 1 in 1 subject. Average UCAS points 26.2.

University and college entrance 90% of 1995 sixth-form leavers went on to a degree course (15% after a gap year); others typically go on to art and media courses. Of those going on to university, 20% went to Oxbridge; 8% took courses in medicine, dentistry and veterinary science, 30% in science and engineering, 7% in law, 46% in humanities and social sciences, 2% in art and design, 7% in combined subjects.

Curriculum GCSE and A-levels. 22 GCSE subjects offered; 18 at A-level. 30% take science A-levels; 30% arts/humanities; 40% both. *Vocational:* Work experience available. *Computing facilities:* 3-server Nimbus network (48 stations plus CD-Rom); Apple Macintosh network (6 stations) and various PCs in departments and in library, which also has 3 CD-Rom stations. *Europe:* French, German and Spanish offered at GCSE, AS and A-level; also Italian in fifth and sixth-forms. Regular exchanges (France, Germany and Spain). European studies offered in sixth-form. European Fellow to foster European links. Work experience scheme for sixth-formers in France and Germany.

The arts (Pupils aged 11 and over) *Music:* Up to 50% of pupils learn a musical instrument; instrumental exams can be taken. Some 8 musical groups including 3 orchestras, wind band, brass ensemble, various other ensembles. *Drama & dance:* Drama offered. GCSE and LAMDA exams may be taken. Some pupils are involved in school productions and house/other productions. *Art:* On average, 45 take GCSE, 12

A-level. Pottery, photography, printing also offered.
Sport, community service and clubs (Pupils aged 11 and over) *Sport and physical activities:* Compulsory sports (first to third form): rugby, cricket. Optional: hockey, cross-country, athletics, tennis, soccer, basketball, golf, shooting, squash. RLSS, RYA exams may be taken. Water polo team in national finals. *Community service:* Pupils take bronze and silver Duke of Edinburgh's Award. CCF and community service optional for 4 years at age 14. Annual old folks' Christmas party; Mencap fun day; wide range of charitable activities, typically raising £30,000 pa. *Clubs and societies:* Over 40 clubs, eg Amnesty, archery, badminton, bridge, canoe, chess, debating, film, jazz, literary, photography, sailing, stamp, science.
Uniform School uniform worn except in the sixth.
Houses/prefects Competitive houses. Prefects, head boy, head of house and house prefects – appointed after consultation. Sixth Form Committee.
Religion Daily assemblies.
Social Extra-curricular activities shared with Haberdashers' Aske's (Girls). Organised trips to Europe and USA. Pupils allowed to bring own bike/motorbike to school. Meals self-service cafeteria. School shop. No tobacco/alcohol allowed.
Discipline Pupils failing to produce homework once might expect extra work; those caught smoking cannabis on the premises could expect exclusion from school pending enquiry and consultation with parents.
Alumni association is run by Jeremy Gibb, Secretary, Old Haberdashers' Association, c/o the School.
Former pupils Rt Hon Leon Brittan PC, QC; Martin Sorrell (WPP); Peter Oppenheimer (economist); Simon Schama (Professor of History, Harvard University); Michael Green (Carlton Communications Group); Nicholas A Serota (Director Tate Gallery); Dennis Marks (Director ENO); Damon Hill (racing driver).

• HABERDASHERS' ASKE'S (Girls)

Haberdashers' Aske's School for Girls, Aldenham Road, Elstree, Hertfordshire WD6 3BT. Tel 0181 953 4261, Fax 0181 953 5663

• Pupils 1141 • Boys None • Girls 4–18 (Day) • Upper sixth 114 • Termly fees £1155-£1380 (Day) • GSA • Enquiries/applications to the Admissions Secretary

What it's like

Founded in 1690, the school moved in 1974 to the Aldenham estate in Elstree. It is on a single, semi-rural site comprising 43 acres of fine park and woodland, adjoining the boys' school. It has first-rate modern facilities. Academic standards are very high and results are consistently excellent. All sixth-formers go on to degree courses, a very high proportion to Oxbridge. Immensely strong in music with a variety of musical groups. Drama and art are also strong. A very good range of games and sports in which high standards are achieved (several representatives at county and national level). A wide variety of activities is available, many organised jointly with the boys' school. It has an outstanding record in the Duke of Edinburgh's Award Scheme.

School profile

Pupils Total age range 4–18; 1141 day girls. Senior department 11–18, 827 girls. Main entry ages 4, 5, 11 and into sixth. Approx 2% are children of former pupils. *State school entry:* 70% main senior intake, plus 50% to sixth.
Entrance Own entrance exam used. All special skills welcomed. Parents not expected to buy textbooks; maximum extras, £100 per term. 26 pa assisted places. 6 pa academic scholarships/bursaries, £300–£1000.
Parents 15+% are doctors, lawyers, etc; 15+% in industry or commerce.
Head and staff *Headmistress:* Mrs Penelope Penney, 6 years in post. Educated at Chatelard School, Switzerland, and Bristol University (English). Previously Headmistress at Putney High and at Prendergast School. Also FRSA; member, Institute of Directors; Fellow, Institute of Management. *Staff:* 72 full time, 23 part time. Annual turnover 10%. Average age 39.
Exam results In 1995, 123 pupils in upper fifth, 114 in upper sixth. *GCSE:* In 1995, 98% upper fifth gained at least grade C in 8+ subjects; 2% in 5–7 subjects. *A-levels:* 12%

upper sixth passed in 4+ subjects; 85% in 3; 2% in 2 subjects. Average UCAS points 26.9.

University and college entrance All 1995 sixth-form leavers went on to a degree course (15% after a gap year), 25% to Oxbridge; 10% took courses in medicine, dentistry and veterinary science, 19% in science and engineering, 5% in law, 62% in humanities and social sciences (including 14% in languages), 1% in art and design, 3% in vocational subjects eg education, pharmacy.

Curriculum GCSE, AS and A-levels. 19 GCSE subjects offered; 21 at A-level. 35% take science A-levels; 35% arts/humanities; 30% both. *Vocational:* Work experience available. *Computing facilities:* Two computer rooms equipped with 70 computers and computers in most departments. *Europe:* French, German and Spanish offered at GCSE, AS and A-level; also GCSE Italian in sixth-form. All girls study French at 11, German or Spanish at 12. Regular exchanges (France, Germany and Spain). Most classes are paired with classes in France and correspond. Links with 5 schools in France, others in Germany and Spain.

The arts (Pupils age 11 and over) *Music:* Over 75% of pupils learn a musical instrument; instrumental exams can be taken. Some 20 musical groups including 3 symphonic orchestras, chamber orchestra, 2 jazz bands, 2 wind bands, 2 chamber choirs, choral society. In 1996, violin soloist in Youth Makes Music, Royal Albert Hall and Oxford organ scholarship. *Drama & dance*: Both offered. GCSE drama may be taken. Some pupils are involved in school productions and all in house/other productions. Dance: represented British Schools in Festival of Youth in Paris. *Art:* GCSE, AS and A-level taken. Design, pottery, photography, screen printing, sculpture also offered.

Sport, community service and clubs (Pupils age 11 and over) *Sport and physical activities:* Compulsory sports: lacrosse, netball, dance, gymnastics, swimming, tennis, athletics. Optional sports: badminton, fencing, trampolining, volleyball, riding, football and rifle shooting (with Haberdashers' Boys). Sixth form only: squash. RLSS exams may be taken. Lacrosse, national, regional and county players, national team finalists U18; swimming, national, county; netball, district players, national team finalists U16, regional finalists U14, U16, U18; fencing, national; athletics, county; gymnastics, national finalists. *Community service:* Pupils take bronze, silver and gold Duke of Edinburgh's Award. Community service optional and heavily subscribed. Frequent visits to local residential homes, Christmas party for 150 local elderly, Mencap Day. *Clubs and societies:* Up to 30 clubs, eg chess, debating, maths, science, Christian Union, poetry, computer, drama, gym, dance.

Uniform School uniform worn except the sixth.

Houses/prefects No competitive houses. Prefects and head girl elected by school. School council.

Religion Compulsory worship. Separate Jewish assembly twice weekly.

Social Debates, quizzes and many extra-curricular activities with Haberdashers' Aske's (Boys). Organised trips abroad. Pupils allowed to bring own car/bike to school. Meals self-service. School shop. No tobacco/alcohol allowed.

Discipline Pupils failing to produce homework might expect a reprimand; a girl smoking cannabis on the premises would be expelled.

• HABERDASHERS' MONMOUTH

Haberdashers' Monmouth School for Girls, Hereford Road, Monmouth, Gwent NP5 3XT. Tel 01600 714214, Fax 01600 772244

• Pupils 648 • Boys None • Girls 7–18 (Day/Board) • Upper sixth 68 • Termly fees £1267–£1507 (Day) £2624–£2982 (Board) • GSA • Enquiries/application to the Headmistress

What it's like

Founded in 1872, it has handsome buildings in delightful semi-rural surroundings high above the town of Monmouth – itself a most attractive place – where the school enjoys a high reputation. The site affords splendid views across the Wye Valley. It retains links with the Habderdashers' Company. It is sister school to Monmouth School, with which it shares a range af activities, not least in musical and dramatic activities and in the sixth-form. It has its own preparatory department. Being a Christian (non-denominational) foundation, there is some emphasis on religious instruction; girls attend the denomination of their choice. It has a favourable staff:pupil ratio of about 1:10. Exam results are very good and the vast majority of leavers go on to degree courses including Oxbridge. The school has a notable record in design and technology. Music is very strong indeed, with a number of ensembles. Art and drama are also very vigorously supported. Considerable emphasis on sport, games and physical education, with an impressive number of representatives at county, district and national level (particularly at lacrosse, rowing and athletics). There is a wide variety of clubs and societies and a substantial commitment to the Duke of Edinburgh's Award Scheme.

School profile

Pupils Total age range 7–18, 648 girls (518 day, 129 boarding). Senior department 11–18, 554 girls. Main entry ages 7, 11, 13 and into the sixth. Approximately 3% are children of former pupils. *State school entry:* 50% senior intake, 33% to sixth.

Entrance Own entrance exam used. No special skills or religious requirements. Parents not expected to buy textbooks; average extras £80 per term. 13 pa assisted places. 6 pa scholarships/bursaries, £311–£1245.

Parents 15% + doctors, lawyers etc; 15% + in industry/commerce. Up to 60% live within 30 miles, up to 10% overseas.

Head and staff *Headmistress:* Mrs Dorothy L Newman, 4 years in post. Educated at Wellington Girls High School and London University (English). Previously Deputy Headmistress at Haberdashers' Monmouth Girls. *Staff:* 63 full time, 16 part time. Annual turnover 3%. Average age 46.

Exam results In 1995, 83 pupils in upper fifth, 70 in upper sixth. *GCSE:* In 1995, 80 upper fifth gained at least grade C in 8 + subjects; 3 in 5–7 subjects. *A-levels:* 6% passed in 4 subjects; 85% in 3; 5% in 2; and 5% in 1 subject. Average UCAS points 20.9.

University and college entrance 93% of 1995 sixth-form leavers went on to a degree course; others typically go on to non-degree courses, art colleges or straight into work. Of those going on to university, 7% went to Oxbridge; 6% took courses in medicine, dentistry and veterinary science, 29% in science and engineering, 57% in humanities and social sciences, 3% in art and design, 7% in other subjects eg music, publishing.

Curriculum GCSE and A-levels offered. 19 subjects to GCSE, 28 to A-level (no A-level general studies). 19% take science A-levels; 52% arts/humanities; 29% both. *Vocational:* RSA CLAIT, RSA text-processing, and GCSE in both computing and IT available; also work experience. *Computing facilities:* 3 computer labs with multi-media (open at lunchtimes); 3 CD-Roms (in library and careers); word processing facilities in sixth-form block. Computer room in prep department. *Europe:* French and German offered at GCSE, AS and A-level (both compulsory aged 11–14); also Spanish GCSE and Italian GCSE and A-level; A-level Spanish and Russian through reciprocal arrangements with Monmouth School. Regular exchanges (France, Germany and Italy). German girls for a term in fifth or sixth-form.

The arts *Music:* Up to 75% pupils learn a musical instrument; instrumental exams can be taken. 14 musical groups (some joint with Monmouth School) including orchestras, choirs (senior, junior, presec and a cappella), concert bands, 4 ensembles and a sax quartet. Winner of 1994 Chandus Young Musician of the Year. 1 member of National Youth Orchestra; 2 members of National Youth Choir; have had finalists in National Youth Chamber Competition. *Drama & dance*: Pupils may take GCSE and A-level drama and theatre studies, and LAMDA. Some pupils involved in school and other productions. Ex-pupil gained Bristol Old Vic Comedy Prize, now works for Hornchurch Rep; in last six years 5 have gone to drama school and 4 in the National Youth Theatre. *Art:* On average, 46 take GCSE, 8 A-level. Design, pottery, textiles, ceramics, photography and fine art also offered. Many pupils go on to art foundation courses. Various successes in design and technology, including work in Livex 94 exhibitition, former pupil winner of De Beers Diamonds International Award.

Sport, community service and clubs *Sport and physical activities:* Compulsory sports: Lacrosse, netball, short tennis, tennis, athletics, rounders, hockey, basketball, football, softball, fitness activities, fencing, swimming, gymnastics, dance, life-saving; badminton and volleyball. Additional options for sixth-form: canoeing, aerobics, trampolining, water polo, rowing, golf, aqua-fitness, body conditioning, self-defence. 16 in U18 Welsh lacrosse team (inc captain); 15 representatives in area and 2 in county athletics (Welsh senior 200m and long jump champions); 3 in county, 1 in Welsh swimming teams; 1 girl in English golf squad and 1 in British Skiing team; U21 British orienteering champion, 2 represent Wales; 5 in British rowing squad, gold medal winners British eights rowing championships (1993–5) and U16 fours title holders. *Community service:* Pupils take bronze, silver and gold Duke of Edinburgh's Award. Community Service optional, including visiting old people in the almshouses and helping PHAB. St John's Ambulance first aid course offered. *Clubs and societies:* Up to 30 clubs including photography, computer, debating, chess, classics, history, junior quiz, public speaking, pottery, snorkelling, life class, environmental, pop, lacrosse, modern languages, Harris Society (sixth-form lecture society).

Uniform School uniform worn throughout, modified in the sixth.

Houses/prefects Competitive houses. Head girl, school and house prefects and heads of houses – elected by staff and sixth-form. School Council.

Religion Boarders encouraged to attend places of worship of their own religion.

Social Musical activities, theatrical productions and debates joint with Monmouth School. Exchanges to Carbonne and Berlin; Italian exchanges on an individual basis. Sixth form may bring cars to school. Meals self-service. School uniform shop. No tobacco/alcohol allowed.

Discipline Serious misdemeanours are treated on an individual basis, with suspension and expulsion as an option.

Boarding Sixth form have own study bedroom; 40% share; 40% in small dormitories of 3–4; 5% in dormitories of 6+. Junior houses of 24, senior of 102. Resident health care staff. Sixth form can provide and cook snacks. 2 fixed exeats each term for juniors plus discretionary ones; any weekend for older pupils. Visits allowed to local town (ranging from escorted visits for first years, to unlimited shopping visits in sixth-form).

Former pupils Jane Glover (musician), Laurie McMillan (radio newsreader)

• HAILEYBURY

Haileybury, Hertford SG13 7NU. Tel 01992 462507, Fax 01992 467603

• Pupils 586 • Boys 11–18 (Day/Board) • Girls 16–18 (Day/Board) • Upper sixth 128 • Termly fees £3075 (Day) £4240 (Board) • HMC • Enquiries/application to the Registrar

What it's like

Founded in 1862, its magnificent buildings are set in a beautiful estate of 500 acres of countryside and playing fields. The main buildings, quadrangle and terrace front were designed by William Wilkins in 1806 for the East India College; the main quadrangle forms the centre and round it are the domed Baroque-style chapel, the library, council chamber and six houses. There have been many recent additions and it has fine modern facilities. In 1942 Haileybury and the Imperial Services College combined. The school maintained the tradition of 'imperial service' well into the 1950s. The religious education aims to prepare pupils for adult membership of the C of E and some chapel services are compulsory. Girls have been admitted to the sixth-form since 1973. A large staff allows a staff:pupil ratio of about 1:8. The teaching is very good, academic standards are high and results are very good. Almost all go on to degree courses, including Oxbridge. The music department is very strong (there are several orchestras and choirs, a concert band and a pop group). Drama is also strong (10 productions are presented annually and the main school play tours Europe); and the art and design centre is very active and produces work of high quality. A wide variety of sports and games is provided and the school is well-known for its successes (numerous representatives at county and national levels). Rugby, cricket, rackets and cross-country are particular strengths. A good deal of emphasis on outdoor pursuits; a flourishing CCF; and a distinguished record in the Duke of Edinburgh's Award Scheme and in the Model United Nations.

School profile

Pupils Age range 11–18; 586 pupils, 186 day (151 boys, 13 girls); 422 boarding (363 boys, 59 girls) – boarding only from age 13. Main entry ages 13 (boys) and into sixth (boys and girls); a single class of day boys admitted at 11. Approx 7% are children of former pupils. *State school entry:* 15 boys at 11, plus 20 into the sixth.

Entrance Common Entrance and own entrance exam used. C of E school but others accepted. Parents expected to buy textbooks; music tuition, expeditions etc also extra.

Assisted places available for day entry at 11. Academic, music, art and all-rounder scholarships, 15 pa.

Parents 70+% live within 50 miles; up to 10% live overseas.

Head and staff *Master*: Stuart Westley, appointed 1996. Educated at Lancaster Royal Grammar and Oxford (law). Previously Principal of King William's College, Isle of Man, Deputy Head of Bristol Cathedral School and Housemaster and Director of Studies at Framlingham. Also member of HMC, of HMC Academic Policy Committee, HMC Inspector of Schools and member of the Institute of Management. *Staff:* 70 full time, 3 part time.

Exam results In 1995, 91 pupils in fifth, 128 in upper sixth. *GCSE:* In 1995, 86 fifth formers gained at least grade C in 8+ subjects; 4 in 6–7; and 1 in 5 or less subjects. *A-levels:* On average, 33% upper sixth pass in 4+ subjects; 53% in 3; 8% in 2 subjects. Average UCAS points 21.8.

University and college entrance 98% of 1995 sixth-form leavers went on to a degree course (30% after a gap year); others typically go on to join family business or the army. Of those going on to university, 10% went to Oxbridge; 10% took courses in medicine, dentistry and veterinary science, 25% in science and engineering, 10% in law, 50% in humanities and social sciences, 5% in art and design.

Curriculum GCSE and A-levels. 16 GCSE subjects offered; 21 at AS and A-level (plus A-level general studies). 17% take science A-levels; 58% arts/humanities; 25% both. *Computing facilities:* Technology centre has a fully-equipped computer room: all pupils do a technology course in their first year; GCSE option thereafter. *Special provision:* Extra coaching in early stages for those mildly dyslexic and overseas pupils whose written English is not strong. *Europe:* French, German and Spanish offered to GCSE, AS and A-level. 3 German boys and girls annually in lower sixth for 1 year, and other European students. Access to European TV satellite broadcasts. Exchanges and professionally-organised school visits to France, Germany and Spain.

The arts *Music:* 35% of pupils learn a musical instrument; instrumental exams can be taken. Some 10 musical groups including choral society, chapel choir, symphony orchestra, brass ensemble, concert band. *Drama & dance*: Drama offered. LAMDA exams may be taken and theatre studies as a part of A-level. Many pupils are involved in school productions and house/other productions (10 a year). Main play is taken on tour to Germany, Belgium and Holland during Easter holidays. *Art:* On average 35 take GCSE and 20 A-level art and design, 10 A-level history of art. Specialist courses for photography and 3D studies also offered for A-level. Several pupils each year gain admittance to art foundation courses.

Sport, community service and clubs *Sport and physical activities:* Games are compulsory for all pupils. Boys play rugby in the autumn term; choose from hockey, soccer, basketball, squash, cross-country and rackets in the spring term; and from cricket, athletics, swimming, tennis and sailing in the summer term. Girls play lacrosse, netball, hockey and squash during both winter terms and rounders, swimming, tennis, sailing and canoeing in the summer term. PE compulsory until upper sixth (gymnastics, athletics, trampolining, health and fitness). Also available: aerobics (step), fitness training, canoeing, fives, real tennis and scuba diving. GCSE and A-level PE and sports studies may be taken. 2 U18 international rugby players; 1 England junior fencer; many county representatives in different sports. *Community service:* Pupils take bronze, silver and gold Duke of Edinburgh's Award. CCF and community service optional. *Clubs and societies:* Over 30 clubs, eg political, Model United Nations, antiquarian, angling, bridge, cathedral, philosophical, opera, international.

Uniform School uniform worn throughout.

Houses/prefects Competitive houses. Prefects, head boy/girl, head of house and house prefects – appointed by The Master.

Religion Daily chapel and one Sunday service compulsory.

Social Geography field trips abroad, cricket tours to Australia and Barbados, orchestra and choir tours to USA and Europe, drama tours to Belgium, Germany, Holland and France. Model United Nations, skiing etc. Meals self-service. School tuck and games-equipment shops. No tobacco allowed; licensed sixth-form centre (wine and beer) for pupils 17+.

Discipline Minor disciplinary problems are dealt with by the housemaster. Bad behaviour punished by detention. Sanctions for smoking and unsupervised drinking

include gating, loss of privileges and regular reporting to authority. A pupil introducing drugs into the school may expect to be expelled.
Boarding A choice of dormitory or study-bedroom accommodation; all upper sixth have single studies or single study-bedrooms. Single-sex houses of approximately 50, same as competitive houses. Resident qualified doctor and nursing staff. Central dining hall. 5 weekends in the school year must be spent at the school: exeats otherwise freely available from 3.30pm on Saturdays until Sunday night. Visits to local town allowed with housemaster's permission.
Alumni association run by Bill Tyrwhitt-Drake, c/o the school.
Former pupils Clement Attlee (former PM); Stirling Moss (racing driver); Alan Ayckbourn (playwright); Rex Whistler (artist); Michael Bonallack (golfer); Philip Franks (actor); Lord Sainsbury (supermarkets); Lord Allenby (soldier); Lord Oaksey (judge at Nuremberg); John McCarthy (former hostage).

• HAMILTON LODGE

Hamilton Lodge School for Deaf Children, Walpole Road, Brighton, East Sussex BN2 2ET. Tel 01273 682362

• Pupils 60 • Boys 5–18 (Day/Weekly Board) • Girls 5–18 (Day/Weekly Board) • Further Education Department 3 • Termly fees £4600-£4865 (Day) £6150-£6415 (Weekly) • Enquiries/application to School Secretary

What it's like

Founded in 1945, this is a small specialist school for children who are severely or profoundly deaf but who do not have significant physical, learning or behavioural difficulties. It uses the Total Communication approach. There is a very large teaching staff, full time and part time, and a large childcare and special support staff. From the age of 16, pupils can choose courses at Brighton College of Technology and attend with support from the school staff.

School profile

Pupils Total age range 5–18, 75 pupils (boys and girls). Main entry ages 5, 7, 11. *State school entry:* 100% intake.
Entrance All pupils' fees are paid by their LEA. All children are profoundly deaf.
Head and staff *Principal:* Mrs A K Duffy, appointed 1996. *Staff:* 12 full time staff, 6 part time; plus special support staff, speech therapist etc.
Destinations Most go on to further education; occasionally to employment.
Curriculum All subjects of National Curriculum, GCSE, RSA. *Computing facilities:* 20 computers.
Sports and clubs *Sport and physical ativities*: Football, swimming, life-saving, basket-ball, hockey, squash. *Other activities*: Include: Scouts, art club, keep-fit, bowling, drama, table-tennis, first-aid, board games, cookery.
Boarding Accommodation for 60 pupils in bedrooms of 1–6. Boarding for Monday to Thursday nights.

• HAMMOND

Hammond School, Hoole Bank House, Mannings Lane, Hoole Bank, Chester CH2 2PB. Tel 01244 328542

• Pupils 120 • Boys 11–16 (Day/Board; dance/drama only) • Girls 11–16 (Day/Board) • Upper sixth for dance pupils • Termly fees £1280 (Day) £3600 (Board) • ISAI

What it's like

Hammond is both an academic school for girls, offering education to girls up to GCSE level, combined with a vocational dance and drama school which is co-educational. At 16+, senior students are specialist dance students who mostly go on to join dance companies or teach. They may be presented for A-level dance and a new academic course has been developed to allow them to study for further A-levels including music, English, art, history, maths and French. Hammond is a small, caring school where students are encouraged to work together and be considerate to others both in school and in the community outside. In addition to dance, a broad, balanced curriculum is offered together with a range of sports.

School profile

Pupils Age range 11–16, 110 pupils; 70 day girls, 40 boarders (5 boys, 35 girls). Dance and drama pupils, boys and girls; other pupils all girls. Main entry age 11. *State school entry:* 50% main intake.
Entrance Own entrance exam and dance/drama audition for specialist pupils only. Grant-aided by most LEAs. Skills in classical ballet required for dance students. 2 pa scholarships (1 academic, 1 music).
Head and staff *Headmistress:* Polly Dangerfield. Educated at Wychwood, and Simon Langton School, Canterbury; Canterbury College of Art and Bristol University (graphics and education). Previously Head of Art at Hammond and Second in Art Department at Queens Park School, Chester. *Staff:* 2 full time, 15 part time, plus dance and drama staff. Annual turnover under 1%. Average age 45.
Exam results In 1995, 34 in upper fifth. *GCSE:* In 1995, 68% fifth achieved grade C or above in 8+ subjects; 32% passed in 5–7 subjects. *A-levels:* 10% passed in 2 subjects, 60% in 1 subject; dance pupils only, who passed all they took.
University and college entrance 95% of upper fifth girls go on to A-levels or further education; senior students, who are all dance specialists, mostly go on to join dance companies or teach.
Curriculum GCSE and A-levels. 15 subjects offered to GCSE level, A-level dance for dance students. *Vocational:* Work experience available; also RSA qualifications. *Computing facilities:* 5 BBCs; network of Nimbus computers. *Europe:* French and German offered to GCSE.
The arts *Music:* Instrumental exams can be taken. Musical groups include choirs, orchestra, instrumental groups. *Drama & dance*: Drama and dance offered as specialist subjects. Majority of pupils are involved in school and house/other productions. *Art:* On average, 28 take GCSE, 2 A-level. 3D design, textiles, photography also offered. Several students accepted on foundation or degree courses in art and design.
Sport, community service and clubs *Sport and physical activities:* Compulsory sports: hockey, netball, tennis, rounders, athletics, gym, dance. BAGA exams may be taken. Welsh International athlete. *Community service:* Fund-raising for many local charities, pupils encouraged to get involved. *Clubs and societies:* Up to 5 clubs, eg explorers, music, art.
Uniform School uniform worn except in the sixth.
Houses/prefects Competitive houses for sport. Prefects, head boy/girl – elected by staff and Year 11.
Religion Attendance at religious worship not compulsory.
Social Musical events and sporting fixtures with other local schools. Biannual trip abroad (eg to Normandy, Netherlands). Meals self-service. No tobacco/alcohol allowed.
Discipline Pupils failing to produce homework once might expect a discussion with their teacher; those caught smoking cannabis on the premises might expect suspension, possibly expulsion, depending on the circumstances.
Former pupils Claire Smith (Miss Great Britain). Errol Pickford (Royal Ballet); plus many dancers.

• HAMPTON

Hampton School, Hanworth Road, Hampton, Middlesex TW12 3HD. Tel 0181 979 5526, Fax 0181 941 7368

• Pupils 940 • Boys 11–18 (Day) • Girls None • Upper sixth 144 • Termly fees £1640 (Day)
• HMC • Enquiries/application to the Headmaster

What it's like

Founded in 1557 and endowed by the will of Robert Hammond, which provided for a school room beside the parish church and for a master's salary. The present buildings, which are on a single site in a suburban area, with adjoining playing fields, date from 1939. Recent extensions and developments provide good facilities and accommodation. It is very well equipped. Staffing allows a staff:pupil ratio of about 1:12. Academic standards are high and results are very good. Most sixth-formers go on to university, including many to Oxbridge each year. An extremely strong music department and about 300 pupils learn an instrument. Considerable strength in drama and art. A high reputation in games and sports; especially rowing at which the school excels. A large number of county and international representatives in sports and games. There is a flourishing CCF and the school has a promising record in the Duke of Edinburgh's Award Scheme.

School profile

Pupils Age range 11–18; 940 day boys. Main entry ages 11, 13 and into sixth. Approx 15% are children of former pupils. *State school entry:* 75% intake at 11 (none at 13), plus 60% to sixth.

Entrance Common Entrance and own exam used. No special skills or religious requirements. Parents not expected to buy textbooks; maximum extras £120 (lunches, insurance). 15 pa assisted places. 12 pa scholarships/bursaries, 15%–35% remission of fees.

Parents 15+% are doctors, lawyers, etc; 15+% in industry or commerce; 15+% in the armed services, 15+% in the Church; 15+% in the theatre, media, music etc.

Head and staff *Headmaster:* Graham Able, in post 8 years. Educated at Worksop and universities of Cambridge (natural sciences; chemistry) and Durham (social sciences). Previously Second Master at Barnard Castle and Housemaster at Sutton Valence Also member HMC academic policy and main committees, ex-Chairman of London Division of HMC. *Staff:* 80 full time, 4 part time. Annual turnover 7%. Average age 38.

Exam results In 1995, 156 pupils in upper fifth, 136 in upper sixth. *GCSE:* in 1995, 153 upper fifth gained at least grade C in 8+ subjects; 2 in 5–7 subjects. *A-levels:* 90% upper sixth passed in 4+ subjects; 7% in 3; and 3% in 2 subjects. Average UCAS points 22.8 (including general studies, 29.9).

University and college entrance 93% of 1995 sixth-form leavers went on to a degree course (2% after a gap year); others typically go on to employment, training or retake A-levels. Of those going on to university, 18% went to Oxbridge; 3% took courses in medicine, dentistry and veterinary science, 40% in science and engineering, 2% in law, 41% in humanities and social sciences, 3% in art and design, 4% in other subjects eg clothing management, town planning, financial management.

Curriculum GCSE, AS and A-levels offered, including A-level general studies. 33% take science A-levels; 33% arts/humanities; 33% both. *Vocational:* Work experience available. *Computing facilities:* 27-station ICL network, ICL DTP system. 45 assorted PCs in different departments; Apple Macintosh (physics). *Special provision:* Some extra help in English where necessary. *Europe:* French (compulsory from 11), German, Russian and Spanish offered to GCSE, AS and A-level; sometimes Portuguese at Institute of Linguists. Regular exchanges to France (age 11–14) and Germany and Spain (sixth-form). Periodic talks from MEPs and senior EU civil servants. Occasional periods of study by European pupils temporarily resident in UK.

The arts *Music:* Over 30% of pupils learn a musical instrument; instrumental exams can be taken. Some 7 musical groups including orchestras, wind bands, choral society, various chamber groups. *Drama & dance*: Drama offered. GCSE drama and A-level theatre studies may be taken. Majority of pupils are involved in school productions. *Art:* On average, 25 take GCSE, 7 AS-level, 6 A-level. Art history also offered. Many pupils have gone on to win prizes in foundation courses and degree shows.

Sport, community service and clubs *Sport and physical activities:* Compulsory sports: one major sport per term from rugby, soccer, rowing and cricket, athletics, tennis, rowing. Optional: table tennis, swimming, fencing, basketball, badminton, squash, volleyball, cross-country. Sixth form only: sailing, golf. Soccer, pupils in Independent Schools XI; rugby, South-east U19 XV, U16 XV; cricket, HMC Schools, England U17; rowing, Great Britain U19, world medallists at least 5 junior world championships. *Community service:* Pupils take bronze, silver and gold Duke of Edinburgh's Award. CCF optional; RAF and Army sections. Community service optional. *Clubs and societies:* Over 30 clubs, from bridge to geographical, debating to war games.

Uniform School uniform worn throughout.

Houses/prefects No competitive houses. All upper sixth act as prefects; head boy and 20 senior prefects.

Religion One traditional religious assembly per week; two church services per year. Active Christian Union.
Social Drama (including joint A-level theatre studies), music, debates etc with Lady Eleanor Holles School. Exchanges with Konstanz (Germany), Fontainebleau (France). Skiing trips, expeditions etc. Pupils allowed to bring own bike/motorbike to school. Meals self-service. School shop selling limited range of tuck. No tobacco/alcohol allowed.
Discipline Pupils failing to produce homework once might expect reprimand or perhaps lunch-time detention; those caught smoking cannabis on the premises might expect expulsion.
Alumni association is run from the school.

• HARROGATE LADIES'

Harrogate Ladies' College, Clarence Drive, Harrogate, North Yorkshire HG1 2QG. Tel 01423 504543, Fax 01423 568893

• Pupils 330 • Boys None • Girls 10–18 (Day/Board/Weekly) • Upper sixth 46 • Termly fees £1995 (Day) £2995 (Board) £2920 (Weekly) • GSA • Enquiries/application to the Headmistress

What it's like

Founded in 1893, it is in a quiet residential area of Harrogate, only ten minutes' walk from the town centre and from open country. The town itself has much to offer culturally. The school's houses (7 formerly privately owned) are all set in their own gardens. It has fine modern facilities including an indoor swimming pool and design studio. A sound all-round education is offered and results are very good. There is a new sixth-form centre which offers GNVQs as well as A-levels and a variety of leisure activities; most sixth-formers go on to degree courses. Priority is given to pastoral care. The school is Church of England and has its own chapel for daily worship. There are high achievement in sports, art and music. Upper sixth-formers have their own boarding house with a greater degree of personal responsibility and freedom. There is substantial interest in the Duke of Edinburgh's Award Scheme.

School profile

Pupils Age range 10–18; 330 girls, 137 day, 193 boarding. Main entry ages 10, 11, 12, 13 and into sixth. *State school entry:* 35% main intake and into sixth.
Entrance Own entrance exam used. No special skills or religious requirements. Parents not expected to buy textbooks; extras include riding, ballet, drama. Up to 14 pa assisted places. Scholarships/bursaries, 17%–33% of fees.
Parents 15+% in industry or commerce. 30+% live within 30 miles; 28% live overseas.
Head and staff *Headmistress:* Dr Margaret J Hustler, appointed 1996. Educated at Marist Convent, London, and at Westfield and Royal Holloway colleges of London University (chemistry and biochemistry). Previously Headmistress of St Michael's, Limpsfield, Deputy Headmistress at Atherley School, Southampton, and Head of Chemistry of Lady Eleanor Holles. Also member of GSA and on National Boarding Committee of GSA. *Staff:* 32 full time, 29 part time. Annual turnover 2%. Average age 40.
Exam results In 1995, 58 in upper fifth, 42 in upper sixth (of whom 4 took GNVQ). *GCSE:* 35 gained at least C in 8+ subjects, 18 in 5–7 subjects. *A-levels:* 23 passed in 4+ subjects; 10 in 3; 2 in 2; and 2 in 1 subject. Average UCAS points 21.8 (including general studies 25.5). GNVQ: 1 distinction, 1 merit, 2 passes.
University and college entrance 90% of 1995 sixth-form leavers went on to a degree course (5% after a gap year); others typically go on to vocational courses. Of those going on to university, 8% went to Oxbridge; 10% took courses in medicine, dentistry and veterinary science, 10% in science and engineering, 6% in law, 30% in humanities and social sciences, 15% in art and design, 16% in vocational subjects eg speech therapy, land management.
Curriculum GCSE, A-levels and GNVQ. 23 subjects offered (including A-level general studies). 37% take science A-levels, 55% arts/humanities, 8% both. *Vocational:* Work experience available; also GNVQ level 3 in business. *Computing facilities:* 26 IBM

compatible stations for class use. Full-school cabled network for general use (55 machines). *Special provision:* for dyslexia and English as a second language. *Europe:* French, German and Spanish offered at GCSE and A-level. Regular exchanges (France and Germany). French, German and Spanish pupils in school. Native speaking assistant for each language.

The arts *Music:* Over 50% of pupils learn a musical instrument; instrumental exams can be taken. Some 7+ musical groups including string, woodwind, orchestra, barbershop, ad hoc. Some pupils in local youth orchestra. *Drama & dance*: Both offered. LAMDA exams may be taken. Majority of pupils are involved in school productions and all in house productions. Major productions annually; junior drama club; inter-house drama competition. *Art:* On average, 25 take GCSE, 8 A-level. Design, pottery, textiles, photography also offered.

Sport, community service and clubs *Sport and physical activities:* Netball, lacrosse, gymnastics, swimming, athletics, squash, tennis, badminton, volleyball, basketball, aerobics, yoga, subaqua, skiing and multigym training available. RLSS exams may be taken. County representatives in eg athletics, tennis, lacrosse; national team, lacrosse. *Community service:* Pupils take bronze, silver and gold Duke of Edinburgh's Award. Community service with local organisations. *Clubs and societies:* Up to 15 clubs, eg photography, amateur radio, science, drama, wind surfing, debating.

Uniform School uniform worn except in the sixth.

Houses/prefects Competitive houses. Prefects, head girl, head of house and house prefects – appointed by staff. Committee of form representatives elected by girls.

Religion Daily assembly compulsory; Sunday C of E services for boarders.

Social BAYS (British Association of Young Scientists), sixth-form society, ski trips, visits to outdoor pursuits centres, industry conference etc. Annual trips to France and Germany. Recent choir concerts in Vienna, Paris, Czech Republic and Slovakia. School shop for small items. No tobacco/alcohol allowed.

Discipline Pupils failing to produce work once might expect more work. Abuse of freedoms means restriction of privileges. Courtesy and consideration for others regarded as essential. Drug abuse would incur expulsion.

Boarding 50% have study bedroom, most shared with one other. Houses of 40–45, divided by age. Separate foundation house for under-13 year olds. 2 qualified nurses, 24-hour cover. Central dining room. Upper sixth can provide and cook some food. 2 weekend exeats each term. Visits to local town allowed.

Alumni association is run by Mrs E Wheatcroft, Westfield Farm, North Wheatley, Retford DN22 9DU.

Former pupils Diane Leather (athlete); Henrietta Shaw (1st woman Cambridge cox); Sheila Burnford (The Incredible Journey); Juliet Bremner (media journalist), Anne McIntosh MEP; Carolyn Reynolds (executive producer, Granada).

• HARROW

Harrow School, Harrow on the Hill, Harrow, Middlesex HA1 3HW. Tel 0181 869 1200

• Pupils 785 • Boys 13–18 (Board) • Girls None • Upper sixth 155 • Termly fees £4475 (Board)
• HMC • Enquiries/application to the Registrar or individual housemasters

What it's like

Founded in 1572 under a royal charter of Queen Elizabeth, it is scattered over Harrow Hill across some 360 acres. There is no campus, the school being in effect a kind of village spread along the High Street and the slopes of the Hill. Only 10 miles from the City of London, this superb environment includes a lake, a conservation area, a golf course and a farm. Several million pounds have been spent over the last 12 years to create first-class accommodation and facilities of every kind. The libraries are exceptionally well-stocked, including many rare books. There are 11 boarding houses, each with its own character, atmosphere and customs. Chapel services are based on the tradition of Anglican worship and most boys are members of the Church of England but other Christian denominations and faiths are represented. Roman Catholics are taught by a visiting Chaplain and Jewish boys by visiting Rabbi. The school has a notable reputation for its teaching and all-round academic achievements. Standards are high and results very good. Most pupils go on to degree courses, many to Oxbridge and the majority after taking a gap year. It is very strong in art and drama, and a high standard is achieved in music. There is a very extensive variety of sports and games, including polo and showjumping and many county and national representatives. There are numerous extra-curricular activities, catering for most interests. A substantial involvement with the local community.

School profile

Pupils Age range 13–18; 785 boarding boys. Main entry age 13, with some into sixth. Approx 30% are sons of former pupils. *State school entry:* 1% main intake and into sixth.

Entrance Common Entrance used. No special skills or religious requirements. Parents not expected to buy textbooks; music tuition only extra. Up to 20 pa scholarships/ bursaries, 10%–50% fees; some supplementable in cases of need.

Parents 15+% in industry or commerce; 25+% are doctors, lawyers etc; 15+% in armed services. 25+% live within 30 miles; up to 10% live overseas.

Head and staff *Head Master*: Nicholas Bomford, 5 years in post. Educated at Kelly College and Oxford (history). Previously Headmaster at Uppingham and at Monmouth, Housemaster at Wellington and Lecturer in History and Contemporary Affairs at BRNC, Dartmouth. Also FRSA; HMC Committee Member (1992); Chairman JSC HMC/IAPS (1990); governor of 5 prep schools and of Roedean and Sherborne Girls'. *Staff:* 80 full time, 36 part time (almost all music). Annual turnover 3%. Average age 37.

Exam results In 1995, 161 pupils in upper fifth, 145 in upper sixth. *GCSE:* In 1995, 147 upper fifth gained at least grade C in 8+ subjects; 13 in 5–7 subjects. *A-levels:* 22 upper sixth passed in 4+ subjects; 107 in 3; 15 in 2; and 1 in 1 subject. Average UCAS points 23.5.

University and college entrance 90% of 1995 sixth-form leavers went on to a degree course (60% after a gap year); others typically go on to armed services, agriculture. Of those going on to university, 17% went to Oxbridge; 8% took courses in medicine, dentistry and veterinary science, 30% in science and engineering, 15% in law, 35% in humanities and social sciences, 5% in art and design.

Curriculum GCSE and A-levels, 25 subjects offered. 30% take science A-levels; 50% arts/humanities; 20% both. *Vocational:* Work experience available. *Computing facilities:* Nimbus networks in computer centre and technology department. Computers in most subject departments and boarding houses. *Europe:* French, German and Spanish offered at GCSE and A-level (French GCSE compulsory); also Italian GCSE. Regular exchanges for sixth-form (France and Germany). European pupils in school.

The arts *Music:* Up to 66% of pupils learn a musical instrument; instrumental exams can be taken. Some 10+ musical groups including orchestra, wind band, concert band, string orchestra, choral society, choirs etc. Finalists in National Schools Chamber Music Competition in the past 4 years. *Drama & dance:* Drama offered. Some pupils are involved in school productions and majority in house/other productions. Strong tradition of Shakespeare production annually. *Art:* On average, 40 take GCSE, 25 A-level. Design, pottery, photography, sculpture also offered. Regular entrants to art college.

Sport, community service and clubs *Sport and physical activities:* Compulsory sports: rugby, cricket, Harrow football, expected in early years. Optional: soccer, shooting, swimming, water polo, athletics, tennis, golf, badminton, fives, rackets, squash, fencing, cross-country, archery, volleyball, basketball, karate, showjumping, polo. Wide national, county representation in various sports. *Community service:* CCF and community service optional. *Clubs and societies:* Up to 30 clubs, eg academic, art, history, aviation, chess, fishing, conservation, film, climbing.

Uniform School uniform worn throughout.

Houses/prefects Each Housemaster appoints head of house, house prefects (house monitors). School monitors appointed by Headmaster. Philathletic Club (senior boys organising games), Guild (senior boys organising cultural activities).

Religion All boys attend weekday chapel twice a week and once on Sunday; Holy Communion celebrated every day. 2 C of E chaplains, 1 part-time RC chaplain, 1 visiting Rabbi.

Social Society meetings open to other local schools; exchanges with schools in Germany, France. Joint choral works, plays with local girls' schools, etc. Visits to London for concerts, plays etc. Trips to eg Jordan, Greece, Austria, France; recent sports

tours to Zimbabwe, South Africa and Japan. Meals self-service. School shops sell clothes, books, tuck and photographic items. No tobacco allowed; sixth-form club over 17 is licensed.
Discipline Pupils failing to produce prep once might expect to repeat it plus extra work; those caught in possession of or smoking cannabis on the premises would expect expulsion.
Boarding 70% have own study bedroom, 30% share with one other. Houses of approximately 70. Resident qualified nurse and house matron. Central dining room. Pupils can use house kitchens for snacks. 2 Sunday exeats per term and half-term. Visits to local town allowed with housemaster's permission.
Alumni association is run by J D C Vargas, c/o the School.
Former pupils Churchill; King Hussein; Crown Prince Hassan; Nehru; Lord Monckton; Duke of Westminster; Sir Keith Joseph; Earl of Lichfield; Lord Deedes; Sir Robin Butler; Earl Alexander of Tunis; Sir John Clark; General Sir Peter de la Billière.

• HEATHFIELD (Ascot)

Heathfield School, London Road, Ascot, Berkshire SL5 8BQ. Tel 01344 882955
• Pupils 215 • Boys None • Girls 11–18 (Board) • Upper sixth 34 • Termly fees £4175 (Board) • GSA, BSA, SHA

What it's like

Founded in 1899 with the object of giving girls a sound education within a religious framework. The buildings consist of a handsome late Georgian house in 34 acres with good teaching facilities, excellent sports hall and comfortable boarding accommodation. Teaching and pastoral care are of a high standard, emphasis always being on individual achievement and breadth. The staff:pupil ratio is about 1:8. Results are very good and all sixth-formers go on to degree courses. There is considerable strength in music, drama and art. Games and sports are well catered for and there are many extra-curricular activities, especially at weekends. Frequent trips to London and elsewhere.

School profile

Pupils Age range 11–18; 215 boarding girls. Main entry ages 11 and into sixth. *State school entry:* 1% main intake, plus 1% to sixth.
Entrance Assessment day (Nov) followed by Common Entrance. Some academic, music and art scholarships.
Head and staff *Headmistress:* Mrs Julia Benammar, 5 years in post. Educated at Adelphi House, Manchester, and at Leeds University (French and Spanish languages and literature) and Université de Lille (L and Mès Lettres). Previously Housemistress at Wellington College (Berkshire). Also Junior Lecturer at the Université de Lille (France) 1981. *Staff:* 25 full time, 20 part time. Annual turnover 1%. Average age 37.
Exam results In 1996, 38 pupils in fifth, 34 in upper sixth. *GCSE:* In 1995, 98% pupils gained grades A–C in 8+ subjects; 2% in 5–7 subjects. *A-levels:* 94% upper sixth passed in 3+ subjects; 5% in 2 subjects. Average UCAS points 23.0.
University and college entrance All 1995 sixth-form leavers went on to a degree course (50% after a gap year), 5% to Oxbridge; 20% took courses in science and engineering, 55% in humanities and social sciences, 10% in art and design, 10% in architecture, 5% in music.
Curriculum GCSE, AS and A-levels. Approx 29 subjects offered; extra languages on demand (Welsh, Italian, Portuguese and Japanese at present). Science/arts mix of A-levels usually preferred. *Vocational:* Work experience available; also City and Guilds qualifications in cookery and RSA in word processing. *Computing facilities:* 12 Apple Macintosh, 5 BBC, 8 Archimedes. *Special provision:* Extra English periods for EFL; little for dyslexia. *Europe:* French, German, Italian and Spanish offered to GCSE, AS and A-level (French compulsory to GCSE, Spanish for 2 years). Private lessons available in Greek, Italian and Welsh. European pupils in school. Exchanges to France.
The arts *Music:* Over 75% of pupils learn a musical instrument; instrumental exams can be taken. Some 6–8 musical groups including orchestra, choirs, various string and wind groups. Pupils in county youth choir. *Drama & dance*: Both offered. GCSE and A-level theatre studies and LAMDA exams may be taken. Majority of pupils are involved in

school productions and all in house/other productions. *Art:* On average, 35 take GCSE, 8 A-level. Design, pottery, textiles, photography, art history, graphics, sculpture, calligraphy also offered. Several prize-winners in Cancer Research Art Competition exhibited at Royal College of Art.
Sport, community service and clubs *Sport and physical activities:* Compulsory sports: lacrosse, netball, gymnastics, swimming, cross-country. Optional: tennis, aerobics, fencing, squash, basketball, badminton, volleyball. BAGA exams may be taken. 7th out of 56 teams at Independent Schools One Day Event (Stonar). *Community service:* Over £8,000 raised for 5 charities at annual Christmas event. *Clubs and societies:* Up to 10 clubs, eg art, environment, photography, opera, riding, badminton, bridge.
Uniform School uniform worn except in upper sixth.
Houses/prefects Competitive houses. Prefects, head girl, head of house and house prefects – elected by school and appointed by Headmistress
Religion Attendance at religious worship compulsory.
Social Theatrical productions jointly with Eton. Upper sixth allowed to bring own car to school. Meals formal. School shop. No tobacco/alcohol allowed except limited alcohol at dinner parties.
Discipline Pupils failing to produce homework might expect extra work, an order mark, then detention. 'Any girl found in possession of drugs, under the influence of drugs or passing drugs to other girls must expect to be expelled immediately' (extract from school policy document).

• HEATHFIELD (Pinner)

Heathfield School, Beaulieu Drive, Pinner, Middlesex HA5 1NB. Tel 0181 868 2346, Fax 0181 868 4405

• Pupils 480 • Boys None • Girls 3–18 (Day) • Upper sixth 30 • Termly fees £1192–£1548 (Day)
• GSA, GPDST • Enquiries/application to the Headmistress

What it's like

Founded in 1900 in Harrow, it moved in 1982 to its present 9-acre site which offers ample playing fields including lacrosse pitches, netball and tennis courts and an athletics track. The buildings are spacious and modern and there are good up-to-date facilities including a new music school. The junior department is housed in a purpose-built wing on the same site. The school provides a strong all-round education and results are very good. Most sixth-formers go on to degree courses. The music and drama departments are strong and there are a number of extra-curricular activities. There is a range of games and sports; a number of county lacrosse players.

School profile

Pupils Total age range 3–18; 480 day girls. Senior department 11–18, 300 girls. Main entry ages 3, 4, 7, 11 and into sixth. Approx 5% are children of former pupils. *State school entry:* 33% senior intake, plus 50% to sixth.
Entrance Own entrance exam used. No special skills or religious requirements. Maximum extras, £84 per term plus lunches. 31 pa assisted places (5 at age 7, 20 at 11, 6 in sixth). Some scholarships/bursaries.
Parents 40% in industry or commerce, 30% are doctors, lawyers, etc.
Head and staff *Headmistress:* Mrs Jean Merritt, 8 years in post. Educated at Notre Dame Collegiate School, Leeds, and Hull University (history). Previously Deputy Head and Head of History at Channing and Lecturer in Education at Chelmer Institute (now Anglia Polytechnic University). *Staff:* 35 full time, 11 part time. Annual turnover 7%.
Exam results In 1995, 51 pupils in Year 11, 37 in upper sixth. *GCSE:* In 1995, 86% in Year 11 gained at least grade C in 8+ subjects; 14% in 6–7 subjects. *A-levels:* 1 upper sixth passed in 4 subjects; 32 in 3; 4 in 2; and 1 in 1 subject. Average UCAS points 20.5.
University and college entrance 95% of sixth-form leavers go on to a degree course; others typically go on to careers (eg banking), non-degree courses or art college. Of those going on to university, 3% take courses in medicine, dentistry and veterinary science, 34% in science and engineering, 60% in humanities and social sciences, 3% in art and design.
Curriculum GCSE, AS and A-levels. 17 GCSE subjects offered; 5 at AS-level; 17 at A-

level (no A-level general studies). 19% take science A-levels; 49% arts/humanities; 33% both. *Special provision:* Extra tuition. *Europe:* French and offered at GCSE, AS and A-level (French compulsory from 11 to GCSE and Spanish to age 14); GCSE German in sixth-form. Regular exchanges to France. French and Spanish nationals in school as assistants. Talks from MEPs and lectures from language department of King's College London.
The arts (Pupils aged 11 and over) *Music:* Up to 25% pupils learn a musical instrument; instrumental exams can be taken. Musical groups include orchestra, choir, string group, recorder group. 6 in LEA music college. *Drama & dance*: GCSE drama offered in sixth-form. Some pupils are involved in school productions, including joint productions with John Lyon School. *Art:* On average 4 take A-level, 2 pa usually accepted for art college.
Sport, community service and clubs (Pupils aged 11 and over) *Sport and physical activities:* Sports available: rounders, tennis, athletics, lacrosse, netball, badminton. 15 county lacrosse players. *Community service:* In sixth-form. *Clubs and societies:* Include computer, social service volunteers, public speaking, drama, discussion and Young Enterprise group.
Uniform School uniform worn except in sixth.
Houses/prefects Competitive houses. Head girl and deputy, and head of house – elected by upper part of school.
Religion Daily assembly.
Social Social service volunteers with local boys' school. Year 8 to France, Year 9 exchange with school in Paris. Trips to Spain and Germany. Pupils allowed to bring own car/bike to school. Meals self-service.
Discipline Punishment given by subject teacher and then in a line through Form Tutor and ultimately to Head. Serious transgressions would lead to parental involvement immediately.
Alumni association is run by Mr J Jethwa, c/o the school.

• HEREFORD CATHEDRAL

Hereford Cathedral School, Old Deanery, Cathedral Close, Hereford HR1 2NG. Tel 01432 363522, Fax 01432 363525

• Pupils 875 • Boys 3–18 (Day/Board) • Girls 3–18 (Day/Board) • Upper sixth 87 • Termly fees £1510 (Day) £2660 (Board) • HMC, CSA • Enquiries/application to the Headmaster's Secretary

What it's like

There is no record of a foundation date but by 1384 a school had been long established and it is a fair presumption that some form of educational establishment had always adjoined the cathedral (founded in the 7th century). It is now fully co-educational, having started as a boys' school and first admitted girls in 1970. Hereford is one of the most beautiful cathedral cities in England and the school is situated right next to the cathedral and housed in a variety of fine buildings of different periods in lovely gardens very near the Wye. A new building, the Portman Centre, housing art, technology and computing opened recently. Large playing fields are nearby. It is a C of E foundation and religious instruction and worship are an essential part of its life. The school uses the cathedral daily for assembly, as well as at other times for special services, and the cathedral choristers are members of the school. Music plays an important part in the life of the school. Academic standards are high and results good; most sixth-formers go on to degree courses. Sports and games also flourish, and there is a wide range of other curricular and extra-curricular activities.

School profile

Pupils Total age range 3–18; 875 pupils, 825 day (465 boys, 360 girls), 50 boarding (35 boys, 15 girls). Senior department 11–18; 626 pupils (333 boys, 293 girls). Main entry ages 3, 5, 7,11, 13 and into sixth. *State school entry:* 50% main senior intake, plus 10% to sixth.
Entrance Common Entrance and own entrance exam used. No special skills required. All pupils attend Christian worship. Parents not expected to buy textbooks; maximum extras £50 per term plus music tuition. 70 pa assisted places. 5 pa scholarships/bursaries at 11+; plus 2 at age 13 and 16; further music exhibitions/scholarships.

Parents 80% live within 30 miles; up to 5% live overseas.
Head and staff *Headmaster:* Dr Howard Tomlinson, 9 years in post. Educated at Ashville College and at the universities of London, Reading and Wales (history). Previously Head of History and Housemaster at Wellington College. Also A-Level Awarder in History, O&C Board. *Publications:* Guns and Government; Before the English Civil War; Religion, Politics and Society in Revolutionary England. *Staff:* 60 full time, 30 part time. Annual turnover 5%.
Exam results Average size of upper fifth 95; upper sixth 85. *GCSE:* On average, 75 pupils in upper fifth gain at least grade C in 8+ subjects. *A-levels:* 75 pupils in upper sixth pass 3 subjects. Average UCAS points 22.5.
University and college entrance 72% of 1995 sixth-form leavers went on to a degree course; others typically go on to non-degree courses eg HND agriculture, business studies, art/drama college or straight into careers. Of those going on to university, 10% went to Oxbridge; 8% took courses in medicine, dentistry and veterinary science, 20% in science and engineering, 48% in humanities and social sciences, 12% in art and design, 12% in other subjects eg music, business.
Curriculum GCSE and A-levels. 35% take science/maths A-levels; 47% take arts and humanities; 18% both. *Computing facilities:* Technology and computing building. *Europe:* French, German and Spanish offered to GCSE, AS and A-level (French compulsory from 11 to GCSE). Regular exchanges.
The arts (Pupils aged 11 and over) *Music:* 40% of pupils learn a musical instrument; instrumental exams can be taken. Over 20 musical groups including Gilbert Consort (medieval instruments), chamber choir. 3 members of National Youth Orchestra in the past 3 years; opera performed at Three Choirs Festival fringe; 3 recent pupils hold organ/choral scholarships at Oxford University; others go on to music courses at universities and music colleges each year. *Drama & dance*: Drama offered and GCSE may be taken. Some pupils are involved in school productions and majority in house/other productions. *Art:* On average, 25 take GCSE, 15 A-level. Design, pottery, textiles, photography offered also and art history A-level. A number go on to study art at university or art colleges each year.
Sport, community service and clubs (Pupils aged 11 and over) *Sport and physical activities:* Athletics, cricket, rugby, rowing, hockey (boys); hockey, netball, athletics, rowing, rounders (girls). Sixth form only: squash, badminton, golf. Several boys and girls at county and national level in various sports. *Community service:* Pupils take bronze, silver and gold Duke of Edinburgh's Award. CCF compulsory for 1 year at age 14, optional thereafter; CCF orienteering champion cadet 1993 and 1994. Community service optional. *Clubs and societies:* Over 40 clubs, eg debating (winners of Observer Mace twice), Austro-Hungarian Society (promoting European awareness), various musical groups.
Uniform School uniform worn; concessions in the sixth-form.
Houses/prefects Competitive houses. Monitors, head boy/girl, head of house and house monitors – appointed by the Headmaster and Housemasters/mistresses. School Council.
Religion Church of England foundation. Daily services at the cathedral.
Social School participates in many Hereford festivals (Three Choirs, etc). Organised trips abroad. Pupils allowed to bring own car/bike to school. Meals self-service. School shop. No tobacco/alcohol allowed.
Boarding 20% have own study bedroom. Single-sex houses, divided by age group. Resident medical staff. Central dining room. Pupils can provide and cook own food. Exeats as required – some weekly boarding. Visits to local town allowed in daylight.
Former pupils Kingsley Martin; Godfrey Winn; Sir David Roberts; Peter and Dick Richardson; Paul Thorburn; Alick Rowe; Air Marshal Sir Geoffrey Dhenin; Michael Walling; Sir Horace Cutler.

• HETHERSETT OLD HALL

Hethersett Old Hall School, Hethersett, Norwich NR9 3DW. Tel 01603 810390, Fax 01603 812094
• Pupils 248 • Boys None • Girls 7–18 (Day/Flexi-Board) • Upper sixth 22 • Termly fees £1450 (Day) £2850 (Flexi-Board) • GSA • Enquiries/application to the Headmistress

What it's like

Founded in 1928 at Hellesdon House near Norwich, it moved to its present site in 1938. The main building is a fine early Georgian house set in beautiful gardens and grounds. It and its associated buildings have been modernised and enlarged. Boarders have comfortable accommodation in the main house or the new sixth-form house. Sports and games facilities include an indoor swimming pool and new sports hall. The school is affiliated to the Church of England, but girls of other denominations are accepted. Each day starts with morning prayers for all and religious instruction is part of the curriculum at all levels. Girls are encouraged to develop Christian attitudes and ideals in their relationships. It has many of the advantages of being a small school and a happy family atmosphere prevails. There is considerable strength in music (which is much encouraged) and also in drama and art. Many sixth-form leavers go on to degree courses. A standard range of sports and games is available and there is a good variety of extra-curricular activities.

School profile

Pupils Total age range 7–18; 248 girls (182 day, 66 boarding). Senior department 11–18, 212 girls. Main entry ages, 7, 8, 11 and into sixth. 5% are children of former pupils. *State school entry:* 50% main intake, 5% to sixth.

Entrance Own entrance exam used. No special skills or religious requirements. Only parents of sixth-form expected to buy textbooks. Average extras, £50 per term. 7 pa scholarships (3 at age 11, 1 at 13, 3 to sixth) up to 50% fees. Also armed forces discount; some bursaries for existing pupils.

Parents 15+% are in the armed services; 15+% are doctors, lawyers, etc; 15% in industry or commerce; 15% farmers. 30+% live within 30 miles, less than 10% live overseas.

Head and staff *Headmistress:* Mrs Victoria Redington, in post for 13 years. Educated at Norwich High and Oxford (geography). Previously Deputy Head at All Hallow's, Ditchingham, Norfolk. Also Academic Adviser, RAF University Cadetship Selection Board; Member of Parochial Church Council and Deanery Synod. *Staff:* 20 full time, 14 part time. Annual turnover 5%. Average age 42.

Exam results On average, 38 pupils in upper fifth, 22 in upper sixth. *GCSE:* On average, 52% upper fifth gain at least grade C in 8+ subjects; 24% in 5–7; and 19% in 1–4 subjects. *A-levels:* 57% upper sixth pass in 3 subjects; 14% in 2; 21% in 1 subject (many with additional AS-level passes). Average UCAS points 15.0.

University and college entrance 88% of sixth-form leavers go on to a degree course (5% after a gap year); others typically go on to nursing, art courses, secretarial or business jobs, travelling. Of those going on to university, 1% go to Oxbridge; 10% take courses in medicine, dentistry and veterinary science, 12% in science and engineering, 6% in law, 40% in humanities and social sciences, 7% in art and design, 24% in vocational subjects eg radiotherapy, nursery nursing, finance, hotel management.

Curriculum GCSE, AS and A-levels. 17 subjects offered at GCSE, 19 at A-level (including fashion design, history of art, textiles and A-level general studies). 31% take a broad area of science/engineering and 36% arts/humanities; 32% both. *Vocational:* Work experience available; also RSA Stages 1 and 2 in word processing and typewriting; also courses in caring skills, modern cookery and IT. *Special provision:* Extra tuition for dyslexic pupils. Extra tuition in English for overseas students. *Europe:* French (taught from age 9), German and Spanish offered at GCSE, AS and A-level. Regular visits to France, Germany and Spain.

The arts (Pupils aged 11 and over) *Music:* Over 50% of pupils learn a musical instrument; instrumental exams can be taken. Several musical groups including orchestra, flute ensemble, recorder group, choirs, madrigals. Annual jazz concert. *Drama & dance*: Both offered. GCSE and A-level drama, Guildhall exams may be taken. Some pupils are involved in school productions and majority in house/other productions. Former pupils in drama school and in stage and TV work. *Art:* On average, 20 take GCSE, 3 AS-level, 5 A-level. Design, pottery, textiles, photography also offered. Pupil illustrated catalogue for exhibition at Norwich Castle Museum; another does illustrations for magazines.

Sport, community service and clubs (Pupils aged 11 and over) *Sport and physical activities:* Compulsory sports: hockey, netball, rounders, orienteering, swimming. Optional: tennis. Sixth form only: aerobics. BAGA, RLSS, CCPR exams may be taken. 2–3 pupils county hockey representatives each year. *Community service:* Pupils take bronze, silver and gold Duke of Edinburgh's Award. Community service optional at age 14+. Fund-raising for science labs for school in Ghana (library already built and stocked). *Clubs and societies:* Up to 15 clubs, eg bridge, judo, robotics, Guides, shooting, Spanish.

Uniform School uniform worn except in sixth.

Houses Competitive houses. Head girl and heads of house – appointed by headmistress and staff.

Religion Attendance at religious worship compulsory.

Social Quizzes/debates – Eastern area; theatre/music with local state and independent schools. Annual visits to Europe. Pupils may bring own car/bike to school. Meals formal for boarders only (evenings/weekends); otherwise self-service. No tobacco/alcohol allowed.

Discipline Those caught smoking or taking drugs on the premises would expect expulsion. Bullying policy in place.

Boarding 10% have own study bedrooms; 40% share with one other; 7% in dormitories of 3-6. Sixth form can provide and cook own food. Half-term plus 2 weekend exeats termly and flexible additional weekends. Visits to the local town allowed weekly from age 14+.

• HIGHGATE

Highgate School, North Road, Highgate, London N6 4AY. Tel 0181 340 1524, Fax 0181 340 7674
• Pupils 1075 • Boys 3–18 (Day) • Girls 3–7 only • Upper sixth 101 • Termly fees £1880–£2375 (Day) • HMC • Enquiries/application to the Admissions Registrar

What it's like

Founded in 1565, the main buildings are in Highgate Village. Together with the extensive grounds and playing fields adjacent to Hampstead Heath, they create a very agreeable environment. The oldest buildings are Victorian. In recent years there has been steady expansion and it is now extremely well equipped. It takes boys who have skills and talents they can contribute to the community. It is well-known for good teaching and high academic attainments. Results are very good and nearly all sixth-form leavers go on to university. Music is particularly strong. A very wide range of sports and games are available and high standards are achieved. An outstanding record in the Duke of Edinburgh's Award Scheme.

School profile

Pupils Total age range 3–18; 1075 day pupils. Senior department 13–18, 615 boys. Main entry ages 3, 7, 11, 13 and into sixth. Approx 5% are children of former pupils. 55% senior intake from own junior school. *State school entry:* 1% at 11, none at 13.

Entrance Common Entrance, interview and own exam used. No special skills or religious requirements but school is a C of E foundation. Main extras are individual music lessons. 11 pa assisted places. 8 pa scholarships, several music awards, 30 pa bursaries, up to full fees.

Parents Mostly professional people; wide social and ethnic mix.

Head and staff *Head Master*: Richard Kennedy, 8 years in post. Educated at Charterhouse and Oxford (maths and philosophy). Previously Acting Headmaster and Deputy Headmaster at Bishop's Stortford and Assistant Master at Westminster and Shrewsbury. Also member of Academy of St Martin-in-the-Fields Chorus; former Great Britain international sprinter. *Staff:* 58 full time, 2 part time.

Exam results In 1995, 124 pupils in upper fifth, 101 in upper sixth. *GCSE:* On average pupils gain at least grade C in 8.8 subjects. *A-levels:* 95% upper sixth passed in 3 or 4 subjects; and 4% in 2 subjects. Average UCAS points 23.3.

University and college entrance Virtually all 1995 sixth-form leavers went on to a degree course

Curriculum GCSE, AS and A-levels. AS-level general studies offered. *Vocational:* Work experience available. *Computing facilities:* Extensive PC and Archimedes networks and separate hardware in most departments; computer-aided design and desktop publishing. *Europe:* French, German, Russian and Spanish offered at GCSE and A-level. Regular exchanges (France and Germany). European studies offered to fifth form.

The arts (Pupils aged 11 and over) *Music:* Over 30% of pupils learn a musical instrument; instrumental exams can be taken. Some 8 musical groups including orchestras, wind band, chamber groups, choirs, dance band, rock groups. Orchestra played at the Proms; pupils appear at Covent Garden, English National Opera etc. *Drama & dance*: Drama offered and GCSE may be taken. Majority of pupils are involved in school productions and some in house/other productions. *Art:* On average, 30 take GCSE, 12 A-level; design, pottery, photography, computer graphics also offered.

Sport, community service and clubs (Pupils aged 11 and over) *Sport and physical activities:* Optional sports: football, fives, cross-country, cricket, athletics, swimming, rugby, basketball, water polo, fencing, golf, hockey, sailing, squash, tennis, canoeing, lifesaving, weight training. BAGA, RLSS exams may be taken. International representatives at athletics, fencing; county representatives at many sports. *Community service:* Pupils take bronze, silver and gold Duke of Edinburgh's Award. CCF and community service optional. Urban survival course. *Clubs and societies:* Up to 30 clubs, eg automobile, chess, debating, film, model engineering.

Uniform School uniform worn throughout.

Houses/prefects Competitive houses. Prefects – elected by pupils and staff; head boy and heads of house appointed by the Head Master and Housemasters. Sixth-form committee.

Religion Chapel once a week; separate assemblies for those of other faiths.

Social Sixth form general studies, drama, music with local girls' school. Exchange with school in Paris. Annual skiing and trips to Mediterranean (cruise), Greece, Italy, Russia (every other year). Pupils allowed to bring own car/bike/motorbike to school. All meals self-service. School shop. No tobacco/alcohol allowed.

Discipline Pupils failing to produce homework once might expect to be judged according to circumstances; those caught smoking cannabis on the premises could expect expulsion.

Alumni association is run by B H G Bennett, 79 The Ridgeway, Northaw, Potters Bar, Herts EN6 4BD.

Former pupils Gerard Manley Hopkins; John Betjeman; Gerard Hoffnung; Anthony Crosland; Howard Shelley; 2 Lord Justices of Appeal; Martin Gilbert; Anthony Green RA; Patrick Procktor RA; Roland Culver; Robin Ellis; Barry Norman; Robin Ray; Geoffrey Palmer; Philip Harben; Christopher Morahan; Robert Atkins MP.

• HOLY CHILD

Holy Child School, Sir Harry's Road, Edgbaston, Birmingham, B15 2UR. Tel 0121 440 4103/0256, Fax 0121 440 3639

• Pupils 310 • Boys 2–11 only • Girls 2–18 (Day) • Upper sixth 11 • Termly Fees £795–£1500 (Day) • GSA • Enquiries/application to the Admissions Secretary.

What it's like

Founded in 1933 by the Society of the Holy Child Jesus, it moved to its present site in 1936. It is two miles from the city centre, a very pleasant site comprising 14 acres of wooded gardens and grounds. The school is very well equipped with up-to-date facilties. As a Catholic foundation the school is committed to Christian education. All pupils attend religious education lessons and school masses on Holy Days. Academically it is very well organised and results are good. Almost all sixth-form girls go to university. Music, drama and art are well supported by a large number of pupils. There is a range of sports, games and extra-curricular activities and a substantial commitment to the Duke of Edinburgh's Award Scheme. A variety of outdoor pursuits are encouraged.

School profile

Pupils Total age range, 2–18; 310 pupils, (35 boys, 275 girls). Senior department, 11–18, girls. Main entry ages 2 (boys and girls), 11 and into sixth (girls). 5% are children of former pupils. *State school entry:* 60% intake at 11; variable to sixth.

Entrance Own entrance exam used. No special skills, but French is an advantage for 11+ entrants. Preference given to RC applications, but all religions accepted. 30 pa

assisted places (5 at age 7, 20 at 11, 2 at 13 and 3 into sixth). Scholarships/bursaries at 11 and for sixth-form; up to half fees.
Parents 15+% doctors, lawyers, etc; 15+% in industry.
Head and staff *Headmistress:* Mrs J M C Hill, 4 years in post. Educated at Rotherham High School for Girls and Cardiff University (history and education). Previously Senior Teacher at Holy Child School. *Staff:* 22 full time, 15 part time. Annual turnover 8%. Average age 40.
Exam results In 1995, 31 pupils in Year 11; 11 in upper sixth. *GCSE:* In 1995, 23 in Year 11 gained at least grade C in 8+ subjects; 9 in 5 – 7 subjects. *A-levels:* Average upper sixth passed in 3.2 subjects. Average UCAS points 19.7.
University and college entrance 90% of 1995 sixth-form leavers went on to a degree course (5% after a gap year); others typically go on to art, music or other vocational courses. Of those going on to university, 5% went to Oxbridge; 11% took courses in medicine, dentistry and veterinary science, 11% in science and engineering, 7% in law, 41% in humanities and social sciences, 4% in art and design, 26% in vocational subjects eg nursing, accountancy, business management, education, pharmacy.
Curriculum GCSE and A level. Subjects include GCSE business studies, AS and A-level Christian theology and general studies. 33% take science A-levels; 33% arts/humanities; 33% both. *Vocational:* Work experience available. *Computing facilities:* PC network; BBCs and Archimedes. *Special provision:* EFL can be arranged. Tutoring for dyslexia. *Europe:* French, German and Spanish offered at GCSE and A-level. Regular exchanges to Germany and France. Pupils from France and Spain in school. Overseas educational visits. Part of network of Catholic schools in Europe .
The arts (Pupils aged 11 and over) *Music:* Over 50% of pupils learn a musical instrument; instrumental exams can be taken. Some 6 musical groups including orchestra, choir, recorder, folk music. Winners of local music contests. *Drama & dance*: Both offered. GCSE drama and LAMDA exams may be taken. Some pupils are involved in school/house productions. LAMDA to silver and gold every year. *Art:* On average, 15 take GCSE, 6 A level.
Sport, community service and clubs (Pupils aged 11 and over) *Sports and physical activities*: Compulsory sports: hockey, netball, rounders, tennis, junior swimming. Optional: table tennis, basketball, volleyball, fencing, judo, badminton. Sixth form only: squash. *Community service:* Pupils take bronze, silver and gold Duke of Edinburgh's Award. Community service optional. *Clubs and societies:* Up to 15 clubs, eg drama, computing, bridge.
Uniform School uniform worn except in the sixth.
Houses/prefects Competitive houses. Head girl, head of house and house prefects – elected by the school. School Council.
Religion Compulsory morning assembly and Masses on Holy Days of Obligation.
Social Debates, theatre workshops. Organised trips, skiing and exchange systems; developing links with Poland and other central/East European countries. Pupils allowed to bring own car/bike to school. Lunch self-service. School shop. No tobacco/alcohol allowed.
Discipline Pupils failing to produce homework once might expect a reprimand/order mark.
Alumni association Friends of Holy Child, Mrs N Broadbridge, President, 104, Edgbaston Road, Birmingham, B12 9QA.
Former pupils Lord Chitnis (leading Liberal Peer); Karen Armstrong (writer/broadcaster); Noelle Walsh (Editor, Good Housekeeping); Ninivah Khomo (designer); Rachel Atkins (theatre/radio); Lolita Chakrabarti (theatre/radio).

• HOLY TRINITY (Bromley)

Holy Trinity College, 81 Plaistow Lane, Bromley, Kent BR1 3LL. Tel 0181 313 0399, Fax 0181 466 0151

• Pupils 550 • Boys 3–5 only. Girls 3–18 (Day) • Upper sixth 25 • Termly fees £1010–£1380 (Day) • GSA • Enquiries/application to the Headmistress

What it's like

Founded in 1886, by a small group of Trinitarian Sisters, it moved in 1888 to a big 18th-century mansion in a landscaped park of 15 acres. Since 1913 the school has expanded at regular intervals to provide increasingly up-to-date facilities and accommodation. It is now very well equipped. It has its own nursery and preparatory department. Pupils are predominantly Roman Catholic but others are accepted; religious worship is compulsory. A sound general education, with a broad curriculum, is provided and results are good. Most sixth-formers go on to degree courses. There is a commitment to local community schemes.

School profile

Pupils Total age range 3–18; 550 day pupils. Senior department 11–18, 300 girls. Main entry ages 3 (boys and girls), 5, 11, 14 and into sixth (girls). Approx 10% are children of former pupils. *State school entry:* 36% main senior intake, plus 10% to sixth.

Entrance Own entrance exam used. No special skills required; most pupils Roman Catholic but others are accepted. Parents not expected to buy textbooks; music tuition only extra (£50). Up to 3 pa academic scholarships in senior school, up to half fees; 1 pa music scholarship.

Parents 15+% in industry or commerce; 15+% are doctors, lawyers, etc. 60+% live within 30 miles.

Head and staff *Headmistress:* Mrs Doreen Bradshaw, 3 years in post. Educated at Loreto College and at the universities of Manchester (English, French, education) and Lancaster (MA). Previously First Deputy at Mount Carmel RC High School, Accrington. *Staff:* 42 full time, 14 part time. Annual turnover 10%. Average age 47.

Exam results On average, 45 pupils in year 11, 25 in year 13. *GCSE:* On average, 92% Year 11 gain at least grade C in 8+ subjects; 6% in 5–7; and 2% in 1–4 subjects. *A-levels:* 10% Year 13 pass in 4+ subjects; 70% in 3; 15% in 2; and 5% in 1 subject. Average UCAS points 17.3.

University and college entrance 92% of 1995 sixth-form leavers went on to a degree course; others typically go straight on to careers eg secretarial. Of those going on to university, 5% took courses in science and engineering, 50% in humanities and social sciences, 20% in art, drama and music, 25% in business and languages.

Curriculum GCSE and A-levels. 16 GCSE subjects offered; 18 at A-level, including general studies. 25% take science A-levels; 45% arts/humanities; 30% both. *Vocational:* Work experience available; also RSA Stage 1 in CLAIT and IT. *Computing facilities:* 25 486 IBM compatibles in 2 specialist rooms, plus 2 with CD-Rom in library and careers room. *Special provision:* Additional help on a one-to-one basis is provided as the need arises. *Europe:* French and German offered GCSE, AS and A-level. Regular exchanges to France and Germany.

The arts (Pupils aged 11 and over) *Music:* Over 30% of pupils learn a musical instrument; instrumental exams can be taken. Some 6 musical groups: orchestra, choirs, madrigal ensemble, clarinet, and recorder. *Drama & dance*: Both offered. GCSE and A-level drama exams may be taken. Majority of pupils are involved in school and house/other productions. *Art:* On average, 20 take GCSE, 4 A-level. Design and pottery also offered. All A-level group usually offered university or art college places.

Sport, community service and clubs (Pupils aged 11 and over) *Sport and physical activities:* Compulsory sports: netball, hockey, gymnastics, dance, swimming, tennis. Optional: badminton, volleyball, trampolining, aerobics, athletics. Sixth form only: bowling, riding, squash, football, lacrosse. GCSE, A-level, BAGA, RLSS exams may be taken. 2 county hockey U16 players, 1 county netball. *Community service:* Pupils take bronze, silver and gold Duke of Edinburgh's Award. Community service optional for 1 year in Year 12: high proportion help young children or the handicapped or visit the elderly. *Clubs and societies:* Up to 30 clubs, eg debating, new scientist, language, faith sharing, pond, drama, maths, careers, technology.

Uniform School uniform worn throughout.

Houses/prefects Prefects, head girl, head of house and house prefects – appointed by Head in consultation with staff and sixth-form.

Religion Religious worship compulsory.

Social Some organised functions with local schools. Trips to Europe, skiing, activity holidays. Pupils allowed to bring own car/bike/motorbike to school. Meals self-service. No tobacco/alcohol allowed.

Discipline Pupils are expected to meet homework deadlines; failure to do so could result in a range of penalties from order marks to detention (after school or Saturday). Pupils committing serious offences (drug/solvent/alcohol abuse) could expect suspension.

• HOWELL'S (Denbigh)

Howell's School, Park Street, Denbigh, Clwyd LL16 3EN. Tel 01745 813631

• Pupils 311 • Boys None • Girls 3–18 (Day/Board) • Upper sixth 32 • Termly fees £875–£2280 (Day) £1895–£3495 (Board) • GSA • Enquiries/application to the Admissions Secretary

What it's like

Its origins date from 1540 when Thomas Howell bequeathed 12,000 gold ducats to the Drapers' Company. In 1852 an Act of Parliament authorised the trust to build two girls' schools in Wales and Howell's School was opened in 1859. The Drapers' Company provides considerable support. It has very pleasant mellow grey stone buildings in delightful grounds and gardens amidst splendid countryside, some 20 miles from Snowdonia. It enjoys comfortable accommodation and excellent modern facilities. The prep department is next to the senior school. The school aims to teach the essentials of the Christian way of life and religious education (in the Anglican tradition) is part of the curriculum. It has a high academic reputation and the large staff allows a staff:pupil ratio of about 1:9. Results are very good and most sixth-formers go on to degree courses. The music, drama and art departments are strong and there is a superb arts and crafts complex. It is very well equipped for sports and games with a fine sports hall. Standards are high; hockey, lacrosse and athletics are all at county and national level. A broad range of extra-curricular activities and some success in the Duke of Edinburgh's Award Scheme.

School profile

Pupils Total age range 3–18; 311 girls (205 day, 106 boarding). Senior department 11–18, 204 girls. Main entry ages, 11 and into sixth. 10% are children of former pupils. Own prep department provides more than 20% of senior intake. *State school entry:* 25% senior intake, plus 10% to sixth.

Entrance Own entrance exam used. No special skills or religious requirements. Rental charge of £22 pa for textbooks. 15 pa assisted places; 12 pa scholarships/bursaries, £450–£5980 pa.

Parents 15+% from industry/commerce. 30+% live within 30 miles, up to 10% live overseas.

Head and staff *Headmistress:* Mrs Mary Steel, 6 years in post. Educated at Cardiff University (modern languages). Previously Deputy Head at St Margaret's, Bushey. *Staff:* 28 full time, 12 part time. Annual turnover less than 10%.

Exam results In 1995, 38 pupils in upper fifth, 24 in upper sixth. *GCSE:* In 1995, 82% upper fifth gained at least grade C in 8+ subjects; 18% in 5–7 subjects. *A-levels:* 13% upper sixth passed in 4+ subjects; 67% in 3; 13% in 2; and 8% in 1 subject. Average UCAS points 23.0.

University and college entrance All 1995 sixth-form leavers went on to a degree course; 50% took courses in science and engineering, 50% in humanities and social sciences..

Curriculum GCSE and A-levels. 20 subjects at GCSE, 19 at A-level. 25% took science A-levels; 44% arts/humanities; 31% both. *Vocational:* Work experience available. *Computing facilities:* 15 Apple Macintosh in computer centre; 6 departmental BBCs. *Special provision:* Tutor for dyslexic pupils. *Europe:* French, German and Spanish offered to GCSE, AS and A-level; also GCSE Italian and Welsh. Regular exchanges to France and Germany. Denbigh twinned with Bierbertal (Germany); school involved in cultural and sporting activities.

The arts (Pupils aged 11 and over) *Music:* 40% of pupils learn a musical instrument; instrumental exams can be taken. Some 12 musical groups including 2 choirs, wind band, orchestra, strings section, string, recorder, wind ensembles. 1 member of National Children's Orchestra, several pupils each year members of county and North Wales orchestras. *Drama & dance*: Both offered. GCSE drama, ESB, Poetry Society, LAMDA exams may be taken. Majority of pupils are involved in school productions and all in house/other productions. Poetry Society silver medals, LAMDA gold, silver and bronze

medals; 5 girls to National Youth Theatre in recent years. *Art:* On average, 58% take GCSE, 28% A-level. Design, pottery, textiles, photography also offered.
Sport, community service and clubs (Pupils aged 11 and over) *Sport and physical activities:* Compulsory sports: lacrosse, hockey, netball, tennis, rounders, athletics, swimming. Optional: badminton, squash, judo, aerobics, canoeing, sailing. GCSE, BAGA exams may be taken. 1–2 each year represent Wales at lacrosse; several county representatives each year at hockey and lacrosse; national athletics representation. *Community service:* Pupils take bronze, silver and gold Duke of Edinburgh's Award; 4 golds this year. Community service optional. *Clubs and societies:* Up to 30 clubs, eg circus, crusaders, drama, gym, art workshops, jewellery making, radio.
Uniform School uniform worn throughout.
Houses/prefects Competitive houses. Head girl and deputy (appointed by the Head), prefects (elected by the school).
Religion Attendance at religious worship compulsory.
Social Debates, dances, dinners and plays with other schools. Exchanges with France, Germany, Australia and the USA. Meals self-service. School shop. No tobacco/alcohol allowed.
Discipline Minor infringements punished by loss of privileges; smoking and drinking alcohol by suspension and possible expulsion; drug abuse by expulsion.
Boarding 12% have own study bedrooms; 25% share (with 1 other); 63% in dormitories of 6+. Houses, of approx 50, same as competitive houses. Resident qualified nurse. Pupils can provide and cook own food for snacks etc. Daily visits to the local town allowed (aged 13+).

• HOWELL'S (Llandaff)

Howell's School, Llandaff, Cardiff CF5 2YD. Tel 01222 562019, Fax 01222 578879

• Pupils 691 • Boys None • Girls 4–18 (Day) • Upper sixth 67 • Termly fees £1328 (Day) • GSA, GPDST • Enquiries/application to the Admissions Secretary

What it's like

Established in 1860, Howell's School occupies a commanding site in the cathedral village of Llandaff, a suburb of Cardiff. The splendid mid-Victorian Gothic building has been enlarged and adapted and includes a concert hall, recording studios, technology centre and indoor swimming pool. There is a sixth-form centre with ample facilities for study, leisure and teaching. A sound education in the grammar school tradition is provided and Welsh is offered throughout the school. Academic standards are high and results very good. Most sixth-formers go on to degree courses. Very strong in music and drama. A good range of games and sports in which high standards are achieved. A plentiful range of activities. Some involvement in local community schemes. Work experience and work shadowing is available, including an opportunity to take part in European work experience in Year 12.

School profile

Pupils Total age range 4–18; 691 day girls. Senior department 11–18, 554 girls. Main entry ages 4, 11 and into sixth. Approx 5–10% are children of former pupils. *State school entry:* 60% main senior intake, plus 5% to sixth.
Entrance Own entrance exam used. No special skills or religious requirements. Parents not expected to buy textbooks. 28 pa assisted places. Some scholarships and bursaries.
Parents 15+% are doctors, lawyers, etc; 15+% in industry or commerce. 80+% live within 30 miles.
Head and staff *Headmistress:* Mrs Jane Fitz, 6 years in post. Educated at Launceston High School, Tasmania, and at universities of Tasmania (biological sciences) and London (chemistry). Previously Headmistress at Notting Hill High, Second Mistress and Head of Chemistry at South Hampstead High, and Head of Chemistry at Bromley High. *Staff:* 44 full time, 17 part time. Annual turnover 5%.
Exam results In 1995, 85 pupils in Year 11, 67 in Year 13. *GCSE:* In 1995, all in Year 11 gained at least grade C in 7+ subjects. *A-levels:* 55 in Year 13 passed in 3 subjects; 8 in 2; and 4 in 1 subject. Average UCAS points 20.2.
University and college entrance 85% of 1995 sixth-form leavers went on to a degree

course, 6% to Oxbridge; 7% took courses in medicine, dentistry and veterinary science, 38% in science and engineering, 5% in law, 50% in humanities and social sciences.

Curriculum GCSE and A-levels. 18 subjects offered (no A-level general studies). 32% take science A-levels; 46% arts/humanities; 22% both. *Vocational:* Work experience available; RSA qualifications in CLAIT. *Computing facilities:* 2 computer rooms, network in maths department and a range of computers in other departments, CAD in technology workshop. *Europe:* French and German offered at GCSE, AS and A-level; also Welsh GCSE and A-level and Italian and Spanish. Regular exchanges (France and Germany). Work experience in Loire Valley for sixth-form.

The arts (Pupils aged 11 and over) *Music:* Over 50% of pupils learn a musical instrument; instrumental exams can be taken. 23 musical groups including 4 choirs, madrigal, 3 large orchestras, jazz groups, 10 chamber groups. 1 pupil member of National Youth Orchestra, 1 in National Youth Choir of GB, 1 in National Youth Orchestra of Wales. *Drama & dance*: Both offered. LAMDA exams may be taken. Majority of pupils are involved in school and house/other productions. Several girls successful in county drama each year. *Art:* Design, pottery, textiles, photography, print making, art history, sculpture, graphics also offered.

Sport, community service and clubs (Pupils aged 11 and over) *Sport and physical activities:* Compulsory sports: gymnastics, dance, hockey, lacrosse, netball, tennis, cricket, swimming, rounders, athletics. Optional: yoga, volleyball, cross-country, fencing, lifesaving, aerobics, aquarobics, football. Sixth form only: badminton, squash, rowing. GCSE sports and RLSS exams may be taken. National representatives at tennis, swimming, lacrosse, trampolining; county representatives at netball, hockey, tennis, swimming. *Community service:* Pupils take bronze, silver and gold Duke of Edinburgh's Award. Community service optional for sixth-form. *Clubs and societies:* Up to 15 clubs, eg BAYS, classics, drama, chess, conservation, various sports.

Uniform School uniform worn except the sixth.

Houses/prefects Competitive houses. Prefects, head girl, head of house; also charity and Eisteddfod secretaries.

Social Meals self-service. No tobacco/alcohol allowed. School uniform shop.

Discipline Relatively minor disciplinary matters dealt with either by the relevant member of staff or Head of Section. For a very serious disciplinary matter, such as the introduction of drugs into school, any pupil concerned will be automatically suspended and the police notified (GPDST procedure).

Alumni association is run by Mrs E. Davies, 12 Sycamore Tree Close, Radyr, Cardiff, CF4 8RT.

Former pupils Baroness Jean McFarlane (Prof of Nursing); Dr Anne-Rosalie David (Egyptologist); Audrey Bates (sport); Trudy Fraser (dress designer); Elaine Morgan (playwright); Felicity Hunt (Cambridge University's Equal Opportunities Officer); Linda Mitchell (TV presenter); Sarah Powell (BBC producer), Meriel Beattie (BBC News Reporter)

• HULME GRAMMAR (Boys)

The Hulme Grammar School for Boys, Chamber Road, Oldham, Lancashire OL8 4BX. Tel 0161 624 4497

• Pupils 810 • Boys 7–18 (Day) • Girls None • Upper sixth 81 • Termly fees up to £1183 (Day) • HMC • Enquiries/application to the Headmaster • (Bursar for financial enquiries – Tel 0161 624 8442)

What it's like

Founded in 1611 and reconstituted in 1887, it occupies a residential urban site with its own playing fields. The present buildings date from 1895, with later additions. In recent years the school has acquired a sixth-form study area, arts centre and sports hall. Facilities are now very good. The girls' school is on the same site and there is collaboration in cultural activities and some shared teaching in the sixth-form. High standards of discipline and behaviour are expected. Academic attainments are high and results good – very many go on to degree courses. Strong in music, games and sports (a lot of county and national representatives). Also strong on outdoor pursuits. Vigorous participation in local community schemes.

School profile

Pupils Total age range 7–18; 810 day boys. Senior department 11–18, 691 boys. Main entry ages 7, 11 and into sixth. Approx 5% are children of former pupils. *State school entry:* 75% main senior intake, plus 5% to sixth.

Entrance Own entrance exam used. No special skills or religious requirements. Parents not expected to buy textbooks nor pay any other extras. 30 pa assisted places plus 5 pa in sixth-form. 6 pa bursaries, £500–£1000.

Head and staff *Headmaster:* Tim Turvey, appointed in 1995. Educated at Monkton Combe and Cardiff University (biology). Previously Deputy Head at Hulme's, Director of Studies and Head of Biology at Monkton Combe and at Edinburgh Academy. *Staff:* 57 full time, 2 part time. Annual turnover 2%. Average age 35.

Exam results In 1995, 84 pupils in upper fifth (Year 11), 87 in upper sixth (Year 13). *GCSE:* In 1995, 91% upper fifth gained at least grade C in 8+ subjects. *A-levels:* 75% upper sixth passed in 4+ subjects; 13% in 3; 9% in 2; and 3% in 1 subject. Average UCAS points 18.8.

University and college entrance 95% of 1995 sixth-form leavers went on to a degree course (none take a gap year); others typically go straight on to careers. Of those going on to university, 7% went to Oxbridge; 8% took courses in medicine, dentistry and veterinary science, 30% in science and engineering, 7% in law, 45% in humanities and social sciences, 2% in art and design, 6% in vocational subjects eg PR, sports coaching.

Curriculum GCSE and A-levels. 20 GCSE subjects offered; 19 at A-level, including philosophy and general studies. 35% take science A-levels; 40% arts/humanities; 25% both. *Vocational:* Work experience available. *Computing facilities:* Computer room and many single computers in departments. *Europe:* French, German and Spanish offered at GCSE and A-level. Regular exchanges (France and Germany).

The arts (Pupils aged 11 and over) *Music:* Over 15% of pupils learn a musical instrument; instrumental exams can be taken. Some 7+ musical groups including dance band, brass band, orchestra, wind ensemble, choirs, ad hoc ensembles. Recent organ scholar (Oxford), instrumental scholars (Oxford, Cambridge, RNCM) and choral scholars. *Drama & dance*: Drama offered. Some pupils are involved in school and other productions. Several pupils are in theatre workshops locally and appear on TV and radio. *Art:* On average, 45 take GCSE, 7 A-level. Pottery, photography also offered. 1 direct entry to art school.

Sport, community service and clubs (Pupils aged 11 and over) *Sport and physical activities:* Compulsory sports: football, swimming, cricket, athletics, badminton, basketball. Optional: hockey, squash, table tennis, volleyball. Numerous sporting achievements including top five in country in swimming, squash, football, table tennis in recent years; 1 sixth-former in county cricket XI. *Community service:* Pupils take bronze, silver and gold Duke of Edinburgh's Award. CCF and community service optional. Regular charitable work by first and fifth years in particular. *Clubs and societies:* Up to 10 clubs, eg debating, cinema, chess, computers, chemistry, voluntary coaching session for sport.

Uniform School uniform worn throughout.

Houses/prefects Competitive houses. Prefects, head boy and head of house – appointed by combination of nominations and elections.

Religion Religious worship not compulsory.

Social Co-operation in music and drama (especially chamber choir) with girls' school, on same site. Skiing trip; visits eg to Austria, Florence and Vienna, and French and German exchange visits annually. Pupils allowed to bring own car to school. Meals self service. No tobacco/alcohol allowed.

Discipline Pupils failing to produce homework once might expect lines; those caught smoking cannabis on the premises could expect expulsion.

Alumni association Mr P Savic (President, OBA), 16 College Avenue, Oldham OL8 4DS.

Former pupils John Stapleton (TV journalist and presenter); Jack Tinker (Daily Mail drama critic); Andy Kershaw (TV pop music presenter); Brian Moffat (Chairman, British Steel).

• HUNTERHOUSE

Hunterhouse College, Finaghy, Belfast BT10 0LE. Tel 01232 612293

• Pupils 800 • Boys None • Girls 5–19 (Day/Board) • Upper sixth 65 • Termly fees Nil (Day – EU residents) £833 (Day – Non-EU parents) £965 (Board/Weekly – EU parents) £1798 (Board/Weekly – Non-EU parents) • Enquiries/application to the Headmistress

What it's like

Founded in 1865, formerly called Princess Gardens, it amalgamated with neighbouring Ashleigh House school in 1987. One of the oldest grammar schools for girls in Northern Ireland, it lies in a beautiful 37-acre estate of wooded parkland, gardens and playing fields 4 miles south of the centre of Belfast. The main boarding house is an elegant listed building, formerly a 'linen mansion'. The purpose-built teaching and recreational accommodation has recently undergone major renovation including a technology suite and a sixth-form centre. The prep department is on the same site. A cheerful, relaxed, but orderly, family atmosphere prevails. The pursuit of excellence is the prime aim. Strong music, art and drama with a significant number of successes in festivals by choirs, orchestral groups and individuals. Very good range of sport, games and activities. Big commitment to local community schemes and education for international understanding. An impressive record in the Duke of Edinburgh's Award Scheme.

School profile

Pupils Total age range 5–19; 800 girls, 730 day, 70 boarding. Senior department 11–19, 670 girls. Main entry ages 5, 11, 14 and into sixth. Own prep provides up to 25% of senior intake. Approx 20% are children of former pupils.

Entrance No special skills or religious requirements – all-rounders welcome. Parents of fee payers expected to buy textbooks; maximum extras approx £65 pa. No tuition fees for pupils whose parents are EU nationals (boarders fulfil resident qualification).

Parents 15+% in industry or commerce. 60+% live within 30 miles; 20+% live overseas (including GB).

Head and staff *Headmistress:* Miss Doreen Hunter, in post for 14 years. Educated at Richmond Lodge, Belfast, and at Queen's University Belfast and Reading (modern history). Previously Headmistress and Head of History, Sixth Form and Careers at Princess Gardens. Also first Chairman (Founder Member) Partnership NI Boarding Schools; Standing Committee member, Council of Queens' University and Schools; and Queen's University Education Faculty; Governor Rockport School; former Director NI Railways. *Staff:* 46 full time, 7 part time. Annual turnover 5%. Average age 42.

Exam results In 1995, 77 pupils in upper fifth, 65 in upper sixth. *GCSE:* In 1995, 70% upper fifth gained at least grade C in 8+ subjects; 20% in 5–7; and 10% in 1–4 subjects. *A-levels:* 24% upper sixth passed in 3+ subjects; 70% in 2; and 6% in 1 subject. Average UCAS points 13.5.

University and college entrance 66% of 1995 sixth-form leavers went on to a degree course (3% after a gap year); others typically go on to further education eg HND, professional training eg accountancy. Of those going on to university, 3% took courses in medicine, dentistry and veterinary science, 30% in science and engineering, 3% in law, 30% in humanities and social sciences, 1% in art and design, 30% in vocational subjects eg speech and occupational therapy.

Curriculum GCSE and A-levels. 47 subjects offered (no A-level general studies). 34% take science A-levels; 52% arts/humanities; 14% both. *Vocational:* Work experience available; also RSA Stages 1 and 2 typing. *Computing facilities:* Industry standard computer network to science, art and technology departments; 80 stations throughout; computers in all departments (designated by ICL a centre of excellence). *Special provision:* Provision made as needed, including EFL. *Europe:* French (compulsory), German and Spanish offered to GCSE and A-level. Regular exchanges to Eire, France and Germany. European studies offered to sixth-form. Active in EU conferences/competitions in Northern Ireland and beyond.

The arts (Pupils aged 11 and over) *Music:* Over 50% of pupils learn a musical instrument; instrumental exams can be taken. Some 8 musical groups: 3 choirs, 2 orchestras, choral group, wind band, recorder group. Regular winners in individual and group classes at local festivals; members of city and regional youth orchestras. *Drama & dance*: Both offered. GCSE drama, Guildhall, New Era Academy exams may be taken. Many pupils are involved in school productions and a number in house/other productions. Top marks in UK in New Era Academy bronze section. *Art:* On average, 27 take GCSE, 12 A-level. Design, pottery, textiles, photography also offered. Recent leaver internationally recognised fashion designer; national award winner in silversmithing and design.

Sport, community service and clubs (Pupils aged 11 and over) *Sport and physical activities:* Compulsory sports (during first 3 years): hockey, netball, tennis, athletics, gymnastics, dance, swimming, rounders, games skills, orienteering, basketball, badminton, table tennis. Additional options: squash, judo, riding. Sixth form only: fitness, golf. Hockey, Northern Ireland senior schools cup semi-finalists in 2 of last 3 years; badminton, semi-finalists; golf, Irish girls championships team winners; swimming, Ulster senior and British Junior Squad member; gymnastics, Commonwealth games competitor. *Community service:* Pupils take bronze, silver and gold Duke of Edinburgh's Award. Community service optional. Winners of Lions and Soroptimists Awards for voluntary service; work with handicapped, old, young and disadvantaged. *Clubs and societies:* Up to 30 clubs, eg drama, public speaking (All-Ireland successes), sports, rambling, music, technology, BAYS, Co-operation North, World Citizenship, Young Enterprise, Guides, school band, driving, work experience.

Uniform School uniform worn except in the upper sixth.

Houses/prefects Competitive houses (in sport and music). No prefects; head girl and house captains – elected by the staff and sixth-form. School Council and Students' Council.

Religion Boarders attend church (if Christian). Morning assembly is Christian but non-denominational.

Social Regular inter-school debates, sports, fund raising for charities etc. Language trips and exchanges (usually through Central Bureau for Educational Visits and Exchanges); cultural trips to Russia, London, Dublin etc; ski trips. Pupils allowed to bring own car to school. Meals formal for boarders, self-service for dayschool. School shop, tuck and second-hand uniforms. No tobacco/alcohol allowed.

Discipline Pupils failing to produce homework once might expect verbal reprimand and detention next day. Those caught smoking or with alcohol or cannabis on the premises should expect the school to take an extremely serious view.

Boarding Most are in dormitories of 4–6; seniors have cubicles for privacy. Sixth-form cottage in grounds. Houses of 40–50, divided by age group. Trained matron. Central dining room. Overseas pupils can provide and cook own food. Weekly boarding available. Visits to local town allowed.

Alumni association is run by The President, c/o the college.

Former pupils Professor Ingrid Allen (professor of neuropathology); Miss Kathleen Robb (former matron Victoria Hospital, Belfast); Miss Suzanne Lowry (journalist); Miss Judith Rodgers (Commonwealth Games athlete); Miss Heather Harper (international opera singer); Mrs Patricia McLaughlin MP; Miss Bessie Machonachie MP; Mrs Linda Steele-Goodwin (toxicologist, Bethseda Naval Hospital, USA); Ms Jane Morrice (Head of European Commission Office in Ulster).

• HURSTPIERPOINT

Hurstpierpoint College, Hurstpierpoint, Hassocks, West Sussex BN6 8JS. Tel 01273 833636

• Pupils 340 • Boys 13–18 (Day/Board) • Girls 13–18 (Day/Board) • Upper sixth 46 • Termly fees £2920 (Day) £3660 (Board) • HMC, Woodard • Enquiries/application to the Headmaster

What it's like

A Woodard school founded in 1849, it has a rural 100-acre site in the mid-Sussex countryside, 2 miles from Hurstpierpoint village and 10 miles north of Brighton. Its very attractive buildings are in the collegiate style, with two pleasant quadrangles. Many additions in the last 25 years, including a new sixth-form house, a science block, design technology centre and a sports hall. It has the advantage of being a compact and unified campus. Everything, including playing fields, is easily accessible. It is now co-educational, girls being admitted for the first time in 1995. It is pledged to C of E tradition and practice. A friendly and orderly atmosphere prevails and there are manifold opportunities for leisure and learning. There are government-sponsored Malaysian students in the sixth-form. Academic attainment is high and results very good. Most sixth-formers go on to university. A high standard also in sport and games (county and national representation). A wide range of extra-curricular activities. Very strong in music, arts and crafts and drama (oldest school Shakespearian Society). A flourishing army section CCF (the first such unit to be formed in England).

School profile

Pupils Age range 13–18; 340 pupils, 100 day, 240 boarding; girls accepted from 1995. Main entry ages 13 and into sixth. Approx 4% are children of former pupils. 20% of intake from own junior school (tel 01273 834975). *State school entry:* 2% main intake, plus 15 girls into sixth.

Entrance Common Entrance used; reports and tests for state school entrants. Pupils mainly, but not exclusively, C of E. Parents not expected to buy textbooks; maximum extras £100 pa plus music tuition and exam fees. 3–4 assisted places. 20 pa scholarships, 25%–100% of fees; plus bursaries if parental need is proven.

Parents 15 + % in industry or commerce. 80 + % live within 1 hour's drive; 10 + % live overseas.

Head and staff *Headmaster:* Stephen Meek, in post since 1995. Educated at St John's, Leatherhead, and St Andrews (history). Previously Housemaster and Head of History at Sherborne. *Staff:* 40 full time, 16 part time. Annual turnover 5%. Average age 40.

Exam results In 1995, 81 pupils in upper fifth, 46 in upper sixth. *GCSE:* In 1995, 80% upper fifth gained at least grade C in 8+ subjects. *A-levels:* Upper sixth passed an average of 3.1 subjects. Average UCAS points 20.3.

University and college entrance 90% of 1995 sixth-form leavers went on to a degree course; others typically go on to art or drama courses or straight into careers (eg banking, surveying). Of those going on to university, 6% took courses in medicine, dentistry and veterinary science, 33% in science and engineering, 60% in humanities and social sciences.

Curriculum GCSE and A-levels. 19 subjects offered (no A-level general studies). 30% took science A-levels; 46% arts/humanities; 24% both. *Vocational:* Work experience available. *Computing facilities:* Apple Macintosh and PCs in two central locations plus others throughout the school; modern multi-media department for inter-active work on video, sound and animation. *Europe:* French, German and Spanish offered at GCSE, AS and A-level. Regular exchanges. French and German pupils welcome; European scholarship to eastern area of Germany.

The arts *Music:* Over 25% of pupils learn a musical instrument; instrumental exams can be taken. Some 10 musical groups including orchestra, choir, saxophone ensemble, wind band, string quartet, brass, wind ensembles. Chapel choir quarter-finalists in Sainsbury's Choir of the Year Competition. *Drama & dance*: Drama offered. Majority of pupils are involved in school productions and house/other productions. *Art:* On average, 30 take GCSE, 5 AS-level, 10 A-level. Design, pottery, sculpture, graphic design also offered.

Sport, community service and clubs *Sport and physical activities:* Compulsory sports: (initially) rugby, hockey, cricket, swimming, athletics, netball, tennis. Optional: fencing, squash, soccer, cross-country, outdoor pursuits, trampolining, basketball, badminton, shooting, volleyball. GCSE, BAGA, RLSS, ASA exams may be taken. 9 county representatives in cricket, 9 in rugby, 7 in hockey, 2 in athletics and 3 in swimming. *Community service:* Pupils take silver Duke of Edinburgh's Award. CCF and community service optional. St John's Ambulance division provides training in first aid; pupils participate in duties in and out of school and most members hold public first aid certificate. *Clubs and societies:* Up to 15 clubs, eg clay-pigeon shooting, debating, woodwork, computing.

Uniform School uniform worn, flexible in final year.

Houses/prefects Competitive houses. Prefects and head boy appointed by Headmaster; head of house/house prefects by housemaster. School Committee.

Religion 2 weekday and 1 weekend service.

Social Theatrical and musical functions with Roedean, Farlington, St Mary's Hall and Burgess Hill schools. German school exchange annually; annual trips to Alps, Dieppe, Greece; cricket team to eg India, Barbados; rugby team to France, Vancouver and Australia; hockey to South Africa, choir to USA. Pupils allowed to bring own bike to school. Meals self-service. School shop. No tobacco allowed. Upper sixth-form bar.

Discipline Sanctions of increasing severity imposed for work and misbehaviour.
Boarding 60% have own study bedroom, 20% share; 20% are in dormitories of 6+. Houses of approximately 45. Upper sixth house of 80 single study bedrooms and social centre. Qualified nurses. Central dining room. Exeats every Sunday for the day and every second Saturday night. Visits to local town (Burgess Hill) and village (Hurstpierpoint) allowed daily; Brighton for special reasons only.
Former pupils Lord Plummer of Marylebone; Sir Brian Cartledge (UK Ambassador, Moscow); Sir Derek Day (High Commissioner in Canada); Michael York (actor); Richard Page MP.

• HUTCHESONS'

Hutchesons' Grammar School, 21 Beaton Road, Glasgow G41 4NW. Tel 0141 423 2933, Fax 0141 424 0251

• Pupils 1870 • Boys 4–18 (Day) • Girls 4–18 (Day) • Higher year 199 • Termly fees £1218 (Day) • HMC • Enquiries/application to the Rector

What it's like

The present school is the result of a merger in 1976 between the boys' school, founded in 1641, with a neighbouring girls' school, founded in 1876. It is situated in a pleasant, quiet, residential area, 3 miles from the city centre. The premises are well equipped with a new science block. Academically it is a very high-powered school with very good results. It sends most pupils to degree courses each year, including 11–12 to Oxbridge which is unusual for a Scottish school. Some vocational qualifications are offered. Very strong indeed in music, drama and art. Equally strong in sports and games with a large number of representatives at county and national level. A good range of extra-curricular activities. Some commitment to local community services.

School profile

Pupils Total age range 4–18; 1870 day pupils, 977 boys, 893 girls. Senior department 12–18, 1210 pupils (642 boys, 568 girls). Main entry ages 4, 9, 12. *State school entry:* 80% at age 12, plus 75% to sixth.
Entrance Own entrance exam used. No special skills or religious requirements. Parents expected to buy some textbooks; extras approx £200 pa (books, sports equipment). Variable number of assisted places (currently 150 in school). Some scholarships/bursaries available.
Parents 21% are in management; 14% doctors, dentists; 9% in education; 7% lawyers; 12% in accounting, finance; 6% engineers; 4% architects, surveyors.
Head and staff *Rector*: David Ward, in post for 9 years. Educated at Sedbergh and Cambridge (history). Previously Headmaster at Hulme Grammar (Boys), Deputy Headmaster at Portsmouth Grammar, Senior History Master and Librarian at City of London (Boys) and History Master and Assistant House Tutor at Wellington College. Also member, Admiralty Interview Board. Publications: Metternich and the Revolution of 1848–49; British Foreign Policy, 1815–1865 Explorations. Also articles in Journal of Contemporary History, History Today and the Contemporary Review. *Staff:* 123 full time, 19 part time. Annual turnover small.
Exam results In 1995, 197 pupils in S-grade year, 204 in Higher year (S5), 160 in A-level/CSYS year. *S-grade:* Many pupils by-pass S-grades. *Highers:* 149 pupils in S5 passed in 5+ or more subjects, 30 in 4; 15 in 3; 8 in 2; 4 in 1 subject. *A-levels:* 6 pupils passed in 4+ subjects; 18 in 3; 33 in 2; and 8 in 1 subject (in addition many take further Highers and/or CSYS).
University and college entrance 97% of 1995 sixth-form leavers went on to a degree course (8% after a gap year); others typically go on to further education or direct into employment. Of those going on to university, 8% went to Oxbridge; 15% took courses in medicine, dentistry and veterinary science, 20% in science and engineering, 8% in law, 23% in humanities and social sciences, 6% in art and design, 28% in vocational subjects eg accountancy, journalism, education, sports science.
Curriculum S-grade, Highers, CSYS and A-levels. 22 subjects offered. 46% take science A-levels; 29% arts/humanities; 25% both. *Vocational:* Work experience available; also Scotvec modules in eg home economics, sport, media studies. *Computing facilities:* Two

computer rooms with machines for S5 pupils plus a number of micros in departments; school is networked. *Europe:* French (taught from age 6), German and Spanish offered at S-grade and A-level. Regular exchanges (Germany and France). Choirs take part in festivals in France and Germany; German school choir stayed in school for 1 week and individual pupils from Europe.

The arts (Pupils aged 11 and over) *Music:* Over 30% of pupils learn a musical instrument; instrumental exams can be taken. Some 14 musical groups including orchestras, string ensemble, wind band, choirs etc. Members of National Youth Orchestra. *Drama & dance*: Both offered. Pupils have taken part in STV, BBC, Scottish Opera, Citizens' Theatre and numerous other productions over the past year. *Art:* On average, 30 take S-grade, 20 Higher, 5 A-level or CSYS. Medals won in Glasgow Art Galleries Competition.

Sport, community service and clubs (Pupils aged 11 and over) *Sport and physical activities:* Compulsory sports (up to 14): swimming, rugby, hockey, cricket, tennis, athletics, netball. Additional options (post-14): rowing, soccer, squash, table tennis, badminton, golf, curling, fencing, judo, volleyball, basketball. Scotvec modules may be taken. International representatives in schools hockey, rugby, swimming, athletics, judo, rowing. *Community service:* Pupils take silver and gold Duke of Edinburgh's Award. Community service optional. *Clubs and societies:* Up to 15 clubs, eg ornithology, literary and debating, photography, drama, media studies, electronics, radio station, Christian Union, bridge, chess.

Uniform School uniform worn throughout.

Houses/prefects Competitive houses. Prefects and head boy/girl – elected by the staff. School Council.

Religion Assembly 4 mornings a week (reading, prayer, hymn). Separate Jewish assembly most days (some 150 Jewish pupils, 50 Muslims in school).

Social Debates with other local schools. Easter trip to Black Forest; skiing trip to Switzerland; exchange with Nürnberg (Germany) for 20 pupils and St Omer (France) for 15 pupils; May trips to Normandy beaches and First World War battlefields. Rugby trip to France. Pupils allowed to bring own car/bike/motorbike to school. Meals self-service. No tobacco/alcohol allowed.

Discipline Detention, report card for parental signature, school-based community work at weekends. For most serious offences, suspension is used, the pupil having to come in for the same number of days in the holidays.

Alumni association run by Mrs Anne Brown, FP Registrar, at the school.

Former pupils Prof Muriel Bradbrook (Shakespearean scholar); John Buchan (novelist); Lord Manuel Kissen (judge); R D Laing (psychotherapist); James Maxton MP; Winnie Wooldridge (tennis international); Ken Bruce (Radio 2 presenter); Prof Robert Crawford (poet); Lady Marion Fraser (Chair, Christian Aid UK); Sir R Russell Hillhouse (Scottish Office); Lord Irvine of Lairg (QC); Lord McColl of Dulwich (Prof of Surgery at Guy's); Lord Macfadyen (judge); Carol Smillie (television personality); Baroness Smith of Gilmorehill; Adair Turner (Director General, CBI).

• HYMERS

Hymers College, Hymers Avenue, Hull HU3 1LW. Tel 01482 343555, 01482 472854

• Pupils 947 • Boys 8–18 (Day) • Girls 8–18 (Day) • Upper sixth 105 • Termly fees £1041–£1185 • HMC • Enquiries/application to the Headmaster

What it's like

Founded in 1893, it is single-site and urban. Solid, late Victorian and Edwardian buildings are situated on a 35-acre estate of the former Hull botanic gardens, half a mile from the centre of the city. There has been a lot of recent development and very good facilities are provided. Firm discipline and high academic standards are insisted on and the need for full parental involvement in the school is stressed. A well-developed pastoral system monitors every pupil's progress. Originally a boys' school, it has been fully co-educational since 1989. Results are very good and most pupils go on to degree courses each year, including Oxbridge. The music, drama and art departments are impressively active and a large number of people are engaged. High standards prevail in sport and games (there are many county representatives). A plentiful range of extra-curricular activities and some emphasis on outdoor pursuits. A distinguished record in the Duke of Edinburgh's Award Scheme.

School profile

Pupils Total age range 8–18; 947 day pupils, 587 boys, 360 girls (fully co-educational from 1989). Senior department 11–18, 747 pupils (452 boys, 295 girls). Main entry ages 8, 9, 11 and into sixth. Approx 20% are children of former pupils. *State school entry:* 20% main senior intake, plus 50% to sixth.

Entrance Own entrance exam used. No special skills or religious requirements. Parents not expected to buy textbooks; trips, theatre etc extra. 25 pa assisted places. Some bursaries.

Parents 15+% are doctors, lawyers, etc; 15+% in industry or commerce.

Head and staff *Headmaster:* John Morris, 6 years in post. Educated at Leighton Park and Oxford (modern history). Previously Deputy Head and Head of History at Hymers and Assistant Teacher, Housemaster and master i/c rugby at Woolverstone Hall, Suffolk. *Staff:* 56 full time, 5 part time. Turnover 3%. Average age 35–40.

Exam results In 1995, 105 pupils in Year 11, 91 in upper sixth. *GCSE:* In 1995, all upper fifth gained at least grade C in 5+ subjects. *A-levels:* 55 upper sixth passed in 4+ subjects; 28 in 3; 6 in 2; and 2 in 1 subject. Average UCAS points 21.8 (including general studies 26.5).

University and college entrance 96% of 1995 sixth-form leavers went on to a degree course; others typically go on to non-degree courses, art colleges or straight into employment. Of those going on to university, 10% went to Oxbridge; 6% took courses in medicine, dentistry and veterinary science, 35% in science and engineering, 50% in humanities and social sciences, 5% in art and design, 4% in other subjects eg music.

Curriculum GCSE and A-levels. 16 subjects offered (including general studies). 35% take science A-levels; 40% arts/humanities; 25% both. *Vocational:* Work experience available; also City and Guilds qualification in computing. *Computing facilities:* 2 computer rooms (30+ machines); computers in most departments. *Europe:* French, German and Spanish offered at GCSE and A-level (French in junior school).

The arts (Pupils aged 11 and over) *Music:* Over 30% of pupils learn a musical instrument; instrumental exams can be taken. Some 17 musical groups including orchestra, wind bands, string groups, many choirs, madrigal group etc. 4 members of National Brass Band, 1 member of National Children's Orchestra. *Drama & dance:* Drama offered and GCSE may be taken. Some pupils are involved in school productions. *Art:* On average, 20 take GCSE, 10 A-level.

Sport, community service and clubs (Pupils aged 11 and over) *Sport and physical activities:* Compulsory sports: rugby, cricket (boys); hockey, netball, rounders (girls). Optional: tennis, basketball, squash, swimming, athletics, badminton, fencing, cross-country. County and regional representatives in rugby, cricket, hockey, U18 national triallist; national finals, fencing. England U18 and U16 rugby representation. *Community service:* Pupils take bronze, silver and gold Duke of Edinburgh's Award. ACF and community service optional. *Clubs and societies:* Up to 30 clubs, eg environment, chess, music, drama, technology, Christian Union, various sports.

Uniform School uniform worn throughout.

Houses/prefects No competitive houses. Prefects, head boy/girl – appointed by Headmaster in consultation with staff.

Religion Daily (non-denominational) assembly for whole school.

Social No organised functions with other schools. Organised trips abroad. Pupils allowed to bring own car/bike/motorbike to school. Meals self-service. School tuck shop. No tobacco/alcohol allowed.

Discipline Pupils failing to produce homework once might expect detention; those caught smoking cannabis on the premises might expect expulsion.

Alumni association is run by Mr J R Fewlass, 10 Hall Walk, Welton, Brough, North Humberside.

I

• INTERNATIONAL (Amsterdam)

International School of Amsterdam, Sportlaan 45, 1185 TB Amstelveen, Amsterdam, The Netherlands. Tel 31 20 642 22 27, Fax 31 20 642 89 28

• Pupils 550 • Boys 3–19 (Day) • Girls 3–19 (Day) • Upper sixth 31 • Fees charged for the year FL 16,000–FL 27,400 • ECIS • Enquiries and applications to the Admission Officer

What it's like

Founded in 1964, it has recently moved to a purpose-built complex on a new campus, minutes from the centre of Amsterdam. It is well-equipped with a theatre, computer centres, large library/media centre and specialised rooms for music, drama and art. There is an on-site gymnasium and excellent sports facilities nearby. The school was founded as a co-educational school and is non-sectarian. The language of instruction is English but the school has many nationalities (36) among pupils and staff. The curriculum follows Anglo-American models with some adaptation, and also offers the International Baccalaureate. The school regards its programmes as an experience in world living and aims to prepare students to enter or re-enter the educational systems of their home countries with minimal adjustment. The staff:pupil ratio is very favourable (about 1:7), which allows individual attention. Standards are high and results most creditable. Most leavers go on to degree courses in countries all over the world. Music and drama are well supported. There is an active physical education programme for all ages. A wide variety of extra-curricular activities is available and there are frequent excursions and trips. Considerable use is made of the cultural resources of Amsterdam. There has been a successful commitment to the Duke of Edinburgh's Award Scheme and pupils participate in local community schemes.

School profile

Pupils Total age range 3–19; 550 day pupils (250 boys, 300 girls). Senior department 12–19; 243 pupils (123 boys, 120 girls). Main entry ages 3, 7, 12 and 15.

Entrance No entrance exams. No special skills or religious requirements. No extras; parents not expected to buy textbooks.

Parents The majority are in business.

Head and staff *Director*: Margaret Armstrong-Law. Educated at North Dakota State, Michigan and California universities. Previously Secondary Head at Vienna International School and Principal of the Secondary School at Taipei American School (Taiwan). *Staff:* 75 full time, 14 part time. Annual turnover 10%. Average age 35.

Exam results On average, 44 in upper fifth, 40 in upper sixth. All pupils pass the IB in 5+ subjects.

University and college entrance 90% of 1995 sixth-form leavers went on to a degree course throughout the world (5% after a gap year); others typically go on to art or music colleges. Of those going on to university, 5% went to Oxbridge; 5% took courses in medicine, dentistry and veterinary science, 10% in science and engineering, 25% in law, 40% in humanities and social sciences, 10% in art and design, 10% in other subjects eg music.

Curriculum IB Middle Years Programme and International Baccalaureate. 19 subjects offered, including Japanese. *Computing facilities:* Over 200 computers in 3 computer labs and 1 ESL computer lab. *Special provision:* ESL programme; special educational needs department. *Europe:* Dutch, French and German IB offered. Many other languages taught at after-school tutorials.

The arts (Pupils aged 11 and over) *Music:* Over 20% of pupils learn a musical instrument; instrumental exams can be taken. 4 musical groups, including an orchestra ensemble and 2 choirs. *Drama & dance*: Both offered. IB level drama exams may be taken. Majority of pupils are involved in school productions. *Art:* On average, 35 take IB level. Design, pottery, photography also offered.

Sport, community service and clubs (Pupils aged 11 and over) *Sport and physical*

activities: PE compulsory. Optional: soccer, basketball, volleyball, athletics, swimming. *Community service:* Pupils take bronze, silver and gold Duke of Edinburgh's Award (4 pupils have completed gold). Community service compulsory in sixth-form. *Clubs and societies:* Up to 15 clubs, eg computer, dance, chess, debating, photography, aerobics, piano, first aid.
Uniform No uniform.
Houses/prefects No competitive houses or prefects. School council.
Religion No religious worship.
Social Mathematics, debating, drama, music and sporting activities with other local schools. Organised trips abroad to eg Denmark (art); Brittany (geography); Austria (skiing); Tasmania (science); summer service trips to Tanzania. Pupils allowed to bring own car/bike/motorbike to school. No tobacco/alcohol allowed.
Alumni association run by Don Morton, c/o the school.

• INTERNATIONAL (Antwerp)

Antwerp International School, Veltwijcklaan 180, B2180 Ekeren, Belgium. Tel 32 3 541 6047
• Pupils 600 • Boys 3–18 (Day) • Girls 3–18 (Day) • Upper sixth Yes • Termly fees BF 261,000 (Day) • ECIS • Enquiries/application to the Admissions Officer

What it's like

Founded in 1967, it enjoys a 7-acre campus in a quiet neighbourhood in the suburbs and comprises five modern, well-equipped and comfortable buildings. It is a community centre for the expatriate community, and is well respected and very active. Pupils are approximately 25% North American, 25% British and the balance from 35 other nationalities. A traditional education is provided. The school year comprises two semesters and four quarters, between September and mid-June. The academic programme of the secondary school tries to meet the needs of those bound for university and those who are not. It includes preparation for the IGCSE and the International Baccalaureate. There is a favourable staff:pupil ratio of 1:10 which permits a good deal of individual attention. Academic results are good and the vast majority go on to universities in Europe or the USA. Art, music and drama are well provided for (a fine arts programme is particularly popular) and three plays a year are presented in the purpose-built theatre. There are plentiful extra-curricular activities. Some 50% of pupils take part in non-compulsory sport and games. Field trips to European destinations are also organised and ample use is made of the cultural facilities of Antwerp.

School profile

Pupils Total age range 3–18; 600 day pupils (310 boys, 290 girls). Entry at any stage.
Entrance No entrance exam. No special skills or religious requirements. Parents not expected to buy textbooks. Bursaries for 7% of pupils, 10%–35% of fees.
Parents Mostly in industry.
Head and staff *Headmaster:* Robert F Schaecher, 12 years in post. Educated at St Mary's College, California, and at California University (economics, education, business and school administration). Previously Vice-Principal at Roosevelt School, Principal at David Avenue School and at the American School in London (lower division). Also Chairman Northwest Council of International Schools; Board Member of American Belgian Association and the European Council of International Schools. *Staff:* 50 full time, 15 part time. Annual turnover 5%. Average age 38.
Exam results 17 subjects offered. *IGCSE:* In 1995, 12% gained grade C or above in 8+ subjects; 53% in 5–7 subjects. IB: 15 attempted, and 13 obtained, the IB diploma.
University and college entrance 95% of sixth-form leavers go on to a degree course in Europe or the United States.
Curriculum IGCSE and International Baccalaureate. *Computing facilities:* Three computer labs, one mini-lab; computers available in classrooms and library. Special provisions: Learning specialists available. EFL programme. *Europe:* Dutch and French offered from age 8, German from 14; one language other than English is mandatory. Model United Nations; week-long European study programmes.
The arts (Pupils aged 11 and over) *Music:* Over 15% of pupils learn a musical instrument. Some 4 musical groups including choirs, vocal ensembles. *Drama &*

dance: Drama offered. Majority of pupils are involved in school productions. Group productions of musicals and plays. *Art:* IB art & design offered. Design, pottery, textiles, photography, art history also offered.
Sport, community service and clubs (Pupils aged 11 and over) *Sport and physical activities:* Compulsory sports: PE up to 10th grade. North European Community of International Schools, and International Schools level in volleyball, soccer, basketball, athletics, swimming, tennis. *Community service:* Community service compulsory. *Clubs and societies:* Some 5 clubs, eg chess, science, yearbook.
Uniform No uniform.
Houses/prefects No competitive houses or prefects. Student Council, with class representatives.
Religion No religious worship during the school day.
Social Interscholastic speech and debate, mathematics, science, chess, orchestra, choir, drama and sports. Grades 6–12 take one-week field trips in Europe. Pupils allowed to bring own car/bike/motorbike to school. Lunch self service. Tobacco allowed with permission; no alcohol.
Discipline Pupils failing to produce homework once might get detention or have to make up work; drugs not tolerated.

• INTERNATIONAL (Milan)

International School of Milan, via Bezzola 6, 20153 Milan, Italy. Tel 39 2 40910067
• Pupils 800 • Boys 3–18 (Day) • Girls 3–18 (Day) • Upper sixth 34 • Termly fees up to Lit 4,500,000 (Day) • ECIS • Enquiries/application to the Headmaster

What it's like

Founded in 1958, as a co-educational school. It has four main urban sites (accommodating kindergarten, elementary, middle and high schools) five minutes from each other; and there are two satellite elementary schools in Monza and Milano 3. All are very well equipped and school buses transport pupils daily. The school has an international curriculum based on the British system and the pupils come from over 50 nationalities. The lower-school classes are self-contained and the emphasis is on small groups and individual instruction. The high-school programme leads to IGCSE and International Baccalaureate. The school year runs from September to late June. The environment is lively and active and the declared aim of the school is to combine a high level of academic attainment with a wide range of activities. A favourable staff:pupil ratio of 1:11. Academic standards are high and results impressive. Almost all sixth-form leavers proceed to degree courses. Music and drama are extremely strong. There is keen interest in sports and games (particularly soccer, basketball, volleyball and athletics). Educational visits are an essential feature of the programme and there is an annual ski week. There is great commitment among pupils to local community schemes.

School profile

Pupils Total age range 3–18; 800+ day pupils (410 boys, 390 girls). Senior department 10–18; 340 pupils (175 boys, 165 girls). Entry at any age, including the sixth. 4% are children of former pupils.
Entrance Own exam for students not previously instructed in English or who have taken exams other than UK-based ones. No special skills nor religious requirements. Average extras Lit 600,000; parents expected to buy textbooks. No scholarships or bursaries.
Parents 25+% are doctors, lawyers, etc; 25+% in industry; 20+% in diplomatic corps.
Head and staff *Headmaster:* Terence Haywood, 11 years in post. Educated at Hyde Grammar School and universities of Oxford (physics) and Cambridge (education). Previously Deputy Head. Also published articles on international education and professional development (International Schools Journal); various offices within British Heads Group of ECIS, member of its accreditation training team and member of its Board of Directors. *Staff:* 69 full time, 8 part time. Annual turnover 8%. Average age 34.
Exam results On average, 39 in upper fifth, 34 in upper sixth. *IGCSE:* On average, 80% upper fifth gained at least grade C in 8+ subjects; 15% in 5–7 subjects. IB: In 1995, average IB score 34.

University and college entrance 95% of 1995 sixth-form leavers went on to a degree course (10% after a gap year); others typically go directly into work or military service. Of those going on to university, 3% went to Oxbridge; 20% took courses in medicine, dentistry and veterinary science, 20% in science and engineering, 10% in law, 20% in humanities and social sciences, 10% in art and design, 20% vocational subjects eg business, economics.
Curriculum IGCSE and International Baccalaureate. 12 subjects offered. *Vocational:* Short work experience available. *Computing facilities:* Computer labs in elementary, middle and high school. *Special provision:* Extensive ESL support available (specialists in every main site). Some help for students with dyslexia and mild learning difficulties, but not for any serious disadvantage. *Europe:* French, German and Italian offered to IGCSE and IB. Private IB tuition for Spanish, Portuguese, Swedish, Dutch and any native language by arrangement. Regular exchanges (France and UK). Many field trips and sports exchanges.
The arts (Pupils aged 11 and over) *Music:* Over 30% of pupils learn a musical instrument. 3 musical groups. *Drama & dance*: Both offered. Drama IGCSE may be taken and also as part of IB. Some pupils are involved in school productions and all in house/other productions. Romeo and Juliet recently taken to Edinburgh Festival Fringe. *Art:* On average, 20 take IGCSE, 10 IB. Design, photography also offered. Several pupils now at art college.
Sport, community service and clubs (Pupils aged 11 and over) *Sport and physical activities:* Compulsory sports: soccer, basketball, volleyball, gymnastics, athletics, swimming. Optional: squash, tennis. Soccer teams in local league; many competitions against other international schools. *Community service:* Community service compulsory for 2 years at age 17. *Clubs and societies:* Up to 10 clubs, eg music, various sports, school newspaper, debating, etc.
Uniform No uniform.
Houses/prefects Competitive houses in lower school only. No prefects. School Council.
Religion Attendance at religious worship not compulsory.
Social Sports and drama exchanges (international), geography/biology fieldwork (to Switzerland/France) and important class trips in middle school. Pupils allowed to bring own car/bike/motorbike to school. Meals self -service. School shop. No tobacco/alcohol allowed.
Discipline Pupils failing to produce homework once would expect detention; those caught smoking cannabis on the premises would be expelled (no possibility of appeal).

• INTERNATIONAL (Paris)

International School of Paris, High School and Business Office, 6, rue Beethoven, 75016 Paris, France. Tel 33 1 42 24 09 54, Fax 33 1 45 27 15 93

• Pupils 350 • Boys 4–18 (Day) • Girls 4–18 (Day) • Upper sixth 50 • Fees charged for the year F 32,000–F 80,500 (Day) • HMC, ECIS, NEASC • Enquiries/application to Headmaster

What it's like

Founded in 1964 with six pupils and two teachers, it has grown swiftly to a strength of 350 pupils with 50–60 staff. The premises (in central Paris, the 16th arrondissement) consist of two handsome private houses and a former art school in the residential area between the Seine and the Bois de Boulogne. Nearby, too, are a sports field, swimming pool and other recreational facilities. It is an HMC school with representatives from forty nationalities (twenty different nationalities on the teaching staff) and offers an Anglo-American international curriculum from kindergarten to 12th grade. Pupils are prepared for the IGCSE and the International Baccalaureate. The language of instruction is English and there is much emphasis on the French programme (language, history and culture). Classes are small (20 maximum); students fluent in English are required to study French as a second language and may study German as a third language in grades 8–10. A very favourable staff:pupil ratio of about 1:7 permits much individual attention. Academic standards are high and results good. Most leavers go on to degree courses. Music, drama and art are all strong. Sports and games are reasonably well catered for and there are many extra-curricular activities which make full use of the resources of the city.

School profile

Pupils Total age range 4–18; 350 pupils, 160 boys, 190 girls. Senior department 11–18.
Entrance Pupils admitted throughout school year on basis of school reports, examples of writing (for native English speakers) and interview; if abroad, by provisional admission confirmed when in Paris.
Parents Very international, at least 40 nationalities.
Head and staff *Headmaster:* Nigel Prentki. Educated at Cheltenham College and Oxford (modern languages). Previously Head of Modern Languages, Housemaster and Master i/c Association Football at Haileybury. Publications: Translations of Huis Clos (J–P Sartre) and Mauser (Hainer Müller). *Staff:* 20 nationalities represented.
Exam results In 1995, 50 pupils in upper sixth. Seniors either take the IB (96% success in 1995) or the ISP (US) High School Diploma.
University and college entrance 95% of 1995 sixth-form leavers went on to a degree course (5% after a gap year); others typically go on to work. Of those going on to university, 2% went to Oxbridge; 5% took courses in medicine, dentistry and veterinary science, 20% in science and engineering, 5% in law, 50% in humanities and social sciences, 5% in art and design, 15% in other subjects eg maths, business.
Curriculum An Anglo-American curriculum leading to the IGCSE and the IB, meeting US High School credit requirements. Seniors either take the IB or the ISP (US) High School Diploma. *Europe:* French (compulsory from age 5) and German offered to IGCSE and IB; Russian and Swedish (as well as Hindi and Japanese) also offered to IB.
The arts (Pupils aged 11 and over) *Music:* Keyboard taught in class music lessons. 1 pupil in International Schools Choir. *Drama & dance*: Drama offered. Some pupils are involved in school productions. Regular participants in International Schools Theatre Association Festivals. *Art:* On average, 15 take GCSE, 12 take IB. Design, pottery, sculpture also offered. Several pupils have gone on to art college in United States and UK.
Sport, community service and clubs (Pupils aged 11 and over) *Sport and physical activities:* Compulsory sports: PE programme including soccer, basketball, athletics, netball and table tennis. *Community service:* Community service compulsory: an integral part of the IB programme for sixth-form. *Clubs and societies:* Up to 10 clubs, eg drama, various sports, yearbook, computing.
Uniform No school uniform.
Discipline Pupils failing to produce homework once might expect to be given a deadline to produce the work; those caught smoking cannabis on the premises might expect expulsion (clearly laid down in school policy).

• INTERNATIONAL (Sotogrande)

International School at Sotogrande, Apartado 15, 11310 Sotogrande, Prov De Cádiz, Spain. Tel 34 56 795902, Fax 34 56 794816

• Pupils 250 • Boys 3–18 (Day/Board) • Girls 3–18 (Day/Board) • Upper sixth 8 • Termly fees £700–£1350 (Day) £2000–£2350 (Board) • ECIS, NABSS • Enquiries/application to school secretary

What it's like

Established in 1978, the single-site school enjoys an unusually beautiful position in the rural development of Sotogrande, a residential area between Gibraltar and Estepona. The surrounding area is pollution-free with extensive woodland. It is housed in an old Spanish Cortijo and the boarding houses together with a chapel are part of the neighbouring buildings. Some 45% of pupils are British, 40% Spanish, and the rest of various nationalities; it has been co-educational since its foundation. A full British curriculum is provided and Spanish is taught throughout. There is a favourable staff:pupil ratio of about 1:10. The school has a commitment to the expressive arts; music is strong and art, drama and dance are well-supported. There are good PE facilities, plus a standard range of extra-curricular activities, sports and games. New children are quickly involved in the active arts and sports programmes.

School profile

Pupils Total age range 3–18; 250 pupils, 236 day (116 boys, 120 girls); 14 boarding.

Senior department 11–18; 90 pupils (40 boys, 50 girls). Entry at any age, including into sixth.

Entrance No entrance exam if satisfactory report from previous school. No special skills nor religious requirements. Public exam fees only extras; parents not expected to buy textbooks.

Parents 15+% are doctors, lawyers, etc. 15+% in industry. Most live within 30 miles.

Head and staff *Headteacher*: George O'Brien, in post since 1995. Educated at Christ's Hospital and at Cambridge and London universities. Previously taught at King's College, Madrid. *Staff:* 24 full time, 5 part time. Annual turnover 10%.

Exam results In 1995, 14 in upper fifth, 8 in upper sixth. *GCSE:* In 1995, 8 upper fifth gained at least grade C in 8+ subjects; 5 in 5–7; 1 in 1–4 subjects. *A-levels:* 4 upper sixth passed in 4+ subjects; 2 in 3; and 2 in 2 subjects. Average UCAS points 19.0.

University and college entrance 95% of 1995 sixth-form leavers went on to a degree course (none take a gap year); others typically go on to further education. Of those going on to university, 15% took courses in science and engineering, 5% in law, 60% in humanities and social sciences, 10% in art and design, 10% in vocational subjects eg tourism.

Curriculum GCSE, AS and A-levels, Spanish elementary and secondary exams for national or fluent Spanish speaker. 11 subjects offered to GCSE and A-level. 38% take science A-levels; 50% arts/humanities; 13% both. *Computing facilities:* Computer room with one Archimedes, 2 A5000, 5 A3000, 6 BBC Masters, and 1 PC, scanner, laser printer, desktop publishing, video interface, three keyboards – software for use in all curriculum areas; all students leave computer-literate. *Special provision:* ESL teacher; qualified teacher in special needs. *Europe:* Spanish (taught throughout) and French offered at GCSE and A-level. Over 75% take GCSE in both.

The arts *Music:* Over 30% of pupils learn a musical instrument; instrumental exams can be taken. Musical groups include woodwind and string groups, choir, recorder group, mixed ensemble, rock band. Ensemble performs in local church and has played in schools in Spain and Gibraltar. *Drama & dance*: Both offered. Majority of pupils are involved in school productions. *Art:* On average, 8 take GCSE, 4 A-level. Ceramics also offered. 2 practising artist-teachers.

Sport, community service and clubs (Pupils aged 11 and over) *Sport and physical activities:* Compulsory sports: hockey, football, tennis, swimming, athletics, basketball, volleyball. Optional: badminton, table tennis. *Community service:* Pupils participate in Duke of Edinburgh's Award Scheme. Charity committee. *Clubs and societies:* Up to 10 clubs, eg karate, creative dance, art, ballet/tap, sports, drama.

Uniform School uniform worn except in the sixth-form.

Houses/prefects Competitive houses. Prefects, head boy/girl, head of house and house prefects – appointed by the Head.

Religion Weekly RE class; also Catholic instruction with preparation for first Holy Communion and Confirmation.

Social Inter-schools sporting activities, especially athletics and swimming. Frequent field trips, concerts, excursions. Pupils allowed to bring own motorbike/bike to school. Meals formal or sandwiches. Uniform shop. No tobacco/alcohol allowed.

Boarding All pupils share study bedrooms (2, 3 or 4 per room). Pupils divided by age and sex into different houses for sleeping. Resident doctor nearby. Unlimited exeats per term.

• IPSWICH

Ipswich School, Henley Road, Ipswich, Suffolk IP1 3SG. Tel 01473 255313, Fax 01473 213831 • Pupils 602 • Boys 11–18 (Day/Board/Weekly) • Girls 11–18 (Day) • Upper sixth 91 • Termly fees £1516–£1684 (Day) £2424–£2884 (Board) £2382–£2802 (Weekly) • HMC • Enquiries/application to the Registrar

What it's like

Founded in 1390 by the Ipswich Merchant Guild of Corpus Christi, its first Charter was granted by Henry VIII and subsequently confirmed by Elizabeth I. In 1852 the school moved into handsome new buildings in the Victorian collegiate style. It stands on high ground overlooking Christchurch Park, with a cricket field and sports hall on that site and 30 acres of other playing fields 10 minutes' walk from the school. Many improvements and additions have been made over the years, including the fine library and performing arts complex, and it now has excellent all-round facilities. The prep school is on the same site, with its own buildings but with the use of the senior school amenities. Religious education is provided at all levels, plus daily chapel services and services on Sunday; all denominations are welcome. The staff:pupil ratio is about 1:12. The school is becoming fully co-educational; there has been a mixed sixth-form for several years and girls aged 11 will be admitted from 1997. A broad general education is provided and results are very good; almost all pupils go on to degree courses. Drama and music are very well supported; there are dramatic productions each year for all age groups and plentiful opportunities for music-making with many musical groups. High standards are achieved in sports and games, with regional representation in large number of sports. A thriving, voluntary CCF contingent, including Army, Navy and Air Force sections; pupils are encouraged to belong to it or undertake some community service and many do so. A wide variety of clubs and societies cater for most needs and a successful record in the Duke of Edinburgh's Award Scheme.

School profile

Pupils Age range 11–18; 602 pupils, 567 day (523 boys, 44 girls), 35 boarding boys. Main entry ages 11, 13 and into sixth (from 1997; previously, girls in sixth-form only). Large intake from own prep, Ipswich Preparatory School (tel 01473 255730). *State school entry:* 50% main intake.

Entrance Own exam or Common Entrance used. 4% from overseas. 15 pa assisted places at 11, plus 10 pa in sixth. 12–15 pa scholarships, including for music and art.

Head and staff *Headmaster:* Ian Galbraith, 4 years in post. Educated at Dulwich and Cambridge (geography). Previously Head of Upper School at Dulwich College. British Schools Exploring Society leader to Iceland and Greenland. *Publications:* Understanding Physical Geography (1995); Ecosystems (1990); Land Forms (1983); Map Reading and Analysis (1974). *Staff:* 48 full time, 6 part time. Annual turnover 2%. Average age 38.

Exam results In 1995, 92 pupils in upper fifth, 91 in upper sixth. *GCSE:* in 1995, 84 upper fifth gained at least grade C in 8+ subjects; 5 in 5–7 subjects. *A-levels:* 5 upper sixth passed in 4+ subjects; 75 in 3; 10 in 2; and 1 in 1 subject. Average UCAS points 21.4.

University and college entrance 95% of 1995 sixth-form leavers went on to a degree course, others typically go on to art or drama college. Of those going on to university, 8% took courses in medicine, dentistry and veterinary science, 27% in science and engineering, 62% in humanities and social sciences, 3% in drama and acting.

Curriculum GCSE and A-levels. General studies for all in sixth but no A-level. On average, 38% take science A-levels; 42% arts/humanities; 20% both. *Vocational:* Work experience offered to upper fifth. *Computing facilities:* Networked PC system. *Europe:* French, German and Russian offered at GCSE and A-level (French compulsory to GCSE); also GCSE Italian and Spanish in sixth. Regular exchanges (France and Germany).

The arts *Music:* About 40% of pupils learn a musical instrument; instrumental exams can be taken. Some 10 musical groups including orchestras, chamber group, chapel choir, wind band, several jazz and pop groups. Daily Telegraph Young Jazz Regional Finalists. *Drama & dance*: Drama offered, as part of English. 10 productions annually involving all school groups. *Art:* On average, 25 take GCSE, 12 A-level. Design, pottery, photography, print-making, sculpture, textiles also offered.

Sport, community service and clubs *Sport and physical activities:* Netball, rugby, hockey, cricket, rounders, soccer, squash, badminton, table tennis, athletics, cross-country, fives, shooting, tennis, polygym and sailing. RLSS, fencing, ASA exams may be taken. Regional and county representatives at rugby, hockey, netball, cricket, cross-country, tennis, athletics. *Community service:* Pupils take bronze, silver and gold Duke of Edinburgh's Award. CCF or community service compulsory for 2–4 years at age 15. *Clubs and societies:* Up to 30 clubs, eg Athenaeum, ornithology, badminton, chess, Viewpoint.

Uniform School uniform worn except in the sixth.

Houses/prefects Competitive and pastoral houses. Head of school and two deputies, prefects, and heads of houses – appointed by the Headmaster in consultation with Housemasters.

Religion Attendance at religious worship compulsory once a week.

Social Part of the Ipswich Initiative, together with 4 other independent and 8 state schools. Many trips abroad eg to Moscow and St Petersburg; classical trips to Mediterranean; exchanges to France and Germany; birdwatching to North Africa. Pupils allowed to bring own car/bike/motorbike to school. Meals self-service. School tuck shop. No tobacco/alcohol allowed.
Discipline Pupils failing to produce homework once might expect a reprimand (parents contacted if other reasons for concern). Those caught smoking cannabis on the premises might expect immediate suspension and contact with parents; probably leading to expulsion.
Former pupils Mark Bailey (England rugby player); Nils Blythe (broadcaster).

• IPSWICH HIGH

Ipswich High School, Woolverstone, Ipswich, Suffolk IP9 1AZ. Tel 01473 780201
• Pupils 670 • Boys None • Girls 3–18 (Day) • Upper sixth 55 • Termly fees £976–£1328 (Day)
• GSA, GPDST • Enquiries/application to the Headmistress

What it's like

The school was founded in 1878 and from 1907 was sited in a residential area of North Ipswich. Planning restrictions prevented further expansion on that site and, in 1992, it moved some four miles south east of Ipswich to Woolverstone Hall, a former boarding school. This has greatly improved facilities. With wide views over the Orwell estuary and the surrounding parkland, covering more than eighty acres, the 18th-century Hall, a Grade I listed mansion, houses the sixth-form centre, libraries, some teaching rooms, and dining rooms. Around the Hall, modern buildings accommodate the senior school and CDT block, sports hall and theatre; a covered, heated swimming pool is planned. The junior department occupies a separate block. Its social spread is wide and it provides a good all-round education with the emphasis on development of individual talents. Results are very good and almost all sixth-form leavers go on to university, including Oxbridge. There is a big commitment to music, intensive dramatic activities and a good range of sports and games. Most pupils are engaged in voluntary service in the district from age 15 or 16.

School profile

Pupils Total age range 3–18; 670 day girls. Senior department 11–18, 470 girls. Main entry ages 3, 4, 7, 9, 11 and into the sixth. *State school entry:* 25% senior intake.
Entrance Own entrance exam used. No special skills or religious requirements. Parents not expected to buy textbooks. 25 pa assisted places. 3–4 pa scholarships awarded on academic merit, 25%–50% fees; bursaries subject to means test.
Head and staff *Headmistress:* Miss Valerie MacCuish, 4 years in post. Educated at Lady Edridge Grammar School and Westfield College, London University (modern languages). Previously Headmistress of Tunbridge Wells Girls' Grammar School and Deputy Head of Surbiton High School and of Aylesbury High School. *Staff:* 42 full time, 16 part time (plus 14 for extras). Annual turnover very small.
Exam results In 1995, 66 pupils in Year 11, 55 in upper sixth. *GCSE:* In 1995, all Year 11 gained at least grade C in 8+ subjects. *A-levels:* 2 upper sixth passed in 4+ subjects; 50 in 3; 1 in 2; and 2 in 1 subject. Average UCAS points 22.0.
University and college entrance 95% of 1995 sixth-form leavers went on to a degree course (20% after a gap year); others typically go on to art foundation courses. Of those going on to university, 10% went to Oxbridge; 7% took courses in medicine, dentistry and veterinary science, 28% in science and engineering, 7% in law, 40% in humanities and social sciences, 9% in vocational subjects eg speech therapy, nursing, 9% in other subjects eg psychology.
Curriculum GCSE and A-level. 20 GCSE and A-level subjects offered (general studies taught but not examined). 18% took science A-levels; 27% art/humanities; 55% both. *Vocational:* Work experience compulsory. *Computing facilities:* 2 rooms with network of 16 computers each; 16 lap tops and stand-alones elsewhere. New facilities in DT. *Europe:* French and German offered at GCSE, AS and A-level; also Italian GCSE. Regular exchanges (France and Germany). Visits to eg Florence and Normandy.
The arts (Pupils aged 11 and over) *Music:* Over 50% of pupils learn a musical

instrument; instrumental exams can be taken. Some 10 musical groups including 2 orchestras, 3 choirs, wind band, chamber groups. Choir and orchestra won 1st prize in their sections at Suffolk Music Festival; choir and orchestra gave concert at Snape Maltings, Aldeburgh 1995. *Drama & dance*: Drama offered. ESB exams may be taken. Majority of pupils are involved in school productions and house/other productions. Recent major production of Half a Sixpence. *Art:* On average, 24 take GCSE, 6 A-level. Design, pottery, textiles, history of art also offered.

Sport, community service and clubs (Pupils aged 11 and over) *Sport and physical activities:* Compulsory sports: swimming, tennis, rounders, netball, hockey. Optional: volleyball, badminton, squash, sailing, fencing. BAGA exams may be taken. 2 members England fencing U18 team – school has won Public Schools Championship for 9 consecutive years; 10 girls represent county in hockey, tennis, netball. *Community service:* Pupils take bronze, silver and gold Duke of Edinburgh's Award. Community service optional; voluntary work in local hospital. *Clubs and societies:* Up to 10 clubs, eg chess, Christian Union, computing, French, debating and engineering.

Uniform School uniform worn except in sixth.

Houses/prefects No competitive houses. All sixth-form are prefects. Head girl elected by sixth-form and staff. School Council.

Religion Daily assembly involves non-denominational worship.

Social Occasional debates and shared lectures or musical performances with local schools. Annual exchange with schools in Chevreuse and Hamburg; visit to Australia in 1995; annual history of art visits to France or Italy; ski trip. Pupils allowed to bring own car/bike to school. Meals self-service. Tuck shop at break. Second-hand uniform sales organised by parents. No tobacco/alcohol allowed.

Discipline Cases of pupils failing to produce homework once would be judged on their merits; those caught smoking cannabis on the premises could expect expulsion.

• ISLAND

Island School, 20 Borrett Road, Hong Kong. Tel 852 2524 7135, Fax 852 2840 1673
• Pupils 1200 • Boys 11–18 (Day) • Girls 11–18 (Day) • Upper sixth 138 • Termly fees HK$21,000 (Day) • HMC, ESF • Enquiries/application to the Principal

What it's like

Founded in 1967, it is urban and single-site, housed in a purpose-built building which makes the most of the crowded Hong Kong conditions, even utilising its roof for sport. Pupils are drawn from the local and international business and professional community, making it a very lively and multi-national school. The staff:pupil ratio is about 1:15. Academic results are good and the vast majority of leavers go on to degree courses around the world. Music and drama are strong. A standard range of sport and games in which high standards are achieved (many Hong Kong representatives). Considerable commitment to the Duke of Edinburgh's Award Scheme and to community services.

School profile

Pupils Age range 11–18; 1200 day pupils, 600 boys, 600 girls. Main entry is 11 and into the sixth. A few are children of former pupils. Peak School and Glenealy School both provide more than 60% of pupils.

Entrance Own entrance test in competence in English. No special skills or religious requirements. Parents expected to buy textbooks for senior pupils; provided for younger pupils. Average extras HK$2000 (school buses, uniform etc.).

Head and staff *Principal:* David J James, 8 years in post. Educated at Hartridge High School and universities of Wales (history) and Hong Kong (education). Previously Housemaster at Mandeville, Jamaica, and teacher of history at Belair School. Also overseas member of HMC. *Staff:* 71 full time, 23 part time. Annual turnover, less than 5%. Average age, mid-30s.

Exam results In 1995, 186 pupils in upper fifth, 138 in upper sixth. *GCSE:* In 1995, 90% of upper fifth gained at least grade C in 5+ subjects. *A and AS-levels*: 16 passed in 4+ subjects; 89 in 3+; 24 in 2+; and 4 in 1 subject. Average UCAS points 22.0.

University and college entrance 95% of sixth-form leavers go on to a degree course; others typically go on to non-degree courses eg Swiss catering, secretarial or art/drama college. Of those going on to university, 3% go to Oxbridge, 5% to Ivy League universities in US; 10% take courses in medicine, dentistry and veterinary science, 25% in science and engineering, 6% in law and psychology, 50% in humanities and social sciences, 5% in art and design, 4% in other subjects eg music, drama.

Curriculum AS and A-levels offered, also American SAT, Australian HSC and GNVQ Intermediate and Advanced Level. 17 AS-level subjects offered; 23 A-level, including Chinese and general studies. 37% take science A-levels; 37% arts/humanities; 25% both. *Vocational:* Work experience available. GNVQ available, also photography qualifications from City & Guilds and secretarial/IT from RSA and BTEC. *Computing facilities:* 3 suites and many micros dispersed around the school – some 100 in all. *Special provisions*: Learning support for minor ESL difficulties (English is second language for some 50% pupils). *Europe:* French, German and Spanish offered at GCSE, AS and A-level (either Mandarin or French compulsory from age 11).

The arts *Music:* Over 30% pupils learn a musical instrument; instrumental exams can be taken. A number of musical groups including 3 choirs, school orchestra, chamber orchestra, dance band. *Drama & dance*: Drama offered; pupils may take GCSE and A-level drama. Majority of pupils involved in school productions, some in house/other productions. Pupils take part in Hong Kong Speech Festival and Fringe for Arts Festival. *Art:* On average, 35 take GCSE, and 12 A-level. Design, pottery, textiles and photography also offered. 1 recent pupil accepted for Chelsea College of Art. School has artist-in-residence.

Sport, community service and clubs *Sport and physical activities:* Compulsory sports: swimming, athletics, cross-country, water polo. *Optional:* cricket, football; sixth-form only: sailing. GCSE sport studies offered, many students represent HK eg swimming in Olympics. *Community service:* Pupils take bronze, silver and gold Duke of Edinburgh's Award. Community service compulsory up to age 16. HK$500,000 raised annually for charity; USA-based Summerbridge Summer School for underprivileged children. *Clubs & societies*: Up to 30 clubs eg social, drama, orchestra.

Uniform School uniform worn except in the sixth.

Houses/prefects Competitive houses. Head boy and girl, house prefects and house captains, appointed by Headmaster and housemasters and student election. School Council.

Religion No compulsory worship. Compulsory study of world religions years 7–9.

Social Links with local schools, including 2 Chinese schools; model UN. Trips abroad eg to Japan, skiing; Philippines, scuba diving; Nepal, trekking; France, language group; and to USA and Taiwan. Meals self-service. School shop. No alcohol/tobacco allowed.

Discipline Pupils failing to produce homework once might expect admonition by staff. Little discipline needed at school; excellent staff student relations.

Former pupils Christine Loh (Member of Hong Kong Legislative Council).

• ITALIA CONTI

Italia Conti Academy of Theatre Arts, Italia Conti House, 23 Goswell Road, London EC1M 7AJ. Tel 0171 608 0047/8, Fax 0171 253 1430

• Pupils 250 • Boys 9–21 (Day) • Girls 9–21 (Day) • Upper Sixth Yes • Termly fees £1599–£2375 (Day) • CDET, ISAI • Enquiries/application to the Principal

What it's like

Founded in 1911 at a church hall in Paddington, it moved to the edge of the City and now occupies a modern 9-floor block next to the Barbican Arts Centre. There are 12 dance and 6 acting/singing studios, plus well-equipped classrooms. The Academy trains young people for professional careers in the media of theatre, screen, radio and television. The secondary school pupil's day is divided between traditional academic lessons and vocational classes. For the academic curriculum, classes are usually of under 18 pupils in mixed-ability year groups and are set within classes. The national curriculum is followed in standard subjects. Stage training classes in ballet, tap, modern, jazz, acting and singing are grouped across narrow age ranges according to grade and ability. Pupils are prepared for external exams set by the ISTD and LAMDA, as preparation for the Teacher's Associate exam offered by these boards to students on the Academy's 16+ course. As part of their training, all pupils are represented by the Italia Conti Agency which organises auditions for professional work. At entrance, pupils are chosen on the basis of their potential for a professional career and their ability to cope academically. In addition to the secondary school, the Academy offers degree courses to students aged 18+ and performing arts and a one-year singing course to students of 16+. Recently introduced is the Sixth Form Performing Arts course which combines A-level study with professional training in ballet, tap, modern, acting and singing. The Academy has trained a formidable number of well-known actors and actresses over the last 80 years.

School profile

Pupils Age range 9–21; 250 day pupils, 35 boys, 215 girls. Main entry at 11 and 16. *State school entry:* 80% at 11, 90% into the sixth.

Entrance Own academic and vocational assessment. Dance, acting and singing talent looked for at entry; no religious requirements. Parents not expected to buy textbooks; average £5 extras. 1 pa scholarship, full fees.

Parents 15+% in theatre/media/music. Most live within 30 miles; up to 10% overseas.

Head and staff *Headmaster:* Clifford Vote, 20 years in post. Educated at universities of New South Wales and London (economics, psychology and education). Previously taught in secondary schools in Australia. Also former prep school governor. *Staff:* 10 full time, 30 part time. Annual turnover, 5%. Average age, 38.

Exam results *GCSE:* On average, 20 pupils in upper fifth: 1 gain at least grade C in 8+ subjects; 7 in 5–7; and 12 in 1–4 subjects.

University and college entrance All leavers enter the professional theatre.

Curriculum *Vocational:* Work experience available. Pupils prepared for ISTD ballet, tap and modern from grade 3 to Associate Teacher's qualification; LAMDA verse and prose and acting exams to Diploma level. *Europe:* French compulsory and offered at GCSE.

The arts *Music:* Singing is taken by all pupils and student. *Drama & dance*: Both offered; pupils may take GCSE drama, LAMDA and ISTD exams. All pupils involved in school productions. Large proportion of 16+ students leave with teaching qualifications in dance in addition to their skills as professional performers. Current and former pupils regularly take major roles in film, television and theatrical productions. *Art:* On average, 15 take GCSE.

Uniform School uniform worn except in the sixth.

Houses/prefects No competitive houses. Head boy/girl and prefects – appointed by the Headmaster.

Religion No compulsory religious worship.

Social Younger pupils travel to France for a week. Meals self-service. No alcohol/tobacco allowed.

Discipline Pupils failing to produce homework once would have an interview with the class teacher concerned, who would decide on the need for further action. Any pupil caught smoking cannabis on the premises might expect expulsion, depending on the overall circumstances (all students are warned on admission about drug taking).

Former pupils Johnny Briggs; Naomi Campbell; Peter Duncan; Jill Gascoine; Olivia Hussey; Bonnie Langford; Millicent Martin; Nanette Newman; Anthony Newley; Anton Rodgers; Tracey Ullman.

J

• JAMES ALLEN'S (JAGS)

James Allen's Girls' School, East Dulwich Grove, London SE22 8TE. Tel 0181 693 1181, Fax 0181 693 7842

• Pupils 740 • Boys None • Girls 11–18 (Day) • Upper sixth 95 • Termly fees £1835–£1900 (Day) • GSA • Enquiries to the Headmistress/Admissions Secretary • Application to the Admissions Secretary

What it's like

Founded in 1741, one of three schools of the Alleyn's College of God's Gift foundation and the oldest girls' school in London. Usually known as JAGS, it moved in 1886 to its present site of 22 acres in the pleasant inner London suburb of Dulwich. There have been massive additions since 1978 to provide excellent modern facilities. Interdenominational, it puts some stress on the inculcation of Christian ethics. Its declared aims are to encourage and promote: intellectual curiosity, enthusiasm and imagination; concern for others; confidence and independence of mind; the pursuit of excellence (whatever the undertaking). A popular school, it is well-known for its good teaching and academic achievements. Results are consistently very good and almost all go on to degree courses, including many to Oxbridge. A partnership is currently being forged with a multi-racial school in South Afrcia. There is a big commitment to music and drama (it has its own theatre designed to professional standards) and art is extremely strong. Collaboration with Dulwich College in cultural enterprises. An unusually wide range of sporting and games activities. Very strong in extra-curricular activities.

School profile

Pupils Age range 11–18, 740 day girls. Main entry ages 11 and into sixth. Own preparatory school provides approx 33% senior intake. *State school entry:* 45% senior intake, plus 40% to sixth.

Entrance Own entrance exam used. No special skills or religious requirements. No compulsory extras. 30 pa assisted places. 20 pa scholarships/bursaries, up to 90% fees according to need.

Head and staff *Headmistress:* Mrs Marion Gibbs, in post since 1994. Educated at Basingstoke High and Pate's Grammar School, Cheltenham, and at Bristol University (classics). Previously an HMI, Head of Sixth Form and Head of Classics at Haberdasher's Aske's and Director of Studies and Head of Sixth Form at Burgess Hill. Also formerly Chief Examiner GCSE (Latin) and Chairman Inter Board A-Level Classics Panel. Publication: Greek Tragedy: An Introduction (Bristol Classical Press). *Staff:* 67 full time, 26 part time. Annual turnover 6%. Average age 37.

Exam results In 1995, 113 pupils in upper fifth, 97 in upper sixth. *GCSE:* In 1995, 108 upper fifth gained at least grade C in 8+ subjects; and 4 in 5–7 subjects. *A-levels:* 9 upper sixth passed in 4+ subjects; 82 in 3; and 5 in 2 subjects. Average UCAS points 24.5.

University and college entrance 93% of 1995 sixth-form leavers went on to a degree course; others typically go on to art and drama colleges or straight into careers eg banking. Of those going on to university, 13% went to Oxbridge; 10% took courses in medicine, dentistry and veterinary science, 22% in science and engineering, 56% in humanities and social sciences, 5% in art and design.

Curriculum GCSE and A-levels. 24 subjects offered, including A-level philosophy; wide general studies programme but not A-level. 20% take science A-levels; 46% arts/humanities; 34% both. *Vocational:* Work experience available in fifth, work shadowing in sixth. *Computing facilities:* Computers in most departments. CAD in design and technology department; 80 computers in four computing rooms. *Special provision:* None, apart from extra general help. *Europe:* French, German, Italian, Russian and Spanish offered to GCSE, A-level and commercial languages (FLAW). Regular exchanges (France, Germany, Italy, Russia and Spain); sixth-form scholarship exchange programme with schools in Milan, Orleans and Nuremburg (pupils spend half-a-term in

each others' schools). European studies compulsory for pupils aged 11 and lower sixth. Use of radio and satellite television; taken part in European pupil radio link. Talks from MEPs, Sir Leon Brittan etc. Much involved in European Youth Parliament.
The arts *Music:* Over 33% of pupils learn a musical instrument; instrumental exams can be taken. Some 10 major musical groups including 3 orchestras, 2 choirs, 2 wind bands, jazz group, pop band, chamber orchestra. 6 pupils currently attend Junior Colleges or Junior Conservatoire. *Drama & dance*: Drama and dance offered. GCSE and A-level drama, ESB exams may be taken. Many pupils are involved in school productions and majority in house/other productions. Sixth form production at Edinburgh Festival 1993. *Art:* On average, 56 take GCSE, 18 A-level. Design, pottery, textiles also offered. 2 pupils to Ruskin College.
Sport, community service and clubs *Sport and physical activities:* Compulsory sports (for 1st 4 years): hockey, netball, swimming, athletics, football, volleyball, squash, basketball, table tennis, rounders, tennis, dance, gym, self defence; PE (for 6 years). Optional: weight-training, trampolining, fencing, skating, sailing, scuba-diving, cross-country, canoeing, riding, golf. BAGA and RLSS (bronze medallion) exams may be taken. 2 regional, 3 county hockey players, county indoor hockey champions; U18 and U14 national fencing champions. *Community service:* Pupils take bronze, silver and gold Duke of Edinburgh's Award. Community service optional; school raised £8,500 for charity in 1995. *Clubs and societies:* Over 30 clubs, eg Amnesty International, conducting class, gardening, Green, polyglots, poetry, photography, scuba diving, synthesiser, Pro Lingua, design and technology.
Uniform School uniform worn except in the sixth.
Houses/prefects House captains and deputies elected by whole school, 10 prefects, head girl and deputy – elected by sixth-form. Year Councils.
Religion Assembly 3 times a week; emphasis on moral values and issues. Non-Christians can be exempted at parents' request (very few are).
Social Joint ventures with Dulwich College (brother school) include integrated general studies in upper sixth; Japanese and Arabic in lower sixth; joint theatre productions and some societies. Windsurfing, skiing and adventure trips abroad; cultural trips and exchanges to France, Germany, Italy, Russia, USA, Jordon, Egypt, Greece, Czech Republic and Slovakia; music tour to South Africa; drama tour to Australasia. Pupils allowed to bring own bike to school. Meals self-service. No tobacco/alcohol allowed.
Discipline Pupils failing to produce homework once might expect order mark (3 means an hour detention); those caught smoking cannabis on the premises could expect suspension, probably expulsion.
Alumni association run by Mrs Brenda Hillier, 27 Beechwood Rise, Edgebury, Chislehurst, Kent BR7 6TF and Mrs Susan Jones, 10 Eastmearn Road, London SE21 8HA.
Former pupils Anita Brookner and Lisa St Aubin de Teran (authors); Frances Line (Controller Radio 2).

• JOHN LYON

The John Lyon School, Middle Road, Harrow, Middlesex HA2 OHN. Tel 0181 422 2046
• Pupils 500 • Boys 11–18 (Day) • Girls None • Upper sixth 62 • Termly fees £1785 (Day)
• HMC • Enquiries to the Headmaster • Application to the Headmaster's Secretary

What it's like

Founded in 1876, it has agreeable premises on the west side of Harrow Hill amidst gardens. There are spacious playing fields nearby. There have been substantial additions and improvements over the years including an assembly hall, laboratories, sports hall and a swimming pool. Some religious education is provided weekly for all pupils throughout the school. There are regular school assemblies. A sound general education is given and this includes Latin in the second year. Academic results are good and most pupils go on to degree courses, including Oxbridge. Music and drama are strong. A fair range of sports and games is provided and there is a plentiful variety of extra-curricular activities.

School profile

Pupils Age range 11–18; 500 day boys. Main entry ages 11, 13 and into sixth. *State school entry:* 50% main intake, plus 10% to sixth.

Entrance Own exam used. 15 pa assisted places. Scholarships at 11 and 13.
Head and staff *Headmaster:* Rev Timothy Wright, in post for 10 years. Educated at Wells Cathedral School and King's College London (theology). Previously Housemaster, Head of Religious Studies and Senior Chaplain at Malvern College, and Assistant Chaplain at Worksop. Also Governor of two prep schools. *Staff:* 40 full time, 3 part time. Annual turnover 7.5%. Average age 41.
Exam results In 1995, 78 pupils in fifth, 62 in upper sixth. *GCSE:* In 1995, 54 upper fifth gained at least grade C in 8+ subjects: 21 in 5–7 subjects. *A-levels:* 4 upper sixth passed in 4+ subjects; 52 in 3; 6 in 2 subjects. Average UCAS points 19.5.
University and college entrance 90% of 1995 sixth-form leavers went on to a degree course (10% after a gap year); others typically go on to professional training. Of those going on to university, 4% went to Oxbridge; 10% took courses in medicine, dentistry and veterinary science, 30% in science and engineering, 10% in law, 50% in humanities and social sciences.
Curriculum GCSE and A-levels. 16 subjects offered (no A-level general studies). 27% take science A-levels; 39% arts/humanities; 34% both. *Vocational:* Work experience available. *Computing facilities:* Computer room – network of 26 486 ICL machines with CD-Rom Multi Media. *Europe:* French and German offered to GCSE and A-level; also French AS-level. Regular exchanges to France.
The arts *Music:* Over 25% of pupils learn a musical instrument; instrumental exams can be taken. Some 6 musical groups including choirs, orchestras, wind band, chamber groups. 1 member of National Youth Orchestra. *Drama & dance*: Drama offered. GCSE drama may be taken. Some pupils are involved in school productions and house/other productions. *Art:* On average, 10 take GCSE, 2 AS-level, 4 A-level. Design, pottery and photography also offered.
Sport, community service and clubs *Sport and physical activities:* Compulsory sports: football, cross-country, cricket, athletics, swimming. Optional: tennis, badminton, table tennis, volleyball, archery, karate, golf, squash. Soccer, 3 in county U19 team; archery, national winner of indoor league; cricket, 2 county schools players. *Community service:* Pupils take bronze, silver and gold Duke of Edinburgh's Award. Community service optional. *Clubs and societies:* Up to 15 clubs, eg computer, stamp, bridge, chess, photography, art, indoor games, debating, karate.
Uniform School uniform worn throughout.
Houses/prefects Competitive houses. Prefects, head boy, head of house and house prefects – appointed by the Headmaster.
Religion All pupils attend assemblies.
Social Choral concerts, theatrical events and community service jointly with other local schools. French exchange with school near Paris; numerous foreign trips to eg Israel, Italy, France, Spain, Germany. Pupils allowed to bring own bike to school; car in upper sixth. Meals self-service. No tobacco/alcohol allowed.
Discipline Pupils failing to produce homework once might expect lines or lunch-time detention; those caught smoking cannabis on the premises might expect expulsion.

K

• KEIL 

Keil School, Helenslee Road, Dumbarton, G82 4AL. Tel 01389 62003

• Pupils 220 • Boys 10–18 (Day/Board/Weekly) • Girls 10–18 (Day/Board/Weekly) • Upper sixth 30 • Termly fees £1600 (Day) £2900 (Board/Weekly) • SHMIS • Enquiries/application to the Headmaster

What it's like

Founded in 1915 at Keil House in Argyll, it moved to its present premises in 1925 where it is under the direction of governors appointed by the Mackinnon-Macneill Trust. It is situated on the north bank of the Clyde at the gateway to the Western Highlands, a few miles away from Loch Lomond. The heart of the school is the handsome mansion house of Helenslee, standing in some 45 acres of grounds – lawns, woodland and playing fields – an altogether beautiful and healthy environment. The original buildings have been adapted and developed and the school is now well-equipped. It has all the advantages of a small school and a lot of care is given to the individual. The accent, where possible, is on self-sufficiency. Much initiative and responsibility is expected of senior pupils through the prefectorial system and almost everyone has some kind of responsibility ultimately. Originally a boys' school, girls have been admitted since 1989. Religious worship is compulsory in daily assemblies and Sunday services. A Church of Scotland foundation, it welcomes those of other faiths. The staff:pupil ratio is about 1:11 and classes are small, always below 20 and often smaller. Exam results are good and most pupils go on to degree courses each year. Vocational qualifications are offered. There is an unusually wide range of sports and games available for a school of this size and high standards are achieved. There is also a plentiful variety of extra-curricular activities and an emphasis on outdoor pursuits for which the environment is ideal. Music, drama and art are all strong and there is regular collaboration with other schools in cultural enterprises. There has been considerable success in the Duke of Edinburgh's Award Scheme.

School profile

Pupils Age range 10–18; 220 pupils, 110 day (59 boys, 51 girls), 110 boarders (86 boys, 24 girls). Main entry ages 10, 11, 12, 13 and into sixth. 4% are children of former pupils. *State school entry:* 90% main intake.

Entrance Own exam used. Skills in music, art, sport looked for and personality. A Church of Scotland foundation but all denominations admitted (RC monastery next door). Parents not expected to buy textbooks; no other compulsory extras. 6 pa assisted places. 6 pa scholarships and 6 pa bursaries, both open and closed (to Highlands and Islands pupils).

Parents 30+% live within 30 miles; up to 10% live overseas.

Head and staff *Headmaster:* John A Cummings, in post since 1993. Educated at Eastbourne Grammar School, and at universities of Kent and London. Previously Head of English and Head of Sixth Form at Wycliffe and taught at Tonbridge School and Glasgow Academy. *Staff:* 20 full time, 3 part time.

Exam results In 1995, 33 pupils in S-grade year, 23 in Higher, 30 in A-level year. *S-grade:* On average, 14 pupils passed in 8 subjects; 14 in 5–7 subjects. *Highers:* 10 pupils passed in 5 subjects; 6 in 4; 9 in 3; 6 in 2; 6 in 1 subject. *A-levels:* 5 pupils pass in 3+ subjects.

University and college entrance 96% of 1995 sixth-form leavers went on to a degree course (3% after a gap year); others typically go on to the services or to art college. Of those going on to university, 3% went to Oxbridge; 10% took courses in medicine, dentistry and veterinary science, 40% in science and engineering, 10% in law, 25% in humanities and social sciences, 15% in art and design.

Curriculum S-grade, Highers, and A-levels. 13 S-grade subjects, 14 Highers, 7 CSYS or A-levels offered (no A-level general studies). 50% take science Highers; 30% arts/humanities; 20% both. *Vocational:* Work experience available; also number of Scotvec modules, including Russian for beginners. *Computing facilities:* Computer lab with 14 Apple Macintosh and CD-Rom; 12 BBC Bs spread among departments. *Special provision:* EFL taught; provision for dyslexic pupils. *Europe:* French and German offered to S-grade and Higher (both compulsory); Spanish and Russian Scotvec module; Gaelic for conversation as a non-examined subject. Regular visits to France and Germany.

The arts *Music:* 20% of pupils learn a musical instrument; instrumental exams can be taken. Some 6 musical groups including 2 choirs, several instrumental, pop group. *Drama & dance*: Drama offered. Most pupils are involved in school productions and majority in house/other productions. *Art:* On average, 20 take S-grade, 2 CSYS. Photography also offered.

Sport, community service and clubs *Sport and physical activities:* Compulsory sports: rugby, hockey, athletics, cricket. Optional: soccer, badminton, volleyball, golf, tennis, basketball, fencing, swimming. *Community service:* Pupils take bronze, silver and gold Duke of Edinburgh's Award. Community service optional. *Clubs and societies:* Up to 20 clubs, eg debating, hill walking, chess, photography, sailing, orienteering, Young Enterprise.

Uniform School uniform worn throughout.

Houses/prefects Competitive houses. Prefects, head boy/girl, head of house and house prefects (named chiefs, deputy chiefs and house deputies) – appointed by the Headmaster.

Religion Daily assembly and Sunday service compulsory (both Church of Scotland and Roman Catholic).

Social Debates, Burns suppers, discos, quizzes. Organised annual French exchange. Meals formal. 3 school shops sell uniform, stationery and tuck. No tobacco/alcohol allowed.

Discipline Pupils failing to produce homework once would receive a warning – repeated failure leads to Saturday afternoon detention; those caught smoking cannabis on or off the premises could expect expulsion.

Boarding 20% have own study bedroom or in doubles, 50% in rooms of 6–8, 30% in larger dormitories. Single-sex houses of up to 40 (one junior, three senior). Resident qualified nurse. Central dining room. Pupils can provide and cook some snacks. Termly exeats (Sat lunch to Sun 9pm) up to parents. Weekly visits to local town (Dumbarton) and Glasgow allowed with permission.

Alumni association is run by Wallace Crawford, 83 Clarence Gardens, Glasgow G11 7JW.

Former pupils Rev James Currie (minister and broadcaster); Alistair Blair (fashion designer); Professor Joseph Thomson (Regius Professor of Law, Glasgow University); Professor Andrew Skinner (Vice-principal, Glasgow University); Alisdair MacCallum (Chairman Scottish CBI).

• KELLY COLLEGE

Kelly College, Tavistock, Devon PL19 OHZ. Tel 01822 613005, Fax 01822 616628

• Pupils 284 • Boys 11–18 (Day/Board/Weekly) • Girls 11–18 (Day/Board/Weekly) • Upper sixth 46 • Termly fees £1695–£2385 (Day) £3796 (Board) £3635 (Weekly) • HMC • Enquiries/application to the Headmaster

What it's like

Founded in 1877 by Admiral Kelly, it has a magnificent site above the River Tavy on the edge of one of the most beautiful parts of Dartmoor. The pleasant market town of Tavistock is nearby. St Michael's, Tavistock, became the Junior School in 1990. Many additions and improvements have been made in recent years and there are plans for further developments. The school is already well-equipped, with its own adventure training centre. Numbers are kept low as a matter of policy. The staff:pupil ratio is about 1:11. A sound general education is provided in a friendly and happy atmosphere. Music, drama and art are all strong. The college has unusually fine playing fields and sports facilities and there is much emphasis on sports and games. Rugby and swimming are particularly strong. High standards are attained and there have been a number of representatives at county, regional and national level. There are many clubs and societies for extra-curricular activities, which include fishing (salmon and trout), riding and printing. Every pupil is taught art, design and technology. The CCF is large, with Royal Navy, Army and Royal Marine sections. The college has maintained its nautical connections and there are close links with the navy in Dartmouth and Devonport. There is a large number of Outward Bound activities, for which the locality is ideal. Overseas trips and expeditions are a regular feature.

School profile

Pupils Age range 11–18; 284 pupils, 150 day (87 boys, 63 girls) 134 boarding (82 boys, 52 girls); fully co-educational since 1991. Main entry ages 11, 13 and into sixth. *State school entry:* 40% main intake, plus 60% to sixth.
Entrance Common Entrance and own exam used. 17 pa scholarships (art, music, science, naval and all-rounder); plus exhibitions and bursaries.
Head and staff *Headmaster:* Mark Turner, in post since 1995. Educated at Rossall and Oxford (geography). Previously Housemaster i/c Hockey and Head of Geography at Oundle. *Staff:* 26 full time, 7 part time. Annual turnover 15%. Average age 38.
Exam results On average, 53 pupils in upper fifth, 46 in upper sixth. *GCSE:* On average, 29 upper fifth gain at least grade C in 8+ subjects; 15 in 5–7; and 7 in 1–4 subjects. *A-levels:* 70% upper sixth pass in 4+ subjects; 18% in 3; 8% in 2; and 3% in 1 subject. Average UCAS points 15.0 (including general studies 23.0).
University and college entrance 85% of 1995 sixth-form leavers went on to a degree course; others typically go on to non-degree courses eg agriculture, secretarial or art/drama colleges. Of those going on to university, 5% went to Oxbridge; 5% took courses in medicine, dentistry and veterinary science, 33% in science and engineering, 58% in humanities and social sciences, 2% in art and design.
Curriculum GCSE and A-levels. 22 subjects offered, including A-level general studies. 14% take science A-levels; 33% arts/humanities; 53% both. *Vocational:* Work experience available. *Computing facilities:* Computing room and computers in various departments. *Special provision:* Individual help is given. *Europe:* French and German offered at GCSE, AS and A-level; also Spanish AS and A-level. Regular exchanges (France and Germany). Several French, German and Spanish pupils in school.
The arts *Music:* Over 50% of pupils learn a musical instrument; instrumental exams can be taken. Some 8 musical groups including choirs, orchestra, wind band, pop group etc. Several pupils play with county youth orchestra. *Drama & dance*: Both offered. Majority of pupils are involved in school/house productions. Recent production of Jonson's The Alchemist. *Art:* On average, 15 take GCSE, 8 A-level. Design, photography and history of art also offered.
Sport, community service and clubs *Sport and physical activities:* Compulsory sports: rugby, hockey, cricket, athletics, cross-county, netball. Optional: swimming, tennis, squash, soccer, basketball. Sixth form only: weight training. A-level sports studies may be taken. Rugby, county champions (XV and sevens); swimming, a number at international level. *Community service:* Pupils take bronze, silver and gold Duke of Edinburgh's Award. CCF compulsory for 3 years at age 13; community service for 2 years at age 16. *Clubs and societies:* Up to 15 clubs, eg debating, public speaking, drama, fishing, chess, bridge.
Uniform School uniform worn throughout.
Houses/prefects Competitive houses. Prefects, head boy/girl, head of house and house prefects – appointed by Headmaster and housemasters.
Religion Attendance at religious worship compulsory.
Social Sharing of music with local community; debating and drama with local schools. Regular visits to France and Germany; adventure training expeditions throughout world; developing links with Ukraine. Day pupils allowed to bring own car/bike to school. Meals self-service. School shop. No tobacco allowed; alcohol only under supervision in sixth-form centre.
Boarding Single-sex houses plus co-educational junior house for 11 – 12 year olds.
Discipline Pupils failing to produce homework once might expect to be referred to the tutor and/or housemaster and be given extra work; those caught smoking cannabis on the premises might expect expulsion. There is a strong framework of discipline.

• KELVINSIDE

Kelvinside Academy, 33 Kirklee Road, Glasgow G12 0SW. Tel 0141 357 3376, Fax 0141 357 5401
• Pupils 550 • Boys 3–18 (Day) • Girls 3–5 only • Higher year 65 • Termly fees £795–£1475 (Day) • HMC • Enquiries/application to the Rector

What it's like

Founded in 1878, it has a fine site with very handsome buildings in a pleasant urban residential area. Ample playing fields are three-quarters of a mile away. It has its own junior department. Excellent modern facilities of all kinds are provided, including a well-stocked new library. One of Scotland's leading schools, it is strongly academic with a high standard of teaching and consistently good results. Most leavers go on to university each year and, in common with a number of other Scottish schools, tend to reject Oxbridge in favour of Scottish universities. The music and drama departments are extremely active; art is strong. There is a big range of sports and games (the school has produced a large number of international and county representatives). An equally good range of activities. There is a flourishing CCF and considerable emphasis on outdoor pursuits (the school has a base in the Cairngorms for skiing, hill-walking and field studies).

School profile

Pupils Total age range 3–18; 550 day pupils. Senior department 11–18, 410 boys. Main entry ages 3 (boys and girls), 4, 7, 8, 11 and into sixth (boys). Approx 15% are children of former pupils. *State school entry:* 95% senior intake, plus 90% to sixth.

Entrance Own entrance exam used. Must have academic ability and fluent English; no religious requirements. Parents not expected to pay for textbooks; music lessons (£105) and lunch (£130) extra. 10 pa assisted places. 7 pa scholarships/bursaries, £400–£900, or up to 50% fees according to parental means.

Parents 25+% in industry or commerce; 25+% are doctors, lawyers, etc.

Head and staff *Rector*: John Duff, in post 16 years. Educated at Edinburgh Academy, and universities of Cambridge (economics), Edinburgh (history) and Oxford (education). Previously Housemaster, Head of History and Master i/c Athletics, Cross-country, Adventure Training and CCF (Army) Training Officer at Kelly College. Also on HMC Committee and Chairman of the Scottish Division. *Staff:* 52 full time, 1 part time. Annual turnover 4%. Average age 39.

Exam results On average, 70 pupils in S-grade year, 65 in Higher, 55 in A-level/CSYS year. *S-grade:* On average 62 pupils pass in 5+ subjects; 8 in 1–4 subjects. *Highers:* 41 pupils pass in 5+ or more subjects; 13 in 4; 13 in 3; 13 in 2; 13 in 1 subject. Pupils take a mixture of Highers, CSYS, A-levels and Scotvec modules. Average leaver has passes in 5+ Highers and 1 CSYS/A-level.

University and college entrance 90% of 1995 sixth-form leavers went on to a degree course (4% after a gap year); others typically go on to HND courses. Of those going on to university, 4% went to Oxbridge; 20% took courses in medicine, dentistry and veterinary science, 25% in science and engineering, 12% in law, 16% in humanities and social sciences, 5% in art and design, 22% in vocational subjects eg accountancy, agriculture, pharmacology.

Curriculum S-grades, Highers, A-levels, CSYS and Scotvec. 18 subjects offered (no A-level general studies). 50% take science A-levels; 25% arts/humanities; 25% both. Pupils take a mixture of Highers, CSYS, A-levels and Scotvec modules. *Vocational:* Work experience available. *Computing facilities:* Laboratory on network system, plus a further room with more sophisticated individual machines. *Special provision:* Help for mild dyslexics. Learning support teacher. *Europe:* French (taught from age 5) and German offered to S-grade, Higher and A-level. Regular exchanges (Germany and France).

The arts (Pupils aged 11 and over) *Music:* Up to 25% of pupils learn a musical instrument in private lessons, all learn instruments in class eg keyboards, recorder, percussion; instrumental exams can be taken. Some 6 musical groups including choirs, orchestras, jazz, rock. *Drama & dance*: Drama offered. Some pupils are involved in school productions. Representatives in 4 major professional productions last year. *Art:* On average, 38 take S-grade, 20 Higher, 4 CSYS. Design also offered. Many successes in external competitions; top prize in 2 out of 3 years in Glasgow Art Galleries Competitions (c 8,000 entrants); annual calendar project sold commercially.

Sport, community service and clubs *Sport and physical activities:* Compulsory sports: rugby, cricket, athletics. Optional: badminton, tennis, golf, shooting, curling, basketball, volleyball, swimming, skiing, climbing, hill walking, hockey, soccer, wrestling, fencing, cross-country. Sixth form only: squash, sailing, water-rafting, gliding, windsurfing, canoeing. Large number of county, regional and national representatives in many sports. *Community service:* CCF compulsory for 1 year at age 14, optional for 3 years at age 15 (CCF celebrated centenary in 1993). Duke of Edinburgh Scheme optional. *Clubs and societies:* Up to 30 clubs, eg various sports clubs, drama, music, chess, computer, electronics, geography, film, Scripture Union, Young Enterprise, debating.
Uniform School uniform worn throughout.
Houses/prefects Competitive houses. Prefects, head boy, head of house and house prefects – appointed by the Rector.
Religion Daily morning assembly. All attend timetabled RE classes.
Social Joint debates, mixed badminton team, social functions with local schools. Organised rugby and cricket tours; ski trips; interest trips to eg Israel/France; CCF camps with BAOR; some exchanges. Pupils allowed to bring own car/bike/motorbike to school. Meals self-service. School tuck shop. No tobacco/alcohol allowed.
Discipline Pupils failing to produce homework once might expect extra work or detention; those caught smoking cannabis on the premises would expect expulsion.
Alumni association run by John A Welsh, Secretary, Kelvinside Academical Club, 18 Grange Road, Bearsden, Glasgow G61.
Former pupils Sir T Risk (Governor of Bank of Scotland); Sir Hugh Fraser (Lord Fraser); Colin Mackay (TV political commentator) Lord Rodger (the Lord Advocate) and many leading figures in the professions.

• KENT COLLEGE (Canterbury)

Kent College, Canterbury, Kent CT2 9DT. Tel 01227 763231

• Pupils 699 • Boys 7–18 (Day/Board) • Girls 7–18 (Day/Board) • Upper sixth 70 • Termly fees £2016 (Day) £3590 (Board) • HMC • Enquiries/application to the Head Master

What it's like

Founded in 1885 and acquired by the Board of Management for Methodist Residential Schools in 1920. It stands on a fine site overlooking the city of Canterbury. The junior school, Vernon Holme, is a mile away. The main campus comprises about 20 acres, with additional playing fields nearby. There is also the school farm on the beautiful Moat Park estate of about 90 acres. The school is about a mile from the city centre and 4 miles from the sea. In recent years there have been major development programmes and the school is now very well equipped. No particular religious affiliation is required but there is an emphasis on regular worship, morning prayers etc. Originally a boys' school, it is now fully co-educational; girls were first admitted to the sixth-form in 1976 and gradually throughout the school thereafter. A sound general education is provided and results are good. Most sixth-formers go on to degree courses, including Oxbridge. A good range of sports and games and high standards are attained. A plentiful variety of clubs and societies for extra-curricular activities, including the Duke of Edinburgh's Awards.

School profile

Pupils Total age range 7–18; 699 pupils, 464 day (244 boys, 220 girls), 235 boarders (154 boys, 81 girls). Senior department, 11–18; 534 pupils (311 boys, 223 girls). Main entry ages 7, 11, 13 and into sixth. *State school entry:* 60% senior intake.
Entrance Own entrance exam used. No special skills or religious requirements. 17 pa assisted places available. Scholarships available (incl music and sixth-form); also bursaries for some boarders.
Head and staff *Head Master*: Edward Halse, appointed in 1995. Educated at Garw Grammar School and Wales University (economics). Previously Second Master at Dauntsey's, Housemaster at Kelly College and Head of Economics at King's (Madrid).
Exam results In 1995, 90 pupils in upper fifth, 75 in upper sixth. *GCSE:* In 1995, 55 upper fifth gained at least grade C in 8+ subjects; 23 in 5–7 subjects. *A-levels:* 6 upper sixth passed in 4+ subjects; 44 in 3; 15 in 2; and 8 in 1 subject. 35 upper sixth passed an AS-level in addition to A-levels. Average UCAS points 18.9.

University and college entrance 87% of 1995 sixth-form leavers went on to a degree course (12% after a gap year); others typically go on to art college or straight into careers. Of those going on to university, 10% went to Oxbridge; 14% took courses in medicine, dentistry and veterinary science, 33% in science and engineering, 30% in humanities and social sciences, 5% in art and design.
Curriculum GCSE, AS and A-levels. 19 GCSE subjects offered; 21 at A-level; several at AS-level. 40% take science A-levels; 41% arts/humanities; 19% both. *Vocational:* Work experience available. *Computing facilities:* Two purpose-built rooms, network extending throughout school. *Special provision:* Dyslexia unit for pupils of sound ability. *Europe:* French (from age 9), German and Spanish offered at GCSE, AS and A-level. Regular exchanges to France and Germany. Exchange programme includes joint musical activities and exchanges with European schools eg orchestra combining with German orchestra to tour France. European studies offered to sixth-form. European pupils for 1–2 years in sixth-form.
The arts (Pupils aged 11 and over) *Music:* Over 30% of pupils learn a musical instrument; instrumental exams can be taken. Some 10+ musical groups including orchestras, wind band, jazz band, rock groups, string quartet, madrigals, close harmony, choral society. Many grade 8 performers. *Drama & dance*: Both offered. Some pupils are involved in school and house/other productions. *Art:* On average, 25 take GCSE, 3 AS-level, 10 A-level. Textiles, photography also offered. Winners of local competitions. Annual arts week.
Sport, community service and clubs (Pupils aged 11 and over) *Sport and physical activities:* Compulsory sports: hockey, netball, tennis, athletics (girls); rugby, hockey, cricket, athletics (boys). Optional: squash, badminton, basketball, volleyball, tennis, swimming, fencing, sailing, orienteering. Many county and regional representatives at rugby, hockey and cricket (boys), netball, hockey and tennis (girls) over recent years. *Community service:* Pupils take bronze, silver and gold Duke of Edinburgh's Award; large numbers involved, 20 training for gold, 40 for bronze. Community service optional. *Clubs and societies:* Up to 10 clubs, eg literature, debating, European.
Houses/prefects Prefects, head of house and house prefects – prefects appointed by Headmaster, house prefects by housemaster/mistress.
Social Music tours abroad – Germany, jointly with German exchange school in France; also sports tours (eg Portugal, Malta, Barbados); skiing tours.

• KENT COLLEGE (Pembury)

Kent College, Pembury, Tunbridge Wells, Kent TN2 4AX. Tel 01892 822006, Fax 01892 820221 • Pupils 382 • Boys None • Girls 3-18 (Day/Board/Weekly) • Upper sixth 20 • Termly fees £2110 (Day) £3528 (Board) £3276 (Weekly) • GSA, BSA • Enquiries/application to the Headmistress.

What it's like

Founded in 1886, it is situated on an attractive open site half a mile from the village of Pembury, three miles from Tunbridge Wells. The main building is a fine Victorian house and in recent years there has been considerable expansion and the facilities now are impressive; including purpose-built boarding houses, an indoor swimming pool and a music school. Originally a Methodist foundation, the school is now inter-denominational. A sound education is given and results are good; most sixth-form leavers go on to degree courses. It is an active school with an extensive extra-curricular programme. Girls are encouraged to aim for high standards in academic studies, and in music, drama and sport. There is a strong emphasis on involvement and all girls are expected to contribute to the school community and accept responsibility.

School profile

Pupils Total age range 3–18; 382 girls, 275 day, 107 boarding. Senior department 11–18, 236 girls. Main entry ages, up to 11; 13 and into sixth. *State school entry:* 35% senior intake, plus 10% to sixth.
Entrance Own exam used (Common Entrance accepted). Average extras £75 for day girls, £150 for boarders. Textbooks supplied by the school. 10 pa scholarships.
Parents 5+% in the armed services. 20+% live overseas.
Head and staff *Headmistress:* Miss Barbara J Crompton, 6 years in post. Educated at

Queen Elizabeth Grammar, Northumberland, and Newcastle University (physics). Previously Deputy Head, Housemistress and Head of Physics at St Anne's, Windermere. Also VSO in Malaysia; School-teacher Fellow Commoner, Sidney Sussex College, Cambridge; Teacher of Physics Award, awarded by Institute of Physics. *Staff:* 27 full time, 12+ part time. Annual turnover 5%. Average age 35–40.

Exam results In 1995, 24 pupils in upper fifth, 38 in upper sixth. *GCSE:* In 1995, 64% upper fifth gained at least grade C in 8+ subjects; 27% in 5–7 subjects. *A-levels:* 18% passed in 4+ subjects; 42% in 3; 29% in 2 subjects. Average UCAS points 16.0.

University and college entrance 90% of 1995 sixth-form leavers went on to a degree course (18% after a gap year); others typically go on to HND or specialised diploma courses eg instrument technology. Of those going on to university, 3% go to Oxbridge; 13% took courses in science and engineering, 10% in law, 37% in humanities and social sciences, 3% in art and design, 37% in vocational subjects eg pharmacy, education, theatre studies, agriculture, textiles.

Curriculum GCSE, AS and A-levels. 21 subjects offered to GCSE; 19 to A-level (including general studies). 14% took science A-levels, 73% arts/humanities and 13% a mixture. *Vocational:* Work experience available; also RSA exams in IT. *Computing facilities:* Computer lab with network of industrial standard computers plus CD ROM and stand-alone multimedia computers in most departments. *Special provision:* ESL tuition available; help for dyslexic pupils. *Europe:* French (from age 7) and German offered at GCSE and A-level. Regular exchanges (France and Germany). Regular 1–2 term visits from European students (usually aged 16).

The arts (Pupils aged 11 and over) *Music:* 60% of pupils learn a musical instrument; instrumental exams can be taken. Musical groups include 2 choirs, orchestra, chamber groups, flute and clarinet choirs. Biannual musical productions with drama department. Regular concerts (in-house and external) including Joint Methodist Schools' London Concerts. Successes in local festivals. Host to Tunbridge Wells International Young Concert Artists' Competition. *Drama & dance*: Both offered. GCSE and A-level drama, Poetry Society, LAMDA, Guildhall exams may be taken. Majority of pupils are involved in school productions and house/other productions. *Art:* On average, 15 take GCSE, 2 AS-level, 6 A-level. Design, pottery, textiles, photography also offered.

Sport, community service and clubs (Pupils aged 11 and over) *Sport and physical activities:* Compulsory sports: hockey, netball, swimming, gymnastics, badminton, tennis, rounders, athletics. Optional: jazz dance, trampolining, archery, sailing, aerobics, riding, volleyball, basketball, squash. BAGA, RLSS exams may be taken. *Community service:* Pupils take bronze, silver and gold Duke of Edinburgh's Award. CCF optional. Community service optional. *Clubs and societies:* Up to 30 clubs, eg photographic, art, cordon bleu, charity committee, self-defence and first aid courses.

Uniform School uniform worn except in the sixth.

Houses/prefects Competitive houses. Head girl and deputy, elected by school; house captains and deputies elected by houses. School Council and Senior Council.

Religion Methodist foundation, now inter-denominational. Morning assembly and Sunday services; everyone attends.

Social Debates, dances, matches with other school; regular theatre visits to London. Day and short trips to France; other visits abroad and field study visits. Self-service meals in central dining-room. School tuck shop. No tobacco/alcohol allowed.

Discipline Detention for poor work. For a serious breach of school rules (eg smoking, alcohol offences), parents are informed and the girl is gated for 2–3 weeks including weekends. Day girls would be expected to report to school on Saturdays and Sundays. Extra work/community service set. Further offences would lead to suspension/expulsion.

Boarding Junior house for 11–13 year olds; others in senior houses. 2 fixed exeats per term. Pupils visit Tunbridge Wells on Saturdays, from age 13 upwards.

• KILGRASTON

Kilgraston School, Bridge of Earn, Perthshire PH2 9BQ. Tel 01738 812257/812973, Fax 01738 813410

• Pupils 270 • Boys 5–8 only • Girls 5–18 (Day/Board/Weekly) • Upper sixth 26 • Termly fees £1230–£1885 (Day) £2965–£3275 (Board/Weekly) • GSA, SHA, BSA, HAS • Enquiries/application to the Headmistress

What it's like

Founded in 1920, it moved in 1930 from Edinburgh to its present splendid site, a little south of Perth, which comprises 70 acres of beautiful gardens, woodlands and playing fields. The main building and focal point of the school is a particularly handsome Georgian house after the style of Robert Adam. There has been a steady programme of building and modernisation which now provides, among other things, comfortable accommodation for boarders and first-rate teaching facilities. Kilgraston is a Roman Catholic foundation and is part of the Society of Sacred Heart network of some 200 schools and colleges throughout the world. Its pupils may be of any religious persuasion and the aim is to create an environment in which Christian ideals and principles may thrive. The chapel is the centre of its spiritual life and prayer and reflection are regarded as important in the development of the pupils. It has many of the advantages of a small school. There is a large staff and a very favourable staff:pupil ratio of about 1:9. A sound, general education is provided, with some strength in modern languages, and vocational qualifications are offered. Results are consistently good and the majority of sixth-form leavers proceed to higher education. Music is strong and drama flourishes. A standard range of sports and games is available, for which there is excellent provision; plus skiing, riding, karate and judo. Community service is particularly well supported and there has been a great deal of success in the Duke of Edinburgh's Award Scheme. Girls have many contacts with other schools for the purpose of debating, dances and public speaking competitions. Extensive use is made of the cultural amenities of neighbouring cities and towns.

School profile

Pupils Total age range 5–18; 252 pupils, 2 day boys, 250 girls (115 day, 135 boarding). Senior department 12–18, 200 girls. Main entry ages, 11, 13 and into the sixth. 10% are children of former pupils. Own junior school provides more than 20% of senior intake. *State school entry:* 30% main intake, 80% to sixth.

Entrance Scholarships and own exam used. No special skills or religious requirements. Parents not expected to buy textbooks. Average extras £325 per term. Approx 7 pa assisted places. Approx 2 pa scholarships/bursaries, £600–£2500 (academic, art, music, tennis and riding scholarships).

Parents 15+% in industry or commerce; 15% farmers/landowners. 30+% live within 30 miles, 10+% live overseas.

Head and staff *Headmistress:* Mrs Juliet L Austin, in post since 1993. Educated at Downe House and Birmingham University (English language and literature). Previously Headmistress of Combe Bank School, Kent, and Head of English and House Mistress at Downe House. *Staff:* 30 full time, 22 part time. Annual turnover 3%.

Exam results In 1995, 41 pupils in S-grade year, 44 in main Higher year, 36 in upper sixth. *S-grade:* In 1995, 13 upper fifth gained at least grade C in 8+ subjects; 24 in 5–7 subjects. *Highers:* 17 lower sixth passed in 4+ subjects; 6 in 3; 7 in 2; and 8 in 1 subject. Upper sixth pupils take further Highers, A-levels or both.

University and college entrance 87% of 1995 British sixth-form leavers went on to a degree course; others typically go on to non-degree coursees.

Curriculum S-grade, Highers and A-levels. 24 subjects offered. 30% took a mixture of arts/science A-levels; 70% took arts/humanities. *Vocational:* Work experience available; also Scotvec modules in graphic communications, fabrics, home economics, computing and drama. *Computing facilities:* 2 computing labs, 1 with Nimbus network (12 stations) and 1 with multi-media facilities. Nimbus and BBCs in other departments. *Special provision:* EFL classes for overseas students. *Europe:* French, German, Italian and Spanish offered to S-grade, Higher and A-Level. French compulsory from primary 1 to S-grade; all pupils are encouraged to study at least one other language. Regular exchanges (France and Germany); the school's international network leads to excellent opportunities for exchange. Small number of European pupils each year. Contact both with French sister school and German school in Perth's twin town.

The arts (Pupils aged 11 and over) *Music:* Over 50% of pupils learn a musical instrument; instrumental exams can be taken. Some 5 musical groups including chamber orchestra, full orchestra, wind trio. Local winners Perthshire Music Festival. *Drama and dance:* Both offered. LAMDA, Scotvec and SEB exams may be taken. Many pupils are involved in school productions. Major productions of musicals (involving staff and pupils) and dramas. *Art:* On average, 20 take S-grade, 12 Higher and 4 A-level. Design, pottery and textiles also offered.
Sport, community service and clubs *Sport and physical activities:* Compulsory sports: hockey, netball, volleyball, swimming, athletics, tennis, badminton, Scottish country dancing. Additional options: highland dancing, curling, aerobics, rounders, cross-country, riding, skiing. Riding and tennis scholarships offered. *Community service:* Pupils take bronze, silver and gold Duke of Edinburgh's Award. Community service optional at age 16. *Clubs and societies:* Up to 15 clubs, eg aerobics, art, karate, gymnastics, orienteering, skiing.
Uniform School uniform worn, including the sixth during class hours.
Houses/prefects Competitive houses. Head girls, prefects, head of house and house prefects, elected by school and ratified by the staff.
Religion Attendance at religious worship compulsory on Sunday. Assemblies three times each week.
Social ESU and Britannic Assurance debates, local newspaper's debates, dances/discos, police quiz competitions, senior citizens' functions, sporting fixtures, Multiple Sclerosis Society and Save the Children Fund functions/flag-selling and fund-raising with other local schools. Trips abroad include exchanges (sister school in France and with German school), ski trips to France/Switzerland, art group to Paris, history group to Russia. Sixth-form day pupils may bring cars. Meals formal on special occasions, usually self-service. School shop. No tobacco; wine allowed at some special functions.
Discipline For those failing to produce a piece of homework for the first time, punishment would be a rebuke or detention, depending on the circumstances. Those caught smoking cannabis on the premises might expect expulsion.
Boarding 60% have own study bedrooms, 40% in dormitories of 6+. Resident qualified nurse; weekly visit by doctor. Pupils can occasionally provide and cook own food, eg for house events. 2 weekend exeats (2 nights) plus half-term (5–11 days). Visits to the local town allowed on Saturday afternoon, from age 14; evening outings for sixth-formers at weekends, as arranged.
Alumnae association is run by Mrs Linda Strachan, 2 West Garleton, Haddington, East Lothian EH41 3SJ.

• KING ALFRED (Hampstead)

King Alfred School, North End Road, London NW11 7HY Tel 0181 457 5200, Fax 0181 457 5249
• Pupils 483 • Boys 4–18 (Day) • Girls 4–18 (Day) • Upper sixth 20 • Termly fees £1260 – £2150 (Day) • Enquiries/application to the Admission Secretary

What it's like

Founded in 1898 as a co-educational school. It is situated on a single urban site, on the edge of Hampstead Garden Suburb, surrounded by 6 acres of woodland gardens. From the beginning, it has been strictly secular, with no religious affiliations. It is kept deliberately small and enjoys a very good staff:pupil ratio of about 1:9. A sound education is provided and academic results are good. Most sixth-formers go on to degree courses. Music and drama are particularly strong and there is a large GCSE drama contingent. Many pupils are involved in both drama and art. Alumni include some distinguished musicians and actors.

School profile

Pupils Total age range 4–18; 483 day pupils (248 girls, 235 boys). Senior department 11–18, 269 pupils (130 boys, 139 girls). Main entry ages 4, 7, a few at 11, 14 and sixth. Many children of former pupils.
Entrance Diagnostic tests, 2-day visit and interview used; good GCSE results required for sixth-form entry. Parents expected to buy textbooks.
Head and staff *Head:* Francis Moran, 13 years in post. Educated at St Ignatius,

Stamford Hill, and at Cambridge University (economics and English) and the Institute of Education. Previously Head of English at Eton. *Staff:* 46 full time, 21 part time. Annual turnover 5%.

Exam results In 1995, 43 pupils in fifth form, 13 in upper sixth. *GCSE:* In 1995, 23 upper fifth gained at least grade C in 8+ subjects; 15 in 5–7 subjects. *A-levels:* 3 upper sixth passed in 4+ subjects; 6 in 3; and 4 in 2 subjects. Average UCAS points 17.4.

University and college entrance 98% of 1995 sixth-form leavers went on to a degree course; others typically go straight in to work. Of those going on to university, 5% went to Oxbridge; 5% took courses in medicine, dentistry and veterinary science, 5% in science and engineering, 2% in law, 58% in humanities and social sciences, 15% in art and design, 10% in other subjects.

Curriculum GCSE and A-levels. 16 subjects offered at GCSE; 17 at A-level including technology, photography, computing, theatre studies and music technology. 50% took a mixture of science and arts A-levels. *Europe:* French (taught from age 9), German and Spanish offered to GCSE and A-level.

The arts (Pupils aged 11 and over) 35% pupils learn musical instruments or take singing lessons. Many musical groups including a large jazz group, baroque strings, a choir, various ensembles, and a number of rock and jazz groups. *Drama & dance*: Drama offered. 50% of pupils take GCSE; A-level theatre studies also offered. *Art:* 50% of pupils take GCSE art. Pottery also offered.

Sport, community service and clubs (Pupils aged 11 and over) *Sport and physical activities* (both girls and boys): football, basketball, hockey, tennis, cricket and rounders. Other activities include: cross-country, volleyball, gymnastics, circuit-training, step aerobics, body conditioning and badminton. 4th and 5th years choice include golf, handball, squash, rugby and weight-training. GCSE PE also offered. Football, basketball, cricket, hockey, tennis and rounders clubs all on offer after school by the PE dept. *Clubs*: Dance, aerobics, squash, computing, CDT, art and craft, music, drama, French, the Bulletin (termly paper) and the sixth-form magazine.

Discipline Punishment is not a feature of the school, though very disruptive students are sent immediately to the deputies or head. Civilised, relaxed behaviour is encouraged. Sanctions will be invoked where drugs are involved.

Alumni association is run by Mrs X Bowlby, Boundary House, Wyldes Close, London NW11.

Former pupils Anthony Pleeth, Janet Craxton, Pamela Moisewitch, Solomon (Musicians); Maggie Norden (radio); Zoe Wanamaker, Stacey Tendeter, Catherine Harrison (actresses); Mamoun Hassan (films); Professor Richard Gregory (psychology).

• KING EDWARD (Bath)

King Edward's School, North Road, Bath, Avon BA2 6HU. Tel 01225 464313, Fax 01225 481363
• Pupils 680 • Boys 11–18 (Day) • Girls 16–18 (Day) • Upper sixth 115 • Termly fees £1431 (Day) • HMC • Enquiries/applications to the Admissions Secretary

What it's like

Founded in 1552 by royal charter of Edward VI, in 1961 it moved to its present premises, which lie on a fine site of 14 acres on the southern slope of the city, just below the university. The Old Building (c1830) houses part of the school, but there are many new buildings from 1961. Modern facilities and accommodation are first-class. There is a high standard of teaching and academic achievement and results are very good. The vast majority of pupils go on to degree courses each year, many to Oxbridge. The music, art and drama departments are very strong. A good range of sports and games and much emphasis on outdoor pursuits. Full use is made of the city's cultural amenities and also those of Bristol.

School profile

Pupils Age range 11–18; 680 day pupils (632 boys, 48 girls). Main entry ages 11 and 13 (boys) and into sixth (boys and girls). Approx 5% are children of former pupils. Own junior school provides 50% of intake. *State school entry:* 45% main intake, plus 50% to sixth.

Entrance Own entrance exam used. No special skills or religious requirements. Parents not expected to buy textbooks; lunch (£93), music tuition (£60–£124 per term) optional extras. 18 pa assisted places. 3 pa first year scholarships (33% fees) and 2 pa sixth-form (50% fees). Bursaries according to need.

Head and staff *Headmaster:* Peter Winter, 4 years in post. Educated at Trinity School, Croydon, and Oxford University (French). Previously Housemaster at the International Centre and Head of Modern Languages at both Sevenoaks and Magdalen College School, and assistant master at Latymer Upper School. *Staff:* 51 full time, 8 part time. Annual turnover 5%. Average age 38.

Exam results In 1995, 98 pupils in fifth, 103 in upper sixth. *GCSE:* In 1995, 84% fifth gained at least grade C in 8+ subjects; 16% in 5–7 subjects. *A-levels:* 8 upper sixth passed in 4+ subjects; 71 in 3; 15 in 2; and 7 in 1 subject. Average UCAS points 20.4

University and college entrance 88% of 1995 sixth-form leavers went on to a degree course; others typically go on to non-degree courses eg HND or art, music colleges. Of those going on to university, 9% went to Oxbridge; 1% took courses in medicine, dentistry and veterinary science, 25% in science and engineering, 65% in humanities and social sciences, 5% in art and design.

Curriculum GCSE and A-levels. 19 subjects offered (general studies offered but not examined). 24% take science A-levels; 50% arts/humanities; 26% both. *Vocational:* Work experience available. *Computing facilities:* A computer centre with 22 Acorn Archimedes A3000 computers linked by Econet system; also computers in most subject areas and in library. *Special provision:* Help arranged for dyslexic pupils offsite. *Europe:* French, German and Spanish offered to GCSE and A-level. Regular exchanges (France, Germany and Spain).

The arts *Music:* Up to 25% of pupils learn a musical instrument; instrumental exams can be taken. Some 12 musical groups including orchestras, wind band, swing band, early music group, brass, choirs. 1 member of National Youth Orchestra. *Drama & dance*: Drama offered. Some pupils are involved in school and house/other productions. School mounts annual arts festival involving a large number of pupils. *Art:* On average, 35 take GCSE, 16–20 A-level. Design, pottery, photography also offered.

Sport, community service and clubs *Sport and physical activities:* Compulsory sports: rugby, hockey, cricket, athletics, basketball. Optional: tennis, fencing, judo, lifesaving, table tennis, volleyball, badminton. Sixth form only: swimming, squash, climbing, golf, netball, aerobics. Athletics, 2 national champions, 2 junior internationals, 12 county representatives; rugby, 3 divisional reps, 9 county; cricket, 6 county reps; badminton, 1 county rep; hockey, 3 divisional reps, 13 county; chess, county U16 champions, 3 county reps; rugby, 1st XV unbeaten tour of Canada. *Community service:* Pupils take own Tudor Rose Scheme. CCF optional at age 13; community service at 16. *Clubs and societies:* Over 30 clubs, eg chess, ornithology, computing, mountain bikes, Amnesty International, astronomical, bowls, Christian Union, mountain walking, ski club.

Uniform School uniform worn except in the sixth-form where there are dress regulations.

Houses/prefects Competitive houses. Prefects, elected by staff after poll of school. Head prefect – appointed by the Headmaster. School Improvements Committee can make suggestions.

Religion Morning assembly compulsory; voluntary communion services twice a term.

Social Pupils belong to joint Sixth Form Societies (eg economics, science) and the Bath Society of Young Musicians with other local schools. Exchange visits to France and Germany; two ski trips a year; music tours abroad. Pupils allowed to bring own car/bike to school. Meals self-service. School shop. No tobacco/alcohol allowed.

Discipline Pupils failing to produce homework once might expect extra work during the lunch break; those caught smoking cannabis on the premises could expect expulsion (but this situation has never occurred).

Alumni association is run by Mr L D L Jones, c/o the school.

Former pupils Viscount Simon, Chancellor of Exchequer 1937–40 and Lord Chancellor 1940–45.

• KING EDWARD (Birmingham: Boys)

King Edward's School, Edgbaston Park Road, Birmingham B15 2UA. Tel 0121 472 1672, Fax 0121 414 1897

• Pupils 870 • Boys 11–18 (Day) • Girls None • Upper sixth 127 • Termly fees £1480 (Day)
• HMC • Enquiries/application to the Chief Master

What it's like

Founded in 1552 by royal charter of Edward VI. It moved from the city centre to its present site at Edgbaston in 1936 to occupy a purpose-built establishment of pleasing design in a big area of parkland and spacious playing fields. The site is shared with King Edward's High School for Girls and there is plenty of collaboration between them. High academic standards are needed for entry. Academically it is one of the leading schools in England and results are consistently excellent. Almost all pupils go on to degree courses, including very many to Oxbridge. It is strong in music, drama and the visual arts and has an excellent all-around record in sports and games, with many recent successes.

School profile

Pupils Age range 11–18; 870 day boys. Main entry ages 11, 13 and into sixth.
Entrance Own entrance exam used. A high academic standard required for entry; no religious requirements. Parents not normally expected to buy textbooks. 40 pa assisted places. Up to 20 pa academic, music and art scholarships, £200 to full fees.
Head and staff Chief Master: Hugh Wright, 5 years in post. Educated at Kingswood and Oxford (Lit Hum). Previously Headmaster at Gresham's and Stockport Grammar, Housemaster and Head of Classics at Cheltenham and Assistant Master at Brentwood. Also FRSA; former Chairman HMC and of NW District; Member, Admiralty Interview Board Panel. *Publications:* Film strips and notes on The Origins of Christianity and the Medieval Church. *Staff:* 67 full time, 10 part time, Annual turnover 5%.
Exam results In 1995, 130 in upper fifth, 127 in upper sixth. *GCSE:* In 1995, 127 upper fifth gained at least grade C in 8+ subjects; 3 in 5–7 subjects. *A-levels:* 119 upper sixth passed in 4+ subjects; 5 in 3 subjects; and 3 in 2 subjects. Average UCAS points 27.5 (including general studies, 35.1).
University and college entrance 99% of 1995 sixth-form leavers went on to a degree course (10% after a gap year, preferably working abroad), 25% to Oxbridge. 20% took courses in medicine, dentistry and veterinary science, 25% in science and engineering, 5% in law, 45% in humanities and social sciences, 5% in art and design.
Curriculum GCSE and A-levels (including A-level general studies). On average, 45% take science/engineering A-levels; 45% take arts and humanities; 10% a mixture. *Vocational:* Work experience available. *Computing facilities:* A new, well-equipped computer laboratory. Computers in most departments. *Europe:* French, German and Spanish offered at GCSE and A-level; also French AS-level and Italian GCSE. Over 75% take GCSE in more than 1 language. Regular exchanges (France, Germany and Spain). Talks from MEPs. Economics study trip to Paris.
The arts *Music:* Over 30% of pupils learn a musical instrument; instrumental exams can be taken. Some 15 musical groups. Strong representation in the Birmingham Schools Symphony Orchestra. *Drama & dance*: Drama offered and GCSE may be taken. All pupils are involved in school productions and some in house/other productions. *Art:* Design, pottery also offered.
Sport, community service and clubs *Sport and physical activities:* Compulsory sports: athletics, basketball, cricket, rugby, swimming. Optional: fives, fencing, tennis, hockey, squash, badminton, table tennis, croquet, sailing, golf. Tennis, winners Midland Bank U15 cup; basketball, 1 member of England Schools U16 team; cricket, 1 English Schools player. *Community service:* CCF and community service optional at age 13. *Clubs and societies:* Up to 30 clubs, eg Shakespeare, mathematics, dramatic, scientific, Star Wars.
Uniform School uniform worn throughout.
Houses/perfects Competitive houses. School prefects.
Social Many activities with King Edward's Girls School. Exchanges; regular ski trips to France, Austria or Switzerland. No tobacco/alcohol allowed.
Discipline Any contact with drugs would result in expulsion.

• KING EDWARD (Birmingham: Girls)

King Edward VI High School for Girls, Edgbaston Park Road, Birmingham B15 2UB. Tel 0121 472 1834

• Pupils 550 • Boys None • Girls 11-18 (Day) • Upper sixth 81 • Termly fees £1410 (Day) • GSA • Enquiries/application to the Headmistress

What it's like

Founded in 1883, it moved to its present buildings in Edgbaston in 1940. Purpose-built and well-equipped, it has spacious playing fields. It shares the site with the boys' school and there is plentiful collaboration between them. It is a non-denominational school. It enjoys good teaching and academic standards are very high. Results are excellent and virtually all leavers go on to degree courses, including many to Oxbridge. Strong in music, drama and art and design. A good range of sport and games and it has particular strength in hockey and netball, with many county and regional representatives. A number of extra-curricular activities. Considerable commitment to local community schemes.

School profile

Pupils Age range 11–18; 550 day girls. Main entry ages 11 and into sixth. Approx 2% are children of former pupils. *State school entry:* 48% main intake, plus 20% to sixth.
Entrance Own entrance exam used. No special skills or religious requirements. Parents not expected to buy textbooks; lunch, outings, music tuition extra. 30 pa assisted places. 25 pa scholarships/bursaries, 25%–100% fees.
Head and staff *Headmistress:* Miss Sarah Evans, appointed 1996. Educated at King James' Grammar School, Knaresborough, and the universities of Sussex, Leicester and Leeds (English). Previously Head at Friends School, Saffron Walden, Deputy Head at Fulneck Girls' School, and Head of English at Leeds High. Also governor of Kings' School, Tynemouth; non-executive director, Essex Ambulance Trust; Vice-Chairman BSA. *Staff:* 36 full time, 12 part time. Annual turnover 3%.
Exam results In 1995, 76 pupils in upper fifth, 73 in upper sixth. *GCSE:* In 1995, all upper fifth gained at least grade C in 8+ subjects. *A-levels:* all upper sixth passed in 4+ subjects. Average UCAS points 27.5.
University and college entrance All 1995 sixth-form leavers went on to a degree course, 15 % to Oxbridge; 9% took courses in medicine, dentistry and veterinary science, 42% in science and engineering, 49% in humanities and social sciences.
Curriculum GCSE and A-levels. 17 subjects offered (including Greek and A-level general studies). 36% took science A-levels, 33% arts/humanities; 31% both. *Vocational:* Work experience available. *Computing facilities:* Nimbus network plus a variety of isolated micros; 2 Archimedes in art and design. *Europe:* French and German offered to GCSE and A-level; also GCSE Italian, Russian and Spanish. Regular exchanges (France, Germany and Austria).
The arts *Music:* Over 50% of pupils learn a musical instrument; instrumental exams can be taken. Some 10 musical groups including orchestra, concert band, choirs, operatic society. Many pupils with Grade 8 with distinction. *Drama & dance*: Both offered. Majority of pupils are involved in school and form/other productions. Pupils take part in dance and drama productions outside school, at Birmingham Hippodrome and Repertory Theatre. *Art:* On average, 24 take GCSE, 4 AS-level, 5 A-level. CAD, design (2D & 3D), pottery, textiles, photography, history and appreciation of art (AS and A-level) also offered. Winners in various national competitions and Eisteddfod.
Sport, community service and clubs *Sport and physical activities:* Compulsory sports: (at different ages) hockey, netball, tennis, swimming, rounders, gym, dance, basketball, badminton, squash, volleyball, athletics. Sixth form only: self-defence, archery, golf. Hockey, 9 county players, 2 regional players, 1994/5 county champions U15, U14, U13, U12; netball, 5 county players U18, U15, U14. *Community service:* Pupils take bronze, silver and gold Duke of Edinburgh's Award. Community service compulsory for 1 term at age 17 and many pupils continue thereafter. *Clubs and societies:* Up to 30 clubs, eg sports, dance, geographical, mathematics, modern languages, debating, classics, Shakespeare, Christian Union, drama.
Uniform School uniform worn except in the sixth.
Houses/prefects Many leadership opportunities throughout the school. School Council.
Social Many joint activities with brother school (King Edward's). Organised trips

abroad. Pupils allowed to bring own car/bike to school. Meals self-service. School shop. No tobacco/alcohol allowed.
Discipline Rules are kept to the minimum necessary for good order and a purposeful working environment. Atmosphere and tradition play an important part in the maintenance of discipline and the encouragement of self-discipline.

• KING EDWARD (Lytham)

King Edward VII School, Lytham St Anne's, Lancashire FY8 1DT. Tel 01253 736459, Fax 01253 731623

• Pupils 570 • Boys 3–18 (Day) • Girls 3–11 only • Upper sixth 60 • Termly fees £1230 (Day) • HMC • Enquiries/application to the Headmaster

What it's like

Founded in 1908, it has an expansive site by the seaside, close to sandhills and in an open and bracing position. Non-denominational, it has good facilities and playing fields. The standards of teaching are high and results are good. Nearly all sixth-formers go on to degree courses, including Oxbridge. It collaborates with its sister school, Queen Mary. Strong sporting tradition, with many county representatives. Use is made of an outdoor pursuit centre at Ribblehead in the Dales. Thre are some imaginative overseas links. Some community service and participation in the Duke of Edinburgh's Award Scheme. Many active clubs and societies. Regular musical and dramatic productions in conjunction with Queen Mary.

School profile

Pupils Total age range 3–18; 570 day pupils. Senior department 11–18, 495 boys. Main entry ages 11, 13 and into sixth. Approx 8% are children of former pupils. Own junior school provides 30% of senior intake. *State school entry:* 60% senior intake.
Entrance Own entrance exam used; occasionally Common Entrance. Overall academic ability required; no religious requirements. Parents not expected to buy textbooks; no essential extras. 32 pa assisted places. 1 or 2 pa open scholarships, 50% fees. 5–6 pa bursaries, 28% fees. 1 music award, 28% fees.
Head and staff *Headmaster:* Julian Wilde, 4 years in post. Educated at Bristol Grammar School and Oxford University (theology). Previously Headmaster at The City School, Lincoln, Deputy Head at Wood Green School, Oxfordshire, and Head of Religious Studies at William Hulme's. *Staff:* 41 full time. Annual turnover 8%. Average age 36.
Exam results In 1995, 85 pupils in upper fifth, 60 in upper sixth. *GCSE:* In 1995, 80% upper fifth gained at least grade C in 8+ subjects; 20% in 5–7 subjects. *A-levels:* 44 upper sixth passed in 4+ subjects; 7 in 3; 5 in 2; and 3 in 1 subject. average UCAS points 16.3.
University and college entrance All 1995 sixth-form leavers went on to a degree course, 10% to Oxbridge.
Curriculum GCSE and A-levels. 16 GCSE subjects offered; 3 at AS-level; 18 at A-level (all students take A-level general studies). 50% take arts/humanities A-levels; 30% science; 20% both. *Vocational:* Work experience compulsory. *Computing facilities:* Network allowing access to computer facilities from every room, plus a main computer base, equipped with Archimedes computers; also plotters and laser colour printers. *Europe:* French and German offered to GCSE, AS and A-level. Regular exchanges (France and Germany). Links with Czech Republic; sixth-form exchange with Ireland.
The arts (Pupils aged 11 and over) *Music:* 20% of pupils learn a musical instrument; instrumental exams can be taken. Some 7 musical groups including orchestra, choir, swing band, brass, opera. *Drama & dance*: A-level theatre studies offered. Some pupils are involved in school and house/other productions. *Art:* On average, 15 take GCSE, 4 A-level. Design, pottery, sculpture and photography also offered. Art exchange with Czech Republic 1996. High proportion of A-level students go on to study architecture.
Sport, community service and clubs (Pupils aged 11 and over) *Sport and physical activities:* Compulsory sports: rugby, cricket, athletics. Optional: badminton, tennis, hockey, squash, table tennis. Sixth form only: swimming, golf, shooting, outdoor pursuits. A-level sports studies may be taken. Rugby, regular representatives at county, divisional and international level; cricket, county reps at U19, U17, U16, U15, U13. Field study/outdoor pursuits centre in Yorkshire Dales; strong on climbing, caving, diving, canoeing, skiing etc. *Community service:* Pupils take bronze, silver and gold Duke

of Edinburgh's Award; D of E combined with sister school – over 100 participants. Community service optional age 14–18. *Clubs and societies:* Up to 30 clubs, eg bridge, aviation, sailing, fell-walking, chess, computing, arts, archery, drama, railway, shooting.
Uniform School uniform worn throughout.
Houses/prefects Competitive houses. Prefects, head boy, head of house and house prefects – appointed by the Headmaster after consultation.
Religion School assemblies, non-denominational.
Social Many activities with sister school, Queen Mary. Organised trips abroad; links with Czech Republic, New Zealand and South Africa. Pupils allowed to bring own car, bike or motorbike to school. Meals self-service. School shop. No tobacco/alcohol allowed.
Alumni association is run by David Barnett, 9 Roseway, Lytham St Anne's FY8 3LU.
Former pupils Sir Alan Leslie (Past Pres, Law Soc.); Peter Shaffer (playwright); Sir Peter Harrop (Permanent Secretary DOE); Mervyn Jones (Chief Constable)

• KING EDWARD (Southampton)

King Edward VI School, Kellett Road, Southampton, Hampshire SO15 7UQ. Tel 01703 704561, Fax 01703 705937

• Pupils 951 • Boys 11–19 (Day) • Girls 11–19 (Day) • Upper sixth 144 • Termly fees £1570 (Day) • HMC • Enquiries/applications to the Registrar

What it's like

Founded in 1553 under Letters Patent of King Edward VI, it has occupied four different sites. It is now housed in buildings erected in 1938 about a mile and a half from the centre of Southampton. Good playing fields adjoin it and there are other playing fields at Swaythling. There have been considerable additions and improvements to the buildings over the years and they are now well-equipped. Founded as a boys' school, girls were accepted into the sixth-form in 1983 and throughout the school from 1994. Pupils of all religious persuasions are accepted, but there is a close association (dating from the 16th century) with St Mary's, Southampton. Assemblies include worship, and religious education forms part of the curriculum. There is a staff:pupil ratio of about 1:11. Academic standards are high and results consistently very good. Almost all sixth-formers go on to degree courses, including many to Oxbridge. Music and drama are well supported. A broad range of games and sports is provided (including squash racquets and Winchester fives). Rugby, netball, hockey, tennis and cricket are strong and foreign tours take place. A very large number of clubs and societies (40 or more) cater for most conceivable extra-curricular needs and interests.

School profile

Pupils Age range 11–19, 951 day pupils (808 boys, 143 girls); school fully co-educational since 1994. Main entry ages 11, 13 and into the sixth. *State school entry:* 55% main intake, plus 40% to sixth.
Entrance Own entrance exam, interview and report. 40 pa assisted places. Scholarships and bursaries.
Head and staff *Head Master*: Peter Hamilton, appointed in 1996. Educated at King Edward's, Southampton, and Oxford University (modern languages). Previously Housemaster and Head of Modern Languages at Westminster. *Staff:* 86 full time, 4 part time. Annual turnover 5%. Average age 33.
Exam results In 1995, 141 pupils in fifth year, 120 in upper sixth. *GCSE:* In 1995, 126 fifth year gained at least grade C in 8+ subjects; 10 in 5–7 subjects. *A-levels:* 17 upper sixth passed in 4 subjects; 92 in 3; 8 in 2; and 3 in 1 subject. Average UCAS points 24.2.
University and college entrance 97% of 1995 sixth-form leavers went on to a degree course (23% after a gap year); others typically go on to employment. Of those going on to university, 10% went to Oxbridge; 9% took courses in medicine, dentistry and veterinary science, 33% in science and engineering, 4% in law, 35% in humanities and social sciences, 3% in art and design, 4% in other subjects eg podiatry, optometry, architecture, music.
Curriculum GCSE and A-levels. 20 subjects offered (no A-level general studies). 53% take science A-levels; 47% arts/humanities. *Computing facilities:* Mostly networked IBM compatible machines with Acorn BBC Micros and AppleMacs for specialist use. *Europe:* French, German and Spanish offered at GCSE and A-level. Regular exchanges (France, Germany and Spain).

The arts *Music:* Over 20% pupils learn a musical instrument; instrumental exams can be taken. 12 musical groups including orchestras, wind band, jazz bands, madrigal, string and woodwind groups, choir, brass groups. Several members of Hampshire County and Southampton Youth orchestras. Winner of recent jazz piano competition. *Drama & dance*: Both offered; GCSE drama may be taken. Some pupils involved in school and house/other productions. Recent productions of Oklahoma, Tin Pan Ali, Hamlet and Oh! What a Lovely War. *Art:* On average, 25 take GCSE, 5 A-level. Design and photography also offered.
Sport, community service and clubs *Sport and physical activities:* Compulsory sports: Rugby, hockey, netball, tennis, cricket; many other options. Sixth only: football. 40+ pupils annually gain county honours, several regional, in a variety of sports; national representatives in sailing, hockey, athletics, cricket, swimming. *Community service:* Pupils take bronze, silver and gold Duke of Edinburgh's Award. Community service optional. *Clubs and societies:* 30 clubs eg aerobics, chess, Christian Union, cookery, debating, essay, film, horse-riding, origami, photography, stamp.
Uniform School uniform worn throughout.
Houses/prefects Competitive houses. Head boy/girl, head of house and house prefects – appointed by the Head Master.
Religion Attendance at religious worship compulsory.
Social Foreign language exchanges; classical tours, ski trips, sports tours (cricket, rugby). Pupils allowed to bring own car/bike/motorbike to school. Meals self-service. School shop. No tobacco/alcohol allowed.
Discipline A high standard of conduct and good manners is expected of all pupils, on and off school premises. Any pupil in breach of School Regulations or failure to complete homework assignments will be liable to be given an appropriate detention. Any pupil found to be supplying or in possession of illegal substances whilst under school jurisdiction must expect serious action to be taken.

• KING EDWARD (Witley)

King Edward's School Witley, Godalming, Surrey GU8 5SG. Tel 01428 682572

• Pupils 500 • Boys 11–18 (Day/Board) • Girls 11–18 (Day/Board) • Upper sixth 65 • Termly fees £2080 (Day) £2990 (Board) • HMC • Enquiries to the Headmaster • Application to the Headmaster's Secretary

What it's like

Founded in 1553 by King Edward VI and, unusually for the period, admitting both genders. It was formerly at the Bridewell Palace and in 1867 moved to its present splendid site of 100 wooded acres near the Surrey/Sussex/Hampshire borders. Strong links with the City and the Lord Mayor of London are retained. The Bridewell Foundation is well-endowed and several million pounds have been spent on facilities in the last 20 years or so. Now extremely well-equipped in every respect. Founded as a co-educational school, pupils come from a wide social background. It is a C of E school and there is pronounced emphasis on religious instruction, and worship in its fine Victorian Gothic chapel. Academic standards are high and results good. The music and art departments are tremendously strong. There is a good range of sport, games and activities and the school has an outstanding record in the Duke of Edinburgh's Award Scheme.

School profile

Pupils Age range 11–18; 500 pupils, 128 day (87 boys, 41 girls), 372 boarding (210 boys, 162 girls). Senior department 13–18, 421 pupils (256 boys, 165 girls). Main entry ages 11, 13 and into sixth. Very few are children of former pupils. *State school entry:* 50% main intake, plus 5% to sixth.
Entrance Own entrance exam used. No special skills required. Parents not expected to buy textbooks; music (£60) extra. 15 pa assisted places. Boarding bursaries, few small forces bursaries, sixth-form scholarship; £400–£1740.
Parents 15+% in industry or commerce; 15+% are doctors, lawyers, etc; 15+% in the armed services. 30+% live within 30 miles; 10+% live overseas
Head and staff *Headmaster:* Rodney Fox, in post 7 years. Educated at Brighton College and universities of Edinburgh (mathematics and natural philosophy) and Oxford (education). Previously Deputy Headmaster, Housemaster and Head of Mathematics

at Brighton College and mathematics and physics teacher at Epsom College. Also Chartered Mathematician and Fellow of the Institute of Mathematics and its Applications. Member of Organising Committee, Surrey Series of Royal Institution Master Classes in Mathematics; previously Secretary, Sussex branch of the Mathematical Association; Chairman of Mathematics Committee of Independent Schools Exam Board; Secretary of Eastern Division of HMC. *Staff:* 53 full time, 28 part time (includes peripatetic teachers). Annual turnover 5%. Average age 40.

Exam results On average, 91 pupils in upper fifth, 65 in upper sixth. *GCSE:* 60 upper fifth gain at least grade C in 8+ subjects; 24 in 5–7; and 6 in 1–4 subjects; in 1995, an average of 7.3 subjects per pupil. *A-levels:* 28 upper sixth pass in 4+ subjects; 18 in 3; 10 in 2; and 8 in 1 subject; an average of 3.2 subjects per pupil. Average UCAS points 17.1.

University and college entrance 95% of 1995 sixth-form leavers went on to a degree course (20% after a gap year), 3% to Oxbridge; 5% took courses in medicine, dentistry and veterinary science, 20% in science and engineering, 5% in law, 30% in humanities and social sciences, 10% in art and design, 5% in vocational subjects eg land management, 2% in eg IT, drama.

Curriculum GCSE and A-levels. 27 subjects offered (including A-level general studies). 30% take science A-levels; 55% arts/humanities; 15% both. *Vocational:* Work experience available. *Computing facilities:* Large computer department; computers used in many departments; GCSE information technology. *Europe:* French and German offered to GCSE, AS and A-level; French compulsory from age 11, German or Latin from 12. Regular exchanges (France and Germany).

The arts *Music:* Over 25% of pupils learn a musical instrument; instrumental exams can be taken. Some 16 musical groups including orchestra, swing band, choir, flute, clarinet, string ensembles etc. *Drama & dance:* Drama offered and GCSE and A-level may be taken. Majority of pupils are involved in school productions and all in house/other productions. *Art:* On average, 100 take GCSE, 10 AS-level, 50 A-level. Design, pottery, textiles and photography also offered.

Sport, community service and clubs *Sport and physical activities:* Compulsory sports: athletics, hockey, soccer, cricket, netball, rounders, tennis. Optional: sailing, shooting, karate, fencing, rugby, cross-country, running, rock-climbing, swimming, squash, basketball. Pupils in county athletics teams, Independent Schools soccer teams. *Community service:* Pupils take bronze, silver and gold Duke of Edinburgh's Award. Community service compulsory for 1 year at age 16. *Clubs and societies:* Up to 30 clubs, eg shooting, sailing, golf, patchwork, computing, aqua-aerobics, cooking, outdoor pursuits.

Uniform School uniform worn throughout.

Houses/prefects Competitive houses. Prefects, head boy and girl, head of house and house prefects – elected by school, approved by Headmaster. School Council.

Religion Religious worship compulsory.

Social Debates, contests, etc with other local schools. Organised trips to France and Germany. Pupils allowed to bring own bike to school. Meals self-service. School shop. No tobacco/alcohol allowed.

Discipline Pupils failing to produce homework once might expect detention; those caught smoking cannabis on the premises could expect expulsion.

Boarding Sixth formers have own study bedroom; fifth formers share with one other; only juniors are in dormitories of 6+. Single-sex houses of about 55, same as competitive houses. Resident qualified nurse. Central dining room. One overnight exeat every 3 weeks. Visits to local town allowed at weekends.

Alumni association run by Mr P Whittle, c/o the school.

• KING GEORGE V (Hong Kong)

King George V School, 2 Tin Kwong Road, Hong Kong. Tel 852 2711 3028, Fax 852 2760 7116 • Pupils 1168 • Boys 11–19 (Day) • Girls 11–19 (Day) • Upper sixth 100 • Termly fees £1750. (Day) • HMC • Enquiries/application to the Principal

What it's like

The school dates from 1902 when Kowloon British School was opened. The name was changed first to the Central British School (in 1923) and then to the King George V (in 1948). It has some 45 nationalities represented; multi-cultural, multi-faith and multi-ethnic and the

PTA is particularly active. In a place where each square metre is at a premium it is fortunate to have a 10-acre site in the dormitory section of the Kowloon peninsula, where it has been since 1936. There have been extensive additions and improvements in the last 30 years and the facilities are first-rate; it is fully air-conditioned. There are sophisticated sporting facilities on site and a purpose-built sixth-form centre was recently completed. It has a reputation for its high standards of discipline, behaviour and a strong work ethos. The staff:pupil ratio is about 1:14. Education is based on the English system in line with the National Curriculum and results are very good. A high proportion of leavers go on to degree courses in many parts of the world. Music and drama flourish. Sport and games are compulsory with a fairly wide range offered; in several games there have been school representatives at national level. A wide variety of extracurricular activities, including the Duke of Edinburgh's Award Scheme. The school displays considerable enterprise in organising expeditions (eg to China, Nepal, Japan, Australia and Taipei). There is a strong commitment to community services and various local charities.

School profile

Pupils Age range 11–19; 1168 day pupils, 570 boys, 598 girls. Main entry is at age 11 and into the sixth. 10% are children of former pupils. 3 ESF primary feeder schools each provide over 30% of the intake.
Entrance Own entrance English test only. No special skills or religious requirements, multi-faith school. Parents expected to buy textbooks in sixth-form only; average extras £250.
Parents Mainly in professions. All live close by.
Head and staff *Principal:* Michael J Behennah, 8 years in post. Educated at St Austell Grammar School and London University (philosophy, politics & economics and education). Previously Deputy Principal at Island School, Hong Kong, and Director of Studies at United World College, Singapore. *Staff:* 86 full time. Annual turnover, less than 5%. Average age, 39.
Exam results On average, 170 pupils in upper fifth, 100 in upper sixth. *GCSE:* In 1995, upper fifth pupils gained grade C or above in an average of 7.9 subjects. *A-levels:* Upper sixth pupils passed an average of 2.6 subjects.
University and college entrance 94% of 1995 sixth-form leavers went on to a degree course; others typically go on to drama, music or art colleges. Of those going on to university, 2% went to Oxbridge; 20% took courses in medicine, dentistry and veterinary science, 10% in science and engineering, 40% in humanities and social sciences, 2% in art and design, 14% in accountancy and business, 4% in drama and music.
Curriculum GCSE, AS and A-levels offered, also American SATs. 14 AS-level subjects offered, 22 A-levels; including Mandarin, computing, theatre studies, psychology; no A-level general studies. 40% take science A-levels; 40% arts/humanities; rest take both. *Vocational:* Work experience available. *Computing facilities:* 240 IBM PCs, networked. *Special provision:* Special needs unit (with 3 staff) for students with specific learning difficulties and moderate learning difficulties; main school co-ordinator of special needs. *Europe:* French and German offered at GCSE, AS-level and A-level. Students must study either Mandarin, French or German. Trips to France every 2 years.
The arts *Music:* Over 50% of pupils learn a musical instrument; instrumental exams and A-level music can be taken. 14 musical groups include orchestras, choirs, jazz band, flute ensemble, quartet, rock band, chamber orchestra. Frequent winners in the Hong Kong Schools Music Competition. *Drama & dance*: Both offered; pupils may take GCSE, AS and A-level drama. Majority of pupils involved in school and house/other productions. Drama groups recently visited Taipei, Kuala Lumpur, Bangkok and Adelaide and appeared on television; Hong Kong School debating champions. *Art:* On average, 9 take GCSE, 2 AS-level, 3 A-level. Design, textiles and photography also offered. Pupils exhibit in Hong Kong art exhibitions.
Sport, community service and clubs *Sport and physical activities:* 17 competitive sports compulsory, including hockey, netball, swimming, rugby, tennis, soccer, cross country. GCSE sports studies available. Hong Kong national teams in tennis, rugby, soccer, cross-country. *Community service:* Pupils take bronze, silver and gold Duke of Edinburgh's Award. CCF and community service optional. Older pupils involved in work with Vietnamese refugees. *Clubs & societies*: Up to 30 clubs including drama, photography, speech, gymnastics, guitar, astronomy, pottery, dance, environment, orienteering.

Uniform School uniform worn throughout.
Houses/prefects Competitive houses for sport. Head boy/girl, prefects, house prefects and house captains. Senior school student council.
Religion No compulsory religious worship.
Social Model United Nations debate with other schools, sixth-form technology/communication conferences. Trekking trips to Nepal, cycling trips to China, skiing to Japan, French trips to Paris, drama to Taipei and Kuala Lumpur. Meals self-service. School shop. No alcohol/tobacco allowed.
Discipline A high standard of behaviour is expected at all times. Pupils failing to produce homework once might expect a verbal reprimand; any case involving drugs would result in compulsory counselling for the pupil and parents; expulsion for repeat offenders.
Alumni association run by Ms Sandra Leckenby, c/o the school.
Former pupils Dr Victor Fung, Chairman TDC Hong Kong.

• KING'S (Bruton)

King's School, Bruton, Somerset BA10 OED. Tel 01749 813326, Fax 01749 813426
• Pupils 332 • Boys 13–18 (Day/Board) • Girls 16–18 (Day/Board) • Upper sixth 59 • Termly fees £2590 (Day) £3655 (Board) • HMC • Enquiries/application to the Headmaster

What it's like

Founded in 1519, it occupies the original site in a very pretty small town. The old school house (1519) is still in use. Modern buildings provide very good accommodation and the school is well-equipped with modern facilities. Recent additions include a physics building (with 2 computing classrooms) and an astroturf pitch. Delightful playing fields adjoin it by the parish church. There are strong, long-standing links with the town and the parish. A balanced all-round education is provided within a strong Christian framework. Academic results are very good and sixth-form leavers are expected to go on to degree courses. The music, drama and art departments are very active. A good range of games and sports (a number of representatives at county level). A big commitment to local community schemes.

School profile

Pupils Age range 13–18; 332 pupils, 74 day (boys), 255 boarding (227 boys, 28 girls). Main entry ages 13 (boys) and into sixth (boys and girls). Approx 5% are children of former pupils. *State school entry:* 2% main intake, plus 3% to sixth.
Entrance Common Entrance; other exams rarely used. No special skills or religious requirements but expected to attend C of E services. Parents not expected to buy textbooks; personal accident insurance (£4 per term) only compulsory extra. 2 pa assisted places. 10 pa scholarships/bursaries, £245 to half fees.
Parents 15+% in industry or commerce. 30+% live within 30 miles.
Head and staff *Headmaster:* R I Smyth, 4 years in post. Educated at Sedbergh and Cambridge (law and modern history). Previously Housemaster at Wellington College and taught at Gresham's and Christ's Hospital (master i/c rugby). Also spent 5 years in business and 1 as lay assistant to Anglican Church in Berne; cricket and rugby blue. *Staff:* 35 full time staff. Annual turnover 3. Average age 37.
Exam results In 1995, 58 pupils in upper fifth, 59 in upper sixth. *GCSE:* In 1995, 96% of upper fifth gained at least grade C in 5+ subjects. *A-levels:* 9 upper sixth passed in 4+ subjects; 38 in 3; 10 in 2; and 2 in 1 subject. Average UCAS points 20.4.
University and college entrance 88% of 1995 sixth-form leavers went on to a degree course (17% after a gap year); others typically go on to further education or HND courses. Of those going on to university, 5% went to Oxbridge; 2% took courses in medicine, dentistry and veterinary science, 33% in science and engineering, 2% in law, 37% in humanities and social sciences, 8% in art and design, 18% in vocational subjects eg tourism, management.
Curriculum GCSE and A-levels. 17 subjects offered (no A-level general studies). 20% took science A-levels; 52% arts/humanities; 28% both. *Vocational:* Work experience available; all pupils take RSA qualifications in CLAIT. *Computing facilities:* 28 booth research machines, Nimbus system and 16 IBM 486 and CD-Roms. *Special provision:*

Learning difficulties unit for small number of pupils with mild dyslexia and to teach EFL. *Europe:* French, German and Spanish offered to GCSE and A-level; also Italian GCSE (in sixth) and London Chamber of Commerce exams; Italian and Spanish non-examined courses. Regular exchanges (France and Germany).

The arts *Music:* Over 50% of pupils learn a musical instrument; instrumental exams can be taken. Some 10 musical groups including choir, orchestra, dance, concert, military bands, brass, jazz, saxophone, etc. *Drama & dance*: Majority of pupils are involved in school productions and some in house/other productions. *Art:* GCSE and A-level taken; design, pottery, textiles and photography also offered.

Sport, community service and clubs *Sport and physical activities:* Compulsory: rugby, hockey, cricket. Optional: soccer, squash, tennis, basketball, fencing, athletics. *Community service:* CCF compulsory for 2 years at age 13 then optional. *Clubs and societies:* Up to 15 clubs, eg archery, book, foreign film, drama, chess, chamber music, beekeeping, archive society.

Uniform School uniform worn throughout.

Houses/prefects Competitive houses. Prefects, head boy/girl, head of house and house prefects – appointed by the Headmaster and housemaster.

Religion Compulsory C of E services (one weekday and Sunday).

Social Many organised local events, trips and exchanges abroad. Meals self-service. School shop. No pupils allowed tobacco; alcohol in supervised sixth-form club.

Discipline Pupils failing to produce homework once would be treated according to teacher; those caught smoking cannabis on the premises must expect expulsion.

Boarding 18% have own study bedroom, 28% share with others, 54% in dormitories of 4+. Single-sex houses of 55–65 (boys); 1 girls house. Resident qualified nurse; 3 doctors in town. Central dining room. 4 weekend exeats each term. Visits to the local town allowed.

Alumni association is run by D Hindley, c/o the school.

• KING'S (Canterbury)

The King's School, Canterbury, Kent CT1 2ES. Tel 01227 595501, Fax 01227 595595

• Pupils 734 • Boys 13–18 (Day/Board) • Girls 13–18 (Day/Board) • Upper sixth 140 • Termly fees £2945 (Day) £4265 (Board) • HMC • Enquiries/application to the Admissions Secretary

What it's like

Founded in 597, the school was first a part of the 6th-century Benedictine monastery. It has been associated with the cathedral for most of its life. Nearly all the buildings are in the cathedral precincts or at the recently purchased St Augustine's Abbey nearby – many dating from the Middle Ages, some from the 16th and 17th centuries. Thus, the school is blessed with an unusually civilised environment and some of the finest architecture in England. Modern facilities are first-class and include exceptionally good libraries, well-equipped laboratories and new sports centre. Originally a boys' school, girls were accepted into the sixth-form in 1971 and the school became fully co-educational in 1990. Religious worship and instruction form an important part of the curriculum. Very well run, it reveals high standards in virtually every enterprise. Academically it is high-powered and achieves excellent results. Nearly all sixth-form leavers go on to degree courses, including many to Oxbridge. The music is of outstanding quality and vigour. Drama is also very strong. Each year the school presents its own festival of music and drama (King's Week) which is attended by thousands. A wide variety of sports and games is available and standards are very high. There are regularly international representatives in various sports and over 30 pupils usually gain county honours or equivalent each year. Thirty or more clubs and societies cater for most extra-curricular activities. There is a flourishing CCF contingent, considerable emphasis on outdoor pursuits and a fine record in the Duke of Edinburgh's Award Scheme.

School profile

Pupils Age range 13–18; 734 pupils, 131 day (78 boys, 53 girls), 603 boarding (365 boys, 238 girls). Main entry ages 13 and into sixth. Intake from some 50 prep/junior schools; some 20% intake from own junior school, Junior King's School (tel 01227 710245). *State school entry:* Minimal; 5% to sixth.

Entrance Common Entrance and own sixth-form entrance exam used. No special skills or religious requirements. Extras include account at school shop. Numerous academic, art and music awards.

Head and staff *Headmaster:* Keith Wilkinson, appointed 1996. Educated at Beaumont Leys College and the Gateway School, Leicester; Hull and Cambridge universities (English and theology). Previously Head Master of Berkhamsted; Senior Tutor and Senior Chaplain at Malvern College; English Master and Chaplain at Eton; Head of Human Sciences at Kelvin Hall High School, Hull; and Head of Religious Studies at Bricknell High School, Hull. *Staff:* 85 full time, 7 part time. Annual turnover 5%.

Exam results In 1996, 148 pupils in upper fifth, 140 in upper sixth. *GCSE:* In 1995, 98% upper fifth gained at least grade C in 9+ subjects; 2% in 5–7 subjects. *A-levels:* 33% upper sixth passed in 4+ subjects; 66% in 3; 1% in 2 subjects. Average UCAS points 27.2.

University and college entrance 97% of 1995 sixth-form leavers went on to a degree course (43% after a gap year); others typically go on to retake A-levels, or to HND or business courses. Of those going on to university, 19% went to Oxbridge; 6% took courses in medicine, dentistry and veterinary science, 49% in science and engineering, 4% in law, 40% in humanities and social sciences, 2% in art and design, 2% in vocational subjects eg nursing, stage management, 9% in other subjects eg business studies.

Curriculum GCSE and A-levels. 23 subjects offered, including A-level general studies. A range of languages (including Japanese) available in sixth-form. *Vocational:* Work experience available. *Computing facilities:* Excellent computing facilities. *Europe:* French (compulsory), German and Spanish offered to GCSE, AS and A-level; also Russian GCSE and A-level, and GCSE Italian and Portuguese in sixth. 75% take GCSE in more than 1 language. Annual involvement in European conferences.

The arts *Music:* Over half of pupils learn a musical instrument; instrumental exams can be taken. Some 18 musical groups including orchestras, choirs, concert, jazz, big bands, chamber music, barbershop, rock. 1 pupil in National Youth Orchestra; 7 in National Youth Choir; 1 in county youth orchestra; choir tours to France and Germany; several Oxbridge choral and organ scholars; Kent Young Musician winner. *Drama & dance*: Both offered. GCSE and A-level drama and LAMDA exams may be taken. Majority of pupils are involved in school and house/other productions. During King's Week 3 plays offered and some dance. *Art:* On average, 50 take GCSE, 12 A-level; design, pottery and textiles also offered. Art facilities open to non-examination pupils.

Sport, community service and clubs *Sport and physical activities:* Compulsory; degree of choice which increases with age. Major sports: rugby, hockey, rowing, cricket (boys), hockey, netball, tennis, rowing (girls). Others available: athletics, badminton, canoeing, climbing, cross-country, fencing, golf, keep fit, lacrosse, sailing, soccer, squash, swimming, tennis, yachting, basketball, dance, gymnastics, judo, karate, rounders, volleyball and water polo. On average 30–40 pa pupils achieve representation at county level or above; recent internationals in fencing, hockey, rugby and rowing (boys and girls). 1993 winners of the Rosslyn Park Festival Competition at the National Schools' Seven-a-Side Rugby tournament. *Community service:* Pupils take bronze, silver and gold Duke of Edinburgh's Award. CCF and community service optional, but some commitment is expected. *Clubs and societies:* Over 30 clubs, eg King's Parliament, Caxton Society, literary, science.

Uniform School uniform worn during school day throughout the school.

Houses/prefects Prefects (school monitors), captain and vice-captain of school, and house monitors – appointed by Headmaster and Housemasters/mistresses. Various school committees.

Religion Compulsory attendance at cathedral or other religious establishments on Sundays.

Social Concerts, plays, debates, quiz programmes with other schools. Many organised trips abroad. Pupils allowed to bring own bike to school. Meals self-service. School shop and restaurant at Recreation Centre. No tobacco allowed. Alcohol available to sixth-form in newly extended social centre.

Boarding Single-sex houses of approximately 60 (6 boys, 5 girls). Resident matrons. Central dining room. Pupils can provide and cook own food on a small scale. Half-term plus 2–3 weekend exeats as required. Visits to local town allowed.

Alumni association run by Mr M Hodgson, Headmaster, St Martin's School, Northwood HA6 2DJ.

• KING'S (Chester)

The King's School, Wrexham Road, Chester CH4 7QL Tel 01244 680026

• Pupils 650 • Boys 7–18 (Day) • Girls None • Upper sixth 70 • Termly fees £973–£1437 (Day)
• HMC • Enquiries/application to the Headmaster

What it's like

Founded in 1541, it was originally in the cathedral precinct. In 1960 it moved to a semi-rural site on the Wrexham Road, a mile from the city. This is an agreeable purpose-built establishment in 32 acres of grounds and playing fields. In 1989 a major development was completed, including new labs, a music school, art room, sixth-form centre and a sports hall. The junior school, which has expanded into new buildings, is combined. A C of E foundation, worship and religious instruction are important. The academic standards are high and results are very good. Almost all sixth-formers go on to degree courses, including many to Oxbridge. Very strong in music and drama. A good range of sports and games and numerous extra-curricular activities. Quite a big commitment to local community services.

School profile

Pupils Total age range 7–18; 650 day boys. Senior department 11–18, 500 boys. Main entry ages 7, 8, 9, 11 and into sixth.

Entrance Own entrance exam used. Pupils should have all-round intellectual ability; Anglican foundation but all denominations and creeds accepted. Parents not expected to buy textbooks. 16 pa assisted places. Several means-tested scholarships/bursaries.

Parents 15+% are doctors, lawyers etc. 90+% live within 30 miles.

Head and staff *Headmaster:* A R D Wickson, in post for 15 years. Educated at Whitgift and Cambridge (history). Previously Headmaster at Shaftesbury Grammar and Head of History and Housemaster at Ardingly. Publications: Britain's Inland Waterways; The Community of the Realm in Thirteenth Century England. *Staff:* 41 full time, 2 part time. Annual turnover 5%.

Exam results In 1995, 73 pupils in upper fifth, 70 in upper sixth. *GCSE:* In 1944, all upper fifth gained grade C or above in 8+ subjects. *A-levels:* 68 pupils passed in 4+ subjects; 2 in 3 subjects. Average UCAS points 23.8.

University and college entrance 97% of 1995 sixth-form leavers went on to a degree course (21% after a gap year); others typically go on to non-degree courses or straight into work. Of those going on to university, 16% went to Oxbridge; 11% took courses in medicine, dentistry and veterinary science, 38% in science and engineering, 6% in law, 31% in humanities and social sciences, 1% in art and design, 14% in vocational subjects eg agriculture, banking, pharmacy, property management.

Curriculum GCSE, AS and A-levels. 14 subjects offered at GCSE, 16 at A-level. 58% take science/engineering A-levels; 25% take arts and humanities; 17% both. *Computing facilities:* A well-equipped computer room; several departments have their own computers. *Special provision:* Mildly visually handicapped pupils are assimilated into normal teaching groups, as are the slightly deaf. *Europe:* French, German and Spanish offered to GCSE, AS and A-level.

The arts (Pupils aged 11 and over) *Music:* Up to 25% pupils learn a musical instrument; instrumental exams can be taken. Musical groups include swing band and choirs. *Drama & dance*: Many pupils are involved in school productions. 2–3 major productions annually. *Art:* On average, 12 take GCSE, 3 A-level.

Sport, community service and clubs (Pupils aged 11 and over) *Sport and physical activities:* Several county representatives (rowing, cricket, football). *Community service:* Pupils participate in the Duke of Edinburgh's Award Scheme. Community service optional. *Clubs and societies:* include a chess club.

Houses/prefects No competitive houses. All sixth-form act as prefects. Head boy appointed by the Headmaster with sixth-form advice. Sixth-form council.

Religion Weekly services, 4 cathedral services a year, plus voluntary communion services in school and cathedral.

Social A variety of activities with Queen's School eg debating society, Christian Union, Gilbert & Sullivan. Regular trips and exchanges abroad. Meals self-service. No tobacco/alcohol allowed. No cars without specific permission, no motorbikes.

Discipline Pupils failing to produce homework once might expect a talking to; those

caught smoking cannabis on the premises would be asked to leave immediately. Serious or repeated offences are punished by community service of various sorts.
Former pupils Ronald Pickup; Nicholas Grace; others in academic or medical spheres.

• KING'S (Ely)

The King's School, Ely, Cambridgeshire, CB7 4DB. Tel 01353 662824, Fax 01353 667485
• Pupils 802 • Boys 2–18 (Day/Board/Weekly) • Girls 2–18 (Day/Board/Weekly) • Upper sixth 65 • Termly fees £620–£2442 (Day) £2300–£3829 (Boarding) £2280–£3739 (Weekly) • HMC, BSA, CSA, SHA • Enquiries/application to the Admissions Secretary or Headmaster's Secretary

What it's like

Founded in 970 and refounded in 1541 by Henry VIII, it has a superb position on the edge of one of the most beautiful cathedral cities in Europe. Much of the school is housed in the buildings of the old Benedictine monastery, which are of great architectural and historical interest and include the 14th-century Monastic Barn (now the school dining hall), the Porta (gateway of the monastery) which is now the art centre, and the Norman Undercroft in School House which contains the library. Since 1960 there has been a massive development and modernisation programme including a library, sports hall and a technology centre. Facilities and accommodation are excellent. The school combines a kindergarten and a junior school, thus providing continuous education for boys and girls from 2–18. Ely is C of E orientated and pupils are expected to attend services. A high standard of teaching prevails and results are good. Most sixth-formers go on to degree courses, including Oxbridge. Very strong indeed in music and drama. A wide range of sports and games (standards are high). A lot of emphasis on outdoor pursuits and adventure training. Full use is made of the city's facilities, and those of Cambridge, fifteen miles away.

School profile

Pupils Total age range 2–18; 802 pupils, 583 day (340 boys, 243 girls), 219 boarding (139 boys, 80 girls; all aged at least 8). Senior department 13–18, 401 pupils (243 boys, 158 girls). Main entry ages 2, 4, 9, 11, 13 and into sixth. Approx 5% are children of former pupils. Own junior school provides more than 75% senior intake. *State school entry:* 25% intake at 11, plus a few at 13, 14 and into sixth.
Entrance Own exam used; also Common Entrance. No special skills required. C of E orientated school and pupils are expected to attend a school service. Parents buy textbooks; other extras include expeditions, music lessons etc (fee structure being revised). Up to 50 pa scholarships/bursaries, maximum 50% fees.
Parents 30+% live within 30 miles; some 10% live overseas.
Head and staff *Headmaster:* Richard Youdale, 5 years in post. Scholar of Winchester and Cambridge (classics and modern and medieval languages). Previously Deputy Headmaster and Second Master at King's (Rochester), Head of Classics and Assistant Housemaster at Christ's Hospital and Classics Teacher at Bradfield and the Perse (Boys). *Staff:* 75 full time, few part time. Annual turnover about 5%. Average age about 40.
Exam results In 1995, 86 pupils in Year 11, 44 in Year 13. *GCSE:* In 1995, 65 pupils gained grade C or above in 8+ subjects; 10 in 5–7 subjects. *A-levels:* 9 pupils passed in 4+ subjects; 25 in 3; 6 in 2; and 2 in 1 subject. Average UCAS points 17.7.
University and college entrance 86% of 1995 sixth-form leavers went on to a degree course (15% after a gap year); others typically go on to non-degree courses eg technician or straight into employment. Of those going on to university, 8% went to Oxbridge; 23% took courses in medicine and science, 12% in engineering and technology, 35% in humanities and social sciences, 30% in art, drama and music.
Curriculum GCSE, AS and A-levels. 18 GCSE subjects offered; 22 at A-level (general education course in sixth-form, no A-level general studies). *Vocational:* Work experience available; also RSA in computer literacy. *Computing facilities:* Computer centre plus computers in most departments. *Special provision:* Some support for dyslexic pupils and for those with learning problems. *Europe:* French (from age 7), German and Spanish to GCSE, AS and A-level. Regular exchanges to France, Germany and Spain (many pupils prefer to make their own family arrangements).
The arts (Pupils aged 11 and over) *Music:* Over 30% of pupils learn a musical

instrument; instrumental exams can be taken. Many musical groups including orchestras, horn ensembles, jazz, various choirs etc. Recent award in regional round of National Chamber Music Competition; concert band tours of Austria and America and in trials for national UK competition; senior orchestra filmed as part of advertisement for Ely Cathedral. *Drama & dance*: Drama offered and GCSE and A-level may be taken. All pupils are involved in school and house/other productions. Successful entrants to National Youth Theatre and to established drama schools. *Art:* On average, 25 take GCSE, 3 AS-level, 5 A-level. Textiles, fine art and history of art also offered. Pupils to art colleges, running own design studios etc.

Sport, community service and clubs (Pupils aged 11 and over) *Sport and physical activities:* rugby, hockey, cricket, athletics, rowing, tennis, netball, rounders, sailing, swimming, squash, adventure training, badminton, golf available. A-level sport studies and Community Sports Leader Award may be taken. County and national representation. *Community service:* Pupils take bronze, silver and gold Duke of Edinburgh's Award. Community service optional. *Clubs and societies:* Few formal clubs and societies but very wide range of activities reflecting the enthusiams of staff and pupils.

Uniform School uniform worn on formal occasions; school dress on other occasions.

Houses/prefects Houses predominantly pastoral. Prefects, head of school and deputies, head of house and house prefects – selected and appointed by the Headmaster. Sixth-form committee.

Religion 4 morning services per week. Sunday service for boarders.

Social Pupils allowed to bring own car/bike/motorbike to school. Some meals formal, most self-service. School-book and tuck shops. No tobacco/alcohol allowed.

Discipline Pupils failing to produce homework once may be put into detention; work-force for minor offences of behaviour; suspension for 1 week or longer if more serious; expulsion if very serious.

Boarding About 10 per house have own study bedroom; most share with 2 or 3 others; few in dormitory of 6. Single-sex houses of 40–50, same as competitive houses in senior school. Resident qualified nurse; doctor local. Central dining room. Pupils can provide and cook own snacks. Exeats each weekend (weekly boarding increasingly popular). Visits to local town allowed out of school time.

Alumni association is run by Hon Sec, Old Elean's Club, c/o the school.

• KING'S (Gloucester)

The King's School, Pitt Street, Gloucester GL1 2BG. Tel 01452 521251

• Pupils 510 • Boys 4–18 (Day/Board/Weekly) • Girls 4–18 (Day/Board/Weekly) • Upper sixth 50 • Termly fees £1700 (Day) £2900 (Board) £2800 (Weekly) • HMC, SHMIS, CSA • Enquiries/application to the Headmaster

What it's like

The first reference to some kind of school attached to the cathedral dates from 1072. The present school was refounded by Henry VIII in 1541. It lies in the cathedral close, in the middle of Gloucester, and is a pleasant combination of ancient and modern buildings with good up-to-date facilities. Originally a boys' school, girls have been admitted since 1975 and it is now fully co-educational. The cathedral is the spiritual and cultural centre of the school and most days begin with worship in it. The school provides a sound general education in the context of the Christian faith. Academically, results are good and most sixth-form leavers go on to degree courses, including Oxbridge. A strong music department has at its core the cathedral choristers who get free tuition. The drama and dance departments are also active. A range of games and sports and an adequate number of clubs and societies. A good record in the Duke of Edinburgh's Award Scheme.

School profile

Pupils Total age range 4–18; 510 pupils, 460 day (310 boys, 150 girls), 50 boarding (39 boys, 11 girls). Senior department 11–18, 453 pupils (342 boys, 111 girls). Main entry ages 4, 11, 13 and into sixth. Approx 20% are children of former pupils. Own junior school provides more than 50% of senior intake. *State school entry:* 50% senior intake, plus 10% to sixth.

Entrance Common Entrance and own exam used. Parents expected to buy textbooks;

maximum extras £100. Some assisted places. 15 pa scholarships, for choristers, academic and music and sport, 40%–full fees.
Parents 45+% in industry or commerce; 30% are professionals. 60+% live within 30 miles; 7% live overseas.
Head and staff *Headmaster:* Peter Lacey, 4 years in post. *Staff:* 47 full time, 9 part time. Annual turnover 4%. Average age 36.
Exam results On average, 70 pupils in upper fifth, 50 in upper sixth. *GCSE:* On average, 37 upper fifth gain at least grade C in 8+ subjects; 19 in 5–7; and 13 in 1–4 subjects. *A-levels:* 8% upper sixth pass in 4+ subjects; 49% in 3; 28% in 2; and 15% in 1 subject. Average UCAS points 18.2.
University and college entrance 90% of 1995 sixth-form leavers went on to a degree course (10% after a gap year); others typically go on to further training. Of those going on to university, 12% went to Oxbridge; 10% took courses in medicine, dentistry and veterinary science, 15% in science and engineering, 15% in law, 30% in humanities and social sciences, 10% in art and design, 20% in vocational subjects eg nursing, education, architecture, agriculture.
Curriculum GCSE, A-levels and GNVQs. 17 subjects offered. including Greek, theatre studies and textiles. 40% take science A-levels; 30% arts/humanities; 30% both. *Vocational:* GNVQ business and design courses offered. Work experience available. *Computing facilities:* Computer centre; computers in most departments. *Special provision:* Mild dyslexia; 1 trained EFL teacher, 1 special needs. *Europe:* French and German (both from age 8) offered at GCSE, AS and A-level. Regular exchanges (France). French and German pupils in sixth-form. Regular choir visit to France.
The arts (Pupils aged 11 and over) *Music:* Over 30% of pupils learn a musical instrument; instrumental exams can be taken. Some 10 musical groups including 2 orchestras, 5 choirs, concert band, chamber groups. *Drama & dance*: Both offered. A-level drama, Poetry Society, RAD exams may be taken. Majority of pupils are involved in school and house/other productions. *Art:* On average, 27 take GCSE, 5 A-level. Design, pottery, textiles also offered.
Sport, community service and clubs (Pupils aged 11 and over) *Sport and physical activities:* Compulsory sports: rugby, hockey, cricket, netball. Optional: squash, tennis, rowing, sailing, swimming. GCSE, RYA exams may be taken. (School is a venue for Gloucestershire County Cricket Club and has its own indoor cricket school.) *Community service:* Pupils take bronze, silver and gold Duke of Edinburgh's Award. CCF optional (ATC). Community service optional. *Clubs and societies:* Up to 15 clubs, eg astronomy, fell walking, debating, poetry, chess.
Uniform School uniform worn throughout.
Houses/prefects Competitive houses. Prefects, head boy/girl. School Council.
Religion Regular worship in cathedral. Sunday service for boarders. Voluntary participation in cathedral services.
Social Joint theatre workshops, choral society productions, dances/discos with other schools. Annual choir trip to France; exchange with France (Metz); expeditions (eg Iceland and Bolivia); annual Pyrenees climbing holiday; skiing trips. Pupils allowed to bring own car/bike/motorbike to school. Meals cafeteria-style. School shop. No tobacco/alcohol allowed.
Discipline Detention system. Pupils failing to produce homework once might expect to complete it by the next day; those caught smoking cannabis on the premises would be asked to leave.
Boarding Sixth formers have own study bedroom; fourth and fifth share with 1 or 2 others; only one dormitory of 6+. Single-sex houses of approximately 30, divided by age. Resident nurse; visiting doctor. Central dining room. Pupils can provide and cook a small amount of their own food. 2 exeats of 24 hours each term. Visits to the local town allowed.
Alumni association is run by The Secretary, The King's School Society, c/o the school.
Former pupils Terry Biddlecombe (champion jockey); Dr Herbert Sumsion (organist); Dr Donald Hunt (organist); Dr Bernard Wood (Professor of Anatomy); Ivan Lampkin (artist); Richard Shephard (composer); John Stafford Smith (composer of The Stars and Stripes).

• KING'S (Macclesfield)

The King's School, Cumberland Street, Macclesfield, Cheshire SK10 1DA. Tel 01625 618586, Fax 01625 614784

• Pupils 1304 • Boys 7–18 (Day) • Girls 7–18 (Day) • Upper sixth 135 • Termly fees £1150–£1465 (Day) • HMC • Enquiries/application to the Admissions Secretary

What it's like

Founded in 1502, the school is situated in the centre of Macclesfield with attractive surroundings. Originally a boys' school, it accepted girls into the sixth-form in 1986 and in 1993 purchased the site of the former High School for Girls, which enabled it to take girls throughout the school. The junior division and the sixth-form remain co-educational but between the ages of 11 and 16, boys and girls are taught separately: the boys on the old site along with the sixth-form; the girls on the new site with the junior division. Earlier developments include a very large library, a fine science block and artificial playing surface. The playing fields are on three sites. The school lays considerable stress on encouraging pupils to develop confidence in their own judgement and to develop their own particular interests to the full within a broad and balanced curriculum. In a secure and supportive environment, the active involvement of parents is much encouraged. Academic standards are high and results are good. The majority of leavers go on to degree courses, including Oxbridge. Very strong in music, drama and art. Wide range of sports and games (again standards are high – many international and county representatives) and outdoor activities. Substantial commitment to local community schemes.

School profile

Pupils Total age range 7–18, 1304 day pupils (906 boys, 398 girls). Senior department 11–18, 1103 pupils (783 boys, 320 girls). Main entry ages 7–11, 13, and into sixth. Approx 15% are children of former pupils. Own junior provides 40% senior intake. *State school entry:* 40% senior intake, plus 50% to sixth.
Entrance Own entrance exam; by interview and GCSE results to sixth-form. Welcomes all talents; no religious requirements. Parents not expected to buy textbooks; few extras. 70 pa assisted places. 8 pa scholarships, £300 pa to half fees.
Head and staff *Headmaster:* A G Silcock, 9 years in post. *Staff:* 100 full time, 17 part time. Annual turnover 3%. Average age mid-30s.
Exam results In 1995, 120 pupils in fifth, 135 in upper sixth. *GCSE:* In 1995, 73% gained at least grade C in 8+ subjects; 22% in 5–7 subjects. A levels: 7 passed in 4+ subjects; 92 in 3; 27 in 2; and 5 in 1 subject. Average UCAS points 18.1.
University and college entrance 90% of 1995 sixth-form leavers went on to a degree course (10% after a gap year); others typically go on to other training courses. Of those going on to university, 8% went to Oxbridge; 5% took courses in medicine, dentistry and veterinary science, 32% in science and engineering, 5% in law, 18% in humanities and social sciences, 7% in art and design, 43% in subjects eg music, business studies, drama.
Curriculum GCSE, AS and A levels. 27 subjects offered, including A-level general studies. *Computing facilities:* 3 fully equipped laboratories with 72 stations. *Special provision:* Extra tuition in English in early years. *Europe:* French and German offered to GCSE and A level; Spanish as a non-examined subject. Regular exchange to Germany (Memmingen) and France (La Rochelle).
The arts *Music:* Some 400 pupils learn a musical instrument; instrumental exams can be taken. Musical groups include choir, chamber orchestra, wind band, orchestra, jazz band, pop group. Occasional pupils accepted for music college. *Drama*: On average 40 take GCSE theatre arts; A-level recently introduced. Many pupils involved in 3 annual school productions, one of which is a musical. *Art:* On average 50 take GCSE, 12 take A-level art & design. Pupils regularly go on to art colleges and study art at universities.
Sport, community service and clubs *Sport and physical activities:* Sports include: football (girls and junior division only), rugby, hockey, cricket, athletics, cross-country, orienteering, swimming, badminton, squash, table tennis, sailing, hill walking, rock climbing, caving, abseiling, basketball, netball, canoeing. Many county and national representative honours won annually by individuals and teams. Hockey, Cheshire champions and NW finalists, U14 Cheshire and NW champions; orienteering, U13 national champions. *Community service:* Optional community service in the sixth. *Clubs and societies:* Computer, chess, ornithology, railways, venturers, debating, aviation,

Christian Union, young scientists, flower arranging, school newspapers.
Uniform School uniform worn except the sixth.
Houses/prefects House system in girls' division, not in boys'. Prefects and School Captain appointed by the Headmaster.
Religion C of E worship encouraged.
Social No organised events with local schools. 5–6 foreign trips and exchanges per year organised on a co-educational basis. Pupils allowed to bring own car/bike/motorbike to school. Meals self-service. School shop. No tobacco/alcohol allowed.
Discipline High standard of conduct expected and maintained. Regular weekly detention after school. Suspension for most serious breaches of school discipline. Those caught smoking cannabis on the premises would probably expect expulsion.
Alumni association is run by P R Mathews, c/o the school.
Former pupils Alan Beith MP; Christian Blackshaw (pianist); C N Booth (Director, Oxford Brookes University); Michael Jackson (Controller BBC2); Steve Smith (rugby international); Graham Turner (journalist); Prof Sir Edward Wrigley.

• KING'S (Madrid)

King's College, Paseo de los Andes, Soto de Viñuelas, 28761, Madrid, Spain. Tel 34 1 803 48 00, Fax 34 1 803 65 57

• Pupils 1206 • Boys 2–19 (Day/Board) • Girls 2–19 (Day/Board) • Upper sixth 23 • Termly fees Ptas 106,000–338,000 (Day) Ptas 567,000–637,000 (Board) • HMC, COBISEC, ECIS, NABSS • Enquiries/application to Headmaster

What it's like

Founded in 1969 as a co-educational school. It is purpose-built and on a 12-acre campus in a pleasant residential development north of Madrid. Open countryside, in a pollution-free zone, surrounds it. The school is well-equipped with up-to-date facilities; a residential wing for boarders was opened in 1985 and there have been many other developments since. There is a parallel infant school (ages 2–7) in the city. The school is privately owned and is non-denominational. It is divided into infant, junior and senior departments and some 40 nationalities are represented in the pupil body. Staff:pupil ratio is roughly 1:15. The curriculum is English leading to IGCSE and A-level, but at the end of the 3rd year pupils can choose to follow a Spanish course leading to the Bachillerato. Music, drama and art are well-supported. A range of sports and games (with good facilities on site) is provided and includes football, tennis, judo, basketball and swimming.

School profile

Pupils Total age range 2–19; 1206 pupils, 599 boys, 607 girls. Senior department 11–19. Entry at any age.
Entrance Tests are given to all over six to establish that a child will be able to follow and benefit from the education provided and to determine appropriate entry level.
Parents Very international – some 40 nationalities.
Head and staff *Headmaster:* Dr Gerald Percy. Educated at Bristol Cathedral School and Keele University (chemistry). Previously Senior Tutor and Head of Science at King's College Madrid, Chemistry Teacher at Nantwich Grammar School and at Crewe Grammar. *Staff:* 84 members (69 of whom are British).
Exam results In 1995, 42 pupils in upper fifth, 23 in upper sixth. *IGCSE:* In 1995, 24 gained grade C or above in 8+ subjects; 11 in 5–7 subjects. *A-levels:* 5 passed in 4+ subjects; 16 in 3; 1 in 2; and 1 in 1 subject. Average UCAS points 21.0.
University and college entrance All 1995 sixth-form leavers went on to a degree course (5% after a gap year), 3% to Oxbridge; 1% took courses in medicine, dentistry and veterinary science, 45% in science and engineering, 3% in law, 20% in humanities and social sciences, 6% in art and design., 25% in vocational subjects eg business and associated subjects, physiotherapy.
Curriculum In the senior department a common British curriculum is followed until the end of the third year. Pupils then either continue with an English curriculum leading to IGCSE and A-level (with special Spanish language lessons if they want to validate their studies in Spain) or join a Spanish course leading to the BUP (Spanish Bachillerato) and

COU (university entrance). The school has been inspected and approved by both the Spanish and British education departments. *Europe:* English and Spanish taught throughout. For pupils not wishing to validate their studies in Spain, French is compulsory from age 11 to GCSE; optional from age 13 for other pupils; GCSE and A-level available. German offered as an extra.
The arts (Pupils aged 11 and over) *Music:* Up to 15% of pupils learn a musical instrument; instrumental exams can be taken. Some 4 musical groups including 3 choirs, musical ensemble. *Drama & dance*: Both offered. RAD exams may be taken. Some pupils are involved in school and house/other productions. *Art:* On average, 15 take GCSE, 6 A-level.
Sport, community service and clubs (Pupils aged 11 and over) *Sport and physical activities:* Compulsory sports: football, basketball, cross-country, volleyball, gymnastics, swimming. Optional: hockey, tennis. *Clubs and societies:* Up to 30 clubs, eg photography, various sports, history, ecology, drama etc.
Uniform Worn throughout school.
Religion Many different religions and denominations. Usually a Christian Minister available and some Christian celebrations but pupils belonging to other faiths are free not to attend.
Discipline Pupils helped and/or disciplined by class tutor, co-ordinator, head of department or Headmaster, depending on circumstances.

• KING'S (Rochester)

King's School, Rochester, Kent ME1 1TF. Tel 01634 843913, Fax 01634 832493
• Pupils 341 • Boys 13–18 (Day/Board/Weekly) • Girls 13–18 (Day/Board/Weekly) • Upper sixth 66 • Termly fees £2370 (Day) £3995 (Board/Weekly) • HMC, CSA, ESHA • Enquiries/application to the Headmaster

What it's like

The school traces its foundation to the early 7th century, but was refounded in 1541. It has a fine site in the precincts of the cathedral, close by the castle and very near the river Medway. The older buildings have historic associations and there has been considerable expansion and modernisation to produce excellent facilities. There are strong links with the cathedral and its life. Religious education is important in the curriculum; attendance at services and chapel is compulsory and all pupils take divinity GCSE. The school has been fully co-educational since 1993, although the sixth-form first admitted girls 15 years earlier. Academic standards are high and results very good; all sixth-formers go on to degree courses. Strong music, art and drama departments. A wide range of sports and games (high standards achieved) and a good range of activities. A vigorous CCF and a lively commitment to local community services.

School profile

Pupils Age range 13–18; 341 pupils, 297 day (287 boys, 54 girls), 44 boarding pupils. Main entry ages 13 and into the sixth. Large intake from own prep school, King's Preparatory School (tel 01634 843657).
Entrance Common Entrance and own exam used. No special skills or religious requirements. Parents not expected to buy textbooks. 10 pa assisted places. 17 pa scholarships/bursaries, £500–full fees (means tested over 50%).
Parents 15+% are doctors, lawyers, etc; 15+% in industry or commerce. 85+% live within 30 miles; up to 10% live overseas.
Head and staff *Headmaster:* Dr I R Walker, in post for 10 years. Educated at Sydney Boys' High, Melbourne College of Divinity and at universities of Bristol and Wales (accountancy, theology, philosophy). Previously Housemaster and Head of Divinity at Dulwich. Also member HMC and Admiralty Interview Board; FRSA, FCP, Associate Bankers' Institute of Australasia. Publications: articles in philosophical journals and reviews; books include Plato's Euthyphro (1984), Christ in the Community (Chairman and ed. 1990), Classroom Classics (1991), Faith and Belief (1995). *Staff:* 43 full time, 15 part time and peripatetic. Annual turnover 2%. Average age 42.
Exam results In 1995, 53 pupils in upper fifth, 63 in upper sixth. *GCSE:* In 1995, 34 upper fifth gained at least grade C in 8+ subjects; 16 in 5–7, subjects. *A-levels:* 60%

upper sixth passed in 4+ subjects; 34% in 3; 3% in 2 subjects. Average UCAS points 23.0.

University and college entrance All 1995 sixth-form leavers went on to a degree course (5% after a gap year), 5% to Oxbridge; 5% took courses in medicine, dentistry and veterinary science, 26% in science and engineering, 5% in law, 49% in humanities and social sciences, 8% in art and design, 7% in vocational subjects eg Christian ministry, psychology.

Curriculum GCSE and A-levels. 17 subjects offered. 14% take science A-levels; 76% arts/humanities; 10% both. *Vocational:* Work experience available; also City & Guilds qualification in computer literacy (basic competence in information technology). *Computing facilities:* Computer centre – Nimbus network. *Europe:* French and German offered to GCSE and A-level (both compulsory for one year); also GCSE Russian in fifth form, Italian in sixth. Regular exchanges (France and Germany). Number of German pupils in school. Number of contacts with eg ministries in Germany, EU bodies; visits to eg European School in Culham, Deutsche Schule in London and Kreisgymnasium Bargteheide, Schleswig-Holstein.

The arts *Music:* Over 25% of pupils learn a musical instrument; instrumental exams can be taken. Some 10 musical groups including orchestras, choirs, brass groups, wind band etc. 2 members county youth orchestra; 2 members county youth choir; Kent Pianist of the Year. *Drama & dance*: Drama offered. Many pupils are involved in school and house/other productions. *Art:* On average, 20 take GCSE, 12 A-level. Design, pottery and photography also offered. Fine art scholarship to Brown University, US; winner of national Child Accident Prevention Trust design competition.

Sport, community service and clubs *Sport and physical activities:* rugby, hockey, netball, athletics; PE (gymnastics, volleyball, basketball, health related fitness), rowing, cross-country, fencing, swimming, 7-a-side rugby, tennis, trampolining, weight training, badminton, squash. BAGA, RLSS exams may be taken. 3 county rugby players, 2 hockey, 1 cricket, 1 athletics, 2 netball, 5 cross-country; 14 district athletes, 19 cross-country; 1 in regional U12 skiing team; 1 shooting international. *Community service:* CCF and community service optional for 4 years at age 14. *Clubs and societies:* Up to 30 clubs, eg geographical, history, art, music, chess, computer, debating, photographic, pottery, technical, bellringing.

Uniform School uniform worn throughout.

Houses/prefects Competitive houses. Prefects, head boy/girl, head of house and house prefects – appointed by the Headmaster after vote/consultation.

Religion Compulsory C of E services and chapel.

Social Organised local events including theatre/music, etc. Organised trips to France, Germany and Russia; clasical tour to Mediterranean. Pupils allowed to bring own car to school. Meals self-service. School shop. No tobacco/alcohol allowed.

Discipline Pupils failing to produce homework once might expect a verbal warning; detention system; anyone involved with drugs can expect expulsion. There is a Commendation system.

Boarding 20% have own study bedroom, 80% share with others; all in one house. Resident qualified nurse. Central dining room. Pupils can provide and cook own food. 4 weekend exeats each term. Visits to the local town allowed after school.

Alumni association is run by Mr M Chesterfield, 01795 890 701

Former pupils John Selwyn Gummer MP; Richard Dadd (artist); Russell Thorndike (novelist); Percy Whitlock (composer); Sir H A Atkinson (PM of New Zealand); Sir Francis Head KCH (privy councillor); Dinsdale Landen (actor); Sir Lionel Dakers (composer); Clive King (children's author).

• KING'S (Taunton)

King's College, South Road, Taunton, Somerset. TA1 3DX. Tel 01823 272708, Fax 01823 334236
• Pupils 442 • Boys 13–18 (Day/Board) • Girls 13–18 (Day/Board) • Upper sixth 94 • Termly fees £2520 (Day) £3830 (Board) • HMC, Woodard • Enquiries/application to the Headmaster

What it's like

Its historical links go back to the medieval grammar school in Taunton which was refounded by Bishop Fox of Winchester in 1522. In 1869 it was moved to its present site half a mile south of the town, in a well-wooded and spacious setting of 110 acres. There are fine playing fields and splendid views of the Blackdown and Quantock Hills: a very attractive and civilised environment. There is a prep and pre-prep school, King's Hall, housed in a handsome Georgian mansion north of the town. Originally a boys' school, girls were first accepted in 1967 and it has been fully co-educational since 1991. A lot of excellent facilities have been added in recent years and the school is very well-equipped. The chapel and its services are an integral part of school life and religious education plays an important part. Standards are high and results are good. Most leavers go on to degree courses each year. Music, drama and art are very strong indeed. Full use is made of the two theatres and there are excellent art and design and CDT centres which produce impressive results. Much use is made, too, of a sophisticated video production unit. Facilities for sports and games are first-rate and there is a high standard of performance (numerous representatives at county and regional level; 4 international rugby caps recently). Many clubs and societies cater for most extra-curricular activities. The CCF is a flourishing contingent and there is a good deal of emphasis on outdoor pursuits. A large number of pupils are involved in local community services. The school is currently working with Exeter University on the conservation of the giant marine turtle, involving the development of a database and a page on the Internet, and field work in the Mediterranean.

School profile

Pupils Age range 13–18; 442 pupils, 97 day (60 boys, 37 girls), 345 boarders (244 boys, 101 girls). Main entry age 13 and into the sixth. 5% are children of former pupils. *State school entry:* 2% main intake, plus 6% to sixth.

Entrance Common Entrance, own entrance scholarship or interview and test. No special skills or religious requirements although Anglican foundation. Parents not expected to buy textbooks. 10 pa assisted places, at 13 and into sixth. 29 pa academic and music scholarships/bursaries at 13 and sixth-form, £1915–£5745.

Parents 15+% in the armed services, 15+% doctors, lawyers etc. 10+% live within 30 miles; 10+% live overseas.

Head and staff *Headmaster:* Simon Funnell, 8 years in post. Educated at King's (Rochester) and at Cambridge (English). Previously Head of English and Housemaster at Shrewsbury, Head of English at Eastbourne. *Staff:* 47 full time, 4 part time. Annual turnover 3%. Average age 35.

Exam results On average, 80 pupils in upper fifth, 95 in upper sixth. *GCSE:* On average, 78% gain at least grade C in 8+ subjects; 17% in 5–7 subjects. *A-levels:* 6% upper sixth pass in 4+ subjects; 73% in 3; 15% in 2; 6% in 1 subject. Average UCAS points 18.0.

University and college entrance 90% of sixth-form leavers go on to a degree course (12% after a gap year); others typically go on to HND courses or straight into employment. Of those going on to university, 7% go to Oxbridge; 5% take courses in medicine, dentistry and veterinary science, 25% in science and engineering, 5% in law, 55% in humanities and social sciences, 6% in art and design, 4% in other subjects eg medical biochemistry, physiotherapy or at universities overseas.

Curriculum GCSE and A-levels. 20 subjects offered, including PE, philosophy, classical civilisation; no A-level general studies. 27% take science A-levels; 41% arts/humanities; 32% both. *Computing facilities:* Computer department; also computers in other departments and houses. CAD/CAM facilities in CDT centre. *Special provision:* EFL tuition available and some help for dyslexic pupils. *Europe:* French, German and Spanish offered to GCSE and A-level. Regular visits to France, Belgium, Germany and Spain. French, German and Spanish pupils in school full-time; hosting groups of French pupils (from Brittany) for 1 week.

The arts *Music:* Over 40% of pupils learn a musical instrument; instrumental exams can be taken. Some 12 musical groups including orchestras, wind band, choirs, brass, show band, string, rock. Rock group won regional and 2nd in national final of Panasonic Rockschool Competition; representatives in Somerset and Devon county orchestras. Recent musicals include, Joseph and His Amazing Technicolour Dreamcoat, Grease, Chicago. Choir sings annually in St Paul's Cathedral and St George's Chapel, Windsor; jazz band recently played at Dartington, in Jersey, France and Luxembourg. *Drama & dance*: Drama offered. Majority of pupils are involved in school and house/other productions eg Bouncers, School for Scandal. *Art:* On average, 45 take GCSE, 20

A-level. Design, ceramics, textiles, photography and printmaking also offered. Numerous pupils go on to study art and design as a career.
Sport, community service and clubs *Sport and physical activities:* Compulsory sports (up to 16; sixth-form have choice): rugby, hockey, cricket (boys); hockey, netball, tennis (girls); plus squash, badminton, cross-country, swimming, golf, sailing, fencing, soccer, athletics, shooting, archery, basketball. GCSE and A-level PE may be taken. Many representatives at national and regional levels: in recent years: 4 rugby internationals, 1 athletic, 1 cricket, 1 fencing; numerous county players; 1995 winners of Rosslyn Park rugby sevens. *Community service:* Pupils take bronze, silver and gold Duke of Edinburgh's Award. Community service and CCF optional for 3 years at age 14; CCF split into 'Chindits', then Army, Navy, RAF or Marines sections. *Clubs and societies:* Up to 30 clubs, eg archery, climbing, cooking, current affairs, debating, fencing, philately, photography, sailing, travel, video.
Uniform School uniform worn, except in the sixth.
Houses/prefects Competitive houses. Head prefect, boy and girl vice-captains, heads of houses and house prefects, prefects (selected after going on a training scheme) – all appointed by the Head.
Religion Compulsory services on two weekdays and on Sundays. Voluntary candlelit communion weekly.
Social Science weekends of lectures and seminars, historical association meetings, general knowledge, debating and public speaking competitions, geographical meetings. Exchanges and visits to Europe; organised trips to eg rain forests of Sierra Leone, to South America, India, Russia, Ethiopia, Greece; fieldwork in Mediterranean 1996 on conservation of giant marine turtle. Pupils allowed to bring own bike to school. Meals self-service. School shop. No tobacco/alcohol allowed; there is a senior social club open on particular evenings.
Discipline Pupils failing to produce homework once would be expected to produce it as soon as possible; those caught smoking cannabis on the premises could expect immediate expulsion. The school takes a specially strong line on stealing, bullying and all forms of drugs.
Boarding 25% have own study bedroom, 25% share (with 1 other); 50% are in dormitories of 6+. Single-sex day and boarding houses, of approx 60, same as for competitive purposes. Resident qualified sister; non-resident doctors, (including lady doctor). Central dining room. Pupils can provide and cook snacks. 2–3 weekend exeats per term, Sunday exeats after chapel. Visits to local town allowed 2 afternoons a week – all ages; Saturday nights – sixth-form.
Alumni association is run by B Sykes, c/o the school.
Former pupils Lord Rippon PC; Professor Anthony Hewish (Nobel prize winner); Simon Jones (actor); Ian Smith (BBC); Gerald Butt (BBC correspondent).

• KING'S (Warwick)

King's High School for Girls, Smith Street, Warwick CV34 4HJ. Tel 01926 494485, Fax 01926 403089

• Pupils 560 • Boys None • Girls 11–18 (Day) • Upper sixth 58 • Termly fees £1365 (Day) • GSA
• Enquiries/application to the Headmistress

What it's like

Founded in 1879, it has an interesting urban site in the town of Warwick, near Warwick Preparatory School and the Warwick School for Boys. It is particularly fortunate in its beautiful buildings which span 600 years and include the town's Eastgate. A sound general academic education is provided and results are very good. Almost all sixth-formers go on to degree courses each year, including Oxbridge. Music and drama are particularly well-supported. There is a fine range of sports and games (in which high standards are attained) and a new sports hall; also a good variety of clubs and societies. Joint events with the boys' school are frequent. Pupils are encouraged to be involved in the organisation of the school. A feature of the school is its vigorous participation in local community schemes.

School profile

Pupils Age range 11–18; 560 day girls. Main entry ages 11 and into sixth. 5% are children of former pupils. Warwick Prep provides 25% pupils. *State school entry:* 50% intake at 11 and into sixth.

Entrance Own entrance exam used. No special skills or religious requirements. Parents not expected to buy textbooks. 30 pa assisted places. 9 pa scholarships/bursaries (at 11 and 16), 50% fees.

Parents 15+% in education, 15+% in industry. 60+% live within 30 miles.

Head and staff *Headmistress:* Mrs Jackie Anderson, in post for 9 years. Educated at Chislehurst and Sidcup Girls' Grammar, and at Keele University (English and history; education). Previously Vice-principal at Cheltenham Ladies' College, Head of English and Sixth Form at Burgess Hill, English teacher and Assistant Housemistress at Bedales and English teacher at Francis Holland (Regent's Park). Also GSA Council Member. Member of RSA and of Court of Warwick University. *Staff:* 40 full time, 13 part time. Annual turnover 5%. Average age 44.

Exam results In 1995, 96 pupils in upper fifth, 58 in upper sixth. *GCSE:* In 1995, 92 upper fifth gained at least grade C in 8+ subjects; and 4 in 5–7 subjects. *A-levels:* 53 upper sixth passed in 3 subjects; 4 in 2; and 1 in 1 subject. Average UCAS points 23.6.

University and college entrance 98% of 1995 sixth-form leavers went on to a degree course (8% after a gap year); others typically go on to HND, art foundation courses or into employment. Of those going on to university, 10% went to Oxbridge; 7% took courses in medicine, dentistry and veterinary science, 45% in science and engineering, 5% in law, 25% in humanities and social sciences, 6% in art and design, 10% in vocational subjects eg physiotherapy, tourism.

Curriculum GCSE and A-levels. 17 GCSE subjects offered; 19 at A-level, including Greek; general studies taught in sixth-form but A-level not taken. 21% took science A-levels; 32% arts/humanities; 47% both. *Vocational:* Work experience available; also RSA exams in CLAIT; St John's Ambulance first aid; Young Enterprise. *Computing facilities:* 3 RML Nimbus networks and additional sixth-form facilities. *Europe:* French, German, Russian and Spanish offered to GCSE, AS and A-level. Regular exchanges (France, Germany and Spain).

The arts *Music:* Over 50% of pupils learn a musical instrument; instrumental exams can be taken. Some 10 musical groups including choirs, orchestra, wind bands. Member of National Youth Orchestra. *Drama & dance*: Drama/theatre studies offered. Majority of pupils are involved in school productions and all in house/other productions. Successful participation in public speaking competitions. *Art:* On average, 33 take GCSE, 4 A-level. Design and art history also offered.

Sport, community service and clubs *Sport and physical activities:* Compulsory sports: gym, dance, swimming, netball, hockey, tennis, athletics, badminton, basketball, health-related fitness. Optional in sixth-form: keep fit, squash and golf. Some county representatives in eg netball and hockey. *Community service:* Pupils take bronze and silver Duke of Edinburgh's Award. Community service optional at age 14+, visiting old people, working with children etc. *Clubs and societies:* Over 30 clubs, eg drama, science (inc electronics), Quo Vadis, classical, computer, chess, bridge, Trivial Pursuits.

Uniform School uniform worn except in sixth (own clothes within guidelines).

Houses/prefects No competitive houses. Prefects, head girl – elected by staff and school. School Council.

Religion Christian and/or inter-denominational assembly daily – not compulsory but all girls choose to attend.

Social BAYS with sixth-formers from local schools; joint music, drama, discussion group, expeditions, social with Warwick Boys' School. Regular trips to Russia, ski trips, exchange visits with French, German, Russian and American schools. Pupils allowed to bring own car/bike/motorbike to school. Meals self-service. No tobacco/alcohol allowed.

Alumni association is run by Mrs J Edwards, 5 Godfrey Close, Radford, Semele, Leamington Spa, Warwickshire CV31 1UH.

Former pupils Kim Hartman (Helga in 'Allo 'Allo); Dr Barbara Ansell (specialist in rheumatology, MRC); Harriet Castor (children's author).

• KING'S (Wimbledon)

King's College School, Southside, Wimbledon Common, London SW19 4TT. Tel 0181 255 5300
Fax 0181 255 5309

• Pupils 720 • Boys 13–18 (Day) • Girls None • Upper sixth 130 • Termly fees £2090 (Day)
• HMC • Enquiries/application to the Registration Secretary

What it's like

Founded in 1829, it occupies 24 acres of grounds on the south side of Wimbledon Common in a very pleasant residential area. Good playing fields; a further 25 acres of fields at Motspur Park, and a boathouse at Putney. Sixth-form centre, theatre/concert hall and music school all on campus. Junior and senior schools share the same campus. Well-designed and comfortable buildings provide first-rate facilities. It is Anglican, but boys of all faiths are accepted. High standards are expected in work and behaviour. Integrity and tolerance are regarded as important qualities. The staff:pupil ratio is about 1:9. A well-run school, it has strong academic traditions and results are excellent. Many leavers go to Oxbridge; almost all the rest go to degree courses. There are strong music, drama and art departments. A good range of sports and games (in which high standards are achieved) and a large number of activities. Considerable emphasis on outdoor pursuits, the CCF and voluntary service.

School profile

Pupils Age range 13–18; 720 day boys. Main entry ages 13 and into sixth. 60% of intake from own junior school, King's College Junior School (tel 0181 255 5335). *State school entry:* 1% main intake at 13, 25% to sixth.

Entrance Common Entrance or own scholarship examination after pre-testing at 11. Oversubscribed. C of E school but boys not required to be of any particular persuasion. Parents expected to buy textbooks but there is a loan scheme; maximum extras lunches (£100), books and stationery (£35). 8 pa assisted places (3 at 13, 5 sixth-form). Up to 18 pa scholarships, including 2 music and 1 sixth-form – up to 50% fees. Also some bursaries.

Parents 15 + % in the theatre, media, music, etc; 15 + % are doctors, lawyers; 15 + % in industry or commerce.

Head and staff *Head Master*: Robin Reeve, in post since 1980. Educated at Hampton and Cambridge (history). Previously Director of Studies and Head of History at Lancing and Assistant History Master at King's (Wimbledon). Also former member HMC Committee; Chairman ISJC Advisory Committee and member of ISJC Governing Council. *Staff:* 76 full time, 4 part time. Annual turnover 5%. Average age 38.

Exam results In 1995, 144 pupils in upper fifth, 131 in upper sixth. *GCSE:* In 1995, all upper fifth gained at least grade C in an average of 10 subjects. *A-levels:* Average upper sixth passed in 3.1 subjects. Average UCAS points 27.0.

University and college entrance Over 99% of 1995 sixth-form leavers went on to a degree course (20% after a gap year); others typically go on to employment. Of those going on to university, 18% went to Oxbridge; 10% took courses in medicine, dentistry and veterinary science, 29% in science and engineering, 10% in law, 46% in humanities and social sciences, 2% in art and design, 3% in combinations of subjects.

Curriculum GCSE, AS and A-levels. 23 GCSE and 19 A-level subjects offered (no A-level general studies). 24% take science/maths A-levels; 31% arts/humanities; 45% both. *Computing facilities:* Nimbus network in 3 large classrooms. Industry standard micro-soft software (Excel and Word) and CD-Rom. *Special provision:* Long experience with gifted pupils. *Europe:* French, German, Russian and Spanish offered to GCSE and A-level; also French AS-level and Italian GCSE. Regular exchanges (France, Germany, Russia and Spain).

The arts *Music:* Some 25% pupils learn a musical instrument; instrumental exams can be taken. Musical groups include orchestra, choir, wind band. *Drama & dance*: Some pupils are involved in school productions. Occasional pupil accepted for drama college. *Art:* On average, 110 take GCSE, 10 A-level. Pupils regularly accepted for art college.

Sport, community service and clubs *Sport and physical activities:* Sport available: rugby, hockey, cricket, athletics, archery, badminton, basketball, cross-country, fencing, golf, riding, rowing, sailing, shooting, soccer, squash, swimming, table tennis and tennis. Regular county representatives (rugby, hockey, cricket, cross-country, fencing). *Clubs and societies:* Include computer, history, English, debating.

Uniform School uniform worn; dark suit in sixth-form.
Houses/prefects Competitive houses. Prefects, head boy, head of house and house prefects – recommended by committee of housemasters for approval by Head Master. School Council.
Religion 3 religious assemblies plus one religious studies period per week; opting out is possible.
Social General studies programme in lower sixth and debating union run jointly with Wimbledon High. Girls recruited from local schools for theatrical productions. Trips and exchanges abroad. Pupils allowed to bring own car/bike/motorbike to school. Meals self-service. School shop. No tobacco/alcohol allowed.
Discipline Pupils failing to produce homework once might expect a prefect-supervised period at lunchtime; those caught smoking cannabis on the premises might expect to be asked to leave.
Alumni association is run by Secretary, Old King's Club, c/o the school.
Former pupils Walter Sickert; John Barrymore; Roy Plomley; Alvar Liddell; Michael Cardew; Jimmy Edwards; Richard Pascoe; Robin Holloway.

• KING'S (Worcester)

The King's School, Worcester WR1 2LH. Tel 01905 23016, Fax 01905 25511
• Pupils 968 • Boys 7–18 (Day/Board/Weekly) • Girls 7–18 (Day/Board/Weekly) • Upper sixth 114 • Termly fees £1697 (Day) £2931 (Board/Weekly) • HMC • Enquiries to the Headmaster • Application to the Headmaster's Secretary

What it's like

Refounded in 1541 by Henry VIII, it comprises an enclave of very fine buildings grouped round College Green on the south side of the cathedral and on the banks of the Severn. The oldest structure is the 14th-century College Hall. There are many 17th, 18th and 19th-century buildings and a large number of modern ones, all in fine grounds and gardens. The junior school, St Albans, occupies separate premises in its own grounds next to the main school. Originally a boys' school, it had a mixed sixth-form for 20 years before becoming fully co-educational in 1991. Academic standards are high and results are very good. Very many go on to degree courses including to Oxbridge. Basic Christian ethics and doctrine are taught and the cathedral plays an important part in the school's life. A very strong music department which gains much from its association with the cathedral. Strong, too, in art and drama (10 or more productions each year). Excellent sport and games and an enormous range of activities. The CCF is vigorous. A fair commitment to local community schemes and a flourishing Duke of Edinburgh's Award Scheme.

School profile

Pupils Total age range 7–18; 968 pupils, 913 day (600 boys, 313 girls), 55 boarding (39 boys, 16 girls). Senior department 11–18, 790 pupils (503 boys, 236 girls). Main entry ages 7, 8, 11, 13 and into sixth. Approx 20% are children of former pupils. Significant proportion of senior department from own junior school, King's Junior School (tel 01905 354906). *State school entry:* 80% at 11; 40% at 13; 40% to sixth.
Entrance Own entrance exam used; some admission by Common Entrance. No special skills or religious requirements. Parents not expected to buy textbooks. 59 pa assisted places. 30 pa scholarships/bursaries, £880 to half fees.
Parents 60+% live within 30 miles; up to 10% live overseas.
Head and staff *Headmaster:* Dr John Moore, in post for 12 years. Educated at Rugby and Cambridge (classics). Previously Director of Sixth Form and Head of Classics at Radley and Assistant Master at Winchester. Also JP; Chairman of HMC Academic Policy Sub-Committee and main committee and various other committees; sometime Chairman Joint Association of Classical Teachers, Chairman MEG Classics Panel. Publications: author of sundry books and articles. *Staff:* 71 full time, 41 part time. Annual turnover 7%.
Exam results In 1995, 123 pupils in upper fifth, 114 in upper sixth. *GCSE:* On average, 76% upper fifth gain at least grade C in 8+ subjects; 23% in 5–7; and 1% in 1–4 subjects. *A-levels:* 12% upper sixth pass in 4+ subjects; 85% in 3; 2% in 2; and 1% in 1 subject. Average UCAS points 22.1.

University and college entrance 94% of 1995 sixth-form leavers went on to a degree course (20% after a gap year); others typically go on to art or music colleges or straight into careers. Of those going on to university, 9% went to Oxbridge; 9% took courses in medicine, dentistry and veterinary science, 26% in science and engineering, 9% in law, 40% in humanities and social sciences, 8% in art and design, 8% in other subjects eg physiotherapy, occupational therapy.

Curriculum GCSE and A-levels. 17 GCSE subjects offered; 24 at A-level (including A-level general studies). 30% take science A-levels; 40% arts/humanities; 30% both. *Vocational:* Work experience available. *Computing facilities:* Widely available throughout the school. *Special provision:* Mildly visually handicapped accepted. Some special provision for mild dyslexia. *Europe:* French (compulsory from age 9), German and Spanish offered to GCSE and A-level; also GCSE Italian and Spanish in sixth. Regular exchanges (France, Germany and Spain); field work trips to Switzerland, Tunisia, Italy and Austria.

The arts (Pupils aged 11 and over) *Music:* Over 30% of pupils learn a musical instrument; instrumental exams can be taken. Some 8 musical groups including orchestras, wind band, choirs; cathedral choristers educated in school. Elgar Festival 1992, cup for most promising choir; cathedral choir – many concerts, broadcasts. Tours including South Africa, USA, Three Choirs Festival. *Drama & dance*: Drama offered and GCSE may be taken. Some pupils are involved in school productions and majority in house/other productions. *Art:* On average, 45 take GCSE, 5 AS-level, 20 A-level. Design, textiles and photography also offered.

Sport, community service and clubs (Pupils aged 11 and over) Sports and physical activities: rugby, football, netball, hockey, rowing, cricket, tennis, athletics, cross-country, badminton, rounders, fencing, squash, golf, swimming, sailing, canoeing. *Community service:* Pupils take bronze, silver and gold Duke of Edinburgh's Award. CCF optional. Community service optional. *Clubs and societies:* Up to 30 clubs, eg sports, shooting, drama, computing, literary, history, science, Christian Union, art, model engineering.

Uniform School uniform worn except the upper sixth.

Houses/prefects Pastoral rather than competitive houses. Prefects, head boy/girl, head of house and house prefects – appointed by the Headmaster.

Religion Worship is encouraged.

Social Regular events organised by development committee; biennial school ball. French/German/Spanish exchanges, skiing trips, geography field trips, other trips to Italy, France, Tunisia and Spain. Pupils allowed to bring own car/bike/motorbike to school. Meals self-service. School shop. No tobacco/alcohol allowed.

Boarding (Full and weekly) Seniors in own or shared studies; juniors in dormitories of 6+. Single-sex houses of approx 35, divided by age group. Resident qualified nurse. Central dining room. Pupils can provide and cook their own food. Visits to local town allowed.

Alumni association is run by Mr M O'Neill, c/o the school.

• KINGSLEY

The Kingsley School, Beauchamp Avenue, Leamington Spa, Warwickshire CV32 5RD. Tel 01926 425127, Fax 01926 831691

• Pupils 578 • Boys 2½–7 only • Girls 2½–18 (Day) • Upper sixth 48 • Termly fees £1415 (Day) • GSA • Enquiries/application to the Admissions Secretary

What it's like

Founded in 1884 by Rose Kingsley, daughter of the writer Charles Kingsley, and by Joseph Wood, who became Headmaster of Harrow. Situated close to the centre of the elegant Regency spa town, the senior school is in Beauchamp Hall (a fine listed building). The junior school is housed in Dilke House, and the early years (up to age 6) close by. There is a well-equipped sixth-form centre at Claremont House. The school has close links with Holy Trinity church. Academic standards and results are good. Each year most sixth-formers go on to higher education. The performing arts flourish in an integrated department and there are numerous productions from small chamber concerts to large scale music-theatre productions. Sports and games are well catered for with regular representation at county level. The show jumping team have twice won the National Schools' Championship at Hickstead. There is a wide variety of clubs and societies and 200 pupils involved in the Duke of Edinburgh's Award Scheme (many silver and over 90 gold awards to date), which involves community services and expeditions in Britain and overseas. Over 20 pupils are taking part in a World Challenge expedition to Zimbabwe.

School profile

Pupils Total age range 2½–18, 578 day pupils (572 girls, 6 boys). Senior department 11–18, 453 girls. Main entry ages 2, 8, 11 and into sixth (a few at 13). Majority of 11+ entrants come from own junior department (tel 01926 425993) or from Warwick Preparatory School (tel 01926 491545). Approx 10% are children of former pupils. *State school entry:* 25% main intake at 11, plus 5% to sixth.

Entrance Own entrance exam used. No special skills or religious requirements. Standard charge for textbooks; extras usually £65 maximum. 30 pa assisted places (5 at age 7, 15 at 11, and 10 to the sixth). 4 pa scholarships/bursaries, £500–£1500; 2 exhibitions (art and music), £450.

Parents 15+% in industry or commerce; 15+% are doctors, lawyers, etc; 15+% in farming; 15+% in education.

Head and staff *Headmistress:* Mrs Margaret A Webster, appointed in 1988. Educated at St Elizabeth's Convent, Ashford Grammar and Manchester University (classics, educational sciences and management of education). Previously Deputy at Altrincham Grammar and Senior Teacher at Whalley Range High. Also FRSA. *Staff:* 35 full time, 18 part time. Annual turnover 5%. Average age 40.

Exam results In 1995, 78 pupils in upper fifth, 33 in upper sixth. *GCSE:* In 1995, 53 upper fifth gained at least grade C in 8+ subjects; 18 in 5–7; and 7 in 1–4 subjects. *A-levels:* 14 upper sixth passed in 4+ subjects; 12 in 3; 5 in 2; and 1 in 1 subject. Average UCAS points 17.8 (including general studies, 21.2).

University and college entrance 94% of 1995 sixth-form leavers went on to a degree course (6% after a gap year); others typically go on to non-degree courses eg HND, nursery nursing, art foundation courses or employment with training eg accountancy. Of those going on to university, 18% took courses in science and engineering, 3% in law, 60% in humanities and social sciences, 3% in art and design, 16% in vocational subjects eg surveying, education.

Curriculum GCSE and A-levels. 20 exam subjects offered, including A-level theatre studies, psychology, business studies and general studies. 6% take science A-levels; 70% art/humanities; 24% both. *Vocational:* Work experience available; also RSA stages 1 and 2 CLAIT. *Computing facilities:* IT centre with Archimedes; PCs in sixth-form centre; CD-Rom Ecctis 2000. *Special provision:* Lessons for dyslexic pupils. *Europe:* French (compulsory) and German offered to GCSE, AS and A-level; also Italian and Spanish GCSE in sixth. Regular exchanges (France and Germany).

The arts New department of performing arts offers music, drama and dance in an integrated course from the age of 4–14. GCSE music, drama and dance are available with A-level music, performing arts and theatre studies. Extra-curricular performing arts activities include 5 dance clubs, 2 orchestras, 3 choirs, flute choir, string ensemble, recorder group, wind band and jazz band, with smaller ensembles within the junior school. Over 30% of pupils learn a musical instrument. Instrumental exams and LAMDA drama exams are taken. The vast majority of girls are involved directly in some aspect of performing arts. 3 recent leavers are members of the National Youth Theatre. *Art:* On average, 18 take GCSE, 6 A-level. Textiles, sculpture, pottery, wood and plastic, computer graphics and screenprinting also offered.

Sport, community service and clubs (Pupils aged 11 and over) *Sport and physical activities:* Compulsory sports: hockey, netball, gymnastics, tennis, rounders, athletics, health-related fitness. Optional: squash, badminton, aerobics, golf, cross-country, riding, swimming, volleyball, table tennis, judo. GCSE and A-level PE and BAGA exams may be taken. Hockey, 3 county U18 representatives, 2 U14; athletics, 8 county representatives; netball, 1 U16 county representative; gymnastics, 1 national rep; tetrathlon, 1 county rep; riding, show jumping national schools champions twice, junior team won ISIS riding competition and Gawcott cross-country in 1995. *Community service:* Pupils take bronze, silver and gold Duke of Edinburgh's Award (90 gold awards to date). Community service optional. Fundraising, some £5000+ pa raised. *Clubs and societies:* Up to 30 clubs, eg

BAYS, chess, computer, drama, gymnastics (Olympic), riding, science, music, Young Enterprise.
Uniform School uniform worn, except in the sixth.
Houses/prefects Competitive houses. Head girls, heads of houses and sports captain – elected by the school. School Council.
Religion Religious worship compulsory unless specifically requested by parents.
Social BAYS, theatrical and musical productions with local boys' independent schools; annual ball. German and French exchanges; skiing, cruises, trips to Russia. Pupils allowed to bring own car/bike/motorbike to school. No tobacco/alcohol allowed.
Discipline Pupils failing to produce homework once might expect an order mark (3 order marks in a half-term means detention); possession of tobacco or alcohol leads to suspension; students are aware that smoking cannabis would mean expulsion.
Former pupils Jane Booker (RSC); Dennis Matthews (pianist); Marie Edgar (European Junior Show Jumping Champion).

• KINGSTON GRAMMAR

Kingston Grammar School, 70 London Road, Kingston Upon Thames, Surrey KT2 6PY. Tel 0181 546 5875, Fax 0181 547 1499

• Pupils 600 • Boys 10–18 (Day) • Girls 10–18 (Day) • Upper sixth 72 • Termly fees £1795 (Day) • HMC • Enquiries/application to the Admissions Secretary

What it's like

The origins of the school are firmly traceable to the Charter issued by Queen Elizabeth in 1561 although it is likely that the school existed c.1300 or earlier. The present site lies on the London Road, opposite the Chapel of St Mary Magdalen, and has an interesting range of buildings representing architectural styles from the 1870s to the present day. It has excellent up-to-date facilities and 22 acres of playing fields near Hampton Court Palace. Originally a boys' school, it first admitted girls in 1978 and is now fully co-educational. Academic standards are high and results are good. Most pupils proceed to degree courses, including Oxbridge. The pastoral organisation is efficient, and pupils are given encouragement to develop their individual talents. Music and drama are strong. There are several orchestras and ensembles, plus a choral society. Several dramatic performances are presented each year. Sports and games are very well catered for, and the school is famous for its hockey (played in both winter terms) and rowing and has a long list of blues and international players. Numerous clubs and societies provide for most extra-curricular needs. Computing, printing, photography and handicrafts have special facilities. The CCF contingent is large and flourishing and comprises Army and Air Force sections.

School profile

Pupils Age range 10–18, 600 day pupils (390 boys, 210 girls). Main entry ages 10, 11, 13 and into the sixth. *State school entry:* 60% main intake, plus 75% to sixth.
Entrance Common entrance and own exam used. Scholarships, bursaries, assisted places.
Head and staff *Headmaster:* C D Baxter, 5 years in post. Educated at Lord Williams' School, Thame, and Oxford University (English language and literature). Previously Academic Director and Head of English and Drama at Wycliffe and Housemaster and Librarian at Gresham's. *Staff:* 51 full time, 3 part time. Annual turnover 5%. Average age 38.
Exam results In 1996, 94 pupils in upper fifth, 73 in upper sixth. *GCSE:* In 1995, 90 upper fifth gained at least grade C in 9+ subjects. *A-levels:* 6 upper sixth passed in 4+ subjects; 54 in 3; 10 in 2; and 3 in 1 subject. Average UCAS points 19.6.
University and college entrance 96% of 1995 sixth-form leavers went on to a degree course (10% after a gap year); others typically go on to resit A-levels. Of those going on to university, 10% went to Oxbridge; 15% took courses in medicine, dentistry and veterinary science, 26% in science and engineering, 5% in law, 38% in humanities and social sciences, 5% in art and design, 5% in vocational subjects eg education, osteopathy, 5% in other subjects.
Curriculum GCSE and A-levels. 22 subjects offered. *Vocational:* Work experience

available. *Computing facilities:* Apple Macs, BBCs and Nimbus in classrooms and library. *Special provision:* All pupils follow a course in basic skills. Extra help available. *Europe:* French, German and Spanish offered to GCSE and A-level. Regular exchanges (France, Germany and Spain). Talks from MEPs. Use of European satellite television. Sporting and musical tours of European countries.

The arts *Music:* Over 30% of pupils learn a musical instrument; instrumental exams can be taken. Some 8–10 musical groups including orchestras, concert band, wind ensemble, various chamber groups, jazz, choirs. 1 pupil co-leader of Guildhall Junior Symphony Orchestra, 1 in National Children's Orchestra, 1 in National Youth Orchestra, 1 soloist in Purcell Room concert. *Drama & dance*: Drama offered. Some pupils are involved in school and house/other productions. Guys and Dolls recently, involving very many pupils and staff. *Art:* On average, 30 take GCSE, 10 A-level. Design, textiles, photography also offered. Pupils regularly gain entry into art colleges; Royal Academy exhibition of sixth-form work.

Sport, community service and clubs *Sport and physical activities:* Compulsory sports (first two years): hockey, cricket, tennis. Optional (third and fourth year): rowing, badminton, squash, table tennis, netball, athletics, cross-country, basketball. Fifth and sixth-form: badminton, swimming, real tennis, squash, golf, table tennis, athletics, cross-country, basketball, shooting. A-level exams may be taken. Hockey, 1992–4 national champions, boys U18; rowing, numerous representatives at all levels (including boys GB U23, girls U21), Schools Head 1993–5. *Community service:* Pupils take bronze, silver and gold Duke of Edinburgh's Award. CCF optional. Community service for sixth-form. *Clubs and societies:* Up to 30 clubs, eg numerous sports, art, Gibbon Society, chess, drama, young engineers, D of E Adventure Society, photography.

Uniform School uniform worn throughout.

Houses/prefects Competitive houses. Prefects, head boy/girl, head of house and house prefects – appointed by the Headmaster.

Religion Attendance at religious worship not compulsory.

Social Language exchanges; hockey tour annually to Holland; geography field trip to Alps; music exchange with school in Germany; annual ski trips. Pupils allowed to bring own bike to school; sixth-form may bring car. Meals self-service. School shop. No tobacco/alcohol allowed.

Discipline Pupils failing to produce homework once might expect to be given a (short) deadline to complete the work; those caught smoking cannabis on the premises might expect to be withdrawn from the school.

Former pupils Michael Frayn (author and playwright); Neil Fox (DJ, Capital Radio); Simon May (composer); Neil Mullarkey (comedian); Edward Gibbon (Decline and Fall of the Roman Empire).

• KINGSWOOD

Kingswood School, Lansdown, Bath, Avon BA1 5RG. Tel 01225 734200, Fax 01225 734205

• Pupils 449 • Boys 11–18 (Day/Board/Weekly) • Girls 11–18 (Day/Board/Weekly) • Upper sixth 66 • Termly fees £2333 (Day) £3720 (Board/Weekly) • HMC • Enquiries/application to the Registrar

What it's like

Founded in 1748 by John Wesley who created its first curriculum and compiled its first textbooks. It has a particularly splendid position on the slopes of Lansdown, a residential area overlooking the city. The main buildings are Victorian Gothic and these remain the heart of the modern school which has a vast campus of 218 acres. Many new buildings have been added, including a sports hall, and art, CDT and information technology centres and a new theatre. In these very civilised surroundings, the facilities and accommodation are first-class. Though ecumenical, the school retains especially strong links with the Methodist Church. Originally a boys' school, it is now fully co-educational having first admitted girls in 1972. An excellent academic education is given and results are good: most go on to universities, including Oxbridge. Very strong music and art departments. An exceptionally fine range of sports, games, clubs, societies and extra-curricular activities. Strong commitment to local community services and an impressive record in the Duke of Edinburgh's Award Scheme.

School profile

Pupils Age range 11–18; 449 pupils, 199 day (114 boys, 85 girls), 250 boarding (146 boys, 104 girls). Main entry ages 11, 13 and into sixth. Many pupils from own prep school, Kingswood Day, and from Prior's Court, near Newbury. *State school entry:* 35% main intake, plus 25% to sixth.
Entrance Common Entrance and own entrance exam used. No special skills or religious requirements, but school has strong links with the Methodist Church. Parents not expected to buy textbooks; other extras agreed with parents. Maximum of 6 pa assisted places. Range of scholarships/bursaries available – up to 50% fees.
Parents 30+% live within 30 miles; 20+% live overseas.
Head and staff *Headmaster:* Gary M Best, appointed in 1987. Educated at South Shields Grammar Technical School and Oxford University (history). Previously Head of History and Head of Sixth Form at Newcastle under Lyme School. Also Methodist local preacher. Publications: Seventeenth Century Europe. *Staff:* 47 full time, 6 part time. Annual turnover 5%. Average age 36.
Exam results In 1995, 74 in Year 11; 66 in upper sixth. *GCSE:* In 1995, 70% in Year 11 gained at least grade C in 8+ subjects; 17% in 5–7 subjects. *A-levels:* 30% upper sixth passed in 4+ subjects; 41% in 3; 20% in 2 subjects. Average UCAS points 18.2.
University and college entrance 90% of 1995 sixth-form leavers went on to a degree course (5% after a gap year), 8% to Oxbridge. Others typically go on to further education or into employment.
Curriculum GCSE, AS and A-levels. 16 GCSE subjects offered; 28 A-level (including general studies). *Vocational:* Work experience available. *Computing facilities:* Information technology centre. *Special provision:* EFL; some special needs support available.
The arts *Music:* 30% of pupils learn a musical instrument; instrumental exams can be taken. Musical groups include orchestra, string group, jazz band, choirs, barbershop, recorder, brass quartet. *Drama & dance*: Both offered. GCSE and A-level drama may be taken. Majority of pupils are involved in school and house/other productions. *Art:* Fine art, design, pottery and art history offered.
Sport, community service and clubs *Sport and physical activities:* Compulsory sports: rugby, hockey, cricket (boys); hockey, netball (girls). Optional: swimming, tennis, squash, badminton, football, fencing, basketball, volleyball, riding, cycling, archery, athletics, cross-country, golf, hiking, multigym, orienteering, rounders, sailing, shooting, trampolining. GCSE may be taken. Orienteering, British Schools U14 winner; cross-country, 2 county reps; hockey, county schools finals 1st XI 2nd, U16 joint winners; athletics, 3 county champions. *Community service:* Pupils take bronze, silver and gold Duke of Edinburgh's Award. Community service optional. *Clubs and societies:* Over 30 clubs, eg country dancing, computers, electronics, photography, art, Greek, orienteering, war games, Christian Fellowship, science.
Uniform School uniform worn except in the sixth.
Houses/prefects Competitive houses. Prefects, senior prefect/deputy senior prefect, head of house and house prefects – appointed by the Headmaster in consultation with staff.
Religion Daily morning assembly and weekly service for all.
Social Local schools joint cricket tour abroad, annual choral production, debating competitions and joint sixth-form activities occasionally. Annual ski trip abroad. Occasional small group trips (for history and art). Annual exchange with German school. Pupils allowed to bring own car to school. Meals self-service. School shop. No tobacco/alcohol allowed.
Discipline Pupils failing to produce homework once might be required to produce it within 24 hours; those caught with illegal drugs would be expelled.
Boarding All sixth-form share (2 or 3); 50% are in dormitories of 6+. Single-sex houses of approximately 50 (2 junior, 6 senior). Resident qualified nurse, visiting doctor. Central dining room. Pupils can provide and cook own snacks. Visits to local town allowed.
Alumni association run by Mr R J Lewis, c/o the school.

• KIRKHAM GRAMMAR

Kirkham Grammar School, Ribby Road, Kirkham, Preston, Lancashire PR4 2BH. Tel 01772 671079, Fax 01772 672747

• Pupils 745 • Boys 4–18 (Day/Board) • Girls 4–18 (Day/Board) • Upper sixth 74 • Termly fees £1225 (Day) £2325 (Board) • SHMIS, BSA • Enquiries/application to the Headmaster

What it's like

Founded in 1549 as a co-educational school, it is attractively situated in more than 30 acres of its own grounds in a semi-rural area between Preston and Blackpool. The main school buildings date from 1910, but there have been many additions. Recently these have included new laboratories, a junior school, sixth-form centre and new boarding accommodation. A technology suite is planned. The school retains traditional links with the Drapers' Company and provides a traditional grammar school education, achieving good examination results at GCSE and A-level. Most sixth-formers go on to university, including Oxbridge. There is a strong sporting tradition, which is complemented by strong art, drama and music departments. Much stress is laid on the Christian ethos of the school, respect for others, courteous behaviour and manners, good order and discipline. Great pains are taken to establish close personal relationships with each pupil, through the tutorial system.

School profile

Pupils Total age range 4–18; 745 pupils, 675 day (355 boys, 320 girls), 70 boarding (39 boys, 31 girls; boarding available from age 11). Senior department 11–18, 540 pupils (280 boys, 260 girls). Main entry ages 4, 9, 11 and into sixth. Approx 5% are children of former pupils. Significant proportion of senior intake from own junior school, Kirkham Grammar Junior School (tel 01772 673222). *State school entry:* 30% at 11, plus 10% to sixth.

Entrance Own entrance exam used. No special skills or religious requirements. Parents not expected to buy textbooks. 10 pa assisted places at 11 and 12 for sixth-form. 10 pa scholarships/bursaries, 20%–50% fees, including 2 music scholarships.

Parents 25+% in industry or commerce; 25+% are doctors, lawyers, etc. 60+% live within 30 miles; up to 10% live overseas.

Head and staff *Headmaster:* Barrie Stacey, 5 years in post. Educated at Holme Valley Grammar School, and universities of Edinburgh (history), Oxford and Bradford (education). Previously Deputy Head and Director of Studies at Birkdale, Senior Deputy Head at Honley High, Huddersfield, Acting Head of History at Holme Valley Grammar and Assistant History Teacher at Bilborough Grammar, Nottingham. Also FRSA. Chairman, Kirklees LEA Secondary Deputy Heads Association (1985). Represented Edinburgh and Oxford for cross-country and athletics; Amateur Athletics Association coach; member of British Milers' Club. *Staff:* 53 full time, 3 part time. Annual turnover 3%. Average age 35.

Exam results In 1995, 74 pupils in upper fifth, 65 in upper sixth. *GCSE:* In 1995, 63% upper fifth gained at least grade C in 8+ subjects; 36% in 5–7 subjects (average of 8.3 per pupil). *A-levels:* 36 upper sixth passed in 4+ subjects; 9 in 3; 7 in 2; and 8 in 1 subject. Average UCAS points 15.5.

University and college entrance 90% of 1995 sixth-form leavers went on to a degree course (5% after a gap year); others typically go on to employment or art foundation courses. Of those going on to university, 5% went to Oxbridge; 2% took courses in medicine, dentistry and veterinary science, 35% in science and engineering, 5% in law, 40% in humanities and social sciences, 1% in art and design, 7% in other subjects.

Curriculum GCSE and A-levels. 18 subjects offered (including A-level general studies). 40% took science A-levels; 40% arts/humanities; 20% both. *Vocational:* Work experience available. *Computing facilities:* 30 computers in specialist rooms; others in departments. Computer studies to GCSE. *Special provision:* EFL help available. Test in English arranged for sixth-formers for whom English is not native tongue. *Europe:* French and German offered to GCSE, AS and A-level. Regular exchanges (France and Germany).

The arts (Pupils aged 11 and over) *Music:* 25% of pupils learn a musical instrument; instrumental exams can be taken. Some 6 musical groups including orchestra, wind band, contemporary, choirs, madrigal group. Members of Northern Cathedral Singers;

member of county youth orchestra. *Drama & dance*: Drama offered. GCSE drama, A-level theatre studies, LAMDA exams may be taken. Some pupils are involved in school productions and majority in house/other productions. *Art:* On average, 30 take GCSE, 6 A-level. A number of students went on to pursue careers in art, design, architecture in 1995.

Sport, community service and clubs (Pupils aged 11 and over) *Sport and physical activities:* Compulsory sports: rugby, hockey, netball, athletics, swimming, tennis, cricket. Optional: squash, badminton, basketball, shooting, golf, volleyball. County representatives at rugby (U15, U16, U17, U18), hockey (U14, U16, U18), athletics, cross-country; national, triathlon and cross-country representatives, England rugby trialist (U18); English Schools U18 girls hockey finalists; Northern representative, hockey and rugby U18. *Community service:* CCF compulsory for 2 years at age 14, optional for sixth-formers. Winners of Battle Initiative Test at NW District Camp 1994. Community service optional for sixth-formers. *Clubs and societies:* Up to 10 clubs, eg drama, Christian Union, electronics, auto, ornithology, chess, fell walking.

Uniform School uniform worn throughout.

Houses/prefects Competitive houses. Prefects, captain and vice captain, senior prefects, head of house and house prefects – appointed by the Headmaster or housemasters.

Religion Non-denominational.

Social Annual Leavers' Ball. Annual activity holidays and ski trips; exchange visits to Germany and France; annual sporting exchange with Wairarapa College, New Zealand; world rugby and hockey tours. Pupils allowed to bring own car/bike/motorbike to school. Meals self-service. School shop. No tobacco/alcohol allowed.

Discipline Firm discipline. On Report system (weekly/daily homework) for pupils underachieving through lack of effort. Detention system – evening (staff and prefect), Saturday morning (Headmaster). Minor offences dealt with by counselling or detention. Major offences lead swiftly to suspension or expulsion. Any pupil caught taking or dealing in drugs would be expelled (no such instances to date).

Boarding 40% have own study bedroom; 50% share with one other; 10% in dormitories of 6+. Resident matrons. Central dining room. One weekend exeat every 3 weeks. Visits to local town allowed.

Alumni association run by Mr G Benstead, 40 Arundel Road, Ansdell, Lytham St Annes FY8 1BL.

Former pupils Prof E R Laithwaite (Imperial College, London); David W H Walton (Director of Research, British Antarctic Survey); Graham Clark (English National Opera); Ian Byatt (Director of Water Services); G Sagar (Professor of Botany, Bangor University); Rt Rev R Brown (Bishop of Birkenhead).

L

• LA SAGESSE

La Sagesse Convent High School, North Jesmond, Newcastle upon Tyne NE2 3RJ. Tel 0191 281 3474, Fax 0191 281 2721

• Pupils 470 • Boys None • Girls 3–18 (Day) • Upper sixth 24 • Termly fees £1285 (Day) • GSA • Enquiries/application to the Headteacher

What it's like

Founded in 1912, by the Sisters of La Sagesse it is now run by a board of governors. The premises lie on the fringe of the city overlooking Jesmond Dene. The nursery, junior and senior departments are all on a single site with 9 acres of grounds. A Christian school with a Roman Catholic foundation, but girls of all religious denominations are welcomed. A sound general academic education is provided and results are good. The majority of sixth-formers go on to degree courses. There is a great deal of emphasis is on careers and guidance in sixth-form (eg understanding industry course). Music, drama and art and a range of sports, games, clubs and societies. Some involvement in local community schemes.

School profile

Pupils Total age range 3–18; 470 day girls. Senior department 11–18, 350 girls. Main entry ages 11 and into sixth. Approx 5% are children of former pupils. Own junior department provides over 30% senior intake. *State school entry:* 40% main intake.

Entrance Own entrance exam used (junior pupils have automatic entrance). Parents not expected to buy textbooks or stationery. 28 pa assisted places. 6 pa scholarships one-third fees; additional bursaries.

Parents 15+% are doctors, lawyers, etc; 15+% in industry or commerce.

Head and staff *Headteacher*: Miss Linda Clark, in post since 1994. Educated at St Josephs Grammar School, Hebburn, and at Trinity and All Saints and the universities of Leeds and Newcastle (Spanish and education). Previously Deputy Head of St Thomas More, Head of Modern Languages at St Aidans and in charge of Spanish at St Anselms. *Staff:* 29 full time. Annual turnover 2%. Average age 45.

Exam results In 1995, 55 pupils in Year 11, 24 in upper sixth. *GCSE:* In 1995, 58% in Year 11 gained at least grade C in 8+ subjects; 36% in 5–7 subjects. *A-levels:* 7 upper sixth passed in 4 + subjects; 13 in 3; 3 in 2; and 1 in 1 subject. Average UCAS points 18.8.

University and college entrance 88% of 1995 sixth-form leavers went on to a degree course (5% after a gap year); others typically go on to management training. Of those going on to university, 10% took courses in medicine, dentistry and veterinary science, 16% in science and engineering, 73% in humanities and social sciences.

Curriculum GCSE and A-levels. 17 subjects offered (including A-level general studies). 38% take science A-levels; 46% arts/humanities; 15% both. *Vocational:* Work experience available; also RSA typing and computer proficiency. *Computing facilities:* 2 computer rooms with 20 computers. Computers used in many areas of the curriculum. *Europe:* French (compulsory from age 11–14) and Spanish offered to GCSE and A-level; also French AS-level and German for Institute of Linguists in sixth. Regular exchanges (France and Spain). Sixth form attend Paris conference.

The arts *Music:* Up to 25% of pupils learn a musical instrument; instrumental exams can be taken. Some 5 musical groups including choirs, orchestra, assembly group, recorder. Local festival winners, soloists and orchestra. *Drama & dance*: Both offered. Some pupils are involved in school productions and majority in house/other productions. *Art:* On average, 20 take GCSE, 8 A-level. Design and textiles also offered. 2nd prize in Schools Industry Link Competition.

Sport, community service and clubs *Sport and physical activities:* Compulsory sports: hockey, netball, tennis, rounders. Optional: badminton, volleyball. Sixth form only: squash. *Community service:* Community service optional, help in special school; Handicapped Club. *Clubs and societies:* Up to 10 clubs, eg dance, drama, art, chess,

debate, Greenhouse conservationist, play reading, stamp collecting, recreational sport.
Uniform School uniform worn, except the sixth.
Houses/prefects Competitive houses. Prefects, head girl, sports captain and house prefects – appointed by the school. School Council.
Religion School prays together once or twice a week.
Social Public speaking and geographical quiz with other local schools. Language and ski trips abroad, individual sixth-formers visit Spain and France; exchange programme. Pupils allowed to bring own bike to school; also cars but not in school grounds. Meals: most bring own food. School shop. No tobacco/alcohol allowed.
Discipline Pupils failing to conform to acceptable standards of behaviour are warned and parents contacted. In a case of a serious breach of discipline a pupil would be suspended. Detention very occasionally used (eg repeated lateness, lack of homework) but in general the warning system and clear rules are sufficient.

• LADY ELEANOR HOLLES

Lady Eleanor Holles School, Hanworth Road, Hampton, Middlesex TW12 3HF. Tel 0181 979 1601, Fax 0181 941 8291

• Pupils 876 • Boys None • Girls 7–18 (Day) • Upper sixth 81 • Termly fees £1680 (Day) • GSA • Enquiries to the Head Mistress • Application to the Registrar

What it's like

Founded in the Cripplegate Ward of the City of London in 1711 under the will of Lady Eleanor Holles, daughter of the second Earl of Clare. It is now housed in modern buildings in Hampton where it moved in 1936. It stands on a pleasant 33-acre site surrounded by gardens and playing fields. All sports facilities are on site. There has been an extensive building programme recently and it is now very well equipped. It is a C of E foundation and has its own chapel where worship in the Anglican tradition is encouraged. Academic standards are high and results are consistently excellent. Most girls go on to degree courses, including many to Oxbridge. Music is very strong (a wind band, string orchestra and chamber groups); as is drama, with 200 or more pupils being involved in annual dramatic competitions and in the productions of neighbouring boys' schools. A good range of sports and games is provided and standards are very high (many representatives at county, regional and national level, especially in netball, rowing and lacrosse). There is much regular social and academic liaison with Hampton School next door. Some commitment to local community services and a modest record in the Duke of Edinburgh's Award Scheme and school involvement in outward bound courses.

School profile

Pupils Total age range 7–18; 876 day girls. Senior department 11–18, 690 girls. Main entry ages 7, 11 and into sixth. 10% are children of former pupils. *State school entry:* 30% senior intake, plus 10% to sixth.
Entrance Own entrance exam used. No special skills required, although music and sport are encouraged; no religious requirements. Parents not expected to buy textbooks. 10 pa assisted places at age 11 and 5 pa at sixth-form. Scholarships (academic and music) at 11 and 16; means tested bursaries at 11, 33%–100% fees.
Head and staff *Headmistress:* Miss Elizabeth Candy, in post for 15 years. Educated at Merrywood Grammar, Bristol, and Westfield College, London (chemistry). Previously Second Mistress, Head of Sixth Form and Head of Science at Putney High and joint Head of Science at Bromley High. Also Governor of two prep schools; Governor of Royal Holloway; Director of Richmond Education Business Partnership. *Staff:* 68 full time, 19 part time (plus 11 full time, 1 part time in Junior school). Annual turnover 10%. Average age 43.
Exam results In 1995, 84 pupils in upper fifth, 87 in upper sixth. *GCSE:* in 1995, 82 upper fifth gained at least grade C in 8+ subjects; 2 in 5–7 subjects. *A-levels:* 85 upper sixth passed in 4+ subjects (incl general studies); 2 in 3 subjects. Average UCAS points 28.2.
University and college entrance 92% of 1995 sixth-form leavers went on to a degree course (15% after a gap year); others typically go on to art foundation courses. Of those going on to university, 12% went to Oxbridge; 14% took courses in medicine, dentistry

and veterinary science, 14% in science and engineering, 2% in law, 67% in humanities and social sciences, 3% in art and design.

Curriculum GCSE, AS and A-levels. 21 GCSE subjects offered; 16 at AS; 27 at A-level (including theatre studies and general studies). 18% take science A-levels; 46% arts/humanities; 36% both. *Vocational:* Work experience available, also RSA stages 1 and 2 in keyboard skills. *Computing facilities:* 12-station Nimbus network plus second network and bank of lap-tops. PCs in several departments. *Special provision:* Additional individual coaching available. *Europe:* French, German (both obligatory to age 14) and Spanish and Russian offered to GCSE, AS and A-level. Foreign Languages for Industry and Commerce and non-examined language courses in French, German and Spanish in sixth-form. Regular exchanges for sixth-form to France, Germany and Spain. Outside speakers, often jointly with Hampton in general studies programme. Occasional German and French girls in sixth-form.

The arts (Pupils aged 11 and over) *Music:* Over 50% of pupils learn a musical instrument; instrumental exams can be taken. Some 35+ musical groups including 2 orchestras, wind band, 2 dance bands, percussion, 3 choirs, baroque consort, cello, brass, recorder ensembles, jazz group. Pupils in Pro Corda and in Stoneleigh Youth Orchestra; scholarship to GSMD and Royal College. *Drama & dance*: Both offered. A-level drama and Guildhall exams may be taken. Some pupils are involved in school productions and majority in house/other productions. Pupils nominated for awards in Richmond Drama Festival; *Art:* On average, 32 take GCSE, 2 AS-level, 16 A-level. Pottery, photography and history of art also offered.

Sport, community service and clubs (Pupils aged 11 and over) *Sport and physical activities:* Compulsory sports: netball, lacrosse, gymnastics, dance, swimming, tennis, athletics, health-related fitness. Optional: badminton, hockey, sport acro, aerobics, squash, real tennis, riding, golf, rowing. Sixth form only: ASA preliminary teachers award. BAGA and RLSS exams may be taken. Rowing, 2 international competitors, national schools champions; athletics, 13 borough champions; gymnastics, regional champions U13 and U16; netball, county champions at U14, U15, U16, U18, 8 girls in U16 county squad, 4 in U18; lacrosse, county champions (senior squad), 12 girls in county teams, 2 in regional, 2 in England U18 (including captain); swimming, LSSA championships winners U13, U16, U17. *Community service:* Pupils take bronze, silver and gold Duke of Edinburgh's Award. Community service optional; girls may attend sign language courses or visit local home for elderly; opportunities to work with mentally and physically disadvantaged children – school organises annual fun day. *Clubs and societies:* Up to 15 clubs, eg chess, gardening, science, debating, Christian Union, Amnesty International, croquet, modern languages.

Uniform School uniform worn, except in the sixth.

Houses/prefects No competitive houses. Head girl, elected by the sixth-form and staff. School Council.

Religion Religious worship encouraged. C of E chapel and chaplain.

Social Service volunteers, drama productions, orchestral and choral performances, debating with neighbouring boys' school. Organised exchange with German school; French, Spanish, Russian, classical trips; 2 ski holidays a year. Pupils allowed to bring own car/bike/motorbike to school. Meals in cafeteria. No tobacco/alcohol allowed.

Discipline Pupils failing to produce homework once might expect to stay in during lunch recess and do the work; those caught smoking cannabis on the premises could expect expulsion.

Alumni association is run by Mrs Ann Roberts, 7 Buttercup Close, Lindford, Bordon, Hampshire GU35 0YR.

Former pupils Charlotte Attenborough; Anne Nightingale; Saskia Reeves; Beattie Edney; Lucy Irvine; Christina Hardyment; Jane Thynne; Joan Hopkins.

• LANCING

Lancing College, Lancing, West Sussex BN15 0RW. Tel 01273 452213, Fax 01273 464720
• Pupils 525 • Boys 13–18 (Day/Board) • Girls 16–18 (Day/Board) • Upper sixth 125 • Termly fees £3015 (Day) £4010 (Board) • HMC, Woodard • Enquiries/application to the Head Master's Secretary

What it's like

Founded in 1848 by the Rev Nathaniel Woodard and the first of the Woodard schools. It has a splendid site on a spur of the South Downs overlooking the sea to the south and the Weald to the north. The superb grounds comprise about 550 acres and include the college farm. The main buildings – handsome examples of the collegiate style of architecture – are grouped round two main quadrangles. There have been many developments in recent years, including a music school, a sixth-form residence, swimming pool, theatre and technology centre. Intended primarily for Church of England pupils, but pupils of other Christian denominations are accepted. Girls were first admitted to the sixth-form in 1971. The college has a magnificent chapel and a strong tradition of choral and orchestral music. A large and well-qualified staff allows a staff:pupil ratio of about 1:9. A broad general education is provided. Academic standards are high and results consistently very good. Most pupils go on to higher education, including many to Oxbridge. Music and art are an important part of the education of all pupils; quite a lot of dramatic work is also done. A good range of sports and games is available and standards are high. There is also a fair variety of extra-curricular activities. There is a flourishing CCF contingent (Army, Naval and RAF sections) and a farming group which helps to run the school farm. A particularly active social services organisation helps the local community and also people in the Camberwell district of London.

School profile

Pupils Age range 13–18; 525 pupils, 49 day (46 boys 3 girls), 476 boarding (423 boys, 53 girls). Main entry ages 13 (boys) and into sixth (boys and girls). *State school entry:* 2% main intake, plus 2% to sixth.

Entrance Common Entrance used. 10 pa assisted places (at 13 and sixth). 30 pa scholarships and exhibitions.

Head and staff *Head Master*: Christopher Saunders, 4 years in post. Educated at Lancing and at universities of Cambridge (geography) and Oxford (education). Previously Headmaster at Eastbourne College, and Housemaster at Bradfield. Also member of FA Council and governor of seven prep schools. *Staff:* 60 full time, 3 part time. Annual turnover 5%. Average age 39.

Exam results In 1995, 94 pupils in fifth, 125 in upper sixth. *GCSE:* In 1995, 82 upper fifth gained at least grade C in 8+ subjects; 7 in 5–7 subjects. *A-levels:* 17 upper sixth passed in 4+ subject; 98 in 3; 7 in 2; and 3 in 1 subject. Average UCAS points 23.7.

University and college entrance 98% of 1995 sixth-form leavers went on to a degree course (35% after a gap year); others typically go on to further education. Of those going on to university, 15% went to Oxbridge; 5% took courses in medicine, dentistry and veterinary science, 30% in science and engineering, 8% in law, 48% in humanities and social sciences, 5% in art and design, 5% in vocational subjects eg business studies, physiotherapy.

Curriculum GCSE and A-levels. Approx 20 subjects offered (including Arabic; no A-level general studies). 24% take science A-levels; 48% arts/humanities; 28% both. *Computing facilities:* Two RML Nimbus networks, 20 machines. *Europe:* French, German (from age 13), Italian and Spanish to GCSE, AS and A-level; also Russian GCSE and A-level. Over 75% take GCSE in more than 1 language. Regular exchanges (France, Germany, Russia, Italy and Spain). Euro-days for fifth and sixth-form to stimulate interest in Europe and give information (careers, political institutions, etc). Work experience for lower sixth linguists.

The arts *Music:* Over 50% of pupils learn a musical instrument; instrumental exams can be taken. Some 7 musical groups including orchestras, chamber group. 1 pupil 2nd in UK in ARCO exams. *Drama & dance*: Some pupils are involved in school productions and majority in house/other productions. *Art:* On average, 15 take GCSE, 12 A-level. Pottery, photography also offered.

Sport, community service and clubs *Sport and physical activities:* No compulsory sports but all must take exercise. Main team games: for boys, soccer (Advent term),

rugby and hockey (Lent term) and cricket (summer); for girls, hockey, netball, lacrosse (winter). Other options: Eton fives, swimming, cross-country, fencing, shooting, basketball, squash, tennis, water polo, wind surfing, sailing, golf and athletics. Squash, county champions; cricket, county champions in Langdale Cup and Sussex Lords Taverners Cup. *Community service:* Pupils take bronze, silver and gold Duke of Edinburgh's Award. CCF or community service compulsory for 3 years. *Clubs and societies:* Up to 30 clubs, eg astronomy, electronics, trout and salmon.
Uniform School uniform worn; more choice in upper sixth.
Houses/prefects Prefects, head boy/girl, head of house and house prefects – appointed after wide consultation with staff and pupils.
Religion Attendance at religious worship compulsory on Sundays and festivals.
Social Rotary debating and public speaking jointly with other schools. Exchanges with France, Germany, Italy, Russia (Kazan) and Spain. Regular expeditions to Malawi (where Malosa school is twinned with Lancing). Pupils allowed to bring own bike to school. Meals self-service. School shop. No tobacco allowed; alcohol only permitted in a licensed club for upper sixth.
Discipline Pupils failing to produce homework once might expect house or teacher's detention; Head Master's detention on subsequent occasion; those caught smoking cannabis on the premises are liable for expulsion after consideration of all circumstances.
Former pupils Tim Rice; Christopher Hampton; David Hare; Tom Sharpe; Charles Anson; Christopher Meyer; Admiral Robert Woodard; Lord Nicholas Browne Wilkinson.

• LANGLEY

Langley School, Langley Park, Norwich NR14 6BJ. Tel 01508 520210, Fax 01508 528058
• Pupils 247 • Boys 10–18 (Day/Board/Weekly) • Girls 10–18 (Day/Board/Weekly) • Upper sixth 27 • Termly fees £1820 (Day) £3500 (Board) £2840 (Weekly) • SHMIS, BSA • Enquiries/application to the Headmaster's Secretary

What it's like

Founded in 1910 (as Norwich High School for Boys), it moved in 1946 to Langley Park, between Norwich and the pleasant town of Beccles. Girls were first admitted in 1978 and it became fully co-educational in 1989. It is housed in a handsome Grade 1, Palladian-style Georgian mansion set in 50 acres of grounds. It is well-equipped, with new computer rooms, laboratories, workshops, studio and a large sports hall. There are extensive playing fields, including a nine-hole golf course. The school belongs to the local squash and sailing clubs. The staff:pupil ratio is about 1:9. It draws pupils from a wide ability range. The aim of the school is to provide a full education, academically, socially and culturally, to encourage pupils to develop their talents and personality, to use time wisely, to achieve a high standard of self-discipline and to draw out and train the qualities of leadership. Careers guidance, study skills and ethical studies are taught to all pupils. Vocational qualifications are offered in the sixth-form. The school offers a caring, secure and disciplined environment. Some 25 clubs and societies cater for most needs.

School profile

Pupils Age range 10–18, 247 pupils, 185 day (147 boys, 38 girls), 62 boarders (44 boys, 18 girls). Main entry ages 10, 11, 12, 13 and into sixth. A number of pupils from own prep school (Langley Preparatory School, tel 01603 433861). *State school entry:* 15% main intake, plus 2% to sixth.
Entrance Common Entrance and own exam used. Parents expected to buy textbooks in sixth. Academic, music, art, technology and sports scholarships and bursaries; discounts for boarding pupils from service families and family discounts.
Parents 30+% live within 30 miles; 10+% live overseas.
Head and staff *Headmaster:* S J W McArthur, in post 7 years. Educated at Coleraine, and at universities of Ulster (geography) and Sussex (education management). Previously Headmaster at Arnold Lodge, Deputy Headmaster at St Bede's and Housemaster, Head of Geography and Head of Careers at Denstone. Also member SHMIS Executive Committee and ISIS (East) Committee. *Staff:* 25 full time, 5 part time. Annual turnover 5%.
Exam results In 1995, 55 pupils in upper fifth, 24 in upper sixth. *GCSE:* In 1995, 53% pupils gained at least grade C in 5+ subjects. *A-levels:* Average pupil passes 2 subjects. Average UCAS points 9.8.

University and college entrance 60% of 1995 sixth-form leavers went on to a degree course (10% after a gap year); others typically go on to further education eg agricultural college or employment. Of those going on to university, 5% took courses in medicine, dentistry and veterinary science, 30% in science and engineering, 5% in law, 30% in humanities and social sciences, 10% in art and design, 20% in other vocational subjects.
Curriculum GCSE, AS and A-levels; GNVQ. 20 subjects offered to GCSE and A-level, and 10 at AS level. Classes are small and a tight monitoring and tutoring system operates at all levels. *Vocational:* Work experience available. GNVQ in business and leisure studies offered in sixth-form. *Computing facilities:* 3 computer rooms with 37 networked computers (486 and Pentium), laser printers and 'stacker' CD-Roms; multi-media facilities including TV/video. All pupils study IT to age 14. *Special provision:* Teachers qualified to teach both dyslexic pupils and English as a foreign language. *Europe:* French, German (both compulsory 11–14), Italian, Russian and Spanish offered to GCSE and A-level; also French, German and Italian to Institute of Linguists. Regular exchanges (France and Germany). Regularly pupils from eg France, Netherlands, Spain.
The arts *Music:* Up to 25% of pupils learn a musical instrument; instrumental exams can be taken. Some 6 musical groups including brass, wind, recorder, choir, strings, *Drama & dance*: Drama offered. GCSE drama and Guildhall exams may be taken. Majority of pupils are involved in school and house/other productions. *Art:* On average, 15 take GCSE, 2 A-level. Design, pottery and photography also offered. Many pupils proceed to art college.
Sport, community service and clubs *Sport and physical activities:* Compulsory sports: rugby, hockey, cricket, athletics, netball. Optional: basketball, badminton, football, tennis, squash, volleyball etc. GCSE and Certificate of Further Studies in sport may be taken. Rugby, representatives in England U16 squad, regional U18, county; hockey, 2 in county U14 XI. *Community service:* Pupils take bronze, silver and gold Duke of Edinburgh's Award. CCF and community service optional. Scouts. *Clubs and societies:* Up to 30 clubs, eg bridge, model railways, drama, sailing, squash.
Uniform School uniform worn throughout.
Houses/prefects Competitive houses. Prefects, head boy and girl, heads of house and house prefects – appointed by the Head.
Religion Attendance at religious worship compulsory.
Social Trips abroad include language exchanges and visits, skiing (Europe and Canada), history (Ypres). Pupils allowed to bring own car, bike or motorbike to school. Meals self-service. School shop (second-hand clothing and tuck). No tobacco/alcohol allowed.
Discipline Pupils failing to produce homework once might expect a warning or work detention; those caught smoking cannabis on the premises would be asked to leave.

• LATYMER UPPER

Latymer Upper School, King Street, London W6 9LR. Tel 0181 741 1851
• Pupils 980 • Boys 11–18 (Day) • Girls 16–18 (Day) • Upper sixth 115 • Termly fees £1934 (Day) • HMC • Enquiries/application to the Registrar

What it's like

Founded by the will of Edward Latymer in 1624, the modern school lies between King Street and the Thames in Hammersmith (West London). The site, which it shares with the prep school, runs down to the river with fine views over Hammersmith Reach. The playing fields are about a mile and a half away. Since 1969, there have been extensive rebuilding and modernisation programmes and it is now very well-equipped. For many years it was one of London's leading direct grant school and draws on boys from a wide area of London. From 1996, girls will be accepted into the sixth-form. It is known as a rigourous but welcoming and tolerant community with high academic standards. Results are very good and almost all pupils go on to degree courses, including to medical schools and to Oxbridge. Music is tremendously strong: 250 learn an instrument; 175 are involved in school orchestras, and about 150 in the choirs. All pupils are encouraged to take part in musical activities. Drama and art are well-supported. There is a good deal of collaboration with Godolphin and Latymer in cultural enterprises and there is a joint orchestra. Many sports and games are provided and standards of achievement are high (a large number of representatives at county and regional level). There is a wide range of extra-curricular activities, including scouts. Many camps, expeditions, sports tours and field courses are organised. The school has also participated very successfully in the Duke of Edinburgh's Award Scheme.

School profile

Pupils Age range 11–18; 980 day pupils. Main entry ages 11, 13 (boys) and into sixth – girls accepted into the sixth-form from 1996, 25 in the first year. Some are children of former pupils. 20% pupils from own prep, Latymer Preparatory School. *State school entry:* 40% at 11, plus a few into sixth.

Entrance Own entrance exam used. Oversubscribed (4–5 applicants per place). Good academic potential looked for; no religious requirements. Parents not expected to buy textbooks. 10 pa assisted places. Scholarships and bursaries.

Parents 20+% are doctors, lawyers, etc. 20+% in the theatre, media, music, etc, 15+% in industry.

Head and staff *Headmaster:* Colin Diggory, 5 years in post. Educated at Durham University (mathematics). Previously Second Master at Latymer, Head of Maths at Merchant Taylors' and Assistant Master at St Paul's and Manchester Grammar. Chief Examiner for A-level maths, London University (1991). *Staff:* 69 full time, 18 music staff. Annual turnover 6%. Average age 35.

Exam results In 1995, 144 in upper fifth, 122 in upper sixth. *GCSE:* In 1995, 132 gained at least grade C in 8+ subjects. *A-levels:* 15 upper sixth passed in 4 subjects; 103 in 3 subjects. Average UCAS points 22.1.

University and college entrance 99% of 1995 sixth-form leavers went on to a degree course (23% after a gap year); others typically go on to eg banking. Of those going on to university, 11% went to Oxbridge; 10% took courses in medicine, dentistry and veterinary science, 35% in science and engineering, 5% in law, 40% in humanities and social sciences, 5% in art and design, 5% in other vocational subjects.

Curriculum GCSE and A-levels. 21 subjects offered at GCSE, 24 at A-level (general studies taught but not examined). 48% take science A-levels; 52% arts/humanities. *Vocational:* Work experience available in Europe and Britain. *Computing facilities:* 65 networked PC 286/386/486 Nimbus and specialist packages such as CD-Roms. *Europe:* French, German and Spanish offered to GCSE and A-level; also Italian A-level. French and German compulsory for a year. Regular exchanges to France and Germany. Work experience and activity courses in France and Germany arranged for fifth and sixth-forms.

The arts (Pupils aged 11 and over) *Music:* Over 40% of pupils learn a musical instrument; instrumental exams can be taken. Some 20 musical groups including 2 full orchestras, 5 string orchestras, bands, choirs. *Art:* On average, 45 take GCSE, 10 A-level. Design, pottery, photography and history of art also offered. Pupils regularly enter art schools.

Sport, community service and clubs (Pupils aged 11 and over) *Sport and physical activities:* Optional sports: rugby, cricket, boats, athletics, soccer, tennis, cross-country. Sixth form only: squash, badminton, swimming. Rugby, 5 in county U18 XV, 1 in London Schools XV, 1st and 2nd XV winners of Middlesex Cup. *Community service:* Pupils take silver and gold Duke of Edinburgh's Award. Community service optional for sixth-form; charity drives to raise money for national and local concerns. *Clubs and societies:* Over 30 clubs, eg chess, debating, drama, photography, various sports, young ornithology, scuba diving.

Uniform School uniform worn except in sixth.

Houses/prefects No houses. Prefects, senior prefects and school captain, appointed by the Headmaster after a trial period of duties. Sixth-form liaison committee.

Religion All pupils whose parents do not request their absence are obliged to attend school assembly (main assembly Christian plus Jewish and other faith assemblies).

Social Annual activities week (700 pupils on 38 different camps, trips or courses). Regular exchanges to Paris and Hamburg; joint orchestra and other activities (eg sub-aqua) with Godolphin and Latymer. Many organised trips abroad eg sports tours, ski trips. Pupils allowed to cycle to school. Meals self-service. Uniform and tuck shops. No tobacco/alcohol allowed.

Discipline Pupils failing to produce homework once would certainly be given an imposition by teacher; thereafter, the school detention system most likely punishment; those caught smoking cannabis on the premises would be expelled.

Alumni association is run by B J Southcott, 9 Kewferry Drive, Northwood HA6 2NT.
Former pupils Lord Walker (former Cabinet Minister); Sir Ian Percival (formerly Solicitor General); Mel Smith (actor, comedian); Andy Holmes (Olympic rowing gold medallist); Alan Rickman (actor); Sir John Killick (formerly Ambassador to Moscow); George Walden MP; Keith Vaz MP; Nigel Spearing MP; Sir James Spicer MP; Sir Roger Moate MP; Hugh Jones (marathon runner); Dr Hilary Jones (TV Doctor); Hugh Grant (actor).

• LAUREL PARK

Laurel Park School, 4 Lilybank Terrace, Glasgow G12 8RX. Tel 0141 339 9127, Fax 0141 357 5530

• Pupils 600 + • Boys 3–4 only • Girls 3–18 (Day) • Higher year Yes • Termly fees £807–£1344 (Day) • GSA • Enquiries/application to the Headmistress

What it's like

A new school, formed in 1996 from the merger of Laurel Bank and Park School and located on Laurel Bank's Lilybank site. This consists of converted terraced houses in the west end of the city and near the university. The nursery, junior school and senior school are combined. Good modern facilities will, subject to planning permission, be augmented by a new sports hall and an all-weather pitch. The teaching staff will be drawn from both schools and class sizes will be in the low 20s. Further details not available at the time of going to press.

School profile

Head and staff *Headmistress:* Mrs Elizabeth Surber, appointed Head of Laurel Bank in 1995. Educated at Tiffin Girls' School, Kingston, and universities of Exeter (French) and Oxford (education). Previously Deputy Head at Bedford High, and French teacher at Cheltenham Ladies College. Member of GSA and of Scottish ISIS.
Uniform A completely new uniform is being designed by parents, staff and pupils.
Former pupils of Laurel Bank School: Frances Cairncross (Economist); Paddy Higson (film producer); Sally Magnusson (TV presenter); Gudrun Ure (actress – Supergran); Moira McLeod (International British Olympic hockey player), Joyce Deans (President Royal Incorporation of Scottish Architects). Former pupils of Park School: Siobhan Redmond (actress); Joanna Isles (artist); Audrey Ajoze (Nigerian Ambassador to Scandanavia).

• LAVANT HOUSE ROSEMEAD

Lavant House Rosemead, Lavant, Chichester, West Sussex PO18 9AB. Tel 01243 527211, Fax 01243 530490; e-mail hm@lhandr.demon.co.uk.

• Pupils 200 • Boys 3–7 only • Girls 3–18 (Day/Board/Weekly) • Upper sixth 18 • Termly fees £475–£1950 (Day) £2775–£3475 (Board/Weekly) • GSA • Enquiries/application to the Headmistress

What it's like

Founded in 1995 through the amalgamation of two girls' schools, Lavant House (founded in 1952) and Rosemead (1919). The main building of the new school is Lavant House, a listed Sussex flintstone house just north of Chichester, between the South Downs and the sea. It is set in 14 acres of gardens, and a further 45 acres of grazing for horses (pupils may bring their own horse). With underground passages and secret doors, there is Girls' Own flavour to the boarding part of the house, emphasised by the family atmosphere. It has many of the advantages of being small. The modern facilities are good and a sound general education is provided. It is charming, academically efficient and climatically healthy but not suited to those who are allergic to horses. The school has an enviable record for bronze and silver in the Duke of Edinburgh's Awards Scheme.

School profile

Pupils Total age range 3–18; 200 pupils, 10 day boys, 190 girls (125 day, 65 boarding).

Senior department 11–18, 135 girls. Entry ages at any age to 14 and into sixth. Approx 2% are children of former pupils. Own junior department provides 80+% senior intake. *State school entry:* 5% at 11.

Entrance Common Entrance and own exam used. No special skills or religious requirements. Parents expected to buy certain A-level books. Scholarships (academic, art and sixth-form); also some bursaries.

Parents 15+% in industry or commerce. 65% live within 30 miles; up to 10% live overseas.

Head and staff *Headmistress:* Mrs S E Watkins, appointed 1996. Educated at Queenswood and at University College London (philosophy) and Surrey University (German and linguistics). Previously Headmistress at Heathfield (Ascot). Has also worked in the diplomatic service and with local educational authorities in Germany, Sussex and Hampshire. *Staff:* Numbers not clear following amalgamation.

Exam results In 1996, 30 pupils in upper fifth, 18 in upper sixth. *GCSE:* In 1995, 93% of upper fifth at Lavant House gained grade C or above in 5+ subjects, 74% at Rosemead; average 9.7 subjects at Lavant House, 6 at Rosemead.

University and college entrance 95% of 1995 sixth-form leavers went on to a degree course.

Curriculum GCSE and A-levels. 15 subjects offered including classical civilisation, business studies and Latin. *Vocational:* Work experience available; also RSA qualifications. *Computing facilities:* 8 PCs (486s) and CD-Roms in computer room. BBCs and PCs in junior school and science labs. *Special provision:* EFL and dyslexia teaching (both extra). *Europe:* French, German and Spanish offered at GCSE and A-level; all subjects taught in French in afternoon in junior school; French and Spanish compulsory from 11–14. Regular exchanges to France and Spain. Year or longer placements for pupils from Europe, especially those with an interest in horses.

The arts (Pupils aged 11 and over) *Music:* Some pupils learn a musical instrument; instrumental exams can be taken. *Drama & dance*: GCSE and A-level may be taken. Many pupils are involved in school productions.

Sport, community service and clubs (Pupils aged 11 and over) *Sport and physical activities:* Sports offered: Lacrosse, netball, swimming, athletics, tennis, squash, badminton, volleyball, gymnastics. rounders and cricket. Sport is compulsory. Some county lacrosse representatives and West Sussex champions. *Community service:* Pupils take bronze and silver Duke of Edinburgh's Award. *Clubs and societies:* Activities include horses, aerobics, karate.

Uniform School uniform worn except the sixth.

Houses/prefects Competitive houses. Prefects, head girl, head of house and house prefects – appointed by Head and staff.

Religion Wide-ranging assembly 3 times per week. Boarders attend village church.

Social Organised trips abroad. Pupils allowed to bring own horse, bike or car to school. Meals self-service. School shop. No alcohol/tobacco allowed.

• LAXTON

Laxton School, North Street, Oundle, Peterborough PE8 4AR. Tel 01832 273569, Fax 01832 273564

• Pupils 199 • Boys 11–18 (Day) • Girls 11–18 (Day) • Upper sixth 28 • Termly fees £1588 (Day) • SHA • Enquiries/application to the Headmaster's Secretary

What it's like

Founded in 1556 when Sir William Laxton left property to the Grocers' Company on condition they paid annual sums to maintain the school he had attended in Oundle. It developed steadily until, in 1876, the Grocers' Company decided to divide it into two schools: Oundle, to prepare boys for entrance to the universities; the other, then called Laxton Grammar School, to offer a wider education for boys who wished to start work at 16. The two schools are now more or less entirely integrated, are co-educational (since 1988) and share a common curriculum and main school facilities, although remaining independent in matters of organisation. Between them, they occupy a large part of the small and extremely attractive town of Oundle. There are exceptionally handsome period buildings, dating from the 16th to the 19th centuries (plus modern additions) and also beautiful precincts and gardens. Pupils are expected to attend Church of England assemblies. The schools are outstandingly well-equipped and a big staff permits a very favourable staff:pupil ratio of about 1:8. Academic standards are high and results very good. The majority of pupils proceed to degree courses, including to Oxbridge. Considerable emphasis is placed on pastoral care through a system of tutors. Music and drama are very strong. There is a very wide range of sports and games (including rowing, golf, fencing, fives, shooting, climbing and clay-pigeon shooting) and some representation at county and national level. Pupils have a remarkable range of extra-curricular activities run in conjunction with Oundle. Much enterprise has been shown in overseas trips, expeditions etc (including Greenland and Australia) and the school has also taken part successfully in the Duke of Edinburgh's Award Scheme.

School profile

Pupils Age range 11–18; 199 day pupils (120 boys, 79 girls). Main entry ages 11, some at 13 and into sixth. 20% are children of former pupils. Own junior school provides 60+% pupils. *State school entry:* 40% at 11, plus 30% to sixth.

Entrance Common Entrance and own exam used. No special skills, but all-round strength looked for; no religious requirements but pupils are expected to attend C of E assemblies. Average extras £250; parents expected to buy textbooks. 3 pa assisted places. 2 pa scholarships at 11, 1 pa in sixth, and 1 music scholarship, 25%–50% of fees; bursaries, 10%–50% fees.

Parents 15+% are doctors, lawyers, etc. 15+% in industry.

Head and staff *Headmaster:* R I Briggs, 6 years in post. Educated at Holgate Grammar School, Barnsley, and at Cambridge University (engineering). Previously Housemaster at Oundle. *Staff:* 100+ full time, 30+ part time (joint teaching staff with Oundle). Annual turnover 5%–7%. Average age 36.

Exam results In 1995, 29 in upper fifth, 29 in upper sixth. *GCSE:* On average, 95% upper fifth gain at least grade C in 8+ subjects; 5% in 5–7 subjects. *A-levels:* 20% upper sixth pass in 4 subjects (only allowed if double maths included); 80% in 3 subjects.

University and college entrance 85% of 1995 sixth-form leavers went on to a degree course; others typically go on to other courses. Of those going on to university, 10% went to Oxbridge; 17% took courses in medicine, dentistry and veterinary science, 30% in science and engineering, 47% in humanities and social sciences, 3% in art and design, 3% in music.

Curriculum GCSE and A-levels. 20 subjects offered (no A-level general studies). 30% take science A-levels; 45% arts/humanities; 25% a mixture of both. *Vocational:* Work experience required of all fifth form after GCSE exams. *Computing facilities:* 2 IT centres, 48 Apple Macs; microelectronics centre, 16 IBM386. Archimedes in maths department. *Special provision:* Part time staff give extra English lessons, for those with learning difficulties. *Europe:* French, German, Greek and Spanish offered to GCSE and A-level; also French AS-level. Regular exchanges (France, Spain and Germany). European studies offered to sixth-form. Annual visit to European Parliament for approx 15 students.

The arts *Music:* Over 30% of pupils learn a musical instrument; instrumental exams can be taken. Some 8 musical groups including 2 orchestras & chamber orchestra, jazz, wind band, brass group, choral society, Schola Cantorum. *Drama & dance*: Drama offered. Some pupils are involved in school and house/other productions. *Art:* (including Oundle) On average, 52 take GCSE, 15 A-level. Pottery, photography also offered.

Sport, community service and clubs *Sport and physical activities:* Optional sports: soccer, rugby, cricket, hockey, netball, fives, rowing, cross-country, tennis, golf, badminton, athletics, squash, swimming, sailing, shooting, sub-aqua. National clay-pigeon champion; England hockey trialist; British junior equestrian trialist; recent leaver played rugby for England Colts. *Community service:* Pupils take bronze and gold Duke of Edinburgh's Award. CCF compulsory for 1 year at age 14, optional for fifth and sixth-form. Community service optional; host (with Oundle) to Mencap Day to provide week's summer holiday to deprived children. *Clubs and societies:* Over 30 clubs, eg bellringing, debating, film, jazz, politics, pottery, theatre, war games, various academically based societies.

Uniform School uniform worn throughout.

Houses/prefects No competitive houses. Prefects and head boy/girl appointed by the Head. School Council.

Religion Attendance at religious worship compulsory.
Social Local newspaper, Oundle Chronicle, involves pupils from local state and independent schools. Organised trips to Russia, Germany, France (visits or exchanges), Amsterdam (art), Australia and South Africa (rugby), Greenland expedition, USA (choir), West Indies (cricket) and many more. Pupils allowed to bring own bike/car/motorbike to school. Meals self-service. School shop. No tobacco allowed; pupils over 17 allowed alcohol in sixth-form club.
Discipline Pupils failing to produce homework once might expect to repeat it, with an extra written imposition; those caught smoking cannabis on the premises could expect to be expelled.
Alumni association is run by I Goldsmith, President, Old Laxtonian Club, 3 Benefield Road, Oundle, PE8 4EU.

• LEEDS GRAMMAR

Leeds Grammar School, Moorland Road, Leeds LS6 1AN. Tel 0113 243 3417, Fax 0113 243 9906
• Pupils 1175 • Boys 7–18 (Day) • Girls None • Upper sixth 120 • Termly fees £1356–£1615 (Day) • HMC • Enquiries/application to the Headmaster's Secretary

What it's like

Founded in 1552 by Sir William Sheafield for the Education of Youths in the Learned Languages. It grew steadily in size and reputation and in 1859 moved to a site near the university. In 1997 it moves to a green field site five miles to the north of the city centre. This new campus has state-ot-the-art buildings and equipment with playing fields on site. It has a traditional and respected role as the city's grammar school and is strongly supported in the city of Leeds. Academic results are very good and the majority of sixth-formers go on to university. Music, drama and art are all vigorously supported and in cultural enterprises there is a good deal of collaboration with the Leeds Girl's High School. There is a wide range of sports and games and high standards are attained. Some 25 clubs and societies cater for most extra-curricular activities. There are also an active scout group and a venture scout unit, plus a large voluntary CCF (RAF and Army). Much emphasis is put on outdoor pursuits and for these the school has a well-equipped outdoor centre in the Pennines near Teesdale. All boys in the lower sixth are involved in local community services. Recently, there has been extensive participation in the Duke of Edinburgh's Award Scheme.

School profile

Pupils Total age range 7–18; 1175 day boys. Senior department 10–18; 1000 boys. Main entry ages 7, 8, 10, 11, 13 and into sixth. *State school entry:* 50% senior intake.
Entrance Own entrance exam used. No special skills or religious requirements. Parents not expected to buy textbooks, maximum extras £70 (including lunches). 35 pa assisted places. 25 pa scholarship/bursaries.
Parents 15+% are doctors, lawyers, etc, 15+% in industry, 15+% academics.
Head and staff *Headmaster:* Bryan Collins, in post for 10 years. Educated at Glyn Grammar, Epsom, and at London and Bristol universities (biological sciences and education). Previously Headmaster at Glyn School, Epsom. Also member of Leeds University Council; member of HMC and of Institute of Biology. *Staff:* 83 full time, 10 part time. Annual turnover 5%. Average age 30–40.
Exam results On average, 125 pupils in fifth form, 120 in upper sixth. *GCSE:* On average, 82% fifth gain at least grade C in 8+ subjects; 17% in 5–7; and 1% in 1–4 subjects. *A-levels:* 87% upper sixth pass in 4+ subjects; 10% in 3; 2% in 2; and 1% in 1 subject. Average UCAS points of 22.8.
University and college entrance 88% of 1995 sixth-form leavers went on to a degree course; others typically go on to non-degree courses eg journalism or into careers eg army. Of those going on to university, 18% went to Oxbridge; 8% took courses in medicine, dentistry and veterinary science, 27% in science and engineering, 62% in humanities and social sciences, 3% in art, drama and music.
Curriculum GCSE and A-levels. 18 GCSE subjects offered; 21 at A-level, including business studies and general studies. 39% take science A-levels; 50% arts/humanities; 11% both. *Vocational:* Work experience available. *Computing facilities:* station network

for CAL, IT, computer studies and private use; plus computers in many departments for CAL electronic blackboard. *Europe:* French (from age 8), German and Russian available at GCSE, AS and A-level. Regular exchanges to France and Germany.
The arts (Pupils aged 11 and over) *Music:* Up to 50% of pupils learn a musical instrument; instrumental exams can be taken. Some 13 musical groups including orchestra, saxophone quartet, choral society, choir, concert band, various chamber groups. Many winners in local music festivals; finalist in Shell/LSO competition; member of National Youth Orchestra. *Drama & dance*: Drama offered. Some pupils are involved in school productions and all in house/other productions. Recent productions include Romeo and Juliet, and Journey's End. *Art:* On average, 25 take GCSE, 4 AS-level, 4 A-level. Design, pottery, textiles and photography also offered.
Sport, community service and clubs (Pupils aged 11 and over) *Sport and physical activities:* Compulsory: squash, basketball. Sixth form only: golf, volleyball. RLSS exams may be taken. Regular national, divisional and regional representation of pupils and teams. *Community service:* Pupils take bronze, silver and gold Duke of Edinburgh's Award. CCF optional at age 14. Community service compulsory for 1 year in lower sixth. *Clubs and societies:* Over 30 clubs, eg philosophy, astronomy, Israel society, bird-watching, model railway, Green.
Uniform School uniform worn, own suit in the sixth.
Houses/prefects Competitive houses. Prefects, head boy, head of house and house prefects – appointed by the Headmaster. Sixth-form committee.
Religion Non-denominational Christian assemblies/separate Jewish assemblies. Sunday chapel optional.
Social Arts programme with Leeds Girls' High (joint-foundation). Many organised trips abroad and exchange systems. Pupils allowed to bring own car/motorbike/bike to school. Meals cafeteria service. School shop. No tobacco/alcohol allowed.
Discipline Pupils failing to produce homework once might expect a warning and requirement to complete; those caught smoking cannabis on the premises could expect expulsion.
Alumni association is run by M J Buswell, Hon Secretary, Old Leodiensian Association, 22 Wynmore Avenue, Bramhope, Leeds LS16 9DE.
Former pupils Tony Harrison; Lord Diamond; Barry Cryer; Colin Montgomerie; Lord Belmin; Professor Tim Frazer; Ian Ritchie; Christopher Price; Harry Gration.

• LEEDS HIGH

Leeds Girls' High School, Headingley Lane, Leeds LS6 1BN. Tel 0113 274 4000, Fax 0113 275 2217

• Pupils 965 • Boys 3–8 only (Day) • Girls 3–18 (Day) • Upper sixth 83 • Termly fees £723–£1412 (Day) • GSA • Enquiries/application to the Admissions Secretary

What it's like

Founded in 1876, it is situated in Headingley, 2–3 miles from Leeds city centre and within walking distance of the university. It has elegant and well-equipped buildings in 10 acres of pleasant grounds with lawns and gardens. The junior school, Ford House, is 3 minutes' walk away; the prep school, Rose Court, is on the same site as the senior school. Academic standards are high and results very good; almost all sixth-form pupils go on to degree courses. A personal and social education programme is in operation for all pupils. The school's industrial liaison officer fosters links with local businesses, runs courses and conferences and arranges work experience/shadowing. Music and drama are strong and the Elinor Lupton Centre provides excellent facilities for work in these subjects, including a suite of individual practice rooms. There is also a modern sports complex with indoor swimming pool on site. A range of extra-curricular activities (including Young Enterprise groups, theatre visits, a school magazine and termly newsletter) develops pupils' awareness beyond the classroom.

School profile

Pupils Total age range 3–18; 965 day pupils, (32 boys, 933 girls). Senior department, 11–18, 600 day girls. Main entry ages 3, 4 (boys and girls), 11 and into sixth (girls). Small proportion are children of former pupils. 50% of senior intake from own junior school,

Ford House (tel 0113 274 4000). Other main feeder schools: Richmond House, Leeds (tel 0113 275 2670), The Froebelian School, Leeds (tel 0113 258 3047) and Moorfield School, Ilkley (tel 01943 607285). *State school entry:* 20% senior intake, plus 3% to sixth.

Entrance Own entrance exam used. No special skills or religious requirements. Parents not expected to buy textbooks. 21 pa assisted places. 7–10 pa scholarships (including 2 music), one-sixth to full fees.

Parents 15+% are doctors, lawyers, etc. 15+% in industry.

Head and staff *Headmistress:* Miss Philippa A Randall, in post for 19 years. Educated at Christ's Hospital and at the LSE (history) and Sussex University (education). Previously Deputy Head at Wolverhampton Girls' High; Head of History and Careers at Marple Hall Grammar School and assistant history teacher and librarian at Purley Grammar School. Also member of GSA Education Committee and governor of local independent junior school. *Staff:* 65 full time, 20 part time.

Exam results In 1995, 94 pupils in upper fifth, 75 in upper sixth. *GCSE:* In 1995, all upper fifth gained at least grade C in 7+ subjects. *A-levels:* 65 pupils passed in 4+ subjects; 6 in 3; 4 in 2 subjects. Average UCAS points 22.2 (including general studies, 29.0).

University and college entrance 99% of 1995 sixth-form leavers went on to a degree course (7% after a gap year); others typically go on to vocational training eg accountancy. Of those going on to university, 10% went to Oxbridge; 10% took courses in medicine, dentistry and veterinary science, 20% in science and engineering, 13% in law, 43% in humanities and social sciences, 2% in art and design, 3% in vocational subjects eg physiotherapy, ophthalmics.

Curriculum GCSE, A-levels and S-levels. 22 subjects offered (including further maths, classical Greek, home economics, theatre studies and A-level general studies). *Vocational:* Work experience available. *Computing facilities:* Purpose-designed computer rooms with 43 machines with networking facilities, plus computers situated in several departments. *Europe:* French and German offered to GCSE, AS and A-level; French compulsory from age 11 to GCSE, German for 2 years at 12. Regular exchanges (France and Germany). 11–12 year olds spend 1 week in France. Many pupils have pen-friends in France/Germany. Visits and twinning with schools in eg France, Germany, Italy.

The arts (Pupils aged 11 and over) *Music:* Over 30% of pupils learn a musical instrument; instrumental exams can be taken. Some 9 musical groups including orchestra, concert band, 2 choirs, wind band, string group, several chamber groups. City choral concerts; local festival, winners of chamber music section, junior choir successful in local competitions. *Drama & dance*: Drama offered. GCSE and A-level drama, LAMDA exams may be taken. Some pupils are involved in school productions and majority in house/other productions. 3 productions a year; interest high and increasing. *Art:* On average, 25 take GCSE, 6 A-level. Design, graphics also offered. Regular acceptances to art schools; some entrants to degree courses without foundation course.

Sport, community service and clubs (Pupils aged 11 and over) *Sport and physical activities:* Compulsory sports: hockey, netball, swimming, gymnastics, tennis, rounders, athletics. Optional: badminton, volleyball, aerobics, lifesaving, basketball, squash, trampolining. BAGA, RLSS, AAA exams may be taken. Tennis, national finals U15, U13 teams; netball, county finals U13 team, county representatives in national tournament U16, U14 teams. *Community service:* Pupils take bronze Duke of Edinburgh's Award. Community service optional for 2 years at age 16. Strong charity fund-raising commitment; links with school in Malawi. *Clubs and societies:* Over 30 clubs, eg various sports, history, French, debating, Christian Union, music, newsletter.

Uniform School uniform worn, except in sixth.

Houses/prefects Competitive houses. Head girl, head of house and house prefects – elected by staff and sixth.

Religion Non-denominational assemblies daily. Pupils may opt for separate Jewish assemblies.

Social Joint social activities, clubs, musical and drama events with other schools particularly Leeds Grammar. Annual ski trip. Pupils allowed to bring own car/bike to school. Meals self-service. No tobacco/alcohol allowed.

Alumni association is run by Mrs K Davis, 38 Becketts Park Drive, Leeds, LS6 3PB.

• LEICESTER GRAMMAR

Leicester Grammar School, 8 Peacock Lane, Leicester LE1 5PX. Tel 0116 291 0500, Fax 0116 291 0505

• Pupils 595 • Boys 10–18 (Day) • Girls 10–18 (Day) • Upper sixth 72 • Termly fees £1440 (Day) • HMC • Enquiries/application to the Headmaster

What it's like

Founded in 1981 as a direct result of the loss of the city's grammar schools through reorganisation. It is housed in two late Victorian buildings in the cathedral precinct in the middle of Leicester. These buildings have been extensively modernised to provide up-to-date facilities. The school's growth has been remarkable, from an original 90 pupils to over 580 in 15 years; a success story which reflects much credit on those involved and highlights the needs of the community. The school has always been co-educational. The curriculum is geared to the academic rather than the average pupil, and a good standard of general education is provided and results are very good. Most sixth-formers go on to university, including many to Oxbridge. Strong departments in music, drama and art. A full range of games, sports (civic amenities are used) and activities. The school enjoys vigorous local support and has a substantial commitment to local social service charity work.

School profile

Pupils Total age range 10–18; 595 day pupils (299 boys, 296 girls). Senior department 11–18, 550 pupils (282 boys, 277 girls). Main entry ages 10, 11, 13 and into sixth. Major intake from own junior school, Leicester Grammar Junior School (tel 0116 241 2000). *State school entry:* 70% senior intake, plus 30% to sixth.

Entrance Own exam used. No special skills or religious requirements; open to all faiths. Meals and non-curricular excursions extra. Assisted places. Scholarships/bursaries, up to full fees.

Head and staff *Headmaster:* John Sugden, 7 years in post. Educated at Bradford Grammar and Cambridge (modern languages). Previously Vice Principal at Newcastle-under-Lyme, Head of Modern Languages and Senior Housemaster at King's (Canterbury) and Modern Languages Teacher at Portsmouth Grammar. *Staff:* 50 full time, 10 part time. Annual turnover 4%. Average age 36.

Exam results In 1995, 84 pupils in upper fifth, 63 in upper sixth. *GCSE:* In 1995, 81 upper fifth gained at least grade C in 8+ subjects; 1 in 5–7; 2 in 4 subjects. *A-levels:* 7 upper sixth passed in 4+ subjects; 48 in 3; 8 in 2 subjects Average UCAS points 21.3.

University and college entrance 90% of 1995 sixth-form leavers went on to a degree course (14% after a gap year); others typically go on to HND, management training or resits. Of those going on to university, 18% went to Oxbridge; 5+% took courses in medicine, dentistry and veterinary science, 32% in science and engineering, 5% in law, 37% in humanities and social sciences, 3% in art and design, 18% in vocational subjects eg marketing, finance, management.

Curriculum GCSE and A-levels. 21 subjects offered, GCSE and A-level (including A-level general studies). 33% take science A-levels; 28% arts/humanities; 38% both. *Computing facilities:* Computer laboratory; IT servicing for other departments. *Europe:* French and German offered at GCSE, AS and A-level; also Russian and Spanish GCSE. Regular exchanges (France, Germany and Russia).

The arts *Music:* Over 50% of pupils learn a musical instrument; instrumental exams can be taken. Musical groups include orchestras, choirs, recorder, jazz, dance bands, pop groups, quartets, wind and brass groups. Large numbers play in county schools orchestras, 11 in national orchestras; regular success at local festivals (including outstanding musician); choral exchange with Strasbourg Conservatoire; 2 Oxbridge choral scholarships, 2 organ. *Drama & dance*: GCSE drama, A-level theatre studies may be taken. Majority of pupils are involved in school productions and in house/other productions. *Art:* 48 take GCSE, 4 A-level. Design, pottery (at junior level), textiles also offered. Regular entry to art foundation courses.

Sport, community service and clubs *Sport and physical activities:* Compulsory sports: rugby, hockey, netball, athletics, tennis, cricket, swimming, health-related PE programme and many other sports. Optional: table tennis. GCSE and A-level PE may be taken. *Community service:* Pupils take bronze, silver and gold Duke of Edinburgh's

Award. Community service optional. *Clubs and societies:* Up to 15 clubs, eg chess, computer, history, literary, model airplane, assertiveness, Christian Union, aerobics.
Uniform School uniform worn except the sixth.
Houses/prefects Competitive houses. Prefects, head boy and girl and head of house; prefects appointed by the Headmaster in consultation with staff and prefects.
Religion Daily assembly, monthly cathedral services for all. Strong links with local Cathedral (servers' guild).
Social Pupils take part in local competitions for debating and academic activities (eg science, geography, classical reading). French, German, Russian exchanges, classical, historical, geographical and language tours and ski trips abroad. Pupils allowed to bring own bike to school Meals self-service. School shop. No tobacco/alcohol allowed.
Discipline Extensive pastoral care through heads of year and houses. Major sanctions: detention and extra work. Bullying and drugs would invite expulsion.
Alumni association is run by R I Longson, c/o the school.

• LEIGHTON PARK

Leighton Park School, Shinfield Road, Reading, Berkshire RG2 7DH. Tel 01734 872065
• Pupils 370 • Boys 11–18 (Day/Board) • Girls 11–18 (Day/Board) • Upper sixth 65 • Termly fees £2490–£2940 (Day) £3333–£3918 (Board) • HMC • Enquiries/application to the Headmaster

What it's like

Founded in 1890, it is situated not far from the middle of Reading but enjoys a most peaceful environment of over 60 acres of lovely wooded grounds, formerly the estates of two large country houses. Some of the well-designed school buildings are 19th-century, some 20th. There has been a major development programme recently, including a science and technology centre, library and study centre and an all-weather pitch, and facilities are excellent. Girls have been accepted in the sixth-form for some time; from 1993 girls of 11 and 13 were also taken and the school has become fully co-educational. A Quaker school, it lays considerable emphasis on Quaker philosophy and adheres to the principles and practice of Quakerism which, of its nature, is both ecumenical and tolerant. Academic standards are high and results very good. Virtually all sixth-formers proceed to degree courses, including Oxbridge. Part of the GCSE course in all subjects is taught at Lycée St Stanislas, Nantes, France. Extremely strong in music; good drama and art. High level of achievement in sports and games (a lot of representatives of county standard). Much emphasis on outdoor pursuits and adventure training. Big commitment to local community services (much post-school voluntary work). Very wide range of activities, including an unusual number of hobby interests.

School profile

Pupils Age range 11–18: 370 pupils, 160 day (120 boys, 40 girls), 210 boarding (165 boys, 45 girls). Main entry ages, 11, 13 and into sixth. Approx 10% are children of former pupils. *State school entry:* 90% intake at 11, 20% at 13, plus 40% to sixth.
Entrance Common Entrance and own exam used. Pupils must be in top 25% of ability range; no religious requirements. Parents only expected to buy sixth-form textbooks (which can be sold back); music tuition extra (£12 per lesson). 10 pa scholarships/ bursaries, 25%–75% of fees.
Parents 15+% in industry or commerce. 30+% live within 30 miles; 10+% live overseas.
Head and staff *Headmaster:* John Chapman, in post for 10 years. Educated at The Beauchamp Grammar, Kibworth, Leicester, and at universities of Oxford (modern history) and Bradford (educational research). Previously Head and Deputy Head at Bishop of Hereford's Bluecoat School, Research Director of the Bloxham Project (1973) and Head of History at Woodhouse Grove. Also Chairman of the Bloxham Project Committee. Publications include Images of Life (SCM Press) with Robin Richardson. *Staff:* 37 full time, 34 part time (including music). Annual turnover under 5%. Average age 35–45.
Exam results In 1995, 60 pupils in the fifth, 65 in upper sixth. *GCSE:* In 1995, 56% fifth gained at least grade C in 8+ subjects; 36% in 5–7 subjects. *A-levels:* 19% upper sixth pass in 4+ subjects; 66% in 3; 11% in 2; and 4% in 1 subject. Average UCAS points 20.2.

University and college entrance 98% of 1995 sixth-form leavers went on to a degree course (50% after a gap year), 10% to Oxbridge; 10% took courses in medicine, dentistry and veterinary science, 20% in science and engineering, 8% in law, 45% in humanities and social sciences, 12% in art and design, 5% in other vocational subjects.
Curriculum GCSE and A-levels. 17 GCSE and A-level subjects offered (no A-level general studies). 33% take science A-levels, 33% arts/humanities; 33% both. *Vocational:* Work experience available. *Computing facilities:* 3 computer rooms, computers in each boarding house and academic department. *Special provision:* Special classes and EFL. *Europe:* French (compulsory 11–16), German and Italian offered to GCSE and A-level; also Russian and Spanish GCSE and German AS-level. Regular exchanges (France and Germany). Part of GCSE course (all subjects) taught at Lycée St Stanislas, Nantes, France; French pupils are taught their syllabus at Leighton Park.
The arts *Music:* Over 50% of pupils learn a musical instrument; instrumental exams can be taken. Some 15 musical groups including jazz band, big band, barbershop, buskers, several orchestras, jazz cats, chamber choir. Concerts given in Philadelphia, South of France and Belgium. *Drama & dance*: Drama offered. Majority of pupils are involved in school productions and some in house/other productions. Recent students star regularly in TV/theatre productions. *Art:* On average, 30 take GCSE, 15 A-level. Design, pottery, photography also offered. Number of art colleges placements.
Sport, community service and clubs *Sport and physical activities:* Compulsory sports (to age 14): rugby, hockey, soccer, tennis, athletics, swimming. Additional options (from age 15): badminton, basketball etc. In 1995: 7 county hockey; 2 county rugby; 2 international canoeing; 1 regional squash champion. *Community service:* Pupils take bronze and silver Duke of Edinburgh's Award. Community service optional. *Clubs and societies:* Over 30 clubs, eg Amnesty International, angling, art, business enterprise, climbing, computer, debating, electronics, golf, Pythagoras, railway, writers' workshop, various sports.
Uniform School dress code followed throughout.
Houses/prefects Competitive houses (which are geographically separate buildings). Prefects head boy/girl, head of house and house prefects – appointed by the Headmaster and school. School Council.
Religion Some compulsory worship in the Quaker manner.
Social Regular conferences at sixth-form level and social events with other schools, also Challenge of Industry events. Organised trips abroad and exchange systems. Meals formal. School shop. No tobacco/alcohol allowed.
Discipline Pupils failing to produce homework once might expect extra prep or detention work; anyone caught smoking cannabis on the premises would be asked to leave.
Boarding 10% have own study bedroom, 20% are in dormitories of 6+. Houses of approximately 70–80. Resident qualified medical staff. Pupils can provide and cook own food. Weekly exeats, if required. Visits to the local town allowed.
Former pupils Michael Foot; David Lean: Richard Rodney Bennett; Lawrence Gowing; Lord Caradon; Bishop Newbigin; Peter Cadbury; Karel Reisz; Tony Baldry; Basil Bunting; Lord Seebohm.

• LEYS (The)

The Leys School, Cambridge CB2 2AD. Tel 01223 355327, Fax 01223 357053.
• Pupils 420 • Boys 13–18 (Day/Board) • Girls 13–18 (Day/Board) • Upper sixth 95 • Termly fees £2900 (Day) £3980 (Board) • HMC, GSA, SHA • Enquiries/application to the Registrar

What it's like

Founded in 1875, it has a compact site on the edge of the city, bounded by common land on two sides and close to the river. The main buildings are late Victorian and very pleasing, and lie in 50 acres of delightful grounds and playing fields. Modern extensions provide excellent facilities, including a big design and technology centre and a sports complex. It is a Methodist foundation but inter-denominational. It first accepted girls in 1984, becoming fully co-educational ten years later. A large well-qualified staff allows a staff:pupil ratio of about 1:9. An informal and friendly atmosphere characterises the school and there is a particularly good tutorial system. Results are good and most leavers go on to university. Very strong in music, drama and art. A wide range of sports and games and a very good variety of activities. Plentiful use is made of the cultural amenities of Cambridge. An outstanding record in the Duke of Edinburgh's Award Scheme.

School profile

Pupils Age range 13–18; 420 pupils, 157 day (140 boys, 17 girls), 263 boarding (161 boys, 102 girls). Main entry ages 13, 14 and into sixth. Approx 14% are children of former pupils. St Faith's Prep School (01223 352073) provides more than 20% of intake; also St John's College School (01223 353532). *State school entry:* 3% main intake, plus 10% to sixth.

Entrance Many enter through Common Entrance but appropriate tests for all ages. Extra-curricular interests, as well as academic potential, taken into account. No special religious requirements, Methodist foundation with ecumenical tradition. 15 pa assisted places (some available at age 11 by arrangement with St Faith's and St John's prep schools). 18 pa scholarships/bursaries, 10%–50% of fees.

Parents 15+% are doctors, lawyers, etc; 15+% in industry or commerce. 30+% live within 30 miles; up to 25% live overseas.

Head and staff *Headmaster:* Rev Dr John C A Barrett, 6 years in post. Educated at Culford and at the universities of Newcastle (economics) and Cambridge (theology). Previously Headmaster at Kent College (Pembury), Chaplain, Housemaster and Head of Religious Studies at Kingswood, Head of Religious Studies at Birches High, Stoke on Trent, and Assistant Tutor at Wesley College, Bristol. Also Lecturer in Divinity at Westminster College, Oxford, and Chairman, World Methodist Council Education Committee. *Staff:* 45 full time, 7 part time. Annual turnover 5%. Average age 40.

Exam results In 1995, 69 pupils in Year 11, 85 in upper sixth. *GCSE:* In 1995, 54 in Year 11 gained at least grade C in 8+ subjects; 9 in 5–7 subjects. *A-levels:* 8 upper sixth passed in 4+ subjects; 59 in 3; 14 in 2; and 3 in 1 subject. Average UCAS points 18.6.

University and college entrance 95% of 1995 sixth-form leavers went on to a degree course (68% after a gap year), 9% to Oxbridge; 1% took courses in medicine, dentistry and veterinary science, 10% in science and engineering, 5% in law, 81% in humanities and social sciences, 2% in art and design.

Curriculum GCSE and A-levels. 20 subjects offered (including business studies, theatre studies, design and technology; no A-level general studies). 19% take science A-levels; 62% arts/humanities; 19% both. *Vocational:* Work experience available. *Computing facilities:* 3 laboratories of 27 computers. Computers in all departments. *Special provision:* Tuition arranged for pupils with special needs eg dyslexia, EFL. *Europe:* French, German and Spanish offered to GCSE and A-level. Exchange programmes with French, German and Spanish schools. Regularly have German pupils in lower sixth.

The arts *Music:* Over 30% of pupils learn a musical instrument; instrumental exams can be taken. Some 11 musical groups including choral society, chapel choir, symphony orchestra, swing band, chamber orchestra. Choir invited to sing evensong at St Paul's Cathedral and Westminster Abbey. *Drama & dance*: Drama offered; GCSE and A-level theatre studies. Majority of pupils are involved in house/other productions. *Art:* On average, 30 take GCSE, 15 A-level; pottery also offered. Art facilities open to non-examination pupils. School holds annual exhibition.

Sport, community service and clubs *Sport and physical activities:* Rugby, hockey, tennis, cricket, sailing, rowing, swimming, squash, badminton, basketball, water polo, shooting, golf, judo, karate, athletics. Hockey, county championships 1993, East of England semi-final; clay-pigeon shooting, national champions 1990-92; cricket, area champions 1992; several county players in all sports. Overseas tours eg rugby (South Africa 1995), cricket (Barbados 1994) and hockey (Spain 1995). *Community service:* Pupils take bronze, silver and gold Duke of Edinburgh's Award. CCF and community service both optional. *Clubs and societies:* Up to 15 clubs, eg debating, maths, science, Moulton Society (philosophy and theology), music, film.

Uniform School uniform worn, modified in the sixth.

Houses/prefects Competitive houses. Prefects, head boy/girl, head of house and house prefects – appointed by the Headmaster or Housemasters/mistresses.

Religion Services on Wednesdays and Sundays.

Social Organised local events include inter-school debates; combined choral concerts; Schools Challenge (inter-schools quiz contests). Visits abroad, cultural visits (art and art

history); individual language exchanges; ski trips, walking holidays in Alps; choir, sports and drama tours. Pupils allowed to bring own bike to school. Meals self-service. School shop.
Discipline A graded system of punishments is available to teachers, from a 30-minute detention to 2 hours on a Saturday night or a Headmaster's detention on a Sunday. The emphasis is on prompt and productive punishments if necessary, but a system of commendations is also an important means of encouraging good work and behaviour; those caught smoking cannabis on the premises can expect expulsion.
Boarding 30% have own study bedroom, 30% share with others; 40% are in dormitories of approx 6. Single-sex houses, of 32–70, same as competitive houses. Resident qualified medical staff. Central dining room. Pupils can provide and cook their own food. Flexible exeats, overnight at least fortnightly. Visits to the local town allowed once or twice a week.
Alumni association is run by the Secretary, OLU: P R Chamberlain; and editor of the OL Directory: G C Houghton – both c/o the school.
Former pupils Sir Alastair Burnet; Martin Bell (BBC TV correspondent); J G Ballard (fiction writer); Richard Heffer (actor); Prof Peter Dickinson (music); D A G Cregan (playwright); Geoffrey Windsor-Lewis (Hon Sec Barbarians); James Hilton (author); Malcolm Lowry (author); Prof David Miller (medicine); Prof TC Smout (history); Prof H B Mattingley (classics); Judge Hollings, Lord Oliver; Lord Weir; Lord McIntosh.

• LICENSED VICTUALLERS' (Ascot)

Licensed Victuallers' School, London Road, Ascot, Berkshire SL5 8DR. Tel 01344 882770, Fax 01344 890648

• Pupils 687 • Boys 4–18 (Day/Boarding) • Girls 4–18 (Day/Boarding) • Upper sixth 32 • Termly fees £1790 (Day) £3190 (Board) £3170 (Weekly) • ISAI • Enquiries/application to the School Secretary

What it's like

Founded in London in 1803, the school has enjoyed royal patronage since 1830. It moved to Slough in 1921, and thence in 1989 to new premises on a 26-acre site at Ascot. The new buildings include boarding houses, a self-contained junior school, sports complex, theatre, chapel and re-equipped teaching facilities; extensive outdoor facilities include a fishing lake. The founders' intention was to cater for pupils of all abilities and it remains the case today. All subjects in the senior school are taught in setted groups and there is a wide range of GCSE and A-level subjects as well as various GNVQs. The underlying aim is to encourage self-motivation and independence across a wide ability range. The sixth-form courses include a general studies course for all, as well as skills courses, driving, cooking, computer skills and sports qualifications.

School profile

Pupils Total age range 4–18, 687 pupils, 456 day (303 boys, 153 girls), 217 boarding (114 boys, 103 girls; all boarders aged 7 or over). Senior department 11–18, 491 pupils (302 boys, 189 girls). Main entry ages 5, 7, 11, 13 and into sixth-form. Some are children of former pupils. 40% senior intake from own junior school. *State school entry:* 60% intake at 11 plus 50% intake into sixth.
Entrance Reports and interviews. No special skills or religious requirements. Parents expected to buy textbooks; maximum £80 extras. 12 pa scholarships/bursaries, £500 to half fees.
Head and staff *Headteacher*: Mrs Pamela Cowley, 4 years in post. Educated at Greenhill Grammar School and Wales University (geography and government). Formerly Deputy Head at Licenced Victuallers', Director of Studies at St Joseph's, Reading, and Head of Junior School at St Christopher's, Nairobi. *Staff:* 68 full time, 4 part time. Annual turnover 10%.
Exam results In 1995, 80 pupils in Year 11, 32 in upper sixth. *GCSE:* In 1995, 69% of pupils in Year 11 gained at least grade C in 5+ subjects. *A-levels:* On average, 53% upper sixth pass in 3 subjects; 7% in 2; and 33% in 1 subject. Average UCAS points 13.9.

University and college entrance 50% of sixth-form leavers go on to a degree course; others typically go on to careers (eg catering, retailing) or non-degree courses (eg business, finance, catering). Of those going on to university, 18% took courses in science and engineering, 36% in humanities and social sciences, 36% in art and design, 9% in drama and acting.
Curriculum GCSE, AS and A-levels and GNVQs. 25 subjects offered (including PE, technology, computing and general studies). 29% take science A-levels; 43% arts/ humanities; 29% both. *Vocational:* GNVQs in sport & leisure, business & finance and health & social care. Work experience compulsory. *Computing facilities:* 3 rooms of 20 stations plus numerous stand-alone computers and department networks. *Special provision:* Special unit for learning difficulties. *Europe:* French, German and Spanish offered to GCSE and A-level (all pupils choose their first European language). Regular exchanges (France, Germany and Spain). Number of European children in school (resident locally).
The arts (Pupils aged 11 and over) *Music:* Instrumental exams are taken. Musical groups include orchestra, wind band, jazz band, 2 choirs. *Drama & dance*: Both offered. GCSE and A-level drama may be taken. Some pupils are involved in school productions and all in house productions. *Art:* On average 25 take GCSE; 6 A-level. Design also offered.
Sport, community service and clubs (Pupils aged 11 and over) *Sport and physical activities:* Compulsory sports: football, rugby, netball, hockey, swimming, athletics, cricket. Optional: tennis, basketball, volleyball. GCSE, A-level, Certificate of Further Studies exams may be taken. *Community service:* Pupils take bronze, silver and gold Duke of Edinburgh's Award. CCF optional. *Clubs and societies:* Up to 20 clubs eg computer, lifesaving, war games, art, cooking, newspaper, sporting; also driving lessons.
Uniform School uniform worn, modified in the sixth.
Houses/prefects Competitive houses. Prefects, head boy and girl, head of house and house prefects – appointed by the Headteacher.
Religion Attendance at religious worship compulsory for boarders.
Social Sports fixtures for all sports with local schools. Exchanges to France, Germany and Spain. School shop. No tobacco/alcohol allowed.
Discipline Pupils failing to produce homework might expect extra work or detention depending on the circumstances. Those caught smoking cannabis on premises would expect to be expelled.
Boarding 10% have own study, 40% share, 25% in dormitories of 6. Houses of up to 60, same as competitive purposes; single sex from Year 9, younger pupils mixed. Resident qualified nurse. 6 exeats per year – Friday afternoon to Sunday evening. Weekend visits to local town allowed at 13 and over.
Former pupils Lord John Moore; William Brake and brothers (Brake Bros. Frozen Foods); Billy Smart (circus).

• LINCOLN SCHOOL

Lincoln School, Upper Lindum Street, Lincoln LN2 5RW. Tel 01522 543764, Fax 01522 537938
• Pupils 425 • Boys 4–18 (Day/Board/Weekly) • Girls 4–18 (Day/Board/Weekly) • Upper sixth 14 • Termly fees £1415 (Day) £2890 (Board) £2665 (Weekly) • CSC • Enquiries/application to the Headteacher

What it's like

Founded by the Church Schools Company in 1996 from the merger of three Lincoln schools – the Cathedral School (a co-educational prep school), Stonefield House (co-educational, up to age 16) and St Joseph's (for girls aged 4–18). The new school takes boys and girls right through from nursery to the sixth-form. The senior department is based on the St Joseph's site, a compact, urban site close to the cathedral precinct. Its handsome buildings, ancient and modern, are well-equipped. The prep department, which educates the cathedral choristers, is on a beautiful site in the cathedral grounds. A range of sports is offered for boys and girls, with competition in local county leagues. The Duke of Edinburgh's Award Scheme and community service are encouraged. Art, drama and music are all offered.

School profile – new school

Pupils Total age range 4–18; 425 pupils, boys and girls. Senior department 225, boys and girls. Boading is available for boys aged 7–14 and girls aged 9–17. Main entry ages 4, 11, 13 into sixth.
Entrance Own entrance exam and interview with Head. A non-selective school, open to all religious denominations.

School profile – St Joseph's

Exam results On average, 35 pupils in St Joseph's Year 11, 14 in upper sixth. *GCSE:* On average, 45% Year 11 pupils gain at least grade C in 8+ subjects; 40% in 5–7; and 15% in 1–4 subjects. *A-levels:* 40% upper sixth pass in 4+ subjects; 40% in 3; 15% in 2; and 5% in 1 subject. Average UCAS points 14.7.
University and college entrance All 1995 sixth-form leavers from St Joseph's went on to a degree course (5% after a gap year); 10% to Oxbridge. 10% took courses in medicine, dentistry and veterinary science, 5% in science and engineering, 10% in law, 20% in humanities and social sciences, 50% in art and design, 5% in other vocational subjects.
Curriculum GCSE and A-levels (including A-level general studies). *Vocational:* Work experience available. GNVQ advanced level in business offered; also RSA stage 3 shorthand, typewriting, wordprocessing. Those taking one or two A-levels usually add RSA examinations. *Computing facilities:* Fully equipped IT room plus computers in subject rooms. *Special provision:* EFL; provision for dyslexic pupils. *Europe:* French and German offered to GCSE, AS and A-level; French compulsory from 4 to GCSE. Regular exchanges and visits.
The arts (Pupils aged 11 and over) *Music:* Over 60% of pupils learn a musical instrument; instrumental exams can be taken. Some 7 musical groups including choirs, orchestras, ensembles, recorder consort. Regular success at Lincoln Music and Drama Festival. *Drama & dance*: Both offered. LAMDA, RAD exams may be taken. Majority of pupils are involved in school and house/other productions. *Art:* On average, 15 take GCSE, 5 A-level. Design, textiles, graphics also offered.
Sport, community service and clubs (Pupils aged 11 and over) *Sport and physical activities:* Compulsory sports: hockey, tennis, netball, rounders, athletics, squash, gymnastics. Optional: judo, badminton, cross-country, outdoor pursuits, skiing. GCSE, BAGA exams may be taken. Netball, 2 county representatives every year on average; tennis, several county players over recent years, recent former pupil now international professional. *Community service:* compulsory for 1 term at age 17, optional for younger pupils – short-term projects. *Clubs and societies:* Up to 30 clubs, eg country dancing, cycling, computer, book, public speaking, charity, Green. Duke of Edinburgh Award Scheme. Young Enterprise offered.
Uniform School uniform worn except in the sixth.
Houses/prefects Competitive houses. Prefects, head girl – elected by the school. School Council.
Religion Interdenominational Christian.
Social Joint sporting activities with other schools. Many organised trips abroad and exchange systems. Meals self-service. No tobacco/alcohol allowed.
Discipline Small size of school meant few problems and school relied on trust building up between staff and pupils. If children play about after lights out they forego some privilege eg miss tennis and go to bed early next night; if they are caught smoking they can be sent home; smoking cannabis would mean instant suspension. Parents are sent for if anything serious occurs.
Boarding All share in rooms of 2–5. Boarding staff (4 including matron). Termly, weekly or flexible boarding available.

• LIVERPOOL COLLEGE

Liverpool College, Mossley Hill, Liverpool L18 8BE. Tel 0151 724 4000, Fax 0151 729 0105
• Pupils 1000 • Boys 3–18 (Day) • Girls 3–18 (Day) • Upper sixth 70 • Termly fees £785–£1360 (Day) • HMC • Enquiries/application to the Principal

What it's like

Founded in 1840, it moved to its present premises at Mossley Hill in the 1930s. It occupies a single, suburban site in 26 acres of grounds and playing fields in a pleasant area. The buildings are mostly modern and well-equipped. The infant (with nursery) junior, middle and upper schools are separate but on the same campus. A C of E foundation (welcoming all faiths), it was originally a boys' school, becoming fully co-educational in 1993. It has high academic standards and good results (most go on to degree courses each year, including Oxbridge). Strong in music, games and sports. The CCF is very active and there is a Scout troop. The school has a good reputation and enjoys vigorous local support.

School profile

Pupils Total age range 3–18; 1000 pupils (700 boys and 300 girls). Senior department 11–18, 620 pupils (410 boys, 210 girls). Entry at any sensible age, mostly 3–5, 7, 11, 13 and into sixth. *State school entry:* most of 11+ intake, plus 10% to sixth.

Entrance Own entrance assessment used. No special skills or religious requirements. Parents expected to buy textbooks in sixth only. 30 pa assisted places plus 5 pa into lower sixth. 12+ pa scholarships (including music), from £100 to half fees.

Parents From a wide variety of backgrounds including substantial numbers from industry or commerce, the law and medicine.

Head and staff *Principal:* Barry Martin, 4 years in post. Educated at Kingston Grammar, and universities of Cambridge (modern languages and economics), Loughborough (business administration) and London (education). Previously Director of Studies, Housemaster and Head of Economics and Business Studies at Mill Hill, Head of Economics at Repton, Head of Economics and Business Studies and Housemaster at Caterham. Also previously worked on EC matters in the Bank of England; Chief Examiner for Cambridge A-level Business Studies. Hockey blue and played cricket for Cambridge. *Staff:* 84 full time, 2 part time. Annual turnover 5%. Average age 40.

Exam results In 1995, 110 pupils in fifth, 70 in upper sixth. *GCSE:* In 1995, 104 fifth gained at least grade C in 5+ subjects. *A-levels:* 46% upper sixth passed in 4+ subjects; 30% in 3; 16% in 2; and 6% in 1 subject. Average UCAS points 16.5 (including general studies, 20.1).

University and college entrance 90% of 1995 sixth-form leavers went on to a degree course; others typically go on to non-degree courses or straight into careers eg armed services, industry. Of those going on to university, 5% went to Oxbridge; 6% took courses in medicine, dentistry and veterinary science, 63% in science and engineering, 25% in humanities and social sciences, 2% in art and design, 3% in drama and music.

Curriculum GCSE and A-levels. 17 GCSE subjects offered; 22 at A-level (including general studies). 40% take science A-levels; 37% arts/humanities; 23% both. *Vocational:* Work experience available. *Computing facilities:* 4-room IT centre, many computers in departments; information technology taught on a cross-curricular basis. *Europe:* French (compulsory from age 4), German and Spanish offered at GCSE, AS-level and A-level.

The arts (Pupils aged 11 and over) *Music:* 30% of pupils learn a musical instrument; instrumental exams can be taken. Some 7 musical groups including 2 string quartets, military band. Recent head chorister at Liverpool Cathedral; 70 prizes or places at Liverpool Music Festival; 7 members of county youth orchestra. *Drama & dance:* Some pupils are involved in school and house/other productions, eg Demon Headmaster and Bugsy Malone 1995/6. *Art:* On average, 20 take GCSE, 8 A-level. Design, pottery, ceramics, sculpture, photography also offered.

Sport, community service and clubs (Pupils aged 11 and over) *Sport and physical activities:* Compulsory sports: rugby, hockey, cricket (boys); lacrosse, netball, rounders (girls). Others sports include: cross-country, swimming, athletics, tennis, squash, badminton, canoeing, basketball. Sixth form only: golf. BAGA and RLSS exams may be taken. Rugby, England U16 XV; hockey, England U15 XI; gymnastics, national final; lacrosse, national U15 semi-finalists and north winners. *Community service:* CCF compulsory for 3 years at age 13. Community service optional. Design technology department makes toys for handicapped children. Sixth formers help those with learning difficulties in local primaries and Barnado's. *Clubs and societies:* Up to 30 clubs, eg classical, pottery, chess, mixed Scout troop, computer, adventure training, debating, weight-lifting.

Uniform School uniform worn throughout.

Houses/prefects Competitive and pastoral houses. Sixth formers act as prefects. Head boy/girl, head of house and house prefects – appointed by the Principal and Common Room.

Religion A C of E foundation welcoming all faiths. All pupils attend unless parents wish them not to.
Social No organised events with local schools. Organised trips abroad. Pupils allowed to bring own car/bike/motorbike to school. Meals self-service. No tobacco/alcohol allowed.
Discipline School emphasis on building up self-discipline and organisation within caring framework. Pupils failing to produce homework once might expect detention; those involved in illegal drugs expect immediate expulsion.
Alumni association run by the Bursar, c/o the college.

• LLANDOVERY

Llandovery College, Llandovery, Carmarthenshire SA20 0EE. Tel 01550 720315, Fax 01550 720168

• Pupils 240 • Boys 11–18 (Day/Board/Weekly) • Girls 11–18 (Day/Board/Weekly) • Upper sixth 44 • Termly fees £1840–£2068 (Day) £2686–£3170 (Board/Weekly) • HMC • Enquiries/ application to the Warden

What it's like

Founded and endowed by Dr Thomas Phillips in 1847, to provide a classical and liberal education in which the Welsh language and the study of Welsh literature and history were to be cultivated. Founded as a boys school, girls were first admitted in 1968. It has a fine site amidst magnificent countryside in the small market town of Llandovery. The extensive grounds and playing fields run alongside the River Towy. The original buildings are handsome and well-appointed and, with recent additions and improvements, it is now well-equipped. There is a daily morning service for all pupils and the Eucharist is celebrated on Saturdays. The staff:pupil ratio is about 1:9; results are good and most pupils proceed to degree courses. Welsh is compulsory for all pupils in the first two years and special provision is made for beginners. It is strong in music and drama and involves the majority of pupils. There is an annual programme of visiting artists and lecturers. Sports and games are compulsory and the college has an outstanding record in these (especially rugby), with representation at county, regional and national level. There is considerable emphasis on outdoor pursuits which include fishing, canoeing, CCF and fell-walking. Considerable success in the Duke of Edinburgh's Award Scheme, with an average of 15 gold awards each year.

School profile

Pupils Age range 11–18; 240 pupils, 72 day (46 boys, 26 girls), 168 boarding (122 boys, 46 girls). Main entry ages, 11, 13 and into sixth. 5% are children of former pupils. *State school entry:* 80% main intakes, 90% to sixth.
Entrance Common Entrance and own exam used. No special skills or religious requirements. Parents not expected to buy textbooks. Average extras £133 per term. 12 pa assisted places. 10 pa scholarships/bursaries, £500 to half fees.
Parents 30+% live with 30 miles, less than 10% live overseas.
Head and staff *Warden*: Dr Claude Evans, 8 years in post. Educated at Llandeilo Grammar School, and universities of Aberystwyth and Cambridge (chemistry). Previously Housemaster at Westminster, Teacher of Chemistry and Mathematics at St Edward's, Oxford. Also Honorary Steward, Westminster Abbey; Co-chairman of UCAS Regional Committee for Wales. *Staff:* 27 full time, 4 part time. Annual turnover 10%. Average age 45.
Exam results In 1995, 37 pupils in upper fifth, 44 in upper sixth. *GCSE:* In 1995, 25 upper fifth gained at least grade C in 8+ subjects; 8 in 5–7 subjects. *A-levels:* 2% upper sixth passed in 4+ subjects; 59% in 3; 24% in 2; and 12% in 1 subject. Average UCAS points 16.4.
University and college entrance 85% of 1995 sixth-form leavers went on to a degree course; others typically go on to careers or to art college or non-degree courses. Of those going on to university, 5% went to Oxbridge; 7% took courses in medicine, dentistry and veterinary science, 39% in science and engineering, 50% in humanities and social sciences, 2% in art and design, 2% in music.
Curriculum GCSE and A-levels. 18 subjects offered (including Welsh). 20% take science

A-levels; 41% arts/humanities; 39% both. *Vocational:* Work experience available in both UK and France. *Computing facilities:* Two computer networks. *Special provision:* Special unit provides teaching for bright, moderately dyslexic pupils, with two fully qualified teachers in charge; individual coaching for any pupil with learning difficulties; EFL for pupils from overseas. *Europe:* French and Welsh offered to GCSE and A-level; also Welsh AS level. Over 75% take GCSE in both languages. Regular exchanges to France.

The arts *Music:* Over 30% of pupils learn a musical instrument; instrumental exams can be taken. Some 8 musical groups including chapel choirs, concert choir, jazz group, numerous chamber groups. Members of county youth orchestra. *Drama & dance:* Drama offered. Majority of pupils are involved in school productions. Variety show; recent productions of The Golden Mask of Agamemnon, Bugsy Malone and Cobblers; series of recitals. *Art:* On average, 12 take GCSE, 2 AS-level, 4 A-level. Design, pottery, textiles and photography also offered.

Sport, community service and clubs *Sport and physical activities:* Compulsory sport: rugby. Optional: cricket, tennis, squash, badminton, basketball, athletics. GCSE, AS and A-level sports studies may be taken. Rugby, national representation at U18, U19, Welsh youth; sailing, 1 boy in national championships U18; shooting, 4 boys, 2 girls, in Welsh youth international team. *Community service:* Pupils take bronze, silver and gold Duke of Edinburgh's Award; on average, 15 pupils gain golds annually. CCF compulsory for 2 years at age 13, optional thereafter. Community service optional. *Clubs and societies:* Up to 10 clubs, eg model; railway, newspaper and journal production, photography, chess.

Uniform School uniform worn throughout.

Houses/prefects Houses arranged by age group. Head pupil appointed by Warden; heads of houses appointed by Warden and Housemasters, house prefects by Housemaster.

Religion Attendance at religious worship compulsory.

Social Local Rotary Clubs debating competitions with other local schools. Exchange scheme with school in France. Regular visits to twinned town in Brittany. Pupils allowed to bring own car/bike/motorbike. Meals self-service. School shop. No tobacco; alcohol allowed only in sixth-form common room.

Discipline Pupils failing to produce a piece of homework once might be asked to repeat it in own free time by next day; those caught smoking cannabis on the premises can expect expulsion.

Boarding Sixth form have own study bedrooms or share with one other. Houses of about 50. Resident qualified nurse. Pupils can provide and cook own food to limited extent. One exeat, 2 leave-out weekends each term. Visits to the local town allowed, frequency depending on age from once/week in forms 1 and 2.

Alumni association is run by S A Richards, c/o Llandovery College.

Former pupils A M Rees, Cliff Jones, Vivian Jenkins (international rugby players); Major General P M Davies (former GOC, Wales); Peter Morgan (former Director General of Institute of Directors); Rod Richards (former Under Sec of State for Wales); David John (Chairman BOC).

• LOMOND

Lomond School, Stafford Street, Helensburgh, Dunbartonshire G84 9JX. Tel 01436 672476, Fax 01436 678320

• Pupils 460 • Boys 3–18 (Day/Board/Weekly) • Girls 3–18 (Day/Board/Weekly) • Higher year 50 • Termly fees £1515 (Day) £3310 (Board) £3205 (Weekly) • SHMIS • Enquiries/application to the Headmaster

What it's like

Founded in 1977 as a result of the amalgamation of Larchfield School for Boys (1845) and St Bride's School for Girls (1895). It has an agreeable split site in the upper part of Helensburgh, a dormitory town a few miles from Loch Lomond and 40 minutes' drive from Glasgow. The three main buildings are quite near each other and have pleasant gardens. The staff:pupil ratio is about 1:10. Academic standards are high and results very good; most sixth-formers go on to degree courses. The music, drama and art departments are all strong. There is a high standard of public performance in drama and music. Sports and games are well catered for (a large number of representatives at county and national level). An unusually wide range and large number of extra-curricular activities is on offer. Good facilities for outdoor pursuits and adventure training for which the neighbouring environment is ideal. Some commitment to local community schemes and an outstanding record in the Duke of Edinburgh's Award Scheme.

School profile

Pupils Total age range 3–18; 460 pupils, 389 day (204 boys, 185 girls), 72 boarding (41 boys, 31 girls). Senior department 12–18, 290 pupils (156 boys, 134 girls). Main entry ages 12 and into sixth. Approx 20% are children of former pupils. *State school entry:* 20% main senior intake, plus 50% to sixth.

Entrance Own entrance exam used. No special skills or religious requirements. Parents not expected to buy textbooks. 7 pa assisted places. 15 pa scholarships/bursaries, £387–£730.

Parents 15+% are doctors, lawyers, etc. 60+% live within 30 miles; up to 10% live overseas.

Head and staff *Headmaster:* Angus Macdonald, in post for 10 years. Educated at Portsmouth Grammar and Cambridge (geography). Previously Deputy Principal and Head of Department at George Watson's, Assistant Master at Edinburgh Academy and Assistant Teacher at Kings School, Parramatta, NSW and at Alloa Academy. Also member of ISIS Committee (Scotland). *Staff:* 46 full time, 8 part time. Annual turnover less than 10%.

Exam results On average, 55 in S-grade year; 50 in Higher year; 40 in A-level year. *S-grades*: In 1995, 89% passed 5–7 subjects. *Highers:* 74% passed 5+ subjects. *A-levels:* 67% passed 3 subjects. (Many pupils take Highers instead.)

University and college entrance 97% of 1995 sixth-form leavers went on to a degree course (5% after a gap year); others typically go on to HND course or straight into work. Of those going on to university, 5% went to Oxbridge; 14% took courses in medicine, dentistry and veterinary science, 43% in science and engineering, 4% in law, 9% in humanities and social sciences, 6% in art and design, 23% in vocational subjects eg education, hotel and leisure management, occupational therapy.

Curriculum S-grades, Highers, A-levels. On average, 23% take science/engineering A-levels; 33% take arts and humanities; 45% a mixture. *Computing facilities:* Computer lab, 15 IBM and 20 Apple Macs with Econet system. *Special provision:* Specialised help in cases of need. *Europe:* French and German offered to S-grade and A-level; also Spanish S-grade. Over 75% take S-grade in more than 1 language. Regular exchanges (France and Germany). French and German assistants in school. European pupils on bursaries every year. S5 pupils on work experience in Germany. Well-established European dimension and tradition.

The arts (Pupils aged 11 and over) *Music:* 40% of pupils learn a musical instrument; instrumental exams can be taken. Musical groups include orchestra, choir, pop group. *Drama & dance*: Some pupils are involved in school productions (5 a year). *Art:* On average, 25 take S-grade, 12 Higher, 2 A-level. Art facilities open to non-examination pupils. 2–3 pa accepted for art college.

Sport, community service and clubs (Pupils aged 11 and over) *Sport and physical activities:* Sports available: rugby, hockey, athletics, tennis, squash, golf, sailing, badminton, table tennis, swimming, cricket, netball. 12 county representatives at rugby, hockey, athletics, tennis, squash, sailing. *Community service:* Pupils take bronze, silver and gold Duke of Edinburgh's Award. Community service optional. *Clubs & societies*: Clubs include computer, Scottish country dancing, dog training, electronics, chess, first aid, art, piping, car maintenance, keep fit, judo, tukido.

Uniform School uniform worn throughout.

Houses/prefects Competitive houses. Prefects, head boy/girl, head of house and house prefects – elected by Headmaster and school.

Social No organised events with local schools. Exchange visits to France and Germany. Pupils allowed to bring own car/bike to school. Meals self-service. School shop. No tobacco/alcohol allowed.

Discipline Pupils failing to produce homework once might expect extra prep; those caught taking drugs on the premises would be expelled. There is a detention system.

Boarding 10% have own study bedroom, 20% share; remainder in dormitories of 6+. Single-sex houses, of approximately 40. Resident qualified nurse and doctor. Central

dining room. Pupils can provide and cook own food. 2 exeats (2 days) each term. Visits to local town allowed.
Alumni association run by Secretary, Lomond Society, c/o the school.

• LONGRIDGE TOWERS

Longridge Towers School, Berwick upon Tweed, Northumberland TD15 2XH. Tel 01289 307584 • Pupils 280 • Boys 4–18 (Day/Board/Weekly) • Girls 4–18 (Day/Board/Weekly) • Upper sixth 18 • Termly fees £1350 (Day) £2700 (Board) £2550 (Weekly) • SHA, ISAI • Enquiries/application to the Headmaster's Secretary

What it's like

Founded in 1983 as a co-educational school, it occupies an impressive Victorian mansion on a fine estate of 80 acres in very beautiful surroundings. A new indoor swimming pool and sports hall have been added recently. With a good staff:pupil ratio of about 1:11, it provides a sound general education and results are good. Most sixth-formers go on to degree courses. There is quite a lot of music, drama, dance and art. A good range of sports and games and a fair range of other activities. A promising record in the Duke of Edinburgh's Award Scheme.

School profile

Pupils Total age range 4–18; 280 pupils, 210 day (110 boys, 100 girls), 70 boarding (36 boys, 34 girls). Senior department 11–18, 200 pupils (105 boys, 95 girls). Main entry ages 4, 8, 11, 13 and into sixth. *State school entry:* 50% senior intake, plus 80% to sixth.
Entrance Common Entrance and own exam used (tests in English and maths). Parents not expected to buy textbooks; £20 maximum extras. 6 pa scholarships, up to half-fees. Scholarships, bursaries and concessions for children of HM Forces, £185–£225 per term.
Parents 17½% in the armed services; 15+% in industry or commerce; 15+% are farmers. 60+% live within 30 miles; 10+% live overseas.
Head and staff *Headmaster:* Dr Michael Barron, in post for 13 years. Educated at Manchester University. Previously Housemaster at the Oratory. *Staff:* 25 full time, 3 part time. Annual turnover 5%. Average age 38.
Exam results On average, 37 pupils in upper fifth, 16 in upper sixth. *GCSE:* 59% upper fifth gain at least grade C in 8+ subjects; 24% in 5–7; and 16% in 1–4 subjects. *A-levels:* 80% upper sixth pass in 3 subjects; 20% in 2 subjects. Average UCAS points 18.9.
University and college entrance 90% of 1995 sixth-form leavers went on to a degree course (10% after a gap year); others typically go on to vocational courses or farming. Of those going on to university, 30% took courses in science and engineering, 10% in law, 50% in humanities and social sciences, 10% in accountancy.
Curriculum GCSE, Highers and A-levels. 15 subjects offered (no A-level general studies). 40% take science A-levels; 40% arts/humanities; 20% both. *Vocational:* Work experience available. *Computing facilities:* Computer lab with 21 Archimedes in Econet. *Special provision:* Some help for dyslexic pupils. *Europe:* French and German offered to GCSE and A-level. Regular exchanges to France.
The arts (Pupils aged 11 and over) *Music:* Over 40% of pupils learn a musical instrument; instrumental exams can be taken. Musical groups include orchestra, swing band, ceilidh band, recorder group, choirs. *Drama & dance*: Both offered. GCSE drama, LAMDA and RAD exams may be taken. Majority of pupils are involved in school productions. Numerous 1st prizes in Musselburgh Festival. *Art:* On average, 10–15 take GCSE, 3–6 A-level. Pottery, clay modelling, photography also offered. Art very popular and successful; pupils have sold clay models and received commissions.
Sport, community service and clubs (Pupils aged 11 and over) *Sport and physical activities:* Compulsory sports: hockey, rounders, athletics, gymnastics, swimming, rugby, cricket. Optional: tennis, canoeing, badminton, archery. BAGA and RLSS exams may be taken. County hockey champions U15 1994, 10 team representatives at hockey, rugby, athletics, cricket, cross-country; national, 2 All-England cross-country championship runners U18. *Community service:* Pupils take bronze, silver and gold Duke of Edinburgh's Award; 52 pupils currently at various stages. Community service optional at age 14+. *Clubs and societies:* Up to 10 clubs, eg computer, chess, bridge, gymnastics, photography, squash.

Uniform School uniform worn except the sixth.
Houses/prefects Competitive houses. Prefects, School Captain, head of house and house prefects – appointed by Headmaster after consultation with staff.
Religion Morning prayers 4 days a week. Sunday service in school chapel.
Social Entries to Musselburgh Festival, drama and debating in competitions. Regular trips abroad eg to Switzerland, Norway, Russia and France. Some meals self-service. School tuck shop for boarders. No tobacco/alcohol allowed.
Discipline Pupils failing to produce homework once might expect a verbal warning; those caught smoking cannabis on the premises would be expelled.
Boarding Sixth form share in pairs; rest in dormitories of 3–5. Single-sex houses of approx 35. Two resident matrons. Central dining room. Four weekend exeats each term. Visits to the local town allowed.
Alumni association is run by Mrs Fletcher, c/o the school.

• LORD WANDSWORTH

Lord Wandsworth College, Long Sutton, Hook, Hampshire RG29 1TB. Tel 01256 862482, Fax 01256 862563

• Pupils 475 • Boys 11–18 (Day/Board/Weekly) • Girls 16–18 (Day/Board/Weekly) • Upper sixth 72 • Termly fees £2460–£2584 (Day) £3152–£3324 (Board/Weekly) • HMC • Enquiries/application to the Headmaster's Secretary or Foundation Registrar

What it's like

Founded in 1920 and endowed by Lord Wandsworth, it has very agreeable buildings in a beautiful part of Hampshire on an estate of 1200 acres. Early links between the school and agriculture have now virtually disappeared but the rural environment remains a strong feature of the school. It is extremely well-equipped in a village environment. It provides a sound education and academic results are good. Many sixth-form leavers go on to degree courses, including Oxbridge. A non-denominational foundation, religious education and attendance at chapel is more or less compulsory. The staff:pupil ratio is good at about 1:11. There is a CCF and a good range of games and sports, with flood-lit all-weather pitches. Music and drama are strong. Weekly boarding is popular.

School profile

Pupils Age range 11–18; 475 pupils, 132 day boys, 343 boarders (298 boys, 45 girls). Main entry ages 11, 13 (boys) and into sixth (boys and girls). *State school entry:* 60% at 11, 3% at 13, 5% to sixth.
Entrance Common Entrance and own exam used. No special skills or religious requirements. Parents not expected to buy textbooks. 27 pa assisted places. 25 pa scholarships of which some are Foundation Awards for sons of single parents (fees according to means).
Parents 75+% live within 30 miles; up to 10% live overseas.
Head and staff *Headmaster:* Guy Waller, 3 years in post. Educated at Hurstpierpoint and Oxford (chemistry). Previously Head of Chemistry, Housemaster and Master i/c Cricket and Hockey at Radley. Also FRSA; Governor of two prep schools; cricket and hockey blue. *Staff:* 45 full time, 4 part time.
Exam results In 1995, 82 in fifth and 72 in upper sixth. *GCSE:* In 1995, 90% fifth gained at least grade C in 8+ subjects; 5% in 5–7; and 5% in 1–4 subjects. *A-levels:* 75% upper sixth passed in 3 subjects and 22% in 2 subjects. Average UCAS points 17.7.
University and college entrance 85% of 1995 sixth-form leavers went on to a degree course; others typically go on to non-degree courses eg agriculture, HND. Of those going on to university, 8% went to Oxbridge; 37% took courses in science and engineering, 63% in humanities and social sciences.
Curriculum GCSE and A-levels (no A-level general studies). 25% take science A-levels; 41% took arts/humanities; 34% both. *Computing facilities:* networked Archimedes, RM Nimbus and Apple Macs in computer centre; many others in academic departments and in computer rooms in houses. *Europe:* French, Spanish and German offered to GCSE and A-level. Regular exchanges (France, Germany and Spain).
The arts *Music:* Over a third of pupils learn a musical instrument; instrumental exams can be taken. Some 12 musical groups including choral society, choirs, orchestra, band,

folk group, jazz band etc. *Drama & dance*: Senior pupils took production of The Winter's Tale to Texas in 1995. *Art:* On average, 4 take A-level. Pottery also offered.
Sport, community service and clubs *Sport and physical activities:* Compulsory sports: (to a small degree) rugby, cricket, hockey. Optional: shooting, sailing, squash, netball, tennis, badminton, athletics, cross-country, basketball, swimming. 11 county rugby players and 11 cricket; 2 England rugby players. *Community service:* Pupils take bronze, silver and gold Duke of Edinburgh's Award. CCF compulsory for fourth form. 140 are involved in community service each week.
Uniform School uniform worn during working day throughout.
Houses/prefects Mildly competitive houses. Head boy and girl and heads of houses appointed by Headmaster and housemaster/mistress in consultation with senior pupils. Sixth-form centre run by an elected committee.
Religion Attendance at religious worship compulsory.
Social Many dramatic and choral functions, dances/discos with local girls' schools. Organised trips abroad and exchange systems. Meals self-service. School shop. No tobacco allowed; some alcohol served in sixth-form centre three times a week.
Boarding Houses of 85 pupils (including day). Resident qualified nurse. Central dining room. Exeats possible each weekend.
Alumni association The Sternian Association, c/o the school.

• LORETTO

Loretto School, Musselburgh, Midlothian EH21 7RE. Tel 0131 665 2567

• Pupils 310 • Boys 13–18 (Day/Board) • Girls 13–18 (Day/Board) • Upper sixth 74 • Termly fees £2580 (Day) £3870 (Board) • HMC • Enquiries/application to the Admissions Office (0131 653 2618)

What it's like

Founded in 1827 by the Rev Thomas Langhorne, it was bought in 1862 by Hely Hutchinson Almond, a distinguished scholar of strong and unconventional convictions. He built up the school and was its Head until he died in 1903. A very distinguished boys' school, it is in the process of becoming co-educational; girls were admitted to the sixth-form in 1981 and from 13 in 1995. It has a fine 80-acre site on the outskirts of the small town of Musselburgh on the Firth of Forth, 6 miles from Edinburgh. The junior school is on the same site. The buildings are handsome and many recent developments have produced excellent facilities (including good boarding accommodation). An ecumenical school, chapel plays an important part in its life. The policy has always been to keep the school small and pupils are expected to give their loyalty and make a general all-round contribution. They are given authority and responsibility from an early age. There is a staff:pupil ratio of about 1:9. Academic standards are high and results consistently good. Most sixth-formers go on to degree courses, including Oxbridge. Very strong in music, drama and art. Much use is made of the cultural amenities of Edinburgh. Loretto has long had a reputation for excellence in sports and games of which there is a wide variety. Many clubs and societies cater for most conceivable extra-curricular needs. There is a very strong CCF (compulsory for every pupil for 2 years) with its own Pipes and Drums. Physical fitness and regular exercise are high priorities and there is an emphasis on adventure training. A substantial commitment to local community services. An outstanding record in the Duke of Edinburgh's Award Scheme.

School profile

Pupils Age range 13–18; 310 pupils, 9 day, 301 boarding; 260 boys, 53 girls. Main entry ages 13 and into sixth. Own junior school (The Nippers) provides more than 20% of intake. Approx 25% are children of former pupils.
Entrance Common Entrance, own entrance and scholarship exams used. General all-round contribution looked for. Parents expected to buy some specialist sixth-form textbooks; other extras variable. 6 pa assisted places. 10–12 pa scholarships/bursaries.
Parents 15+% are doctors, lawyers, etc; 15+% in industry or commerce. A number live overseas.
Head and staff *Headmaster:* Keith J Budge, in post since 1995. Educated at Rossall and Oxford (English). Previously Housemaster at Marlborough and Assistant English Master

at Eastbourne College. Considerable experience of planning and managing the transition to co-education, gained at Marlborough. *Staff:* 35 full time, 4 part time.

Exam results In 1995, 53 in upper fifth, 74 in upper sixth. *GCSE:* In 1995, 46 pupils in upper fifth passed 8+ subjects; 7 in 5–7 subjects. *A-levels:* In 1995, 6 pupils passed in 4 subjects; 48 in 3; 7 in 2 (5 also passed 2+ Highers); and 7 in 1 subject (3 also passed 2+ Highers). Average UCAS points 18.1.

University and college entrance 90% of 1995 sixth-form leavers went on to a degree course; others typically go on to non-degree courses (eg agriculture) or straight into careers eg army, family business. Of those going on to university, 10% went to Oxbridge; 8% took courses in medicine, dentistry and veterinary science, 34% in science and engineering, 54% in humanities and social sciences, 2% in art and design, 2% in drama and acting.

Curriculum GCSE, Highers and A-levels. Pupils on an A-level course may take 1 or more Highers to broaden their course; a minority of pupils concentrate more on Highers. On average 32% take science/engineering A-levels; 35% take arts and humanities; 33% a mixture. *Vocational:* Work experience available. *Computing facilities:* Computer centre in new industry and business centre; departmental computers/word processors. *Special provision:* For mild dyslexia; cystic fibrosis, diabetes. *Europe:* French and German offered to GCSE and A-level. Regular exchanges to France and Germany. Pupils from France, Germany, Lithuania, Romania and Spain in school for varying periods of time. Language tapes for those not studying academic languages.

The arts *Music:* Over 50% of pupils learn a musical instrument; instrumental exams can be taken. Some 8 musical groups including chamber choir, sax quartet, swing band, pipes and drums, instrumental ensemble. Pipes and drums tours, winners of international piping competitions. *Drama & dance*: Drama GCSE offered. Majority of pupils are involved in school productions and all in other productions. *Art:* On average, 50 take GCSE, 12+ A-level. Design, pottery, textiles, photography and art history also offered.

Sport, community service and clubs *Sport and physical activities:* Compulsory sports: Boys: rugby (autumn), hockey (spring), cricket (summer). Girls: hockey (autumn), lacrosse (spring), tennis (summer). Optional: athletics, swimming, squash, sailing, fives, archery, badminton, softball etc. *Community service:* Pupils take gold Duke of Edinburgh's Award. CCF compulsory for 2 years at age 13, optional at other times. Community service compulsory for 1 year at age 16, optional for 2nd year. *Clubs and societies:* Various debating groups, Amnesty International, conservation etc.

Uniform School uniform worn throughout.

Houses/prefects No competitive houses. Prefects, head of school, head of house/room/table (graduated system of responsibility) and house prefects – appointed by Headmaster and housemasters/mistresses. Committees for eg messing, charities. Regular leadership seminars on service and management.

Religion Sunday chapel and mid-week services compulsory.

Social Joint community service committee with Musselburgh Grammar School; involved with local club for disabled. Sharing of school and local facilities eg sports hall, swimming pool, squash club, theatre. Carol service for town. Some organised trips abroad. Pupils allowed to bring own bike to school (summer term). Meals formal. School shop. No tobacco/alcohol allowed.

Discipline Pupils failing to produce homework once might expect to do it in their own time and detention; rigorous framework of discipline leading to suspension with tripartite pupil/parent/school discussions about the future, and expulsion for the most serious of offences.

Boarding 30% have own study bedroom; 50% are in dormitories of 6+; 20% in rooms of 2 or 3. Single-sex houses of 50–60. Resident qualified sanatorium sister. Central dining room. Overnight exeats in autumn and spring terms plus half-term. Visits to local town (Musselburgh) at specific times allowed according to age.

Former pupils Jim Clark (motor racing); Alistair Darling MP; Lord Laing of Dunphail (former Chairman, United Biscuits); Sir Denis Forman (former Chairman, Granada TV); Sandy Carmichael (Scotland XV – 50 caps); Lord Fraser of Carmyllie (Minister of State, Scottish Office); Andrew Marr (the Independent); Michael Mavor (Headmaster, Rugby); David McMurray (Headmaster, Oundle); The Rt Hon Norman Lamont MP; Sir Nicholas Fairbairn; Professor John Hunter (Grant Professor of Dermatology, Edinburgh University); Professor I M Murray-Lyon (Consultant Physician and Gastroenterologist, Charing Cross Hospital).

• LOUGHBOROUGH GRAMMAR

Loughborough Grammar School, 6 Burton Walks, Loughborough, Leicestershire LE11 2DU. Tel 01509 233233, Fax 01509 218436

• Pupils 940 • Boys 10–18 (Day/Board/Weekly) • Girls None • Upper sixth 134 • Termly fees £1497 (Day) £2772 (Board) £2439 (Weekly) • HMC • Enquiries/application to the Headmaster

What it's like

Founded in 1495 by Thomas Burton, Merchant of the Staple of Calais, though it is likely that a school existed well before that date – one of the oldest schools in the country. It moved to its present site in 1852 where it is blessed with most attractive grounds, gardens and playing fields. The buildings of the Victorian period are handsome and in the collegiate style. Three main buildings form three sides of a quadrangle. There have been a number of additions in the past 30 years, including a sixth-form centre, art & design centre, sports hall and theatre. In general, the school is exceptionally well-equipped and the playing fields are outstanding. It prides itself on its family atmosphere, and very active house system. Academic results are consistently very good and almost all pupils go on to university each year, including many to Oxbridge. Music and drama are very strongly supported and there is much enterprise in these cultural activities (frequent collaboration with the sister school). A wide range of sports and games is available and the school has long been known for its excellence in these, providing a substantial number of representatives at county, regional and national level. A large variety of clubs and societies cater for most conceivable needs. The big CCF (Army, Navy and Air Force) is voluntary with about 250 senior members. There is considerable emphasis on outdoor pursuits and the school has a distinguished record in the Duke of Edinburgh's Award Scheme.

School profile

Pupils Age range 10–18; 940 boys (870 day, 70 boarding). Main entry ages 10, 11, 13 and into sixth. Small proportion are children of former pupils. *State school entry:* 50% main intake.

Entrance Common Entrance and own entrance exam used. No special skills or religious requirements. Parents not expected to buy textbooks. 23 pa assisted places (at 11, 13, 16). A number of scholarships (including music), exhibitions, boarding bursaries, armed forces and clergy.

Parents 60+% live within 30 miles; up to 10% live overseas.

Head and staff *Headmaster:* David Neville Ireland, in post for 13 years. Educated at Lancaster Royal Grammar, and at Cambridge University and King's College London (history). Previously Head of Sixth and Director of Studies at University College School, Head of Department at Roundhay Grammar and History Teacher at Leeds Grammar. *Staff:* 74 full time, 3 part time. Annual turnover 5%. Average age 35.

Exam results In 1995, 144 pupils in fifth, 134 in upper sixth. *GCSE:* In 1995, 138 upper fifth gained at least grade C in 8+ subjects; 6 in 5–7 subjects. *A-levels:* 124 upper sixth passed in 4+ subjects; 5 in 3; 2 in 2; and 2 in 1 subject. Average UCAS points 20.8 (including general studies, 29.0).

University and college entrance 98% of 1995 sixth-form leavers went on to a degree course (1% after a gap year); others typically go on to art foundation courses. Of those going on to university, 20% went to Oxbridge; 6% took courses in medicine, dentistry and veterinary science, 31% in science and engineering, 7% in law, 26% in humanities and social sciences, 2% in art and design, 28% in vocational subjects.

Curriculum GCSE and A-levels. 22 subjects offered (ancient Greek, Arabic and A-level general studies). 45% take science A-levels; 55% arts/humanities. *Computing facilities:* 2 computer laboratories containing a network of IBM PCs and compatibles; PCs in most other departments. *Europe:* French and German offered to GCSE and A-level; Spanish and Italian GCSE in sixth. Regular exchanges (France and Germany).

The arts *Music:* Up to 25% of pupils learn a musical instrument; instrumental exams can be taken. Numerous musical groups including orchestras, concert band, big band, choir. Concert band and big band won silver award in national concert bands area finals 1994; regular overseas choir tour. *Drama:* Joint productions with Loughborough High. *Art:* On average, 24 take GCSE, 10 A-level. Design, printing and photography also offered.

Sport, community service and clubs *Sport and physical activities:* Compulsory sports: rugby, cricket, swimming, athletics. Optional: hockey, tennis, badminton, basketball, volleyball, cross-country, fencing, golf, squash. Recent schoolboy internationals in rugby, athletics, badminton. *Community service:* Pupils take bronze, silver and gold Duke of Edinburgh's Award. CCF and community service both optional. *Clubs and societies:* A wide range of clubs, eg science, debating, karting, board games, rifles, radio aircraft, bridge, Scouts, photography.
Uniform School uniform worn throughout.
Houses/prefects Competitive houses. Head boy, deputy head boy, head of house and house prefects – appointed by Headmaster and staff.
Religion Assembly compulsory – Sunday chapel for boarders.
Social Debates, music and drama, clubs and societies, are joint with sister school (Loughborough High). Many organised trips abroad and exchange systems. Pupils allowed to bring own car/bike to school. Meals formal. School shop. No tobacco/ alcohol allowed.
Discipline Pupils failing to produce homework once might expect a warning.
Boarding Sixth have own study bedroom, fourth and fifth share (2–4); others in dormitories of 6+. Houses of 25–35, junior and senior. Resident qualified medical staff. Central dining room. 2 exeats each term. Daily visits to local town allowed. Weekly boarding allowed.
Former pupils include: 1 Vice-Chancellor, 1 General, 1 Air Marshal, Editor of the Guardian, 5 FRS, 1 Government Minister.

• LOUGHBOROUGH HIGH

Loughborough High School, Burton Walks, Loughborough, Leicestershire LE11 2DU. Tel 01509 212 348, Fax 01509 21086

• Pupils 529 • Boys None • Girls 11–18 (Day) • Upper sixth 70 • Termly fees £1338 (Day) • GSA
• Enquiries/application to the Headmistress

What it's like

The school is part of the foundation originally provided by Thomas Burton who, in 1495, endowed a chantry with which was connected a grammar school for boys. The foundation was extended to girls in 1849. The girls' upper school moved to its present site in 1879. There are spacious and very pleasant grounds on the edge of the town. There have been many modern additions to the late Victorian buildings and facilities are now excellent. Religious instruction is non-denominational but the school has a Christian basis and all pupils are expected to attend RS lessons and assembly. The aim is to provide an academic education of the traditional grammar school type in a disciplined atmosphere of steady work. Standards are high and results very good. Most girls go on to degree courses each year, including many to Oxbridge. The school is very strong in music, drama and art. There are also high standards in sports and games (there are always representatives at county and international level). There is a full range of extra-curricular activities. There is a strong commitment to local community schemes and a good record in the Duke of Edinburgh's Award Scheme and in the Young Enterprise Scheme.

School profile

Pupils Age range 11–18; 529 day girls. Main entry ages 11 and into sixth. Own junior school, shared with Loughborough Grammar. *State school entry:* 40% main intake.
Entrance Own exam used. Assisted places. Academic scholarships and bursaries, including some music awards.
Head and staff *Headmistress:* Miss J E L Harvatt, in post for 18 years. Educated at Sheffield High and London University (German and French). Previously Second Mistress and Head of German at Bolton Girls' School and German Mistress, Housemistress and Fourth Year Tutor at Ecclesfield Grammar School. Also served on North West Committee of the Association of Teachers of German, The Joint Four, the Council of the GSA and its Midland Region. Recently represented the GSA on the Women's Advisory Committee; now member of the Loughborough University Court and Council, and of the Admiralty Interview Board. *Staff:* 39 full time, 12 part time. Annual turnover 4%.

Exam results In 1995, 80 pupils in upper fifth, 76 in upper sixth. *GCSE:* In 1995, all upper fifth gained at least grade C in 8+ subjects. *A-levels:* 71 upper sixth passed in 4+ subjects; 4 in 3; and 1 in 2 subjects. Average UCAS points 24.2 (including general studies, 31.6).

University and college entrance 92% of 1995 sixth-form leavers went on to a degree course (12% after a gap year); others typically go on to art foundation courses. Of those going on to university, 12% went to Oxbridge; 4% took courses in medicine, dentistry and veterinary science, 39% in science and engineering, 1% in law, 57% in humanities and social sciences, 6% in art and design, 4% in vocational subjects eg physiotherapy, nursing.

Curriculum GCSE and A-levels (A-level general studies offered.) 18% took science A-levels; 45% arts/humanities; 37% both. *Vocational:* Work experience available. *Computing facilities:* School-wide network, linking 2 computer rooms, library, careers, science and music departments; CD-Rom in library; access to Internet. *Europe:* French and German to GCSE and A-level (French compulsory from 11 to GCSE); also Spanish to GCSE. Many regular exchanges (France and Germany). European studies offered to pupils aged 11–12. Several sixth-formers work in Europe in holidays. French assistantes each year.

The arts *Music:* Almost all pupils learn one or more musical instruments; instrumental exams can be taken. Some 15+ musical groups including 3 orchestras, 2 choirs, woodwind ensembles, concert band, 2 big bands, chamber groups. *Drama & dance*: Both offered. GCSE dance may be taken. Some pupils are involved in school productions and many in house/other productions. *Art:* On average, 18 take GCSE, 6 A-level. Textiles also offered.

Sport, community service and clubs *Sport and physical activities:* Compulsory sports: netball, hockey, swimming, athletics, dance, gymnastics, tennis, rounders. Optional: golf, lacrosse, volleyball, new image rugby, aerobics, fencing. Hockey and netball teams frequent county champions at all levels, moving into regional rounds, national finalists (netball), many county players at all levels; tennis, county champions, regional players, national finalists; athletics, national finalists, English schools' competitors; squash and fencing, county representatives. *Community service:* Pupils take bronze, silver and gold Duke of Edinburgh's Award. Community service optional. *Clubs and societies:* Over 30 clubs, eg drama, debating, bellringing, chess, Young Enterprise, Christian Society, computer, musical.

Uniform School uniform worn, except in the sixth when dress guidelines are followed.

Houses/prefects Competitive houses. All upper sixth are prefects. Head girl and two deputies (selected by staff) and head of house and house prefects (selected by girls).

Religion Attendance at religious worship not compulsory (all attend currently).

Social Music and sporting events locally, regionally and nationally. Joint play/musical/opera with Loughborough Grammar (brother school). School also involved in voluntary service, work experience and shadowing, Young Enterprise, Institute of Management competitions. Exchange visits with twin towns Epinal and Schwäbisch-Hall; many other trips organised by department. Pupils allowed to bring own car/bike to school. Meals cafeteria style. School uniform shop. No tobacco/alcohol allowed.

Discipline Pupils failing to produce homework once might expect a firm cautionary talking to; those truanting will be cautioned and serve a detention on a Saturday. Any involvement with drugs will be closely investigated and will normally lead to suspension, pending further enquiries.

• LYCÉE

Lycée Français Charles de Gaulle, 35 Cromwell Road, London SW7 2DG. Tel 0171 584 6322, Fax 0171 823 7684

• Pupils 2800 • Boys 4–19 (Day) • Girls 4–19 (Day) • Upper sixth 150 • Termly fees £749-£1118 (Day) • Enquiries/application to the Headmaster

What it's like

Founded in 1915 it first opened in Buckingham Palace Road and in 1939 moved to its present location in South Kensington. It is one of over 400 French Lycées set in 120 different countries. Most of the pupils are French or British, but it is a remarkably cosmopolitan school with pupils from as many as 60 different countries. Its fees are subsidised by the French Government. One of the largest schools in Britain, it has a huge staff of 180 (140 French and 40 British) which allows a staff:pupil ratio of about 1:14. Its main asset lies in the virtual guarantee of bi- or tri-lingualism which all pupils achieve under the French system up to the end of the third year of the secondary school (six languages, including Arabic, are taught). At this stage, pupils may opt for either the English or French streams. It is divided into four different buildings, according to the ages of the pupils: the primary school; the first to third years of the secondary school in the Petit Lycée; the fourth and fifth secondary school years are in the Grand Lycée; sixth-formers are in a separate block. Everyone is in a highly concentrated area which has well-equipped buildings. The teaching is of a high standard and results are very good in both GCSE and A-levels and in the Baccalauréat. Very many leavers go on to degree courses, including Oxbridge. There are close links with French cultural organisations and the Lycée is run by the French Ministry of Foreign Affairs. Physical education is part of the curriculum and there is some sport; rugby and cross-country are strong, with county representation. The playing fields are at Raynes Park. A wide range of activities, including drama, music and art is available. Many outings are organised each year.

School profile

Pupils Total age range 4–19; 2800 day pupils (1350 boys, 1450 girls). Senior department 11–19; 1400 pupils (700 boys, 700 girls). Main entry ages 4, 14 and into the sixth. 10% are children of former pupils.

Entrance Own entrance exam used. Fluency in French looked for; no special religious requirements. Parents only expected to buy A-level textbooks; maximum extras £50.

Head and staff *Headmaster:* Henri-Laurent Brusa, 5 years in post. Educated at Lycée Massena (Nice), Nice University (literature) and La Sorbonne (law). Previously Headmaster at the Naval College, Brest, Headmaster at Lycée de Charlieu and Deputy Headmaster at Lycée de Vitry sur Seine (France). Also lecturer at Brest University; Teacher at the French Telecommunications Engineering School (Brest); member of the Institut des Hautes Etudes de la Defense Nationale. French Naval Reserve Officer. *Staff:* 180 full time, 20 part time. Annual turnover less than 10%. Average age 35.

Exam results In 1995, 49 pupils in upper fifth, 41 in the British section upper sixth; 118 in French section preparing for the Baccalauréat. *GCSE:* In 1995, 33 gained grade C or above in 8+ subjects; 16 in 5–7 subjects. *A-levels:* 16 passed in 4+ subjects; 17 in 3; 5 in 2; and 2 in 1 subject. Average UCAS points 28.0. Baccalauréat: 99% pass.

University and college entrance 80% of 1995 sixth-form leavers went on to a degree course; others typically go on to art, drama or music colleges. Of those going on to university, 10% went to Oxbridge; 35% took courses in science and engineering, 40% in humanities and social sciences, 25% in economics and business.

Curriculum GCSE, A-levels or French Baccalauréat. 17 subjects offered at AS and A-level (including Arabic; no A-level general studies). *Vocational:* Work experience available. *Europe:* French (taught from age 4), German, Italian, Russian and Spanish (all offered from 13) offered to GCSE, AS and A-level. Over 75% take GCSE in more than 1 language. Regular exchanges (Belgium, France, Germany, Italy, Russia and Spain).

The arts (Pupils aged 11 and over) *Music:* Over 50% pupils learn one or more musical instruments. 3 musical groups: chamber, orchestral and jazz. *Drama & dance*: Drama offered. A few pupils are involved in school productions and other productions. *Art:* On average, 30 take GCSE, 6 A-level.

Sport, community service and clubs (Pupils aged 11 and over) *Sport and physical activities:* PE compulsory. Optional: tennis, basketball, rugby, handball. Winner of English schools' volley championships, regional winners in tennis. Pupils represent county at rugby and cross-country. *Clubs and societies:* Up to 10 clubs, eg drama, photography, chess, video, jazz, magazine.

Uniform School uniform not worn.

Houses/prefects No competitive houses or prefects. School Council, with elected pupil representatives.

Religion No compulsory worship.

Social Organised local events from time to time eg theatre visits, international conferences, lectures, geography and biology field trips etc. Organised trips abroad.

Pupils allowed to bring own bike to school. Meals self-service. No tobacco/alcohol allowed.

Discipline Pupils failing to produce homework once might expect school to contact the parents so they may co-operate in ensuring that work is done; a pupil caught taking illegal drugs on the premises can expect expulsion.

M

• MAGDALEN COLLEGE SCHOOL

Magdalen College School, Oxford OX4 1DZ. Tel 01865 242191, Fax 01865 240379

• Pupils 520 • Boys 9–18 (Day) • Girls None • Upper sixth 78 • Termly fees £1603 (Day) • HMC, CSA • Enquiries/application to the Master

What it's like

Founded in 1478 by William of Waynflete as part of Magdalen College, it was a distinguished school in Tudor times and produced some famous grammarians. William Tyndale was a pupil and so, in all probability, were Thomas More and Richard Hooker. Cardinal Wolsey was one of its Masters. Formerly, the famous choristers had their own separate school but from the nineteenth century or earlier have been incorporated in the grammar school. It is situated near Magdalen Bridge and is well-equipped with up-to-date facilities, most buildings having been built during a period of steady expansion in the last thirty years. A wide range of subjects is provided for a sound general education. Academic standards and results are consistently very good and most pupils go on to universities each year, many to Oxbridge. Music is, of course, very strong; there is strength, too, in art, drama and chess. A good range of sports and games is provided on the large playing fields surrounded by the River Cherwell. Standards in sports and games are high (a large number of county representatives). There is also a plentiful variety of extra-curricular activities.

School profile

Pupils Age range 9–18; 520 boys (including 16 choristers). Main entry ages 9, 11, 13 and into sixth. *State school entry:* 60% main intake.

Entrance Common Entrance and own exam used. 31 pa assisted places. 5 pa academic scholarships, 2 pa music scholarships and bursaries.

Head and staff *Master*: P M Tinniswood, 6 years in post. Educated at Charterhouse and Oxford (PPE) and INSEAD (MBA). Previously Housemaster and Head of Business Studies at Marlborough. Also Trustee, Cambridge Business Studies Project Trust. Publications: Marketing Decisions, Marketing and Production Decisions. *Staff:* 41 full time, 7 part time. Annual turnover 3%. Average age 40.

Exam results In 1995, 69 pupils in upper fifth, 78 in upper sixth. *GCSE:* In 1995, 92% upper fifth gained at least grade C in 8+ subjects; 6% in 5–7 subjects. *A-levels:* 21% upper sixth passed in 4+ subjects; 68% in 3; 6% in 2; 4% in 1 subject. Average UCAS points 24.3.

University and college entrance 96% of 1995 sixth-form leavers went on to a degree course, 25% to Oxbridge; 7% took courses in medicine, dentistry and veterinary science, 32% in science and engineering, 58% in humanities and social sciences, 3% in music.

Curriculum GCSE and A-levels. 22 subjects offered (no A-level general studies). 29% took science A-levels; 36% arts/humanities; 36% both. *Computing facilities:* 2 computer rooms, 33 Acorn Risc machines linked by Ethernet and Econet. *Europe:* French and German offered to GCSE, A-level and as non-examined subjects; also Spanish and Russian GCSE and A-level French for Professional Use. Frequently 1 or 2 German boys for 1 term at lower sixth. Regular hockey exchanges with Hamburg Johanneum.

The arts *Music:* Over 25% of pupils learn a musical instrument; instrumental exams can be taken. Some 11 musical groups including 2 orchestras, 2 choirs, jazz band, wind band, close harmony group, various chamber groups. National Chamber Music for Schools finalists; members of National Youth Orchestra, National Children's Orchestra, National Youth Choir and National Youth Musical Theatre; organ and choral awards to Oxbridge. *Drama & dance*: Drama offered. Some pupils are involved in school and house/other productions. *Art:* On average, 25–30 take GCSE, 6–8 A-level. Design, pottery, photography, sculpture, theory, European art and architecture also offered. A-level pupils regularly accepted onto art and design foundation courses.

Sport, community service and clubs *Sport and physical activities:* Major games: rugby, cricket, hockey, tennis, rowing. Minor: cross-country, basketball, volleyball, soccer, fencing, golf, sailing, swimming. Several boys reach divisional hockey and rugby; many reach county levels in hockey, rugby, cricket, tennis. *Community service:* All pupils involved in either CCF or community service for 3 years from age 15. *Clubs and societies:* Over 30 clubs, eg archaeological, bridge, Christian Union, computing, general knowledge, natural history, politics, debating, stage, history.
Uniform School uniform worn.
Houses/prefects Competitive houses. Head boy, prefects (appointed by the Master); head of house and house prefects appointed by housemaster.
Religion Attendance at religious worship compulsory unless there are known religious objections. Voluntary weekly eucharist. RC prayers weekly.
Social Debates, BAYS lectures, history society, plays with other local schools. Ski trips abroad. Pupils allowed to bring own car/bike to school. Meals self-service. No tobacco/alcohol allowed.
Discipline Pupils failing to produce homework once might expect to hand it in the following morning or detention in the afternoon; those caught smoking cannabis on the premises might expect expulsion.
Former pupils Will Wyatt (BBC managing director, TV); John Caird and Sam Mendes (theatre directors/producers); Nigel Starmer-Smith and Jim Rosenthal (sports commentators); John Parsons (sports commentator/writer); Adam Lively (novelist).

• MALVERN COLLEGE

Malvern College, Malvern, Worcestershire WR14 3DF. Tel 01684 892333, Fax 01684 572398
• Pupils 640 • Boys 13–18 (Day/Board) • Girls 13–18 (Day/Board) • Upper sixth 160 • Termly fees £2960 (Day) £4070 (Board) • HMC • Enquiries/application to the Registrar

What it's like

Founded in 1865 as a boys' school, Malvern became co-educational in 1992. It has a most beautiful setting: the elegant, well-appointed buildings are arranged in a horse-shoe around the grounds on the eastern slope of the Malvern Hills, with magnificent views over the Severn Valley and the Vale of Evesham. It has first-class facilities of every kind, including excellent boarding accommodation. The town is 10 minutes' walk away and the college benefits greatly from its position by a town which has become an important centre of education. The aims of the house system and the tutorial arrangements are to ensure that pupils learn to live in a community and develop their potential. It is an Anglican foundation but all faiths are welcome; all pupils are obliged to attend certain chapel services. Academic standards are high and results very good. Most leavers go on to university each year, including many to Oxbridge. It is very strong indeed in music (many pupils learn an instrument), drama, art, science and technology. Also very strong in sport and games, with many county representatives and some internationals. The CCF is optional; there are Army, RAF and Royal Marine sections. Adventure training is compulsory in the sixth-form. There is a substantial commitment to local community services for the old, disabled and homeless. A fine record in the Duke of Edinburgh's Award Scheme.

School profile

Pupils Age range 13–18; 640 pupils, 115 day (76 boys, 39 girls), 525 boarding (379 boys, 146 girls). Main entry ages 13 and into sixth. Approx 8%–10% are children of former pupils. Large intake from own junior department, Hillstone (tel 01684 573057). *State school entry:* 1% main intake, plus 20% to sixth.
Entrance Common Entrance and own entrance exam used. No special skills or religious requirements. Parents expected to buy textbooks; no other extras. 20 pa assisted places. 20 pa scholarships/bursaries, £500–£7500; plus sixth-form scholarships.
Parents 15 + % are doctors, lawyers, etc. Up to 10% live within 30 miles; up to 10% live overseas.
Head and staff *Headmaster:* Roy Chapman, in post for 13 years (retires 1997). Educated at Dollar Academy and St Andrews University (modern languages). Previously Rector at Glasgow Academy, Head of Modern Languages and CCF at Marlborough. Also former

Chairman of Common Entrance Board and HMC. Publications: Le Français Contemporain (with D Whiting). *Staff:* 75 full time, 10 part time.

Exam results In 1995, 127 pupils in upper fifth, 153 in upper sixth (of whom 16 took the IB). *GCSE:* In 1995, 100 upper fifth gained at least grade C in 8+ subjects; 20 in 5–7 subjects. IB: 16 took and passed the Diploma, 60% getting the equivalent of A and B A-level grades. *A-levels:* 45 upper sixth passed in 4+ subjects; 70 in 3; 16 in 2; and 6 in 1 subject. Average UCAS points 21.4.

University and college entrance 90% of 1995 sixth-form leavers went on to a degree course; others typically go on to careers (eg army, retailing), art or drama courses or resit A-levels. Of those going on to university, 11% went to Oxbridge; 8% took courses in medicine, dentistry and veterinary science, 25% in science and engineering, 64% in humanities and social sciences (including 6% in languages), 3% in art and design, 1% in music.

Curriculum GCSE, A-levels and International Baccalaureate. 22 GCSE subjects offered; 26 at A-level (including Greek and technology). Most A-level subjects also offered in the IB. 12% took science A-levels; 58% arts/humanities; 30% both. *Vocational:* Work experience available. *Computing facilities:* 180 Apple Macintosh, 24 Nimbus and 24 BBC computers. *Special provision:* Extensive English courses for pupils with special writing difficulties in lower English sets; qualified part-time SLD and ESL teachers who will teach on one-to-one basis. *Europe:* French, German and Spanish offered to GCSE, AS and A-level or IB; also Italian and Russian GCSE. Regular exchanges for junior pupils to France and for sixth-form to Germany. Regular visits France and Spain. Some European pupils, particularly in sixth-form.

The arts *Music:* Over 30% of pupils learn a musical instrument; instrumental exams can be taken. Some 10 musical groups including symphony orchestra, chamber orchestra, wind band, jazz band, choirs etc. Local piano competition winner; King's Cambridge organ scholar. *Drama & dance*: Drama offered. GCSE drama and LAMDA exams may be taken. Some pupils are involved in school productions and majority in house/other productions. Regular admission to National Youth Theatre; regular appearances on Fringe of Edinburgh Festival; annual production in Festival Theatre, Malvern. *Art:* On average, 75–80 take GCSE, 30 A-level. History of art, ceramics, photography also offered. On average 8–9 enter foundation courses in art; regular prizewinners of NADFAS award.

Sport, community service and clubs *Sport and physical activities:* Compulsory sports: soccer, rugby, cricket, lacrosse, hockey, tennis – PE/games to fifth year. Optional: range of some 20 including judo, fencing, sailing, shooting, rackets, fives. Sixth form only: outdoor pursuits. Rugby, over a dozen county players; hockey international; Queens rackets winner; athletics, 3 county representatives, public schools champion; cricket, 4 county representatives, 1 U19 England player. *Community service:* Pupils take bronze, silver and gold Duke of Edinburgh's Award (97 golds gained in past 10 years). CCF and community service both optional at age 14. *Clubs and societies:* Up to 15 clubs, eg bridge, car restoration, debating, chess, electronics, photography, polo, clay-pigeon shooting.

Uniform School uniform worn throughout.

Houses/prefects Competitive houses. Prefects and head boy – appointed by the Headmaster; head of house and house prefects – appointed by housemasters/mistresses.

Religion Some compulsory chapel services.

Social Joint general studies classes, debates, dances, discos, plays, concerts with local schools. Organised trips abroad (eg to USA). Exchanges with French/German pupils on individual basis. Pupils allowed to bring own bike to school. Meals formal. School shop. Sixth-form bar. No smoking.

Boarding 40% have own study bedroom, 60% in dormitories of up to 6. Houses, of approximately 60, same as competitive houses. Resident qualified nurse, doctors on call. No central dining room. Pupils can provide and cook own food at times. 2 fixed leave weekend exeats each term plus half-term. Visits to the local town allowed.

Alumni association run by G H Chesterton, c/o the school.

Former pupils Bernard Weatherill (former Speaker of the House of Commons); Denholm Elliott (actor); Sir Ian Maclaurin (Chairman of Tesco); Jeremy Paxman (TV presenter); C S Lewis (author).

• MALVERN (Girls)

Malvern Girls' College, Avenue Road, Malvern, Worcestershire WR14 3BA. Tel 01684 892288, Fax 01684 566204

• Pupils 465 • Boys None • Girls 11–18 (Day/Board) • Upper sixth 83 • Termly fees £2600 (Day) £3900 (Board) • GSA • Enquiries/application to the Registrar

What it's like

Founded in 1893, it has a splendid site at the foot of the Malvern Hills in the town. Seven school houses are scattered near the main buildings. It is extremely well-equipped and has excellent sports facilities including an all-weather games pitch. There is a high standard of teaching and academic standards and results are excellent. Almost all sixth-formers go on to degree courses each year, including to Oxbridge. It is tremendously strong in music and over 75% of girls learn an instrument. Games and sports are of a high standard and girls regularly reach county, district and national levels. A plentiful range of extra-curricular activities and quite a lot of emphasis on outdoor pursuits. Full use is made of Malvern's cultural and festival events. Worship and prayer in the Anglican tradition are encouraged.

School profile

Pupils Age range 11–18; 465 girls, 60 day, 405 boarding. Main entry ages 11, 12, 13 and into sixth. Approx 8% are children of former pupils. Close links with Croftdown Prep School (also known as Malvern Girls' Prep School).

Entrance Common Entrance and own entrance/scholarship exam used. No special skills or religious requirements but majority C of E. Parents expected to buy some textbooks. 10 pa scholarships/exhibitions (including music and art scholarship), half fees.

Parents 15+% are doctors, lawyers, etc; 15+% in industry or commerce; 4% in armed services. 15+% live within 30 miles; 20% live overseas.

Head and staff *Acting Headmistress:* Rev Pauline Newton, who has been Deputy Head since 1986. *Staff:* 70 full time, 30 part time. Annual turnover 5%.

Exam results In 1995, 70 pupils in upper fifth, 83 in upper sixth. *GCSE:* In 1995, 96% pupils in upper fifth gained at least grade C in 8+ subjects; 4% in 5–7 subjects. *A-levels:* 52% pupils in upper sixth passed in 4+ subjects; 42% in 3; 5% in 2; and 1% in 1 subject. Average UCAS points 25.7 (including general studies 29.8).

University and college entrance 95% of 1995 sixth-form leavers went on to a degree course, 14% to Oxbridge; approximately one third study science, engineering or medicine. Others typically go on to other higher education courses.

Curriculum GCSE and A-levels. 26 take science/maths A-levels; 42 take arts and humanities; 12 take a mixture. *Vocational:* Work experience available. *Computing facilities:* Computer centre plus 12 computers in library (on-line to CD-Rom data-bases) plus 2 multi-media for using interactive discs; computers in all boarding houses. *Special provision:* for dyslexic pupils. *Europe:* French, German and Spanish offered to GCSE and A-level; also AS-level French and German and GCSE Italian. Regular exchanges to France, Germany and Spain.

The arts *Music:* 75% of pupils learn a musical instrument; instrumental exams can be taken. Some 11 musical groups including orchestras, wind bands, choirs, choral society, brass, recorder ensembles. Regular musical productions. 3 girls in national orchestras; success in chamber music for schools competition. *Drama & dance*: Both offered. All pupils are involved in house/other productions. *Art:* On average, 40 take GCSE, 5 AS-level, 18 A-level. Graphics, fine art, ceramics, design, jewellery and textiles also offered; plus facilities for metalwork, plastics, wood. Girls regularly accepted to art schools.

Sport, community service and clubs *Sport and physical activities:* Compulsory sports (at different ages to end of fifth form): gym, dance, hockey, lacrosse, swimming, tennis, athletics, rounders, basketball, lifesaving, squash, netball, cricket, volleyball, aerobics. Sixth form only: badminton. Hockey, girls in county teams, U16, U18; lacrosse, girls in county, Midland and international teams. *Community service:* Pupils take bronze, silver and gold Duke of Edinburgh's Award. Compulsory week of community service for sixth-formers; girls and staff run fortnightly sports club for disabled; weekly coffee mornings for the elderly, hosted by 11-year-olds; £16,000 raised recently in charity weekend (including fashion show). *Clubs and societies:* Over 30 clubs, eg journalists, electronics,

bridge, earth action, Young enterprises, CDT, music, natural history, sporting.
Uniform School uniform worn except in the sixth.
Houses/prefects Prefects, head girl, head of house and house prefects – appointed by Headmistress after consultation with staff and pupils.
Religion Worship encouraged; members of other faiths welcomed.
Social Debating and regular social events with local schools. Organised trips abroad. Sixth form allowed to bring own bike to school. Meals all self-service. School shop sells books and second-hand uniforms. No tobacco/alcohol allowed.
Discipline Pupils caught smoking cannabis on the premises would expect instant dismissal. Each girl is given a house handbook which includes guidelines on conduct expected. A sixth-form council composed of girls and staff deals with some offences in the sixth-form.
Boarding Sixth form mainly have own study bedroom (may share if they wish). 15% middle school have own study bedrooms, 85% share with 1–3 others. 1 house for 11–12 year olds; 4 for 13–16 (60 pupils), 2 sixth-form houses. 1 resident qualified nurse. Sixth form can provide and cook own food. 2 long exeats a term; pupils may go home on most weekends. Visits to local town allowed.
Alumni association is run by the Old Girls' Secretary, Mrs P Wilkinson, Syke House, Saddleworth Road, Greetland, Halifax HX4 8PA.

• MANCHESTER GRAMMAR

The Manchester Grammar School, Rusholme, Manchester M13 OXT. Tel 0161 224 7201, Fax 0161 257 2446

• Pupils 1420 • Boys 11–18 (Day) • Girls None • Upper sixth 200 • Termly fees £1380 (Day)
• HMC • Enquiries/application to the Admissions Secretary

What it's like

Founded in 1515 by Hugh Oldham, Bishop of Exeter, it moved in 1931 to Fallowfield where it grew to its present size. The buildings have been constantly added to (most recently, the Mike Atherton Sports Hall) and facilities are first-class. The playing fields are adjacent and the whole area covers 36 acres. As its founder intended, it is a predominantly academic school and has long been one of the most distinguished in the country. Each year over 200 boys join it from widely differing backgrounds and from a wide area of the north-west. Intellectually and academically very high-powered, its results are consistently excellent and a large number of boys go on to Oxbridge. All the major religions are represented and religious studies, taught as an academic discipline, forms a fundamental part of the curriculum. A large number of boys represent the country in various scientific olympiads. Very strong in music, drama, art and CDT. An excellent range of games and sports in which high standards are attained. There is an immense range of out-of-school activities – many carried to remarkable levels of achievement. Considerable emphasis on outdoor pursuits: the school owns two sites, one in the Peak District and one near Grasmere; in addition several other camp sites are used each year. Local community schemes are active. It has a very high reputation locally and far afield.

School profile

Pupils Age range 11–18; 1420 day boys. Main entry ages 11 and into sixth. *State school entry:* 55% main intake, plus 35% to sixth.
Entrance Common Entrance and own exam used. Oversubscribed. High ability in English and mathematics looked for; no religious requirements. Parents not expected to buy textbooks. 45 pa assisted places. Bursaries, on scale similar to government assisted places scheme.
Head and staff *High Master*: Dr G M Stephen, in post since 1994. Educated at Uppingham and universities of Leeds and Sheffield (English and history). Previously Headmaster at The Perse School, Second Master at Sedbergh, Housemaster at Haileybury and Teacher of English and House Tutor at Uppingham. Publications: author of 13 books and over 100 reviews and articles. *Staff:* 108 full time, 12 part time. Annual turnover 5%. Average age 40.
Exam results In 1995, 200 pupils in fifth and in upper sixth. *GCSE:* In 1995, all in fifth

gained at least grade C in 8+ subjects. *A-levels:* 25 upper sixth passed in 4+ subjects; 175 in 3 subjects. Average UCAS points 27.8.

University and college entrance 96% of 1995 sixth-form leavers went on to a degree course; others typically go on to art or drama colleges or straight into careers. Of those going on to university, 30% went to Oxbridge; 42% took courses in science and engineering, 58% in humanities and social sciences.

Curriculum GCSE and A-levels. 18 subjects offered (not including A-level general studies). 43% take science A-levels; 43% arts/humanities; 14% both. *Vocational:* Work experience available. *Computing facilities:* Micro-computer laboratories plus department micros. *Europe:* French (compulsory), German, Russian and Spanish offered at GCSE and A-level; Greek (modern) and Italian as non-examined subjects.

The arts *Music:* 20% of pupils learn a musical instrument; instrumental exams can be taken. Musical groups include orchestra, senior strings, brass ensemble, wind band, choir, madrigals etc. 2 members of Pro Corda national chamber music group; 1 member of National Youth Orchestra; recent finalists in national chamber music competition; organ scholarships to Oxford, Cambridge and St George's Chapel, Windsor. *Drama & dance*: Drama offered. Many pupils are involved in school productions and a few in house/other productions. 1996, production to the Edinburgh Festival. Two major awards in regional drama competition. Leading actors in recent TV series. *Art:* Design, pottery, graphics also offered.

Sport, community service and clubs *Sport and physical activities:* Compulsory sports (years 1 to 3): soccer, rugby, cricket, athletics, tennis, swimming. Additional options: basketball, water polo, lacrosse, golf, squash, badminton, climbing. Sixth form only: ice skating, martial arts. Rugby, 2 county U18 representatives; cricket, 2 England schoolboy players; soccer, 5 Independent Schools FA players; water polo, 2 GB schools U18 representatives. *Community service:* Community service optional; long-standing links with local special needs school and inner-city community scheme; annual fund-raising activities for local and national charities. *Clubs and societies:* Over 30 clubs, eg philosophy, debating, dungeons and dragons, astronomical, railways.

Uniform School uniform; specific dress regulations in the sixth.

Houses/prefects No competitive houses. Prefects, head boy – appointed by High Master. Staff/pupils committee.

Religion School is multi-faith community, which is reflected in all aspects of religion within it. Religion is taught as an academic subject. Weekly assemblies for the major religious traditions represented.

Social Joint society meetings, productions, other activities with local girls' schools. Trips abroad, exchange systems. Pupils allowed to bring own car/bike/motorbike to school. Meals self-service. No tobacco/alcohol allowed.

Discipline Pupils failing to produce homework once might expect verbal warning. For more serious offences there is a staff-supervised Punishment School, both after school and on Saturday mornings. Drug offences are treated seriously, and are likely to result in suspension/expulsion.

Alumni association run by Mr W T Hall, c/o the school.

Former pupils Sir William Barlow; Lord Sieff; Lord Winstanley; Lord Tordoff; Lord Lever; Ben Kingsley; Robert Powell; Robert Bolt; Nick Hytner; Sir Michael Atiyah; Alan Garner; Howard Davies; Martin Sixsmith; Michael Atherton; John Crawley.

• MANCHESTER HIGH

Manchester High School for Girls, Grangethorpe Road, Manchester M14 6HS. Tel 0161 224 0447, Fax 0161 224 6192

• Pupils 912 • Boys None • Girls 4–18 Day • Upper sixth 102 • Termly fees £875–£1305 (Day) • GSA • Enquiries/application to the Head Mistress

What it's like

Founded in 1874, it moved to its present 11-acre wooded site in central Manchester, close to Manchester Grammar School and the universities, in 1940. The main buildings, which were built in the 1940s and 1950s, have been frequently updated and recent additions include a music school, laboratories and classrooms. The prep school is on the same site. Originally established to promote the extension of educational opportunities to women, it was a pioneering institution preparing girls for university entrance. The early emphasis on academic strength continues: standards are high and results are very good. The seven-year academic programme is planned to lead to university entrance and almost all go on to degree courses including to Oxbridge. There is a strong pastoral care system. The school is un-denominational and welcomes girls of any religious faiths or none. There are assemblies for religious services. Music is strong and there is a variety of musical groups. There is a standard range of sports and some participation in the Duke of Edinburgh's Award Scheme. Joint activities with Manchester Grammar include debates, drama and lectures.

School profile

Pupils Total age range 4–18; 912 day girls. Senior department 11–18, 701 girls. Main entry ages 4, 7, 8, 9, 11 and into sixth. *State school entry:* 50% senior intake, plus 80% to sixth.

Entrance Own entrance exam used. No special skills or religious requirements. Parents not expected to buy textbooks. 40 pa assisted places. 3 pa scholarships, 17%–33% fees.

Parents 15+% are doctors, lawyers etc; 15+% in industry and commerce.

Head and staff *Headmistress:* Miss E M Diggory, appointed 1994. Educated at Shrewsbury High and at Westfield College, London (history) and Cambridge University (education). Previously Head of St Albans High and Head of History at King Edward VI High School for Girls, Birmingham. Also former President GSA and Chairman of its Professional Committee, Director of General Teaching Council for England and Wales; FRSA. *Staff:* 66 full time, 14 part time. Annual turnover 5%. Average age 43.

Exam results In 1995, 94 pupils in upper fifth; 102 in upper sixth. *GCSE:* In 1995, all in fifth gained at least grade C in 8+ subjects. *A-levels:* 56 upper sixth passed in 4+ subjects; 39 in 3; 5 in 2; and 2 in 1 subject. Average UCAS points 23.6 (including general studies, 28.3).

University and college entrance 95% of 1995 sixth-form leavers went on to a degree course (10% after a gap year), 10% to Oxbridge; 19% took courses in medicine, dentistry and veterinary science, 22% in science and engineering, 4% in law, 39% in humanities and social sciences, 3% in art and design, 2% in vocational subjects eg equine studies, physiotherapy.

Curriculum GCSE and A-levels. 21 GCSE subjects offered, 22 A-level (including A-level general studies). 28% take science A-levels; 24% arts/humanities; 48% both. *Vocational:* Work experience available. *Computing facilities:* 2 networked PC suites, PCs with CD-Roms and wordprocessors in library and for individual subjects. *Europe:* French (compulsory 11–16), German, Russian and Spanish offered at GCSE and A-level; also GCSE Italian and AS-level French. Regular exchanges (France and Germany).

The arts *Music:* 50% of pupils learn a musical instrument; instrumental exams can be taken. 12 musical groups include orchestras, choirs, string ensembles, flute and guitar groups, wind band. *Drama & dance*: Drama offered. Guildhall exams may be taken. *Art:* 44 take GCSE, 10 A-level. Design, textiles also offered.

Sport, community service and clubs *Sport and physical activities:* Compulsory sports: hockey, netball, tennis, rounders, athletics, gymnastics. *Community service:* Pupils take bronze, silver and gold Duke of Edinburgh's Award Scheme. *Clubs and societies:* Up to 15 clubs, eg philosophy, debating, art.

Uniform School uniform except in the sixth.

Houses/prefects No competitive houses or prefects. Head girl – elected by the school. School council.

Religion Attendance at religious worhip not compulsory.

Social Joint society meetings, productions, debates etc with Manchester Grammar. Trips abroad include French and German exchanges, art visits to eg Florence, New York, Barcelona, Prague. Pupils allowed to bring own car, bike or motorbike to school. Meals self-service. No tobacco/alcohol allowed.

Discipline All punishments depend on the nature and circumstances of the offence.

Alumni association Apply to the school.

• MARLBOROUGH

Marlborough College, Marlborough, Wiltshire SN8 1PA. Tel 01672 892200, Fax 01672 892207 • Pupils 800 • Boys 13–18 (Day/Board) • Girls 13–18 (Day/Board) • Upper sixth 165 • Termly fees £2995 (Day) £4250 (Board) • HMC, SHA • Enquiries/application to the Senior Admissions Tutor

What it's like

Founded in 1843 as a school for the Sons of Clergy of the Church of England, it has a delightful setting on the edge of one of the most agreeable market towns in southern England. The Marlborough Downs lie to the north, Savernake Forest to the east, and the Kennet runs through the school grounds. Its elegant and well-appointed buildings lie amidst fine lawns and gardens, with large playing fields adjoining them. All facilities are of a high standard. It pioneered the admission of girls into the sixth-form in 1968, and became fully co-educational in 1989. It is said to combine strenuous activity with relaxed personal relations. In line with the terms of its foundation, there is quite a lot of emphasis on Anglican worship and instruction and some services are compulsory. Academic standards are high and results consistently very good. Almost all leavers go on to degree courses each year, many to Oxbridge and Edinburgh. Tremendously strong involvement in music (about 350 pupils learn an instrument). Also very strong in art and drama (over 20 dramatic productions a year, at every level of the school). There are 34 sports and games on offer and an outstanding record in these with many county and national representatives. An excellent range of extra-curricular activities – 42 clubs and societies cater for virtually everyone's interests. A flourishing CCF contingent and the Duke of Edinburgh's Award Scheme is also run. There is splendid provision for outdoor activities with centres both in the college and Snowdonia; a pack of beagles is managed entirely by pupils. There is a very substantial commitment to local and overseas community schemes.

School profile

Pupils Age range 13–18; 800 pupils, 30 day (20 boys, 10 girls), 770 boarding (510 boys, 260 girls). Main entry ages 13 and into sixth. Approx 14% are children of former pupils. *State school entry:* Less than 1% main intake, plus 6% to sixth.
Entrance Common Entrance used; own exam for sixth-form entrance. No special skills or religious requirements but is an Anglican foundation. Parents expected to buy textbooks; average extras £180 per term. No assisted places. At least 18 pa scholarships at 13+ (13 academic, 1 art, 4 music) and 6 pa sixth-form scholarships (music, art and academic); up to 50% of fees on merit (can be supplemented by bursaries up to 90%).
Parents 20% live overseas.
Head and staff *Master*: Edward Gould, 4 years in post. Educated at St Edward's (Oxford) and Oxford University (geography). Previously Headmaster of Felsted and Housemaster and Head of Geography at Harrow. Also JP and FRGS. Served on HMC Committee, HMC Academic Policy Sub-Committee and Common Entrance Board; and as Chairman of ISCC and ISIS (East); quadruple rugby blue. *Staff:* 90 full time, 9 part time. Annual turnover 6%. Average age 38.
Exam results In 1995, 162 pupils in upper fifth, 165 in upper sixth. *GCSE:* In 1995, 157 pupils gained at least grade C in 8+ subjects; 5 in 5–7 subjects. *A-levels:* 19 upper sixth passed in 4+ subjects; 120 in 3; 18 in 2; and 7 in 1 subject. Average UCAS points 20.8.
University and college entrance 95% of 1995 sixth-form leavers went on to a degree course (64% after a gap year); others typically go on to HND, art foundation courses or straight into work. Of those going on to university, 12% went to Oxbridge; 2% took courses in medicine, dentistry and veterinary science, 26% in science and engineering, 4% in law, 38% in humanities and social sciences, 14% in art and design, 12% in vocational subjects eg land management, 4% in other subjects eg computing.
Curriculum GCSE and A-levels. 17 GCSE subjects offered; 23 at A-level, including design, theatre studies, business studies; no A-level general studies. Arabic, Chinese and Japanese courses in the sixth-form. *Vocational:* Work experience available. *Computing facilities:* 28-station RML Nimbus network centre; also more than 100 micros in academic and administrative departments; facilities available to pupils in and outside curriculum six days a week. *Special provision:* Individual remedial help with dyslexia; English as a Second Language. *Europe:* French, German, Russian and Spanish offered to

GCSE and A-level; also French AS-level. French compulsory to GCSE, a second language for most in first year. Regular exchanges (France, Germany and Spain). Pupils from most European countries, for 1–5 years. Periodic talks by MEP.
The arts *Music:* Up to 50% of pupils learn a musical instrument; instrumental exams can be taken. Musical groups include at least 8 orchestras, bands and choral groups plus innumerable jazz and pop groups. Major scholarship to Royal Academy of Music. *Drama & dance*: GCSE and A-level drama offered. All pupils are involved in school and house/other productions. *Art:* On average, 40 take A-level. Design, pottery, photography also offered.
Sport, community service and clubs *Sport and physical activities:* Compulsory sports: cricket, hockey, rugby (boys); athletics, hockey, netball, tennis (girls). Optional: 29 other sports and games. *Community service:* Pupils take bronze, silver and gold Duke of Edinburgh's Award. CCF/outdoor activities compulsory for 1 term at age 14, optional thereafter. Community service optional. *Clubs and societies:* Over 30 clubs, eg Arabic, campanology, folk song, law, natural history, psychology, social anthropology.
Uniform School uniform worn by lower school; dress regulations in upper school.
Houses/prefects Prefects, head boy/girl, head of house and house prefects – appointed by the Master.
Religion Religious worship encouraged. Compulsory services thrice weekly in first year; some compulsory services each term thereafter.
Social Day School organised periodically with St John's Comprehensive; week-long exchanges annually with a comprehensive school in Birmingham; Third World Development link with the Gambia. A number of trips abroad and exchanges (eg France, Germany, Spain, Ukraine); growing contact with Latvia. Pupils allowed to bring own bike to school. Meals self-service. School shop. No tobacco allowed; some supervised house bars.
Discipline Pupils failing to produce homework automatically earn extra work; expulsion for any drugs offence, or sexual misconduct.
Boarding About 400 have own study bedroom, about 150 share with 1 other, 250 are in small dormitories. Houses of about 60; most single-sex, some for boys and 10 sixth-form girls. Qualified nurses in sanatorium; doctors local. Central dining room. Pupils can provide and cook own supplementary food. 2 weekend exeats each term plus half-term. Afternoon visits into town allowed.
Alumni association run by Robert Smith, c/o the college.
Former pupils Captain Mark Phillips; Sir John Betjeman; Norris McWhirter; The Hon Peter Brooke; Lord Hunt; Norman Del Mar; Sir Nicholas Goodison; Julian Pettifer; Chris De Burgh; Christopher Martin-Jenkins.

• MARY ERSKINE

The Mary Erskine School, Ravelston, Edinburgh EH4 3NT. Tel 0131 337 2391, Fax 0131 346 1137
• Pupils 657 • Boys None • Girls 12–18 (Day/Board/Weekly) • Higher year 110 • Termly fees £1380 (Day) £2760 (Board/Weekly) • GSA • Enquiries/application to the Admissions Secretary

What it's like

Founded in 1694 as the Merchant Maiden Hospital by Mary Erskine and the Company of Merchants of the City of Edinburgh. It was one of the first schools in Britain to be endowed specifically for girls. There is now a particularly close association with Daniel Stewart's and Melville boys' school (they share a common Principal and junior school), intended to ensure that pupils of both schools have the advantages of both single-sex and combined education. It has occupied its present site at Ravelston since 1966. The modern and well-equipped buildings are set in pleasant grounds. Morning assemblies are non-denominational; religious, moral and social education forms part of the curriculum at all levels. Academic results are most creditable and almost all leavers go on to university although, in the Scottish tradition, not large numbers to Oxbridge. Music is very strong and plays an important part in the life of the school; drama and art are well supported. There are excellent facilities for sports and games in which good standards are attained. Sports include shooting, riding, curling, fencing, rowing and skiing. There is much emphasis on other open-air activities (eg orienteering, mountaineering and Outward Bound training), extensive participation in the Duke of Edinburgh's Award Scheme and a joint CCF contingent with Stewart's Melville. A large number of activities are run jointly between the two schools. Full use is made of the cultural amenities of Edinburgh.

School profile

Pupils Age range 12–18, 657 girls (627 day, 30 boarding). Main entry ages 12, 14 and into the sixth. 5% are children of former pupils. Many pupils from own junior school (Mary Erskine and Stewart's Melville Junior School). *State school entry:* 75% of main intake, 100% into sixth.

Entrance Own entrance exam used. No special skills or religious requirements. Average extras, £70 for books, plus stationery and uniform. Variable number of assisted places. Some 5 pa scholarships, £120–£1592.

Head and staff *Principal:* Patrick F J Tobin, 7 years in post. Educated at St Benedict's, Ealing, and Oxford University (history). Previously Headmaster at Prior Park, Head of History at Tonbridge and Christ College, Brecon, and Head of Economics at St Benedict's. Also Member of Scottish Consultative Council for the Curriculum and Results and of Scottish Council of Independent Schools and Chairman of HMC Professional Sub-Committee; Assessor for the National Educational Assessment Centre. *Staff:* 58 full time, 2 part time. Annual turnover 8%. Average age 40.

Exam results In 1995, 112 pupils in SIV (main S-grade year), 110 in SV (Higher year) and 79 in SVI (CSYS year). *S-grade:* In 1995, 97% of SIV passed in 8 + subjects; 3% in 5–7 subjects. *Highers:* Average of 4 subjects passed.

University and college entrance 93% of 1995 sixth-form leavers went on to a degree course (5% after a gap year); others typically go on to non-degree courses. Of those going on to university, 2% went to Oxbridge; 9% took courses in medicine, dentistry and veterinary science, 21% in science and engineering, 4% in law, 45% in humanities and social sciences, 7% in art and design, 7% in other vocational subjects eg business management.

Curriculum S-grade, Highers and CSYS. 20 subjects offered. 23% took science Highers/CSYS; 31% arts/humanities; 46% took both (all take a mixture in SV). *Vocational:* Work experience available. 10 Scotvec modules offered. *Computing facilities:* 22 networked machines in technology; 20 machines in business studies; 12 in humanities block; stand-alones in other departments. *Special provision:* Assessment by educational psychologist; some group withdrawal. *Europe:* French and German (both compulsory) offered at S-grade, Higher and CSYS. Regular exchanges (France and Germany). European studies offered as Scotvec module. Member of European Movement; trips to Strasbourg.

The arts *Music:* Over 30% of pupils learn a musical instrument; instrumental exams can be taken. 7 main musical groups, including orchestras, choirs, wind bands, pipe band, plus many small chamber groups and ensembles. Members of Edinburgh Youth Orchestra, Scottish Sinfonia, National Youth Wind Orchestra GB. *Drama & dance:* Drama offered. 1 pupil in National Youth Music Theatre. *Art:* On average, 40 take S-grade, 25 Higher, 8 CSYS. Design, pottery, textiles, photography, printmaking and ceramics also offered. In 1995, all 7 applicants gained places at art colleges.

Sport, community service and clubs *Sport and physical activities:* Compulsory sports: hockey, basketball, short tennis, swimming, cross-country, badminton, athletics, tennis. Fifth and sixth-form: squash, volleyball, aerobics, golf. Pupils may take S-grade, Higher and Scotvec PE and RLSS exams. County and national representatives in running; county representatives in orienteering; Scottish reps in hockey and fencing. *Community service:* Pupils take bronze, silver and gold Duke of Edinburgh's Award. CCF and community service optional. Liaison with Royal Blind School. *Clubs and societies:* Up to 30 clubs including choir, curling, fencing, debating, maths, orienteering, rowing, bridge, chess.

Uniform School uniform worn throughout.

Houses/prefects Competitive houses. Head girl, prefects, head of house and house prefects – both appointed by the Principal and elected by the school. School Council.

Religion Attendance at (non-denominational) religious worship compulsory.

Social Many extra-curricular events twinned with Stewart's Melville; Carbisdale 10-day project in northern Scotland. Exchanges and Young Reporters trip to Germany or France. Pupils may bring own car/bike/motorbike to school (but park cars off-site). Meals self-service. School shop. No alcohol/tobacco allowed.

Discipline Pupils failing to produce prep/homework once might expect a warning (detention for repeated offence); those caught smoking cannabis on the premises might expect expulsion.

Boarding 10% have own study bedrooms; 10% share; 20% in dormitories of 6. All in single house. No resident qualified medical staff. Pupils may provide and cook own food. Weekend exeats, or visits to local town from third year onwards.
Alumni association run by Mrs E Kelly, 31 Grigor Avenue, Edinburgh EH4 2PG.
Former pupils Caroline Kaart-Rairt (singer in Netherlands); Audrey Innes (Scottish concert pianist); Lynda Cochrane (pianist); Catherine Young (artistic director for Andrew Lloyd-Webber).

• MARYMOUNT

Marymount International School, George Road, Kingston upon Thames, Surrey KT2 7PE. Tel 0181 949 0571, Fax 0181 336 2485.

• Pupils 200 • Boys None • Girls 11–18 (Day/Board/Weekly) • Upper sixth 50 • Annual fees £6900–£7700 (Day) £12550–£13350 (Board) £12350–£13150 (Weekly) • GSA, ECIS, MSA
• Enquiries/application to the Admissions Officer

What it's like

Founded in 1955, it derives from an educational movement inaugurated by the Roman Catholic Institute of the Religious of the Sacred Heart of Mary in Beziers which established international schools in four continents. Known as Marymount schools, the first was in New York. This, like its sister schools in Rome and Paris, aims to provide continuity of education in an international environment. Many pupils have parents in the diplomatic corps or international commerce and pupils come from 40 nations. Its 7-acre campus of pleasant grounds lies on the outskirts of the town. The original main building is a mock-Tudor private house, with recent buildings adjoining it. It is extremely well-equipped (excellent art, computer, library and sports facilities) and provides comfortable boarding accommodation (a new boarding extension was recently opened). It is one of the few schools in the UK offering the International Baccalaureate. It also offers the IB Middle Years programme for those aged 11–16, together with the American College Preparatory curriculum, designed to meet the needs of an international student body. The staff:pupil ratio is about 1:8 plus specialist academic tutors for eg Japanese, German and Korean pupils. High academic standards are achieved with most pupils going on to degree courses. Strong in music, drama and design. A compulsory religious study programme includes the study of world religions: a multi-faith approach. There are strong international links with educational bodies and with other Marymount schools. Its cosmopolitanism is pervasive and very constructive.

School profile

Pupils Age range 11–18; 200 girls (100 day, 100 boarding). Entry age 11 onwards; entrance possible throughout academic year.
Entrance Good working knowledge of English required; no religious requirements. Parents expected to buy some specialist textbooks. Limited financial help at Principal's discretion.
Parents 15+% are from the diplomatic service; 20+% in industry or commerce. 30+% live within 30 miles; 50% live overseas.
Head and staff *Principal:* Sister Rosaleen Sheridan, 6 years in post. Educated at Marymount College, New York, Fordham University, New York, and University College, Dublin (psychology) and Perugia University (Italian). Previously Guidance Counsellor/Psychology at Marymount International Schools in both London and Rome. *Staff:* 24 full time, 8 part time. Annual turnover 4%. Average age 38.
Exam results Average size of upper fifth (10th grade) 52; upper sixth (12th grade) 50. School offers no external examination at age 16. Students in 12th grade sit for IB Diploma or IB Certificate (Higher and Subsidiary level) exams. 90% of pupils entering gain full IB Diploma.
University and college entrance 95% of 1995 sixth-form leavers went on to a degree course (2% after a gap year); others typically go on to art school. Of those going on to university, 5% went to Oxbridge; 4% took courses in medicine, dentistry and veterinary science, 4% in science and engineering, 64% in humanities and social sciences, 8% in art and design, 20% in other subjects eg business studies.
Curriculum International Baccalaureate (including any IB language). The IB pro-

gramme covers 6 subjects to be chosen from 5 subject areas including 2 languages, humanities, science, maths, arts. *Computing facilities:* New laboratory with 15 IBM PC compatibles. Computer studies is a compulsory part of all student programmes in first 3 years. *Special provisions*: EFL. Learning resource specialist. *Europe:* French and Spanish offered at IB; other languages are available on a private basis. Educational tours to European countries.

The arts (Pupils aged 11 and over) *Music:* Over 30% of pupils learn a musical instrument; instrumental exams can be taken. Musical groups include 3 choral groups, chamber choir. *Drama & dance*: Drama offered. IB theatre arts may be taken. Majority of pupils are involved in school productions. Regular participants at International Schools Theatre Association. *Art:* On average, 10 take IB higher level, 4 subsidiary level. Design – fashion, theatre, fabric, interior design – and art history also offered.

Sport, community service and clubs (Pupils aged 11 and over) *Sport and physical activities:* Compulsory sports: badminton, volleyball, basketball, softball, tennis, gymnastics. Optional: golf, soccer, self-defence, yoga, table tennis, racketball. Volleyball, basketball, tennis teams compete in International Schools' Sports Association Tournament. Community service. Pupils take bronze, silver and gold Duke of Edinburgh's Award Scheme. *Clubs and societies:* 5 clubs: Model United Nations, National Honor Society, drama, social services.

Uniform School uniform worn throughout.

Houses/prefects No competitive houses. Student council elected by the school.

Religion Religious studies programme includes study of world religions: a multi-faith approach. Students are encouraged to bear witness to their own faith and to learn to respect and understand the beliefs of others.

Social Drama, sports and maths competitions with other ECIS members all over Europe; participate in the Model United Nations in The Hague. Annual educational tours week (several destinations each year eg Russia, Egypt, France, Greece, US). Pupils allowed to bring own bike to school. Meals self-service. School tuckshop. No tobacco/alcohol allowed.

Discipline Punishment for pupils failing to abide by the rules of the school eg drug abuse, alcohol, smoking; those smoking cannabis on the premises could expect immediate expulsion.

Boarding Some upper sixth have single rooms; most share with 1, 2, or 3. Qualified nurse and doctor during school hours, then on call. Central dining room. Pupils can provide and cook snacks. Exeats any weekend. Visits to local town allowed, but not alone.

Alumnae association run by Sister Mary Catherine Walsh, c/o the school.

• MAYNARD

The Maynard School, Denmark Road, Exeter, Devon EX1 1SJ. Tel 01392 73417

• Pupils 550 • Boys None • Girls 7–18 (Day) • Upper sixth 63 • Termly fees £1391 (Day) • GSA, SHA, NAHT • Enquiries/application to the Headmistress

What it's like

Founded in 1658, it moved to its present site in 1882. A short distance from the centre of Exeter, it occupies high ground overlooking the Cathedral. The main building is a handsome edifice in the Victorian collegiate style. It enjoys fine gardens and grounds, in which also stands Traceyville, the junior school. Overall, the school's facilities are good, with purpose-built technology and computer rooms and a sixth-form centre. The school is non-denominational but is committed to the inculcation of sound Christian principles. Every opportunity is given for the development of talents and aptitudes and for the maturing of social skills. The staff:pupil ratio is about 1:12 and a thorough general education is provided. Results are very good and each year most girls go on to degree courses (including Oxbridge). Music, art and drama are particular strengths (a large number of girls are involved in theatrical presentations). There are excellent facilities for sports and games and the school has a distinguished reputation, especially in tennis, netball, basketball, hockey and indoor hockey. A fair range of clubs and societies and some participation in community service and the Duke of Edinburgh's Award Scheme.

School profile

Pupils Total age range 7–18; 550 day girls. Senior department 11–18, 490 girls. Main entry ages 7, 10, 11 and into sixth. *State school entry:* 50% main intake at 11, plus 50% to sixth.

Entrance Own entrance exam used. No special skills or religious requirements. Parents not expected to buy textbooks; maximum extras, £100 per term (1 extra per pupil). 31 pa assisted places. 2 pa music scholarships (1 for sixth-form), 50% fees; 4pa music exhibitions. 4+ sixth-form bursaries for isolated cases of hardship, £150–£2000.

Head and staff *Headmistress:* Miss Felicity Murdin, in post for 16 years. Educated at The High School for Girls, Brackley, and at Oxford Unversity (French and Spanish). Previously Second Mistress and Head of Spanish at North London Collegiate. Also GSA Public Relations Committee; one of the first women to be admitted to Rotary. *Staff:* 48 full time, 10 part time. Annual turnover 6%. Average age 40.

Exam results In 1995, 68 pupils in upper fifth, 54 in upper sixth. *GCSE:* In 1995, 66 upper fifth gain at least grade C in 8+ subjects; 2 in 5–7 subjects. *A-levels:* 49 upper sixth pass in 3 subjects (18 with A-level general studies or an AS-level in addition); 3 in 2; and 2 in 1 subject. Average UCAS points 20.9.

University and college entrance 90% of 1995 sixth-form leavers went on to a degree course (18% after a gap year); others typically go on to employment, A-level retakes or non-degree courses. Of those going on to university, 6% went to Oxbridge; 4% took courses in medicine, dentistry and veterinary science, 18% in science and engineering, 2% in law, 56% in humanities and social sciences, 7% in art and design, 11% in other vocational courses eg pharmacy, speech therapy, 2% in combined subjects.

Curriculum GCSE and A-levels. 20 GCSE subjects offered; 25 at A-level (including general studies). 20% take science A-levels; 40% arts/humanities; 40% both. *Vocational:* Work experience available; also RSA stages 1 and 2 typing, and wordprocessing. *Computing facilities:* 1 fully-equipped room for IT, plus single computers in junior form rooms and specialist department rooms. *Special provision:* Sympathetic attention and help given as required to any pupil in special difficulties (must be able to pass selective entrance test). *Europe:* French (compulsory), German, Russian and Spanish offered at GCSE and A-level; also non-examined French. Language awareness course for 10-year olds. Regular exchanges (France, Germany and Spain; Russia for A-level students). Biennial trip to Greece or Italy.

The arts (Pupils aged 11 and over) *Music:* Over 30% of pupils learn a musical instrument; instrumental exams can be taken. Some 13 musical groups including orchestras, choirs, jazz, wind band, clarinet, string quartet. 1 pupil 1st in regional Young Musician of the Year; choir, 1st in Exeter Music Festival. *Drama & dance*: Both offered. GCSE and A-level drama may be taken. Almost all pupils are involved in school productions. Regional finalists in two public-speaking competitions (Rotary and BPWA). *Art:* On average, 35 take GCSE, 4 A-level. Pottery, textiles, photography also offered. 1 pupil won trip to United States for poster for tobacco company; recent pupil at Courtauld Institute for history of art degree.

Sport, community service and clubs (Pupils aged 11 and over) *Sport and physical activities:* Compulsory sports: (at different age levels) hockey, indoor hockey, netball, gymnastics, tennis, swimming, rounders, athletics, dance, basketball, badminton, volleyball, aerobics, health related fitness. Optional: squash, canoeing, indoor hockey. Sixth form only: archery. BAGA, RLSS exams may be taken. National: netball finals U14 and U16, indoor hockey finals U18, tennis Midland Bank finals U13 (runners-up and 3rd), Aberdare Cup finals (occasionally champions), basketball finals U16; county representation in hockey, basketball, cross-country, athletics, netball, swimming, tennis, badminton, judo. *Community service:* Pupils take bronze, silver and gold Duke of Edinburgh's Award. Community service optional for 2 years at age 16. Youth award scheme. *Clubs and societies:* Up to 30 clubs, eg literary, drama, geography, classics, cookery, German, science/technology, chess, Japanese, Ten Tors, various sporting.

Uniform School uniform worn except in the sixth.

Houses/prefects Competitive houses for sports activities. No prefects; head girl – appointed by sixth-form and staff in secret ballot. House captains elected by house members. School Council.

Religion Attendance at religious worship compulsory.

Social Annual inter-school public-speaking, modern languages, classical reading events with local schools, many local quizzes, etc sponsored by eg fire service, local radio and TV, road safety; sports fixtures. Exchanges with schools in Moscow, Rennes, Hildesheim; biennial ski trip (Alps); classical trips (Greece, Rome), history of art (Paris, Amsterdam); activities holidays (Mediterranean). Pupils allowed to bring own bike/moped to school. Second-hand uniform shop. Meals self-service. No tobacco/alcohol allowed.

Discipline Pupils failing to produce homework once might expect a reprimand by teacher and early deadline for production of work; those caught smoking cannabis on school premises would be sent to the Headmistress and kept out of lessons and from all contact with other pupils until the matter had been discussed with parents, preferably at school and with the offender present. Further action would be unlikely to be necessary (a persistent offender would be regarded as a medical rather than a moral problem).

Alumni association is run by Mrs T Baker, Rowan Oak, Muchelney, Langport, Somerset TA10 ODN.

Former pupils Professor Margaret Turner-Warwick (first woman President of Royal College of Physicians); Penelope Campbell, Rosemary Goodridge, Heather Wakefield (hockey internationals); Alison Hill (tennis international).

• MERCHANT TAYLORS' (Crosby)

Merchant Taylors' School, Crosby, Liverpool L23 OQP. Tel 0151 928 3308, Fax 0151 928 0434

• Pupils 843 • Boys 7–18 (Day) • Girls None • Upper sixth 77 • Termly fees £843–£1248 (Day)
• HMC • Enquiries/application to the Registrar (Tel 0151 928 5759)

What it's like

Founded in 1620 by John Harrison, citizen and Merchant Taylor of London, it moved in 1878 to its present site in a residential suburb. It is well-equipped with modern facilities. A separate junior school is attached to the main school. Academic standards are high and results are very good. Most sixth-formers go on to degree courses, including Oxbridge. Very strong in music; and the drama and art departments are also active. Good range of sports and games (high standards and a lot of county representatives) plus activities. Some participation in the Duke of Edinburgh's Award Scheme.

School profile

Pupils Total age range 7–18; 843 day boys. Senior department 11–18, 729 boys. Main entry ages 7, 11, 13 and into sixth. *State school entry:* 75% main senior intake, plus 90% to sixth.

Entrance Own entrance exam used. No special skills or religious requirements. Parents not expected to buy textbooks; £62 maximum extras. 30 pa assisted places. 10 pa grants, up to full fees.

Parents 15+% in industry or commerce; 15+% are doctors, lawyers, etc.

Head and staff *Headmaster:* Simon Dawkins, in post for 10 years. Educated at Solihull School, and at the universities of Nottingham (economics, politics and philosophy), Cambridge (education) and London (management). Previously Boarding Housemaster and Head of Economics at Dulwich and Head of Economics at Eltham College. *Staff:* 55 full time, 5 part time. Annual turnover 7%. Average age 40.

Exam results In 1995, 113 pupils in upper fifth, 77 in upper sixth. *GCSE:* In 1995, 99% upper fifth gained at least grade C in 8+ subjects; 1% in 5–7 subjects. *A-levels:* 75% upper sixth passed in 4+ subjects; 20% in 3; and 5% in 2 subjects. Average UCAS points 22.5 (including general studies, 30.4).

University and college entrance 95% of 1995 sixth-form leavers went on to a degree course (8% after a gap year); others typically go on to employment, retake A-levels, armed forces. Of those going on to university, 10% went to Oxbridge; 20% took courses in medicine, dentistry and veterinary science, 13% in science and engineering, 16% in law, 41% in humanities and social sciences, 4% in art and design, 8% in other subjects eg pharmacy, sports science, music.

Curriculum GCSE and A-levels. 22 subjects offered (including A-level philosophy and general studies). 40% take science A-levels; 40% arts/humanities; 20% both. *Vocational:* Work experience available. *Computing facilities:* 40 Archimedes plus 15 in separate departments. *Special provision:* Dyslexic counselling. *Europe:* French, German and

Spanish at GCSE and A-level. Regular exchanges (France and Germany).
The arts (Pupils aged 11 and over) *Music:* Over 30% of pupils learn a musical instrument; instrumental exams can be taken. Some 10–12 musical groups including orchestras, bands, string, wind brass ensembles. Finalist Choirboy of the Year competition; organ scholarship; 5 pupils in regional youth orchestra; 2 in National Youth Orchestra. *Drama & dance*: Drama offered. A-level theatre studies may be taken. Some pupils are involved in school and house/other productions. *Art:* On average, 15 take GCSE, 5 A-level. Design, pottery, photography also offered.
Sport, community service and clubs (Pupils aged 11 and over) *Sport and physical activities:* Compulsory: in winter, rugby/hockey/cross-country/rowing; in summer, tennis/cricket/athletics. Optional: swimming, golf. Rugby, last 16 in Daily Mail cup, last 8 in Rosslyn Park sevens, 8 county representatives at various ages; hockey, county champions 5 of past 6 years, 22 county representatives at various ages; tennis, 3 nationally ranked players; cricket, county representatives. *Community service:* Pupils take bronze, silver and gold Duke of Edinburgh's Award. CCF and community service optional. *Clubs and societies:* Many clubs, eg drama, debating, model railway, science, philosophy, classics, photography, chess, bridge, economics, history, geography, theatre, film.
Uniform School uniform worn throughout.
Houses/prefects Competitive houses. Prefects, head boy, head of house and house prefects – appointed by the Headmaster.
Religion Non-denominational Christian assemblies involve prayers and readings and RS classes explain (amongst other things) the meaning and purpose of Christian worship. Parents may opt their children out; very few do.
Social Drama, music, several societies with sister girls' school. Organised trips abroad. Pupils allowed to bring own car/bike/motorbike to school. Meals informal. School shop. No tobacco/alcohol allowed.
Discipline Pupils failing to produce homework once might expect a verbal warning; those caught smoking cannabis on the premises would be expelled.
Alumni association run by J A Sparrow, 32 Freshfield Road, Formby, Liverpool, L37 3HN.

• MERCHANT TAYLORS' (Girls)

Merchant Taylors' School for Girls, Crosby, Liverpool L23 5SP. Tel 0151 924 3140
• Pupils 915 • Boys 4-7 (Day) • Girls 4–18 (Day) • Upper sixth 72 • Termly fees £777-£1248 (Day) • GSA • Enquiries/application to the Headmistress

What it's like

Founded in 1888, it is suburban and single-site in the centre of Crosby which is on the coast, 10 miles from Liverpool and 12 from Southport. Its well-designed and pleasant buildings lie in gardens, with playing fields nearby. The junior school is close. It is non-denominational. There are strong traditional links with Merchant Taylors' Boys' School, especially in cultural activities. It is a well-run school with high academic standards and very good results. Almost all sixth-formers go on to universities, including Oxbridge. The music department is extremely strong; theatre studies are offered to A-level. There is a good range of extra-curricular activities and sports, where high standards are achieved. In the sixth-form there is a very substantial commitment to local community services and 80 girls are members of the joint CCF.

School profile

Pupils Total age range 4–18; 915 day pupils (850 girls, 65 boys). Senior department 11–18, 650 girls. Main entry ages 4 (boys and girls), 11 and into sixth (girls). Approx 3% are children of former pupils. Own junior school, Stanfield, provides approx 25% of senior intake. *State school entry:* 75% main senior intake, plus several to sixth.
Entrance Own entrance exam used. No special religious requirements; music and sports skills looked for. Parents not expected to buy textbooks; dinner and music extra. 38 pa assisted places. 6–7 pa scholarships/bursaries, some depending upon parents' income.
Parents 15+% are doctors, lawyers, etc; 15+% in industry or commerce.
Head and staff *Headmistress:* Mrs J I Mills, in post since 1994. Educated at West

Norfolk and King's Lynn High School, and at York University (chemistry). Previously Deputy Head at St Martin's Solihull and Housemistress at Frensham Heights. Represented Norfolk in hockey; university colours for hockey, tennis and badminton. *Staff:* 52 full time, 28 part time (including music). Annual turnover 3%. Average age 40+.

Exam results In 1995, 85 pupils in upper fifth, 76 in upper sixth. *GCSE:* In 1995, 98% upper fifth gained at least grade C in 8+ subjects; 2% in 5–7 subjects. *A-levels:* 51% upper sixth passed in 4+ subjects; 41% in 3; 5% in 2; and 3% in 1 subject. Average UCAS points 23.1 (including general studies, 27.4).

University and college entrance 90% of 1995 sixth-form leavers went on to a degree course (5% after a gap year); others typically go on to non-degree courses eg HND, art foundation or resit A-levels. Of those going on to university, 10% went to Oxbridge; 10% took courses in medicine, dentistry and veterinary science, 10% in science and engineering, 10% in law, 48% in humanities and social sciences, 4% in art and design, 18% in other subjects eg pharmacy, psychology, business, accountancy.

Curriculum GCSE and A-levels. 20 subjects offered (including Russian, theatre studies and A-level general studies). 40% take science A-levels; 40% arts/humanities; 20% both. *Vocational:* Work experience available; City and Guilds computing qualifications. *Computing facilities:* Acorn Archimedes networked (19 terminals) and Acorn Masters networked. *Special provision:* A preliminary screening test for dyslexia is available and examination concessions arranged; all-round awareness of the condition though no specific dyslexia unit. *Europe:* French and German offered to GCSE, AS and A-level; Spanish to GCSE. Work experience links for sixth-formers through Lingua programme.

The arts (Pupils aged 11 and over) *Music:* Over 30% of pupils learn a musical instrument; instrumental exams can be taken. Some 8 musical groups: 4 choirs, 2 orchestras, 2 bands. 1 pupil in National Youth Choir; several girls in regional youth orchestra; 1 National Youth Orchestra; 2 National Children's Orchestra; BBC Radio 4, Radio Merseyside recordings of choirs for morning service etc. *Drama & dance:* Drama offered. A-level theatre studies, ESB exams may be taken. Majority of pupils are involved in school productions and all in form/other productions. *Art:* On average, 25 take GCSE, 6 A-level. Design, pottery, textiles, graphics also offered.

Sport, community service and clubs (Pupils aged 11 and over) *Sport and physical activities:* Compulsory sports: hockey, netball, athletics, tennis, swimming, dance, gymnastics, cross-country. Optional: leisure sports eg squash, badminton, step aerobics. County and regional representatives in hockey, cross-country, athletics; national, several swimmers, English Schools athletics finalists, modern dance national finalist. *Community service:* Pupils take bronze and silver Duke of Edinburgh's Award. CCF optional for 4–5 years at age 14+; 80 girls are members of joint CCF. Community service optional for sixth-form (120 girls participate). *Clubs and societies:* Up to 15 clubs, eg chess, dance, drama, debating etc, some joint with the boys' school.

Uniform School uniform worn, modified in sixth.

Houses/prefects No house system or prefects – school affairs run by sixth-form committees. Head girl and 2 deputies, elected by staff and seniors, confirmed by Headmistress. School Council.

Religion Compulsory, non-denominational morning assembly.

Social Work closely with brother school. Regular trips abroad. Pupils allowed to bring own car/bike/motorbike to school (but not use car park). Meals self-service. Tuck facilities at break. No tobacco/alcohol allowed.

Discipline Those involved in serious breaches of rules (eg caught smoking on the premises) might expect immediate suspension until facts were verified; those with drugs may be expelled.

Alumni association is run by Mrs S Duncan, Fairhaven, Serpentine South, Blundellsands, Liverpool L23 6UQ.

Former pupils Beryl Bainbridge.

• MERCHANT TAYLORS' (Northwood)

Merchant Taylors' School, Sandy Lodge, Northwood, Middlesex HA6 2HT. Tel 01923 821850, Fax 01923 835110

• Pupils 750 • Boys 11–18 (Day/Board) • Girls None • Upper sixth 125 • Termly fees £2217 (Day) £3680 (Board) • HMC • Enquiries/application to the Headmaster

What it's like

Founded in 1561 by the Merchant Taylors' Company. It moved to its present premises at Sandy Lodge in 1933 where it occupies a superb 250-acre estate of gardens, wooded grounds and lakes. The Merchant Taylors' Company continues to support the school financially. The handsome, well-equipped brick buildings are dominated by the Great Hall. Facilities are very good indeed and there is a superb new library. The school provides a highly academic and competitive environment and results are consistently excellent; a high proportion of leavers goes on to Oxbridge. Music, drama and art are all very well supported. A wide range of games and sports is available and standards are high. There is a wide range of activities including a very big CCF, a strong commitment to local community services and a fine record in the Duke of Edinburgh's Award Scheme.

School profile

Pupils Age range 11–18; 750 boys (690 day, 60 boarding). Main entry ages 11, 13 and into sixth. Approx 5% are children of former pupils. *State school entry:* 18% main intake, few to sixth.

Entrance Own entrance exam (13+ exam based on Common Entrance). Excellence in all fields is welcomed; no religious requirements. Parents not expected to buy textbooks; extras rarely exceed £50 (fees include lunch). 18 pa assisted places. 22 pa scholarships (including 5 music). Various bursaries available in case of need, supplementing up to full day fees.

Parents 15+% in industry or commerce; 15+% are doctors, lawyers, etc. 60+% live within 30 miles; 10+% live overseas.

Head and staff *Headmaster:* Jon Gabitass, 6 years in post. Educated at Plymouth College and Oxford University (English). Previously Second Master and Head of English at Abingdon and English Teacher at Clifton. *Staff:* 69 full time, 14 part time. Annual turnover 5%. Average age 36.

Exam results In 1995, 140 pupils in upper fifth, 125 in upper sixth. *GCSE:* In 1995, all in fifth year gained at least grade C in 5+ subjects. *A-levels:* 12 upper sixth passed in 4+ subjects; 111 in 3; and 2 in 2 subjects. Average UCAS points 25.1.

University and college entrance 99% of 1995 sixth-form leavers went on to a degree course (25% after a gap year); others typically go on to retake A-levels. Of those going on to university, 16% went to Oxbridge; 12% took courses in medicine, dentistry and veterinary science, 18% in science and engineering, 8% in law, 45% in humanities and social sciences, 2% in art and design, 6% in vocational subjects eg banking, optometry, 9% in joint courses.

Curriculum GCSE and A-levels offered (including Greek and Latin). 36% take maths/science A-levels; 36% arts/humanities; 28% take both. *Vocational:* Work experience available, some abroad. *Computing facilities:* New computer centre with Windows 95 and networked to all departments. Further computer facilities in departments and the boarding house. *Special provision:* Academically suitable children with special educational needs considered (medical advice sought as appropriate). Pupils must be able to cope with teaching in English without remedial help. *Europe:* French, German, Spanish and Russian offered to GCSE and A-level; also non-examined Italian. 65% take GCSE in more than 1 language. Regular exchanges (France, Spain and Germany).

The arts *Music:* Over 30% of pupils learn a musical instrument; instrumental exams can be taken. Some 10 musical groups including orchestras, symphonic wind band, choir. Recent Cambridge choral award and Guildhall and Royal College of Music entry; member of National Youth Orchestra. *Drama & dance*: A-level theatre studies may be taken. Large numbers involved in school and house/other productions. *Art:* On average, 13 take GCSE, 3 A-level. Design, pottery, art appreciation, printing, graphic techniques, photography, computer graphics also offered. Work of 4 pupils published by WH Smith in book of student poetry and verse.

Sport, community service and clubs *Sport and physical activities:* Compulsory sports:

rugby (to 15), cricket (to 14), hockey (to 13). Optional: squash, fives, soccer, golf, cross-country, shooting, tennis, badminton, fencing, croquet, judo, sailing, athletics, windsurfing, climbing, multi-gym, swimming, fishing. Sixth form only: croquet. BAGA, RLSS personal survival exams may be taken. Recently international shooting team members, rugby 1 U16, cricket 1 U18; regional golfers; county hockey, rugby, athletics, cricket representatives. *Community service:* Choice of Duke of Edinburgh's Award, CCF, community service compulsory for 2 years. 30 sixth-formers completing gold D of E; 2 Army scholarships (1996); 3 England B international shooters. *Clubs and societies:* Up to 30 clubs, eg chess, Scrabble, bridge, astronomy, philosophy, film, modern languages, railway, debating, computers, war games, science, clay-pigeon shooting, arts & craft.

Uniform School uniform worn throughout.

Houses/prefects Competitive houses. Prefects, head boy, head of house and house prefects – selected by the Headmaster, housemasters and by sixth-form as a whole after consultation.

Religion Assembly most days of the week.

Social Choral works, concerts, debates, drama, field work, careers conventions, industrial conferences, academic lectures with local schools; particularly ski trips, dances, musicals etc with sister school, St Helens. Organised exchanges to France, Germany and Russia; German orchestral exchange visit; sports tours. Pupils allowed to bring own car/bike/motorbike to school. Meals self-service. No tobacco/alcohol allowed.

Discipline Discipline aims to be simple and consistent; boys are kept well-informed of the school's expectations, and are required to have high expectations of themselves. Pupils failing to produce homework would expect to have to do it satisfactorily by the following day; those persistently refusing to obey school rules could expect expulsion.

Boarding 25 have own study bedroom, 25 share (2), others in dormitories of 5 +, all in one house. Resident qualified nurse; doctor visits regularly and always on call. Central dining room. Pupils can provide and cook their own food. Weekly boarding available and weekend arrangements flexible. Visits to the local town allowed conditionally.

Alumni association is run by Gavin Brown, Chairman OMT Society, Hill Farm House, Hill Farm Lane, Chalfont St Giles, Bucks. (OMT Society has its own clubhouse and grounds near the school.)

Former pupils Rt Rev Donald Coggan; Reginald Maudling; Michael Peschardt; Lynn Chadwick.

• MERCHISTON CASTLE

Merchiston Castle School, Colinton, Edinburgh EH13 0PU. Tel 0131 441 1722, Fax 0131 441 6060 • Pupils 400 • Boys 10–18 (Day/Board) • Girls None • Upper sixth 73 • Termly fees £2480 (Day) £3835(Board) • HMC • Enquiries to the Headmaster • Applications to the Admissions secretary.

What it's like

Founded in 1833 in the centre of Edinburgh, it moved in 1930 to Colinton House and the ruins of Colinton Castle, 4 miles south-west of Edinburgh. Set in a fine estate of gardens, sports fields and parkland, beside the Water of Leith and close to the Pentland Hills, the original house is now the science block; all the other buildings are purpose-built. In the 1980s there were a number of additions and the facilities are now very good. The school prides itself on its adherence to Scottish values and traditions and there is emphasis on striving for excellence, a belief in the value of the individual, in hard work, integrity and good manners. The Scottishness is exemplified in the wearing of a kilt on Sundays and formal occasions, the fine pipe band, and social occasions such as a Highland Ball and Scottish country dancing. There is also emphasis on the practice of Christianity (it is inter-denominational but services are based on the Church of Scotland) and the importance of service to the community. There is a substantial commitment to local community services and considerable sums are raised for charity. A staff:pupil ratio of about 1:8, academic standards are high and the teaching very good. Results are consistently good and a high proportion of pupils goes on to degree courses, including Oxbridge. Music is particularly strong and the choir has recorded for the BBC and regularly goes on tour abroad. Art, design, drama and debating are also strong. A wide range of sports and games is available and the school has long had a reputation for excellence, particularly rugby. Also a good range of extra-curricular activities with emphasis on outdoor pursuits for which the environment is ideal. There is a flourishing CCF, overseas expeditions and an impressive record in the Duke of Edinburgh's Award Scheme.

School profile

Pupils Age range 10–18; 400 boys, 120 day, 280 boarding. Senior department 13–18, 330 boys. Main entry ages 10, 11, 12, 13 and into sixth. Approx 25% are children of former pupils. *State school entry:* 25% main intake, plus 10% to sixth.
Entrance Common Entrance and own exam used. A breadth of interest and talents looked for; inter-denominational. Parents charged £25 per term towards textbooks; maximum extras approx £80 for eg music. 5 pa assisted places. Various scholarships/bursaries, 10%–75% of fees.
Parents 40% are doctors, lawyers, etc; 40% in industry or commerce. 20% live within 30 miles; 20% expatriates.
Head and staff *Headmaster:* David Spawforth, in post for 14 years. Educated at Silcoates and Oxford (modern languages). Previously Housemaster at Wellington and Assistant Master at Winchester. *Staff:* 52 full time, 5 part time. Annual turnover 6%. Average age 35.
Exam results In 1995, 66 in GCSE year; 73 in A-level/Higher year. *GCSE:* In 1995, 48 gained at least grade C in 8+ subjects; 11 in 5–7; 6 in 1–4 subjects. *Highers:* 9 passed in 5+ subjects; 17 in 4; 10 in 3; and 2 in 2 subjects. *A-levels:* 2 passed in 4+ subjects; and 27 in 3 subjects.
University and college entrance 90% of 1995 sixth-form leavers went on to a degree course (6% after a gap year); others typically go on to non-degree courses eg art, music, agriculture. Of those going on to university, 8% went to Oxbridge; 3% took courses in medicine, dentistry and veterinary science, 36% in science and engineering, 10% in law, 43% in humanities and social sciences, 6% in art and design, 2% in vocational subjects eg agriculture.
Curriculum GCSE, Highers, AS and A-levels. 17 GCSE subjects offered; 13 at Higher; 17 at A-level (including Mandarin Chinese in the sixth, electronics and computing; general studies taught but not examined). *Vocational:* Work experience available. *Computing facilities:* 2 purpose-built labs; computing department. All pupils undergo basic computing (age 10–13); also available at GCSE, A-level and as an activity. *Special provision:* Extra English/maths classes and tutoring. *Europe:* French, German and Spanish offered at GCSE and A-level and as non-examined subjects; also Portuguese. Exchanges organised for linguists and others in lower sixth. Regular study trips mainly to France and Germany. A number of pupils from eg Belgium, France, Germany and Holland. Conference every second year on EU/NATO.
The arts *Music:* Over 30% of pupils learn a musical instrument; instrumental exams can be taken. Some 7 musical groups including choirs, orchestra, ensemble, pipes, jazz band. On average 2 pupils a year go on to study music at university; choir has recorded for BBC, recent tours to Far East and United States. *Drama & dance*: Drama offered. Majority of pupils are involved in school and house/other productions. *Art:* On average, 25 take GCSE, 8 AS-level, 4 A-level art & design technology. Design also offered. Finalist Engineering Council Young Engineer for Britain 1992; winner CBI/Toshiba Year of Invention 1993, all age groups.
Sport, community service and clubs *Sport and physical activities:* Compulsory sports: rugby, cricket, athletics, swimming. Optional: golf, tennis, squash, fives, hockey, football, shooting, skiing. Sixth form only: sub-aqua. Rugby, 3 members Scottish Schools senior XV, 1 U16 XV. *Community service:* Pupils take bronze, silver and gold Duke of Edinburgh's Award. CCF compulsory for 2 years at age 14; CCF expedition to Kenya summer 1993. Community service compulsory for 1 year at age 16; school raised £25,000 for Edinburgh hospital. *Clubs and societies:* Up to 30 clubs, eg art, drama, debating, chess, Young Enterprise, literary, history, music, reel, flying.
Uniform School uniform worn except the upper sixth.
Houses/prefects No competitive houses. Prefects, head boy, head of house and house prefects – appointed by the Headmaster. Various committees and councils, eg food, charities, chapel.

Religion Daily morning act of worship; Sunday morning service for whole school.
Social Debates, plays, concerts, charity fund-raising events, dances, Scottish reel evenings and some guest speakers organised with local girls' schools. Tours to France, Germany, Spain, Italy; ski trips; rugby tours eg recently to Japan; choir (eg Far East, USA); expeditions (eg to Canadian Rockies, Kenya, USA). Meals self-service. School shops sell sports equipment, books and second-hand school wear. No tobacco allowed; sixth-form club with beer bar at weekends under housemaster's control.
Discipline Pupils failing to produce homework once might expect to re-do; also detentions, suspensions or expulsion for very serious offences.
Boarding 50% have own study bedroom, 30% are in dormitories of 4+, 20% in cubicles. Houses, of approximately 60, divided by age. Resident nurse and assistant matron; doctor on call. Central dining room. Pupils can provide and cook own food in house kitchen. 1 exeat each term (3 days to 1 week). Visits to local town allowed, dependent on age.
Alumni association run by President of the Merchistonian Club, c/o the school.
Former pupils Rt Hon John MacGregor MP; Lord Craigavon; Sir James Robertson; Sir Donald Acheson (formerly Government Chief Medical Officer); Lt Gen Sir Alexander Boswell; Roger Baird John Jeffrey (ex-Scotland XV); Sir Eric Campbell Geddes.

• METHODIST COLLEGE

The Methodist College, 1 Malone Road, Belfast BT9 6BY. Tel 01232 669558, Fax 01232 666375
• Pupils 2436 • Boys 4–19 (Day/Board) • Girls 4–19 (Day/Board) • Upper sixth 268 • Termly fees £55 (Day) £1886 (Board) • HMC • Enquiries/application to the Principal

What it's like

Founded in 1868 as a co-educational school, it is urban and single-site in landscaped grounds close to Queen's University and a mile from the city centre. The principal buildings are Victorian Gothic, with suggestions of Scottish baronial and hotel de ville. There are many modern buildings including a splendid chapel. It is a superbly well-equipped establishment with very high academic attainments. Many leavers go on to degree courses, including Oxbridge. It has two large prep schools. Strong in music and drama. Very high standards in sport and games. An enormous number of clubs and societies catering for virtually every need. Big commitment to local community schemes and an outstanding record in the Duke of Edinburgh's Award Scheme.

School profile

Pupils Total age range 4–19; 2436 pupils, 2251 day (1210 boys, 1041 girls), 185 boarding (115 boys, 70 girls). Senior department 11–19, 1853 pupils (988 boys, 865 girls). Main entry ages 11 and into sixth. Approx 35% are children of former pupils.
Entrance NI children sit transfer test; school reports used for others; 11+ exam for boarding scholars. All EU pupils exempted from tuition fees. Oversubscribed. No special skills or religious requirements. Parents not expected to buy textbooks; £150 pa maximum extras. 10 pa scholarships/ bursaries, from £200–£400.
Parents 15+% are doctors, lawyers, etc; 15+% in industry or commerce; 15+% are teachers/lecturers. 60+% live within 30 miles; 5% live overseas.
Head and staff *Principal:* Wilfred Mulryne, in post for 8 years. Educated at Methodist College and Cambridge University (classics). Previously Principal at Royal School (Armagh) and Head of Classics at Methodist College. Formerly President, Ulster Heads Association and Chairman, Partnership of NI Boarding Schools and Colleges; Member of GBA Excecutive. Publications: Homer's Odyssey Book 9; The Acropolis; The Roman Forum. *Staff:* 135 full time, 25 part time. Annual turnover 3%. Average age 42.
Exam results Average size of upper fifth 230; upper sixth 270. *GCSE:* On average, 190 upper fifth gain at least grade C in 8+ subjects; 25 in 5–7; 15 in 1–4 subjects. *A-levels:* On average, 28 upper sixth pass in 4 subjects; 174 in 3; 42 in 2; 26 in 1 subject.
University and college entrance 87% of 1995 sixth-form leavers went on to a degree course (8% after a gap year); others typically go on to repeat A-levels or into employment. Of those going on to university, 8% went to Oxbridge; 12% took courses in medicine, dentistry and veterinary science, 14% in science and engineering, 6% in law,

48% in humanities and social sciences, 2% in art and design, vocational subjects eg education, pharmacy.
Curriculum GCSE and A-levels (including classical Greek). On average, 33% take science/engineering A-levels; 30% take arts and humanities; 37% take a mixture. *Vocational:* Work experience available; also RSA Stage 1 CLAIT and IT. *Computing facilities:* 18-station 480Z network, two 30-station Nimbus networks, three 15-station Nimbus networks. 16-station Nimbus network for word processing and business studies. *Europe:* French, German, Russian and Spanish offered to GCSE and A-level. Regular exchanges (France). European studies offered in sixth. Member of European Studies Project.
The arts (Pupils aged 11 and over) *Music:* Over 20% of pupils learn a musical instrument; instrumental exams can be taken. Some 10 musical groups including choir, orchestra, recorder consort, band, brass ensemble. 1 member of National Youth Orchestra. *Drama & dance*: Drama offered and GCSE may be taken. Some pupils are involved in school and other productions. School teams of public speakers have won cups in competitions over the past year. *Art:* On average, 34 take GCSE, 15 A-level. Design, photography also offered. Art facilities open to non-examination pupils.
Sport, community service and clubs (Pupils aged 11 and over) *Sport and physical activities:* Optional sports: rugby, hockey, netball, rowing, athletics, squash, badminton, cricket etc. Pupils represent Ulster and Ireland at rugby, hockey, squash, swimming, rowing, athletics, fencing, judo, golf, tennis, cricket, badminton. *Community service:* Pupils take bronze, silver and gold Duke of Edinburgh's Award. Community service optional. *Clubs and societies:* Over 30 clubs, eg current affairs, conservation, chess, history, BAYS.
Uniform School uniform worn throughout.
Prefects Prefects, head boy and girl, deputy head boy and girl – appointed by the Principal in consultation with staff. Sixth Form Council.
Religion Sunday evening service compulsory for boarders (in school chapel); brief act of worship at morning assemblies for all pupils.
Social Current affairs, debates, public speaking, Christian Union, chess and sports with other local schools. Exchanges to France; links with Romania. Pupils allowed to bring own car/bike/motorbike to school. Meals self-service. Small school tuck shops. No tobacco/alcohol allowed.
Discipline Pupils failing to produce homework once might expect reprimand; those caught smoking cannabis on the premises might expect expulsion.
Boarding 40% have own study bedroom; up to 18% share with 1 or 2 others; remainder (mostly boys) in dormitories of 6+. Single-sex houses, of 11–30, divided by age. Resident qualified medical staff. Central dining room. Pupils can provide and cook their own food (senior girls at supper, boys in specified rooms). 2 weekend exeats each term. Visits to local town allowed.
Alumni association Old Boys' Association, Mr D Wilson, 22 Netherleigh Park, Belfast BT4 3GR. Old Girls' Association, Mrs R Gibson, 9 Casaeldona Crescent, Belfast, BT6 9RE.
Former pupils Barry Douglas (winner of Tchaikovsky Piano Competition); James Ellis (actor); Dr Robin Eames (present Primate of All Ireland); George Hamilton (sports commentator); Jack Siggins (British Lions Manager); Roger Young (British Lion); Prof Ernest Walton (winner of Nobel Prize 1951); Sir Ewart Bell (ex-head NI Civil Service); Field Marshal Sir John Dill (CIGS World War II); Edith Major (Mistress of Girton).

• MICHAEL HALL

Michael Hall Steiner School, Kidbrooke Park, Forest Row, East Sussex RH18 5JB. Tel 01342 822275

• Pupils 620 • Boys 3–18 (Day/Board/Weekly) • Girls 3–18 (Day/Board/Weekly) • Upper sixth 30 • Termly fees £745–£1225 (Day) £2675 (Board) £2525 (Weekly) • Steiner • Enquiries/application to the Secretary for Admissions

What it's like

Founded in 1925, this is the oldest, biggest and most established of the Steiner schools in the UK. It has a fine rural site in its own parkland on the edge of Ashdown Forest and a mile from the village centre of Forest Row. It offers a very broad education to boys and girls 3–18, which is based on the educational philosophy of Rudolf Steiner. The curriculum embodies cultural studies, sciences, general arts and humanities, crafts, music and movement and foreign languages. Art, music and drama are very important elements in the school life. A remedial dept and EFL is available. Steiner's fascinating educational theories, philosophy and methods need to be looked at in detail by prospective parents. The teaching is of a high standard. A fair range of sports, games and extra-curricular activities is offered.

School profile

Pupils Total age range 3–18; 620 pupils, 560 day (270 boys, 290 girls), 60 boarding (30 boys, 30 girls). Senior department 14–18, 240 pupils (118 boys, 122 girls). Open entry. Approx 10% are children of former pupils. *State school entry:* Less than 5% senior intake and to sixth.

Entrance Knowledge of French and/or German an advantage; no particular religious requirements. Parents expected to pay for textbooks, outings, meals, laboratory materials, etc; maximum extras, £275. Means-tested bursaries available (after first year of school).

Parents 60 + % live within 30 miles; up to 10% live overseas.

Head and staff *Chairman of the College of Teachers*: Elected biannually. *Staff:* 44 full time, 4 part time. Annual turnover 10%. Average age 36.

Exam results On average, 40 pupils in upper fifth, 30 in upper sixth. *GCSE:* On average, 20 upper fifth gain at least grade C in 5–7 subjects; and 18 in 1–4 subjects. *A-levels:* 44% upper sixth pass in 3 subjects; 32% in 2; and 24% in 1 subject.

University and college entrance 58% of 1995 sixth-form leavers went on to a degree course; others typically go on to art, drama courses, non-degree courses or straight into careers. Of those going on to university, 9% went to Oxbridge; 14% took courses in science and engineering, 64% in humanities and social sciences, 7% in art and design, 14% in drama, music.

Curriculum GCSE and A-levels. 20 subjects offered to GCSE and A-level (including integrated science; general studies course but not A-level). 8% take science A-levels; 52% arts/humanities; 40% both. *Vocational:* Work experience available; also City and Guilds foundation programme, GNVQ. *Computing facilities:* Apple Mackintosh laboratory with 8 computers. *Special provision:* Special EFL programme; remedial one-to-one coaching. *Europe:* French and German (from age 6) offered at GCSE and A-level. Regular exchanges (France, Germany and other countries).

The arts (Pupils aged 11 and over) *Music:* 40% of pupils learn a musical instrument; instrumental exams can be taken. Some 6 + musical groups including orchestras, choirs, several chamber ensembles. *Drama & dance*: Both offered. Majority of pupils are involved in school productions (several annually) and all in house/other productions. *Art:* On average, 19 take GCSE, 5 A-level. Design, pottery also offered. Stage design by large number of non-exam pupils, also costume design, practical landscaping and individual arts projects.

Sport, community service and clubs (Pupils aged 11 and over) *Sport and physical activities:* Compulsory sports depending on age (and optional in sixth): archery, fencing, basketball, volleyball, gymnastics, orienteering, cross-country, athletics, softball, tennis, cricket, climbing, canoeing, sailing. County basketball league, cross-country and tennis player. *Clubs and societies:* Up to 10 clubs, eg various sports, drama, photography.

Uniform School uniform not worn.

Houses/prefects No competitive houses; no prefects or head boy/girl.

Religion Attendance at non-denominational Sunday service in school is encouraged.

Social Some musical productions with other local schools. Art history trip to Italy, and opportunities for exchanges with sister schools (over 600 worldwide). Pupils allowed to bring own bike/motorbike to school. Lunch self-service. No tobacco/alcohol allowed.

Boarding One hostel of 30 pupils; most rooms are shared with a few others; also boarding in homes of families with children at the school. Exeats by arrangement. Visits to local town allowed.

Alumni association c/o the school.

Former pupils Martyn Boysens (mountaineer); Oliver Tobias (actor); Sean Yates (international cyclist); Bella Freud (Young Designer of the Year); Estella Freud (actress, writer).

• MICKLEFIELD WADHURST

Micklefield Wadhurst, Mayfield Lane, Wadhurst, East Sussex TN5 6JA. Tel 01892 783193, Fax 01892 783638

• Pupils 170 • Boys 10–18 (Ballet pupils only) • Girls 10–18 (Day/Board/Weekly) • Upper sixth 22 • Termly fees £2140 (Day) £3370 (Board) 3340 (Weekly) • Enquiries/application to the Registrar

What it's like

Micklefield Wadhurst is the result of an amalgamation in 1994 of two established girls' schools: Micklefield School, previously at Seaford on the south coast, and Wadhurst College. An integral part of the school is the Legat School of Classical Ballet, which offers an academic programme combined with a highly specialised training for students aiming for a professional dance career. Facilities include sports hall, sixth-form centre, ballet studios, heated indoor swimming pool. Some co-educational sixth-form classes with Mayfield College. Strong music, drama, dance and art departments. Sport is strong for a school this size, particularly lacrosse.

School profile

Pupils Age range 10–18, 170 pupils 92 day (3 boys, 89 girls), 78 boarding (3 boys, 75 girls). Main entry ages 10, 11, 12, 13 and into sixth-form (boys accepted only as ballet pupils). *State school entry:* 30% main senior intake plus 10% to sixth.

Entrance Common Entrance and own exam used; ballet audition for dance pupils. Scholarships (including for music, science, ballet, drama, art, sport); bursaries (for service children and some for daughters of clergy or missionaries).

Head and staff *Headmaster:* Eric Reynolds, in post since the school's foundation in 1994. Educated at St Alban's Boys' Grammar and Swansea University (French and Italian). Previously Head of Micklefield School, Deputy Head of Wadhurst College, Principal of St Giles College, Eastbourne and Housemaster at Frensham Heights,

Exam results On average, 36 pupils in upper fifth, 22 in upper sixth. *GCSE:* Average pupil gained grade C or above in 5+ subjects. *A-levels:* Average pupil passed in 1.8 subjects. Average UCAS points 11.4.

University and college entrance 60% of 1995 sixth-form leavers went on to a degree course; others typically go on to non-degree courses, art, music or drama colleges.

Curriculum GCSE and A levels. 18 subjects offered (no A-level general studies). 25% take science A-levels; 25% arts/humanities, 50% both. Some sixth-form classes taught in association with Mayfield College. *Vocational:* City & Guilds levels 1 & 2 in cookery available, also RSA keyboarding/word processing; also childcare qualifications. Work experience available. *Computing facilities:* Computer laboratory with 12 RKM Nimbus and computers in departments. *Special provision:* Special needs teacher, specialist EFL teacher. *Europe:* French and German offered to GCSE and A-level; Spanish to GCSE. Regular exchanges (France).

The arts *Music:* Over 30% of pupils learn a musical instrument; instrumental exams can be taken. Musical groups include orchestra, school choir, chamber choir. Choir has featured on Radio Sussex and Classic FM. *Drama & dance*: Both offered. GCSE and A-level drama, LAMDA, RAD ballet exams may be taken. All pupils are involved in school and house/other productions. 1 pupil with major part in West End show, Crazy for You. *Art:* On average, 10 take GCSE, 6 A-level. Design, textiles also offered. Exhibitions locally.

Sport, community service and clubs *Sport and physical activities:* Compulsory sports: lacrosse, netball, gym, swimming, tennis, rounders in lower school. Optional: riding, sailing, volleyball, basketball, trampolining. Sixth form only: squash. GCSE/A-level sport may be taken. Representatives in county lacrosse, tennis and netball teams. *Community service:* Pupils can take Duke of Edinburgh's Award. *Clubs and societies:* Several regular activities including drama, various sports, guides, pottery, computers.

Uniform Uniform worn, except in the sixth.

Houses/prefects Competitive houses. Prefects, head girl, head of house and house prefects appointed by Headteachers. School Council.

Religion Attendance at religious worship compulsory.

Social Other schools occasionally invited to sixth-form suppers with guest speaker. Exchanges to co-ed school in Paris. Pupils allowed to bring own bike/car. Meals self-service. School shop. No alcohol/tobacco allowed.

Discipline Pupils failing to produce homework once might expect an order mark; those caught smoking cannabis on the premises might expect suspension or expulsion.

• MILL HILL

Mill Hill School, The Ridgeway, London NW7 1QS. Tel 0181 959 1176, Fax 0181 201 0663
• Pupils 530 • Boys 13–18 (Day/Board) • Girls 16–18 (Day/Board) • Upper sixth 94 • Termly fees £2510 (Day) £3880 (Board/Weekly) • HMC • Enquiries/application to the Director of Admissions

What it's like

Founded in 1807 by a group of non-conformist Christian ministers and City merchants. In 1827 it moved to the buildings which form the central part of the main school. Palatial, neo-classical, magnificently designed within and without, they lie in 120 acres of wooded parkland in the green belt 10 miles from the middle of London. There has been much development in recent years and facilities and accommodation are first-class. Belmont, the junior school, is a few hundred metres away and a pre-prep school, Grimsdell, opened in 1995 so education is provided from 3–18. A boys' school until 1975, when girls were admitted to the sixth-form, it is set to become completely co-educational in 1997 with the admission of girls at age 13. A well-run school with long-established high standards, it regards hard work, self-criticism, enthusiasm and loyalty as paramount virtues. Chapel services are compulsory for all. Academic results are good and most sixth-form leavers go on to universities, including Oxbridge. There is a large business studies centre, pioneering business and IT. Strong in music, drama and art. Very broad range of games and sports (the standards are high). Substantial commitment to local community schemes. CCF for 14–16 age group and appreciable success in the Duke of Edinburgh's Award Scheme.

School profile

Pupils Age range 13–18; 530 pupils, 335 day (320 boys, 15 girls), 195 boarding (175 boys, 20 girls). Main entry ages 13 (boys, and girls from 1997) and into the sixth (boys and girls). Approx 5% are children of former pupils. Own junior school, Belmont, provides 40% of intake. *State school entry:* 12% main intake, plus 25% to sixth.
Entrance Common Entrance and own entrance exam used. No special skills or religious requirements (but all are expected to attend chapel services). Parents not expected to buy textbooks; £50 average extras. 15 pa assisted places. 12 pa scholarships (musical and academic) up to half fees. 15% fees reduction for service children; variable number of other bursaries.
Parents 30% in industry or commerce. 60% live within 30 miles; 10+% live overseas.
Head and staff *Headmaster:* William R Winfield, appointed 1996. Educated at William Ellis School, Highgate, at the Royal Academy of Music and Cambridge University (modern and medieval languages). Previously Deputy Headmaster, Director of Studies and Head of Modern Languages at Mill Hill. Publications: CILT languages articles; school's Section Bilingue; various articles in journals. Member of HMC and Modern Languages working parties; GCSE and A-level examiner. *Staff:* 55 full time, 15 part time. Annual turnover 4%. Average age 35.
Exam results In 1995, 106 pupils in fifth form, 94 in upper sixth. *GCSE:* In 1995, 90% fifth form gained at least grade C in 8+ subjects. *A-levels:* 10% upper sixth passed in 4+ subjects; 72% in 3; 14% in 2; and 5% in 1 subject. Average UCAS points 19.6.
University and college entrance 95% of 1995 sixth-form leavers went on to a degree course; others typically go on to non-degree courses, art or music colleges or into careers. Of those going on to university, 5% went to Oxbridge; 2% took courses in medicine, dentistry and veterinary science, 22% in science and engineering, 3% in law, 25% in humanities and social sciences, 19% in business and finance.
Curriculum GCSE and A-levels. 16 GCSE subjects, 21 at A-level offered (including design technology GCSE/A-level, business studies with IT A-level; no A-level general studies). 45% take science A-levels; 55% arts/humanities. *Vocational:* Work experience available. *Computing facilities:* 50 Apple Macintosh machines networked in three computer rooms. *Special provision:* Extra English and EFL for boys with overseas educational background. *Europe:* French, Spanish and German offered at GCSE and A-level; also French and German AS-level. Regular exchanges (France, Germany and Spain). Pupils from all over Europe in school.
The arts *Music:* Up to 25% of pupils learn a musical instrument; instrumental exams can be taken. Some 10 musical groups including choirs, orchestras, jazz, wind band, chamber ensembles. *Drama & dance*: Drama offered and GCSE may be taken. Majority

of pupils are involved in school and house/other productions. *Art:* On average, 15 take GCSE, 6 A-level. Design, pottery also offered.
Sport, community service and clubs *Sport and physical activities:* Compulsory sports: rugby, hockey, cricket, athletics, cross-country. Optional: badminton, basketball, croquet, fencing, fives, golf, karate, riding, shooting, scuba, squash, swimming, table tennis, volleyball. *Community service:* Pupils take bronze, silver and gold Duke of Edinburgh's Award. CCF compulsory for 2 years at age 14, community service optional for 4. *Clubs and societies:* Up to 30 clubs, eg computing, debating, military modelling, video filming.
Uniform School uniform worn, modified in the sixth.
Houses/prefects Competitive houses. Prefects, head boy/girl, head of house and house prefects – appointed by the Headmaster and housemasters, taking into account votes from upper sixth. School Council.
Religion Chapel compulsory for all (about once a week).
Social Extensive use of field study centre at Dent in Cumbria. Exchanges with France, Germany and Spain; involves about 100 boys a year. Pupils allowed to bring own car/bike to school. Meals self-service. School shop. No tobacco allowed. Alcohol on occasion.
Discipline Pupils failing to produce homework once might expect a warning; any pupils involved with drugs must expect to be expelled.
Boarding All upper sixth have own study bedroom, most lower sixth and fifth form share with one other; juniors in study bedrooms for 2–6 boys. Houses, of approximately 50, same as competitive houses; some single-sex, some mixed. Resident SRN, doctor visits daily. Central dining room. Pupils can provide and cook own snacks. Exeats most weekends (weekly boarding allowed). Visits to local town allowed.
Alumni association is run by Mrs Janet Scott, c/o the school.
Former pupils Dennis Thatcher; Francis Crick (Nobel prize – structure of DNA); Simon Jenkins; Richard Dimbleby; Lord Salmon of Sandwich; Sir Michael Bishop.

• MILLFIELD

Millfield School, Street, Somerset BA16 0YD. Tel 01458 442291, Fax 01458 447276

• Pupils 1258 • Boys 13–18 (Day/Board) • Girls 13–18 (Day/Board) • Upper sixth 242 • Termly fees £2940 (Day) £4595 (Board) • HMC • Enquiries/application to Tutor for Admissions

What it's like

Founded in 1935 by R J O Meyer as a boys' school, girls were admitted in 1947 and it is now fully co-educational. It has a fine campus of 67 acres, plus 97 acres of playing fields. It is in beautiful countryside, with 26 boarding houses in the town of Street and surrounding villages. The pre-prep and junior school are in nearby Glastonbury. Large, diverse and complex, Millfield is a well-run school which enjoys a very high staff:pupil ratio (about 1:7), and this is one of its many strengths. Since 1970 a massive building programme has provided superb facilities. It caters for virtually every need and displays energy, organisation and purposefulness in every activity. The vast majority of sixth-formers go on to degree courses each year, including to Oxbridge. A very wide range of languages offered and includes Japanese, Russian, Dutch, modern Greek and Portuguese. Over 40 sports and games are available and the school has excelled in many. It produces an average of 25 international representatives each year in 19 different sports. Since 1960 it has produced over 20 Olympic competitors. Music is strong. The school turns itself into an activity holiday centre during the summer.

School profile

Pupils Age range 13–18; 1258 pupils, 310 day (174 boys, 136 girls), 948 boarding (546 boys, 402 girls). Main entry ages 13 and into sixth. Approx 5% are children of former pupils. Own junior school, Edgarley Hall (tel 01458 832446) provides approx 50% of intake. *State school entry:* 10% main intake, plus 25% to sixth.
Entrance Common Entrance and own entrance exam used. Good all-round academic and sporting abilities looked for; no special religious requirements. Parents not expected to buy textbooks; stabling of horses etc extra. 50 pa scholarships/bursaries, 5%–50% of fees; possibility of further remission where need is established.

Parents 15+% are doctors, lawyers, etc; 65+% in industry or commerce. 30+% live within 30 miles; 15+% live overseas.

Head and staff *Headmaster:* Christopher Martin, 6 years in post. Educated at Westminster and St Andrews (modern languages). Previously Headmaster at Bristol Cathedral School. Also National Representative on HMC Committee; previously Chairman, Choir Schools' Association and Chairman HMC/SHA Working Party on Teacher Supply. *Staff:* 165 full time. Annual turnover 11%. Average age 35.

Exam results In 1995, 246 pupils in upper fifth, 242 in upper sixth. *GCSE:* In 1995, 142 upper fifth gained at least grade C in 8+ subjects; 51 in 5–7 subjects. *A-levels:* 149 upper sixth passed in 4+ subjects; 49 in 3; 29 in 2; and 10 in 1 subject. Average UCAS points gained 18.9 (including general studies, 22.3).

University and college entrance 92% of 1995 sixth-form leavers went on to a degree course; others typically go on to non-degree courses eg cordon bleu, secretarial, art or drama or straight into careers. Of those going on to university, 11% went to Oxbridge; 8% took courses in medicine, dentistry and veterinary science, 43% in science and engineering, 35% in humanities and social sciences, 8% in art and design, 6% in drama and music.

Curriculum GCSE, A-levels and GNVQ. Subjects include Chinese, Japanese and A-level general studies. 30% take science A-levels; 40% arts/humanities; 30% both. *Vocational:* Work experience available; also GNVQ in business studies and in art & design; RSA stages 1–3 typing and word processing. *Computing facilities:* Computer centre with classroom and office layout. *Special provision:* Language development unit for dyslexics; FE department for English as a second language. *Europe:* French, German and Italian offered at GCSE, AS and A-level. Dutch, Greek and Portuguese at GCSE; Spanish at GCSE and A-level. Regular exchanges (France, Germany and Spain). Study scholarships for languages other than French.

The arts *Music:* Over 30% of pupils learn a musical instrument; instrumental exams can be taken. Some 15 musical groups including orchestras, brass band, string quartets, wind octet, symphonic wind band, jazz band, choirs, early music group. Members of National Youth Orchestra past 2 years. *Drama & dance*: Both offered. GCSE and A-level drama, ESB, LAMDA exams may be taken. Some pupils are involved in school and majority in house/other productions. Recent productions include Candide, Oedipus, Guys and Dolls. *Art:* On average, 60 take GCSE, 35 A-level. Design, pottery, textiles, photography also offered.

Sport, community service and clubs *Sport and physical activities:* Games compulsory from options: soccer, rugby, hockey, cricket, athletics, tennis (boys); rounders, hockey, netball, athletics, tennis (girls). Sixth form only: 40 choices. On average 25 international representatives a year and countless county representatives. *Community service:* Pupils take bronze, silver and gold Duke of Edinburgh's Award. Community service optional for 1 year at age 16. Annual Mencap day (school open to 600 Mencap members guided and coached by pupils). *Clubs and societies:* Over 30 clubs, eg bridge, conservation, school newspaper, photography, video workshop, Young Enterprise.

Uniform Suits, sports jackets for boys; school skirt/trousers and jumper for junior girls.

Houses/prefects Competitive houses. Prefects, head boy/girl, head of house and house prefects – appointed by prefect committee and staff. School Council.

Religion Worship is compulsory on special occasions eg carol service, start of term multi-faith service plus regular services for Catholics, Jews, Muslims, etc.

Social No organised local events. German/French exchange, games tours (eg Germany, Hong Kong, Zimbabwe); cultural tours to eg China, Russia; geography field trip to Malaysia (1992). Pupils allowed to bring own bike/horse to school. Meals self-service. School shop. No tobacco/alcohol allowed.

Discipline Pupils failing to produce homework once might expect a warning and a deadline; those caught smoking cannabis on the premises can expect immediate expulsion.

Boarding Few seniors have own study bedroom, most share double study bedrooms; juniors in dormitories of 3+. Single-sex houses, 10–50 (most small), same as competitive houses. Resident qualified nurse. Central dining room. 3 weekend exeats each term. Visits to the local town allowed.

Alumni association is run by Mr J H Davies, The Millfield Society, c/o the school.

Former pupils Sir John L Standing (actor); John Sargeant (BBC parliamentary correspondent); Charles Burton (explorer: circumnavigated world via North and South Poles); Gareth Edwards (international rugby); Duncan Goodhew and Mary Rand (Olympic gold medallists); Jeremy Thomas (film producer, The Last Emperor); Michael Ridpath (novelist, Free To Trade).

• MILTON ABBEY

Milton Abbey School, Blandford, Dorset DT11 0BZ. Tel 01258 880484, Fax 01258 881194

• Pupils 203 • Boys 13–18 (Day/Board) • Girls None • Upper sixth 43 • Termly fees £2582 (Day) £3686 (Board) • SHMIS • Enquiries/application to the Headmaster

What it's like

Founded in 1954, it has an exceptionally beautiful site in a large area of parkland near Blandford. The main building is a large 18th-century country house which incorporates some of the buildings of the original Benedictine monastery of the Middle Ages. The magnificent medieval abbey church is the outstanding architectural feature. There are many modern additions and extensions and the accommodation and facilities are first-rate. It is a C of E school and the abbey church is the co-ordinating focus of the life of the community and a considerable influence on it. Worship and religious instruction are an important part of the general curriculum. Self-discipline, courtesy, self-respect and a sense of responsibility are deemed to be of prime importance in a pupil's development. A sound general education is provided and a large staff permits a staff:pupil ratio of about 1:7. Drama is strong; music and art flourish. Natural history has a particularly keen following. The CCF is very strong and there are close links with service units in the region. A good range of sports and games and outdoor pursuits (sailing is particularly strong). The school's local community services are long established.

School profile

Pupils Age range 13–18; 203 boys (12 day, 191 boarding). Main entry ages 13 and into sixth. Approx 3% are children of former pupils. Pupils come from a large number of prep schools and a wide geographical range. *State school entry:* 3% main intake, plus 6% to sixth.

Entrance Common Entrance exam used. No special skills or religious requirements. Parents expected to buy textbooks; £250 average extras. 8 pa scholarships/bursaries (academic, all-round, music, art), 25%–50% of fees.

Parents 30+% live within 30 miles; up to 15% live overseas.

Head and staff *Headmaster:* W J Hughes-D'Aeth, in post since 1995. Educated at Haileybury and universities of Liverpool (geography) and Cambridge (education). Previously Housemaster at Rugby and 1 year teaching in Australia. *Staff:* 30 full time, 7 part time. Annual turnover 3%. Average age 40.

Exam results In 1995, 39 pupils in upper fifth, 43 in upper sixth. *GCSE:* In 1995, 14 upper fifth gained at least grade C in 8+ subjects; 15 in 5–7 subjects. *A-levels:* 11 upper sixth passed in 4+ subjects; 9 in 3; 11 in 2; and 6 in 1 subject. Average UCAS points 12.4.

University and college entrance 56% of 1995 sixth-form leavers went on to a degree course (37% after a gap year); others typically go on to HND, other diploma or foundation courses, repeat A-levels or straight into employment. Of those going on to university, 3% took courses in medicine, dentistry and veterinary science, 25% in science and engineering, 66% in humanities and social sciences, 6% in art and design.

Curriculum GCSE, AS and A-levels. 14 GCSE subjects offered: 18 at AS and A-level. 24% took science A-levels; 60% arts/humanities; 17% both. *Vocational:* Work experience available. *Computing facilities:* Main centre with modern networked computers. Separate facilities in individual departments eg CAD, science dept. *Special provision:* Remedial English and mathematics; EFL. *Europe:* French and Spanish offered at GCSE and A-level; also French AS-level and French for business studies at AO-level for sixth-form. Regular exchanges (France) and sixth-form French pupils visit Paris. MEP visits occasionally. German and Spanish pupils regularly in school.

The arts *Music:* Over 25% of pupils learn a musical instrument; instrumental exams can be taken. Some 7+ musical groups including brass, woodwind ensembles, plainsong choir, chamber choir. *Drama & dance*: Drama offered. GCSE drama, A-level theatre

studies may be taken. Some pupils are involved in school productions and majority in house/other productions. 2 pupils accepted into National Youth Theatre. *Art:* On average, 10 take GCSE, 5 A-level. Design, pottery, photography also offered.
Sport, community service and clubs *Sport and physical activities:* Compulsory: rugby, hockey/cross-country, cricket/tennis/athletics/sailing. Optional: canoeing, golf, squash, shooting, swimming, fencing, basketball. RYA exams may be taken. County representatives at rugby, hockey, cricket, cross-country, athletics; members of British Pony Club polo team. *Community service:* Pupils take bronze, silver and gold Duke of Edinburgh's Award; average of 100 boys involved; expeditions in Britain, France, Germany. CCF or community service compulsory for 2 years at age 14 (140 boys involved). *Clubs and societies:* Up to 30 clubs, eg motor engineering, chess, computing, clay-pigeon shooting, debating, electronics, modelling, music, printing, sub-aqua.
Uniform School uniform worn throughout.
Houses/prefects Competitive houses. Prefects, head boy, head of house and house prefects – appointed by the Headmaster.
Religion Religious worship compulsory
Social Theatrical productions and dances with other local schools. Modern languages trips abroad, Himalayan adventures. Meals self-service. School shop. No tobacco allowed; alcohol allowed in sixth-form club.
Discipline Pupils failing to produce homework once might expect warning and repeat work; those caught smoking cannabis on the premises must expect expulsion.
Boarding 22% have own study bedroom, 50% share with up to 3 others; 18% are in dormitories of 6+. Houses, of approximately 45, same as competitive houses. Resident qualified nurse. Central dining room. 2 weekend exeats per term plus half-term. Visits to local town allowed at weekends.
Alumni association run by A P Nicholson, c/o the school.
Former pupils Alastair Boyd (who parachuted off the Empire State Building); Anthony Geffen (BBC producer).

• MOIRA HOUSE

Moira House School, Upper Carlisle Road, Eastbourne, East Sussex BN20 7TE. Tel 01323 644144, Fax 01323 649720

• Pupils 350 • Boys None • Girls 3–18 (Day/Board/Weekly) • Upper sixth 35 • Termly fees £2300 (Day) £3570 (Board/Weekly) • GSA, BSA • Enquiries/application to the Headmaster

What it's like

Founded in 1875, situated near Beachy Head with grounds and gardens opening on to the Downs. The buildings are well-designed and comfortable and provide good accommodation and facilities. Religious education and worship are compulsory. Academic standards are high and results are good and almost all sixth-formers go on to degree courses. It enjoys a high staff:pupil ratio of about 1:8. The music and drama departments are flourishing and the school particularly prides itself on its very strong careers counselling service. Good sports and games, plus an enormous range of activities. Some commitment to local community schemes.

School profile

Pupils Total age range 3–18; 350 girls (240 day, 110 boarding). Senior department 11–18, 280 girls. Main entry ages 3–13 and into sixth. Approx 5% are children of former pupils. A significant proportion of the senior intake comes from the junior school and from both St Andrew's and St Bede's prep schools in Eastbourne. *State school entry:* 10% senior intakes, plus 2% to sixth.
Entrance Common Entrance and own exam used. No special skills or religious requirements. Parents not expected to buy textbooks; maximum extras approx £100. 15 pa scholarships/bursaries, 50%–75% of fees.
Parents 70+% live within 30 miles; 30+% live overseas.
Head and staff *Headmaster:* Adrian Underwood, in post for 21 years. Educated at Dulwich College and at the universities of Kent and Dalhousie, Nova Scotia (English). Previously Housemaster and Senior English Master at Kingham Hill. Also chairman of BSA and member of the executive of the English Speaking Union Scholarship Scheme; ran

in 2 London marathons. *Staff:* 43 full time, 34 part time. Annual turnover 7%. Average age 35.
Exam results In 1995, 42 pupils in upper fifth, 34 in upper sixth. *GCSE:* In 1995, 24 upper fifth gained at least grade C in 8+ subjects; 18 in 5–7 subjects. *A-levels:* 27 upper sixth passed in 3 subjects; 5 in 2 subjects. Average UCAS points 19.1.
University and college entrance All 1995 sixth-form leavers went on to a degree course (15% after a gap year), 4% to Oxbridge; 15% took courses in medicine, dentistry and veterinary science, 35% in science and engineering, 10% in law, 30% in humanities and social sciences, 5% in art and design, 5% in other vocational subjects.
Curriculum GCSE, AS and A-levels. 20 GCSE and A-level subjects offered; 15 at AS-level (no A-level general studies). 50% take science A-levels; 40% arts/humanities; 10% both. *Vocational:* Work experience available. *Computing facilities:* Olivetti computer room (20 units plus CD- Rom). *Special provision:* Special tutoring for dyslexic pupils and EFL. *Europe:* French, German and Spanish offered at GCSE, AS and A-level. Regular exchanges (France, Germany and Spain).
The arts (Pupils aged 11 and over) *Music:* Over 50% of pupils learn a musical instrument; instrumental exams can be taken. Some 6 musical groups including orchestra, chamber groups, woodwind. Many successes in Eastbourne Festival. *Drama & dance*: Both offered. GCSE, AS and A-level drama and LAMDA exams may be taken. Majority of pupils are involved in school and house/other productions. Many successes in Eastbourne Festival. *Art:* On average, 15 take GCSE, 3 A-level. Design also offered.
Sport, community service and clubs (Pupils aged 11 and over) *Sport and physical activities:* Compulsory sports: hockey, netball, swimming, athletics, gymnastics, tennis. Optional: cricket, squash, badminton, golf, sailing, windsurfing, orienteering, riding. BAGA, RLSS, RYA exams may be taken. Biennial hockey tour to West Indies and US. *Community service:* Pupils take bronze, silver and gold Duke of Edinburgh's Award. Community service optional. *Clubs and societies:* Over 30 clubs, eg sports clubs, drama, tapestry/origami, computing, Young Enterprise.
Uniform School uniform worn except the sixth.
Houses/prefects Competitive houses. Prefects, 2 head girls, house councils – elected by girls and staff.
Religion Morning prayers and Sunday church compulsory; confirmation, Christian Unions.
Social Public speaking, Eastbourne Festival with other local schools. Organised trips abroad. Pupils allowed to bring own car/bike to school. Some meals formal, some self-service. School shop. No tobacco/alcohol allowed.
Discipline Pupils failing to produce homework once will repeat their work; those caught with cannabis on the premises will be expelled.
Boarding 50% have own study bedroom, 50% share with others. Houses of approximately 55, divided by age. Resident RGNs. Central dining room. Sixth-form pupils can provide and cook their own food. 2 weekend and half-term exeats. Visits to local town allowed at weekends.
Former pupils Rumer Godden (novelist); Prunella Scales (actress); Joy Finzi (artist).

• MONKTON COMBE

Monkton Combe School, Monkton Combe, Bath, Avon BA2 7HG. Tel 01225 721102, Fax 01225 721181

• Pupils 324 • Boys 11–18 (Day/Board) • Girls 11–18 (Day/Board) • Upper sixth 65 • Termly fees £2195–£2695 (Day) £3215–£3895 (Board) • HMC • Enquiries/application to the Head Master

What it's like

Founded in 1868, and merged with Clarendon School, Bedford, in 1992. It lies in a very attractive village 3 miles from Bath, overlooking the Avon valley. The buildings are in Cotswold stone and there have been many modern and well-equipped extensions. Extensive playing fields adjoin the school. Active Christian teaching, with both chapel and a range of informal activities. Academic standards are high and results are good. There is a staff:pupil ratio of about 1:9. The majority of pupils go on to degree courses each year. It is strong in music, drama, art and computing. A good record in sports and games with a large number of representatives at county level. The CCF contingent is large and active. There are numerous clubs and societies and a community service group.

School profile

Pupils Age range 11–18; 324 pupils, 54 day (42 boys, 12 girls), 270 boarding (179 boys, 91 girls). Main entry ages 11, 13 and into sixth. Approx 6% are children of former pupils. Own junior school provides more than 25% of intake. *State school entry:* 5% main intake, plus 40% to sixth.

Entrance Common Entrance and own entrance exam used. No religious requirements but must be willing to attend chapel. Parents expected to buy textbooks which can be sold back after use; £150 maximum extras. 10 pa assisted places. 12 pa scholarships, 10%–50% fees (can be increased by bursaries in cases of need). 6–8 pa bursaries for children of clergy and missionaries, up to one-third fees.

Parents 15+% in the armed services. 20+% live within 30 miles; 15+% live overseas.

Head and staff *Headmaster:* Michael Cuthbertson, 5 years in post. Educated at Merchant Taylors' and Cambridge (history, education). Previously Director of Sixth Form Studies and Head of History at Radley and Head of History at Bradfield. Also Governor, St Piran's School, Maidenhead, and Castle Court School, Dorset; formerly lay member, Bath and Wells Diocesan Board of Education; member, Admiralty Interview Board. *Staff:* 35 full time, 8 part time. Annual turnover 8%. Average age 35.

Exam results In 1995, 59 pupils in upper fifth, 65 in upper sixth. *GCSE:* In 1995, 63% of upper fifth gained at least grade C in 8+ subjects; 19% in 5–7 subjects. *A-levels:* Average UCAS points 19.6.

University and college entrance 75% of 1995 sixth-form leavers went on to a degree course; others typically go on to non-degree courses or straight into careers eg banking. Of those going on to university, 5% went to Oxbridge; 32% took courses in science and engineering, 52% in humanities and social sciences, 16% in vocational subjects.

Curriculum GCSE and A-levels. 20 subjects offered. *Vocational:* Work experience available. *Computing facilities:* Industry-standard PCs in IT centre, others in departments; computer aided design in CDT department. *Special provision:* Specialist EFL teacher; teacher from Bath Dyslexic Institute. *Europe:* French (compulsory for a year) and German offered to GCSE, AS and A-level. Regular exchanges to France and Germany. Occasional European pupils in school.

The arts *Music:* 40% of pupils learn a musical instrument or singing; instrumental exams can be taken. Musical groups include choir, choral society, big band, orchestra, several ensembles. Big band gives many concerts outside school and toured France summer 1996. *Drama & dance*: Drama offered. GCSE and Guildhall exams may be taken. Many pupils are involved in school and house plays and musicals. *Art:* On average, 25 take GCSE, 15 A-level. Design, printmaking, photography also offered. Pupil in top 6 bird illustrators of the year.

Sport, community service and clubs *Sport and physical activities:* Major games are rugby, hockey, cricket, tennis, netball, rowing. Minor sports: volleyball, aerobics, swimming, squash, judo, fencing, athletics, cross-country, basketball. District and county representation at hockey, rugby, cricket. *Community service:* Pupils take silver and gold Duke of Edinburgh's Award. All encouraged to join CCF at age 14. Community service optional. Annual visit to Julian House in Bath to help with homeless. *Clubs and societies:* Over 30 clubs, eg chess, Christian Union, climbing, judo, bridge, dance, basketball.

Uniform School uniform worn, modified in the sixth.

Houses/prefects Competitive houses. Prefects: senior prefect, heads of house and house prefects – appointed by the Head Master or houseparent after consultation with staff and pupils. All new pupils help with general chores.

Religion Attendance at chapel is compulsory and Christian activities are encouraged. Active voluntary Christian Union.

Social Sponsored Activity Day in support of a local or national charity. Ski trip abroad each year. Pupils allowed to bring own bike to school. Meals self-service. School shop. No tobacco/alcohol allowed.

Discipline Report card system or detention for pupils failing to produce work. Estate work for most other offences. Expulsion for any offence involving drugs or serious sexual misconduct.

Boarding 15% have own study bedroom, 20% share with one; 40% in dormitories of 6+. Single-sex houses of 40–50, same as competitive houses (separate junior house for 11–12 year olds). 2 qualified nurses. Central dining room. Pupils can provide and cook own food. 3 Saturday night exeats each term, and half-term. Visits to local town allowed once a week.
Alumni association is run by John Gedge, 17 Partis Way, Bath BA1 3QG.
Former pupils Bernard Cornwell; Richard Stilgoe; Martin Adeney; a number of bishops including Rt Rev G Leonard (former Bishop of London) and Rt Rev M A P Wood (former Bishop of Norwich); Sir Timothy Lankester; Air Chief Marshall Sir Michael Stear; Major-General Sir Philip Ward.

• MONMOUTH

Monmouth School, Monmouth, Gwent NP5 3XP. Tel 01600 713143, Fax 01600 772701
• Pupils 569 • Boys 11–18 (Day/Board/Weekly) • Girls None • Upper sixth 80 • Termly fees £1636 (Day) £2725 (Board/Weekly) • HMC • Enquiries/application to the Headmaster

What it's like

Founded in 1614, it is on a single site on the edge of the town by the Wye; a very fine position. The present buildings, in the collegiate style, date from 1865 and there has been much modernisation in the last twenty years. A distinguished and well-run school, with a high reputation locally and further afield. It shares with its sister school, Haberdashers' Monmouth School for Girls, the benefits of strong links with the Haberdashers' Company and provides excellent facilities and a first-rate education on terms that few schools can match. Closely integrated with the historic town of Monmouth, there is a strong local flavour with a third of the pupils coming from Monmouth or the neighbouring villages. Academic results are very good and most leavers go on to degree courses, many to Oxbridge. Very strong in music and also in drama and art. Also very strong in sports and games (especially rugby, cricket and rowing); a large number of county and international representatives. Notable emphasis on extra-curricular activities. Strong participation in the Duke of Edinburgh's Award Scheme.

School profile

Pupils Age range 11–18; 569 boys (387 day, 182 boarding). Main entry ages 11, 13 and into sixth. Approx 10% are children of former pupils. Own junior day school, The Grange, provides about 30% of intake at 11. *State school entry:* 60% at 11, 10% at 13, and 80% to sixth.
Entrance Common Entrance at 13; own exam at 11. Good academic standard and good all-round contributors, especially in music and sport; no religious barriers. Parents not expected to buy textbooks; average extras £50, excluding music lessons. 26 pa assisted places. Scholarships/bursaries, up to 50% fees.
Parents 60+% live within 30 miles; up to 10% live overseas.
Head and staff *Headmaster:* Timothy Haynes, in post since 1995. Educated at Shrewsbury and Reading University (history). Previously Surmaster at St Paul's School. *Staff:* 55 full time, 5 part time. Annual turnover 4%. Average age 35–40.
Exam results In 1995, 84 pupils in fifth form, 86 in upper sixth. *GCSE:* In 1995, 81 in fifth gained at least grade C in 8+ subjects; 3 in 5–7 subjects. *A-levels:* 9 upper sixth passed in 4+ subjects; 66 in 3; 8 in 2 subjects. Average UCAS points 22.3.
University and college entrance 98% of 1995 sixth-form leavers went on to a degree course (25% after a gap year); others typically go on to art or drama college or other non-degree courses.
Curriculum GCSE and A-levels. 20 GCSE subjects offered, 18 at AS-level; 28 at A-level (including geology) General studies compulsory for sixth but not examined. 33% take science A-levels; 40% arts/humanities; 27% both. *Vocational:* Work experience available. *Computing facilities:* New computer centre with 32 IBM compatibles, with VGA graphics; about 30 other machines in departments, eg DTP in English, CAD in technology and for simulations in science. IT studied by all in years 1 and 2, also in sixth AS-level group. *Europe:* French (from 11), German and Spanish offered at GCSE and A-level; also French and Spanish AS-level and Italian and Russian A-level. 50% take Regular exchanges (France, Germany and Spain). Some sixth-formers undertake work experience in France.

The arts *Music:* 50% of pupils learn a musical instrument; instrumental exams can be taken. Many musical groups including orchestras, 4 choirs, 3 wind bands and many smaller ensembles. 12 groups in 1995 National Chamber Music Competition with septet playing in final concert. Currently 5 choral/organ scholars at Oxbridge. Live performances of Britten's Spring Symphony with BBC National Orchestra of Wales, Turandot with Welsh National Opera, and Britten's War Requiem with Swansea Philharmonic Society. *Drama & dance*: Drama offered and A-level may be taken. Majority of pupils are involved in school and house/other productions. *Art:* On average, 30 take GCSE, 12 A-level. Printing, drawing, 3D studies, printmaking, textiles, ceramics, photography and mixed media are offered. Art workshops (some in Cornwall) involving established artists.

Sport, community service and clubs *Sport and physical activities:* Main sports are rugby, cricket and rowing. Also offered: Golf, tennis, shooting, soccer, badminton, squash, swimming, cross-country, athletics, canoeing, sailing, fencing, sub-aqua diving, archery, riding, karate, climbing. Athletics, 1 in Welsh junior team; Cricket, 1 England U19, 2 ex-pupils currently playing first-class cricket; Fencing, 2 Welsh internationals; Rowing, 4 in Welsh international junior 8, Welsh junior coxless pair, 1 British junior B team. Rugby, 3 Welsh schoolboy caps recently, 1 Welsh youth, 1 U21, winners of West of England, runners-up in Oxford and Marches competitions; Skiing, 1 in GB squad. *Community service:* Pupils take silver and gold Duke of Edinburgh's Award. CCF compulsory for 2 years at age 14+. Community service optional. Many charity fund-raising activities eg walks, cycle rides, swimming etc. *Clubs and societies:* Up to 30 clubs, eg chess, debating, aero-modelling, astronomy, table tennis, electronics, Mah Jong, herpetology, Christian Fellowship, bridge.

Uniform School uniform worn throughout.

Houses/prefects Day and boarding houses. Prefects, head boy, head of house and house prefects – appointed by the Headmaster or housemaster.

Religion 2 chaplains. School chapel follows the rites of the Church in Wales.

Social Plays, concerts, Challenge of Industry Conference with local schools, particularly sister school, Haberdashers' Monmouth. Organised exchanges with French, Spanish, German and Japanese schools; art gallery visits in UK an Europe. Pupils allowed to bring own bike to school. Meals self-service. School shop. No tobacco/alcohol allowed.

Discipline Pupils failing to produce homework once might expect to have to explain why; those caught in possession of drugs could expect explusion.

Boarding All sixth-formers share study bedrooms, 33% of juniors in dormitories of 6+. Houses of approximately 45, divided by age. Qualified school nurse. Central dining room. Cooking facilities in houses. Flexible boarding arrangements, with special activity weekends. Visits to the local town allowed.

Alumni association is run by H C Toulouse, 3 Monkswell Close, Monmouth, Gwent NP5 3PH.

Former pupils Lord Ezra of Horsham (former Chairman NCB); Lord Brecon; K Jarrett, A M Jorden and E T Butler (rugby internationals); F J Davies (managing director, Rockware); R J Herd (engineer, racing car designer); Glyn Worsnip (TV presenter); Victor Spinetti (actor); M W Barnes QC; Hon Colin Moynihan (ex-Minister for Energy); David Broome (showjumper).

• MORETON HALL

Moreton Hall, Weston Rhyn, Oswestry, Shropshire SY11 3EW. Tel 01691 773671, Fax 01691 778 552

• Pupils 280 • Boys None • Girls 10–18 (Day/Board) • Upper sixth 40 • Termly fees £2530 (Day) £3650 (Board) • GSA, SHA, BSA • Enquiries/application to the Principal

What it's like

Founded in 1913, it occupies an attractive rural site of 100 acres of splendid grounds and gardens. The campus is a village-like community and the buildings are a mixture of the modern and the venerable. Completely refurbished and extremely well equipped with modern facilities. A sports complex (with floodlit tennis courts) and a theatre centre are the latest additions; it also has its own golf course and cross-country eventing course. The school looks for all-round ability and a happy purposeful atmosphere prevails. It is neither consciously progressive nor traditional in its approach. It is not academically exclusive but all girls are expected to be able to make a positive contribution to their own growth and that of the school. The teaching is good (a high staff:pupil ratio of about 1:8) and results are very good, with all sixth-form leavers going on to degree courses (including Oxbridge). The school prides itself on its careers department. Strong music and drama departments. A good range of sports and games (high standards) and a wide range of activities. Moreton Enterprises and Moreton Travel (own travel agency with a £250,000 turnover) give girls opportunities to learn business and entrepreneurial skills

School profile

Pupils Age range 10–18; 280 girls, 15 day, 265 boarding. Main entry ages 11, 12, 13 and into sixth. Approx 3%–5% are children of former pupils. *State school entry:* 10%-15% main intake, plus 10% to sixth.

Entrance Own entrance exam or Common Entrance used. All-round abilities looked for; no particular religious requirements. Parents not expected to buy textbooks or stationery; maximum extras £200 including music tuition. 14 pa assisted places. Up to 10 pa scholarships (academic, tennis and music) for half-fees at 11–13; 4 pa sixth-form. Bursaries for children of clergy, school teachers and armed forces.

Parents 25+% in industry or commerce; 25% from professions. 50+% live within 50 miles; 15+% live overseas (expatriates).

Head and staff *Principal:* J Forster, 4 years in post. Educated at Shrewsbury, and Leeds University (English). Previously Housemaster i/c Girls and Head of English at Strathallan. *Staff:* 37 full time, 11 part time. Annual turnover 5%. Average age 38.

Exam results In 1995, 45 pupils in upper fifth, 58 in upper sixth. *GCSE:* In 1995, 84% upper fifth gained at least grade C in 8+ subjects; 9% in 5–7 subjects. *A-levels:* 8 upper sixth passed in 4+ subjects; 41 in 3; 8 in 2; and 1 in 1 subject. Average UCAS points 20.0.

University and college entrance 90% of 1995 sixth-form leavers went on to a degree course (40% after a gap year), 10% to Oxbridge; 10% took courses in medicine, dentistry and veterinary science, 25% in science and engineering, 10% in law, 25% in humanities and social sciences, 10% in art and design, 25% in vocational subjects eg nursing, physiotherapy.

Curriculum GCSE, A-levels and GNVQs. 24 GCSE subjects offered; 20 at A-level (including general studies). 30% take science A-levels; 40% arts/humanities; 30% both. *Vocational:* GNVQ leisure & tourism offered; plus RSA course in CLAIT. Work experience available; all lower sixth involved in Moreton Enterprises or Moreton Hall Travel. *Computing facilities:* New IT network of PCs with CD-Rom and Internet link; all departments have their own computers. Technology introduced in year 7; optional courses to GCSE and in sixth-form. *Special provision:* Full time learning support teacher (dyslexia and related disorders). *Europe:* French, German and Spanish offered at GCSE and A-level; also Italian and Russian GCSE and non-examined, French and Italian for Institute of Linguists exams. Partner schools/exchange scheme with Germany and France. All second and fourth years visit France and Spain annually.

The arts *Music:* Over 50% of pupils learn a musical instrument; instrumental exams can be taken. Some 10–15 musical groups including two orchestras, jazz bands, blues, wind bands, string groups, choirs. Director of Music from Chetham's. Members of Shrewsbury Choir and Orchestra; winners of local entry to BBC carol competition. *Drama & dance*: Both offered. GCSE and A-level drama, ESB, LAMDA exams may be taken. Some pupils are involved in school productions and majority in house/other drama. Recently joint production with Shrewsbury; one production taken to Edinburgh Festival (written by a pupil); also include Shakespeare, Oliver!, The Mikado. *Art:* On average, 20 take GCSE, 6 A-level. Design, costume design, history of art, pottery, textiles, photography also offered. 4 gained places at art colleges in 1995.

Sport, community service and clubs *Sport and physical activities:* Compulsory sports (initially): lacrosse, netball, tennis, swimming. Optional: hockey, cricket, golf (own golf course), riding, basketball, dance, self defence. GCSE, BAGA exams may be taken. 9 members of county and regional lacrosse teams, 1 England U18 lacrosse, 2 Welsh U18 and U16 teams. *Community service:* Pupils take bronze, silver and gold Duke of Edinburgh's Award (50+ involved). Community service optional at age 13 (200 participate). *Clubs and societies:* Up to 30 clubs, eg archery, farm, croquet, weaving, debating. All lower sixth involved in Moreton Enterprises or Moreton Hall Travel

(include farm, art gallery, golf course, travel agency, bank).
Uniform School uniform worn except the sixth.
Houses/prefects Junior and upper sixth houses; others competitive. Prefects, including head and second prefects – appointed by the Principal after consultation. Lower sixth are house prefects. School council and sixth-form council.
Religion Compulsory daily assembly and Sunday church in the Anglican tradition. Relaxation of Sunday requirements for upper sixth.
Social Boarding houses twinned with houses at Shrewsbury School; many joint social activities/outings. Annual ski trip, visits to Germany, France and Spain to stay with families. Meals self service. School shop. No tobacco allowed; alcohol only permitted on restricted basis, in sixth-form club (to which girls may invite visitors, including boys).
Discipline Punishments range from order marks to expulsion eg for drugs. Pupils failing to produce homework at any time would expect an enquiry as to why and be expected to remedy the situation at once.
Boarding All sixth-formers have single or double bedrooms. 6 houses of 50–55 (2 junior, 3 senior, 1 upper sixth). Resident qualified nurse; separate sanatorium. Central dining room. Sixth-form pupils can provide and cook own snacks. 2–4 weekend exeats each term (flexible). Visits to local towns allowed, according to age.
Alumni association Secretary is Miss D Gittins, 42 Roman Road, Shrewsbury, Shropshire.
Former pupils Thea Musgrave (composer), Shanaz Pakravan (broadcaster).

• MORRISON'S

Morrison's Academy, Ferntower Road, Crieff, Perthshire PH7 3AN. Tel 01764 653885
• Pupils 529 • Boys 5–18 (Day/Board) • Girls 5–18 (Day/Board) • Higher year 93 • Termly fees £750–£1215 (Day) £3173–£3530 (Board) • HMC, GSA • Enquiries to the Rector • Application to the Admissions Secretary

What it's like

Founded in 1860, it has a pleasant, semi-rural, 10-acre site on the lower slopes of the Knock in Crieff. Regular development over the years has produced a fine and well-equipped campus. Originally separate boys' and girls' school, these merged in 1979 to form a single co-educational school. The primary school is an integral part of the Academy. Since the 1980s the school has reserved a proportion of places for non-British pupils so that students can learn from cultural diversity; celebrations now include the major Christian and Muslim festivals, Christmas, New Year, Burns Supper and St Andrew's Night. A thorough, traditional Scottish education is provided and academic results are good. Many pupils go on to degree courses each year. Very strong indeed in music, and there are flourishing drama groups. A good range of sports and games and high standards are achieved. Over 40 clubs and societies cater for most conceivable needs. A vigorous CCF and a good record in the Duke of Edinburgh's Award Scheme. A lot of emphasis on outdoor pursuits for which the environment is very suitable.

School profile

Pupils Total age range 5–18; 529 pupils, 424 day (228 boys, 196 girls), 105 boarding (75 boys, 30 girls). Senior department 12–18, 451 pupils (260 boys, 191 girls). Main entry ages 5, 12 and into sixth. Approx 20% are children of former pupils. *State school entry:* 43% main senior intake, plus 20% to sixth.
Entrance Own entrance exam and interview. No special skills or religious requirements. Parents not expected to buy textbooks, stationery, etc. Variable number of assisted places (currently 140 in school). 6 pa scholarships/bursaries, half fees.
Parents 60+% live within 30 miles; up to 12% live overseas.
Head and staff *Rector and Principal:* Harry Ashmall, in post for 17 years. Educated at Kilsyth Academy and Glasgow (history). Previously Rector at Forfar Academy, Principal Teacher of History at Glasgow High and Principal Teacher of History and Modern Studies at Lochend Secondary. Also Chairman of ISIS (Scotland); Vice Chairman, UNICEF UK Committee; member of ISJC Public Affairs Committee, of SCIS Governing Board and Management Committee, and of Malaysian Institute of Management; Fellow of the IMgt. *Staff:* 52 full time, 3 part time. Annual turnover 1%. Average age 42.

Exam results In 1995, 85 pupils in S-grade year, 94 in Higher year, 77 A-level/CSYS year. *S-grade:* In 1995, 83 pupils achieved grade 3 or above in 5–9 subjects; and 2 in 1–4 subjects. *Highers* (form 5 only): 42 pupils passed in 5 subjects; 17 in 4; 5 in 3; 13 in 2; 9 in 1 subject. *CSYS and A-levels:* 16 pupils passed in 3 subjects; 18 in 2; and 4 in 1 subject.
University and college entrance 78% of 1995 sixth-form leavers went on to a degree course (8% after a gap year); others typically go on to the services, commerce or banking. Of those going on to university, 1% went to Oxbridge; 10% took courses in medicine, dentistry and veterinary science, 35% in science and engineering, 5% in law, 25% in humanities and social sciences, 5% in art and design, 20% in vocational subjects eg business, physiotherapy.
Curriculum S-grade, CSYS, Highers and A-levels. 15 subjects offered (no A-level general studies). 58% take science A-levels; 30% arts/humanities; 12% both. *Vocational:* Work experience available; also Scotvec modules in eg modern languages, economics, computing, maths. *Computing facilities:* 5 networked labs plus individual machines in some departments. *Special provision:* Small group tuition for English as a second language. Special examination. *Europe:* French, German and Spanish offered at S-grade and Higher (French and German compulsory to age 14). Regular exchanges to Germany. Some German pupils in school.
The arts (Pupils aged 11 and over) *Music:* Over 20% of pupils learn a musical instrument; instrumental exams can be taken. Some 14 musical groups including choirs, orchestra, wind band, brass group, recorder ensembles, ceilidh band, jazz, percussion. *Art:* On average, 20 take S-grade, 10 Higher. 2–3 pupils go on to art college each year.
Sport, community service and clubs (Pupils aged 11 and over) *Sport and physical activities:* Compulsory sports, rugby, cricket, (boys), hockey, tennis (girls). Optional: cross-country, golf, badminton, swimming, softball, athletics, netball, basketball, hockey (boys) tennis (boys). Regular rugby and hockey representation at district level, occasionally national. *Community service:* Pupils take bronze, silver and gold Duke of Edinburgh's Award. CCF and community service optional. *Clubs and societies:* Some 42 clubs, eg basketball, fencing, orienteering, sailing, chess, debating, table tennis, Young Enterprise, music.
Uniform School uniform worn throughout.
Houses/prefects Competitive houses. Prefects, head boy and girl, head of house and house prefects.
Religion Morning prayers.
Social Discos and debates with other schools. Organised trips and exchange systems with schools abroad. Lunch self-service; other meals formal. No tobacco/alcohol allowed.
Boarding Single sex-sleeping accommodation. Central dining room. Seniors can provide and cook own supper. 7 weekend exeats during session. Visits to local town allowed.
Former pupils Sir Andrew McCance; Sir James Henderson Stewart; Dr Gavin Strang; Air Vice-Marshal MacGregor; Sir Ross Belch; Dennis Lawson; Ewan McGregor.

• MOUGINS

Mougins School, 615 Avenue Dr Maurice Donat, 06250, Mougins, France. Tel 33 93 901547, Fax 33 93 753140

• Pupils 200 • Boys 3–18 (Day) • Girls 3–18 (Day) • Upper sixth 8 • Termly fees FF16,000–FF23,000 • COBISEC, ECIS • Enquiries/application to Headmaster

What it's like

It is a few miles from Cannes, situated in a wooded corner of the huge Sophia Antipolis science park, in purpose-built premises. It was previously named the Anglo-American School of Mougins but, with a new Headmaster, it changed its name in 1992 to emphasise its pan-European outlook. The curriculum is British, leading to GCSE and A-level and meeting the entrance requirements of universities world-wide. All the staff are qualified professionals, the staff:student ratio is about 1:8. The official language is English but most pupils speak French.

School profile

Pupils Total age range 3–18; 200 day pupils (100 boys, 100 girls).
Entrance Open entrance. Some assisted places, up to 30%.
Parents Drawn largely from the local international community, partly transient and partly established. About one third are British or American, 20% French and the remainder drawn from a wide range of nationalities.
Head and staff *Headmaster:* Brian Hickmore, appointed 1995. Educated at Sussex University. Previously Deputy Head at Mougins and Deputy Head of a large London comprehensive school. *Staff:* 26 full time staff, all of whom speak French.
Exam results On average, 16 pupils in upper fifth, 8 in upper sixth. *GCSE:* 19% of pupils gain at least grade C in 8+ subjects; 69% in 5–7 subjects. *A-levels:* 2 pass in 4+ subjects; 3 in 3; 1 in 2; and 1 in 1 subject. Average UCAS points 15.0.
University and college entrance Most leavers go on to university.
Curriculum GCSE and A-levels and the US College Board SAT and ACH. The school is a local centre for Cambridge and London universities. *Special provision:* Special help with ESL and learning difficulties provided. *Vocational:* Work experience available.
The arts (Pupils aged 11 and over) *Music:* Tuition in musical instruments available. Drama & dance: Both offered. *Art:* On average, 8 take GCSE, 3 A-level.
Sport, community service and clubs (Pupils aged 11 and over) *Sport and physical activities:* Compulsory sports: athletics, orienteering, basketball, tennis, football. Optional: gymnastics. GCSE exams may be taken. 1 former pupil on international tennis circuit; regional gymnastics, orienteering victories. *Community service:* Optional at age 16. *Clubs and societies:* Up to 5 clubs, eg dance, ballet.
Uniform No uniform worn.
Religion No religious affiliation.
Discipline The school expects high levels of tolerance, respect and international understanding; committed to a safe, healthy and honest community with a code of conduct to show what is expected of all its members.

• MOUNT (York)

The Mount School, Dalton Terrace, York YO2 4DD. Tel 01904 667500, Fax 01904 667524
• Pupils 349 • Boys 3–11 only • Girls 3–18 (Day/Board/Weekly) • Upper sixth 44 • Termly fees £2085 (Day) £3390 (Board/Weekly) • GSA, BSA • Enquiries/application to the Headmistress's Secretary

What it's like

Founded in 1831, it moved to its present site in 1857. A very pleasant compact wooded campus with splendid gardens, mature trees and playing fields. The buildings are a combination of 19th-century architecture and new blocks. Facilities are good. Tregelles, the junior school (3–11), uses the main school's swimming pool and sports facilities. A Quaker school, its ethos is to encourage and develop the individual within a small, caring community. It prides itself on a welcoming atmosphere but aims, also, for academic excellence. It has all the advantages of a small school, with a good staff:pupil ratio. Results are good and the great majority of sixth-form leavers go on to degree courses, including Oxbridge. Very strong in music, drama and art (talent in these is looked for in candidates). Much involvement in local cultural activities and full use is made of the city's amenities, plus expeditions further afield. A wide range of sport and games and extra-curricular activities. Big commitment to local community services and an outstanding record in the Duke of Edinburgh's Award Scheme.

School profile

Pupils Total age range 3–18; 349 pupils, 221 day (boys and girls), 103 boarding girls, 25 weekly boarding girls; boarding available in senior department (occasionally in Year 6). Senior department 11–18, 248 girls. Main entry ages 11 (also 12, 13 and 14) and into sixth. Approx 7% are children of former pupils. *State school entry:* 50% main intakes, plus 50% to sixth.
Entrance Own entrance exam used. No special skills or religious requirements but school is Quaker. Parents not expected to buy textbooks; minimum of extras. 15 pa

assisted places (10 at age 11, 3 at 13 and 2 in sixth-form). Scholarships (academic) up to 50% fees; smaller scholarships for music and art. Bursaries for Quakers according to need and limited help to children of old pupils.

Parents 10+% are doctors, lawyers, etc; 10+% in industry or commerce; 5+% in the armed service; 10+% are farmers. 10+% live within 30 miles; 15% live overseas.

Head and staff *Headmistress:* Miss Barbara J Windle, in post for 10 years. Educated at Tapton House and Cambridge (English Literature). Previously Head of Sixth Form and Curriculum at Bolton Girls School and Head of English at Clapham County. Also Convenor, Quaker Schools' Heads Conference and Committee Member, Peace Education Advisory Group. *Staff:* 28 full time, 39 part time. Annual turnover 5%. Average age 37.

Exam results In 1995, 41 pupils in Year 11, 39 in upper sixth. *GCSE:* In 1995, 92% upper fifth gained at least grade C in 8+ subjects. *A-levels:* 25 upper sixth passed in 4+ subjects; 11 in 3; 2 in 2 subjects. Average UCAS points 22.6 (including general studies 25.6).

University and college entrance 99% of 1995 sixth-form leavers went on to a degree course (15% after a gap year); others typically go on to drama or Montessori teaching. Of those going on to university, 10% went to Oxbridge; 8% took courses in medicine, dentistry and veterinary science, 19% in science and engineering, 8% in law, 32% in humanities and social sciences, 3% in art and design, 30% iin vocational subjects eg sports studies, education, management, physiotherapy.

Curriculum GCSE and A-levels. 20 subjects offered at A-level, including general studies. 40% take science A-levels; 60% arts/humanities. *Vocational:* Work experience available; also RSA stages 1 and 2 typewriting. *Computing facilities:* Computer room with access at all times; computers in most departments. *Special provision:* Assessed by local branch of Dyslexia Institute and attend as advised. Extra English provided for limited number by qualified EFL teacher. *Europe:* French and German offered to GCSE, AS and A-level (French compulsory to GCSE); also GCSE Spanish and Italian (by arrangement). Regular visits to Europe; classical trips to Italy periodically. European girls accepted (1 term or more).

The arts (Pupils aged 11 and over) *Music:* Over 50% of pupils learn a musical instrument; instrumental exams can be taken. Some 5+ musical groups including choir, orchestras, rock band. *Drama & dance*: Both offered. GCSE drama, LAMDA and RAD exams may be taken. Majority of pupils are involved in school and house/other productions. Annual joint dramatic/musical production with Bootham for all lower six form. *Art:* On average, 20 take GCSE, 8 A-level. History of art, pottery, textiles (GCSE available) and photography also offered.

Sport, community service and clubs (Pupils aged 11 and over) *Sport and physical activities:* Compulsory sports: (at different ages) gymnastics, swimming, hockey, netball, athletics, tennis, rounders. Optional: fencing, volleyball, badminton, rowing. Sixth form only: squash. RLSS, ASA swimming exams may be taken. Fencing, area, regional representatives; hockey, area representatives; athletics, county, area representatives. *Community service:* Community service optional at age 14 upwards. *Clubs and societies:* Up to 30 clubs, eg trampolining, lifesaving, fencing, photography, debating, creative writing, poetry, jewellery, pottery.

Uniform School uniform worn except the sixth.

Houses/prefects No competitive houses. School prefects and head girls elected by the school. House prefects, appointed by house staff. School council.

Religion Quaker; attendance at daily act of worship and Sunday evening meetings.

Social Social events with other local schools; debates, theatrical productions with Bootham (sibling school) and joint meeting for worship, dances. Foreign language exchanges; trips abroad for language study, art and art history, religious education. Older pupils allowed to bring own bike to school. Meals, self-service; special meals for boarders remaining at dispersed weekends. School shop. No alcohol allowed.

Discipline Firm guidelines laid down along with encouragement of self-discipline. Pupils failing to produce homework once might expect discussion and completion of work; if anyone were caught smoking cannabis on the premises they would be excluded, immediately.

Boarding Houses of 60–75, divided broadly by age. 85% share with 2–6 others. Separate sixth-form house. Resident qualified medical staff. Central dining room. Sixth formers sometimes allowed to cook own food. Flexible system of exeats. Visits to local town allowed.

Alumni association is run by The Secretary, MOSA, c/o the school.

Former pupils Dame Judi Dench; Margaret Drabble; A S Byatt; Isobel Barnett; Dame Elaine Kellett-Bowman; Jocelyn Burnell (astronomer); Mary Ure; Jenny Killick; Hilary Wainwright; Rose Neil (Ulster TV); Anna Walker (ITV holiday programme); Kate Bellingham (Tomorrow's World and Radio 5).

• MOUNT CARMEL

Mount Carmel School, Wilmslow Road, Alderley Edge, Cheshire SK9 7QE. Tel 01625 583028

• Pupils 390 • Boys None • Girls 11–18 (Day) • Upper sixth 43 • Termly fees £1196 (Day) • ISAI • Enquiries/application to the Headmistress

What it's like

Founded in 1945 by the Congregation of the Sisters of St Joseph of the Apparition, the main school building is set in agreeable surroundings in the village of Alderley Edge. It is well equipped with a modern library and resource centre, and new sixth-form and language learning centres opened in 1995. Children of all faiths are welcome, and separate provision is made for religious instruction for Catholic pupils. There is some emphasis on regular worship, prayers, mass etc. A broad general education is given. Academic results are good and most sixth-form leavers go on to degree courses. Music is very well supported and there are several choirs, plus orchestras, ensembles, etc. Drama and dance are popular and flourishing and are taught as part of the curriculum. There are good facilities for sports and games of which there is the usual range. Plenty of societies and clubs cater for extra-curricular activities and the school organises a wide range of residential courses and participation in the Duke of Edinburgh's Award Scheme. Senior girls are involved in local community services.

School profile

Pupils Age range 11–18, 390 day girls. Main entry age 11. *State school entry:* 40% main intake.

Entrance Own entrance exam used. Bursaries and assisted places.

Head and staff *Headmistress:* Mrs Kathleen Mills, appointed in 1995. Educated at University of Wales.

Exam results In 1995, 69 pupils in upper fifth, 43 in upper sixth. *GCSE:* In 1995, 50% upper fifth gained at least grade C in 10+ subjects; 46% in 5–9 subjects. AS and *A-levels:* 35% upper sixth passed in 4+ subjects; 39% in 3/3½; 16% in 2; 7% in 1 subject. Average UCAS points 15.5.

University and college entrance 90% of sixth-form leavers go on to a degree course; others typically go on to non-degree courses or straight into careers.

Curriculum GCSE and A-levels. 18 subjects offered (including A-level general studies). 39% take science A-levels; 42% arts/humanities; 19% both. *Vocational:* Work experience available. *Europe:* French and German offered at GCSE, AS and A-level; Italian and Spanish as certificate courses in sixth. Regular exchanges (France and Germany). Work experience for sixth-formers in French or German speaking countries.

The arts *Music:* Over 40% of pupils learn a musical instrument; instrumental exams can be taken. Some 11 musical groups including flute, woodwind, guitar groups, string ensembles, orchestras etc. Many cups in local festivals; 1 pupil won Sheila Mossman award for highest mark in grade 8 ABRSM piano exam. *Drama & dance*: Both offered. ESB exams may be taken. Majority of pupils are involved in school productions and all in house/other productions. *Art:* On average, 22 take GCSE, 2 AS-level, 5 A-level.

Sport, community service and clubs *Sport and physical activities:* Compulsory sports: Tennis, rounders, hockey, athletics, fencing. Sixth form only: squash. 2 county netball representatives; 2 county hockey representatives. *Community service:* Community service optional. *Clubs and societies:* Up to 10 clubs, eg bridge, poetry, debating, dance, drama, gym.

Uniform School uniform worn; pupils' own version in sixth.

Houses/prefects Competitive houses. Prefects, head girl, head of house and house prefects – appointed by Headmistress and staff.

Religion Attendance at religious worship compulsory except Mass for non-Catholics. **Social** Competitions of all kinds, including public speaking with other local schools. Annual exchange with St Joseph's College and Lycée Dax in France. Meals self-service. School stationery shop run by pupils. No tobacco/alcohol allowed.

• MOUNT ST MARY'S (Spinkhill)

Mount St Mary's College, Spinkhill, Derbyshire S31 9YL. Tel 01246 433388, Fax 01246 435511 • Pupils 300 • Boys 13–18 (Day/Board/Weekly) • Girls 13–18 (Day/Board/Weekly) • Upper sixth 43 • Termly fees £1964 (Day) £2906 (Board) £2689 (Weekly) • HMC • Enquiries/application to the Headmaster.

What it's like

Founded in 1842 and run under the direction of the Society of Jesus, which has had a presence at Spinkhill from 1580. The school lies in the village and has a fine estate of playing fields and farmlands. Originally a boys' school, girls have been admitted as pupils since 1977. Most pupils are Roman Catholics but other denominations are welcome. There is strong emphasis on religious instruction in Catholic doctrine; mass and some other services are compulsory for Catholic pupils. It has a good staff:pupil ratio of about 1:9. Academic standards are high and results are good. Most leavers go on to degree courses each year. There are strong music, drama and art departments. Considerable strength in sport and games with many county representatives in rugby. A very good variety of clubs and societies. About a quarter of the pupils are involved in local community services and the school has an outstanding record in the Duke of Edinburgh's Award Scheme.

School profile

Pupils Age range 13–18; 300 pupils, 96 day (75 boys, 21 girls), 204 boarding (131 boys, 73 girls). Main entry ages 13 and into sixth. Approx 15% are children of former pupils. Own prep school, Barlborough Hall, provides more than 20% of intake. *State school entry:* 10% main intake, plus 20% to sixth.
Entrance Common Entrance and own exam used (with interviews and IQ tests). Sport and music skills looked for; pupils expected but not required to be RC. Parents do not buy textbooks. 15 pa assisted places. 10 pa scholarships, £100 to full fees depending on need. Bursaries added to assisted places to enable pupils to board.
Parents 15+% are doctors, lawyers, etc; 25+% in industry or commerce; 10+% in the armed services. 50 +% live within 30 miles; up to 10% live overseas.
Head and staff *Headmaster:* Paul Fisher, 6 years in post. Educated at St Ignatius College, Enfield, and Oxford University (classics). Previously Housemaster and Head of Classics at Prior Park and Assistant Master at Marlborough. Also member of MCC; former professional cricketer with Middlesex and Worcestershire. *Staff:* 33 full time, 13 part time. Annual turnover 5%. Average age 36.
Exam results In 1995, 60 pupils in fifth, 43 in upper sixth. *GCSE:* In 1995, 50% fifth gained at least grade C in 8+ subjects; 23% in 5–7 subjects. *A-levels:* 10% upper sixth passed in 4+ subjects; 58% in 3; 25% in 2; and 7% in 1 subject. Average UCAS points 18.3.
University and college entrance 96% of 1995 sixth-form leavers went on to a degree course (15% after a gap year); others typically go on to business or other employment. Of those going on to university, 7% went to Oxbridge; 10% took courses in medicine, dentistry and veterinary science, 30% in science and engineering, 10% in law, 30% in humanities and social sciences, 10% in art and design, 15% in other vocational subjects eg leisure, sports.
Curriculum GCSE and A-levels. 23 GCSE subjects offered; 22 at A-level (including sports studies; no A-level general studies). 14% take science A-levels; 60% arts/humanities; 26% both. *Vocational:* Work experience available. *Computing facilities:* Computer laboratory and desktop publishing facilities. *Special provision:* Specialist teaching for dyslexia and EFL. *Europe:* French, German and Spanish offered to GCSE, AS and A-level. Regular exchanges to France (schools in Lille and Orleans). Pupils from France (St Louis de Gonzague in Paris), and Spain (Barcelona). Contact with activity/outdoor centre in south of France.

The arts *Music:* Over 30% of pupils learn a musical instrument; instrumental exams can be taken. Some 3 musical groups including orchestra, band, quartets. *Drama & dance*: Some pupils are involved in school and house/other productions. *Art:* On average, 20 take GCSE, 4 AS-level, 6 A-level. Design also offered.
Sport, community service and clubs *Sport and physical activities:* Compulsory sports: rugby, cricket, hockey, netball. Optional: athletics, rounders, tennis. Fifth and sixth only: badminton, swimming, table tennis. GCSE and A-level sport may be taken. More than 20 boys represent county at rugby, 4 represent region. *Community service:* Pupils take bronze, silver and gold Duke of Edinburgh's Award. CCF compulsory for 1 year at age 15, community service at 17. *Clubs and societies:* Up to 30 clubs, eg many minor sports, fencing, weight-training, aerobics etc, chess, bridge, TV & video, radio, astronomy.
Uniform School uniform worn in lower school.
Houses/prefects Competitive houses. Prefects, head boy/head girl, head of house and house prefects – appointed by the Headmaster.
Religion Compulsory mass for Catholics. Other denominations welcomed.
Social No organised local events. Exchanges with Jesuit schools in Australia, Zimbabwe and France. Day pupils allowed to bring own car/bike/motorbike to school. Meals self-service; lunch separate sittings. School shop. No tobacco/alcohol allowed.
Discipline Strong emphasis throughout the school on growth to self-discipline.
Boarding Sixth form have own study bedrooms; remainder in study cubicles. Single-sex houses of 50–60, for first 3 years. Resident SRN. Central refectory. 2 weekend exeats each term. Visits to local town allowed for upper school.
Former pupils Rt Hon Lord Wheatley PC; Sir Martin Melvin; Air Marshal Sir Francis Fresanges; Rt Hon Sir Denis Henry; Sir David Rose; Sir Diarmaid Conroy; Major General McGinness.

• MPW (Birmingham)

Mander Portman Woodward, 38 Highfield Road, Birmingham B15 3ED. Tel 0121 454 9637, Fax 0121 454 6433

• Pupils 100 • Boys 13–19 (Day) • Girls 13–19 (Day) • Upper sixth 66 • Termly fees up to £2850 (Day) • CIFE, BAC • Enquiries/application to the Principal

What it's like

Founded in 1980, it is a tutorial college with single-site premises in the suburb of Edgbaston. The staff of 12 (plus 10 part-timers) provide standard MPW college courses. Traditionally a sixth-form college, it now takes pupils from age 13 for GCSE and A-level courses. Some 80% of pupils go on to degree courses. See also MPW (London) for information on the MPW group.

School profile

Pupils Age range 13–19; 100 day pupils (50 boys, 50 girls). Main entry ages 13 and 16.
Entrance No entrance exams. No special skills or religious requirements. Parents expected to buy textbooks. 3 pa scholarships, 25%–50% fees.
Parents 15+% are doctors, lawyers, etc. 15+% in industry.
Head and staff *Principal:* Keith Munnings, in post from 1994. Educated at Malton Grammar School, UMIST (polymer science) and Bolton College of Education (PGCE). Previously Vice-Principal of MPW (Bristol). *Staff:* 12 full time, 10 part time. Annual turnover 10%. Average age 30.
Exam results *A-levels:* 66 pupils in upper sixth. 35% passed in 3 subjects; 48% in 2; and 17% in 1 subject. Most pupils are re-taking some subjects.
University and college entrance 80% of 1995 sixth-form leavers went on to a degree course; others typically go on to non-degree courses eg HND or art or drama college. Of those going on to university, 25% took courses in medicine, dentistry and veterinary science, 35% in science and engineering, 40% in humanities and social sciences.
Curriculum GCSE and *A-levels:* 21 subjects offered (including accounting and A-level general studies). *Europe:* French, German and Spanish offered to GCSE and A-level.
Uniform No uniform.
Houses/prefects No competitive houses or prefects.
Religion Attendance at religious worship not compulsory.

Social Pupils allowed to bring own car/bike/motorbike to school. No meals; vending machines available. No tobacco/alcohol allowed.
Discipline All members of college community expected to show mutual respect.

• MPW (Bristol)

Mander Portman Woodward, 10 Elmdale Road, Clifton, Bristol BS8 1SL. Tel 0117 925 5688
• Pupils 85 • Boys 15–21 (Day/Board) • Girls 15–21 (Day/Board) • Upper sixth 41 • Termly fees £2163 (Day) • CIFE • Enquiries/application to the Principal

What it's like

A co-educational tutorial college founded in 1990, it has agreeable premises in Clifton, a quiet district of the city where the university is also sited. The main building is a large Victorian house. Facilities are good. It is a small, hardworking college with a friendly atmosphere. It is stressed that there is a very rigorous approach to work and to attendance and a strict policy is enforced to ensure high academic standards. There are a few boarders who have supervised accommodation with local families. The staff of 10 (plus 12 part-timers) has an average age of 40. Academic results are good. The college caters for A-level and GCSE, plus AS-level courses. Most of the upper sixth are retaking and the pattern of results reflect this. Almost all students go on to degree courses. Some sport and games (eg squash and badminton) is available. Pupils may use the catering services and refectory of the university. See also MPW (London) for information on the MPW group of colleges.

School profile

Pupils Age range 15–21; 85 pupils, 75 day (45 boys, 30 girls), 10 boarding with families. Main entry age 15–18. Transfer from maintained schools: 15%.
Entrance No entrance exams. No special skills or religious requirements. Boarding £75 per week with private families. Parents expected to buy textbooks. 6 pa scholarships.
Parents 15+% are doctors, lawyers, etc. 15+% in industry. 60+% live within 30 miles, 10% overseas.
Head and staff *Principal:* Fiona Eldridge, 5 years in post. Educated at Ralph Allen School and Hayesfield School (Bath) and London University (biological sciences and education). Previously Deputy Principal at MPW (London). *Publications:* co-author, A-level Practical Biology. *Staff:* 10 full time, 12 part time. Annual turnover 5%. Average age 40.
Exam results *A-levels:* 41 pupils in upper sixth: 9 passed in 3 subjects; 10 in 2; and 19 in 1 subject (most students were retaking and already had 1 or 2 A-levels).
University and college entrance 96% of 1995 sixth-form leavers went on to a degree course (2% after a gap year); others typically go on to employment. Of those going on to university, 1% went to Oxbridge; 10% took courses in medicine, dentistry and veterinary science, 30% in science and engineering, 5% in law, 50% in humanities and social sciences, 1% in art and design, 4% in vocational subjects eg osteopathy, physiotherapy.
Curriculum GCSE and A-levels. 12 GCSE, 25 A-level subjects offered (including environmental science A-level, but not general studies). 25% take science A-levels; 60% arts/humanities; 15% a mixture of both. *Vocational:* Work experience available. *Computing facilities:* Multi-media CD-Rom. *Special provision:* Links developing with Clifton dyslexia unit; specialist teaching arranged. *Europe:* French, German, Italian and Spanish offered at GCSE and A-level and as non-examined subjects.
Sport Range of activities including swimming, badminton and squash – all off-site.
Uniform No uniform.
Houses/prefects No competitive houses or prefects.
Religion Attendance at religious worship not compulsory.
Social Pupils allowed to bring own car/bike to school but there are no parking facilities. No meals. No tobacco/alcohol allowed.
Discipline Pupils failing to produce homework once might expect to be put on morning report system – all work to be handed in at a daily (pre-9 am) meeting with personal tutor. Those caught smoking cannabis on the premises would be expelled.
Boarding All pupils with local private families. Students (with permission from the Principal) can go home each weekend. Visits to local town allowed.

• MPW (Cambridge)

Mander Portman Woodward, 3/4 Brookside, Cambridge CB2 1JE. Tel 01223 350158, Fax 01223 366429

• Pupils 85 • Boys 14–19 (Day/Board) • Girls 14–19 (Day/Board) • Upper sixth 70 • Termly fees up to £2950 (Day) £4200 (with accommodation) • CIFE • Enquiries/application to the Principal

What it's like

Founded in 1987 as a tutorial college. The premises comprise two large, attractive collegiate-style houses a mile from the city centre. There are good laboratory facilities etc. Family accommodation for boarders is available nearby. The college prides itself on having a friendly, informal atmosphere but emphasises that the regime is tough. Lateness, absenteeism and uncompleted work are not acceptable. The predominantly young staff of 15 (plus 20 part-timers) provides one and two-year A-level courses, GCSE and AS-level courses, as well as retake courses for GCSE and A-levels. This college also runs secretarial courses. Staff are available outside formal lessons for discussion and supervised extra work. See also MPW (London) for information on MPW group.

School profile

Pupils Age range 14–19; 85 pupils, 54 day (33 boys, 21 girls); 31 boarding (20 boys, 11 girls). Main entry ages 14 and 16. *State school entry:* 15% of intake.
Entrance No entrance exam. No special skills or religious requirements. Parents expected to buy textbooks. 6 pa scholarships, 15%–100% fees.
Parents 40+% live within 30 miles. Up to 15% overseas.
Head and staff Co-Principals: Nick Marnott and David Musgrove, first year in post. *Staff:* 15 full time, 20 part time. Annual turnover 5%. Average age 28.
Exam results In 1995, 15 in upper fifth, 64 in upper sixth. *GCSE:* In 1995, 30% gained at least grade C in 5–7 subjects; 70% in 1–4 subjects. *A-levels:* 60% upper sixth passed in 3 subjects, 35% in 2 subjects.
University and college entrance 95% of 1995 sixth-form leavers went on to a degree course; others typically go on to non-degree courses. Of those going on to university, 2% went to Oxbridge; 5% took courses in medicine, dentistry and veterinary science, 45% in science and engineering, 50% in humanities and social sciences.
Curriculum GCSE and A levels. 30 subjects offered. 35% took science A levels; 40% arts/humanities; 25% a mixture of both. *Vocational:* Work experience available; also RSA Stages 1–3 word processing/shorthand; and RSA (Stages 1–3) and Pitman (elementary, intermediate and advanced) word processing/secretarial practice. *Computing facilities:* 18 IBM compatible micro-computers. *Special provision:* EFL provision. *Europe:* French, German, Russian and Spanish offered to GCSE, AS and A-level; also Greek A-level and Italian GCSE and A-level. Less than 10% take GCSE in more than 1 language. Language tuition provided for secretarial students.
The arts *Art:* On average, 6 take GCSE, 3 A-level.
Sport, community service and clubs *Clubs and societies:* Up to 5 clubs.
Uniform No uniform worn.
Houses/prefects No competitive houses or prefects
Religion Attendance at religious worship not compulsory.

• MPW (London)

Mander Portman Woodward, 108 Cromwell Road, London SW7 4ES. Tel 0171 835 1355

• Pupils 400 • Boys 14–20 (Day) • Girls 14–20 (Day) • Upper sixth 200 • Termly fees £3057 (Day) • CIFE • Enquiries/application to the Principals

What it's like

The college was founded in London in 1973 to offer an alternative to conventional education and to cater for pupils needing to retake A-level exams and those trying Oxbridge entrance. It now consists of a group of colleges based in four centres – Birmingham, Bristol, Cambridge and London. The group offers a very wide range of courses at A-level and GCSE; its reputation is based on exam results and the number of pupils who gain entrance to university and medical school. Many of the pupils are retaking exams. The colleges have managed to create environments in which those pupils who have lost motivation or confidence in the past are able to rediscover and enjoy the traditional values of hard work and academic discipline. The colleges have large full-time and part-time staffs. This permits unusually favourable staff:pupil ratios. At A-level there is an absolute maximum of seven pupils in each teaching group. The method is based on rigorous tuition with great emphasis placed on the demands of syllabuses and on examination techniques. Full-time pupils follow a general academic curriculum and also have the opportunity to pursue cultural activities and sport in local facilities. Academic progress is closely monitored by personal tutors who write regular reports and who will arrange a meeting between parents and subject tutors when necessary. These personal tutors have few, if any, teaching commitments.

MPW London has handsome and well-equipped premises. A predominantly young staff of 35 plus 25 part-timers cater for 400 pupils, about half of whom are retaking exams. A full range of courses is available and very good exam results are achieved. Some 85% of pupils go on to degree courses. There is some sport available (eg squash, badminton, swimming). The college arranges a variety of trips abroad, to the theatre etc. A new building opened in 1995 to provide additional leisure and sporting facilities.

School profile

Pupils Age range 14–20; 400 day pupils (200 boys, 200 girls). 50% doing retakes. Entry at 14–18. *State school entry:* 5% of intake.

Entrance No entrance exam. High motivation and appropriate academic ability looked for; no religious requirements. Parents expected to buy textbooks. 10 pa scholarships, including 1 for a student from the maintained sector (up to full fees).

Head and staff Joint-Principals: Fiona Dowding and Dr Nigel Stout, 4 years in post. Fiona Dowding educated at Convent of St Helen and St Katherine, at Radley and Oxford (English). Nigel Stout educated at Magdalen College School and Oxford (philosophy and psychology); previously Joint-Principal at MPW (Bristol) and MPW (Cambridge). *Staff:* 35 full time, 25 part time. Annual turnover 10%. Average age 28.

Exam results In 1995, 45 in upper fifth, 200 in upper sixth, about half of whom are retaking exams. *GCSE:* In 1995, 55% upper fifth gained at least grade C in 5–7 subjects; and 45% in 1 subject. *A-levels:* 48% of all subject entries were at A or B grade.

University and college entrance 85% of 1995 sixth-form leavers went on to a degree course; others typically go on to other courses. Of those going on to university, 5% went to Oxbridge; 8% took courses in medicine, dentistry and veterinary science, 19% in science and engineering, 73% in humanities and social sciences.

Curriculum GCSE and A-levels. 35 subjects offered, including Russian, philosophy, environmental science. 30% take science A-levels; 50% arts/humanities; 20% a mixture of both. *Computing facilities:* Combination of desk-top and lap-top PCs enabling all members of a computer science group to work on their own computer. *Special provision:* Specialist teacher and counsellor for dyslexia.

The arts *Art:* 15 take GCSE; 20 A-level; on average,10 accepted for art college each year.

Sport No facilities on site; use of local clubs; squash, badminton, weight-training, swimming and other indoor sports – informal outdoor team sports available.

Uniform No uniform worn.

Houses/prefects No competitive houses or prefects.

Religion No religious worship at the college.

Social Geography and biology field trips, art history trip to Paris/Rome; theatre visits. Pupils allowed to bring own car/bike to school. Small self-service cafeteria. Smoking allowed in designated rooms; no alcohol allowed. New leisure and sporting facilities.

Discipline Strict rules on punctuality, attendance and homework. Pupils failing to produce homework required to see personal tutor. Pupils caught smoking cannabis on (or off) the premises would be expelled.

N

• NEW HALL

New Hall, Chelmsford, Essex CM3 3HT. Tel 01245 467588, Fax 01245 467188

• Pupils 545 • Boys 4–11 only • Girls 4–18 (Day/Board/Weekly) • Upper sixth 42 • Termly fees £1020–£2201 (Day) £2388–£3438 (Board) £2388–£3370 (Weekly) • GSA, BSA • Enquiries/application to the Registrar

What it's like

Founded at Liège in 1642 and run by the English Canonesses of the Holy Sepulchre. When the nuns were compelled to leave during the French Revolution, it was reopened at its present site in 1798–99. The present buildings are handsome and provide excellent facilities. The main building is New Hall, formerly a Tudor palace (once the home of Mary Tudor) and it is set in a beautiful 120-acre estate with excellent playing fields and sporting amenities. It is a Catholic school centred on a religious community and with a cosmopolitan intake; about half the pupils are Roman Catholics but many others are welcomed. Its essential aim is that staff and pupils should experience Christian community together. The life of the school is closely associated with the liturgy of the Church, of which Sunday Mass is an important element. Academic standards are high and results very good; most sixth-formers go on to degree courses each year. There is a massive commitment to music. It is very strong indeed in drama and dance (many productions) and art (sixth-form students exhibit locally). A wide range of sport and games (high standards attained) and a variety of activities caters for most needs. Voluntary service activities have gained national awards. There is an impressive record in the Duke of Edinburgh's Award Scheme. Justice and peace issues are important to the school's ethos. A co-educational prep school opened in 1994 on the same site.

School profile

Pupils Total age range 4–18; 545 pupils, 30 day boys, 515 girls (323 day, 192 boarding). Senior department 11–18; 405 girls. Main entry ages 4, 11 and into sixth; also 12, 13, 14. Small number are children of former pupils (but school has grown 5-fold in last 30 years). *State school entry:* 25% main intake, plus 50% to sixth.

Entrance Own entrance exam used. Variety of skills and a commitment to Christian values (half pupils are RC, but many other Christians and some non-Christians welcomed). Parents expected to buy only a few textbooks that are to be kept; extras usually under £100 per term, maximum £250. Some scholarships and bursaries.

Parents 20+% in industry or commerce. 50% live within 30 miles; 20% live overseas.

Head and staff *Headmistress:* Sister Anne Marie Brister CRSS, appointed 1996. Educated at New Hall and at the universities of Cambridge (history), Oxford (theology) and Newcastle (education). Previously Head of History and taught classics, Latin and RE at New Hall; has also worked in personnel management with British Leyland. *Staff:* 46 full time. Annual turnover 1%.

Exam results In 1995, 70 pupils in upper fifth, 60 in upper sixth. *GCSE:* In 1995, 48 upper fifth gained at least grade C in 8+ subjects; 18 in 5–7 subjects. *A-levels:* 54 upper sixth passed in 3+ subjects; 3 in 2; and 3 in 1 subject. Average UCAS points 20.4.

University and college entrance 92% of 1995 sixth-form leavers went on to a degree course (33% after a gap year); others typically go on to HND or secretarial courses or straight into employment. Of those going on to university, 7% went to Oxbridge; 10% took courses in medicine, dentistry and veterinary science, 14% in science and engineering, 5% in law, 30% in humanities and social sciences, 6% in art, design and architecture, 11% in other vocational subjects eg education, speech therapy, 17% in business, economics and accounting, 7% in other subjects.

Curriculum GCSE, AS and A-levels. Approx 20 GCSE subjects offered; 4 at AS; 19 at A-level. Approx 15% take science A-levels; 58% arts/humanities; 27% both; sixth-form is mixed ability, offering other courses eg GCSE courses in psychology, expressive arts, health & hygiene etc. *Vocational:* Work experience available. *Computing facilities:* IBM compatibles for IT GCSE, including desktop publishing and CD-Rom; plus PCs in business studies; Apple Macs (English and music); computer aided design and colour printing (art). *Special provision:* Special teaching and ancillary help for physically handicapped; specialist EFL staff; specialist dyslexia staff. *Europe:* French, German and Spanish offered at GCSE and A-level; also French AS-level; Italian GCSE as an extra. Regular exchanges (to France, Germany and Spain).

The arts *Music:* Over 50% of pupils learn a musical instrument; instrumental exams can be taken. Some 15 musical groups including year-based ensembles, choirs, orchestras, wind ensembles, pop groups. Liturgical choir has appeared at Westminster Cathedral and Brentwood Cathedral; various pupils are members of county youth orchestra and National Youth Choir. *Drama & dance*: Both offered. GCSE and A-level drama and expressive arts exams may be taken. Majority of pupils are involved in school productions and all in house/other productions. Pupils have gained places at LAMDA, Guildford, E15, Oxford, Mountview as well as numerous drama/English honours degrees. *Art:* On average, 30 take GCSE, 1 AS-level, 12 A-level. Pottery, textiles, photography also offered. A number continue art to degree level.

Sport, community service and clubs *Sport and physical activities:* Compulsory sports: (first to third forms) netball, hockey, gym, health related fitness, tennis, rounders, swimming. Optional: badminton, volleyball, trampolining, aerobics, short tennis, golf, squash, windsurfing, riding, cricket, football, fencing. BAGA, RLSS, BTF, ESA, ESAA exams may be taken. Netball, regional level teams, 3 representatives in county U19, U16 teams; hockey, 1 representative in regional team, 2 in county, 1 in national squad U19, U16; swimming, 1 British Schools. *Community service:* Pupils take bronze, silver and gold Duke of Edinburgh's Award. Community service optional at age 14. Voluntary service runs playgroups, visiting the elderly, handicapped club; Justice & Peace group works with homeless, adult literacy group etc. *Clubs and societies:* Over 30 clubs, eg all sports, crafts, chess, bridge, maths, dressmaking, ballet, drama, music, French, riding.

Uniform School uniform worn; formal occasions only in sixth.

Houses/prefects Competitive houses. All members of upper sixth have positions of responsibility.

Religion Compulsory attendance at Eucharist on Sundays, Assemblies, House Prayers, etc. Many other opportunities.

Social Debates, choirs, social events with other schools. Trips abroad arranged most half-terms and holidays. Pupils allowed to bring own bike/caged pet to school. Meals self-service. No tobacco allowed; sixth-form permitted limited alcohol under supervision and on special occasions.

Discipline Pupils failing to produce homework once might expect help from tutor; any involvement in illegal drugs can lead to expulsion.

Boarding Upper sixth have own study bedroom, some lower sixth share; all others in individual cubicles in dormitories (each with own basin). 2 houses for ages 13–16, plus separate houses for 11–12 year olds and for sixth-form. Resident SRN. Central dining room. Pupils can provide and cook some own food at weekends. Exeats – vary with age (on the principle that some weekend time at school allows pupils to benefit from boarding but contact with home encouraged). Weekend visits to local town allowed, dependent on age.

Former pupils Cindy Buxton (natural history film maker); Ciaran Madden (actress); Nadine Beddington (past president, ARIBA); Anya Hindmarch (businesswoman).

• NEWCASTLE CHURCH HIGH

Newcastle Upon Tyne Church High School, Tankerville Terrace, Jesmond, Newcastle Upon Tyne NE2 3BA. Tel 0191 281 4306, Fax 0191 281 0806

• Pupils 668 • Boys None • Girls 3–18 (Day) • Upper sixth 37 • Termly fees £1245 (Day) • GSA • Enquiries/application to the School Secretary

What it's like

Founded in 1885, it stands in a pleasant residential district in one of the older suburbs, close to the city centre and university. The original buildings (completed in 1890) are well designed and there are many modern additions. These are surrounded by pleasant gardens and grounds. The senior and junior schools are on the same site and there is a nursery school for 3-year-olds. It caters for varying degrees of academic ability and lays considerable stress on a Christian atmosphere and education. Exam results are good and most sixth-formers go on to degree courses. There are flourishing music, art and drama departments and a fair range of sports, games (good district and county representation) and activities. Strong commitment to local community schemes.

School profile

Pupils Total age range 3–18; 668 day girls. Senior department 11–18, 367 girls. Main entry ages 3, 4, 7, 9, 11 and into sixth. Approx 5% are children of former pupils. *State school entry:* 65% senior intake, plus minimal proportion to sixth.

Entrance Own entrance exam used. No special skills or religious requirements. Parents not expected to buy textbooks. 5 pa assisted places. 12 pa scholarships/exhibitions, plus 2 music, 25%–50% of fees.

Head and staff *Headmistress:* Mrs L G Smith, appointed 1996. Educated at Colston's Girls' School and London University (medieval and modern history). Previously at St Nicholas School, Fleet. Also FRSA. *Staff:* 49 full time, 13 part time.

Exam results In 1995, 63 pupils in upper fifth, 47 in upper sixth. *GCSE:* In 1995, 97% upper fifth gained at least grade C in 8+ subjects. *A-levels:* 36 upper sixth passed in 3+ subjects; 8 in 2; and 2 in 1 subject. Average UCAS points 18.0.

University and college entrance 99% of 1995 sixth-form leavers went on to a degree course (5% after a gap year); others typically go on to retail management schemes. Of those going on to university, 11% went to Oxbridge; 5% took courses in medicine, dentistry and veterinary science, 8% in science and engineering, 11% in law, 24% in humanities and social sciences, 8% in art and design, 11% in other vocational subjects eg physiotherapy, nursing, sports studies, 33% in other subjects eg media, town planning. .

Curriculum GCSE and *A-levels:* 19 GCSE and A-level subjects offered. *Vocational:* Work experience available; also RSA qualifications in CLAIT. *Computing facilities:* 18 computers in labs. *Special provision:* EFL tutor (senior school). *Europe:* French and German offered at GCSE, AS and A-level. Regular exchanges (France and Germany).

The arts (Pupils aged 11 and over) *Music:* Over 30% of pupils learn a musical instrument; instrumental exams can be taken. Some 7 musical groups including orchestra, madrigal group, chamber ensembles, recorder group etc. *Drama and dance:* Both offered. Central School exams may be taken. Some pupils are involved in school and house/other productions. *Art:* On average, 12 take GCSE, 4–5 A-level.

Sport, community service and clubs (Pupils aged 11 and over) *Sport and physical activities:* Compulsory sports: netball, tennis, hockey, athletics, swimming, rounders. Optional: table tennis. Sixth form only: badminton. Netball, county and city U18 champions; 30 girls represent county and city in various sports; 3 girls in regional YSA team, 1 in national team; swimming, 1 girl in national youth team. *Community service:* Pupils take bronze, silver and gold Duke of Edinburgh's Award. Community service optional. *Clubs and societies:* Up to 15 clubs, eg music, drama, Christian Union, debating, computer, chess, first aid, cookery, fencing, aerobics.

Uniform School uniform worn, optional in the sixth.

Houses/prefects Competitive houses. Prefects and head girl, appointed by sixth-form and staff; head of house and house prefects by girls. Sixth-form council meets twice a term.

Religion Daily assembly. 3 or 4 church services a year.

Social Summer fair, debates and music with local schools. Trips for skiing, art and languages; sports weeks in holidays (riding, canoeing, orienteering). Pupils allowed to bring own car to school. Meals cafeteria-style. No tobacco/alcohol allowed.

Discipline Detention is given for three consecutive pieces of work not produced.

Alumni association is run by Mrs A Horrocks, Heugh Mill House, Mill Lane, Stamfordham, Northumberland NE18 OPS.

• NEWCASTLE-UNDER-LYME

Newcastle-under-Lyme School, Mount Pleasant, Newcastle-under-Lyme, Staffordshire ST5 IDB. Tel 01782 633604, Fax 01782 632765

• Pupils 1295 • Boys 8–18 (Day) • Girls 8–18 (Day) • Upper sixth 155 • Termly fees £1026-£1180 (Day) • HMC • Enquiries/application to the Principal

What it's like

Founded in 1981 through the amalgamation of Newcastle High School (1874) and Orme Girls' School (1876). The school is set in some 30 acres of grounds in a quiet residential suburb close to the centre of the town. The original buildings still form part of the school and a number of extensions provide good, modern facilities. The school has built up a strong academic reputation and results are very good; most sixth-formers go on to degree courses, including many to Oxbridge. Music and drama are strong and it is also well known for its high standards in games. There is a vigorous voluntary CCF and a mixed Scout troop. The school's structure combines predominantly single-sex teaching between the ages of 11 and 16, with full co-education in the sixth-form.

School profile

Pupils Total age range 8–18; 1295 day pupils (635 boys, 660 girls). Senior department 11–18, 1150 pupils (572 boys, 578 girls). Main entry ages 8, 11, 13 and into sixth. Approx 10% are children of former pupils. *State school entry:* 50% senior intake.

Entrance Own exam used. No special skills or religious requirements. Parents not expected to buy textbooks. 82 pa assisted places (including 5 at age 8). 6 pa scholarships at age 11, £800–£1200 plus sixth-form maths scholarships (£1000) and physics scholarship (£250).

Parents 15+% in industry or commerce; 15+% are doctors, lawyers, etc.

Head and staff *Principal:* Dr Ray Reynolds, 6 years in post. Educated at Bangor Grammar and Belfast University (physics and mathematics). Previously Head of Physics and Head Master of the Upper Sixth at Millfield, Head of Physical Sciences at Royal Forest of Dean Grammar, Physics Master at Royal Belfast Academical Institution and Lecturer in Physics at Belfast University. Also formerly Chief Examiner O-level physics and Reviser in GCSE physics. Publications: papers in international scientific journals on gaseous electronics and atomic collision physics. *Staff:* 85 full time, 17 part time. Annual turnover 5%. Average age 40.

Exam results In 1995, 173 pupils in fifth, 151 in upper sixth. *GCSE:* In 1995, 98% fifth gained at least grade C in 8+ subjects; 2% in 5–7 subjects. *A-levels:* 75% upper sixth passed in 4+ subjects; 15% in 3; 9% in 2 subjects. Average UCAS points 20.3 (including general studies, 26.2).

University and college entrance 93% of 1995 sixth-form leavers went on to a degree course; others typically go on to art courses or retake A-levels. Of those going on to university, 10% went to Oxbridge; 5% took courses in medicine, dentistry and veterinary science, 35% in science and engineering, 57% in humanities and social sciences, 2% in art and design.

Curriculum GCSE and A-levels. 24 subjects offered at A-level (including Greek); all sixth-form take A-level general studies. 32% take science A-levels; 36% arts/humanities; 32% both. *Vocational:* Work experience available. *Computing facilities:* 2 computer rooms. *Europe:* French and German offered to GCSE, AS and A-level; also Russian GCSE and A-level and Spanish GCSE. Regular exchanges to France and Germany, occasionally to Russia.

The arts (Pupils aged 11 and over) *Music:* 25% of pupils learn a musical instrument; instrumental exams can be taken. Some 11 musical groups including 2 orchestras, 4 choirs, wind band, jazz band, recorder groups, guitar ensemble. *Drama and dance:* Drama offered. Many pupils are involved in school productions. *Art:* On average, 35 take GCSE; 10 A-level. Design, pottery, textiles, photography also offered.

Sport, community service and clubs (Pupils aged 11 and over) *Sport and physical activities:* Compulsory sports: swimming; rugby, hockey, cricket (boys to 16); swimming, netball, rounders, hockey (girls to 16). Optional: cross-country, athletics, basketball, water polo, shooting, judo, badminton, table tennis. Sixth form only: aerobics, squash, golf. BAGA, RLSS exams may be taken. International representatives in badminton (2 pupils), rugby, squash, swimming, water polo; county reps in badminton, hockey, swimming, squash, cricket, rugby, netball; county/league champion teams, rugby, hockey (girls), netball, tennis. *Community service:* Pupils take bronze, silver and gold Duke of Edinburgh's Award. CCF and community service optional. *Clubs and societies:* Over 15 clubs, eg art, calligraphy, computing, debating, history, literary, school magazine, Scouts, BAYS.

Uniform School uniform worn throughout.

Houses/prefects Competitive houses. Head boy and girl, their deputies and senior prefects are elected by the lower sixth and staff.

Religion Daily assemblies

Social 6 organised trips abroad and exchange systems with schools abroad annually. Pupils allowed to bring own car/bike/motorbike to school. Meals self-service. School shop. No tobacco/alcohol allowed.

Discipline Pupils failing to produce homework once might expect a repeat or detention; those caught smoking cannabis on the premises could expect expulsion.

Former pupils Sir Richard Bailey; Sir David Barritt; 6 professors; 2 generals; an admiral.

• NORTH FORELAND LODGE

North Foreland Lodge, Reading Road, Sherfield-on-Loddon, Hook, Hampshire RG27 0HT. Tel 01256 882431

• Pupils 150 • Boys None • Girls 11–18 (Day/Board) • Upper sixth 15 • Termly fees £2200 (Day) £3600 (Board) • GSA, BSA • Enquiries/application to the Head Mistress

What it's like

Founded 1909, it occupies a pleasant rural site near Basingstoke. The buildings are pleasant and facilities and accommodation are up to date. A sound education is given, based on the teaching of the Church of England. Results are good and many sixth-form leavers go on to degree courses. Vocational qualifications are offered. There is a staff:pupil ration of 1:7. A standard range of sports, games and extra-curricular activities.

School profile

Pupils Age range 11–18; 150 boarding girls; a few day girls accepted from 1995. Main entry ages 11–12. *State school entry:* None.

Entrance Common Entrance exam used plus own assessment day. No special skills or religious requirements. Parents not expected to buy textbooks; music and sport coaching extra. A variety of scholarships at 11, 12 and sixth-form.

Head and staff *Headmistress:* Miss Diana Matthews, in post for 13 years. Educated at Stamford High, and at universities of Nottingham, London and Paris (history/archaeology). Previously Housemistress, Senior Mistress and Head of History at The Abbey, Reading. *Staff:* 23 full time, 17 part time. Annual turnover 10%. Average age 42.

Exam results In 1995, 28 pupils in upper fifth, 22 in upper sixth. *GCSE:* In 1995, 24 upper fifth gained at least grade C in 8+ subjects; 3 in 5–7 subjects. *A-levels:* 18 upper sixth passed in 3 subjects; 3 in 2 subjects. Average UCAS points 18.8.

University and college entrance 70% of 1995 sixth-form leavers went on to a degree course; others typically go on to non-degree courses eg secretarial.

Curriculum GCSE and A-levels (A-level general studies offered). 14% took science A-levels; 86% arts/humanities. *Vocational:* Work experience for one week a year, organised by parents; City and Guilds professional cooks certificate (upper sixth) and RSA qualifications in CLAIT and typewriting 1 and 2. *Computing facilities:* RM Nimbus network. *Europe:* French and Spanish offered at GCSE, AS and A-level; German to GCSE. Regular exchanges for sixth-form to Spain; visits most years to eg France, Italy or Spain.

The arts *Music:* Over 50% of pupils learn a musical instrument; instrumental exams can be taken. Some 6 musical groups including choirs, orchestra, chapel players, various woodwind groups. *Drama & dance*: Both offered. GCSE drama may be taken. All pupils are involved in school and house/other productions. *Art:* On average, 10 take GCSE, 2–3 AS-level, 2–3 A-level. Design, pottery, textiles, photography also offered.

Sport, community service and clubs *Sport and physical activities:* Compulsory sports: lacrosse, netball, tennis, swimming. Optional: gymnastics, trampolining, fencing, basketball, badminton. BAGA and RLSS exams may be taken. Lacrosse, 3 county players;

fencing, various national qualifiers, trampolining, gold and silver medals in reading competition. *Community service:* Pupils take bronze, silver and gold Duke of Edinburgh's Award. Community service optional. *Clubs and societies:* Up to 10 clubs, eg art, crafts, drama, debating, gymnastics, bridge, chess.
Uniform Uniform throughout, except in sixth.
Houses/prefects No competitive houses. Head girl, elected by lower sixth. School Council.
Religion Attendance at certain services is compulsory.
Social Educational trips organised annually. Upper sixth allowed to bring own car to school. Meals self-service. School shop. No tobacco/alcohol allowed except for upper sixth.

• NORTH LONDON COLLEGIATE

North London Collegiate School, Canons, Edgware, Middlesex HA8 7RJ. Tel 0181 952 0912, Fax 0181 951 1391

• Pupils 998 • Boys None • Girls 4–18 (Day) • Upper sixth 106 • Termly fees £1616 (Day) • GSA • Enquiries/application to the Headmistress

What it's like

Founded in 1850 by Miss Frances Buss, the first woman to use the title 'headmistress'. In 1929 it bought Canons, the former home of the Duke of Chandos, a magnificent 18th-century house with fine terraces and gardens, which is now the heart of the school for the sixth-form. A modern school was added in the 30 acres of parkland, including a music school, a drawing school, a theatre, a new library, an indoor swimming pool and a junior school – its facilities are very good. Strongly traditional, it is an energetic, purposeful school. Standards are very high and the results obtained are excellent. Almost all pupils go to university including many to Oxbridge. The school has a strong musical tradition (300 girls learn an instrument), and many opportunities for drama. A range of sports, games and extra-curricular activities, including the Duke of Edinburgh's Award Scheme.

School profile

Pupils Total age range 4–18; 998 day girls. Senior department 11–18, 744 girls. Main entry ages 4, 7, 11 and into sixth. Approx 10% are children of former pupils.
Entrance Own entrance exam used. No special skills or religious requirements. Parents not expected to buy textbooks. 13 pa assisted places. 7 pa bursaries, 4 pa scholarships, £4848.
Head and staff *Headmistress:* Mrs Joan Clanchy, in post for 10 years. Educated at St Leonards School, St Andrews, and Oxford University (history). Previously Headmistress at St George's (Edinburgh), Head of History and Head of Sixth at Park School and Assistant Teacher at Glasgow High and Woodberry Down Comp. *Staff:* 60 full time, 35 part time. Annual turnover 6%.
Exam results In 1995, 100 pupils in upper fifth, 106 in upper sixth. *GCSE:* In 1995, all in upper fifth gained at least grade C in 8+ subjects. *A-levels:* 36 upper sixth passed in 4+ subjects; 70 in 3 subjects. Average UCAS points 28.7.
University and college entrance All 1995 sixth-form leavers went on to a degree course (45% after a gap year); 26% to Oxbridge. 16% took courses in medicine, dentistry and veterinary science, 25% in science and engineering, 5% in law, 40% in humanities and social sciences, 2% in art and design, 10% in vocational subjects eg nursing, business studies, artchitecture, education, 2% in drama and music.
Curriculum GCSE and A-levels. *Vocational:* Work experience available. *Computing facilities:* Network of 12 BBC + 4 stand-alone BBCs; a network of 14 Nimbus (RM), plotters, printers, etc; network of 20 Apple Macs. *Europe:* French, German and Spanish offered at GCSE, AS and A-level; also Russian at GCSE and A-level, and Italian GCSE. Regular exchanges (to France and Germany). Membership of Young Europeans; regular information on Erasmus.
The arts (Pupils aged 11 and over) *Music:* Over 30% of pupils learn a musical instrument; instrumental exams can be taken. Many musical groups including 2 orchestras, concert band, 2 choirs, chamber groups. Finalists in National Chamber Music Competition; 4 major concerts in school each year. *Drama and dance:* Both

offered. 2 major productions a year. *Art:* On average, 30+ take GCSE, 18 A-level. Design, pottery, photography also offered. Murals at National Audit Office and at Royal Society.
Sport, community service and clubs (Pupils aged 11 and over) *Sport and physical activities:* Compulsory sports: lacrosse, tennis, netball, swimming, athletics. Optional: badminton, trampolining, cross-country. RLSS examinations may be taken. English Schools cross-country selection. *Community service:* Pupils take bronze, silver and gold Duke of Edinburgh's Award. *Clubs and societies:* Up to 15 clubs, eg debating, chess, polyglot, Jewish, science, Young Enterprise, Earth Action, charity, electronics.
Uniform School uniform worn except in the sixth.
Houses/prefects Senior student committee elected by sixth-form.
Religion Religious worship compulsory.
Social Some debates, drama, lectures with other schools. Exchange with a French and German school, skiing trips, visits to France, Russia, Italy, Greece, etc. Outdoor education week for 3rd year each summer. Pupils allowed to bring own bike to school; upper sixth allowed to bring cars. Meals self-service.
Discipline Codes of practice made clear to the student body. Strong pastoral care.
Former pupils Stevie Smith, Stella Gibbons, Marie Stoppes, Barbara Amiel, Susie Orbach, Eleanor Bron, Esther Rantzen, Natasha Walters.

• NORTHAMPTONSHIRE GRAMMAR

Northamptonshire Grammar School, Pitsford, Northamptonshire NN6 9AX. Tel 01604 880306, Fax 01604 882212

• Pupils 180 • Boys 7–18 (Day) • Girls None • Upper sixth 19 • Termly fees £1660 (Day)
• Enquiries/application to the Headmaster's Secretary

What it's like

Founded in 1989, this new school has for its premises Pitsford Hall, in a fine 26-acre park 5 miles north of Northampton. The school, which is interdenominational, was created by parents to fill a gap, as there was no academic boys' day school in Northamptonshire. It aims eventually to have 360 pupils. A full range of subjects is provided, from classics to technology. The first sixth-formers left in 1994 and most pupils are expected to go on to higher education. There is a standard range of sports and games and it is gaining a national reputation at rugby.

School profile

Pupils Age range 7–18; 180 day boys. Main entry ages, 7, 8, 9, 11 and 13. *State school entry:* 50% at main intake at 11.
Entrance Common Entrance and own exam used. Christian foundation; sympathetic to others. Parents not expected to buy textbooks; maximum extras, £100 for lunches. 7 pa scholarships, 10 pa bursaries, value 10%–50% fees.
Head and staff *Headmaster:* Dan Hanson, in post since 1995. Educated at Durham University. Previously Acting Headmaster and Deputy Head at Birkdale School. *Staff:* 18 full time, 5 part time. Average age 33.
Exam results In 1995, 39 pupils in fifth year, 19 in upper sixth. *GCSE:* In 1995, 23 fifth year gained at least grade C in 8+ subjects; 10 in 5–7; and 5 in 1–4 subjects. *A-levels:* 3 passed in 4+ subjects; 8 in 3; and 6 in 2 subjects. Average UCAS points 14.6.
University and college entrance 95% of 1995 sixth-form leavers went on to a degree course (15% after a gap year), 5% went to Oxbridge; 30% took courses in medicine, dentistry and veterinary science, 30% in science and engineering, 10% in law, 20% in humanities and social sciences, 10% in other vocational subjects eg phsyiotherapy, equine studies.
Curriculum GCSE and *A-levels:* 18 GCSE subjects offered, 15 A-level. 50% take science A-levels; 10% arts/humanities; 40% both. *Vocational:* Work experience mandatory. *Computing facilities:* Archimedes, Apple Macs, PCs. *Europe:* French (from age 10), German (from 13) offered to GCSE and A-level; also Spanish GCSE in sixth-form. Regular exchanges (France and Germany).
The arts (Pupils aged 11 and over) *Music:* 20% of pupils learn a musical instrument; instrumental exams can be taken. School choir. Several pupils in county bands and

orchestras. *Drama & dance:* Drama offered. Many pupils are involved in school productions. Boys in professional productions at Royal Theatre, Northampton, and Birmingham Royal Ballet. *Art:* On average, 10 take GCSE. Boys design sets for school productions.
Sport, community service and clubs (Pupils aged 11 and over) *Sport and physical activities:* Compulsory sports: rugby, cricket, athletics. Optional: hockey, cross-country, golf, sailing, badminton, tennis. Sixth form only: squash. County and regional representation in cricket, golf and rugby (30 in 1994). All rugby teams reached at least the semi-finals of the county competition, 2 in England squads; U15 team in last eight of national cup competition. *Community service:* Pupils take bronze, silver and gold Duke of Edinburgh's Award.
Uniform School uniform worn; dress regulations in the sixth.
Houses/prefects Competitive houses. Prefects, head of school and heads of houses – appointed by the Headmaster.
Religion Regular religious school assemblies. Occasional atendance at local parish church.
Social Musical events, debating, general knowledge competitions, and dances with Northampton High School. Annual visits to Hadrian's Wall, and to France, Germany and Italy/Greece; skiing holiday. Pupils allowed to bring own bike/car to school. Meals formal. School shop. No tobacco/alcohol allowed.
Discipline Pupils failing to produce homework once would be asked to produce it next day (failure to do so results in detention); those caught smoking cannabis on the premises would be expelled.

• NORTHFIELD

Northfield School, Church Road, Watford, Hertfordshire WD1 3QB. Tel 01923 229758
• Pupils 120 • Boys 2½–7 only (Day) • Girls 2½–18 (Day) • Upper sixth 5 • Termly fees £1440 (Day) • SHA, AHIS, ISAI • Enquiries/application to the Secretary

What it's like

Founded c. 1870, it has occupied its present urban, single-site premises since 1944. It combines a nursery class and kindergarten. The main building is a large private house with very agreeable grounds. Modern extensions provide good facilities. A pleasant, happy school which has all the advantages of being small. It prides itself on a caring and supportive atmosphere and has very small learning groups. All girls in the upper school are expected to take 8 or 9 subjects at GCSE. Sixth-form courses fall into 3 categories: AS and A-levels in a range of subjects; GCSE one-year courses, eg business studies, sociology, child care, human biology; and vocational courses, eg Pitman foundation course, typing, office practice, bookkeeping, pre-nursery nursing course. A decent range of sports, games and activities.

School profile

Pupils Total age range 2½–18; 120 day pupils (15 boys, 105 girls). Senior department 11–18, 94 girls. Main entry ages 3 (boys and girls), 7, 11 and into sixth (girls). *State school entry:* 50% senior intake.
Entrance Own entrance exam used. No special skills or religious requirements. Sixth form scholarships/bursaries.
Head and staff *Headmistress:* Mrs Pamela Hargreaves, in post 6 years. Educated at The Collegiate School, Blackpool, and at Hull University (physics and pure mathematics) and Hatfield Polytechnic (education). Previously Assistant Deputy Head at St Albans High, Head of Physics at Hatfield Girls' Grammar and Physics and Mathematics Teacher at Cheadle County Grammar School. Also Committee Member, AHIS, ISAI National Executive Council; Hertfordshire Science Teaching Association; member of SHA. *Staff:* 5 full time, 20 part time. Annual turnover negligible.
Exam results In 1995, 14 pupils in fifth, 5 in upper sixth. *GCSE:* In 1995, 88% fifth gain at least grade C in 5+ subjects. *A-levels:* 5 upper sixth passed in 3 subjects. Average UCAS points 18.8.
University and college entrance All 1995 sixth-form leavers went on to a degree course (20% after a gap year); 60% took courses in science and engineering, 20% in art

and design, 20% in other subjects.
Curriculum GCSE and A-levels plus vocational courses. 17 subjects offered (no A-level general studies). *Vocational:* Work experience available; also Pitman intermediate level typing, text production, office practice and shorthand. *Computing facilities:* computer in every lower school classroom; computer room available for all age groups. *Europe:* French (from age 11), German (from 13) offered to GCSE, AS and A-level.
The arts (Pupils aged 11 and over) *Music:* Over 15% of pupils learn a musical instrument; instrumental exams can be taken. 2 musical groups – orchestra and choir. *Drama & dance*: Both offered. GCSE drama, LAMDA exams may be taken. Majority of pupils are involved in school and house/other productions. Every year girls go to drama school, others continue interest through eg amateur dramatic society. *Art:* On average, 12 take GCSE, 2 AS-level, 3 A-level. Art history also offered. Girls go on to art school each year.
Sport, community service and clubs (Pupils aged 11 and over) *Sport and physical activities:* Compulsory sports: swimming, netball, tennis, rounders, athletics, gym. Optional: badminton. *Community service:* Pupils take bronze, silver and gold Duke of Edinburgh's Award. Community service optional, mainly fourth form but some other ages. Regular charity fund-raising; third-form pupils liaise with school for handicapped children each year.
Uniform School uniform worn except in the sixth.
Houses/prefects Competitive houses. Prefects, head girl, head of house and house prefects – elected by the school and staff. School council (head girl chairs meetings of class reps and some staff; broad range of non-curricular matters discussed).
Religion Daily prayers.
Social Public speaking and road safety competitions with other local schools. Week in France for fourth and fifth forms. Pupils allowed to bring own car/bike to school. No tobacco/alcohol allowed.
Discipline Discipline is dealt with at an appropriate level, being brought to the attention of the Deputy Head or Headmistress only if repeated or of a serious nature. The parents of any girl found smoking at school would be contacted, asked to escort her home and keep her there until consultation between Headmistress and family had produced a satisfactory outcome and necessary assurances from the individual concerned.

• NORTHWOOD

Northwood College, Maxwell Road, Northwood, Middlesex HA6 2YE. Tel 01923 825446

• Pupils 661 • Boys None • Girls 4–18 (Day) • Upper sixth 34 • Termly fees £1612 (Day) • GSA
• Enquiries/application to the Head Mistress

What it's like

Founded in 1878, it is single-site on the outskirts of London. The college consists of the original main building (1892) and several modern buildings erected during the last 25 years. These provide good, up-to-date facilities in a pleasant environment including a fully-equipped science block, indoor swimming pool and sports hall. Academic standards and results are very good. Most sixth-form leavers go on to degree courses each year, including Oxbridge. Girls have much opportunity to participate in music and drama. There is a good range of sports and games, a wide variety of clubs and activities and some commitment to local community schemes; the Duke of Edinburgh's Award Scheme is available and there is an Air Training Corps.

School profile

Pupils Total age range 4–18; 661 day girls. Senior department 11–18, 407 girls. Main entry ages 4, 7, 11 and into sixth. *State school entry:* 25% senior intake, plus 25% to sixth.
Entrance Own entrance exam used. No special skills or religious requirements. Parents not expected to buy textbooks; £200 maximum extras. Assisted places. 3 pa sixth-form scholarships, one third tuition fees.
Parents 30% in industry or commerce; 30% are doctors, lawyers, etc.
Head and staff *Headmistress:* Mrs Ann Mayou, 5 years in post. Educated at City of Bath Girls' School and Oxford University (PPE). Previously Head of Sixth Form, Head of

Economics and Head of Careers at Oxford High. *Staff:* 41 full time, 12 part time. Annual turnover 5%. Average age 40.

Exam results In 1995, 47 pupils in upper fifth and 34 in upper sixth. *GCSE:* In 1995, all upper fifth gained at least grade C in 6+ subjects. *A-levels:* 31 upper sixth passed in 3+ subjects. Average UCAS points 20.6.

University and college entrance 95% of 1995 sixth-form leavers went on to a degree course (20% after a gap year), 5% to Oxbridge; 20% took courses in medicine, dentistry and veterinary science, 20% in science and engineering, 10% in law, 20% in humanities and social sciences, 10% in art and design, 10% in other vocational subjects eg education, 10% in eg drama and music.

Curriculum GCSE and A-levels; 27 subjects offered. *Computing facilities:* 43 machines in computing centre plus ECCTIS 2000 facility in careers room. *Europe:* French (compulsory from 7), German and Spanish offered at GCSE and A-level. Regular exchanges (France and Germany). Sixth-form attend language courses in France; sixth-form representatives attend EU Conference in Luxembourg.

The arts (Pupils aged 11 and over) *Music:* Over 40% of pupils learn a musical instrument; instrumental exams can be taken. Musical groups include orchestra, 2 choirs, concert band. *Drama & dance*: both offered as part of the curriculum, ballet as an extra. GCSE and A-level drama, ESB and Central exams may be taken. Majority of pupils are involved in school productions. Recent production of The Merchant of Venice. *Art:* On average, 15 take GCSE, 5 A-level. Design technology, textiles, graphic design also offered.

Sport, community service and clubs (Pupils aged 11 and over) *Sport and physical activities:* Compulsory sports (at various ages): rounders, hockey, netball, dance, swimming, gymnastics, tennis. Optional: volleyball, badminton, judo. County and borough representatives at hockey, netball and swimming; borough team winners at hockey, netball and rounders; county hockey and netball tournament entrants. *Community service:* Pupils participate in the Duke of Edinburgh's Award Scheme. Community service optional. ATC available. *Clubs and societies:* Clubs include debating, science, maths, music, art, drama, sports.

Uniform School uniform worn except in the sixth.

Houses/prefects Competitive houses. Prefects, head girl, heads of houses – appointed by Head Mistress, nominated by senior pupils and staff.

Religion Assembly compulsory for all.

Social Joint conferences with local independent boys' schools. Organised skiing trips, classical tours, choir tour in France, hockey course, geography field trips. Pupils allowed to bring own car/bike to school. Meals self-service. No tobacco/alcohol allowed.

Discipline Those caught using drugs on the premises could expect expulsion.

Former pupils Dame Margaret Booth (judge).

• NORWICH

Norwich School, The Close, Norwich, NR1 4DQ. Tel 01603 623194

• Pupils 780 • Boys 8–18 (Day) • Girls 16–18 (Day) • Upper sixth 115 • Termly fees £1510 (Day) • HMC, CSA • Enquiries/application to the Headmaster

What it's like

An ancient foundation, it was re-founded and granted a charter by Edward VI in 1547 and moved to its present site in the Cathedral Close a few years later. Its buildings are very handsome, in some cases magnificent – including the early 14th-century Chapel. Overall, the school is very well equipped with modern facilities and since 1949 has been strongly supported by the Worshipful Company of Dyers. It is non-denominational but has a C of E chaplain and enjoys daily assemblies in the cathedral. Cathedral choristers are educated at the school and there is a certain amount of emphasis on ecumenical religious instruction. Girls were admitted to the sixth-form in 1994. A broad, general education is provided and results are very good. Most sixth-form leavers go on to a degree course, a good number to Oxbridge. Music is very strong and all pupils are encouraged to take part; a large number is involved in orchestras, choirs and bands. Drama is also strong and there is close co-operation with Norwich High in theatrical activities. There are excellent facilities for sport and games and high standards are attained in rugby, cricket and hockey (numerous representatives at county level) as well as other games. Many clubs and societies cater for most conceivable needs. There is considerable emphasis on outdoor activities which include cycling, shooting, sailing, and rowing. There is a flourishing group of Sea Scouts and the Duke of Edinburgh's Award Scheme has been well supported over the years. Plentiful use is made of Norwich's cultural amenities.

School profile

Pupils Total age range 8–18; 780 day pupils (755 boys, 25 girls). Senior department 11–18, 630 pupils (605 boys, 25 girls). Main entry ages, 8, 9, 11, 12 (boys) and into sixth (boys and girls). 5% are children of former pupils. *State school entry:* 50% main intake, plus 30% to sixth.

Entrance Common Entrance and own exam used. No special skills or religious requirements. Parents not expected to buy textbooks; public exam fees are only extras. 18 pa assisted places. 8 pa scholarships/bursaries, £300 to full tuition fees (means tested).

Parents 15+% are doctors, lawyers, etc. 80+% live within 30 miles.

Head and staff *Headmaster:* C D Brown, in post for 12 years. Educated at Plymouth College and Cambridge (English). Previously Head of English and Director of Sixth Form at Radley. Also member of the National Committee of the Choir Schools Association; member of the Editorial Board of HMC Magazine (1988); HMC Committee. *Staff:* 58 full time, 4 part time. Annual turnover 8%. Average age 42.

Exam results In 1995, 104 pupils in upper fifth, 94 in upper sixth. *GCSE:* In 1995, 93% upper fifth gained at least grade C in 8+ subjects; 7% in 5–7 subjects. *A-levels:* 6% upper sixth passed in 4+ subjects; 85% in 3; 8% in 2; and 1% in 1 subject. Average UCAS points 22.1.

University and college entrance 98% of 1995 sixth-form leavers went on to a degree course (50% after a gap year); others typically go on to retake A-levels or straight into jobs. Of those going on to university, 12% went to Oxbridge; 5% took courses in medicine, dentistry and veterinary science, 35% in science and engineering, 5% in law, 48% in humanities and social sciences, 7% in art and design.

Curriculum GCSE and *A-levels:* 19 subjects offered (no A-level general studies). 37% take science A-levels; 34% arts/humanities; 29% both. *Vocational:* Work experience available. *Computing facilities:* 60 IBM compatible PCs (Novelle-networked and stand-alone); Acorn, Archimedes, Master and Micros, plus various peripherals. *Europe:* French and German offered at GCSE and A-level. Regular exchanges (to France and Germany).

The arts (Pupils aged 11 and over) *Music:* 40% of pupils learn a musical instrument; instrumental exams can be taken. Some 16 musical groups including chamber groups, jazz bands, orchestras, guitar, recorder groups, choirs. Recent choral and organ scholarships to Oxbridge. *Drama*: Many pupils are involved in school and house/other productions. Recent pupil accepted at LAMDA. *Art:* On average, 40 take GCSE, 3–4 AS-level, 9 A-level. Design, pottery, photography also offered. A number of pupils have obtained direct entry to art degree courses.

Sport, community service and clubs (Pupils aged 11 and over) *Sport and physical activities:* Compulsory sports: rugby, hockey, cricket. Optional: athletics, badminton, cross-country, cycling, fencing, golf, judo, rowing, self-defence, shooting, soccer, sailing, squash, swimming, table tennis and tennis. Sixth form only: volleyball. 2 England rugby players U16A; independent clay-pigeon shooting champions (1994); national schools squash champions (1992); national and regional achievements in squash, golf, fencing, tennis, shooting; regular county representation in hockey, cricket, rugby. *Community service:* Pupils take bronze, silver and gold Duke of Edinburgh's Award. Community service optional. Sea scout troup. *Clubs and societies:* Up to 30 clubs, eg electronics, debating.

Uniform School uniform worn throughout; more choice in sixth-form.

Houses/prefects Houses are pastoral units with some competitive games. Head of school, prefects, head of house and house prefects, appointed by the Headmaster. School consultative committee.

Religion Attendance at daily assembly compulsory; chapel services are voluntary.

Social Debating, theatre, music, Young Enterprise with other schools. German and French exchanges and music trips abroad. Pupils allowed to bring own bike/motorbike. Meals self-service. School tuck shop. No tobacco/alcohol allowed.

Discipline Pupils failing to produce homework once could expect detention; those caught smoking cannabis on the premises could expect expulsion.
Alumni association is run by R Thompson, Hon Sec, Old Norvicensian Club, c/o the school.
Former pupils Sir John Quinton (Barclays Bank), Lord Blake, Clive Radley (England cricketer).

• NORWICH HIGH

Norwich High School for Girls GPDST, 95 Newmarket Road, Norwich, Norfolk NR2 2HU. Tel 01603 453265, Fax 01603 259891

• Pupils 900 • Boys None • Girls 4–18 (Day) • Upper sixth 87 • Termly fees £976–£1328 (Day)
• GSA, GPDST • Enquiries/application to the Admissions Secretary

What it's like

Founded in 1875, it is single-site in the middle of the city. The senior school is housed in a fine Georgian mansion in spacious wooded grounds and beautiful gardens. There are numerous purpose-built extensions and facilities are excellent. It enjoys a wide social spread of pupils drawn from Norfolk and north Suffolk. Non-denominational, it provides a very good education in the grammar school tradition. Results are very good and most leavers proceed to degree courses, including many to Oxbridge. Tremendously strong in music (most are involved) and also strong in drama and art. High standards in sport and games. An outstanding record in the Duke of Edinburgh's Award Scheme. Full advantage is taken of the city's cultural amenities. It has a high reputation locally and is well supported.

School profile

Pupils Total age range 4–18; 900 day girls. Senior department 11–18, 657 girls. Main entry ages 4, 7, 11 and into sixth. *State school entry:* 60% senior intake, plus 40% to sixth.
Entrance Own entrance exam used. All-rounders welcome; no religious requirements. Parents not expected to buy textbooks; no other extras. 50 pa assisted places (5 at age 7, 35 at 11, 10 to sixth). Scholarships, including music, 10%–50% fees. Also bursaries.
Head and staff *Headmistress:* Mrs Valerie Bidwell, in post 11 years. Educated at Harrogate Ladies College and at Newcastle and London universities (French and German). Previously Senior Mistress and Head of Modern Languages at Framlingham. Also GSA Council Member. *Staff:* 55 full time, 11 part time.
Exam results In 1995, 102 pupils in upper fifth, 87 in upper sixth. *GCSE:* In 1995, 98 upper fifth gained at least grade C in 9 subjects; 4 in 5–8 subjects. *A-levels:* 84 upper sixth passed in 4+ subjects; 2 in 3; 1 in 1 subject. Average UCAS points 22.3.
University and college entrance 94% of sixth-form leavers go on to a degree course; others typically go on to non-degree courses in eg art, drama or straight into careers. Of those going on to university, 12% went to Oxbridge; 8% took courses in medicine, dentistry and veterinary science, 48% in science and engineering, 40% in humanities and social sciences, 3% in art and design, 1% in music.
Curriculum GCSE and A-levels. 21 subjects offered (including A-level general studies). 14% take science A-levels; 40% arts/humanities; 45% both. *Vocational:* Work experience available; also RSA qualification in CLAIT. *Computing facilities:* Networked and free-standing machines. *Europe:* French (from age 11) and German (from 12) offered at GCSE, AS and A-level; also Spanish GCSE and A-level, and Italian GCSE in sixth. Regular exchanges (France and Germany).
The arts (Pupils aged 11 and over) *Music:* Over 50% of pupils learn a musical instrument; instrumental exams can be taken. Some 14+ musical groups including jazz, 3 orchestras, wind band, recorder, chamber ensembles, 3 choirs etc. *Drama & dance*: Both offered. GCSE theatre arts may be taken. Some pupils are involved in school productions and majority in house/other productions. ESU regional finalists. *Art:* On average, 25 take GCSE, 3–4 AS-level, 3–4 A-level. Design, photography also offered.
Sport, community service and clubs (Pupils aged 11 and over) *Sport and physical activities:* Compulsory sports: lacrosse, netball, swimming, gym, rounders, athletics, tennis. Optional: badminton, lifesaving, fencing. Sixth form only: volleyball, golf, riding,

aerobics. BAGA, RLSS exams may be taken. 2 pupils in national lacrosse team; regular county representation. *Community service:* Pupils take bronze, silver and gold Duke of Edinburgh's Award; several golds each year. Community service optional. *Clubs and societies:* Up to 30 clubs, eg camera, stamp, debating (3 societies), Christian Union, computer, technology, chess.
Uniform School uniform worn except in the sixth.
Houses/prefects Competitive houses. Prefects, head girl, head of house and house prefects – elected by staff and sixth-form.
Religion Morning assembly (parents may withdraw their children on religious grounds).
Social Debates, Young Enterprise, theatrical productions, BAYS with other local schools. Organised trips abroad. Pupils allowed to bring own bike/motorbike to school. Meals self-service. School shop sells uniform. No tobacco/alcohol allowed.
Discipline Pupils failing to produce homework once might expect to make up work promptly; those caught smoking cannabis on the premises could expect suspension, probable expulsion.
Alumni association run by Mrs F Williams, 7 Wheatfields, Drayton, Norwich NR8 6EU.
Former pupils Beryl Bryden (international jazz singer); Pat Barr (novelist); Anne Weale (authoress); Jane Manning (opera singer); Jenny Lane (BBC); Ann Tyrell (dress designer); Dr Jennifer Moyle (scientist).

• NOTRE DAME (Cobham)

Notre Dame Senior School, Burwood House, Cobham, Surrey KT11 1HA. Tel 01932 863560
• Pupils 350 • Boys None • Girls 11–18 (Day) • Upper sixth 19 • Termly fees £1500–£1575 (Day)
• GSA • Enquiries/application to the Headmistress

What it's like

Founded in 1937 and run by the Sisters of the Company of Mary, an international teaching order. The original building is Burwood House, a mansion on a fine estate. A large number of modern additions provide good facilities and equipment. Both senior and junior schools are on the same site, approximately 1 mile from Cobham. A sound general education is provided and results are good. Most sixth-formers go on to degree courses. Drama and art are strong. There is a range of sports and games and good facilities on site, including an indoor swimming pool. The sports complex is open to parents, as are art, language and word processing classes.

School profile

Pupils Age range 11–18; 350 day girls. Main entry ages 11 and into sixth (other ages by agreement). Own junior school, 3-11 years.
Entrance Own entrance exam used; on basis of GCSE results to sixth. No special skills or religious requirements. Parents not expected to buy textbooks. No assisted places. Some scholarships/bursaries.
Head and staff *Headmistress:* Sister Faith Ede, in post for 9 years. *Staff:* 33 full time, 26 part time. Annual turnover 5%. Average age 39.
Exam results In 1995, 56 pupils in Year 11, 19 in upper sixth. *GCSE:* In 1995, 94% gained grade C or above in 8+ subjects. *A-levels:* 2 upper sixth passed in 4+ subjects; 13 in 3; 2 in 2; and 2 in 1 subject. Average UCAS points 21.4.
University and college entrance 89% of sixth-form leavers go on to a degree course (13% after a gap year); others typically go on to nursery nursing, resits or secretarial courses. Of those going on to university, 2% go Oxbridge; 2% take courses in medicine, dentistry and veterinary science, 26% in science and engineering, 2% in law, 58% in humanities and social sciences, 2% in art and design, 10% in other vocational subjects eg speech therapy, physiotherapy, hotel and catering management.
Curriculum GCSE and A-levels. *Vocational:* Work experience available; also RSA computing/IT; London Chamber of Commerce private secretary's certificate; possibility of GNVQ in art/design, business/finance, and healthcare. *Computing facilities:* 20 Nimbus network system. *Europe:* French (compulsory age 11–13), German and Spanish offered to GCSE, AS and A-level.

The arts *Music:* Over 10% of pupils learn a musical instrument; instrumental exams can be taken. Some 4 musical groups: orchestra, choir, chamber, recorder. Several pupils play in county youth orchestra and other local orchestras; pupils study at junior depts of Royal Academy and Guildhall. *Drama & dance*: Drama offered. GCSE drama, LAMDA exams may be taken. Majority of pupils are involved in school productions and some in house/other productions. Sixth form have written or adapted plays and performed them for charity. *Art:* On average, 28 take GCSE, 2 AS-level, 3 A-level. Design, textiles, photography also offered.
Sport, community service and clubs *Sport and physical activities:* Compulsory sports: netball, tennis, athletics, swimming. Optional: squash, badminton, gymnastics, aquarobics. Sixth form only: aerobics. GCSE may be taken. Regular competitor in county netball, tennis and swimming tournaments; 1 member county netball team; winners or close 2nd in netball and tennis tournaments. *Community service:* Pupils take bronze, silver and gold Duke of Edinburgh's Award. Community service optional. Extensive charity activities, £3000 raised in 1995; Christmas party for local senior citizens; community work with elderly and handicapped. *Clubs and societies:* Up to 15 clubs, eg computer, gardening, debating, environment, science, various sports.
Uniform School uniform worn except in the sixth.
Houses/prefects Competitive houses. Prefects, head girl, head of house and house prefects – appointed by Headmistress and staff or by vote.
Religion All girls attend Mass twice a term; assemblies reflect Christian beliefs.
Social Organised trips abroad. Sixth formers allowed to bring own cars to school. Meals self-service. School tuck shop. No tobacco/alcohol allowed.
Discipline Pupils failing to produce homework once might expect parents to be informed, threatening detention (after-school detention rarely necessary).
Alumni association run by Headmistress.

• NOTRE DAME (Lingfield)

Notre Dame School, Lingfield, Surrey RH7 6PH. Tel 01342 833176, Fax 01342 836048
• Pupils 450 • Boys 2½–18 (Day) • Girls 2½–18 (Day) • Upper sixth 20 • Termly fees £1425 (Day) • ISAI • Enquiries/application to the Principal's Secretary

What it's like

Founded in 1940 by the School Sisters of Notre Dame; they withdrew in 1987 and it is now a corporate charity under lay management. It combines nursery through to senior school on the edge of the attractive village of Lingfield. The senior school is in the process of becoming co-educational. Boys are now accepted at age 11 and into the sixth-form; in 1998 they will also be acepted at 13 and so the school will be mixed by the year 2000. The pleasant buildings are well equipped and occupy a campus which comprises 20 acres of lawns, formal gardens, orchards and playing fields. An historic country house on site has been developed as a sixth-form centre. The school is ecumenical and its philosophy is based on a firm belief in the development of the whole person encompassing maximum care and support for the individual. A sound general education is provided and results are good; a high proportion of the sixth-form goes on to degree courses. It is strong in music and drama. A range of sports, games and extra-curricular activities, including the Duke of Edinburgh's Award Scheme are enjoyed. There is a diverse programme of sporting activities in the sixth-form.

School profile

Pupils Total age range 2½–18; 450 day pupils. Senior department 11–18, 300 girls. Main entry ages 2½–10, 11 and into sixth; also intake at 13, for girls only until 1998. School is in the process of becoming co-ed. Approx 5% are children of former pupils. *State school entry:* 15% main senior intake.
Entrance Own entrance exam used, interview and report from previous school; sixth-form entry, 5 GCSE grades A-C and interview. Parents expected to buy maths textbooks; maximum extras, £50. Assisted places at age 8, 11, 13 and into the sixth. Scholarships at 11, 13 and 16.
Parents From the professions, industry and commerce.
Head and staff *Principal:* Mrs N E Shepley, 5 years in post. Educated at St Louis Convent, Ballymena (Northern Ireland) and Birmingham University (mathematics,

history). Previously Deputy Head and Head of Mathematics at Ruskin High School, Crewe. *Staff:* 33 full time, 13 part time. Annual turnover 5%.

Exam results In 1995, 43 pupils in fifth year, 15 in upper sixth. *GCSE:* In 1995, 67% pupils gained grade C or above in 8+ subjects; 23% in 5–7 subjects. *A-levels:* 1 upper sixth passed in 4 subjects; 6 in 3; 6 in 2; and 1 in 1 subject. Average UCAS points 17.0.

University and college entrance 95% of 1995 sixth-form leavers went on to a degree course; others typically go on to non-degree courses eg agriculture, nursery nursing, or straight into careers eg food research, banking.

Curriculum GCSE and A-level, 16 subjects offered; plus sixth-form secretarial course and non-examination subjects. *Vocational:* Work experience available; also RSA CLAIT. *Computing facilities:* Full suite of PCs, CD-Roms, and access to the Internet. *Special provision:* Help for dyslexic pupils. *Europe:* French (compulsory) and German offered at GCSE, AS- level and A-level; Italian and Russian as non-examined subjects. Exchanges to France and Germany.

The arts (Pupils aged 11 and over) *Music:* Over 40% of pupils learn a musical instrument; instrumental exams can be taken. Musical groups include orchestras, wind band, flute ensemble, choirs. Choir winner of local festival; pupils go on to music degrees etc. *Drama & dance*: Both offered. GCSE drama, LAMDA exams may be taken. Majority of pupils are involved in school and house/other productions. Participation in local festivals; audition for National Youth Theatre. *Art:* On average, 4 pupils take GCSE, 2 A-level. Design, textiles also offered.

Sport, community service and clubs (Pupils aged 11 and over) *Sport and physical activities:* Compulsory sports: hockey, netball, athletics, rounders, gym, tennis, squash, badminton. Optional: aerobics, golf. Sixth form only: sailing, canoeing, archery, orienteering, dry skiing and many others. GCSE, BAGA exams may be taken. International squash; county hockey, netball, athletics, district champions regularly. *Community service:* Pupils take bronze and silver Duke of Edinburgh's Award. Community service optional. *Clubs and societies:* Some 5 clubs, eg dance, drama, Latin, Italian.

Uniform School uniform worn, modified in the sixth.

Houses/prefects Competitive houses. Prefects, head girl and heads of houses – appointed in consultation with staff. School council and sixth-form council.

Religion Compulsory morning assembly, occasional voluntary ecumenical services.

Social Drama, debates, orchestral and choral concerts; sixth-form social events with local independent schools. Exchanges; educational and sporting holidays. Sixth-formers allowed to bring own car to school. Hot school lunches served, plus snack bar. School shop sells stationery. No tobacco/alcohol allowed.

Discipline Pupils failing to produce homework once might expect to repeat it plus extra work on same topic; detention for persistent offenders. Parental involvement in disciplinary procedure is regarded as very important; any pupil caught smoking cannabis on the premises would be expelled.

Alumni association Contact school secretary.

• NOTTING HILL HIGH

Notting Hill and Ealing High School, 2 Cleveland Road, Ealing, London W13 8AX. Tel 0181 997 5744, Fax 0181 810 6891

• Pupils 830 • Boys None • Girls 5–18 (Day) • Upper sixth 70+ • Termly fees £1548 (Day)
• GSA, GPDST • Enquiries/application to the Headmistress

What it's like

Founded in 1873 by the Girls' Public Day School Company (now the Girl's Public Day School Trust) in Notting Hill. The move to Ealing took place in 1931. Suburban and single-site, it lies in a pleasant and quiet residential area. The core consists of several large (formerly private) houses to which modern blocks have been added. There are playgrounds and large gardens. It has its own junior school. A sound general education is provided and results are very good. From a large sixth-form, virtually all go on to degree courses, including many to Oxbridge. There is a school-wide policy of personal development and pupils are encouraged to gain confidence through public speaking, discussion, and the Duke of Edinburgh's Award Scheme. Art, drama and music are strong throughout the school. European links are strong. A range of games, sports and activities. Good commitment to local social services.

School profile

Pupils Total age range 5–18; 830 day girls. Senior department 11–18, 560 girls. Main entry ages 5, 7, 11 and into sixth. Approx 5%–10% are children of former pupils. Own junior provides 50% senior intake. *State school entry:* 50% new senior intake, plus 10% to sixth.

Entrance Own entrance exam and interview used. Academic ability looked for; no religious requirements. Parents not expected to buy textbooks. Assisted places (at 11 and 16). 3 pa scholarships (1 academic at 11, 1 music, 1 sixth-form), 10%–50% fees. Bursaries for current pupils depending on family income.

Parents 15+% in industry or commerce; 15+% are doctors, lawyers, etc and 15+% in the theatre, media, music, etc.

Head and staff *Headmistress:* Mrs Susan Whitfield, 5 years in post. Educated at Westonbirt and Cambridge (natural sciences and physical anthropology). Previously Biology Teacher at St Paul's Girls' School. Also Education Consultant to the Multiple Births Foundation. *Staff:* 50 full time, 19 part time. Annual turnover 5%–10%.

Exam results In 1995, 80 pupils in upper fifth, 73 in upper sixth. *GCSE:* In 1995, 79 upper fifth gained at least grade C in 8+ subjects; 1 in 5–7 subjects. *A-levels:* 7 upper sixth passed in 4+ subjects; 57 in 3; 9 in 2 subjects. Average UCAS points 22.4.

University and college entrance Almost all sixth-form leavers go on to a degree course, 20% to Oxbridge; 18% took courses in medicine, dentistry and veterinary science, 27% in science and engineering, 55% in humanities and social sciences.

Curriculum GCSE and A-levels. 16 GCSE subjects offered; 19 at A-level. 19% take science A-levels; 54% arts/humanities; 27% both. Sixth form may also take Diploma in IT, French for business use. *Computing facilities:* 2 computer rooms, with PCs and CD-Rom; further developments planned. *Special provision:* Visiting teacher gives assistance to mild dyslexics of all ages. *Europe:* French, German and Spanish offered to GCSE and A-level. All study 2 languages to age 16. Regular exchanges (France, Germany and Spain); other visits, including musical.

The arts (Pupils age 11 and over) *Music:* Over 50% of pupils learn a musical instrument; instrumental exams can be taken. A number of musical groups, including several choirs, 3 orchestras, madrigal choir (which tours in Europe every summer). *Drama & dance*: Both offered. RAD exams may be taken as an extra. Many pupils are involved in school productions. Public speaking and debating groups. *Art:* On average, 30% take GCSE, 10% A-level. Painting, drawing, graphics, collage, printing (lino, screen, drypoint, monoprints) also offered.

Sport, community service and clubs (Pupils age 11 and over) *Sport and physical activities:* Sports available: Netball, hockey, tennis, athletics, gym, dance, badminton, volleyball, yoga, aerobics, squash. Sixth form only: golf. Successful netball team; county and regional representation in gym, netball, tennis and badminton. *Community service:* Pupils take Duke of Edinburgh's Award. Community service optional; each form has charity work to raise money (£6000 in 1995). *Clubs & societies*: Include computers, literary, BAYS, lighting, speakers club, photography, life drawing, embroidery.

Uniform School uniform worn except in the sixth.

Houses/prefects No competitive houses. No prefects; head girl and deputies chosen by Headmistress, staff and sixth-form. School Council.

Religion Non-denominational – morning assembly with variable content.

Social Trips to Spain, France, Germany, Italy and Austria; skiing in Alps and activity holidays in the UK. Pupils allowed to bring own car/bike to school. Meals self-service.

Former pupils Angela Rumbold; Eve Matheson.

• NOTTINGHAM HIGH (Boys)

Nottingham High School, Waverley Mount, Nottingham NG7 4ED. Tel 0115 978 6056, Fax 0115 979 2202

• Pupils 838 • Boys 11–18 (Day) • Girls None • Upper sixth 123 • Termly fees £1548 (Day) • HMC • Enquiries/application to the Headmaster

What it's like

Founded in 1513 by Dame Agnes Mellers, widow of Richard Mellers – a bell-founder and Mayor of Nottingham. She was granted a royal charter from Henry VIII. It had early links with Oxford and Cambridge to which many boys went as scholars. From the turn of the 19th century it expanded steadily to its present size and in 1868 moved to its present position between the Arboretum and the Forest – a very agreeable bosky, urban site with fine gardens. The large campus is both well designed and well equipped, with many recent developments. It is a well-run school with motivated pupils and staff. Its academic standards are high and results are excellent. Almost all sixth-form leavers proceed to universities, many to Oxbridge. Music is very strong with a range of musical groups. There is much activity in drama throughout the school. Sports and games are compulsory for everyone and high standards are attained each year (the school has an outstanding record at county and national level). Numerous clubs and societies cater for most conceivable needs. Chess is especially strong (it has won the national final of The Times competition; the zonal final many times). A large and flourishing CCF and a small, but active, scout group. At any one time there are over a hundred pupils taking part in the Duke of Edinburgh's Award Scheme for silver and gold awards. Outdoor pursuits, eg orienteering, canoeing, rock-climbing, are widely encouraged and expeditions and foreign trips are frequent. The school combines with Nottingham Girls' High School in joint theatrical productions etc. A large number of boys are actively engaged in local community work.

School profile

Pupils Age range 11–18; 838 day boys. Main entry ages, 11 and into sixth. Own prep provides 45% of intake. *State school entry:* 45% main intake, 60% to sixth.

Entrance Own entrance exam used. All skills besides academic ability are recognised; no special religious requirements. Parents expected to buy textbooks. 25 pa assisted places. 15 pa scholarships/bursaries.

Head and staff *Headmaster:* Christopher Parker, in post from 1995. Educated at Windsor Grammar School, and at universities of Bristol (geography) and Cambridge (education). Previously Headmaster of Batley Grammar School, Deputy Head of Goff's School, and Senior Geography Master at Bradford Grammar. Also FRSA; Member of HMC/GSA working party for assisted places scheme and also of ISJC working party for assisted places. Member of the Admiralty Interview Board. Publications: The Choice Between Fairness and Envy (a parliamentary brief). *Staff:* 77 full time, 16 part time (including peripatetic music teachers). Annual turnover 5%. Average age 38.

Exam results In 1995, 113 pupils in Year 11, 123 in upper sixth. *GCSE:* In 1995, 98% of Year 11 gained at least grade C in 8+ subjects. *A-levels:* 22% of upper sixth passed in 4+ subjects; 75% in 3; 2% in 2; and 2% in 1 subject. Average UCAS points 25.8 (including general studies, 32.2).

University and college entrance 95% of 1995 sixth-form leavers went on to a degree course (5% after a gap year); others typically go on to non-degree courses or into employment. Of those going on to university, 17% went to Oxbridge; 17% took courses in medicine, dentistry and veterinary science, 35% in science and engineering, 11% in law, 35% in humanities and social sciences, 2% in art and design.

Curriculum GCSE and A-levels. 14 GCSE subjects offered, 18 A-level (including general studies). 26% take science A-levels; 28% arts/humanities; 46% both. *Vocational:* Work experience available. *Computing facilities:* Information technology centre. *Europe:* French and German offered to GCSE and A-level; Italian as a non-examined subject. Regular exchanges (France and Germany).

The arts *Music:* Over 30% of pupils learn a musical instrument. Musical groups include 2 orchestras, 2 bands, a number of choirs and ensembles. National wind band championships, finalists. *Drama & dance:* Drama offered. Some pupils are involved in school productions. *Art:* On average, 20 take GCSE, 3 A-level. Design also offered.

Sport, community service and clubs *Sport and physical activities:* Compulsory sports (in 1st year): rugby, athletics, cricket. Sixth form only: football, badminton, golf, squash, shooting, riding, weight training. Recent national representatives at cross-country. *Community service:* Pupils take silver and gold Duke of Edinburgh's Award. CCF and Community Action both optional at age 14. *Clubs and societies:* Up to 25 clubs, eg canoe, climbing, shooting, drama, music, politics, debating, Scout, stage staff, fencing, design technology, poetry, chess, modern languages, Christian Union, juggling, role play, photography.

Uniform School uniform worn throughout.

Houses/prefects Competitive houses. Head boy, prefects, head of house and house prefects, appointed by the Headmaster based on recommendations from housemasters and prefects.
Religion Attendance at non-denominational religious assemblies compulsory, unless parents request exemption.
Social Joint theatrical productions, politics society, Venture Scouts with Nottingham High (Girls). French and German exchange visits; Mediterranean educational cruise. Pupils allowed to bring own car/bike. Meals formal. School shop. No tobacco/alcohol allowed.
Discipline Pupils failing to produce a piece of prep/homework once would receive a warning; those caught smoking cannabis on the premises would be suspended or expelled.
Alumni association is run by Simon Jackson, Lenton House, Cropwell Bishop, Nottingham NG12 3BQ.
Former pupils Kenneth Clarke, Lord Richardson, Reg Simpson, Sir Peter Gregson, Sir Douglas Wass.

• NOTTINGHAM HIGH (Girls)

Nottingham High School for Girls, GPDST, 9 Arboretum Street, Nottingham, NG1 4JB. Tel 0115 941 7663, Fax 0115 924 0757
• Pupils 1099 • Boys None • Girls 4–18 (Day) • Upper sixth 118 • Termly fees £976–£1328
• GSA, GPDST, SHA • Enquiries/application to the Headmistress

What it's like

Founded in 1875, it is single-site in the middle of Nottingham. The original Victorian houses have been modernised and there have been extensive additions to create a well-equipped school. The junior school is housed in new buildings adjacent to the senior school. Pupils come from a wide range of backgrounds. Religious worship is encouraged. An academic education is provided in all areas, including technology. Results are very good and most girls go on to degree courses, many to Oxbridge. Very strong in music, as well as in art and drama. High standards are achieved in games and sports. A substantial commitment to local community schemes and an outstanding record in the Duke of Edinburgh's Award Scheme. Frequent collaboration with Nottingham High (Boys) in drama, debating, joint community service and Christian Union.

School profile

Pupils Total age range 4–18; 1099 day girls. Senior department 11–18, 824 girls. Main entry ages 4, 7, 11 and into sixth. *State school entry:* 61% at 11 and 42% to sixth-form.
Entrance Own entrance exam. No special skills or religious requirements. Extras include lessons from peripatetic staff and meals. 70 pa assisted places (5 at age 7, 30 at 11 and 35 to sixth). Scholarships up to half fees. Bursaries in cases of financial need.
Head and staff *Headmistress:* Mrs Angela Rees, appointed in 1996. Educated at Cleveland Grammar, Cheadle Grammar and the universities of Oxford (physics) and Bristol (education). Previously Deputy Head at Sheffield High. *Staff:* 69 full time, 40 part time (including visiting musicians). Annual turnover 5%–10%.
Exam results In 1995, 115 pupils in upper fifth, 118 in upper sixth. *GCSE:* In 1995, 114 upper fifth gained at least grade C in 8+ subjects; 1 in 5–7 subjects. *A levels*: 63 upper sixth passed in 4+ subjects; 48 in 3; and 6 in 2 subjects. Average UCAS points 24.2 (including general studies 28.6).
University and college entrance 80% of 1995 sixth-form leavers went on to a degree course (14% after a gap year); others typically go on to art foundation courses or straight into careers. Of those going on to university, 15% went to Oxbridge; 6% took courses in medicine, dentistry and veterinary science, 28% in science and engineering, 51% in humanities and social sciences, 15% in other vocational subjects.
Curriculum GCSE, AS and A-levels. 26 GCSE subjects offered (including Russian and Greek); 11 at AS; 25 at A-level (including general studies). 29% take science A-levels, 36% arts, 35% both. *Vocational:* Work experience compulsory. *Computing facilities:* 3 networked computer rooms and departmental computers (PCs, BBC, Archimedes). Fully computerised library system with CD-Rom. *Europe:* French, German and Spanish

offered to GCSE, AS and A-level; also GCSE Russian in sixth. Regular exchanges (France and Germany).

The arts (Pupils aged 11 and over) *Music:* Over 50% of pupils learn a musical instrument; instrumental exams can be taken. Some 10 musical groups including choirs, orchestras, music theatre group, concert band, flute choir, many chamber music ensembles. Chamber groups regularly successfully enter National Chamber Music Competition. *Drama & dance*: Both offered as class lessons. Some pupils are involved in school productions and all in house/other productions. Pupils participate in Central Television drama workshops. *Art:* On average, 30 take GCSE, 9 A-level. Design, pottery, textiles, photography also offered. Pupils regularly go on to art foundation courses.

Sport, community service and clubs (Pupils aged 11 and over) *Sport and physical activities:* hockey, netball, gym, dance, tennis, swimming, athletics, rounders, football, aerobics, basketball. Sixth form only: ice skating, bowling, yoga, self-defence, squash. GCSE, RLSS exams may be taken. Players at all ages in county netball, hockey, cross-country. *Community service:* Pupils take bronze, silver and gold Duke of Edinburgh's Award. Community service optional in sixth: visiting old people locally, old people's party at Christmas, holiday for disadvantaged children, charity fund-raising for homeless. *Clubs and societies:* Up to 30 clubs, eg Christian Union, debating, drama, computing, engineering, modern languages, guitar group, public speaking.

Uniform School uniform worn except in the sixth.

Houses/prefects New house system. Head girl and deputies elected by the school. Elected sixth-form executive committee and school council.

Religion Religious worship encouraged (assembly).

Social Debating and drama activities with Nottingham High (Boys), also joint community service and Christian Union. Annual skiing holiday; educational cruises and holidays; exchanges with schools in France and Germany. Pupils allowed to bring own cars to school. Meals self-service. No tobacco/alcohol allowed.

Discipline Based on a clear understanding of mutual consideration and self-discipline. Lunchtime and after-school detentions if necessary.

O

• OAKHAM 

Oakham School, Chapel Close, Oakham, Rutland, Leicestershire LE15 6DT. Tel 01572 722487, Fax 01572 755786

• Pupils 1016 • Boys 11–18 (Day/Board) • Girls 11–18 (Day/Board) • Upper sixth 147 • Termly fees £2150 (Day) £3890 (Board) • HMC, BSA, SHA • Enquiries/application to the Registrar

What it's like

Founded in 1584 by Robert Johnson, Archdeacon of Leicester, it remained, until about 1960, a small and comparatively local boys' school. In the next 10 years the number of boys almost doubled and co-education was introduced in 1971. To meet this rapid expansion the amenities were transformed and a massive building programme undertaken. It is now extremely well-equipped, with a theatre furnished to professional standards, a computer centre, sports hall and new library and study centre. The houses are scattered in the very attractive, mellow, small country town of Oakham and extend into the countryside. There are fine gardens and playing fields. The practice of Christianity is an essential part of the life of the community and there are regular chapel services. A happy, friendly school in which a lot of attention is given to the individual. The large staff allows a staff:pupil ratio of about 1:9. Academic standards are high and results very good. Each year very many pupils go on to degree courses (many to Oxbridge). It is very strong indeed in music and drama (annual spring drama festival and tour of play to USA). There is a very high standard in sports and games (a large number of county and national representatives in hockey, rugby, cricket, squash and shooting). Numerous extra-curricular activities cater for most interests. There is a large and flourishing CCF and an exploration society has sent expeditions to Iceland, the Sahara, Papua New Guinea and Madagascar. A substantial commitment to local community services and a phenomenal record in the Duke of Edinburgh's Award Scheme.

School profile

Pupils Age range 11–18; 1016 pupils, 497 day (269 boys, 228 girls), 519 boarding (250 boys, 269 girls). Main entry ages 11, 13 and into sixth. Approx 7% are children of former pupils. *State school entry:* 5% main intake, plus 5% to sixth.

Entrance Common Entrance and own exam used. Skills in music and art welcomed; no particular religious requirements. Parents not expected to buy textbooks; maximum extras, £150 per term. Assisted places available. 35 pa scholarships/bursaries, one-third to full fees.

Parents 30+% live within 30 miles; 10+% live overseas.

Head and staff *Headmaster:* Anthony R M Little, appointed in 1996. Educated at Eton and Cambridge (English). Previously Headmaster of Chigwell, Head of English and Housemaster at Brentwood and taught English at Tonbridge. *Staff:* 108 full time, 30 part time. Annual turnover 3%. Average age 35.

Exam results In 1995, 167 pupils in Year 11, 147 in Year 13. *GCSE:* In 1995, 96% of Year 11 gained at least grade C in 8+ subjects; 3% in 5–7 subjects. *A-levels:* 18 in Year 13 passed in 4+ subjects; 112 in 3; 15 in 2; and 2 in 1 subject. Average UCAS points 21.7.

University and college entrance 94% of 1995 sixth-form leavers went on to a degree course (15% after a gap year); others go on to various jobs and courses including the forces. Of those going on to university, 12% went to Oxbridge; 9% took courses in medicine, dentistry and veterinary science, 40% in science and engineering, 3% in law, 40% in humanities and social sciences, 4% in art and design, 5% in other subjects eg education, psychology, sports science, archaeology.

Curriculum GCSE and A-levels. 28 subjects offered (including theatre studies, textiles; no A-level general studies). On average, 31% take science A-levels; 35% arts/humanities; 34% both. *Vocational:* Work experience available. *Computing facilities:* Comprehensive networked and stand-alone computers in all departments. *Special provision:* Some specialised teaching. *Europe:* French, German, Russian and Spanish offered to GCSE

and A-level; also Italian GCSE and French for Professional Use (modular A-level). Over 80% take GCSE in more than 1 language. Regular exchanges (Germany, Spain, France and Russia). Frequent cultural visits to France, Germany and Spain.
The arts *Music:* Over 30% of pupils learn a musical instrument; instrumental exams can be taken. 10+ musical groups including orchestras, big band, concert band, choirs, numerous chamber ensembles. Winners of Founders Trophy in National Chamber Music for Schools Competition (1991); several pupils in National Youth Orchestra in recent years; choral awards to Oxbridge; some 10 pupils perform solo in concerts each year; annual musicals written by members of staff (2 per year) performed by pupils. *Drama & dance*: Drama offered (and dance, as part of musical theatre). GCSE and A-level drama, LAMDA exams may be taken. Majority of pupils are involved in school productions and house/other productions. 1 pupil in National Youth Theatre, 3 study drama at university each year; regular tours of United States with main production. *Art:* On average, 90 take GCSE, 30 A-level. Design, pottery, textiles, print making, sculpture, technology, CAD, CAM also offered.
Sport, community service and clubs (Pupils aged 11 and over) *Sport and physical activities:* No compulsory sports. Optional: rugby, cricket, tennis, netball, athletics, swimming, shooting, fencing, water polo, fives, table tennis, squash, basketball, soccer, lacrosse. BAGA, BHS, RLSS, RYA exams may be taken. In 1995/96 numerous county players in main games; 1 England cricket U15, 1 HMC cricket U19; 1 England girls hockey U16 and U21; 1 regional rugby U16, 1 U18; boys' and girls' squash teams to finals of Woolwich National; national finalists Golf Foundation schools' competition, England schools golf captain and winner of Carris Trophy. *Community service:* Pupils take bronze, silver and gold Duke of Edinburgh's Award (over 600 golds awarded since 1976). CCF and community service optional. *Clubs and societies:* A number of clubs and activities, eg computers, chess, exploration, observing, debating.
Uniform School uniform worn except in the upper sixth.
Houses/prefects Competitive houses. Prefects, head boy and girl, head of house and house prefects – elected. School Council.
Religion Regular chapel services.
Social Debating in local and national competitions. Regular German, Spanish, Russian and French school exchanges. Pupils allowed to bring own bike to school. Meals self-service. School shop. No tobacco allowed; supervised licensed bar for upper sixth.
Discipline Pupils failing to produce homework once might expect detention; those caught smoking cannabis on the premises will be expelled.
Boarding 90% share a study bedroom with 1 or 2, 10% are in dormitories of 3–4. Single-sex houses, of approximately 70, divided by age. Resident qualified nurse. 2 central dining rooms. Pupils can provide and cook own snacks. 1 termly exeat, 4–7 days. Visits to local town allowed in free time.
Alumni association run by Mr Jon Wills, c/o the school.
Former pupils Thomas Merton (religious philosopher); A P F Chapman (cricketer); R Jacobs (rugby); Matthew Manning (psychic); Sir John Cope (Paymaster General); Prof Robert Stevens (Master, Pembroke College Oxford); Dr Peter North (Vice-Chancellor, Oxford University).

• OLD PALACE

Old Palace School of John Whitgift, Old Palace Road, Croydon, Surrey, CRO 1AX.
Tel 0181 688 2027

• Pupils 800 • Boys None • Girls 4–18 (Day) • Upper sixth 84 • Termly fees £975–£1326 (Day)
• GSA • Enquiries/Applications to the Headmistress

What it's like

Founded in 1889 by the Sisters of the Church, it became an independent day school in 1974. The school is now a member of the Whitgift Foundation, which administers the Whitgift and Trinity Boys Schools. The Old Palace, from which the school takes its name, was a former residence of the Archbishops of Canterbury. The chapel, Great Hall and library which date back to the 15th-century, are used by the school. The historic buildings are complemented by modern ones, including a new arts and technology block. The preparatory and infant departments are on the same site. It aims to provide a sound education based on Christian ideas. Academic standards are high and results very good; almost all the sixth-form go on to university. There is some drama and art and lively musical activity. There is a standard range of sports and games (the netball and tennis teams have achieved some local success), plus a variety of clubs and societies for extra-curricular activities.

School profile

Pupils Total age range 4–18; 800 day girls. Senior department 11–18, 600 girls. Main entry ages 11 and into sixth. *State school entry:* 60% main intake, 12% to sixth.
Entrance Own entrance examination. No charge for textbooks. 35 pa assisted places. Up to 12 pa scholarships, 50% fees; where appropriate, parents may be helped with fees by a Whitgift Bursary.
Head and staff *Headmistress:* Miss Kathleen Hilton, 19 years in post. Educated at Queen Mary, Lytham, and Royal Holloway College London (history). Previously Senior Mistress and Head of History at Manchester High and also taught at Malvern Girls College and Levenshulme Grammar School. Also School Governor, former Chairman of Advanced General Studies committee of JMB and member of Schools Council. *Staff:* 51 full time, 10 part time.
Exam results In 1995, 87 pupils in upper fifth and 72 in upper sixth. *GCSE:* 86 pupils gained at least grade C in 8+ subjects; 1 in 5–7 subjects. *A-levels:* 46 upper sixth passed in 4+ subjects (including general studies); 16 in 3; 6 in 2; 4 in 1 subject. Average UCAS points 23.8 (including general studies, 28.4).
University and college entrance 92% of 1995 sixth-form leavers went on to a degree course (1% after a gap year); others typically go on to art foundation courses. Of those going on to university, 1% went to Oxbridge; 1% took courses in medicine, dentistry and veterinary science, 46% in science and engineering, 1% in law, 35% in humanities and social sciences, 1% in art and design, 15% in vocational subjects eg education.
Curriculum GCSE and A-levels. 26 subjects offered at A-level. 30% take science A-levels; 24% arts/humanities; 46% both. *Computing facilities:* Two Nimbus networks; desk top publishing facilities. Computing lessons start at 4+. *Europe:* French, German, Italian and Spanish offered to GCSE and A-level; also Russian GCSE; all pupils take French from age 7 to GCSE; over 75% take more than 1 language. Regular exchanges (France, Germany, Spain and Italy). Russian politics studies at A-level. French, Spanish and Italian taught by foreign nationals.
The arts *Music:* 50% of pupils learn musical instruments. Many musical groups, including choirs, orchestras, various chamber music ensembles. Many pupils play in local orchestras. Regular concerts. *Drama and dance:* Drama offered and GCSE may be taken. 2 productions a year and regular drama workshops. Great attention given to public speaking and debating. *Art:* On average, 25 take GCSE, 8 A-level. Photography, textile design and screen printing and jewellery also offered; art department works closely with technology department in creating design awareness.
Sport, community service and clubs *Sport and physical activities:* Netball, hockey, swimming, tennis, dance, fitness, county netball players. *Community service:* Pupils take bronze, silver and gold. Duke of Edinburgh's Award Scheme. Caritas Society for raising money for charity. *Clubs and societies:* include debating, Christian Union, Young Enterprise, musical, drama, chess.
Uniform School uniform worn except in the sixth.
Houses/prefects Competitive houses. Head girl, prefects, head of house and house prefects, elected by the school and staff.
Social Debates with local schools. Combined music and drama activities with Whitgift. Organised visits abroad. Visits to lectures, concerts, plays etc.

• OLD SWINFORD

Old Swinford Hospital, Stourbridge, West Midlands DY8 1QX. Tel 01384 370025, Fax 01384 441686

• Pupils 560 • Boys 11–18 (Day/Board/Weekly) • Girls None • Upper sixth 71 • Termly fees Nil (Day) £1400 (Board/Weekly) • SHMIS, BSA, STABIS • Enquiries/application to the Admissions' Secretary

What it's like

Founded in 1670 by Thomas Foley, a local industrialist. It is still sometimes known locally as the Bluecoat School (though the traditional uniform was abandoned in 1928). It has a fine site on the edge of Stourbridge on a spacious campus with excellent playing fields: handsome and extremely well-equipped and comfortable buildings and boarding accommodation is particularly good. There has been rapid development over the last 10 years including a new technology centre and a computer network. The school has grant-maintained status: parents pay nothing for education costs and the boarding fees are low. It is a very energetic, well-run school with a civilised and purposeful atmosphere. Religious worship and instruction is in the Anglican tradition, but all denominations are welcome. Academic standards are high and results very good; almost all boys go on to degree courses each year. Tremendously strong in music, drama and art. A wide range of sports and games is provided and an unusually large number of clubs and societies cater for most conceivable needs. There is a CCF contingent and also much emphasis on adventure training of various kinds. The school has an excellent record in the Duke of Edinburgh's Award Scheme. A strong, competitive spirit pervades the school.

School profile

Pupils Age range 11–18; 560 boys (184 day, 376 boarding). Main entry ages 11, 13 and into sixth. Recruits from state and prep schools in the Birmingham and Midlands area and further afield.

Entrance Boarders chosen after day's interview at school; prep school candidates also take Common Entrance. Always oversubscribed. Skills in music, drama and sport an advantage. No religious requirements. Parents not expected to buy textbooks, no other extras. Scholarships and sixth-form bursaries available.

Parents 6% in the armed services.

Head and staff *Headmaster:* Christopher Potter, in post for 18 years. Educated at March Grammar and Cambridge University (classics). Previously Head of Classics and Archaeology and also Housemaster at Ardingly. Also formerly Chief Examiner in Archaeology, London Board. Publications: The Romano-British Village at Grandford (British Museum); Parish Registers of Romsley, Worcs; Parish Registers of Stone, Worcs. *Staff:* 40 full time, 15 part time, plus artist in residence, musician in residence, games coaches, etc. Annual turnover 5%. Average age approx 35.

Exam results In 1995, 82 pupils in fifth, 76 in upper sixth. *GCSE:* In 1995, 68 fifth gained at least grade C in 8+ subjects; 9 in 5–7 subjects. *A-levels:* 50 upper sixth passed in 4+ subjects; 17 in 3; 5 in 2; and 3 in 1 subject. Average UCAS points 22.4.

University and college entrance 95% of 1995 sixth-form leavers went on to a degree course (12% after a gap year); others typically go on to further education or family business. Of those going on to university, 2% went to Oxbridge; 6% took courses in medicine, dentistry and veterinary science, 44% in science and engineering, 6% in law, 31% in humanities and social sciences, 7% in art and design, 6% in vocational subjects eg pharmacy, surveying.

Curriculum GCSE and A-levels. 20 subjects offered (including A-level sports studies and general studies). *Vocational:* Work experience available; also City and Guilds radio amateur's novice and A and B licences exams. *Computing facilities:* 150 stations, campus-wide 5km network, including all boarding houses: Archimedes and multimedia PC systems; most sixth-form study bedrooms on line. *Europe:* French (from age 11), German and Spanish (from 13) offered at GCSE and A-level. Over 30% take GCSE in more than 1 language.

The arts *Music:* Over 40% of pupils learn a musical instrument; instrumental exams can be taken. Some 10 musical groups including orchestras, brass, concert, swing bands, choir, rock groups. Winners of U16 brass ensemble regional competition. *Drama & dance*: A flourishing theatre workshop. LAMDA exams may be taken. *Art:* On average,

18 take GCSE, 9 A-level. Design, pottery also offered.
Sport, community service and clubs *Sport and physical activities:* Compulsory sports; rugby, cricket, athletics, fitness training, gymnastics, basketball. Optional: soccer, hockey, golf, tennis, badminton, weight training, volleyball, sailing. County school rugby champions U15, U16 for past 7 years; many county and regional representatives in all sports particularly rugby, cricket, soccer. *Community service:* Pupils take bronze, silver and gold Duke of Edinburgh's Award. CCF compulsory for 2 years at age 13; at least 1 cadet each year enters Sandhurst. Community service optional. *Clubs and societies:* Up to 30 clubs, eg video production, archery, sailing, amateur radio, fishing, electronics, Young Enterprise, computing, kung fu, shooting, bridge, chess, photography.
Uniform School uniform worn, modified in the sixth; school prefects wear gowns.
Houses/prefects Competitive houses. Prefects, head boy, head of house and house prefects.
Religion All boys go to assemblies. All boarders attend Sunday service. School Chaplain.
Social Girls take part in drama productions. Organised trips abroad include annual adventure week. Sixth-form day boys allowed to bring car; bikes allowed. Meals self-service. School shop and bookshop. No tobacco on premises. Sixth-form club licensed bar for 17+ boys with permission; girl friends are invited.
Discipline Pupils failing to produce homework once would expect a warning by subject teacher, and report to personal tutor; anyone caught being involved with drugs, etc on the premises could expect expulsion, even for first offence, regardless of previous record in school.
Boarding All sixth-form, and some fifth, have own study bedroom; others are in dormitories of 2–11. Houses of 60–70 (11 year olds separately). Resident qualified sanatorium staff; doctor visits. Central dining room. Pupils can provide and cook snacks within boarding houses to a limited extent (some have microwave cookers.) Number and length of exeats varies. Visits to local town allowed with restrictions.

• ORATORY ☨

The Oratory School, Woodcote, Reading RG8 OPJ. Tel 01491 680207

• Pupils 412 • Boys 11–18 (Day/Board) • Girls None • Upper sixth 69 • Termly fees £2225–£2740 (Day) £3085–£3920 (Board) • HMC • Enquiries/application to the Headmaster

What it's like

Founded in 1859 to meet the educational needs of the Catholic laity. The Venerable John Henry Newman was very much responsible for establishing the school and his views and beliefs about education are still its driving force. It was originally founded in Birmingham and settled at Woodcote during the Second World War. It has a very agreeable rural site with spacious grounds and purpose-built accommodation. Facilities are excellent. Religious education is an important part of the curriculum. Sunday mass and daily house prayers are compulsory. Very good teaching is provided and academic standards are high. Results are very good and most sixth-formers proceed to degree courses, including Oxbridge. European links are exceptionally strong: the school runs a property in Normandy and has links with a Jesuit College in Paris. It is outstandingly strong in music and there is a considerable commitment to drama and art. A big range of games and sports is available (a lot of representatives at county level) and the newly constructed sports centre includes a real tennis court (the first in the country for eighty years), and the school has recently opened a new golf course. Also a wide variety of extra-curricular activities and a strong CCF. A promising record in the Duke of Edinburgh's Award Scheme.

School profile

Pupils Age range 11–18; 412 boys, 132 day, 280 boarding. Senior department 13–18, 381 boys. Main entry ages 11, 13 and into sixth. Approx 7% are children of former pupils. Own prep school provides more than 20% of intake. *State school entry:* 3% main intake, plus 2% to sixth.
Entrance Common Entrance exam and informal tests used. No special skills required; overwhelming majority of boarders are Roman Catholic, some day boys not. Parents expected to pay a termly flat-rate charge for books. Scholarships/bursaries available.

Parents 15+% in the armed services; 15+% are doctors, lawyers, etc; remainder are professional, commercial and industrial. 10+% live within 30 miles; up to 10% live overseas.

Head and staff *Headmaster:* S W Barrow, in post for 5 years. Previously Deputy Head, Housemaster and History Teacher at the school. *Staff:* 37 full time, 17 part time. Annual turnover under 5%. Average age 37.

Exam results In 1995, 78 pupils in upper fifth, 69 in upper sixth. *GCSE:* In 1995, 67% upper fifth gained at least grade C in 8+ subjects; 26% in 5–7 subjects. *A-levels:* 85% upper sixth passed in 3 subjects; 13% in 2 subjects. Average UCAS points 21.9.

University and college entrance 84% of 1995 sixth-form leavers went on to a degree course; others typically go on to non-degree courses eg art foundation. Of those going on to university, 8% went to Oxbridge; 3% took courses in medicine, dentistry and veterinary science, 39% in science and engineering, 50% in humanities and social sciences, 7% in art and design.

Curriculum GCSE and A-levels. 22 subjects offered (including GCSE photography; no A-level general studies). 33% take science A-levels; 47% arts/humanities; 20% both. *Computing facilities:* Computer centre (Nimbus), two computer study rooms. *Special provision:* Specialist tuition for mildly dyslexic children only. *Europe:* French (from age 11), German, Italian, Portuguese and Spanish offered to GCSE and A-level. 75% take GCSE in more than 1 language. Regular exchanges (France, Spain and Germany). Strong links with a Jesuit college in Paris. Range of European pupils in school. Property in Normandy used for language visits, lay pupils, history study groups, geography field work and base for musical and sporting pursuits.

The arts *Music:* Over 30% of pupils learn a musical instrument; instrumental exams can be taken. Some 8 musical groups including orchestras, choirs, string quartets, jazz, various ensembles. *Drama & dance*: Drama offered. LAMDA exams may be taken. Majority of pupils are involved in school and house/other productions. *Art:* On average, 45 take GCSE, 15 A-level. Design, pottery, photography also offered.

Sport, community service and clubs *Sport and physical activities:* No compulsory sports. Optional sports: rugby, cricket, soccer, rowing, lawn tennis, hockey, athletics, cross-country, real tennis, squash, swimming, sailing, canoeing, table tennis, badminton, basketball, windsurfing, shooting, volleyball, weight training, golf available. RLSS, RYA exams may be taken. British U14 real tennis champion; 1 England U18 cricketer, 4 county, 1 regional; 6 county U16 rugby players, 4 U18; *Community service:* Pupils take bronze, silver and gold Duke of Edinburgh's Award. CCF compulsory for 2 years at age 13, optional thereafter. Community service optional. *Clubs and societies:* Up to 15 clubs, eg debating, drama, cultural affairs, war games.

Uniform School uniform worn, modified in the sixth.

Houses/prefects Competitive houses. Prefects, school captain, house captains and house prefects – appointed by the Headmaster with housemasters.

Religion Sunday Mass and twice-termly house Mass compulsory; weekday Masses optional; daily house prayers compulsory.

Social Debates, dances, other social/educational ventures with other local schools. Organised ski trips, sailing trips, tennis, rugby and soccer tours, some exchanges – usually to Spain, France and Germany. Pupils allowed to bring own bike to school. Meals self-service. School tuck shop and paperback bookshop. Smoking is not permitted. Boys over 18 may visit local inns; some social functions and informal occasions where boys between 16 and 18 may be allowed alcohol under staff supervision.

Discipline Pupils failing to produce homework once might expect additional work to be set; those caught smoking cannabis on the premises or off would be asked to leave.

Boarding 25% have own study bedroom, 35% share double studies; 20% share with 2–4 others; 20% are in dormitories of 6+. 5 houses (1 junior, 4 senior) of some 60 boarders (and 15 day). 2 resident qualified nurses, doctor lives very close. Central dining room. Pupils can provide and cook own food. Exeats to suit parental convenience. Occasional visits to the local town allowed for sixth-form for specified reasons.

Former pupils Sir James Comyn (High Court judge); Sir Michael Levey (National Gallery); Mgr V F J Morgan (ex-Vicar General of Royal Navy); J J Hayes MP; Michael Berkeley (composer); Christopher Hurford (Australian government minister); Joseph Connolly (Times columnist); Nicholas Bicat (composer); Igor Judge QC; Paul Purnell QC; Nicholas Purnell QC; E Leigh MP.

• OSWESTRY

Oswestry School, Oswestry, Shropshire SY11 2TL. Tel 01691 655711, Fax 01691 671194

• Pupils 385 • Boys 8–18 (Day/Board) • Girls 8–18 (Day/Board) • Upper sixth 40 • Termly fees £1772 (Day) £3030 (Board) • SHMIS • Enquiries/application to the Headmaster

What it's like

Founded in 1407 and one of the oldest continous foundations in England. The agreeable, well-designed, red-brick buildings occupy pleasant grounds and playing fields on the edge of the market town of Oswestry and overlooking the Shropshire Plain. The junior school and pre-prep are self-contained but nearby. Facilities are very good. A good all-round education is provided in a supportive family atmosphere and every effort is made to accommodate families' needs. Academic standards and results are good and the great majority of sixth-form leavers go on to degree courses each year. The music department is thriving, and drama and art are also lively. Sport and games are encouraged and high standards are attained (many county representatives annually). A very large number of clubs and societies cater for every need. The CCF is vigorous and the school has an impressive record in the Duke of Edinburgh's Award Scheme.

School profile

Pupils Total age range 8–18; 385 pupils, 276 day (163 boys, 113 girls), 109 boarding (69 boys, 40 girls). Senior department 13–18, 246 pupils (150 boys, 96 girls). Main entry ages 11, 13 and into sixth. *State school entry:* 50% senior intakes, plus 80% to sixth.

Entrance Common Entrance and own exam used. No religious requirements. Parents expected to buy textbooks. 10 pa scholarships/bursaries available (including sport, art and music), 10%–50% of tuition fees.

Parents 15+% in the armed services. 60+% live within 30 miles; 10+% live overseas.

Head and staff *Headmaster:* Paul K Smith, in post from 1995. Educated at Aylesbury Grammar School and universities of Cambridge (geography) and Bath. Previously Deputy Head at Royal Grammar, Worcester. Also FRGS. *Staff:* 29 full time, 4 part time. Annual turnover 5%. Average age 40.

Exam results In 1995, 70 pupils in upper fifth, 39 in upper sixth. *GCSE:* In 1995, 23 upper fifth gain at least grade C in 8+ subjects; 46 in 5–7 subjects. *A-levels:* 23 upper sixth passed in 3 subjects; 4 in 2; and 4 in 1 subject. Average UCAS points 14.2.

University and college entrance 70% of 1995 sixth-form leavers went on to a degree course; others typically go on to non-degree courses (eg art, drama, catering, agriculture) or into careers (eg banking, retailing). Of those going on to university, 4% went to Oxbridge; 9% took courses in medicine, dentistry and veterinary science, 22% in science and engineering, 45% in humanities and social sciences, 15% in art and design, 9% in other subjects eg drama, music.

Curriculum GCSE, AS and A-levels. 15 subjects offered (including sports studies and business studies). 30% take science A-levels; 50% arts/humanities; 20% both. *Computing facilities:* New RM Nimbus machines in 2 computer rooms; others in departments. *Special provision:* EFL teaching and help for dyslexic pupils (on withdrawal from classes basis), usually three times a week. *Europe:* French and German offered to GCSE, AS and A-level. Regular exchanges (France and Germany).

The arts (Pupils aged 11 and over) *Music:* Over 30% of pupils learn a musical instrument; instrumental exams can be taken. Musical groups include orchestras, choirs, pop group. Many pupils in county orchestra. *Drama & dance:* Majority of pupils are involved in school productions. *Art:* On average, 30 take GCSE, 6 A-level. Photography also offered. Pupils regularly accepted for art college and to read architecture.

Sport, community service and clubs (Pupils aged 11 and over) *Sport and physical activities:* Boys: rugby, soccer, cricket; Girls: hockey, netball; Both: athletics, cross-country, swimming, badminton, tennis. BAGA, ASA exams may be taken. Regular county representation (cricket, swimming, athletics, hockey, football). *Community service:* Pupils take bronze, silver and gold Duke of Edinburgh's Award. Active social service and charitable works. *Clubs and societies:* Clubs include computer, chess, angling, clay-pigeon shooting, outdoor pursuits.

Uniform School uniform worn except in the sixth (smart business dress).

Houses/prefects Competitive houses. Prefects, head boy and girl, head of house and house prefects – appointed after consultation.

Religion Non-denominational. Compulsory chapel. Boarders must attend unless attending own (eg Roman Catholic) church.
Social Organised exchanges in France, Germany; trips to Russia, France, Spain, Italy. Pupils allowed to bring own bike to school. Meals self-service. School shop. No tobacco allowed; beer allowed in sixth-form club supervised by staff.
Discipline Pupils failing to produce homework once might expect a reminder, then work detention for persistent failure. Should anyone be caught with drugs, they would be expelled (has never arisen).
Boarding 5% have own study bedroom; 50% share (1 or 2); 45% in dormitories of 5–8. Single-sex houses of approximately 50, same as competitive houses; separate mixed sixth-form house. Resident qualified medical staff. Central dining room. Pupils can provide and cook own snacks. 3 or 4 overnight exeats each term. Visits to local town allowed.
Alumni association run by J F Tilley, Herschell House, Whittington, Oswestry, Shropshire SY11 4DB.

• OUNDLE

Oundle School, Oundle, Peterborough PE8 4EN. Tel 01832 273536, Fax 01832 274967
• Pupils 844 • Boys 11–18 (Board) • Girls 11–18 (Board) • Upper sixth 178 • Termly fees £4285 (Board) • HMC • Enquiries/application to the Headmaster

What it's like

The school originated from the bequest of Sir William Laxton, to the Grocers' Company in 1556. In 1876 the Grocers' Company divided the school, founding Oundle (and leaving the grammar school in close association, as Laxton School). Girls were first accepted throughout the school in 1990. The school is extremely well equipped and its buildings (from 17th to 20th century) are scattered through the small and very agreeable town. There is a close town and gown relationship. Religious instruction accords with the teaching of the Church of England and there is some emphasis on regular worship. A very large staff allows a staff:pupil ratio of about 1:8. Academic standards are high and results are consistently excellent; practically all leavers go on to university (including many to Oxbridge). There is an extremely strong music department and many of the pupils are involved in numerous musical activities in the school and beyond it. There is also an excellent and very active art department. Large numbers of pupils are also engaged in dramatic activities and professional companies often visit. It has long had a reputation for high achievements in sports and games (a number of county and national representatives). A very large CCF contingent with an ambitious and enterprising programme each year. There is also emphasis on outdoor pursuits and there is a large adventure training section whose members have made expeditions to Ecuador, Afghanistan, China, Pakistan, Belize, Greenland and Kenya. Over 100 pupils are engaged in local community services.

School profile

Pupils Age range 11–18; 844 boarding pupils, 640 boys, 204 girls. Main entry ages 11 and 13 and a small number into sixth and at other stages. *State school entry:* 8% main intake.
Entrance Common Entrance and own exam used. Some scholarships (including music, art and design & technology).
Head and staff *Headmaster:* David McMurray, in post for 13 years. Educated at Loretto and Cambridge (English). Previously Headmaster at Loretto, Housemaster and Head of English at Fettes. *Staff:* 105 full time, 46 part time. Annual turnover 9%. Average age 36.
Exam results On average, 155 pupils in fifth form, 180 in upper sixth. *GCSE:* On average, 96% fifth gained at least grade C in 8+ subjects; 4% in 5–7 subjects. *A-levels:* 15% upper sixth passed in 4+ subjects; 84% in 3; 1% in 2 subjects. Average UCAS points 26.4.
University and college entrance 94% of 1995 sixth-form leavers went on to a degree course (45% after a gap year); others typically go on to art or music courses, management training, advertising, the forces or to own business. Of those going on to university, 15% went to Oxbridge; 9% took courses in medicine, dentistry and veterinary science, 32% in science and engineering, 5% in law, 42% in humanities and social sciences, 4% in art and design, 8% in other subjects eg media studies, estate management.

Curriculum GCSE and A-levels (including Mandarin; no A-level general studies). 28% took science A-levels; 23% arts/humanities; 44% both. All thirteen-year-olds spend an afternoon a week for a whole year on technology. *Vocational:* Work experience available; also City and Guilds qualification in IT. *Computing facilities:* Three fully-equipped IT rooms with approx 100 machines. Additional machines in all departments and houses. CAD in workshops. *Special provision:* Extra English. Dyslexic tuition by qualified team (limited in numbers). *Europe:* French (from age 11), German and Spanish (from 13) offered to GCSE and A-level; also beginners' German, Spanish and Russian available in sixth-form. 70% take GCSE in more than 1 language; 65% take a language to AS or A-level. Regular exchanges (France, Germany, Spain, Hungary, Poland and Russia); work experience for lower sixth in Germany and France.
The arts *Music:* Over 50% of pupils learn a musical instrument; instrumental exams can be taken. Some 12 musical groups including choirs, choral groups, orchestras, brass, concert band, jazz orchestras, blues, string and wind ensembles. 3 members of National Youth Orchestra; 1 National Youth Chamber Orchestra; 5 Cambridge choral scholarships; 3 National Youth Jazz Orchestra; 2 National Youth Choir; 1 on European Youth Brass Ensemble tour; 3 take regular instrumental tuition in London; 1 attends RAM intermediate academy. *Drama and dance:* Both offered. GCSE and A-level drama may be taken. About half of all pupils are involved in school and house/other productions in some capacity during their career; drama classes for all third form. *Art:* On average, 70 take GCSE, 15 A-level. Design, pottery, textiles, photography, printmaking, sculpture also offered. Art facilities open to non-examination pupils.
Sport, community service and clubs *Sport and physical activities*: Sports compulsory in first year only. 20 choices from sailing to netball; emphasis on rugby, hockey, cricket, rowing. Sixth form only: soccer. RLSS, RYA exams may be taken. Some county and national representatives. *Community service:* Pupils take bronze, silver and gold Duke of Edinburgh's Award. CCF compulsory for 1 year at age 14, optional thereafter; wide range of activities. Community service optional for 2 years at age 15; 2 summer holidays, 1 for mentally handicapped children, 1 for inner city children; 4-week summer school for adults with learning difficulties, run by Social Services with school volunteers. *Clubs and societies:* 46 clubs, eg archaeology, astronomy, bellringing, bridge, croquet, law, politics, science, war games, creative writing.
Uniform School uniform worn throughout.
Houses/prefects Competitive houses. Prefects, head boy/girl, head of house and house prefects – appointed by the Headmaster.
Religion Attendance at chapel service compulsory for C of E pupils. Those of other faiths encouraged to be instructed in and to worship according to their own religion.
Social Debates, choral society, community service, local newspaper, theatre productions with other schools, locally and abroad. Exchanges and visits abroad to France, Germany, Russia, Poland, Hungary; trips abroad for sports, rugby, sub-aqua; geography field trips; history trips to Somme battlefields, Berlin and Strasbourg. Pupils allowed to bring own bike to school. Meals formal. School shop. No tobacco allowed; alcohol only in licensed sixth-form club for those 17+, and with ID card for 18+ in pubs.
Discipline Pupils failing to produce homework once might expect to re-write it or a house detention; those caught smoking cannabis on the premises should expect dismissal.
Former pupils Al Alvarez; David Edgar; Arthur Marshall; Sir Peter Scott; Maxwell Hutchinson; Stephen Dawking.

• OUR LADY'S (Abingdon)

Our Lady's Convent Senior School, Radley Road, Abingdon, Oxfordshire OX14 3PS. Tel 01235 524658

• Pupils 310 • Boys None • Girls 11–18 (Day) • Upper sixth 28 • Termly fees £1325 (Day)
• ISAI, SHA • Enquiries/application to the Headmistress

What it's like

Founded in 1860 and administered by the Sisters of Mercy. It is situated in the market town on a single site with playing fields opposite. Pleasant buildings and good modern facilities. A new building programme has provided extensive additions. There is a junior school. It has a reputation for a friendly and caring approach and aims to provide a thorough education by a combination of traditional and modern methods, in the atmosphere of a Catholic community and according to Christian principles (not all pupils are Catholic). Standards of teaching are good and so are results. Each year some girls go on to degree courses. Very strong in music; a third of the school is involved. Some drama and art. A wide range of sports and games and plentiful activities. Some commitment to local community schemes and an impressive record in the Duke of Edinburgh's Award Scheme.

School profile

Pupils Age range 11–18; 310 day girls. Main entry ages 11 and into sixth. Approx 2% are children of former pupils. *State school entry:* 30% main intake, plus 2% to sixth.
Entrance Own entrance exam used. No special skills required; Catholics and other Christian denominations accepted. Parents not expected to buy textbooks; no extras. Assisted places at age 11 and into sixth. Some scholarships/bursaries.
Head and staff Acting *Headmistress:* Mrs Glynne Butt, in post from 1996. *Staff:* 25 full time, 18 part time. Annual turnover 1%. Average age mid-40s.
Exam results In 1995, 55 pupils in upper fifth, 31 in upper sixth. *GCSE:* In 1995, 38 upper fifth gained at least grade C in 8+ subjects; 13 in 5–7 subjects. *A-levels:* 17 upper sixth passed in 3 subjects; 7 in 2; and 7 in 1 subject. Average UCAS points 20.5.
University and college entrance 75% of 1995 sixth-form leavers went on to a degree course (15% after a gap year); others typically go on to non-degree courses. Of those going on to university, 2% took courses in medicine, dentistry and veterinary science, 25% in science and engineering, 70% in humanities and social sciences, 3% in vocational subjects.
Curriculum GCSE and A-levels (no A-level general studies). 10% take science A-levels; 65% arts/humanities; 25% both. *Vocational:* Work experience available. *Computing facilities:* Fully-equipped computer room with 12 BBC computers. *Europe:* French, German and Spanish offered to GCSE, AS and A-level; Italian to A-level if requested. Regular exchanges to France and Germany.
The arts *Music:* Over 30% of pupils learn a musical instrument; instrumental exams can be taken. Some 5 musical groups including 2 orchestras, 2 choral, 1 chamber group. *Drama & dance*: Drama offered. LAMDA exams may be taken. Some pupils are involved in school productions. *Art:* On average, 50+ take GCSE, 6 A-level. Pottery, textiles also offered.
Sport, community service and clubs *Sport and physical activities:* Compulsory sports: netball, tennis, hockey, swimming. Optional: badminton, squash. Fifth and sixth-form only: scuba. GCSE, BAGA, RLSS exams may be taken. *Community service:* Pupils take bronze, silver and gold Duke of Edinburgh's Award. CCF optional. Community service compulsory at age 16, optional at other ages. *Clubs and societies:* Up to 30 clubs, eg music, PE, swimming and diving, French and German, science, art.
Uniform School uniform worn, modified in the sixth.
Houses/prefects Competitive houses. Prefects and head girl – appointed by Headmistress following suggestions by staff and sixth-form. School Council.
Religion All pupils join in daily assembly and school services (once or twice a term).
Social Lectures and activities with other sixth-forms. French exchange scheme; German exchange with school in Munich. Pupils allowed to bring own car/bike/motorbike to school (but no parking provided). Meals formal. School shop. No tobacco/alcohol allowed.
Discipline Pupils failing to produce homework once might expect to be kept in to make it up at break, lunch time or after school; those caught smoking cannabis on the premises could expect expulsion.

• OXFORD HIGH

Oxford High School, Belbroughton Road, Oxford OX2 6XA. Tel 01865 59888, Fax 01865 52343 • Pupils 650 • Boys None • Girls 9–18 (Day) • Upper sixth 75 • Termly fees £1268 (Day) • GSA, GPDST • Enquiries/application to the Headmistress

What it's like

Founded in 1875, in the decade which saw the foundation of the first women's colleges at Oxbridge. Its early pupils were among the first women to obtain university degrees. It has expanded steadily during the 20th century and now occupies a large, well-equipped urban site two miles from the city centre. All playing fields are on site. Assemblies are frequently (but not always) in the form of religious worship. There is some emphasis on religious education, during which major world faiths are studied. A sound general education is provided, in the high school tradition, and academic results are excellent. Almost all girls go on to degree courses each year, a high proportion to Oxbridge. Music, drama and art are very strong. So are sports and games (there have been a large number of representatives at county level). The school provides some local community service volunteers and it has an outstanding record in the Duke of Edinburgh's Award Scheme and Young Enterprise. There is collaboration with other schools (such as Magdalen College School) in various activities.

School profile

Pupils Total age range 9–18; 650 day girls. Senior department, 11–18, 550 girls. Main entry ages 9, 11 and into sixth. Small number are children of former pupils.
Entrance Own entrance exam used. Academic ability looked for; no religious requirements. Parents not expected to buy textbooks. 19 pa assisted places (14 at 11, 5 to sixth). Up to 8 pa scholarships (including music) at 11 and 16, 12%–25% fees.
Parents 15+% are doctors, lawyers etc. 15+% university dons.
Head and staff *Headmistress:* Mrs Joan Townsend, in post for 15 years. Educated at Wigan Girls' High and Hawarden Grammar and universities of Oxford and Swansea (mathematics). Previously Head of Mathematics at School of St Helen and St Katherine, Abingdon, and Tutor and Lecturer both at the Open University and Oxford Poly. Also Trustee Westminster Centre, Oxford; FRSA. Publications: papers in Quarterly Journal of Mathematics and Applied Mechanics; various articles on education. *Staff:* 55 staff, both full time and part time.
Exam results Average size of upper fifth 80; upper sixth 75. *GCSE:* In 1995, all upper fifth gained at least grade C in 8+ subjects. *A-levels:* Average UCAS points 25.7.
University and college entrance 95% of 1995 sixth-form leavers went on to a degree course (23% after a gap year); others typically go on to employment, travel, secretarial course. Of those going on to university, 20% went to Oxbridge; 10% took courses in medicine, dentistry and veterinary science, 15% in science and engineering, 2% in law, 45% in humanities and social sciences, 10% in art, design, art history and architecture, 5% in vocational subjects eg stage management, hospitality management, sports science, 14% in business, accounting or combinations of subjects.
Curriculum GCSE and A-levels (subjects include design technology GCSE). *Vocational:* Work experience available. *Computing facilities:* Whole school network; stand-alone PCs. *Special provision:* No formal provision; can provide for pupils with eg hearing aids, crutches (difficult because of stairs), mild dyslexia if academically sound. *Europe:* French, German, Spanish and Russian offered to GCSE and A-level; also French AS-level, Italian GCSE and A-level in sixth. Many regular exchanges (France, Germany, Russia and Spain). Periodically, German students from exchange school in Bonn spend a term in lower sixth. Visits to Russia and Italy.
The arts (Pupils aged 11 and over) *Music:* Over 50% of pupils learn a musical instrument; instrumental exams can be taken. Musical groups include 4 orchestras, 4 choirs, many chamber groups, several recorder groups, jazz group. *Drama & dance*: Both offered. GCSE drama, ESB, Guildhall exams may be taken. All pupils are involved in school and house/other productions. Speech and drama awards at Buckinghamshire Festival; 1 pupil's plays written and performed for BBC Radio, finalist in BP Speech and Poem Competition. *Art:* On average, 30–40 take GCSE, 4–9 A-level; design, pottery, textiles, photography, sculpture also offered. Art facilities open to non-examination pupils. Many go on to art foundation courses; several recent pupils have given one-man shows and are self-supporting artists; some doing postgraduate art and design work.
Sport, community service and clubs (Pupils aged 11 and over) *Sport and physical activities:* Compulsory/optional sports (at different ages): hockey, netball, gymnastics, tennis, dance, athletics, swimming, badminton, trampolining, volleyball, softball. Sixth form only: squash, fitness exercise, ice skating. RLSS, ASA exams may be taken. Several county tennis representatives; netball, 7 county players, county U16 and U18 runners-up; hockey, county U18 champions; athletics, 2 county reps; 1 regional gymnast; swimming, several Oxford reps. *Community service:* Pupils take bronze, silver and gold Duke of

Edinburgh's Award; 1 pupil completed gold by volunteer teaching at school in Himalayas. Community service optional for 1 year at age 15. *Clubs and societies:* Up to 30 clubs, eg literary, meditation, drama, technology, computing, bridge, chess, sports, maths, debating, Christian Union, Young Enterprise.

Uniform School uniform worn except in the sixth.

Houses/prefects No competitive houses. Prefects, head girl and deputy – elected by sixth and staff. School Council.

Religion Religious worship encouraged. Assemblies frequently in form of religious worship. Christian Union flourishes.

Social Debates with eg Magdalen College School and joint theatrical productions; parents organise occasional dances. Organised trips abroad to Russia, France, Germany, Spain and Italy. Pupils allowed to bring own bike to school. Meals self-service. Parents organise sale of second-hand uniforms. No tobacco/alcohol allowed.

Discipline Pupils failing to produce homework once might expect a reprimand and to produce work later; those caught smoking cannabis on the premises could expect expulsion.

Alumni association Jane Birch, The Secretary, Oxford High School Old Girls' Association, c/o the school.

Former pupils Maggie Smith; Miriam Margolyes; Sian Edwards (conductor); Elizabeth Jennings (poet); Lucinda Leech (furniture designer); Emma Bridgewater (potter); Ursula Buchan (journalist); Sophie Grigson; Louise Williams (violinist); Dame Josephine Barnes; Eleanor Oldroyd (Radio 4, Sport).

P

• PADWORTH

Padworth College, Padworth, Near Reading, Berkshire RG7 4NR. Tel 01734 832644, Fax 01734 834515

• Pupils 120 • Boys None • Girls 14–20 (Day/Board/Weekly) • Upper sixth 35 • Termly fees £1823 (Day) £3645 (Board) £3545 (Weekly) • BAC, CIFE, ARELS • Enquiries/application to the Bursar

What it's like

Founded in 1963 as an international sixth-form college for girls, it is set in beautiful parkland. The main building on campus is a large and handsome 18th-century mansion in the neo-classical idiom, Padworth House. Four miles away, there is Mortimer Hall – a large Victorian country house in its own grounds. The former houses 80 pupils in two buildings, the latter 45. Accommodation and facilities are first rate. The vast majority of pupils are from overseas or expatriates, and the age range is 14 to 20+. Pupils are treated more as students than as school children and discipline and organisation are informal (no house system, uniform or prefects). There is an exceptional staff:pupil ratio of about 1:6 and classes average 5–6 students. There is a free selection of subjects (all combinations are possible). Exam results are good and a high proportion of leavers go on to degree courses, one or two to Oxbridge. It also offers GNVQ levels 2 and 3 in business/finance, hotel studies and art and design. Some 25% of students are following English language courses only. A fair range of optional sports and games (tuition for British Horse Society exams is offered) and some commitment to the Duke of Edinburgh's Award Scheme. There are no formal societies or clubs but several social functions are organised with other schools/colleges, and social engagements include attendance at Royal Ascot, Wimbledon, and the Badminton Horse Trials.

School profile

Pupils Age range 14–20; 120 girls (3 day and 117 boarding). Main entry is into the sixth.
Entrance No entrance exam except for scholarships. No special skills or religious requirements; college is multi-denominational and cultural. Parents are expected to buy textbooks; extras average £100–£150 termly. 6–8 pa scholarships, value £2500–£10,935.
Parents 15+% are in industry/commerce; 15+% are doctors/lawyers; 15+% diplomatic/foreign service. Up to 10% live within 30 miles of the school; over 60% overseas.
Head and staff *Principal:* Dr Sheila Villazon, in post for 13 years. Educated at George Watson's and Edinburgh University (fine art). Previously taught art history at Padworth, lectured at university and worked at the National Gallery of Scotland. Publications: The Vanishing Landscape; and Development of the English Watercolour. Also AEB Art History Moderator. *Staff:* 21 full time, 11 part time. Average age, 41.
Exam results On average, 12 in upper fifth, 35 in upper sixth. *GCSE/GNVQ level 2*: On average, 65% upper fifth gain at least grade C in 5–7 GCSE subjects or GNVQ level 2 (equivalent to 5 GCSE subjects). *A-levels/GNVQ level 3*: 96% pass in 3 subjects at A-level or GNVQ level 3 (equivalent to 2 A-level); 3% in 2; and 1% in 1 subject. Average UCAS points 19.3.
University and college entrance On average, 95% of A-level/GNVQ level 3 leavers go on to a degree course (2% after a gap year); others typically go on to HND, art or nursery nursing courses, American colleges. Of those going on to university, 2% go to Oxbridge; 5% take courses in medicine, dentistry and veterinary science, 10% in science and engineering, 15% in law, 10% in humanities and social sciences, 15% in art and design, 45% in othr vocational subjects eg pharmacy, agriculture, accountancy, financial management.
Curriculum GCSE, AS and A-levels and GNVQ levels 2 and 3 offered. 16 GCSE subjects offered, 15 A-level; also AS-level general studies. 30% take science A-levels; 30% arts/humanities; 40% both. *Vocational:* Work experience available; BTEC GNVQ level 2 and 3 in business and finance and business and hotel studies; Pitmans and RSA stages 1, 2 and

3 typing and secretarial exams. *Computing facilities:* Acorn and PCs. *Special provision:* Full EFL department; all overseas students follow English for Academic Purposes and enter for a range of exams eg Cambridge (PET, First Certificate, Certificate in Proficiency) JMB Test in English, Oxford Prelim and Higher exams, ARELS orals and Pitmans English exams. Individual tuition and specialised English tuition. *Europe:* French, German and Spanish offered to GCSE and A-level, plus Italian AS-level (none compulsory). European studies offered throughout. 90% students are from overseas, up to 50% from Europe.

The arts *Music:* 10% pupils learn a musical instrument; instrumental exams can be taken. Some musical groups. *Drama & dance*: Dance offered as an evening activity. *Art:* On average, 5 take GCSE, 4 A-level; 9 taking GNVQ level 3 in art and design. Design, pottery, photography and textiles also offered.

Sport, community service and clubs *Sport and physical activities:* Optional: tennis, swimming, aerobics, callanetics, horse riding, squash, badminton, table tennis, self-defence, volleyball, rounders. Students may enter for BHS exams. *Community service:* Pupils take bronze and silver Duke of Edinburgh's Award. Community service optional. *Clubs and societies:* No formal societies but full range of activities including cookery, theatre, video, concerts, drama, pottery, ice skating, swimming, 10-pin bowling, and social events such as Royal Ascot, Badminton Horse Trials, Wimbledon.

Uniform None.

Houses/prefects No competitive houses or prefects.

Religion No compulsory worship.

Social Debates, parties and social functions with other local schools/colleges. Art history trips to Paris and Amsterdam. Students may bring own car/horse to school. Meals self-service. School shop. Senior pupils allowed to smoke in restricted areas.

Discipline Pupils failing to produce homework once might expect a verbal warning; expulsion if evidence of any involvement with drugs

Boarding 30% have own study bedrooms; other share 2–4 per room. Three houses (of 40–45), divided by course. No resident medical staff but nurse attends daily, doctor twice weekly. Senior house has cooking facilities. Unlimited weekend exeats plus 3 long weekends. Visits to the local town allowed with parental permission at 14-18; at students' discretion at 18+.

• PANGBOURNE

Pangbourne College, Pangbourne, Reading, Berkshire RG8 8LA. Tel 01734 842101, Fax 01734 845443

• Pupils 400 • Boys 11–18 (Day/Board) • Girls 11–18 (Day/Board) • Upper sixth 45 • Termly fees £1915–£2640 (Day) £2750–£3770 (Board) • HMC • Enquiries/application to the Registrar

What it's like

Founded in 1917, the school has a very fine site of 230 acres in beautiful Berkshire countryside a mile from Pangbourne village and near the river. There have been many improvements and additions in recent years and the college is now extremely well equipped. It was founded to train boys for a career at sea but since then it has developed into a fully-fledged public school and a broad general education is provided. The school began admitting girls to its sixth-form in 1991 and throughout the age range from 1996. There is a favourable staff:pupil ratio of about 1:9 and nearly all leavers go on to degree courses. The college has a strong tradition of success in music and drama. There is a chapel choir, a choral society, an orchestra and a military band. Each year there is a major annual dramatic production plus a house drama festival and work by the modern theatre group. Sports and games are well provided for (rugby and hockey are strong) and the school has a national reputation for rowing and sailing. The CCF is voluntary but there are army and naval contingents and a Royal Marine section. There is an emphasis on outdoor pursuits for which the environment is most suitable. A good range of clubs and societies caters for most extra-curricular activities. Pupils are engaged in a lot of charity fund-raising.

School profile

Pupils Age range 11–18; 400 pupils (100 day, 300 boarding); girls accepted from age 11 in 1996. Main entry ages 11, 13 and into sixth. 3% are children of former pupils. Pupils drawn from Pangbourne Junior School (tel 01734 843225); St Piran's, Maidenhead (tel 01628 27316); Moulsford Preparatory School (tel 01491 651438); St Andrew's School, Buckhold (tel 01734 744276); St Edward's, Tilehurst (tel 01734 574342); and Eagle House, Sandhurst (tel 01344 772134). *State school entry:* 20% main intake, plus 1% to sixth.

Entrance Common Entrance and own exam used. No special skills or religious requirements, but C of E predominates. Parents not expected to buy textbooks. 5 pa assisted places. 12 pa scholarships (academic, music and art) at 11, 13 and into the sixth, value £950–£5655.

Parents 15+% in the armed services. 15+% in industry or commerce. 30+% live within 30 miles; up to 10% live overseas.

Head and staff *Headmaster:* Anthony Hudson, in post for 8 years. Educated at Tonbridge and universities of Grenoble (French) and Oxford (modern history), and at Institute of Education. Previously Housemaster and Sub-Warden at Radley, and Head of English at La Roseraie (France). *Staff:* 43 full time, 15 part time (including music). Annual turnover 10%. Average age 37.

Exam results In 1995, 74 pupils in upper fifth, 44 in upper sixth. *GCSE:* In 1995, 32 upper fifth gained at least grade C in 8+ subjects; 21 in 5–7 subjects. *A-levels:* 4 upper sixth passed in 4+ subjects; 24 in 3; 12 in 2; and 4 in 1 subject. Average UCAS points 14.5.

University and college entrance 85% of 1995 sixth-form leavers went on to a degree course (20% after a gap year); others typically go on to art foundation courses. Of those going on to university, 4% went to Oxbridge; 5% took courses in medicine, dentistry and veterinary science, 20% in science and engineering, 50% in humanities and social sciences, 20% in art and design, 5% in drama and acting.

Curriculum GCSE and A-levels. 16 GCSE subjects offered; 19 at A-level, including drama & theatre arts and sports studies; no general studies. 27% take science A-levels; 44% arts/humanities; 29% both. *Vocational:* Work experience available. *Computing facilities:* Network of 10 terminals for computer science and other subjects; various departments have computers as teaching aids; including CAD and computer animation. *Special provision:* Full-time specialist supervises a number of part-time teachers providing extra tuition in English and maths for dyslexics and EFL for foreigners. *Europe:* French and German offered at GCSE and A-level (French compulsory from age 11 to GCSE); also GCSE Italian, Spanish and Portuguese. Some exchanges to France and Germany. Some European pupils in school.

The arts *Music:* 40% of pupils learn a musical instrument; instrumental exams can be taken. Some 5 musical groups: orchestra, choir, chamber, jazz band, marching band. Biennial European tour of choir and orchestra. *Drama & dance:* Theatre studies offered and GCSE and A-level may be taken; dance is an extra. Some pupils are involved in school productions and majority in house/other productions. *Art:* On average, 32 take GCSE, 12 A-level. Design, pottery, photography also offered. Good uptake from A-level into art college.

Sport, community service and clubs *Sport and physical activities:* No compulsory sports, but most play rugby. Optional: hockey, rugby, sailing, cricket, rowing, athletics, squash, judo, tennis, golf, cross-country. GCSE may be taken. Rowing, 1st VIII won at Henley Regatta, 2 boys rowed for Great Britain B; sailing, VI finalists in national championships, 3 boys sailed for Great Britain; rugby, U15 won county cup; hockey, 1st XI county indoor runners-up. Judo, national champions 1995. *Community service:* Pupils take bronze Duke of Edinburgh's Award. CCF and community service optional. Recent expedition to Kenya to build clinic and large dam for water. *Clubs and societies:* Up to 30 clubs: magic to bridge; ballroom dancing to leaf and bean; Eclectics to Philistines; electronics to watercolours.

Uniform School uniform worn by day.

Houses/prefects Competitive houses. Prefects, head boy, head of house and house prefects – appointed by the Headmaster.

Religion Daily morning prayers for the whole school, or by houses. Sunday chapel.

Social Debates, music, dancing, drama frequently organised jointly with local schools. Organised choir and orchestra tours abroad; also sports tours, ski trips, French language trips. Sixth formers allowed to bring bike to school. Meals self-service. School shop. Some alcohol allowed in upper sixth social club.

Discipline Pupils failing to produce homework once might expect detention, ie one hour

of compulsory extra study time; those caught smoking cannabis on the premises could expect expulsion.
Boarding 30% have own study bedroom, 50% share (from 1–4); 20% are in dormitories of 6+. Houses, of approximately 65, same as for competitive purposes. Resident qualified nurse. Central dining room. Pupils can provide own food (some cooking). 2 weekend exeats termly and any Sunday. Visits to local village allowed when free – all ages.
Alumni association is run by L C Stephens, Hon Secretary OP Society, c/o the college.
Former pupils Ken Russell (film director); Mike Hailwood (racing motor cyclist); Lord Vinson (life peer and industrialist); John Ridgway (transatlantic oarsman); Jeffrey Bernard (journalist).

• PARSONS MEAD

Parsons Mead School, Ottways Lane, Ashtead, Surrey KT21 2PE. Tel 01372 276401, Fax 01372 278796

• Pupils 350 • Boys None • Girls 3–18 (Day/Weekly board) • Upper sixth 20 • Termly fees £1675 (Day) £2943 (Weekly) • GSA • Enquiries/application to the Headmistress

What it's like

Founded in 1897, it is in the greenbelt with well-designed modern buildings and good facilities in 12 acres of wooded gardens. Recent additions include a new science block, sports hall and drama studio. Senior and junior schools are combined. It is C of E by tradition but girls of all faiths are welcome. There is close cooperation between parents and staff. A sound education is given and exam results are good. Drama, music and art are popular and well supported. A good range of sports and games (regular county representation); also Duke of Edinburgh's Award Scheme, a flourishing Young Enterprise and a number of clubs and societies.

School profile

Pupils Total age range 3–18; 350 girls (340 day, 10 weekly boarding). Senior department 11–19, 230 girls. Main entry ages 3, 7, 11 and into sixth. Approx 5% are children of former pupils. *State school entry:* 10% intake at 11.
Entrance Own entrance exam used. No special skills or religious requirements. Parents not expected to buy textbooks; extras include ballet, piano etc. Up to 6 pa scholarships/bursaries at 11 plus others in sixth, 20%–30% fees.
Parents 15+% in industry or commerce. 80+% live within 30 miles.
Head and staff *Headmistress:* Miss Elizabeth Plant, 6 years in post. Educated at Bolton Girls School and Westfield College, London (classics). Previously Deputy Headmistress, Senior Mistress and Head of Classics at Bolton Girls and Head of Lower School at Manchester High. *Staff:* 36 full time, 10 part time. Annual turnover up to 10%. Average age 35–48
Exam results In 1995, 44 pupils in upper fifth, 10 in upper sixth. *GCSE:* In 1995, 29 upper fifth gained at least grade C in 8+ subjects; 12 in 5–7 subjects. *A-levels:* 5 upper sixth passed in 4 subjects; 4 in 3; 1 in 2 subjects. Average UCAS points 21.0 (including general studies 25.0).
University and college entrance All 1995 sixth-form leavers went on to a degree course (20% after a gap year); 20% took courses in medicine, dentistry and veterinary science, 10% in science and engineering, 70% in humanities and social sciences.
Curriculum GCSE and *A-levels:* 18 GCSE subjects offered; 24 at A-level (including A-level general studies). 30% took science A-levels; 50% arts/humanities; 20% both. *Vocational:* Work experience available; also RSA stages 1 and 2, CLAIT, and Pitmans typing qualifications. *Computing facilities:* Computer room with 12+ Nimbus network; 3 multimedia PCs. *Special provision:* Extra coaching possible. *Europe:* French taught from age 9, German from 12; both offered at GCSE and A-level, also Spanish GCSE in sixth. Regular exchanges and visits (France and Germany).
The arts (Pupils aged 11 and over) *Music:* Over 30% of pupils learn a musical instrument; instrumental exams can be taken. Some 6+ musical groups including orchestra, wind band, choir, form and year group ensembles. 1 pupil member of National Children's Orchestra. *Drama & dance:* Both offered and GCSE and A-level

may be taken. Majority of pupils are involved in school productions. Pupils often go on to drama school. *Art:* On average, 10 take GCSE, 3 A-level. Textiles also offered. Pupils regularly gain places at art colleges.
Sport, community service and clubs (Pupils aged 11 and over) *Sport and physical activities:* Compulsory sports: hockey, netball, swimming, rounders, athletics, tennis. Optional: badminton, volleyball, table tennis. Sixth form only: squash, sailing, golf. GCSE PE may be taken. Netball and hockey teams regularly win local leagues and tournaments; girls represent county in swimming, tennis, netball, athletics and hockey. *Community service:* Pupils take bronze, silver and gold Duke of Edinburgh's Award (activities include police service, fire service, working in charity shops, making jewellery, playing music). Community service and CCF optional. *Clubs and societies:* Up to 15 clubs, eg Young Engineers, science, maths, computers, table tennis, Young Enterprise, technology, cookery, Christian Union.
Uniform School uniform worn except in the sixth.
Houses/prefects No competitive houses. Head girl – elected by sixth-form. All upper sixth are prefects. School Council.
Religion Religious worship encouraged.
Social Various organised local events. Skiing and other educational trips abroad. Day pupils allowed to bring own bike to school (minibus to/from local station). Uniform shop. Meals self-service. No tobacco/alcohol allowed.
Discipline Pupils failing to produce homework once might expect 1 demerit; those caught smoking cannabis on the premises could expect suspension/expulsion.
Boarding Weekly only. Most have own study bedroom, some in pairs, some in dormitories of 3-4. Qualified nurse during day, then on call. Central dining room. Sixth form can provide and cook own snacks. Visits to local town allowed. Day boarding available.
Alumni association is run by Miss Louise Firth, c/o the School.

• PERSE (Boys)

The Perse School, Hills Road, Cambridge CB2 2QF. Tel 01223 568300.
• Pupils 495 • Boys 11–18 (Day) • Girls 16–18 (Day) • Upper sixth 71 • Termly fees £1508 (Day)
• HMC • Enquiries/application to the Headmaster's Secretary

What it's like

Founded in 1615, and originally in Free School Lane, it moved to its present 30-acre green field site on the outskirts of Cambridge in 1960. It has pleasant buildings and excellent modern facilities. Recent developments include a new 180-seater drama studio/lecture theatre and an astroturf pitch; new laboratories and sports hall are planned. While it has the advantages of being a comparatively small school, it is undergoing a controlled expansion and, for the first time in 1995, it admitted girls into the sixth-form. It is Christian but non-denominational. There is much emphasis on management by pupils and there is a very efficient pastoral care scheme. Naturally there are strong links with the university. The teaching is good, academic standards are high and results excellent. Almost all leavers go on to degree courses and a large proportion to Oxbridge. There is a staff:pupil ratio of about 1:11. Very strong indeed in music and drama, which are often undertaken as a joint venture with the Perse (Girls) and also strong in art. A notable record in sports and games (a very large number of representatives at county and national level) and an excellent range of extra-curricular activities, including an unusually large and energetic CCF. Some commitment to local community services. Much use is made of Cambridge's cultural amenities.

School profile

Pupils Age range 11–18; 495 day boys; girls admitted to the sixth-form since 1995. Main entry ages 11, 13 (boys) and into sixth (boys and girls). Own prep school (Perse Preparatory School; tel 01223 568270) provides 60% of intake at 11. *State school entry:* 40% at 11, some at 13.
Entrance Own entrance exam used. No special skills or religious requirements. Parents not expected to buy textbooks. 11 pa assisted places. Variable number of scholarships/ bursaries.

Parents 25 + % have links with Cambridge University; 15 + % are doctors, lawyers etc; 15 + % in industry or commerce.
Head and staff *Headmaster:* Nigel Richardson, in post since 1994. Educated at Highgate and Cambridge (history). Previously Deputy Head of King's, Macclesfield; Head of the Dragon School, Oxford, and Second Master at Uppingham. *Staff:* 44 full time, 3 part time. Annual turnover 5%.
Exam results In 1995, 75 pupils in fifth, 71 in upper sixth. *GCSE:* In 1995, 71 fifth gained at least grade C in 8 + subjects; 4 in 5–7 subjects. *A-levels:* 11 upper sixth passed in 4-5 subjects; 55 in 3; and 5 in 2 subjects. Average UCAS points 25.6.
University and college entrance 95% of sixth-form leavers go on to a degree course, up to 33% go to Oxbridge; 10% take courses in medicine, dentistry and veterinary science, 50% in science and engineering, 40% in humanities and social sciences.
Curriculum GCSE and A-levels. On average, there is a 50/50 split between science/engineering and arts/humanities. *Vocational:* Work experience available. *Computing facilities:* 50 + networked Archimedes plus various others; whole school on Econet network system. New system being installed 1996. *Europe:* French and German offered to GCSE and A-level; Spanish and Russian as a non-examined subjects, occasionally to GCSE on demand. Over 75% take GCSE in more than 1 language. Regular exchanges (France and Germany). Significant number of sons of visiting academics in school for 1–3 terms. Establishing Young Enterprise Scheme with French schools.
The arts *Music:* Over 50% of pupils learn a musical instrument; instrumental exams can be taken. Some 20 musical groups including orchestras, wind band, brass group, choirs, up to 10 chamber music groups. National chamber group brass award. *Drama & dance:* Majority of pupils are involved in school productions and all in other productions; very large number of plays plus form drama evenings. *Art:* On average, 26 take GCSE, 10 A-level. Photography also offered.
Sport, community service and clubs *Sport and physical activities:* Compulsory sports (to 14): rugby, hockey, cricket. Optional: tennis, basketball, athletics available; off site – golf, squash, swimming, cross-country, soccer. Many sporting successes: old boy gained Cambridge blue, place in Oxford Greyhounds and Cambridge reserve team; county champions at hockey and many other sports at numerous levels; England schoolboy hockey representatives; county squash champion; winner of novice 4s rowing at schools' Head of the Thames; and many more. *Community service:* Pupils take bronze, silver and gold Duke of Edinburgh's Award. CCF and community service both optional. Young Enterprise scheme awards. *Clubs and societies:* Up to 30 clubs, eg astronomy, aero-modelling, bridge, chess, Christian Union, drama, debating, electronics, fencing, judo, charity, computing, music, war games, medical.
Uniform School uniform worn, dress code in sixth.
Houses/prefects No competitive houses. Prefects, head boy – appointed by the Head after nomination by staff and pupils. School Council.
Religion Compulsory religious worship (unless opted out).
Social Music and drama (including master classes) often joint with Perse (Girls) plus debates, discos, plays. Organised trips abroad. Pupils allowed to bring own car/bike to school. Meals self-service. School tuckshop. No tobacco/alcohol allowed.
Discipline Pupils failing to produce homework once may not be punished. Pupils using banned substances likely to be expelled.
Alumni association run by Mr T D Plumridge, c/o the School.
Former pupils Sir Peter Hall; 2 Nobel prizewinners; many notable university figures.

• PERSE (Girls)

Perse School for Girls, Union Road, Cambridge CB2 1HF. Tel 01223 359589

• Pupils 720 • Boys None • Girls 7–18 (Day) • Upper sixth 70 • Termly fees £1335-£1552 (Day) • GSA • Enquiries/application to the Headmistress

What it's like

Founded in 1881 under the scheme for the management of the Perse Trust, it is well sited in the centre of Cambridge, in agreeable and very well-equipped buildings. Recent developments include a music wing, new science and technology facilities and a sixth-form centre. The junior school is nearby. It has a high reputation academically; it prides itself on providing a first-class, balanced education for girls from all sectors of society and the opportunity to develop talent and individuality in any field. The GCSE and A-level results are consistently excellent, and each year most sixth-formers go on to degree courses, including a high proportion to Oxbridge. Music, drama and art are all strong, especially music. The senior school has three choirs, two orchestras, a wind band and a variety of music groups, including jazz. The school combines with other schools in Cambridge for various extra-curricular activities (of which there are many), in drama, music, Young Enterprise and Youth Action etc. Sports and games are played to a high standard (the playing fields are ten minutes from the school). Hockey and tennis are especially strong (a high number of representatives at county and regional level). The Duke of Edinburgh's Award Scheme is well supported. Extensive use is made of Cambridge's cultural amenities.

School profile

Pupils Total age range 7–18; 720 day girls. Senior department 11–18, 540 girls. Main entry ages 7 to 11 and into sixth. Very few are children of former pupils. Significant number of senior intake is from its own junior department (tel 01223 357322). *State school entry:* 35% of main intake at 11, and 50% into sixth.

Entrance Own entrance exam used. All-round ability looked for; no religious requirements. Parents not expected to buy textbooks; maximum extras, £112 (for individual music/speech lessons). 20 pa assisted places. 15 pa scholarships and bursaries £600–£1,800.

Parents Up to 10% live overseas.

Head and staff *Headmistress:* Miss Helen Smith, in post for 7 years. Educated at King Edwards High School for Girls, Birmingham, and Oxford University (mathematics). Previously Deputy Head, Head of Department at the Perse (Girls) and Mathematics Teacher both at the International School, Brussels, and at Cheltenham Ladies' College. *Staff:* 60 full time, 16 part time. Annual turnover 5%. Average age 40.

Exam results In 1995, 84 pupils in upper fifth, 51 in upper sixth. *GCSE:* In 1995, all upper fifth gained at least grade C in 8+ subjects. *A-levels:* 8 upper sixth passed in 4+ subjects; 38 in 3; 4 in 2; 1 in 1 subject. Average UCAS points 26.9.

University and college entrance 98% of 1995 sixth-form leavers went on to a degree course (35% after a gap year); others typically go on to management training or to foundation courses. Of those going on to university, 18% went to Oxbridge; 18% took courses in medicine, dentistry and veterinary science, 25% in science and engineering, 3% in law, 40% in humanities and social sciences, 3% in art and design, 11% in other subjects eg textile design, maths, economics .

Curriculum GCSE and *A-levels:* 22 GCSE subjects offered; 24 at A-level (not general studies). 31% take science A-levels; 29% arts/humanities; 40% both. *Vocational:* Work experience available. *Computing facilities:* 2 well-equipped computer rooms; individual computers in specialist rooms. *Special provision:* Any necessary provision arranged on individual basis. *Europe:* French, German, Italian, Russian and Spanish offered at GCSE and A-level; also French AS-level. All girls take French from age 7, a second language from 12 to 14. 98% take GCSE in 2 or more languages. Regular exchanges (France, Germany, Italy, Spain and Russia).

The arts (Pupils aged 11 and over) *Music:* Over 75% of pupils learn a musical instrument; instrumental exams can be taken. Some 30 musical groups including 4 choirs, 2 orchestras, brass, jazz, wind, chamber, recorder. Several groups winners of National Chamber Music Competition for Schools; 4 recent Oxbridge choral awards; 1 member National Youth Orchestra; several members National Children's Orchestra. *Drama & dance*: Drama offered. GCSE and A-level drama, Poetry Society and LAMDA exams may be taken. Some pupils are involved in school productions and majority in house/other productions. Medal successes every year in Cambridge Festival; regular medals in LAMDA and Poetry Society exams. *Art:* On average, 20 take GCSE, 2–4 AS-level, 4 A-level. Design, pottery, textiles, photography, costume, jewellery, sculpture etc also offered.

Sport, community service and clubs (Pupils aged 11 and over) *Sport and physical activities:* Compulsory sports: gymnastics, dance, swimming, hockey, netball, tennis, rounders, athletics. Optional: squash, aerobics, basketball, badminton, trampolining, jazz, dance, table tennis. Sixth form only: golf. BAGA exams may be taken. County

netball U14 B team winners at regional tournament 1992–1994; several county and regional tennis players; county hockey players, U14, U16, U18; regional sports acrobatics U13 winners. *Community service:* Pupils take silver and gold Duke of Edinburgh's Award. Community service optional; close involvement with local old people's home. *Clubs and societies:* Up to 30 clubs, eg chess, bridge, debating, dance, gymnastics, maths, computing, CDT, science, Christian Union.
Uniform School uniform worn, except in sixth.
Houses/prefects Competitive houses. Prefects, head girl, head of house and house prefects – elected by the school. School Council.
Religion Attendance at assembly compulsory, except for conscientious objectors and sixth-form.
Social Joint with Perse (Boys): windband, theatrical productions, debates, Young Enterprise, some societies. Exchanges with schools in France, Germany, Italy, Spain and Russia. Organised trips to Pompeii, Italy (skiing), France, Russia. Pupils allowed to bring own bike (car in sixth). Meals self-service. No tobacco/alcohol allowed.
Discipline Pupils failing to produce homework once might expect discussion with relevant staff; those caught smoking cannabis on the premises could expect to be expelled.
Alumni association Old Persean Guild, Mrs J Waters, 12 Garner Close, Milton, Cambridge CB4 6DY.

• PIPERS CORNER

Pipers Corner School, Great Kingshill, High Wycombe, Buckinghamshire HP15 6LP. Tel 01494 718255, Fax 01494 715391

• Pupils 340 • Boys None • Girls 4–18 (Day/Board/Weekly) • Upper sixth 23 • Termly fees £935–£1936 (Day) £2688–£3234 (Board) £2648–£3194 (Weekly) • GSA, BSA, AHIS • Enquiries/application to the Headmistress

What it's like

Founded in 1930, it has been on its present site since 1945. It stands in most agreeable, rural surroundings, high in the Chilterns, with some 36 acres of grounds and gardens. The main building reflects the 17th-century farmhouse out of which the school has grown. It is well equipped with good modern facilities, including a new technology/performing arts development, and comfortable accommodation. A C of E foundation, it is ecumenical in spirit and policy. Boarders are expected to attend Sunday service either in the school chapel or at the local parish church of Hughenden with which the school has close links. Most sixth-formers go on to degree courses. Drama is strong. A variety of sports and games is available and there are plentiful extra-curricular activities. Local community services flourish and the school achieves success at bronze level in the Duke of Edinburgh's Award Scheme.

School profile

Pupils Total age range 4–18; 340 girls (270 day, 70 boarding). Senior school 11–18, 270 girls. Main entry ages 4, 7, 11, 12 and into sixth. 5% are children of former pupils. *State school entry:* 20% senior intake.
Entrance Own entrance exam used. No special skills or religious requirements. Parents not expected to buy textbooks. Sixth-form scholarships; service and academic bursaries available.
Parents 10+% in the armed services. 60+% live within 30 miles; up to 10% live overseas.
Head and staff *Headmistress:* Dr Mary Wilson, in post for 10 years. Educated at St Joseph's, Olney and Wolverton Grammar, and at London, Paris, Caen, and Oxford universities (French, Spanish, management). Previously Deputy Head at Sexey's School, Bruton, Lecturer in French at Milton Keynes College of Education, and Associate Lecturer at Caen University. *Staff:* 25 full time, 15 part time. Annual turnover 8%. Average age 40.
Exam results In 1995, 52 pupils in upper fifth, 23 in upper sixth. *GCSE:* In 1995, 77% upper fifth gained at least grade C in 8+ subjects; 12% in 5–7 subjects. *A-levels:* 4% upper sixth passed in 4 subjects; 52% in 3; 26% in 2; and 13% in 1 subject. Average UCAS points 13.9.

University and college entrance 97% of 1995 sixth-form leavers went on to a degree course (17% after a gap year); others typically go on to work. Of those going on to university, 5% went to Oxbridge; 9% took courses in science and engineering, 50% in humanities and social sciences, 14% in art and design, 27% in vocational subjects eg physiotherapy, accounting.
Curriculum GCSE, AS-levels, A-levels (including AS and A-level general studies) and GNVQ. 57% take arts/humanities A-levels, 43% both arts and sciences. *Vocational:* GNVQ level 3 business studies (equivalent to 2 A-levels). *Computing facilities:* 19-station network of research machines; including one multi-media system and 7-station network extension. 20 Acorn computers in IT rooms and in classrooms. Computerised library system. *Special provision:* Private EFL. *Europe:* French, German and Spanish to GCSE and A-level. All girls take GCSE in 2 languages. Exchanges can be arranged.
The arts *Music:* Over 30% pupils learn a musical instrument; instrumental exams taken automatically. Musical groups include choir, orchestra, wind band, recorder, string groups. *Drama & dance*: Both offered. GCSE drama and A-level theatre studies, Poetry Society, LAMDA examinations may be taken. Majority of pupils are involved in school productions (Alice, 1995).
Sport, community service and clubs *Sport and physical activities:* Compulsory sports (to different ages): gymnastics, netball, hockey, tennis, athletics, rounders, lacrosse. Fifth and sixth-form only: aerobics, basketball, badminton, volleyball. Netball, national round of All England tournament U14. *Community service:* Pupils can take bronze Duke of Edinburgh's Award. Community service optional. *Clubs and societies:* Up to 30 clubs, eg debating, computers, music, Christian Fellowship, Young Enterprise, sports, Guides, bridge, photography, art, riding.
Uniform School uniform worn except in sixth-form.
Houses/prefects Competitive houses. Prefects, head girl, head of house and house prefects – selected by Headmistress, staff and sixth-form. School council. Charity committee.
Religion C of E foundation; confirmation, church and chapel.
Social Debates, dances with local boys' schools; public speaking, Youth Speaks (Rotary) and English Speaking Union, Observer Mace Debating. Some organised trips abroad. Upper sixth day pupils allowed to bring own cars to school. Lunch self-service; other meals formal. No tobacco/alcohol allowed.
Discipline Pupils failing to produce homework once would be asked to produce work by next day to tutor.
Boarding Upper sixth have own study bedroom, lower sixth share (2); others in dormitories of 4–6. Houses divided by year groups. Resident nurse; doctor visits. Central dining room. Sixth form can provide and cook snacks. 3 exeats for full boarders, weekly boarding available. Visits to local town allowed by sixth-form in groups of 2 or 3 at the weekend.

• POCKLINGTON

Pocklington School, West Green, Pocklington, York YO4 2NJ. Tel 01759 303125, Fax 01759 306366

• Pupils 753 • Boys 7–18 (Day/Board) • Girls 7–18 (Day/Board) • Upper sixth 78 • Termly fees £1614 (Day) £2896 (Board) • HMC, BSA • Enquiries/application to the Headmaster.

What it's like

Founded in 1514, its fine Victorian buildings are sited on the outskirts of the small market town in ample grounds. There have been extensive modern developments and facilities are very good. The standard of teaching is high and the academic results are good; most sixth-formers go on to degree courses. Very strong in art, music, drama and dance; almost all participate school and house productions. Wide range of sports and games including riding, show jumping, cross-country to county standard. High standards achieved in hockey, rugby and badminton (a lot of county players). Numerous societies and clubs and the Duke of Edinburgh's Award Scheme. The school is well supported in the area and is much involved with its local community: it has designed a town plan for Pocklington and it runs the talking newspaper for the blind in the East Riding.

School profile

Pupils Total age range 7–18; 753 pupils, 610 day (468 boys, 285 girls), 143 boarding (96 boys, 47 girls); boarding available from age 11 only. Senior department: 11–18, 628 pupils (390 boys, 238 girls). Main entry ages 11, 13 and into sixth. Approx 15% are children of former pupils. *State school entry:* 50% senior intake, plus 40% to sixth.

Entrance Common Entrance and own exam used. No special skills required. C of E school but accepts all denominations. Parents not expected to buy textbooks; maximum £100 extras. 26 pa assisted places. Various scholarships for academic excellence and for art and music. Means tested bursaries, £150 to full tuition fees.

Parents 15+% are doctors, lawyers, etc; 15+% in armed services, 15+% in agriculture. 60+% live within 30 miles; up to 10% live overseas.

Head and staff *Headmaster:* David Gray, 4 years in post. Educated at Fettes and Bristol University (English). Previously Head of General Studies at Dulwich and Head of English at Leeds Grammar. Also former co-owner and now partner and recruitment officer of Key English Language Institute, Athens. *Staff:* 61 full time, 6 part time. Annual turnover 5%. Average age 35–40.

Exam results In 1995, 78 pupils in upper fifth, 84 in upper sixth. *GCSE:* In 1995, 50 upper fifth gained at least grade C in 8+ subjects; 19 in 5–7; and 9 in 1–4 subjects. *A-levels:* 47 upper sixth passed in 4+ subjects; 14 in 3; 17 in 2; and 4 in 1 subject. Average UCAS points 16.2.

University and college entrance 90% of 1995 sixth-form leavers went on to a degree course; others typically go on to HND or art courses or straight into careers. Of those going on to university, 2% went to Oxbridge; 3% took courses in medicine, dentistry and veterinary science, 40% in science and engineering, 55% in humanities and social sciences, 2% in art and design.

Curriculum GCSE and *A-levels:* 21 GCSE subjects offered; 24 at A-level (including general studies). 35% took science A-levels; 50% arts/humanities; 15% both. *Vocational:* Work experience available. *Computing facilities:* Computer lab with 20 IBM compatible 286 VGA systems, 15 BBC, 4 Archimedes, Apple, Amstrad, 2 Acorns. *Special provision:* EFL for foreign students; dyslexic help, facilities for children with cerebral palsy. *Europe:* French and German offered at GCSE, AS and A-level; also Spanish GCSE. Regular exchanges (France and Germany).

The arts (Pupils aged 11 and over) *Music:* Over 30% of pupils learn a musical instrument; instrumental exams can be taken. Musical groups include wind, classical guitar, early music, jazz, swing. Member of National Children's Orchestra. *Drama and dance:* Both offered. A-level theatre studies may be taken. Majority of pupils are involved in school productions and all in house/other productions. Recent productions of As You Like It, Christmas Carol, The Hobbit and Peer Gynt. *Art:* On average, 40 take GCSE, 20 A-level. Design, pottery, textiles, photography, video, graphic design also offered. Winner of National Road Safety Video award; designer of winning trophies for North of England's Businessmen's award.

Sport, community service and clubs (Pupils aged 11 and over) *Sport and physical activities:* Compulsory sports: hockey, netball, rounders, cricket, rugby, gymnastics, swimming, cross-country. Optional: badminton, basketball, athletics, golf, riding, squash, tennis, volleyball, orienteering, gliding. RLSS exams may be taken. Hockey, girls regional U16 champions, 2 boys represent county U15; rugby, county U18 representative; badminton, county representatives; showjumping, member of national junior team; cross-country, county champions boys and girls, individual champion. *Community service:* Pupils take bronze, silver and gold Duke of Edinburgh's Award. CCF compulsory for 1 year at age 15, community service for 1 year at age 17. School runs the talking newspaper for the blind in East Riding; pupils have won regional awards in recent years for community projects. *Clubs and societies:* Up to 30 clubs, eg board games, bridge, chess, computer, debating, conservation, film, karate, orienteering, street theatre, school newspaper, electronics, first aid.

Uniform School uniform worn throughout.

Houses/prefects Competitive houses. Prefects, head boy/girl, head of house and house prefects – appointed by the Headmaster and housemasters/mistresses.

Religion Sunday morning service and daily assembly.

Social No organised events with local schools. Organised trips abroad to France and Germany. Day pupils allowed to bring own car/bike/motorbike to school. Meals self-

service. School shop. Upper sixth allowed some alcohol; no tobacco allowed.
Discipline Pupils failing to produce homework once might expect to re-write it or get detention. Those caught smoking cannabis on the premises would expect expulsion, but would be helped to move to another school to make a new start if this was appropriate.
Boarding 25% have own study bedroom, 50% share with others; 25% are in dormitories of 5 or 6. Single-sex houses, of approximately 50, divided by age group. Resident qualified nurse. Central dining room. Pupils can provide and cook own food. Cottage in grounds run by adults as boarders' social area with snooker, TV, games room, kitchen. 2 weekend exeats and half-term. Visits to local town allowed frequently.
Alumni association is run by M G Milne Esq, c/o the school.
Former pupils Sir James Cobban; Tom Stoppard; Adrian Edmondson; William Wilberforce.

• POLAM HALL

Polam Hall School, Grange Road, Darlington, Durham DH1 5PA. Tel 01325 463383, Fax 01325 383539

• Pupils 420 • Boys None • Girls 4–18 (Day/Board/Weekly) • Upper sixth 16 • Termly fees £1422 (Day) £2903 (Board) £2888 (Weekly) • GSA • Enquiries/application to the Headmistress

What it's like

Originally a Friends' school under personal ownership, founded in 1884; the present school dates from 1888. The main building (and the heart of the place) is a very elegant late 18th-century house in a beautiful garden and wooded park of 19 acres on the edge of Darlington. Kindergarten and junior school are combined with the main school. The buildings have been much improved recently and facilities and accommodation are now excellent. Great importance is attached to pastoral life and to the creation of a happy family atmosphere. A good general academic education is given and results are excellent. Most sixth-formers proceed to degree courses, including Oxbridge. Very strong music, art and drama departments. Good range of sports, games and activities. Substantial commitment to local community service. Quite an impressive record in the Duke of Edinburgh's Award Scheme.

School profile

Pupils Total age range 4–18; 420 girls, 360 day, 60 boarding. Senior department 11–18, 310 girls. Main entry ages 4, 9, 11, 13 and into sixth. Approx 5%–10% are children of former pupils. *State school entry:* 30% senior intakes, plus 10% to sixth.
Entrance Own entrance exam used. No special skills or religious requirements. Parents not expected to buy textbooks; maximum extras £90, plus £74 per term lunch for day girls. 18 pa assisted places. Scholarships/bursaries available, 10%–50% fees.
Parents 80+% live within 30 miles; up to 10% live overseas.
Head and staff *Headmistress:* Mrs Helen Hamilton, in post for 10 years. Educated at West Norfolk and Kings Lynn High School for Girls and at London University (mathematics). Previously Deputy Head and Head of Mathematics at Polam Hall and Head of Mathematics at Teesside High. Also member of GSA Boarding Committee.
Exam results In 1995, 55 pupils in upper fifth, 16 in upper sixth. *GCSE:* In 1995, 44 upper fifth gained at least grade C in 8+ subjects; 5 in 5–7 subjects. *A-levels:* 15 upper sixth passed in 4+ subjects; 1 in 3 subjects. Average UCAS points 26.3 (with general studies, 32.1).
University and college entrance 94% of 1995 sixth-form leavers went on to a degree course (12% after a gap year); others typically go on to art college. Of those going on to university, 6% went to Oxbridge; 25% took courses in medicine, dentistry and veterinary science, 12% in science and engineering, 6% in law, 50% in humanities and social sciences, 6% in art and design.
Curriculum GCSE and *A-levels:* 20 GCSE subjects offered; 18 at A-level (including statistics, theatre studies and general studies). 30% take science A-levels; 40% arts/humanities; 30% both. *Vocational:* Work experience available; also RSA qualifications in CLAIT and typing. *Computing facilities:* 12 BBC Masters and 13 Archimedes. *Special provision:* Dyslexia Institute visits; ESL lessons provided in school; special needs unit. *Europe:* French, German and Spanish offered to GCSE, AS and A-level (French

compulsory from age 11, German from 12).

The arts (Pupils aged 11 and over) *Music:* 40% of pupils learn a musical instrument; instrumental exams can be taken. Some 10 musical groups including choir, wind band, chamber groups, recorder. Members National Children's Orchestra, National Youth Wind Orchestra, Northern Junior Philharmonic etc. *Drama & dance*: Both offered. GCSE drama, A-level theatre studies, ESB, LAMDA exams may be taken. Majority of pupils are involved in school productions and all in house/other productions. Recent production of Kiss Me Kate. *Art:* On average, 18 take GCSE, 1 AS-level, 3 A-level. Design, pottery, textiles also offered. Recent pupil to foundation course at Central Saint Martin's.

Sport, community service and clubs (Pupils aged 11 and over) *Sport and physical activities:* Compulsory: lacrosse, hockey, netball, swimming, athletics, tennis, rounders. Optional: badminton, self-defence, fencing, squash, basketball, volleyball. Sixth form only: rock climbing. GCSE and BAGA exams may be taken. Representatives in county and area hockey teams; regional lacrosse squads; area netball teams. *Community service:* Pupils take bronze, silver and gold Duke of Edinburgh's Award. Community service optional in sixth. *Clubs and societies:* Up to 15 clubs, eg debating, country dance, fencing, creative writing, chess, drama.

Uniform School uniform worn except the sixth.

Houses/prefects Competitive houses. No prefects, head girl and head of house elected by school and staff.

Religion Morning assembly (reading) compulsory at all ages, as is church for boarders except in sixth-form.

Social Social functions and occasional joint musical activities with local independent schools. Organised trips abroad. Pupils allowed to bring own car/bike to school. Some meals formal, some self-service. No tobacco/alcohol allowed.

Discipline Pupils failing to produce homework once might expect a late mark; those caught smoking cannabis on the premises may expect expulsion.

Boarding 2% have own study bedroom, 98% share, up to 5. Houses of 25–40, divided by age. Resident qualified nurse. Central dining room. Pupils can provide and cook limited food. 2 weekend exeats each term. Limited visits to local town allowed.

Alumni association run by Mrs D Bateman, Honey Cottage, 6 West Street, Gayles, Richmond, N Yorkshire DL11 7JA.

• PORTSMOUTH GRAMMAR

The Portsmouth Grammar School, High Street, Portsmouth, Hampshire PO1 2LN. Tel 01705 819125, Fax 01705 870184

• Pupils 822 • Boys 11–18 (Day) • Girls 11–18 (Day) • Upper sixth 101 • Termly fees £1495 (Day) • HMC • Enquiries/application to the Headmaster

What it's like

Founded in 1732 by Dr William Smith. The present buildings, in an agreeable, plain design, were opened in 1927 and stand in the High Street of Old Portsmouth. Recent developments include a theatre, music school, sports hall, sports pavilion and sixth-form centre. The school is closely connected with Portsmouth Cathedral (whose choristers are mainly pupils), but religious instruction, in accordance with the principles of the Christian faith, is non-denominational. Originally a boys' school, girls were admitted to the sixth-form in 1976 and the school became fully co-educational in 1991. A large, well-qualified staff allows a staff:pupil ratio of about 1:12. A sound general education is provided and there is a large sixth-form. Academic standards are high and results consistently very good. Nearly all sixth-form leavers go on to degree courses, a number to Oxbridge. Music and drama are strong. There is a good range of sports and games, including judo, fencing, rowing (at sea) and sailing, for which the facilities are first-rate. A strong CCF contingent comprises Navy, Army and Air Force sections. Considerable emphasis on open-air pursuits and on the Duke of Edinburgh's Award Scheme (which involves local community services and charity work). The school has vigorous local support.

School profile

Pupils Age range 11–18, 822 day pupils (609 boys, 213 girls) Main entry age 11. Large proportion from own junior school (The Lower School; tel 01705 819125). *State school entry:* 35% main intake, plus 20% to sixth.

Entrance Common Entrance or own exam (including pupils of own junior). Assisted places; scholarships (including art and music) and bursaries.

Head and staff *Headmaster:* A C V Evans, in post for 13 years. Educated at De la Salle Grammar School, London, and at the Sorbonne, Oxford University and University College London (modern languages). Previously Head of Humanities and Head of Modern Languages at Dulwich and Assistant Master at Winchester and Eastbourne. Chairman of HMC, 1996. Publications: on Georges Duhamel; co-writer of HMC Modern Languages Report No. 3, 1992. *Staff:* 69 full time, 13 part time. Annual turnover 5%. Average age 40.

Exam results In 1995, 127 pupils in fifth, 101 in upper sixth. *GCSE:* In 1995, 40% fifth gained at least grade C in 10+ subjects, 58% in 8+; 2% in 6+ subjects. *A-levels:* 28% upper sixth passed in 4+ subjects; 69% in 3; 3% in 2 subjects. Average UCAS points 24.6.

University and college entrance All 1995 sixth-form leavers went on to a degree course (12% after a gap year), 7% to Oxbridge; 16% took courses in medicine, dentistry and veterinary science, 35% in science and engineering, 1% in law, 33% in humanities and social sciences, 1% in art and design, 3% over vocational subjects eg podiatry, physiotherapy, 11% in combined courses.

Curriculum GCSE, AS-levels and A-levels (general studies taught but not as examination subject; GCSE Japanese on offer to sixth-form). 30% take science A-levels; 40% arts/humanities; 30% both. *Vocational:* Work experience available. *Computing facilities:* Well-equipped IT centre and computers in various departments. *Europe:* French, German and Spanish offered to GCSE, AS and A-level. Regular exchanges.

The arts *Music:* Over 30% of pupils learn a musical instrument; instrumental exams can be taken. Some 15 musical groups including orchestra, concert band, rock bands, choirs, swing groups. A number of distinctions at music festivals; 1 pupil in National Youth Orchestra. *Drama & dance*: Drama offered. GCSE theatre arts may be taken; also LAMDA exams (private lessons). Pupils are involved in school and house/other productions. 2 recent pupils have gone on to study drama full time. *Art:* On average, 20 take GCSE, 3 AS-level, 7 A-level. Design, pottery, sculpture, photography also offered. 75% A-level candidates enter foundation courses.

Sport, community service and clubs *Sport and physical activities:* Compulsory sports: rugby, hockey, cross-country, tennis, athletics (boys); netball, hockey, cross-country, rounders, tennis (girls). Optional: rowing, fencing, basketball, squash, badminton, swimming, judo. Sixth form only: sailing. GCSE sport, BAGA, RLSS exams may be taken. 1994: rugby, Daily Mail semi-final, 8 in county team, 1 in England squad; swimming, 1 international representative, 3 county; fencing, 1 regional representative; hockey, 2 county representatives, regional captain; athletics, 1 national-level runner; cross-country, national 1st Oxford relay, 3rd Coventry road relay; rowing, 1st pair winners junior event, Nottingham championships. *Community service:* Pupils take Duke of Edinburgh's Award (in 1995/6, 86 bronze, 25 silver and 3 gold awards). CCF and community service optional. *Clubs and societies:* Over 30 clubs, eg photography, technology, electronics, debating, bridge, judo, computers, fencing, wildlife, war games, dance, creative writing, Christian Union, radio-controlled models.

Uniform School uniform worn throughout.

Houses/prefects Competitive houses. Senior prefects (appointed by the Head), head of house and house prefects. School sixth-form Council, elected by the sixth-form.

Religion Attendance at religious worship compulsory.

Social Debates, choirs, orchestras and foreign trips jointly with other local schools. Exchanges with France, Germany, Spain and USA; visits to Italy and Russia; choir and concert band trips to Europe and USA; ski and white water rafting holidays. Pupils allowed to bring own car/bike/motorbike to school. Meals self-service. No tobacco/ alcohol allowed.

Discipline Pupils failing to produce homework once might expect an oral warning; those caught smoking cannabis on the premises could expect suspension certainly, expulsion probably.

Former pupils Roger Black (athlete); Jon Ayling (cricketer); Paul Jones (pop singer, Manfred Mann).

• PORTSMOUTH HIGH

Portsmouth High School, 25 Kent Road, Southsea, Hampshire PO5 3EQ. Tel 01705 826714, Fax 01705 814814

• Pupils 505 • Boys None • Girls 11–18 (Day) • Upper sixth 57 • Termly fees £1326 (Day)
• GSA, GPDST • Enquiries/application to the Headmistress

What it's like

Founded in 1882, it has pleasant premises close to Southsea Common and the sea which have been greatly extended over the years. Modern facilities are good and include a fine sports hall, excellent labs and art and technology accommodation. The junior school at Dovercourt is a few minutes away. Pupils are drawn from all parts of Portsmouth and surrounding districts. Academic standards are very high and results very good. Most of the sixth-form go on to degree courses each year, a number to Oxbridge. Music, drama and art departments are strong. A good range of sports and games (quite a few representatives at county and national level) and a varied range of extra-curricular activities. A promising record in the Duke of Edinburgh's Award Scheme.

School profile

Pupils Age range 11–18; 505 day girls. Main entry ages, 11, 14 and into the sixth. Small number are children of former pupils. Own junior school provides over 40%. *State school entry:* 40% main intakes, plus 80% to sixth.

Entrance Own entrance exam used. No special skills or religious requirements. Parents not expected to buy textbooks. 29 pa assisted places. 6 pa scholarships and bursaries, 33%–50% fees.

Parents 15+% are doctors, lawyers etc; 15+% in industry or commerce.

Head and staff *Headmistress:* Mrs J M Dawtrey, in post for 12 years. Educated at Frome Grammar and London University (French with Spanish). Previously Senior Mistress and Head of Modern Languages at Rickmansworth Masonic. *Staff:* 31 full time, 13 part time. Annual turnover 4%.

Exam results In 1995, 84 pupils in upper fifth, 57 in upper sixth. *GCSE:* In 1995, 82 upper fifth gained at least grade C in 7+ subjects. *A-levels:* 5 upper sixth passed in 4+ subjects; 49 in 3; and 1 in 2; and 2 in 1 subject. Average UCAS points 21.5.

University and college entrance 97% of 1995 sixth-form leavers went on to a degree course (9% after a gap year); others typically go on to music college or art foundation course. Of those going on to university, 10% went to Oxbridge; 11% took courses in medicine, dentistry and veterinary science, 14% in science and engineering, 12% in law, 55% in humanities and social sciences (including 21% languages), 3% in art and design, 4% in vocational subjects eg physiotherapy.

Curriculum GCSE and A-levels. 17 subjects offered (no A-level general studies). 23% take science A-levels; 56% arts/humanities; 21% both. *Vocational:* Post-GCSE work experience compulsory. *Computing facilities:* RM Nimbus network plus Archimedes and Elonex in mathematics and technology departments. *Special provision:* Coaching as necessary. *Europe:* French, German and Spanish offered to GCSE, AS and A-level; also GCSE Italian in sixth. All pupils take GCSE in French and/or Spanish. Regular exchanges to France, Germany and Spain. European work experience in sixth-form.

The arts *Music:* Over 50% of pupils learn a musical instrument; instrumental exams can be taken. Some 10+ musical groups including string orchestra, wind band, chamber choir, orchestras, other choirs and groups. School ensemble selected for final concert in National Chamber Music Competition for Schools. 6 pupils in county youth orchestra; 5 in county training orchestras; 1 in county youth band; 1 in Southampton Youth Orchestra. *Drama & dance*: Dance offered. GCSE theatre studies, LAMDA and New Era exams may be taken. Some pupils are involved in school productions. *Art:* On average, 45 take GCSE, 3 AS-level, 6 A-level. Pottery and textiles also offered.

Sport, community service and clubs *Sport and physical activities:* Compulsory sports (age 11–14): Lacrosse, netball, tennis, rounders, swimming. Optional: Distance running, football, hockey, cricket. Additional options (14–18): Badminton, volleyball, table tennis,

ice-skating. 2 pupils in county lacrosse team, 3 in county netball, 4 in county cricket, 1 county swimming, 3 in county athletics, 1 in Southern Region gymnastics, 2 in British junior sailing team; national U19 pole vault champion, Southern counties synchronised swimming champion (12–14 age group). *Community service:* Pupils take bronze, silver and gold Duke of Edinburgh's Award. Community service optional in sixth-form. *Clubs and societies:* Up to 15 clubs, eg aerobics, chess, computing, current events, debating, drama, environment, judo, pottery, as well as music and sports.
Uniform School uniform worn except in the sixth.
Houses/prefects No competitive houses or prefects. Head girl and 2 deputies, elected by senior girls.
Religion Morning assembly unless withdrawn for religious reasons.
Social Concerts, debates, musicals, lectures with local boys' schools; BAYS, Young Enterprise etc. Exchanges with France, Germany, Spain; group cultural visits; skiing trips. Pupils allowed to bring own car/bike to school (no parking provided for cars). Meals self-service. School tuckshop. No tobacco/alcohol allowed.
Discipline Pupils failing to produce homework once will be required to do it; those caught smoking cannabis on the premises can expect immediate suspension and probable expulsion.
Alumni association Contact: The Secretary of the PHS Guild c/o the school.

• PRINCESS HELENA

The Princess Helena College, Preston, Hitchin, Hertfordshire SG4 7RT. Tel 01462 432100, Fax 01462 431497

• Pupils 150 • Boys None • Girls 10–18 (Day/Board/Weekly) • Upper sixth 20 • Termly fees £1932–£2320 (Day) £2776–£3330 (Board) • GSA, BSA • Enquiries/application to the Headmaster

What it's like

Founded in 1820, it was the first academic school for girls (day or boarding). After a series of moves it settled at its present site at Temple Dinsley. The main building is a delightful Queen Anne mansion (1712), enlarged by Lutyens in 1909. This and the Dower House lie in fine Gertrude Jekyll gardens and 183 acres of parkland. Considerable modern developments now provide first-rate accommodation and all-round facilities. It has all the advantages of a small school and a happy family atmosphere prevails. Worship is compulsory at morning prayers and Sunday services. A staff:pupil ratio of 1:7, plus a large number of part-time staff. A good all-round education is given and results are good. Most sixth-formers proceed to degree courses. It is very strong in music. A good range of sports, games and activities is available. There is a substantial commitment to local community schemes and an impressive record in the Duke of Edinburgh's Award Scheme.

School profile

Pupils Age range 10–18; 150 girls (40 day, 110 boarding). Main entry ages 11, 12, 13 and into sixth. Approx 5% are children of former pupils. *State school entry:* 10% main intake.
Entrance Common Entrance and own examination used. Music skills looked for. Maximum extras £150. Scholarships 4 pa (including 2 sixth-form), 50% fees; minor income-related awards; bursaries for clergy and armed forces, 15% fees.
Parents 70% in industry or commerce. 70+% live within 30 miles; up to 15% live overseas.
Head and staff *Headmaster:* John Jarvis, appointed in 1995. Educated at Lydney Grammar, and universities of Birmingham (geography and economics), London (law), Loughborough (management and behavioural sciences); also at RAF School of Education (mathematics and science). Previously Governor and Director of Development, Princess Helena College; Chief Education Officer and Director of RAF Training and Head of RAF School of Education. Formerly Member of Council BTEC and NFER. Also FIPD, FIMgt and FRGS. *Staff:* 15 full time, 20 part time.
Exam results In 1995, 27 pupils in upper fifth, 18 in upper sixth. *GCSE:* In 1995, 11 upper fifth gained at least grade C in 8+ subjects; 13 in 5–7 subjects. *A-levels:* 4 upper sixth passed in 4+ subjects; 8 in 3; 3 in 2; and 3 in 1 subject. Average UCAS points 17.9.

University and college entrance 95% of 1995 sixth-form leavers went on to a degree course (70% after a gap year); others typically go on to secretarial or art foundation courses. Of those going on to university, 5% went to Oxbridge; 4% took courses in medicine, dentistry and veterinary science, 33% in science and engineering, 4% in law, 49% in humanities and social sciences, 7% in art and design, 4% in vocational subjects.
Curriculum GCSE and A-levels. 18 subjects offered. *Vocational:* Work experience available; also City and Guilds levels 1, 2 and 3 in business administration and RSA qualifications in CLAIT. *Computing facilities:* 15 computers (1 to a girl in each set). *Special provision:* Individual and group lessons by dyslexia specialists. EFL exams (Cambridge First Certificate and Certificate of Proficiency). *Europe:* French, German, Italian and Spanish offered at GCSE, AS and A-level. Regular exchanges to France and with school in Hamburg. European girls visit school. French, Italian and Spanish teachers are native speakers.
The arts *Music:* Over 75% of pupils learn a musical instrument; instrumental exams can be taken. Some 8 musical groups including choirs, orchestras, madrigal, jazz, ensembles. Pupils in county youth orchestra. *Drama & dance*: Both offered. GCSE drama, Poetry Society and LAMDA exams may be taken. Majority of pupils are involved in school and house/other productions. *Art:* On average, 50% take GCSE, 1 AS-level, 5 A-level. Pottery, photography, glass engraving also offered.
Sport, community service and clubs *Sport and physical activities:* Compulsory sports: lacrosse, netball, swimming, tennis, rounders, gymnastics. Optional: squash, badminton, hockey, trampolining. RLSS and BAGA exams may be taken. GCSE sports science offered in sixth-form. *Community service:* Pupils take bronze, silver and gold Duke of Edinburgh's Award. Community service compulsory for sixth-form. *Clubs and societies:* Up to 15 clubs, eg art, photography, wildlife, gardening, dance, aerobics, sailing, riding, debating.
Uniform School uniform worn except in the sixth.
Houses/prefects Competitive houses. Prefects, head girl, head of house and house prefects – appointed by the Head, consulting colleagues and head girl. School Council.
Religion Attendance at religious worship is expected: daily prayers; village church on Sunday (or Catholic church in Hitchin).
Social Participation in social events with other schools. Regular visits abroad plus Outward Bound. Sixth form allowed to bring own car/bike to school. Meals combination of self-service and formal. School shop. No tobacco/alcohol allowed.
Discipline Pupils failing to produce prep might expect a detention; anyone caught smoking cannabis on the premises would be suspended (although this has never had to happen); for smoking cigarettes, suspension after first and final warning.
Boarding Fifth and sixth-forms have own study bedrooms; others in small dormitories. New sixth-form house. Resident qualified nurse. Central dining room. Flexible exeats including weekly boarding. Visits to local town allowed for senior girls; London and Cambridge for sixth-formers.
Alumni association is run by Mrs C Murray, c/o the school.
Former pupils Governesses to the children of Queen Victoria and the Kaiser; Dr Helena Wright (pioneer of birth control); Mary Allen (founder of Women's Auxiliary Police); Dorothea Lambert Chambers (six times Wimbledon champion); Kathleen Archer (M15, who rumbled Philby); Lady Trumpington (Government minister); Cindy Shelley (actress).

• PRIOR PARK

Prior Park College, Ralph Allen Drive, Bath, Avon BA2 5AH. Tel 01225 835353, Fax 01225 835753

• Pupils 490 • Boys 11–18 (Day/Board) • Girls 11–18 (Day/Board) • Upper sixth 70 • Termly fees £1778–£1857 (Day) £3358 (Board) • HMC • Enquiries/application to the Headmaster

What it's like

Founded in 1830 by Bishop Peter Augustine Baines, and for a long time governed by the bishops of Clifton, it changed to lay administration in 1981. Girls were accepted in 1985, making it one of the few lay Roman Catholic co-educational schools in the country. The school enjoys a splendid position on the southern hills of Bath, looking down on the city.

Its particularly beautiful and well-appointed 18th-century Georgian buildings are set in 57 acres of fine grounds and playing fields. There have been many recent additions, including a new library, theatre, music school and an astroturf hockey pitch and it is now well equipped. It provides an education rooted in the values of the Catholic Church, and two priests serve as full-time chaplains. Considerable importance is attached to religious education (all pupils study this to GCSE) and practice. The staff:pupil ratio is about 1:11. Results are good and most sixth-formers go on to degree courses. Music is strong and there are two orchestras, six choirs and a band. Drama is also strong, and both drama and debating feature prominently. The college has a notable sporting tradition, and games and sports are well provided for; hockey and rugby are strong. There is a wide range of extra-curricular societies and clubs. A flourishing CCF includes all three services, plus REME and signals platoons. There is keen participation in the Duke of Edinburgh's Award Scheme and an extensive community service programme and Young Enterprise scheme.

School profile

Pupils Age range 11–18; 490 pupils, 332 day (192 boys, 140 girls), 158 boarding (109 boys, 49 girls); boarding for girls only from age 12. Main entry age 11, 13 and into sixth. Own prep school provides large intake (Prior Park Preparatory School). *State school entry:* 40% main intake, plus 15% to sixth.

Entrance Common Entrance and own exam used. Assisted places. Academic, music and art scholarships.

Head and staff *Headmaster:* Jeremy Goulding, in post 7 years. Educated at The Becket School, Nottingham, and Oxford University (classics, philosophy and theology). Previously Housemaster and Head of Divinity at Shrewsbury and House Tutor and Head of Divinity Department at Abingdon. *Staff:* 46 full time, 9 part time. Annual turnover 4%. Average age 36.

Exam results On average, 77 pupils in upper fifth, 70 in upper sixth. *GCSE:* On average, 61 upper fifth gain at least grade C in 8+ subjects; 10 in 5–7; and 4 in 1–4 subjects. *A-levels:* 8% upper sixth pass in 4+ subjects; 75% in 3; 13% in 2; and 2% in 1 subject. Average UCAS points 19.0.

University and college entrance 86% of 1995 sixth-form leavers went on to a degree course (3% after a gap year); others typically go on to vocational courses, art college or straight into work. Of those going on to university, 13% went to Oxbridge; 4% took courses in medicine, dentistry and veterinary science, 30% in science and engineering, 60% in humanities and social sciences, 3% in art and design, 1% in other vocational subjects.

Curriculum GCSE and A-levels. 19 subjects offered (including philosophy, history of art, classical civilisation, politics and economics). 23% take science A-levels; 71% arts/humanities; 6% both. *Vocational:* Work experience available. *Computing facilities:* Computing department; computers in other departments. *Special provision:* Language support centre; extra English lessons for foreign pupils. *Europe:* French, German and Spanish offered at GCSE and A-level; French compulsory from 11 to GCSE. Regular exchanges (France, Germany and Spain).

The arts *Music:* Over 50% of pupils learn a musical instrument; instrumental exams can be taken. Some 10 musical groups including various choirs, madrigals, jazz band, orchestras etc. Local success in Young Musician of the Year award. *Drama & dance:* Both offered. Many pupils are involved in school productions and some in house/other productions. Recent productions include Godspell, Romeo and Juliet, and Iolanthe. *Art:* On average, 16 take GCSE, 7 A-level. Design, pottery, history of art also offered.

Sport, community service and clubs *Sport and physical activities:* Compulsory sports: rugby, hockey, cricket (boys); hockey, netball, tennis (girls). Optional: cross-country, swimming, basketball. Hockey, county champions U18, U16, U14 (boys), county champions U16, regional runners-up (girls); rugby, 4 county representatives, 1 national junior. *Community service:* Pupils take bronze, silver and gold Duke of Edinburgh's Award. CCF and community service both optional for 2 years at age 14+. *Clubs and societies:* Up to 15 clubs, eg archery, chess, cookery, maths, science, drama, debating, choral, photography, bridge.

Uniform School uniform worn throughout.

Houses/prefects Competitive houses. Prefects, head boy and girl, head of house and house prefects – appointed by Head and staff.

Religion Regular attendance at religious worship compulsory including Sunday Mass for boarders.
Social Annual participation in Bath Schools Model United Nations; sixth-formers undertake careers experience in locality; local residents participate in concert choir; support for local charities eg fun runs, musical events. Annual exchanges to France, Spain. Meals self-service. School clothes shop and tuck shop in each house. No tobacco/alcohol allowed.
Discipline Pupils failing to produce homework once might expect to be asked to produce it by a stated deadline; those caught smoking cannabis on the premises might expect immediate expulsion.
Former pupils Cameron Mackintosh, Damian Cronin, Peter Levi, Hugh Scully, 2 Catholic bishops and the Archbishop of Cardiff.

• PRIOR'S FIELD

Prior's Field School, Godalming, Surrey GU7 2RH. Tel 01483 810551, Fax 01483 810180
• Pupils 218 • Boys None • Girls 11–18 (Day/Board/Weekly) • Upper sixth 23 • Termly fees £2185 (Day) £3270 (Board/Weekly) • GSA • Enquiries/application to the Headmistress

What it's like

Founded in 1902 by Mrs Leonard Huxley, mother of Julian and Aldous Huxley, it retains links with the Huxley family which has been a guiding influence since the foundation. The main buildings, which include a Voysey house, are in a delightful and peaceful rural site of 25 acres (including formal gardens) in the green belt outside Guildford. Apart from the sixth-form house and music school, the whole school is under one roof. A small school, it has a congenial family atmosphere and enjoys comfortable accommodation and good modern facilities. The staff:pupil ratio is about 1:7. Academic standards and results are creditable and vocational qualifications are offered. Most sixth-formers go on to degree courses each year. Music, art and drama are strong. All girls play some sport on a regular basis. There is a wide range of extra-curricular activities, including the Duke of Edinburgh's Award Scheme.

School profile

Pupils Age range 11–18; 218 girls, 100 day, 118 boarding. Main entry ages 11, 12, 13 and into sixth. 1% are children of former pupils. *State school entry:* 12% main intake, plus 5% to sixth.
Entrance Common Entrance or own exam used. No special skills or religious requirements. Parents not expected to buy textbooks. 5 pa scholarships (academic, art, music and drama) 25%–50% fees; plus some sixth-form scholarships and bursaries according to need, 10%–50% fees. 10% forces discount and old girls' bursary.
Parents 15+% are doctors, lawyers etc; 15+% are in industry or commerce. 60+% live within 30 miles; 10+% live overseas.
Head and staff *Headmistress:* Mrs Jennifer McCallum, in post for 9 years. Educated at Park Place, Hampshire, and Bristol University (philosophy and English literature). Previously Sixth Form Housemistress at Cheltenham Ladies College and Head of Sixth Form and Head of Department at St Catherine's Comprehensive, Bexley Heath. *Staff:* 22 full time, 12 part time. Annual turnover 8%. Average age 40.
Exam results On average, 40 pupils in upper fifth, 25 in upper sixth. *GCSE:* On average, 75% upper fifth gain at least grade C in 8+ subjects; 25% in 5–7 subjects. *A-levels:* 6% upper sixth pass in 4 subjects; 60% in 3; 34% in 2 subjects. Average UCAS points 15.0.
University and college entrance 73% of 1995 sixth-form leavers went on to a degree course; others typically go on to art/drama college, non-degree courses in eg accountancy or straight into careers eg personnel. Of those going on to university, 6% took courses in medicine, dentistry and veterinary science, 24% in science and engineering, 52% in humanities and social sciences, 12% in art and design, 6% in drama and acting.
Curriculum GCSE and *A-levels:* 19 subjects offered (no A-level general studies). On average, 36% take science A-levels; 56% arts/humanities; 8% both; *Vocational:* Work experience available; also RSA stages 1 and 2 in typewriting, French typewriting; wordprocessing (English and French), Pitmans elementary and intermediate levels in typing, wordprocessing, shorthand and IT. *Computing facilities:* Networked Archi-

medes. *Special provision:* One-to-one tuition with specialist teachers on the staff for dyslexic pupils and for EFL. *Europe:* French and Spanish offered at GCSE, AS and A-level (French compulsory to 16, Spanish to 14). German, Italian and Russian lessons by arrangement. Regular exchanges.
The arts *Music:* Over 50% of pupils learn a musical instrument; instrumental exams can be taken. Some 9 musical groups including 3 choirs, 2 orchestras, flute group, strings, chamber orchestra. Solo singing entrants and chamber choirs won at Woking and Godalming Festivals. *Drama & dance*: Both offered. GCSE and A-level drama, LAMDA exams may be taken. Majority of pupils are involved in school productions and all in house/other productions. Open-air Shakespeare productions of using professional costume design and choreography; recently, The Insect Play. More than 50% distinctions and honours for LAMDA. *Art:* On average, 20 take GCSE, 3 A-level. Design, pottery, textiles, photography, history of art, sculpture also offered. All past year's A-level students now at art college, including main London colleges.
Sport, community service and clubs *Sport and physical activities:* Compulsory sports: lacrosse, hockey, netball, badminton, volleyball, tennis, gymnastics, swimming, dance, basket-ball, athletics, rounders. Optional: squash, trampolining, table tennis, golf, football, aerobics, riding. RLSS exams may be taken. County lacrosse, tennis and athletics representatives. *Community service:* Pupils take bronze, silver and gold Duke of Edinburgh's Award. Liaison with local home for the elderly. *Clubs and societies:* Over 30 clubs, eg lacemaking, computers, gymnastics, chess, photography.
Uniform School uniform worn except the sixth.
Houses/prefects Competitive houses. Prefects and head girl – appointed by the Head after secret ballot of sixth-form and staff. School Council.
Religion Compulsory church on some Sundays for all Christians.
Social Skiing holidays and exchange with school in France. Sixth form allowed to bring own bike/car to school. Meals self-service (include vegetarian menu). School shop. No tobacco/alcohol allowed.
Discipline Pupils failing to produce homework once might expect to do it in their own time by the following day; those caught smoking cannabis on the premises expect expulsion.
Boarding 50% have own study bedroom, 50% share with 1 or 2, occasionally 4. Houses, of 40–65, divided by age group. Resident qualified nurse. Central dining room. Sixth form can provide and cook own food. 4 weekend exeats each term. Visits to local town allowed (twice a term for juniors, weekly for seniors, by arrangement for sixth-form).
Alumni association run by Mrs V Wright, 10 Putney Heath Lane, London SW15 3JG.
Former pupils Baroness Warnock; Jill Bennett (actress), Victoria Hamilton.

• PURCELL

The Purcell School, Mount Park Road, Harrow on the Hill, Middlesex. Tel 0181 422 1284, Fax 0181 423 0526

• Pupils 152 • Boys 8–18 (Day/Board) • Girls 8–18 (Day/Board) • Upper sixth 25 • Termly fees £2838 (Day) £4800 (Board) • SHMIS, SHA, NAGC, ISM • Enquiries/application to the Registrar

What it's like

Founded in 1962, as a co-educational specialist school for young musicians and was the first of its kind in Britain. It began in Conway Hall and, after two relocations, moved in 1975 to its present, agreeable semi-rural site in pleasant grounds on Harrow Hill. It is the only specialist music school in the Greater London area and academic results are also very good. Almost all sixth-formers go on to degree courses in music, many of them to Oxbridge. It is a multi-racial and non-denominational school with a very high staff:pupil ratio of about 1:7. It can therefore pay particular attention to the needs – musical, academic or pastoral – of the individual and reduce to a minimum the pressures which often threaten a musically gifted child. Drama is strong and there is a fair range of sports and games and extra-curricular activities.

School profile

Pupils Total age range 8–18; 152 pupils, 56 day (19 boys, 37 girls), 96 boarders (39 boys, 57 girls). Senior department, 12–18; 140 pupils (50 boys, 90 girls). Main entry ages 8, 11, 12, 13 and into sixth.

Entrance By musical audition only. Exceptional musical promise essential; no religious requirements (international intake). Parents are expected to buy textbooks only in the sixth. Government aided pupil scheme; LEA awards from some authorities, some school bursaries and scholarships, income related.
Parents 15+% are doctors, lawyers, teachers; 15+% in industry; 15+% in music. 10+% live within 30 miles; up to 15% live overseas.
Head and staff *Headmaster:* John Bain, in post for 13 years. Educated at Bancroft's and Oxford (classics). Previously Housemaster at Cranleigh, Assistant Master at Stanbridge Earls. Also member of SHMIS Education Committee. Publications: occasional articles in educational journals. *Staff:* 20 full time, 5 part time. Annual turnover 4%. Average age 40.
Exam results Average size of upper fifth 27; upper sixth 25. *GCSE:* most pupils gain at least grade C in 5–7 subjects (must take 6 or 7). *A-levels:* on average, 5 upper sixth pass in 3 subjects; 18 in 2; 2 in 1 subject (norm is for pupils to take 2 subjects). Average UCAS points 19.8.
University and college entrance 97% of 1995 sixth-form leavers went on to a degree course (7% after a gap year), 16% to Oxbridge; almost all study music. Others typically go on to study abroad.
Curriculum GCSE and A-levels. Most pupils take 2 A-levels, in arts and humanities including A-level music. *Computing facilities:* Computer studies may be taken to GCSE on request. Facilities being developed. *Special provision:* EFL teaching as required. *Europe:* French and German offered to GCSE and A-level. Exchanges with music schools in many countries eg Russia, Germany, Poland, Israel.
The arts (Pupils aged 11 and over) *Music:* All pupils learn a musical instrument; instrumental exams can be taken. 40+ musical groups include chamber groups, several choirs, orchestras, jazz group. Pupil winner Royal Overseas League string competition and ESU Tanglewood Scholar; 8 members of National Youth Orchestra, 6 members of National Children's Orchestra. Orchestral and concert tours to Germany, Malta and Israel. *Drama & dance*: Majority of pupils are involved in school productions. *Art:* On average, 12 take GCSE, 4 A-level.
Sport, community service and clubs (Pupils aged 11 and over) *Sport and physical activities:* Optional sports: football, swimming, badminton, squash, rounders, basketball. *Community service:* Community service optional. *Clubs and societies:* Up to 5 clubs, eg chess, gym.
Uniform School uniform not worn.
Houses/prefects No competitive houses. Prefects ('deputies'); head boy/girl ('senior deputies') – appointed by the Headmaster, in consultation with sixth-form tutors. School Council.
Religion Religious worship on a private basis.
Social Occasionally provides whole orchestra or some players for other schools' productions. Regular organised trips abroad, including orchestral and concert tours to Germany, Malta and Israel; exchanges with Russian and United States. Pupils allowed to bring own car/bike/motorbike to school, by arrangement. Meals self-service. School tuck shop. No tobacco/alcohol allowed.
Boarding Most share in groups of 4. Single-sex houses. Resident matron. Central dining room. Pupils can provide own snacks. 1 or 2 weekend exeats termly. Visits to local town allowed with permission, in pairs or small groups.
Former pupils Robert Cohen (cellist); Oliver Knussen (composer and conductor); Nicholas Daniel (oboist); Janice Graham (violinist).

• PUTNEY HIGH

Putney High School, 35 Putney Hill, London SW15 6BH. Tel 0181 788 4886, Fax 0181 789 8068
• Pupils 841 • Boys None • Girls 4–18 (Day) • Upper sixth 77 • Termly Fees £1192-£1548
• GSA, GPDST • Enquiries to the Headmistress

What it's like

Founded in 1893, it is single-site on Putney Hill and has the bonus of unusually beautiful gardens. The main buildings are three large late-Victorian houses to which there have been important additions in recent years. Facilities are good and include laboratories, a technology and computing centre and a new sports hall. The junior department is separate in Lytton House within the school grounds. Academic results are very good and most girls go on to degree courses each year, including to Oxbridge. Tennis and netball are very strong, with courts on site; pupils attend a local leisure centre for swimming and multi-gym. Music is very strong and there is also considerable strength in drama, dance and art. Several girls within the school are highly gifted at music and sport: they benefit from a curriculum which enables them to further their talents alongside their academic subjects.

School profile

Pupils Total age range 4–18, 841 day girls. Senior department 11–18, 572 girls. Main entry ages 4, 7, 11 and into sixth-form. *State school entry:* 28% senior intake.

Entrance Own entrance examination used. No special religious requirements or skills (but academically competitive). Parents not expected to buy textbooks; music tuition extra £120 per term. 20 pa assisted places at 11 and at sixth-form entry. Scholarships, including one for music, available at 11 and sixth-form entry, up to 50% fees. GPDST bursary scheme.

Parents Mainly professional.

Head and staff *Headmistress:* Mrs Eileen Merchant, 5 years in post. Educated at St Angela's Ursuline Convent, London, and Sheffield University (chemistry). Previously Deputy Head at Latymer School, Edmonton, and Director of Studies at Bedford High. *Staff:* 36 full time, 10 part-time in the senior department.

Exam results In 1995, 85 pupils in Year 11, 70 in Year 13. *GCSE:* In 1995, 82 Year 11 gained at least grade C in 8+ subjects; and 3 in 5–7 subjects. *A-levels:* 57 Year 13 passed in 3+ subjects; 11 in 2; and 2 in 1 subject. Average UCAS points 21.7.

University and college entrance 95% of 1995 sixth-form leavers went on to a degree course (39% after a gap year); others typically go on to physiotherapy, art, drama or music schools. Of those going on to university, 12% went to Oxbridge; 6% took courses in medicine, dentistry and veterinary science, 10% in science and engineering, 6% in law, 60% in humanities and social sciences, 4% in art and design, 14% in other vocational subjects eg publishing, opthalmics, drama, tourism, computing.

Curriculum GCSE and A-levels. 22 subjects offered (including history of art; no A-level general studies). 17% took science A-levels; 49% arts/humanities; 34% a combination. *Vocational:* Work experience available. *Computing facilities:* Large computing room with network for whole class; computers in departments, classrooms and sixth-form block also on the network; CD-Roms in library resource centre. *Europe:* French from age 11, German or Spanish from 13 – all at GCSE and A-level; Italian in sixth-form (one-year to GCSE, one-year to A-level). Exchanges (to France, Germany and Italy; annual visit to Spain.

The arts (Pupils aged 11 and over). *Music:* Over 50% of pupils learn a musical instrument; instrumental exams can be taken. Some 18 musical groups, including 3 orchestras, 3 choirs, saxophone and guitar groups, chamber groups, small choirs. 2 members National Youth Orchestra; several county standard youth orchestras; finalists in Youth and Music; winners of National Chamber Music competition, Choir of the Day, Sainsbury Competition; recordings; tours of Canada and South Africa; composition winners and commissions; large in-school music festival. Choral works performed include Requiems, Carmina Burana and Ellijah. *Drama & dance*: Both offered. Majority of pupils are involved in school and group productions. Drama and dance competitions; recent productions include The Crucible and Guys and Dolls. *Art:* On average, 30 take GCSE, 8 A-level; A-level course can include work in 3D design, textiles, sculpture. Regular entrants to art school.

Sport, community service and clubs (Pupils aged 11 and over) *Sport and physical activities:* Compulsory sports: netball, gym, dance, tennis, swimming, athletics, badminton, aerobics, sports acrobatics, rhythmic gym, volleyball, games foundation course, hockey, trampolining. Optional: touch rugby, girls soccer, rowing. Sixth form only: multigym. Community Sports Leader Award, LTA. Tennis Leaders Award, ESNA Netball Leaders Award. Tennis, county league champions 1994/5, county players each year; runners up in national finals Midland Bank competition 1995, winner county league 1992 and 1994; netball county league finalists 1993-6, national finalists 1996; gymnastics, British rhythmic gym junior champion. *Community service:* Duke of Edinburgh's Award.

£3500 raised by school activities last year for charities. *Clubs and societies:* Over 20 clubs eg gym, fencing, sports acrobatics, drama, Christian Union, Amnesty International, public speaking, debating, bridge.

Uniform School uniform worn except in the sixth-form.

Houses/prefects No competitive houses. Prefects and head girl – elected by staff and girls. School Council.

Religion No compulsory worship.

Social Visits to sporting events, galleries, museums, artists' studios and places of historical interest. Large numbers involved in annual drama and music festivals. Technology race, ski trips and residential activity holidays are regular events.

Discipline School aims to encourage pupils to be self-reliant and self-disciplined; number of rules is kept to a minimum but all are expected to behave with courtesy and tolerance towards others.

Alumni association run by Mrs Sweetingham, c/o the school.

Q

• QUEEN ANNE'S (Caversham)

Queen Anne's School, Caversham, Reading RG4 6DX. Tel 01734 471582, Fax 01734 461498

• Pupils 322 • Boys None • Girls 11–18 (Day/Board) • Upper sixth 52 • Termly fees £2460 (Day) £3750 (Board) • GSA • Enquiries to the Headmistress

What it's like

Founded in 1894, it has a semi-rural, single site near the village of Caversham, a few minutes' journey from Reading. The absolute origins of the school go back to 1698, when the Grey Coat Hospital was founded for the children of Westminster, and Queen Anne granted the Foundation a charter a few years later. In 1894 the governors decided to use part of the endowment for a boarding school for girls at Caversham. The school retains links with the Hospital and Westminster and every 3 years has its own service in Westminster Abbey. In fact, there is a pronounced emphasis on Christian teaching and principles at the school and the fine chapel has a central place in its daily life. The buildings are most agreeable and lie in delightful grounds and gardens. Modern facilities are extensive and include excellent libraries, a new performing arts centre and comfortable quarters for boarders. There is an unusually favourable staff:pupil ratio of about 1:7. Academic standards are high and results very good: the vast majority of pupils go on to university, including to Oxbridge. Music and drama are strong. The school has an outstanding record at national level in lacrosse and athletics and sixth-formers may play real tennis (most unusual for a school). A plentiful range of clubs and societies provides for most needs and the Duke of Edinburgh Award Scheme is well supported.

School profile

Pupils Age range 11–18; 322 girls (118 day, 203 boarding). Main entry ages 11, 13 and into sixth. Approx 3% are children of former pupils. *State school entry:* 30% at 11, and 1% at sixth-form.

Entrance Common Entrance used; own exam for scholarships and post-CE entry. All-rounders encouraged but no special skills or religious requirements. Parents expected to buy textbooks only in sixth-form; average extras £100. Approx 12 pa scholarships (including 6 sixth-form), £600–£7100.

Parents 15+% in industry or commerce; 15+% doctors, lawyers etc. Up to 30% live within 30 miles of the school, up to 30% live overseas.

Head and staff *Headmistress:* Mrs Deborah Forbes, in post for 3 years. Educated at Bath High and Oxford (English). Previously Head of English at Cheltenham Ladies' College. *Staff:* 39 full-time, 9 part-time. Annual turnover approx 10%. Average age 40.

Exam results In 1995, 66 pupils in upper fifth, 52 in upper sixth. *GCSE:* In 1995, 54 pupils gained at least grade C in 8+ subjects; 9 in 5–7 subjects. *A-levels:* 14% upper sixth passed in 4 subjects; 59% in 3; 17% in 2; and 3% in 1 subject. Average UCAS points 21.1.

University and college entrance 94% of 1995 sixth-form leavers went on to a degree course (40% after a gap year); others typically go on to art foundation courses. Of those going on to university, 8% went to Oxbridge; 10% took courses in medicine, dentistry and veterinary science, 10% in science and engineering, 5% in law, 45% in humanities and social sciences, 10% in art and design, 20% in other vocational subjects eg business, hospitality management, PE.

Curriculum GCSE and A-levels. 18 GCSE subjects offered, 21 A-level (including general studies). 30% took science A-levels; 40% took arts/humanities; 30% took both. *Vocational:* Work experience available. RSA stages 1 & 2 offered in WP, CLAIT 1 and IT2. *Computing facilities:* 2 computer rooms, 21 Apple Macs, 10 PCs. *Special provision:* Extra coaching in English and specialist EFL teaching. *Europe:* French (compulsory from age 11), German and Spanish offered at GCSE and A-level; also French and German AS-level and Italian GCSE. Regular exchanges (to France and Germany).

The arts *Music:* Over 25% learn a musical instrument; instrumental exams can be taken. 6 musical groups including choirs, orchestra and wind band. 1 member of National Children's Orchestra and 5 members County Youth Orchestra. *Drama & dance*: Both offered. GCSE and A-level drama and Guildhall exams may be taken. All pupils are involved with school and house productions. Junior team won Rotary Youth Speak competition. School second in ESU competition. Participated in World Debating and Public Speaking Championships. Strong connections with Globelink. *Art:* On average, 25 pupils take GCSE and 6 take A-level. Textiles also offered.
Sport, community service and clubs *Sport and physical activities:* Compulsory: lacrosse, swimming, tennis, gym, dance, athletics. Optional: squash, rowing, badminton, basketball, volleyball, trampolining. Sixth form only: aerobics, sailing, real tennis, golf, weight training. Lacrosse: National Schools' champions many times, county, West of England and international players. County tennis, cross country and athletics representatives. *Community service:* Pupils take bronze, silver and gold Duke of Edinburgh's Award. Clubs: Over 20 clubs including art, debating, photography, Young Enterprise, Ju-te-Do, computing, science, cross-country plus music and sports clubs.
Uniform School uniform worn except in the sixth.
Houses/prefects Competitive houses. Two head girls, heads of houses and deputies – elected by Head. School Council.
Religion Compulsory attendance at religious worship.
Social Debates, opera/musical, sports, social events, business and conferences with other local schools. Annual exchange with a school in Toulouse. Sixth-form French study trip. Annual art/art history trips. Ski trip, choir and lacrosse tour. Spanish study trip. Pupils allowed to bring own car to school. Meals self-service. No tobacco/alcohol allowed.
Discipline Pupils failing to produce homework once might expect a reprimand; those smoking cannabis would be expelled.
Boarding 20% have own study bedrooms, 10% share with one other. Houses of 30–40, plus sixth-form houses. Resident nurse. Sixth formers can cook own food. 2 exeat weekends each term, 2 additional Sundays and half-term. Visits to local town allowed, varying with age.
Alumni association is run by Mrs D Hall, Bank House, Cropthorne, Pershore, Worcs WR10 3NB.
Former pupils Frances Heaton (Director General, Panel on Takeovers & Mergers and Director, Bank of England); Celia Haddon (columnist); Posy Simmonds (cartoonist); Margaret Wolfit, Juliet Aubrey, Jenny Seagrove (actresses).

• QUEEN ELIZABETH (Blackburn)

Queen Elizabeth's Grammar School, Blackburn, Lancashire BB2 6DF. Tel 01254 59911, Fax 01254 692314

• Pupils 1080 • Boys 7–18 (Day) • Girls 16–18 (Day) • Upper sixth 135 • Termly fees £1314 (Day) • HMC, SHA • Enquiries/application to the Headmaster

What it's like

Originally founded in 1509, it was refounded in 1567 under royal charter by Elizabeth I and moved to its present site in 1882. The solid, well-designed and well-equipped buildings make a compact campus of about 16 acres in the north-west outskirts of Blackburn. Its junior school is on the same site. There have been very considerable developments over the years, including recently a sports hall and a new sixth-form centre. Girls were first admitted to the sixth-form in 1978. The school has high standards of teaching and good academic results. Most pupils go on to degree courses each year, including Oxbridge. Christian in emphasis, the school is interdenominational in practice. There are close links with the cathedral. Very strong in music and art. Also much strength in sports and games. Active commitment to community services and a good record in the Duke of Edinburgh's Award Scheme.

School profile

Pupils Total age range 7–18; 1080 day pupils (1030 boys, 50 girls). Senior department 11–18, 940 pupils (890 boys, 50 girls). Main entry ages 7–11 (boys) and into sixth (boys and girls). *State school entry:* 90% senior intake, plus 85% to sixth.

Entrance Common Entrance and own exam used. No special skills or religious requirements. Parents not expected to buy textbooks; maximum £400 extras. 39 pa assisted places.

Parents 15+% are doctors, lawyers etc.

Head and staff *Headmaster:* Dr David Hempsall, in post since 1995. Educated at Manchester Grammar and Cambridge (history). Previously Headmaster of Scarborough College, Head of History at Rugby, and Assistant Master at Sir William Nottidge School. Also SHMIS Committee Member; Trustee, St Catherine's Hospice; Vice Chairman and Non-executive Director, Scarborough NHS Trust. *Staff:* 92 full time, 6 part time. Annual turnover 3%. Average age 40.

Exam results In 1995, 140 pupils in upper fifth, 135 in upper sixth. *GCSE:* In 1995, 70% upper fifth gained at least grade C in 8+ subjects; 28% in 5–7; and 2% in 1–4 subjects. *A-levels:* 70% upper sixth passed in 4+ subjects; 30% in 3 subjects. Average UCAS points 19.5.

University and college entrance 92% of 1995 sixth-form leavers went on to a degree course (3% after a gap year); others typically go on to vocational training. Of those going on to university, 12% went to Oxbridge; 10% took courses in medicine, dentistry and veterinary science, 50% in science and engineering, 6% in law, 30% in humanities and social sciences, 2% in art and design, 2% in other vocational subjects.

Curriculum GCSE and A-levels. 24 subjects offered (including A-level general studies). 68% take science A-levels; 30% arts/humanities; 2% both. *Vocational:* Work experience available. *Computing facilities:* 22 networked Nimbus. *Europe:* French and German offered to GCSE and A-level; Spanish to GCSE and Italian as a non-examined subject. Regular exchanges (France, Germany, Greece and Italy).

The arts (Pupils aged 11 and over) *Music:* 20% of pupils learn a musical instrument; instrumental exams can be taken. Some 10 musical groups: 3 choral groups, 2 orchestral, piano trio, swing band, 2 pop groups, brass ensemble. 6 members county school symphony orchestra; 2 members county wind band. *Drama & dance*: Drama offered and GCSE may be taken. Some pupils are involved in school and house/other productions. Recent entrant to RADA; at least 2 major school drama productions a year. *Art:* On average, 20 take GCSE, 10 A-level. Design also offered. Recent entrant to Courtauld Institute; success in national competitions eg Electricity Council (Energy) Competition.

Sport, community service and clubs (Pupils aged 11 and over) *Sport and physical activities:* Compulsory sports: PE, choice of seasonal games eg swimming, soccer, rugby, squash, cricket. Sixth form only: sailing, skiing, ice skating, climbing, martial arts. GCSE PE exams may be taken. International junior swimmer; regular representatives in county teams at various sports; leading croquet school with current world champion; county soccer champions U19. *Community service:* Pupils take bronze, silver and gold Duke of Edinburgh's Award. Community service optional. Scout troop. *Clubs and societies:* Up to 30 clubs, eg art, chess, Christian Union, computer, debating and public speaking, drama, geography, maths, model railway, sailing, war games, Young Amnesty.

Uniform School uniform worn throughout.

Houses/prefects Competitive houses. Prefects, head boy/girl, head of house and house prefects – appointed by the Headmaster and school.

Religion Religious worship encouraged.

Social Pupils allowed to bring own car/bike to school. Meals self-service. School shop. No tobacco/alcohol allowed.

Discipline Weekly detention for serious misbehaviour.

Former pupils Russell Harty; Bishop Peter Hall (Bishop of Woolwich); the late Vic Whitsey (Bishop of Chester); Sir Kenneth Durham (former Chairman of Unilever); Professor K Miller (Head of Engineering, Sheffield University).

• QUEEN ELIZABETH (Wakefield)

Queen Elizabeth Grammar School, Northgate, Wakefield, West Yorkshire WF1 3QX. Tel 01924 373943, Fax 01924 378871

• Pupils 975 • Boys 7–18 (Day) • Girls None • Upper sixth 100 • Termly fees £1374 (Day) • HMC • Enquiries/application to the Admissions Secretary

What it's like

Founded in 1591 by royal charter, it is single-site and close to the city centre. The main building (an example of early Gothic revival) has been in use since 1854. Many extensions in the last 30 years have provided first-rate modern facilities. The junior school is in the main grounds. It has a wide catchment area and the pupils are of a wide social background. High standards of work and conduct are expected and academic results are very good. Almost all sixth-formers go on to degree courses, including many to Oxbridge. Increasingly strong in music (there are traditional links with the cathedral and the school provides many of the choristers), drama and art. Very strong tradition of excellence in games and sports (many county representatives) and an impressive range of activities and societies. Much collaboration with Wakefield Girls' High School.

School profile

Pupils Total age range 7–18; 975 day boys. Senior department 11–18, 750 boys. Main entry ages 7, 9, 11, 12, 13 and into sixth. Approx 10% are children of former pupils. Own junior school provides almost 60% of senior intake. *State school entry:* 45% senior intake.

Entrance Common Entrance and own exam used. No special skills or religious requirements. Parents not expected to buy textbooks; all extras optional including music tuition, £86.50 per term. 22 pa assisted places. 6 pa scholarships/bursaries (up to 25% tuition fees), 12 pa sixth-form scholarships (including music).

Parents 15+% are doctors, lawyers, etc; 15+% in industry or commerce.

Head and staff *Headmaster:* Robert Mardling, in post for 11 years. Educated at Nottingham High and Oxford (German and French). Previously Deputy Head and Head of German Department at Arnold and Assistant Modern Languages Master at Gelding County Secondary and at Nottingham High. Also Principal, Wakefield Grammar School Foundation; Chairman HMC Professional Development Committee. *Staff:* 59 full time, 3 part time. Annual turnover 5%. Average age mid-30s.

Exam results On average, 112 pupils in Year 11, 100 in upper sixth. *GCSE:* on average, 105 Year 11 gain at least grade C in 8+ subjects; 6 in 5–7; and 1 in 1–4 subjects. *A-levels:* 80% upper sixth pass in 4+ subjects; 16% in 3; 2% in 2 subjects. Average UCAS points 20.2.

University and college entrance 91% of 1995 sixth-form leavers went on to a degree course (6% after a gap year); others typically go on to art foundation courses. Of those going on to university, 8% went to Oxbridge; 11% took courses in medicine, dentistry and veterinary science, 32% in science and engineering, 8% in law, 40% in humanities and social sciences, 6% in art and design, 3% in other vocational subjects eg architecture, accountancy, town planning.

Curriculum GCSE and *A-levels:* 20 GCSE subjects offered; 25 at A-level (all take A-level general studies). 51% take science A-levels; 29% arts/humanities; 19% both. *Vocational:* Work experience available. *Computing facilities:* Network of 14 BBC master compact computers with disk drive and printer facilities, plus 16 IBM compatible computers. Domesday equipment. Computerised library database. *Europe:* French, German and Spanish offered to GCSE and A-level; also French and German AS-level, Italian and Russian GCSE.

The arts (Pupils aged 11 and over) *Music:* Over 30% of pupils learn a musical instrument; instrumental exams can be taken. 22 on a joint A-level course with Wakefield High. Some 14 musical groups including orchestras, concert bands, swing bands, choirs. Swing band successes. *Drama & dance*: All pupils study drama in Year 7. Senior and junior school productions. *Art:* On average, 40 take GCSE, 16 A-level. Painting and drawing, graphics, illustration, design, photography and print-making offered. Lunchtime art activities. Large uptake to art colleges and universities.

Sport, community service and clubs (Pupils aged 11 and over) *Sport and physical activities:* Compulsory sports (initially): rugby, hockey, cross-country, cricket, tennis,

athletics. Optional: wide range including swimming, basketball, table tennis, squash etc. Fifth and sixth-form only: badminton, sailing. Rugby, Daily Mail national U15 semi-finalists and U18 finalists, county champions U14 and U15; cricket, county champions U14, U15 and U16; athletics, county champions. *Community service:* Pupils take bronze, silver and gold Duke of Edinburgh's Award. Community service optional. *Clubs and societies:* Over 30 clubs, eg angling, bridge, computer, golf, mountain bike, outdoor pursuits, shooting, debating, travel.
Uniform School uniform worn throughout.
Houses/prefects No competitive houses. Prefects elected; head boy appointed by Headmaster and staff. School Council.
Religion Compulsory school assembly (non-denominational).
Social Theatrical productions with Wakefield Girls High. Organised trips abroad. Pupils allowed to bring own car/bike/motorbike to school. Meals self-service. School shops selling tuck and games kit. No tobacco/alcohol allowed.
Discipline Pupils failing to produce homework once might expect either a verbal warning or Bad Record (a note in the pupil's school diary); suspension/expulsion would be considered for those caught smoking cannabis on the premises.
Alumni association is run by Mr S Chamberlain, c/o the school.
Former pupils Mike Harrison (rugby); Prof Sir Hans Kornberg (Master of Christ College, Cambridge); Kenneth Leighton; Peter Dews (playwright/theatrical producer); Ronald Eyre; Lord Marshall; Lord Wolfenden; Most Rev and Rt Hon David Hope (Archbishop of York); Rt Rev Robert Hardy (Bishop of Lincoln).

• QUEEN ELIZABETH'S HOSPITAL

Queen Elizabeth's Hospital, Berkeley Place, Clifton, Bristol BS8 1JX. Tel 0117 929 1856, Fax 0117 929 3106

• Pupils 510 • Boys 11–18 (Day/Board) • Girls None • Upper sixth 60 • Termly fees £1305 (Day) £2319 (Board) • HMC • Enquiries/application to the Headmaster

What it's like

Founded in 1590, it is a Blue Coat school along the lines of Christ's Hospital. Since 1847, it has occupied its present urban site, near the university and city centre. The buildings are imposing and very well-equipped, including a new theatre and a technology department. There is daily Christian worship. It is socially comprehensive while being academically selective. Academic standards are high and results very good; almost all pupils go on to degree courses each year. Generous endowment permits support of many pupils. Very strong music department, good drama and art. Strong on games, and plentiful activities. Emphasis on outdoor pursuits. Some commitment to local community schemes and the Duke of Edinburgh's Award Scheme. It enjoys vigorous local support. Full use is made of the cultural amenities of the city.

School profile

Pupils Age range 11–18; 510 boys, 430 day, 80 boarding. Main entry ages 11, 13 and into sixth. Approx 5–10% are children of former pupils. *State school entry:* 60% main intakes, plus 80% to sixth.
Entrance Bristol area entrance exam used. Oversubscribed. No special skills or religious requirements. Parents not expected to buy textbooks; extras include music tuition and lunch (£1.30 per day). 25 pa assisted places. 6 pa scholarships/bursaries, £500–£2200 based on entrance exam; others related to family income.
Parents 60+% live within 30 miles; up to 5% live overseas.
Head and staff *Headmaster:* Dr Richard Gliddon, in post for 11 years. Educated at Queen's, Taunton, and at King's College London and Bristol University (zoology). Previously Housemaster and Head of Biology at Clifton and Assistant Master at Winchester. Also Fellow of Institute of Biology; Governor of Downs School, Clifton High and Cheltenham Ladies College. *Staff:* 38 full time, 6 part time. Annual turnover 10%. Average age 35.
Exam results On average, 75 pupils in upper fifth, 60 in upper sixth. *GCSE:* On average, 75% upper fifth gain at least grade C in 8+ subjects; 25% in 5–7 subjects. *A-levels:* 19% upper sixth pass in 4+ subjects; 63% in 3; 15% in 2; and 4% in 1 subject. Average UCAS

points 20.2.
University and college entrance 95% of 1995 sixth-form leavers went on to a degree course, 10% to Oxbridge; 50% took courses in science and engineering, 46% in humanities and social sciences, 4% in music.
Curriculum GCSE and *A-levels:* 18 GCSE subjects offered; 14 at A-level (no A-level general studies). 40% take science A-levels; 45% arts/humanities; 15% both. *Vocational:* Work experience available; also YAS. *Computing facilities:* BBC micros, Apple Mac and IBM compatible; network of latter. Two computer rooms as well as various department facilities. *Special provision:* As necessary for public examinations. *Europe:* French and German offered at GCSE and A-level; also Spanish GCSE. Regular exchanges. French and Spanish assistants teach in school. Visits to Europe by second year (to Brittany), fourth year history (Belgium and Northern France) and classics pupils (Italy). Sixth form involved in European conference.
The arts *Music:* Over 20% of pupils learn a musical instrument: instrumental exams can be taken. Some 9 musical groups including choir, orchestra, wind band, brass, strings, woodwind groups. *Drama & dance*: Drama offered; GCSE and A-level may be taken. Some pupils are involved in school and house/other productions. *Art:* On average, 20 take GCSE, 5 A-level. Design, pottery, also offered.
Sport, community service and clubs *Sport and physical activities:* Compulsory sports: rugby and cricket (first 2 years). Optional: swimming, athletics, tennis, soccer, badminton, squash. Sixth form only: rowing. Regular county and regional representatives at rugby and cricket. *Community service:* Pupils take bronze and silver Duke of Edinburgh's Award. Community service optional. *Clubs and societies:* Some 30 clubs eg archery, computer, film, Scrabble, war games, gardening and apiary.
Uniform School uniform worn, modified in the sixth.
Houses/prefects Competitive houses. Prefects, head boy, head of house and house prefects – some elected, some appointed.
Religion Morning assembly, Sunday service for boarders.
Social Drama and music (choral and orchestral) with three local girls' schools; debates (Bristol Rotary Club event). Organised trip to France (French and history), Germany (German and rugger), winter ski trip. Meals self-service. School tuckshop (at break). No tobacco/alcohol allowed.
Discipline Pupils failing to produce homework once might expect a reprimand or detention; those caught smoking cannabis could expect suspension or expulsion.
Boarding 25% have study bedroom (in pairs), others share (up to 6). Houses (of 35 and 55), divided by age group. Resident qualified nurse, doctor visits. Central dining room. Senior pupils can provide and cook own food. 3–4 weekend exeats each term plus half-term. Visits to the local town allowed.
Alumni association is run by Mr M J Stoodley, The Old Orchard, Lower Stanton Street, Quinton, Chippenham, Wilts SN14 6DB.

• QUEEN ETHELBURGA'S

Queen Ethelburga's College, Thorpe Underwood Hall, Ouseburn, York, North Yorkshire Y05 9SZ. Tel 01423 331480, Fax 01423 331007

• Pupils 300 • Boys 2½–11 only • Girls 2½–18 (Day/Board/Weekly) • Upper sixth 15 • Termly fees £449–£2259 (Day) £2359–£3499 (Board/Weekly) • GSA • Enquiries/application to the Registrar

What it's like

Founded in 1912, it has a fine rural site between York and the very agreeable spa town of Harrogate. Pleasant gardens and ample playing fields surround it and beyond lies beautiful Yorkshire countryside. The buildings are well-designed and spacious and the boarding accommodation is comfortable. The prep school (Chapter House) and the senior school are on the same site. Queen Ethelburga's has all the advantages of being small; a happy, purposeful, family atmosphere prevails. There is considerable emphasis on Christian values, and religious practice in the Anglican tradition, plus a firm belief in the merits of a single-sex education. Academic standards are creditable and most sixth-formers go on to degree courses each year. The music, art and drama departments are very active. A good standard is attained in sports and games. The school has a high reputation locally, a commitment to local community schemes and an outstanding record in the Duke of Edinburgh's Award Scheme. It has its own BHS Approved Equestrian centre and cross-country course. Full use is made of cultural amenities of Harrogate and York.

School profile

Pupils Total age range 2½–18; 300 pupils, 24 boys (day), 276 girls (116 day, 160 boarding). Senior department 11–18, 200 girls (145 boarders, 55 day). Main entry ages, 2½ and 5 (boys and girls), 11, 13 and into the sixth (girls). Own junior department provides over 20% senior intake. *State school entry:* 20% intake at 11, plus 10% to sixth.
Entrance Common Entrance and own exam used. No special skills or religious requirements. Parents not expected to buy textbooks. Scholarships (including music) and bursaries available, up to 20% fees; sixth-form scholarships, up to full fees.
Head and staff *Principal:* Mrs G L Richardson, 4 years in post. Previously Director of Studies and Head of Modern Languages at Queen Ethelburga's. *Staff:* 19 full time, 14 part time. Annual turnover 10%. Average age 40.
Exam results In 1995, 29 pupils in upper fifth, 15 in upper sixth. *GCSE:* In 1995, 52% upper fifth gained at least grade C in 8+ subjects; and 40% in 5–7 subjects. *A-levels:* 67% upper sixth passed in 3 subjects; 20% in 2; and 13% in 1 subject. Average UCAS points 12.6.
University and college entrance 90% of sixth-form leavers go on to a degree course (occasionally after a gap year); others typically go on to secretarial courses or family business. Of those going on to university 25% take courses in medicine, dentistry and veterinary science, 25% in science and engineering, 5% in law, 25% in humanities and social sciences, 10% in art and design. 10% in other subjects eg physiotherapy.
Curriculum GCSE, AS and A-levels. 17 subjects offered. 50% take science A-levels; 50% arts/humanities. *Vocational:* Work experience available; also City and Guilds qualifications in basic competence in IT. BHS Associate Instructors Awards in riding; NNEB Diploma; Leith's basic certificate in food and wine; and RSA office studies. *Computing facilities:* Range of BBC model B and IBM compatible Nimbus machines; also Pentium 586 with CD-Rom. *Special provision:* Special needs unit. English as a foreign language. *Europe:* French and German offered at GCSE, AS and A-level; also Italian and Spanish GCSE. Regular exchanges (France). Pupils in school from variety of European countries.
The arts (Pupils aged 11 and over) *Music:* Over 50% of pupils learn a musical instrument; instrumental exams can be taken. 4 musical groups: choir, chamber, madrigals, handbells. *Drama & dance*: Both offered. GCSE and A-level drama and LAMDA exams may be taken. Majority of pupils are involved in school productions and all in house/other productions. *Art:* On average, 9 take GCSE, 3 AS-level, 3 A-level. Design, art history, printmaking also offered.
Sport, community service and clubs (Pupils aged 11 and over) *Sport and physical activities:* Compulsory sports: lacrosse, tennis, netball, rounders. Optional: riding. Sixth form only: fitness, gym. Indoor Olympic size riding school and cross country course. Pupils can take BHS Associate Instructors Awards. *Community service:* Pupils take bronze, silver and gold Duke of Edinburgh's Award. CCF and community service optional. *Clubs and societies:* Up to 15 clubs, eg riding, computer, art, bridge.
Uniform School uniform worn except sixth.
Houses/prefects Competitive houses. Prefects, head girl, head of house and house prefects.
Religion Religious worship encouraged.
Social Debates, dances, choir, literary studies outings, French trips and exchanges. Meals formal. School shop. No tobacco allowed; alcohol occasionally on controlled basis.
Discipline Pupils failing to produce homework once might expect reprimand; those caught smoking cigarettes on the premises might expect expulsion after warnings.
Boarding Most sixth-formers have own study bedroom. Houses, of approximately 50, plus sixth-form house. Qualified nurse, visiting doctor. 2 weekend exeats each term. Visits to local town allowed: on a regular basis at weekends.

• QUEEN MARGARET'S (York)

Queen Margaret's School, Escrick Park, York YO4 6EU. Tel 01904 728261, Fax 01904 728150
• Pupils 365 • Boys None • Girls 11–18 (Day/Board) • Upper sixth 54 • Termly fees £2158 (Day) £3406 (Board) • GSA, BSA • Enquiries/application to the Headmaster's Secretary

What it's like

Founded in 1901, it moved to its present site in 1949. The main building is a huge and magnificent country house built in 1758 in 65 acres of splendid parkland. A C of E foundation, its pupils come from a wide social and geographic background. It has many of the advantages of a small school, with friendly, happy, well-motivated girls. There is a good staff:pupil ratio of 1:8. It is strong academically and results are very good. There is a part-time special needs department. A notable feature is the big parental involvement in many areas of school life (eg organisation, cultural, work experience etc). Strong in music, drama and art with a wide range of sports, games and activities. Good record in the Duke of Edinburgh's Award Scheme.

School profile

Pupils Age range 11–18; 365 girls, 30 day, 335 boarding. Main entry ages 11–13 and into sixth. 5% are children of former pupils.
Entrance Common Entrance used. No special skills or religious requirements. 9 pa scholarships, plus music scholarship, £300 to one third fees; some bursaries.
Parents 15+% are doctors, lawyers, etc; 20+% in industry or commerce. 10+% live within 30 miles, up to 10% live overseas.
Head and staff *Headmaster:* Dr Geoffrey A H Chapman, 4 years in post. Educated at St Bartholomew's Grammar, Newbury, and Oxford University (classics). Previously Head of Classics at Christ's Hospital and Professor of Classics at University of Natal. Also member of Council of Society for Promotion of Roman Studies. Publications: Several articles in international classics journals. *Staff:* 47 full time, 10 part time. Annual turnover 10%. Average age 40.
Exam results In 1995, 57 in upper fifth, 44 in upper sixth. *GCSE:* In 1995, 91% upper fifth gained grade C or above in 8+ subjects; 9% in 5–7 subjects. *A-levels:* 39 upper sixth passed in 3+ subjects; 5 in 2 subjects. Average UCAS points 21.0.
University and college entrance 95% of 1995 sixth-form leavers went on to a degree course (30% after a gap year). Of those going on to university, 8% went to Oxbridge; 5% took courses in medicine, dentistry and veterinary science, 8% in science and engineering, 5% in law, 50% in humanities and social sciences, 12% in art and design, 20% in other vocational subjects eg education, nursing, accountancy, estate management.
Curriculum GCSE and A-levels. 23 subjects offered at A-level. *Vocational:* Work experience available; also City and Guilds cookery course and RSA stages 1 and 2 in typing. *Computing facilities:* 3 dedicated rooms with additional computers in nine departments. *Special provision:* Part time special needs department. *Europe:* French, German and Spanish offered at GCSE, AS and A-level. Over 60% take GCSE in more than 1 language. Regular exchanges (France).
The arts *Music:* Over 60% of pupils learn a musical instrument; instrumental exams can be taken. Some 16+ musical groups including 3 orchestras, 3 bands, vocal, choral groups, rock band etc. Members of National Children's Orchestra. *Drama & dance:* Both offered. GCSE and A-level drama may be taken. Majority of pupils are involved in school and house/other productions. *Art:* On average, 25 take GCSE, 12 A-level. Design, pottery, textiles, photography also offered. Recently, 2 pupils accepted at Chelsea Art College; exhibition York Art Gallery.
Sport, community service and clubs *Sport and physical activities:* Compulsory sports: lacrosse, hockey, netball, swimming, tennis, athletics, gym, rounders. Optional: squash, badminton, golf, tennis, fencing, riding, canoeing. Sixth form only: aerobics. BAGA, BHS, RLSS exams may be taken. Member England lacrosse U18 team; county representatives at lacrosse, hockey and athletics. *Community service:* Pupils take bronze and gold Duke of Edinburgh's Award. Community service optional. *Clubs and societies:* Up to 15 clubs, eg chess, astronomy, Guides, Amnesty, modern studies, choral.
Uniform School uniform worn except sixth.
Houses/prefects Competitive houses. Prefects, head girl and heads of houses – appointed by the Headmaster. School Committee.

Religion Compulsory worship; all denominations welcome.
Social Mission work locally, debates, social events, musical events (village invited). Organised trips abroad – skiing and to Florence, Paris, Greece, Moscow, Venezuela. Pupils allowed to bring own bike/horse to school. Meals self-service. School shop. No tobacco/alcohol allowed.
Boarding Upper sixth have own study bedroom, lower sixth may share with one other. Houses, of approximately 60, divided by age. Resident qualified medical staff. Central dining room. 1–2 weekend and half-term exeats each term. Visits to local town allowed from 13 upwards.
Alumni association is run by Mrs Judith Cooke, Old House Farm, Stubbs Walden, Doncaster DN6 9BU.
Former pupils Winifred Holtby; Joan Hall (MP); Ann Jellicoe (writer); Dorothy Hutton (RA); Elizabeth Poston (musician).

• QUEEN'S (Chester)

The Queen's School, City Walls Road, Chester CH1 2NN. Tel 01244 312078, Fax 01244 321507
• Pupils 634 • Boys None • Girls 4–18 (Day) • Upper sixth 53 • Termly fees up to £1440 (Day)
• GSA, SHA • Enquiries/application to the Secretary

What it's like

Founded in 1878, it has a pleasant urban site with gardens and playing fields on the west side of the city wall, near the Watergate. A combination of late Victorian and modern buildings. The school still uses the original assembly hall given by the Duke of Westminster in 1882 when Queen Victoria became the first patron. The junior and prep departments are housed in separate buildings in Liverpool Road. The school is interdenominational with strong Christian emphasis. A sound general education is provided and results obtained are very good. Almost all leavers go on to degree courses, including many to Oxbridge. Considerable strength in music, drama and art. An adequate range of sports and games, in which high standards are achieved, and a fair range of extra-curricular activities.

School profile

Pupils Total age range 4–18; 634 day girls. Senior department 11–18, 458 girls. Main entry ages 5, 8, 11 and into sixth. *State school entry:* 38% senior intake, plus 90% to sixth.
Entrance Own entrance exam used. Good all-round academic ability sought; no religious requirements. Parents not expected to buy textbooks. 11 pa assisted places. Bursaries available, dependent on need.
Head and staff *Headmistress:* Miss Diana Skilbeck, 7 years in post. Educated at Wirral County Grammar School for Girls and London University (geography). Previously Head at Sheffield High, Deputy Head at West Kirby Grammar and Head of Geography at Wirral County Grammar. *Staff:* 41 full time, 27 part time.
Exam results In 1995, 69 pupils in upper fifth, 53 in upper sixth. *GCSE:* In 1995, all upper fifth gained at least grade C in 8+ subjects. *A-levels:* 33 upper sixth passed in 4+ subjects; 20 in 3 subjects. Average UCAS points 23.3 (including general studies, 29.6).
University and college entrance Typically, all leavers go on to degree courses (18% to Oxbridge).
Curriculum GCSE and A-levels (including A-level general studies). 30% take science A-levels; 30% arts/humanities; 40% both. *Vocational:* Work experience available. *Computing facilities:* Well-equipped room with BBC and A3000 computers. *Special provision:* Some individual help. *Europe:* French and German offered at GCSE and A-level; also French AS-level, Italian and Spanish GCSE. Over 75% take GCSE in more than 1 language. Regular exchanges (France). Native speakers as conversation assistants.
The arts (Pupils aged 11 and over) *Music:* Up to 50% of pupils learn a musical instrument; instrumental exams can be taken. Some 7 musical groups including choirs, orchestras, wind band, recorder group. *Drama & dance*: Drama offered. ESB, LAMDA exams may be taken. Some pupils are involved in school productions and majority in house/other productions. *Art:* On average, 14 take GCSE, 3 AS-level, 5 A-level. Design also offered.

Sport, community service and clubs (Pupils aged 11 and over) Sport and physical activities Compulsory sports: netball, cross country, hockey, lacrosse, gymnastics, dance, swimming, tennis, rounders, athletics. Sixth form only: badminton, squash, weightlifting, yoga, ice skating. BAGA awards may be taken. *Community service:* Pupils take bronze, silver and gold Duke of Edinburgh's Award. Community service optional in sixth-form. Young Enterprise. *Clubs and societies:* Up to 10 clubs, eg Christian Union, Quest, debating, drama, computers, electronics, table tennis, other sports etc.
Uniform School uniform worn except the sixth.
Houses/prefects Competitive houses for games, music and drama. Head girl and deputies appointed by Head and staff. School Committee.
Religion Short Christian assembly every morning.
Social Organised local events and joint functions with other schools from time to time. French and German exchanges; ski trips and adventure holidays abroad. Pupils allowed to bring own bike to school. Meals self-service. Twice-weekly tuckshop. No tobacco/alcohol allowed.
Alumni association run by Mrs Susan Seys-Llewellyn, c/o the school.

• QUEEN'S (London)

Queen's College London, 43-49 Harley Street, London W1N 2BT. Tel 0171 580 1533, Fax 0171 436 7607

• Pupils 370 • Boys None • Girls 11–18 (Day) • Upper sixth 45 • Termly fees £1940 (Day) • GSA • Enquiries/application to the College Registrar (tel 0171 636 2446)

What it's like

Founded in 1848, it was the pioneer college for the higher education of women and the first institution to provide both a sound academic education and proper qualifications for women. Queen Victoria herself was interested in its foundation and contributed personally to funds. The main buildings date from 1762 and consist of three handsome Georgian houses. There have been many additions and improvements over the years and there are excellent modern facilities, particularly for science and IT, music, art and drama. There is a staff:pupil ratio of about 1:11. Results are very good and the majority of the sixth-form proceed to degree courses each year including to Oxbridge. Great emphasis is placed on careers. Music, drama and art are all strongly supported. There is a standard range of games and sports available (easy access to playing fields in the nearby Regent's Park); very strong in fencing including at national level.

School profile

Pupils Age range 11–18; 370 day girls. Main entry ages 11, 13, 14 and into sixth. 5% are children of former pupils. *State school entry:* 50% main intake at 11.
Entrance London Consortium entrance exam and interview. No special skills or religious requirements. Parents expected to buy textbooks. Some assisted places and scholarships.
Head and staff *Principal:* The Hon Lady (Celia) Goodhart. Educated at St Michael's Limpsfield and Oxford University (history). Previously History Tutor at Westminster Tutors and civil servant (1966). Also Hon Fellow St Hilda's College, Oxford; President, Schoolmistresses and Governesses Benevolent Institution. SDP National and Policy Committees and Liberal Democrat Federal Executive. Stood for Parliament. Member: Data Protection Committee (1978); National Gas Consumer Council; Elizabeth Nuffield Education Fund; Oxford University Nuffield Medical Trustees. *Staff:* 35 full time, 16 part time.
Exam results In 1995, 54 pupils in upper fifth, 45 in upper sixth. *GCSE:* In 1995, 96% of upper fifth gained grade C or above in 8+ subjects. *A-levels:* All upper sixth passed in 3 subjects. Average UCAS points 21.3.
University and college entrance 97% of 1995 sixth-form leavers went on to a degree course (15% after a gap year); 24% took courses in science and engineering, 9% in law, 39% in arts and humanities, 15% in vocational subjects, 9% in combined courses.
Curriculum GCSE and A-levels. 23 subjects offered (including classical Greek, history of art, computing and theatre studies). *Computing facilities:* New computer laboratory with facilities for A-level computing. *Europe:* French (from age 11), German, Italian, Russian

and Spanish offered to GCSE, AS and A-level. Regular exchanges (France).
The arts *Music:* Over 10% pupils learn a musical instrument; instrumental exams may be taken. Musical groups include various chamber ensembles, orchestra and choir. *Drama & dance*: Some pupils involved in school productions. Occasionally pupils accepted for drama colleges. *Art:* On average 33 take GCSE; 17 A-level. Regular entrants to art college.
Sport, community service and clubs *Sport and physical activities:* Sports available: netball, hockey, rounders, tennis, gymnastics, fencing, swimming. 2 pupils in English fencing team. *Clubs and societies:* Clubs include computers, debating society, drama, maths, writing.
Uniform No school uniform.
Houses/prefects No houses. Prefects, head girl – elected by staff, Principal and pupils.
Religion Anglican tradition with many religions included. Separate Jewish prayers.
Social Regular trips abroad. Meals self-service. School bookshop and art shop. No tobacco/alcohol allowed.
Alumni association is run by Mrs L Bernard, Old Queens Society, c/o the College.

• QUEEN'S (Taunton)

Queen's College, Trull Road, Taunton, Somerset TA1 4QS. Tel 01823 272559, Fax 01823 388430
• Pupils 684 • Boys 3–18 (Day/Board) • Girls 3–18 (Day/Board) • Upper sixth 63 • Termly fees £2118 (Day) £3231 (Board) • HMC • Enquiries/application to the Headmaster

What it's like

Founded in 1843, as a Methodist foundation. Its premises are single-site and semi-rural in 30 acres on the southern outskirts of Taunton. Very pleasant buildings and fine playing fields. Originally a boys' school, it first admitted girls in the eighties and is now fully co-educational. The junior school and nursery are combined. There has been much development in the last 30 years, including a fine concert/assembly hall and music school. Facilities are good and the school is well positioned for field work and expeditions to Exmoor, Dartmoor and the Quantocks. An exceptionally strong music department; good drama and art. Academic results are good and most sixth-formers go on to university, including Oxbridge. A good range of games, sports and activities and a distinguished record in the Duke of Edinburgh's Award Scheme. The school enjoys vigorous local support.

School profile

Pupils Age range 3–18; 684 pupils, 448 day (197 boys, 194 girls), 236 boarding (147 boys, 89 girls). Senior department 12–18, 450 pupils, (246 boys, 204 girls). Main entry ages 8, 12, 13 and into sixth. More than 70% of intake from own junior school. *State school entry:* 20% main intake, plus 30% to sixth.
Entrance Common Entrance and own exam used. Musical skills looked for; all denominations welcome. Parents not expected to buy textbooks. 10 pa assisted places. Various scholarships/bursaries, means-tested if over half-fees.
Head and staff *Headmaster:* Christopher Bradnock, 5 years in post. Educated at Eltham College and Cambridge (English and theology). Previously Deputy Head at Ashville, Housemaster at Eltham College and Assistant Master at King's College, Budo, Uganda and at Bradford Grammar. *Staff:* 45 full time, 6 part time.
Exam results In 1995, 78 pupils in Year 11, 63 in Year 13. *GCSE:* In 1995, 72% Year 11 gained at least grade C in 8+ subjects; 17% in 5–7 subjects. *A-levels:* 14% Year 13 passed in 4 subjects; 61% in 3; 18% in 2; and 7% in 1 subject. Average UCAS points 17.2.
University and college entrance 95% of 1995 sixth-form leavers went on to a degree course (10% after a gap year); others typically go straight into careers. Of those going on to university, 11% went to Oxbridge; 6% took courses in medicine, dentistry and veterinary science, 20% in science and engineering, 2% in law, 40% in humanities and social sciences, 1% in art and design, 30% in vocational subjects eg physiotherapy, hotel and catering.
Curriculum GCSE and A-levels. 21 GCSE and 19 A-level subjects offered, including A-level music; no A-level general studies. 39% took science A-levels; 61% arts/humanities. *Vocational:* Work experience available. *Special provision:* Specialist help for dyslexics.

Europe: French and Spanish offered at GCSE and A-level; also French AS-level. Regular exchanges to France, Spain and Sweden.

The arts *Music:* 30% of pupils learn a musical instrument; instrumental exams can be taken. Some 15 musical groups including choir, 3 orchestras, wind band, madrigal, rhythm & blues. 3 recent members of National Youth orchestra, 5 of National Children's Orchestra. *Drama & dance*: Drama offered; GCSE and A-level drama and theatre studies may be taken. Some pupils are involved in school productions; 3 in National Youth Theatre. *Art:* On average, 20 take GCSE, 5 A-level. Design, pottery, textiles, photography also offered.

Sport, community service and clubs *Sport and physical activities:* Compulsory sports: rugby, hockey, netball, cricket. Optional: swimming, tennis, rounders, athletics, cross-country, fencing. Sixth form only: football. GCSE and A-level sport and RLSS exams may be taken. *Community service:* Pupils take bronze, silver and gold Duke of Edinburgh's Award. Community service optional. *Clubs and societies:* Up to 10 clubs, eg war games, model making, sixth-form society, canoeing.

Uniform School uniform worn throughout.

Houses/prefects Competitive houses. Prefects, head boy/girl, head of house and house prefects – appointed by the Head.

Religion Part of a group of Methodist schools.

Social Organised trips abroad. Pupils allowed to bring own car/bike to school. Meals self-service. School shop. No tobacco/alcohol allowed.

Discipline Fines and suspension used. Pupils failing to produce homework are detained to do it.

Boarding Upper sixth have own study bedroom, lower sixth share with 2; 50% are in dormitories of 6+. Houses of 40, same as competitive houses; one mixed house. Resident qualified nurse. Central dining room. Visits to local town allowed for older pupils.

• QUEENSWOOD

Queenswood, Shepherds Way, Brookmans Park, Hatfield, Hertfordshire AL9 6NS. Tel 01707 652262, Fax 01707 649267

• Pupils 400 • Boys None • Girls 11–18 (Day/Board) • Upper sixth 54 • Termly fees £2256 (Day) £3658–£3814 (Board) • GSA, BSA • Enquiries/application to the Admissions Secretary

What it's like

Founded in 1894 at Clapham Park by two Methodist ministers, it moved to its present site in 1925. This is in an exceptionally pleasant area of the green belt and comprises 420 acres of farmland, woodland and sports fields. There has been much recent expansion and the school is now very well equipped. Being within easy reach of London, its pupils make frequent visits to theatres, concerts and exhibitions. The school prides itself on its friendly atmosphere and general community spirit. It has a strong Christian foundation and the chapel plays a significant part in the life of the school. The staff:pupil ratio is about 1:8 and high academic standards can be achieved by good and average pupils and exam results are very good. There is a great deal of emphasis on drama, with high standards of performance; music is very strong and there is a variety of musical groups. High standards are attained in sport, with numerous representatives at county level and some at national level in tennis, hockey and athletics; it is an LTA national tennis centre. There are many clubs and societies for other extra-curricular activities. The school has a substantial commitment to local community schemes and has an impressive record in the Duke of Edinburgh's Award Scheme. It also runs its own exploration society.

School profile

Pupils Age range 11–18; 400 girls (350 boarders, 50 day boarders). Main entry ages 11, 12, 13 and into sixth. 6% are children of former pupils. Pupils recruited in significant numbers from Duncombe School, Hertford (tel 01992 582653), Maltman's Green School, Gerrards Cross (tel 01753 883022), Stormont School, Potters Bar (tel 01707 654037) and Riddlesworth Hall, Diss (tel 0195 381246). *State school entry:* 3% main intake, plus 10% to sixth.

Entrance Common Entrance exam used except under exceptional circumstances. No special skills required except motivation to make good use of opportunities offered; no religious requirements. 8 pa scholarships (academic, music, tennis) at 11, 12, 13, 16, all means tested, 50% of fees.

Parents 30+% are doctors, lawyers etc. 30+% in industry and commerce 15+% live within 30 miles; 30% live overseas, half of whom are foreign nationals.

Head and staff *Principal:* Clarissa Farr, appointed 1996. Educated at Bruton School for Girls and Exeter University (English). Previously Deputy Head (Academic) at Queenswood and Senior Mistress at Leicester Grammar School. *Staff:* 52 full time, 9 part time. Annual turnover 10%. Average age 35.

Exam results In 1995, 51 pupils in Year 11, 54 in upper sixth. *GCSE:* In 1995, 49 Year 11 gained at least grade C in 8+ subjects; 2 in 5–7 subjects. *A-levels:* 1 upper sixth passed in 4+ subjects; 47 in 3 (including 3 pupils with an additional AS-level); 3 in 2 subjects; and 2 in 1 subject (1 with and AS-level). Average UCAS points 22.3.

University and college entrance 97% of 1995 sixth-form leavers went on to a degree course (35% after a gap year); others typically go on to other higher education courses. Of those going on to university, 10% went to Oxbridge; 4% took courses in medicine, dentistry and veterinary science, 20% in science and engineering, 66% in humanities and social sciences, 4% in art and design, 4% in drama and acting, 2% in music.

Curriculum GCSE, AS and A-levels. 16 GCSE subjects offered; 8 at AS; 17 at A-level (including economics, theatre studies, business studies, history of art; no A-level general studies). 27% take science/maths A-levels; 48% arts/humanities; 24% both. *Vocational:* Work experience available. 5 girls involved in Education for Engineering Scheme. *Computing facilities:* Campus-wide network, via fibre optic links, of RM PCs including computer room, multi-media studio and departmental machines; CD-Rom server. *Special provision:* Specialist help for intelligent dyslexic pupils only. EFL teaching. *Europe:* French, German and Spanish offered at GCSE and A-level; also French AS-level. Over 75% take GCSE in more than one language; all sixth-form take a certificated language course (eg GCSE, A-level, business French). Regular exchanges to Germany (Years 9–11 to Munich), France (sixth-form to Paris including 2-week work experience), Denmark and Spain. European studies compulsory (Years 7 and 8); school was UK representative at Eurencounter conference in Brussels. Variety of European trips and visits.

The arts *Music:* Over 50% of pupils learn a musical instrument; instrumental exams can be taken. Some 12 musical groups including 2 choirs, string and chamber orchestras, wind, flute ensembles, big band. Upper school choir has appeared at St John's Smith Square in Choral Spectrum and with the chamber orchestra toured Belgium, Germany and France. *Drama & dance*: Drama offered; GCSE, A-level and LAMDA exams may be taken. School production annually. *Art:* Design, pottery, textiles, photography, print-making offered. 2–4 students to foundation art courses each year.

Sport, community service and clubs *Sport and physical activities:* Compulsory sports; hockey, netball, gym, swimming, health related fitness, dance, aerobics, tennis, athletics. Optional: trampolining, volleyball, canoeing, golf. Sixth form only: shooting, sailing, windsurfing, skiing, weight training. GCSE sports, BAGA, RLSS, BTF exams may be taken. National, county and regional tennis players; county and regional hockey; county swimming. LTA National Centre. *Community service:* Pupils take bronze, silver and gold Duke of Edinburgh's Award. Community service compulsory for 1 year at age 16. *Clubs and societies:* Up to 20 clubs, eg pottery, chess, art, aerobics, Young Enterprise, Queenswood Raven Exploration Society, English Society, debating.

Uniform School uniform worn except in upper sixth.

Houses/prefects Competitive houses. Prefects and head girl (upper sixth) appointed after wide consultation; head of house and house prefects (fifth years) selected within house. School Council, members chosen by girls. Prefects share a managerial role in music, sport, chapel, computing.

Religion Both compulsory and voluntary worship exist. Majority of girls choose to be confirmed.

Social Debating (Observer Mace & Rotary Competitions), tennis, socials, discos, annual ball (various schools). Organised trips abroad for skiing, tennis, music (choral), language (French and Spanish), art, exploration society. Meals self-service (2 formal meals annually). School shop and school bank. Wine with meals with adults present; no other alcohol or tobacco allowed.

Discipline Pupils failing to produce homework once after being given an extension would be disciplined by their tutor; any girl caught smoking cannabis on the premises could expect to be expelled.

Boarding 60 have own study bedroom, 72 share with 1 or 2; 80 in dormitories of 4, 182 in dormitories of 6+. Houses, of 40–58, divided by age. 2 resident SRNs. Central dining room. Lower sixth pupils can provide and cook snacks (own kitchen); upper sixth given budget to cover all meals except lunch (own large kitchens). 4 exeats annually plus half terms, extra for seniors if no school commitments. Visits to local town allowed for third year and above (usually Saturday); sixth allowed into London in groups.

Alumni association is run by Mrs C Astles, 1 Mead Field, Fetcham, Leatherhead, Surrey KT22 9XB.

Vocational Work experience available. *Computing facilities:* 50 Apple Macintosh machines networked in three computer room)

R

• RADLEY

Radley College, Abingdon, Oxfordshire OX14 2HR. Tel 01235 543000

• Pupils 600 • Boys 13–18 (Board) • Girls None • Upper sixth 120 • Termly fees £4100 (Board)
• HMC • Enquiries/application to the Warden

What it's like

Founded in 1847 by the Rev William Sewell, Fellow of Exeter College, Oxford, to provide a public school education on the principles of the Church of England. Its agreeable and well-equipped buildings lie in a beautiful 700-acre estate, 2½ miles from Abingdon and 5 miles from Oxford. It is a very successful boarding school for boys and has first-class facilities of all kinds and comfortable boarding accommodation. It retains strong links with Oxford and the Church of England. The chapel and religious education are an important part of the college's life. Two resident chaplains and the Warden are responsible for chapel services etc. A large and well-qualified staff permits a staff:pupil ratio of about 1:10. Academic standards are high and results excellent. Most leavers go on to degree courses, many to Oxbridge, and the aim is that every sixth-former should be fluent in a European language and feel European before they leave. The music department is very strong and there is extensive activity in drama (annual school productions, shorter plays by dramatic societies, a production by the Gilbert and Sullivan society and house plays). There is a fine design centre in which work of high quality is produced. Sports facilities are exceptionally good and the college is well known for its achievements in rugby, cricket, hockey and rowing (there are boathouses on the Thames, a mile away). Numerous clubs and societies cater for virtually every extra-curricular need. There is also a golf course and the college runs its own beagle pack. The CCF is a large contingent and there is considerable emphasis on outdoor pursuits. There is an impressive record in the Duke of Edinburgh's Award Scheme; community service is central to the Radleian's education.

School profile

Pupils Age range 13–18; 600 boarding boys. Main entry ages 13, a few into sixth. Approx 20% are children of former pupils. *State school entry:* None in main intake, 1% to sixth.

Entrance Common Entrance and own scholarship exam used. Oversubscribed. No special skills required; C of E preferred, other denominations welcome. Maximum extras £180 – theatre trips, account at school shop etc. 20 pa scholarships/exhibitions (7 pa for music), £1,000 to half fees.

Parents 15+% are doctors, lawyers etc; 15+% in industry or commerce. 10+% live within 30 miles; up to 10% live overseas.

Head and staff Warden: Richard Morgan, 6 years in post. Educated at Sherborne and Cambridge (economics and law). Previously Headmaster at Cheltenham, Housemaster and Assistant Master at Radley. *Staff:* 62 full time, 8 part time plus musicians. Annual turnover 6%. Average age 37.

Exam results In 1995, 121 pupils in upper fifth, 127 in upper sixth. *GCSE:* In 1995, 119 upper fifth gained at least grade C in 8+ subjects; 2 in 5–7 subjects. *A-levels:* 16 upper sixth passed in 5 subjects; 15 in 4; 90 in 3; 6 in 2 subjects. Average UCAS points 27.2.

University and college entrance 97% of 1995 sixth-form leavers went on to a degree course (55% after a gap year); others typically go in to the forces or other employment. Of those going on to university, 19% went to Oxbridge; 5% took courses in medicine, dentistry and veterinary science, 15% in science and engineering, 1% in law, 71% in humanities and social sciences, 8% in art and design.

Curriculum GCSE and A-levels. 27 subjects offered (no A-level general studies; Mandarin offered in sixth-form). 24% took science A-levels; 38% arts/humanities; 38% both. *Vocational:* Work experience available. *Computing facilities:* Computer department plus individual machines in departments and houses. *Europe:* French,

German and Spanish offered to GCSE, AS- and A-level. All study a language in the sixth-form.

The arts *Music:* Over 30% of pupils learn a musical instrument; instrumental exams can be taken. Some 12 musical groups including orchestra, choral society, madrigal society, Radley Clerkes, wind band, dance band, jazz group, various chamber groups. *Drama & dance*: Drama offered. Majority of pupils are involved in school and house/other productions. School play invited to Fringe at 1993 Edinburgh Festival. *Art:* On average, 26 take GCSE, 7 A-level. Design, pottery, photography also offered.

Sport, community service and clubs *Sport and physical activities:* Optional sports: Rugby, rowing, hockey, cricket, tennis, diving, sub-aqua, windsurfing, gymnastics, athletics, squash, swimming, basketball, judo, karate, fencing, fives, rackets, sailing, golf. Boys have represented county and national teams in various sports. *Community service:* Pupils take bronze, silver and gold Duke of Edinburgh's Award. CCF compulsory for 4 terms at age 14, optional thereafter. Community action programme compulsory until upper sixth when it is optional; initiatives across the country and in Romania. *Clubs and societies:* Up to 30 clubs, eg Amnesty International, bridge, electronics, film production, debating, political, literary, natural history, printing, racing, trout fishing.

Uniform School uniform worn throughout.

Houses/prefects Competitive houses. Prefects, head boy, head of house and house prefects – appointed by the Head and housemasters. Chores performed by junior boys; no fagging.

Religion Attendance compulsory at 4 short evening services a week plus one of a choice of Sunday services.

Social Debating, concerts etc with other schools. Oriental summer school in summer holidays (pupils can act as guides and develop links for their gap year). Annual skiing trip abroad. Pupils allowed to bring own bike to school. Meals self-service. School shop. No tobacco/alcohol allowed.

Discipline A firm and clear structure. Instant dismissal for use or possession of illegal drugs.

Boarding One year in a Social Hall; one in a shared study, 3 in single study bedroom. Houses, of approximately 75, same as competitive houses. Resident qualified nurses. Central dining room. Pupils can provide and cook own food. Half-term plus 1 or 2 Saturday night exeats each term. All encouraged to make best pssible use of Oxford (special Oxford calendar provided termly)

Alumni association run by J K Mullard, c/o the college.

• RANNOCH

Rannoch School, Rannoch, by Pitlochry, Perthshire PH17 2QQ. Tel 01882 632332, Fax 01882 632443

• Pupils 230 • Boys 10–18 (Day/Board) • Girls 10–18 (Day/Board) • Upper sixth 35 • Termly fees £1830 (Day) £2900–£3450 (Board) • SHMIS, Round Square • Enquiries/application to the Headmaster

What it's like

Founded in 1959 by three masters from Gordonstoun, it has a marvellous site in 120 acres of grounds on the south shore of Loch Rannoch in a spectacular setting of Highland scenery. The main building was built in 1855, by a chief of the Robertson clan, and is a towered and turreted Scottish baronial mansion. Modern facilities, including converted farm buildings, provide excellent additional accommodation. A well-run and enterprising school, it has very strong links and contacts with the local community which gives vigorous support. Its international spread of intake includes some 140 pupils from Scotland, 40-odd from England and 50 from overseas (mostly the children of expatriates). It has high academic standards and reasonable results. The staff:pupil ratio is about 1:9. Chapel services are compulsory and there is quite a lot of emphasis on religious education. Strong in music, drama and art, and considerable strength in games and sports. A big commitment to local community schemes. The fine range of clubs and societies caters for many needs. The environment is ideal for outdoor pursuits and a lot are available (including fishing, skiing, mountaineering, camping, sailing and canoeing).

The school has a most remarkable record in the Duke of Edinburgh's Award Scheme (over 500 gold awards in 28 years).

School profile

Pupils Age range 10–18; 230 pupils, 8 day (4 boys, 4 girls), 222 boarding (171 boys, 51 girls). Main entry ages 10, 11, 12, 13 and into sixth. Approx 10% are children of former pupils. *State school entry:* 60+% main intake, plus 50% to sixth.

Entrance Common Entrance and own exam used. Pleasant young people looked for; no religious requirements. Parents expected to pay a small charge per session for textbooks; minimal standard extras. 6 pa assisted places. Up to 10 pa scholarships/bursaries, up to three-quarters of fees.

Parents Parents drawn from a wide range of occupations. About 140 live in Scotland, 40 in England and 50 overseas.

Head and staff *Headmaster:* Michael Barratt, in post for 13 years. Educated at George Watson's and Merchiston Castle, and at universities of St Andrew's and Oxford (English). Previously Housemaster at Strathallan and Assistant Master at Epsom. Formerly committee member SHMIS, ISIS (Scotland) Committee and ISCO Scotland Committee. *Staff:* 22 full time, 8 part time. Average age 30–40.

Exam results In 1995, 45 pupils in S-grade year, 40+ in Higher/A-level years. *S-grade:* In 1995, 82% pupils passed in 5–7 subjects; 15% in 1–4 subjects. *Highers:* 75% passed in 5+ or more subjects; 25% in 3 subjects. *A-levels:* All passed in 3 subjects.

University and college entrance 50% of 1995 sixth-form leavers went on to a degree course; others typically go on to non-degree courses eg art and drama, or straight into careers eg nursing, farming, the armed services. Of those going on to university, 5% went to Oxbridge; 14% took courses in medicine, dentistry and veterinary science, 43% in science and engineering, 14% in humanities and social sciences, 21% in art and design, 7% in music.

Curriculum S-grades, Highers and A-levels offered (including Higher/A-level geology and computer studies; no A-level general studies). Some pupils take Highers, some A-levels; there is an even spread of pupils taking science exams and arts/humanities. *Vocational:* Work experience available; also Scotvec modules in geology and physical education. *Computing facilities:* 14 networked Acorn Archimedes, 6 IBM compatibles (of which 1 is 486, 2 Pentium 90s, 1 multimedia); Internet connection. Further computers in most departments and in houses. *Special provision:* Small remedial department for those with mild learning difficulties in English and mathematics. *Europe:* French and German offered to S-grade, Higher and A-level. Regular exchanges.

The arts *Music:* Over 50% of pupils learn a musical instrument; instrumental exams can be taken. Some 5 musical groups including wind group, strings, rock band, chapel choir. Choir regularly sings around Scotland – summer tours (Iona Abbey, Dunkeld Cathedral, etc), Malta (1994), Spain (1996). *Drama & dance*: Both offered. Scottish Highland dancing exams may be taken. Majority of pupils are involved in school productions and some in house/other productions. Recent productions of Oliver and an Alan Ayckbourn play. *Art:* On average, 25 take S-grade, 20 Higher, 3 A-level. Pottery also offered.

Sport, community service and clubs *Sport and physical activities:* Compulsory sports: rugby, athletics (boys); hockey, netball (girls). Optional: wide range including skiing, football, cricket, rounders, swimming, squash, tennis, golf, sailing. BAGA, RLSS, RYA, S-grade and Highers may be taken. Pupils have competed at national level in rugby and cross-country. *Community service:* All pupils take bronze, most silver and gold Duke of Edinburgh's Award; special reputation in the scheme, with some 500 gold award winners. Community service optional at age 15. *Clubs and societies:* Up to 30 clubs, eg archery, aero-modelling, auto-mechanics, Bible study, bridge, chess, cookery, computing, dress-making, karate, hairdressing, photography, Scottish country dancing, shooting.

Uniform School uniform worn throughout.

Houses/prefects Competitive houses. Prefects, head boy/girl, head of house and house prefects – appointed by the Head after consultation. Various school committees.

Religion Compulsory religious worship.

Social Very strong contact with local community (large sum raised recently to save the village hall). Organised trips abroad and exchange systems to France, Germany, Australia and Canada. Pupils allowed to bring own bike to school. Meals self-service. School shop. No tobacco/alcohol allowed.

Boarding All sixth-form have own study bedroom, some fifth formers share. Single-sex houses of approx 50, same as competitive houses. Resident qualified medical staff. Central dining room. Pupils can provide and cook own food within limits. Exeats permitted each term, number varies. Visits to the local town allowed.
Alumni association run by Mr Allan Hartley, Elliott McDougall Ltd, 6/8 Dewar Place Lane, Edinburgh. Tel 0131 553 5549 (work), 0131 337 6976 (home).

• RATCLIFFE

Ratcliffe College, Fosse Way, Ratcliffe on the Wreake, Leicestershire LE7 4SG. Tel 01509 817000, Fax 01509 817004

• Pupils 489 • Boys 10–18 (Day/Board/Weekly) • Girls 10–18 (Day/Board/Weekly) • Upper sixth 63 • Termly fees £2022 (Day) £3032 (Board/Weekly) • HMC • Enquiries/application to the Headmaster

What it's like

Founded in 1847 by priests of the Institute of Charity as a school for Catholic boys. Set in splendid grounds of a hundred acres of rural Leicestershire, the main buildings (designed by Pugin) form a compact block round a quadrangle with the old chapel, now converted, occupying a central position. Recent additions include a new chapel, science and music buildings and a fine sports centre. In 1977 girls were admitted to the sixth-form and in 1984 a junior house for day boys and girls was inaugurated. Most pupils are Catholics, but an increasing number of Christians of other persuasions and some non-Christians have been accepted. Religious instruction is given at all levels and Mass, daily prayers etc are an integral part of the school's life. The aim of the school is summed up by its motto *Legis plenitudo charitas* (Charity is the fulfilment of the law). Academically, morally, socially and spiritually it aims to equip pupils to succeed and to make the sort of contribution to society which is the ideal of the Christian life. A sound general education is provided and academic results are good; most sixth-form leavers go on to degree courses. Music, drama and art are all strongly supported and there is a successful film club. Some pupils have achieved success in sports and games at county and district levels. A number of clubs and societies cater for most extra-curricular activities. The CCF has strong Army and RAF contingents and there is a Scout group and a voluntary service unit. Much emphasis is put on adventure training, Outward Bound courses, Duke of Edinburgh's Award Scheme and skiing.

School profile

Pupils Age range 10–18; 489 pupils, 356 day (252 boys, 104 girls), 133 boarding (83 boys, 50 girls). Main entry ages 10, 11, 12, 13 and into sixth. Own prep, Grace Dieu Manor. *State school entry:* 42% main intake, plus 12% to sixth.
Entrance Own entrance exam and Common Entrance used. Assisted places, scholarships and bursaries.
Head and staff *Headmaster:* Fr K A Tomlinson, 4 years in post. Educated at Ratcliffe and at Rome University (theology). Previously Head of Year and Deputy Head at Ratcliffe. Also School Chaplain and Chairman of Governors, St Richard's School, Bexhill-on-Sea; Parish Priest in Wisbech and Prison Chaplain at Whitemoor Prison. *Staff:* 48 full time, 11 part time. Annual turnover 5%. Average age 35.
Exam results On average, 90 pupils in fifth form, 60 in upper sixth. *GCSE:* On average, 41% fifth formers gain at least grade C in 8+ subjects; 51% in 5–7 subjects. *A-levels:* 71% upper sixth pass in 3+ subjects; 29% in 2 subjects. Average UCAS points 15.6.
University and college entrance 90% of 1995 sixth-form leavers went on to a degree course; others typically go on to art courses or straight into careers eg retailing. Of those going on to university, 5% went to Oxbridge; 4% took courses in medicine, dentistry and veterinary science, 35% in science and engineering, 45% in humanities and social sciences, 14% in art and design.
Curriculum GCSE and *A-levels:* 23 GCSE subjects offered (no A-level general studies). 24% take science A-levels; 66% arts/humanities; 10% both. *Vocational:* Work experience available. *Computing facilities:* 16-station RML Nimbus network; some 30 BBC micros. *Special provision:* EFL tuition available; some special needs provision for those with minor specific learning difficulties including link with the Dyslexia Institute in

Nottingham. *Europe:* French, German and Spanish offered to GCSE and A-level. Regular exchanges (France). Work experience can take place in France; reciprocal arrangement for French students in UK.

The arts *Music:* 30% of pupils learn a musical instrument; instrumental exams can be taken. Some 6 musical groups including orchestral, jazz, brass band, string quartets and trios. A-level music can be taken. *Drama & dance*: Drama offered up to A-level. Some pupils are involved in school and house/other productions. Number of awards in local theatre festivals; close links with Loughborough Drama Centre. *Art:* On average, 30 take GCSE, 10 A-level; design also offered. Art facilities open to non-examination pupils.

Sport, community service and clubs *Sport and physical activities:* Compulsory sports: Rugby, hockey, cricket (boys); Hockey, netball, tennis, rounders (girls). Optional: squash, badminton, basketball, rowing, athletics. GCSE and A-level sports science may be taken. *Community service:* Pupils take bronze, silver and gold Duke of Edinburgh's Award. CCF and service optional. *Clubs and societies:* Up to 10 clubs, eg chess, debating, quiz, film (has won national and international awards).

Uniform School uniform worn; sixth-form may wear dark suits as an alternative.

Houses/prefects Competitive houses. Prefects, head boy and girl and head of house appointed by the Headmaster. Year Councils.

Religion Attendance at religious worship compulsory on Sundays and Holy Days.

Social Visits to Russia, Eastern Europe, Germany, France and Italy; exchanges with 2 French schools. Pupils allowed to bring own car/bike to school. Some meals formal; most self-service. School shop. Bar for sixth-form, run by staff.

Discipline Pupils failing to produce homework once might expect detention; those caught smoking cannabis on the premises, expulsion.

• RBAI

The Royal Belfast Academical Institution, College Square, Belfast BT1 6DL. Tel 01232 240461
• Pupils 1050 • Boys 11–19 (Day) • Girls None • Upper sixth 116 • Termly fees £130 (Day)
• HMC, SHA • Enquiries/admissions to the Principal

What it's like

Founded in 1810, the Institution was originally a university level institution, with faculties of arts and medicine, as well as a school. It is now a voluntary grammar school situtated on an 8-acre city-centre site where the first buildings were erected. These are fine buildings after the design of Sir John Soane. Many major additions have been made, the most recent of which is a new technology and design centre. Academic standards are high and results very good; each year the majority of leavers go on to degree courses. Music and drama are strongly supported. The main sports and games are rugby, hockey, cricket, lawn tennis, rowing and athletics. Many pupils have participated in games and sports at national and international level. A large number of clubs and societies cater for most conceivable interests. There is a CCF contingent, a Scout troop (with a Venture Scout section) and a community service group.

School profile

Pupils Age range 11–19, 1050 day boys. Main entry age 11. Own junior school.

Entrance Entry through transfer procedure arranged by LEAs in Northern Ireland, together with Department of Education (NI). Foundation and leaving scholarships.

Head and staff *Principal:* Michael Ridley, 6 years in post. Educated at Clifton and Oxford (English). Previously Headmaster at Denstone, Head of English at Merchiston Castle and Housemaster at Wellington College. *Staff:* 61 full time. 2 part time. Annual turnover 3%. Average age 40.

Exam results In 1995, 154 pupils in fifth, 116 in upper sixth. *GCSE:* In 1995, 85% upper fifth gained at least grade C in 8+ subjects; 15% in 5–7 subjects. *A-levels:* 10 upper sixth passed in 4+ subjects; 93 in 3; 8 in 2; and 1 in 1 subject. Average UCAS points of 21.0

University and college entrance 85% of 1995 sixth-form leavers went on to a degree course (20% after a gap year); others typically go on to careers, art/drama/music colleges or non-degree courses.. Of those going on to university, 10% went to Oxbridge; 10% took courses in medicine, dentistry and veterinary science, 40% in science and engineering, 10% in law, 30% in humanities and social sciences, 5% in art and design, 5% in music.

Curriculum GCSE, AS and A-levels. 18 GCSE subjects offered; 2 AS-level; 20 at A-level. Italian and Japanese offered in sixth-form. 45% took science A-levels; 20% arts/ humanities; 35% both. *Vocational:* Work experience available. *Computing facilities:* 2 suites of computer rooms (Amstrad, Nimbus) and facility for computer studies to A-level and IT Certificate of Competence. *Europe:* French, German and Spanish offered to GCSE and A-level; also French AS-level. Italian offered in sixth-form. Regular exchanges.
The arts *Music:* Up to 25% of pupils learn a musical instrument; instrumental exams can be taken. Some 7 musical groups including orchestra, choir, jazz band, string, brass ensembles. Winners of 4 categories of Belfast Music Festival. *Drama & dance*: Drama offered. Many pupils are involved in school productions. *Art:* On average, 30 take GCSE, 10 A-level. Winners of NI USPCA competition.
Sport, community service and clubs *Sport and physical activities:* Optional sports: rugby, hockey, cricket, rowing, athletics, tennis, badminton, golf, soccer, table-tennis, swimming, fencing. 44 pupils in 1995 represented Ulster/Northern Ireland and/or Ireland; All-Ireland Champions in hockey 1995–96; winner Ulster schools hockey, cricket and rugby 1995. *Community service:* Pupils take bronze, silver and gold Duke of Edinburgh's Award. CCF and community service optional; winners of 1991 Webb Ivory Award for fundraising in NI. *Clubs and societies:* Over 30 clubs, eg industry, role-playing, current affairs, debating, electronics, computing, media, foreign languages, classical.
Uniform School uniform worn throughout.
Houses/prefects Competitive houses. Prefects/Head boy, heads of houses and house prefects appointed by the Head, following discussions with staff and a poll of the lower sixth.
Social Drama and music with girls' schools; quizzes, debates, Christian Union with local schools. Trips abroad for skiing, Scouting, music (every 2 years); German school exchange. Pupils not allowed to bring own car/bike to school. Meals self-service. School shop. No tobacco/alcohol allowed.
Discipline Pupils failing to produce homework once might expect to be kept in or given detention; those caught smoking cannabis on the premises would be suspended immediately, followed by expulsion.
Former pupils Dawson Stelfox (Irish Everest Expedition 1993); Dr Brian Mawhinney (Minister of Health); Michael Longley (poet); Keith Crossan (Irish rugby winger); Sammy Nelson (Arsenal Double winning team).

• READ

Read School, Drax, Selby, North Yorkshire YO8 8NL. Tel 01757 618248, Fax 01757 617432, e-mail Jenny @ Handson.telme.com

• Pupils 220 • Boys 4–18 (Day/Board/Weekly) • Girls 4–18 (Day/Board/Weekly) • Upper sixth 12 • Termly fees £865–£1205 (Day) £2260–£2485 (Board) £2115–£2325 (Weekly) • ISAI, BSA • Enquiries/application to the Headmaster

What it's like

Founded in 1667, it has a very pleasant rural site in the village of Drax. Teaching is on two sites – the main campus for the senior department and the junior campus for 4–11; and boarding accommodation is on one site. Most of the buildings are early 19th century. There have been extensive developments in the last 30 years and facilities are good. A small school, it is caters for a wide range of ability, skills and interests. Strong music, drama and art departments. It gives a sound all-round education. Now co-educational, it was founded as a boys' school and admitted girls in 1991. A good range of sport, games and activities including CCF. Some involvement in local community services.

School profile

Pupils Total age range 4–18; 220 pupils, 160 day (115 boys, 45 girls) 60 boarding boys (boarding only from age 8). Senior department 11–18, 160 pupils (150 boys, 10 girls); girls have been admitted since1991. Main entry ages 4, 8, 11, 13 and into sixth. Approx 5% are children of former pupils. *State school entry:* 5% senior intake, plus 5% to sixth.
Entrance Admission by interview. No special skills or religious requirements. Parents not expected to buy textbooks; maximum compulsory extras, £5 plus trips etc. School

assisted places. 8 pa scholarships/bursaries, up to half tuition fee.
Parents 10+% in the armed services. 60% live within 30 miles; 15+% live overseas.
Head and staff *Headmaster:* Richard Hadfield, appointed 1996. Educated at Lancaster Royal Grammar School and York University. Previously Head of Sixth Form, Housemaster and Head of Chemistry at Gordonstoun. *Staff:* 18 full time, 4 part time. Annual turnover 5%. Average age 40.
Exam results In 1995, 26 pupils in upper fifth, 12 in upper sixth. *GCSE:* In 1995, 37% upper fifth gained at least grade C in 8+ subjects; 38% in 5–7; and 25% in 1–4 subjects. *A-levels:* 67% upper sixth passed in 3+ subjects; 17% in 2; and 17% in 1 subject. Average UCAS points 15.2.
University and college entrance 75% of 1995 sixth-form leavers went on to a degree course (very few after a gap year); others typically go on to commissions in armed services or other employment. Of those going on to university, 40% took courses in science and engineering, 30% in humanities and social sciences, 20% in art and design, 10% in other subjects eg agriculture.
Curriculum GCSE and *A-levels:* 15 subjects offered (including A-level general studies). 33% take science A-levels; 33% arts/humanities; 33% both.
Vocational Work experience available. *Computing facilities:* Nimbus 16-computer network plus several individual PCs. *Special provision:* Some extra English lessons provided. *Europe:* French and German offered at GCSE, French to AS and A-level.
The arts (Pupils aged 11 and over) *Music:* Up to 20% of pupils learn a musical instrument; instrumental exams can be taken. Some 4 musical groups: recorders, wind band, orchestra, choir. *Drama & dance*: Drama offered and GCSE and A-level may be taken. Some pupils are involved in school and house/other productions. *Art:* On average, 20 take GCSE, 2–3 A-level. Design also offered.
Sport, community service and clubs (Pupils aged 11 and over) *Sport and physical activities:* Compulsory sports: rugby, hockey, tennis, netball, cricket, cross-country. Optional: athletics, swimming, football, badminton. GCSE, A-level may be taken. *Community service:* CCF compulsory for 2 years from age 14, optional thereafter; strong involvement. Community service optional. *Clubs and societies:* Up to 10 clubs, eg YFC, fishing, tae kwan do, electronics, aerobics.
Uniform School uniform worn, except the sixth.
Houses/prefects Competitive houses for some sports. Prefects and head boy appointed by the Headmaster.
Religion C of E worship. RC worship also available in local church.
Social Many local events organised; some trips abroad. Pupils allowed to bring own bike/car to school. Meals self-service. School shop. No tobacco/alcohol allowed.
Discipline High standards expected. Suspension or expulsion for serious offences.
Boarding 10% have own study bedroom, 50% share with 1 other; 40% are in dormitories of 3–4. Resident qualified medical staff. Central dining room. 36 hour exeats on request. Visits to local town allowed with parental permission for pupils of 14+.
Alumni association run by its own officers, c/o Headmaster.
Former pupils John Sherwood (Olympic bronze medalist); Sir L V Appleyard (Ambassador to China).

• READING BLUE COAT

Reading Blue Coat School, Holme Park, Sonning, Berkshire RG4 6SU. Tel 01734 441005, Fax 01734 442690

• Pupils 540 • Boys 11–18 (Day/Board/Weekly) • Girls 16–18 (Day) • Upper sixth 64 • Termly fees £1838 (Day) £3350 (Board) £3245(Weekly) • HMC, BSA • Enquiries/application to the Headmaster

What it's like

Founded in 1646 by Richard Aldworth, a merchant of London and Reading. In 1947 it moved to its present premises at Holme Park. The main buildings comprise a magnificent brick-and-flint mansion in the Tudor collegiate style of architecture. It lies in a beautiful 45-acre wooded estate with a most agreeable frontage along the River Thames at Sonning Lock. The school is well appointed and comfortable and there are good modern facilities, including a new drama studio and IT centre. The school has kept close links with the Church of England but the main concern is that pupils are taught and learn in an atmosphere where Christian values and standards are recognised and established within the community. The staff:pupil ratio is about 1:11. A broad, sound and general education is provided and results are good. Most sixth-formers go on to degree courses, some to Oxbridge. Music is very strong and there is a variety of orchestral and choral groups. Art is also well supported. Facilities for games and sports (of which there is a standard range) are very good. The CCF is a large voluntary unit with Army, Navy and Air Force sections. A wide range of clubs and societies caters for most needs. Activities include archery, fencing and community work. Considerable enterprise is shown in organising expeditions, excursions and tours overseas.

School profile

Pupils Age range 11–18, 540 pupils, 485 day (455 boys, 30 girls), 55 boarding boys. Main entry ages 11, 13 (boys) and into sixth (boys and girls). *State school entry:* 50% main intakes, plus 25% to sixth.

Entrance Own entrance exam used. 6 pa scholarships, including music.

Head and staff *Headmaster:* Reverend Allan Sanders, in post for 22 years. Educated at Peter Symonds' School, Winchester, and Oxford University (chemistry). Previously Headmaster at Alliance High School, Kenya, and chemistry teacher at Monkton Combe. Also past chairman of Christians Abroad. *Staff:* 48 full time, 4 part time. Annual turnover 5%. Average age 39.

Exam results In 1995, 92 pupils in fifth, 64 in upper sixth. *GCSE:* In 1995, 95% fifth gained grade C or above in 7+ subjects. *A-levels:* 83% upper sixth passed in 3+ subjects. Average UCAS points 18.0.

University and college entrance 95% of 1995 sixth-form leavers went on to a degree course, others typically go directly to careers or art or drama colleges. Of those going on to university, 3% took courses in medicine, dentistry and veterinary science, 40% in science and engineering, 45% in humanities and social sciences, 6% in art and design, 6% in music.

Curriculum GCSE and *A-levels:* 20 subjects offered (including general studies). 40% took science A-levels, 42% arts/humanities; 17% in both. *Vocational:* Work experience in fourth year. *Computing facilities:* Nimbus network with 30 stations, 12 stations in resource area; new IT centre. *Europe:* French, German and Spanish offered to GCSE and A-level. Regular exchanges to France. European studies offered.

The arts *Music:* 25% of pupils learn a musical instrument; instrumental exams can be taken. Some 7 musical groups including orchestra, wind band, jazz band, choir. Some pupils in regional youth orchestra. *Drama & dance*: Theatre studies and drama offered. Pupils are involved in school and house/other productions. Pupils with parts in recent TV productions and films. *Art:* On average 27 take GCSE, 10 A-level. Design and photography also offered.

Sport, community service and clubs *Sport and physical activities:* No compulsory sports. Optional: rugby, soccer, hockey, cricket, athletics, rowing, squash, tennis etc. A-level sports studies may be taken. Represented national teams in rowing, county in hockey, cricket, swimming, triathlon. *Community service:* Pupils take bronze, silver and gold Duke of Edinburgh's Award. CCF and community service both optional from age 13. *Clubs and societies:* Up to 15 clubs, from chess to clay pigeon shooting.

Uniform School uniform worn except in sixth.

Houses/prefects Competitive houses. Prefects, head boy/girl, head of house and house prefects – appointed by Headmaster on the recommendation of staff and sixth-form. School Council.

Religion Attendance at religious worship compulsory.

Social Conferences (sixth-form) and lectures jointly with other local schools. Annual excursion for skiing; trips to France or Germany; pupil exchange with Canadian school. Pupils allowed to bring own car/bike/motorbike to school. Meals formal. No tobacco/alcohol allowed.

Discipline Pupils failing to produce homework once might expect to repeat the work; those caught smoking cannabis on the premises, expulsion.

• RED MAIDS'

The Red Maids' School, Westbury-on-Trym, Bristol BS9 3AW. Tel 0117 962 2641, Fax 0117 962 1687

• Pupils 500 • Boys None • Girls 11–18 (Day/Board) • Upper sixth 57 • Termly fees £1240 (Day) £2480 (Board) • GSA • Enquiries/application to the Headmistress

What it's like

Founded in 1634 through a bequest by John Whitson. It was originally a 'hospital for forty poor women children, daughters of Burgesses who were deceased or decayed'. The school owes its name to the fact that the inmates wore a costume of red cloth (still worn on ceremonial/traditional occasions). Today it occupies a fine 12-acre site in a north-west suburb of Bristol. It has handsome buildings, ancient and modern, set in beautiful gardens and grounds. Many modern additions provide comfortable accommodation and good up-to-date facilities. A sound general education is provided. Academic results are very good and most sixth-formers go on to degree courses each year. Music, drama and art are strongly supported. An impressive range of sports and games is available and high standards are attained (not a few girls represent the school at county level each year). There is some commitment to local community services and participation in the Duke of Edinburgh's Award Scheme and Young Enterprise.

School profile

Pupils Age range 11–18; 500 girls (400 day, 100 boarding). Main entry ages 11 and into sixth. *State school entry:* 75% main intake, plus a few to sixth.

Entrance Own entrance exam used. No special skills or religious requirements. Parents not expected to buy textbooks. 25 pa assisted places. 8 pa scholarships/bursaries (including 2 for music), up to 50% tuition fees.

Parents 15+% in the armed services; smaller percentage are doctors, lawyers or in industry.

Head and staff *Headmistress:* Miss Susan Hampton, in post for 9 years. Educated at Haberdashers' Monmouth Girls School and at London and Cambridge universities (mathematics and PGCE). Previously Deputy Head Kingsfield School and Senior Mistress at Redland High. Also past President, Soroptimist International of Bristol; Avon Outward Bound Council; Chairman GSA South-west and South Wales Region 1991–3. *Staff:* 35 full time, 16 part time. Annual turnover 6%. Average age late 30s.

Exam results In 1995, 74 pupils in upper fifth, 57 in upper sixth. *GCSE:* In 1995, 71 upper fifth gained at least grade C in 9 subjects; 3 in 5–8 subjects. *A-levels:* 4 upper sixth passed in 4+ subjects; 47 in 3; 4 in 2 subjects. Average UCAS points 23.3.

University and college entrance 90% of 1995 sixth-form leavers went on to a degree course; others typically go on to art, drama or music colleges. Of those going on to university, 9% took courses in medicine, dentistry and veterinary science, 28% in science and engineering, 60% in humanities and social sciences, 4% in art and design.

Curriculum GCSE, AS and A-levels. 19 subjects offered (including classical civilisation; AS-level general studies taken by all sixth-form). Approx 50% took science A-levels; 25% arts/humanities; 25% both. *Vocational:* Work experience available. *Computing facilities:* Osborne network, several standalone RM Nimbus and Apple Macs: Dartcom satellite system. *Special provision:* Extra English if needed for overseas pupils. *Europe:* French and Spanish to GCSE and A-level; also German, Italian and Russian GCSE. Regular exchanges (to France, Russia and Spain).

The arts *Music:* Over 50% of pupils learn a musical instrument; instrumental exams can be taken. Some 7 musical groups including choirs, orchestra, various instrumental ensembles. Pupils in 3 county orchestras. *Drama & dance*: Drama (first year only) and dance (first 3 years) offered. Majority of pupils are involved in school and house/other productions. Joint production of The Boy Friend with Queen Elizabeth's Hospital, 1995. *Art:* On average, 30 take GCSE, 2 AS-level, 10 A-level. Design technology, pottery and textiles also offered. Limited access to art facilities for non-examination pupils.

Sport, community service and clubs *Sport and physical activities:* Compulsory sports: hockey, netball, cross-country running, tennis, athletics, swimming (first 3 years). *Optional:* squash, badminton, fencing, volleyball, keep fit, weight training. GCSE exams may be taken. Pupils represent county in athletics, cross country, netball and hockey. *Community service:* Pupils take bronze and silver Duke of Edinburgh's Award.

Two head almoners organise charity events. *Clubs and societies:* Up to 10 clubs, eg music, sport, chess, Scrabble, Christian Union, Amnesty International, Guides.
Uniform School uniform worn, more flexible in sixth.
Houses/prefects Competitive houses. No prefects but head girls (1 day, 1 boarder) and heads of houses – elected by senior school. School Council.
Religion Compulsory worship.
Social Music/drama, joint Sunday service with brother school twice a term. Organised trips to Greece, Italy, France (choir tour and watersports); exchanges (including with school in Moscow 1996); Russian students from Moscow Languages Institute. Pupils allowed to bring own car/motorbike/bike to school. Meals formal at weekend lunchtimes, self-service weekday lunchtimes. School tuck shop. Sixth-form boarders may entertain friends in their common rooms during certain hours at weekends.
Boarding Upper sixth have own study bedroom; lower sixth in single study cubicles; rest in dormitories of 4+. Houses of up to 36, divided by age. SRN on duty/call. Central dining room. Upper sixth can provide and cook specified weekend meals. 5 exeats per term, and half-term; very flexible for sixth-form. Visits to local town allowed, accompanied until aged 13.
Alumni association is run by Mrs M Stone, c/o the school.

• REDLAND HIGH

Redland High School, Redland Court, Bristol BS6 7EF. Tel 0117 924 5796

• Pupils 650 • Boys None • Girls 3–18 (Day) • Upper sixth 52 • Termly fees £1400 (Day) • GSA, SHA • Enquiries/application to the Headmistress

What it's like

Founded in 1882 in Redland Grove as a small independent school. In 1885 it moved to its present site, where the main building is a handsome 18th-century mansion in pleasant gardens. The playing fields are a few minutes' walk away and the junior school opposite. Pupils come from all areas of Bristol and Avon and from all sections of the community. The sixth-form plays an important part in the running of the school. Academic standards high and results very good. Almost all sixth-formers go on to degree courses, including Oxbridge. Flourishing music, drama, arts and science. A full range of sports and games and a good variety of extra-curricular activities. Some commitment to local community services and an impressive record in the Duke of Edinburgh's Award Scheme. Every year there is a Young Enterprise Company in the School. Full use is made of Bristol's cultural amenities.

School profile

Pupils Total age range 3–18; 650 day girls. Senior department 11–18, 470 girls. Main entry ages 11 and into sixth.
Entrance Own entrance exam used. No special skills or religious requirements. Parents not expected to buy textbooks. Some assisted places. Scholarships and bursaries at 11 and in sixth-form.
Head and staff *Headmistress:* Mrs Carol Lear, 7 years in post. Educated at Colston's Girls' School and universities of London (classics) and Bristol (education). Previously Deputy Head and Head of Classics at Redland High and Examination Secretary at Red Maids'. Also President of Bristol Soroptomist and Secretary of Bristol Association of Classical Teachers. *Staff:* 41 full time, 19 part time. Annual turnover 8%. Average age 33.
Exam results In 1995, 75 pupils in upper fifth and 64 in upper sixth. *GCSE:* In 1995, 96% gained grade C or above in 8+ subjects. *A-levels:* 13% upper sixth passed in 4+ subjects; 79% in 3; and 7% in 2 subjects. Average UCAS points 22.0.
University and college entrance 99% of 1995 sixth-form leavers went on to a degree course, others typically go on to art or drama colleges. Of those going on to university, 5% went to Oxbridge; 5% took courses in medicine, dentistry and veterinary science, 45% in science and engineering, 43% in humanities and social sciences, 7% in art and design.
Curriculum GCSE and A-levels (including A-level history of art). 30% take science/engineering A-levels; 40% take arts/humanities; 30% a mixture. *Vocational:* Work experience available. *Computing facilities:* Computer room with 14 machines; compu-

ters also in technology, music and art & design departments. *Europe:* French, German and Spanish offered at GCSE and A-level. Regular exchanges and visits (France and Germany). Sixth formers attended Paris conference on Europe 1994.
The arts (Pupils aged 11 and over) *Music:* 25% of pupils learn a musical instrument; instrumental exams can be taken. Musical groups include orchestras, wind bands, choirs. Some members of National Youth Orchestra and county schools orchestra; 3 members of county school symphonic wind band. *Drama & dance*: Both offered. Majority of pupils are involved in school productions. Recent productions include A Midsummer Night's Dream and Le Petit Prince in French. *Art:* On average, 31 take GCSE, 13 A-level history of art, 7 art & design. Design, pottery, textiles also offered. Group prize won in secondary schools art competition in Bristol Cathedral.
Sport, community service and clubs (Pupils aged 11 and over) *Sport and physical activities:* Compulsory sports: hockey, netball, tennis, athletics, swimming, gymnastics, dance. Optional: cricket, soccer, squash, badminton, table tennis, weight training, outdoor pursuits. GCSE, BAGA exams may be taken. Tennis, netball and hockey teams regularly compete at national and county level. *Community service:* Pupils take bronze, silver and gold Duke of Edinburgh's Award. Community service optional. Fund-raising for numerous charities; parties for the elderly and children from local school for handicapped. *Clubs and societies:* Up to 10 clubs, eg drama, maths, computer, art history, various music and sports.
Uniform School uniform worn except in the sixth-form.
Houses/prefects No competitive houses or prefects but sixth-form executive committee; head girl – elected by staff and sixth. School Council.
Religion Daily school assembly
Social Occasional joint meetings, musical performances and drama productions with other city schools. Exchanges with schools in Bordeaux and Marburg (German); skiing trips abroad; history of art trip to Italy, Paris, Moscow and St Petersburg; visits to Italy and Greece. Pupils allowed to bring own car/bike to school. No tobacco/alcohol allowed.
Discipline High expectation of behaviour eventually leading to self-discipline.
Alumni association run by Mrs Sue Perry, c/o the school.

• REED'S

Reed's School, Sandy Lane, Cobham, Surrey KT11 2ES. Tel 01932 863076, Fax 01932 869046
• Pupils 330 • Boys 11–18 (Day/Board) • Girls 16–18 (Day/Board) • Upper sixth 35 • Termly fees £2162–£2580 (Day) £2893–£3413 (Board) • HMC • Enquiries/application to the Headmaster's Secretary

What it's like

Founded in 1813 by Andrew Reed for the purpose of educating boys whose fathers had died. In 1958 the school expanded and all boys became eligible for entrance, but Foundation awards are still granted each year to boys who have lost the support of one or both parents. Girls are now accepted into the sixth-form. It has a very agreeable semi-rural site of about 45 acres of heath, woodland and playing fields near Esher. There have been many developments and extensions as a result of which the school now well equipped. It is situated on a compact campus where the original buildings blend in with the modern. It is proud of its charitable foundation and the Christian principles of the founder live on. Ecumenical in spirit and policy, it has some emphasis on worship in chapel and religious education is part of the curriculum. There is a favourable staff:pupil ratio of about 1:10. Exam results are creditable and many pupils go on to degree courses each year. There are close ties with Holland and a Dutch school has separate premises on campus. Music, art and drama are strong. There is an adequate range of sports and games and a CCF contingent with both RAF and Army sections. Considerable emphasis on outdoor pursuits, practical skills and self-reliance. The Duke of Edinburgh's Award Scheme is well supported and there is some commitment to local community services.

School profile

Pupils Age range 11–18; 330 boys (190 day, 140 boarders). In addition, 25 Dutch pupils (15 boys, 10 girls), at a separate school on same campus, who join in certain activities.

Main entry ages, 11, 12, 13 (boys); into sixth (boys and girls). 3% are children of former pupils. Own junior school. *State school entry:* 40% main intakes.
Entrance Common Entrance and own exam. No special skills required. Parents not expected to buy textbooks; extras £50 maximum. 8 pa assisted places. Scholarships/bursaries, £100 to half-fees.
Parents 15+% in industry. 50+% live within 30 miles; up to 10% live overseas.
Head and staff *Headmaster:* D E Prince, in post for 13 years. Educated at Carres Grammar School, Sleaford, and Cambridge University (English). Previously Housemaster and CO of CCF at Uppingham and Assistant Housemaster and master i/c cricket at Reeds. Also Member HMC Committee and of ISCO Council, Chairman HMC Small Schools Group and Chairman of HMC East Division. *Staff:* 34 full time, 9 part time (including 6 music). Annual turnover 8%. Average age 36.
Exam results In 1995, 70 pupils in upper fifth, 35 in upper sixth. *GCSE:* In 1995, 42 upper fifth gained at least grade C in 8+ subjects; and 14 in 5–7 subjects. *A-levels:* 1 upper sixth passed in 4+ subjects; 18 in 3; 11 in 2; and 1 in 1 subject. Average UCAS points 14.8.
University and college entrance 70% of 1995 sixth-form leavers went on to a degree course; others typically go on to non-degree courses eg management, art or drama, or straight into careers (15%). Of those going on to university, 60% took courses in science and engineering, 30% in humanities and social sciences, 10% in art and design.
Curriculum GCSE and *A-levels:* 16 GCSE subjects offered; 15 at A-level. 20% take science A-levels; 55% arts/humanities; 25% both. *Vocational:* Work experience available. *Computing facilities:* 16 Nimbus Ethernet; 2 Apple Macintosh SEs, Dartcom, satellite software on Viglen DX486/33. *Special provision:* Part-time dyslexia specialist. *Europe:* French and German offered to GCSE, AS-level and A-level. Regular exchanges (France, Holland and Germany). Unique link with Rijnlands Lyceum – a Dutch school for some 30 pupils (some are children of Dutch businessmen and diplomats living in the UK), which has a classroom block on the Reeds campus; its pupils follow their Dutch curriculum but join Reeds classes for art, music, technology, PE and all extra-mural activities; strong links maintained between Reeds and the parent school in Holland.
The arts *Music:* 30% of pupils learn a musical instrument; instrumental exams can be taken. Some 5 musical groups including choral, brass, wind, string, popular. Recent pupil won prize for composition at Royal College of Music. *Drama & dance*: Drama offered and GCSE may be taken. Some pupils are involved in school productions and majority of pupils in house/other productions. *Art:* On average, 30 take GCSE, 8 A-level. Design also offered.
Sport, community service and clubs *Sport and physical activities:* Compulsory sports: rugby, hockey, cricket (first year only). Optional: tennis, badminton, swimming, karate, squash, athletics. 2 in county hockey squad. *Community service:* Pupils take silver and gold Duke of Edinburgh's Award. CCF available; 19 RAF flying scholarships in last 25 years. *Clubs and societies:* Up to 10 clubs, eg chess, photography, printing.
Uniform School uniform worn; sixth-form may wear 'office dress'.
Houses/prefects Competitive houses. Prefects (elected by sixth-form and staff), head boy (appointed by the Head), head of house, house prefects. School Committee – no executive powers.
Religion Compulsory chapel.
Social Debates and outings with several local girls' schools. Organised trips abroad. Day pupils allowed to bring own car/motorbike/bike to school. Meals self service. No tobacco/alcohol allowed.
Discipline Pupils failing to produce homework once might expect a comment in record book and to do it again; those caught smoking cannabis on the premises might expect expulsion.
Boarding Sixth form have own house with single study bedrooms. Years 3–5 are in dormitories of 4–8; years 1–2 are in a separate house. Resident qualified nurse. Central dining room. Pupils can provide and cook own food – limited facilities. Visits to local town allowed, strict control to age 13.
Former pupils John Alvey (Chairman of Alvey Committee); Brian Miles (Director RNLI); Simon Keenlyside (opera singer); Tim Henman (Davis Cup tennis player).

• REIGATE GRAMMAR

Reigate Grammar School, Reigate Road, Reigate, Surrey RH2 0QS. Tel 01737 222231, Fax 01737 224201

• Pupils 800 • Boys 10–18 (Day) • Girls 10–18 (Day) • Upper sixth 120 • Termly fees £1624 (Day) • HMC • Enquiries/application to the Headmaster

What it's like

Founded in 1675 as a free school for ten poor boys and endowed through a bequest of Henry Smith, Alderman of the City of London. The buildings are situated in pleasant surroundings to the east of Reigate town centre within easy reach of local public transport. Recent additions include the art and technology centre, opened in 1995. There are 33 acres of playing fields, including an all-weather surface, two miles away at Hartswood. The school seeks to provide an education based on sound Christian principles and all pupils are expected to attend school services and religious education lessons unless exempted. The school has been fully co-educational since 1993 (there have been girls in the sixth-form since 1976). The staff:pupil ratio is about 1:12. A sound, general education is provided, academic standards are high and results are very good; most sixth-formers go on to university. Music and drama are very strongly supported and large numbers of pupils take part. There is much strength in sports and games and the school has a long record of success in district, county and national competitions. A wide variety of clubs and societies is available and a flourishing CCF contingent and a Sea Scout group. The Duke of Edinburgh's Award Scheme has always been well supported and the school has gained over 200 gold awards. Social and community service is a major feature of this scheme at Reigate.

School profile

Pupils Age range 10–18, 800 day pupils, 650 boys, 150 girls. Main entry ages 10, 11, 13 and into the sixth. *State school entry:* 50% main intake, plus 15% to sixth.

Entrance Common Entrance and own exam used. 30 pa assisted places. Scholarships at 10, 11 and 13; bursaries.

Head and staff *Headmaster:* Paul Dixon, appointed 1996. Educated at Bexhill County Grammar School and Oxford University (zoology). Previously Second Master at Stockport Grammar and has taught at St Dunstan's, Brighton College and at Winchester. *Staff:* 67 full time, 3 part time. Annual turnover less than 10%

Exam results In 1995, 128 pupils in fifth, 96 in upper sixth. *GCSE:* In 1995, 115 upper fifth gained at least grade C in 8+ subjects; 13 in 5–7 subjects. *A-levels:* 13 upper sixth passed in 4+ subjects; 74 in 3; 7 in 2; and 2 in 1 subject. Average UCAS points 20.9.

University and college entrance 90% of 1995 sixth-form leavers went on to a degree course (15% after a gap year); others typically go on to art foundation courses, HNDs etc. Of those going on to university, 10% went to Oxbridge; 6% took courses in medicine, dentistry and veterinary science, 34% in science and engineering, 58% in humanities and social sciences, 2% in art and design.

Curriculum GCSE and *A-levels:* 22 subjects offered (no A-level general studies). 25% take science A-levels; 60% arts/humanities; 15% both. *Vocational:* Work experience available. *Computing facilities:* 35 Archimedes and 12 PCs. *Europe:* French, German and Spanish offered to GCSE and A-level. Regular exchanges.

The arts *Music:* Up to 15% of pupils learn a musical instrument; instrumental exams can be taken. Some 8 musical groups including orchestra, wind band, choir, vocal, brass ensemble. Recent full performances with orchestra of The Creation, Elijah, St John's Passion and Messiah. *Drama & dance*: Drama offered and A-level theatre studies may be taken. Many pupils are involved in school productions (recently include Journey's End, Bugsy Malone, Brecht's Good Person of Setzuan, Euripides' Hecuba). *Art:* On average, 35 take GCSE, 7 A-level. Design, pottery, photography also offered. Separate sixth-form studio area.

Sport, community service and clubs *Sport and physical activities:* Compulsory sports (to certain ages): hockey, netball (girls), rugby (boys). Optional: cross-country, cricket, swimming, athletics, tennis, badminton, gymnastics. Sixth form only: soccer, sailing, golf. GCSE and A-level sports studies may be taken. Final four of national squash inter-schools tournament. *Community service:* Pupils take bronze, silver and gold Duke of Edinburgh's Award; about 15 golds each year. CCF and community service both

optional. *Clubs and societies:* Up to 30 clubs, eg debating, Christian Union, history, Model United Nations, philately, model railway, science, sports.
Uniform School uniform worn throughout.
Houses/prefects Competitive houses. Prefects, school captain, head of house and house prefects – appointed by the Headmaster in consultation with staff.
Religion Attendance at religious worship compulsory.
Social Rotary public speaking competition with other local schools. Numerous visits abroad; in 1995–6 to Switzerland, Ireland, France, South Africa. Pupils allowed to bring own car/bike/motorbike to school. Meals self-service. No tobacco/alcohol allowed.
Discipline Pupils failing to produce homework once might expect to have to do the work by the next lesson or during lunch break; for those caught smoking cannabis on the premises expulsion would be likely, unless there were exceptionally strong mitigating circumstances. There are published school policies on behaviour, bullying and the disciplining of students who may become involved with drugs.
Former pupils Lord Sterling of Plaistow (Chairman P & O); Mr Justice Hidden (High Court judge); Bill Frindall (cricket statistician).

• RENDCOMB

Rendcomb College, Cirencester, Gloucestershire GL7 7HA. Tel 01285 831213, Fax 01285 831331

• Pupils 250 • Boys 11–18 (Day/Board/Weekly) • Girls 11–18 (Day/Board/Weekly) • Upper sixth 40 • Termly fees from £2144–£2814 (Day) £2769–£3558 (Board) • HMC • Enquiries/application to the Headmaster

What it's like

Founded in 1920 as a boys' school, it has been co-educational since 1992. It has very handsome buildings and is part of a tiny village in a superb 200-acre estate of Gloucestershire countryside. Generously endowed, it has excellent modern facilities and recent developments include new boarding houses and modern languages classrooms. A very friendly atmosphere prevails; it has all the advantages of a small school and describes itself as unpretentious, business-like, hardworking and caring. A good staff:pupil ratio of about 1:10. Academic results are good and almost all sixth-form leavers go on to degree courses, including some to Oxbridge. Very strong music, drama and art departments. Big commitment to local community schemes and an impressive record in the Duke of Edinburgh's Award Scheme.

School profile

Pupils Age range 11–18; 250 pupils, 40 day (20 boys, 20 girls), 210 boarding (155 boys, 55 girls). Main entry ages 11, 13 and into sixth. Approx 5% are children of former pupils. *State school entry:* 40% main intake, plus 25% to sixth.
Entrance Common Entrance and own exam used. No special skills or religious requirements. Music tuition extra (£50 per term). 5 pa assisted places. 12 pa scholarships (academic, art, music and sport), £800 to full fees. Bursaries for children of HM forces.
Parents 15+% in industry or commerce; 15% in armed services. 50+% live within 30 miles; up to 10% live overseas.
Head and staff *Headmaster:* John Tolputt, in post for 9 years. Educated at Ardingly and Cambridge (English). Previously Head of English and Drama at Bromsgrove and at Cranleigh. *Staff:* 26 full time, 10 part time. Annual turnover 2%. Average age 35.
Exam results On average, 40 pupils in upper fifth, 40 in upper sixth. *GCSE:* On average, 54% upper fifth gain at least grade C in 8+ subjects; 28% in 5–7; and 10% in 1–4 subjects. *A-levels:* 8% upper sixth pass in 4+ subjects; 78% in 3; 9% in 2; and 5% in 1 subject. Average UCAS points 15.6.
University and college entrance 90% of 1995 sixth-form leavers went on to a degree course (50% after a gap year); others typically go on to HND and foundation courses. Of those going on to university, 10% went to Oxbridge; 10% took courses in medicine, dentistry and veterinary science, 25% in science and engineering, 10% in law, 40% in humanities and social sciences, 10% in art and design, 5% in other vocational subjects.
Curriculum GCSE and A-levels offered (no A-level general studies). 33% take science A-levels; 33% arts/humanities; 33% both. *Vocational:* Work experience available. *Computing*

facilities: Computer room, network. *Europe:* French and German offered to GCSE and A-level; French also a non-examined subject. Regular exchanges. German students regularly in sixth-form, for 1–2 years. Satellite-receiving equipment in languages department.

The arts *Music:* Over 50% of pupils learn a musical instrument; instrumental exams can be taken. Some 8 musical groups including orchestra, Dixieland, wind, string band, chamber group, choir, choral society, several rock groups. *Drama & dance*: Both offered. AS-level and A-level performing arts and LAMDA exams may be taken. Majority of pupils are involved in school and house/other productions. *Art:* On average, 20 take GCSE, 10 A-level; design, pottery, textiles and photography also offered. Art facilities open to non-examination pupils. About 4 per year go on to art schools.

Sport, community service and clubs *Sport and physical activities:* Optional sports: rugby, hockey, cricket, tennis, squash, badminton, netball, archery, judo. 2 in county U18 rugby, 2 U14 hockey squad. *Community service:* Pupils take bronze and gold Duke of Edinburgh's Award. Community service optional for 2 years at age 16. Several local awards for community service. *Clubs and societies:* Up to 30 clubs, eg stamps, skiing, fishing, ballroom, dancing, debating, shooting.

Uniform School uniform worn throughout (except by sixth-form in free time).

Houses/prefects No competitive houses. Prefects, head boy and girl, head of house and house prefects – appointed by the Headmaster and staff. School Council.

Religion Compulsory assembly twice a week, church service on Sundays.

Social Numerous social events with other schools. Exchanges with France and Germany. Pupils allowed to bring own bike to school. Meals self-service. Village shop in grounds. No tobacco allowed; alcohol allowed in sixth-form bar.

Discipline Pupils failing to produce homework once might expect to be kept back to do it; those caught smoking cannabis on the premises may expect expulsion.

Boarding Fifth and sixth-forms have own study bedrooms, others share with up to 4. Single-sex houses, of approximately 50. Resident qualified nurses; doctor in village. Central dining room. Pupils can provide and cook own food. Half-term and 2 long weekend exeats each term. Visits to local town allowed with permission.

Alumni association is run by Christopher Wood, c/o the College.

Former pupils David Vaisey (Bodleian Librarian); Richard Dunwoody (Grand National winning jockey).

• REPTON

Repton School, The Hall, Repton, Derby DE65 6FH. Tel 01283 702375

• Pupils 560 • Boys 13–18 (Day/Board) • Girls 13–18 (Day/Board) • Upper sixth 130 • Termly fees £2910 (Day) £3868 (Board) • HMC • Enquiries to the Headmaster • Application to the Registrar

What it's like

Founded in 1557 as a boys' school and with a decade of experience of girls in its sixth-form, Repton became fully co-educational in 1992. Two purpose-built houses have been built to accommodate girls. The school is an integral part of the village of Repton and vice versa. A civilised environment in which the architecture is very pleasing, as are the beautiful surroundings. Facilities are extremely good. It is a C of E foundation and emphasis is given to Anglican worship and practice. Results are very good and nearly all leavers proceed to degree courses each year, including Oxbridge. Very strong music and art departments, and an outstanding record of dramatic presentations of many kinds. A very wide range of sports and games is on offer and standards are high (many representatives at county level). Tennis is particularly strong (recognised by the LTA as one of the best schools). The CCF is strong and outdoor pursuits and adventure training have vigorous support. A high commitment to local community services in and around Repton and an impressive record in the Duke of Edinburgh's Award Scheme.

School profile

Pupils Age range 13–18; 560 pupils, 170 day (125 boys, 45 girls), 390 boarding (300 boys, 90 girls). Main entry ages 13 and into the sixth. Approx 10% are children of former pupils. 50% intake from own prep school (Foremarke Hall, tel 01283 703269). *State school entry:* 5% main intake, plus some into sixth.

Entrance Common Entrance exam used. Credit given for extra-curricular activities; all denominations and religions welcomed. Parents not expected to buy textbooks; £50 maximum extras. 12 pa assisted places. Numerous scholarships, exhibitions, music and art awards, up to 50% fees.

Head and staff *Headmaster:* G E Jones, in post for 9 years. Educated at Birkenhead and Cambridge (economics). Previously Housemaster, Head of Economics and Politics at Charterhouse and on secondment at BP. Also Chairman HMC Midlands Division; formerly Awarder in Economics, O&C Examining Board and Reviser for JMB. *Staff:* 69 full time, 4 part time. Annual turnover 5%

Exam results In 1995, 119 pupils in upper fifth, 134 in upper sixth. *GCSE:* In 1995, 112 upper fifth gained at least grade C in 8+ subjects; 6 in 5–7 subjects. *A-levels:* 10 upper sixth passed in 4+ subjects; 97 in 3 subjects (all excluding general studies). Average UCAS points 22.0.

University and college entrance 95% of 1995 sixth-form leavers went on to a degree course (2% after a gap year); others typically go on to other courses eg art. Of those going on to university, 10% went to Oxbridge; 7% took courses in medicine, dentistry and veterinary science, 26% in science and engineering, 63% in humanities and social sciences, 3% in art and design, 1% in music.

Curriculum GCSE and *A-levels:* 23 GCSE subjects offered; 19 at A-level (including A-level general studies). 30% took science A-levels; 30% arts/humanities; 40% both. *Vocational:* Work experience available. *Computing facilities:* 8 BBC Masters; 45 Apple Macs; 20 Archimedes, 7 IBM PCs, laser/colour printers, scanner, modems, CD-Rom drives etc. *Special provision:* Special tutor for dyslexic pupils. *Europe:* French and German offered at GCSE and A-level; usually Italian and Spanish as non-examined subjects.

The arts *Music:* Over 30% of pupils learn a musical instrument; instrumental exams can be taken. Some 15 musical groups including concert band, choral society, chapel choir, brass, string orchestra, chamber ensembles. *Drama & dance*: Drama offered and GCSE may be taken. Some pupils are involved in school productions and majority in house/other productions. *Art:* On average, 30 take GCSE, 20 A-level. Design, pottery and photography also offered.

Sport, community service and clubs *Sport and physical activities:* Compulsory sports: football, hockey, cricket, netball. Optional: tennis, cross-country, athletics, rugby, swimming, fencing, squash, sailing, badminton, golf. GCSE sports studies may be taken. *Community service:* Pupils take bronze, silver and gold Duke of Edinburgh's Award. CCF compulsory for 2 years at age 14; community service optional. *Clubs and societies:* Up to 30 clubs, eg chess, debating, geographical, Wildfowl Trust, historical, musical, video, dramatic, art society.

Uniform School uniform worn except in the sixth.

Houses/prefects Competitive houses. Prefects, head boy/girl, head of house and house prefects – appointed by the Headmaster and the Housemaster/mistress. No personal fagging; some communal services.

Religion Friday morning assembly, Sunday matins. Frequent voluntary services.

Social Modern languages exchanges can be arranged. Overseas trips have included cricket, mountaineering, hockey, skiing, music, art, athletics etc. Meals formal, by house. School shop. No pupils allowed tobacco. Upper sixth-form allowed limited amount of alcohol three evenings/week.

Discipline Pupils failing to produce homework once might expect extra work; those caught smoking cannabis on the premises would be required to leave the school.

Boarding 10% have own study bedroom, 19% share (2 or 3); 71% are in dormitories of 4+. Single sex houses, of 55–60. Resident qualified nurse and doctor. Each house has its own dining room. Pupils can provide and cook own food. Half-term plus 1 weekend exeat each term and as many Sundays as required. Visits to the local town allowed, mostly for sixth-formers.

Alumni association is run by J R Muir, 6 Chestnut Way, Repton, Derby.

Former pupils Sir John Tooley (Royal Opera House); Robert Sangster (racehorse owner); Ian Grist MP; Sir John Stanley MP (Minister of State, Northern Ireland); Graeme Garden (TV); Roald Dahl (author); James Fenton (poet); Richard Heller (political journalist); Donald Carr and Richard Hutton (cricketers); Lord Ramsey (Archbishop of Canterbury); Sir J Grindrod (Archbishop of Australia).

• RICKMANSWORTH MASONIC

The Rickmansworth Masonic School, Rickmansworth Park, Rickmansworth, Hertfordshire WD3 4HF. Tel 01923 773168, Fax 01923 896729

• Pupils 690 • Boys None • Girls 4–18 (Day/Board) • Upper sixth 70 • Termly fees £1787 (Day) £2937 (Board) £2912 (Weekly) • GSA • Enquiries to the Headmistress • Applications to the Admissions Secretary

What it's like

Founded in 1788, it moved in 1934 from Central London to the Chilterns. Here there is an exceptionally fine purpose-built establishment of elegant and well-appointed buildings, in 315 acres of superb grounds. Extremely comfortable accommodation and first-rate facilities, including an unusually fine library. The teaching is of a high standard with a staff:pupil ratio of about 1:12. Many sixth-formers go on to degree courses. Strong in music, drama and art. There is much emphasis on debating and public speaking. A feature is the school drill: a display of callisthenics and movement. A good range of games, sport and activities. A fine record in the Duke of Edinburgh's Award Scheme.

School profile

Pupils Total age range 4–18; 690 girls, 430 day, 260 boarding (boarding from age 7 only). Senior department 11–18, 490 girls. Main entry age 4–7, 11 and into sixth.
Entrance Own entrance exam and interview used. No special skills required; school is a Christian foundation but accepts pupils of all faiths and none. Parents not expected to buy textbooks, nor pay for field trips or exams; extras include music, drama, dancing, sport etc. 22 pa scholarships and plentiful bursaries for masonic families in need; scholarships £1000–£5303 pa.
Parents 15 + % in industry or commerce. 30 + % live within 30 miles; up to 10% live overseas.
Head and staff *Headmistress:* Mrs I M Andrews, 3 years in post. Educated at Oxford University (English) and Institute of Education. Previously Deputy Head (Academic) at Rickmansworth Masonic, Head of English at St Margaret's (Bushey), English Teacher at Haberdashers' Aske's (Girls') and Tutor and Counsellor at the Open University. *Staff:* 54 full time, 13 part time plus music staff. Annual turnover 5–10%. Average age 38.
Exam results In 1995, 75 pupils in upper fifth, 70 in upper sixth, of whom 63 took A-levels. *GCSE:* 55% pupils gained grade C or above in 8 + subjects; and 21% in 5-7 subjects. *A-levels:* 31 pupils in upper sixth passed in 3 subjects; 16 in 2; and 14 in 1 subject. Average UCAS points 15.2.
University and college entrance 75% of sixth-form leavers go on to a degree course (17% after a gap year); others typically go on to foundation courses, NNEB or other vocational courses or into employment. Of those going on to university, 2% go to Oxbridge; 4% take courses in medicine, dentistry and veterinary science, 22% in science and engineering, 2% in law, 40% in humanities and social sciences, 20% in art and design, 20% in vocational subjects eg physiotherapy, hospitality management.
Curriculum GCSE, A-levels and advanced GNVQ. Subjects include A-level psychology, economics, politics and geology. 28% take science A-levels; 50% arts/humanities; 22% both. *Vocational:* Work experience available; also RSA and Pitman wordprocessing, shorthand, typewriting and secretarial skills and T-line shorthand. Advanced GNVQ in business studies. *Computing facilities:* 2 laboratories with 20 working computers. Individual computers in other departments. *Special provision:* for mildly dyslexic pupils. *Europe:* French (compulsory from age 9) and German offered at GCSE, AS-level and A-level; also Spanish GCSE and A-level. Regular exchanges to France.
The arts (Pupils aged 11 and over) *Music:* Over 50% of pupils learn a musical instrument; instrumental exams can be taken. Some 8 musical groups including 3 choirs, orchestra, brass & woodwind ensembles, recorder consorts. Senior choir, tours in Canada and United States; chapel choir, evensong in St Paul's and other cathedrals; senior and junior choirs in national finals McDonald's Music in the Community and in West End production of Joseph and his Amazing Technicolor Dreamcoat. *Drama & dance:* Both offered. GCSE, AS-level, A-level drama and Poetry Society exams may be taken. Majority of pupils are involved in school productions and all pupils in house/other productions. 2 major productions annually; some pupils in National Youth Theatre. *Art:* On average, 30 take GCSE, 10 A-level. Design, pottery, textiles and photography also

offered. Design awards in national competitions organised by Sock Shop and BBC TV's Clothes Show.
Sport, community service and clubs (Pupils aged 11 and over) *Sport and physical activities:* Compulsory sports: netball, tennis, hockey, swimming, rounders. Optional: aerobics, trampolining, badminton, squash, fencing, riding. Sixth form only: golf. BAGA and RLSS exams may be taken. *Community service:* Pupils take bronze, silver and gold Duke of Edinburgh's Award. CCF and community service optional. *Clubs and societies:* Up to 30 clubs.
Uniform School uniform worn, modified in sixth.
Houses/prefects Competitive houses. Prefects, head girl, head of house and house prefects appointed by the Headmistress with recommendations from staff and senior pupils. School council with elected chair.
Religion Attendance at religious worship compulsory on Sundays.
Social Joint debates, theatrical productions, musicals, games etc with other schools; also with the general public. Organised trips abroad. Pupils allowed to bring own car to school. A few meals formal, most self-service. School shop. No tobacco/alcohol allowed.
Discipline Pupils failing to produce homework once might expect a warning; persistent offenders, a detention; anybody caught smoking or drinking on premises after a first warning could expect a letter home followed by suspension/expulsion for repeated offenders.
Boarding 32% have own study bedroom, 8% share; 60% are in dormitories of 6+. Houses of 40-48; separate houses for juniors and for sixth-formers. 2 qualified sisters and 1 nursing assistant. Central dining room. Seniors can provide and cook own food. 2 weekend exeats each term, plus half-term; more flexible exeats for sixth-formers. Visits to the local town allowed weekly for juniors; more often and unaccompanied for 16+.
Alumni association is run by Mrs Rosemary Turney, Hon Sec OMGA, c/o the school.
Former pupils First female president of Cambridge Union.

• RISHWORTH

Rishworth School, Rishworth, Sowerby Bridge, West Yorkshire HX6 4QA. Tel 01422 822217, Fax 01422 823231

• Pupils 530 • Boys 3–18 (Day/Board/Weekly) • Girls 3–18 (Day/Board/Weekly) • Upper sixth 42 • Termly fees £830–£1622 (Day) £2960-£3220 (Board) • SHMIS • Enquiries/application to the Headmaster's Secretary

What it's like

Founded in 1724, as a boys' school, it is now co-educational (girls were first admitted in 1968). It has occupied its present site since 1826, in a beautiful valley (20 miles from Manchester and Leeds) with extensive gardens and grounds. The buildings are handsome, solid, stone-built and there have been many modern additions which provide good accommodation and up-to-date facilities. The original school has become the chapel and there is some emphasis on worship and religious instruction. A good deal of attention is given to the principles and practice of Christianity. A broad general education is provided and the aim is to create a social and scholastic society in which boys and girls contribute as fully as possible to each other's education. Academic standards are high and results are good. Many sixth-formers go on to degree courses each year. Strong music and drama departments. A good range of games and sports, and also extra-curricular activities. Considerable emphasis on outdoor pursuits for which the surroundings are ideal. The school has an outstanding record in the Duke of Edinburgh's Award Scheme.

School profile

Pupils Total age range 3–18; 530 pupils, 446 day (244 boys, 202 girls), 84 boarding (52 boys, 32 girls); boarding only from age 11. Senior department 11–18. Main entry ages, 4, 7, 11 and into the sixth. 10% are children of former pupils. Own prep department provides 50% of senior intake. *State school entry:* 40% senior intake, plus 70% to sixth.
Entrance Common Entrance and own exam used. No special skills or religious requirements. Parents not expected to buy textbooks. 5 pa scholarships at 11, more for sixth-form based on GCSE performance, all 33% tuition fee. 10% reductions for children of C of E priesthood or the armed services.

Parents 15+% in industry or commerce. 30+% live within 30 miles; 10+% live overseas.

Head and staff *Headmaster:* Michael Elford, 4 years in post. Educated at Queen Elizabeth's Grammar, Wakefield, St Luke's College, Exeter, and Bradford University (applied educational studies). Previously Director of Physical Education at Bradford Grammar and Deputy Head at Silcoates. Also former rugby coach to the Yorkshire Senior XV and the Yorkshire and England Schools XVs. *Staff:* 48 full time, 3 part time. Annual turnover 4%. Average age 38

Exam results In 1995, 89 pupils in upper fifth, 42 in upper sixth. *GCSE:* In 1995, 49% of fifth formers gained at least grade C in 8+ subjects; 24% in 5–7 subjects. *A-levels:* 33% upper sixth passed in 4+ subjects; 38% in 3; 18% in 2; and 7% in 1 subject. Average UCAS points 14.8 (including general studies 18.0).

University and college entrance 90% of 1995 sixth-form leavers went on to a degree course (5% after a gap year); others typically go on to employment. Of those going on to university, 6% went to Oxbridge; 6% took courses in medicine, dentistry and veterinary science, 44% in science and engineering, 3% in law, 21% in humanities and social sciences, 6% in art and design, 20% in other subjects.

Curriculum GCSE and *A-levels:* 24 GCSE and A-level subjects offered (including Chinese, performing arts; A-level general studies for all sixth). 30% take science A-levels; 40% arts/humanities; 30% both. *Vocational:* Work experience available. *Computing facilities:* 25 Nimbus, 10 Autocad, 12 Acorn. *Special provision:* Some help from qualified staff for dyslexics. EFL tuition available. *Europe:* French, German and Spanish offered to GCSE and A-level; also French AS-level, French and German to Institute of Linguists. Regular exchanges.

The arts (Pupils aged 11 and over) *Music:* Over 10% of pupils learn a musical instrument; instrumental exams can be taken. Some 6 musical groups including choirs, chamber music groups (strings, wind, brass etc). Finals of Young Singer of the Year competition, auditions for National Youth Orchestra etc. *Drama & dance*: Drama offered; GCSE drama and A-level performing arts may be taken. Some pupils are involved in school and house/other productions. *Art:* On average, 20 take GCSE, 6 A-level. Design also offered.

Sport, community service and clubs (Pupils aged 11 and over) *Sport and physical activities:* Optional sports: rugby, hockey, netball and cricket are main sports, plus many others. GCSE and A-level sports studies may be taken. Many pupils represent county in various sports, some at national levels in athletics and cross-country, 1 international junior tri-athlete. *Community service:* Pupils take bronze, silver and gold Duke of Edinburgh's Award. *Clubs and societies:* Up to 10 clubs, eg chess, radio amateurs, various sports, debating.

Uniform School uniform worn throughout.

Houses/prefects Non-competitive houses. Head of school, prefects, head of house and house prefects – appointed by Headmaster.

Religion Religious worship encouraged; chapel attendance not compulsory in senior school.

Social Joint musical competition with local schools. 3 trips to France, 1 to Spain, 2 skiing trips. Day pupils allowed to bring own car to school. Meals self-service. School shop. No tobacco/alcohol allowed.

Boarding 45% have own study bedroom, 50% share with 2 and 5% in dormitories of 6+. Central dining room. Pupils can provide and cook some own food. 2 or 3 weekend exeats each term. Seniors allowed weekly visits to local towns.

Discipline Each incident dealt with on its merits, extenuating circumstances, if any, taken into consideration. Late work/work not done may be re-done, possibly twice or individual members of staff would detain pupils. For serious matters the Headmaster reserves the right to suspend or expel.

• RNIB NEW COLLEGE

RNIB New College Worcester, Whittington Road, Worcester WR5 2JX. Tel 01905 763933, Fax 01905 763277

• Pupils 120 • Boys 11–18 (Day/Board) • Girls 11–18 (Day/Board) • Upper sixth 13 • Termly fees £5020 (Day) £7531 (Boarding) – Fees normally payable by LEA • HMC • Enquiries/application to the Principal

What it's like

A national and international specialist school for blind students or those with seriously defective sight, who are academically able. Very well equipped for teaching and for learning skills: there are six boarding houses, a sixth-form hostel, swimming pool, football pitch, on-site ski slope and a multi-sensing maze. Founded as a boys' school, it has accepted girls since 1986. All pupils follow the National Curriculum, combined with a thorough programme of mobility and living skills and an extensive range of outdoor and leisure activities, including outward bound. Almost all sixth-formers go on to degree courses, many to Oxbridge. A very large staff allows a staff:pupil ratio of better then 1:4. Most teaching groups have a maximum of 10 and the average class size is 6. Administered by the RNIB, fees are normally paid by the pupil's local education authority or, in the case of some post-16 pupils, the Further Education Funding Council (FEFC). The aim of the school is to enable pupils to advance to the chosen course of higher education, having the confidence to take their place in society on equal terms with their sighted counterparts.

School profile

Pupils Age range 11–18 (exceptionally, younger children accepted); 120 pupils, 3 day (1 boy, 2 girls), 117 boarding (68 boys, 49 girls). Main entry ages 11 and into sixth but also at any age or time appropriate to the pupil.

Entrance Own assessment used but all pupils must be able to benefit from GCSE and A-level courses. Most pupils' fees covered by their LEA or in some cases the FEFC.

Head and staff *Principal:* Helen Williams, in post since 1995. Educated at Redland High and Cambridge (English). Previously High Mistress of St Paul's Girls School, Headmistress of Blackheath High School and lecturer in English at Edinburgh University. Also on governing body of SOAS and Stowe School. *Staff:* 33 full time, plus a number of part time. All teaching staff are experienced teachers in their own subject, who have qualified to teach the visually impaired; care staff also with specialist qualifications.

University and college entrance 95% of 1995 sixth-form leavers went on to a degree course (5% after a gap year); others typically go on to further education or straight into employment. Of those going on to university, 10% went to Oxbridge; 15% took courses in science and engineering, 5% in law, 55% in humanities and social sciences, 5% in art and design, 5% in other vocational subjects.

Curriculum GCSE, AS and *A-levels:* 20 subjects offered (if students want to study unusual subjects eg Urdu or Japanese, this can be arranged). Most pupils take 8 GCSEs before joining the sixth-form. *Vocational:* Work experience available. *Computing facilities:* 4 IT rooms, and equipment in library/electronic classrooms etc. *Special provision:* All pupils are severely visually handicapped and may have other disabilities. Small teaching groups and teaching adapted to cater for pupils' needs. Short-term arrangements can be made for those who have just experienced the onset of blindness. *Europe:* French and German offered to GCSE and A-level. Regular exchanges.

The arts *Music:* Over 30% of pupils learn a musical instrument; instrumental exams can be taken. Some 4 musical groups: choral, wind, rock, folk. *Drama & dance*: GCSE expressive arts and A-level theatre studies may be taken. Some pupils are involved in school productions and the majority in house/other productions. *Art:* Art and design offered.

Sport, community service and clubs *Sport and physical activities:* Compulsory sports: Athletics, swimming; boys – football, cricket; girls – gym, dance, trampoline. Optional: canoeing, cycling/tandeming. BAGA, RLSS, ASA and BTF exams may be taken. *Community service:* Pupils take bronze, silver and gold Duke of Edinburgh's Award. *Clubs and societies:* Up to 15 clubs, eg choir, chess, craft, swimming, radio, aerobics, trampolining.

Uniform School uniform worn up to Year 10.

Houses/prefects No competitive houses. Head boy/girl jointly elected by staff and pupils. School Council.

Religion All denominations accepted. Religious education is given on a broad basis with Christianity at its centre.
Social Pupils live in family units, moving on to a sixth-form student hostel when older. Special attention is given to the needs of the visually impaired in the curriculum, where mobility, keyboard skills, and daily living skills feature on the syllabus as well as the usual academic subjects; in the house, where they practice their daily living skills on a regular basis, and in the leisure activities where there is a wide choice of activities offered by the school. Pupils free to join local organisations. Language trips and skiing trips abroad. Meals self-service.
Discipline Pupils are expected to behave in a way that is considerate to the community.
Boarding Family units in six boarding houses, mostly new and purpose-built. 16 to each house, mixed or single-sex. Sixth-form hostel on the lines of a university student hostel. Daily living skills learnt in class are put into practice.

• ROBERT GORDON'S

Robert Gordon's College, Schoolhill, Aberdeen AB9 1FE. Tel 01224 646346, Fax 01224 630301
• Pupils 1360 • Boys 5–17 (Day) • Girls 5–17 (Day) • Higher year 160 • Termly fees £1300 (Day)
• HMC • Enquiries/application to the Headmaster

What it's like

Founded in 1732 by Robert Gordon, a wealthy Aberdonian merchant. In fact, the first occupants were the Hanoverian troops of the Duke of Cumberland, on their way to Culloden in 1746, but the first boys were admitted 4 years later. In 1881 the college was converted into a day school. Girls were first admitted in 1989 and have been successfully integrated throughout the school. It is now fully co-educational. The senior and junior schools are on the original city centre site; the 40-acre playing fields are 3 miles away. The main school buildings are magnificent and solid, in the 18th-century classical tradition, with elegant interiors. Extensive development has been possible over the years and the college is now very well equipped. It is a non-denominational school; all pupils take a class in religious education and there are occasional religious services. The staff:pupil ratio is about 1:15. Academic standards are high and results consistently good. The majority of sixth-formers proceed to degree courses. Music is strong and treated as a practical subject in the curriculum. Art is also well supported, as is drama and ballroom and country dancing have a sizeable following. A wide range of sports and games (including orienteering, angling and curling) is provided. Considerable emphasis on outdoor activities such as climbing, angling and ornithology. Some 30 clubs and societies cater for most needs; debating, chess, charities and the CCF (which includes a pipe band) are particularly popular. Some community services and a high rate of success in the Duke of Edinburgh's Award Scheme.

School profile

Pupils Total age range 5–17; 1360 day pupils (910 boys, 450 girls). Senior department 11–17, 965 pupils (665 boys, 300 girls). Main entry ages, 5, 9, 11 and into sixth. 10%–15% are children of former pupils. 50% senior department from own junior. *State school entry:* 45% main intake.
Entrance Own entrance exam. No special skills or religious requirements. Parents expected to buy textbooks. Average £14 extras. 15 pa assisted places. 35 pa scholarships/bursaries, £1100 to full fees.
Parents 15+% are doctors, lawyers etc, 25+% from industry/commerce, 15+% farming.
Head and staff *Headmaster:* Brian Lockhart, appointed 1996. Educated at Leith Academy and George Heriot's and the universities of Aberdeen (history) and Edinburgh (education). Previously Deputy Rector at Glasgow High and Head of History at George Heriot's. Also Council Member of Headteachers' Association of Scotland; member of UCAS Scottish Committee and ex-council member of SHA. *Staff:* 85 full time, 13 part time. Annual turnover 3%. Average age 43.
Exam results In 1995, 172 pupils in fourth year (S-grade), 160 in fifth year (Higher), 115 in CSYS year. S-grades: In 1995, 99% fourth years gained at least grade 1–4 in 3+ subjects. *Highers:* 80% fifth years gained grade A-C in 3+ subjects.
University and college entrance 90% of 1995 sixth-form leavers went on to a degree course (1% after a gap year); others typically go on to further education or direct to jobs.

Of those going on to university, 2% went to Oxbridge; 7% took courses in medicine, dentistry and veterinary science, 36% in science and engineering, 9% in law, 19% in humanities and social sciences, 10% in art, design and architecture, 20% to accountancy, business studies etc.

Curriculum S-grades, Highers, CSYS: 20 subjects offered. 6% take arts/humanities Highers; 94% a mixture of science/engineering and arts/humanities. *Vocational:* Work experience available. *Computing facilities:* 2 computer rooms and small word-processing unit. Computers in classrooms/laboratories as teaching aids. *Special provision:* 1 part-time teacher of learning support; 1 qualified EFL teacher. *Europe:* French, German and Italian offered to S-grade and Higher (French compulsory from age 12, German from 13). Annual exchange with school in Austria; some private exchange scheme with individual families.

The arts (Pupils aged 11 and over) *Music:* Over 15% of pupils learn a musical instrument; instrumental exams can be taken. Some 8 musical groups including choir, concert band, jazz ensemble, rock group. 1 member of National Youth Orchestra of Scotland, 1 member of National Youth Music Theatre Co. *Drama & dance*: Both offered. Some pupils are involved in school productions. *Art:* On average, 24 take S-grade, 25 Higher, 3 CSYS. Design, pottery and photography also offered.

Sport, community service and clubs (Pupils aged 11 and over) *Sport and physical activities:* Compulsory sports: hockey, rugby, cricket, tennis, athletics. Optional: cross-country, rock-climbing, skiing, badminton, basketball, volleyball, curling, table tennis, lacrosse BAGA and RLSS exams may be taken plus Scottish Swimming Awards Scheme, Scottish Thistle Awards (athletics). Gold, silver and bronze medals in Scottish Schools Swimming Championships; finalists in British Schools Skiing Championships; 9 in regional rugby XV. *Community service:* Pupils take bronze, silver and gold Duke of Edinburgh's Award. CCF optional for 4 years at age 13, community service for 1 year at age 17. *Clubs and societies:* Up to 30 clubs, eg ornithology, angling, aviation, debating, chess, Christian Union, environmental.

Uniform School uniform worn throughout.

Houses/prefects Competitive houses. Head boy/girl, prefects, house prefects, appointed by the head from nominations from staff and pupils.

Religion Attendance at religious worship compulsory (unless excused at parental request).

Social Debates, drama, music, dance with two local independent girls' schools. Debates with local maintained schools. Tours to Switzerland, Italy, Russia, Austria (skiing), France (Paris and St Malo), Belgium (concert band). Exchanged with school in Graz (Austria). Pupils allowed to bring own bike. Meals self-service. School shop. No tobacco/alcohol allowed.

Discipline Pupils failing to produce homework once could expect warning from teacher and work to be handed in without fail the next day; those caught smoking cannabis on the premises could expect expulsion.

Alumni association is run by Mr Philip G Dawson, James & George Collie, Advocates, 1 East Craibstone Street, Aberdeen.

• ROEDEAN

Roedean School, Brighton, East Sussex BN2 5RQ. Tel 01273 603181, Fax 01273 680791

• Pupils 444 • Boys None • Girls 10–18 (Day/Board) • Upper sixth 82 • Termly fees £2455 (Day) £4325 (Board) • GSA • Enquiries/application to the Admissions Secretary

What it's like

Founded in 1885, the school moved to its present site in 1898. It has a splendid position above the cliffs and overlooking the sea, between Brighton and Rottingdean. It is a purpose-built school with attractive and very well-equipped buildings on a large estate of which about 40 acres are given to playing fields and leisure activities. One of the most distinguished schools in Britain, it is well run and its large and well-qualified staff permits a staff:pupil ratio of about 1:9. Standards are very high and results each year are very good. Almost all the sixth-formers go on to degree courses, many to Oxbridge. Great emphasis is placed on careers advice and the teaching of leadership skills. Extremely strong in art, music and drama; virtually all pupils are involved in these activities. A wide range of games and sports is available and high standards are achieved. There is a high commitment to local community services. The school has an outstanding record in the Duke of Edinburgh's Award Scheme and the Young Enterprise Business Scheme.

School profile

Pupils Age range 10–18; 440 boarding girls, plus 4 day girls. Main entry ages 10, 11, 12, 13 and into sixth. Approx 5% are children of former pupils. *State school entry:* Very small.

Entrance Common Entrance used; interviews for entry to sixth. Wide range of interests and skills looked for; no religious requirements. Parents not expected to buy textbooks until sixth-form. 6 pa scholarships/bursaries. 15 pa assisted places.

Parents 15+% are doctors, lawyers etc; 15+% in industry or commerce. 30+% live within 30 miles; 10+% live overseas.

Head and staff *Headmistress:* Mrs Ann Longley, in post for 12 years. Educated at Walthamstow Hall, and at Edinburgh and Bristol universities (modern languages and education). Previously Headmistress at Vivian Webb School (California), Residential Teacher at Choate School (Conn, USA), Housemistress at Peninsula C of E School (Victoria, Australia) and teacher at Toorak College (Victoria, Australia). Also FRSA; Sussex University (Hon D Univ). Trustee, Central Bureau for Educational Visits and Exchanges; Deputy Chairman ESU Education Committee and member of GSA Council. *Staff:* 50 full time, 15 part time. Annual turnover 10%. Average age 44.

Exam results In 1995, 68 pupils in upper fifth, 83 in upper sixth. *GCSE:* In 1995, all upper fifth gained at least grade C in 5+ subjects. *AS/A-levels:* 18% upper sixth passed in 4 subjects; 75% in 3; 6% in 2; and 1% in 1 subject. Average UCAS points 24.0.

University and college entrance 95% of 1995 sixth-form leavers went on to a degree course (8% after a gap year); others typically go on to art foundation courses, hotel management. Of those going on to university, 14% went to Oxbridge; 7% took courses in medicine, dentistry and veterinary science, 11% in science and engineering, 6% in law, 28% in humanities and social sciences, 6% in vocational subjects eg optometry, architecture, PE, 26% in other subjects eg classics, maths, combined arts subjects.

Curriculum GCSE, AS and *A-levels:* 22 subjects offered at A-level (no A-level general studies), 22 subjects at AS-level. 18% took science AS/A-levels; 34% arts/humanities; 48% both. *Vocational:* Work experience available; also RSA information technology (Stage 1 for all, Stage 2 optional). *Computing facilities:* 3 computer rooms; 1 for computer studies and IT (IBM based); 1 for computer assisted learning (BBC based) plus an IBM-based sixth-form unit for maths education; and 1 for DT, with desktop publishing facilities (Apple Mac based). At least 1 BBC in each department. *Europe:* French, German and Spanish offered to GCSE, AS and A-level; also beginners' Spanish crash course in sixth (GCSE after 1 year, AS- or A-level after 2). Regular exchanges (France and Germany).

The arts *Music:* Over 50% of pupils learn a musical instrument; instrumental exams can be taken. Some 10 musical groups including orchestra, string orchestra, choir, chamber choir, jazz band. Winner piano concerto class, winner concerto class, Brighton Competitive Festival. Finalists National Schools Chamber Music Competition. *Drama & dance:* Both offered. GCSE and A-level drama, ESB, LAMDA, RAD and ISTD exams may be taken. Majority of pupils are involved in school and house/other productions. In 1995, 3 pupils accepted for drama/theatre related courses at university, 2 to National Youth Theatre. *Art:* On average, 26 take GCSE, 6 A-level; also design and technology GCSE and A-level. Design, pottery, textiles and photography also offered. Numbers taking GCSE and A-level design and technology rapidly growing. In 1995, 2 gained places at Wimbledon Art School, 2 places to read architecture (Cambridge and Architectural Association)

Sport, community service and clubs *Sport and physical activities:* Compulsory sports (to lower fifth): lacrosse, netball, swimming, tennis, rounders, gymnastics, athletics; also, at various stages, dance, hockey. Upper fifth and sixth: PE, and games include aerobics, archery, badminton, basketball, cricket, volleyball, squash, yoga, fitness room, golf, riding, fencing, ten-pin bowling, rock climbing. RLSS exams may be taken. Lacrosse (U15, U18), hockey (U16, U18), netball (U16, U19), cricket (U15, U18) at county and national levels; U19 National Cricket Tournament winners 1995. *Community service:* Pupils take bronze, silver and gold Duke of Edinburgh's Award; gold award, girls undertake challenging mountain expedition in France. Community service optional.

Clubs and societies: Over 30 clubs, eg Cecilian Singers, debating societies, political societies, Project Physics, creative pottery, Roedean Amateur Theatrical Society (RATS).
Uniform School uniform worn except in the sixth-form.
Houses/prefects Competitive houses. Head girl, prefects and head of house – appointed by Head, staff and sixth; house prefects – elected by school. Sixth-form committee and school council.
Religion Compulsory C of E morning assembly and Sunday chapel, except for practising members of other faiths; Roman Catholics attend own church and Jewish girls have tuition from local Rabbi.
Social Joint musical events, debates, quizzes, dances with local boys' schools. Occasional organised trips to France; annual skiing holiday. Sixth form allowed to bring own bike to school. Meals self-service. School bookshop, tuckshop and stationery store. No tobacco/alcohol allowed.
Discipline All rules, and penalties for breaking these, are clearly defined in the Student Handbook issued to each girl each year.
Boarding Sixth form have own study bedroom, upper fifth share bedroom with 2 and study with 2–3. Houses of approx 80; separate houses for 10–12 year olds and for upper sixth. Resident qualified sister, 2 visiting doctors. Central dining rooms. Upper sixth may cook own food some of the time. Half-term plus 2–3 exeats termly; others by arrangement with housemistress. Visits to local town allowed – escorted for younger girls.
Alumni association run by Mrs P Graham, President, The Old Roedeanian Association, c/o the school.
Former pupils Baroness Chalker of Wallasey; Verity Lambert (actress and director); Sarah Miles (actress); Sally Oppenheimer MP; Dame Cecily Saunders (founder of hospice movement).

• ROSSALL

Rossall School, Fleetwood, Lancashire FY7 8JW. Tel 01253 774201, Fax 01253 772052

• Pupils 412 • Boys 11–18 (Day/Board) • Girls 11–18 (Day/Board) • Upper sixth 65 • Termly fees £1400 (Day) £2570–£3800 (Board) • HMC • Enquiries/application to the Registrar

What it's like

Founded in 1844 as a C of E foundation. Built as a school for the purpose of giving a sound education to the sons of clergy and lay people. It is well sited on the Lancashire coast between Cleveleys and Fleetwood, semi-rural on an estate of 155 acres. The addition of new buildings and the refitting of the solid Victorian buildings has been a constant process and much of the modern structure dates from the 1970s. Religious worship is encouraged and the chapel used daily. A well-qualified teaching staff allows a staff:pupil ratio of about 1:9. Academic standards are high and good results are achieved; most sixth-formers go on to degree courses. Music is strong and drama is well supported. There is a good range of sports and games and a high level of attainment. Extra-curricular activities are plentiful. There are many opportunities for outdoor pusuits, with emphasis on self-reliance and practical skills; this is complemented by an extensive programme of community service to assist the less advantaged. The CCF contingent is the most senior, having been formed in 1860 and the Duke of Edinburgh's Award Scheme is well supported.

School profile

Pupils Age range 11–18; 412 pupils, 115 day (64 boys, 51 girls), 297 boarders (198 boys, 99 girls). Main entry ages 11, 13 and into sixth. 15% are children of former pupils. Own prep provides 47% of intake at 11. *State school entry:* 53% of intake at 11, plus 15% to sixth.
Entrance Own exam used; Common Entrance occasionally. No special skills or religious requirements, though school is C of E foundation. 7 pa assisted places. 15+ pa scholarships, up to 100% fees; 10 Governors awards for sixth-form entrants; clerical and service bursaries.
Parents Some 65% live within 30 miles; 20% live overseas.
Head and staff *Headmaster:* Richard Rhodes, in post for 9 years. Educated at Durham

and Oxford universities. Previously Headmaster (introduction of co-educational boarding) and Deputy Headmaster responsible for sixth-form at Arnold, and Housemaster at St John's (Leatherhead). Also JP; governor of a prep school (Terra Nova School, Jodrell Bank); member HMC Boarding Sub-Committee. *Staff:* 42 full time, 16 part time (including music). Annual turnover less than 10%.

Exam results In 1995, 75 pupils in upper fifth, 63 in upper sixth. *GCSE:* In 1995, 82% upper fifth gained at least grade C in 5+ subjects. *A-levels:* 34% upper sixth passed in 4+ subjects; 40% in 3; 12% in 2; and 12% in 1 subject. Average UCAS points 16.1 (19.4 including general studies).

University and college entrance 90% of 1995 sixth-form leavers went on to a degree course (5% after a gap year); others typically go in to careers (armed forces, computing, retail management). Of those going on to university, 7% went to Oxbridge; 32% took courses in science and engineering, 44% in humanities and social sciences, 2% in art and design, 2% in music, 20% in business studies.

Curriculum GCSE, AS and *A-levels:* 20 subjects offered (including A-level general studies and PE). 20% take science A-levels; 64% arts/humanities; 16% both. *Computing facilities:* Specialist IT department with 24 terminal computer network. Computer support in all major departments. *Special provision:* Support units for specific learning difficulties and overseas pupils requiring help with English. *Europe:* French and German offered at GCSE and A-level. Exchange visits to France and Germany. Several European pupils for 1 term or more.

The arts *Music:* Over 30% of pupils learn a musical instrument; instrumental exams can be taken. Numerous musical groups including orchestral, brass, wind jazz, choral. Member of National Jazz Youth Orchestra. *Drama & dance*: Both offered. Some pupils are involved in school and house/other productions. *Art:* Pottery also offered.

Sport, community service and clubs *Sport and physical activities:* Sports available: Rugby, cricket, hockey, athletics, netball, squash, fives, cross-country, shooting, swimming available. GCSE and A-level may be taken. *Community service:* Pupils take bronze and silver Duke of Edinburgh's Award. CCF and community service both optional. *Clubs and societies:* Up to 30 clubs, eg chess, Christian Union, drama, outdoor pursuits, sub-aqua, fencing, debating.

Uniform School uniform worn throughout.

Houses/prefects Competitive houses. School captain, house captains, monitors.

Religion Daily chapel compulsory, to provide school's multi-racial, multi-cultural community with a period of reflection.

Social Occasional (irregular) events with local schools. Regular sports tours abroad; exchange visits with German school. Meals cafeteria style. Sixth-form centre with bar; no tobacco allowed.

Discipline Pupils failing to produce prep complete work under supervision on half holidays; minor misdemeanors dealt with by community sevice within school. Any pupil in possession of cannabis must expect expulsion.

Boarding Sixth formers have own study bedroom; remainder in dormitories of 4–10. Houses of 35–59, single-sex except junior house (11–13). Resident qualified nurses. Central dining room. Pupils can provide and cook own snacks. Flexible policy on exeats. Visits to local town allowed, twice weekly.

Alumni association is run by John Gill, General Secretary, Rossallian Club, c/o the School.

Former pupils Sir Thomas Beecham; Leslie Charteris; General Sir Thomas Hutton; Sir David Brown; Professor F R Smith.

• ROUGEMONT

Rougemont School, Llantarnam Hall, Malpas Road, Newport, Gwent NP9 6QB. Tel 01633 855560, Fax 01633 855598

• Pupils 500 • Boys 3–18 (Day) • Girls 3–18 (Day) • Upper sixth 30 • Termly fees £850–£1478 (Day) • SHMIS • Enquiries/application to the Admissions Secretary

What it's like

Founded in 1920, the school was established as a co-educational junior school to feed local grammar schools. The present school took shape after a parental buy-out in 1974 and a charitable trust was formed. The first sixth-form opened in 1981. Recently most of the school moved to a new site at Llantarnam Hall, where it offers education from 7–18. Staff:pupil ratio of about 1:12. Academic results are very good and most sixth-formers go on to degree courses each year. There is some music, drama and art. Sport is good with several county and national representatives. A most impressive record in the Duke of Edinburgh's Award Scheme.

School profile

Pupils Total age range 3–18; 500 day pupils (250 boys, 250 girls). Senior department 11–18, 250 pupils (128 boys, 122 girls). Main entry ages 3–4, 11 and into sixth. Approx 10% are children of former pupils. *State school entry:* 60% senior intake, plus 50% to sixth.
Entrance Own exam used. No special skills or religious requirements. No extras. 9 pa scholarships/bursaries, maximum 50% fees.
Parents 15+% are doctors, lawyers, etc.
Head and staff *Head:* Ian Brown, appointed 1995. *Staff:* 40 full time, 7 part time. Annual turnover 3%. Average age 43.
Exam results On average 40 pupils in upper fifth, 30 in upper sixth. *GCSE:* On average, 76% upper fifth gain at least grade C in 8+ subjects; 20% in 5–7; and 4% in 1–4 subjects. *A-levels:* 93% upper sixth passed in 3+ subjects; 7% in 2 subjects. Average UCAS points 21.9.
University and college entrance 95% of 1995 sixth-form leavers went on to a degree course (5% after a gap year); others typically go on to resit or enter family business. Of those going on to university, 10% went to Oxbridge; 20% took courses in medicine, dentistry and veterinary science, 30% in science and engineering, 10% in law, 30% in humanities and social sciences, 3% in art and design, 7% in other vocational subjects.
Curriculum GCSE and *A-levels:* 16 GCSE subjects offered; 12 at A-level (AS but no A-level general studies). 30% take science A-levels; 35% arts/humanities; 35% both. *Vocational:* Work experience available. *Computing facilities:* Apple Mac; PCs; Amstrad PCW 8256s. *Special provision:* Individual tuition on withdrawal basis. Dyslexia unit. *Europe:* French and German offered to GCSE, AS and A-level. Over 60% take GCSE in both languages. German exchange, with a school in Koblenz.
The arts (Pupils aged 11 and over) *Music:* 30% of pupils learn a musical instrument; instrumental exams can be taken. 3 musical groups: orchestra, chamber, choral. *Drama & dance*: Both offered. GCSE drama may be taken. Majority of pupils are involved in school and house/other productions. *Art:* Art facilities open to non-examination pupils.
Sport, community service and clubs (Pupils aged 11 and over) *Sport and physical activities:* Compulsory sports: rugby, soccer, cricket, netball, rounders. Optional: tennis, squash, cross-country, rowing. RLSS, AAA and ARA exams may be taken. Pupils in Welsh national teams: badminton (U16), hockey (U19), cricket (U19). *Community service:* Pupils take bronze, silver and gold Duke of Edinburgh's Award: more than 45 gold awards over the past 10 years. Community service optional. *Clubs and societies:* Over 30 clubs, including chess, computer, debating and environmental care.
Uniform School uniform worn throughout.
Houses/prefects Competitive houses. Prefects, head boy/girl, head of house and house prefects – appointed by the Headmaster, with staff consultation.
Religion Non-denominational.
Social Three sets of debating competitions (Rotary, Business Women, English-Speaking Union). At least three organised trips abroad each year. Pupils allowed to bring own car/bike/motorbike to school. Meals self-service. School shop.

• ROYAL (Bath)

The Royal School, Lansdown, Bath BA1 5SZ. Tel 01225 313877, Fax 01225 420338
• Pupils 301 • Boys 2½–7 only • Girls 2½–18 (Day/Board) • Upper sixth 42 • Termly fees £927–£1962 (Day) £2731–£3560 (Board) • GSA • Enquiries/application to the Headmistress

What it's like

Founded in 1864 to educate 'the Daughters of necessitous Officers of the Army at the lowest possible cost' and to help widows whose husbands had died in the Crimean War. Its pupils now come from a wide range of backgrounds, but the daughters of servicemen still form the largest group in the school. It is on a singlesite in the very pleasant residential district of Lansdown, on the north side of the city. It prides itself on being a happy community which welcomes day pupils for all its activities. All pupils are expected to have serious career intentions and particular care is given to individual needs. It is a C of E foundation but ecumenical in spirit and policy. All girls attend chapel daily and boarders attend most Sundays. A broad general education is provided and results are good. The majority of girls go on to degree courses each year, including Oxbridge. Very strong in music and drama. A decent range of sports and games (very strong in lacrosse) and plentiful leisure activities. Growing commitment to local community services.

School profile

Pupils Total age range 2½–18; 301 pupils, 138 day (17 boys, 138 girls), 163 boarding girls. Senior department, 11–18, 219 girls. Main entry ages 2½ and 5 (boys and girls), 7, 9, 11, 13 and into sixth (girls). 5% are children of former pupils. *State school entry:* 2% senior intake, plus 2% to sixth.

Entrance Own assessment procedure and scholarship examination used. All skills taken into account. No religious requirements but C of E foundation; broadly Christian with some other faiths. Parents not expected to buy textbooks; individual music, drama, sports coaching extra. 20+ pa scholarships, 17% to 33% fees; exhibitions, 8% fees.

Parents 15+% in the armed services; 15+% are doctors, lawyers, etc; 15+% are in industry. 10+% live within 30 miles; 10+% live overseas.

Head and staff *Headmistress:* Mrs Emma McKendrick, in post from 1994. Educated at Bedford High and at Liverpool and Birmingham universities (German and Dutch). Previously Deputy Head, Head of Sixth Form and Senior Housemistress at The Royal School.

Exam results On average, 50 pupils in Year 11, 40 in Year 13. *GCSE:* In 1995, 75% Year 11 gained at least grade C in 8+ subjects; 18% in 5–7; and 7% in 1–4 subjects. *A-levels:* 14% Year 13 passed in 4+ subjects; 76% in 2 or 3 subjects. Average UCAS points 15.4.

University and college entrance 85% of 1995 sixth-form leavers went on to a degree course (12% after a gap year); others typically go on to nursing, secretarial, or art foundation courses. Of those going on to university, 7% went to Oxbridge; 5% took courses in medicine, dentistry and veterinary science, 25% in science and engineering, 65% in humanities and social sciences, 5% in art and design.

Curriculum GCSE, AS and *A-levels:* 25 subjects offered (including AS-level general studies). 25% take science A-levels; 50% arts/humanities; 25% both. *Vocational:* Work experience available Years 11 and 13; GNVQ level 2 business studies taught with local FE college. *Computing facilities:* IT centre; computers in all departments for use both in class and in pupils' free time. *Special provision:* Individual needs department offers basic skills and EFL to small minority of students. *Europe:* French, German and Spanish offered to GCSE, AS and A-level. Regular exchanges. International students in the sixth-form. Resident foreign language assistants.

The arts (Pupils aged 11 and over) *Music:* Over 50% of pupils learn one or more musical instrument; instrumental exams can be taken. Musical groups including 3 choirs, wind ensembles, string ensemble, recorder ensemble. Many winners at mid-Somerset Festival (13 trophies in 1996, including solo vocal, solo instrumental, chamber music and choral); 1 recent piano exhibition to Oxford. *Drama & dance*: Both offered. GCSE and A-level drama, ESB, LAMDA and RAD exams may be taken. Majority of pupils are involved in school productions and house competitions. Large number participate in dance productions and competitions. Ballet lessons with local studio. *Art:* On average, 19 take GCSE, 1 AS-level, 6 A-level. Design, pottery, textiles, photography, painting, sculpture and life drawing also offered.

Sport, community service and clubs (Pupils aged 11 and over) *Sport and physical activities:* Sports: lacrosse, hockey, netball, swimming, tennis, cricket, rounders, athletics, aerobics, trampolining. Sixth form only: squash. BAGA exams may be taken. 8 players in county lacrosse teams; recent lacrosse tours to Scotland and United States; gymnastics team competes locally. *Community service:* Pupils take bronze, silver and gold Duke of Edinburgh's Award. Community service optional at age 16. ATC unit linked to Bath ATC squadron. *Clubs and societies:* Over 50 clubs operate at lunchtime or in the evenings with a huge range of cultural, academic, recreational and sporting opportunities and Young Enterprise; outdoor activities a speciality of school life.

Uniform School uniform, except in the sixth.
Houses/prefects Competitive houses. Head of school elected, heads of houses and prefects appointed by Head; heads of boarding elected by school. School Council.
Religion Christian worship compulsory.
Social Young Engineers and Scientists, joint theatrical productions, open meetings, conferences and social events with other schools. Organised trips abroad and exchange systems. Pupils allowed to bring own car/bike to school. Meals self-service. School shop. No tobacco/alcohol allowed.
Discipline Pupils failing to produce homework once might expect a detention; those caught smoking cannabis on the premises (unprecedented) could expect serious consequences.
Boarding 15% have own study bedroom, 85% share (with 1, 2 or 3). Houses, of about 50, divided by age group. Resident qualified nurse, visiting doctor. Central dining room. Pupils can provide and cook own food by arrangement. 2 weekend exeats termly plus half-term. Weekend visits to local town allowed, depending on age.
Alumni association is run by Mrs Unity Marriott, c/o the school.
Former pupils Jean Nunn (Under Secretary, Cabinet Office; first woman to receive the Order of the Bath); Veronica Sutherland (British Ambassador to Eire).

• ROYAL (Dungannon)

The Royal School, Dungannon, Northland Row, Dungannon, County Tyrone, Northern Ireland DT71 6AP. Tel 01888 722710

• Pupils 750 • Boys 4–19 (Day/Board/Weekly) • Girls 4–19 (Day/Board/Weekly) • Upper sixth 84 • Termly fees £29 or £931 (Day) £2050 (Board/Weekly) • SHM1S • Enquiries/application to the Headmaster

What it's like

Founded in 1614 as a boys' school and became co-educational in 1986 when it assimilated the Dungannon High School for Girls. Its ancient and modern buildings (the Old Building of the school is listed) lie on the edge of the town in a fine 45-acre estate in beautiful surroundings. The preparatory department is combined. The whole establishment is extremely well equipped with excellent facilities. Results are good and most pupils proceed to university each year, including some to Oxbridge. Flourishing music, art and drama departments. A very good range of sport and games, with many national and county representatives, particularly in rugby and hockey (All-Ireland Schools Trophy 1995). Plentiful extra-curricular activities. Quite a good record in the Duke of Edinburgh's Award Scheme.

School profile

Pupils Total age range 4–19; 750 pupils, 643 day (309 boys, 334 girls), 45 boarding (30 boys, 15 girls). Senior department 11–19, 684 pupils (334 boys, 350 girls). Main entry ages 11 and into sixth. Approx 15% are children of former pupils. Dungannon and Howard primary schools both provide more than 20% of intake. *State school entry:* 95% senior intake, plus 2% to sixth.
Entrance NI eleven plus and interview used. No special skills or religious requirements. Parents expected to pay a deposit of £25 for books; no other extras. 7 pa scholarships of £200–£750; 3 pa bursaries of £150.
Parents 25+% in industry or commerce; 15+% are doctors, lawyers, etc. 85+% live within 30 miles; up to 10% live overseas.
Head and staff *Headmaster:* P D Hewitt, in post for 13 years. Educated at RBAI and at Queens University Belfast and London University (French, English and education). Previously Sixth Form Master and Form Master at Belfast Royal Academy. Also member of SHA, Admiralty Interview Board and also of Board of Visitors, HM Prisons. *Staff:* 40 full time, 6 part time. Annual turnover 1%. Average age 40.
Exam results In 1995, 105 pupils in upper fifth, 84 in upper sixth. *GCSE:* In 1995, 83% upper fifth gained at least grade C in 8+ subjects; 15% in 5–7 subjects. *A-levels:* 85% upper sixth passed in 3 subjects; 12% in 2; and 3% in 1 subject. Average UCAS points19.0.
University and college entrance 85% of 1995 sixth-form leavers went on to a degree course (8% after a gap year); others typically go on to further education, farming or

family business. Of those going on to university, 4% went to Oxbridge; 5% took courses in medicine, dentistry and veterinary science, 25% in science and engineering, 20% in law, 40% in humanities and social sciences, 5% in art and design, 5% in other vocational subjects.

Curriculum GCSE and *A-levels:* 18 subjects offered (including Japanese for lower sixth; no A-level general studies). 58% took science A-levels; 25% arts/humanities; 17% both. *Vocational:* Work experience available (3–5 days in lower sixth); also RSA stages 1 and 2 keyboarding. *Computing facilities:* 6 BBCs, 3 networked 15-station RM Nimbus laboratories; 2 Internet lines. *Special provision:* Extra EFL tuition, 3 days a week after school. *Europe:* French and German offered to GCSE, AS and A-level; also as non-examined subjects. Regular exchanges; twinned with a German school in Bavaria and a French school outside Nantes.Visits to EU office in Belfast; talks from MEPs.

The arts (Pupils aged 11 and over) *Music:* Over 30% of pupils learn a musical instrument; instrumental exams can be taken. Some 6 musical groups including symphonic band, strings, woodwind quartet, barbershop, senior choir (100). Runner up in regional band competition 1995. 15 in National Youth Orchestra. *Drama & dance*: Majority of pupils are involved in school productions and some in house/other productions. Annual production (Gilbert & Sullivan in 1995). *Art:* on average, 50 take GCSE, 12 A-level. Design, ceramics, textiles, photography also offered. Several A-level and GCSE candidates selected to exhibit nationally. Pupils regularly accepted for art college.

Sport, community service and clubs (Pupils aged 11 and over) *Sport and physical activities:* Compulsory sports (except in sixth): Rugby, hockey, cricket, athletics, golf, swimming, tennis, rambling, basketball, volleyball, cross-country, indoor soccer, table tennis, weights. Rugby, 3 played for Ulster, 3 for Ireland; hockey, won Ulster Schools and All-Ireland cups, 3 played for Ulster, 1 for Ireland. *Community service:* Pupils take bronze, silver and gold Duke of Edinburgh's Award. ATC and community service optional. *Clubs and societies:* Up to 15 clubs, eg debating, public speaking, quiz, photography, SU, library, computing, art.

Uniform School uniform worn throughout; boarders wear own clothes out of class.

Houses/prefects Competitive houses. Prefects, head boy/girl, head of house and house prefects – appointed by the Headmaster after election by sixth-form and recommendation of staff.

Religion Compulsory morning assembly, Sunday morning and evening service for boarders. Exceptions made if parents request. Muslim, Hindu and Jewish preferences respected. No sects permitted access to pupils.

Social Debates, discos, sports meetings, quizzes, academic lectures. Annual European trip plus trips eg to Paris, skiing. Pupils allowed to bring own car/bike/motorbike to school. Some meals formal, some self-service. School shop. No tobacco/alcohol allowed.

Discipline Pupils falling to produce homework once might expect to have to repeat it; those caught smoking cannabis on the premises could expect expulsion.

Boarding All boarders share a modern cubicle for 2 or 4. Dormitories divided by age and sex. Resident qualified nurse/doctor. Central dining room. Exeats every 3–4 weekends. Visits to the local town allowed. Mixing with day pupils' families encouraged.

Alumni association is run by Mr Howard McLean, (OBA President), The Park, Moy Road, Dungannon, Co Tyrone; Mrs Joyce Espie, (OGA President), Drumgold, Dungannon, Co Tyrone BT71 7EN.

Former pupils Ken Maginnis MP, Allen Clarke and Paddy Johns (Ireland rugby XV), Darren Clark (professional golfer), Edmund Curren (editor, Belfast Telegraph).

• ROYAL (Guildford)

The Royal Grammar School, High Street, Guildford, Surrey GU1 3BB. Tel 01483 502424
• Pupils 840 • Boy 11–18 (Day) • Girls None • Upper sixth 125 • Termly fees £1985 (Day)
• HMC • Enquiries/application to the Headmaster's Secretary

What it's like

Founded in 1509 and established in 1552 by King Edward VI's Royal Charter, it is in the centre of Guildford, on both sides of the Upper High Street. The original buildings are handsome examples of Tudor architecture in the Oxbridge collegiate style and have been in continuous use for over 400 years. A large 1960s building on the other side of the High Street contains modern facilities including the recent addition of laboratories, technology workshops and a new library. Religious education is an integral part of the curriculum and RE periods are compulsory at all levels. Assemblies are Christian, and the school is closely linked with Holy Trinity Church nearby. Academic standards are high and results excellent; nearly all the large sixth-form go on to degree courses, including very many to Oxbridge. The staff:pupil ratio is about 1:12. Music and drama are strong. Many boys learn an instrument; there is an orchestra, several instrumental ensembles, a chamber choir and a choral society. At least one school play is presented each term (usually in conjunction with one of the local girls' schools). A wide variety of sports and games is available, including sailing, rowing and golf, and pupils have recently won national and international honours in rugby, cricket and rifle shooting. An impressive range of clubs and societies caters for most extra-curricular activities. The CCF contingent and a scout group flourish. A number of pupils take part in the Duke of Edinburgh's Award Scheme, there is an environmental group and many pupils contribute to local community services.

School profile

Pupils Age range 11–18; 840 day boys. Main entry ages 11, 13 and into sixth. Approx 5% are children of former pupils. *State school entry:* 40% main intake at 11 (not 13), plus 50% to sixth.

Entrance Common Entrance and own entrance exam used. No special skills or religious requirements. Parents not expected to buy textbooks. 20 pa assisted places. 20 pa scholarships/bursaries, full fees.

Head and staff *Headmaster:* Timothy Young, 4 years in post. Educated at Eton and at universities of Cambridge and Bristol (history and education). Previously Housemaster at Eton and Social Studies Teacher at Harvard School, Los Angeles, California. Also taught in New Zealand. Publications: chief researcher for Cambridge Between Two Wars; historical consultant to The Royal Horse of Europe. *Staff:* 69 full time, 8 part time. Annual turnover 5%. Average age 39.

Exam results On average, 140 pupils in upper fifth, 125 in upper sixth. *GCSE:* All upper fifth gain at least grade C in 8+ subjects. *A-levels:* 15% upper sixth pass in 4+ subjects; 77% in 3; 6% in 2; and 2% in 1 subject. Average UCAS points 29.0.

University and college entrance 98% of 1995 sixth-form leavers went on to a degree course, 25% to Oxbridge; others typically go on to art or music colleges.

Curriculum GCSE, AS- and A-levels. 21 subjects offered. 42% take science A-levels; 25% arts/humanities; 33% both. *Vocational:* Work experience available. *Computing facilities:* Nimbus science network. Many Apple Macs. *Europe:* French and German offered to GCSE and A-level; also as non-examined courses. Regular exchanges to France and Germany.

The arts *Music:* Over 30% of pupils learn a musical instrument; instrumental exams can be taken. Some 10+ musical groups including chamber orchestra, big band, string orchestra, choir, choral society etc. Many boys in county Youth Orchestra; winner of Bach Choir Competition for 2 years; finalist in BBC Song for Christmas; 12 at Music College Junior Dept. *Drama & dance*: Drama offered. Some pupils are involved in school and house/other productions. *Art:* On average, 20 take GCSE, 6 A-level. Design, calligraphy, art history and typography also offered.

Sport, community service and clubs *Sport and physical activities:* Compulsory sports: swimming (1st year) rugby, cricket, athletics (1st/2nd year). Optional: (3rd year onwards) rugby, cricket, hockey, basketball, sailing, cross-country, tennis. Sixth form only: squash, badminton, shooting, soccer, golf. RLSS and RYA exams may be taken. County representatives at rugby, cricket, athletics, sailing, shooting; school international rugby, athletics, shooting. Daily Mail National finalists (rugby) 1993. *Community service:* Pupils take bronze, silver and gold Duke of Edinburgh's Award. Community service optional for fifth and sixth-forms. Either CCF, Scouts, Environmental Group or D of E compulsory for 13–14 year olds; wider choice for 15+. Visually Handicapped Club outings; visits to Day Centre for Children of Single Parents (aged 3–5). *Clubs and societies:* Up to 30 clubs, eg technology, Christian Union, philosophy, feature film, radio, chess, bridge, writers' workshop, drama, music.

Uniform School uniform worn except upper sixth who wear suits.

Houses/prefects Competitive houses. Prefects, head boy and four other senior prefects

(appointed by the Headmaster); head of house (appointed by housemaster).
Religion Non-denominational.
Social Music, drama and sixth-form general studies programme with girls' schools. French and German exchanges; ski holidays. Pupils allowed to bring own car/bike/motorbike to school. Meals self-service. No tobacco/alcohol allowed.
Discipline Pupils failing to produce homework once might expect a detention. Anyone involved with drugs can expect expulsion.
Alumni association is run by D H B Jones, c/o the school.
Former pupils R G D Willis (England cricket captain); Terry Jones (Monty Python).

• ROYAL (Haslemere)

The Royal School, Farnham Lane, Haslemere, Surrey GU27 1HQ. Tel 01428 605415, Fax 01428 607451

• Pupils 250 • Boys None • Girls 11–18 (Day/Board/Weekly) • Upper sixth 57 • Termly fees £1854 (Day) £3004 (Board/Weekly) • GSA • Enquiries/application to the Headmaster

What it's like

The result of a merger between the Royal Naval School for Girls and the Grove School in 1995. The new school occupies handsome buildings in 50 acres of pleasant wooded grounds. It has excellent modern facilities which are being expanded. A sound education is provided and results are good. Most sixth-form leavers go on to degree courses. It is very strong in music, sport and drama. Big commitment to local community services and to adventure education. Good range of sports, games (some country representatives) and extra-curricular activities. A fine record in the Duke of Edinburgh's Award Scheme.

School profile

Pupils Age range 11–18; 250 girls (100 day, 150 boarding). Main entry ages 11, 13, 14 and into sixth.
Entrance Common Entrance and own exam used. No special skills required, C of E school but other religions accepted. 6 pa scholarships, 15%–33% fees
Parents 15+% are doctors, lawyers, etc; 20+% in industry or commerce; 15+% in the armed services. 30+% live within 30 miles; up to 8+% live overseas.
Head and staff *Headmaster:* Colin Brooks, appointed in 1995 but Headmaster of Grove School for 12 years. Educated at Darwen Grammar School, Lancashire, and the universities of Liverpool and Surrey (geography and psychology). Previously Head of Geography and Housemaster of Pierrepont School, Surrey. Also Member of Associated Examining Board's Education Committee and of IACCE (government independent arbitration panel on GCSE and GCE results). *Staff:* 32 full time, 14 part time. Annual turnover 6%. Average age 39.
Exam results Average size of upper fifth 40, upper sixth 30. *GCSE:* On average, 26 upper fifth gain at least grade C in 8+ subjects; 11 in 5–7; 3 in 1–4 subjects. *A-levels:* 10 upper sixth pass in 4 subjects; 16 in 3; 3 in 2; 1 in 1 subject. Average UCAS points 19.7.
University and college entrance 92% of 1995 sixth-form leavers went on to a degree course (some after a gap year); 4% took courses in medicine, dentistry and veterinary science, 29% in science and engineering, 67% in humanities and social sciences.
Curriculum GCSE and A-levels. *Vocational:* Cambridge certificate in IT available. *Computing facilities:* PC with IBM network. *Special provision:* Visiting remedial teachers and extra coaching. *Europe:* French, German, Italian and Spanish offered at GCSE and A-level. Regular exchanges to France and Germany; visits to Spain; choir exchange and work experience exchange with Germany.
The arts *Music:* Over 50% of pupils learn a musical instrument; instrumental exams can be taken. Musical groups include choirs, wind ensemble, orchestra, various groups formed for musical productions etc. Music technology and composition taught. *Dance & drama*: LAMDA and Poetry Society exams may be taken. Many pupils are involved in school productions and majority in house/other productions. Dance trophies at Chichester and Godalming festivals. *Art:* On average, 10 take GCSE, 6 A-level. Design, pottery, textiles, also offered.
Sport, community service and clubs *Sport and physical activities:* Sports: lacrosse, hockey, netball, rounders, tennis, swimming, gymnastics, volleyball, athletics, dance.

Optional: riding. Sixth form only: golf, squash, fencing. Athletics, 2 county schools champions qualified for English schools, 8 district representatives; 2 lacrosse county squad members. *Community service:* Pupils take bronze, silver and gold Duke of Edinburgh's Award. Community service optional. All houses adopt charities and fundraise; school sponsored walks for charity; personal development and leadership training. *Clubs and societies:* Up to 15 clubs, eg QUEST, dance, debating, technology, science, ballet, astronomy, IT.
Uniform School uniform worn, except in the sixth-form.
Houses/prefects Competitive houses. Prefects, head girl, head of house and house prefects – elected by the school. School Council
Religion Morning assembly; weekly communion (optional).
Social Dances, debates and social evenings with local schools. Regular school exchanges and skiing trips. Sixth form allowed to bring own car to school. Meals self-service; salad bar. School shop. No tobacco allowed; alcohol only in sixth-form bar.
Discipline Pupils failing to produce homework once might expect a talking to; those in possession of, or using, prohibited drugs would be expelled.
Boarding Sixth formers have own or twin study bedroom. Houses of approx 50+, divided by age. Central dining room. Sixth formers can provide and cook own snacks. 2 weekend exeats each term. Visits to local town allowed at weekends. Range of weekend activities and visits (mountain biking, canoeing).

• ROYAL (Newcastle)

Royal Grammar School, Eskdale Terrace, Newcastle upon Tyne NE2 4DX. Tel 0191 281 5711, Fax 0191 212 0392

• Pupils 1100 • Boys 8–18 (Day) • Girls None • Upper sixth 140 • Termly fees £1203 (Day) • HMC • Enquiries/admissions to the Headmaster

What it's like

Founded and endowed early in the 16th-century by Thomas Horsley. By virtue of Queen Elizabeth's charter in 1600 it became the Free Grammar School of Queen Elizabeth in Newcastle upon Tyne. It is one of the most distinguished schools in the north of England. For over 400 years it has enjoyed close links with the city and the region and its governing body consists largely of representatives from local authorities and universities. It is well sited near the civic and city centres and the two universities. Its pupils are drawn from a wide area. Most of the premises date from 1907 and there have been numerous extensions, including a junior school, a music centre and a sports centre; a new science and technology building opens in 1997. Academic standards have always been high and results excellent. Almost all the upper sixth go on to degree courses, including many to Oxbridge. Music, drama, art and technical studies are very strong indeed. There are three school orchestras, plus wind bands and choirs. About a dozen concerts are given each year and five or six main productions in the theatre (one in a foreign language). A wide range (20 in all) of sports and games is available; high standards are achieved and there have been many representatives at county, regional and national level. Chess and debating are especially notable activities. There is a flourishing voluntary CCF and considerable emphasis on adventure training. The school has vigorous support in the city and locality.

School profile

Pupils Total age range 8–18, 1100 day boys. Senior department 11–18, 950 boys. Main entry age 11, 13 and into sixth. *State school entry:* 50% main intake, plus 50% to sixth.
Entrance Own entrance exam and Common Entrance used. 50 pa assisted places.
Head and staff *Headmaster:* James F X Miller, 3 years in post. Educated at Douai and Oxford (PPE). Previously Headmaster at Framlingham and Housemaster, Head of Economics, Master i/c cricket at Winchester. Also member of Winchester City Council (1983); Chairman of both its Health and Welfare Committee and Traffic Management Sub-Committee. HMC Academic Policy Committee. *Staff:* 75 full time, including junior school, 11 part time. Annual turnover 5%. Average age 38.
Exam results On average, 140 in fifth form, 140 in upper sixth. *GCSE:* all fifth form

take 10–11 GCSEs, with very few results below grade C. *A-levels:* Average sixth-formers pass 3 A-levels. Average UCAS points 26.9.

University and college entrance 98% of 1995 sixth-form leavers went on to a degree course (10% after a gap year). 20% went to Oxbridge; 10% took courses in medicine, dentistry and veterinary science, 38% in science and engineering, 7% in law, 38% in humanities and social sciences, 2% in art and design, 5% in other vocational subjects eg accountancy, hotel and catering, quantity surveying.

Curriculum GCSE, AS and A-levels. 19 GCSE and A-level subjects offered; 15 at AS-level; also Arabic (Schools Arabic Project – Certificate); several other languages as part of general studies options; some A-level general studies. Most upper sixth take a combination of A and AS-levels, usually a mix of arts and sciences. *Computing facilities:* 2 designated computing rooms; departmental equipment as required. *Europe:* French and German offered to GCSE, AS and A-level (French compulsory to GCSE); Italian and Spanish occasionally as non-examined subjects. Regular exchanges.

The arts *Music:* Over 25% of pupils learn a musical instrument; instrumental exams can be taken. Some 10 musical groups including orchestras, choirs, wind bands. 1 in National Youth Orchestra; several every year in Northern Junior Philharmonic Orchestra. *Drama & dance*: Drama offered. Some pupils are involved in school and other productions. Euripides play performed in Greek for national conference of the Classical Association. *Art:* On average, 40 take GCSE, 6 AS-level, 10 A-level. Pottery, photography also offered.

Sport, community service and clubs *Sport and physical activities:* Compulsory sports: rugby, cricket, athletics, swimming. Optional: badminton, basketball, fencing, gymnastics, hockey, judo, karate, orienteering, rowing, cross-country, tennis, table tennis, volleyball. GCSE may be taken. At or near top nationally in swimming, running, athletics, gymnastics, hockey; one of best rugby schools in North of England; individual national achievements in fencing, orienteering. *Community service:* CCF and community service both optional. *Clubs and societies:* Up to 15 clubs, eg debating, chess (often in finals of Times schools tournament), model railway, bee-keeping.

Uniform School uniform worn except in sixth.

Houses/prefects Competitive houses. Prefects, head prefect, heads of house and senior prefects – appointed by a committee of staff with pupil representation.

Religion Attendance at religious worship not compulsory.

Social 2 neighbouring girls' schools involved in music, drama, debating and other societies; some jointly-run general studies courses in sixth-form. Annual ski trips, sports tours, exchanges with schools in France and Germany. Pupils allowed to bring own car/bike/motorbike to school. Meals self-service. No tobacco/alcohol allowed.

Discipline Action taken in the case of pupils failing to produce homework once is at the discretion of the subject teacher. It is made clear that any trafficking in illegal drugs is an expellable offence.

Former pupils Brian Redhead; Lord Chief Justice Taylor.

• ROYAL (Wolverhampton)

Royal Wolverhampton School, Penn Road, Wolverhampton WV3 0EG. Tel 01902 341230
• Pupils 548 • Boys 2½–18 (Day/Board/Weekly) • Girls 2½–18 (Day/Board/Weekly) • Upper sixth 43 • Termly fees £830-£1725 (Day) £2370-£3015 (Board) £2900 (Weekly) • SHMIS, SHA
• Enquiries/application to the Headteacher

What it's like

Founded in 1850 and co-ed virtually from the outset, it moved to its present site, a large wooded area a mile from the town centre, in 1854. There are fine gardens and ample playing fields. The main buildings are of an agreeable neo-Tudor design. Modernisation and extension of the buildings has included a new technology block; accommodation and facilities are good. The junior school is on the same site. Christian faith and values are central to the life of the school. Daily services are compulsory, as is religious education. The teaching is of a high standard and results are good. Many leavers go on to degree courses each year. The senior school staff:pupil ratio is about 1:11. Strong in music, drama and art. An impressive range of sports and games. Quite a high commitment to local community services, and a strong CCF with Army and RAF sections.

School profile

Pupils Total age range 2½–18; 548 pupils, 374 day (234 boys, 140 girls), 174 boarding (113 boys, 61 girls). Senior department 11–18, 301 pupils (201 boys, 100 girls). Main entry ages 2½, 4, 11 and into sixth. Approx 15% are children of former pupils. *State school entry:* 20% main senior intake, plus 20% to sixth.
Entrance Own entrance exam used. No special skills or religious requirements although an Anglican school. Parents not expected to buy textbooks; maximum extras £25 per term. Scholarships and bursaries, for music, sport, maths and sixth-form.
Parents 15+% in armed services; 15+% in industry or commerce. 30+% live within 30 miles; 10+% live overseas.
Head and staff Headteacher: Mrs B A Evans, in post since 1995. *Staff:* 30 full time, 2 part time. Annual turnover under 5%. Average age 35.
Exam results On average, 55 pupils in upper fifth, 43 in upper sixth. *GCSE:* On average, 9% upper fifth gain at least grade C in 8+ subjects; 61% in 5–7; and 28% in 1–4 subjects. *A-levels:* 5% upper sixth pass in 4+ subjects; 75% in 3; 15% in 2; and 5% in 1 subject. Average UCAS points 15.2.
University and college entrance 75% of 1995 sixth-form leavers went on to a degree course; others typically go on to non-degree courses eg physiotherapy, or straight into careers. Of those going on to university, 3% went to Oxbridge; 7% took courses in medicine, dentistry and veterinary science, 52% in science and engineering, 41% in humanities and social sciences.
Curriculum GCSE and A-levels offered (including A-level general studies). 45% take science A-levels; 35% arts/humanities; 20% both. *Vocational:* Work experience available; also BTEC diploma in IT. *Computing facilities:* Network system and several standalone PCs. *Special provision:* One member of staff helps very few children. *Europe:* French and German offered to GCSE, AS and A-level. Regular exchanges (to Germany). Several bilingual pupils in school.
The arts (Pupils aged 11 and over) *Music:* Over 50% of all pupils learn a musical instrument; instrumental exams can be taken. Some 6 musical groups including orchestra, string ensemble, wind group etc. *Drama & dance*: Drama offered. Some pupils are involved in school and house/other productions. Recent production of Annie. *Art:* On average, 20 take GCSE, 10 A-level. Design, pottery and photography also offered.
Sport, community service and clubs (Pupils aged 11 and over) *Sport and physical activities:* Compulsory sports: football, rugby, cricket or tennis (boys); hockey, tennis (girls). Optional sports: basketball, netball, volleyball, swimming. 2 pupils run cross-country at national level; pupils have represented county in rugby, hockey, swimming, badminton, athletics, cross-country. *Community service:* CCF optional for 2 years at age 14: strong CCF with Army and RAF sections. *Clubs and societies:* Up to 15 clubs, eg chess, drama, public speaking, stamp.
Uniform School uniform worn throughout.
Houses/prefects Competitive houses. Prefects, head boy/girl, head of house and house prefects – appointed by Head after consultation.
Religion Compulsory daily service, Sunday service for boarders.
Social Debating competitions and games matches with other schools. 2 or more trips abroad annually. Some meals formal, some self-service. School shop. No tobacco/alcohol allowed.
Discipline Pupils failing to produce homework once might expect remonstration or reprimand; those caught smoking on the premises might expect suspension after warning, use of drugs will lead to expulsion.
Boarding 80% have own study bedroom, 20% share. Single-sex houses, of approximately 35. Resident qualified nurse. Central dining room. Unlimited weekend exeats. Visits to local town allowed once a week.
Alumni association is run by A Sharpe, President ORA, c/o the school.
Former pupils Eric Idle (Monty Python); Gilbert Harding (actor); Philip Oakes (author).

• ROYAL (Worcester)

Royal Grammar School, Upper Tything, Worcester WR1 1HP. Tel 01905 613391

• Pupils 927 • Boys 7–18 (Day) • Girls None • Upper sixth 97 • Termly fees £1446 (Day) • HMC • Enquiries/application to the Registrar

What it's like

Founded before 1291 (one of the oldest schools in England) and given a charter by Elizabeth I in 1561. In 1868 it moved to its present site, near the city centre, with fine buildings in spacious gardens. Playing fields are close by and the prep school is on the same site. Very good modern facilities and recently a new sixth-form centre, a lecture theatre, drama theatre and design centre have been built. A friendly, civilised and well-disciplined environment in which pupils receive a thorough education. Results are very good and almost all sixth-form leavers go on to degree courses, including Oxbridge. Music and drama expanding. There is a strong tradition of excellence in games, especially cricket. The CCF is vigorous and there is much emphasis on outdoor pursuits. Big commitment to local community schemes and an impressive record in the Duke of Edinburgh's Award Scheme. The school has a high reputation locally and is well supported. Full use is made of Worcester's amenities, cultural and otherwise. The school has close links with industry.

School profile

Pupils Total age range 7–18; 927 day boys. Senior department 11–18, 777 boys. Main entry ages 7–13 and into sixth. Approx 5% are children of former pupils. *State school entry:* 44% senior intake, plus 5% to sixth.

Entrance Own entrance exam used. School looks for potential contributors to its wide range of extra-curricular activities. Parents not expected to buy textbooks; individual music tuition and lunches are extra. Assisted places. Scholarships/bursaries.

Parents 20+% are doctors, lawyers, etc; 50+% in industry or commerce. 80+% live within 30 miles.

Head and staff *Headmaster:* W A Jones, 4 years in post. Educated at Campbell College, Belfast, and Cambridge University. Previously Second Master at King's School Bruton and Head of Economics at Kings College School, Wimbledon. *Staff:* 70 full time. Annual turnover 8%. Average age 35.

Exam results In 1995, 127 pupils in upper fifth, 103 in upper sixth. *GCSE:* In 1995, 80% of fifth gained at least grade C in 8+ subjects; 19% in 5–7 subjects. *A-levels:* 20% upper sixth pass in 4+ subjects; 63% in 3; 13% in 2; and 3% in 1 subject. Average UCAS points 23.9.

University and college entrance 98% of 1995 sixth-form leavers went on to a degree course (after a gap year); others typically go on to art/drama colleges or straight into eg banking or the services. Of those going on to university, 12% went to Oxbridge; 4% took courses in medicine, dentistry and veterinary science, 26% in science and engineering, 33% in humanities and social sciences, 37% in other subjects eg business, languages, building, law.

Curriculum GCSE, AS and *A-levels:* 21 GCSE and A-level subjects offered, 14 at AS (including A-level general studies). 21% take science A-levels; 50% arts/humanities; 29% both. *Vocational:* Work experience available. *Computing facilities:* Two computing rooms; 60+ micros used within academic departments. *Europe:* French (compulsory from age 11), German and Russian offered to GCSE, AS and A-level. Regular exchanges (France, Germany and Russia).

The arts (Pupils aged 11 and over) *Music:* Over 20% of pupils learn a musical instrument; instrumental exams can be taken. Some 15 musical groups including joint orchestra, big band, madrigal group, early music consort, barbershop quartet, string ensemble. *Drama & dance*: Drama offered and AS-level may be taken. Majority of pupils are involved in school and house/other productions. Recent productions include Into The Woods, Epsom Downs, and She Stoops To Conquer. *Art:* On average, 20 take GCSE, 5 AS-level, 5 A-level. Design, photography also offered.

Sport, community service and clubs (Pupils aged 11 and over) *Sport and physical activities:* Compulsory sports: rugby, football, cricket. Optional: rowing, cross-country, athletics, badminton, tennis, swimming. Sixth form only: hockey, squash, golf. A-level PE may be taken. *Community service:* Pupils take bronze, silver and gold Duke of

Edinburgh's Award. CCF and community service both optional at age 14. Ten Tors Competition, winner of Black Mountain Challenge. *Clubs and societies:* Over 30 clubs, eg historical, geographical, general knowledge quizzes, glass engraving, war games, natural history, CAD.
Uniform School uniform worn throughout.
Houses/prefects Competitive houses. Prefects appointed by the Headmaster in consultation with the staff.
Religion Morning worship is non-denominational.
Social Frequent links with Alice Ottley School, especially for drama and music. German, French and Russian exchanges; cricket tour to Malaysia and Singapore; rugby to South Africa; music USA; trips to Normandy and Prague. Pupils allowed to bring own car/bike/motorbike to school. Meals self-service. School shop. No tobacco/alcohol allowed.
Former pupils Imran Khan, Tim Curtis, John Carter, Professor I R Christie.

• ROYAL BALLET

The Royal Ballet School, White Lodge, Richmond Park, Surrey TW10 5HR. Tel 0181 876 5547 (for age 11–16); 155 Talgarth Road, London W14 9DE. Tel 0181 748 6335 (for ages 16+)
• Pupils 244 • Boys 11–18 (Board to 16; Day thereafter) • Girls 11–18 (Board to 16; Day thereafter) • Upper sixth 43 • Termly fees £3058 + lodgings (Day 16+) £5257 (Board 11–16) • BSA • Enquiries/application to the Auditions Secretary at Talgarth Road.

What it's like

Started as the Academy of Choreographic Art in 1929 by Ninette de Valois. Under the auspices of Lilian Baylis, it became The Sadler's Wells Ballet School in 1931, and the Royal Ballet School at the granting of the Queen's 1956 charter. It provides most of the soloists and corps de ballet of the Royal Ballet and Birmingham Royal Ballet. Although the majority of pupils are girls, there is an increasing number of boys. The Lower School is a boarding school for pupils aged age 11–16. It is housed in White Lodge, built as a Royal Hunting Lodge (1727), and set in idyllic surroundings in the middle of Richmond Park. The Upper School provides tuition in West London for students living at home or in rented accommodation. The school puts on an annual performance at The Royal Opera House followed by a week at Holland Park Theatre. Dance classes are built up from one a day until pupils study dance for 17 hours a week. The curriculum includes classical ballet, character dancing, English folk dancing, Scottish social and highland dancing, classical Greek and national dancing, dalcroze eurythmics and drama. Although nearly all pupils go on to become professional dancers, the school aims to provide an education that will be useful for fields outside dancing as well.

School profile

Pupils Age range 11–18. 134 boarding pupils aged 11–16 in Lower School; 110 students aged 16+ in Upper School, including a teachers' course. Main entry age 11, and significant intake to Upper School at 16.
Entrance Audition and one year's trial. Potential talent and physical suitability looked for. Pupils are eligible for the DFEE's Aided Places Scheme.
Head and staff *Director*: Dame Merle Park. Educated at Elmhurst Ballet School. Also principal ballerina with the Royal Ballet; founder of the Ballet School, St Peter's Square. Assistant Director: Nigel Grant. *Academic and Pastoral Principal:* John Mitchell.
Exam results In 1995, 24 pupils in upper fifth, 43 in upper sixth. *GCSE:* In 1995, 12 passed in 8+ subjects; 8 in 5–7 subjects. *A-levels:* 22 passed in 2 subjects; 8 in 1 subject. Average UCAS points 11.0.
Careers Lower School pupils graduate to Upper School in Talgarth Road at 16+. Many then join the Royal Ballet or Birmingham Royal Ballet.
Curriculum GCSE and A-levels. Most pupils take 8 GCSEs and 2 A-levels including dance. *Computing facilities:* ICL network of IBM-compatible PCs. *Special provision:* for EFL.
Social Meals self-service. Shop selling dancewear and makeup.
Boarding Qualified nursing sister; termly orthopaedic examinations for Upper School. Student counsellor, physiotherapist attends daily.

Former pupils include Lesley Collier; Sir Anthony Dowell; Dame Margot Fonteyn; Dame Merle Park; Lynne Seymour; Wayne Sleep; Darcy Bussell; Viviana Durante; Jonathan Cope.

• ROYAL HOSPITAL

Royal Hospital School, Holbrook, Ipswich, Suffolk IP9 2RX. Tel 01473 328342

• Pupils 630 • Boys 11–18 (Board) • Girls 11–18 (Board) • Upper sixth 80 • Termly fees £2550 (Board) £1350 (Day, sixth-form only) • SHMIS, BSA • Enquiries/application to the Registrar

What it's like

Founded in 1712 at Greenwich, it moved in 1933 to its present exceptionally well-equipped new complex with 200 acres of beautiful grounds overlooking the River Stour, just south of Ipswich. It is now fully co-educational, the first girls' being admitted in 1991. The school enjoys first-rate facilities and accommodation in a civilised and healthy environment. Religious worship is compulsory. A large staff allows a staff:pupil ratio of about 1:10. Academic standards and results are good and the majority of sixth-formers go on to degree courses each year. Very strong indeed in music. It has high standards also in sports and games (many representatives at county and national level). Its naval tradition is continued in the large CCF contingent and with sailing.

School profile

Pupils Age range 11–18; 630 pupils (400 boys, 230 girls); all pupils board except a few sixth-formers. Main entry ages 11, 12, 13 and into sixth. Approx 10% are children of former pupils. *State school entry:* 60% main intake, 60% to sixth.

Entrance Own exam used. No special skills or religious requirements. Parents not expected to buy textbooks; maximum extras, £40. Fees for all pupils already subsidised; further subsidies available for children and grandchildren of seafarers, according to means test. Academic, music and art scholarships available.

Parents 15+% in armed services. Up to 30% live within 40 miles; up to 10% live overseas.

Head and staff *Headmaster:* Nicholas Ward, in post from 1995. Educated at Leicester University (engineering and law). Previously Headmaster at Bentham School, Lancaster, and Housemaster and Bursar at Framlingham. *Staff:* 71 full time, 5 part time. Annual turnover 4%. Average age 40.

Exam results In 1995, 95 pupils in upper fifth, 72 in upper sixth. *GCSE:* In 1995, 82% upper fifth gained at least grade C in 5+ subjects. *A-levels:* 19 upper sixth passed in 4+ subjects; 18 in 3; 27 in 2; and 6 in 1 subject. Average UCAS points 16.0.

University and college entrance 89% of 1995 sixth-form leavers went on to a degree course (15% after a gap year); others typically go on to employment. Of those going on to university, 10% went to Oxbridge; 13% took courses in medicine, dentistry and veterinary science, 20% in science and engineering, 4% in law, 45% in humanities and social sciences, 11% in art and design, 6% in other vocational subjects.

Curriculum GCSE and *A-levels:* 18 subjects offered (including industrial studies, politics, electronics, technology and A-level general studies). 24% take science A-levels; 18% arts/humanities; 58% both. *Vocational:* Work experience available. *Computing facilities:* 30 computers in 2 rooms; plus 20+ PCs and 18 departmental computers. *Special provision:* Local dyslexia centre available. Special needs teacher. *Europe:* French and German offered to GCSE and A-level. Some German and Spanish pupils in school.

The arts *Music:* Up to 50% of pupils learn a musical instrument; instrumental exams can be taken. Some 10 musical groups including choir, chamber choir, orchestra, wind ensemble, concert band, marching band, brass ensemble, corps of drums, pop groups. *Drama & dance*: Drama and dance offered. GCSE media studies, ISTD and RAD exams may be taken. Some pupils are involved in school productions and the majority in house/other productions. Recent productions of The Boyfriend, HMS Pinafore and Arsenic And Old Lace. *Art:* On average, 25 take GCSE, 15 A-level. Design, pottery, textiles, photography, print techniques, art history also offered. Students have been publicly and privately commissioned to produce work.

Sport, community service and clubs *Sport and physical activities:* Major sports:

soccer, rugby, cricket, netball, hockey, rounders. Optional: swimming, squash, badminton, tennis, shooting, athletics, croquet, life-saving, cross-country, basketball, trampolining, gymnastics. All pupils learn to sail. RLSS and RYA exams may be taken. 1994: rugby, U16 England 'A' captain, county XVs (various ages), U18 Eastern Counties; Suffolk cross-country; National Lifesaving Championships; national cross-country trialists; swimming, county U14 and relay champions. *Community service:* 150+ pupils take bronze, silver and gold Duke of Edinburgh's Award. CCF compulsory for 3 years at age 14; optional in upper sixth. Community service optional. St John Ambulance Corps within school. *Clubs and societies:* Over 30 clubs, eg riding, clay-pigeon shooting, model railway, rambling, computing, electronics, photography, drama, ballet, modern/tap dance, astronomy, music, table tennis, sailing, public speaking, debating. (Some 75 activities take place weekly.)

Uniform School uniform worn throughout, provided by school at no cost.

Houses/prefects Competitive houses. Prefects, head of school, head of house and house prefects – appointed by Headmaster. Sixth Form Committee and School Council.

Religion Compulsory attendance at religious worship; separate C of E and RC chapels. Facilities for CSFC pupils.

Social Theatre, debates. Organised trips abroad including skiing, adventure training, France (battlefields etc). Pupils allowed to bring own bike to school. Meals self-service. School shop. No tobacco allowed; upper sixth bar.

Discipline Weekday detentions are given to those who fail to produce work, Saturday night detentions for misbehaviour. Sliding scale of fines/punishment for smoking. Drugs or solvent abuse leads to expulsion.

Boarding 15% have own study bedroom, 85% are in rooms of 2–4. Houses of approximately 60, same as competitive houses; upper sixth separate. Resident qualified nurse. Central dining room. Pupils can provide and cook own food in a limited way. 1 week's exeat at half-term; other exeats by arrangement. Sixth form allowed visits to local town.

Alumni association is run by L Dryden, c/o the school.

• ROYAL RUSSELL

Royal Russell School, Coombe Lane, Croydon, Surrey CR9 5BX. Tel 0181 657 4433, Fax 0181 657 0207

• Pupils 690 • Boys 3–18 (Day/Board/Weekly) • Girls 3–18 (Day/Board/Weekly) • Upper sixth 44 • Termly fees £1850 (Day) £3510 (Board/Weekly) • SHMIS • Enquiries/application to the Headmaster

What it's like

Founded in 1853, by a committee of textile workers to provide free education for the sons and daughters of 'necessitous' employees in the trade. Almost from the outset it was under the patronage of the royal family; since 1901 each succeeding monarch has been patron. In 1924 the school moved to its present site two miles south-east of Croydon where it stands in beautiful gardens in a delightful 100-acre, rural, wooded estate. Its elegant and well-appointed buildings include a fine chapel and excellent modern facilities. The school is affiliated to the Church of England, and the approach to daily life is founded on Christian principles, but pupils of all persuasions are welcome. The senior school staff:pupil ratio is approximately 1:12. A sound general education is provided and results are good, bearing in mind the wide range of ability. Most of those that stay on into the sixth-form go on to university. Music, drama and art are strong. There are very good facilities for sports and games, including a large sports hall and a new indoor swimming pool. A plentiful range of clubs and societies. The CCF has an Army unit open to both boys and girls. Full use is made of the estate and a good deal of enterprise is shown in cultural visits, expeditions abroad etc. The school is greatly involved in the Model United Nations programmes: there is an annual four-day conference at the school and delegations are sent each year to the international conference in The Hague, with several honours for best delegations.

School profile

Pupils Total age range 3–18, 690 pupils: 560 day (380 boys, 180 girls), 121 boarding (81 boys, 40 girls; bording only in senior department). Senior department 11–18, 450 pupils (310 boys, 140 girls). Main entry age 11. *State school entry:* 10% main intake, plus 5% to sixth.

Entrance Own entrance exam used, report and interview. Scholarships and bursaries available.

Head and staff *Headmaster:* Dr John Jennings, appointed in 1996. Educated at West Buckland and London University. Previously Vice Master of Queen Elizabeth's Grammar School, Blackburn. *Staff:* 38 full time in senior school, 13 part time. Annual turnover 9%. Average age 44.

Exam results In 1995, 96 pupils in fifth, 44 in upper sixth. *GCSE:* In 1995, 23 fifth gained at least grade C in 8+ subjects; 24 in 5–7 subjects. *A-levels:* 4 upper sixth passed in 4+ subjects; 20 in 3; 12 in 2; and 5 in 1 subject. Average UCAS points 15.8.

University and college entrance 95% of 1995 sixth-form leavers went on to a degree course (14% after a gap year); others typically go on to retakes or art foundation courses. Of those going on to university, 3% went to Oxbridge; 2% took courses in medicine, dentistry and veterinary science, 23% in science and engineering, 7% in law, 32% in humanities and social sciences, 2% in art and design, 28% in vocational subjects.

Curriculum GCSE and A-levels. 22 GCSE subjects offered; 17 at A-level (no A-level general studies). 25% take science A-levels; 70% arts/humanities; 5% both. *Vocational:* Work experience available; also City and Guilds cookery certificate and professional cook's course. *Computing facilities:* Network of 60 PCs; whole-school network planned. *Special provision:* EFL for foreign pupils; help for dyslexics. *Europe:* French, German and Spanish offered to GCSE, AS and A-level. Regular exchanges to France and Germany. Number of Euroboarders in school for 1 term to 2 years.

The arts (pupils aged 11 and over) *Music:* Over 30% of pupils learn a musical instrument; instrumental exams can be taken as well as GCSE and A-level. Musical groups include chapel choir, chamber choir, various other occasional ensembles. *Drama & dance*: Drama offered; GCSE, A-level and LAMDA exams may be taken. Frequent school productions. 2 pupils currently in National Youth Theatre, 1 National Youth Music Theatre; former pupil playing lead in Miss Saigon. *Art:* On average, 30 take GCSE, 3 AS-level, 8 A-level. Design, pottery, graphics, IT and 3-D design offered. Extra-curricular art and design always available. Several students accepted on foundation courses.

Sport, community service and clubs (Pupils aged 11 and over) *Sport and physical activities:* Compulsory sports: Cricket (boys), netball, rounders (girls), football, hockey, swimming, basketball, badminton, athletics, tennis, softball, trampolining, cross-country, gymnastics. Optional: squash, volleyball, aerobics, judo, fencing, dry slope skiing, orienteering, table tennis. Fifth and sixth-form only: weight training. 5 county cricketers. *Community service:* Pupils take bronze, silver and gold Duke of Edinburgh's Award. CCF and community service optional. *Clubs and societies:* Up to 15 clubs, eg art, chess, drama, photography, Model United Nations, computing, young engineers, Young Enterprise.

Uniform School uniform worn except in the sixth.

Houses/prefects Competitive houses. Prefects, head boy/girl, appointed by the Headmaster. Heads of houses and house prefects appointed by house staff.

Religion Attendance at religious worship compulsory.

Social Annual ski trips, French trip and German exchange with Augsburg. Sixth form allowed to bring own car to school, subject to strict controls. Meals self-service. School uniform shop. No tobacco/alcohol allowed.

Discipline Pupils failing to produce homework once might expect a reprimand and extra time to complete it. Those caught smoking pursue a smokers' reform programme and pay a fine which goes to cancer research. For serious offences, suspension and expulsion would be considered.

• RUGBY

Rugby School, Rugby, Warwickshire CV22 5EH. Tel 01788 543465, Fax 01788 579745

• Pupils 710 • Boys 12–18 (Day/Board) • Girls 12–18 (Day/Board) • Upper sixth 139 • Termly fees £3330 (Day) £4240 (Board) • HMC • Enquiries application to the Registrar

What it's like

Founded in 1567, it moved in 1750 to an old manor house on the site of the present School House. By the end of the 18th century it was established as a major public boarding school. Dr Arnold became Head in 1828 and added much to its fame. Substantial growth in the 19th century led to the addition of many of the buildings which give the school its distinctive character. Twentieth-century development includes the design centre with a media studio, theatre and micro-electronics centre. There are also fine gardens, 80 acres of playing fields, plus the amenities of Rugby town on the doorstep. A traditional school, but also warm, friendly and extremely open. It became co-educational in 1993. It is a C of E foundation and a certain amount of worship and religious education are compulsory. A large and very well-qualified staff allows a staff:pupil ratio of about 1:8. Academically, it is a high-powered school and standards are very high. Results are excellent and each year a very large number of pupils go on to degree courses, including many to Oxbridge. The music, drama, media and art departments are tremendously strong. About half the pupils have some involvement in music and virtually everyone is engaged in dramatic presentations at some time or another. Everybody takes a modular general studies course which includes IT, media and careers. It is renowned for its achievements in sports and games of which a great variety is available and with numerous representatives at county and international level. A very large number of clubs and societies cater for virtually every need. The Tawney Society is a most important academic society for visiting speakers on political, historical and cultural topics. There is a large voluntary CCF contingent involving about 300 boys and girls in Army, Navy and Air Force sections. The school has a considerable commitment to local community services and initiates a wide range of holiday courses of all kinds.

School profile

Pupils Age range 12–18, 710 pupils, 151 day (98 boys, 53 girls), 559 boarding (400 boys, 159 girls). Junior department for day pupils aged 12. Senior school 13–18; 697 pupils. Main entry ages 13 and into sixth. Approx 25% are children of former pupils. *State school entry:* into junior department, plus 10% to sixth.

Entrance Common Entrance used; interviews for 16+ intake. No special skills or religious requirements. Parents expected to buy textbooks; clothes and music lessons also extra. 16 pa scholarships including music and art; 16 major and 28 minor foundationerships (day pupils).

Parents are largely professional; others in industry, finance, commerce or the services. 20+% live within 30 miles; up to 20% live overseas. Remainder widely spread over British Isles.

Head and staff *Head Master*: M B Mavor, 6 years in post. Educated at Loretto and Cambridge (English and education). Previously Headmaster at Gordonstoun, Course Tutor (drama) at Open University, Assistant Master at Tonbridge and Woodrow Wilson Teaching Fellow at Northwestern University, Evanston, Illinois. *Staff:* 80 full time, 14 part time. Annual turnover 5%. Average age 36.

Exam results In 1995, 113 pupils in upper fifth, 141 in upper sixth. *GCSE:* In 1995, all upper fifth gained at least grade C in 8+ subjects. *A-levels:* 27% upper sixth passed in 4+ subjects; 67% in 3; 5% in 2; and 1% in 1 subject. Average UCAS points 25.5.

University and college entrance 87% of 1995 sixth-form leavers went on to a degree course; others typically go on to art or music colleges, non-degree courses eg agriculture or into careers (eg City). Of those going on to university, 14% went to Oxbridge; 10% took courses in medicine, dentistry and veterinary science, 27% in science and engineering, 60% in humanities and social sciences, 1% in art and design, 2% in drama and music.

Curriculum GCSE and A-levels. 20 subjects offered, including Japanese; no A-level general studies. 35% take science A-levels; 55% arts/humanities; 10% both. *Vocational:* Work experience available. *Computing facilities:* Information technology centre. *Special provision:* Qualified teacher for dyslexia gives regular lessons; foreign pupils can receive

timetabled extra English lessons. *Europe:* French, German, Russian and Spanish offered to GCSE and A-level; also non-examined Italian and Welsh. Regular exchanges for sixth-form to France, Germany and Spain. Talks from MEPs and other distinguished European visitors. Biennial colloquium, Educating Europe.
The arts *Music:* 40% of pupils learn a musical instrument; instrumental exams can be taken. Some 6 musical groups including chapel choir, orchestra, sinfonia, brass and chamber ensembles. *Drama & dance*: Drama offered. Many pupils are involved in school productions and the majority in house/other productions. *Art:* Art and design offered.
Sport, community service and clubs *Sport and physical activities:* Optional sports: rugby, hockey, cricket, athletics, tennis, swimming and most other sports. 1995: 1 pupil national rugby U19 XV; 5 national hockey; very substantial county representation in various sports. *Community service:* Pupils take bronze, silver and gold Duke of Edinburgh's Award. CCF and community service optional. *Clubs and societies:* Up to 15 clubs, eg Tawney Society (politics and current affairs), debating, chess, philately, model railway.
Uniform School uniform worn throughout.
Houses/prefects Competitive houses. Prefects (The Levée) and head of school – appointed by Head; head of house, house prefects – appointed by housemaster/housemistress. No school council but Levée takes some decisions.
Religion Compulsory 10-minute chapel 3 times/week; 4–5 compulsory Sunday services each term; other Sundays choice between Forum (speaker from a charity or social organisation) or Chapel Eucharist.
Social Musical co-operation including the sinfonia orchestra with other local schools. 2 ski trips abroad a year, 1 sports trip, natural history expeditions every other year (eg Galapagos, Hindu Kush); annual exchanges (Vienna, Madrid, France). Pupils allowed to bring own bike to school (other vehicles rarely). All meals in house dining halls; lunch formal. Regular dances. School shops. No tobacco; sixth-form bar 3 nights/week (2 drinks limit).
Discipline Pupils failing to produce homework might expect verbal reproof, 1½ hr detention for repeated offence; those caught in possession of drugs on the premises should expect immediate expulsion.
Boarding 10% have own study bedroom, 15% share with 1 other, 70% are in dormitories of 6+. Studies from entry; 50% have study to themselves. Houses of approximately 55, are main social unit. Resident qualified medical staff. Pupils can provide and cook own snacks, 3 termly exeats (1 week, 2 weekends), unlimited Sundays after Chapel/Forum. Visits to restricted area of local town allowed after lunch each day.
Alumni association is run by Mr John Inglis, 115 Dunchurch Road, Rugby, CV22 6BU.
Former pupils Tom King and Ian Lang (MPs); A N Wilson and Salman Rushdie (novelists); Marmaduke Hussey (former Chairman of BBC Governors); David Croft (TV scriptwriter); Sir Ewen Fergusson (former UK Ambassador, Paris); Robert Hardy, Francesca Hunt (actors); Bishop Hugh Montefiore; Sir Campbell Adamson (former Director of the CBI); Chris Brasher; Zia Mahmood (current World Bridge Champion); Andrew Rawnsley and Isabel Wolff (journalists).

• RUNNYMEDE

Runnymede College, Camino Ancho 87, La Moraleja, 28109 Madrid, Spain. Tel 34 1 650 83 02, Fax 34 1 650 82 36

• Pupils 462 • Boys 3–18 (Day) • Girls 3–18 (Day) • Upper sixth 23 • Termly fees £1105–£2240 (Day) • Enquiries/application to the Assistant Headmaster

What it's like

Founded in 1967, the school moved in 1990 to purpose-built premises on a large site in La Moraleja, an elegant residential area north of Madrid. It is well equipped with libraries, laboratories and a hall-cum-gymnasium. The fine and spacious grounds permit basket-ball courts, a football pitch and two tennis courts. It is a British primary and secondary day school, 40% of whose pupils come from the UK, 14% from the USA and the rest from all over the world. As a matter of principle only a limited number of Spanish pupils are admitted, not because the school is anti-Spanish but in order to maintain the ethos and the linguistic and academic standards of a British school. Runnymede is somewhat unusual in that it was founded and is privately owned by the Headmaster and his wife and one of their sons who is the Assistant Headmaster. It is very much a British school abroad, but with many of the features of an international school. A favourable staff:pupil ratio of about 1:12 permits much individual attention. Spanish is taught throughout. Academic standards are good and many sixth-formers proceed to degree courses. Music, art and drama are very well supported and there is a fair range of extra-curricular activities. Sports and games are encouraged and there are plentiful inter-school fixtures and tournaments.

School profile

Pupils Total age range 3–18; 462 day pupils (250 boys, 212 girls). Senior department 11–18; 202 pupils (102 boys, 100 girls). Main entry ages 3, 5, 11 and 16. Some are children of former pupils.
Entrance Own entrance exam used. No special skills or religious requirements; children with obvious learning difficulties not accepted. No extras; parents not expected to buy textbooks. Some scholarships.
Parents Mainly business, diplomatic corps and professional.
Head and staff *Headmaster:* Arthur Powell, 29 years in post. Educated at King's College Wimbledon, and School of Slavonic and East European Studies. Previously Assistant Director of Studies at the British Council Institute in Milan, and Director of Studies at the English Institute, Naples. Also Lecturer in English Language, Universitá Cattolica, Milan, and Director of English Language Courses, Radiotelevisione Italiana. Author of a number of English textbooks. Founder of National Association of British Schools in Spain. *Staff:* 40 full time, 10 part time. Annual turnover 5%. Average age 35.
Exam results In 1995, 30 in upper fifth, 23 in upper sixth. *IGCSE:* In 1995, 23 upper fifth gained at least grade C in 8+ subjects; 7 in 5–7 subjects. *A-levels:* 1 upper sixth passed in 5 subjects; 4 in 4; 14 in 3; 1 in 2 subjects. Average UCAS points 23.5.
University and college entrance 85% of 1995 sixth-form leavers went on to a degree course, others typically go on to eg tourism courses. Of those going on to university, 47% took courses in science and engineering, 53% in humanities and social sciences.
Curriculum IGCSE, AS and A-levels. 13 subjects offered (no A-level general studies). 32% took science A-levels; 47% arts/humanities; 21% a mixture of both. *Vocational:* Work experience available. *Computing facilities:* Computer room with 12 Macintosh. *Special provision:* EFL classes available; access to 2 educational psychologists. *Europe:* French and Spanish offered to IGCSE and A-level
The arts (Pupils aged 11 and over) *Music:* Up to 50% of pupils learn a musical instrument (clarinet, saxophone, piano or guitar). 3 musical groups: choir, recorder, instrumental ensemble. *Art:* On average, 15 take GCSE, 5 A-level. Photography also offered.
Sport, community service and clubs (Pupils aged 11 and over) *Sport and physical activities:* Compulsory sports: basketball, football, volleyball, hockey, athletics. Optional: swimming, tennis, riding, skiing, rounders. *Clubs and societies:* Up to 10 clubs, eg debating, chess, art, photography, drama, music.
Uniform School uniform worn except in sixth (and nursery).
Houses/prefects Competitive houses. Prefects, head boy/girl, head of house and house prefects appointed by the Head and Deputy.
Religion None.
Social Sports events with other international or English-medium schools in cross-country, swimming, athletics, basketball, soccer. Course at Centre de Culture Européenne (France) for lower sixth French students; several take summer language courses (Montpellier, Tours or Paris). Annual ski trip; field trips to Merida (Latin studies), Jerez de la Frontera (geography); day excursions to museums, concerts, plays, archaeological sites and Spanish towns of historic and artistic interest. Sixth form allowed to bring own car/bike to school. Meals formal. No tobacco/alcohol allowed.
Discipline Pupils failing to produce homework once might expect admonition (then detention; report after the third; then suspension). Pupils who make life very unpleasant for pupils or teachers are expelled.
Former pupils David Broza (singer); Vicki Larraz (pop group, Olé Olé); Mari Kumamoto (concert pianist); Gabino Diego (Spanish actor); Dr Charles Powell (Oxford historian).

• RYDAL PENRHOS (Co-ed)

Rydal Penrhos Senior School (Coeducational Division), Pwllycrochan Avenue, Colwyn Bay, Clwyd LL29 7BT. Tel 01492 530155, Fax 01492 531872

• Pupils 412 • Boys 11–18 (Day/Board) • Girls 11–18 (Day/Board) • Upper sixth 59 • Termly fees £2068–£2408 (Day) £2835–£3328 (Board) • HMC • Enquiries/application to the Headmaster

What it's like

Formerly Rydal School, this is the co-educational division of Rydal Penrhos School, which was recently formed from a merger between two Colwyn Bay schools - Rydal School and Penrhos College. Rydal was founded in 1885 as a boys' school and became co-educational in 1977. Its agreeable and well-designed buildings occupy a fine site on the edge of the resort and overlooking the Irish Sea. It has excellent facilities and accommodation. Rydal Penrhos preparatory school is combined but has a distinctive atmosphere of its own. As a Methodist school, religious services and religious education are an important part of the curriculum. The teaching is good with a staff:pupil ratio of about 1:8. Results are good and most pupils go on to degree courses, including some to Oxbridge. A very strong tradition in drama, art and music; and an excellent record in games and sports, including county and international representatives. There is a wide range of other activities are offered, with emphasis on outdoor pursuits (ideal because of the proximity of the sea and Snowdonia) and the Duke of Edinburgh's Award Scheme. Very active in charity fundraising and community service. A school-based club, Rydal Focus, enables the local senior citizens to join the school in the use of sports, CDT and art facilities.

School profile

Pupils Age range 11–18; 412 pupils, 210 day (135 boys, 75 girls), 202 boarding (146 boys, 56 girls). Main entry ages 11, 13 and into the sixth. 6% are children of former pupils. Rydal Penrhos Prep School (Tel 01492 530381) provides over 75%. *State school entry:* 5% main intake, plus 5% to sixth.

Entrance Common Entrance and own tests used. Welcomes skills in music, sports, art; no religious requirements but school has a Methodist foundation. Parents expected to buy textbooks. 16 pa assisted places. 12–15 pa scholarships, 10%–50% fees. Bursaries for clergy children (50%) and for service children (up to 20%).

Parents 40% in industry or commerce. 10+ % live overseas.

Head and staff *Headmaster:* Nigel Thorne, 5 years in post. Educated at Bishop Wordsworth, Salisbury, and at Westminster College (Oxford), and Birkbeck College, London (geography and education). Previously Deputy Head at Caterham and Head of Geography and Assistant Housemaster at Harrow. *Staff:* 35 full time, 8 part time. Annual turnover 2 or 3. Average age 40.

Exam results In 1995, 71 pupils in Year 11, 58 in upper sixth. *GCSE:* In 1995, 59 in Year 11 gained at least grade C in 8+ subjects; 7 in 5–7 subjects. *A-levels:* 6 upper sixth passed in 4+ subjects; 30 in 3; 14 in 2; and 6 in 1 subject. Average UCAS points 18.0.

University and college entrance 88% of 1995 sixth-form leavers went on to a degree course (18% after a gap year); others typically go on to HND or other courses in eg engineering, business, tourism. Of those going on to university, 5% went to Oxbridge; 8% took courses in medicine, dentistry and veterinary science, 18% in science and engineering, 4% in law, 52% in humanities and social sciences, 6% in art and design, 9% in other subjects eg Japanese, dietetics, nursing, accountancy.

Curriculum GCSE, AS and A-levels: 37 subjects offered (including AS level general studies, not A-level; Japanese offered by arrangement). 10% take science A-levels; 52% arts/humanities; 38% both. *Vocational:* Work experience available. *Computing facilities:* Nimbus PC network. *Special provision:* Specialist EFL teaching plus special help for dyslexics. *Europe:* French and German offered at GCSE, AS and A-level; also business French; Italian in the sixth-form. Regular exchanges; also sports exchanges to France.

The arts *Music:* Over 30% of pupils learn a musical instrument; instrumental exams can be taken. Numerous musical groups including orchestra, blues/rock group, chamber and several choirs. *Drama & dance*: Many pupils are involved in school productions and house/other productions. Recent productions include To Kill a Mockingbird, Macbeth, Oh What a Lovely War; past pupils include actors in Coronation Street and RSC. *Art:* On average, 23 take GCSE, 2 AS-level, 11 A-level. Design, pottery, textiles, photography, 3D,

history of art, graphics also offered. Many pupils go to art and design colleges.
Sport, community service and clubs *Sport and physical activities:* Compulsory sports: rugby, cricket, hockey, netball, tennis. Optional: athletics, swimming, cross-country, basketball, volleyball, trampolining. GCSE, BAGA, RLSS exams may be taken. 2 county players in netball, 1 in swimming, 2 in cross country, 3 hockey; county champions in cross country and sailing; 2 trialists in Welsh netball finals, 2 Welsh international runners and 2 in Welsh youth sailing squad. *Community service:* Pupils take bronze, silver and gold Duke of Edinburgh's Award. Community service compulsory for 1 year at age 14, and 1 year at 16. Outdoor activities programme includes climbing, canoeing, sailing, windsurfing, mountain biking, skiing, orienteering. *Clubs and societies:* Up to 30 clubs, eg chess, debating, canoeing, charity, shooting, music, golf and other sports.
Uniform School uniform worn except in sixth (when suits or equivalent are worn).
Houses/prefects Competitive houses. Prefects, head boy/girl, head of house and house prefects – appointed by the Headmaster after consultation. School Council elected by pupils.
Religion Compulsory morning prayers and Sunday morning service.
Social Social events with local schools. Exchange visits with European schools; skiing party abroad at Easter; climbing party in summer eg to Austrian Alps; rugby tours to Canada and Zimbabwe; netball to Barbados. Day pupils allowed to bring own car/motorbike to school. Meals self-service. Several school shops (tuck, stationery, books, second-hand clothes). No tobacco/alcohol allowed.
Discipline Pupils failing to produce homework once would be expected to do it; those caught smoking cannabis could expect to be expelled.
Boarding 10% have own study bedroom, 78% share (2–4); 9% are in dormitories of 6+. Single-sex houses of approximately 27, same as competitive houses. 3 non-resident qualified nurses, local doctor. Central dining room. Pupils can provide and cook snacks. Flexible boarding arrangements. Visits to the local town allowed.
Alumni association run by M T Leach, Secretary of the Old Rydalian Club, c/o the school.
Former pupils Wilfred Wooller (sportsman); Professor Sir G R Elton (historian); Professor Sir Michael Thompson (Vice-Chancellor of Birmingham University); Professor Peter Butterworth (Pro-Vice-Chancellor, Surrey University); William Roache (actor in Coronation Street), Linus Roache (actor), Duncan Kenworthy (film producer).

• RYDAL PENRHOS (Girls)

Rydal Penrhos Senior School (Girls' Division), Llannerch Road East, Colwyn Bay, Clwyd LL28 4DA. Tel 01492 530333, Fax 01492 533198

• Pupils 225 • Boys None • Girls 11-18 (Day/Board/Weekly) • Upper sixth 30 • Termly fees £1995-£2135 (Day) £2755-£3115 (Board/Weekly) • GSA • Enquiries/application to the Headmaster

What it's like

Formerly Penrhos College (founded 1880), this is now the girls' division of Rydal Penrhos School, which was recently formed from a merger between two Colwyn Bay schools – Rydal School and Penrhos College. It provides single-sex education from 11–18. It has a pleasant campus in the town, by the sea, with well-designed buildings and good boarding accommodation. The co-educational prep school is half a mile away. A forward looking school with a happy atmosphere, it is interdenominational but basically Christian. A sound general education is provided and results are good. The majority of girls go on to degree courses. It is very strong indeed in music, drama and art. Considerable strength in sport and games (a number of county representatives). There is an extensive activities programmes – between 25–30 activities are available each term – there is also a comprehensive programme for outdoor pursuits (eg sailing, canoeing, mountaineering).

School profile

Pupils Age range 11–18; 225 girls (104 day, 121 boarders) Main entry ages, 11–14 and into sixth. Approx 5% are children of former pupils. Large number of pupils from Rydal Penrhos Prep school (tel 01492 530381). *State school entry:* 50% main intake, plus 50% to sixth.

Entrance Own entrance exam used. No special skills or religious requirements. Parents not expected to buy textbooks; no compulsory extras. 13 pa assisted places. 5 pa scholarships/bursaries available, up to 50% of fees.
Parents 30+% live within 30 miles; 10+% live overseas.
Head and staff *Headmaster:* Christopher M J Allen, 4 years in post. Educated at The Judd School, Tonbridge, and at the universities of Durham, London, York (Toronto), and Oxford (geography, economics, management). Previously Deputy Head at United World College of SE Asia and Head of Department and Housemaster at Steyning Grammar School. *Staff:* 30 full time, 13 part time. Annual turnover 1 or 2. Average age 42.
Exam results On average, 40 pupils in upper fifth, 30 in upper sixth. *GCSE:* In 1995, all upper fifth gained at least grade C in 5+ subjects. *A-levels:* On average 1 upper sixth passes in 4+ subjects; 16 in 3; 10 in 2; and 3 in 1 subject. Average UCAS points 18.0.
University and college entrance 95% of 1995 sixth-form leavers went on to a degree course (1% after a gap year); others typically go on to nursing, secretarial, hotel and catering. Of those going on to university, 1% went to Oxbridge; 9% took courses in medicine, dentistry and veterinary science, 30% in science and engineering, 5% in law, 30% in humanities and social sciences, 20% in art and design, 6% in other vocational subjects.
Curriculum GCSE, AS and A-levels (A-level general studies offered but preferred as a non-examined subject). 42% take science A-levels; 42% arts/humanities; 17% both. *Vocational:* Work experience available; also RSA qualifications in word processing. *Computing facilities:* 13 Nimbus, CD-Rom plus various computers in subject rooms. Word processing room. *Special provision:* Specialist one-to-one tuition for dyslexics. ESL available. *Europe:* French and German offered to GCSE and A-level. Regular exchanges for pupils to Germany. Second year spend one week at chateau in Normandy and third year goes to Germany (cost included in fees). School hosts 1 overseas student each year. Various European pupils have spent 1 term in school.
The arts *Music:* Over 50% of pupils learn a musical instrument; instrumental exams can be taken. Some 6 musical groups including orchestras, choirs, wind band. *Drama & dance*: Drama offered; GCSE and LAMDA exams may be taken. All pupils are involved in school and house/other productions. Recent production of The Golden Flute. *Art:* On average, 17 take GCSE, 4 AS-level, 11 A-level; design, pottery, textiles, photography also offered. Art facilities open to non-examination pupils. Pupil winner of Zoological Society of Wales art competition.
Sport, community service and clubs *Sport and physical activities:* Compulsory sports: hockey, gymnastics, netball, tennis, rounders, athletics. Sixth form only: golf, weight training. GCSE, BAGA, RYA exams may be taken. County champions, hockey U16 and athletics U16; 1 pupil sails for Wales, 2 train for Welsh sailing squad. *Community service:* Pupils take bronze, silver and gold Duke of Edinburgh's Award. Community service optional for 2 years at age 16. *Clubs and societies:* Over 30 clubs, eg ballet, sailing, calligraphy, welding, car maintenance, puppet making, skiing, rock climbing, canoeing.
Uniform School uniform worn, optional in sixth-form.
Houses/prefects Competitive houses. Prefects, head girl, head of house and house prefects – some appointed, some volunteer.
Religion Interdenominational. Range of visiting lay and clerical people for Sunday service (compulsory for boarders).
Social Social functions – sports, dances, debates, sixth-form dinner – with local boys and co-ed schools. Cultural trips, individual exchanges for staff and pupils from time to time. Pupils allowed to bring own bike to school. Meals self-service. Pupils run school shop. No tobacco/alcohol allowed.
Discipline Sanctions include work detention, conduct detention. Use of drugs, or illicit use of alcohol are regarded as grounds for expulsion.
Boarding Sixth-form study bedrooms for most, some share (2, 3, 4). No large dormitories. Houses, of approx 35, same as for competitive purposes. Resident qualified nurses. Central dining room. Upper sixth pupils can provide and cook own food. 1 long weekend exeat per term (pupils' choice); unlimited short weekends. Visits to local town allowed.
Former pupils Paula Yates; Prof Alison Fairlie (Professor of French, Cambridge); Janet Hargreaves (actress); Roberta Lamming (author); Dr Kathleen Sherry (gynaecologist); Marjorie Young (golf); Moya Jackson (social work, Philippines), Katy Cropper ('One Man and His Dog' TV series winner), Angela Knight MP.

• RYDE

Ryde School with Upper Chine, Queen's Road, Ryde, Isle of Wight PO33 3BE. Tel 01983 562229, Fax 01983 564714.

• Pupils 658 • Boys 3–18 (Day/Board/Weekly) • Girls 3–18 (Day/Board/Weekly) • Upper sixth 59 • Termly fees £598–£1450 (Day) £2725-£2959 (Board) £2570-£2780 (Weekly) • HMC, SHMIS • Enquiries/application to the Headmaster

What it's like

Founded in 1921 as a boys' school, it has been co-educational since 1985 and recently merged with Upper Chine School for Girls. Ryde moved to its present site on the edge of the town in 1928. For the most part there are elegant buildings amidst fine gardens and playing fields on a site overlooking the Solent. There have been many additions to the buildings and the school is now very well equipped. Boarding accommodation is provided at Bembridge School, which is governed by the same charitable trust. Academic standards and results are good and the majority of sixth-form leavers go on to degree courses. Drama is strong as are music and art. There is a good range of sports and games (regular representatives at county level) and a variety of extra-curricular activities.

School profile

Pupils Total age range 3–18; 658 pupils, 620 day (349 boys, 271 girls), 38 boarding (24 boys, 14 girls); boarding from age 11 only. Senior department 11–18, 462 pupils (253 boys, 209 girls). Main entry ages 9, 11, 13 and into sixth. Approx 5% are children of former pupils. *State school entry:* 80% main senior intake, plus 20% to sixth.

Entrance Common Entrance sometimes used, otherwise by interview. No special skills or religious requirements. Parents not expected to buy textbooks; individual music tuition extra (£76 per term) and lunch for day pupils (£112 per term). 23 pa assisted places. 9 pa scholarships/bursaries.

Parents 90+% live within 30 miles; up to 5% live overseas.

Head and staff *Headmaster:* M D Featherstone, in post for 6 years. Educated at Whitgift and Oxford (modern languages). Previously Housemaster and Head of Modern Languages at Radley. *Staff:* 49 full time, 9 part time. Annual turnover 8%. Average age 38.

Exam results In 1995, 109 pupils in fifth, 56 in upper sixth. *GCSE:* In 1995, 75 fifth gained at least grade C in 8+ subjects; 18 in 5–7; and 15 in 1–4 subjects. *A-levels:* 7 upper sixth passed in 4+ subjects; 30 in 3; 13 in 2; and 6 in 1 subject. Average UCAS points 18.0.

University and college entrance 85% of 1995 sixth-form leavers went on to a degree course, others typically go on to eg art or drama courses. Of those going on to university, 5% took courses in medicine, dentistry and veterinary science, 40% in science and engineering, 45% in humanities and social sciences, 10% in art and design.

Curriculum GCSE, AS and A-levels offered. 20% took science A-levels; 46% arts/humanities; 34% both. *Vocational:* Work experience available. *Computing facilities:* Archimedes. *Europe:* French, German and Spanish offered at GCSE and A-level. Regular exchanges.

The arts (Pupils aged 11 and over) *Music:* Over 30% of pupils learn a musical instrument; instrumental exams can be taken. Some 6 musical groups including orchestra, concert band, swing band. Choir recently toured United States and France. *Drama*: A-level theatre studies and ESB exams may be taken. *Art:* On average, 30 take GCSE, 15 A-level.

Sport, community service and clubs (Pupils aged 11 and over) *Sport and physical activities:* Compulsory sports: rugby, cricket, hockey, netball, swimming, athletics, cross-country. Optional: trampolining, volleyball, basketball, weight training, table tennis, indoor athletics. Sixth form only: ice skating, aerobics. GCSE and A-level may be taken. Pupils regularly selected to represent county in a wide variety of sports. *Community service:* CCF compulsory for 1 year at age 14. Community service optional for 1 year at age 15. *Clubs and societies:* Up to 15 clubs, eg computers, hobbies, video, BAYS, fencing, shooting and other sports, debating.

Uniform School uniform worn throughout.

Houses/prefects Competitive houses. Prefects, head boy/girl, head of house and house prefects – appointed by staff and pupils. Sixth form committee.

Religion Compulsory religious assembly.
Social Organised trips abroad. Sixth-form pupils allowed to bring own car/bike to school. Meals formal. School shop. No tobacco/alcohol allowed.
Discipline A pupil failing to produce homework might expect detention; those caught smoking cannabis on the premises could expect expulsion.
Boarding Boarding is available on the Bembridge School site; transport provided to and from Ryde.
Alumni association is run by I J Clark, c/o the school.
Former pupils Philip Norman (journalist and author).

• RYE ST ANTONY

Rye St Antony School, Pullen's Lane, Headington Hill, Oxford OX3 0BY. Tel 01865 62802, Fax 01865 63611

• Pupils 400 • Boys None • Girls 5–18 (Day/Board/Weekly) • Upper sixth 40 • Termly fees £1750 (Day) £2850 (Board) £2725 (Weekly) • GSA • Enquiries/application to the Headmistress

What it's like

Founded in 1930, the school moved in 1939 to its present site on Headington Hill, a mile or so from the city centre. In the last 30 years there has been a continuous building programme which now provides good modern facilities of all kinds. Modern buildings harmonise with Victorian houses in 12 acres of grounds with beautiful gardens. Christian principles are fundamental to the life and work of the school. It is the only girls' Roman Catholic independent school which is a lay foundation. The staff:pupil ratio is a favourable 1:10, and there is considerable emphasis on personal attention and tuition. Results are good and most girls go on to university, including some to Oxbridge. Music is strong; half the girls learn one or more instruments. Art is very strong throughout the school; a range of options is available in design, textiles and ceramics. Drama is vigorously supported and is treated as a curriculum subject. Games and sports facilities are good and a wide range of sport is available. Good standards are attained with regular representation at city, county and regional level. Many girls are involved in local community services, parish work etc. The Duke of Edinburgh's Award Scheme is very popular, and each year an average of 20 girls complete the Gold Award. Extensive use is made of Oxford's cultural amenities.

School profile

Pupils Total age range 5–18; 400 girls (250 day, 150 boarding). Senior department 11–18, 340 girls. Main entry ages 5, 7, 11, 13 and into sixth. 10% are children of former pupils. *State school entry:* 40% main intake.
Entrance Common Entrance used at 11, own exam for other years. No special skills required. Parents not expected to buy textbooks. Average extras £100 a term. Some scholarships/bursaries available.
Parents 50+% live within 30 miles, less than 10% live overseas.
Head and staff *Headmistress:* Miss Alison Jones, 6 years in post. Educated at Northampton Girls School and York University (English). Previously Head of English and Head of Sixth Form at St Mary's (Cambridge). *Staff:* 37 full time, 33 part time. Annual turnover 2%. Average age 42.
Exam results In 1995, 53 pupils in upper fifth, 40 in upper sixth. *GCSE:* In 1995, 60% upper fifth gained at least grade C in 9+ subjects; 27% in 5–8 subjects. *A-levels:* 80% upper sixth passed in 3 subjects; 15% in 2 subjects. Average UCAS points 17.0.
University and college entrance 90% of 1995 sixth-form leavers went on to a degree course (12% after a gap year); others typically go on to art foundation courses or to nursing. Of those going on to university, 10% went to Oxbridge; 5% took courses in medicine, dentistry and veterinary science, 10% in science and engineering, 5% in law, 56% in humanities and social sciences, 6% in art and design, 5% in vocational subjects eg therapeutic radiography and midwifery, 3% in music.
Curriculum GCSE and A-levels. 28 subjects offered (not including A-level general studies). 15% take science A-levels; 58% arts/humanities; 27% both. *Computing facilities:* 10 Risc PCs, 20 Archimedes, 8 IBM PCs. *Europe:* French (from age 9), German, Italian and Spanish to GCSE and A-level. Regular exchanges to France and

Spain. 1 year and 1 term places for European pupils.
The arts (Pupils aged 11 and over) *Music:* 50% pupils learn one or more musical instrument; instrumental exams can be taken. Musical groups include orchestra, ensembles and choirs. *Drama & dance*: Many pupils are involved in school productions. *Art:* On average 40% take GCSE, 15% A-level. Pupils regularly accepted for art college.
Sport, community service and clubs (Pupils aged 11 and over) *Sport and physical activities:* Sports available: athletics, badminton, fencing, fitness training, gymnastics, football, hockey, netball, rounders, squash, swimming, table-tennis, tennis, touch rugby. Regular city, county and regional representatives in tennis, hockey and netball. *Community service:* Pupils take bronze, silver and gold Duke of Edinburgh's Award.
Uniform School uniform worn, except in the sixth.
Houses/prefects Competitive houses for sport. Head girl and prefects, elected by the school.
Religion All girls attend school Masses and morning assembly.
Social Debates and social events with various local schools. Organised trips abroad, including sports tours and exchanges. Meals formal. School tuck shop. No tobacco/alcohol allowed.
Discipline The aim is to teach the girls to recognise their responsibilities as members of the school community.
Boarding Sixth form have own study bedrooms in separate house. Others in 2–5 bedded rooms. Houses of 25–50. SRN cover 24 hours; doctor visits. 3 weekend exeats each term. Visits to the local town allowed – arrangements depend on age.
Alumni association is run by the Headmistress.

S

• ST ALBANS

St Albans School, Abbey Gateway, St Albans, Hertfordshire AL3 4HB. Tel 01727 855521, Fax 01727 843447

• Pupils 655 • Boys 11–18 (Day) • Girls 16–18 (Day) • Upper sixth 110 • Termly fees £1820 (Day) • HMC • Enquiries/application to the Headmaster

What it's like

Its origins date to the pre-Norman monastic school which, by 1100, occupied buildings near its present site and was controlled by the Abbot of St Albans. In c.1570 Elizabeth I granted it a charter and late in the 19th century it moved into the Abbey Gateway. It is urban and single-site and the playing fields are a mile away. Architecturally, it comprises a very interesting mixture of buildings dating from the late Middle Ages to the 1980s. Very well equipped with modern facilities, its main aim is to develop talent and responsibility and it retains close links with the Abbey. Girls have been accepted in the sixth-form since 1991. Academic standards are high and results are very good; most sixth-formers go on to degree courses, including many to Oxbridge. It has flourishing music, art and drama departments, a good range of sport and games and a thriving CCF. A good deal of use is made of its field study centre in South Wales. A big commitment to local community services, and an outstanding record in the Duke of Edinburgh's Award Scheme.

School profile

Pupils Age range 11–18; 655 day pupils, 625 boys; approx 30 girls. Main entry ages 11, 13 (boys) and into sixth (boys and girls). Approx 3% are children of former pupils. Pupils are drawn from a range of schools at all entry ages. *State school entry:* 80% intake at 11, 5% at 13, plus 50% to sixth.

Entrance Common Entrance and own exam used. No special skills or religious requirements. Parents not expected to buy textbooks; £15 maximum extras. 25 pa assisted places. Up to 12 pa scholarships/bursaries.

Parents 15+% are from industry or commerce.

Head and staff *Headmaster:* Andrew Grant, 4 years in post. Educated at Southend High School and Cambridge (English). Previously Second Master at The Royal Grammar School, Guildford, and Head of English at Whitgift. *Staff:* 55 full time staff, 10 part time staff. Annual turnover 3%. Average age 38.

Exam results On average, 100 pupils in upper fifth, 110 in upper sixth. *GCSE:* On average, 85% upper fifth gain at least grade C in 8+ subjects. *A-levels:* 13% upper sixth pass in 4+ subjects; 72% in 3 subjects. Average UCAS points 20.5 (including general studies, 22.2).

University and college entrance 95% of 1995 sixth-form leavers went on to a degree course (6% after a gap year); others typically go on to management training or direct to careers. Of those going on to university, 17% went to Oxbridge; 4% took courses in medicine, dentistry and veterinary science, 39% in science and engineering, 10% in law, 22% in humanities and social sciences, 5% in art and design, 20% other subjects (eg ophthalmics, business studies).

Curriculum GCSE, AS and A-levels offered (including AS-level general studies). 35% take science A-levels; 45% arts/humanities; 20% both. *Vocational:* Work experience available. *Computing facilities:* 2 computer rooms; 24 Archimedes, 12 Apple Macs, 9 PCs; hard disk networked to science and technology department computers; portable computers; Atari music systems. *Special provision:* for mild dyslexia. *Europe:* French, German and Spanish offered to GCSE and A-level (French compulsory to GCSE); Italian as non-examined subject. Regular exchanges; work experience in France. Satellite TV in all classrooms.

The arts *Music:* 30% of pupils learn a musical instrument; instrumental exams can be taken. Some 10 musical groups including wind bands, string groups, rock bands, jazz

bands, choir, chamber orchestra. *Drama & dance*: Both offered. GCSE and A-level drama may be taken. Large number of pupils involved in all productions. Recently major rock musical, written and produced in-house for local junior schools. *Art:* On average, 15 take GCSE, 6 A-level. Design, photography, printmaking including etching also offered.
Sport, community service and clubs *Sport and physical activities:* Compulsory sports (at various stages): rugby, hockey, cricket, athletics, tennis, badminton, gymnastics, basketball, football, volleyball, cross-country, softball, health-related fitness, table tennis. Optional: golf, mountaineering, sailing, squash, swimming, karate, aerobics and netball. Regular county representatives each year, in rugby, football, hockey, cricket, athletics, tennis, badminton, golf, swimming, cross-country; regional reps each year, cricket and rugby; national, swimming, table tennis, golf and curling. Major rugby, cricket and hockey tours. *Community service:* Pupils must choose one of 4 options for 2 years at age 15: Duke of Edinburgh's Award, CCF, community service, conservation. Pupils take silver and gold D of E. *Clubs and societies:* Up to 10 clubs, eg orienteering, Christian Union, bridge, chess, aeromodelling, skiing.
Uniform School uniform worn, except the sixth.
Houses/prefects Competitive houses. Prefects, head of school – appointed by the Headmaster after consultation with staff and sixth-form.
Religion Compulsory services, unless parents request otherwise.
Social Joint theatrical productions, oratorios, general studies, community service camp, fêtes etc with other local schools. Skiing trips; mountaineering trips; exchanges to France, Germany and the USA; classics trips to Italy and Greece; sports tours to eg Holland, West Indies, Argentina. Pupils allowed to bring own car/bike/motorbike to school. Meals self-service. School shop. No tobacco/alcohol allowed.
Discipline Pupils caught smoking cannabis on the premises could expect expulsion.
Former pupils Professor Lord Renfrew (Master of Jesus College, Cambridge); Professor S Hawking, Tim Rice; Nicholas Breakspeare (Pope Adrian IV); James Shirley (playwright); Mike Newell (film producer: Four Weddings and a Funeral).

• ST ALBANS HIGH

St Albans High School for Girls, 3 Townsend Avenue, St Albans, Hertfordshire AL1 3SJ. Tel 01727 853800, Fax 01727 845011

• Pupils 532 • Boys None • Girls 11-18 (Day) • Upper sixth 70 • Termly fees £1570 (Day) • GSA • Enquiries/applications to the Headmistress

What it's like

Founded in 1889 the school is situated on a pleasant urban site. The buildings are mainly purpose-built with some modern additions. It is Christian by tradition and ethos and tries to put this into practice as a caring community. Closely connected with St Albans Abbey, there is regular worship in the Anglican tradition. A broad academic education is provided and examination result are very good. Girls go on to a wide variety of careers, most via degree courses. Extra-curricular activities are plentiful and varied; music and drama are particularly strong and there are joint orchestral, choral and dramatic activities with St Albans (Boys) School. Facilities for PE and games include playing fields and a new sports hall. There is keen participation in the Duke of Edinburgh's Award Scheme. Parents are very much involved in the activities of the school.

School profile

Pupils Age range 11–18; 532 day girls. Main entry ages 11 and into sixth. Own prep school. *State school entry:* 45–50% main intake.
Entrance Own exam used. No special skills or religious requirements. Parents not expected to buy textbooks. 15 pa assisted places (10 at age 11, 5 at sixth-form). Scholarships (at 11 and 16), 8%–17% fees. Also bursaries and special terms for daughters of clergy.
Parents 15+% doctors, lawyers, etc; 15+% in industry or commerce.
Head and staff *Headmistress:* Mrs Carol Y Daly, in post from 1994. Educated at High Wycombe High School and Nottingham University (chemistry and geology). Previously Headmistress at Forest Girls School, Deputy Head at Netherhall School (Cambridge-

shire) and Housemistress and Head of Chemistry at Kings School, Ely. Also FRSA. *Staff:* 40 full time, 15 part time.

Exam results On average, 76 pupils in upper fifth, 70 in upper sixth. *GCSE:* On average, 99% upper fifth gain at least grade C in 8+ subjects. *A-levels:* 93% upper sixth pass in 2+ subjects; average upper sixth passes 3 subjects. Average UCAS points 23.9.

University and college entrance 91% of 1995 sixth-form leavers went on to a degree course (9% after a gap year); others typically go on to art foundation courses. Of those going on to university, 5% went to Oxbridge; 5% took courses in medicine, dentistry and veterinary science, 36% in science and engineering, 4% in law, 27% in humanities and social sciences, 11% in art and design, 16% in other vocational subjects eg nursing, media and business studies.

Curriculum GCSE and A-levels. 20 subjects offered (no A-level general studies). *Computing facilities:* 50 Apple Macs, 7 PCs, some BBC micros. *Special provision:* Some special provision in certain circumstances. *Europe:* French (from age 11), German and Spanish (from 13) offered at GCSE, AS and A-level. Regular visits and exchanges.

The arts *Music:* Musical groups include: orchestra (joint with St Albans), 2 wind bands, string ensembles, chamber ensembles, and 4 choirs. Annual choral concert in the Abbey (with St Albans). Competes in St Albans Music Festival and regularly records for the BBC. *Drama & dance:* Drama offered at GCSE and A-level. Several clubs, frequent workshop productions, annual house drama festival and at least one major production a year. *Art:* Pottery and screen printing also taught.

Sport, community service and clubs (Pupils aged 11 and over) *Sport and physical activities:* Compulsory: lacrosse, netball, tennis, gymnastics, dance, athletics and swimming. Optional (from 4th year): badminton, volleyball, trampolining and fencing. Sixth form only: squash, judo, aerobics, weight training and golf. *Community service:* Pupils take bronze, silver and gold Duke of Edinburgh's Award. Community service strongly encouraged; lot of fund-raising for charities. *Clubs and societies:* Clubs include Young Enterprise, computing, ecology, dance, photography and technology.

Uniform School uniform worn, except in the sixth.

Houses/prefects Competitive houses. Head girl, prefects, head of house and house prefects – elected by the school. School Council.

Religion Attendance at religious worship compulsory except on certain occasions. Church of England school but girls of other faiths welcomed.

Social Theatrical productions with St Albans School, debating competitions with other schools. Exchanges with Dijon, Lüneberg and Vermont; visits to eg Russia, Florence. Regular skiing trip. Frequent visits to theatres, museums and exhibitions in London. Sixth form allowed to bring car/bike/motorbike. Meals self-service. School shop. No tobacco/alcohol allowed.

• ST AMBROSE

St Ambrose College, Wicker Lane, Hale Barns, Altrincham, Cheshire WA15 OHE. Tel 0161 980 2711, Fax 0161 980 2323

• Pupils 910 • Boys 4–18 (Day) • Girls None • Upper sixth 66 • Termly fees £1150 (Day) • HMC • Enquiries/application to the Head Master or Secretary

What it's like

Opened by the Christian Brothers in 1946, this is a modern purpose-built school in extensive parkland. It is a Roman Catholic foundation and most of the pupils are RCs although pupils of other denominations are welcome. There is a good deal of emphasis on religious instruction and worships: Mass, prayers (public and private), retreats. A sound general education is provided and academic results are good. Most sixth-formers go on to degree courses each year, including Oxbridge. Music and drama are flourishing. A good range of sports and games and a wide variety of extra-curricular activities. The school has some commitment to local community services.

School profile

Pupils Total age range 4–18; 910 day boys. Senior department 11–18, 720 boys. Main entry ages 4, 7, 11 and into sixth. Approx 15% are children of former pupils. Own prep department provides more than 20% of intake. *State school entry:* 70% senior intake.

Entrance Own entrance exam used. No special skills; RC school but admits others. Parents not expected to buy textbooks. 14 pa assisted places. About 10 pa scholarships/bursaries.
Parents 15+% are doctors, lawyers, etc; 15+% in industry or commerce; 15+% are teachers.
Head and staff *Head Master*: G E Hester, 5 years in post. Educated at Thornleigh Salesian College and King's College, London (English). Previously Head Master at St Joseph's, Horwich, Deputy Head Master at St Michael's, Stevenage and Head of English at Royal Russell and also at St Peter's Grammar, Prestwich. Also experienced Chief Examiner for English Literature at O-level and GCSE; current Chairman of inter-board A-level English syllabus revision committee. *Staff:* 57 full time, 4 part time. Annual turnover 2%. Average age 34.
Exam results In 1995, 118 pupils in fifth, 80 in upper sixth. *GCSE:* In 1995, 95 fifth gained at least grade C in 8+ subjects; 13 in 5–7 subjects. *A-levels:* 49 passed in 4+ subjects; 18 in 3; 5 in 2; and 5 in 1 subject. Average UCAS points (6.0 including general studies).
University and college entrance 90% of sixth-form leavers went on to a degree course; others typically go on to HND courses, careers in broadcasting, banking or surveying. Of those going on to university, 10% went to Oxbridge; 40% took courses in science and engineering, 60% in humanities and social sciences.
Curriculum GCSE and *A-levels:* 14 subjects offered (including A-level general studies). 35% took science A-levels; 36% arts/humanities; 29% both. *Vocational:* Work experience available. *Computing facilities:* Well-equipped laboratory. *Europe:* French and German offered at GCSE and A-level; Italian to GCSE and AS-level. Regular exchanges.
The arts (Pupils aged 11 and over) *Music:* Up to 25% of pupils learn a musical instrument; instrumental exams can be taken. Some 3 musical groups including orchestra, other ensembles. Choir has sung in Worcester and Chester cathedrals, York Minster and appeared on TV. *Drama & dance:* Majority of pupils are involved in school productions. *Art:* On average, 25 take GCSE, 8 A-level.
Sport, community service and clubs (Pupils aged 11 and over) *Sport and physical activities:* Optional sports: rugby, cross-country, cricket, athletics, swimming, tennis, badminton, squash. Sixth form only: golf. BAGA, RLSS exams may be taken. *Community service:* Community service optional for sixth-form. St Vincent de Paul Society. *Clubs and societies:* Up to 30 clubs, eg debating, art, science, chess, fell-walking, politics, philately.
Uniform School uniform worn throughout.
Houses/prefects Prefects, head boy – elected by school and staff.
Religion Worship encouraged; Mass, prayers (private and assembly), retreats.
Social Drama, theatre and swimming gala with Loreto Convent School; local festivals. Organised visits to France, Germany, Austria. Pupils allowed to bring own car/bike/motorbike to school. Meals self-service. School shop. No alcohol/tobacco allowed.
Discipline Pupils failing to produce homework once might expect detention; suspension and expulsion for serious offences. School is proud of positive discipline leading to self-discipline.

• ST ANNE'S (Windermere)

St Anne's School, Browhead, Windermere, Cumbria LA23 1NW. Tel 015394 46164, Fax 015394 88414

• Pupils 369 • Boys 2–11 only (Day) • Girls 2–18 (Day/Board) • Upper sixth 30 • Termly fees £2110 (Day) £3180 (Board) • GSA, Round Square • Enquiries/application to the Headmaster

What it's like

Founded in 1863, it has a magnificent situation in the Lake District National Park, on a site of 80 acres with splendid views over Lake Windermere and the fells. Its pleasant and well-equipped buildings are spread over two main sites. The co-educational junior department, Elleray, is in its own large grounds, closer to Windemere. It is Christian in outlook but non-denominational. It attracts girls from all over the world and endeavours to provide a liberal and progressive education in which activities such as sailing, canoeing, fell walking, music, art, drama and voluntary service play an important part. It is a member of the Round Square – a group of internationally based schools following the Kurt Hahn traditions – which allows an unusually wide range of exchanges in Europe, the Commonwealth and the USA. The teaching and exam results are good. Most leavers proceed to degree courses each year. It has a very strong music department, also drama. Very good range of sports and games, societies and clubs. Much emphasis on outdoor pursuits and field studies (unusual among girls' schools); also a very big commitment to local community schemes and an outstanding record in the Duke of Edinburgh's Award Scheme.

School profile

Pupils Total age range 2–18; 369 pupils, 177 day (35 boys, 142 girls), 192 boarding girls. Senior department 11–18, 240 girls. Main entry ages 3 (boys and girls), 11, 13 and into sixth (girls). Approx 5% are children of former pupils. *State school entry:* 30% senior intakes, plus 5% to sixth.

Entrance Own entrance exam used. No special skills or religious requirements; children with allergies, asthma, diabetes and epilepsy can be accommodated. Parents not expected to buy textbooks; maximum extras £150–£200 for boarders, less for day girls. Scholarships and bursaries available.

Parents 15+% are doctors; lawyers, farmers, etc; 15+% in industry or commerce. 20+% of senior school parents live within 30 miles; up to 20% live overseas.

Head and staff *Headmaster:* Ross Hunter, appointed 1996. Educated at Haberdashers' Aske's and Cambridge (geography). Previously Housemaster and Head of Geography at Aiglon College (a Round Square school in Switzerland) and Head of Economics at Canon Slade School, Bolton. *Staff:* 39 full time, 15 part time. Annual turnover 2%. Average age 40.

Exam results In 1995, 43 pupils in fifth, 29 in upper sixth. *GCSE:* In 1995, 34 upper fifth gained at least grade C in 8+ subjects; 5 in 5–7 subjects. *A-levels:* 14 upper sixth passed in 4+ subjects; 5 in 3; 7 in 2 subjects. Average UCAS points 17.5 (21.3 including general studies).

University and college entrance All 1995 sixth-form leavers went on to a degree course (46% after a gap year), 8% to Oxbridge. 4% took courses in medicine, dentistry and veterinary science, 19% in science and engineering, 27% in humanities and social sciences, 46% in art and design, 4% in vocational subjects eg physiotherapy.

Curriculum GCSE and A-level subjects offered (including theatre studies and A-level general studies). 20% take science A-levels; 58% arts/humanities; 22% both. *Vocational:* Work experience available; also RSA level 1 and 2, typewriting and word processing. *Computing facilities:* 16 station RM Nimbus network and Apple Macs. *Special provision:* English for foreign students and specialist help for dyslexic pupils. *Europe:* French, German, Italian and Spanish offered to GCSE, AS and A-level; also Spanish and Portuguese. Over 75% take GCSE in more than 1 language. Regular exchanges (France, Germany and Spain) and with European schools in Round Square Group.

The arts (Pupils aged 11 and over) *Music:* Over 30% of pupils learn a musical instrument; instrumental exams can be taken. Some 8 musical groups including wind band, choirs, orchestra, flute choir, various chamber groups. Recent oratoria performances of Belshazzar's Feast and Dido and Aeneas; chamber music group semi-finalists in National Chamber Music Competition; choral awards in Oxbridge college choirs. *Drama & dance*: Both offered. GCSE and A-level drama, ESB, LAMDA and other speech and drama exams may be taken. Majority of pupils are involved in school productions and all in house/other productions. Cumbria Drama Trophy (school sections); students accepted at Old Vic Theatre School. *Art:* On average, 16 take GCSE, 8 A-level. Design, pottery, textiles also offered.

Sport, community service and clubs (Pupils aged 11 and over) *Sport and physical activities:* Compulsory sports: hockey, netball, athletics, tennis. Optional: volleyball, basketball, canoeing, sailing, gymnastics, fencing, self-defence. BAGA, RYA exams may be taken. Winners S Cumbria U18 hockey; runners-up Cumbria U18 netball; winners South Lakes junior cross-country; tennis, junior doubles championships; county representatives in hockey, cross-country, netball, athletics. *Community service:* Pupils take bronze, silver and gold Duke of Edinburgh's Award. Community service optional; work with Age Concern, Cheshire Home and Scope. *Clubs and societies:* Over 30 clubs, eg community service, bridge, debating, photography, riding, archery.

Uniform School uniform worn throughout.

Houses/prefects Competitive houses. No prefects. Head girl, deputies and heads of houses elected by the school. School Council.
Religion Morning assembly. Sunday evening service.
Social Organised events with local independent schools. Language exchanges and with other Round Square schools (eg Australia, New Zealand, South Africa, USA, Canada, India). Pupils allowed to bring own car/bike to school. Meals self-service. School shop. No tobacco/alcohol allowed.
Discipline Pupils failing to produce homework once can expect extra work; those involved with drugs can expect expulsion.
Boarding Sixth form have own study bedrooms; 60% others share, 40% in dormitories of 6+. Houses of about 50. Resident qualified staff. Central dining room. Pupils can provide and cook own food in the senior house. 2 weekend exeats each term. Visits to local town allowed.
Alumni association is run by Mrs M Beard, Flowerdale, Church Street, East Markham, Nr Newark, Notts.
Former pupils Dodie Smith (author), Frances Hay-Smith (England equestrian team), Teddi Thompson (actress).

• ST ANTONY'S-LEWESTON

St Antony's-Leweston School, Sherborne, Dorset DT9 6EN. Tel 01963 210691, Fax 01963 210786
• Pupils 285 • Boys None • Girls 11–18 (Day/Board) • Upper sixth 30 • Termly fees £2287 (Day) £3505 (Board) • GSA • Enquiries to the Development Officer • Application to the Admissions Tutor

What it's like

Founded in 1891 as a Roman Catholic school, it is situated 3 miles south of the historic abbey town of Sherborne, in beautiful Dorset countryside. It is based around an elegant 18th-century manor house set in 40 acres of grounds and parkland. The manor house has been enhanced in recent years by the addition of a sixth-form wing and the provision of a sports hall, arts centre, design and technology centre and a senior science centre. There are two chapels, one Jacobean and a modern RC church. The school accepts pupils from many religious backgrounds. It aims to provide strong pastoral care allied to high academic standards and results are good. There is a strong tradition in the creative arts and in sport, both inside the school and at competitive level outside. A centre for help with dyslexia has recently been established. The school has flexible boarding arrangements; day girls are welcome to join in weekend activities.

School profile

Pupils Age range 11–18; 285 girls, 130 day, 155 boarding. Main entry ages 11, 12, 13 and into sixth. St Antony's-Leweston Prep School (01963 210790) is the main feeder school.
Entrance Common Entrance, interview and own exam. No special skills or religious requirements, although a Roman Catholic school. Parents not expected to buy textbooks; maximum £240 for extras. Assisted places. Scholarships (including academic, music, sport and art) at 11, 12, 13 and 16, up to 66% fees; some bursaries available.
Parents Strong links with the armed services (particularly Army and Navy). Boarders include those from Europe, America and Far East.
Head and staff *Headmistress:* Miss Brenda A King, 3 years in post. Educated at London University (divinity and theology) and Maria Assumpta Catholic College, Kensington. Previously Deputy Head at Cardinal Newman School, Hove, Head of Religious Studies at Farnborough Hill School and taught at various secondary schools in both state and independent sector. Before moving into education, worked in the Department of Economic Affairs and Ministry of Defence. *Staff:* 43 full time, 13 part time. Annual turnover 10%. Average age 40.
Exam results In 1995, 50 pupils in upper fifth, 30 in upper sixth. *GCSE:* In 1995, 63% upper fifth gained at least grade C in 8+ subjects; 24% in 5–7 subjects. *A-levels:* 73% upper sixth passed in 3 subjects; 23% in 2; and 5% in 1 subject. Average UCAS points 16.5.
University and college entrance 90% of sixth-form leavers go on to a degree course (3% go to Oxbridge); others typically go on to HND, professional or art foundation courses.

Curriculum GCSE and A-levels. 22 subjects offered (no A-level general studies). 17% take science A-levels; 65% arts/humanities; 19% both. *Vocational:* Work experience available; also RSA diploma, stages 1 and 2, and Pitmans level 1, both in word processing. *Computing facilities:* Computers in all departments; computer studies taught. *Special provision:* Specialist centres for EFL and dyslexia. *Europe:* French, German and Spanish offered to GCSE and A-level; GCSE Italian and Spanish in sixth-form. Regular exchanges (France and Germany).
The arts *Music:* Over 50% of pupils learn a musical instrument (22% learn more than one); instrumental exams can be taken. A number of musical groups including string ensembles, flute group, folk band, orchestras (2 joint with Sherborne Schools), choirs and chamber music groups. Annual choral concert eg St Matthew Passion. In 1996, winner of Rayne Foundation award for chamber music and finalists in Chamber Music Competition for Schools; one pupil in National Youth Orchestra, 10 in Dorset county orchestra. *Drama & dance*: Both offered. GCSE drama (joint with Sherborne), LAMDA, RAD and Guildhall exams may be taken. Majority of pupils involved in frequent school and house productions. Regular successes in Bath, Mid-Somerset and Taunton Festivals. *Art:* Painting, drawing, graphic design, ceramics, sculpture, jewellery, fabric painting and photography offered.
Sport, community service and clubs *Sport and physical activities:* Main games - hockey, netball, rounders, tennis, athletics and swimming. Optional extras include riding, squash, gymnastics, fencing, karate; for seniors, rugby, skiing, lacrosse and golf. Several county runners; 2 former pupils karate black belts. *Community service:* Pupils take bronze Duke of Edinburgh's Award. Community service optional (help in local home for the elderly). *Clubs and societies:* Up to 15 clubs, eg riding, orienteering, shooting, bell ringing, aerobics, also driving lessons.
Uniform School uniform worn until final term in upper sixth.
Houses/prefects Competitive houses. Prefects, senior prefects, head girl, head of house and house secretary – elected by staff and prefects.
Religion Pupils expected to attend Chapel once a week. Preparation for confirmation available for Catholic and Anglican pupils. Anglican Communion once a term.
Social Close links with Sherborne, Milton Abbey and Downside, with many social and cultural activities shared. Italian art and history of art trip. No tobacco/alcohol allowed.
Discipline Any drugs-related offence leads to automatic expulsion.
Boarding Older pupils have own study bedroom. Houses divided by age. 2 long weekend exeats each term, short (24-hour) weekends when required. Flexi-boarding available and popular.
Alumni association Old Antonians Association, run by Mrs R Berry c/o the school.
Former pupils Sarah Payne; Erin Pizzey; Kristin Scott-Thomas; Colette Burke (née Halligan); Serena Scott-Thomas; Serena de la Hey; Angela Hickey; Louise Innes (née Nicholson).

• ST AUGUSTINE'S (London)

St Augustine's Priory, Hillcrest Road, London W5 2JL. Tel 0181 997 2022
• Pupils 420 • Boys None • Girls 4–18 (Day) • Upper sixth 18 • Termly fees £835-£1265
• Enquiries to the Headmistress • Applications to the Secretary

What it's like

It has an urban site in a pleasant residential area in west London, with extensive grounds and ample playing fields. It is an RC school owned by a community of nuns. Academic results are good and most sixth-formers go on to degree courses. Music is particularly strong (especially choral work) and there is extensive drama. Media studies is compulsory in the sixth-form. Many extra-curricular activities are available and there is a good range of sport and games (quite a lot of hockey representatives at county and regional level).

School profile

Pupils Total age range 4–18; 420 day girls. Senior department 11–18, 250 girls. Main entry ages 4, 11 and into sixth.
Entrance Own entrance exam used. No special skills looked for; school mainly RC but

others accepted. Parents not expected to buy textbooks until sixth-form; extras £84 maximum. 17 pa assisted places. 2–4 pa sixth-form scholarships.
Head and staff *Headmistress:* Mrs F Gumley-Mason, in post from 1995. Educated at St Augustine's and Cambridge (classics). Previously journalist, author and broadcaster (BBC and Channel 4). *Staff:* 29 full time, 13 part time. Annual turnover 5% or less.
Exam results In 1995, 39 pupils in upper fifth, 20 in upper sixth. *GCSE:* In 1995, 72% upper fifth gained at least grade C in 8+ subjects; 26% in 5–7 subjects. *A-levels:* 80% upper sixth passed in 3 subjects; 20% in 2 subjects. Average UCAS points 16.7.
University and college entrance All sixth-form leavers usually go on to a degree course.
Curriculum GCSE and *A-levels:* 15 subjects offered. 15% take only science A-levels; 55% arts/humanities; 35% both. *Vocational:* Work experience available. *Computing facilities:* IT taught throughout. *Europe:* French (compulsory from age 10) and Spanish (from 12) offered at GCSE and A-level.
The arts (Pupils aged 11 and over) *Music:* 30% of pupils learn a musical instrument; instrumental exams can be taken. Some 7 musical groups including choirs, instrumental groups. *Drama & dance*: Both offered. GCSE drama and Trinity exams may be taken. Some pupils are involved in school and house/other productions. *Art:* On average, 15 take GCSE, 4 A-level. Design, textiles also offered.
Sport, community service and clubs (Pupils aged 11 and over) *Sport and physical activities:* Compulsory sports: hockey, netball, rounders, swimming, athletics, tennis, gymnastics. Optional: dance, football. Sixth form only: badminton, squash, riding. GCSE may be taken. 13 county hockey representatives at different ages; 1 regional U16 rep and 1 U18 trialist; joint county champions U15. *Community service:* Community service optional; different forms of CS encouraged at all ages. *Clubs and societies:* Up to 15 clubs, eg sports, music, dance, computers.
Uniform School uniform worn except in the sixth.
Houses/prefects Competitive houses. Head girl, deputy prefects, head of house and house prefects – appointed by Headmistress.
Religion Morning assembly and Mass four times a term.
Social Organised events with other schools. Trips abroad include choir tours, skiing, etc. Pupils allowed to bring own car/bike to school.
Discipline Periodic detentions as required.

• ST BEDE'S (Hailsham)

St Bede's School, The Dicker, Hailsham, East Sussex BN27 3QH. Tel 01323 843252
• Pupils 450 • Boys 12–19 (Day/Board) • Girls 12–19 (Day/Board) • Upper sixth 80 • Termly fees £2250 (Day) £3800 (Board) • SHMIS • Enquiries/application to the Headmaster.

What it's like

Founded in 1978 as a co-educational school, it is set in the village of Upper Dicker in the countryside. The buildings and playing fields occupy four sites around this small village. The main building is a large country house situated in 20 acres (formerly the home of the egregious and notorious Horatio Bottomley). Nearby Camberlot Hall is one of three residences for boy boarders; in all, the school covers some 170 acres. There has been steady expansion and the school has increased from 22 pupils at its foundation to the present 450, with a deliberate policy to increase the sixth-form. Other developments are under way and its facilities are already very good. It enjoys a staff:student ratio of 1:8. The academic standards are high and most sixth-formers go on to degree courses. It is strong in music, drama and art, and has a very wide range of games (particularly strong in tennis), sports and activities. There are over 80 clubs and societies providing for almost every conceivable interest. Outdoor pursuits are very popular and the school has its own riding stables, competition-size swimming pool and practise golf course.

School profile

Pupils Age range 12–19; 450 pupils, 160 day (95 boys, 65 girls), 290 boarding (175 boys, 115 girls). Main entry ages 12, 13 and into sixth.
Entrance Common Entrance or own exam used. No special skills or religious requirements. Up to 12 pa scholarships/bursaries (academic, musical, artistic, sporting and for all-rounders), 20%–75% of fees.

Parents 15+% are in industry or commerce. 10+% live within 30 miles; 30+% live overseas.

Head and staff *Headmaster:* Roger Perrin, in post for 18 years. Educated at Ardingly and Oxford (history and law). Previously Housemaster and Medieval Historian at Brentwood and Head of History at the Dragon School, Oxford. *Staff:* 47 full time, 10 part time. Annual turnover 10%. Average age 38.

Exam results Average size of upper fifth 90; upper sixth 80. *GCSE:* Students gain at least grade C in an average of 7 subjects. *A-levels:* Students pass an average of 3 subjects. Average UCAS points 15.7.

University and college entrance 85% of 1995 sixth-form leavers went on to a degree course (15% after a gap year); others typically go on to HND courses or directly into employment. Of those going on to university, 5% went to Oxbridge; 5% took courses in medicine, dentistry and veterinary science, 25% in science and engineering, 3% in law, 44% in humanities and social sciences, 14% in art and design, 9% in other subjects (eg acting, agriculture, drama).

Curriculum GCSE, AS and A-levels, also some GNVQs. 30 subjects at GCSE (including Arabic, Japanese, rural studies, food and nutrition, commerce and photography). *Vocational:* Work experience available. RSA course in IT; GNVQ advanced level in business and art/design. *Computing facilities:* RM Nimbus network. *Special provision:* for EFL and specific learning difficulties. *Europe:* French, German, Italian and Spanish offered to GCSE, AS and A-level; also Dutch GCSE, French and Spanish for business use. Regular exchanges.

The arts *Music:* Over 50% of pupils learn a musical instrument; instrumental exams can be taken. Some 9 musical groups including orchestra, choir, chamber groups, brass, woodwind, jazz, pop groups etc. 5 cups and trophies in Eastbourne Festival 1994. *Drama & dance*: Both offered. GCSE drama, A-level theatre studies may be taken. Majority of pupils are involved in school productions and all in house/other productions. Former pupils currently at Central, Mountview and Crouch Hill; annual Shakespeare tour through south-east; annual theatrical gala; 3 principal school productions annually. *Art:* On average, 45 take GCSE, 15 A-level. Design, pottery, textiles, photography, history of art also offered. All applicants gained entry to art college in past 3 years.

Sport, community service and clubs *Sport and physical activities:* No compulsory sports – all pupils advised to take part in physical activity once a week. Optional: soccer, rugby, squash, tennis, cricket, athletics, hockey, netball, rounders, swimming, fencing, badminton, archery, golf, cross-country, riding, dry skiing, sailing, windsurfing, aikido, canoeing, rock-climbing, fly fishing, step aerobics, shooting, volleyball, basketball, gymnastics, weight training, and table tennis. GCSE and A-level sports studies, BHS, RYA exams may be taken. County players in tennis, soccer, netball, cricket, rugby; county champions in squash and soccer; national final 16, volleyball; world silver medal, skiing. *Community service:* Pupils take bronze, silver and gold Duke of Edinburgh's Award. ACF and community service both optional. *Clubs and societies:* Over 80 clubs, including scientific, engineering, literary, art/craft, music, film, debating, social activities.

Uniform Uniformity of dress, except for girls in the sixth.

Houses/prefects Prefects, head of school, head of house and house perfects – appointed by the Headmaster and housemasters.

Religion Multi-religious school meetings on Sundays and mid-week; plus C of E, RC and Free Church services.

Social Musical and termly theatrical productions with local schools. Annual school skiing trip, French, German and Spanish visits. Meals self-service. Sixth-form common room sells beer and cider twice a week. Weekend outings for boarders.

Discipline Pupils failing to produce homework once might expect work detention; detention and gating for misdemeanours; expulsion for any drug offence.

Boarding All sixth and upper fifth have study bedrooms, usually shared with 1 other; 35 in dormitories of 6+. Single-sex houses of 40–70. School doctor visits every morning. Central dining room. 3–4 weekend exeats each term. Visits to local towns allowed.

Former pupils Clare Wood (Wightman Cup Player 1987 and Federation Cup 1989); Julie Salmon (Federation Cup player 1989).

• ST BEES

St Bees School, St Bees, Cumbria CA27 ODS. Tel 01946 822263, Fax 01946 823657

• Pupils 290 • Boys 11–18 (Day/Board/Weekly) • Girls 11–18 (Day/Board/Weekly) • Upper sixth 46 • Termly fees £2406 (Day) £3497 (Board) £3331 (Weekly) • HMC • Enquiries/application to the Registrar

What it's like

Founded in 1583 by Edmund Grindal, Archbishop of Canterbury, it has a particularly fine site of 150 acres in the pleasant valley of St Bees. The sea and a magnificent beach are within half a mile and it has easy access to the Lake District. There are fine gardens and ample playing fields The buildings are handsome, the older ones made of St Bees sandstone; the original school building (1587) is now the dining hall. There have been substantial developments. Originally a boys' school, it became fully co-educational in 1976. The aim of the school is to develop the individual talents of each pupil while providing an education based on Christian principles. Self-reliance, individuality and consideration for others are encouraged. The chapel is used frequently and worship in the Anglican tradition is compulsory. The staff:pupil ratio is about 1:11. Academic standards are high and results consistently good. Almost all sixth-formers proceed to degree courses each year. Considerable strength in music, drama and art. An excellent range of sports and games, including Eton fives and golf (the school has its own course). Plentiful extra-curricular activities are available. There is a large and flourishing CCF; many pupils take part in the Duke of Edinburgh's Award Scheme or the school's own Challenge Award. Considerable emphasis is placed on outdoor pursuits for which the environment is ideal.

School profile

Pupils Age range 11–18; 290 pupils, 175 day (98 boys, 77 girls), 115 boarding (58 boys, 57 girls). Main entry ages 11, 13 and into sixth. Approx. 5% are children of former pupils. *State school entry:* 80% main intakes, plus 80% to sixth.

Entrance Common Entrance and own exam used. Good all-round ability looked for; no religious requirements. Parents expected to buy textbooks; maximum extras £300, including music, excursions, clothing, GCSE sundries. 18 pa assisted places. Scholarships/bursaries available.

Parents 15% in industry or commerce. 30% live within 30 miles; up to 10% live overseas.

Head and staff *Headmaster:* P A Chamberlain, 8 years in post. Educated at Verdin Grammar, Cheshire, and Durham University (zoology). Previously Housemaster at Haileybury. *Staff:* 26 full time, 5 part time. Annual turnover 6%. Average age 42.

Exam results In 1995, 47 pupils in upper fifth, 46 in upper sixth. *GSCE:* On average, 98% upper fifth gain at least grade C in 5+ subjects. *A-levels:* 40% upper sixth pass in 4+ subjects; 25% in 3 subjects. Average UCAS points 19.5.

University and college entrance 90% of sixth-form leavers go on to a degree course, others typically go on to non-degree courses, art colleges etc. Of those going on to university (some to Oxbridge most years), 9% take courses in medicine, dentistry and veterinary science, 40% in science and engineering, 45% in humanities and social sciences, 2% in art and design, 4% in drama and music.

Curriculum GCSE and *A-levels:* 21 GCSE and A-level subjects offered (including photography and A-level general studies). 40% take science A-levels; 40% arts/humanities; 20% both. *Vocational:* Work experience available. *Computing facilities:* Full facilities for computer studies and information technology. *Europe:* French and German offered at GCSE, AS and A-level. Regular exchanges. European students regularly on short stays in school.

The arts *Music:* Over 30% of pupils learn a musical instrument; instrumental exams can be taken. Some 8 musical groups including choir, orchestra, string group, brass. 3 pupils in National Children's Orchestra. *Drama & dance*: Drama offered. Majority of pupils are involved in school productions and all in house/other productions. 2 pupils recently won ESU Shakespeare competition. *Art:* On average, 12 take GCSE, 8 A-level. Design, textiles, photography and graphics also offered.

Sport, community service and clubs *Sport and physical activities:* Compulsory sports: rugby, cricket, hockey, netball, tennis. Optional: cross-country, athletics, squash, fives, golf, soccer, basketball, badminton, etc. *Community service:* Pupils take bronze, silver

and gold Duke of Edinburgh's Award. CCF compulsory for 3 years at age 14. Community service optional. St Bees Challenge Award in sixth-form. *Clubs and societies:* Up to 30 clubs, eg chess, bridge, classics, squash, shooting, Japanese, heritage, fives, lifesaving, film, electronics, YFC.
Uniform School uniform worn throughout.
Houses/prefects Prefects, head boy/girl, head of house and house prefects – appointed by the Head.
Religion Religious worship compulsory.
Social Debates and lectures with other local schools. Trips abroad and exchanges with schools abroad. Pupils allowed to bring own bike to school. School shop. No tobacco allowed; alcohol only at supervised sixth-form social events.
Discipline High standards of conduct are expected and enforced. The scale of punishments varies according to the nature of the offence; pupils may be suspended or expelled for breaches of major school rules.
Boarding Single-sex houses of approximately 60, divided by age. Resident qualified medical staff. Central dining room. Pupils can provide and cook own food. Termly exeats. Visits to local town allowed.
Former pupils Professor R A McCance; Air Chief Marshal Sir Augustus Walker; Rowan Atkinson.

• ST BENEDICT'S

St Benedict's School, 54 Eaton Rise, London W5 2ES. Tel 0181 862 2010, Fax 0181 862 2199
• Pupils 571 • Boys 11–18 (Day) • Girls 16–18 (Day) • Upper sixth 57 • Termly fees £1620 (Day)
• HMC • Enquiries/application to the Headmaster

What it's like

Founded in 1902 by monks from Downside Abbey. The school is attached to the Benedictine Abbey and monastery created in Ealing, and is governed by the Abbot and the Community. Both junior and senior schools are on the same urban site, with some gardens; the playing fields are a mile away. The buildings are mostly 20th century and provide good accommodation and facilities. The education is Benedictine and inculcates the values and ethos of the order. The study of religion, Roman Catholic and ecumenical, is compulsory. Academic standards are high and results very good. Almost all sixth-formers go on to degree courses each year, including Oxbridge. Exceptionally strong in music and art. A good record in sports and games. Plentiful clubs and societies. A substantial commitment to local community schemes and a creditable record in the Duke of Edinburgh's Award Scheme.

School profile

Pupils Age range 11–18; 571 day pupils (539 boys, 32 girls). Main entry ages 11 and 13 (boys); into sixth (boys and girls). Approx 8% are children of former pupils. Own junior school provides more than 20% of intake. *State school entry:* 45% main intakes, plus 8% to sixth.
Entrance Common Entrance and own exam used. All-round and academic skills required; pupils largely Roman Catholic. £100 maximum extras. 15 pa assisted places. Discretionary scholarships/bursaries.
Head and staff *Headmaster:* Dr Anthony Dachs, in post for 10 years. Educated at St George's College, Zimbabwe, and at London and Cambridge universities (history). Previously Deputy Head at Stonyhurst. Also university lecturer for ten years. *Staff:* 52 full time, 10 part time.
Exam results In 1995, 92 pupils in upper fifth, 57 in upper sixth. *GCSE:* In 1995, 92% upper fifth gained at least grade C in 8+ subjects; 3% in 5–7 subjects. *A-levels:* 2% upper sixth passed in 4+subjects; 95% in 3 subjects. Average UCAS points 21.3.
University and college entrance 94% of 1995 sixth-form leavers went on to a degree course, others typically go on to eg art college or apprenticeships. Of those going on to university, 6% went to Oxbridge; 8% took courses in medicine, dentistry and veterinary science, 25% in science and engineering, 64% in humanities and social sciences, 3% in art and design.
Curriculum GCSE and A-levels. 17 subjects offered (general studies taught but not

examined). 32% take science A-levels; 44% arts/humanities; 24% both. *Vocational:* Work experience available. *Computing facilities:* Research machines, Nimbus network. *Special provision:* Tailored to individual needs within school's capability. *Europe:* French, German and Spanish offered to GCSE, AS and A-level (French compulsory from 11–16). Regular exchanges.

The arts *Music:* 30% of pupils learn a musical instrument; instrumental exams can be taken. Some 7 musical groups including choir, orchestra, big band, glee group. *Drama & dance*: Drama offered and GCSE may be taken. Some pupils are involved in school productions. *Art:* On average, 24 take GCSE, 10 A-level. On average, 4 art school entrants per year.

Sport, community service and clubs *Sport and physical activities:* Compulsory sport: rugby, cricket (for 3 years). Optional: tennis, swimming, athletics, golf, badminton, squash, basketball, volleyball, aerobics. Sixth form only: weight training. Finalists in Daily Mail U15 national rugby competition. *Community service:* Pupils take bronze, silver and gold Duke of Edinburgh's Award. CCF and community service optional from age 14. Mountaineering club. *Clubs and societies:* Up to 10 clubs, eg debating, drama, chess, badminton, fencing.

Uniform School uniform worn throughout.

Houses/prefects No competitive houses. Prefects and head boy/girl – appointed by the Headmaster.

Religion Roman Catholic services.

Social Debating and other regional competitions. Ski trips, art visits, language trips, and exchanges. Pupils allowed to bring own car/bike/motorbike to school. Meals self-service. No tobacco/alcohol allowed.

Discipline Pupils failing to produce homework once might expect to have to do it under supervision on Saturdays.

Alumni association is run by Mr J Harvey, Hon Sec, Old Priorian Association, c/o the school.

• ST CATHERINE'S

St Catherine's School, Bramley, Guildford, Surrey GU5 0DF. Tel 01483 893363, Fax 01483 893003

• Pupils 600 • Boys None • Girls 4–18 (Day/Board/Weekly) • Upper sixth 40 • Termly Fees £970-£1960 (Day) £2785-£3210 (Board/Weekly) • GSA, BSA • Enquiries/application to the Headmistress

What it's like

Founded in 1885, it shares the same Royal Charter and Council as Cranleigh Boys' School though each has a separate governing body. It has a compact campus in the village of Bramley in the Surrey hills, three miles south of Guildford. The school is set in attractive grounds and gardens, with excellent playing fields and sports/games facilities. The buildings are predominantly modern, red-brick and pleasant and include a recent building with facilities and accommodation for sixth-form boarders. It is a Church of England school with its own chapel. Religious knowledge is taught throughout the school to all girls, and there are regular services in chapel. There is a large staff allowing a good staff:pupil ratio of about 1:10. Academic standards are high and results very good; most sixth-formers go on to degree courses. There is a considerable emphasis on music, which is strong with choirs, an orchestra, concert band and jazz group. Drama and ballet also flourish. A range of sports and games is available and teams have been successful in recent county and national championships. A number of clubs and societies cater for extra-curricular activities. The Duke of Edinburgh's Award Scheme is well supported.

School profile

Pupils Total age range 4–18, 603 girls (462 day, 141 boarding). Senior department 11–18, 465 girls. Main entry age, 4, 7, 11. Own junior school provides 33% intake. *State school entry:* 20% main intake.

Entrance Common entrance at 11, own entrance exam at other ages. Scholarships 11 pa (3 at age 11, 4 at U5, 4 at sixth-form), other music awards, 1 old girl bursary, one-sixth to half fees. Assisted places 13 pa (5 at age 11, 3 at 12, 5 at sixth-form).

Head and staff *Headmistress:* Mrs C M Oulton, 3 years in post. Educated at Oxford University (history). Previously Head of History at Charterhouse. *Staff:* 62 full-time, 13 part-time. Annual turnover 12%.
Exam results In 1995, 74 pupils in upper fifth, 36 in upper sixth. *GCSE:* In 1995, 72 upper fifth gained at least grade C in 8+ subjects. *A-levels:* 8 upper sixth passed in 4 subjects; 24 in 3; 4 in 2 subjects. Average UCAS points 23.0.
University and college entrance 93% of sixth-form leavers went on to a degree course (50% after a gap year); others typically go on to art foundation course. Of those going on to university, 13% went to Oxbridge; 10% took courses in medicine, dentistry and veterinary science, 3% in science and engineering, 3% in law, 73% in humanities and social sciences, 3% in art and design, 6% in other vocational subjects eg opthalmology, education.
Curriculum GCSE and A-levels. 23 GCSE subjects offered, 24 for A-level; also AS-level general studies. 3% take science A-levels; 64% arts/humanities; 33% both. *Vocational:* Work experience available (one week in lower sixth); also RSA qualifications in CLAIT. *Computing facilities:* 2 computer rooms, 50 RM Nimbus machines on a network and several stand alone machines in some labs and classrooms. *Europe:* French (from 11), German and Spanish (from 14) offered to GCSE and A-level; also French AS-level and Italian GCSE and A-level in sixth. Regular exchanges (to France).
The arts *Music:* Over 40% of pupils learn a musical instrument; instrumental exams can be taken. Some 10+ musical groups including 7 choirs, orchestra, concert band, jazz group, chamber groups. *Drama & dance*: Both offered (about 33% particiate). LAMDA and RAD exams may be taken. Many pupils are involved in school productions and the majority in house/other productions. *Art:* Pottery, textiles, photography, print-making, sculpture, drawing, painting and graphics offered.
Sport, community service and clubs *Sport and physical activities:* Compulsory sports: netball, lacrosse, rounders, athletics, swimming, tennis. Optional: squash, tennis coaching. Sixth form only: basketball, volleyball. GCSE and A-level sport, BAGA and RLSS exams may be taken. Teams successful in recent county championships. *Community service:* Pupils take bronze, silver and gold Duke of Edinburgh's Award. Community service optional. *Clubs and societies:* Up to 30 clubs, eg dancing, self-defence, swimming, art, ceramics, needlecraft, cookery, lifesaving, computer, Christian Union, musical activities.
Uniform School uniform worn except in sixth.
Houses/prefects Competitive houses. Prefects, head girl (appointed by the Headmistress), head of house and house prefects. School Council.
Religion Attendance at religious worship compulsory.
Social Some joint events with other local schools. Annual French exchange; trips abroad annually to Germany, Spain or Italy. Pupils allowed to bring own bike to school; upper-sixth day girls may bring own car. Most meals self-service. School shop. No tobacco allowed; alcohol in sixth-form bar.
Discipline Pupils failing to produce homework once might expect to have to catch it up at a later date; those caught smoking cannabis on the premises might expect suspension or expulsion.
Former pupils Dorothy Tutin, Joan Greenwood, Zena Skinner, Francine Stock, Sarah Crowe, Juliet Stevenson.

• ST CHRISTOPHER (Letchworth)

St Christopher School, Barrington Road, Letchworth, Hertfordshire SG6 3JZ Tel 01462 679301, Fax 01462 481578

• Pupils 452 • Boys 2½–18 (Day/Board) • Girls 2½–18 (Day/Board) • Upper sixth 41 • Termly fees £2062 (Day) £3640 (Board) • Enquiries/application to the Admissions Secretary

What it's like

Founded in 1915 as a co-educational school, in Ebenezer Howard's Garden City, it was a pioneering concept in education that attracted progressive causes. For the first few years it was controlled by the Theosophical Educational Trust which practised ecumenicism long before such a movement became established. In the 1920s the school was developed to give expression to the child-centred ideals of the World Education Fellowship, becoming very much a family school under the guidance of Lyn and Eleanor Harris whose son continued their regime until 1980. They provided continuity of purpose and fostered what the Quakers call 'an answering to that of God in every child'; this is the central purpose of the school. There is a domestic village atmosphere with most of the buildings in the Garden City idiom, surrounded by attractive grounds. The school provides a complete education from infancy to adulthood and a large number of the teaching staff have children at the school. The staff:pupil ratio is about 1:9 and there are also 26 part-time teachers. The school has long been noted for the value it places on the individual. It attracts children (and parents) with strongly independent attitudes, those who find pressures elsewhere restrictive and those who need special care and attention. The school does not believe in artificial competition in academic work; thus there are no subject or form orders and no prizes. The teaching is of a high standard and academic results are good. The school is very strong in drama and art. There is a very wide range of sports, games and extra-curricular activities, with special emphasis on outdoor pursuits such as rock-climbing, orienteering, canoeing and hill-walking. The school has strong local support and its pupils are involved in a range of ventures among the local community, including the young, the old and the mentally ill. There are strong international links and visits by sixth-formers to development projects in Rajasthan. The school is entirely vegetarian.

School profile

Pupils Total age range 2½–18; 452 pupils, 289 day (182 boys, 107 girls), 163 boarders (98 boys, 65 girls). Senior department 11–18, 326 pupils (202 boys, 124 girls). Main entry ages 2½, 9, 11 and into sixth (boarding from age 7). 10% are children of former pupils. Own junior department provides 50% senior intake. *State school entry:* 25% senior intake, plus 15% to sixth.

Entrance Own informal tests at an interview day. Selection based on the ability to respond to opportunities, not only academic but in the creative arts, in outdoor pursuits and to participate in the school's unusual system of self-government. No religious requirements (no communal worship at the school so attractive to parents who do not want this for their children). Parents expected to buy only examination set textbooks for literature.

Parents 15+% in the theatre, media, music etc; 15+% are doctors, lawyers etc; 15+% in industry; 15+% in education. 30+% live within 30 miles; 10+% live overseas.

Head and staff *Headmaster:* Colin Reid, in post for 15 years. Educated at Brentwood and Cambridge (history). Previously Housemaster and Head of History at Atlantic College and History Teacher at Tonbridge. Also ex-Chairman of the BSA; Director of the Atlantic College Peace Studies Project. Publications: General editor of Teaching Matters (a series of books for teachers). *Staff:* 50 full time, 26 part time. Annual turnover 8%. Average age 37.

Exam results In 1995, 64 pupils in upper fifth, 40 in upper sixth. *GCSE:* In 1995, 65% upper fifth gained at least grade C in 8+ subjects; 20% in 5–7 subjects. *A-levels:* 21% upper sixth passed in 4 subjects; 63% in 3; 17% in 2 subjects. Average UCAS points 16.9.

University and college entrance 95% of 1995 sixth-form leavers went on to a degree course (20% after a gap year); others typically go on to art or drama college. Of those going on to university, 5% went to Oxbridge; 4% took courses in medicine, dentistry and veterinary science, 30% in science and engineering, 4% in law, 40% in humanities and social sciences, 12% in art and design, 8% in other subjects eg business, journalism, hotel management, drama, technical theatre.

Curriculum GCSE, AS-levels and *A-levels:* 19 subjects offered (including A-levels theatre studies, classical civilization, history of art, design and technology, business studies; no A-level general studies). 20% took science A-levels; 70% arts/humanities; 10% both. *Vocational:* Work experience available. *Computing facilities:* Pilot school for the Education 2000 project; Over 80 RM Nimbus machines on three networks with open access until 10pm. *Special provision:* for limited number of pupils of good general ability requiring dyslexic or EFL help (both categories greatly oversubscribed). *Europe:* French, German and Spanish offered to GCSE and A-level; also French and German AS-level. Regular exchanges. Some 12 European pupils in school for 1–3 terms.

The arts (Pupils aged 11 and over) *Music:* Instrumental exams can be taken. Some 6 musical groups including jazz band, madrigal group, junior singers, recorder consort.

Pupils in National Youth Orchestra and National Children's Orchestra. *Drama & dance:* Drama offered to a high standard and GCSE and A-level may be taken. All pupils are involved in school and house/other productions. Students regularly move on to drama school, including RADA and Guildhall. *Art:* On average, 50% take GCSE, 30% A-level. Design, pottery, photography also offered. Pupils regularly accepted at top art colleges eg Courtauld, Chelsea, Middlesex, Farnham.

Sport, community service and clubs (Pupils aged 11 and over) *Sport and physical activities:* Compulsory sports: soccer, hockey, lacrosse, tennis, athletics. Optional: basketball, swimming, croquet. Represented at national level at lacrosse; regional, athletics, county, volleyball. *Community service:* Pupils take bronze, silver and gold Duke of Edinburgh's Award. Community service optional for 1 year at age 14 and 16. Opportunities for all students to do community service; all fourth group required to do Guilds; Active Relief Committee as part of student government. *Clubs and societies:* Up to 30 clubs, eg film, debating, jazz, sailing, theory of music, meditation, badminton, physics, beekeeping, aerobics.

Uniform School uniform not worn apart from games and PE.

Houses/prefects Competitive houses for games. Prefects ('major officials'), head boy and girl – all elected by single transferable vote. School Council in existence since 1920 with much importance attached to its debates and decisions.

Religion No communal worship. Significant period of silence in each assembly and staff meeting. Some education about religions.

Social Occasional sixth-form conferences with other schools. Strong links with a German school (3 exchanges a year and joint theatrical/expeditions, projects) and 2 French schools (3 exchanges a year). Pupils allowed to bring own bike to school. Meals self-service. Diet is entirely wholefood vegetarian (no meat or fish allowed on campus). School shop (managed by students). Alcohol allowed occasionally under staff supervision; no tobacco.

Discipline School strongly inclined towards non-violent and pacifist solutions to conflict. For pupils failing to produce homework once there are extra work sessions twice a week after school so they may repeat the work or catch up.

Boarding Nearly all sixth-form have own study bedroom, younger pupils in rooms (2–3 sharing). 7 houses, of 12–50 divided by age group, mixed sex. Resident qualified nurse. Central dining room for lunch; breakfast and supper in own houses. Fifth and sixth-form allowed to provide and cook own food. Overnight exeats any weekend except 7 closed weekends a year. Visits to local town allowed daily after school from age 11.

Alumni association c/o the School.

Former pupils Paul Hamlyn, Ralph Halpern (entrepreneurs); Michael Winner (film producer); Neil Coles (golfer); Shaun Slovo, Jonathan Croall, Jenny Diski (authors); Gavin Campbell (actor).

• ST COLUMBA'S (Kilmacolm)

St Columba's School, Duchal Road, Kilmacolm, Renfrewshire, PA13 4AU. Tel 01505 872238

• Pupils 580 • Boys 3–18 (Day) • Girls 3–18 (Day) • Higher year 50 • Termly fees £1212 (Day)
• SHA, HAS • Enquiries/application to the Rector

What it's like

Founded in 1897 as a girls' school, it became fully co-educational in 1978. Its site is in the small village of Kilmacolm. The primary and secondary buildings are about a quarter of a mile apart. The surrounding countryside is delightful. The main building was erected in 1897 and there have been many extensions since, including a games hall and new science classrooms. Facilities and accommodation are now very good. Some religious services are compulsory. A sound general education is provided and results are good. Most leavers go on to degree courses each year. There is music, drama and art, and a range of games, sports and extra-curricular activities. The school has an excellent record in the Duke of Edinburgh's Award Scheme.

School profile

Pupils Total age range 3–18; 580 day pupils (270 boys, 310 girls). Senior department 11–18, 356 pupils (167 boys, 189 girls). Main entry ages 3, 11 and into sixth. Own primary

dept provides more than 80% of senior intake. *State school entry:* 15% senior intake, plus 5% to sixth.
Entrance Own entrance exam used. No special skills or religious requirements. Parents not expected to buy textbooks. 6 pc assisted places.
Parents 70+% are in industry or commerce.
Head and staff *Rector*: Andrew H Livingstone, in post for 9 years. Educated at Campbeltown Grammar and at universities of Aberdeen and Glasgow (mathematics). Previously Depute Rector at Paisley Grammar, Assistant Rector at Williamwood High and Principal Teacher of Mathematics at Paisley Grammar. *Staff:* 43 full time, 7 part time. Annual turnover 2%. Average age 42.
Exam results On average, 53 pupils in S-grade year, 50 in Higher year, 40 in 6th year. *S-grade:* On average, 9 pupils pass in 8+ subjects; 44 in 5–7 subjects. *Highers:* 19 pupils pass in 5+ or more subjects; 16 in 4; 7 in 3; 5 in 2; 3 in 1 subject. *CSYS*: 2 pupils pass in 3 subjects; 14 in 2; and 10 in 1 subject.
University and college entrance 93% of 1995 sixth-form leavers went on to a degree course (2% after a gap year); others typically go on to HND courses. Of those going on to university, 8% took courses in medicine, dentistry and veterinary science, 37% in science and engineering, 5% in law, 15% in humanities and social sciences, 5% in art and design, 3% in music, 27% in other subjects (eg accountancy, business studies).
Curriculum S-grade and Highers, CSYS: 15 subjects offered. 67% take science CSYS; 33% arts/humanities. *Vocational:* Work experience available; also RSA typing and Scotvec modules in computing, word processing and cooking. *Computing facilities:* Computer laboratory. *Europe:* French (from age 5) and German (from 13) both offered at S-grade, Higher and CSYS; also Spanish to Higher grade.
The arts (Pupils aged 11 and over) *Music:* Over 30% of pupils learn a musical instrument; instrumental exams can be taken. Some 9 musical groups: 4 orchestras and 5 choirs. Pupils gained 30 1st prizes in last Inverclyde Music Festival; senior choir and orchestra taken part in two services recorded for BBC (1993) and on TV (1994). *Drama & dance*: Drama offered. ESB exams may be taken. Majority of pupils are involved in school and house/other productions. *Art:* On average, 12 take S-grade, 4 Higher. Pottery and textiles also offered.
Sport, community service and clubs (Pupils aged 11 and over) *Sport and physical activities:* Compulsory sports: rugby, hockey, tennis, athletics, badminton. Optional: netball, volleyball, squash, cricket. Sixth form only: windsurfing. BAGA exams may be taken. National players athletics (U16), rugby (U16), hockey (U16, U18). *Community service:* Pupils take bronze, silver and gold Duke of Edinburgh's Award. Community service optional. *Clubs and societies:* Up to 15 clubs, eg chess, public speaking, sporting, musical.
Uniform School uniform worn throughout.
Houses/prefects Competitive houses. Prefects, head boy/girl, head of house and house prefects – elected by fifth and sixth-forms.
Religion Compulsory morning prayers 3 times a week.
Social School dances, Burns Supper with neighbouring school. Organised trips to France, Germany and skiing; annual sixth-form trip; rugby and hockey tours. Meals self-service. School tuck shop. No tobacco/alcohol allowed.
Discipline Pupils failing to produce homework once might expect additional work or order marks; those caught smoking cannabis on the premises could expect to be excluded.

• ST DAVID'S (Ashford)

St David's School, Church Road, Ashford, Middlesex TW15 3DZ. Tel 01784 252494, Fax 01784 248652

• Pupils 450 • Boys None. Girls 3–18 (Day/Board/Weekly) • Upper sixth (run jointly with Halliford Boys School) 30 • Termly fees £1725 (Day) £2995 (Board) £2820 (Weekly) • GSA, BSA • Enquiries/application to the Headmistress

What it's like

Founded in 1716 by the Most Honourable and Loyal Society of Ancient Britons in order to provide an education for the children of Welsh parentage in London. In 1857 it moved to its present site in Ashford. The junior and senior schools are on the same site of 30 acres, with a lake, on the outskirts of Ashford. The main building, a very handsome one of stone in the collegiate style of architecture, stands in beautiful gardens. There is also a fine chapel and additional modern buildings which are well-appointed and well-equipped. A broad, general education is provided and the sixth-form is run jointly with Halliford Boys' School. Music is strong, drama is also well-supported. A standard range of sports and games is available (sports acrobatics is particularly successful). There is a notable commitment to the Duke of Edinburgh's Award Scheme and many pupils have been highly successful. A good deal of local community service work is done.

School profile

Pupils Total age range 3–18, 450 girls (410 day, 40 boarding); boarding only from age 8. Senior department 11–18, 250 girls; sixth-form joint with Halliford Boys' School. Main entry ages 4 and 11. Many senior pupils from own junior department and numerous local primary schools. *State school entry:* 30% main intake at 11, plus 20% to sixth.

Entrance Own assessment used. 14 pa assisted places (2 at aged 5, 2 at 8, 5 at 11 and 5 into sixth). 6 pa academic scholarships at 11, plus sixth-form and gymnastics scholarships, value negotiable.

Head and staff *Headmistress:* Mrs Judith Osborne, in post for 11 years. Educated at Leeds High and Allerton High schools and at Leeds University (French). Previously Headmistress at Manor House School (Little Bookham) and Housemistress at Harrogate Ladies College; has also taught at Queen's University, Ontario.

Exam results In 1995, 57 pupils in Year 11, 16 girls in an upper sixth operated joint with Halliford Boys' School. *GCSE:* In 1996, 54% in Year 11 gained at least grade C in 8+ subjects; 44% in 5–7 subjects. *A-levels:* 2 upper sixth girls passed in 4+ subjects; 6 in 3; 4 in 2; and 2 in 1 subject. Average UCAS points gained 12.7.

University and college entrance 85% of 1995 sixth-form leavers went on to a degree course; others typically go straight on to careers (eg banking) or non-degree courses eg NNEB, secretarial or HND.

Curriculum GCSE and A-levels. 20+ GCSE subjects offered; 20 at A-level, including theatre studies, business studies, government and politics, economics and psychology; no A-level general studies. 33% take science A-levels; 66% arts/humanities. *Vocational:* work experience available; also City and Guilds course in cookery and RSA word processing. *Computing facilities:* Computer network, IT facility. *Special provision:* 4 (private) tutors for EFL and dyslexia; provision for pupils with hearing impairment. *Europe:* French (compulsory for 2 years), German and Spanish offered to GCSE, AS and A-level. Regular exchanges to France, Germany and Spain. Annual short visit by Spanish girls and ad hoc arrangements for European girls in sixth.

The arts *Music:* Over 30% of pupils learn a musical instrument; instrumental exams can be taken. 5 musical groups – orchestra, 2 choirs, chamber group, flute ensembles. *Drama & dance*: Drama offered at GCSE, AS and A-level, LAMDA exams may be taken. Some pupils are involved in school productions and the majority in house/other productions. LAMDA silver medals and other passes. *Art:* On average, 15 take GCSE, 4+ A-level. Pottery, textiles also offered. Winner Spelthorne in Bloom poster competition, several years.

Sport, community service and clubs *Sport and physical activities:* Compulsory sports: swimming, tennis, hockey, netball, athletics, rounders, gym. Optional: badminton, volleyball, sports-acrobatics, football. Sixth form only: squash, golf. BAGA, RLSS, ASA, AAA, Milk in Action (athletics) exams may be taken. Borough cross-country and national sports-acrobatic champions 1994; county, hockey U16. *Community service:* Pupils take bronze, silver and gold Duke of Edinburgh's Award. Community service optional. *Clubs and societies:* Up to 10 clubs, eg chess, trampolining, computing, drama, gymnastics, canoeing.

Uniform Uniform worn except in the sixth.

Houses/prefects Competitive houses. Prefects, head girl, head of house and house prefects – mixture of election by school and appointment by Headmistress. School council.

Religion Compulsory attendance at school assemblies in chapel 4 days/week.

Social Debates, lectures, drama productions with Halliford Boys' School. French, German and Spanish exchanges jointly with 3 local schools. Annual ski trip, bi-annual

holiday to France. Pupils allowed to bring own car/bike to school. Formal meals. Tuck shop run by pupils. No alcohol/tobacco allowed.
Discipline Pupils failing to produce homework once might expect a verbal warning (negative house points and involvement of parents thereafter). Those caught smoking cannabis on the premises might expect suspension pending investigation; then expulsion.

• ST DENIS AND CRANLEY

St Denis and Cranley School for Girls, Ettrick Road, Edinburgh EH10 5BJ. Tel 0131 229 1500, Fax 0131 229 5753

• Pupils 180 • Boys 3–9 only • Girls 3–18 (Day/Board/Weekly) • Higher year 25 • Termly fees £1495 (Day) £3050 (Board/Weekly) • GSA • Enquiries/application to the Headmistress

What it's like

The school is a result of an amalgamation in 1979 of St Denis (founded in 1855) and Cranley (founded in 1871). The school is sited in a pleasant, residential district of Edinburgh. All buildings are on one site forming, with three boarding houses, a compact campus with fine lawns, trees, gardens and playing fields. It is quiet, spacious and well-equipped. It is a small school and enjoys a happy, friendly and family atmosphere. The staff:pupil ratio is about 1:10. A sound, general education is provided and results are good. Many pupils go on to degree courses each year. There is a big commitment to music, drama and art. There is a good range of sports and games and a plentiful variety of extra-curricular activities. Quite a substantial commitment to local community services and an impressive record in the Duke of Edinburgh's Award Scheme.

School profile

Pupils Total age range 3–18; 180 girls, 120 day, 60 boarding. Senior department 12–18, 130 girls. Main entry ages 5, 9, 12 and into sixth. Approx 5% are children of former pupils. *State school entry:* 50% senior intake.
Entrance Own entrance exam used. No special skills or religious requirements but pupils expected to participate in morning assembly and RE classes. Parents not expected to buy textbooks; maximum extras £100 (lunch, day girls), £150 (boarders, pocket money, expeditions etc), plus music tuition, riding, skiing etc. 3 pa assisted places. 5 pa scholarships including art, music and sixth-form, £735 per term. Reductions for daughters of clergy and forces.
Parents 15+% in armed services; 15+% are doctors, lawyers etc; 15% in industry or commerce. 30+% live within 30 miles; 10+% live overseas.
Head and staff *Headmistress:* Mrs Sally Duncanson, appointed in 1996. Educated at Dundee High, at Madras College, St Andrews, and Edinburgh University (German, French and Latin). Previously Head of Modern Languages and Assistant Headteacher at Mary Erskine. Also SEB marker and setter; committee member of German Teachers' Association; award leader of Duke of Edinburgh's Award Scheme. *Staff:* 18 full time, 11 part time plus music staff. Annual turnover 2%.
Exam results On average, 30 pupils in S-grade year, 25 in Higher year, 15 in A-level/CSYS year. *S-grade:* on average, 25 pupils gain at least grade 3 in 5–7 subjects; 5 in 1–4 subjects. *Highers:* 8 pupils pass in 5+ subjects; 3 in 4, 8 in 3, 3 in 2, 1 in 1 subject. *A-levels and CSYS:* 3 pupils pass in 3 subjects; 7 in 2; and 4 in 1 subject.
University and college entrance 60% of 1995 sixth-form leavers went on to a degree course; others typically go on to art/music colleges, non-degree courses or straight into careers (eg armed services or music or drama). Of those going on to university, 4% took courses in medicine, dentistry and veterinary science, 42% in science and engineering, 35% in humanities and social sciences, 12% in art and design, 4% in drama and acting.
Curriculum S-grade, Highers, A-levels and CSYS. 17 subjects offered including Japanese; no A-level general studies. 40% take science A-levels; 40% arts/humanities; 20% both. *Vocational:* Work experience available; also Scotvec National Certificate modules in computing, communications, photography, health and home economics; RSA stages 1–3 in typewriting and word processing. *Computing facilities:* Apple Mac computers. *Special provision:* Qualified learning support teacher and EFL help. *Europe:* French, Spanish and German offered to S-grade, Highers and A-level (French compulsory for 6 years from age 8); also Italian as a Scotvec module. Regular exchanges to France, Spain

and Germany. Short European studies course for ages 16–18. Various European country weeks in school (eg music, history, art, literature of a country, including school lunch).
The arts (Pupils aged 11 and over) *Music:* Over 50% of pupils learn a musical instrument; instrumental exams can be taken. Some 7 musical groups including orchestra, wind band, various ensembles, choir, madrigal group. Distinction in grade 8 piano; member of regional wind band; Stockbridge Youth Recital series – selected players went on to Queen's Hall Edinburgh. *Drama & dance*: Drama offered. LAMDA exams may be taken. Some pupils are involved in school productions and majority in house/other productions. *Art:* On average, 12 take GCSE, 8 Higher, 3 A-level. Pottery, textiles, photography also offered. A number of girls have exhibited.
Sport, community service and clubs (Pupils aged 11 and over) *Sport and physical activities:* Compulsory sports (at different stages): athletics, hockey, tennis, badminton, basketball, swimming. Optional: squash, judo, keep fit. BAGA, RLSS exams may be taken. Some county representation (skiing, hockey, tennis, squash). *Community service:* Pupils take bronze, silver and gold Duke of Edinburgh's Award. Community service optional. *Clubs and societies:* Up to 10 clubs, eg debating, Scripture Union.
Uniform School uniform worn; optional in the sixth-form.
Houses/prefects Competitive houses. Prefects, head girl and head of house – elected by peers, staff and Headmistress. School Council.
Religion Compulsory morning assembly (Hindus, Muslims etc may opt out but in practice do not).
Social ESU debates, sporting fixtures, occasional joint production, combined careers talks, Geographical Association etc with other schools. Trips to Germany, France, Spain; visiting schools from USA, New Zealand, Italy. Meals formal. School shop twice-weekly. No tobacco/alcohol allowed.
Discipline Pupils failing to produce homework once would have a warning; expulsion could follow a serious offence but it could depend on the effect of the offence on others.
Boarding 4% have own study bedroom. Houses include a junior and a sixth-form one. Daytime nurse, usually one medically-trained house staff member. Central dining room. 3 weekend exeats plus mid-term. Visit to local town allowed.
Alumni association run by The Secretary, St Denis & Cranley Association, c/o the school.
Former pupils Hannah Gordon (actress); Dr Jacqueline Mok (leading consultant).

• ST DOMINIC'S (Brewood)

St Dominic's School, 32 Bargate Street, Brewood, Stafford ST19 9BA. Tel 01902 850248

• Pupils 430 • Boys 2½–7 only • Girls 2½–18 (Day) • Upper sixth 20 • Termly fees £750–£1300 (Day) • GSA • Enquiries/application to Secretary .

What it's like

Founded in 1920 by the English Dominican Sisters and administered by them until 1975 when a Board of Directors took over the organisation and in 1984 bought the school from the Dominican order. It has a 9-acre site in the very attractive village of Brewood. It has good buildings, accommodation and facilities, including sport facilities and a purpose-built junior school. A sound general education is given and many sixth-form leavers go on to degree courses. The Christian ethos underpins all school activities. It is very strong in music and drama. An impressive range of sport, games and activities. Successful participation in the Duke of Edinburgh's Award Scheme, Young Enterprise and sports tournaments, local and national.

School profile

Pupils Total age range 2½–18; 430 day pupils, 15 boys, 415 girls. Senior department 11–18, 241 girls. Main entry ages 2½ (boys and girls); 11 and into sixth (girls). Approx 4% are children of former pupils. *State school entry:* 28% senior intake, plus 4% to sixth.
Entrance Own examination used. No special skills. Parents not expected to buy textbooks. A number of scholarships at 11 and 16.
Parents 15+% in industry or commerce; 15+% are doctors, lawyers, etc.
Head and staff *Headmistress:* Mrs Krysia Butwilowska, 6 years in post. Educated at Birmingham University (education). Previously Headmistress at Holy Trinity, Kidder-

minster, and Deputy Head at Coppice High School, Wolverhampton Also JP; Chair Catholic Secondary Heads, Birmingham Archdiocese. *Staff:* 32 full time, 13 part time. Annual turnover 8%. Average age 40.

Exam results In 1995, 56 pupils in upper fifth, 22 in upper sixth. *GCSE:* In 1995, 49 upper fifth gained at least grade C in 8+ subjects; 4 in 5–7 subjects. *A-levels:* 5 upper sixth passed in 4+ subjects; 12 in 3; 5 in 2 subjects. Average UCAS points 15.0.

University and college entrance 80% of sixth-form leavers go on to a degree course; others typically go on to non-degree courses or straight into careers (eg industry, civil service, music/drama). Of those going on to university, 10% go to Oxbridge; 9% take courses in medicine, dentistry and veterinary science, 28% in science and engineering, 63% in humanities and social sciences.

Curriculum GCSE and A-levels, including A-level general studies. 41% take science A-levels; 27% arts/humanities; 32% both. *Vocational:* Work experience available. *Computing facilities:* Facilities for groups of 20 pupils. GCSE; AEB practical and City & Guilds exams. *Europe:* French and German offered to GCSE, AS and A-level. Regular exchanges to France and Germany.

The arts (Pupils aged 11 and over) *Music:* Over 30% of pupils learn a musical instrument; instrumental exams can be taken. Some 5 musical groups including choir, recorder group, flute, clarinet ensembles. Member of BFYC; senior and junior choirs won Lichfield, Dudley and Brownhills Festivals. *Drama & dance:* Drama offered. GCSE and ESB exams may be taken. Majority of pupils are involved in school productions and all in house/other productions. *Art:* On average, 20 take GCSE, 3 A-level; history of art A-level also offered.

Sport, community service and clubs (Pupils aged 11 and over) *Sport and physical activities:* Compulsory sports: netball, hockey, rounders, athletics, gymnastics. Optional: tennis, aerobics, badminton. Sixth form only: swimming, squash, ice skating. BAGA exams may be taken and 5 star athletic awards, 10 step awards. 2 district hockey U14, 2 county tennis. *Community service:* Pupils take bronze, silver and gold Duke of Edinburgh's Award. Community service compulsory for 2 years at age 16. *Clubs and societies:* Up to 5 clubs, eg information technology, gymnastics, guitar.

Uniform School uniform worn throughout.

Houses/prefects Competitive houses. Prefects, head girl and head of house – elected by the school.

Religion Assembly compulsory. Optional prayer group.

Social Trips to France, Austria, Germany and Belgium. Sixth-form pupils allowed to bring own car to school. Meals formal. No tobacco/alcohol allowed.

Discipline Merits/demerits system operates, unethical conduct leads to expulsion.

• ST DOMINIC'S (Stone)

St Dominic's Priory School, 21 Station Road, Stone, Staffordshire ST15 8EN Tel 01785 814181
• Pupils 370 • Boys 3–8 only (Day) • Girls 3–18 (Day) • Upper sixth 14 • Termly fees £1141 (Day) • ISAI, CTF • Enquiries/application to the Secretary

What it's like

Founded in 1934 and conducted by the English Dominican Sisters, this is an ecumenical school welcoming all denominations. It has an agreeable urban site with gardens and well-appointed buildings. There are two main buildings: the senior school and the Croft (juniors), plus the nearby Croftside (nursery). The moral and religious education of the pupils has a high priority. All pupils take religious studies at GCSE level. There is an unusually large part-time staff. A sound general education is provided and results are good. From those who stay on into the sixth-form, almost all proceed to degree courses each year. There is a strong music tradition, and drama is popular. A range of sports and games and extra-curricular activities are offered. There is an indoor tennis centre of LTA match standard. Commitment to local community services and a promising record in the Duke of Edinburgh's Award Scheme.

School profile

Pupils Total age range 3–18; 370 day pupils (27 boys, 343 girls). Senior department 11–18, 220 girls. Main entry ages 3 (boys and girls); 11 and into sixth (girls). Approx 10% are

children of former pupils. *State school entry:* 30% senior intake.
Entrance Own entrance exam used. No special skills or religious requirements. Parents expected to buy textbooks; other extras optional. Assisted places. Few bursaries, value according to need.
Parents 15+% are doctors, lawyers etc; 15+% in industry or commerce. 60+% live within 30 miles.
Head and staff *Headmistress:* Mrs Jacqueline Hildreth, in post since 1994. Educated at Olton Convent, Solihull, and at the Open University and Warwick University (geography and biology). Previously Deputy Head at Cardinal Wiseman, Birmingham. Lecturer with Open University. *Staff:* 8 full time, 23 part time. Annual turnover 1%.
Exam results In 1995, 41 pupils in fifth, 14 in upper sixth. *GCSE:* In 1995, 32 fifth gained at least grade C in 8+ subjects; 8 in 5–7; and 1 in 1–4 subjects. *A-levels:* 9 upper sixth passed in 4+ subjects; 1 in 3; 2 in 2; and 2 in 1 subject. Average UCAS points 17.5.
University and college entrance All 1995 sixth-form leavers went on to a degree course (5% after a gap year), 5% to Oxbridge. 10% took courses in medicine, dentistry and veterinary science, 20% in science and engineering, 10% in law, 30% in humanities and social sciences, 10% in art and design, 20% in vocational subjects.
Curriculum GCSE and A-levels. 19 subjects offered, including A-level general studies. 29% take science A-levels; 71% arts/humanities. *Vocational:* Work experience available. *Computing facilities:* Nimbus RM network for senior use. BBC computers in various classrooms; meteosat receiver. *Special provision:* Visits to Dyslexia Institute (5 minutes' walk). *Europe:* French (compulsory from age 9) and German offered to GCSE and A-level; also GCSE Italian. Regular exchanges to Belgium, France and Germany.
The arts (Pupils aged 11 and over) *Music:* Almost all pupils learn a musical instrument; instrumental exams can be taken. Some 4 musical groups including orchestra, choir, recorder group. Many in Staffordshire Youth Orchestra. *Drama & dance*: Both offered. LAMDA exams may be taken. Some pupils are involved in school and house/other productions. *Art:* On average, 18 take GCSE, 6 A-level. Textiles also offered.
Sport, community service and clubs (Pupils aged 11 and over) *Sport and physical activities:* Compulsory sports: tennis, netball, rounders, badminton, cross-country, gymnastics. Optional: swimming, hockey. Sixth form only: squash. Winners & runners-up, badminton, Staffordshire tournament 1994; winners Midlands Tennis Tournament U16. *Community service:* Pupils take bronze, silver and gold Duke of Edinburgh's Award. Community service optional. *Clubs and societies:* Up to 10 clubs, eg chess.
Uniform School uniform worn throughout.
Houses/prefects Competitive houses. Prefects, head girl, head of house and house prefects elected by staff.
Religion Compulsory morning assembly; regular Mass.
Social French language and Italian and classics trips abroad. Art trips abroad. Meals self-service. No tobacco/alcohol allowed.
Discipline Pupils failing to produce homework once might expect extra work in lunch hour or detention.
Alumni association run by Miss Caroline Handforth, Coppice Farmhouse, Longton Road, Stone, Staffordshire.
Former pupils Lord Stafford; Hilaire Belloc's daughters; Hilary Pepler's grandchildren.

• ST DUNSTAN'S (Catford)

St Dunstan's College, Stanstead Road, Catford, London SE6 4TY. Tel 0181 690 1274, Fax 0181 314 0242

• Pupils 900 • Boys 4–18 (Day) • Girls 4–18 (Day) • Upper sixth 100 • Termly fees £1155-£1790 (Day) • HMC • Enquiries/application to the College Registrar

What it's like

Founded in 1888, it is urban and single-site and surrounded by big playing fields. Many additions have been made to the original and striking Victorian building and facilities are good; a sports hall complex has recently opened. The pre-prep and prep schools have combined into the junior school and the whole school became co-educational with the introduction of girls in 1994. The main emphasis in the school is on the need to develop the all-round qualities of a pupil in and out of the classroom. There is much stress on individual pastoral care and close links between home and school. The academic standards are high and results very good. Most sixth-form leavers go on to degree courses each year, including several to Oxbridge. There is a very strong music department (musicians are especially welcome) and lively drama and art. There is a good range of sport and games, with high standards (quite a lot of representatives at county level), a strong CCF contingent and a very substantial commitment to local community schemes.

School profile

Pupils Total age range 4–18; 900 day pupils (774 boys, 126 girls). Senior department 11–18, 700 pupils. Main entry ages 4, 7, 11 and into sixth. Approx 10% are children of former pupils.

Entrance Own entrance exam used. Musicians and genuine all-rounders especially welcome. Parents not expected to buy textbooks; extras include subscriptions, music and some sports coaching. 30 pa assisted places (at 7, 11, 13 and 16). Scholarships/bursaries 12 pa, 17%–50% fees.

Parents 15+% in industry or commerce; 15+% are doctors, lawyers, etc.

Head and staff *Headmaster:* J D Moore, 4 years in post. Educated at Bradford Grammar School and Cambridge University (classics). Previously Headmaster at Ilford County High School, and taught at King's, Macclesfield, and at The Judd School and Skinner's School in Kent. *Staff:* 70 full time, 6 part time. Annual turnover 5%. Average age 35–40.

Exam results In 1995, 90 pupils in upper fifth, 100 in upper sixth. *GCSE:* In 1995, 82% upper fifth gained at least grade C in 8+ subjects; 14% in 5–7 subjects. *A-levels:* 10% upper sixth passed in 4+ subjects; 84% in 3; 6% in 2 subjects. Average UCAS points 21.0.

University and college entrance 95% of 1995 sixth-form leavers went on to a degree course (5% after a gap year); others typically go on to art school, armed forces or financial services. Of those going on to university, 7% went to Oxbridge; 2% took courses in medicine, dentistry and veterinary science, 25% in science and engineering, 11% in law, 53% in humanities and social sciences, 2% in art and design, 2% in other vocational subjects.

Curriculum GCSE and A-levels: 21 subjects offered (no A-level general studies). 40% take science A-levels; 60% arts/humanities. *Vocational:* Work experience available (for 2 weeks after GCSE). *Computing facilities:* Well-equipped IT centre, with 24 workstations; on-line facilities for most departments (also for lower school, prep and pre-prep departments). *Special provision:* Private tuition for dyslexic pupils with specialist. *Europe:* French and German offered at GCSE and A-level; also German AS-level; Spanish A-level; Italian as a non-examined subject. Over 50% take GCSE in more than 1 language. Modern languages society. Regular lectures by European nationals about their respective countries and the EU. Annual trip to Strasbourg for all lower sixth.

The arts (Pupils aged 11 and over) *Music:* Over 25% of pupils learn a musical instrument; instrumental exams can be taken. Some 6 musical groups including orchestra, chamber choir, brass ensembles, woodwind, various informal groups. Choral scholarship to Oxford; 2 members of RSCM Southern Cathedral Singers. *Drama & dance*: A-level theatre studies may be taken. Majority of pupils are involved in school and house/other productions. *Art:* On average, 15 take GCSE, 7 A-level. Stage design and history of art A-level also offered. On average, 6 go on to art college or art-related FE course each year.

Sport, community service and clubs (Pupils aged 11 and over) *Sport and physical activities:* Compulsory sports: hockey, rugby, cricket. Optional: tennis, squash, swimming, fives, judo, golf, sailing, shooting, athletics, table tennis, netball, basketball, rackets, indoor hockey, cross-country. Sixth form only: soccer. GCSE and A-level may be taken. Numerous sporting achievements: regular representation in a variety of sports at all levels. International and county rugby representatives, county champions U15, U16, national champions colts singles and doubles in rugby fives. *Community service:* Pupils take bronze, silver and gold Duke of Edinburgh's Award. CCF and community service both optional for 2+ years at age 14. *Clubs and societies:* Up to 25 clubs, eg electronic workshop, classical, bridge, shooting, Christian Union, debating, hill & moor walking, climbing.

Uniform School uniform worn throughout.
Houses/prefects Competitive houses. Prefects, head boy/girl, head of house and house prefects – appointed by the Headmaster after consultation with staff and prefects. Separate councils for middle school and sixth-form.
Religion Religious worship compulsory, subject to parental right to withdraw.
Social Close links with local independent schools for music, drama, debating, films. Visits to USA, Australia, Canada, Romania, Russia, France, Germany, Italy and Zimbabwe recently taken place. Pupils allowed to bring own bike/motorbike to school. Meals self-service. School shop. No tobacco allowed; wine at sixth-form tutorial and society dinners (formal).
Discipline Discipline aims to be fair but strict. Pupils failing to produce homework once might expect work to be repeated, usually under supervision; those caught involved with illegal drugs could expect severe treatment.
Alumni association is run by Mr W White, Flat 6, Crown House, School Hill, Lamberhurst, Kent TN3 8HY.
Former pupils Matthew D'Ancona (Deputy Editor, Sunday Telegraph); Dr Walter Hamilton (Master of Magdalene College, Cambridge); Dr David Jenkins (formerly Bishop of Durham); Sir Paul Judge; Bill Muirhead (Managing Director, Saatchi); Wing Commander Stanford Tuck DSO, DFC; Major Johnson VC; Hubert Gregg (broadcaster); Michael Grade (Channel 4).

• ST DUNSTAN'S (Plymouth)

St Dunstan's Abbey, The Mill Fields, Plymouth, Devon PL1 3JL. Tel 01752 201350, Fax 01752 201351

• Pupils 330 • Boys 4–7 only • Girls 4–18 (Day/Board/Weekly) • Upper sixth 26 • Termly fees £1500 (Day) £2670 (Board) £2370 (Weekly) • GSA • Enquiries/application to the Headmaster

What it's like

Founded in 1867 by Anglican sisters, it now has secular Heads in both the senior and prep schools. It has recently moved to a new site, using the buildings of the old Royal Naval Hospital. Added facilities now include a theatre, drama studio and squash courts and much improved boarding accommodation. The school plans to expand across the age range until it reaches a total of about 400 girls. Religious worship is encouraged. Academic standards are high and results good; most sixth-formers go on to degree courses including Oxbridge. A very strong art department; considerable strength in music and drama. Some commitment to local community schemes.

School profile

Pupils Total age range 4–18; 330 pupils, 298 day, 38 boarding. Senior department 11–18, 201 girls. Main entry ages 3, 4 (boys and girls); 11 and into sixth (girls). Approx 8% are children of former pupils. *State school entry:* 35% senior intake, plus 5% to sixth.
Entrance Own entrance exam used. No special skills or religious requirements. Parents not expected to buy textbooks; music tuition extra (£50 per term). 7 pa scholarships, 30%–100% fees.
Parents 15+% in industry or commerce; 15+% are doctors, lawyers, etc; 15+% in the armed services. 60+% live within 30 miles.
Head and staff *Headmaster:* Robin Bye, 5 years in post. Educated at Clee Humberstone Foundation, Cleethorpes, and at Reading, the Open and Durham universities (biology, chemistry, educational management). Previously Director of Studies at Wadhurst, Head of Year at Frankfurt International School and Boarding Housemaster at De Aston School. *Staff:* 25 full time, 17 part time. Annual turnover 3%. Average age 40.
Exam results In 1995, 42 pupils in upper fifth, 26 in upper sixth. *GCSE:* In 1995, 94% upper fifth gained at least grade C in 8+ subjects; 6% in 5–7 subjects. *A-levels:* 4% upper sixth passed in 4+ subjects; 92% in 3; 4% in 2 subjects. Average UCAS points 19.2.
University and college entrance 85% of sixth-form leavers go on to a degree course; others typically go on to non-degree courses eg nursing. Of those going on to university, 7% go to Oxbridge; 7% took courses in medicine, dentistry and veterinary science, 31% in science and engineering, 52% in humanities and social sciences, 10% in art and design.
Curriculum GCSE and A-levels (including Chinese). 24% take science A-levels; 24%

arts/humanities; 52% both. *Vocational:* Work experience available; also RSA level 1 in CLAIT. *Computing facilities:* BBC computers. *Special provision:* Extra help available; English as second language. *Europe:* French and German offered to GCSE and A-level. Regular exchanges.

The arts (Pupils aged 11 and over) *Music:* Over 15% of pupils learn a musical instrument; instrumental exams can be taken. Some 5 musical groups including choirs, flute choir, band. Choirs recently won all sections entered in Plymouth Music Festival. *Drama & dance*: Both offered. GCSE and A-level drama, LAMDA and RAD exams may be taken. Some pupils are involved in school productions and the majority in house/other productions. *Art:* On average, 12 take GCSE, 3 A-level. Textiles, also offered.

Sport, community service and clubs (Pupils aged 11 and over) *Sport and physical activities:* Compulsory sports: netball, gym, hockey, tennis, athletics. Optional: archery, dry-slope skiing, sailing, badminton. BAGA and RYA exams may be taken. *Clubs and societies:* Up to 15 clubs, eg archery, dry-slope skiing, sailing, walking, chess, badminton.

Uniform School uniform worn, different uniform in sixth.

Houses/prefects Competitive houses. Prefects appointed by Headmaster and staff; head girl, head of house and house prefects – appointed by the Headmaster and elected by the school.

Religion Religious worship encouraged but not compulsory. One compulsory lesson a week up to sixth-form.

Social Some organised events with local schools. Some organised trips abroad including exchanges to Poland. Meals formal. No tobacco/alcohol allowed.

Discipline Pupils failing to produce homework once might expect warning/demerit mark; those caught smoking cannabis on the premises could expect expulsion.

Boarding All have own study bedroom (may share with one other if wished). Central dining room. Visits to local town allowed (in sixth). Flexible boarding arrangements: 5 or 7 nights a week; also single nights or longer for day girls.

Former pupils Dawn French; Lady Judith Wilcox (Chairman National Consumer Council).

• ST EDMUND'S (Canterbury)

St Edmund's School, St Thomas' Hill, Canterbury, Kent CT2 8HU. Tel 01227 454575, Fax 01227 471083

• Pupils 490 • Boys 3–18 (Day/Board/Weekly) • Girls 3–18 (Day/Board/Weekly) • Upper sixth 50 • Termly fees £1960–£2620 (Day) £2805–£4010 (Board/Weekly) • HMC, CSA • Enquiries/ application to the Headmaster

What it's like

Founded in 1749, on the same foundation as St Margaret's School for Girls at Bushey. It moved from London to its present site in 1855 where it lies on a spur of the Downs in 60 acres of fine grounds a mile from Canterbury, with a magnificent view of the city and its cathedral. It enjoys substantial and well-designed buildings (the main structure, in Kentish ragstone, dates from 1855) and there has been much expansion since 1975. It is now very well equipped indeed. The junior department is housed in a self-contained wing of the main building. The original purpose of the school was to provide an education for the sons of deceased clergy of the Church of England and the Church of Wales but the school is now fully co-educational (girls were first admitted in 1983). The Christian basis of the school continues to be of prime importance and the chapel plays a central role in the life of the school. The declared aim is to provide the widest possible opportunities for the individual, to develop his or her talents to the utmost and to provide a high level of pastoral care within a framework of firm but understanding discipline. Academic standards are high and results good. Music is very strong indeed and there are numerous ensembles (thirty Cathedral choristers are members of the junior school). A large number of pupils learn an instrument. Sports and games are well catered for. A wide variety of extra-curricular activities is provided. The strong CCF (Army section) is compulsory for one year and is run to a high standard. Involvement with the British Association of Young Scientists and Young Enterprise. Substantial commitment to local community services.

School profile

Pupils Total age range 3–18; 490 pupils, 330 day (210 boys, 120 girls) 160 boarding (125 boys, 35 girls); boarding only for boys from age 7, girls from 10. Senior department 13–18; 280 pupils (190 boys, 90 girls). Main entry ages 3, 7, 11, 13 and into sixth. *State school entry:* 7% senior intake.

Entrance Common Entrance and own exam used. 23 pa assisted places. Scholarships and bursaries; chorister scholarships for boys 7–9. Fee reductions for children of service/diplomatic personnel, clergy and former pupils. Full fees normally remitted for children of deceased clergy.

Head and staff *Headmaster:* A Nicholas Ridley, in post from 1994. Educated at Clifton and Oxford (modern languages). Previously Senior Housemaster at Fettes.

Exam results In 1995, 69 pupils in upper fifth, 46 in upper sixth. *GCSE:* In 1995, 31 upper fifth gained at least grade C in 8+ subjects; 22 in 5–7 subjects (average of 7+ subjects). *A-levels:* 2 upper sixth passed in 4+ subjects; 29 in 3; 9 in 2; and 6 in 1 subject. Average UCAS points 17.7.

University and college entrance 80% of 1995 sixth-form leavers went on to a degree course (10% after a gap year); others typically go on to employment, HND or art foundation courses. Of those going on to university, 5% went to Oxbridge; 8% took courses in medicine, dentistry and veterinary science, 20% in science and engineering, 10% in law, 50% in humanities and social sciences, 5% in art and design, 5% other vocational subjects.

Curriculum GCSE and *A-levels:* 21 GCSE subjects offered; 18 at A-level (no A-level general studies). 28% take maths/science A-levels; 41% arts/humanities; 31% both. *Computing facilities:* Network of RM Nimbus microcomputers. *Special provision:* Skilled individual help. *Europe:* French and German offered (from age 10) to GCSE and A-level; also Spanish GCSE and French for business studies. European studies GCSE for sixth-form. Links with schools in France and Germany; annual sixth-form business studies trip to Strasbourg or Paris.

The arts *Music:* Over 75% of pupils learn a musical instrument; musical exams can be taken. 16 musical groups including choral society, chapel choirs, madrigal group, symphony and string orchestras, wind and jazz band, percussion ensemble. Regional winners of B&H National Concert Band Festival; 7 in county youth orchestras; several individual festival winners; 2 competed in Young Musician of the Year, winner in 1992. *Dance & drama*: Drama offered. GCSE and A-level drama can be taken. Some pupils involved in school and house productions. Recent productions of Pirates of Penzance, The Boy Friend, The Mikado. *Art:* Pottery, textiles, photography and printing also offered.

Sport, community service and clubs (Pupils aged 11 and over) *Sport and physical activities:* Sport is compulsory; choice of soccer, hockey, cricket, tennis, athletics, swimming, cross-country, badminton, basketball, netball, rounders, squash, volleyball, aerobics, dance, fitness training, gymnastics. Optional: golf, judo, fencing, table tennis, riding, ice-skating. GCSE and A-level sports studies offered, also BAGA and CFS sports studies. Current representatives: 1 county hockey, 1 county golf, 1 county squash, 1 cross-country; 1 England athlete; many district cross-country and athletics reps. *Community service:* Pupils take bronze, silver and gold Duke of Edinburgh's Award. CCF compulsory for 1 year at age 14, optional at other ages over 13. Community service optional at ages 13 and 15. *Clubs and societies:* Over 50 clubs or activities including photography, film, natural history, model railway, chess, brewing, CD, rock band workshop, science, debating, literary, geographical, choreography.

Discipline Pupils failing to produce homework once might expect a revised deadline.

Former pupils Robin Jackman (test cricketer); Roger Royle (TV and radio cleric); Frederick Kempf (BBC Young Musician of the Year, 1992).

• ST EDWARD'S (Cheltenham)

St Edward's School, Ashley Road, Charlton Kings, Cheltenham GL52 6NT. Tel 01242 526697, Fax 01242 260986

• Pupils 665 • Boys 2½–18 (Day) • Girls 2½–18 (Day) • Upper sixth 40 • Termly fees up to £1795 (Day) • ISAI • Enquiries/application to the Admissions Secretary

What it's like

Formed in 1987, as a co-educational school, by the amalgamation of two independent Catholic schools – Charlton Park and Whitefriars. The school occupies two large sites on the outskirts of town; the junior school on one and the senior on the other. Both are well-equipped and have plenty of space and playing fields. St Edward's is a Roman Catholic foundation but open to pupils of all denominations. The Christian faith is central to the school, not simply as a taught subject but as a way of living. Academic standards and results are good although the school aims at being a family school taking pupils of a broad range of ability. Each year most go on to degree courses, including Oxbridge. Amongst the strengths of the school are the creative arts and sport. Both parts of the school produces a major drama production and musical concerts. In sports, high standards are achieved and the school regularly competes in national competitions with success. There is a considerable number of clubs and extra-curricular activities.

School profile

Pupils Total age range 2½–18; 665 day pupils (338 boys, 327 girls). Senior school 11–18; 470 pupils. Main entry ages, 4, 7, 11 and into the sixth. Own junior school provides 60% of senior intake. *State school entry:* 20% at 11, 5% to sixth.

Entrance Own exam used; Common Entrance accepted. No special skills or religious requirements – a Catholic foundation which welcomes pupils of other denominations. Parents not expected to buy textbooks or pay for normal school outings; meals and transport extra. 18 pa scholarships (at 11 and 16); discretionary awards.

Head and staff *Headmaster:* Anthony Martin, 6 years in post. Educated at Morecambe Grammar and at Reading, Newcastle and the Open universities (classics and education). Previously Head of Middle School at St Edward's and at Whitefriars School and Head of Classics at St Chad's College, Wolverhampton. *Staff:* 52 full time, 16 part time. Annual turnover 5%. Average age 40.

Exam results On average, 80 pupils in upper fifth, 45 in upper sixth. *GCSE:* On average, 34% upper fifth gain at least grade C in 8+ subjects; 47% in 5–7 subjects. *A-levels:* 5% upper sixth pass in 4+ subjects; 73% in 3; 10% in 2; and 12% in 1 subject. Average UCAS points 15.0.

University and college entrance 90% of 1995 sixth-form leavers went on to a degree course (5% after a gap year); others typically go on to art foundation courses. Of those going on to university, 10% went to Oxbridge; 5% took courses in medicine, dentistry and veterinary science, 20% in science and engineering, 5% in law, 50% in humanities and social sciences, 10% in art and design, 10% in other subjects.

Curriculum GCSE and A-levels. 20+ subjects offered (including theatre studies and A-level general studies). 38% take science A-levels; 44% arts/humanities; 18% both. *Vocational:* Work experience available. *Computing facilities:* 3 rooms equipped with computers (2 computer science, 1 business studies); plus a range of computers in subject departments. *Special provision:* Two trained special needs teachers. *Europe:* French, German and Spanish offered at GCSE, AS and A-level. Regular exchanges. Visits arranged abroad.

The arts (Pupils aged 11 and over) *Music:* Over 50% of pupils learn a musical instrument; instrumental exams can be taken. Some 8 musical groups including flute, string, clarinet groups, jazz/pop band, orchestra, recorder. Music/drama productions. *Drama & dance*: Both offered. GCSE and A-level drama may be taken. All pupils are involved in school productions and some in house/other productions. One recent pupil to Guildhall. *Art:* On average, 50 take GCSE, 2 AS-level, 5 A-level. Textiles also offered. A recent 3D study chosen by Cambridge Board as example of excellence in A-level work.

Sport, community service and clubs (Pupils aged 11 and over) *Sport and physical activities:* Compulsory sports: rugby, soccer, hockey, cricket, tennis, rounders, athletics, basketball, netball, swimming. Optional: squash, badminton, cross-country, volleyball, skiing, aerobics. GCSE and A-level sports studies may be taken. *Community service:*

Pupils take bronze, silver and gold Duke of Edinburgh's Award. Community service optional. *Clubs and societies:* Up to 30 clubs, eg chess, camera, choir, speech and drama, judo, art, music, food and fabric, model, sports.
Uniform School uniform worn throughout, varied in sixth.
Houses/prefects Competitive houses. Prefects, head boy/girl and deputies, house captains – voted by sixth-form and staff, appointed by Headmaster. School Council.
Religion Daily assembly, Mass at beginning and end of term compulsory.
Social Joint concerts with Cheltenham College, and Cheltenham Ladies' College. Trips abroad to France, Greece etc, also skiing; exchanges to France and Germany. Pupils allowed to bring own car/bike/motorbike to school. Meals self-service. School shop. No tobacco/alcohol allowed.
Discipline Detentions used when necessary. Minor misdemeanours dealt with by form tutor, more serious are referred to Year Head.
Alumni association run by Mr Ablett, c/o the school.
Former pupils Lucy Soutter (international squash player).

• ST EDWARD'S (Liverpool)

St Edward's College, North Drive, Sandfield Park, Liverpool L12 1LF. Tel 0151 228 3376, Fax 0151 252 0219

• Pupils 1100 • Boys 3–18 (Day) • Girls 3–18 (Day) • Upper sixth 93 • Termly fees £800–£1166 (Day) • HMC • Enquiries/application to the Registrar.

What it's like

Founded in 1900 by the Christian Brothers it is sited in a fine 30-acre wooded park in a residential district of the City and caters for a wide area of Merseyside. First-rate modern facilities are available. The school has been fully co-educational since 1991, although girls were accepted in the sixth-form in the early eighties. About 98% of the pupils are Roman Catholic. A full course of religious education is an integral part of the curriculum. Academic standards are high and results are good; most pupils go on to degree courses, many to Oxbridge. It is the choir school to the Metropolitan Cathedral (approx 36 choristers). Partly as a result there is immense strength in music. There are many well-known alumni in the musical world. Drama is strong. Very high standards in sports and games (a large number of county representatives, especially track and field athletes). A substantial commitment to local community services and an impressive record in the Duke of Edinburgh's Award Scheme.

School profile

Pupils Total age range 3–18; 1100 day pupils (613 boys, 487 girls). Senior department 11–18, 747 pupils (464 boys, 283 girls). Main entry ages 3, 5, 11 and into sixth. Own junior department provides more than 35% of senior intake. Approx 40% are children of former pupils.
Entrance Own entrance exam used. No special skills or religious requirements (but 98% of pupils are Roman Catholic). Parents not expected to buy textbooks; no other extras. 55 pa assisted places. 18 pa scholarships/bursaries, £250–£1000.
Parents 15+% are manual workers; 15+% are doctors, lawyers etc; 15+% in industry or commerce.
Head and staff *Headmaster:* John Waszek, 4 years in post. Educated at St Joseph's, Stoke-on-Trent, and at City, Leicester and Loughborough universities (economics and PGCE). Previously Housemaster and Head of Economics at Rugby and Head of Economics at Hedingham School, Essex. Publications: Three O-level economics texts. *Staff:* 77 full time, 23 part time. Annual turnover 1%. Average age 40.
Exam results In 1995, 90 in Year 11, 72 in Year 13. *GCSE:* In 1995, 69 in Year 11 gained at least grade C in 8+ subjects; and 11 in 5–7 subjects. *A-levels:* 33 in Year 13 passed in 4+ subjects; 27 in 3; 10 in 2; and 1 in 1 subject. Average UCAS points 19.72.
University and college entrance 92% of 1995 sixth-form leavers went on to a degree course (3% after a gap year); others typically go on to repeat A-levels. Of those going on to university, 6% went to Oxbridge; 9% took courses in medicine, dentistry and veterinary science, 28% in science and engineering, 3% in law, 46% in humanities and social sciences, 2% in art and design, 9% other vocational subjects (eg accountancy, tourism).

Curriculum GCSE and A-levels. 53% take science/engineering, 38% take arts and humanities, 9% a mixture. *Computing facilities:* IT suite with 32 PCs, and further 29 PCs. *Special provision:* for EFL, dyslexic and mildly visually handicapped. *Europe:* French and Spanish offered at GCSE, AS and A-level; Portuguese AS-level. Regular exchanges.
The arts *Music:* Over 30% of pupils learn a musical instrument; instrumental exams can be taken. Some 9 musical groups including Cathedral choir, chamber choir, orchestras, brass ensemble, early music group, string quartet. Several members of Merseyside youth orchestra and Metropolitan Cathedral Choir, Oxbridge choral scholarships etc. *Drama & dance*: Drama offered. A-level theatre studies may be taken. Pupils are involved in a variety of school productions. *Art:* On average, 50 take GCSE, 7 A-level. Fine art, painting and drawing, printmaking and 3D design also offered. All A-level students accepted for art foundation courses and then degree courses.
Sport, community service and clubs *Sport and physical activities:* Sports available: rugby, cross-country, cricket, athletics, swimming, tennis, basketball, hockey, badminton, weight-training, rounders, netball, climbing. All experience a wide range of sports and can concentrate on those they prefer. A-level PE, RLSS exams may be taken. Rugby, normally U15 7 represent Merseyside, 2 county, 2 region; swimming, 2 county; athletics, 3 county; cross-country, 6 city, 3 county; hockey, 3 city, 2 county; netball, 2 city, 1 county. *Community service:* Pupils take bronze, silver and gold Duke of Edinburgh's Award. Community service compulsory for 6 months at age 16–18. Clubs and societies; Up to 30 clubs, eg amateur radio, bridge, French, debating, drama, model railway, philately, poetry.
Uniform School uniform worn throughout.
Houses/prefects Prefects, head boy and girl – appointed by the Head.
Religion Morning assembly/prayer compulsory. Daily eucharistic service is encouraged.
Social Debates, public speaking and sporting events with local schools. Frequent trips and exchanges abroad arranged by modern language departments. Pupils allowed to bring own car/bike to school. Meals self-service. No tobacco/alcohol allowed.
Discipline Pupils failing to produce homework once might be told to produce it next day; those caught possessing illegal substances on the premises may expect suspension. Merits and distinctions for good work; impositions and detentions for poor work.
Former pupils Sir Brian Pearse (Chairman Lucas Aerospace and Housing Trust); Michael Williams (actor); Michael Slemen and Edward Rudd (England Rugby players), Terry Leahy (Tesco's), Kevin McCarten (Sainsbury's) and numerous musicians.

• ST EDWARD'S (Malta)

St Edward's College, Cottonera, Malta. Tel Malta 356 825978/827077, Fax 356 681557

• Pupils 950 • Boys 5–18 (Day) • Girls 16–18 (Day) • Upper sixth 50 • Termly fees £M195–£M270 (Day) • HMC • Enquiries/application to the Headmaster

What it's like

Founded in 1929, it has a suburban site. A school with strong local roots. Boys mainly enter at age 5, while girls are admitted only into the sixth-form. The staff:pupil ratio is about 1:15. Roughly 50% of sixth-form leavers go on to degree courses, most of them to the University of Malta. Some musical and dramatic activity; also clubs and societies, including a Young Enterprise group.

School profile

Pupils Total age range 5–18; 950 day pupils. Senior department 11–18; 500 pupils, 430 boys, 70 girls. Main entry is 5 (boys) and into the sixth (boys and girls). 50% are the children of former pupils. *State school entry:* 5% of the intake to the sixth.
Entrance No special skills or religious requirements; Catholic school but all denominations accepted. Parents expected to buy textbooks; no other extras. 8 pa sixth-form scholarships, 33% fees.
Parents 50% in industry/commerce; 35% doctors/lawyers etc. More than 60% live within 30 miles; fewer than 10% overseas.
Head and staff *Headmaster:* Gerald Briscoe, 7 years in post. Educated at Oswestry High School, and at Bristol and Oxford universities (geography). Previously Headmaster of Mayfield and Head of Humanities at Seaford. Also member of National Council of Independent Schools Associations. *Staff:* 63 full time, 3 part time. Annual turnover, 5%. Average age, 40.

Exam results On average, 70 pupils in upper fifth, 50 in upper sixth. *IGCSE:* 20 upper fifth pass in 5–7 subjects; and 40 in 1–4 subjects. *A-levels:* 30 pass in 3 subjects; 10 in 2; and 10 in 1 subject.
University and college entrance 50% of sixth-form leavers go on to a degree course, most to the university of Malta; others typically go on to courses in eg tourism management. Of those going on to university, 20% took courses in medicine, dentistry and veterinary science, 40% in science and engineering, 40% in humanities and social sciences.
Curriculum IGCSE, A-levels and Maltese Matriculation offered. 15 IGCSE subjects, 13 A-level, including Maltese; no A-level general studies but Systems of Knowledge for Maltese matric. 30% take science A-levels; 60% arts/humanities; 10% both. *Computing facilities:* Computer laboratory with network of 18 Archimedes; separate sixth-form lab; some classroom computers. *Special provision:* Some EFL teaching. *Europe:* English and Maltese (both compulsory from 5), Italian (from 10) and French (from 11) all offered at IGCSE and A-level; over 50% pupils take IGCSE in more than one language.
The arts *Music:* More than 25% pupils learn a musical instrument. Junior recorder group. *Drama & dance*: Drama offered, not examined. Majority of pupils involved in school productions. *Art:* Art offered at all ages.
Sport, community service and clubs *Sport and physical activities:* All pupils participate in PE programme, which introduces many sports and games which they then may choose. National representatives in football and tennis. *Community service*: optional. *Clubs and societies:* Up to 10 clubs in senior school including Young Enterprise, Mini-European Assembly.
Uniform School uniform worn throughout.
Houses/prefects Competitive houses. Head boy/girl, house prefects and house captains, appointed by Headmaster and housemasters.
Religion Religious worship compulsory unless exemption requested by parents.
Social Sports fixtures and debates with other local schools. Usually 2 overseas trips annually; groups of foreign students visit the school. Pupils allowed to bring own car/bike to school. Meals self-service. School shop. No tobacco/alcohol allowed.
Discipline Pupils failing to produce homework once might expect to complete it in detention; pupils caught smoking cannabis on the premises might expect expulsion.
Alumni association run by Dr Noel Arrigo, 186 St Margaret Street, Siggiewi, Malta.
Former pupils Dr Edward De Bono (lateral thinking).

• ST EDWARD'S (Oxford)

St Edward's School, Woodstock Road, Oxford OX2 7NN. Tel 01865 319204, Fax 01865 319202 • Pupils 565 • Boys 13–18 (Day/Board) • Girls 13–18 (Day/Board) • Upper sixth 128 • Termly fees £3070 (Day) £4090 (Board) • HMC • Enquiries/application to the Registrar (01865 319200)

What it's like

Founded in 1863, the original buildings were in the centre of Oxford. In 1873 the school moved to Summertown, two miles north of the city. There it enjoys a site of about 100 acres. The agreeable original buildings are in the Victorian collegiate style. There has been a comprehensive programme of renovation and development and the school is now very well equipped. Girls have been admitted to the sixth-form since 1983 and the school is going fully co-educational in 1997. The staff:pupil ratio is very favourable – nearly 1:8. Academic standards are high and results are good. Each year most sixth-form leavers proceed to degree courses including many to Oxbridge. Music is well supported (two orchestras, a concert band, a jazz band and choir). There is a very strong dramatic tradition and each year there are numerous small-scale productions, plus two major ones. For many years there has been strength in sports and games which are very well provided for with fine playing fields and a superb sports hall. A large number of clubs and societies cater for a wide range of interest. The CCF includes Air Force and Naval sections and there is a good deal of emphasis on open-air adventure training. Ample use is made of the cultural facilities of Oxford.

School profile

Pupils Age range 13–18, 565 pupils, 125 day (120 boys, 5 girls), 440 boarding (385 boys,

55 girls). Main entry ages 13 and into sixth; girls admitted throughout from 1997. *State school entry:* 2% main intake, plus 2% to sixth.

Entrance Common Entrance exam used. Assisted places (at age 13 and into sixth). Up to 13 pa scholarships including art and music. Also scholarship schemes jointly with nominated prep schools for pupils age 9–11, including one for a state school pupil. Some bursaries.

Head and staff *Warden*: David Christie, in post for 8 years. Educated at Dollar Academy and universities of Strathclyde and London (economics). Previously Head of Economics at Winchester and has taught at European School, Luxembourg. Also member of HMC Inspection Working Party and Professional Development Sub-Committee, Scottish Committee of IBA. Publications: text book (with Prof A Scott); numerous contributions to journals and books on education. *Staff:* 67 full and part time.

Exam results In 1995, 90 pupils in fifth; 128 in upper sixth. *GCSE:* In 1995, 67 gained at least grade C in 8 + subjects; 18 in 5–7 subjects. *A-levels:* 16 passed in 4 + subjects; 104 in 3; 6 in 2; and 2 in 1 subject. Average UCAS points 20.8.

University and college entrance 90% of sixth-form leavers went on to a degree course; others typically go on to other courses or straight into careers. Of those going on to university, 17% went to Oxbridge; 1% took courses in medicine, dentistry and veterinary science, 29% in science and engineering, 66% in humanities and social sciences, 2% in art and design, 2% in music or drama.

Curriculum GCSE and A-level. 18 GCSE subjects offered, 21 at A-level (no A-level general studies). 17% took sciences, 34% arts/humanities, 49% both. *Computing facilities:* 12 networked Apple Macs, 6 networked Nimbus; stand-alone Apple Macs or PCs in most departments and all boarding houses. *Special provision:* available for pupils with mild dyslexia. *Europe:* French, German and Spanish offered to GCSE, AS and A-level. Regular exchanges. Small intake of European pupils.

The arts *Music:* Over 30% pupils learn a musical instrument; instrumental exams can be taken. Musical groups, include orchestra, concert band, big band, choral society, chapel choir, chamber music groups, string quartets. *Drama & dance*: Some pupils are involved in school productions; all first year in house/other productions. 10 productions a year; recently included Equus (which toured America), Jumpers, South Pacific, As You Like It and Marriage of Figaro. House festival directed by senior boys. *Art:* On average 40 take GCSE, 20 A-level. Design, woodwork, metalwork, plastics, ceramics, graphics, art history and photography also offered.

Sport, community service and clubs *Sport and physical activities:* Major sports: rugby (autumn), hockey, rowing (spring and summer), cricket, athletics (summer term). Also squash, tennis, sailing, fencing, cross-country, swimming, golf, weight training, badminton, basketball, volleyball, 5-a-side soccer, 6-a-side hockey, gymnastics, judo, table tennis. *Community service:* CCF compulsory at age 14, voluntary thereafter. *Clubs and societies:* A wide range.

Discipline Pupils failing to produce homework once might expect a reprimand and to produce the work by the next day or earlier; those caught smoking cannabis on the premises might expect expulsion.

Former pupils George Fenton (film music eg. Gandhi, Shadowlands); Peter Rawlins (Chief Executive, Stock Exchange); Jon Snow (news journalist); Judge Stephen Tumim.

• ST ELPHIN'S

St Elphin's School, Darley Dale, Matlock, Derbyshire DF4 2HA. Tel 01629 733263

• Pupils 230 • Boys 3–7 only • Girls 3–18 (Day/Board/Weekly) • Upper sixth 19 • Termly fees £1886 (Day) £3237 (Board) £3075 (Weekly) • GSA, SHA, BSA • Enquiries/application to the Headmistress.

What it's like

Founded in 1844 for the daughters of Anglican clergy, it moved to its present premises in Derbyshire in 1904. Its main original buildings, handsome in local stone, stand in beautiful gardens and grounds. There has been a number of recent additions, including a new nursery/infants/junior school, sixth-form boarding house and music centre. Boys are admitted from 3–12 only. The school has its own chapel and this is central to its life. Pupils are encouraged to develop their Christian faith and life as fully as possible through prayer, corporate worship and teaching. The staff:pupil ratio is about 1:12. A sound general education is provided and results are very good. Almost all girls go on to degree courses. Music is strong and drama is popular. There are good facilities,for sports and games on site and a standard range is available. A choice of off-site sports (eg sailing, canoeing, abseiling) is available. A variety of clubs and societies caters for extra-curricular activities. There is keen participation in the Duke of Edinburgh's Award Scheme, the debating society and a very active social services society which works for the local community and for national causes. The Young Enterprise groups have achieved notable successes with presentations of their companies to the Derby Area Board.

School profile

Pupils Total age range 3–18, 230 pupils, 155 day (12 boys, 143 girls), 75 boarding girls. Senior department 11–18. Main entry age 11. *State school entry:* 20% main senior intake, plus 10% to sixth.

Entrance Own entrance exam used. Scholarships, exhibitions and awards, including 2 performing arts scholarship (£1500 and free tuition on 2 instruments or speech & drama).

Head and staff *Headmistress:* Mrs Valerie Fisher, appointed 1994. Educated at Bolton School and Manchester University (theology). Previously Head of the Assumption School, Richmond, North Yorkshire. *Staff:* 16 full time, 19 part time. Annual turnover 1%. Average age: 44.

Exam results In 1995, 32 pupils in Year 11, 19 in Year 13. *GCSE:* In 1995, 24 in Year 11 gained at least grade C in 8+ subjects; 6 in 5–7 subjects. *A-levels:* 11 in Year 13 passed in 4+ subjects; 7 in 3; 1 in 2 subjects. Average UCAS points 20.8 (including general studies, 23.3).

University and college entrance Almost all sixth-form leavers go on to a degree course (10% after a gap year); others typically go on to art foundation courses. Of those going on to university, 5% go to Oxbridge; 7% take courses in medicine, dentistry and veterinary science, 12% in science and engineering, 7% in law, 28% in humanities and social sciences, 10% in art and design, 28% in vocational subjects (eg pharmacy, business, nursing), 7% in other subjects eg drama.

Curriculum GCSE and A-levels: 21 subjects offered (including A-level general studies). 11% took science A-levels, 63% arts/humanities, 26% both. *Vocational:* Work experience available; also RSA information technology. *Computing facilities:* A fully equipped computer room, plus computers in various departments. *Special provision:* Dyslexia unit and EFL teachers. *Europe:* French and German offered to GCSE and A-level; Spanish and Italian offered as extras. Regular exchanges in Paris and the Loire Valley; also with Würzburg (Germany) and Trinec (Czech Republic).

The arts (Pupils aged 11 and over) *Music:* Over 50% pupils learn a musical instrument; instrumental exams may be taken. Some 8 musical groups: 4 choirs, choral society, orchestra, wind group, brass group. *Drama & dance*: Drama offered. A-level drama, LAMDA and Guildhall exams may be taken. Majority of pupils are involved in school and house/other productions. LAMDA gold medals for several pupils. *Art:* On average, 17 take GCSE, 3 A-level. Pottery and textiles also offered. 1st prize in Derbyshire competition.

Sport, community service and clubs (Pupils aged 11 and over) *Sport and physical activities:* Compulsory sports: netball, hockey, tennis, rounders, athletics, swimming, cross-country, gymnastics, volleyball, badminton, aerobics, lifesaving. Optional: riding, carriage driving. Sixth form only: rock climbing, sailing, wind-surfing, bowling, skiing, ice skating, abseiling, canoeing, caving, cycling. BHS and RLSS exams may be taken. *Community service:* Pupils take bronze, silver and gold Duke of Edinburgh's Award. Community service optional. *Clubs and societies:* Up to 15 clubs, including, biology, Scottish country dancing, Amnesty International, trampolining, diving, Young Enterprise, music, games, drama, debating, public speaking.

Uniform School uniform worn; only rarely (eg Speech Day) in sixth.

Houses/prefects Competitive houses. Prefects, head girl, head of house and prefects appointed by the Head in consultation with staff and sixth-form.

Religion Attendance compulsory at 4 short weekday services, Sunday service for boarders.

Social Regular debating competitions and sporting activities with other local schools. Exchange visits to France, Germany and Czech Republic. Trips abroad include tennis holiday (Austria), music (France), classics department trips, skiing. Sixth-form girls only allowed to bring own car to school. Meals self-service. No tobacco/alcohol allowed.

• ST FELIX

St Felix School, Southwold, Suffolk IP18 6SD. Tel 01502 722175, Fax 01502 722641

• Pupils 230 • Boys None • Girls 11–18 (Day/Board/Weekly) • Upper sixth 25 • Termly fees £2345 (Day) £3605 (Board/Weekly) • GSA

What it's like

Founded in 1897 by Margaret Isabella Gardiner, it is one of the few schools of its period actually designed and built as a boarding school. It stands in 75 acres of beautiful gardens, lawns and playing fields near the Suffolk coast and within walking distance of Southwold. It is well equipped, with a fine library, a modern DT, art and science block and a new covered swimming pool. The junior school, St George's, stands in its own grounds next to the main school. Non-denominational in its foundation, it welcomes girls of every religious faith. St Felix has a broad-based academic curriculum. Standards are high and results are good; most upper sixth go on to degree courses. Music, drama and art & design play an important part in the school's life. All instruments are taught and there are orchestras, a choir and ensemble groups. Inter-house music and drama competitions are held regularly. A large and well-equipped art department produces work of high quality. Many sports and games are available, as well as riding, shooting and water sports. Girls regularly represent Suffolk and East Anglia in hockey, tennis and athletics. There is a wide range of extra-curricular activities, including Young Enterprise with Danish and German schools in the lower sixth; most girls involved in the Duke of Edinburgh's Award Scheme – many achieve gold award before they leave.

School profile

Pupils Age range 11–18; 230 girls (87 day, 127 boarding, 16 weekly). Main entry ages 11, 12 and into sixth but entry at 13 and 14 too. Own junior school. *State school entry:* 16% main intakes, plus 23% to sixth.

Entrance Common Entrance exam used. 9 pa assisted places at 11, 12, 13 and 16. Scholarships, including music awards.

Head and staff *Headmistress:* Mrs Sue Campion, 5 years in post. Educated at Lycée Français de Londres and Cambridge University (modern languages). Previously Headmistress at Woodford County High, Deputy Head at Edmonton School and Senior Teacher at Dereham Neatherd High. Also President and Founder of the Association of Maintained Girls' Schools (1991). *Staff:* 25 full time, 6 part time.

Exam results In 1995, 44 pupils in upper fifth, 25 in upper sixth. *GCSE:* In 1995, 34 upper fifth gained at least grade C in 8+ subjects; 7 in 5–7 subjects. *A-levels:* 3 upper sixth passed in 4+ subjects; 19 in 3; 2 in 2; 1 in 1 subject. Average UCAS points 19.1.

University and college entrance 90% of 1995 sixth-form leavers went on to a degree course (20% after a gap year); others typically go on to art or music colleges. Of those going on to university, 5% went to Oxbridge; 5% took courses in medicine, dentistry and veterinary science, 10% in science and engineering, 5% in law, 40% in humanities and social sciences, 10% in art and design, 25% in other subjects eg English, drama, classics.

Curriculum GCSE, AS and A-levels: 22 GCSE subjects offered; 20 at A-level (including theatre studies and business studies). 20% take science A-levels; 80% arts/humanities. *Vocational:* Work experience available. *Computing facilities:* 30 RM Pentium PCs with CD-Rom, network facilities and Internet access on one machine; additional facilities in CDT and science. *Special provision:* for mild dyslexia; international centre provides EFL programme for foreign students. Provision for gifted children. *Europe:* French, German and Spanish offered to GCSE, AS-level and A-level; also Russian and Italian for seniors. Regular exchanges. German and Spanish girls attend school for 1–3 terms. School has EU funding to run multinational Young Enterprise (lower sixth) with Danish and German schools.

The arts *Music:* Over 50% of pupils learn a musical instrument; instrumental exams can be taken. Some 15 musical groups including choirs, choral society, orchestra, chamber orchestra, piano trio, baroque ensemble, string quartets. National Children's Orchestra, 2 members; Guildhall Junior, 1; North Suffolk Youth Orchestra, leader; Suffolk Youth

Orchestra, many members. *Drama & dance*: Both offered. A-level theatre studies may be taken. Majority of pupils are involved in school and house/other productions. National winner, Shakespeare on the Platform; National Youth Theatre members. *Art:* Design, pottery and photography also offered. Art facilities open to non-examination pupils.
Sport, community service and clubs *Sport and physical activities:* Compulsory sports: hockey, netball, swimming, tennis, rounders, athletics, gymnastics, trampolining, volleyball. Optional to seniors: athletics, hockey/netball. Sixth form only: golf. RLSS, RYA and Sports Leadership exams may be taken. Regular county and regional representatives, particularly in hockey, tennis and athletics. *Community service:* Pupils take bronze, silver and gold Duke of Edinburgh's Award. *Clubs and societies:* Over 30 clubs, eg wine society, drama, gym, soft toy making, embroidery, cookery, korfball, newspaper production, t-shirt design, aerobics, yoga, Amnesty International, Bronze Crest (science), karate.
Uniform School uniform worn except in sixth.
Houses/prefects Competitive houses. Prefects, head girl, head of house and house prefects appointed by the Head and staff, after consultation with upper sixth. School Council.
Religion Attendance at religious worship expected.
Social Debates and music jointly with other local schools. Modern language and Duke of Edinburgh's Award trips abroad. Sixth form allowed to bring cars to school. Meals self-service. School tuck shop. Sixth-form social centre with bar and multigym. No tobacco allowed; wine tasting course for sixth-form.
Discipline Pupils failing to produce homework once might expect an extension, on request and the problem would be investigated by the tutor; those caught bringing cannabis onto the premises might expect to be expelled.

• ST GEORGE'S (Ascot)

St George's School, Ascot, Berkshire SL5 7DZ. Tel 01344 20273, Fax 01344 874213

• Pupils 289 • Boys None • Girls 11–18 (Day/Board) • Upper sixth 31 • Termly fees £2275 (Day) £3875 (Board) • GSA • Enquiries/application to the Admissions Secretary •

What it's like

Founded at the turn of the century it has a fine site close to Windsor Great Park and opposite the Ascot racecourse. The grounds comprise 30 acres of fields, woods, streams and heathland and the handsome brick buildings have an elevated position with good views. The school is well equipped and has good sports facilities, including a new sports hall. There is a recently completed general teaching block with art, design and technology facilities and the computer system has been renewed. St George's is Christian in outlook and has its own chapel hall. A sound general education is provided with good academic standards. Results in public examinations are very good and almost all sixth-form leavers go on to degree courses. Music, drama and art are an important part of the curriculum. There is a wide range of sports, games and extra-curricular activities.

School profile

Pupils Age range 11–18; 289 girls, 110 day, 179 boarding. Main entry ages 11, 12, 13 and into sixth. Approx 2% are children of former pupils. *State school entry:* 1% intakes.
Entrance Common Entrance used. No compulsory extras; charges for extra games and music. Some bursaries for day girls. Scholarships (sixth-form and 1 academic); music awards.
Head and staff *Headmistress:* Mrs Anthea M Griggs, 8 years in post. Educated at North Foreland Lodge and at Homerton, Cambridge, and Edinburgh University (religious studies). Previously Housemistress and Careers Adviser at Harrogate Ladies College and Deputy Head at Oxenford Castle School. Also FRSA.
Exam results In 1995, 45 pupils in upper fifth, 36 in upper sixth. *GCSE:* In 1995, 40 upper fifth gained at least grade C in 8+ subjects; 5 in 5–7 subjects. *A-levels:* 1 upper sixth passed in 4+ subjects; 30 in 3; 4 in 2; and 1 in 1 subject. Average UCAS points 22.9
University and college entrance 95% of sixth-form leavers went on to a degree course (60% after a gap year).
Curriculum GCSE and A-levels: 16 GCSE subjects offered; 19 at A-level (no A-level general studies). 10% took science A-levels; 60% arts/humanities; 30% both. *Vocational:*

Work experience available. *Computing facilities:* One computer room with network of Acorn Archimedes computers; PCs in other departments. *Special provision:* Support teaching is arranged as an extra one-to-one. *Europe:* French, Spanish and offered to GCSE and A-level (German as an intensive course in sixth); other languages by special arrangement. Regular exchanges.

The arts *Music:* 60% of pupils learn a musical instrument; instrumental exams can be taken. Some 10 musical groups including choirs, woodwind, strings, jazz group, orchestra. *Drama & dance*: Both offered. GCSE drama, A-level theatre studies and LAMDA exams may be taken. Some pupils are involved in school productions and majority in house/other productions. *Art:* On average, 20 take GCSE, 5 A-level. Textiles, photography, ceramics and history of art A-level also offered.

Sport, community service and clubs *Sport and physical activities:* Compulsory sports: netball, lacrosse, gymnastics, tennis, swimming, rounders, athletics, squash. Optional: badminton, volleyball, table tennis, fitness, fencing, ballet, aerobics, modern stage, tap, basketball. County and region lacrosse teams members. *Community service:* Pupils take bronze and silver Duke of Edinburgh's Award. *Clubs and societies:* Clubs include bridge, pet keeping, pottery, photography and cookery.

Uniform School uniform worn except in sixth.

Houses/prefects Competitive houses. School Council.

Religion Compulsory morning assembly in chapel, 4 days a week. One compulsory Sunday service; Roman Catholics attend Mass; other religions may participate in their practices.

Social Contact with local schools encouraged; annual skiing trip, occasional visits to Russia and Australia. Frequent European music tours.

Boarding Resident qualified nurses; doctor visits twice-weekly.

• ST GEORGE'S (Edinburgh)

St George's School for Girls, Garscube Terrace, Edinburgh EH12 6BG. Tel 0131 332 4575

• Pupils 900 • Boys 3–5 only • Girls 3–18 (Day/Board) • Higher year 80 • Termly fees £1365 (Day) £2885 (Board) • GSA • Enquiries/application to the Headmistress

What it's like

Founded in 1888 by a committee of distinguished women who were inspired by the new ideals for women's education. It has an attractive 11-acre urban site with excellent facilities, including a purpose-built art block, music centre, an all-weather pitch, a centenary sports hall and good boarding accommodation. The primary school is on the same site. The school is non-denominational, with a Christian foundation. Christian assemblies are held daily. Academically a distinguished school, it has high standards of teaching and results are consistently very good. Most leavers go on to university each year, including Oxbridge. Both the Scottish Higher and a 2-year A-level course are offered. It is very strong indeed in music, drama and art, with many successes in these fields. An excellent record in games and sports (a large number of county representatives each season). It also has an outstanding record in the Duke of Edinburgh's Award Scheme.

School profile

Pupils Total age range 3–18; 900 pupils. Senior department 11–18, 550 girls (469 day, 81 boarding). Main entry ages 3, 5, 9, 10, 11, 13 and into sixth. Approx 10% are children of former pupils. State school entry: 20% senior intake, plus 54% to sixth.

Entrance Own entrance exam used. Academic potential to cope with the courses provided is sought; no religious requirements. Parents not expected to buy textbooks; extra charges include lunch for day girls (£1.80/day), music tuition £120). 31 pa assisted places. 2 pa sixth-form scholarships for girls from maintained schools.

Parents 15+% are doctors, lawyers etc; 15+% in industry or commerce. 60+% live within 30 miles, up to 10% live overseas.

Head and staff *Headmistress:* Dr Judith McClure, appointed 1994. Educated at Newlands Grammar School, Middlesbrough, and Oxford University (history and research in early medieval history). Previously Headmistress at The Royal School, Bath; Assistant Head and Director of Studies, Kingswood School; Head of History, School of St Helen and St Katharine, Abingdon; Lecturer in Medieval Latin, Liverpool University; Lecturer in History at Jesus, Somerville and Worcester colleges and Research Fellow at Lady Margaret Hall, Oxford. Publications: various articles on early medieval history. *Staff:* 68 full time, 16 part time. Annual turnover 1%–5%. Average age 41

Exam results In 1995, 79 pupils in upper fifth, 83 in Higher and A-level year (L6); 80 in A-level/CSYS year (U6). *GCSE/S-Grade*: In 1995, nearly all gained at least grade C (or 3) in 8+ subjects. *Highers/A-levels/CSYS*: Over the two years in the sixth, pupils gain an average of 6 subjects at Higher, A-level and/or CSYS. Average UCAS points 24.5.

Curriculum GCSE, S-grade, Highers, A-levels and CSYS. 26 subjects offered. Pupils in the sixth either choose the English curriculum (3 A-levels) or the Scottish system (5 Highers in L6, followed by a year in U6 taking extra Highers, converting a Higher to an A-level or taking other qualifications such as Scotvec). 37% take science A-levels; 51% arts/humanities; 12% both. *Vocational:* All lower sixth have one week's work experience; also RSA stage 1 and 2, desktop publishing and CLAIT and Scotvec modules in statistics, Spanish and Italian. *Computing facilities:* Senior school: network of BBC B and A3000 computers covers the computer room and many classrooms. *Europe:* French, German and Spanish offered to GCSE, Higher and A-level (French or German from age 11, second language at 13); sixth-form can take beginner's S-grade Spanish, Italian (Scotvec), RSA business and secretarial French and German for professional use. Regular exchanges.

The arts (Pupils aged 11 and over) *Music:* Over 50% of pupils learn a musical instrument or take singing lessons; instrumental exams can be taken. Some 15 musical groups including 3 orchestras, concert band, choirs, choral group, brass consort, wind band, recorder groups, chamber ensembles. Girls in National Youth Orchestra of Scotland, Edinburgh Youth Orchestra; regular entrants to specialist music colleges and university music departments. *Drama & dance*: Drama offered. GCSE or Higher drama may be taken. Majority of pupils are involved in school productions and all in house/other productions. Recent productions of Patience, Gang Aft Agley, A Winter's Tale. Winners of local drama competition; drama clubs every week. *Art:* On average, 40 take GCSE, 20 Higher, 9 A-level. Design, pottery, textiles and photography also offered. Prizewinners in regional ISIS art exhibition. Several girls go on to study art or design at colleges and university each year.

Sport, community service and clubs (Pupils aged 11 and over) *Sport and physical activities:* Compulsory sports: hockey, lacrosse, gym, dance, swimming, volleyball, basketball, tennis, athletics, badminton. Optional: squash, orienteering, aerobics, skating, rock climbing, lifesaving, windsurfing, judo, fencing, curling, netball. Sixth form only: cycling, golf, soccer. Higher PE, Scotvec, RLSS and RYA exams may be taken. Pupils form more than half of Scottish Schools' lacrosse team; last 12 of national lacrosse championships and only Scottish representatives; regional and national hockey teams; Scottish athletics champions; runners-up national tennis championship and regional squash competitons; British skiing champions. *Community service:* Pupils take bronze, silver and gold Duke of Edinburgh's Award. One of largest D of E Award centres in Scotland; 48 bronze, 25 silver and 40 gold participants in 1994. *Clubs and societies:* Up to 30 clubs, eg European, history, debating (2), Amnesty International, chess, drama, art, maths, Scrabble, computing, photography, Young Enterprise, archaeology, law.

Uniform School uniform worn except the sixth.

Houses/prefects Competitive houses. Prefects, head girl, heads of houses – elected by the sixth-form and staff.

Religion Christian assembly each morning (not compulsory, but no one has asked to withdraw).

Social Balls, Scottish reel evenings, Burns suppers, discos, musical and dramatic productions with other local independent schools. Skiing trips, visits to Italy, Greece, Germany, Belgium, Spain and Russia, language exchanges and with Germantown Friends' School (Philadelphia). Pupils allowed to bring own car/bike to school. Meals formal in boarding houses, self-service in school. No tobacco/alcohol allowed.

Boarding 25% have own study bedroom, 20% share with another, 55% are in dormitories of 5+. Houses of 30 and 52, divided by age. Weekends home by arrangement with Housemistress. Visits to local town allowed. Flexible boarding and after school care offered.

Alumnae association Secretary: Miss E M Mackintosh, 41 Netherby Road, Edinburgh EH5 3LP.

• ST GEORGE'S (Rome)

St George's English School, Via Cassia, La Storta, 00123 Rome, Italy. Tel 39 6 3089 0141/3, Fax 39 6 3089 2490

• Pupils 650 • Boys 3–18 (Day) • Girls 3–18 (Day) • Upper sixth 55 • Termly fees up to £2590 (Day) • HMC, COBISEC, ECIS • Enquiries/application to the Principal

What it's like

Founded in 1958 as a co-educational school, it is in a 27-acre site in pleasant countryside on the Via Cassia north of Rome. It was originally a Catholic seminary attached to the cathedral next door, which commemorates the place where St Ignatius Loyola dreamed of founding the Jesuits. It comprises three buildings and has good playing fields and other sports facilities. It provides a British system of education and runs a traditional house system. From 1996 the International Baccalaureate will replace A-levels. Some 65 nationalities are represented, the majority having English as their first language. It prides itself on possessing a stimulating but tolerant atmosphere. A staff:pupil ratio of about 1:11 permits plenty of individual attention. Academic standards are good and results very good. About 88% of leavers go on to degree courses. There is a rigorous ESL programme for small sets. Music is particularly strong and drama is well supported. A fair range of sports and games is available, plus usual extra-curricular activities. All members of the school are involved in local charity/community schemes.

School profile

Pupils Total age range 3–18; 650 pupils (330 boys, 320 girls) – most day, but family boarding provided. Senior department 11–18, 350 pupils. Main entry ages 3, 5, 11, 14 and into sixth. 570

Entrance Based on interviews, tests and past reports. No special skills or religious requirements. Average extras £900 for optional school transport plus private tuition/individual lessons if desired; parents not expected to buy textbooks. Limited bursaries available. Reduction for third and fourth child at school; plus discretionary awards.

Parents 15+% are in industry; 15+% in diplomatic service; 15+% in international organisations/agencies.

Head and staff *Principal:* Brigid Gardner, 3 years in post. Educated at Alice Ottley and Cambridge (history and English). Previously Headmistress at James Allen's Girls School, London. Also Governor, Whitgift Foundation (Croydon) and of Oundle. Publications: Guardian article on education for 14–19 year olds, book for Nelson A-level series. Ran the London marathon (1986). *Staff:* 64 full time, 6 part time. Annual turnover 3%. Average age 42.

Exam results In 1995, 53 in upper fifth, 51 in upper sixth. *GCSE:* In 1995, 60% upper fifth gained at least grade C in 8+ subjects; 26% in 5–7 subjects. *A-levels:* 26% upper sixth passed in 4+ subjects; 53% in 3; 12% in 2 and 7% in 1 subject. Average UCAS points 21.6.

University and college entrance 88% of 1995 sixth-form leavers went on to a degree course (7% after a gap year); others disperse worldwide. Of those going on to university, 5% went to Oxbridge; 10% took courses in medicine, dentistry and veterinary science, 20% in science and engineering, 12% in law, 56% in humanities and social sciences, 2% in art and design.

Curriculum GCSE, IGCSE, AS and A-levels, IB (replacing A-levels in 1996). 15 A-levels offered and 15 GCSEs (including classical civilisation). 21% take science A-levels; 43% arts/humanities; 36% a mixture of both. *Computing facilities:* Approx 30 IBM PCs in computer room and elsewhere. *Special provision:* Considerable ESL provision (5 staff). *Europe:* Italian (from age 7), French, German and Spanish to GCSE and A-level; also AS-level French, German and Spanish; and exams in many pupils' home language, eg Dutch, Russian. Over 80% take GCSE in more than 1 language.

The arts (Pupils aged 11 and over) *Music:* Over 30% of pupils learn a musical instrument; instrumental exams can be taken. Some 7 musical groups – 4 orchestras, strings, wind band, choir. Students go to British music colleges post A-level; music tour of Malta recent. *Drama & dance*: Both offered. Majority of pupils are involved in school and house/other productions. School productions recently include The Crucible, Trial by Jury, Murder in the Cathedral. *Art:* On average, 30 take GCSE, 9 A-level. Design, pottery, textiles, photography also offered. One former student recently accepted by RCA.

Sport, community service and clubs (Pupils aged 11 and over) *Sport and physical activities:* Compulsory sports: soccer, netball, hockey, basketball, tennis, swimming, dance, gymnastics, rounders, volleyball, athletics, cross-country. *Optional:* badminton, squash, table tennis, ballet, karate, aerobics. BAGA, ASA, ESAA exams may be taken. Generally good performance in Rome International Schools Association competitions and leagues. *Clubs and societies:* Over 30 clubs, eg expeditions, karate, computer, ballet, puppet, music, ecology, sport, debating, maths, design and technology, Scouts.
Uniform School uniform worn except in sixth when a dress code is followed.
Houses/prefects Competitive and pastoral houses. Head boy and girl, house captains, appointed by Principal, in consultation with staff and year group. Active School Council.
Religion None.
Social Joint music concert with Sir James Henderson School (Milan); joint art exhibition with Rome international schools. Organised trips to USA and UK universities; some activities-week trips abroad. Pupils allowed to bring own bike/motorbike to school. Meals self-service. Several discos every year. No tobacco/alcohol allowed.
Discipline Pupils failing to produce homework once might expect lunchtime detention and note in pupil-parent diary; those caught smoking cannabis on the premises might expect to be expelled.
Alumni association Gerry Firth c/o the school.
Former pupils Paul Getty, Eddie Cheever, Vittorio Gassman, Olga Fernando.

• ST GEORGE'S (Weybridge)

St George's College, Weybridge Road, Addlestone, Surrey KT15 2QS. Tel 01932 854811, Fax 01932 851829

• Pupils 525 • Boys 11–18 (Day) • Girls 16–18 (Day) • Upper sixth 65 • Termly fees £2085 (Day) • HMC, SHMIS, SHA • Enquiries/application to the Headmaster's Secretary

What it's like

Founded in 1869 by the Josephite Fathers, it moved to its present site in 1884 at Woburn Park where there are 100 acres of fine grounds, gardens and playing fields. Many extensions and developments have taken place over the years and the school is now very well equipped, with recent work in the music, science, English and languages areas. A Roman Catholic school into which all Christian denominations are welcomed, the religious life is an integral part of its existence and religious instruction and regular worship are compulsory. There is a good range of sports and games and high standards are achieved in hockey, rugby, cricket, rowing and tennis. A good range of extra-curricular activities includes commitment to local community services through the St Vincent de Paul Society. The Duke of Edinburgh's Award Scheme and Young Enterprise Scheme are well supported.

School profile

Pupils Age range 11–18; 525 pupils (450 boys, 75 girls). Main entry ages 11, 13 (boys) and into sixth (boys and girls). Approx 15% are children of former pupils. St George's College Junior School provides 50+% of intake. *State school entry:* 15% main intakes, plus 5% to sixth.
Entrance Common Entrance and/or own exam used. No special skills; Catholic school but other Christian denominations welcome. Parents not expected to buy textbooks; other extras vary. 6 pa assisted places. 15 pa scholarships available; bursaries at discretion of school, depending on parental circumstances.
Head and staff *Headmaster:* J A Peake, in post from 1994. Educated at Oxford University (chemistry). Previously Director of Curriculum at Millfield, teacher at Manchester Grammar School and in West Africa. *Staff:* 51 full time, 3 part time. Annual turnover 10%. Average age 40.
Exam results In 1995, 72 pupils in upper fifth, 65 in upper sixth. *GCSE:* 82% of upper fifth gained grade C or above in 8+ subjects; 11% in 5–7 subjects. *A-levels:* 4% upper sixth passed in 4+ subjects; 77% in 3; 15% in 2; and 4% in 1 subject. Average UCAS points 17.9.
University and college entrance 85% of 1995 sixth-form leavers went on to a degree course (20% after a gap year); others typically go on to art college or vocational non-

degree courses. Of those going on to university, 12% went to Oxbridge; 5% took courses in medicine, dentistry and veterinary science, 30% in science and engineering, 10% in law, 40% in humanities and social sciences, 10% in art and design, 5% in other vocational subjects.
Curriculum GCSE and A-level offered: 21 A-level subjects. *Vocational:* Work experience available. Computing facilites: Fully equipped computer suites and other computers throughout the school. *Special provision:* for mild dyslexia. *Europe:* French, Spanish and German offered to GCSE, AS and A-level; also Italian to GCSE. 70% take GCSE in more than 1 language. A-level pupils visit relevant countries.
The arts *Music:* Over 30% of pupils learn a musical instrument; instrumental exams can be taken. Musical groups including small and large choirs, various orchestras and ensembles. *Drama & dance*: Drama offered and A-level may be taken. Some pupils are involved in school and house productions. *Art:* On average, 50 take GCSE, 12 A-level. Design and ceramics also offered.
Sport, community service and clubs *Sport and physical activities:* Compulsory sports: rugby, hockey, cricket. Optional: rowing, tennis. National champions indoor hockey U16; county representatives hockey and cricket, all ages. *Community service:* Pupils take bronze, silver and gold Duke of Edinburgh's Award. Community service optional for all ages. Accompanying handicapped and sick in the Across Scheme. *Clubs and societies:* Many clubs, eg table tennis, play reading, bridge, chess, cinema, debating, Amnesty International.
Uniform School uniform worn with a dress code in the sixth-form.
Religion All follow religious studies throughout the school. Religious assemblies occasionally; Mass on major feasts; various voluntary and compulsory services.
Social Organised trips to London museums, galleries and theatres, sports team tours (UK, Europe, Africa and Australia), annual skiing trip, history of art and geography expeditions to Europe, Africa and India, history department tours and choir tour.
Discipline Discipline aims to be firm and fair with an emphasis on personal responsibility and high standards of behaviour.
Alumni association Old Georgians Association run by Father Francis Owen, CJ, Secretary c/o the school.

• ST GERARD'S

St Gerard's School Trust, Ffriddoedd Road, Bangor, Gwynedd LL57 2EL. Tel 01248 351656

• Pupils 350 • Boys 3–18 (Day) • Girls 3–18 (Day) • Upper sixth 17 • Termly fees £890 (Day)
• ISAI • Enquiries/application to the Headmistress

What it's like

Founded in 1915, it was in the care of the Sisters of Mercy until transferred to lay management in 1990; a lay Head was appointed in January 1991. Now co-educational, it was founded as a girls' school and first accepted boys in 1983. Single-site and semi-rural, it has pleasant buildings in wooded grounds. A Roman Catholic foundation, it is ecumenical and its ethos is firmly based on Christian principles. An increasing number of full-time members of staff and many part-time teachers. Fees are low and a good general education is given. Results are good and almost all sixth-formers go on to degree courses. French, German and Welsh are offered to A-level and there are regular exchanges to France.

School profile

Pupils Total age range 3–18; 350 day pupils (150 boys, 200 girls). Senior department 11–18, 205 pupils (85 boys, 120 girls). Main entry ages 3, 7, 11, 13 and into sixth. Approx 5% are children of former pupils. *State school entry:* 3% senior intakes, plus 10% to sixth.
Entrance Own entrance exam used. No special skills or religious requirements. Parents not expected to buy textbooks; other extras £60 per term per subject. Assisted places. Means tested bursaries for Catholic pupils.
Parents Farmers, hoteliers, medical and other professionals.
Head and staff *Headmistress:* Miss Anne Parkinson, 6 years in post. Educated at Llanrwst Grammar and University of Wales (modern languages). Previously Senior Mistress at More House School, London. *Staff:* 25 full time, 15 part time. Average age 41.

Exam results In 1995, 30 pupils in Year 11, 17 in upper sixth. *GCSE:* In 1995, 77% Year 11 gained at least grade C in 5+ subjects. *A-levels:* 15 pupils passed in 3 subjects; 2 in 1 subject. Average UCAS points 16.5.
University and college entrance 90% of 1995 sixth-form leavers went on to a degree course (none took a gap year); others typically go on to training or employment eg banking. Of those going on to university, 15% took courses in medicine, dentistry and veterinary science, 10% in science and engineering, 60% in humanities and social sciences, 10% in art and design, 5% in other vocational subjects (eg physiotherapy).
Curriculum GCSE, AS and A-levels: 19 subjects offered (no A-level general studies). *Computing facilities:* Fully equipped technology room. *Special provision:* Children with learning problems are assessed, language therapist arranged for dyslexics. *Europe:* French, German and Welsh offered to GCSE and A-level. Regular exchanges.
The arts (Pupils aged 11 and over) *Music:* Over 10% of pupils learn a musical instrument; instrumental exams can be taken. 2 musical groups: choir and orchestra. *Drama & dance*: Both offered. GCSE drama and LAMDA exams may be taken. Some pupils are involved in school and house/other productions. *Art:* Design and textiles also offered.
Sport, community service and clubs (Pupils aged 11 and over) *Sport and physical activities:* Compulsory sports: netball (girls), football (boys), basketball, hockey, tennis, athletics, volleyball. National and county badminton and rugby players.
Uniform School uniform worn, except in sixth-form.
Houses/prefects Competitive houses. Prefects, head boy/girl, head of house and house prefects – elected by the sixth-form.
Religion Compulsory assembly (parents have right of withdrawal).
Social Games fixtures and occasional joint skiing holidays with other schools. French exchange. Meals: packed lunches. School shop. No tobacco/alcohol allowed.
Discipline Pupils failing to produce homework once might expect a warning; subsequent action might involve detention. More serious infringements of school code of behaviour would lead to an interview with pupil, and informing of parents. Persistent transgression would lead to suspension and possible exclusion.

• ST HELEN'S

St Helen's School, Eastbury Road, Northwood, Middlesex HA6 3AS. Tel 01923 828511, Fax 01923 835824

• Pupils 960 • Boys None • Girls 4–18 (Day/Board/Weekly) • Upper sixth 80 • Termly fees £1012–£1591 (Day) £2643–£2998 (Board) £2536–£2891 (Weekly) • GSA • Enquiries to the Head • Application to the Registrar.

What it's like

Founded in 1899, it occupies an attractive semi-rural site of some 22 acres of gardens and playing fields in north-west London. It comprises a pre-prep department, a junior school and a senior school housed in well-equipped buildings which are being constantly upgraded. It has an excellent academic record with very good results. Almost all sixth-formers go on to degree courses each year, including many to Oxbridge. There is strong emphasis on music and drama and impressive art and design technology facilities. A very good range of sports and games in which high standards are attained, particularly in lacrosse and swimming. There is a plentiful range of extra-curricular activities and a promising record in the Duke of Edinburgh's Award Scheme. Regular use is made of London's cultural amenities. Strong links with Merchant Taylors' Boys School.

School profile

Pupils Total age range 4–18; 960 girls (900 day, 60 boarding). Senior department 11–18, 610 girls. Main entry ages 4, 7, 11, 12 and into sixth. Many senior pupils from own junior department, as well as a range of other schools. *State school entry:* 50% intake at 11, 3% to sixth.
Entrance Part of North London Consortium for entry at 11; own exam at 12 and 16. All talents considered; no religious requirements. Parents expected to buy sixth-form textbooks. Assisted places at 7, 11, 12 and 16. 7 pa scholarships at 11 and 16; also bursaries.

Parents 6% in armed services; 40% in industry or commerce. 70% live within 30 miles; up to 15% live overseas.

Head and staff *Head:* Mrs Diana Jefkins, in post from 1995. Educated at North London Collegiate and universities of Cambridge (natural sciences) and Southampton (education). Previously Deputy Head at Henrietta Barnett School and Head of Science at Dr Challoner's High School; has also taught at a range of other schools and worked as a Scientific Office in the Civil Service. *Staff:* 70 full time, 18 part time. Annual turnover 6%. Average age 44.

Exam results In 1995, 82 pupils in Year 11, 80 in Year 13. *GCSE:* In 1995, 99% of Year 11 gained at least grade C in 8+ subjects. *A-levels:* 4% upper sixth passed in 4+ subjects; 88% in 3; 7% in 2; and 1% in 1 subject. Average UCAS points 24.3.

University and college entrance 97% of 1995 sixth-form leavers went on to a degree course (18% after a gap year); others typically go on to management training. Of those going on to university, 12% went to Oxbridge; 11% took courses in medicine, dentistry and veterinary science, 13% in science and engineering, 13% in law and economics, 26% in humanities and social sciences, 7% in art and design, 5% in other vocational subjects eg education, physiotherapy, 25% in other subjects eg business and management.

Curriculum GCSE and A-levels: 20 subjects offered (including Japanese in sixth). 21% take science A-levels; 44% arts/humanities; 35% both. *Vocational:* Work experience available in UK and Europe. *Computing facilities:* 24 station PC 386/486 Novell network (2Gbyte server) plus 3 RM Nimbus networks (18 PC 386/486 stations) plus peripherals eg laser printers and scanner; PCs in other specialist areas. *Special provision:* Extra English lessons given on 1 to 1 basis for dyslexia and EFL. *Europe:* French (from age 7), German and Spanish (from age 11) to GCSE, AS-level and A-level; Italian offered in sixth. Over 50% take GCSE in more than 1 language and all pupils may continue language study in the sixth. Regular exchanges. European Youth Parliament annually. Work experience in Europe for sixth-formers.

The arts (Pupils aged 11 and over) *Music:* Over 35% of pupils learn a musical instrument; instrumental exams can be taken. Some 9 musical groups: 2 choirs, 2 orchestras, wind ensemble, flute and string quartets. *Drama & dance*: Drama and ballet offered. GCSE and A-level theatre studies, ESB and LAMDA exams may be taken. Majority of pupils are involved in school and house/other productions and joint productions with Merchant Taylors' School. *Art:* On average, 28 take GCSE, 9 A-level. Design & technology A-level.

Sport, community service and clubs (Pupils aged 11 and over) *Sport and physical activities:* Compulsory sports: lacrosse, netball, tennis, swimming, athletics etc. Sixth form only: golf, volleyball, badminton, squash, step aerobics; multigym at local leisure centre. Lacrosse, winners of U12 and U15 county tournaments, 30 in county teams, 1 in regional and 2 in junior England team; tennis, regional finalists in Midland Bank competition; swimming, district winners. *Community service:* Pupils take bronze, silver and gold Duke of Edinburgh's Award. CCF optional at age 14 (with Merchant Taylors'). Community service optional in sixth-form: also runs residential holiday for disabled each year with Merchant Taylors'. *Clubs and societies:* Up to 30 clubs, eg Amnesty International, Christian Union, debating, French, green, Japanese, mathematics, photography, science.

Uniform School uniform worn except the sixth.

Houses/prefects Competitive houses. Prefects, head girl, head of house and house prefects – head girl and deputies appointed after selection process involving external interviewers; prefects elected.

Religion Girls of all faiths welcomed within the framework of school's Christian foundation; compulsory morning assembly, weekend services for boarders, other chapel services voluntary.

Social Debates, theatrical and choral productions, local conferences with other school. Many activities shared with Merchant Taylors' school. Trips abroad: language exchanges eg Germany, France, Spain; educational eg Greece, Russia, Italy, Turkey; sporting eg USA lacrosse tour, skiing. Pupils allowed to bring own car/bike to school. Meals self-service. No alcohol/tobacco allowed.

Discipline High standards of behaviour expected and achieved; punishment for minor offences includes detentions or some form of service to school which would be generally

useful. Serious offences such as smoking or drug-taking can lead to temporary or permanent exclusion.
Boarding Year 13 have own study bedroom; Years 11 and 12 share; ages 14 and below in rooms of up to 7. Houses of approx 30 (all have computers for girls' use). Sanatorium with resident qualified nurse. Central dining room. Sixth form can provide and cook snacks and breakfast in house at weekend. Half-term and 2 weekend exeats per term; flexible arrangements for sixth. Visits to local towns allowed and to London for sixth-form.
Alumni association run by Miss M R Seldon, 26 Grove Lane, Camberwell, London SE5.
Former pupils Patricia Hodge (actress); Commandant D M Blundell, CB, WRNS; Julia Allan (sculptress); Josephine Buchan (TV); Barbara Mills (DPP); Penelope Marshall (TV).

• ST HILARY'S (Alderley Edge)

St Hilary's School, Alderley Edge, Cheshire SK9 7AG. Tel 01625 583532, Fax 01625 586110
• Pupils 250 • Boys None • Girls 3–18 (Day) • Upper sixth 15 • Termly fees £725–£1347 (Day)
• GSA, Woodard • Enquiries/application to the Head Mistress

What it's like

Founded in 1876, a Woodard school with a strong Christian ethos. It is semi-rural, in a residential area on the lower slopes of Alderley Edge, 15 miles south of Manchester. Senior, junior and nursery schools share the single site and have attractive and well-equipped buildings. It aims to develop a girl's abilities to the full, giving maximum opportunity for higher education and other avenues of professional training. Strong in music, drama and public speaking. Many clubs and activities and some participation in local community services.

School profile

Pupils Total age range 3–18; 250 day girls. Senior department 11–18, 140 girls. Main entry ages 3, 4, 7, 11 and into sixth.
Entrance Own entrance exam used. C of E school but other denominations are accepted. Lunch extra £107 per term. Scholarships and bursaries.
Head and staff *Headmistress:* Mrs Gillian Case, in post from 1995. Educated at Ormskirk Grammar School and Newcastle University. Previously Head of Upper Sixth at Bolton Girls' School. *Staff:* 15 full time, 13 part time.
Exam results In 1995, 33 in Year 11, 10 in upper sixth. *GCSE:* In 1995, 18 Year 11 gained grade C or above in 8+ subjects; 12 in 5–7 subjects. *A-levels:* 3 upper sixth passed in 4 subjects; 4 in 3; 2 in 2; and 1 in 1 subject. Average UCAS points 20.0.
University and college entrance 90% of 1995 sixth-form leavers went on to a degree course, others typically go on to employment. Of those going on to university, 45% took courses in science and engineering, 44% in humanities and social sciences, 11% in other subjects.
Curriculum GCSE and A-levels. 40% take science A-levels; 30% take arts; 30% a mixture. *Vocational:* Work experience available. *Computing facilities:* Computer suite and use of computers in subject areas; CD-Rom and satellite dish. *Europe:* French (compulsory from 11-16), German (compulsory for 1 year) offered at GCSE and A-level; also French AS-level and Italian GCSE. Regular exchanges to France.
The arts (Pupils aged 11 and over) *Music:* 15% of pupils learn a musical instrument; instrumental exams can be taken. Some 10 musical groups including orchestras, choirs, flute, wind and recorder ensembles and steel band. Pupils in local youth orchestras. *Drama & dance*: Both offered. Some pupils are involved in school productions and all in house/other productions. Zone winners of Rotary Public Speaking Competition. *Art:* On average, 15 take GCSE, 2 A-level. Design, pottery, textiles also offered.
Sport, community service and clubs (Pupils aged 11 and over) *Sport and physical activities:* Compulsory sports: netball, hockey, tennis, rounders, gym, athletics. Royal Navy aero-gymnastic awards may be taken. *Clubs and societies:* Up to 20 clubs, eg dance, drama, embroidery, cake decorating, media, table tennis, photography, art, jewellery, gym, cookery, Caledonian dancing.

Uniform School uniform worn except in sixth-form.
Houses/prefects Competitive houses. Prefects, head girl and head of house – appointed by the Head. School Forum.
Religion Strong Christian ethos.
Social Organised ski trips abroad, foreign exchanges, adventure holidays, theatre visits.

• ST HILDA'S (Whitby)

St Hilda's School, Sneaton Castle, Whitby, North Yorkshire, YO21 3QN Tel 01947 600051, Fax 01947 603490

• Pupils 232 • Boys 3–18 (Day/Board/Weekly) • Girls 3–18 (Day/Board/Weekly) • Upper sixth 24 • Termly fees £970–£1600 (Day) £2475–£2950 (Board/Weekly) • ISAI • Enquiries/application to the Headmistress

What it's like

Founded in 1915, the school stands on twin sites in the historic harbour town of Whitby. The upper school occupies Sneaton Castle, an imposing castellioned building, overlooking the town towards the Abbey of St Hilda's. The lower school is at Carr Hall, in 30 acres of fine gardens in the Esk valley. A notable feature of the school is its pastoral care. A good general education is provided and most sixth-form leavers go on to degree courses. Music, drama and art are important parts of the curriculum. A wide of sports, games and activities. Some commitment to local community schemes and a good record in the Duke of Edinburgh's Award Scheme.

School profile

Pupils Total age range 3–18; 232 pupils, 147 day (42 boys, 105 girls), 85 boarding (19 boys, 66 girls). Senior department 13–18, 85 pupils (13 boys, 72 girls). Main entry ages 3–11, 13 and into sixth. Approx 2% are children of former pupils. *State school entry:* 20% main intakes at 11 and 13, plus 30% to sixth.
Entrance Own entrance exam used. All special gifts are welcome; no religious requirements. Scholarships available (academic, art, drama and music); some bursaries.
Parents 15+% in the armed services; 15+% in industry or commerce. 50+% live within 30 miles; 10 +% live overseas.
Head and staff *Headmistress:* Mrs Mary Blain, in post from 1995. Educated at Our Lady of Mercy Grammar, Wolverhalmpton, and Birmingham University (theology and education). Previously Senior Housemistress and Head of Department at Cheltenham College, Acting Deputy Head at Winchcombe School and taught at Queensbury School Dunstable. *Staff:* 24 full time, 21 part time. Annual turnover 2%. Average age about 38.
Exam results On average, 23 pupils in upper fifth, 14 in upper sixth. *GCSE:* On average, 14 upper fifth gain at least grade C in 8+ subjects; 6 in 5–7; and 3 in 1–4 subjects. *A-levels:* 2 upper sixth pass in 4+ subjects; 4 in 3; 5 in 2; and 3 in 1 subject. Average UCAS points 14.5.
University and college entrance 88% of 1995 sixth-form leavers went on to a degree course; others typically go on to non-degree courses or art colleges. Of those going on to university, 50% took courses in science and engineering, 40% in humanities and social sciences, 10% in art and design.
Curriculum GCSE and A-levels. 24 GCSE subjects offered; 22 at A-level, including A-level general studies. 30% take science A-levels; 50% arts/humanities; 20% both. *Computing facilities:* Computer lab. *Special provision:* Dyslexia tuition. EFL assistance. *Europe:* French and German offered to GCSE, AS and A-level. Regular exchanges to Germany. German pupils regularly attend school for one term (French and Spanish occasionally).
The arts (Pupils aged 11 and over) *Music:* Over 50% of pupils learn a musical instrument; instrumental exams can be taken. Some 5 musical groups including madrigal group, chapel choir, wind band. *Drama & dance*: Both offered. LAMDA and BBS exams may be taken. Some pupils are involved in school productions and all in house/other productions. *Art:* On average, 10 take GCSE, 5 A-level. Design, pottery, textiles and photography also offered.
Sport, community service and clubs (Pupils aged 11 and over) *Sport and physical activities:* Compulsory sports: rugby, football, hockey, netball, athletics, cross-country,

swimming, tennis, rounders. Optional: squash, badminton, table tennis, riding, sailing, judo, weightlifting. GCSE sport can be taken. A number of pupils in county and district teams, including 1 representing county in British schools cross-country championship and 1 athletics. *Community service:* Pupils take bronze and gold Duke of Edinburgh's Award. Community service optional. *Clubs and societies:* Extra-curricular activities include astronomy, rocketeering, engineering, drama, debating, orienteering, canoeing, abseiling, photography, dance, theatre.

Uniform School uniform worn throughout.

Houses/prefects Prefects in upper sixth. Student Council (represented by all year groups).

Religion Church of England school. All denominations welcome.

Social Debates and socials with local schools. Occasional trips abroad; exchange with St Hilda's (Perth, Australia); travel awards to Austalia and Canada. Sixth form allowed to bring own bike to school. Meals formal. School shop. No tobacco/alcohol allowed.

Discipline Pupils failing to produce homework once might expect reprimand or detention; any possession or use of illegal drugs will result in expulsion.

Boarding 15% have own study bedroom. All boarders over age 13 in single house. Resident qualified nurse. Central dining room. Sixth form can provide and cook own food. 2 weekend exeats each term. Occasional visits to local town allowed (daily in sixth).

• ST JAMES'S AND THE ABBEY

St James's and The Abbey, West Malvern, Worcestershire WR14 4DF. Tel 01684 560851, Fax 01684 569252

• Pupils 200 • Boys None • Girls 11–18 (Day/Board/Weekly) • Upper sixth 27 • Termly fees £2436 (Day) £3654 (Board/Weekly) • GSA • Enquiries/application to the Headmistress

What it's like

Founded in 1979 from the amalgamation of The Abbey School and St James's, it merged in 1994 with Lawnside. The school stands on the western slopes of the Malvern Hills and is set in 47 acres of beautiful gardens and parkland. Its handsome buildings are well equipped and there have been many developments, including most recently a purpose-built theatre. It is predominantly, though not exclusively, a Church of England school; the whole life of the school is an attempt to express Christian principles. A sound general education is provided with emphasis on developing every aspect of learning and personality. A large staff permits a staff:pupil ratio of about 1:7. Academic standards and results are good; most leavers go on to degree courses. Music, drama and art are curricular and extra-curricular strengths. Facilities for sports are good and a standard range of games and sports is provided; levels of performance are high and school teams have won county and regional competitions, particularly in hockey and athletics. An adequate range of clubs and societies for extra-curricular activities.

School profile

Pupils Age range 11–18, 200 girls (30 day, 170 boarding). Main entry age 11. *State school entry:* 1% main intake, plus 1% to sixth.

Entrance Common Entrance or own exam. Scholarships (general academic, science, art, music, drama and PE); also some bursaries.

Head and staff *Headmistress:* Elizabeth Mullenger, in post for 10 years. Educated at Bolton School (Girls' Division) and at the universities of Wales, Birmingham and Bristol (English, education and drama). Previously Head of English at King Edward VI Camp Hill School for Girls, Birmingham, and Joint Head of Intake Year at Falmer High, Sussex. Also FRSA; governor of three schools/colleges; ABM Selector (Educational) for C of E ministry. *Staff:* 18 full-time, 18 part-time. Annual turnover 2%. Average age 37.

Exam results In 1995, 35 pupils in upper fifth, 27 in upper sixth. *GCSE:* In 1995, 66% of upper fifth gained grade C or above in 8 subjects; 20% in 5-7 subjects. *A-levels:* 11% upper sixth pass in 4+ subjects; 48% in 3; 30% in 2; and 11% in 1 subject. Average UCAS points 15.0.

University and college entrance 96% of 1995 sixth-form leavers went on to a degree course, others typically go on to art and other non-degree courses. Of those going on to university, 4% took courses in medicine, dentistry and veterinary science, 15% in science and engineering, 65% in humanities and social sciences, 16% in other subjects eg art, music, drama..

Curriculum GCSE and A-levels. 22 subjects offered (including Japanese, theatre studies). 25% take science A-levels; 50% arts/humanities; 25% both. *Vocational:* Work experience available. Also GNVQ in business studies; typing and office skills (RSA and LCC). *Computing facilities:* Well-equipped computer room with BBCs and Amstrads; Internet link. *Special provision:* Provision for mildly dyslexic girls and EFL teaching. *Europe:* French, German, and Spanish offered to GCSE, AS and A-level; Italian to GCSE. Regular exchanges (France, Germany, Italy and Spain). Some European pupils for various periods. Compulsory extended European language and study in sixth-form.

The arts *Music:* Almost all pupils learn a musical instrument; instrumental exams can be taken. Some 5+ musical groups including choral, jazz group, ensemble. *Drama & dance*: Drama offered. GCSE, AS and A-level theatre studies and ESB exams may be taken. Majority of pupils are involved in school and other productions. *Art:* On average, 18 take GCSE, 12 A-level. Design, pottery, textiles and photography also offered.

Sport, community service and clubs *Sport and physical activities:* Compulsory sports: hockey, netball, volleyball, tennis, swimming, dance, athletics. Optional: squash, cricket, lifesaving. Sixth form only: golf. GCSE, BAGA, BHSL and RLSS exams may be taken. County hockey and athletics representatives. *Community service:* Pupils take bronze, silver and gold Duke of Edinburgh's Award. Community service optional at age 16. *Clubs and societies:* Up to 15 clubs, eg ceramics, squash, science, ballroom dancing, craft, computer, performing arts, riding, pottery, gym, debating, self-defence.

Uniform School uniform worn except in sixth.

Houses/prefects Competitive houses – 'ships'. Prefects, head girl and head of house elected by the school. School Council.

Religion Compulsory attendance at a short daily act of religious worship and on some Sundays.

Social Debates, lectures, societies and social events with other local schools. Educational trips to Italy and France and exchange with German school. Most meals semi-formal, supper self-service. School shop. No tobacco allowed; wine only for special occasions, with permission and under supervision (sixth-form wine society).

Discipline The school aims at firm guidelines and an atmosphere of mutual respect. Three basic school rules: adherence to the law of the land; observance of safety of others and self; consideration and regard for others at all times. Anyone caught in possession of, or using, drugs on the premises, might expect certain suspension and probably expulsion.

• ST JOHN'S (Leatherhead)

St John's School, Leatherhead, Surrey KT22 8SP. Tel 01372 372021, Fax 01372 386606

• Pupils 400 • Boys 13–18 (Day/Board/Weekly) • Girls 16–18 (Day/Board/Weekly) • Upper sixth 90 • Termly fees £2550 (Day) £3700 (Board/Weekly) • HMC • Enquiries/application to the Secretary

What it's like

Founded 1851, originally as a small boarding school for the sons of clergy, it moved to its present site in 1872. A very pleasant campus on the edge of the town, it comprises 50 acres of delightful grounds dominated by the handsome late Victorian buildings to which there have been many modern additions providing excellent facilities and accommodation. Although the school looks for all-rounders, the aim is for academic excellence and results are good. Most sixth-form leavers go on to degree courses. It is a C of E foundation with a lively chapel life that supports the strong pastoral framework of the house system; attendance at worship is both compulsory and encouraged. The music, drama and art departments are very active and many boys are involved in theatrical presentations each year. The school has a long-standing reputation for achievement in games and sports, and games are held 5 days a week. A very substantial commitment to local community schemes and an outstanding record in the Duke of Edinburgh's Award Scheme.

School profile

Pupils Age range 13–18; 400 pupils, 283 day (263 boys, 20 girls), 117 boarding (98 boys,

19 girls). Main entry ages, 13 (boys) and into the sixth (boys and girls). Some children of former pupils. *State school entry:* Very few in main intake; 1 or 2 to sixth.

Entrance Common Entrance and own tests used. School looks for all-rounders; C of E school – all other religions accepted. Parents expected to buy textbooks (often available secondhand). 6 pa assisted places. 10–15 pa scholarships/exhibitions (including for art, music and all-rounder), 25%–50% day fees; also academic and music awards at 16; foundationerships for sons of clergy.

Parents 5+% are clergy. 60+% live within 30 miles; less than 10% live overseas.

Head and staff *Headmaster:* Christopher Tongue, 4 years in post. Educated at Kingswood and at universities of Cambridge (engineering) and East Africa (education, London University external). Previously Headmaster at Keil, Housemaster and Master i/c Rugby at Felsted and Housemaster and Head of Physics at Kagumo High, Kenya. Also member Council of Scottish ISCO. *Staff:* 35 full time; 5 part time staff plus 12 music. Average age 39.

Exam results On average, 80 pupils in upper fifth, 90 in upper sixth. *GCSE:* on average, 75 upper fifth gain at least grade C in 7+ subjects. *A-levels:* 85 upper sixth pass in 2+ subjects. Average UCAS points 18.2.

University and college entrance 75% of sixth-form leavers go on to a degree course, 5% to Oxbridge; others typically go on to art or drama courses or other non-degree courses.

Curriculum GCSE and A-levels. 20 subjects offered (no A-level general studies). 21% take science A-levels; 60% arts/humanities; 19% both. *Vocational:* Work experience available. *Computing facilities:* Computer suite with Nimbus Network. *Special provision:* Dyslexic classes. *Europe:* French, German and Spanish offered to GCSE, AS and A-level. Regular exchanges to France, Germany and Spain.

The arts *Music:* Up to 25% of pupils learn a musical instrument; instrumental exams can be taken. Some 4 musical groups: orchestra, wind band, brass group, jazz. 2 pupils played at Royal Albert Hall in Schools Prom. *Drama & dance*: Some are involved in school productions and majority in house/other productions. *Art:* On average, 27 take GCSE, 14 A-level. Pottery also offered.

Sport, community service and clubs *Sport and physical activities:* Compulsory sports: rugby, cricket. Optional: soccer, athletics, swimming, golf, fencing, sailing, netball, hockey, lacrosse, tennis, shooting, rounders, badminton, basketball, table tennis, karate. *Community service:* Pupils take bronze, silver and gold Duke of Edinburgh's Award. CCF compulsory for 4 terms at age 14+. Community service optional. *Clubs and societies:* Up to 10 clubs, eg theatre (including regular West End visits), Christian Union, ethical discussion etc.

Uniform School uniform worn; upper sixth may wear own suit.

Houses/prefects Competitive houses. Prefects, head of school (appointed by Headmaster); head of houses and house prefects (by housemasters).

Religion Attendance at chapel compulsory; full involvement encouraged.

Social Sixth form club; debates, music, discussion groups, occasional dances, charity rock concerts and annual conference on industry and business management. Organised trips/exchanges to France, Germany, Spain and America; sports tour to Holland, Belgium and West Indies; field trips to France, North Africa and Norway. Upper sixth allowed to bring own car to school; others, bikes. Meals, cafeteria style. School shop. No tobacco/alcohol allowed.

Discipline Pupils failing to produce homework, do it in detention. Anyone caught smoking cannabis would be expelled.

Boarding Senior pupils have own study bedroom, juniors in dormitories of 3–6. Houses of 50–55. Resident qualified nurse. Central dining room. Pupils can provide and cook their own food. Weekly exeats. Daily visits to local town allowed (juniors with permission, seniors on trust).

Alumni association run by Rev Philip Morgan, c/o the school.

Former pupils Richard Rogers; Anthony Hope; David Hatch; Guy Michelmore; Gavin Hewitt.

• ST JOSEPH'S (Ipswich)

St Joseph's College with the School of Jesus and Mary, Birkfield, Belstead Road, Ipswich, Suffolk IP2 9DR. Tel 01473 690281, Fax 01473 602409

• Pupils 750 • Boys 3–18 (Day/Board/Weekly) • Girls 3–18 (Day/Board/Weekly) • Upper sixth 80 • Termly fees £998–£1610 (Day) £2522–£2812 (Board) £2270–£2531 (Weekly) • BSA
• Enquiries/application to the Academic Registrar

What it's like

Founded in 1995 from the merger of two established Roman Catholic schools: a boys' school, St Joseph's College (founded 1937); and a girls' school, the School of Jesus and Mary (1860). Set in 55 acres of wooded parkland and based on two Regency country houses, Birkfield Lodge and Goldrood House. Its facilities include a boarding house, CDT centre, science centre and a sports hall. The school ethos is Christian and firmly embedded in the foundations of the original teaching orders, although there are no longer any Brothers or Sisters on the teaching staff. Religious education, including personal and social education, is taught throughout. Pupils and staff from all faiths are welcomed. Pastoral care is particularly good and the community is built around a concern for each individual. In the grammar school tradition, the best possible results for each pupil irrespective of ability are sought. A strong sporting tradition (many county representatives) and a number of extra-curricular activities and a considerable commitment to support the less fortunate, both locally and abroad. Some involvement with the Duke of Edinburgh's Award Scheme and a new CCF detachment.

School profile

Pupils Total age range 3–18, 750 pupils: 700 day (530 boys, 170 girls), 50 boarding boys. Senior department 11–18. Main entry ages 5, 11 and into sixth. Approx 15% are children of former pupils. Own junior department provides more than 20% of intake. *State school entry:* 50% main intake, plus 25% to sixth.

Entrance Common Entrance, own exam and current school reports. No special skills; school Roman Catholic but majority of pupils are not. Parents expected to buy some sixth-form textbooks; £100 maximum extras. 30 pa assisted places (5 at age 8, 15 at 11 and 10 into sixth). Scholarships at 11 and 16.

Parents Drawn from a complete cross-section of employment backgrounds and social groups. Up to 5% live overseas.

Head and staff *Headmaster:* John Regan, appointed in 1995. Educated at St Michael's College, Leeds, and Leeds University. Previously Deputy Head at St Joseph's College. *Staff:* 61 full time, 9 part time. Annual turnover 10%. Average age 39.

Exam results In 1995, 104 pupils in fifth, 62 in upper sixth. *GCSE:* In 1995, 62% upper fifth gained at least grade C in 8+ subjects; 25% in 5–7 subjects. *A-levels:* 80% of upper sixth passed in 3+ subjects; 17% in 2; and 3% in 1 subject. Average UCAS points 19.0.

University and college entrance All 1995 sixth-form leavers went on to a degree course (27% after a gap year), 5% to Oxbridge. 14% took courses in medicine, dentistry and veterinary science, 32% in science and engineering, 8% in law, 39% in humanities and social sciences, 3% in art and design, 4% in other vocational subjects eg architecture, agriculture, media.

Curriculum GCSE and A-levels. 31% took science A-levels; 27% arts/humanities; 42% both. *Vocational:* Work experience available; also RSA information technology. *Computing facilities:* 3 computer networks; own stand-alones in each department; connected to the Internet. Computers used as curricular tool in each subject. *Special provision:* EFL; small special unit for dyslexic pupils. *Europe:* French, German and Spanish offered to GCSE, AS and A-level (French in junior school, others from 11). Regular exchanges. French and Spanish pupils often in school.

The arts *Music:* Up to 25% of pupils learn a musical instrument; instrumental exams can be taken. Some 5 musical groups – orchestral, choral, jazz, pop. Annual music competition. Regular successes in Suffolk Schools Festival. *Drama & dance*: Variety of productions annually, including classics, musicals, improvisation. *Art:* On average, 15–20 take GCSE, 10 A-level. Design, pottery and photography also offered. Regular prize-winners in competitions.

Sport, community service and clubs *Sport and physical activities:* Main sports: rugby, cricket, netball, hockey, athletics, squash. Other sports include swimming, football,

sailing, basketball, golf, tennis, badminton, rounders, volleyball. *Community service:* Pupils take bronze, silver and gold Duke of Edinburgh's Award. Many sixth-formers involved with community service projects. *Clubs and societies:* Clubs include railway society, chess, music, theatre, debates, history, sixth-form society.
Uniform School uniform worn; dress code in sixth.
Houses/prefects Competitive houses. Prefects, head boy and girl and house prefects appointed by the Head in consultation with staff. Pupils have corporate responsibility for areas in common.
Religion Weekly school assemblies; regular assemblies for house and year groups. Mass for whole school on important occasions; Sunday Mass for boarders; voluntary daily Mass, confessions, vigils and prayers.
Social Annual skiing trips abroad; exchanges; community service projects in summer holidays in Togo and Kenya; sixth-form tours of Europe. Day pupils allowed to bring own car/bike/motorbike to school. Meals self-service. Uniform shop (including secondhand).
Discipline Pupils failing to produce homework once might expect a warning. Detention/litter duty are standard sanctions. Expulsion only in extreme cases.
Boarding 50 places available; each with own study bedroom. Attendant qualified matron; weekly doctor's visit – local doctor on call. Central dining room. Kitchen facilities available. Frequent weekend exeats. Visits to local town allowed.
Alumni association run by Mike Davey, c/o the school
Former pupils Earl Nelson; Christopher Mullin, MP; Brian Eno; Sean Blowers.

• ST JULIAN'S

St Julian's School, 2777 Carcavelos, Codex, Portugal. Tel 351 1 4570140

• Pupils 703 • Boys 3–18 (Day) • Girls 3–18 (Day) • Upper sixth 41 • Termly fees Esc 227,000–Esc 735,000 • COBISEC, ECIS • Enquiries/application to the Admissions Officer

What it's like

Founded in 1932 as a co-eductional school, it is on a single, suburban site, close to the sea about 10 miles from Lisbon. The heart of the school is a very handsome 18th-century palace which has been adapted. Modern extensions and additions provide good facilities. The buildings lie in attractive grounds and gardens. It is a Christian foundation and non-denominational. There are Portuguese and English sides to the school, following their respective national education systems; the English side has both junior and senior sections and a house system operates. The staff:pupil ratio is about 1:10 which permits a good deal of individual attention. Pupils are prepared for GCSE and the International Baccalaureate. Music and drama form part of the curriculum, and extra-curricular activities include music, sport and drama. Sports and games facilities are on site, and tennis, volleyball, basketball, hockey, athletics, football and karate are available. The school is part of an inter-school sports league with other international schools.

School profile

Pupils Total age range 3–18; 703 day pupils on the English side (350 boys, 353 girls). Senior department 11–18, 341 pupils (167 boys, 174 girls). Main entry ages 3, 7, 11 and into sixth. 25% are children of former pupils. *State school entry:* variable number from NATO base.
Entrance Own entrance exam. Ability to follow an academic curriculum looked for; no religious requirements. Parents not expected to buy textbooks. 10 pa scholarships for residents in Portugal, 50% fees.
Parents 15+% are doctors, lawyers, etc. 15+% in armed services; 15+% in industry or commerce.
Head and staff *Headmaster:* David Styan, in post from 1994. Educated at the universities of London (geography and economics), Oxford (education) and York (management). Previously led the School Management Task Force at the DES, Director of Education: North West and Headmaster at Marple Ridge High School, Stockport. *Staff:* 77 full time, 11 part time. Annual turnover under 10%. Average age 40+.
Exam results In 1995, 45 in upper fifth, 41 in upper sixth. *GCSE:* In 1995, 82% upper fifth gained at least grade C in 5+ subjects. *IB:* 95% pass the IB diploma with 6 subjects; average of 33 IB points.

University and college entrance 90% of 1995 sixth-form leavers went on to a degree course (10% after a gap year); others typically go on to family business. Of those going on to university, 9% went to Oxbridge (others to Edinburgh, LSE, Stanford etc); 10% took courses in medicine, dentistry and veterinary science, 30% in science and engineering, 10% in law, 20% in humanities and social sciences, 10% in art and design, 20% in other subjects.
Curriculum GCSE and International Baccalaureate. 16 subjects offered to GCSE, 16 to IB. *Computing facilities:* 3 labs plus computers for teaching aids. *Special provision:* special English classes provided in junior and senior school. *Europe:* Portuguese (compulsory from age 6) and French to GCSE and IB; beginning German, Italian and Spanish. Regular school trips (1995 to Italy).
The arts (Pupils aged 11 and over) *Music:* 15% pupils learn a musical instrument. Musical groups include school orchestra. *Drama & dance*: Many pupils are involved in school productions. *Art:* On average, 15 take GCSE, 7 IB. Some 3 pa accepted for art college.
Sport, community service and clubs (Pupils aged 11 and over) *Sport and physical activities:* Sports available: Soccer, volleyball, basketball, tennis, trampolining, athletics, cross-country. *Community service:* Community service as part of the IB. *Clubs and societies:* Clubs include computers, drama, music, karate, gym.
Uniform School uniform worn except in sixth.
Houses/prefects Competitive houses. Prefects, head boy/girl, appointed after consultation.
Religion Attendance at religious worship not compulsory.
Social Part of an inter-school sports league with other international schools in the area. Regular trips abroad eg to Kenya, Russia, Greece, and skiing. Pupils allowed to bring own car/bike/motorbike to school. Meals formal. School tuck shop.
Discipline Pupils failing to produce homework once might expect to receive a warning, followed by detention; those caught smoking cannabis on the premises might expect to be expelled.

• ST LAWRENCE

St Lawrence College in Thanet, Ramsgate, Kent CT11 7AE. Tel 01843 592680, Fax 01843 851123 • Pupils 540 • Boys 4–19 (Day/Board/Weekly) • Girls 4–19 (Day/Board/Weekly) • Upper sixth 65 • Termly fees £1940–£2480 (Day) £2960–£3720 (Board/Weekly) • HMC • Enquiries/ application to the Headmaster

What it's like

Founded in 1879 to provide a public school education within the evangelical tradition of the Church of England. A boys' school until 1968, it is now fully co-educational. It enjoys a fine site of 150 acres (with sea on three sides) between Broadstairs and Ramsgate. The junior and senior schools are on the same campus and their agreeable buildings, in traditional collegiate style, are set in splendid gardens. The chapel is an important focus of school life and there is some emphasis on Christian education; the college has long-standing bonds with mission societies and many Lawrentians have entered Holy Orders. Academic standards are high and results very good. Most leavers proceed to degree courses, including some to Oxbridge. Art, music and drama are all strongly supported. Excellent games and sports facilities include 36 acres of playing fields and a new flood-lit astroturf hockey pitch and tennis courts. There is a good range of games and sports (including rifle-shooting and sailing) and sporting standards are high, especially in hockey and athletics. A wide range of clubs and societies cater for most needs. The flourishing CCF is one of the oldest in Britain (founded in 1898) and has Navy, Army and Air Force sections. The Duke of Edinburgh's Award Scheme is also popular and there has been much success in it. Local community service is vigorously supported.

School profile

Pupils Age range 4–19; 540 pupils, 270 day (140 boys, 130 girls), 270 boarding (170 boys, 100 girls). Senior school 11–19, 370 pupils (215 boys, 155 girls). Main entry ages 4–7, 11, 13 and into sixth. Approx 5% are children of former pupils. Over 20% senior intake from own junior school (Tel 01843 591788). *State school entry:* 20% at 11, plus 8% to sixth.

Entrance Common Entrance and own entrance exam. No special skills required but talent in music, languages, sport, art and technology welcomed. No religious requirements; evangelical Church of England foundation but other faiths welcomed. Parents not expected to buy textbooks; cost of extras low, eg exam fees, insurance, excursions. 5 pa assisted places (at age 11). 15–20 pa scholarships/bursaries at 8, 11, 13 and sixth, 20%–50% (plus a further 50% if proven need).
Parents 15+% in armed services; 15+% in industry/commerce; 15+% are doctors, lawyers etc. 40% live within 30 miles; 15% live overseas.
Head and staff *Headmaster:* John Binfield, 13 years in post. Educated at Sloane School, Chelsea, and Oxford University (English). Previously Senior Master, Housemaster and Head of English and Drama at St Lawrence College, and Captain in British Army. Also Chief Awarder at A-level for O&C Board. *Staff:* 35 full time, 5 part time (+ 6 part time musicians). Annual turnover, up to 5%. Average age 40.
Exam results In 1995, 51 pupils in upper fifth, 47 in upper sixth. *GCSE:* In 1995, 75% upper fifth gained at least grade C in 8+ subjects, 18% in 5–7 and 7% in 1–4 subjects (average of 8.57 subjects). *A-levels:* 20% passed in 4+ subjects; 60% in 3; 15% in 2; and 5% in 1 subject. Average UCAS points 20.1.
University and college entrance 98% of sixth-form leavers go on to a degree course (15% after a gap year); others typically go on to Sandhurst, secretarial courses. Of those going on to university, 4% go to Oxbridge; 6% take courses in medicine, dentistry and veterinary science, 24% in science and engineering, 6% in law, 44% in humanities and social sciences, 6% in art and design, 14% in other vocational subjects eg architecture, accounting, pharmacy, hotel management.
Curriculum GCSE, AS-level and A-level. 20 subjects offered (including Ancient Greek A-level; no A-level general studies). 31% took science A-levels; 45% arts/humanities, 24% mixture. *Vocational:* Work experience available, one week after GCSEs. *Computing facilities:* 1 network of 26, 1 of 20, plus science network and various in CDT. Computers in all boarding houses. Telecommunication centre with internet, e-mail, weather satellite retrieval etc. All lower sixth take an IT course in addition to A-levels. *Special provision:* Bright, mildly dyslexic pupils accepted, 3 part time qualified staff. EFL, 4 part time qualified staff. *Europe:* French, German and Spanish offered to GCSE, AS-level and A-level (French compulsory from age 8 to GCSE); also German, Italian and Spanish for Institute of Linguists. All lower sixth must study a modern language in addition to A-levels. Regular exchanges (France and Belgium). Also a European 2000 conference room; TV available from several European countries.
The arts (Pupils aged 11 and over) *Music:* 30% of pupils learn a musical instrument; instrumental exams can be taken. Some 8 musical groups, including orchestra, choirs, stage band and other smaller groups. Recent winner of BBC Choir Girl of the Year, plus a finalist. *Drama & dance*: Drama offered. LAMDA exams may be taken. Some pupils are involved in school productions (usually 3 a year) and majority in house productions (7 a year). *Art:* On average, 20 take GCSE, 2 AS-level, 6 A-level. Pottery also offered.
Sport, community service and clubs (Pupils aged 11 and over) *Sport and physical activities:* Compulsory sports: hockey, netball, tennis (girls); rugby, hockey, cricket (boys). Optional: badminton, squash, golf, shooting, athletics, swimming, tennis, cross-country, football, adventure training. Several representatives in county and south east teams, especially in hockey and athletics. *Community service:* Pupils take bronze, silver and gold Duke of Edinburgh's Award (very popular). CCF compulsory for 5 terms at age 13 (many stay on). Most take life saving and first aid qualifications in CCF; services sixth-form scholarships to a boy and a girl in each of last 4 years, 2 flying scholarships 1995. Community service optional but popular. *Clubs and societies:* Up to 15 clubs, eg bridge, cookery, Christian Union, debating, electronics, film, model railways, stamps, Out and About Club (with Gourmet section).
Uniform School uniform worn, modified in sixth.
Houses/prefects Competitive houses. Prefects, head girl and boy, heads of houses and house prefects – appointed by the Head and Housemasters/mistresses, in consultation with current prefects.
Religion Compulsory attendance at worship except those of other faiths.
Social Orchestral concerts, numerous debates, and career conferences with local schools. Trips abroad include ski trip, exchanges with schools in France and Belgium, hockey tours to Holland. Day pupils allowed to bring own car/bike. Meals self-service.

School shop. No tobacco/alcohol allowed.
Discipline Pupils failing to produce homework once might be expected to produce it the next day; those caught smoking cannabis on the premises would be asked to leave.
Boarding 50% have own study bedrooms; 20% share with one other; 30% are in dormitories of 6. Single-sex houses of about 45. Resident qualified nurse (plus part-time nurses); doctor visits daily. Pupils can provide and cook own food. Half-term and 2 weekend exeats each term. Visits to local town allowed twice a week, sixth-formers more frequently.
Alumni association Old Lawrentian Society, run by Andrew Jackson, Holtwood, Onslow Crescent, Woking, Surrey.
Former pupils Sir Kirby and Sir Maurice Laing (John Laing PLC), Sir David Hunt (Mastermind winner and diplomat); erstwhile bishops of Winchester and Colchester, various generals, opera singers, MPs etc.

• ST LEONARDS

St Leonards School, St Andrews, Fife, Scotland KY16 9QU. Tel 01334 472126, Fax 01334 476152 • Pupils 274 • Boys None • Girls 12–18 (Day/Board) • Upper sixth 46 • Termly fees £2075 (Day) £3925 (Board) • GSA • Enquiries/application to the Headmistress

What it's like

Founded in 1877, it is situated on the edge of the historic town which is the seat of Scotland's oldest university. It has a very fine campus with 34 acres of gardens and playing fields, set against the background of the ruined cathedral and old harbour. It has excellent accommodation and facilities, including a fine computer centre. A large staff permits a staff:pupil ratio of about 1:8. The teaching is of a high standard and academic results are consistently impressive. Virtually all sixth-form leavers go on to degree courses each year. A wide range of languages is taught: Arabic, Japanese and Chinese as well as European languages. The school is very strong in music, drama and art and there have been many successes in these fields. Also very strong in games and sports (there are many county and international representatives, especially in hockey, fencing and lacrosse). The range of extra-curricular activities is wide and there is an outstanding record in the Duke of Edinburgh's Award Scheme.

School profile

Pupils Age range 12–18; 274 girls, 51 day, 223 boarding. Main entry ages 12, 13, 14 and into sixth. Approx 5% are children of former pupils. Over 25% intake from own prep school, St Katharines. *State school entry:* 5% at 12–13, plus 4% to sixth.
Entrance Common Entrance and own entrance test used. No special skills or religious requirements. Parents expected to buy some textbooks in sixth-form; house accounts £35 average. 38 pa assisted places. 30 pa scholarships/bursaries available, £50–£3000 pa.
Parents 15+% in industry or commerce; 15+% are doctors, lawyers etc. 30+% live within 30 miles; 20+% live overseas.
Head and staff *Headmistress:* Mrs Mary James, 8 years in post. Educated at St Leonards School and at York and Oxford universities (history). Previously Headmistress at Queen Ethelburga's and Head of History at Casterton. Also member of Scottish ISCO Council and of SCIS PR Committee. *Staff:* 34 full time, 11 part time. Annual turnover 5 to 10%. Average age mid-late 30s.
Exam results In 1995, 52 pupils in GCSE year, 47 in A-level/Higher year. *GCSE:* In 1995, 22 upper fifth gained at least grade C in 8+ subjects, 25 in 5–7 subjects. *Highers:* 4 passed in 4+ subjects; 4 in 4. *A-levels:* 1 passed in 4 subjects; 21 in 3; 13 in 2; 6 in 1 subject; A-levels are taken in association with Highers.
University and college entrance 87% of 1995 sixth-form leavers went on to a degree course (30% after a gap year); others typically go on to art foundation courses. Of those going on to university, 9% go to Oxbridge; 4% take courses in medicine, dentistry and veterinary science, 23% in science and engineering, 5% in law, 48% in humanities and social sciences, 9% in art and design, 2% in other vocational subjects eg occupational therapy.
Curriculum GCSE, AO-levels, Highers and A-levels. 19 subjects offered (no A-level general studies). 14% take science A-levels; 63% arts/humanities, 23% both. *Vocational:*

Work experience available; also Scotvec modules. *Computing facilities:* 2 computing labs (Nimbus network and Apple Macs), laser printer. Computers in each boarding house. *Special provision:* Tutoring for dyslexic pupils. *Europe:* French, German, Spanish offered to GCSE and A-level; Italian to GCSE. A language is compulsory to GCSE (usually French); continuation courses compulsory for sixth-formers not studying a language at A-level/Higher. Regular exchanges.

The arts *Music:* Over 50% of pupils learn a musical instrument; instrumental exams can be taken. Some 10 musical groups, plus numerous chamber groups, including chamber orchestra, string orchestra, 2 wind ensembles, brass ensemble, jazz band, 3 choirs. Winners in ESTA composition competition; winners in local festivals: tours to Austria, Italy and Russia. *Drama & dance*: Drama offered. A-level theatre studies exams may be taken. Award at Edinburgh Festival 1995. *Art:* On average, 20 take GCSE, 8 A-level. Design, pottery, textiles and printing also offered. Pupils regularly accepted for top art schools.

Sport, community service and clubs *Sport and physical activities:* Compulsory sports: hockey, lacrosse, tennis, athletic, gymnastics, dance, swimming. Optional: basketball, badminton, squash, rugby, skiing, golf, sailing, netball. Sixth form only: shooting, BAGA and RLSS exams may be taken. 6 Scottish lacrosse players, 1 national athletics, 3 regional hockey, 1 fencing international, 1 Scottish cross country. *Community service:* Pupils take bronze, silver and gold Duke of Edinburgh's Award. CCF and community service optional. *Clubs and societies:* Up to 15 clubs, eg orchestral, choir, golf, skiing, sailing, other sports, ecology, philosophy.

Uniform School uniform worn until upper sixth.

Houses/prefects Competitive houses. No prefects. Head girl and heads of houses – appointed by the Head and Housemistress. Vice heads (2) elected by pupils. School Council, run by head girl.

Religion Girls must attend a local church on Sundays. 2 or 3 school services are arranged each term.

Social Official link with Merchiston Castle and other independent schools for social and academic events; occasional links with local schools (music, debates). Many organised trips (recently to Nepal, Tanzania, Egypt, Italy, Spain and Greece) plus annual skiing trip and eg choir trip to Russia, hockey tour to Barbados. Senior pupils allowed to bring own bike to school. Meals self-service. No school shop, very near to local ones. No tobacco/alcohol allowed.

Discipline Pupils failing to produce homework once might be expected to produce it and perhaps do some additional work; those caught smoking cannabis on the premises would be expelled immediately. Rules are given in pupil handbook.

Boarding Sixth have own study bedrooms; occasionally pupils share; 50% are in dormitories of 6+. Houses of 27–35; separate upper sixth house. 2 resident SRNs, doctor visits every day. Central dining room. Upper sixth can provide and cook own food at weekends. Half-term and 2 weekend exeats each term. Visits to local town allowed.

Alumni association run by Mrs M Boulter c/o the school.

• ST LEONARDS-MAYFIELD

St Leonards-Mayfield School, The Old Palace, Mayfield, East Sussex TN20 6PH. Tel 01435 873055, Fax 01435 872627

• Pupils 525 • Boys None • Girls 11–18 (Day/Board/Weekly) • Upper sixth 84 • Termly fees £2300 (Day) £3450 (Board) £3425 (Weekly) • GSA, ACSC • Enquiries/application to the Headmistress

What it's like

Started in 1863 when the Duchess of Leeds presented to the foundress of the Society of the Holy Child Jesus the property which comprised the ruins (and the surrounding land) of the Old Palace of the medieval archbishops of Canterbury. These and the synod hall were restored and the school opened in 1872. Besides the original buildings there are extensive modern facilities and accommodation in delightful grounds and gardens. A Roman Catholic foundation (boarders must be Catholic), the doctrines and practice of the church (attendance at Mass etc) are an important part of the curriculum. A staff:pupil ratio of about 1:10. Good academic standards prevail and vocational qualifications are offered. Results are very good and the majority of sixth-formers go on to degree courses, including Oxbridge. Drama and art departments are well supported and music is particularly strong. A wide range of sports, games and activities is available. The Duke of Edinburgh's Award Scheme is popular. Pupils are encouraged to participate in local community schemes.

School profile

Pupils Age range 11–18; 525 girls (205 day, 320 boarding). Main entry ages 11, 13 and into sixth. *State school entry:* 33% main intakes, plus 20% to sixth.

Entrance Common Entrance and own scholarship exams used. Special gifts welcomed; boarders must be Roman Catholic. Parents are expected to buy a few textbooks. Means-tested scholarships and bursaries, up to full fees.

Parents 35% live within 30 miles; 30% live overseas.

Head and staff *Headmistress:* Sister Jean Sinclair, in post for 15 years. Educated at Wycombe Abbey and London University (mathematics). Previously Deputy Head at Convent of the Holy Child, Edgbaston, and Head of Department at Convent of the Holy Child, Preston. Also Past President GSA and of the Conference of Catholic Schools and Colleges; member ISJC Advisory Committee, Trustee Joint Educational Trust; Governor of Dunottar and Royal School, Haslemere; member of the Oxford and Cambridge Catholic Education Board. *Staff:* 53 full time, 12 part time. Annual turnover varies.

Exam results In 1995, 78 pupils in upper fifth, 80 in upper sixth. *GCSE:* In 1995, 67 upper fifth gained at least grade C in 8+ subjects; 11 in 4–7 subjects. *A-levels:* 13 upper sixth passed in 4+ subjects; 52 in 3; 8 in 2 subjects. Average UCAS points 20.3.

University and college entrance 96% of 1995 sixth-form leavers went on to a degree course (15% after a gap year); others typically go on to retail, secretarial, nursing. Of those going on to university, 8% went to Oxbridge; 10% took courses in medicine, dentistry and veterinary science, 10% in science and engineering, 5% in law, 55% in humanities and social sciences (including 17% on language-related courses), 10% in art and design, 10% in other vocational subjects (eg physiotherapy, pharmacy, occupational therapy).

Curriculum GCSE and A-levels: 26 subjects offered (no A-level general studies). 11% took science A-levels; 49% arts/humanities; 40% both. *Vocational:* Work experience available; also City and Guilds cookery certificate and Pitmans shorthand, typing and word processing (elementary and intermediate). *Computing facilities:* 1 Dell and 2 RM Nimbus networks (one in general use, one in science and geography, one in maths department). *Special provision:* Specialist help for dyslexia. EFL: teaching for Cambridge First Certificate and Certificate of Proficiency. *Europe:* French, German, Italian, Russian and Spanish offered to GCSE, AS and A-level and Institute of Linguists; French compulsory from 11 to GCSE. Regular individual exchanges.

The arts *Music:* Over 50% of pupils learn a musical instrument; instrumental exams can be taken. Some 15+ musical groups including 5 choirs, 2 orchestras, woodwind, ensemble, flute ensemble, brass ensemble, various string groups, recorder. *Drama & dance*: Both offered. GCSE and A-level drama, RAD, Guildhall and ISTD exams may be taken. Majority of pupils are involved in school productions and all in house/other productions. *Art:* On average, 25 take GCSE art, 20 ceramics, 10 design & realisation, 8 A-level art, 7 history of art. Design, pottery, textiles also offered. Ceramics and design prizes in East Sussex Guild of Craftworkers.

Sport, community service and clubs *Sport and physical activities:* Compulsory sports (at different stages): hockey, netball, tennis, rounders, athletics, swimming, gymnastics, cross-country, dance, aerobics, fitness activities. Optional: volleyball, fencing, self-defence & judo, lifesaving, equestrian, canoeing, archery, badminton, ballet, table tennis, snooker. Sixth form only: sailing, golf, squash. BAGA, BHS, RLSS exams may be taken. National, team in sports aerobics and tumbling finals; riding teams; county team members in hockey, netball, tennis, volleyball at different ages. *Community service:* Pupils take bronze, silver and gold Duke of Edinburgh's Award. Community service optional. Adventure Service Challenge Scheme for younger pupils. *Clubs and societies:* Some 15+ clubs, eg drama, debating, gymnastics, chess, bridge, Young Enterprise, engineering, modern languages, video, photography, computer.

Uniform School uniform worn except in upper sixth.

Houses/prefects Competitive houses. Prefects and head girl elected by main school and

staff, approved by Head; house prefects, elected by house, approved by housemistress. School Council.
Religion Girls are expected to fulfil requirements of Roman Catholic Church; voluntary forms of prayer encouraged.
Social Debates, socials, joint musical competitive performances with other schools. Trips abroad, skiing (annual), to Greece (biennial for classicists), Russia (for those studying Russian), individual exchanges to France, Germany, Spain and Italy. Sixth form allowed to bring own car/bike to school with good reason. Meals mainly self-service. Book stall, vending machine. Alcohol allowed in controlled situations (eg at meal with tutor); no tobacco.
Discipline Pupils failing to produce homework once might expect to discuss reason for failure and to produce it; those caught smoking cannabis on the premises could expect immediate suspension, probably without return. The school operates a system of trust, believing that if the girls are treated as reasonable human beings, they will respond responsibly.
Boarding All upper sixth have own study bedroom, lower sixth and fifth share in pairs; remainder in small dormitories or ones partitioned into cubicles. Houses divided broadly by age. Resident nurse; accessible local practice. Pupils can provide and cook food to limited extent at weekends. 3 or 4 optional Sat/Sun exeats termly plus half-term. Visits to local town allowed on Saturdays (lower sixth up); all ages to local village.

• ST MARGARET'S (Aberdeen)

St Margaret's School for Girls, 17 Albyn Place, Aberdeen AB10 1RU. Tel 01224 584466, Fax 01224 585600

• Pupils 417 • Boys 3–5 only (Day) • Girls 3–18 (Day) • Higher year 44 • Termly fees £1234 (Day) • GSA, HAS, SHA • Enquiries/application to the Headmistress

What it's like

Founded in 1846, it is one of the oldest all-through girls' schools in Scotland. It occupies a pleasant landscaped site in the west end of Aberdeen, based on two large 19th-century buildings with other more recent additions. Playing fields are two miles away. An integrated education is provided from nursery to the sixth year. A school with a family atmosphere, small enough to care about the individual but large enough to provide a full and varied curriculum. Girls are prepared for living and working in the 21st century. They are encouraged to aim high, assume responsibility and have fun whilst showing courtesy and self discipline. Over 80% leavers go on to degree courses, including some to Oxbridge. There are lively music and drama departments and a range of extra-curricular activities, including the Duke of Edinburgh's Award Scheme.

School profile

Pupils Total age range 3–18; 417 day pupils (6 boys, 411 girls). Senior department 12–18, 231 girls. Main entry ages 3 (boys and girls), 5, 11, 12 (girls). *State school entry:* 55% intake at 11 and 12.
Entrance Own test and interview. No special skills or religious requirements. Parents expected to buy textbooks; maximum extras, £65. Around 20 pa assisted places. 1 pa scholarship for entry to sixth year.
Parents 25+ % are doctors, lawyers etc; 30+ % in industry or commerce.
Head and staff *Headmistress:* Miss Lorna Ogilvie, 8 years in post. Educated at Mary Erskine and at universities of Edinburgh and Calgary, Canada (geography). Previously Assistant Head Teacher at Morrison's, Head of Geology and Sixth Form Housemistress at Royal Russell. Former Chairman of GSA Scottish Region and on GSA council; and on Governing Body of Scottish Council for Independent Schools. *Staff:* 32 full time, 17 part time. Annual turnover 1%.
Exam results On average, 44 pupils in S-grade year, 40 in Higher, 28 in A-level/CSYS year. *S-grade:* In 1995, 30 passed 8 subjects; 13 in 5–7; and 1 in 1–4 subjects. *Highers:* 19 passed in 5+ subjects, 7 in 4, 8 in 3, 3 in 2, 4 in 1 subject.
University and college entrance 85% of 1995 sixth-form leavers went on to a degree course (8% after a gap year); others typically go on to nursing, HNDs in leisure, tourism, media studies. Of those going on to university, 10% went to Oxbridge; 14% took courses

in medicine, dentistry and veterinary science, 29% in science and engineering, 16% in law, 24% in humanities and social sciences, 4% in art and design, 14% in other vocational subjects eg physiotherapy, dietetics, education.

Curriculum S-grades, Highers and CSYS (plus 1 subject at A-level). 15 subjects offered. *Vocational:* Work experience available; also RSA level 1 and 2 word processing and Scotvec modules in calculus, accounting, computer studies. *Computing facilities:* 15 machines in senior computer room; others in subject and primary departments. *Special provision:* Dyslexic testing available and exam provision made; magnifiers provided for visually handicapped. *Europe:* French (compulsory from age 6) and German to S-grade, Higher and CSYS; also German Scotvec modules. Biannual exchanges to Germany; visits to France.

The arts (Pupils aged 11 and over) *Music:* All pupils learn a musical instrument; instrumental exams can be taken. Some 6 musical groups including choirs, orchestras, woodwind, recorder. Pupils have played with Scottish National Repertoire Orchestra, regularly selected for regional orchestra. *Drama & dance*: Both offered (including Scottish country dancing). S-grade drama, ESB exams may be taken. Some pupils are involved in school and house/other productions. Recent productions include The Lion, the Witch and the Wardrobe, Daisy Pulls It Off and A Midsummer Night's Dream; girls regularly act with local dramatic companies and act and dance with visiting theatre. *Art:* On average, 8 take S-grade, 6 Higher, 1 CSYS; design also offered. Pupils' works selected for annual Scottish independent schools art exhibition.

Sport, community service and clubs (Pupils aged 10 and over) *Sport and physical activities:* Compulsory sports: hockey, tennis, athletics, gymnastics, badminton, swimming. Optional: volleyball, netball, squash, skiing, basketball, cross-country, golf, rowing and curling. RLSS exams may be taken. Pupils selected for district hockey teams and national trials; successes at Scottish Schools' Championship in swimming and athletics; British skiing team member. *Community service:* Pupils take bronze, silver and gold Duke of Edinburgh's Award. Community service optional at age 15. Pupils help with Riding for the Disabled scheme and with handicapped children. *Clubs and societies:* Up to 30 clubs, eg debating/public speaking, gym, Young Enterprise, Young Investigators, Scottish country dancing, bridge, Scripture Union, computer.

Uniform Uniform worn throughout.

Houses/prefects Competitive houses. Prefects, head girl, senior prefect and heads of house elected by the senior pupils and staff. School Council.

Religion Compulsory attendance at daily assembly.

Social Regular debating, public speaking and sporting fixtures held with local schools; also occasional quiz competitions; instrumentalists participate with other Grampian schools. Biannual ski trip (Europe/USA), cruises (Mediterranean), French visits, German exchange, choir and orchestra (Europe, USA). Pupils allowed to drive own car to school (but not park in grounds). Packed lunch. Tuck shop and uniform sales. No tobacco/alcohol allowed.

• ST MARGARET'S (Edinburgh)

St Margaret's School Edinburgh Ltd, East Suffolk Road, Edinburgh EH16 5PJ Tel 0131 668 1986, Fax 0131 662 0957

• Pupils 680 • Boys 3–7 only (Day) • Girls 3–18 (Day/Board) • Higher year 88 • Termly fees £685-£1380 (Day) £2371-£2785 (Board/Weekly) • GSA • Enquiries/application to the Principal

What it's like

Founded in 1890, it is urban with the school houses around the site within a quarter of a mile of each other. There are pleasant buildings and grounds. The nursery and preparatory departments are combined. Very good facilities and comfortable boarding accommodation are provided. A limited amount of religious worship is compulsory. Results are good and many sixth-formers go on to degree courses. Vocational qualifications are offered. The music, drama and art departments are very strong indeed. The school also has a good reputation in sports and games (10–15 representatives at county level). The record in the Duke of Edinburgh's Award Scheme is outstanding.

School profile

Pupils Total age range 3–18; 680 pupils, 630 day (15 boys, 615 girls), 50 boarding girls. Senior department 12–18, 360 girls. Main entry ages 3, 5 (boys and girls), 12 and into the sixth (girls). 5% are children of former pupils. Own prep department provides over 40% senior intake. *State school entry:* 25% senior intake, plus 2% to sixth.

Entrance Own entrance exam used (plus interview and school references). No special skills or religious requirements. Parents not expected to buy textbooks. 15 pa assisted places. 5 pa scholarships/bursaries available, 50%–100% day fees.

Parents 15+% are in industry or commerce; 15+% are doctors, lawyers etc; 15+% are academics, lecturers etc. 60+% live within 30 miles; up to 10% live overseas.

Head and staff *Principal:* Miss Anne C Mitchell, 3 years in post. Educated at Lossiemouth High School, Elgin Academy and Aberdeen University (English). Previously Depute Head Teacher at Dunbar Grammar School, Principal Teacher of English at Balerno High School and at North Berwick High School and Assistant Housemistress at St Leonards School. Also former Arts Coordinator, Lothian Region (1992). Publications: co-author of Heinemann Core English series. *Staff:* 60 full time, 20 part time. Annual turnover 2%. Average age 45.

Exam results S-grade, Highers, A-levels, CSYS. 24 subjects offered (including A-level general studies). On average, 77 in S-grade year, 88 in Higher, 73 in A-level/CSYS year. *S-grade:* On average, 39 pupils pass in 8+ subjects; 30 in 5–7; and 8 in 1–4 subjects. *Highers:* 30 pass in 5+ subjects, 24 in 4, 13 in 3, 10 in 2, 7 in 1 subject. *A-levels and CSYS:* 1 passes in 4 subjects; 3 in 3; 7 in 2; and 21 in 1 subject. 65 took Highers as well as, or instead of, A-levels and CSYS.

University and college entrance 64% of 1995 sixth-form leavers went on to a degree course; others typically go on to other courses or careers eg nursing. Of those going on to university, 4% took courses in medicine, dentistry and veterinary science, 9% in science and engineering, 23% in humanities and social sciences, 6% in art and design, 58% in other subjects eg agriculture, business studies.

Curriculum 56% take science A-levels/CSYS; 44% arts/humanities. *Vocational:* Work experience for S5 along with Challenge of Industry conference; also Scotvec National Certificate in a range of subjects eg art, business studies, computing, home economics, photography, theatre arts. *Computing facilities:* 12 computers in each of 2 labs, plus computers in many classrooms. *Special provision:* Learning support; exam dispensations for dyslexics; EFL lessons. *Europe:* French, German and Spanish offered to S-grade, Higher and CSYS (either French or German from age 5); Italian offered in after school club. Regular exchanges.

The arts (Pupils aged 11 and over) *Music:* Over 30% of pupils learn a musical instrument; instrumental exams can be taken. Some 11 musical groups including 6 choir groups, 2 wind, orchestra, junior strings, recorder, jazz group. Junior choir won national final of Saltire Society of Scotland Choral Competition; senior choir 3rd prize at Llangollen International Eisteddfod. *Drama & dance*: Drama offered at S-grade. Some pupils are involved in school productions and majority in house/other productions. *Art:* On average, 6 take A-level, plus Scotvec modules in drawing, CSYS. Design, pottery, jewellery, photography also offered; art appreciation as part of social education programme. Art facilities open to non-examination pupils. Pupils' CSYS sculptures used as examples of excellence by Scottish examination board.

Sport, community service and clubs (Pupils aged 11 and over) *Sport and physical activities:* Compulsory sports: swimming, gymnastics, dance, netball, hockey, lacrosse, badminton, rounders, tennis, athletics. Optional: aerobics, keep fit, skiing, judo, fencing. Sixth form only: golf, squash, self-defence. BAGA and RLSS exams may be taken and community sports leader award. Hockey, Scottish U16 team, players in district team; lacrosse, Scottish U18 team; squash, Scottish squad, GB squad; fencing, tennis, skiing, Scottish representatives. *Community service:* Pupils take bronze, silver and gold Duke of Edinburgh's Award. Community service optional. *Clubs and societies:* Up to 30 clubs, eg sports, musical, drama, history, debating, wildlife, French, video, electronics, art, country dancing, gym, swimming.

Uniform School uniform worn except in the sixth.

Houses/prefects Competitive houses. New prefect system. School Council.

Religion Compulsory assembly and church on Sunday for boarders under 16.

Social Reel club, debates, productions with other local schools. Trips of various kinds

including to France and Germany. Pupils allowed to bring own car/bike/motorbike to school. Meals self-service. School shop. No tobacco/alcohol allowed.
Discipline Emphasis on self-discipline and on high standards of behaviour and courtesy in a caring environment.
Boarding 10% have own study bedroom; 90% share with 1. Central dining room. Various exeats each term, up to every weekend for seniors. Visits to the local town allowed. Flexible boarding arrangements.
Alumni association run by Ms Diana Tudhope, c/o the school.

• ST MARY'S (Ascot)

St Mary's School, St Mary's Road, Ascot, Berkshire SL5 9JF. Tel 01344 23721
• Pupils 336 • Boys None • Girls 11–18 (Day/Board) • Upper sixth 47 • Termly fees £2367 (Day) £3945 (Board) • GSA • Enquiries/application to the Admissions Secretary

What it's like

Founded in 1885, it is semi-rural, single-site and purpose-built in 45 acres of very pleasant gardens and grounds. The buildings are well designed and accommodation comfortable. Very good modern facilities. It is owned and managed by a RC charitable trust and some of the staff are Sisters of the Institute of the Blessed Virgin Mary. All pupils must be RCs and the doctrines and practices of the Church (attendance at Sunday Mass etc) are an essential part of the curriculum. Academically the standards are high and results are very good. Each year virtually all sixth-formers go on to degree courses, including Oxbridge. An impressive array of European languages is offered. Strong in music, drama and art. A wide range of games, sports and activities. Commitment to local community schemes and a promising record in the Duke of Edinburgh's Award Scheme.

School profile

Pupils Age range 11–18; 336 girls, 13 day, 323 boarding. Main entry ages 11, 13 and into sixth. Approx 5% are children of former pupils. Very few from state schools.
Entrance Own entrance exam used. No special skills required but pupils should be Roman Catholic. Parents expected to buy textbooks in sixth-form: £300 maximum extras. 2 pa scholarships (music and sixth-form science), 60% tuition fees. Some discretionary bursaries.
Parents 15+% in industry or commerce. 30+% live within 30 miles; 10+% live overseas.
Head and staff *Headmistress:* Sister Frances Orchard, in post for 14 years. Educated at St Mary's (Ascot) and London University (history). Previously Head of History at St Mary's (Ascot) and History and RE Teacher at St Mary's (Cambridge) *Staff:* 44 full time, 20 part time. Annual turnover 5%. Average age 40.
Exam results In 1995, 48 pupils in Year 11, 44 in upper sixth. *GCSE:* In 1995, 99% gained grade C or above in 8+ subjects; 1% in 5–7 subjects. *A-levels:* In 1995, 98% passed in 3 subjects; 2% passed in 2 subjects. Average UCAS points 23.7.
University and college entrance 99% of 1995 sixth-form leavers went on to a degree course (65% after a gap year); others typically go on to vocational training, fashion or design. Of those going on to university, 7% went to Oxbridge; 7% took courses in medicine, dentistry and veterinary science, 12% in science and engineering, 7% in law, 61% in humanities and social sciences, 12% in art and design.
Curriculum GCSE and A-levels: 19 subjects offered (including AS-level general studies). *Vocational:* Work experience available; also RSA computing. *Computing facilities:* 12 Archimedes computers; 4 BBC Masters; 2 CD-Rom; Compass 2000; 6 PCs. *Europe:* French, German, Italian, Portuguese, Russian and Spanish offered to GCSE, AS and A-level (French compulsory from age 11 to GCSE). Talks from MEP. Second recently in European Youth Parliament Competition.
The arts *Music:* Almost all pupils learn a musical instrument; instrumental exams can be taken. Some 12 musical groups including orchestra, choir, various chamber ensembles, pop band. 1995 Ascot Young Strings Player of the Year, Singer of the Year; 2 members of National Youth Choir; 3 members of Junior RA/Guildhall. Musical appreciation group to concerts and opera in London. *Drama & dance*: Both offered. A-level drama, LAMDA and Guildhall exams may be taken. Majority of pupils are involved in school and house/

other productions. LAMDA gold medal with distinction. *Art:* On average, 25 take GCSE, 2 AS-level, 10 A-level. Design, pottery, textiles and photography also offered.
Sport, community service and clubs *Sport and physical activities:* Compulsory sports: (to 14) gym, hockey, netball, swimming, tennis, rounders, athletics, trampolining, fencing. Optional: (from 14) as above plus squash, golf, ice skating, jazz dancing, aerobics, canoeing. Midland Bank Tennis 1995 U15, U13 South of England champions. *Community service:* Pupils take bronze, silver and gold Duke of Edinburgh's Award. Community service compulsory for 1 year at age 16/17, optional for those on D of E bronze. *Clubs and societies:* Up to 30 clubs, eg debating, Friends of the Earth, science, art, theatre, human rights, music, winetasting, Young Enterprise, video, writers workshop, photography, candlemaking, bridge, chess, backstage, computer.
Uniform School uniform worn, except the sixth.
Houses/prefects Competitive houses. Prefects, head girl, head of house and house prefects – mixture of appointment by Head and election by school.
Religion Compulsory worship in accordance with requirements of RC Church.
Social Occasional debates, sports events, theatrical performances with other schools. Organised skiing trips abroad; A-level French/history of art trip to Paris and Italy; classics trip to Greece. Senior pupils allowed to bring own bike to school. Juniors may keep pets. Meals self-service. No tobacco/alcohol allowed.
Discipline Pupils failing to produce homework once might expect their tutor to be informed ('on report' on second occasion; detention on third). Those caught taking illicit drugs on the premises may expect immediate expulsion; those caught smoking are fined £20 for first offence, suspension for second.
Boarding 35% have own study bedroom, 55% share with 1 other; 10% are in dormitories of 6+. Houses of 60, divided by age; upper sixth have own purpose-built courtyard. Resident qualified nurse. Central dining room. 2 termly exeats. Visits to local town allowed.
Alumni association run by Sister Bridget Geoffrey-Smith, c/o the school.
Former pupils Sarah Hogg; Marina Warner, Antonia Fraser.

• ST MARY'S (Calne)

St Mary's School, Calne, Wiltshire SN11 0DF. Tel 01249 815899, Fax 01249 822432
• Pupils 307 • Boys None • Girls 11–18 (Day/Board) • Upper sixth 43 • Termly fees £2275 (Day) £3850 (Board) • GSA • Enquiries/application to the Secretary

What it's like

Founded in 1873 by Canon Duncan, the Vicar of Calne. It occupies an agreeable site of 25 acres on the outskirts of the small town at the edge of the Wiltshire Downs. All the school buildings are within the grounds which include attractive gardens. Since 1950 there has been a continuous development programme and the school is now very well equipped with modern facilities. An Anglican foundation, it puts some emphasis on worship and religious education (a chapel was built in the seventies). It is a personal school structured for the individual and has a friendly atmosphere. Quite a large staff allows a staff:pupil ratio of about 1:9. Exam results are very good and for a school of this size a very large number of sixth-formers go on to degree courses, including Oxbridge. The school is strong in pastoral care. Music is vigorously supported (many girls learn at least one instrument; many study two or more). Drama and art are major activities – a new theatre was opened in 1990 and the art school has been recently extended. A standard range of sports and games is available and there are plentiful extra-curricular activities. A considerable number of girls take part in local community schemes and the Duke of Edinburgh's Award Scheme has become increasingly important.

School profile

Pupils Age range 11–18; 307 girls (38 day, 269 boarding). Main entry ages 11, 12 and occasionally into the sixth. Many entrants from own junior school (St Margaret's School, tel 01249 815197).
Entrance Common Entrance exam used (at 11 and 12). No special skills or religious requirements. Parents not expected to buy textbooks. 6 pa scholarships (academic, music, art, sixth); some bursaries for current pupils.

Parents 15+% in industry. 10+% live within 30 miles; up to 10% live overseas.
Head and staff *Headmistress:* Mrs C J Shaw, appointed 1996. Educated at West Kirby Grammar School for Girls and London University (English). Previously University Adviser at Cheltenham Ladies' College and Head of English at Mount St Agnes Academy (Bermuda); also marketing manager in an export company. *Staff:* 37 full time, 22 part time. Annual turnover low but variable.
Exam results In 1995, 52 pupils in upper fifth, 43 in upper sixth. *GCSE:* In 1995, 51 gained grade C or above in 8+ subjects, 1 in 5–7 subjects. *A-levels:* 2 upper sixth passed in 4+ subjects; 40 in 3; 1 in 2 subjects. Average UCAS points 26.7.
University and college entrance 98% of 1995 sixth-form leavers went on to a degree course (37% after a gap year); others typically go on to full or part time employment, courses eg secretarial. Of those going on to university, 21% went to Oxbridge; 5% took courses in medicine, dentistry and veterinary science, 2% in science and engineering, 91% in humanities and social sciences, 2% in art and design.
Curriculum GCSE and *A-levels:* 19 subjects offered (no A-level general studies). 4% take science A-levels; 83% arts/humanities; 13% both. *Vocational:* Work experience available; RSA level 1 keyboard for sixth-form. *Computing facilities:* 10 BBC Masters, 29 IBM computers (4 with CD-Rom). *Special provision:* Tutors can be arranged. *Europe:* French, Spanish or German offered to GCSE and A-level (French compulsory to GCSE); also Italian GCSE in sixth-form.
The arts *Music:* 80% of pupils learn a musical instrument; instrumental exams can be taken. Some 8+ musical groups including orchestra, string orchestras, wind band, choirs, jazz band, flute choir and many chamber groups. Chamber choir recently recorded CD and sings at festivals and cathedrals. *Drama & dance*: Drama offered. GCSE drama, A-level theatre studies, LAMDA and ESB exams may be taken. Recent school productions include Jesus Christ Superstar, Amadeus and West Side Story. Links with visiting theatre companies and professionals. *Art:* On average, 25 take GCSE, 5 A-level, 6 A-level history of art. Design, pottery, textiles, photography, screenprinting/etching, sculpture and life drawing also offered. 80% of A-level students go on to foundation courses; close links established with a number of local professional artists and craftsmen.
Sport, community service and clubs *Sport and physical activities:* Compulsory sports: lacrosse, hockey, netball, tennis, swimming, athletics, gym, dance. Optional: Water-sports, riding, squash, fitness, ballet, golf, fencing. Sixth form only: football, touch rugby. BAGA, RLSS and BTF (trampolining) exams may be taken. County players in netball, athletics, lacrosse and tennis. *Community service:* Pupils take bronze, silver and gold Duke of Edinburgh's Award; all lower fifth involved in bronze award; half of upper fifth and lower sixth in silver; flourishing sixth-form gold group. Community service optional. *Clubs and societies:* Up to 30 clubs, eg aerobics, computing, cookery, debating, fencing, photography, pottery, trampoline, woodwork.
Uniform School uniform worn; dress code for sixth-form.
Houses/prefects Competitive companies. No prefects. Head girl, head of house and house prefects – selected by staff and school. School Council.
Religion Morning assembly. Sunday chapel.
Social Organised trips abroad to Normandy. Fifth form upwards allowed to bring own bike to school. Meals self-service. Tuck shop. No tobacco/alcohol allowed.
Discipline Pupils failing to produce homework once might get a warning.
Boarding 50% have own study bedroom; 4% share; 15% in dormitories of 6+. Houses of approx 38–70, divided by age. Resident qualified nurse. Central dining room. Upper sixth can provide and cook own snacks, but main meals compulsory. Two fixed exeats each term plus others. Visits to local town allowed at lunchtime.

• ST MARY'S (Cambridge)

St Mary's School, Bateman Street, Cambridge CB2 1LY. Tel 01223 353253

• Pupils 565 • Boys None • Girls 11–18 (Day/Weekly) • Upper sixth 56 • Termly fees £1290 (Day) £2310 (Weekly) • GSA • Enquiries/application to the Admissions Secretary

What it's like

Founded in 1898, it is sited in the city centre, overlooking the university botanic garden, within easy walking distance of museums, theatres and colleges. It is a Catholic school which also admits pupils of other denominations. There is a purposeful working atmosphere, and a broad-based curriculum designed to develop individual skills and talents. Academic standards are high and results very good. Virtually all sixth-formers go on to higher education each year, including Oxbridge. Talents for music, art, drama and sport are encouraged and the school is strong in drama, art and music. There is a wide variety of sports, games and extra-curricular activities; very successful Young Enterprise and thriving Duke of Edinburgh Award Scheme.

School profile

Pupils Age range 11–18; 565 girls, 505 day, 60 weekly boarding. Main entry ages 11–14, and into sixth. Approx 5% are children of former pupils. *State school entry:* 45% main intake, plus 45% to sixth.

Entrance Own entrance exam used. Special consideration given to candidates with talents in music and art. Catholic school but other denominations welcomed. Parents not expected to buy textbooks; no compulsory extras. 20 pa assisted places, plus 5 pa for sixth.

Head and staff *Headmistress:* Miss Michele Conway, 7 years in post. Educated at Ursuline Convent, Wimbledon, and Oxford University (mathematics). Previously Head of Mathematics and Computing at St Leonard's-Mayfield. *Staff:* 48 full time, 10 part time plus music and drama staff. Average age 40.

Exam results In 1995, 86 pupils in fifth year, 50 in upper sixth. *GCSE:* In 1995, 93% fifth years gained at least grade C in 8+ subjects; 7% in 5–7 subjects. *A-levels:* 1 upper sixth passed in 4+ subjects; 40 in 3; 9 in 2 subjects. Average UCAS points 20.5.

University and college entrance 98% of 1995 sixth-form leavers went on to a degree course (10% after a gap year); others typically go on to secretarial courses or direct to employment. Of those going on to university, 7% went to Oxbridge; 7% took courses in medicine, dentistry and veterinary science, 14% in science and engineering, 5% in law, 20% in humanities and social sciences, 4% in art and design, 50% in other subjects eg equine studies, agriculture, physiotherapy, classics.

Curriculum GCSE, AS and A-levels. On average 15% take science A-levels; 54% arts/humanities; 30% both. *Vocational:* Work experience available (Years 11–13). *Computing facilities:* Large network of Archimedes and A3000s with laser, colour and dot-matrix printers. *Special provision:* School copes with mild dyslexia. *Europe:* French (compulsory), German, Italian and Spanish offered to GCSE, AS and A-level. Regular exchanges.

The arts *Music:* Over 50% of pupils learn a musical instrument; instrumental exams can be taken. Some 11 musical groups including string quartet, jazz, brass, wind band, guitar group, choirs, string orchestra, recorder, chamber music group. 1 member of National Youth Orchestra, 4 in county youth orchestra. *Drama & dance*: Both offered. GCSE drama, A-level theatre studies, LAMDA, Guildhall exams may be taken. Some pupils are involved in school productions and all in house/other productions. 1 pupil recent gold medal in verse & prose. *Art:* On average, 35 take GCSE, 5 AS-level, 8 A-level. Design, pottery, textiles also offered.

Sport, community service and clubs *Sport and physical activities:* Compulsory sports: netball, hockey, swimming, tennis, athletics, rounders, volleyball, badminton, dance. Optional aerobics, jogging, table tennis. Sixth form only: squash, archery, golf, rowing, multi-gym course. ASA and personal survival exams may be taken. 8 national representatives – tennis, hockey, cross-country, athletics; 2 county, netball, tennis; regional, tennis U16 champions; cross-country schools winning team; athletics district schools winning team. *Community service:* Pupils take bronze, silver and gold Duke of Edinburgh's Award. Community service optional. Girls help with Diocesan pilgrimage to Lourdes and raise some £11,000 per year for charity. *Clubs and societies:* Up to 10 clubs, eg computing, pottery, debating.

Uniform School uniform worn except in sixth.

Houses/prefects No competitive houses. No prefects; duties shared by upper sixth. Head girl and group of deputies – elected by staff and sixth-form. Sixth Form Council.

Religion All attend daily assembly and Christmas carol service. Mass and other services attended by majority of pupils on a voluntary basis. RE curriculum followed by all pupils.

Social Debating, theatrical productions with other schools. Regular trips to France; Spanish, German, Italian exchanges; other excursions abroad. Pupils allowed to bring own bike to school. Meals self-service. School shop. No tobacco/alcohol allowed.

Discipline No penal code; pupils are expected to work hard and to respect the aims of the school. Parents would be consulted in serious cases, and decisions would depend on circumstances.
Boarding 45 have own study bedroom, 35 share (2–5 beds per room). Central dining room. All pupils return home at weekends. Visits to local town allowed, according to age.
Alumni association run by Mrs S de Backer, c/o the school.

• ST MARY'S (Crosby)

St Mary's College, Crosby, Merseyside L23 3AB. Tel 0151 924 3926
• Pupils 915 • Boys 3–18 (Day) • Girls 3–18 (Day) • Upper sixth 70 • Termly fees £1248 (Day)
• HMC • Enquiries/application to the Secretary

What it's like

Founded in 1919 by the Christian Brothers. It is urban and single-site, except the playing fields which are on a separate site. The first school buildings were erected in 1923 and there has been regular expansion and development since and facilities are now good. There is a recently opened kindergarten and a preparatory department. Originally a boys' school, it has been fully co-educational since 1989. It is a Roman Catholic foundation and 80% pupils are RCs but other denominations are welcome. A sound general education is provided and results are good; 95% of sixth-formers go on to degree courses, including Oxbridge. There is music and drama, and very considerable strength in art. A good range of sports and games in which high standards are achieved. Good range of extra-curricular activities including Duke of Edinburgh's Award and a flourishing CCF.

School profile

Pupils Total age range 3-18; 915 day pupils (516 boys, 399 girls). Senior department 11–18, 600 pupils (345 boys, 280 girls). Main entry ages 3, 7, 11, 13 and into sixth. Approx 20% are children of former pupils. *State school entry:* 52% senior intake, plus 63% to sixth.
Entrance Own entrance exam used. No special skills required; RC school, other practising Christians admitted. Parents not expected to buy textbooks, nor pay for extras such as music lessons. 45 pa assisted places. 12 pa bursaries, £150–£1800; sixth-form scholarships.
Parents 15+% are doctors, lawyers etc; 15+% in industry or commerce.
Head and staff *Headmaster:* Wilfred Hammond, 5 years in post. Educated at Dudley Grammar and Cambridge (history). Previously Deputy Head at Prior Park and Head of Sixth Form, Director of Studies, Head of History and Housemaster at Durham School. *Staff:* 47 full time, 7 part time. Annual turnover 5%. Average age 35.
Exam results In 1995, 96 pupils in upper fifth, 57 in upper sixth. *GCSE:* In 1995, 79 upper fifth gain at least grade C in 8+ subjects; 10 in 5–7 subjects. *A-levels:* 31 upper sixth pass in 4+ subjects; 13 in 3; 7 in 2; and 5 in 1 subject. Average UCAS points 19.0.
University and college entrance 95% of 1995 sixth-form leavers went on to a degree course (5% after a gap year); others typically go on to armed forces, banking etc. Of those going on to university, 5% went to Oxbridge; 15% took courses in medicine, dentistry and veterinary science, 30% in science and engineering, 8% in law, 30% in humanities and social sciences, 5% in art and design, 12% in other vocational subjects eg nursing, para-medical.
Curriculum GCSE and A-levels (including A-level general studies). 14% take science A-levels; 35% arts/humanities; 51% both. *Vocational:* Work experience available; also City and Guilds IT. *Computing facilities:* Mainly networked ICL 486s. *Europe:* Either French, Spanish and German offered to GCSE and A-level. Regular exchanges.
The arts (Pupils aged 11 and over) *Music:* All Year 7 pupils learn a musical instrument; instrumental exams can be taken. Some 10 musical groups including school bands, orchestra, choir, woodwind, jazz, folk groups. School band silver award winners in National Concert Band Festival, concert tours of Holland, Australia and Austria. *Drama & dance*: Both offered. Some pupils are involved in school productions. *Art:* On average, 30 take GCSE, 8 A-level. A-level candidates' work kept by exam board as example of highest standard in 2 successive years.

Sport, community service and clubs (Pupils aged 11 and over) *Sport and physical activities:* Compulsory sports: rugby, netball. Optional: cricket, hockey, swimming, basketball, athletics, rounders. Sixth form only: golf, squash. *Community service:* Pupils take bronze, silver and gold Duke of Edinburgh's Award. CCF optional at age 14+. Extensive opportunities for community service in sixth-form. Flourishing SVP group; more than 50 sixth-formers working with Handicapped Children's Pilgrimage Trust (Lourdes). *Clubs and societies:* Over 30 clubs, eg debating, Justice & Peace, Pro Life, horticulture, chess, design, art, jazz, Amnesty, music, dance, French.
Houses/prefects Competitive houses. Prefects, head boy/girl – elected by the school. School Council.
Religion Worship encouraged.
Social Debating competitions. French/German/Spanish language exchanges, skiing and other trips abroad. Pupils allowed to bring own car/bike/motorbike to school. Meals self-service. School shop selling uniform. No tobacco/alcohol allowed.
Discipline Pupils failing to produce homework would be detained; those caught in possession of cannabis would be automatically expelled.
Alumni association run by T. White, Chairman, St Mary's College Association, Moor Lane, Crosby.
Former pupils John Birt (Director General, BBC); Kevin McNamara MP; Kevin Dunn (ITN correspondent); William Hanrahan (BBC), Bishop Vincent Nichols; Roger McGough (poet), John Price (News Editor, Independent); Prof Laurie Taylor; Prof David Crystal.

• ST MARY'S (Gerrards Cross)

St Mary's School, Packhorse Road, Gerrards Cross, Buckinghamshire SL9 8JQ. Tel 01753 883370

• Pupils 280 • Boys None • Girls 3–18 (Day) • Upper sixth 19 • Termly fees £885-£1695 (Day)
• GSA • Enquiries/application to the Admissions Secretary

What it's like

Founded in 1874 and originally run by the Anglican Sisters of the Community of St Mary the Virgin, Wantage, it began life in London and moved to its present premises in 1937. The main building is a country house in ample gardens and grounds. Many modern extensions now provide good facilities. The junior and senior schools are on the same site on the north edge of Gerrards Cross. It adheres to Anglican practice and tradition although it is non-denominational. Academic standards and results are good and most sixth-form leavers go on to degree courses each year. Good opportunities for drama, speech and music. A good range of games, sports and activities. An impressive record in the Duke of Edinburgh's Award Scheme.

School profile

Pupils Total age range 3–18; 280 day girls. Senior department 10–18, 180 girls. Main entry ages 11, 12 and into the sixth. Own junior school provides some 80% senior intake. *State school entry:* 20% main senior intake, 10% into sixth.
Entrance Common Entrance and own exam. No special skills or religious requirements. 7 pa scholarships, including 1 music, 50% fees; plus 3 internal and 2 external scholarships and 2 bursaries for sixth-form.
Head and staff *Headmistress:* Mrs Fanny Balcombe, in post from 1995. Educated at Southampton University. Previously Senior Mistress at South Hampstead High School and English teacher at St Helen's, Northwood. *Staff:* 25 full time, 15 part time. Annual turnover 2%.
Exam results In 1995, 20 pupils in Year 11, 12 in upper sixth. *GCSE:* In 1995, 82% of Year 11 gained at least grade C in 8+ subjects; 11% in 5–7 subjects. *A-levels:* 64% upper sixth passed in 3 subjects; 9% in 2 subjects. Average UCAS points 15.3.
University and college entrance 82% of sixth-form leavers go on to a degree course, others typically go on to eg nursing. Of those going on to university, 36% take courses in science and engineering, 54% in humanities and social sciences, 18% in art and design.
Curriculum GCSE and A-levels. 18 GCSE subjects offered; 17 at A-level (including theatre studies, no A-level general studies). 36% took arts/humanities A-levels; 9%

science; 55% both. *Vocational:* Work experience available. *Computing facilities:* Computer room equipped with 8 stand-alone Nimbus PC486; 2 Nimbus PC286 and 15 Nimbus PC486. (BBCs in all junior classrooms.) *Special provision:* Practical help (eg enlarged papers for visually handicapped) and some remedial teaching. *Europe:* French (from age 5), Italian, German and Spanish offered to GCSE and A-level. Most pupils take GCSE in more than 1 language. Regular exchanges (France and Germany); individually to Italy. First and second years visit France.

The arts (Pupils aged 11 and over) *Music:* Over 30% of pupils learn a musical instrument; instrumental exams can be taken. Some 5 musical groups including madrigal, choirs, wind, recorder. Winners of local arts festival choral shield; senior choir exchange visit to Stuttgart 1995. *Drama & dance*: Drama offered. GCSE, A-level and LAMDA exams may be taken. Majority of pupils are involved in school and house/other productions. *Art:* On average, 8 take GCSE, 4 A-level. Design, textiles, 3-dimensional work in glass, metal and plaster also offered. Admissions to art college and university.

Sport, community service and clubs (Pupils aged 11 and over) *Sport and physical activities:* Compulsory sports: badminton, basketball, tennis, trampolining, gymnastics, dance, hockey, netball, athletics, swimming, rounders. Optional: squash, self-defence, skiing. Sixth form only: dry skiing, weight training, step aerobics, windsurfing. GCSE sport may be taken. Netball, county representatives; athletics, county finalists; swimming, national junior squad member. *Community service:* Pupils take bronze and gold Duke of Edinburgh's Award. *Clubs and societies:* Up to 15 clubs, eg computers, dancing, board games, Christian, gymnastics.

Uniform School uniform worn except the sixth.

Houses/prefects Competitive houses. Prefects, head girl, head of house and house prefects – appointed by Headmistress and staff and election by pupils.

Religion Compulsory non-denominational assembly.

Social Debates, Young Enterprise with other local schools; organised trips abroad. Pupils allowed to bring own car to school. Meals self-service. No tobacco/alcohol/make-up/jewellery allowed.

Discipline Pupils failing to produce homework once might expect detention; those caught smoking cigarettes on the premises would be liable to expulsion.

Alumni association run by Mrs Sarah Simpson, c/o the school.

• ST MARY'S (Shaftesbury)

St Mary's School, Shaftesbury, Dorset SP7 9LP. Tel 01747 854005, Fax 01747 851557

• Pupils 310 • Boys None • Girls 9–18 (Day/Board) • Upper sixth 31 • Termly fees £2050 (Day), £3200 (Board) • GSA, BSA • Enquiries/application to the Headmistress

What it's like

Founded in 1945 by the Institute of the Blessed Virgin Mary in the tradition of its 17th-century foundress Mary Ward who said 'There is no such difference between men and women that women may not do great things, as we have seen by example of many saints. And I hope in God it will be seen that women in time to come will do much.' The school has a handsome site of 55 acres about a mile outside the Saxon town of Shaftesbury. It has fine buildings and excellent facilities, including comfortable boarding accommodation and a new purpose-built sixth-form house. It aims to educate girls of all Christian denominations, but primarily Roman Catholics, in an environment which develops Christian values and prepares girls for any walk of life. Religious education is part of the core curriculum and there is considerable emphasis on worship and prayer. The staff:pupil ratio is about 1:10. Academic standards are creditable and results very good; most sixth-formers go on to degree courses, including Oxbridge. Music is very strong indeed. Speech and drama exams are taken to Gold Medal level. Ballet and modern dance are well supported. There is a fair range of clubs and societies and participation in the Duke of Edinburgh's Award Scheme. A wide and increasing range of sports and games and the new sports hall is in regular use.

School profile

Pupils Total age range 9–18; 310 girls (80 day, 230 boarding). Senior department 11–18,

270 girls. Main entry ages 9-13 and into sixth. Approx 5% are children of former pupils. State shoool entry: 50% main intake, plus 1–2 pa into sixth.

Entrance Common Entrance (at 12 or 13) or own entrance examination plus interview and testimonial. For sixth-form entry, 5 GCSEs with at least grade C (grades A or B in subjects to be taken at A-level.) Parents expected to buy a few textbooks in sixth-form. Maximum extras around £150 per term. 7 pa assisted places (5 at age 11, 2 for sixth-form). 7 pa scholarships, 30%–50% fees.

Parents 15+% in the armed services. 10+% live within 30 miles; up to 10% live overseas.

Head and staff *Headmistress:* Sister M Campion Livesey, in post for 11 years. Educated at Lady Eleanor Holles and Cambridge (history and theology). Also Governor of Prior Park. Council Member ISIS South and West. *Staff:* 30 full time, 12 part time. Annual turnover 5%. Average age 40–45.

Exam results In 1995, 44 pupils in upper fifth, 37 in upper sixth. *GCSE:* In 1995, 43 upper fifth gained at least grade C in 8+ subjects; 1 in 5–7 subjects. *A-levels:* 31 upper sixth passed in 3 subjects; 5 in 2 subjects. Average UCAS points 20.7.

University and college entrance 92% of 1995 sixth-form leavers went on to a degree course (45% after a gap year); others typically go on to secretarial courses or straight into work. Of those going on to university, 6% went to Oxbridge; 3% took courses in medicine, dentistry and veterinary science, 8% in science and engineering, 5% in law, 56% in humanities and social sciences, 3% in art and design, 8% in other vocational subjects eg business and finance.

Curriculum GCSE and A-levels. 18 GCSE subjects offered; 19 at A-level. 20% take science A-levels; 50% arts/humanities; 30% both. *Vocational:* Work experience available. *Computing facilities:* Information technology resource room plus computers in a range of departments. All pupils learn information technology. *Europe:* French (compulsory from 9 to 16), German and Spanish offered to GCSE and A-level; Italian to GCSE. Regular exchanges on an individual basis (France and Spain).

The arts *Music:* Over 50% of pupils learn a musical instrument; instrumental exams can be taken. Some 10 musical groups including brass groups, recorder consort, woodwind ensemble, orchestra, folk group, 4 choirs. Sainsbury Choir of the Year competition, regional winner; Bath music festival, trophy winners; Choir Girl of the Year, finals; choir trips to Salzburg, Bavaria, Italy and Budapest. *Drama & dance*: Both offered. GCSE drama, A-level theatre studies and LAMDA exams may be taken. Majority of pupils are involved in school and house/other productions. Many achieve gold medal speech & acting with honours. *Art:* On average, 15 take GCSE, 5 A-level. Design, pottery, textiles, photography also offered.

Sport, community service and clubs *Sport and physical activities:* Compulsory sports: netball, hockey, swimming, athletics, tennis, rounders. Optional: badminton, fencing, keep fit, riding, volleyball, basketball, gymnastics. County netball champions, regular finalists at all age groups; county hockey finalists, cross-country champions. *Community service:* Pupils take bronze, silver and gold Duke of Edinburgh's Award. Community service optional. *Clubs and societies:* Up to 10 clubs, eg debating, wine tasting, photography.

Uniform School uniform worn (sold on premises); varied in sixth.

Houses/prefects Competitive houses. Prefects, head girl, head of house and house prefects – appointed by Head after consultation with staff, lower sixth and previous upper sixth.

Religion Attendance at religious worship compulsory.

Social Regular debates and joint concerts. Trips abroad typically: second year one week in France; history of art trips to Paris (sixth), Florence and Venice; choir concert to Hungary; general trip to Russia. Pupils allowed to bring own bike for Duke of Edinburgh scheme; upper sixth may bring own cars. Meals self-service. School tuck shop. No tobacco/alcohol allowed.

Discipline Pupils failing to produce homework once might expect to re-do it in own time, followed by re-do in weekly detention slot for this purpose. Drug or solvent abuse of any kind will result in expulsion.

Boarding All sixth-form have own study bedroom, upper sixth in separate house; fifth form share in pairs, fourth 2–4. Houses same as competitive, 40–45 boarders and 15–20 day girls. Sixth form can provide and cook own food to limited extent. Qualified nurse by day (and at night when required). 2 weekend exeats termly (3 in sixth). Visits to the local town range from 3rd year (2 Saturdays per term) to sixth (any Saturday and during week if free and with tutor's permission).

• ST MARY'S (Wantage)

St Mary's School, Wantage, Oxfordshire OX12 8BZ. Tel 01235 763571, Fax 01235 760467
• Pupils 220 • Boys None • Girls 11–18 (Day/Board) • Upper sixth 40 • Termly fees £2400 (Day) £3620 (Board) • GSA • Enquiries/application to the Registrar

What it's like

Founded in 1872 by William Butler, vicar of Wantage, and run until 1975 by the Sisters of the Anglican Community of St Mary the Virgin. It remains an Anglican foundation and most of the pupils are Anglicans, although girls of other denominations and faiths are welcomed. The well-appointed buildings are on a continuous site in the middle of the small, market town. The modern facilities are of a high standard. There is a large staff, creating a ratio of about 1:6 pupils. Academic standards are high and results good. Most upper sixth leavers go on to degree courses each year. Very strong in art, music and drama. A wide range of games, sports and activities. An impressive record in the Duke of Edinburgh's Award Scheme.

School profile

Pupils Age range 11–18; 220 girls, mostly boarders (max 20 day girls). Main entry ages 11, 12, 13, 14 and into sixth. Approx 8% are children of former pupils. *State school entry:* 2% intake.

Entrance Common Entrance used. No special skills or religious requirements. Parents expected to buy some sixth-form textbooks; £120 average extras. 4 pa scholarships, 33% fees.

Parents From a wide range of occupations. Up to 10% live within 30 miles; up to 10% live overseas.

Head and staff *Headmistress:* Mrs Susan Bodinham, in post since 1994. Educated at King's College, London (geography and PGCE) and Open University (educational management). Previously second Deputy Head, Head of Lower Sixth and head of a day-girl house at Headington School, Oxford. Also Senior Assistant Chief Examiner for NEAB A-level geography. Reader in the Church of England. *Staff:* 41 full time, 6 part time. Annual turnover 5%. Average age 40.

Exam results In 1995, 47 pupils in upper fifth, 36 in upper sixth. *GCSE:* In 1995, 24 upper fifth gained at least grade C in 8+ subjects; 16 in 5–7 subjects. *A-levels:* 3 upper sixth passed in 4+ subjects; 21 in 3; 5 in 2; and 5 in 1 subject. Average UCAS points 15.1.

University and college entrance 80% of sixth-form leavers go on to a degree course (65% after a gap year); others typically go on to art, drama or music (12%) or vocational courses in secretarial, horsemanship (8%). Of those going on to university, 1% go to Oxbridge; 1% take courses in medicine, dentistry and veterinary science, 30% in science and engineering, 2% in law, 26% in humanities and social sciences, 31% in art and design, 10% in other vocational subjects eg fashion, agriculture.

Curriculum GCSE and A-levels. 15 GCSE subjects offered; 19 at A-level (including history of art, theatre studies, economics, politics). 23% take science A-levels; 46% arts/humanities; 30% both. *Vocational:* Work experience organised; also RSA level 1 and 2 word processing, 1–3 typing and Pitman office procedures Diploma of Achievement. *Computing facilities:* Network of Archimedes computers plus office technology centre with IBM-compatible machines; minimum of one computer per department and study area. *Special provision:* Extra coaching available for mild dyslexia. EFL teaching available. *Europe:* French (compulsory to GCSE), Spanish and German offered to GCSE, AS and A-level. Regular exchanges (France and Germany).

The arts *Music:* Over 50% of pupils learn a musical instrument; instrumental exams can be taken. Some 6 musical groups including choirs and orchestras. 1 National Youth Wind Band; 1 National Choir Girl of the Year regional finalist; Oxford and Cheltenham festival successes; 3 girls in semi-final of National Chamber Music Competition. Recent scholarship to Birmingham Conservatoire. *Drama & dance*: Both offered. GCSE, A-level drama and LAMDA exams may be taken. Majority of pupils are involved in school/

house productions. 2 A-level groups performed at Edinburgh Festival and nominated for Fringe First, also appeared on Channel 4's Edinburgh Special; 1 old girl runs drama therapy group, 1 selected for Pro-Am Drama, 1 running a circus; many girls go to drama school. *Art:* On average, 25 take GCSE, 1 AS-level, 8 A-level. Design, pottery, textiles, photography, theatre design and fine art also offered. Many girls go on to art colleges.
Sport, community service and clubs *Sport and physical activities:* Compulsory sports: lacrosse, netball, tennis, swimming, rounders, gym, athletics. Optional: badminton, cross-country, riding, squash, judo, keep fit. Sixth form only: golf. BAGA and RLSS exams may be taken. 1 pupil in county lacrosse and netball teams. *Community service:* Pupils take bronze and gold Duke of Edinburgh's Award. Community service optional. World Challenge Expedition to Zimbabwe 1996. Sixth form undertake a variety of residential projects in holidays for Gold D of E including Pony Club camps, helping at centre for homeless, National Trust projects etc. *Clubs and societies:* Up to 15 clubs, eg science, music, art, games, needlecraft, art, debating, jazz dance, country dancing, drama.
Uniform School uniform worn except the sixth.
Houses/prefects Competitive houses (socials). Prefects and head girl – appointed by Headmistress in consultation with staff and girls. School Council.
Religion Compulsory daily C of E service and Sunday eucharist.
Social Organised dances, parties, singing, drama with local boys' public schools; some activities (eg careers convention) with local comprehensive. Exchanges with Germany and France; sixth-formers to Paris, Florence and Washington; skiing trips. Pupils over 15 allowed to bring own bike to school. Meals self-service. School bookshop. No tobacco/ alcohol allowed.
Discipline Those caught involved with drugs would be expelled, as would persistent smokers.
Boarding 33% have own study bedroom, 5% share with 1 other, 10% are in dormitories of 6+. Houses of approximately 50, divided by age group. Resident qualified nurse; doctors visits regularly. Central dining room. Sixth form can provide and cook their own snacks. 1 or 2 weekend exeats each term plus 2 days and half-term. Visits to local town allowed.
Alumni association Magazine edited by Mrs D Webb, c/o the school.
Former pupils Emma Nicholson MP; Lucinda Green (3-day eventer); Dame Ruth Railton (founder, National Youth Orchestra); Presily Baxendale, QC.

• ST MARY'S MUSIC

St Mary's Music School, Coates Hall, 25 Grosvenor Crescent, Edinburgh EH12 5EL. Tel 0131 538 7766

• Pupils 52 • Boys 9–18 (Day/Board) • Girls 9–18 (Day/Board) • Upper sixth 9 • Termly fees: apply to school • CSA • Enquiries/application to the Headteacher

What it's like

Founded in 1880 as the boys' choir school of St Mary's Episcopal Cathedral. In 1972 it widened its scope to become a specialist music school, accepting both boys and girls as instrumentalists; later girl choristers were admitted too. While it continues its choral tradition, the bulk of its pupils are now instrumentalists. Composition, singing, counterpoint, harmony and aural training are also taught. The core of the curriculum is music making. But a sound general education is also provided and exam results are good – academic work takes two-thirds of the timetable in the early years and about half from S3. The school moved in 1995 to new premises at Coates Hall, 5 minutes walk from the cathedral, where it has good facilities and accommodation. There is a range of sports and the Duke of Edinburgh's Award Scheme. All pupils go on to higher education, most to music college or to degree courses in music.

School profile

Pupils Total age range 9–18; 52 pupils, 26 day, 26 boarding. Senior department 11–18, 31 pupils. Main entry ages 9–11 and into sixth.
Entrance Admission by audition. Good musical skills required; no religious requirements. Parents not expected to buy textbooks. 39 pa means-tested aided places (35 instrumental, 4 chorister); 16 cathedral scholarships for choristers.

Parents 10+% live within 30 miles; up to 10% live overseas.
Head and staff Headteacher: Mrs J J Rimer, appointed in 1996. *Staff:* 5 full time, 33 part time. Annual turnover 1–10%. Average age mid-30s.
Exam results On average, 9 in fourth form, 9 in sixth. All take arts and humanities A-levels; most pass 4–6 S-grades, 2–4 Highers and 1 A-level.
University and college entrance 63% of 1995 sixth-form leavers went on to a degree course (10% after a gap year), over 90% to courses in music; others typically go on to music college.
Curriculum S-grade, Highers, CSYS and A-levels. *Europe:* French, German and Italian offered to S-grade and Higher.
The arts (Pupils aged 11 and over) *Music:* All pupils learn a musical instrument; instrumental exams can be taken. Some 15+ musical groups including chamber music groups, orchestras, choirs, cathedral choir etc. Violinist, finalist of Young Musician of the Year (strings); violinist, finalist in Audi competition; several members of National Youth Orchestra of Scotland. *Drama & dance*: Drama offered. Some pupils are involved in school productions. *Art:* On average, 1–2 take S-grade, 1–2 Higher 1–2 A-level. Design, pottery, textiles, photography, stained glass and silk screen printing also offered. Recent prizes in national art competitions.
Sport, community service and clubs (Pupils aged 11 and over) *Sport and physical activities:* Compulsory sports: general PE. Optional: badminton, unihoc, football, short tennis, squash, sailing, riding, hillwalking. *Community service:* Participation in Duke of Edinburgh Awards.
Uniform School uniform not worn.
Houses/prefects No competitive houses. Prefects and head boy/girl.
Religion Compulsory attendance at school assembly.
Social Occasional musical activities with other local schools and musical tours. Pupils allowed to bring own car/bike/motorbike to school. Meals self-service. No tobacco/alcohol allowed.
Discipline Pupils failing to produce homework once would be asked why; those caught smoking cannabis on the premises should expect expulsion.
Boarding 1 has own study bedroom, others share (1 or 2 others). Central dining room. 3 exeats each term, 3–10 days. Visits to the local town allowed.

• ST MAUR'S

St Maur's, Thames Street, Weybridge, Surrey KT13 8NL. Tel 01932 851411, Fax 01932 842037
• Pupils 700 • Boys 2–4 only (Day) • Girls 2–18 (Day) • Upper sixth 24 • Termly fees £1400–£1500 • GSA • Enquiries/application to the Headmistress

What it's like

Founded in 1898, it is semi-rural, single-site with spacious and pleasant grounds. The main school building dates from 1897 and there have been many modern additions. About 40% of the pupils are Roman Catholics and the school welcomes those from other denominations. Results are good and most sixth-form leavers go on to degree courses. Strong in music and vigorous drama and art departments. A good range of sports, games and activities. Some participation in local community schemes and the Duke of Edinburgh's Award Scheme.

School profile

Pupils Total age range 2–18; 700 day pupils (20 boys, 680 girls). Senior department 11–18, 400 girls. Main entry ages 4, 11 and into sixth. *State school entry:* 30% senior intakes.
Entrance Own entrance exam used. No special skills or religious requirements but about 50% are Roman Catholic. 15 pa assisted places. Scholarships and bursaries available including 1 for physically handicapped pupil.
Parents Professions and business backgrounds.
Head and staff *Headmistress:* Mrs Maureen Dodds, 5 years in post. Educated at Convent of the Sacred Heart Grammar, Newcastle-upon-Tyne, and at Durham and Reading universities (French and philosophy; educational administration and institutional management). Previously Headmistress at More House School, London; Deputy Head at Amery Hill Comprehensive, Hampshire, and taught at four other comprehensive

and two grammar schools. Also, governor of Sacred Heart High School, Hammersmith. *Staff:* Annual turnover 5%. Average age 45.

Exam results In 1995, 69 pupils in Year 11, 16 in upper sixth. *GCSE:* In 1995, 94% of Year 11 gained at least grade C in 8+ subjects. *A-levels:* Most upper sixth pass in 3 subjects. Average UCAS points 21.1.

University and college entrance 95% of 1995 sixth-form leavers went on to a degree course (5% after a gap year); others typically go on to HND, secretarial courses. Of those going on to university, 5% went to Oxbridge; 12% took courses in medicine, dentistry and veterinary science, 10% in science and engineering, 15% in law, 40% in humanities and social sciences, 15% in art and design, 5% in other vocational subjects eg physiotherapy, computer studies.

Curriculum GCSE and A-levels: 24 A-level subjects offered. *Vocational:* Strong emphasis on work experience including sixth-form placements in Europe. *Computing facilities:* Nimbus networked system, 18 stations. *Europe:* French (from age 7), German and Spanish offered to GCSE, AS and A-level; also Italian GCSE and A-level. Over 50% take GCSE in more than 1 language. Regular exchanges to France, Germany and Italy. Strong links with sister schools in Toulouse.

The arts (Pupils aged 11 and over) *Music:* 50% of pupils learn a musical instrument; instrumental exams can be taken. Musical groups including orchestral, choral. *Drama & dance*: Both offered. GCSE, AS and A-level drama exams may be taken. Majority of pupils are involved in school and house/other productions. *Art:* Textiles, photography also offered. Art facilities open to non-examination pupils.

Sport, community service and clubs (Pupils aged 11 and over) *Sport and physical activities:* Lacrosse, tennis, netball, swimming, gymnastics, athletics. *Community service:* Pupils take bronze, silver and gold Duke of Edinburgh's Award. Community service for all sixth-form.

Uniform School uniform worn; dress code in sixth-form.

Houses/prefects Competitive houses. Prefects, head girl, head of house and house prefects – appointed by the Head after consultation with the school and staff. School Forum.

Religion RS is compulsory part of the curriculum.

Social Several organised trips. Meals self-service.

Discipline School has strong pastoral structure emphasising partnership with students and parents.

Alumni association Mrs R Wilson, c/o the school

• ST PAUL'S (Boys)

St Paul's School, Lonsdale Road, Barnes, London SW13 9JT. Tel 0181 748 9162, Fax 0181 748 9557

• Pupils 785 • Boys 13–18 (Day/Board/Weekly) • Girls None • Upper sixth 160 • Termly fees £2694 (Day) £4119 (Board/Weekly) • HMC • Enquiries to the High Master • Applications to the Admissions Office

What it's like

Founded in 1509 by John Colet, Dean of St Paul's. A grammar school had previously existed for centuries in connection with the cathedral and Colet probably absorbed this in the new foundation. It moved from the cathedral site in 1884 and to purpose-built premises in Barnes in 1968. To the original buildings, serviceable but lacking distinction, have been added a new technology building and art block, which have greatly improved facilities and enhanced the environment. It is governed by the Mercers' Company, and has its own prep school, Colet Court (founded in 1881) on the same site. Religious instruction is in accordance with the C of E but attendance at services is voluntary. The academic reputation of the school remains formidable with the classics still prospering. A very high-powered teaching staff is strong in pastoral care (thanks to the well-established tutorial system) and produces outstanding results. All leavers go on university, exceptional numbers to Oxbridge. The school is tremendously strong in music, drama, technology and art and these departments work closely together and form an integral part of the academic and social life of the school. In music there are orchestras, choirs, jazz groups, instrumental ensembles and about a third of pupils learn an instrument.

Several plays are produced each year and there are a number of minor workshop productions. The school has a notable record in sports and games (there is a fine sports hall and separate gymnasium and fencing salle) and most pupils are involved in one or more of them. Some 30 extra-curricular activities are available.

School profile

Pupils Age range 13–18; 785 boys, 734 day, 51 boarding. Main entry age 13, maximum of 12 into sixth. Approx 10% are children of former pupils. Own prep, Colet Court, provides 45% of intake. *State school entry:* None in main intake, a few into sixth.

Entrance Common Entrance and own scholarship exam used. Selection interviews at age 11/12. No special skills or religious requirements. Parents expected to buy some textbooks; £100 maximum extras. 11 pa assisted places. 24 pa scholarships, 15%–100% of fees plus bursaries.

Parents 60+% live within 30 miles.

Head and staff *High Master*: R S Baldock, 4 years in post. Educated at St Paul's and Cambridge (classics and theology). Previously Surmaster, Housemaster and Assistant Master at St Paul's. *Staff:* 78 full time, 4 part time. Annual turnover 3–4%. Average age 42.

Exam results In 1995, 154 pupils in upper fifth, 141 in upper sixth. *GCSE:* In 1995, over 99% upper fifth gained at least grade C in 8+ subjects. *A-levels:* 24% upper sixth passed in 4+ subjects; 72% in 3; 4% in 2 subjects. Average UCAS points 31.8.

University and college entrance 99% of 1995 sixth-form leavers went on to a degree course (42% after a gap year); others typically travel and apply later. Of those going on to university, 32% went to Oxbridge; 9% took courses in medicine, dentistry and veterinary science, 27% in science and engineering, 4% in law, 41% in humanities and social sciences, 2% in art and design.

Curriculum GCSE, AS and A-levels (subjects include a 1-year Japanese course; no A-level general studies). 28% take science A-levels; 52% arts/humanities (including maths); 20% both. *Vocational:* Work experience available. *Computing facilities:* 120 Apple Macs, 10 PCs. *Europe:* French, German and Italian offered to GCSE, AS and A-level; also Spanish at AS-level. Regular exchanges to France, Germany and Italy. Special link with Collège Stanislas (Paris). Modern language assistants in French (2), German (1) and Italian (1). Lectures by eg Sir Leon Brittan on future of Europe; satellite TV from Europe.

The arts *Music:* Over 40% of pupils learn a musical instrument; instrumental exams can be taken. Some 15 musical groups including choir, orchestras, concert band, jazz group, saxophone ensemble, string quarters, wind octet, many other chamber groups. Member of National Youth Wind Orchestra; finalists Schools Chamber Music Competition; semi-finalists Schools Jazz Competition; finalist Audi Competition; organ scholars to Cambridge and Bristol universities and Windsor (St George's). *Drama & dance*: Drama offered at GCSE. Some pupils are involved in school and other productions. 1 pupil in production of Arcadia at the Theatre Royal; 1 starred in recent film of The Browning Version; 2 recent old boys in Royal Shakespeare Company. *Art:* On average, 87 take GCSE, 5 AS-level, 12 A-level. Design, pottery, photography, silkscreen printing and sculpture also offered. Own art gallery for professional and internal exhibitions. Many pupils go onto art colleges eg Slade, Royal College of Art.

Sport, community service and clubs *Sport and physical activities:* Compulsory sports: PE programme for juniors. Optional: aikido, athletics, badminton, basketball, cricket, cross-country & orienteering, fencing, fives, fitness, centre, golf, judo, riding, rowing, rugby, soccer, squash, swimming, table tennis, tennis, volleyball, water polo. RLSS exams may be taken. 8 county rugby players; 1 national fencer, 3 regional; 2 county tennis; NAGC swimming champion; 1 county squash; 1 international chess master; 2 national independent schools judo champions; rowing team Head of the River. Community Service: Pupils take Duke of Edinburgh's Award. *Clubs and societies:* Up to 30 clubs, eg art appreciation, bridge, chess, debating, Christian Union, classical, drama, English, cookery, electronics, European, geography, film-making, history, politics, natural history, BAYS.

Houses/prefects Competitive houses. Prefects, head boy – appointed by Head.

Religion Voluntary worship.

Social Central atrium for social gathering. Debates, concerts and joint theatrical productions with St Paul's Girls and other schools. Organised trips abroad. Day pupils allowed to bring own bike/car/motorbike to school. Meals self-service. School shop (uniform and tuck). No tobacco/alcohol allowed.

Discipline Pupils failing to produce homework once might expect a warning, those caught smoking cannabis on the premises might expect expulsion.

Boarding One-third have own study bedroom, others share with up to 5. Houses of approx 35. Resident matrons. Central dining room. Pupils can provide and cook own food. Exeats every weekend. Visits to local town allowed 4.00–5.30 pm.

Alumni association run by M K Seigel, c/o the school.

Former pupils Kenneth Baker, MP: Clement Freud; Admiral Treacher; Sir Robin Renwick; Magnus Pyke; Dr Jonathan Miller; Lord McColl; W Galen Weston; Peter Shaffer (playwright); Eric Newby (travel writer); Max Beloff; Sir Kenneth Dover; Professor R F Gombrich; Chris Barber (musician); John Simpson (BBC foreign correspondent); John Cavanagh (fashion designer); Sir Isaiah Berlin; Oliver Sacks.

• ST PAUL'S (Girls)

St Paul's Girls' School, Brook Green, London W6 7BS. Tel 0171 603 2288, Fax 0171 602 9932

• Pupils 618 • Boys None • Girls 11–18 (Day) • Upper sixth 106 • Termly fees £2094 (Day)

• GSA • Enquiries/application to the High Mistress

What it's like

Like its counterpart for boys, it belongs to the Christian Foundation originally provided by Dean Colet in 1509. The trustees are the Worshipful Company of Mercers. Its handsome Edwardian buildings lie in a pleasant part of Hammersmith and are outstandingly well equipped with, among other things, first-class art rooms and workshops, excellent libraries, laboratories and IT facilities and a fine theatre named in memory of Dame Celia Johnson. Games and sports facilities are all provided on site and include a fine swimming pool. Religious instruction is in accordance with the principles of the Church of England. A large and extremely well-qualified full-time staff as well as many part-timers. Academically it is formidably high-powered, equally strong in arts and sciences. Considerable importance is attached to girls establishing from the outset good habits of work and learning to read and think independently. Academic results are consistently excellent. Almost all leavers go on to degree courses; a very high proportion to Oxbridge. Since the appointment of the school's first director of music, Gustav Holst, music has been an important activity. There is a specially built music wing with a concert hall and the Great Hall has an organ. There are four orchestras, two wind bands and several choirs and a high proportion of girls learn one or more instruments. A great deal of drama is done each year, including workshop productions, and the standards are high. They are equally high in a wide variety of sports and games and physical education. There are demonstrations of self-defence in one of the martial arts. There are numerous extra-curricular activities, clubs and societies.

School profile

Pupils Age range 11–18; 618 day girls. Main entry ages 11 and into the sixth-form.

Entrance Own exam used. Assisted places. Foundation awards include scholarships for art and music.

Head and staff *High Mistress*: Janet Gough, 4 years in post. Educated at Ludlow High School and Cambridge (history and English). *Staff:* 50 full time, 11 part time plus 40 music staff, full and part time.

Exam results On average, 83 in Year 11, 106 in Year 13. *GCSE:* On average Year 11 pupils gain grade C or above in 9.23 subjects. *A-levels:* Year 13 pupils pass an average of 3.2 subjects. Average UCAS points 28.2.

University and college entrance All 1995 sixth-form leavers went on to a degree course (64% after a gap year), 47% to Oxbridge; 13% took courses in medicine, dentistry and veterinary science, 15% in science and engineering, 4% in law, 24% in humanities and social sciences, 3% in art and design, 41% in maths, languages, English, music.

Curriculum GCSE and A-level. *Vocational:* Work experience available. *Computing facilities:* Acorn Archimedes and Nimbus PCs. *Europe:* French and German offered to GCSE and A-level; also Italian and Spanish A-level. Regular exchanges.

The arts *Music:* Over 60% of pupils learn a musical instrument; instrumental exams can be taken. Some 20 musical groups including 4 orchestras, 4 choirs, jazz group, very many ensembles. Pupils regularly offered Royal College places or choral/instrumental scholarships at Oxbridge. Many pupils in National Youth Orchestra; school regular finalist in National Schools' Chamber Music Competition. *Drama & dance*: Drama part of curriculum for first three years, later an option. All pupils are involved in school productions. *Art:* On average, over half of pupils take school-directed course with GCSEs. Design, pottery, photography, printmaking, critical and historical studies also offered. 4 students on average go on to art colleges each year.

Sport, community service and clubs *Sport and physical activities:* Compulsory sports (to 14): lacrosse, netball, gym, dance, swimming, volleyball, keep fit etc. Optional: golf, squash, rowing. RLSS exams may be taken. England junior, Scotland junior, regional and country junior representatives at lacrosse; London Schools athletics. *Community service:* Pupils take bronze, silver and gold Duke of Edinburgh's Award. Community service optional. *Clubs and societies:* Up to 30 clubs, eg literary, philosophy, photography, classics, politics, economics, drama, modern languages, history, geography.

Uniform No school uniform.

Houses/prefects No competitive houses or prefects. School Council.

Religion Attendance at religious worship compulsory. Separate Jewish and Moslem assemblies weekly; weekly celebration of communion.

Social Joint activities with St Paul's School (boys): concerts and plays, literary and political discussion groups, modern languages group. Regular exchanges with schools in Bonn, Paris, Marseilles, Sydney, Washington and New York. History of art, skiing and cultural trips to Greece, Italy, France, Spain and Holland. Pupils allowed to bring own car/bike to school. Meals self-service. School shop. No tobacco/alcohol allowed.

Discipline Pupils failing to produce homework once might expect to complete the work within the day/by the next day.

Former pupils Brigid Brophy, Harriet Harman, Professor Catherine Peckham, Jessica Rawson, Natasha Richardson, Anne Sofer, Emma Tennant.

• ST PETER'S (York)

St Peter's School, York YO3 6AB. Tel 01904 623213, Fax 01904 670407

• Pupils 479 • Boys 13–18 (Day/Board) • Girls 13–18 (Day/Board) • Upper sixth 97 • Termly fees £1963–£2061 (Day) £3372–£3462 (Board) • HMC • Enquiries/application to the Head Master

What it's like

Founded in 627 and thus one of the oldest schools in Europe. Alcuin was a pupil and headmaster; its first head was a saint (Paulinus) and Guy Fawkes was an old boy (now a C of E school). It is urban, single-site by the Ouse and is exceptionally well equipped in fine buildings dating from the 1830s to the present day. The prep school, St Olave's, is on the same site. Academic standards are high and results very good. The majority of leavers proceed to degree courses each year, including to Oxbridge. Strong in the drama and art departments and particularly in music. Wide variety of sports and games, in which good standards are attained, and a big range of activities with particular emphasis on outdoor pursuits. There is a vigorous CCF contingent, considerable commitment to local community schemes and a creditable record in the Duke of Edinburgh's Award Scheme.

School profile

Pupils Age range 13–18; 479 pupils, 317 day (203 boys, 114 girls), 162 boarding (100 boys, 62 girls). Main entry ages 13 and into sixth. Approx 10% are children of former pupils. Own junior school (St Olave's) provides more than 70% of intake. *State school entry:* 10% main entry, plus 20% to sixth.

Entrance Own exam used. No special skills or religious requirements but all attend chapel (C of E). Parents not expected to buy textbooks. 29 pa assisted places. 6–8 pa scholarships/bursaries, up to half tuition fees.

Parents 15+% in industry or commerce. 60+% live within 30 miles; up to 10% overseas.

Head and staff *Head Master*: Andrew Trotman, in post from 1995. Educated at Alleyne's Grammar School, Stevenage, and Oxford University (English). Previously

Deputy Rector at Edinburgh Academy, Housemaster and English teacher (and rowing, rugby and CCF) at Abingdon and at Radley. Also Secretary, Oxford Conference in Education. *Staff:* 43 full time. Annual turnover 6%. Average age 35.

Exam results In 1995, 95 pupils in fifth, 97 in upper sixth. *GCSE:* In 1995, 97% pupils in fifth gained at least grade C in 8+ subjects. *A-levels:* 86 upper sixth passed in 4+ subjects; 9 in 3; 1 in 2 subjects. Average UCAS points 21.9.

University and college entrance All 1995 sixth-form leavers went on to a degree course (25% after a gap year), 9% to Oxbridge; 11% took courses in medicine, dentistry and veterinary science, 26% in science and engineering, 6% in law, 48% in humanities and social sciences, 6% in art and design, 3% in eg food marketing, information technology.

Curriculum GCSE and A-levels: 16 GCSE subjects offered; 20 at A-level (including A-level general studies for all). 41% take science A-levels; 40% arts/humanities; 19% both. *Vocational:* Work experience available. *Computing facilities:* Computer laboratory plus computers in specialist areas. *Special provision:* Extra English provision for the few pupils that need it. *Europe:* French, German and Spanish to GCSE, AS and A-level. Regular exchanges France and Germany.

The arts *Music:* Over 30% of pupils learn a musical instrument; instrumental exams can be taken. Some 10+ musical groups including orchestra, string orchestra, bands, choirs, choral society, swing band, string ensemble, barbershop quartet. Regular members of National Youth Orchestra. Regular productions, eg Dream of Gerontius. *Drama & dance*: Some pupils are involved in school and house/other productions, including recently Roots, Look Back in Anger and Twist. *Art:* On average, 45 take GCSE, 12 A-level. Pottery, textiles also offered.

Sport, community service and clubs *Sport and physical activities:* Sport is compulsory; choice from some 15 options: rugby, cricket, hockey, rowing, squash, fencing, swimming, cross-country, netball, gymnastics, golf etc. Regular national and county representatives. *Community service:* Pupils take bronze silver and gold Duke of Edinburgh's Award. CCF and community service optional. *Clubs and societies:* Up to 10 clubs, eg chess, debating, electronics, art.

Uniform School uniform worn except in sixth.

Houses/prefects Prefects, head boy/girl, head of house and house prefects – appointed by the Head Master and staff.

Religion Compulsory attendance at C of E services during the week.

Social Many holiday expeditions to eg Florence, Greece, Northern France battlefields; rugby tour to Paris, skiing to France. Pupils allowed to bring own car to school. Meals self-service. School shop.

Discipline Discipline founded on self-discipline and respect for others.

Boarding Sixth form in own study bedrooms or share with up to 2 others. Single-sex houses of up to 50, mixed ages. Resident SRN. Central dining room. Pupils can provide and cook own food. 28-hour exeats each weekend. Regulated visits to York.

Alumni association is run by Mr E G Thompson, 4 Moor Lane, Haxby, York YO3 8PH.

Former pupils C Northcote Parkinson (of Parkinson's Law); Norman Yardley (England cricket captain); Guy Fawkes; Jeremy Beadle (music critic); Christopher Hill (hitorian); Thomas E Albert (inventor of clinical thermometer); John Barry (composer); Basil Radford (actor).

• ST SWITHUN'S

St Swithun's School, Alresford Road, Winchester, Hampshire SO21 1HA. Tel 01962 861316, Fax 01962 841874

• Pupils 450 • Boys None • Girls 11–18 (Day/Board/Weekly) • Upper sixth 52 • Termly fees £2240 (Day) £3710 (Board/Weekly) • GSA, BSA • Enquiries/application to the School Secretary

What it's like

Founded in 1884, it moved in 1931 to its present magnificent site on the edge of Winchester. It is set in some 19 acres, 5 minutes east of the centre of the city overlooking open country. The school is now very well equipped with modern, purpose-built buildings for science, technology, sport and the arts. The separate junior school is close by. It is a Church of England foundation, with close ties with the cathedral and, while pupils of other denominations and faiths are welcome, all are expected to attend the school's regular acts of worship. Academic education has aways been strong – its original aims were 'sound learning and true religion' – and the curriculum is flexible. Exam results are excellent and almost all sixth-formers go on to degree courses, a very high proportion to Oxbridge. Music, drama and art are all strong. So is sport (with regular representation at county, regional and national levels), coupled with an emphasis on enjoyment and an active life-style. There is a strong tradition of service to the community, ranging from fund-raising for charities, community work in Winchester and an active Amnesty group. There is a good range of activities and participation in the Duke of Edinburgh's Award Scheme.

School profile

Pupils Age range 11–18; 450 girls (227 day, 223 boarding). Main entry age 11 but also 12, 13 and into sixth. 15+% pupils from own junior school (tel 01962 852634). *State school entry:* 5% main intake, plus 10% to sixth.

Entrance Common Entrance used; own exam for those who miss CE entry. No special skills or religious requirements. Parents expected to buy some sixth-form course books only; average extras £300. 4 pa assisted places (2 at 11, 2 in sixth). 15 pa scholarships (at 11, 12, 13 and sixth) 10%–50% fees. Occasional bursaries for pupils already in the school.

Parents 15+% are from industry or commerce, 15% doctors, lawyers etc. Over 30% live within 30 miles; under 10% live overseas.

Head and staff *Headmistress:* Dr H L Harvey, appointed 1995. Educated at Lordswood Girls' School, Birmingham, and London University (physiology). Previously Headmistress and Head of Biology at Upper Chine School, Isle of Wight. *Staff:* 52 full time staff, 18 part time staff. Annual turnover 5%. Average age 45.

Exam results On average, 76 pupils in upper fifth, 52 in upper sixth. *GCSE:* In 1995, 100% upper fifth gain at least grade C in 8+ subjects. *A-levels:* 92% upper sixth pass in 4+ subjects; 8% in 3 subjects. Average UCAS points 25.2 (including general studies, 31.7).

University and college entrance 98% of 1995 sixth-form leavers went on to a degree course (50% after a gap year); others typically go on to nursing or art/drama foundation courses. Of those going on to university, 25% went to Oxbridge; 20% took courses in medicine, dentistry and veterinary science, 10% in science and engineering, 5% in law, 50% in humanities and social sciences (including 15% in languages), 5% in art and design, 10% other vocational subjects (eg occupational therapy, physiotherapy).

Curriculum GCSE and A-levels offered: 19 subjects at GCSE, 21 at A-level (including A-level general studies). 14% take science A-levels; 57% arts/humanities; 29% both. *Vocational:* Work experience available. RSA Typing and text-processing qualifications available. *Computing facilities:* Networked suite of Acorn machines; some departments linked to network; other PCs. *Special provision:* Specialist staff for dyslexia and teaching EFL. *Europe:* French, German and Spanish offered to GCSE and A-level (French and German compulsory for 3 years); also Russian GCSE. Regular exchanges (France and Germany).

The arts *Music:* Over 50% of pupils learn a musical instrument; instrumental exams can be taken. Some 25 musical groups including orchestras, choirs, wind bands, brass and recorder ensembles, jazz band and many chamber groups. Chamber group in finals of National Chamber Music Competition; many girls in Hampshire County Orchestra and other county ensembles. *Drama & dance*: Both offered. A-level theatre studies, Poetry Society and Guildhall exams may be taken. Some pupils involved in school and house productions. Recent productions include Animal Farm and Dandy Dick. Pupil won junior championship at Southampton Drama Festival; Shakespeare day to raise funds for The Globe. *Art:* On average, 22 take GCSE, 3 A-level. Design, ceramics, textiles, photography, silk-screen and dry-point printing, paper-making, mono-printing also offered.

Sport, community service and clubs *Sport and physical activities:* Compulsory sports: Lacrosse, netball, badminton, swimming, tennis, rounders, gymnastics, dance. Optional: Volleyball, judo, fencing, karate, self-defence, cross-country, running aerobics. Sixth form only: Trampoline. RLSS exams may be taken. 11 in county lacrosse team, 3 in regional team, Junior England vice-captain; tennis, U13 and U15 Midland Bank County

winners; 1 county cross-country runner. *Community service:* Pupils take bronze, silver and gold Duke of Edinburgh's Award. Community service optional; first aid and life-saving courses. *Clubs and societies:* Up to 15 clubs, eg Young Enterprise, Green Society, Christian Union, Amnesty International, science, technology, cooking, drama.
Uniform School uniform worn, except the sixth.
Houses/prefects Competitive houses. Head girl and house prefects – appointed by the Head and teaching staff. School council.
Religion Attendance at religious worship compulsory.
Social Joint music, drama, dances and societies, primarily with Winchester College. Language exchanges, skiing trips, classics trip (eg Provence), choir tour (Florence and Venice). Upper sixth day girls allowed to bring own car. Meals self-service. School shop. No tobacco/alcohol allowed.
Discipline Pupils failing to produce homework once might expect advice on becoming more organised; those caught smoking cannabis on the premises would expect expulsion.
Boarding Sixth form and some upper fifth have own study-bedroom; 11 and 12-year-olds only in dormitories of 7. Divided into houses, 28–50, same as for competitive purposes. 2 resident nurses. Pupils may cook their own snacks. Exeats: half term plus 4 nights per term (6 for lower sixth); upper sixth make own weekend arrangments; weekly boarding also available. Visits to local town allowed.
Alumni association run by Mrs A Chester, Flat 4, 11 Chester Street, London SW1X 7BB.
Former pupils Baroness (Mary) Warnock; Vivienne Parry.

• ST TERESA'S

St Teresa's School, Effingham Hill, Dorking, Surrey RH5 6ST. Tel 01372 452037/454896, Fax 01372 450311

• Pupils 340 • Boys None • Girls 11–18 (Day/Board/Weekly) • Upper sixth 39 • Termly fees £1690 (Day) £3595 (Board/Weekly) • GSA, SHA, CCSS, BSA • Enquiries to the Headmaster • Application to the Admissions Secretary

What it's like

It was founded by the Religious of Christian Instruction in 1928. The main house, dating from 1799, is the centre of the school, now greatly extended to provide modern facilities. The preparatory school, from which very many pupils are drawn, is about 1½ miles away. It is situated amid beautiful, rural surroundings, 22 miles from London, in 45 acres of grounds amongst the Surrey hills. Its prime aim is to provide a broad education based on Christian principles in a happy, caring atmosphere. A Roman Catholic foundation, it welcomes other denominations. Classes are small and a broad curriculum provides an all-round education. Results are good and almost all sixth-formers go on to university, including Oxbridge. Pupils are involved in a wide range of extra-curricular activities – music, drama, arts and crafts, public speaking, debating, the Duke of Edinburgh's Award Scheme, Girl Guides and Young Enterprise; facilities for sports and games include an open-air heated swimming pool, tennis courts, all-weather hockey pitch and a multi-purpose sports hall. There is much emphasis on travel, foreign exchanges and visits.

School profile

Pupils Age range 11–18; 340 girls (230 day, 110 boarding). Main entry ages 11, 12, 13 and into sixth. Own preparatory school (Grove House) provides 80% intake; many others from Rowan, Halstead, Downsend, Stanway, Rydes Hill and Holy Cross prep schools. State school entriy: 4% main intake.
Entrance Own entrance exam used. No special skills or religious requirements. Parents not expected to buy textbooks. Scholarships/bursaries available, up to full day fees.
Head and staff *Headmaster:* Mr Leslie Allan, in post for 9 years. Educated at Edinburgh and Stirling universities (fine art and education). Previously Deputy Head at Kilgraston and Head of Department and Senior Master at La Sainte Union, London. Publications: The Role of the Deputy Head (Scottish Council for Research in Education). *Staff:* 30 full time, 14 part time. Annual turnover 10%. Average age 40.
Exam results In 1995, 63 in upper fifth, 28 in upper sixth. *GCSE:* In 1995, 63% upper fifth gained at least grade C in 8+ subjects; 25% in 5–7 subjects. *A-levels:* 4% upper sixth

passed in 4+ subjects; 64% in 3; 25% in 2; and 4% in 1 subject. Average UCAS points 15.5.

University and college entrance 96% of 1995 sixth-form leavers went on to a degree course (21% after a gap year); others typically go on to vocational training in nursing, drama or art courses. Of those going on to university, 10% went to Oxbridge; 4% took courses in medicine, dentistry and veterinary science, 29% in science and engineering, 3% in law, 56% in humanities and social sciences, 4% in art and design, 4% in other vocational subjects eg accountancy, business studies.

Curriculum GCSE and A-levels: 19 GCSE subjects offered, 20 A-level. 20% take science A-levels; 32% arts humanities; 50% both. *Computing facilities:* Computer lab plus computers in all subject areas and sixth-form centre. *Special provision:* Lessons in EFL by specialist teacher; small groups or individual teaching. *Europe:* French, German and Spanish at GCSE, AS and A-level (French compulsory from 11, one other from 12). Over 75% take GCSE in more than 1 language. Regular exchanges. French and Spanish boarders.

The arts *Music:* Over 30% of pupils learn a musical instrument; instrumental exams can be taken. 12 taking GCSE music. Musical groups include orchestra, choirs, string groups, woodwind groups, recorder. *Drama & dance:* Both offered. Majority of pupils are involved in school productions. *Art:* On average, 19 take GCSE, 8 A-level. Photography also offered. On average, 4 accepted for art college each year.

Sport, community service and clubs *Sport and physical activities:* Hockey, netball, cricket, tennis, rounders, basketball, volleyball, athletics, cross-country, badminton, riding, football, swimming, gymnastics, trampolining, swimming, judo. Exams may be taken. County and regional hockey representatives. *Community service:* Pupils take bronze, silver and gold Duke of Edinburgh's Award. *Community service:* Geriatric visits, Riding for the Disabled etc. *Clubs and societies:* Over 60 extra-curricular activities; clubs include Guides, computer, driving lessons, riding, debating, public speaking.

Uniform School uniform worn except in the sixth, who wear it for special occasions.

Houses/prefects Competitive houses. Prefects, head girl, head of house and house prefects elected by school, ratified by Headmaster and staff. School Council.

Religion All girls attend assemblies and chapel.

Social Debates, theatre trips, modern languages events and social events with local boys' independent schools. Organised trips abroad include classics trip to Italy, sport to Spain and music to Czech Republic. Meals self-service. School bank and shop. No tobacco/alcohol allowed.

Discipline Clearly understood grade system of discipline. Grades decided at weekly staff meeting. Pupils failing to produce homework once would be given the lowest grade or warning; those caught with drugs or alcohol on the premises would be expelled immediately.

Boarding Fifth and sixth have own study bedrooms; others share or in dormitories. Houses divided by age group. Resident qualified nurse. Central dining room. Pupils can provide and cook own food on special occasions. One week half-term. Weekly boarding and flexible boarding offered; also extended day for day girls. Visits to local town allowed once a week, 11–16; sixth-form by arrangement.

Alumni association St Teresa's Old Girls' Association (STOGA) – information from Sister Catherine c/o the school.

Former pupils Lynne Reid-Banks (author); Faye Maschler (restaurateur and food critic); Jennifer Michelmore (actress).

• SCARBOROUGH

Scarborough College, Filey Road, Scarborough, North Yorkshire YO11 3BA. Tel 01723 360620, Fax 01723 377265

• Pupils 359 • Boys 11–18 (Day/Board) • Girls 11–18 (Day/Board) • Upper sixth 38 • Termly fees £1702 (Day) £3140 (Board) • SHMIS, SHA • Enquiries/application to the Headmaster's Secretary

What it's like

Founded in 1898, it has a splendid site south of Scarborough on the eastern slopes of Oliver's Mount, overlooking Scarborough Castle and the South Bay. The main Victorian building is a fine example of its kind. In the last 25 years there have been many developments and facilities are good. Girls were first admitted in 1993 and it is now fully co-educational. It is a Christian and interdenominational establishment with high academic standards and good results. The music, drama and art departments are well supported. A good record in games and sports (several county and regional representatives). Many extra-curricular activities cater for most needs. A flourishing CCF and some emphasis on outdoor pursuits. Some involvement in the Duke of Edinburgh's Award Scheme.

School profile

Pupils Age range 11–18; 359 pupils, 323 day (180 boys, 143 girls), 36 boarding (18 boys, 18 girls). Main entry ages, 11, 13, and into the sixth. Own junior school, Lisvane School (tel 01723 361595) provides 50% of intake. 10% are children of former pupils. *State school entry:* 50% intake.
Entrance Common Entrance and own exam used. Pupils with high potential in music and art encouraged; college is Christian and interdenominational. Parents not expected to buy textbooks. 45 pa assisted places. Scholarships/bursaries, £850–£2200.
Parents 55 + % in industry or commerce. 60 + % live within 30 miles; 15% live overseas.
Head and staff *Headmaster*: T L Kirkup, appointed in 1996. Educated at Brentwood and Cambridge (English). Previously Housemaster at Christ's Hospital and Head of English at King Edward VI, Southampton. Also organ scholar at Magdalene College (Cambridge); visiting Professor of English, University of North Texas (1994/95); ARCM. *Staff:* 33 full time, 5 part time. Annual turnover 5%. Average age 39.
Exam results In 1995, 78 pupils in upper fifth, 33 in upper sixth. *GCSE:* In 1995, 86% upper fifth gained at least grade C in 8 + subjects; 7% in 5–7 subjects. *A-levels:* 18 upper sixth passed in 4 + subjects; 7 in 3; 5 in 2; and 3 in 1 subject. Average UCAS points 16.5 (including general studies 20.6.).
University and college entrance 95% of 1995 sixth-form leavers went on to a degree course (10% after a gap year); others typically go on to business or HM Forces. Of those going on to university, 5% went to Oxbridge; 15% took courses in medicine, dentistry and veterinary science, 15% in science and engineering, 10% in law, 40% in humanities and social sciences, 10% in art and design, 10% in vocational subjects eg physiotherapy.
Curriculum GCSE and A-levels. 17 subjects offered, including A-level psychology and general studies. 40% take science A-levels; 40% arts/humanities; 20% both. *Vocational:* Work experience available; possibility of RSA or City and Guilds qualifications in IT. *Computing facilities:* Computers in departments and IT laboratories. *Special provision:* Specialist tuition for dyslexia. *Europe:* French and German offered to GCSE, AS and A-level and Institute of Linguists; also non-examined courses in both languages and in Spanish. Regular exchanges to France and Germany, including some extended exchanges, half term to whole academic year. Some European pupils in school. Work placements in Europe for students in gap year.
The arts *Music:* Over 30% of pupils learn a musical instrument; instrumental exams can be taken. Musical groups include orchestra, string group, wind bands, choir. Various regional competition victories; Eskdale/Ryedale festivals. *Drama & dance*: Many pupils involved in school and house/other productions. *Art:* On average, 15 take GCSE, 5 A-level. Design, photography also offered. Several pupils go on to art and design courses.
Sport, community service and clubs *Sport and physical activities:* Compulsory sports: wide range of sports including hockey, netball, rounders, athletics (girls); rugby, hockey, cricket (boys); tennis, cross-country, badminton, gym etc. Optional: squash, riding, swimming, golf available. GCSE sport may be taken. 6 county and 20 + regional champions/representatives. *Community service:* Pupils take bronze, silver and gold Duke of Edinburgh's Award. CCF compulsory for 1 year at age 13. *Clubs and societies:* Up to 30 clubs, eg aerobics, art, chamber music, chess, electronics, expeditions, orienteering and rambling, photography, public speaking, shooting.
Uniform School uniform worn except in the sixth, where smart dress required.
Houses/prefects Competitive houses. Prefects, head boy/girl – appointed by Headmaster following recommendations made by housemasters/mistresses. Head of house and house prefects appointed by housemaster/mistress.
Religion Assemblies compulsory; additional services voluntary; Bible study sessions; Christian Union.

Social Debates, industrial conferences, departmental lectures with local schools. Exchanges to France and Germany; other trips abroad, skiing, junior languages, CCF. Pupils allowed to bring own car/bike/motorbike to school. Meals self-service. School shop. No tobacco allowed; alcohol when approved by house staff.
Discipline Pupils failing to produce homework without satisfactory reason might expect detention; those caught smoking cannabis on the premises could expect expulsion.
Boarding 60% have own study bedroom, 40% share. Single-sex houses of 30. Qualified nurse. Central dining room. Pupils can provide and cook own food. Exeats at discretion of house staff. Visits to the local town allowed.
Alumni association run by Secretary to the OSA, c/o the college.
Former pupils Ian Carmichael (actor); Brian Reading; David Byas; Mark Precious.

• SCARISBRICK HALL

Scarisbrick Hall School, Scarisbrick, Ormskirk, Lancashire L40 9RQ. Tel 01704 880200, Fax 01704 880032

• Pupils 532 • Boys 3–18 (Day) • Girls 3–18 (Day) • Upper sixth 15 • Termly fees £593–£894 (Day) • ISAI • Enquiries/application to the Headmaster

What it's like

Founded in 1964, it was a boys' school until 1971 when girls were admitted. It is now fully co-educational. It lies 3 miles from Ormskirk in a superb private estate of 440 acres comprising gardens, woodland, pastures and a lake. The main building is Scarisbrick Hall itself: a vast listed country mansion designed by Pugin. New buildings include a chapel, classroom blocks and a gym. The school is Christian, non-denominational and there is strong emphasis on evangelical faith and practice. Results are good and nearly all sixth-form leavers proceed to degree courses. Some music, art and drama. Fees are low.

School profile

Pupils Total age range 3–18; 532 day pupils (266 boys, 266 girls). Senior department 11–18, 230 pupils (109 boys, 121 girls). Main entry ages 3, 4, 7, 11 and into sixth. Some are children of former pupils (school not old enough to have many).
Entrance Own exam used. No special skills or religious requirements. Parents not expected to buy textbooks; music tuition £60 extra. Some 5 pa scholarships, 25%–75% of fees.
Head and staff *Headmaster:* David Raynor, in post for 19 years. Educated at King George V School, Southport, and Manchester University (English and General BA). Previously Assistant Master in English, French and Latin at Kingswood. *Staff:* 30 full time, 14 part time. Annual turnover less than 5%. Average age 43.
Exam results In 1995, 37 pupils in upper fifth, 13 in upper sixth. *GCSE:* In 1995, 29 upper fifth gained at least grade C in 8+ subjects; 4 in 5–7 subjects. *A-levels:* 9 upper sixth passed in 4+ subjects; 3 in 3 subjects. Average UCAS points 18.0 (24.3 including general studies).
University and college entrance 92% of 1995 sixth-form leavers went on to a degree course (10% after a gap year); others typically go on to vocational courses or family business.
Curriculum GCSE and A-levels: 15 subjects offered (including A-level general studies). *Vocational:* Work experience available. *Computing facilities:* 20 computers and VDUs, 6 printers. *Europe:* French (compulsory) and German to GCSE and A-level. Regular exchanges to Germany.
The arts (Pupils aged 11 and over) *Music:* Over 30% of pupils learn a musical instrument; instrumental exams can be taken. Musical groups include an orchestra and choir. *Art:* On average, 6–10 take GCSE.
Sport, community service and clubs (Pupils aged 11 and over) *Sport and physical activities:* Compulsory sports: soccer, athletics, cross-country, basketball, netball, swimming. Optional: cricket, tennis, squash, badminton, volleyball. *Clubs and societies:* Up to 10 clubs, eg chess, Christian Fellowship.
Uniform School uniform worn throughout.
Houses/prefects Competitive houses. Prefects, head boy and girl, head of house and house prefects – appointed by staff.

Religion Compulsory school assembly
Social Trips abroad: skiing in the Alps, exchange with German school, visits to France, soccer tour to Malta. Annual sixth-form visit to London. No bikes allowed. School shop selling stationery and uniform. No tobacco/alcohol allowed.
Discipline Corporal punishment (rarely used) for serious misbehaviour. Pupils failing to produce homework once might expect reprimand/warning/work to be done at lunch-time; those caught smoking cannabis on the premises might expect expulsion.

• SEAFORD

Seaford College, Petworth, West Sussex GU28 0NB. Tel 01798 86392, Fax 01798 867606
• Pupils 330 • Boys 11–18 (Day/Board) • Girls 11–18 (Day) • Upper sixth 50 • Termly fees £1975 (Day) £3210 (Board) • SHMIS • Enquiries/application to the Registrar

What it's like

Founded in Seaford in 1884, it moved to West Sussex in 1946 and has a fine site in 320 acres of splendid wooded parkland below the Downs between Petworth and Chichester. Many staff live on the park to produce a community atmosphere. Originally a boys' school, it has accepted girls into the sixth-form since 1993 and is now moving towards full co-education. There are excellent modern facilities including a design technology art centre and a junior house (11+). A generous staff:pupil ratio of about 1:10 enables a good general education to be provided and, from those who stay on into the sixth-form, most go on to university. Specialist tuition for dyslexia (on a one-to-one basis) and for EFL is provided. Religious worship and practice is compulsory in the school chapel which dates to pre-Norman times. The declared aims of the school are to promote all that is best in the ethos and atmosphere in an English independent school while infusing a modern and progressive spirit into all its activities. Good music, technology and art departments. An excellent boys' choir with international reputation. Wide range of sport, games and extra-curricular activities, including a thriving CCF.

School profile

Pupils Age range 11–18; 330 pupils, 318 boys (70 day, 248 boarding), 12 day girls (girls accepted since 1993). Main entry ages 11, 13 and into sixth.
Entrance Common Entrance and own exam used. Most pupils are C of E but not essential. Parents expected to buy textbooks in sixth; compulsory extras £10. About 20 pa scholarships/bursaries (academic, art, choral, music, games, sixth-form and forces), 10% –70% fees.
Parents 15+% in industry/commerce. 30+% live within 30 miles; up to 10% live overseas.
Head and staff *Headmaster:* Charles Hannaford, 6 years in post. Educated at Durham and Cambridge universities (biology and education). Previously Head of Biology and Housemaster at Rendcomb, Housemaster at Millfield and Assistant Master at Sherborne and at Clifton. *Staff:* 32 full time, 15 part time. Annual turnover 4%. Average age 38.
Exam results In 1995, 63 pupils in upper fifth, 36 in upper sixth. *GCSE:* In 1995, 13 in upper fifth gained at least grade C in 8+ subjects; 19 in 5–7; 29 in 1–4 subjects. *A-level:* 14 upper sixth passed in 3 subjects; 13 in 2; 8 in 1 subject. Average UCAS points 11.7.
University and college entrance 80% of 1995 sixth-form leavers went on to a degree course (10% after a gap year); others typically go on to art or technology foundation courses. Of those going on to university, 10% took courses in medicine, dentistry and veterinary science, 40% in science and engineering, 30% in humanities and social sciences, 10% in art and design, 10% in drama, acting or music.
Curriculum GCSE, A-levels and GNVQ Advanced level. 38% upper sixth take science/maths A-levels, 52% arts/humanities, 10% both. *Vocational:* BTEC Advanced level GNVQ in business and finance; also work experience available. *Computing facilities:* 20 networked 486s plus stand-alones in new department; CD-Rom; 12 386s for juniors. *Special provision:* Specialist teaching for both dyslexia (one-to-one basis) and for EFL. *Europe:* French, German and Spanish offered to GCSE and A-level (French compulsory from age 11 to GCSE); French also included in GNVQ course. Visits arranged to France and Germany.
The arts *Music:* 25% learn a musical instrument; instrumental exams may be taken (as

well as GCSE and A-level). Several musical groups including a small orchestra and chapel choir. Several choristers have gone on to National Youth Choir. *Drama and dance:* Annual dramatic production. *Art:* On average, 40 take GCSE, 20 A-level. Design, pottery, textiles, photography, silkscreen printing also offered. All pupils who apply for foundation courses each year have been accepted.

Sport, community service and clubs *Sport and physical activities:* Option system, most do rugby and hockey; cross-country, cricket, athletics, squash, swimming, shooting, tennis. Badminton, basketball, archery, canoeing, fencing, trampolining also available. GCSE, A-level may be taken. County hockey champions U16, U14, 1993; county rugby champions U18 1994, international rugby representative U16; national awards for schools at clay pigeon shooting and athletics. *Community service:* CCF compulsory for 1 year at age 14 (optional thereafter), community service for 1 year at 15. Lifesaving scheme; RLSS bronze, silver and instructors courses. *Clubs and societies:* Up to 15 clubs, eg debating, electronics, natural history, military history, CDT/art workshop, chess, fly fishing, parascending, photography, stock market, creative writing.

Uniform School uniform worn, modified in sixth.

Houses/prefects Competitive houses. School prefects and head pupil appointed by Headmaster; head of house and house prefects by housemaster.

Religion C of E: attendance at religious worship compulsory.

Social Tennis, lacrosse, debates and dances with local girls' school; social visits to sixth-form club. Organised trips abroad. Pupils allowed to bring own bike to school (prefects can bring cars). Meals self-service. School shop. Beer and wine allowed in sixth-form club; no tobacco.

Discipline Pupils failing to produce homework once might expect a reprimand, detention for further failure. Those caught smoking could expect a fine which would be sent to a cancer charity; parents would be informed. Drug taking would result in expulsion.

Boarding All sixth-form have own study bedroom; all in forms 4 and 5 in single or double study bedrooms. Houses of 60+. Resident qualified nurses. Central dining room. Some basic cooking facilities in boarding houses. Half-term and 3 weekend exeats termly. Visits to Chichester allowed. Many parents watch matches.

• SEDBERGH

Sedbergh School, Sedbergh, Cumbria LA10 5HG. Tel 0153 96 20535

• Pupils 350 • Boys 11–18 (Day/Board) • Girls None • Upper sixth 73 • HMC • Termly fees £2715 (Day) £3880 (Board) • Enquiries/application to the Headmaster's Secretary/Registrar

What it's like

Founded in 1525, it is in a small market town with the boarding houses scattered over a big rural site in a setting of the Cumbrian hills which is superb by any standards. Excellent modern facilities and comfortable accommodation. Religious services are essentially Anglican and all attend regular worship in chapel. A strong all-round education is provided and results are consistently good. Nearly all leavers go on to degree courses, including many to Oxbridge. There is a tremendously strong music department (many boys learn an instrument); also very strong in drama and art. It has an outstanding record in sports and games (especially rugby and cricket) with many county representatives. Plentiful activities and much emphasis on outdoor pursuits (eg fell walking, climbing, fishing and caving) for which the environment is ideal. Frequent expeditions into the Lake District. The CCF is strong and compulsory for two years at age 13. A big commitment to local community schemes (numerous charity events) and a remarkable record in the Duke of Edinburgh's Award Scheme.

School profile

Pupils Age range 11–18; 350 boys (10 day, 340 boarding). Main entry ages 11, 13 and into sixth. Approx 10% are children of former pupils.

Entrance Common Entrance and own scholarship entrance exam used. Good all-rounders looked for at entry; specialist scholarships available in music and art. No religious requirements. Parents expected to buy textbooks; maximum extras £150 excluding instrumental tuition. 5 pa assisted places at 11, 5 into sixth. Scholarships/bursaries, up to full fees.

Parents Up to 10% live within 30 miles; up to 10% live overseas.
Head and staff *Headmaster:* Christopher Hirst, in post from 1995. Educated at Merchant Taylors, Northwood, and Cambridge University (history). Previously Headmaster of Kelly College, and Housemaster at Radley. Involved in formulation of HMC policy for training and for sport. *Staff:* 40 full time, 15 part time. Annual turnover 8.5%. Average age 40.
Exam results In 1995, 62 pupils in upper fifth, 73 in upper sixth. *GCSE:* In 1995, 48 upper fifth gained at least grade C in 8+ subjects; 13 in 5–7 subjects. *A-levels:* 14 upper sixth passed in 4+ subjects; 44 in 3; 11 in 2 subjects. Average UCAS points 19.0 (including general studies, 22.2).
University and college entrance 97% of 1995 sixth-form leavers went on to a degree course (10% after a gap year); others typically go direct into employment or retake examinations. Of those going on to university, 12% went to Oxbridge; 7% took courses in medicine, dentistry and veterinary science, 36% in science and engineering, 5% in law, 43% in humanities and social sciences, 5% in art and design.
Curriculum GCSE and A-levels (including CDT technology, and design and realisation). *Vocational:* Work experience available. *Computing facilities:* Nimbus-AX network in lab plus computers in a number of departments and all boarding houses. *Europe:* French and German offered to GCSE and A-level; also French AS-level. Regular exchanges (France, Austria and Germany).
The arts *Music:* Over 40% of pupils learn a musical instrument; instrumental exams can be taken. Some 10 musical groups including orchestras, string and brass groups, CCF marching band, choral society, informal singing groups, rock bands. Winner of Andrew Lloyd Webber Memorial Prize for cello; school band winners of Mary Wakefield Festival. *Drama & dance*: Some pupils are involved in school productions and majority in house/other productions. *Art:* On average, 40 take GCSE, 10 A-level. Design, pottery, photography also offered.
Sport, community service and clubs *Sport and physical activities:* Compulsory sports (up to 16): rugby and cricket. Optional: football, swimming, water polo, tennis, fives, squash, athletics, cross-country, running, hockey, golf, basketball, badminton, table tennis, shooting, archery, yard soccer. *Community service:* Pupils take bronze, silver and gold Duke of Edinburgh's Award. CCF compulsory for 2 years at age 13. Community service optional for 1 year at age 16. *Clubs and societies:* Up to 15 clubs, eg science, music, literary, history, astronomy, debating.
Uniform School uniform worn throughout the school, except at weekends.
Houses/prefects Competitive houses. Prefects, head boy and head of house and house prefects – appointed by the Headmaster or housemaster.
Religion Religious worship compulsory. Chapel every Sunday, assembly each day. House prayers in evening. Confirmation services for Church of England, Church of Scotland and Roman Catholics.
Social Organised local events with girls schools for all age groups: activities (sailing, climbing etc), debates, theatre, music, dances, roller skating, dinners, English/history lectures. Many organised trips, recently include expedition to Arctic, Sahara, Iceland; skiing to France and Italy; cricket to Holland, West Indies; rugby to Canada, Portugal; Chapel choir to Belgium and Germany. Exchanges with schools in Germany (sixth-form), France and Austria (3 weeks, all age groups). Some pupils allowed to bring own bike to school. Meals formal, in houses. School shops (games equipment, books, tuck). No tobacco allowed; upper sixth bar.
Discipline Pupils failing to produce homework once might expect a repeat on special paper – signed before and after by housemaster; those caught smoking cannabis on the premises could expect expulsion.
Boarding All sixth-form have own study bedroom, a few fifth formers share; only third form are in dormitories of 6+. Houses of approximately 55, same as competitive houses. Resident qualified nurse and full-time school doctor. One half-term break per term and voluntary exeats (Sat. night) in the Michaelmas and Lent terms. Visits to the local town allowed daily.
Alumni association is run by The Secretary, The Old Sedberghian Club, Malim Lodge, Sedbergh School, Sedbergh, Cumbria LA10 5RY.

• SEVENOAKS

Sevenoaks School, Sevenoaks, Kent TN13 1HU. Tel 01732 455133, Fax 01732 456143

• Pupils 939 • Boys 11–18 (Day/Board) • Girls 11–18 (Day/Board) • Upper sixth 195 • Termly fees £2358 (Day) £3873 (Board) • HMC • Enquiries/application to the Registrar

What it's like

Founded in 1432 by Sir William Sevenoke, Mayor of London and friend of Henry V, by way of thank offering for his share in the victory at Agincourt. It is one of the three oldest lay foundations in England. The school has a compact and attractive 100-acre campus, adjoining Knole Park on the edge of town. The first building of note was designed by the Earl of Burlington in 1718 (now used as a boarding house) and there have been numerous 20th-century additions. These include international houses for sixth-formers, a purpose-built theatre and music centre, and a sports hall and complex of covered tennis courts. The school is interdenominational and, since 1984, fully co-educational. The staff:pupil ratio is about 1:10 and it consistently gets very good results; almost all sixth-formers go on to degree courses, including many to Oxbridge. The school is one of the very few offering the International Baccalaureate (IB), and 10% of parents live overseas. A large number of languages are offered and an exceptionally high proportion of pupils takes GCSE in more than one. The music, drama and art departments are all tremendously strong and active, and the school runs a local arts festival. High standards are attained in a wide variety of sport and games, particularly in rugby, sailing, shooting and tennis, with many representatives at county and national level each year. A wide range of extra-curricular activities and a large and flourishing CCF contingent. Sevenoaks was one of the pioneers of school-based community services in Britain; there is now a federal unit comprising over 30 local schools with 600 volunteers, 250 of these from Sevenoaks. The school also has a remarkable record in the Duke of Edinburgh's Award Scheme.

School profile

Pupils Age range 11–18; 939 pupils (512 boys, 427 girls), 619 day and 320 boarders. Main entry ages 11, 13 and into sixth. *State school entry:* 30% main intakes, plus 18% to sixth.

Entrance Common Entrance at 13; own exam at 11 and 13; interview at sixth-form level. All special skills and all faiths welcomed. Parents have an option on the purchase of textbooks. 10 pa assisted places. Over 50 pa scholarships and bursaries, 50% fees to £1400; special awards for art, music, sport, and all round ability.

Parents 50+% in industry or commerce. 65% live within 30 miles; 10+% live overseas.

Head and staff *Headmaster:* T R Cookson, appointed 1996. Educated at Winchester and Oxford (English literature). Previously Headmaster of King Edward VI , Southampton, Housemaster and Head of English at Winchester. Publications: John Keats (Edward Arnold); Bernard Shaw (Edward Arnold). *Staff:* 90 full time, 40 part time. Annual turnover 5%. Average age under 40.

Exam results In 1995, 142 pupils in upper fifth, 195 in upper sixth. *GCSE:* In 1995, 137 upper fifth gained at least grade C in 8+ subjects, 4 in 5–7 subjects. *A levels and IB*: (35% of the sixth-form took the IB instead of A levels.) 37% A-level candidates passed in 4+ subjects; 54% in 3; 8% in 2; and 1% in 1 subject. Average UCAS points 22.9.

University and college entrance 98% of 1995 sixth-form leavers went on to a degree course (25% after a gap year); others typically go on to employment. Of those going on to university, 14% went to Oxbridge; 7% took courses in medicine, dentistry and veterinary science, 29% in science and engineering, 4% in law, 54% in humanities and social sciences, 4% in art and design, 1% combined courses eg PPE.

Curriculum GCSE, A-levels, International Baccalaureate (IB). 26 subjects offered (including a wide range of languages eg Japanese). *Computing facilities:* Computing department with some 40 computers on two networks and PDP 11/34A miniframe computer. IBM compatible hardware/software allows students to investigate business uses as well as educational software. Many other departments have own computers, some have links to the computing department, with access to its large database. Courses range from information technology GCSE to programming for beginners; desktop publishing to information systems; business studies and computing to electronic painting. Computing facilities available for use by the Computing Society (280 members) 12 hours a day and during holidays. *Special provision:* Some special provisions made. *Europe:* French, German and Spanish offered to GCSE, IB and A-level. Dutch, Italian, Norwegian, Russian and Swedish to IB. Over 75% take GCSE in more than 1 European language. Regular exchanges. Some 80 overseas pupils, predominantly European. Participated in Model United Nations at the Hague and in Dublin. Regular tours (eg sport, drama) talks from MEPs, embassy officials etc.

The arts *Music:* 40% of pupils learn a musical instrument; instrumental exams can be taken. Some 23 musical groups including 4 choirs, 3 orchestras, 2 wind bands, jazz group, percussion group, numerous chamber groups, wind quintet, string ensembles, recorder, saxophone, guitar groups. Pupils study GCSE, A-level and IB in music. *Drama & dance*: Both offered. GCSE and IB drama, Guildhall and LAMDA may be taken. Majority of pupils are involved in school/house productions (12 a year). Tours of Europe. Drama club for actors and technicians. *Art:* On average, 20 take GCSE and 20 A-level or IB; design, sculpture, stained glass, ceramics, textiles, printmaking, photography and video also offered.

Sport, community service and clubs *Sport and physical activities:* Compulsory sports: hockey, netball, tennis, athletics, rounders (girls); rugby, soccer, athletics, cricket (boys). Optional: racquet sports, cricket (girls), cross-country, rowing, sailing, shooting, swimming. Sixth form only: riding, golf, weight training, aerobics. Hockey, girls, Kent U15 champions 1992; rugby, 2 England XV member 1996; tennis, public schools champions; shooting, 3 Athelings 1995; sailing, won UK nationals 1991–95, international/worlds 1991, 1992 and 1994. *Community service:* Pupils take bronze, silver and gold Duke of Edinburgh's Award. CCF compulsory at age 14/15 then optional; includes sub-aqua training, rock climbing, abseiling, shooting, canoeing, sailing. Community service compulsory at age 14/15 then optional. *Clubs and societies:* Up to 30 clubs, eg needlework, photography, MUN, debating, war games, art, poetry, film.

Uniform School uniform worn throughout.

Houses/prefects Houses/pastoral groups in upper, middle and junior divisions. Prefects, head boy/girl, head of house and house prefects – appointed by Headmaster. School Council.

Religion Compulsory assemblies, some with religious content. Services largely voluntary including communion services; annual confirmation 25–35. Pupils' depth of spirituality more remarkable than their enthusiasm for attending services; spirituality is what the school seeks to develop.

Social Occasional ventures with other schools eg Young Enterprise Scheme. Exchanges with variety of schools in UK, France, Germany and Spain. Pupils allowed to bring own car/bike/motorbike to school. Meals self-service. School shops for tuck, stationery, second-hand clothes. No tobacco/alcohol allowed.

Discipline Pupils failing to produce homework once might expect verbal reprimand; very strict drug punishment.

Boarding 20% have own study bedroom, 70% share, 5% are in dormitories of 6+. Single-sex houses of approximately 50. Separate, co-educational house of 18 for 11–12 year olds. Central dining room. Pupils can provide and cook own food. Flexible weekend policy for exeats but houses close at half term. Visits to local town allowed.

Alumni association run by Dr R Hackett, c/o the school.

• SHEFFIELD HIGH

Sheffield High School, 10 Rutland Park, Sheffield S10 2PE. Tel 0114 266 0324

• Pupils 797 • Boys None • Girls 4–18 (Day) • Upper sixth 62 • Termly fees £976–£1328 (Day) • GSA, GPDST • Enquiries/application to the Headmistress

What it's like

Founded in 1878, it moved in 1884 to its present premises in spacious grounds in the pleasant suburb of Broomhill. The Junior school at Melbourne House is combined. Many additions have been made to the original Victorian buildings and facilities are first-rate. It provides a sound general education and results are very good. Most sixth-form leavers go on to degree courses each year, many to Oxbridge. A good range of sports, games and activities and a full programme of music, drama and art. A promising record in the Duke of Edinburgh's Award Scheme and substantial commitment to local community services.

School profile

Pupils Total age range 4–18; 797 day girls. Senior department 11–18, 545 girls. Main entry ages 4, 11 and into sixth. Approx 40% are children of former pupils.

Entrance Own entrance exam used. No special skills or religious requirements. Parents not expected to buy textbooks; music tuition extra. 21 pa assisted places. Scholarships and bursaries.

Head and staff *Headmistress:* Mrs Margaret Houston, 6 years in post. Educated at St Hilda's, Whitby, and Leeds University (English). Previously Deputy Head i/c curriculum and senior school at Harrogate Grammar School. *Staff:* 50 full time, 10 part time. Annual turnover 2%. Average age 41.

Exam results In 1995, 66 pupils in upper fifth, 68 in upper sixth. *GCSE:* In 1995, 100% upper fifth gained at least grade C in 5+ subjects. *A-levels:* 52 upper sixth passed in 4+ subjects; 11 in 3; 4 in 2; 1 in 1 subject. Average UCAS points 22.9 (29 with general studies).

University and college entrance 93% of 1995 sixth-form leavers went on to a degree course (6% after a gap year), 9% to Oxbridge. 13% took courses in medicine, dentistry and veterinary science, 14% in science and engineering, 9% in law, 54% in humanities and social sciences, 6% in art and design, 4% in other vocational subjects.

Curriculum GCSE and A-levels. Greek, geology, IT offered to GCSE and A-level. On average, 50% take science/engineering A-levels; 40% take arts and humanities; 10% a mixture. *Vocational:* Work experience compulsory at age 16 and 17. RSA level 1 and 2 CLAIT available. *Computing facilities:* Research machine network. 2 IT laboratories. *Europe:* French, Russian, German and Spanish offered to GCSE, and A-level. 80% take GCSE in more than 1 language. Regular exchanges (to France and Germany). European Society, industrial seminars in Paris.

The arts (Pupils aged 11 and over) *Music:* Almost all pupils learn a musical instrument; instrumental exams can be taken. Some 9 musical groups including wind band, chamber orchestra, school orchestra, choirs, madrigal groups. 2 members of National Youth Orchestra. *Drama & dance*: Drama offered. Poetry Society and LAMDA exams may be taken. Some pupils are involved in school productions and all in house/other productions. *Art:* On average, 16 take GCSE, 6 A-level. Design, pottery and textiles also offered.

Sport, community service and clubs (Pupils aged 11 and over) *Sport and physical activities:* Compulsory sports: hockey, netball, tennis, athletics. Optional: squash, volleyball, table tennis. Sixth form only: outdoor activities. GCSE sport may be taken. 1 national representative at netball; national athletics championship, 1 girl 5th; county finalists and champions in hockey, netball, tennis; regional finalists in tennis. *Community service:* Pupils take bronze, silver and gold Duke of Edinburgh's Award. CCF compulsory for 1 year at age 17, community service at age 18. *Clubs and societies:* Up to 30 clubs, eg chess, debating, rock and fossil, physics, Christian Union.

Uniform School uniform worn except in the sixth.

Houses/prefects Competitive houses. Prefects, head girl and head of house – elected by sixth-form and staff. School Council.

Religion Compulsory religious assembly on four mornings a week.

Social Games fixtures with local schools, debating with schools, joint music and drama with local boys' independent school. Skiing trips, exchanges and visits to France, Germany and Russia. Educational cruises. Pupils allowed to bring own car/bike/motorbike to school. School tuck shop. No tobacco/alcohol allowed.

Discipline Pupils failing to produce homework once might expect detention; those caught smoking cannabis on the premises could expect exclusion.

Former pupils Margaret Drabble; Baroness Oppenheimer; A S Byatt; Angela Knight MP.

• SHERBORNE (Boys)

Sherborne School, Dorset DT9 3AP. Tel 01935 812249, Fax 01935 816628
• Pupils 610 • Boys 13–18 (Day/Board) • Girls None • Upper sixth 135 • Termly fees £3190 (Day) £4185 (Board) • HMC • Enquiries/application to the Registrar (tel 01935 813242, fax 01935 817511)

What it's like

Its origins date back to the 8th century when some kind of school at Sherborne was begun by St Aldhelm and was refounded by Edward VI in 1550. It was linked with the Benedictine Abbey. The library, chapel and Headmaster's block were once Abbey buildings and the whole school forms an architectural complex which is delightful and lies in the centre of one of the most attractive country towns in England. Some of the houses are dispersed in the town (but all are within 5 minutes' walk of the main buildings) and there is a close town and gown relationship. There have been numerous modern extensions and facilities are excellent (including outstandingly good libraries). It is a happy school with a strong pastoral care/tutorial system built round a traditional boarding house structure. Emphasis on religious practice in the Anglican tradition is considerable and some services are compulsory. There is a wide range of voluntary community and other services. Academic standards are high and results very good. Almost all leavers go on to degree courses each year, including to Oxbridge. A staff:pupil ratio of 1:8. There is a very strong tradition in music (about half the school is involved) and a wide variety of dramatic activity. A good range of sports and games is available and standards are high (a lot of representatives at county and national level). There is an unusually large range of extra-curricular activities. The CCF is large (about 200). Boys also help with the running of a 25-acre nature reserve near the town. There is a field centre on Exmoor.

School profile

Pupils Age range 13–18; 610 boys, 35 day, 575 boarding. Main entry ages 13; 25 a year into sixth. Approx 10% are children of former pupils.
Entrance Common Entrance and own exam used. No special skills or religious requirements. Few extras. 25 pa scholarships/exhibitions 20%–50% fees (may be increased in case of financial need).
Parents 15+% in the armed services; 15+% are doctors, lawyers etc. 30+% live within 30 miles; up to 10% live overseas.
Head and staff *Headmaster:* P H Lapping, in post for 8 years. Educated at St John's College, Johannesburg, and at the universities of Natal and Oxford (history and PPE). Previously Headmaster at Shiplake, Housemaster and Head of History at Loretto and Assistant Master at Reed's. *Staff:* 78 full time, 17 part time (mainly music). Annual turnover 5%. Average age 39.
Exam results In 1995, 127 pupils in upper fifth, 123 in upper sixth. *GCSE:* In 1995, 95% of upper fifth gained at least grade C in 8+ subjects; 5% in 5–7 subjects. *A-levels:* 5% upper sixth passed in 4+ subjects; 88% in 3; and 7% in 2 subjects. Average UCAS points 22.5.
University and college entrance 98% of 1995 sixth-form leavers went on to a degree course (25% after a gap year), 10% to Oxbridge; 10% took courses in medicine, dentistry and veterinary science, 29% in science and engineering, 5% in law, 40% in humanities and social sciences, 3% in art and design, 11% in vocational subjects eg business, hotel management.
Curriculum GCSE and A-levels. General studies taught (with Sherborne Girls) but A-level not taken. 25% take science A-levels; 40% arts/humanities; 35% both. *Vocational:* Work shadowing available. *Computing facilities:* 24 Acorn Archimedes for class and individual use. 12 computers in technical activity centre for CAD. Computers in most departments. *Europe:* French, German and Spanish offered to GCSE and A-level; continuation language courses available in sixth-form. Regular exchanges for lower sixth linguists to France, Germany, or Spain for half-term. European studies offered as part of general studies.
The arts *Music:* Over 50% of pupils learn a musical instrument; instrumental exams can be taken. Some 12 regular musical groups including orchestras, choirs, concert band, swing band, jazz band, guitar orchestra, several chamber music groups. Regular house concerts; others periodically. Members in National Youth Orchestra, County Youth

Orchestra; organ and choral awards to Cambridge; success with musical diplomas such as ARCO, ARCM, LRAM; winners of national composition prize; finalist in BBC Young Musician of the Year competition. *Drama & dance*: Drama offered and GCSE may be taken. Some pupils are involved in school productions and majority in house/other productions. About 200 involved in all aspects of school and house drama productions in recent years. 3 accepted by National Youth theatre. *Art:* On average, 20 take GCSE, 12 A-level. Design and photography also offered. 6 places in recent years to Ruskin College, Oxford.

Sport, community service and clubs *Sport and physical activities:* Rugby, hockey, soccer, squash, fives, athletics, basketball, cross-country, fencing, golf, swimming, tennis, badminton: National level, 4–8 pupils pa; county level, 30–40 pa, rugby, hockey, cricket, athletics, cross-country, sailing. *Community service:* Pupils take Duke of Edinburgh's Award. CCF and community service optional. *Clubs and societies:* Over 30 clubs, eg all academic fields, debating, film, typing, chess, bridge, instrument making, Christian Forum, ornithology, Young Enterprise, sea-angling.

Uniform School uniform worn, modified in sixth.

Houses/prefects Nine competitive houses. Prefects, head boy, head of house and house prefects – appointed by Headmaster.

Religion Compulsory Sunday service and chapel twice-weekly. Wide range of voluntary communion and other services.

Social Regular concerts, debates, dances with Sherborne (Girls) and St Antony's-Leweston. Pupils allowed to bring own bike to school. Meals self-service. School shop sells uniform and sports kit. No tobacco/alcohol allowed.

Discipline Pupils failing to produce homework once might expect repetition of similar exercise; failing that, they would do a Saturday evening detention. Those caught smoking cannabis on the premises could expect expulsion.

Boarding 25% have own study bedroom, 50% share; 25% are in dormitories of 6+. Houses, of approximately 70. Resident qualified sanatorium sister; local medical practitioner. Central dining room. Pupils can provide and cook light snacks and coffee/tea in houses. 2 weekend exeats termly. Visits to local town allowed.

Alumni association run by J R Tozer, Hon Sec Old Shirburnian Society, c/o the school.

Former pupils David Sheppard (Bishop of Liverpool); Christopher Chataway MP; Jeremy Irons; Nigel Dempster; Generals Sir Stewart Pringle and Sir Martin Garrod (both Commandants General Royal Marines); Gen Sir John Wilsey (GOC N. Ireland); Maj General Patrick Cordingley (7 Armoured Brigade in the Gulf); Michael McCrum (Former Vice Chancellor, Cambridge); Jonathan Powell (Director, BBC1); John Le Carre; Richard Eyre (Director of National Theatre); Sir Michael Hopkins (architect); the King of Swaziland.

• SHERBORNE (Girls)

Sherborne School for Girls, Sherborne, Dorset DT9 3QN. Tel 01935 812245, Fax 01935 814973 • Pupils 423 • Boys None • Girls 11–18 (Day/Board) • Upper sixth 80 • Termly fees £2650 (Day) £3850 (Board) • GSA, BSA • Enquiries/application to the Headmistress

What it's like

Founded in 1899, it is on a 40 -acre site on a hill overlooking open country and on the edge of the delightful town of Sherborne. Pleasant buildings and first-class accommodation. A C of E foundation, its services are compulsory. A distinguished and civilised establishment with an exceptional staff:pupil ratio of 1:7. Academic standards are high and results very good; all leavers go on to degree courses, including many to Oxbridge. A tremendously strong music department; good drama and art. First-rate games facilities and a high standard in sports and games (a very large number of representatives at county level). Wide range of societies, clubs etc catering for most needs. Big commitment to local community schemes and an impressive record in the Duke of Edinburgh's Award Scheme. There is frequent co-operation with Sherborne's Boys' School.

School profile

Pupils Age range 11–18; 423 girls (18 day, 405 boarding). Main entry ages 11, 12, 13 and into sixth. Approx 7% are children of former pupils.

Entrance Common Entrance and scholarship exams used. No special skills or religious requirements but school is C of E. Parents not expected to buy textbooks; average extras £170 per term. 11 pa scholarships/exhibitions.

Parents 15+% in the armed services; 15+% are doctors, lawyers, etc. 10+% live within 30 miles; up to 10% live overseas.

Head and staff *Headmistress:* Miss June Taylor, in post for 11 years. Educated at Grittleton House, at Sherborne and at universities of Sussex and Oxford (mathematics and education). Previously Senior Housemistress at Sherborne (Girls). Member of Common Entrance Board and GSA Council. *Staff:* 61 full time, 10 part time. Annual turnover 5%. Average age 43.

Exam results On average, 90 in upper fifth, 80 in upper sixth. *GCSE:* On average, 85 upper fifth gain at least grade C in 8+ subjects. *A-levels:* 4 upper sixth pass in 4 subjects; 71 in 3; 5 in 2 subjects. Average UCAS points 23.2.

University and college entrance All 1995 sixth-form leavers went on to a degree course (35% after a gap year), 12% to Oxbridge. 8% took courses in medicine, dentistry and veterinary science, 15% in science and engineering, 5% in law, 57% in humanities and social sciences, 10% in art and design, 5% in vocational subjects eg physiotherapy, speech science, education.

Curriculum GCSE and A-levels: 25 subjects offered, including history of art and social biology at A-level. 10% take science A-levels; 54% arts/social sciences; 35% a mixture. *Vocational:* Work experience sometimes available; RSA course in CLAIT for sixth-form. *Computing facilities:* Major upgrading in progress. Currently 36 Archimedes (RISC processors) plus other machines, scanners, printers in 2 central rooms; other Archimedes and multimedia PCs in departments; computers in some boarding houses. *Special provision:* for mild dyslexia. *Europe:* French, German and Spanish offered to GCSE and A-level (over 75% take GCSE in more than one); Italian and Russian A-level; sixth-form continuation languages in French, German, Spanish and Russian. Regular exchanges (to France, Russia and Germany). Some European pupils in school.

The arts *Music:* Over 66% pupils learn a musical instrument; GCSE, AS- and A-level may be taken. Musical groups include orchestras, choirs, madrigal society, swing band, jazz groups and many ensembles. Pupils in National Youth Orchestra and Dorset County Youth Orchestras. Madrigal Society tours; public concerts in eg Sherborne Abbey; joint musical activity with Sherborne (boys) and St Antony's-Leweston; involved in eg Sherborne Musical Society annual oratorio and Dorset Opera. *Drama & dance*: Drama offered and Guildhall exams may be taken. Many pupils are involved in school productions (including Sherborne Boys) and some in house/other productions. 1 member of National Youth Theatre. *Art:* On average, 25 take GCSE, 7 AS-level, 6 A-level. Design, pottery, textiles, photography, printmaking also offered. Girls have gone on to Ruskin and other art colleges.

Sport, community service and clubs *Sport and physical activities:* Compulsory sports: lacrosse, hockey, tennis, athletics, swimming. Optional: volleyball, basketball, badminton, squash, aerobics, indoor hockey, trampolining, ballroom and Scottish dancing, fencing, canoeing, cricket, fencing, lifesaving, squash awards may be taken. Hockey, county champions U16, district winners 1st XI; lacrosse, county schools winners 1st XII, West Rally winners 1st XII, U15, runners-up U14, 8 county players, junior regional players; cross-country junior team winners. *Community service:* Pupils take bronze, silver and gold Duke of Edinburgh's Award. Community service optional. *Clubs and societies:* Up to 15 clubs, eg debating, drama, gym, photography, music.

Uniform School uniform worn except in the sixth.

Houses/prefects Competitive houses. Head girl and vice heads appointed by Head; head of house and house prefects appointed by housemistresses. Elected upper sixth committee for administration.

Religion Religious worship compulsory.

Social Joint orchestra, joint drama, languages club (with Sherborne and St Antony's-Leweston), youth social services with local schools. Trips abroad and exchange systems with schools abroad. Pupils allowed to bring own bike to school. Meals formal; self-service in upper sixth house. No tobacco/alcohol allowed.

Discipline Pupils failing to produce homework once might expect to do it in own time; those caught smoking cannabis on the premises could expect expulsion.

Boarding Upper sixth have own study bedrooms; majority of remainder in cubicles in

dormitories of 6–10. Houses of some 50 pupils of all ages, plus upper sixth house. Resident qualified nurse and visiting doctor. 1- or 2-night exeat per term and half-term. Visits to local town allowed.
Alumni association run by Mrs D Prain, The Grange, Tilford, near Farnham, Surrey, GU10 2EB.
Former pupils Dame Diana Reader Harris; Maria Aitken, Emma Kirkby.

• SHERRARDSWOOD

Sherrardswood School, Lockleys, Welwyn, Hertfordshire AL6 0BJ. Tel 01438 714282, Fax 01438 840616

• Pupils 365 • Boys 3–18 (Day/Board/Weekly) • Girls 3–18 (Day/Board/Weekly) • Upper sixth 6 • Termly fees £1479 (Day) £2795 (Board/Weekly) • ISAI • Enquiries/application to the Headmaster

What it's like

Founded in 1928 as a co-educational school. The main building is a fine 18th-century house in 25 acres of delightful parkland shared by the junior school and the boarders. A new senior department complex opened on the same site in 1995. Accommodation is comfortable and modern facilities plentiful. A sound general education is provided. From a small sixth-form, most go on to degree courses. Music, art and drama are on the curriculum. A good range of sport, games and activities.

School profile

Pupils Total age range 3–18; 365 pupils, 333 day (180 boys, 153 girls), 32 boarding (17 boys, 15 girls). Senior department 11–18, 123 pupils (79 boys, 44 girls). Main entry ages 4, 11 and into sixth. *State school entry:* 10% senior intakes.
Entrance Parents expected to buy textbooks for sixth-formers. 2 pa scholarships/bursaries, up to one-third fees.
Head and staff *Headmaster:* M C Lloyd, 3 years in post. Previously Director of School at Mostyn House School, South Wirral, and Senior School co-ordinator at Abbeygate College. *Staff:* 27 full time, 6 part time.
Exam results In 1995, 24 pupils in upper fifth, 6 in upper sixth. *GCSE:* In 1995, 16% upper fifth gained at least grade C in 8+ subjects; 77% gained 5–7 subjects. *A-levels:* 3 upper sixth passed in 3 subjects; 2 in 2; 1 in 1 subject. Average UCAS points 10.5.
University and college entrance From a small sixth-form, 80% go on to a degree course (5% after a gap year); others typically go on to vocational courses. Of those going on to university, 5% took courses in medicine, dentistry and veterinary science, 40% in science and engineering, 5% in law, 25% in humanities and social sciences, 15% in art and design, 10% other vocational subjects.
Curriculum GCSE and A-levels, 15 subjects offered; Certificate of Further Studies courses also offered in sixth-form. 30% take science A-levels; 60% arts/humanities; 10% both. *Vocational:* Work experience available; RSA level 1 and 2 typing offered. *Computing facilities:* classics ICL, IBM. *Special provision:* Provision for dyslexics. Small amount of EFL. *Europe:* French and German offered to GCSE, AS and A-level; at least one must be taken to upper fifth.
The arts (Pupils aged 11 and over) *Music:* 20% of pupils learn a musical instrument; instrumental exams can be taken. Some musical groups including 2 choirs. *Drama & dance*: Some pupils are involved in school productions. *Art:* On average, 14 take GCSE, 2 A-level. Design, pottery, textiles, photography also offered.
Sport, community service and clubs (Pupils aged 11 and over) *Sport and physical activities:* Compulsory sports: hockey, netball, football, cross-country, athletics, tennis, cricket, swimming. Optional: basketball, badminton, table tennis, volleyball. National, regional ISAI competition success in cross-country, swimming, athletics. *Clubs and societies:* Up to 15 clubs, eg sports, chess, drama, bridge, computing.
Uniform School uniform worn except in the sixth.
Houses/prefects Competitive houses. Prefects, head boy/girl, head of house and house prefects – appointed by the Headmaster. School Council.
Social Pupils allowed to bring own car/bicycle/motorbike to school.

• SHIPLAKE

Shiplake College, Henley-on-Thames, Oxfordshire RG9 4BW. Tel 01734 402455

• Pupils 310 • Boys 13–18 (Day/Board) • Girls None • Upper sixth 55 • Termly fees £2510 (Day) £3725 (Board) • SHMIS • Enquiries/application to the Headmaster

What it's like

Founded in 1959, it has a very attractive site on the north bank of the Thames, 2½ miles upstream from Henley. It is based on the historic Shiplake Court, around which first-rate facilities and comfortable accommodation have been created. C of E services take place in the adjoining 12th-century village church. There is a broad academic mix of pupils of whom about half proceed to degree courses. Strong in art, public speaking, debating, drama and music. Very good record in sports (especially rowing and squash), with many representatives at national and county level. Sport/games is compulsory four afternoons a week; CCF for 3 years. Emphasis on outdoor pursuits and adventure training (expeditions to Himalayas, Kenya and the Alps). About 20 minor extra-curricular activities available. Considerable participation in local community schemes and an impressive record in the Duke of Edinburgh's Award Scheme.

School profile

Pupils Age range 13–18; 310 boys, 70 day, 240 boarding. Main entry ages 13 and into sixth. *State school entry:* 5% main intake (such pupils welcomed).

Entrance Common Entrance and own exam used. C of E school but other denominations and religions welcomed. Parents not expected to buy textbooks; maximum extras £250 pa. Some scholarships (academic and sports) available. Service bursaries

Parents 15+% in industry or commerce. 30+% live within 30 miles, up to 12% live overseas.

Head and staff *Headmaster:* N H Bevan, 8 years in post. Educated at Shrewsbury and at Oxford and Cambridge universities (geography and education). Previously Housemaster at Shrewsbury and Master i/c Rowing at Westminster. Also Chairman-elect of SHMIS. *Staff:* 36 full time, 4 part time. Annual turnover 7%. Average age 34.

Exam results In 1995, 64 pupils in fifth, 50 in upper sixth. *GCSE:* In 1995, 52 fifth gained at least grade C in 5+ subjects; and 12 in 1–4 subjects. *A-levels:* 9 upper sixth passed in 3+ subjects; 18 in 2; and 16 in 1 subject. Average UCAS points 13.0.

University and college entrance 51% of 1995 sixth-form leavers went on to a degree course; others typically go on to non-degree courses (HND, business studies, agriculture, A-level retakes) or straight into careers. Of those going on to university, 34% took courses in science and engineering, 44% in humanities and social sciences, 22% in art and design.

Curriculum GCSE and A-levels: 26 subjects offered. 25% take science A-levels; 35% arts/humanities; 40% both. *Vocational:* Work experience available. *Computing facilities:* Networked computer room – 17 RM Nimbus 486 (multi-media); similar machines in houses. *Special provision:* up to 24 dyslexic pupils accepted each year; specialist tuition available (free of charge) within remedial English department (Amstrads used). *Europe:* French and Spanish offered to GCSE, AS and A-level; also German GCSE and as a non-examined subject.

The arts *Music:* Many pupils learn a musical instrument; instrumental exams can be taken. Some musical groups band, wind, string, choral, orchestra, Glee Club etc. *Drama & dance*: Drama offered. At least 4 major productions a year, involving over half the school. *Art:* On average, 16 take GCSE, 8 A-level. Art and ceramics popular.

Sport, community service and clubs *Sport and physical activities:* Sports include rowing, rugby, hockey, cricket, tennis, squash, sailing, cross-country, athletics, soccer, badminton, basketball. 4–8 county rugby players each year. *Community service:* Pupils take silver and gold Duke of Edinburgh's Award. CCF compulsory for 3 years at age 14, optional in upper sixth. Community service compulsory for 1 year at age 13/14, optional thereafter. *Clubs and societies:* Clubs include computer, tree-climbing, mountaineering, Christian Forum and sixth-form society.

Uniform School uniform worn throughout.

Houses/prefects Competitive houses. Prefects, head boy, head of house and house prefects – appointed by housemasters and Headmaster.

Religion Regular chapel services.

Social Conferences, composite crews for national/international reg... drama and dances with local schools. Annual expeditions, art and French ... trip to Paris, skiing trip to Alps. 40% of pupils go on trip or expedition in holidays... self-service. School shop. No tobacco allowed; beer allowed in Junior Common Roo... for boys over 17 with parents' permission.
Discipline Pupils failing to produce homework once might expect to repeat it; failure to live up to acceptable standards results in withdrawal of privileges; those caught smoking cannabis on the premises can expect expulsion.
Boarding 20% have own study bedroom, 30% share with 1 or 2; 10% are in dormitories of 6+. Houses of 65, same as competitive houses. Resident qualified nurse. Central dining room. Minimum of 2 exeat weekends each term. Occasional visits to local town allowed, weekly for seniors.
Alumni association run by R A Esau, c/o the college.

• SHREWSBURY

The Schools, Shrewsbury, Shropshire SY3 7BA. Tel 01743 344537, Fax 01743 243107
• Pupils 680 • Boys 13–18 (Day/Board) • Girls None • Upper sixth 136 • Termly fees £2900 (Day) £4125 (Board) • HMC • Enquiries/application to the Headmaster

What it's like

Founded in 1552 by charter of Edward VI, it occupies a splendid site of 105 acres on a loop of the Severn on a high bluff overlooking the old town of Shrewsbury. Its buildings, ancient and modern, are very fine indeed and include a Jacobean library. This is one of the very few important scholarly libraries in a public school and possesses valuable medieval manuscripts and the entire collection of books owned by the school in Stuart times. It is a local and national school with about 50 boys are from overseas. A sixth-form annexe caters for a few senior boys where the bar and common room function as a club. New buildings include a new gym, a computer room and the purpose-built Ashton theatre. Religious worship is in the Anglican tradition and all boys are expected to attend one mid-week service and one Sunday service. A large staff allows a staff:pupil ratio of about 1:9. Academic standards are high and results excellent. Nearly all sixth-form leavers go on to degree courses, including Oxbridge. There is a very strong tradition in music. Tuition in every orchestral instrument is available. There are 2 orchestras, a wind band, jazz band, chapel choir, concert choir and madrigal choir. Concerts are frequent and there is regular contact with local musical groups. The art school and workshops are very well equipped and many activities are catered for. Frequent dramatic productions are presented by the school and by individual houses. Facilities for sports and games are first rate and high standards are achieved. Many societies and clubs provide for most extra-curricular needs. Clubs include printing, electronics and canoe-building. Open-air activities such as hill-walking and mountaineering are encouraged. There is a flourishing CCF contingent.

School profile

Pupils Age range 13–18; 700 boys (140 day, 560 boarding). Main entry ages 13 and into sixth. *State school entry:* mainly scholars.
Entrance Common Entrance and own exam used. Scholarships include 17 pa academic, 4 pa music, 1 art and 4 pa sixth-form scholarships. Also 1–2 junior scholarships for boys under 11, attending state schools; covers 2–3 years at prep school (places at Packwood Haugh, Kingsland Grange, Prestfelde and Yarlet Hall schools) as well as the 5 years at Shrewsbury.
Head and staff *Headmaster:* Ted Maidment, in post for 8 years. Educated at Pocklington and Cambridge. Previously Headmaster and Housemaster at Ellesmere and Assistant Master at Lancing. *Staff:* 76 full time.
Exam results In 1995, 138 in fifth, 126 in upper sixth. Average sixth-former passes 3 subjects at A-level. Average UCAS points 25.6.
Curriculum GCSE and A-levels, 21 subjects offered. *Europe:* French and German offered to GCSE and A-level. All sixth-formers continue with a modern language. Full-time European awareness officer – promotes cross-curricular projects and fosters links and exchanges.
The arts *Music:* Some 25% pupils learn a musical instrument. Musical groups include

...tras, jazz band, big band and various ensembles. *Drama & dance*: GCSE ... drama may be taken. Most pupils involved in school/house productions. ... pupils have been accepted for drama college. *Art:* On average, 48 take GCSE, 9 A-level. Printmaking, photography, ceramics and history of art also offered. Regular entrants to art college.

Sport, community service and clubs *Sport and physical activities:* Principal sports: football, fives, cross country, rugby, rowing, cricket, tennis, athletics, swimming. Also available: badminton, squash, canoeing, gymnastics, fencing, judo. *Community service:* Pupils take bronze and silver Duke of Edinburgh's Award. Community service and CCF optional. *Clubs*: Many societies including chess, bridge, debating, bee-keeping, diving, mountaineering, European.

Social Boys allowed into town in the afternoons and, with permission, in the evenings. Close links with several local girls' schools.

Former Pupils Anthony Chenevix-Trench, Nevil Shute, Richard Ingrams, John Peel, Charles Darwin, William Rushton, Paul Foot, Michael Heseltine MP.

• SHREWSBURY HIGH

Shrewsbury High School, 32 Town Walls, Shrewsbury, Shropshire SY1 1TN Tel 01743 62872, Fax 01743 364942

• Pupils 585 • Boys None • Girls 4–18 (Day) • Upper sixth 40 • Termly fees £1328 (Day) • GSA, GPDST • Enquiries/application to the Headmistress

What it's like

Founded in 1885, it transferred to its present site in 1897. Over the years it has expanded steadily, the most recent building being a performing arts centre. Pleasant grounds slope down to the Severn. A sound general education is given and academic results are very good. Almost all sixth-formers go on to degree courses each year, including Oxbridge. A range of sports, games and extra-curricular activities including art, drama and Duke of Edinburgh's Award. Strong in music and over half the pupils learn a musical instrument. School's own junior department is 10 minutes away.

School profile

Pupils Total age range 4–18; 585 day girls. Senior department 11–18, 408 girls. Main entry ages 4–9, 11 and into sixth. Several are children of former pupils. Own junior department provides approximately 60% of senior intake.

Entrance Own entrance exam used (English and maths). No special skills or religious requirements. Parents not expected to buy textbooks. 19 pa assisted places in senior school, 5 in junior.

Parents 15+% are doctors, lawyers etc; 15+% farmers.

Head and staff *Headmistress:* Miss Susan Gardner, 6 years in post. Educated at Enfield County and at University College, London (history) and the Institute of American Studies (US studies). Previously Deputy Head at St Edward's Church of England School, Romford. *Staff:* 33 full time, 18 part time.

Exam results In 1995, 76 pupils in fifth, 40 in upper sixth. *GCSE:* In 1995, 93% fifth gain at least grade C in 8+ subjects; 7% in 5–7 subjects. *A-levels:* 59% upper sixth pass in 4+ subjects; 33% in 3; 5% in 2; and 3% in 1 subject. Average UCAS points 20.8 (27.6 including general studies).

University and college entrance 91% of 1995 sixth-form leavers went on to a degree course (28% after a gap year); others typically go on to HND, nursing (Project 2000), or work. Of those going on to university, 10% went to Oxbridge; 13% took courses in medicine, dentistry and veterinary science, 22% in science and engineering, 9% in law, 28% in humanities and social sciences, 9% in art and design, 12% vocational subjects eg planning, business information, applied psychology, 9% in other subjects eg music.

Curriculum GCSE and A-levels: 19 GCSE subjects offered (A-levels include general studies). 15% take science A-levels; 50% arts/humanities; 35% both. *Vocational:* Work experience available. Computing facilities; 21 Archimedes; 1 laser, 2 ink jet colour, 6 dot matrix printers, 4 Master 128. Site licence for desktop publishing, graphics, word processing systems. Purpose-built computer room. *Europe:* French and German offered to GCSE and A-level; also Italian GCSE. 66% take GCSE in more than 1 language.

Regular exchanges. Local MEP visits school occasionally. Some work experience abroad.
The arts (Pupils aged 11 and over) *Music:* Over 60% of pupils learn a musical instrument; instrumental exams can be taken. Musical groups include an orchestra and 2 choirs. *Drama & dance*: Both offered. LAMDA exams may be taken. Majority of pupils are involved in school productions and house/other productions. Students have been in National and Northern Youth Theatres. *Art:* On average, 20 take GCSE, 6 A-level. Design, pottery, textiles and photography also offered.
Sport, community service and clubs (Pupils aged 11 and over) *Sport and physical activities:* Compulsory sports: hockey, netball, volleyball, tennis, athletics, rounders, gym, dance, badminton. Optional: table tennis. Sixth form only: rowing, multi-gym, swimming. BAGA exams may be taken. Tennis, pupils competing at all levels; gymnastics and hockey at national level; cross-country, netball, badminton, county level. *Community service:* Community service optional at age 16. Many charity fund-raising events; each form organises an event each term. *Clubs and societies:* Up to 10 clubs, eg debating, chess, keep fit, badminton, Amnesty International, aerobics, art, drama, gardening.
Uniform School uniform worn except in the sixth.
Houses/prefects Competitive houses. No prefects; head girl – elected by staff and school. House captains.
Religion Regular non-denominational morning assembly.
Social Drama, music, debating, dances with local schools; organised trips abroad, eg skiing. Pupils allowed to bring own bike to school. No tobacco/alcohol allowed.
Discipline Minor misdemeanors dealt with according to the circumstances. No regular detentions necessary; emphasis on positive self-discipline and co-operation.

• SIBFORD

Sibford School, Sibford Ferris, Banbury, Oxfordshire OX15 5QL. Tel 01295 780441, Fax 01295 788444

• Pupils 310 • Boys 5–18 (Day/Board/Weekly) • Girls 5–18 (Day/Board/Weekly) • Upper sixth 14 • Termly fees £1025 – £1695 (Day) £2295 – £3200 (Board/Weekly) £690 (learning difficulties supplement) • SHMIS, BSA • Enquiries/application to the Admissions Secretary

What it's like

Founded in 1842, it has a 70-acre campus in a small village a few miles from Banbury. The oldest building is a 17th-century manor house and it is set in very pleasant surroundings in the north Oxfordshire countryside. Its Quaker background is of great importance and the philosophy and principles of Quakerism are central to the school life. The intake is cosmopolitan. The sixth-form offers academic courses leading to A-levels and vocational courses leading to GNVQ, as well as other general studies. There is a well-established Specific Learning Difficulties unit. A sound general training is given and the staff:pupil ratio is about 1:8. A range of sports, games and activities. Some participation in local community services, the Duke of Edinburgh's Award Scheme is very popular and work experience is undertaken by sixth-formers.

School profile

Pupils Total age range 5–18, 310 pupils. Senior department 11–18, 256 pupils, 92 day (60 boys, 32 girls), 164 boarding (110 boys, 54 girls). Main entry ages 5–11, 13, 14 and into the sixth. Large senior intake from own junior school (Orchard Close). Approx 3% are children of former pupils. *State school entry:* 50% senior intake, plus 10% to sixth.
Entrance Own tests used, school reports and interview (also an educational psychologist's report for dyslexic pupils). No religious requirements. Parents not expected to buy textbooks. Scholarships including music scholarships; bursaries available on the basis of need, particularly for members of the Society of Friends.
Parents 30+% live within 30 miles; 25% live overseas.
Head and staff *Head:* John Dunston, 6 years in post. *Staff:* 35 full time, 11 part time plus visiting music staff. Annual turnover 5%. Average age 38–40.
Exam results In 1995, 64 pupils in upper fifth; 14 in upper sixth. *GCSE:* In 1995, 39% of upper fifth passed in 5–10 subjects. *A-levels:* Students take A-levels or GNVQs.
University and college entrance 5% of sixth-form leavers go on to a degree course;

others typically go on to art, drama or music colleges, to other non-degree courses or some straight into careers eg retail management or training schemes.
Curriculum GCSE, A-levels and GNVQs. *Special provision:* Highly regarded Specific Learning Difficulties Unit (dyslexia) provides specialised support. *Europe:* French, German and Spanish offered to GCSE and A-level.
The arts (Pupils aged 11 and over) *Music:* 25% of pupils learn a musical instrument; instrumental exams may be taken. Musical groups include choirs, orchestra, various ensembles of different sizes and styles. Music competitions and recitals. *Drama & dance:* Many pupils involved in school productions. *Art:* On average, 48 take GCSE. Recent sculpture exhibited at Taiwan British Exhibition.
Sport, community service and clubs (Pupils aged 11 and over) *Sport and physical activities:* Sports available: Rugby, soccer, cricket, hockey, netball, squash, tennis, volleyball, swimming, athletics, basketball, badminton, sailing, skiing, golf, orienteering. *Community service:* Pupils take bronze and silver Duke of Edinburgh's Award. Community service optional.
Uniform School uniform worn except in sixth.
Houses/prefects Houses are non-competitive. Head boy and girl, head of house and house prefects – appointed by the Head or house staff.
Religion School has Quaker ethos and welcomes pupils of all faiths.
Social Theatre visits, visits organised to Oxford, Stratford, Banbury weekly. Organised trips abroad. Pupils allowed to bring bike to school. School shop and tuck shop.
Discipline Clear system of sanctions.
Boarding Sixth formers in single or double study bedroom; 12% younger pupils in dormitories of 4+. Houses of approximately 35, most single-sex; sixth-form house mixed. Resident qualified nurse. Central dining room; some meals formal, some self-service. Pupils can provide and cook supplementary food. Weekly boarding available. Visits to the Oxford, Stratford etc allowed weekly from Year 10 upwards.
Alumni association run by Margaret Fairnington, c/o the school.
Former pupils Paul Eddington; Sir John Berg.

• SIDCOT

Sidcot School, Winscombe, Avon, North Somerset BS25 1PD. Tel 01934 843102, Fax 01934 844181

• Pupils 410 • Boys 9–18 (Day/Board/Weekly) • Girls 9–18 (Day/Board/Weekly) • Upper sixth 45 • Termly fees £1906 (Day) £3187 (Board/Weekly) • SHMIS • Enquiries/application to the admissions secretary.

What it's like

Founded in 1808, one of the oldest co-educational schools in the country, it has a very pleasant rural site of 110 acres in the Mendips, 8 miles from Weston-super-Mare. Its buildings are an agreeable mixture of the old and modern and a library, health centre, sports complex, science block, horse stabling and refectory have recently been completed. A Quaker school, the principles and philosophy of Quakerism guide the school in all its activities. A sound general education is given and general vocational qualifications are offered. Most of the sixth-form proceed to degree courses each year. Very strong indeed in music, drama and art departments. There is an international programme for overseas pupils. A good range of sport and games and plentiful emphasis on outdoor pursuits.

School profile

Pupils Total age range 9–18; 410 pupils, 210 day (107 boys, 103 girls), 200 boarding (110 boys, 90 girls). Senior department 11–18; 380 pupils (203 boys, 177 girls). Main entry ages 9, 11, 13 and into the sixth. Many senior pupils from own junior departments (The Hall School, Sidcot and St Christopher's, Burnham on Sea). *State school entry:* 50% of senior intake, plus 50% of sixth-form intake.
Entrance Common Entrance or own exam used. Average intellectual ability or above looked for; no religious requirements. Parents not expected to buy textbooks. 40 pa scholarships/bursaries and special scheme helps children from Quaker families, £300–£4500.
Parents 30+% live within 30 miles; 10+% live overseas.

Head and staff *Headmaster:* Christopher Greenfield, in post for 10 years. Educated at Kingswood Grammar and at Leeds, Michigan State, Bristol and Cambridge universities (English/history and education). Previously English teacher at Salendine Nook High, English teacher and Junior High Co-ordinator at Bahrain International School and administrator at Brummana School, Lebanon. Also former Chairman of Conference of Heads of Quaker Schools and member of Leeds City Education Committee; parliamentary candidate on three occasions; Deputy Chairman of Citizenship Institute's Education Committee.

Exam results In 1996, 60 pupils in upper fifth, 45 in upper sixth. *GCSE:* In 1995, 40% upper fifth gained at least grade C in 8+ subjects, 33% in 5–7 subjects. *A-levels:* 19% upper sixth passed in 4 subjects; 67% in 3 subjects; 11% in 2 subjects; and 3% in 1 subject. Average UCAS points 17.2.

University and college entrance 83% of 1995 sixth-form leavers went on to a degree course (6% after a gap year); others typically go on to non-degree courses (eg HND geology or business). Of those going on to university, 46% took courses in science and engineering, 42% in humanities and social sciences, 6% in education.

Curriculum GCSE and A-levels: 20 subjects offered (including theatre studies, business studies and geology at A-level). 46% took arts/humanities A-level; 29% took science A-levels; and 25% took both. *Vocational:* GNVQ business studies (levels 2 and 3) offered. Work experience available. *Computing facilities:* 18 Amstrads in computer centre; 10 Amstrads and 40 BBCs (and others) in other departments. *Special provision:* Supplementary education programme (including dyslexia); EFL programme. *Europe:* French, German and Spanish offered to GCSE, AS and A-level (French compulsory to Year 9). Regular exchanges. European studies offered. International club. Visits to Europe. Links with MEP. Approx 20 European pupils in school and 3 members of staff.

The arts (Pupils aged 11 and over) *Music:* Over 50% of pupils learn a musical instrument; instrumental exams can be taken. Some 12 musical groups including full symphony orchestra, swing band, string ensembles, folk, rock groups, choirs etc. *Drama & dance*: Both offered. GCSE and A-level drama, LAMDA and RAD exams may be taken. Majority of pupils are involved in school productions and house/other productions. 4 major productions a year eg Midsummer's Night Dream, Oliver; 8 LAMDA gold medals in past 4 years; recent old scholars appearing in national productions. *Art:* On average, 15 take GCSE, 10 A-level. Design, pottery, textiles, photography and graphics also offered. High proportion of leavers take art at higher level.

Sport, community service and clubs (Pupils aged 11 and over) *Sport and physical activities:* Compulsory sports: rugby, soccer, hockey, netball, swimming, athletics. Optional: squash, tennis, basketball, volleyball, judo, riding, fencing. GCSE sport may be taken. Hockey, cross country and athletics - several at county level each year, 1 regional representative. *Community service:* Pupils take bronze, silver and gold Duke of Edinburgh's Award. Community service encouraged, as with ASDAN scheme. Links with community clean-up campaigns, etc. *Clubs and societies:* Over 50 clubs, eg Social Action, Amnesty International, canoeing, caving, conservation, international, riding.

Uniform School uniform worn except in the sixth.

Houses/prefects Eight pastoral houses (five boarding, three day) and three competitive houses. All sixth-form and some upper fifth have prefectorial duties. Head boy/girl, head of house and house prefects – names recommended by ballot, and appointed by the Head. Head of School Council elected by pupils.

Religion Boarders expected to attend Quaker Meeting for worship about once a month but most religions represented in the school.

Social Biennial joint concerts with other schools. Two or three visits abroad each year. Senior pupils allowed to bring own car/bike to school. Most meals self-service. School shop. School aims to be alcohol and tobacco-free zone.

Discipline 'Returned work' deals with academic indolence, while punishments escalate from gating to suspension to expulsion. Expulsion for any drugs offence.

Boarding Single-sex houses of 25–40, divided by age group. Qualified nurses. Central refectory. Leave any weekend (midday Sat to Sun evening.) Visits to local town allowed for pupils over 14, Saturday afternoons.

Alumni association is run by Marion Coleman, Tregennys, Harewood Road, Calstock, Cornwall PL18 9QN.

• SIERRA BERNIA

Sierra Bernia School, Apartado 121, La Cañeta S/N, 03580 Alfaz Del Pi, Alicante, Spain. Tel and Fax 34 96 6875149

• Pupils 180 • Boys 3–18 (Day) • Girls 3–18 (Day) • Upper sixth 5 • Termly fees Pts 102,000–181,000 (Day) • COBISEC, NABSS • Enquiries/application to the Headmaster

What it's like

Established in 1973, it is situated near Alicante and some 5 km from Benidorm. Single-site and semi-rural, it comprises a two-storey building in attractive gardens with adequate playground facilities and space. The primary section occupies the ground floor; senior pupils work upstairs. A cosmopolitan establishment, it is run on lines similar to a small private school in England and follows the British system of education. Term dates and holidays are like those in English schools but Spanish national holidays are honoured. There are at present no catering arrangements and pupils bring packed lunches. Weekly boarding arrangements can be made with members of staff or families living locally. A favourable staff:pupil ratio of 1:14 allows small classes and a good deal of individual attention. Academic results are respectable and a sixth-form has recently opened. Art is very strong; ballet, music and drama are well supported. There are very good on-site facilities for a variety of sports and games including basketball, volleyball, hockey, rounders, mini-tennis, gymnastics and athletics. The school also has the use of Olympic-standard municipal sports installations. A wide variety of extra-curricular activities is catered for and there are organised trips and cultural outings.

School profile

Pupils Total age range 3–18; 180 day pupils (90 boys, 90 girls). Senior department 11–18; 90 pupils (45 boys, 45 girls). Entry at any age, including into sixth.
Entrance No entrance exam; no special skills or religious requirements. Parents are not charged for textbooks or other extras.
Parents 15+% are in industry. 60+% live within 30 miles; less than 10% overseas.
Head and staff *Headmaster:* Duncan M Allan, 19 years in post; educated at Munkwearmouth Grammar School, Sunderland, and at Durham University and the Open University. *Staff:* 14 full time, 2 part time. Annual turnover 10%. Average age 43.
Exam results On average, 12 in Year 11, 5 in upper sixth. *GCSE:* on average, 75% of Year 11 gain at least grade C in 8+ subjects. *A-levels:* In 1995, of an upper sixth of 4, 1 passed in 4 subjects; 1 in 3 and 1 in 1 subject.
University and college entrance 40% of leavers go on to a degree course (either direct, or after taking a sixth-form course elsewhere); others typically go on to secretarial, art or drama courses. Of those going on to university, 25% took courses in science and engineering, 50% in humanities and social sciences, 25% in art and design.
Curriculum GCSE and A-levels. 9 GCSE subjects offered; 6 to A-level. All take arts/humanities A-levels. *Computing facilities:* 3 PCs and 4 Spectrum for secondary pupils. *Special provision:* small classes allow constant monitoring. *Europe:* French and Spanish offered to GCSE, AS and A-level; Dutch also offered.
The arts (Pupils aged 11 and over) *Music:* Up to 50% of pupils learn a musical instrument; instrumental exams can be taken. Some 4 musical groups including choral, popular mix. 2nd place Yamaha championship. *Drama & dance*: Both offered. RAD and ISTD exams may be taken. Majority of pupils are involved in school productions. *Art:* On average, 15 take GCSE. Printing – silk screen, batik – also offered.
Sport, community service and clubs (Pupils aged 11 and over) *Sport and physical activities:* Compulsory sports: hockey, football, netball, basketball, volleyball, rounders, gymnastics, athletics, swimming. BAGA exams may be taken. *Clubs and societies:* Up to 10 clubs, eg Brownies, Girl Guides, rock music, computers.
Uniform School uniform worn throughout except in sixth.
Houses/prefects Competitive houses. Prefects (monitors) and house captains appointed by the Headmaster.
Religion None.
Social Organised skiing trip. Pupils allowed to bring own bike to school. School shop. No tobacco/alcohol allowed.
Alumni association run by the Secretary, c/o the School.

• SIR JAMES HENDERSON

Sir James Henderson British School of Milan, Viale Lombardia 66, 20131 Milano, Italy. Tel 39 2 26 13 299, Fax 39 2 26 11 05 00

• Pupils 400 • Boys 3–18 (Day) • Girls 3–18 (Day) • Upper sixth 22 • £625–£1850 (Day) • HMC, COBISEC, ECIS • Enquiries/application to the Principal

What it's like

Founded in 1969 to serve the educational needs of the British and international community in Milan, it is the only HMC school in northern Italy and operates a fully British system. A truly international school, with approximately one-third British pupils, one-third Italians and one-third representing 35 other nationalities. A regular member of ECIS, it is also a founder member of COBISEC. It has two inner city sites within five minutes' walk of each other. The lower school is housed in very handsome 15th-century monastic buildings which have been extensively modernised; the upper school is accommodated in recently renovated and redesigned premises. Facilities are good and include three laboratories, libraries and specialised music and art complexes. The school has the use of modern sports halls and fields nearby. A favourable staff:pupil ratio of about 1:10 permits a good deal of individual attention. Italian is taught throughout. Academic standards are high and results are very good. Some 95% of leavers go on to degree courses (10% to Oxbridge). Music is an important and integral part of the programme: all children have music lessons from age 4 and many learn to play an instrument. Drama is well supported. A standard range of sports and games is available, including cricket (cricketers may join the Milan Cricket Club whose grounds lies in the Alps above Lake Como). Most pupils take part in non-compulsory sport and several have performed at national level in swimming and skiing. A fair variety of extra-curricular activities.

School profile

Pupils Total age range 3–18; 400 day pupils (195 boys, 205 girls). Senior department 11–18; 167 pupils (75 boys, 92 girls). Entry at any age including into sixth. A significant proportion of pupils are drawn from Sir James Henderson Lower School (Via Mancinelli 3, 20131 Milano; tel 39 2 26 19 717, fax 39 2 26 14 17 03).

Entrance By previous school record/recommendation. No entrance exam but English language assessment if necessary. English language ability preferred; no religious requirements. Parents expected to buy textbooks in upper school only.

Parents 15+% are doctors, lawyers, etc. 15+% in industry.

Head and staff *Principal:* Christopher T Gill Leech, 10 years in post; educated at St Lawrence, Ramsgate, and Cambridge University (French and Spanish). Previously Headmaster at St George's (Argentina), Head of Modern Languages at St Edmund's (Canterbury) and Assistant Master at Colston's. Also Chief Examiner French A-level, Moderator French for Business Studies, Setter CE French Paper. Publications: 3 French textbooks (Macmillan and Heinemann). *Staff:* 39 full time, 8 part time. Annual turnover 10–15%. Average age 35.

Exam results In 1995, 22 in upper fifth, 15 in upper sixth. *GCSE:* In 1995, 73% upper fifth gained at least grade C in 8+ subjects; 23% in 5–7 subjects. *A-levels:* 27% upper sixth passed in 4 subjects; 33% in 3; 40% in 2 subjects. Average UCAS points 20.1.

University and college entrance 95% of 1995 sixth-form leavers went on to a degree course; others typically go on to art or music colleges. Of those going on to university, 10% went to Oxbridge; 35% took courses in science and engineering, 60% in humanities and social sciences, 5% in art and design.

Curriculum GCSE and A-levels. 13 subjects offered (AS, but not A-level general studies). 40% take science A-levels; 55% arts/humanities; 5% a mixture of both. *Computing facilities:* One computer specialist room, Archimedes A3000, computers (BBC) in classrooms and labs in upper school. *Special provision:* Full-time ESL teacher in each section. *Europe:* French, German, Italian and Spanish offered to GCSE and A-level (Italian compulsory for ages 6–16, French for 11–16). Various trips within Italy and other European countries.

The arts (Pupils aged 11 and over) *Music:* Over 10% pupils learn a musical instrument; instrumental exams can be taken; musical groups include orchestra, choir, pop group. Recent pupil accepted for music college. *Drama & dance*: Some pupils are involved in

school productions. *Art:* On average, 8 take GCSE, 6 A-level. Design, pottery, textiles and photography also offered. 3–4 pa go on to art college.
Sport, community service and clubs (Pupils aged 11 and over) *Sport and physical activities:* Sports available: soccer, hockey, basketball, athletics, swimming, tennis, volleyball, trampoline, aerobics. Several national representatives (swimming, skiing, horseriding). *Clubs and societies:* Clubs include computers, karate, chess.
Uniform No uniform.
Houses/prefects Competitive houses. Prefects, head boy/girl, head of house and house prefects elected by school and appointed by the Head.

• SIR WILLIAM PERKINS'S

Sir William Perkins's School, Guildford Road, Chertsey, Surrey KT16 9BN Tel 01932 562161/ 560264, Fax 01932 570841

• Pupils 590 • Boys None • Girls 11–18 (Day) • Upper sixth 65 • Termly fees £1365 (Day) • GSA • Enquiries/application to the Registrar

What it's like

Founded in 1725 by Sir William Perkins, in Chertsey, it moved to its present site in 1819. This comprises 12 acres of attractive gardens and playing fields. It has handsome buildings which are very well equipped. Religious education is non-denominational. A sound general education is provided and results are very good. The staff:pupil ratio is about 1:12. Nearly all sixth-formers go on to degree courses, a number to Oxbridge. Music is very strong: many girls play an instrument and the school has an orchestra, wind and chamber ensembles, recorder groups and five choirs. Drama is also strong and there is a variety of productions each year. A range of games and sports is available. Young Enterprise and the Duke of Edinburgh's Award Scheme are well supported and there are numerous clubs and societies. Girls are encouraged to contribute to community services in local hospitals and day centres. Each form adopts a charity and works for its support.

School profile

Pupils Age range 11–18, 590 day girls. Main entry age 11. *State school entry:* 40% main intake, plus some to sixth.
Entrance Own entrance exam used. 20 pa assisted places (15 at 11, 5 to sixth). Scholarships, academic and music.
Head and staff *Headmistress:* Miss Susan Ross, in post from 1994. Educated at West Hartlepool High, and at universities of Manchester (physics) and Cambridge (PGCE). Previously Deputy Head and Head of Science at Godolphin and Latymer and Assistant Physics teacher at Putney High. *Staff:* 39 full time, 16 part time. Annual turnover 1%. Average age 37.
Exam results In 1995, 82 pupils in Year 11, 74 in upper sixth. *GCSE:* In 1995, 81 upper fifth gained at least grade C in 8+ subjects. *A-levels:* 65 upper sixth passed in 3+ subjects, 7 in 2 subjects. Average UCAS points 24.7.
University and college entrance 99% of 1995 sixth-form leavers went on to a degree course (18% after a gap year); others typically go on to employment. Of those going on to university, 6% went to Oxbridge; 5% took courses in medicine, dentistry and veterinary science, 15% in science and engineering, 5% in law, 35% in humanities and social sciences, 1% in art and design, 10% in vocational subjects eg fashion, pharmacy, accountancy, education, 25% in other subjects eg maths, languages or combinations.
Curriculum GCSE, AS and A-levels. 17 GCSE subjects offered; 20 A-level; several AS-levels, including general studies. 25% take science A-levels; 30% arts/humanities; 45% both. *Vocational:* Work experience available. *Computing facilities:* 21 Archimedes in computer room; new computer suite with 25 multimedia PCs and connection to Internet; machines in other specialist rooms. *Europe:* French (from Year 7), German (Year 8) and Spanish (Year 10) offered to GCSE and A-level; also French and German AS-level. All take one language to GCSE, over 50% take more than one. Regular exchanges. Spanish work experience exchange for sixth-form.
The arts *Music:* 68% of pupils learn a musical instrument; instrumental exams can be taken. Musical groups include orchestras, wind band, 5 choirs (including madrigal, chamber, gospel), baroque and early music groups, saxophone, clarinet and flute

ensembles. Messiah and Fauré's Requiem recently performed by senior choir and orchestra. *Drama & dance*: Drama and dance offered (Year 7). LAMDA and Guildhall exams may be taken. Many pupils involved in school productions; recent examples Midsummer Night's Dream, Into the Woods, An Ideal Husband. *Art:* On average, 25 take GCSE, 6 A-level. Design, photography also offered.
Sport, community service and clubs *Sport and physical activities:* Compulsory sports: hockey, netball, athletics, tennis, gym. Optional: indoor hockey, badminton, volleyball, trampolining, cross-country, fencing, rugby, football. Sixth form only: squash, wight-training, golf, swimming. Surrey swimming finals; winners Southern indoor hockey competition. *Community service:* Pupils take bronze, silver and gold Duke of Edinburgh's Award (strongly supported and a number win gold). Community service optional. *Clubs and societies:* Clubs include young engineers, history, French, debating, computing, dance, technology.
Uniform Uniform worn apart from sixth.
Houses/prefects No competitive houses or prefects. Head girl and deputies elected by the school. School Council.
Religion Attendance at religious worship compulsory but pupils may be withdrawn at parents' request.
Social Some events with local schools including debates, art and music. Regular ski trips and other educational visits. Pupils allowed to bring own car/bike/motorbike to school. Meals formal. School shop. No alcohol or tobacco allowed.
Discipline Pupils failing to produce homework once might expect a warning, if no adequate explanation; those caught smoking cannabis on the premises would expect suspension pending governors' decisïon.

• SOLIHULL

Solihull School, Warick Road, Solihull, B91 3DJ. Tel 0121 705 0958/4273, Fax 0121 711 4439
• Pupils 972 • Boys 7–18 (Day) • Girls 16–18 (Day) • Upper sixth 131 • Termly fees £1428
• HMC • Enquiries/application to the Admissions Secretary

What it's like

Founded in 1560, it has occupied its 50-acre urban site close to the town centre, since 1882. The original Victorian building (in the collegiate idiom) was modernised in 1989, and during the last thirty years substantial developments have included facilities for music, art, design and technology as well as a chapel, sports hall and a drama studio. The junior school is an integral part of the school. The moral and spiritual welfare of pupils is regarded as very important: attendance at religious worship (in the Anglican tradition) is compulsory. A broad, traditional education is provided and there is a favourable staff:pupil ratio of about 1:13. Results are very good and almost all sixth-formers go on to university. Music is very strong indeed – musical groups include chapel choir, orchestras and jazz band. Drama and art are also well supported. There is a good deal of emphasis on competitive sport and games and these are pursued to a high standard. A normal range of field and court games; also sailing and golf, and soccer for sixth-formers. There is a large CCF and scout group and considerable commitment to the Duke of Edinburgh's Award Scheme. Service to the community and to others in the school is a valued part of the regime involving some 200 pupils. Numerous clubs and societies cater for virtually all interests. Much enterprise is shown in the arrangement of overseas tours and trips.

School profile

Pupils Total age range 7–18, 972 day pupils (915 boys, 57 girls). Senior department 11–18, 814 pupils (757 boys, 57 girls). Main entry ages 7, 9, 10, 11, 13 (boys) and into the sixth (boys and girls). 6% are children of former pupils. *State school entry:* 53% main intake, 47% to sixth.
Entrance Own entrance exam used (Common Entrance rarely). Ability in key academic subjects (especially English and maths) looked for at entry and encouraging school reports; no religious requirements. Parents not required to buy textbooks. Average extras £55 per term. 30 pa assisted places (5 at 7, 10 at 11, 5 at 13 and 10 at 16). 30 pa scholarships, £910–£4284 pa.

Parents 15+% doctors, lawyer etc; 15+% in industry/commerce and 15+% in teaching.
Head and staff *Headmaster:* Patrick Derham, appointed in 1996. Educated at Pangbourne and Cambridge (history). Previously Head of History and Housemaster at Radley. *Staff:* 76 full time, 6 part time. Annual turnover 4%. Average age 44.
Exam results In 1995, 113 pupils in upper fifth, 131 in upper sixth. *GCSE:* In 1995, 94% of upper fifth gained at least grade C in 8+ subjects; and 5% in 5–7 subjects. *A-levels:* 80% passed in 4 subjects; 18% in 3; and 2% in 2 subjects. Average UCAS points 21.4.
University and college entrance 95% of 1995 sixth-form leavers went on to a degree course, others typically go on to art college. Of those going on to university, 8% went to Oxbridge; 10% took courses in medicine, dentistry and veterinary science, 25% in science and engineering, 10% in law, 49% in humanities and social sciences, 2% in art and design, 4% in other subjects eg music.
Curriculum GCSE and A-levels offered: 17 subjects to GCSE, 18 to A-level (including business studies, design and general studies). 28% take science A-levels; 44% arts/humanities; 28% both. *Vocational:* Work experience available. *Computing facilities:* Over 40 Archimedes in IT centre plus provision in science departments (1 Archimedes in each classroom in junior school). *Europe:* French (compulsory from 11) and German (from 12) offered to GCSE and A-level; also sixth-form GCSE in Italian and Spanish, AS-levels French and Spanish. Up to 75% pupils take GCSE in more than 1 language. Regular exchanges.
The arts *Music:* Over 30% pupils learn a musical instrument; instrumental exams can be taken. 15 musical groups, including chapel choir, 2 orchestras, wind ensemble, jazz band, jazz singers, choral society, junior school orchestra. Piano quartet in final of 1993 National Chamber Music Competition; 5 places at music academies and a choral and two organ scholarships since 1994; 3 members of National Youth Orchestra. *Drama & dance*: Drama offered and GCSE may be taken. Some pupils involved in school and in house/other productions. 2 pupils in National Youth Theatre. *Art:* On average, 21 take GCSE, 10 A-level. Design, pottery and photography also offered. 2 ex-pupils at London art colleges and a number go on to art foundation courses.
Sport, community service and clubs *Sport and physical activities:* Compulsory for boys: rugby, hockey, cricket, gymnastics, cross-country, swimming, lifesaving, basketball, athletics, tennis, badminton, fitness training, weight training and water polo. Optional for boys: sailing, squash, and soccer. Compulsory for girls: hockey, netball, tennis and rounders. Optional for girls: Squash, aerobics, badminton, athletics, swimming, trampolining. Pupils may take RLSS, RYA and ASA exams. Recently: county champions in badminton (U15 Warwick), athletics (W Midlands super schools), cross-country (Birmingham league), cricket (Warwickshire U18); semi-finalists, Rosslyn Park 7s; runners-up HMC golf foursomes; 3 country cricket players (Warwicks U18, 1993); 7 England rugby players (2 U18 in 1995, 5 U16 in 1994-6). *Community service:* Pupils take bronze, silver and gold Duke of Edinburgh's Award (300 awards in last 11 years). CCF and community service optional. All 12-year-olds spend a week in school's cottage in Snowdonia, also used by other pupils. *Clubs & societies*: Up to 35 clubs including sports, art and design, printing, Christian discussion circle, computer, drama, physics and technology.
Uniform School uniform worn throughout.
Houses/prefects Competitive houses. Head boy/girl, school prefects and heads of houses, appointed by Headmaster.
Religion Religious worship compulsory.
Social Participates in many local competitions (team games, chess, public speaking etc). Regular exchanges with pupils in Cologne and Lyon; World Challenge expedition to Zanskar (1992), Bolivia in 1995; classical tours of Greece; French trips to Normandy; skiing parties. Pupils may bring own car/bike to school. Meals self-service. School shop. No alcohol/tobacco allowed.
Discipline Pupils failing to produce homework could expect detention; those caught smoking cannabis on the premises could expect expulsion.
Alumni association Run by B Allen, 32 Stonebow Avenue, Solihull, West Midlands B91 3UP.
Former pupils Michael Buerk (BBC news reader and reporter); David Briggs (organist); Lord Butterfield (former Vice-Chancellor of Cambridge University); Sir Oliver Wright (ex-ambassador to USA); Mr Justice Owen.

• SOUTH HAMPSTEAD HIGH

South Hampstead High School, 3 Maresfield Gardens, London NW3 5SS Tel 0171 435 2899, Fax 0171 431 8022

• Pupils 915 • Boys None • Girls 4–18 (Day) • Upper sixth 69 • Termly fees £1548 (Day) • GSA, GPDST • Enquiries/application to the Registrar

What it's like

Founded in 1876, it has occupied its present premises since 1882. The core is the original Victorian building on a single urban site. Well-equipped new buildings include a theatre and sports hall and a separate sixth-form house. The junior school is nearby. It is a selective and highly academic school and results are very good. Almost all leavers go on to degree courses each year, including very many to Oxbridge. Strong in music and in drama and art. Very good range of games and sports. Numerous activities, clubs and societies. It has flourishing local connections and a substantial commitment to local community schemes. A fine record in Young Enterprise and the Duke of Edinburgh's Award Scheme.

School profile

Pupils Total age range 4–18; 915 day girls. Senior department 11–18, 628 girls. Main entry age 4, 7, 11 and into sixth. Approx 4% are children of former pupils. *State school entry:* 45% senior intake.

Entrance Own entrance exam used. Oversubscribed. No special skills or religious requirements. Parents not expected to buy textbooks; only music tuition extra. 12 pa assisted places including 2 sixth-form. 1–4 scholarships pa, 25%–50% fees, including music scholarships at 11 and 16.

Parents 15+% are doctors, lawyers, etc; 15+% in industry or commerce; 15+% in the theatre, music, media etc.

Head and staff *Headmistress:* Mrs Jean Scott, 4 years in post. Educated at George Watson's Ladies' College, Wellington School, Ayr, and at Glasgow University (zoology) and Institute of Education (PGCE). Previously Headmistress of St George's, Edinburgh, Senior Mistress and Head of Biology at Ipswich High, Biology Teacher at Northgate Grammar, Ipswich, and taught biology part time at other schools and colleges. Also research biologist (Glaxo, ICI); teacher moderator for A-level Social Biology and member of Biology Committee (1986). *Staff:* 55 full time, 14 part time.

Exam results In 1995, 87 pupils in upper fifth, 74 in upper sixth. *GCSE:* In 1995, all upper fifth gained at least grade C in 8+ subjects. *A-levels:* 8 upper sixth passed in 4+ subjects; 60 in 3; 5 in 2 subjects. Average UCAS points 24.4.

University and college entrance All 1995 sixth-form leavers went on to a degree course (33% after a gap year), 25% went to Oxbridge; 10% took courses in medicine, dentistry and veterinary science, 17% in science and engineering, 8% in law, 55% in humanities and social sciences (20% languages), 8% in art and design, 2% in vocational subjects eg nursing.

Curriculum GCSE and *A-levels:* 15 GCSE subjects offered; 20 at A-level (general studies taught but not examined). 14% take science A-levels; 46% arts/humanities; 40% both. *Vocational:* Work experience encouraged. *Computing facilities:* Newly networked computer room with Pentium PCs (multi-media and CD-Rom); other machines in departments. *Europe:* French, German and Spanish offered to GCSE, AS- and A-level; also Italian and Russian GCSE. Regular exchanges. Active European club; economics, government and politics students trips to Europe; work experience in France, Germany and Spain for sixth-formers; talks from MEPs and others with European interests in sixth-form general studies course.

The arts (Pupils aged 11 and over) *Music:* Over 60% of pupils learn a musical instrument; instrumental exams can be taken termly. Some 64 take GCSE music and 9 A-level. Some 15 musical groups including 3 orchestras, 4 choirs, and 2 big bands, groups for most instrumentalists, chamber & jazz groups. Choir 2nd at International Eisteddfod, quarter-finalists Sainsbury's Choir of the Year; tours (USA in 1994) and broadcasts. *Drama & dance*: Both offered. Majority of pupils are involved in school productions and some in club productions. *Art:* On average 30 take GCSE, 12 A-level. Graphic design, 3D, textile work, photography, photo-silkscreen work and computer image manipulation also offered. 8 students went to art school/fine art university courses

in 1994; all 5 A-level candidates gained grade A in 1995.
Sport, community service and clubs (Pupils aged 11 and over) *Sport and physical activities:* Compulsory sports: netball, hockey, health-related fitness, dance, tennis, rounders, athletics, gym, football, basketball, pop lacrosse. Optional: volleyball, badminton, squash, trampolining, aerobics, self-defence. Regular county representatives, netball, U16, U18; tennis, U14, U16, U18. *Community service:* Pupils take bronze, silver and gold Duke of Edinburgh's Award. Community service compulsory at age 15, optional thereafter. *Clubs and societies:* Up to 30 clubs, eg 3 drama, 2 dance, yoga, aerobics, philosophy, computing, 2 debating, bridge, gardening, pop, lacrosse, trampolining and other sports, archives, history, politics.
Uniform School uniform worn except the sixth.
Houses/prefects No competitive houses. Head girl and other positions of responsibility – submit cv and are interviewed. School Council.
Religion Everyone attends a non-denominational assembly.
Social Joint choral concert annually with boys' public school; joint drama productions; shared societies/speakers/debates. Trips to Europe (eg Greece, Italy, Turkey), choir tours (USA 1994), skiing. Pupils allowed to bring own car/bike/motorbike to school. Meals self-service. No tobacco/alcohol allowed.
Discipline Pupils failing to produce homework once might expect reprimand; those caught smoking cannabis on the premises might expect expulsion. (The policy of the Council is to suspend the pupil and inform the police.)
Former pupils Rabbi Julia Neuberger; Fay Weldon (author); Miriam Karlin, Helena Bonham-Carter and Angela Lansbury (actresses); Nina Milkina, Sarah Francis and Joanna Macgregor (musicians); Baroness Birk (politician); Harriet Mena Hill (painter); Professors Jennifer Temkin, Tessa Goldsmith and many other academics.

• SOUTHBANK INTERNATIONAL

Southbank International School, 36/38 Kensington Park Road, London W11 3BU. Tel 0171 229 8230, Fax 0171 229 3784

• Pupils 250 • Boys 3–18 (Day) • Girls 3–18 (Day) • Upper sixth 60 • Termly fees £1200–£3160 (Day) • ISAI, ECIS • Enquiries/application to the Assistant to the Headmaster

What it's like

Founded in 1979, as a co-educational school. It is located in a handsome Victorian building in Kensington, close to Notting Hill Gate underground station. A primary section was opened in 1992 and a second campus for pupils aged 3–14 opened in Hampstead in 1995. A large number of nationalities are represented among the pupils. The school offers the International Baccalaureate so that the curriculum is broad throughout. All the main European languages are offered (and many minority languages such as Serbo-Croat and Hungarian), in addition to Japanese, Arabic, Farsi and Swahili – an altogether exceptional variety. A very high proportion of pupils takes more than one European language. The teaching is of high standard and results are very good. Almost all sixth-formers go on to degree courses. ESL teaching available. Good drama, art and music, including orchestra and choir. Fair range of games, clubs and societies. Full use is made of the capital's cultural amenities.

School profile

Pupils Total age range 4–18. Senior department (middle and high school), 11–18, 250 day pupils (140 boys, 110 girls). Main entry ages 4 and into sixth. Large number of high school intake from own 2 primary/middle sections – one at Kensington, on the same site as the senior school; one in Hampstead (tel 0171 229 8230).
Entrance No special skills or religious requirements. 15 pa scholarships/bursaries, £1000 to £3000
Parents 15+% are doctors, lawyers etc; 60+% in industry or commerce; 20% diplomatic. Many overseas parents are on a fixed term posting in London.
Head and staff *Headmaster:* Milton E Toubkin, in post for 16 years. Educated at CBC Pretoria and Guinea Fowl School (Zimbabwe) and at Rhodes, Witwatersrand, London and Bristol universities (Latin, English, education). Previously Principal at American Community School (London), Director at Lycée des Nations (Geneva), Head of Anglo-

American section at Rosenberg International School (St Gallen, Switzerland) and Head of Latin at Churchill School (Harare, Zimbabwe). Past Chairman of the London International Schools Association. *Staff:* 22 full time, 25 part time. Annual turnover 5%.
University and college entrance 98% of 1995 sixth-form leavers went on to a degree course (10% after a gap year); others typically go on to work, military service. Of those going on to university, 5% went to Oxbridge; 10% took courses in medicine, dentistry and veterinary science, 30% in science and engineering, 5% in law, 45% in humanities and social sciences, 10% in art and design.
Curriculum International Baccalaureate (IB) is taken in six subjects; all include creative arts, experimental science, social science, language and maths. 12 subjects offered plus 18 different languages – Farsi, Japanese, Arabic, Swahili, in addition to European languages. On average, 48 pupils in upper fifth, 60 in upper sixth. *Computing facilities:* 16 Apple Macintosh computers in computer room plus 10 in classrooms and library (with Internet and e-mail connections). *Special provision:* ESL teaching available at all levels. *Europe:* German (from age 4) and French (from 11) to IB. Danish, Dutch, Finnish, Hungarian, Italian, Portuguese, Norwegian, Russian, Serbo-Croat, Swedish and Spanish offered as mother tongue or second language to IB, as extras.
The arts (Pupils aged 11 and over) *Music:* Over 50% of pupils learn a musical instrument (violin compulsory in primary section); instrumental exams can be taken. Some musical groups including orchestra, choir, musical ensemble. *Drama & dance*: Both offered. Majority of pupils are involved in school productions and some in house/other productions. *Art:* Art facilities open to non-examination pupils.
Sport, community service and clubs (Pupils aged 11 and over) *Sport and physical activities:* Optional sports: soccer, volleyball, basketball, tennis, self-defence, swimming. *Community service:* Community service compulsory for 2 years at age 16. *Clubs and societies:* Up to 5 clubs, eg Student Council, MUN, ISTA.
Uniform None.
Houses/prefects No competitive houses, prefects or head boy/girl. School Council.
Religion No compulsory religious worship.
Social Major events include annual sponsored walk, international dinner, art show, science fair, school prom (joint activities between Kensington and Hampstead branches). Organised trips abroad. Pupils allowed to bring own car/bike/motorbike to school. Meals self-service. School canteen. No alcohol/tobacco allowed.
Discipline Pupils failing to produce homework once might expect reprimand and warning; those involved with drugs would be referred to school's Drugs Committee and counselling before re-admission.
Alumni association is run by Miss Mary Langford, c/o the school.

• STAMFORD

Stamford School, St Paul's Street, Stamford, Lincolnshire PE9 2BS. Tel 01780 62171, Fax 01780 480120

• Pupils 920 • Boys 4–18 (Day/Board) • Girls None • Upper sixth 106 • Termly fees £1355 (Day) £2710 (Board) • HMC • Enquiries/application to the Headmaster

What it's like

Founded in 1532 by William Radcliffe and in the 19th-century endowed by the Trustees of Browne's Hospital, as was the High School. The two schools remain separate but share many cultural, social and educational activities, as well as a Board of Governors. Over the centuries both have played a major part in the life of the town and neighbourhood and there is a close 'town and gown' relationship. Stamford School's buildings lie to the north-east of the town in some 34 acres of agreeable grounds and playing fields. The chapel was originally part of the 12th-century St Paul's Church. Much of the school was rebuilt in 1875 and a continuous programme of modernisation and extension has resulted in excellent facilities. An Anglican foundation, it follows the liturgy of the Church of England but welcomes boys of other faiths. A large staff permits a staff:pupil ratio of about 1:12. Academic standards are high and results good; the majority of sixth-formers go on to degree courses each year. Music is very strong indeed (up to half the pupils learn an instrument; choirs and orchestras are vigorously supported). Drama is also strong. A standard range of sports and games is provided and there are many successful teams (a large number of representatives at county level; some at national level). The CCF contingent is unusually big (RN, Army and RAF sections) and local community services are a popular alternative (one group produces a weekly newspaper for the blind). Many clubs and societies cater for most needs. A successful Young Enterprise group and a traditional commitment to the Duke of Edinburgh's Award Scheme in which the school has an outstanding record of success. Each year a large number of overseas trips is organised (eg Himalayas, South America) plus sporting tours all over the country and beyond eg Australia, Zimbabwe, South Africa.

School profile

Pupils Total age range 4–18; 920 boys (700 day, 220 boarding). Senior department 13–18, 570 boys. Main entry ages 4, 7, 8, 11, 13 and into sixth. 5% are sons of former pupils. *State school entry:* 50% of the intake at 11 and to sixth.

Entrance Common Entrance and own exam used. No special skills or religious requirements. Parents not expected to buy textbooks. 15 pa assisted places. Approx 15 pa scholarships/bursaries, £250 to full fees.

Parents 15+% in the armed services; 15+% in industry. 60+% live within 30 miles; up to 10% live overseas.

Head and staff *Headmaster:* Geoffrey Timm, in post for 18 years. Educated at Spalding Grammar School and Cambridge University (modern and medieval languages). Previously Head of Modern Languages and Housemaster at Bishops Stortford, and Modern Languages Master (French, German, Spanish) and Master i/c Cricket at Fettes. Also HMC Committee and formerly Chairman of Midlands Division and Chairman ISIS; member, Board of Visitors, HM Prison Stocken. *Staff:* 75 full time, 28 part time. Annual turnover 5%. Average age 37.

Exam results In 1995, 135 pupils in fifth, 106 in upper sixth. *GCSE:* in 1995, 92% fifth gained at least grade C in 8+ subjects; 6% in 5–7 subjects. *A-levels:* 8% upper sixth passed in 4+ subjects; 78% in 3; 13% in 2; and 1% in 1 subject. Average UCAS points 20.0.

University and college entrance 90% of sixth-form leavers go on to a degree course; others typically go on to non-degree courses or directly into careers (banking, armed forces, retailing). Of those going on to university, 5% go to Oxbridge; 5% take courses in medicine, dentistry and veterinary science, 30% in science and engineering, 5% in law, 50% in humanities and social sciences, 5% in art and design, 5% in drama and music.

Curriculum GCSE, AS and A-levels. 21 GCSE subjects offered; 2 at AS-level; 20 at A-level. General studies at AS-level, not A-level. 13% take science A-levels; 47% arts/humanities; 40% both. *Vocational:* Well-established links with business and industry include a two-day sixth-form industrial conference, industry day for 14-year-olds, careers conferences and practice interview arrangements. Work experience encouraged – pupils make their own arrangements with guidance from the school. *Computing facilities:* 2 Econet networks with 60 BBCs, Masters and Archimdedes computers, plus 386 PC with CD-Rom in careers library. *Special provision:* Two teachers give individual lessons to dyslexic pupils. *Europe:* French, German and Russian offered at GCSE and A-level (French compulsory from age 11 to GCSE). Regular exchanges for sixth-form to France and Germany.

The arts (Pupils aged 11 and over) *Music:* Up to 50% of pupils learn a musical instrument; instrumental exams can be taken. Some 8 musical groups including symphony orchestra, wind band, choral society, chapel choir, chamber groups, jazz band etc. Pupils have achieved Oxbridge choral scholarships; pop group finalist in national competition. *Drama & dance*: Much extra-curricular drama. Many pupils are involved in school productions and some in house/other productions. Recent drama includes Volpone, Macbeth; musicals, Mikado, Oliver, Cabaret, West Side Story. *Art:* On average, 33 take GCSE, 16 A-level. Design, pottery, photography and sculpture also offered.

Sport, community service and clubs (Pupils aged 11 and over) *Sport and physical activities:* Compulsory sports – boys choose from: rugby, hockey, cricket, cross-country, athletics, soccer, tennis, squash, canoeing, golf, table tennis, shooting, basketball, ski trips, fencing, chess. GCSE and Community Sports Leadership Awards may be taken. Rugby, hockey, cricket, strong county representation; athletics, frequent county champions; cross-country, national finalists; canoe, national youth champions last five years; shooting, Bisley every year. *Community service:* Pupils take bronze, silver and gold Duke of Edinburgh's Award; 20 or so gold each year. CCF optional (over 300 boys) and community service (eg visiting, Talking News for the Blind). Drama groups perform in local primary schools; school newspapers – Daily Telegraph prizewinners 1992. *Clubs and societies:* Up to 30 clubs, eg science, history, chess, air rifle, quizzes, computing, art, debating, Young Enterprise.

Uniform School uniform worn throughout.

Houses/prefects Competitive houses. Prefects, head boy, head of house and house prefects. School prefects appointed by Head, house prefects by housemasters.

Religion Christian worship compulsory.

Social Plays, musical events, choir, certain sixth-form studies with sister school. Various organised trips abroad (fieldwork, skiing etc); rugby tours (eg Australia, South Africa) and cricket tours (eg Zimbabwe); teacher exchange with Camberwell Grammar School, Australia; pupil exchange with St Albans School, Washington DC. Pupils allowed to bring own car/motorbike/bike to school. Meals self-service except in junior boarding houses. School shop. No tobacco/alcohol allowed.

Discipline Pupils failing to produce homework once might expect to be admonished and kept in if persistent; those caught smoking cannabis on the premises would be suspended, while all factors considered – expulsion likely.

Boarding 7% have own study bedroom, 35% share; 58% in dormitories of 6+. Houses of 36–83, divided by age group (8–12; 13–18). Resident qualified nurse. Central dining room for senior boarders. Pupils can provide and cook coffee, tea and toast. Exeats for seniors most weekends; juniors, two weekends per term. Seniors allowed to local town daily with permission; juniors, rationed.

Alumni association is run by B M McKenzie, 11 Rutland Terr, Stamford, PE9 2QD (Membership and Information Sec).

Former pupils M J K Smith (England cricket captain/England rugby too); John Terraine (historian); Sir Malcolm Sargent; Sir Michael Tippett; Robert Clift (Olympic Gold Medallist, hockey); Simon Hodgkinson (England rugby); Mark James (golfer); the Bishop of Worcester; Colin Dexter (Insp Morse creator).

• STAMFORD HIGH

Stamford High School, St Martin's, Stamford, Lincolnshire PE9 2LJ. Tel 01780 62330, Fax 01780 481100

• Pupils 942 • Boys 4–8 only • Girls 4–18 (Day/Board/Weekly) • Upper sixth 90 • Termly fees £1091–£1363 (Day) £2454–£2726 (Board) £2428–£2700 (Weekly) • GSA, BSA • Enquiries/ application to the Headmistress

What it's like

Founded in 1877, it belongs to the Stamford Endowed Schools which also includes Stamford School. They are run separately but work in close conjunction, sharing many cultural, social and educational activities, as well as a board of governors. Their daily life is interwoven with that of the town and there is a close 'town and gown' relationship. Stamford High School has a fine site in the centre of town. Facilities are very good and boarding accommodation comfortable. The school is non-denominational but there is some emphasis on religious education and daily assembly for all pupils. The school's academic aim is to avoid early specialisation and to encourage the best of traditional and modern methods of learning. Academic standards are high and results consistently good. The vast majority of girls go on to university, including Oxbridge. Music and drama are strongly supported (new purpose-built performing arts studio). Some 350 girls learn a musical instrument. Drama is part of the curriculum and there are several productions each year. Sports and games are well catered for and include, besides the standard range, tae kwon do, fencing and Olympic gymnastics. There is a wide variety of clubs and societies. Girls are encouraged to take part in community and social services. The school has an outstanding record of success in the Duke of Edinburgh's Award Scheme, which is very popular.

School profile

Pupils Total age range 4–18; 942 pupils, 828 day (59 boys, 769 girls), 114 boarding girls. Senior department 11–18, 717 girls. Main entry ages 4 (boys and girls), 8, 11 and into sixth (girls). Approx 5% are children of former pupils. *State school entry:* 50% of senior intake, plus 10% into sixth.

Entrance Own entrance exam used. Musical and sporting ability welcomed; no religious requirements. Parents not expected to buy textbooks; no compulsory extras. 30 pa assisted places. 25 pa LEA scholarships. 6 pa scholarships and foundation awards, £300 to full tuition.

Parents 15+% in industry or commerce; 15+% in the armed services, 15+% are doctors, lawyers, etc. 60+% live within 30 miles; up to 10% live overseas.

Head and staff *Headmistress:* Miss Gladys Bland, in post for 18 years. Educated at Tottenham High School and at Queen Mary College, London (history) and Oxford University (research student). Previously Senior Mistress, Head of History and Resident Sixth Form Tutor at Malvern Girls' College, and Assistant Mistress at Manchester High and at Casterton. Also GSA – previously member of Education Committee, Chairman Eastern Branch and member of Council, member of Membership Committee. Chairman Stamford Civic Society. *Staff:* 56 full time, 12 part time. Annual turnover 3%. Average age 38.

Exam results In 1995, 115 pupils in upper fifth, 77 in upper sixth. *GCSE:* In 1995, 105 upper fifth gained at least grade C in 8+ subjects; 7 in 5–7; and 3 in 1–4 subjects. *A-levels:* 62 upper sixth passed in 3+ subjects; 9 in 2; and 3 in 1 subject. Average UCAS points 19.3.

University and college entrance 95% of 1995 sixth-form leavers went on to a degree course, others typically go on to non-degree courses or careers eg banking. Of those going on to university, 9% went to Oxbridge; 10% took courses in medicine, dentistry and veterinary science, 36% in science and engineering, 50% in humanities and social sciences, 4% in art and design.

Curriculum GCSE, AS and A-levels: 21 GCSE subjects offered; 21 at A-level (no A-level general studies). *Computing facilities:* Main computer centre, linked to computers in CDT centre; plus computers in arts and science departments. *Special provision:* Testing and special tuition arranged for dyslexic pupils. *Europe:* French, German and Spanish offered to GCSE and A-level. Regular exchanges.

The arts (Pupils aged 11 and over) *Music:* Over 30% of pupils learn a musical instrument; instrumental exams can be taken. Some 18 musical groups including choral society, orchestras, concert band, chamber singers, chamber groups. *Drama & dance*: Both offered. LAMDA, RAD, GCSE drama and A-level performing arts exams may be taken. Some pupils are involved in school productions and house/other productions. *Art:* On average, 40 take GCSE, 10 A-level; design, pottery, textiles, photography also offered. Art facilities open to non-examination pupils.

Sport, community service and clubs (Pupils aged 11 and over) *Sport and physical activities:* Compulsory sports: hockey, netball, tennis, aerobics, rounders. Sixth form only: ten-pin bowling, golf, fencing, squash, trampolining, self-defence. RLSS exams may be taken. *Community service:* Pupils take bronze, silver and gold Duke of Edinburgh's Award. *Clubs and societies:* Over 30 clubs, eg band, lifesaving, creative writing, Christian Union, tae kwon do, Young Naturalists, science.

Uniform School uniform worn throughout.

Houses/prefects No competitive houses. Prefects, head girl, head of house and house prefects – elected by the sixth, except in boarding houses. School Council.

Religion Religious worship compulsory, though exemption allowed on grounds of conscience.

Social Joint activities with Stamford School include film, Brazenose Society, historical lectures, science society, joint musical and dramatic performances and dances. Trips abroad include ski trips, visits to Switzerland, Russia, Eastern Europe, classical tours to Greece and Italy; linked school in Bonn, exchange visits to France and Spain. Pupils allowed to bring own car/bike/motorbike to school. Meals self-service. School shop. No tobacco/alcohol allowed.

Discipline Pupils failing to produce homework once might expect to be admonished and asked to produce it; those caught smoking cannabis on the school premises could expect expulsion.

Boarding 1% have own study bedroom, 27% share – mainly 2; 72% in dormitories of 6+. Houses of 50–60, divided by age. Sixth-form pupils can provide and cook own food. 2 weekend exeats termly plus unlimited day exeats. Visits to the local town: special shopping expeditions by juniors, ranging to daily visits for upper fifth and sixth.
Alumni association is run by Mrs A Marshall c/o the school.

• STANBRIDGE EARLS

Stanbridge Earls, Romsey, Hampshire SO51 0ZS. Tel 01794 516777, Fax 01794 511201
• Pupils 180 • Boys 11–18 (Day/Board/Weekly) • Girls 11–18 (Day/Board/Weekly) • Upper sixth 15 • Termly fees £2665–£2915 (Day) £3550–£3885 (Board/Weekly) • SHMIS, BSA, BDA
• Enquiries/application to the Headmaster

What it's like

Founded in 1952, it is largely housed in a beautiful building of medieval origins and Tudor appearance and is of considerable architectural and historical interest (King Alfred is thought to have lived on the site and King Ethelwolf to have been buried there in the 9th century). The 13th-century chapel is at the heart of the building. The mansion lies in 50 acres of splendid landscaped grounds and gardens, with woodland and a chain of small lakes. Religious worship is in the Anglican tradition. It has all the advantages of being a small school, and its most particular feature is its large special needs department staffed by a dozen teachers. The school tends to specialise in pupils who for various reasons have underachieved, especially those with dyslexia. There is much emphasis on personal attention and the large staff (including a lot of part-timers) permits an unusually generous staff:pupil ratio of about 1:5. Class sizes are very small (ten pupils or fewer). Much is achieved academically and though the sixth-form is small, several pupils go on to degree courses each year. Art and drama are particular strengths. There is an excellent range of sports and games (including fishing and riding) and a plentiful variety of extra-curricular activities.

School profile

Pupils Total age range 11–18; 180 pupils, 20 day (15 boys, 5 girls); 160 boarding (140 boys, 20 girls). Main entry ages, 11, 13 and into the sixth. *State school entry:* 10% main intakes, plus 2% to sixth.
Entrance Common Entrance sometimes used. No special skills or religious requirements although C of E predominates. Parents not expected to buy textbooks. 10 pa scholarships, 33% fees.
Parents 15+% in armed services; 15+% in industry or commerce; 15+% in farming. Up to 10% live within 30 miles; 10+% live overseas.
Head and staff *Headmaster:* Howard Moxon, in post for 12 years. Educated at Ecclesfield Grammar, Yorkshire, and Cambridge University (geography). Previously Senior Boarding Housemaster and Head of Geography at Highgate and Assistant Master at Forrest School. Also ISJC Special Needs Sub-Committee; SHMIS Committee (Chairman 1993). *Staff:* 30 full time, 16 part time. Annual turnover 4%. Average age 33.
Exam results In 1995, 29 pupils in upper fifth, 14 in upper sixth. *GCSE:* In 1995, 15% upper fifth gain at least grade C in 5–7 subjects; and 65% in 1–4 subjects. *A-levels:* 15% upper sixth pass in 3 subjects; 20% in 2; and 50% in 1 subject. Average UCAS points 6.0.
University and college entrance 10% of sixth-form leavers went on to a degree course, others typically go on to non-degree courses or straight into careers. Of those going on to university, 20% took courses in science and engineering, 20% in humanities and social sciences, 60% in art and design.
Curriculum GCSE and *A-levels:* 20 subjects offered (including photography, motor vehicle engineering; no A-level general studies). 40% take science A-levels; 40% arts/humanities; 20% both. *Vocational:* GNVQ, work experience available. *Computing facilities:* Computer room – networked Archimedes BBCs. *Special provision:* School has been a leader in the field of specific learning difficulties for 30+ years. Special unit with 12 specialist trained staff; lessons on one-to-one basis. *Europe:* French offered to GCSE and A-level; also Italian GCSE. Regular exchanges to Germany. French department visit to France at least once a year.
The arts *Music:* Over 30% of pupils learn a musical instrument; instrumental exams can

be taken. Musical groups include pop, brass band, choir. *Drama & dance*: Both offered. GCSE drama and RAD exams may be taken. Majority of pupils are involved in school and house/other productions. *Art:* On average, 35 take GCSE, 10 A-level. Design, textiles and photography also offered. On average 5 pupils get into art college each year.
Sport, community service and clubs *Sport and physical activities:* Compulsory sports (initially, then optional): rugby, hockey, cricket, swimming. Optional: squash, badminton, netball, athletics, basketball, judo, sailing, riding, fishing, archery, shooting. GCSE and RYA exams may be taken. Rugby, 2 represent county, U16, U18; cricket, 2 represent county. *Community service:* Pupils take bronze Duke of Edinburgh's Award. Community service optional at age 16. *Clubs and societies:* Up to 15 clubs, eg models, skate board, debating, angling, photographic, computer, chess, motor vehicle maintenance, welding, radio-controlled cars.
Uniform School uniform worn except the sixth.
Houses/prefects Competitive houses. Prefects, head boy/girl, head of house and house prefects – appointed by the Headmaster after discussion with housemasters.
Religion School chapel. Daily assembly by form. Full school once a week. Interdenominational Sunday service. Communion once a month. Preparation for confirmation.
Social Debates and speaking competitions with other local schools; some trips abroad. Pupils allowed to bring own bike to school. Meals self-service. School shop. No tobacco allowed; alcohol (no spirits) at limited times in staff/sixth-form bar.
Discipline Pupils failing to produce homework once might expect reprimand and discussion; those caught experimenting with illegal substances would probably expect expulsion.
Boarding Senior school, 5% have own study bedroom, 95% share; junior school are in dormitories of 4+. Single-sex houses. Resident qualified nurse. Central dining room. Pupils can provide and cook own food. 3 termly exeats (up to a week). Visits to local town allowed.
Alumni association run by Secretary to the Wyvern Society, c/o the school.
Former pupils Paul Cox (artist); Marc Sinden (actor); Michael Blodgett (sculptor); Christopher Neame (actor/producer); Charles Balchin (TV producer).

• STOCKPORT GRAMMAR

Stockport Grammar School, Buxton Road, Stockport, Cheshire SK2 7AF. Tel 0161 456 9000
• Pupils 1265 • Boys 4–18 (Day) • Girls 4–18 (Day) • Upper sixth 128 • Termly fees £1299
• HMC • Enquiries to the Headmaster; applications to Headmaster's secretary

What it's like

Founded in 1487 by Sir Edmond Shaa, the 100th Lord Mayor of London and leading goldsmith of his era, to 'teche allman persons children the science of grammer', the school has been in continuous existence under the patronage of The Goldsmiths' Company and is the second oldest school of secular foundation in the country. Like many traditional grammar schools it is very much a part of the community, by which it is strongly supported. The junior school is on the same site. The school is now co-educational, having admitted girls since 1980. There have, since then, been a number of additional buildings and it is now very well equipped. The school is non-denominational, but the approach is predominantly Christian in style. The vast majority of leavers go on to degree courses (including many to Oxbridge). Music is exceptionally strong, with choirs, orchestras, wind bands and several chamber groups. Art and drama also have vigorous support. A traditional range of sports and games for which there are first-class facilities on site, including an all-weather pitch. Many pupils regularly gain representative honours at county and regional level. A large number of clubs and societies cater for a range of extra-curricular interests; numerous overseas trips are organised. There is a substantial commitment to community services and a thriving Duke of Edinburgh's Award Scheme.

School profile

Pupils Age range 4–18, 1265 day pupils (650 boys, 615 girls). Senior department 11–18, 1005 pupils, (510 boys, 495 girls). Main entry ages 4, 7, 11 and into the sixth. Over 20% senior intake is from own junior school. *State school entry:* 50% senior intake.

Entrance Own entrance exam used. Academic potential looked for at entry; no religious requirements. Parents not expected to buy textbooks; average extras £72 per term (for lunch). 40 pa assisted places at age 11, 5 at 16.
Parents Great variety of occupations and social groups represented.
Head and staff *Headmaster:* I Mellor, appointed 1996. Educated at Manchester Grammar School and Cambridge (modern languages). Previously Headmaster at Sir Roger Manwood's School, Kent, and Deputy Head at Sale Grammar School for Boys. *Staff:* 77 full time, 4 part time. Annual turnover 6%. Average age 38.
Exam results In 1995, 143 pupils in fifth, 127 in upper sixth. *GCSE:* In 1995, 93% fifth gained at least grade C in 8+ subjects; and 7% in 5–7 subjects. *A-levels:* 85% passed in 4 subjects; 6% in 3; 6% in 2 subjects. Average UCAS points 22.0.
University and college entrance 98% of 1995 sixth-form leavers went on to a degree course (10% after a gap year), 15% to Oxbridge. 12% took courses in medicine, dentistry and veterinary science, 30% in science and engineering, 10% in law, 35% in humanities and social sciences, 5% in art and design, 8% in other subjects eg medical computing, pharmacy.
Curriculum GCSE and A-levels offered: 19 subjects offered, including A-level general studies. *Computing facilities:* 2 specialist computer rooms; CD-Rom facilities and access to Internet. *Europe:* French and German (both compulsory from 11) offered at GCSE and A-level; also GCSE Spanish (in fifth form) and Italian (in sixth). Regular exchanges. Teacher exchanges; holidays in France and Germany, plus cultural visits to Spain and Greece.
The arts *Music:* Over 30% pupils learn a musical instrument; instrumental exams can be taken. Many musical groups including 4 orchestras, 3 wind bands, chamber groups, big band, 4 choirs. Member of World Youth Choir and National Youth Choir; regular success in the Daily Telegraph Young Jazz Competition and in NW Region Daily Telegraph Big Band Competition; regular wind band and choir tours to US. *Drama & dance*: Many pupils involved in termly school productions. *Art:* On average, 45 take GCSE, 12 A-level. Design, pottery, textiles, sculpture and ceramics also offered. Range of general studies options in sixth.
Sport, community service and clubs *Sport and physical activities:* Compulsory sports (boys and girls): athletics, swimming, cross-country; (boys) rugby, lacrosse, cricket, tennis, squash, basketball; (girls) netball, hockey, tennis, squash, rounders. Many representative honours in Cheshire, Greater Manchester and the north. *Community service:* Many pupils take bronze, silver and gold Duke of Edinburgh's Award including service option. Community service optional in sixth. *Clubs & societies*: Up to 30 clubs including animal, chess, climbing, computer, dance, debating, Christian, Grammarail, gym, jewellery, lasers, model United Nations, photography, timewatch, trampolining, Young Enterprise.
Uniform School uniform worn throughout.
Houses/prefects Competitive houses. Head boy/girl, school prefects, house captains, appointed by Headmaster.
Religion Attendance at daily assembly compulsory; usually with Christian theme. Chaplain attached from local church. Regular Jewish assemblies.
Social Active Parents Association organise regular social events. Annual sixth-form ball.
Discipline Pupils failing to produce homework once might expect a detention; those in possession of a controlled substance on the premises should expect immediate suspension and possible exclusion.
Alumni association is run by M H Bown, 13 Brampton Road, Bramhall, Stockport, Cheshire SK7 3BS.
Former pupils Peter Boardman (mountaineer); Admiral Back (Artic explorer); Professor Sir Frederick Williams (inventor of the computer); Toby Box (athlete); John Amaechi (basketball).

• STONAR

Stonar, Cottles Park, Atworth, Melksham, Wiltshire SN12 8NT. Tel 01225 702309, Fax 01225 790830

• Pupils 480 • Boys None • Girls 5–18 (Day/Board/Weekly) • Upper sixth 50 • Termly fees £1763 (Day) £3182 (Board/Weekly) • GSA • Enquiries/applications to the Registrar

What it's like

Founded in 1921 at Sandwich, it moved to its present site in 1939. The main building is a very handsome listed 19th-century country house set in 40 acres of splendid parkland. Facilities are very good and boarding accommodation is comfortable. Religious worship is compulsory in the Anglican tradition but all denominations are welcome. A large staff allows a staff:pupil ratio of nearly 1:9 (and there is quite a large part-time staff). A good general education is provided and vocational qualifications are offered. There is a big commitment to music, drama and art. A fine range of sports and games is available and there is an excellent variety of extra-curricular activities (including riding: the school has its own stables, indoor and an outdoor riding school and a number of horses and ponies). A promising record in the Duke of Edinburgh's Award Scheme.

School profile

Pupils Total age range 5–18; 480 girls (220 day, 260 boarding). Senior department 11–18, 401 girls. Main entry ages 5, 11, 13 and into sixth. Less than 5% are children of former pupils. *State school entry:* 20% senior intake, plus 10% to sixth.

Entrance Own entrance exam used. No special skills or religious requirements. Parents not expected to buy textbooks; maximum extras £100. Scholarships available plus bursaries for music, riding, art, sport.

Parents 15+% in industry or commerce. 30+% live within 30 miles; 10+% live overseas.

Head and staff *Headmistress:* Mrs Sue Hopkinson, in post for 11 years. Educated at Howell's, Llandaff, and Oxford University (modern history). Previously Deputy Head/Acting Head at Queen Ethelburga's, Head of History at Skipton Girls High and Head of Enviromental Studies at West Leeds Girls High. *Staff:* 53 full time, 25 part time. Annual turnover 3%. Average age 36.

Exam results On average, 60 pupils in upper fifth, 50 in upper sixth. *GCSE:* On average, 72% upper fifth gain at least grade C in 8+ subjects; 13% in 5–7; and 15% in 1–4 subjects. *A-levels:* 69% upper sixth pass in 3 subjects; 24% in 2; and 7% in 1 subject. Average UCAS points 14.0.

University and college entrance 70% of 1995 sixth-form leavers went on to a degree course, others typically go on to non-degree courses eg nursing, HND or art, or direct into careers.

Curriculum GCSE, AS and A-levels. 20 GCSE subjects offered (including Latin); 26 at A-level. 20% take science A-levels; 40% arts/humanities; 40% both. *Vocational:* Some BTEC and RSA qualifications offered; work experience available. *Computing facilities:* Archimedes network; labs, library, music school fully equipped. *Special provision:* Help with dyslexia. Specialist teacher for EFL. *Europe:* French, German, Italian and Spanish offered to GCSE, AS and A-level.

The arts (Pupils aged 11 and over) *Music:* Over 50% of pupils learn a musical instrument; instrumental exams can be taken. 5 musical groups including choir, brass and wind bands, orchestra. *Drama & dance*: Both offered. GCSE, AS and A-level drama and LAMDA exams may be taken. All pupils are involved in school and house/other productions. *Art:* On average, 22 take GCSE, 28 A-level. Photography and history of art also offered.

Sport, community service and clubs (Pupils aged 11 and over) *Sport and physical activities:* Compulsory sports: hockey, netball, tennis, athletics, swimming. Optional: volleyball, golf, riding, tetrathlon. GCSE, BAGA and BHS exams may be taken. Hockey teams, county champions, U16, U14, 1994. *Community service:* Pupils take bronze, silver and gold Duke of Edinburgh's Award. CCF and community service optional at age 16. *Clubs and societies:* Some 20 clubs, eg various sports, various music, CDT.

Uniform School uniform worn except in the sixth.

Houses/prefects Competitive houses. Prefects, head girl, head of house and house prefects – appointed by the Headmistress. School Council.

Religion Attendance at religious worship compulsory.
Social Organised local events and trips abroad. Pupils allowed to bring own bike/horse to school. Meals self-service. School shop. No tobacco/alcohol allowed.
Discipline Pupils failing to produce homework once might expect a warning; those caught smoking cannabis on the premises would expect expulsion.
Boarding Sixth have study bedrooms, rest share with 2–6. Houses of approximately 35. Resident qualified nurse. Central dining room. 2 weekend exeats and a week at half-term. Visits to local town allowed.
Former pupils Katharine Schlesinger (actress).

• STONYHURST

Stonyhurst College, Stonyhurst, Lancashire BB7 9PZ. Tel 01254 826345, Fax 01254 826013
• Pupils 400 • Boys 13–18 (Day/Board) • Girls 16–18 (Day/Board) • Upper sixth 80 • Termly fees £2375 (Day) £3824 (Board) • HMC • Enquiries/application to the Director of Admissions

What it's like

Founded in 1593 at St Omers, it moved to Bruges in 1762 and to Liège in 1773. Forced to leave the continent at the outbreak of the French Revolution, it established itself at the Hall of Stonyhurst in 1794. It has very fine buildings in a beautiful setting in the Ribble Valley on the slopes of Longridge Fells. It has two prep schools: St Mary's Hall at Stonyhurst and St John's Beaumont at Windsor. Extremely well equipped with modern facilities, the college is a foundation of the Society of Jesus (a number of whose priests are on the staff) and describes itself as a community of young people, parents, Jesuits, lay staff, old boys and friends. It undertakes to provide instruction in Catholic doctrine and to educate boys in the principles and practice of their faith; enquiries from other Christians are also welcome. Girls have been accepted into the sixth-form since 1989. Its large staff permits a ratio of about 1:9 pupils. Excellent teaching is provided and results are very good. Most leavers go on to degree courses. Very strong indeed in music and drama and there is a wide range of games, sports and activities. Excellent standards in games with a number of county and national representatives. Considerable emphasis on outdoor pursuits for which the environment is ideal. A big cadet corps contingent. Very substantial commitment to local community schemes and charities and a good record in the Duke of Edinburgh's Award Scheme.

School profile

Pupils Age range 13–18; 400 pupils, 65 day (59 boys, 6 girls), 335 boarding (330 boys, 5 girls). Main entry ages 13 (boys) and into sixth (boys and girls). St Mary's Hall, Stonyhurst (tel 01254 826242) and St John's Beaumont, Windsor (tel 01784 432428) provide more than 65% of intake.
Entrance Common Entrance and own exam used. Special skills taken into account. Pupils are largely Roman Catholic although Christians of other denominations are encouraged to apply. Parents are not expected to buy textbooks; other extras variable. 5 pa assisted places. 10–12 pa academic, art, design and music scholarships, up to half fees; college bursaries (for some 65 pupils).
Parents 15+% in industry or commerce; 14+% are doctors, lawyers, etc. 10+% live within 30 miles; 20+% live overseas; 21% from Home Counties/London.
Head and staff *Headmaster:* Adrian Aylward, appointed 1996. Educated at Worth School and Oxford University (Greats) and King's College London (education). Previously Housemaster, Head's Deputy and Director of Admissions at Downside. Prior to starting teaching, he worked for a number of years in corporate finance, with Samuel Montague, County NatWest and as chief executive of a public company. *Staff:* 43 full time, 10 part time. Annual turnover 3.
Exam results In 1996, 82 pupils in fifth, 80 in upper sixth. *GCSE:* In 1995, 96.4% upper fifth gained at least grade C in 5+ subjects (average number was 9 subjects). *A-levels:* 15% upper sixth passed in 4+ subjects; 56% in 3; 21% in 2; and 7% in 1 subject. Average UCAS points 20.5
University and college entrance All 1995 sixth-form leavers eventually go on to degree courses (17% after a gap year; 9% after national service, particularly Singapore). Of those going on to university, 6% go to Oxbridge; 6% took courses in medicine, dentistry

and veterinary science, 25% in science and engineering, 4% in law, 35% in humanities and social sciences, 8% in art and design, 22% in vocational subjects (eg agriculture, property management).
Curriculum GCSE and *A-levels:* 21 GCSE subjects offered (plus astronomy and psychology in sixth); 23 at A-level (including general studies; Chinese and Japanese as extras). 35% took science A-levels; 35% arts/humanities; 30% both. *Vocational:* Some work experience available. *Computing facilities:* 16-station computer network in design and technology department. IT workshop with 24 IBM compatible machines. *Special provision:* EFL classes outside the timetable (small groups). Specialist teaching for pupils with dyslexia and other special needs. *Europe:* French, German and Spanish offered to GCSE and A-level (and Italian, as an extra); also non-examined French in sixth.
The arts *Music:* Over 30% of pupils learn a musical instrument; instrumental exams are taken. Musical groups include orchestras, concert band, training band, string and wind chamber groups, jazz band, dance band etc. *Drama & dance*: Pupils and staff in school productions; majority of pupils in house/other productions. 4–5 productions each year; successes in local speaking competitions. *Art:* On average, 20 take GCSE, 6–8 A-level. Design and pottery also offered; separate design and technology department. 2–3 entries each year to art and design foundation courses.
Sport, community service and clubs *Sport and physical activities:* Compulsory sports: rugby, cricket, athletics. Optional: soccer, badminton, squash, tennis, cross-country, basketball, fencing, swimming. Many county and national representatives in rugby and other sports. Strong outdoor pursuits. *Community service:* Pupils take bronze, silver and gold Duke of Edinburgh's Award. Cadet Corps compulsory for 1 year in fourth form, optional thereafter. Community service optional at all ages. *Clubs and societies:* Up to 12 clubs, eg astronomy, maths, debating, fishing, hillwalking, video, science, computing, scuba diving.
Uniform School uniform worn by all (home clothes for part of weekend).
Houses/prefects Competitive houses for sports only. Prefects and head boy – appointed by the Headmaster.
Religion Compulsory Sunday Mass, year group Mass weekly, Sunday evening service. Morning and evening prayers.
Social Links with Jesuit colleges in Reims, Sydney, Melbourne and Zimbabwe. Pupils allowed to bring own bike to school (from second year). Some meals formal, some self-service. School shop. No tobacco allowed; occasional alcoholic drinks allowed at sixth-form socials.
Discipline Pupils failing to produce work assignments once might expect some loss of free time.
Boarding 117 sixth-formers have own study bedroom; own cubicle in dormitory for third and fourth form. Houses divided by age group; separate house for sixth-form girls. Resident qualified full and part time nursing staff. Central dining room. Exeats on application to Headmaster. Visits to the local town allowed, with permission, for older boys.
Alumni association The Stonyhurst Association, c/o the College.
Former pupils General Vernon Walters (former US Ambassador to UN); Arthur Conan Doyle; Charles Laughton; Paul Johnson; Sir Cecil Clothier; Bruce Kent; Bill Cash MP; Kyran Bracken; Lord Chitnis; Patrick McGrath; Bishop Crispian Hollis.

• STOVER

Stover School, Newton Abbot, Devon TQ12 6QG. Tel 01626 54505

• Pupils 160 • Boys None • Girls 10–18 (Day/Board/Weekly) • Upper sixth 17 • Termly fees £1385 (Day) £2640 (Board) £2575 (Weekly) • GSA, BSA • Enquiries to the School Secretary • Application to the Headmaster.

What it's like

Founded in 1932, it lies in 64 acres of grounds, part of the original Stover Park. There are beautiful landscaped gardens and fine playing fields with splendid views across Dartmoor. The main building is a superb 18th-century Palladian mansion, formerly the home of the Duke of Somerset. Since foundation there have been several additions and developments. A relaxed and friendly atmosphere prevails and there is a policy of trying to suit the needs of the individual. Worship is in the Anglican tradition. A sound general education is provided, with a good range of music, performing arts and art. A standard range of games and sports is available, and there is a variety of extra-curricular activities. Considerable emphasis on outdoor pursuits for which the environment is ideal, and an impressive record in the Duke of Edinburgh's Award Scheme. Very successful Young Enterprise.

School profile

Pupils Age range 10–18; 160 girls, 80 day, 80 boarding. Main entry ages 10, 11 and into sixth. Own nursery and junior departments from 1996. *State school entry:* 50% main intakes, plus occasional pupil to sixth.

Entrance Own entrance exam and standardised tests. No special skills or religious requirements but strong Anglican links. Parents not expected to buy textbooks. 4 pa scholarships/bursaries, 10%–50% of fees.

Parents 10+% live within 30 miles; 5+% live overseas.

Head and staff *Headmaster:* Philip Bujak, in post from 1995. Educated at Attleborough High School, King's Lynn College, and at University of East Anglia and Trinity College (history). Previously Head of Lower and Middle School at Langley. *Staff:* 15 full time, 12 part time. Average age 40.

Exam results In 1995, 44 pupils in Year 11, 17 in upper sixth. *GCSE:* 57% gained grade C or above in 8+ subjects; 30% in 5–7 subjects. *A-levels:* 1 pupil passed in 4 subjects; 9 in 3 subjects; 3 in 2 subjects; and 2 in 1 subject. UCAS points 15.6.

University and college entrance All 1995 sixth-form leavers went on to a degree course (5% after a gap year), 5% to Oxbridge. 5% took courses in medicine, dentistry and veterinary science, 25% in science and engineering, 5% in law, 25% in humanities and social sciences, 20% in art and design, 20% in vocational subjects eg physiotherapy, radiography.

Curriculum GCSE and A-levels; also RSA basic computer literacy. *Vocational:* Work experience compulsory. *Computing facilities:* RM network. *Europe:* French and German offered to GCSE and A-level. Regular exchanges to France and Germany.

The arts *Music:* Over 50% of pupils learn a musical instrument; instrumental exams can be taken. Musical groups include ensembles, groups, choirs eg string, flute, madrigal, brass. Some pupils play with the Devon Schools Orchestra. *Drama & dance:* Both offered. GCSE drama, A-level theatre studies, ESB, LAMDA, gymnastics and modern dance awards exams may be taken. Some pupils are involved in school productions and all in house/other productions. *Art:* On average, 28 take GCSE, 8 A-level. Design, pottery, textiles, photography also offered.

Sport, community service and clubs *Sport and physical activities:* Hockey, cross-country, swimming, tennis, netball, rounders, athletics, riding. Sports are compulsory, options vary with age group. Sixth form only: squash. GCSE, BAGA, RLSS exams may be taken. Regular county team members; Ten Tors teams at 35 and 45 miles; riding, national side-saddle winners. *Community service:* Pupils take bronze, silver and gold Duke of Edinburgh's Award. Developing community service scheme. *Clubs and societies:* Up to 30 clubs: Young Enterprise area winners 4 times in past 7 years, Tycoon business game (2nd of 75 schools), national maths olympiads.

Uniform School uniform worn except in the sixth.

Houses/prefects Competitive houses. Prefects, head girl, head of house and house prefects – appointed by the Headmaster after consultation with staff and prefects.

Religion Morning service compulsory.

Social Young Enterprise scheme with other local schools; some organised trips abroad. Sixth form allowed to bring own car/bike/motorbike to school. Meals self-service. School shop.

Discipline Removal of privileges is the normal sanction. Pupils failing to produce homework expect prep detention.

Boarding Head girl has own study bedroom, sixth-form in doubles; remainder in dormitories of 5+. Houses of approximately 50, are divided by age. Resident qualified nurse. Central dining room. Sixth form can provide and cook own food. 2 weekend exeats and half-term. Visits to local town allowed.

Alumni association run by Mrs A Morley-Smith, c/o the school.

• STOWE

Stowe School, Buckingham MK18 5EH. Tel 01280 813164, Fax 01280 822769.

• Pupils 547 • Boys 13–18 (Day/Board) • Girls 16–18 (Day/Board) • Upper sixth 137 • Termly fees £2990 (Day) £4260 (Board) • HMC, SHA, Allied • Enquiries/application to the Registrar (01280 816518)

What it's like

Founded in 1923, it lies in a magnificent park of 750 acres landscaped by Vanbrugh, Bridgman, Kent and Brown. The main building – the original Stowe House is a huge and elegant country house furnished in 1770 to designs by Adam. It now has modern facilities of every conceivable kind and is exceedingly well equipped. Academic standards are high and results good; over 90% of sixth-formers go on to degree courses each year. Pupils are expected to work hard and display good manners. There is a strong emphasis on the availability of personal help and guidance. High standards are achieved in a wide variety of sports and games and the school is tremendously strong in music, drama and art. A very large number of clubs and societies caters for almost every extra-mural interest. There is a strong commitment to local community schemes and the Duke of Edinburgh's Award Scheme. Health education and environmental issues form integral parts of the general studies programme and there is a visual education course, which fosters visual appreciation of architecture and the built environment.

School profile

Pupils Age range 13–18; 547 pupils, 32 day (27 boys, 5 girls), 515 boarding (447 boys, 100 girls). Main entry ages 13 (boys) and into sixth (boys and girls). 10% are children of former pupils. *State school entry:* 3% main intake.

Entrance Scholarships and Common Entrance used; own exam where CE is inappropriate. Any special skill is of interest; no religious requirements but pupils must attend religious services. Parents expected to buy textbooks; other extras variable. 4 pa assisted places (sixth-form only). Up to 18 pa scholarships and exhibitions available (academic, music, art and leadership potential) up to half fees; successful candidates may apply for a bursary to supplement an award.

Parents 75+% in industry or commerce; 20+% in the professions. 10+% live within 30 miles; 10+% live overseas.

Head and staff *Headmaster:* Jeremy Nichols, 7 years in post. Educated at Lancing and at universities of Cambridge and Perugia (English). Previously Housemaster at Eton, English Teacher at Rugby and Teacher at Livorno Naval Academy and at Gilman (Baltimore). Also Governor of eight schools. *Staff:* 58 full time, 24 part time. Annual turnover of staff 5%.

Exam results In 1995, 105 pupils in upper fifth, 127 in upper sixth. *GCSE:* In 1995, 75% upper fifth gained at least grade C in 8+ subjects; 20% in 5–7; and 5% in 1–4 subjects. *A-levels:* 16% upper sixth passed in 4+ subjects; 65% in 3; 13% in 2; and 4% in 1 subject. Average UCAS points 19.2.

University and college entrance 92% of sixth-form leavers go on to a degree course, others typically go straight into careers or to art or other non-degree courses. Of those going on to university, 5% go to Oxbridge; 4% take courses in medicine, dentistry and veterinary science, 25% in science and engineering, 62% in humanities and social sciences, 7% in art and design, 2% in eg drama, music.

Curriculum GCSE and A-levels. 16 GCSE subjects offered; 17 at A-level (AS-level general studies offered). 17% take science A-levels; 54% arts/humanities; 29% both. *Vocational:* Work experience available. *Computing facilities:* 16 IBM PC compatibles, laser printer, scanner, CD-Rom in computer room and desktop publishing studio; IBM compatible PCs in design and biology departments; BBCs or equivalent in each maths classroom and most other departments. *Special provision:* Regular part-time support for those with special learning difficulties. *Europe:* French, German and Spanish offered to GCSE and A-level; also French AS-level. Regular individual exchanges for sixth-formers to France and Germany, occasionally Spain and Russia. European pupils in school; French, German and Spanish nationals as assistant teachers. Subsidiary Russian and Eurolingua Society in sixth-form.

The arts *Music:* Almost 50% of pupils learn a musical instrument; instrumental exams can be taken. Some 15 musical groups including orchestra, choral society, jazz bands, rock bands, chapel choir. Members of National Youth Orchestra. *Drama & dance:* Both offered. Theatre studies GCSE and A-level may be taken. Some pupils are involved in school and house/other productions. Stowe Theatre Company; full-time crews learning stagecraft, stage-management. Regular entrants to drama school and National Theatre Company. *Art:* On average, 25 take GCSE, 20 A-level. Graphic design, pottery, textiles, photography, sculpture and theatre design also offered.

Sport, community service and clubs *Sport and physical activities:* Major sports: rugby, hockey, cricket (boys); netball, lacrosse, hockey (girls). Optional: wide range of sports/activities (school very strong at several minor sports). Sixth form only: self-defence. *Community service:* Pupils take bronze, silver and gold Duke of Edinburgh's Award. CCF and community service optional. *Clubs and societies:* Over 30 clubs, eg bell-ringing, choral, drama, debating, literary, photographic, Christian Union, Young Farmers. Expeditions: Himalayas, Amazonia.

Uniform School uniform not worn, but dress regulations exist.

Houses/prefects Prefects, head boy/girl, head of house and house prefects – appointed by the Headmaster.

Religion Compulsory attendance at religious worship.

Social Industrial Conference (with Royal Latin School), public speaking with other schools. Organised trips abroad – to Nepal most years and eg South America and skiing parties to Europe. Pupils allowed to bring own bike to school. Meals self-service. School shop. No tobacco or alcohol allowed except beer, cider and wine in supervised bar for top year.

Discipline Pupils failing to produce satisfactory work once should expect to do it again properly with possible further sanctions; those found taking drugs at school can expect expulsion (the dangers of drug and alcohol abuse are discussed in health and safety education programme).

Boarding All sixth-form have own study bedroom. Houses of 50–60 pupils, full age range. Resident qualified nurse; doctor visits daily. Two central dining rooms. Pupils can provide and cook their own food. Exeats at half-term and up to two other weekends each term. Visits to the local town allowed.

Alumni association is run locally by Mr C J G Atkinson, c/o the school, who is in touch with over 6000 former pupils.

Former pupils Grp Capt Lord (Leonard) Cheshire; Lord Quinton; Sir Nigel Broackes; Robert Kee; David Scott Cowper; Richard Branson; David Wynne; David Shepherd; David Fanshawe; Howard Goodall; Sir Nicholas Henderson; Lord Sainsbury; Lord McAlpine; Laurence Whistler; Lord Annan; Lord Boyd Carpenter; Sir Nicholas Lyell; Lord Stephens; Algy Cluff; Tommy Sopwith; Garfield Weston; Bobby Butlin; John Asprey; Sir Jack Hayward; David Niven; George Melly; Peregrine Worsthorne; Gavin Maxwell; Michael Ventris.

• STRATHALLAN

Strathallan School, Forgandenny, Perth PH2 9EG. Tel 01738 812546, Fax 01738 812549

• Pupils 500 • Boys 10–18 (Day/Board) • Girls 10–18 (Day/Board) • Upper sixth 75 • Termly fees £2570 (Day) £3685 (Board) • HMC • Enquiries/application to the Headmaster

What it's like

Founded in 1912 at Bridge of Allan, and moved to its present site in 160 acres in 1920. The centre of the school is a splendid 19th-century country house, with modern boarding houses and classrooms surrounding it. Facilities are first-rate. Religious practice follows the Church of Scotland, but the school is interdenominational. A high standard of teaching is provided (the staff:pupil ratio is about 1:8) and results are good. Each year many pupils go on to degree courses, including to Oxbridge. The school offers Highers and A-levels. The music, drama and art departments are very strong. A good range of games, sports and activities. The CCF is voluntary and well supported. Considerable emphasis on outdoor pursuits for which the environment is ideal. A promising record in the Duke of Edinburgh's Award Scheme.

School profile

Pupils Total age range 10–18; 500 pupils, 40 day (15 boys, 25 girls), 460 boarding (310 boys, 150 girls). Senior department 13–18, 425 pupils (280 boys, 145 girls). Main entry ages 11, 13 and into sixth. Approx 10% are children of former pupils. Own prep (Riley House) provides large proportion of intake. *State school entry:* 30% main intakes over

11, plus 33% to sixth.
Entrance Common Entrance and own exam used. No special skills required. Parents not expected to buy textbooks; £150 maximum extras. 6 pa assisted places. 6 pa scholarships/ bursaries at 11, 13 and 16, 20%–80% of fees. Also art and music scholarships.
Parents Up to 10% live within 30 miles; 25+% live overseas.
Head and staff *Headmaster:* Angus W McPhail, 4 years in post. Educated at Abingdon and Oxford. Previously Housemaster and Head of Economics at Sedburgh, teacher at Glenalmond, and with the Bank of England. *Staff:* 57 full time, 12 part time. Annual turnover 3%. Average age 38.
Exam results On average, 85 in GCSE year, 75 in Higher/A-level year. *GCSE:* In 1995, 65% fifth form gained grade C or above in 8+ subjects; 22% in 5-7 subjects. *Highers/A-levels:* Average UCAS points 18.8.
University and college entrance 75% of sixth-form leavers went on to a degree course, others typically go on to art, drama or other non-degree courses.
Curriculum GCSE, S-grade, Highers and A-levels. 16+ subjects offered, no A-level general studies. *Vocational:* Work experience available. *Computing facilities:* Special department, and machines in virtually all departments. *Special provision:* for remedial English. *Europe:* French, German and Spanish offered to GCSE, AS and A-level. Annual exchanges (to France and Germany).
The arts *Music:* 40% of pupils learn a musical instrument; instrumental exams can be taken. Musical groups include orchestra, string group, dance band, jazz group, brass group, choir and choral society. Members of National Youth Orchestra of Scotland. *Drama & dance*: Both offered; expressive arts are part of the core syllabus pre-GCSE. Majority of pupils are involved in school/house productions. Recent production (Tartuffe) at Edinburgh Fringe Festival. *Art:* On average, 85 take GCSE, 35 Higher, 40 A-level. Painting, drawing, ceramics and printmaking also available.
Sport, community service and clubs *Sport and physical activities:* Compulsory sports: rugby (boys), hockey/netball (girls). Optional: Skiing, hockey, squash, shooting, badminton, swimming, lacrosse, cross-country, curling, basketball, horse riding, football, multi-gym, aerobics, cricket, athletics, tennis, golf, cycling, climbing, canoeing, sailing and croquet. Recent Scottish Schools internationalists in rugby, hockey, cricket, cross-country, golf, skiing, athletics and shooting. *Community service:* Pupils take bronze, silver and gold Duke of Edinburgh's Award. CCF (Army, Navy and Marines sections) and community service optional. *Clubs and societies:* Up to 15 clubs, eg chess, bridge, drama, falconry, land management.
Uniform Dress regulations throughout.
Houses/prefects Competitive houses. Prefects, head boy/girl, head of house and house prefects – appointed by the Headmaster after consultation.
Religion Attendance at religious worship compulsory.
Social Theatre excursions, debates, musical events with other local schools. Annual French and German exchanges; recent organised trips to France, Australia, Hong Kong, China, Barbados, Austria and South America. Meals self-service. School tuck shop and shop in each house for basics. No tobacco/alcohol allowed.
Discipline Discipline administered at house level for minor offences and Headmaster or Deputy for major ones. Pupils failing to produce homework satisfactorily would be given Sunday afternoon detention.
Boarding All girls and most senior boys in own study bedroom. Single-sex houses of approximately 75, same as competitive houses. Resident qualified nursing sister. Central dining room. Pupils allowed to provide and cook own food. Half-term and three Saturday night exeats each term. Visits to Perth for upper sixth; with adult supervision for others.

• STREATHAM HIGH

Streatham Hill & Clapham High School, 42 Abbotswood Road, London SW16 1AW. Tel 0181 677 8400/2904, Fax 0181 677 2001.

• Pupils 620 • Boys None • Girls 4–18 (Day) • Upper sixth 45 • Termly fees £1192–£1548 (Day) • GSA, GPDST • Enquiries/applications to the Headmistress

What it's like

Opened in 1887 as Brixton Hill High School, in 1938 it amalgamated with Clapham High

School. The senior school moved to a new site adjacent to Tooting Bec Common in 1994 while the junior school remains in adapted buildings at the old Streatham site. Both sites now provide first-class accommodation and resources. Interdenominational worship is encouraged. A sound, well-balanced, general education is provided. Academic results are good and most sixth-formers go on to university. There is a substantial commitment to music, drama, art and overseas visits.

School profile

Pupils Total age range 4–18; 620 day girls. Senior department 11–18, 425 girls. Main entry ages 4, 11 and into the sixth. Own junior department provides over 90% of the senior intake.

Entrance Own entrance exam used. Musical skill looked for; no religious requirements. Parents not expected to buy textbooks. 24 pa assisted places. 10 pa scholarships; also bursaries.

Parents 15+% in theatre, media, music etc; 20+% are doctors, lawyers etc; 20+% in industry or commerce.

Head and staff *Headmistress:* Miss Gillian Ellis, in post for 17 years. Educated at Glasgow University (chemistry). Previously Senior Mistress at Croydon High and Assistant Science Teacher at St Margaret's. Also Liveryman of Goldsmiths' Company; Freedom of the City of London; Chairman of Standing Committee of GPDST Headmistresses (1990). *Staff:* 42 full time, 8 part time. Annual turnover 5%. Average age 34.

Exam results Average size of upper fifth 70; upper sixth 45. *GCSE:* On average 65 pupils in upper fifth pass 8+ subjects. *A-levels:* 3% upper sixth passes in 4 subjects; 78% in 3; and 13% in 2 subjects. Average UCAS points 18.8.

University and college entrance 90% of 1995 sixth-form leavers went on to a degree course, others typically go on to non-degree courses or straight into careers (eg retail management). Of those going on to university, 5% went to Oxbridge; 15% took courses in medicine, dentistry and veterinary science, 20% in science and engineering, 60% in humanities and social sciences, 5% in art and design.

Curriculum GCSE and A-levels. 30% take science/engineering A-levels; 30% arts and humanities; 40% a mixture. *Computing facilities:* Information technology centre networked with library, 16 extra machines in science, geography and CDT departments; whole school being networked. *Europe:* French, German and Spanish offered to GCSE, AS and A-level; also Italian A-level. Regular exchanges. Regular visits from MEPs; conversation lessons and visits abroad.

The arts (Pupils aged 11 and over) *Music:* 50% of pupils learn a musical instrument; instrumental exams can be taken. Musical groups include orchestra, wind band, chamber groups, choirs. *Drama & dance*: Both offered. GCSE drama may be taken. Majority of pupils are involved in school productions and all in house/other productions. *Art:* On average, 45% take GCSE, 10% A-level; design, pottery, photography also offered.

Sport, community service and clubs (Pupils aged 11 and over) *Sport and physical activities:* Compulsory sports: netball, tennis, swimming, athletics, cricket. Optional: skating. *Community service:* Pupils take bronze, silver and gold Duke of Edinburgh's Award. World Challenge Expedition 1996. *Clubs and societies:* Up to 70 clubs, eg classical, debating, photography, gym, dance, drama, public speaking, science, astronomy, languages, history, international affairs, army challenge.

Uniform School uniform worn except in the sixth.

Houses/prefects Competitive houses. No prefects; head girl – elected by staff and senior girls.

Religion Worship encouraged.

Social Frequent visits to France, Austria, Italy, Greece. Pupils allowed to bring own bike to school. Meals self-service. No tobacco/alcohol allowed.

Discipline Pupils failing to produce homework once might expect detention after school; those caught smoking cannabis on the premises might expect expulsion.

Former pupils June Whitfield (actress); Norman Hartnell (fashion designer); Angela Carter (novelist); Carol Royle (actress).

• SUNDERLAND HIGH

Sunderland High School, Mowbray Road, Sunderland. SR2 8HY. Tel 0191 567 4984, Fax 0191 510 3953

• Pupils 550 • Boys 3–18 (Day) • Girls 3–18 (Day) • Upper sixth 20 • Termly fees £750–£1305 (Day) • SHMIS, CSCo • Enquiries/application to the Head

What it's like

Founded as a co-educational school in 1993, from a merger between the existing Church Schools Company girls' school, founded in 1884, with a boys' school, Tonstall House. It has an agreeable urban campus with pleasant grounds. The junior school is close by. The senior school is housed in the original building and has been extensively modernised over the years; it is now well equipped. The Centenary Building nearby provides classrooms, laboratories and a music centre and there is a new sixth-form centre. Pupils from all parts of the school share the sports facilities which include a sports hall and all-weather pitch. Being a Church school it lays stress on the creation of a Christian atmosphere but is ecumenical in spirit and in policy. A sound general education is provided. Most sixth-formers go on to degree courses each year. Music, drama and art are well supported. There is a good range of sports and a variety of extra-curricular activities including the Duke of Edinburgh's Award Scheme.

School profile

Pupils Total range 3–18; 550 day pupils, 250 boys, 300 girls. Senior department 11–18; 230 pupils (100 boys, 130 girls). Main entry ages 11, 13 and into sixth. 2% are children of former pupils. Many pupils from own Junior School (tel 0191 514 3278). *State school entry:* 30% senior intake, 10% to sixth.

Entrance Own entrance exams used. No special skills or religious requirements. Parents not expected to buy textbooks; music lessons extra, £75 per term. 16 pa assisted places (at age 5, 7, 11, 13 and into sixth). Scholarships at 11+ and sixth-form, one term's fees; plus music scholarship; bursaries available depending on pupil needs.

Head and staff *Head:* Ms Charlotte Rendle-Short, 3 years in post. Educated in Australia – Melbourne and New England universities (maths). Previously Deputy Head at the Perse School for Girls and Head of Senior School and Housemaster at Geelong Grammar. *Staff:* 37 full time, 12 part time. Annual turnover 4% Average age 37.

Exam results In 1995, 31 pupils in Year 11, 20 in Year 13. *GCSE:* in 1995, 27 in Year 11 gained at least Grade C in 8+ subjects; 3 in 5–7 subjects. *A-levels:* 4 passed in 4+ subjects; 8 in 3; 3 in 2 subjects. Average UCAS points 13.4.

University and college entrance 95% of sixth-form leavers go on to a degree course (10% after a gap year); others typically go on to HND courses or to employment. Of those going on to university, 5% went to Oxbridge; 5% took courses in medicine, dentistry and veterinary science, 4% in science and engineering, 4% in law, 50% in humanities and social sciences, 15% in art and design, 20% in vocational subjects.

Curriculum GCSE and A-levels. 20 GCSE and A-level subjects offered, including Latin and A-level general studies. 25% take science A-levels; 40% arts/humanities, 35% both. *Vocational:* Work experience available; also RSA computing. *Computing facilities:* 2 fully networked RM rooms; other Acorn, Amstrad, and BBC computers in classrooms, careers room and library. *Special provision:* Some extra tuition for pupils with special needs; one or two pupils with severe dyslexic or visual problems. *Europe:* French, German and Spanish offered to GCSE and A-level (German compulsory from age 4; French from 10 to GCSE); all sixth-form students have the opportunity to continue language study. Regular exchanges to France, Germany and Denmark.

The arts *Music:* Up to 50% of pupils learn a musical instrument; instrumental exams can be taken. Musical groups include instrumental groups, choirs, chamber group, wind group, ceilidh band. *Drama & dance*: Dance offered. LAMDA, RAD exams may be taken. Pupils are involved in school, house and other productions. *Art:* On average 12 take GCSE, 4 A-level. Design, pottery, photography also offered. School invited annually to nominate a sixth-form candidate to have work exhibited in London by Worshipful Company of Painter Stainers.

Sport, community service and clubs *Sport and physical activities:* Compulsory sports: (mixed where appropriate) hockey, football, athletics, swimming, tennis, netball, cricket. Sixth-form games include a variety of leisure activities. Several pupils playing sport at

county level. *Community service:* Duke of Edinburgh's Award. Fund-raising involves the whole school – normally raise £4000 annually by events; annual party for the elderly. *Clubs and societies:* Include public speaking, art, drama, stage lighting, computer, music, karate, photography.
Uniform School uniform worn.
Houses/prefects Competitive houses. Prefects, senior prefects, head prefect, house prefects – appointed by Head, taking views of peer group and staff into account.
Religion Regular church services in local parish church; attendance at religious worship compulsory (non-Christians may be withdrawn; few are).
Social Organised trips abroad and exchange systems. Pupils allowed to bring own car to school. Meals self-service. No tobacco/alcohol allowed.
Discipline Pupils failing to produce homework receive a verbal warning; a detention on the second occasion. Those caught smoking cannabis on the premises would be asked to leave.
Former pupils Kate Adie; Jane Grigson.

• SURBITON HIGH

Surbiton High School, Surbiton Crescent, Kingston Upon Thames, Surrey KT1 2JT. Tel 0181 546 5245, Fax 0181 547 0026

• Pupils 913 • Boys 4–11 only (Day) • Girls 4–18 (Day) • Upper sixth 57 • Termly fees £1613 (Day) • GSA, CSCL • Enquiries/application to the Headmistress

What it's like

Founded in 1884 and owned by the Church Schools Company, it stands in a quiet part of Surbiton in pleasant grounds. The buildings are well designed and facilities are good. A new junior girls school and redesigned sixth-form centre were opened recently and it has acquired Surbiton Assembly Rooms for use as a theatre and music block. Basically it is a C of E establishment but all faiths are welcome. A friendly school where individuals are valued and encouraged to develop their talents. Academic results are very good and most sixth-formers proceed to degree courses each year, including Oxbridge. It has strong music, drama and art departments and a fair range of games, sports and activities.

School profile

Pupils Total age range 4–18; 913 day pupils (114 boys, 799 girls). Senior department 11–18, 553 girls. Main entry ages 4, 5, 8 (boys and girls); 11 and into sixth (girls). Approx 3% are children of former pupils. *State school entry:* 30% senior intake.
Entrance Own entrance exam used. No special skills or religious requirements. Variable extras. Assisted places at 11 and into the sixth. Scholarships (including academic, music, sport and sixth-form) and bursaries available, up to half fees. Reduced fees for clergy children.
Head and staff *Headmistress:* Miss Gail Perry, 4 years in post. Educated at Newport High School, Gwent, and at Bristol University and King's College London (science). Previously deputy headmistress at Putney High School. *Staff:* 68 full time, 19 part time.
Exam results In 1995, 86 pupils in upper fifth, 51 in upper sixth. *GCSE:* In 1995, 94% upper fifth gained at least grade C in 8+ subjects; 5% in 5–7 subjects. *A-levels:* 9% passed in 4+ subjects; 91% in 3 subjects. Average UCAS points 22.9.
University and college entrance 98% of 1995 sixth-form leavers went on to a degree course (10% after a gap year); others typically go on to vocational courses. Of those going on to university, 16% went to Oxbridge; 7% took courses in medicine, dentistry and veterinary science, 15% in science and engineering, 2% in law, 57% in humanities and social sciences, 5% in art and design, 14% in vocational subjects eg drama, fashion management.
Curriculum GCSE and A-levels. 24 subjects offered (no A-level general studies) Japanese offered in sixth. 21% take science A-levels; 26% arts/humanities; 53% both. *Vocational:* Work experience available. *Computing facilities:* Computer room with network throughout the school. Specialist desktop publishing facilities including laser and colour printers. All sixth-form take computer awareness course. *Europe:* French (taught from age 4), German and Spanish offered to GCSE, AS and A-level; also French to Institute of Linguists and non-examined German. All sixth-formers study at least one foreign

language as part of their general studies programme. Regular exchanges to France and Germany. European studies offered; talks from MEPs etc.
The arts (Pupils aged 11 and over) *Music:* Up to 50% of pupils learn a musical instrument. Some 10 musical groups including orchestras, wind band, choirs, chamber ensembles, recorder consort. Some pupils participate in ENO productions; success in local music festivals. *Drama & dance*: Drama offered. GCSE drama, A-level theatre studies and LAMDA exams may be taken. Some pupils are involved in school productions and majority in house/other productions. Great success in local festivals. *Art:* On average, 50 take GCSE, 8 A-level. Design, pottery, textiles, product design and photography also offered. National competition success eg Woolwich Collage Competition.
Sport, community service and clubs (Pupils aged 11 and over) *Sport and physical activities:* Compulsory sports: hockey, netball, tennis, athletics. Optional: squash, rowing, badminton, dry skiing, keep fit, aerobics. Sixth form only: weights, swimming, BAGA exams may be taken. *Community service:* Community service optional; sixth-form Community Awareness option. *Clubs and societies:* Up to 30 clubs, eg technology, science, drama, music, debating, classics, opera, theatre, sport, computer.
Uniform School uniform worn except in sixth.
Houses/prefects No competitive houses. No prefects but permanent sixth-form committee. Head girl – appointed by Headmistress after discussion with staff and pupils. School Council.
Religion Compulsory attendance at daily assembly, pupils often taking participatory role in leading prayers.
Social Observer Mace Debating Competition with other schools; sixth-form theatre club and opera club; inter-sixth-form public speaking competition. Organised visits to Russia, France, Belgium; regular skiing holidays; French and German exchanges. Pupils allowed to bring own car/bike to school. Meals self-service. Cafeteria for seniors. No tobacco/alcohol allowed.
Discipline Pupils failing to produce homework once might expect a reprimand; those caught smoking cannabis on the premises could expect expulsion.

• SUTTON HIGH

Sutton High School, 55 Cheam Road, Sutton, Surrey SM1 2AX. Tel 0181 642 0594, Fax 0181 642 2014

• Pupils 750 • Boys None • Girls 4–18 (Day) • Upper sixth 53 • Termly fees £1548 (Day) • GSA, GPDST • Enquiries/application to the Headmistress

What it's like

Founded in 1884, it is located on a 5-acre site near the centre of Sutton and occupies what were six adjacent family houses in Cheam Road and Grove Road. There has been much recent development, including purpose-built accommodation which is well-equipped for science, art, design and technology. The junior school is in three houses nearby. Overall it is a pleasant campus with some games facilities on site. Playing fields are at Cheam. Years 11 and sixth-form have their own common room and do not have to wear uniform. A high value is placed on academic study both as an end in itself and as a preparation for adult life and work. A sound general education is provided. Academic results are excellent and the vast majority of sixth-formers go on to degree courses each year. There is a considerable commitment to music and much strength in drama (the school has an open-air theatre built by parents and pupils). A good range of games and sports (high standards are achieved) and plentiful extra-curricular activities. Senior girls are encouraged to contribute to local social services and the school has an impressive record in the Duke of Edinburgh's Award Scheme.

School profile

Pupils Total age range 4–18; 750 day girls. Senior department 11–18, 500 girls. Main entry ages 4, 6, 11 and into sixth. *State school entry:* 45% senior intakes.
Entrance Own entrance exam used. Good academic ability looked for; no religious requirements. Parents not expected to buy textbooks; extras include instrumental studies, speech and drama. 34 pa assisted places. 9 pa scholarships, 5%–100% of fees; bursaries in cases of financial need.
Head and staff *Headmistress:* Mrs Anne Coutts, in post from 1995. Educated at King's

High, Warwick, Apsley Grammar and Warwick University (microbiology, virology and education). Previously Headmistress of Eothen, Deputy Head of Edgbaston College and Head of Department at Trent College. Also member of Midlands Business Women's Association. *Staff:* 33 full time, 16 part time. Annual turnover approx 5%.

Exam results In 1995, 83 pupils in Year 11, 65 in upper sixth. *GCSE:* In 1995, 74 Year 11 gain at least grade C in 8+ subjects; 8 in 5–7 subjects. *AS/A-levels:* 6 upper sixth pass in 4+ subjects; 53 in 3–3½; 6 in 2 subjects. Average UCAS points 25.7.

University and college entrance 94% of 1995 sixth-form leavers went on to a degree course (19% after a gap year), 9% to Oxbridge; 26% took courses in medicine, dentistry and veterinary science, 4% in science and engineering, 2% in law, 23% in humanities and social sciences, 6% in art and design, 39% in vocational subjects eg radiography, education, speech therapy.

Curriculum GCSE and A-levels. 21 subjects offered (no A-level general studies). *Vocational:* Work experience available. *Computing facilities:* Well-equipped computer laboratory. *Europe:* French and German offered to GCSE and A-level; also AS-level French and GCSE Spanish in sixth. Regular exchanges to France and Germany.

The arts (Pupils aged 11 and over) *Music:* Over 30% of pupils learn a musical instrument; instrumental exams can be taken. Musical groups include choirs, 2 orchestras, wind band and string orchestra. *Drama & dance*: Drama offered. Some pupils are involved in school productions. 2 drama competitions annually. *Art:* On average, 30 take GCSE, 12 A-level. Design, pottery, textiles, photography, sculpture and print-making also offered.

Sport, community service and clubs (Pupils aged 11 and over) *Sport and physical activities:* Compulsory sports: hockey, netball, tennis, rounders, swimming, gymnastics, badminton, volleyball. Optional: aerobics. Sixth form only: squash. GCSE exams may be taken. some pupils in county squads. *Community service:* Pupils take bronze, silver and gold Duke of Edinburgh's Award. Community service optional. Involvement in Sutton Borough's Youth Action. Upper sixth Christmas revue raises some £1,300 pa. *Clubs and societies:* Up to 30 clubs, eg computer, wildlife, chess, debating, drama, Christian Union.

Uniform School uniform worn except in Year 11 and the sixth.

Houses/prefects No competitive houses. 2 head girls and 4–5 deputies – elected by staff and seniors. School Council.

Religion Attendance at daily assembly expected unless parents request otherwise.

Social Inter-sixth society with local schools, occasional joint activities with Sutton Grammar School. Organised trips abroad. Pupils allowed to bring own car/bike/ motorbike to school. Meals self-service. No tobacco/alcohol allowed.

Discipline Pupils failing to produce homework once might expect a kindly reproof; those caught smoking cannabis on the premises should expect automatic suspension.

• SUTTON VALENCE

Sutton Valence School, Sutton Valence, Maidstone, Kent ME17 3HL Tel 01622 842281, Fax 01622 844093

• Pupils 640 • Boys 3–18 (Day/Board/Weekly) • Girls 3–18 (Day/Board/Weekly) • Upper sixth 64 • Termly fees £1085–2365 (Day) £2800–3695 (Board/Weekly) • HMC, SHA, BSA • Enquiries/ application to the Admissions Secretary

What it's like

Founded in 1576 as a boys' school, it has been co-educational since 1983. The senior school occupies about 100 acres on the slopes of a high ridge overlooking the Weald and above a beautiful and safe village. There is excellent accommodation, delightful gardens and extensive playing fields. The boarding facilities have recently been up-graded. Modern teaching facilities are first-rate. The junior school, Underhill, is on a 20-acre site in the neighbouring village of Chart Sutton. Sutton Valance has a reputation for close pastoral care, and the staff:pupil ratio of about 1:10 helps to produce good academic standards and results. Pupils from a broad academic range aim high and achieve well: over 90% go on to university. Flourishing music and art departments; strong in drama. An impressive range of games and sports in which high standards are achieved (20 plus representatives at county level). A very large number of clubs and societies provide for most conceivable needs. Big commitment to local community schemes.

School profile

Pupils Total age range 3–18; 640 pupils, 524 day (282 boys, 242 girls), 116 boarding (79 boys, 37 girls). Senior department 11–18, 370 pupils (225 boys, 145 girls). Main entry ages 11, 13 and into sixth. Approx 8% are children of former pupils. Many senior pupils from own junior school, Underhill. *State school entry:* 90% at 11, 5% at 13, plus 5% to sixth.
Entrance Common Entrance and own exam used. All-rounders looked for; Anglican foundation but others accepted. Parents expected to buy textbooks; £300 maximum extras. 10 pa assisted places. Scholarships for academic, sport, music, drama and art, up to 50% fees pa; bursaries according to need.
Parents 15% in the professions. 15+% in industry or commerce 60+% live within 30 miles; 15% live overseas.
Head and staff *Headmaster:* Nicholas Sampson, in post from 1994. Educated at Howard School and at universities of Cambridge (English) and Oxford (PGCE). Previously Housemaster at Wells Cathedral School, English teacher at Rydal and at St Aloysius' College, Sydney. Has also worked in publishing and the Civil Service; Member of Area Training Board; FRSA. *Staff:* 34 full time, 7 part time. Annual turnover 2–3. Average age 36.
Exam results On average, 60 pupils in fifth, 60 in upper sixth. *GCSE:* On average, 45 in fifth gain at least grade C in 8+ subjects; 8 in 5–7 subjects. *A-levels:* 8% upper sixth pass in 4+ subjects; 64% in 3; 24% in 2; and 3% in 1 subject. Average UCAS points 17.2.
University and college entrance 92% of 1995 sixth-form leavers went on to a degree course (15% after a gap year); others typically go on to employment or other higher education courses. Of those going on to university, 1% went to Oxbridge; 10% took courses in medicine, dentistry and veterinary science, 15% in science and engineering, 10% in law, 20% in humanities and social sciences, 5% in art and design, 20% in other vocational subjects (eg physiotherapy, hotel/catering, sports studies, teaching), 20% in other subjects (eg business, media, leisure studies).
Curriculum GCSE and A-levels: 22 subjects offered. All pupils sit diploma in information technology. 32% take science A-levels; 38% arts/humanities; 29% both. *Vocational:* Work experience available – one week for all fifth formers. *Computing facilities:* 40 IBM compatible PCs; 10 BBC Bs. *Special provision:* Specialist support for mild dyslexics; EFL classes for non-English speakers. *Europe:* French and German offered to GCSE, AS and A-level; Spanish to GCSE. Regular exchanges. Music and art tours (France, Benelux countries, Italy and Eastern Europe). Some European pupils in sixth-form.
The arts *Music:* 50% of pupils learn a musical instrument; instrumental exams can be taken. Some 11 musical groups including 3 choirs, orchestra, wind band, recorder groups, string and wind ensembles, jazz band, pop group. Choirgirl of the Year 1994; European music tour. *Drama & dance*: Both offered. LAMDA exams may be taken. Majority of pupils are involved in school and house/other productions. Theatre workshop. *Art:* On average, 20 take GCSE, 2 AS-level, 8 A-level. Design, pottery, photography and history of art also offered. Lively creative arts magazine.
Sport, community service and clubs *Sport and physical activities:* Compulsory sports – pupils choose from: rugby, cricket, hockey, netball, swimming, tennis, athletics, cross-country, badminton, squash, basketball, shooting, fives, golf. National representatives in hockey, cross-country; county and regional, rugby, hockey, athletics, tennis, cricket. *Community service:* Pupils take bronze, silver and gold Duke of Edinburgh's Award. CCF optional for 2 years at age 13+, community service optional at 15+. *Clubs and societies:* Up to 30 clubs, eg shooting, art, birdwatching, riding, model-making, chess, photography, typing, video filming, yoga.
Uniform School uniform worn throughout; special sixth-form uniform.
Houses/prefects Non-competitive houses. Prefects, head boy/girl, head of house and house prefects – appointed by the Housemasters and Headmaster.
Religion Daily chapel, Sunday service (boarders).
Social Debates, dances, business conferences, choral activities with local schools. Organised exchanges to France and Germany. Day pupils allowed to bring own car/bike/motorbike to school. Meals self-service. School shop. No tobacco or private alcohol allowed; sixth-form licensed club.
Discipline Pupils failing to produce homework once would expect to do extra work; those caught smoking cannabis on the premises should expect expulsion.

Boarding 60+% have own study bedroom, 40% are in dormitories of 6+. Single-sex houses of approx 60. Resident qualified nurse. Central dining room. Weekly boarding an option. Visits to the local town allowed, at housemaster's discretion.
Alumni association is run by Mr C R G, Shaw, c/o the school.
Former pupils Sir Charles Groves; Compton Rennie; Sir Rustam Feroze; Peter Fairley; Terence Cuneo; Mark Benson; Ben Brown; Sidney Wooderson; Robert Fisk.

• SYDENHAM HIGH

Sydenham High School for Girls, 19 Westwood Hill, Sydenham London SE26 6BL. Tel 0181 778 8737, Fax 0181 776 8830

• Pupils 700 • Boys None • Girls 4–18 (Day) • Upper sixth 50 • Termly fees £1288–£1640 (Day)
• GSA, GPDST • Enquiries/application to the Headmistress

What it's like

Founded in 1887, the school developed rapidly and now occupies a 5½-acre site well served by public transport. The main building is a handsome Victorian house to which has been added modern purpose-built premises which provide excellent facilities. Academic standards and results are good and the majority of sixth-form leavers go on to degree courses. Music is very well supported: choirs, orchestras and bands flourish and pupils are involved in wide range of music-making enterprises. Drama is also popular, a high proportion of pupils are successful in drama examinations. There is a range of sports and games (including hockey, trampolining, karate, fencing, archery) for which there are excellent facilities on site. There have been many representatives in hockey, tennis, swimming, trampolining and gymnastics at county and national level. A wide variety of extra-curricular activities is available; the school takes part successfully in the Duke of Edinburgh's Award Scheme.

School profile

Pupils Total age range 4–18, 700 day girls. Senior department 11–18, 480 girls. Main entry ages 4, 5, 7, 11, 13 and into sixth. Own junior department provides 60% of senior intake. *State school entry:* 40% at 11.
Entrance Own entrance exam (10 and 16; interim test papers at other stages); interview. Good standard of English and mathematics required, with an enthusiasm for learning; no religious requirements. Parents not expected to buy textbooks. 42 pa assisted places (5 at age 7, 30 at 11 and 7 to sixth). 8 scholarships pa (4 at age 11, 4 to sixth), 25% fees.
Parents Most parents are professional or business people.
Head and staff *Headmistress:* Mrs Geraldine Baker, 9 years in post. Educated at Hafod-y-Ddol Grammar and London University (zoology). Previously Deputy Headmistress at South Hampstead High. Also Scientific Fellow – Royal Zoological Society. *Staff:* 45 full time, 15 part time. Annual turnover less than 10%.
Exam results In 1995, 77 pupils in upper fifth, 50 in upper sixth. *GCSE:* 86% upper fifth gained at least grade C in 5 subjects. *A-levels:* Upper sixth pass an average of 2.8 subjects. Average UCAS points 16.4.
University and college entrance 90% of 1995 sixth-form leavers went on to a degree course (10% after a gap year); others typically go on to vocational courses, to art or music colleges. Of those going on to university, 8% went to Oxbridge; 5% took courses in medicine, dentistry and veterinary science, 15% in science and engineering, 5% in law, 70% in humanities and social sciences, 10% in art and design and vocational subjects eg hotel management.
Curriculum GCSE, AS and A-levels. 20 subjects offered at GCSE, 22 to A-level; (general studies for all lower sixth but no A-level. *Computing facilities:* 3 research machine networks; individual department computers. *Europe:* French, German and Spanish offered at GCSE, AS and A-level; also conversation classes for all sixth-form in French, German and Spanish. Regular exchanges to France and Germany, occasionally to Spain. Recent cultural visits to Paris, Rome, Provence, Barcelona and Berlin.
The arts (Pupils aged 11 and over) *Music:* Many pupils learn a musical instrument; instrumental exams can be taken. Over 9 musical groups including orchestra, chamber group, jazz band, flute group, wind band, wind ensemble, string ensemble, choirs. Prizes

in Beckenham Festival; girls sing in Ernest Read Choir, Bach Choir; students have won place at Royal College of Music. *Drama & dance*: Both offered. A-level theatre studies, ESB, LAMDA exams may be taken. Pupils are involved in a range of school productions. *Art:* On average, 30 take GCSE, 8 A-level; design, technology, CDT, pottery, textiles, photography also offered. Art college applications always successful.
Sport, community service and clubs (Pupils aged 11 and over) *Sport and physical activities:* Compulsory sports (at different ages): gym, netball, hockey, dance, swimming, athletics, rounders, tennis, volleyball, netball. Optional: fencing, trampolining, archery, squash, racket-ball, aerobics, badminton, karate, basketball. GCSE, BAGA exams may be taken. Highly placed in London Schools trampolining; diving, regional champion; gymnastics, national squad; tennis, county players; fencing, national championships; hockey, district player. *Community service:* Pupils take bronze, silver and gold Duke of Edinburgh's Award. Community service optional: stress on charity activities, both in school and participation in national events. *Clubs and societies:* Up to 20 clubs, eg modern languages, pottery, CDT, computer, Christian Union, textiles, Model United Nations.
Uniform School uniform worn except in the sixth.
Prefects Prefects, head girl, elected by staff and peers. School Council.
Religion Non-denominational assembly compulsory.
Social Close contact with Dulwich College. Organised ski trips, water sports holidays, French exchanges; trips to Paris (art), Berlin; biology/geography field trips. Sixth form allowed to bring own car to school. Meals self-service. No tobacco/alcohol allowed.
Discipline Pupils failing to produce homework once would be asked by teachers what the problem was; consistent failure to produce work would incur a detention and report home. Those caught smoking cannabis on the premises could expect suspension, then expulsion.
Alumni association Mrs Jenny Holmes, 1 Shelford Rise, London SE19 2PX.
Former pupils Kathleen Halpin; Margaret Lockwood.

• SYLVIA YOUNG

Sylvia Young Theatre School, Rossmore Road, London NW1 6NJ. Tel 0171 402 0673
• Pupils 129 • Boys 9–16 (Day) • Girls 9–16 (Day) • Upper sixth No • Termly fees £956–£1175 (Day) • ISAI • Enquiries/application to the Director

What it's like

Founded in 1981, as a co-educational theatre school. It has agreeable premises on a single site in north London. The school is committed to providing a balanced theatrical and academic curriculum to ensure that students have a wide range of career and higher education options open to them. Besides the basic academic subjects they are taught speech, singing, tap, jazz, ballet and drama. Most pupils go on to drama or acting courses or straight into the theatre and film industries. It is a happy school with an enthusiastic staff. The pupils are highly motivated and are encouraged to express themselves and contribute on all levels. There is close communication between parents and staff and a flourishing PTA. Pastoral care is taken very seriously. Form tutors liaise closely with parents. Spare time is spent in rehearsals for school shows and charity events.

School profile

Pupils Total age range 9–16; 129 day pupils (53 boys, 76 girls). Main entry ages 9, 11, 14, but also at any age up to year 10.
Entrance Audition, interview, written assessment used. Potential in performing arts looked for; no religious requirements. Parents not expected to buy textbooks; maximum extras £25. LEA grants available.
Head and staff *Director*: Miss Maggie Melville, in post for 11 years. Educated at Les Oiseaux, Westgate-on-Sea, Kent and at New College of Speech and Drama (English, speech and drama) and the Open University. Previously taught at IFPP; Ecole Active Bilingue, Paris; International Section, Lycee de Sevres; Ecole Pigier, Paris. Publications: Towards the Creative Teaching of English (Heinemann 1980). Seminars at British Council and for RSA course. *Staff:* 1 full time, 20 part time. Age range 20s–50s.
Exam results *GCSE:* In 1995, 26 pupils in Year 11, 1 gained at least grade C in 7+ subjects; 8 in 5–7 subjects.

University and college entrance On average, 50% leavers go on to courses in drama/acting; 25% take other courses; 25% straight into careers in films or theatre.
Curriculum GCSE only offered, an addition to drama (see under The arts). *Computing facilities:* BBC B micro. *Special provision:* A visiting tutor. *Europe:* French offered to GCSE.
The arts *Drama and dance:* Pupils take LAMDA acting, verse and prose exams. Pupils regularly accepted for drama and dance colleges, enter competitions, go on to work in theatre or musicals. Current pupils in cabaret groups and charity shows. *Art:* GCSE taken. All extra time is spent in rehearsals for school shows and charity events.
Uniform School uniform worn.
Houses/prefects School Council.
Religion Religious worship not compulsory.
Social Day trips to France. Many educational outings organised. Meals self-service or packed lunch. School shop. No tobacco/alcohol allowed.
Discipline Pupils failing to produce homework once might expect to complete it by the next day or do a detention; those caught smoking on the premises could expect their parents to be called in and to be asked to leave.
Former pupils Tisha Dean (East Enders); Frances Ruffelle (Tony Award winner 1987 – Les Miserables); Danni Behr; Danniella Westbrook; Nicola Stapleton; John Pickard.

T

• TALBOT HEATH

Talbot Heath, Rothesay Road, Bournemouth, Dorset BH4 9NJ. Tel 01202 761881, Fax 01202 768155

• Pupils 550 • Boys 3–7 only • Girls 3–18 (Day/Board/Weekly) • Upper sixth 43 • Termly fees £1750 (Day) £3050 (Board) £2970 (Weekly) • GSA, SHA • Enquiries/application to the Headmistress.

What it's like

Founded in 1886 it moved to its present site in 1935. It has purpose-built premises on a single site in woodlands 1½ miles from the town centre and 2 miles from the coast. It has very good facilities, including a new music school, sports hall and heated swimming pool. Broad and balanced curriculum. Academic standards are high and results very good. Most sixth-form leavers proceed to degree courses. Flourishing art and drama departments and a tremendously strong music department. Excellent range of sports and games (numerous county representatives) and fine variety of extra-curricular activities. Some local community service. Church of England foundation but pupils of all faiths welcomed.

School profile

Pupils Total age range 3–18; 550 pupils, 521 day (3 boys, 518 girls), 29 boarding girls. Main entry ages 3, 6 (boys and girls); 7, 11, 12, 13 and into sixth (girls). *State school entry:* 50% senior intake plus 10% sixth.

Entrance Own entrance examination used. Academic and personal potential looked for. Parents not expected to buy textbooks. 60 pa assisted places. Scholarships and bursaries available.

Parents Majority of parents live within 30 mile radius, 5+% live overseas.

Head and staff *Headmistress:* Mrs Christine Dipple, 5 years in post. Educated at Barnard Castle Grammar and at universities of Leeds (modern languages), Lille III (Maitrise) and Oxford (education). Previously Head of Modern Languages and Head of House for day girls at St Swithun's, Head of Modern Languages at Sherborne (Girls), Head of Italian Department and Fifth Form Careers at Millfield and also taught modern languages at comprehensive school in the North East. *Staff:* 46 full time, 16 part time plus visiting staff for extra subjects.

Exam results In 1995, 70 pupils in upper fifth, 43 in upper sixth. *GCSE:* In 1995, 55 upper fifth gained grade C or above in 8+ subjects; 13 in 5–7 subjects. *A-levels:* 37 passed in 3 subjects; 4 in 2; and 2 in 1 subject. Average UCAS points 22.3.

University and college entrance Majority go on to higher education and/or other professional training. Several Oxbridge places every year. Gap year is increasingly popular.

Curriculum GCSE and A levels; 21 subjects offered. *Computing facilities:* Integrated information technology network for use throughout the curriculum. *Vocational:* Work experience available. *Special provision:* Individual support for pupils with specific language difficulties. *Europe:* French (from age 7), German, Italian and Spanish offered to GCSE, AS and A-level. Regular exchanges to France. European studies for sixth-form.

The arts (Pupils aged 11 and over) *Music:* Over 30% of pupils learn at least one musical instrument; instrumental exams may be taken. Some 15–20 musical groups including orchestra, 3 choirs, flute choir, clarinet choir, handbells, early music, recorder consort, concert band, string groups. Strings finalist BBC Young Musician of the Year 1994. *Drama & dance*: LAMDA exams may be taken. Majority of pupils are involved in school productions. *Art:* Offered to GCSE and A-level with use of varied media.

Sport, community service and clubs (aged 11 and over) *Sport and physical activities:* Compulsory sports: athletics, badminton, dance, gymnastics, health-related exercise, hockey, netball, orienteering, rounders, swimming, tennis, volleyball. Optional sports for older pupils: aerobics, archery, fencing, squash, table tennis, yoga. Currently international representation in netball and tennis; national finalists/winners in netball, tennis; regional representation in badminton, netball, tennis, volleyball; county representation in badminton, hockey, netball, squash, tennis. *Community service:* Many pupils take bronze and silver Duke of Edinburgh's Award Scheme. Police service and first aid courses followed. Numerous fundraising projects for wide range of causes undertaken by whole school, form/year groups or individuals. Sixth-form outreach scheme in retirement homes, special needs schools, etc. Art projects (open to all senior pupils) to decorate local children's wards and clinics. *Clubs and activities*: include Amnesty International, Christian Focus, debating, computing.

Uniform School uniform worn, except in sixth-form. Uniform exchange shop – second-hand clothing shop run by parents.

Houses/prefects 2 head girls, 2 deputies, 6 prefects with special responsibilities. Democratic election, final confirmation by Headmistress. All sixth-formers share general school duties. School Council.

Religion Religious studies lessons (general) at all levels; daily morning assembly. Girls of other faiths may be excused with parental permission. Regular visits from (Anglican) chaplain.

Social Regular history of art visits to Florence and Venice; skiing trips. Pupils allowed to bring own car/bike to school. Meals self-service. No tobacco/alcohol allowed.

Discipline 'Firm but fair' ethos with necessary minimum of formal rules. Privileges granted according to age.

Boarding Boarding houses on main campus. Younger pupils share dormitories (maximum 6); older students in single or shared; study bedrooms for sixth. Resident nurse. 2 general weekend exeats each term, other outings may be permitted.

Alumni association run by the Headmistress.

Former pupils Judge Daffodil Cosgrave; Lady Faithfull; Dilys Powell; Pat Smythe; Virginia Wade.

• TEESSIDE HIGH

Teesside High School, The Avenue, Eaglescliffe, Stockton-on-Tees, Cleveland TS16 9AT. Tel 01642 782095, Fax 01642 791207

• Pupils 553 • Boys None • Girls 3–18 (Day) • Upper sixth 39 • Termly fees £1312 (Day) • GSA, SHA • Enquiries/application to the Headmistress

What it's like

Founded in 1970, through the amalgamation of the Queen Victoria High School and the Cleveland School. It is situated in 19 acres of beautiful wooded grounds on the banks of the River Tees, thus having the benefit of a rural setting while being near a residential centre. It is a purpose-built school with excellent modern facilities including a school hall, sixth-form centre, sports hall and music wing. The staff:pupil ratio is about 1:15, with smaller groups for practical subjects. Academic standards and results are good and most sixth-formers go on to degree courses. Music, drama and art are all well supported and plentiful use is made of the cultural facilities of Newcastle, Durham and York. The school is well provided with playing fields and standards in games and sports are high (representatives at county, regional and national level). The Duke of Edinburgh's Award Scheme is popular and there is a good deal of emphasis on outdoor activities for older girls. Community service is encouraged.

School profile

Pupils Total age range 3–18; 553 day girls. Senior department 11–18, 350 girls. Main entry ages 3, 5, 7, 11 and into sixth. Small percentage are children of former pupils. *State school entry:* One-third main intake at 11, plus small percentage into sixth.

Entrance Own entrance exam used. Academic ability looked for; no religious requirements. Parents not expected to buy textbooks. Assisted places at age 8, 11 and sixth-form. Discount fees available in sixth, variable value.

Parents 15+ % parents are in industry or commerce, 15+ % are doctors, lawyers, etc.

Head and staff *Headmistress:* Miss Jane Hamilton, appointed 1995. Educated at Cartrefle College of Education (PE) and University College London (mathematics). Previously Deputy Head at City of London School for Girls, Head of Mathematics at The

Maynard School and City of London School. *Staff:* 37 full time, 14 part time. Average age 45.

Exam results In 1995, 64 pupils in upper fifth, 39 in upper sixth. *GCSE:* In 1995, 56 upper fifth gained at least grade C in 8+ subjects; 7 in 5–7 subjects. *A-levels:* On average, 14% upper sixth pass in 4+ subjects; 65% in 3; 14% in 2; 7% in 1 subject. Average UCAS points 20.0.

University and college entrance 98% of 1995 sixth-form leavers went on to a degree course (59% after a gap year); others typically go on to further professional training. Of those going on to university, a small proportion go to Oxbridge; 7% took courses in medicine, dentistry and veterinary science, 20% in science and engineering, 5% in law, 55% in humanities and social sciences, 3% in art and design, 10% in other subjects (eg radiography, physiotherapy, education).

Curriculum GCSE and A-levels: 26 subjects offered (including Greek and A-level general studies). 25% take science/maths A-levels; 50% arts/humanities; 25% both. *Vocational:* Work experience for all in sixth-form. *Computing facilities:* 52 computers and 26 printers. *Special provision:* Dyslexic, mildly visually and physically handicapped pupils accepted; private EFL coaching arranged. *Europe:* French, German and Spanish offered to GCSE, AS and A-level (French compulsory from age 9, German from 12). MEP gives talks to sixth-form. Regular visits to France (working holidays with specific language assignments); German exchange.

The arts (Pupils aged 11 and over) *Music:* Over 75% of pupils learn a musical instrument; instrumental exams can be taken. Musical groups include orchestra, choir, windband, flute and string quartets, 2 recorder ensembles. several in county youth orchestra and choir; 1 in Young Musician of the Year competition: 3 in Scottish Independent Schools Orchestra. *Drama & dance*: Both offered. GCSE drama, Poetry Society and Guildhall exams may be taken. Majority of pupils are involved in school and house/other productions. *Art:* On average, 25 take GCSE, 5 A-level. Design, pottery, textiles and photography also offered.

Sport, community service and clubs (Pupils aged 11 and over) *Sport and physical activities:* Compulsory sports: hockey, netball, gymnastics, dance, tennis, athletics, rounders, swimming. Optional: indoor hockey, badminton, aerobics, orienteering, volleyball, table tennis. AAA and ASA exams may be taken. District and county levels in hockey, cross-country, athletics. *Community service:* Pupils take bronze, silver and gold Duke of Edinburgh's Award. Community service optional. *Clubs and societies:* Up to 10 clubs, eg drama, public speaking, aikado, aeroplane modelling.

Uniform School uniform worn, except in sixth.

Houses/prefects Competitive houses. Prefects, head girl, head of house and house prefects – elected by the school.

Religion All, except strict orthodox, attend multi-faith assembly.

Social Debates, concerts; community work. Trips abroad include French, German, classics visits, ski visit, individual exchanges. Pupils allowed to bring own car/bike to school. Meals self-service. No tobacco/alcohol allowed.

Discipline Pupils failing to produce homework once might expect to be seen by staff; those caught taking drugs would be expelled.

Alumni association is run by Mrs J Sellars, c/o the school.

• TETTENHALL

Tettenhall College, Wolverhampton, West Midlands WV6 8QX. Tel 01902 751119, Fax 01902 741940

• Pupils 340 • Boys 7–19 (Day/Board/Weekly). Girls 7–19 (Day/Board/Weekly) • Upper sixth 40
• Termly fees £1504–£1880 (Day) £2503–£3049 (Board) £2030–£2537 (Weekly) • HMC, SHMIS
• Enquiries/application to the Headmaster

What it's like

Founded in 1863 by a group of Wolverhampton businessmen to provide a school for the sons of non-conformists. It is now inter-denominational and, since 1982, co-educational. It has a most agreeable site in the old village of Tettenhall in 33 acres of attractive grounds three miles from Wolverhampton. The original building contains the boys' boarding houses, dining hall, chapel and big school. Playing fields are on site. Tettenhall has many of the advantages of a small school and enjoys a staff:pupil ratio of about 1:11. A broad general education is provided and academic results are good; most sixth formers go on to degree courses. Music, art and drama are well supported. A standard range of sports and games is available and there are numerous clubs and societies for extra-curricular activities. A social services group is very active and pupils participate in the Duke of Edinburgh's Award Scheme.

School profile

Pupils Total age range 7–19, 340 pupils, 267 day (182 boys, 85 girls), 73 boarding (44 boys, 29 girls). Senior department 13–19, 238 pupils. Main entry age 7, 11, 13 and into sixth. *State school entry:* 90% main intake.
Entrance Common Entrance or test places, interviews used. 7–9 pa scholarships (including 2 music) plus other awards for art, drama or sport.
Head and staff *Headmaster:* Dr P C Bodkin, 3 years in post. Educated at Bradfield and St Andrew's University. Previously Senior Housemaster at Bradfield. *Staff:* 30 full time, 3 part time. Annual turnover 2%. Average age 44.
Exam results In 1995, 54 pupils in upper fifth, 35 in upper sixth. *GCSE:* In 1995, 27 upper fifth gained at least grade C in 8+ subjects; 11 in 5–7; and 13 in 1–4 subjects. *A-levels:* 17 upper sixth passed in 4+ subjects; 7 in 3; 8 in 2 subjects. Average UCAS points 14.6.
University and college entrance 95% of 1995 sixth-form leavers went on to a degree course, others typically go on to eg HND business studies or direct into careers. Of those going on to university, 3% took courses in medicine, dentistry and veterinary science, 21% in science and engineering, 76% in humanities and social sciences.
Curriculum GCSE and A-levels: 18 GCSE and A-level subjects offered (including general studies). 10% took science A-levels; 80% arts/humanities; 10% both. *Vocational:* Work experience available. *Computing facilities:* Extensive. *Special provision:* EFL department. *Europe:* French (compulsory from age 7) and German (offered from age 13) GCSE and A-level. Exchanges to Germany and Czech Republic.
The arts (Pupils aged 11 and over) *Music:* A third of pupils learn a musical instrument; instrumental exams can be taken. Some 6 musical groups including chamber choir, concert band. Numerous successes at regional level plus occasional national level. *Drama & dance*: Both offered. GCSE drama and AS-level performing arts may be taken. Some pupils are involved in school productions and many in house/other productions. Productions include Joseph and Dracula Spectacular (both 1995), The Boyfriend (1996). *Art:* On average, 12 take GCSE, 6 A-level. Design, pottery, textiles, photography, graphics also offered.
Sport, community service and clubs (Pupils aged 11 and over) *Sport and physical activities:* Sports: wide range including rugby, football, hockey, netball, tennis, swimming, cricket, squash, athletics – guided choice at all levels. County and regional level, numerous players in rugby, hockey, cricket, squash, athletics; national, squash, athletics. *Community service:* Pupils take bronze, silver and gold Duke of Edinburgh's Award. Community service optional. *Clubs and societies:* Over 30 clubs, eg canoeing, typing, ballet, pottery, photography, computing, electronics, drama, discussion group, karate, chess.
Uniform School uniform worn, some concessons in sixth-form.
Houses/prefects Competitive houses. Prefects, head boy/girl, head of house and prefects appointed by the Headmaster.
Religion Attendance at (non-sectarian) religious worship compulsory.
Social Regular skiing trips. Pupils allowed to bring own bike to school. Meals self-service. School shop.
Discipline Minor offences usually result in a reprimand; detention used and more serious offences (bullying, stealing, illegal drugs) result in suspension/expulsion).

• TONBRIDGE

Tonbridge School, Tonbridge, Kent TN9 1JP. Tel 01732 365555

• Pupils 680 • Boys 13–18 (Day/Board) • Girls None • Upper sixth 139 • Termly fees £3051 (Day) £4323 (Board) • HMC • Enquiries/application to the Admissions Secretary

What it's like

Founded in 1553 by Sir Andrew Judde, it expanded considerably during the 19th century to become one of the major public schools. It retains close links with the Worshipful Company of Skinners. The fine campus lies on the northern edge of the town. There are many handsome Victorian buildings to which there have been numerous additions in recent years to provide first-class facilities and accommodation. A major five-year development programme is due for completion in 1997. Beautiful playing fields lie next to the school. A C of E foundation, there are some compulsory services and some emphasis on Anglican tradition and practice. There is a high standard of teaching, and academic results are extremely good. Almost all pupils go on to university each year, many to Oxbridge. The music department is very strong. Art and drama are good too. The school has long had a wide reputation for excellence in sports and games. There is a wide variety of these and many boys have achieved county and international recognition. The CCF has a big contingent and there are numerous clubs and societies which cater for most needs. Very substantial commitment to local community schemes and a fine record in the Duke of Edinburgh's Award Scheme.

School profile

Pupils Total age range 13–18; 680 boys, 250 day, 425 boarding. Main entry at age13; a few into sixth. Approx 10% are children of former pupils.

Entrance Common Entrance and own scholarship exam used. No special skills or religious requirements (C of E foundation, but other faiths welcomed). 3 pa assisted places to sixth. 35 pa scholarships for academic, music, art or technology; foundation bursaries for individuals in need of assistance.

Parents 15+% are doctors, lawyers, etc; 15+% in industry or commerce. 30+% live within 30 miles; 10+% live overseas.

Head and staff *Headmaster:* J M Hammond, 6 years in post. Educated at Winchester and Oxford (Lit Hum). Previously Headmaster at City of London School, Master in College (Housemaster of Scholars) and Head of Classics at Eton. Publications: Translation of Homer: The Iliad (Penguin 1987). *Staff:* 73 full time, 4 part time. Annual turnover 5%. Average age 40.

Exam results In 1995, 128 in upper fifth, 123 in upper sixth. *GCSE:* In 1995, 127 upper fifth gained at least grade C in 8+ subjects; 1 in 5–7 subjects. *A-levels:* 30 upper sixth passed in 4+ subjects; 87 in 3; 5 in 2; and 1 in 1 subject. Average UCAS points 25.2.

University and college entrance 98% of 1995 sixth-form leavers went on to a degree course (34% after a gap year); others typically go on to courses in the City. Of those going on to university, 16% go to Oxbridge; 8% take courses in medicine, dentistry and veterinary science, 30% in science and engineering, 4% in law, 58% in humanities and social sciences, 1% in art and design. 30% go to honours courses combining two of these categories.

Curriculum GCSE and A-levels (computer science and electronics offered to GCSE and A-level). On average, 24% take science/engineering A-levels; 50% take arts and humanities; 26% take a mixture. *Vocational:* Work experience available. *Computing facilities:* Several 30 Mbyte Winchester file servers serving 3 Econet networks with some 140 computers; Archimedes, IBMs and BBCs, all the usual word-processing, spread sheet, desktop publishing and CAD packages. *Special provision:* for mildly dyslexic pupils with above average IQs. *Europe:* French, German and Spanish offered to GCSE and A-level (French compulsory for 2 years). Regular exchanges (Austria, France, Germany and Spain).

The arts *Music:* 60% of pupils learn a musical instrument; instrumental exams can be taken. Some 12 musical groups including symphony, chamber and wind orchestras, chapel choir, choral society, concert band, string, wind and brass ensembles. Several Oxbridge choral scholarships; pupils in county youth orchestra, National Youth Wind Orchestra. *Drama & dance*: Drama offered and GCSE may be taken. Some pupils are involved in school and house/other productions. *Art:* On average, 23 take GCSE, 12 A-level. History of art, photography also offered.

Sport, community service and clubs *Sport and physical activities:* Boys choose from wide range of sports, including cricket, rugby, hockey, athletics, cross-country, rackets, climbing, sub-aqua, riding, plus judo, golf, rowing, shooting, fives, squash, fencing, sailing, swimming, tennis etc. RLSS, RYA, BSAC scuba diving exams may be taken. Squash, shooting, county schools champion teams for many years; judo, golf, public schools champion teams in recent years; several county representatives at cricket, hockey, athletics. *Community service:* Pupils take silver and gold Duke of Edinburgh's Award; 18 golds in past 3 years. CCF optional; 1 RN, 5 army and 2 RAF flying scholarships in 1995. Community service optional, as are Certificated First Aid exams. *Clubs and societies:* Over 30 clubs, eg most academic disciplines; hobbies such as bridge, chess, photography; activities such as sub-aqua, field sports; interests such as astronomy, war games, conservation.
Uniform School uniform worn throughout.
Houses/prefects Competitive houses. Prefects and head boy (appointed by Headmaster); head of house and house prefects (appointed by house masters).
Religion Compulsory chapel, Sundays and 4 mornings per week.
Social Major choral performances, combined band concerts. Weekly lectures by distinguished speakers, girls from local schools for drama productions and dances; industry courses. School exchange arrangements. Holiday exchanges, organised trips to Italay, Greece, Russia, France etc, plus orchestral/choral tours to USA/Germany etc. Pupils allowed to bring own bike to school. Meals formal in houses. Sixth-form centre and social centre with café. School shop. No tobacco/alcohol allowed.
Discipline Pupils failing to produce homework once might expect to do it, plus some extra, in own time; those involved with drugs on or off the premises may expect expulsion.
Boarding 50% have own study bedroom, 50% in dormitories of about 6. About 60 in each house. Sanatorium sister and assistance. Pupils can provide and cook own food. At least 2 exeats (24-hour) plus half-term each term. Visits to local town allowed.
Former pupils Colin Cowdrey; Frederick Forsyth; Sir Patrick Mayhew; Richard Ellison; Bill Bruford; Maurice Denham; Benjamin Whitrow; David Tomlinson; Christopher Cowdrey; Vikram Seth.

• TORMEAD

Tormead School, Cranley Road, Guildford, Surrey GU1 2JD. Tel 01483 575101, Fax 01483 450592

• Pupils 650 • Boys None • Girls 4–18 (Day) • Upper sixth 40 • Termly fees £800-£1700 (Day) • GSA • Enquiries/application to the Headmistress

What it's like

Founded in 1905, as a non-denominational school, it is set in an attractive site of some 4 acres, close to the centre of Guildford. The junior school has its own buildings opposite the main school. Results are good and most sixth-formers go on to higher education. A sixth-form general studies programme is run in conjunction with Guildford High and the Royal Grammar School. Drama and music are well supported and a wide range of sports and games is available. The school takes part in the Duke of Edinburgh's Award Scheme and most pupils participate. Pupils have regularly joined in British Schools' Exploration Society expeditions. There is a large number of clubs and societies and regular exchange visits to Europe and America.

School profile

Pupils Total age range 4–18, 650 day girls. Senior department 11–18. Main entry ages 4, 7, 8, 11 and into sixth. *State school entry:* 10% senior intake.
Entrance Own entrance exam used. Scholarships/exhibitions, bursaries and assisted places at 11+.
Head and staff *Headmistress:* Mrs Honor Alleyne, 4 years in post. Educated at Victoria College (Belfast), and at Queen's University, Belfast, and Marburg University (German, theology). Previously Deputy Head at St Swithun's, Winchester. *Staff:* 48 full time, 20 part time. Annual turnover 10%. Average age 45.
Exam results In 1995, 62 pupils in upper fifth, 37 in upper sixth. *GCSE:* In 1995, 94% upper fifth gained at least grade C in 8+ subjects. *A-levels:* 3% upper sixth passed in 4

subjects; 92% in 3; 5% in 1–2 subjects. Average UCAS points 19.7.
University and college entrance 95% of 1995 sixth-form leavers went on to a degree course (20% after a gap year); others typically go on to HND courses or retail management. Of those going on to university, 10% went to Oxbridge; 5% took courses in medicine, dentistry and veterinary science, 35% in science and engineering, 5% in law, 35% in humanities and social sciences, 5% in art and design, 15% in other vocational subjects eg nursing, meteorology, catering management, physiotherapy.
Curriculum GCSE and A-levels. 24 subjects offered (including A-level general studies). 38% take science A-levels; 38% arts/humanities; 24% both. *Vocational:* Work experience available: also RSA English exams; CLAIT. *Computing facilities:* Fully equipped computer room, plus computers in all laboratories, libraries and some classrooms. *Europe:* French, German and Spanish GCSE and A-level. French compulsory from age 11 to GCSE; German or Spanish from age 12. 65% take GCSE in more than 1 language. Regular exchanges
The arts (Pupils aged 11 and over) *Music:* Over 50% pupils learn a musical instrument; instrumental exams can be taken. Some 10+ musical groups, including orchestras, jazz group, big band, chamber ensembles, choirs. Several pupils play with Surrey Youth Orchestra. *Drama & dance*: Both offered. A-level theatre studies, LAMDA exams may be taken. Some pupils are involved in school productions, majority in house/other productions. *Art:* On average, 30 take GCSE, 6 A-level. Design, pottery and textiles also offered.
Sport, community service and clubs (Pupils aged 11 and over) *Sport and physical activities:* Compulsory sports: gym, netball, hockey, swimming, basketball, volleyball, badminton, athletics, tennis, rounders. Optional: squash, cross-country. Sixth form only: aerobics, golf, sailing, horseriding, fencing, weight training, ice skating. Gymnastics – aerobics national finals BAGA. *Community service:* Pupils take bronze, silver and gold Duke of Edinburgh's Award. Community service optional. Girls selected for BSES summer expedition to northern Europe and North America. *Clubs and societies:* Up to 30 clubs eg Christian Union, Young Engineers, speakers society, computers, drama, chess, debating, various sports.
Uniform School uniform worn except in sixth.
Houses/prefects Competitive houses. Head girl, heads of houses and games captain – all apply for the job and are selected on the basis of their application and staff recommendation. School Committee.
Religion Attendance at school assembly compulsory.
Social Debates, lectures, theatrical and musical productions with other local schools, and shared sixth-form general studies. Regular French, German and North American exchanges; annual skiing trip. Meals self-service. No tobacco/alcohol allowed.

• TRINITY (Croydon)

Trinity School of John Whitgift, Shirley Park, Croydon, Surrey CR9 7AT. Tel 0181 656 9541, Fax 0181 655 0522

• Pupils 850 • Boys 10–18 (Day) • Girls None • Upper sixth 107 • Termly fees £1768 (Day) • HMC • Enquiries/application to Admissions Registrar

What it's like

Founded in 1596 by Archbishop John Whitgift, it moved from central Croydon to its present site in 1965: a complex of buildings and playing fields in a parkland site of 27 acres. Recent developments are a sports complex including two sports halls, a design building for all aspects of art, design and technology, and a sixth-form centre. It has excellent facilities and comfortable accommodation. The standard of teaching is high and the results are very good. Most leavers proceed to degree courses each year, including many to Oxbridge. Religious worship is broadly conceived and religious education continues up to the end of the fifth year. There is a very strong musical tradition and the choirs frequently take part in national events. Considerable strength also in drama, with numerous productions in two well-equipped theatres. A very good record in sports and games and considerable emphasis on outdoor pursuits. A wide variety of clubs and societies cater for most needs. There is an active CCF contingent and a very active community service unit. A notable record in the Duke of Edinburgh's Award Scheme.

School profile

Pupils Total age range 10–18; 850 day boys. Senior department 11–18, 800 boys. Main entry ages 10, 11, 13 and into sixth. Approx 5% are children of former pupils. *State school entry:*70% main intakes.

Entrance Own entrance exam used. No special skills or religious requirements. Parents not expected to buy textbooks. 25 pa assisted places. Scholarships 30 pa, 10%–50% fees. Bursaries available to all families with an income below £30,000.

Parents 15+% in industry or commerce.

Head and staff *Headmaster:* Barnaby Lenon, in post from 1995. Educated at Eltham College and at universities of Oxford (geography) and Cambridge (PGCE). Previously Deputy Head Master at Highgate and Deputy Director of Studies, Master i/c Athletics and Head of Geography at Eton. *Staff:* 65 full time, 6 part time. Annual turnover 6. Average age 40.

Exam results On average, 118 pupils in upper fifth, 107 in upper sixth. *GCSE:* most upper fifth gain at least grade C in 10+ subjects. *A- and AS-levels*: 42 upper sixth pass in 4+ subjects; 65 in 3 subjects. Average UCAS points 21.0.

University and college entrance 95% of sixth-form leavers go on to a degree course, 20% to Oxbridge; 10% take courses in medicine, dentistry and veterinary science, 40% in science and engineering, 50% in humanities and social sciences.

Curriculum GCSE and A-levels: 18 GCSE subjects offered; 20 at A-level (general studies taught but not examined). 30% take science A-levels; 30% arts/humanities; 40% both. *Vocational:* Work experience available. *Computing facilities:* 30-booth lab, plus research lab. *Special provision:* Extra tuition for dyslexic pupils. *Europe:* French, German and Spanish offered to GCSE and A-level. Regular visits/exchanges.

The arts *Music:* Up to 50% of pupils learn a musical instrument; instrumental exams can be taken. Some 20+ musical groups including choirs, orchestras, concert band, brass group, numerous quarters, trios. Trinity Boys Choir has many public professional engagements, eg Glyndebourne, English National Opera, Queen's 40th anniversary celebrations etc; several finalists in National Chamber Music Competition. *Drama & dance*: Drama offered. All pupils are involved in school and house/other productions. *Art:* Art and photography offered.

Sport, community service and clubs Compulsory sports: (initially): rugby, hockey, cricket. Optional: a very wide range including the above. 12 in international squads, 74 county representatives, various sports. *Community service:* Pupils take bronze, silver and gold Duke of Edinburgh's Award. CCF and community service optional. *Clubs and societies:* Up to 30 clubs.

Uniform School uniform worn except in the sixth-form.

Houses/prefects Prefects and head boy – appointed by the Headmaster and the school. Sixth form School Council.

Social Sixth-form society, dramatic and musical productions with local girls' schools. Lots of organised trips abroad. Pupils allowed to bring own car/bike/motorbike to school. Meals self-service. School tuck shop. No pupils allowed tobacco/alcohol.

Discipline Pupils failing to produce homework once might expect a mild punishment; those caught in possession of cannabis on the premises might expect expulsion.

Alumni association is run by The Secretary, Lime Meadow Avenue, Sanderstead, Croydon.

• TRINITY (Teignmouth)

Trinity School, Buckeridge Road, Teignmouth, Devon TQ14 8LY. Tel 01626 774138, Fax 01626 775491

• Pupils 325 • Boys 3–18 (Day/Board/Weekly) • Girls 3–18 (Day/Board/Weekly) • Upper sixth 5
• Termly fees £860-£1370 (Day) £2500-£2780 (Board) £2430-£2710 (Weekly) • SHA, ISAI
• Enquiries/application to the Headmaster

What it's like

Founded in 1901 under the Order of Notre Dame, as a girls' convent, it was refounded in 1979 as a co-educational school, Trinity School. It is a joint Roman Catholic and Anglican foundation and has a very pleasant single site of over 13 acres in remarkably beautiful surroundings, overlooking Lyme Bay. It also enjoys most attractive buildings and has excellent boarding accommodation. Other facilities are of a high order and include three libraries, a music centre and a new science and resource block. It has many of the advantages of a small family school and prides itself on its in-depth pastoral care system. Some emphasis on religious instruction and worship. A favourable staff:pupil ratio of about 1:10. GNVQs (intermediate and advanced) are offered as well as A-levels. Strong music, drama and art. On-site sports and games facilities and an large number of extra-curricular activities for a school of this size. Some commitment to the Duke of Edinburgh's Award Scheme and community services; CCF introduced in 1996.

School profile

Pupils Age range 3–18; 325 pupils, 220 day (120 boys, 100 girls), 105 boarding (68 boys, 37 girls). Senior department 11–18, 180 pupils (100 boys, 80 girls). Entry at any age, including the sixth. Some 7% are children of former pupils. *State school entry:* 20%–30% of main intake.

Entrance Common Entrance and own entrance exam used. No special skills or religious requirements. Parents expected to buy few textbooks (eg atlas). No compulsory extras; optional extras £20–£30 per term. 5–10 pa bursaries/scholarships available, eg academic and for sport, music, drama; also forces bursaries.

Parents 15% in armed services; 15+% doctors/lawyers; 15+% in industry/commerce; 15+% in financial sector. 60+% live within 30 miles; up to 15% overseas.

Head and staff *Headmaster:* Colin J Ashby, 3 years in post. Educated at Sir Thomas Rich's School, Gloucester, and at universities of Birmingham (chemistry) and Oxford (PGCE). Previously Housemaster and master i/c rugby and swimming at Bromsgrove and assistant chemistry master at Epsom College. Also ISAI Regional Co-ordinator, member of National Executive Council of ISAI and ISIS south and west; Oxford rugby blue and Captain of Birmingham University RFC. *Staff:* 26 full time, 16 part time. Annual turnover 5%. Average age, 40.

Exam results In 1995, 33 pupils in upper fifth, 5 in upper sixth. *GCSE:* In 1995, 56% gained at least grade C in 8+ subjects; 26% in 5–7; 18% in 1–4 subjects. *A-levels:* Mixture of GNVQ and A-levels taken; all upper sixth passed the equivalent of 2 A-levels. Average UCAS points 10.0.

University and college entrance 70% of sixth-form leavers go on to a degree course (8% after a gap year); others typically go on to training and employment. Of those going on to university, 5% take courses in medicine, dentistry and veterinary science, 10% in science and engineering, 5% in law, 10% in humanities and social sciences, 15% in art and design, 30% in business, 13% in other vocational subjects, 12% other forms of training.

Curriculum GCSE, GNVQ (intermediate and advanced in business), A-levels offered. 19 GCSE subjects (including Chinese and Japanese); A-level subjects may be combined with the advanced GNVQ or studied separately. *Vocational:* GNVQ and Advanced Certificate in Business; also intermediate (RSA) and advanced (BTEC) in business; also RSA stages 1, 2 and 3 in CLAIT and in word processing. Work experience available. *Computing facilities:* Total of 70 computers: 2 laboratories with 20 computers; 486 IBM computers in senior department; othrs in business centre, careers library etc. *Special provision:* Three qualified EFL teachers, three special needs teachers. *Europe:* French, German, Spanish, Dutch and Russian offered at GCSE; also A-level, depending on demand. French compulsory from 5–16, German 9–14. Exchanges to France and Germany. European pupils spend 1–6 terms in the school.

The arts (Pupils aged 11 and over) *Music:* Over 30% pupils learn a musical instrument; instrumental exams can be taken. 5–7 musical groups – small musical groups, orchestra, choir, big band. Pupils in South West Schools Orchestra and Torbay Light Orchestra; involvement in Devon & Exeter Festival. *Drama & dance*: Both offered as extra-curricular subjects. Majority of pupils involved in school and house/other productions. *Art:* On average, 30 take GCSE. Pottery and textiles also offered. 3 pupils were winners of the local schools art competition; two regional winners and two national art prize winner.

Sport, community service and clubs (Pupils aged 11 and over) *Sport and physical activities:* Choice from: cross country, cricket, rugby, football, hockey, netball, rounders, swimming. Optional sports: judo, horse riding, sailing, tennis, volleyball, basketball, windsurfing, golf, squash, archery, off-road driving. GCSE physical education offered,

maybe A-level and BAGA. 1 international rugby player; U16 girls netball team, cross-country runners, and athletes represented ISAI south west at national finals; 2 national ISAI swimming champions. *Community service:* Pupils take bronze Duke of Edinburgh's Award; silver may be available. CCF optional with local cadet group; community service optional. *Clubs and societies:* Over 30 clubs including chess, art, drama, music, computing, workshop, gardening, aerobics, handicraft and many sports clubs.
Uniform School uniform worn except in sixth, where a dress code applies.
Houses/prefects Competitive houses. Head boy/girl prefects, house prefects and house captains. School Council.
Religion Religious worship compulsory; certain exemptions for boarders on Sundays.
Social Joint concerts with local churches and local choral society; recent Rotary Club Youth Speaks Competitions winners at U13 level. French and German exchanges. Pupils may bring own bikes to school. School shop. No alcohol/tobacco allowed, except limited wine or beer for senior pupils for special occasions.
Discipline Pupils failing to produce homework once might expect a warning and a 'forgetfulness slip'; any pupil caught smoking cannabis on the premises would expect permanent or temporary exclusion from school, certainly until a full investigation and report produced.
Boarding 30% have own study bedrooms; 70% share with 1 other. Houses of approx 20, divided by age and sex. Pupils allowed to provide and cook own food. 2–3 exeats allowed termly and extra ones possible. Visits to local town allowed from age 11 in small groups.
Alumni association run by Alison Twose, Patricia Galli and Victoria Hulbert, c/o the school.

• TRURO

Truro School, Trennick Lane, Truro, Cornwall TR1 1TH. Tel 01872 72763, Fax 01872 223431.
• Pupils 795 • Boys 11–18 (Day/Board) • Girls 11–18 (Day/Board) • Upper sixth 109 • Termly fees £1536 (Day) £2860 (Board) • HMC • Enquiries/application to the Headmaster

What it's like

Founded in 1880 by Cornish Methodists. It is on a fine 50-acre site overlooking the cathedral and the Fal estuary. It has strong roots in the county and is its only HMC school. Ample facilities include on-site playing fields, sports halls, IT and CDT centres and a pottery. A Christian Methodist school, aiming to ensure that Christian values permeate school life, it regards parents as partners in educating children, especially in the moral and spiritual components of school life. Originally a boys' school, girls were admitted (aged 11) since 1991 and it is now fully co-educational. The staff:pupil ratio is about 1:12. Academic results are very good and almost all sixth-formers go to university, including Oxbridge. Music is strong (several recent prize winners at the Corwall Music Festival). Sport is very successful, with regular regional and county honours, especially in rugby, soccer, cricket and athletics. A strong emphasis on outdoor education, making full use of the sea, cliffs and moorland of the West Country. Strong participation in the Duke of Edinburgh Award Scheme.

School profile

Pupils Age range 11–18; 795 pupils, 647 day (451 boys, 196 girls), 148 boarding (91 boys, 57 girls). Main entry ages 11, 13 and into sixth. 30% pupils from own prep, Treliske Prep School (tel 01872 72616). *State school entry:* 70% main intake, plus 75% to sixth.
Entrance Common Entrance and own exam used. No special religious or other requirements. Parents not expected to buy textbooks. Average extras £10–£20 per term. 40 pa assisted places (25 on entry, 15 in sixth). Scholarships for about 20% pupils, available at 11 and 16, 10%–50% fees (occasionally more but then means-tested).
Parents 15% parent are doctors, lawyers etc; 15% self-employed or in the holiday industry. 60+% live within 30 miles, under 10% live overseas.
Head and staff *Headmaster:* G A G Dodd, 3 years in post. Educated at Cheltenham and Cambridge (history). Previously Headmaster of Lord Wandsworth College and Housemaster at Cheltenham. *Staff:* 65 full time, 21 part time. Annual turnover 4%. Average age 41.

Exam results In 1995, 127 pupils in fifth form, 109 in upper sixth. *GCSE:* In 1995, 115 pupils in fifth gained at least grade C in 8 subjects; 10 in 5–7; 2 in 1–4 subjects. *A-levels:* 10 upper sixth passed in 4+ subjects; 83 in 3; 12 in 2; and 3 in 1 subject. Average UCAS points 23.2
University and college entrance 98% of 1995 sixth-form leavers went on to a degree course, others typically go on to farming, secretarial or into business. Of those going on to university, 9% went to Oxbridge; 10% took courses in medicine, dentistry and veterinary science, 30% in science and engineering, 10% in law, 35% in humanities and social sciences, 10% in art and design, 5% in other vocational subjects eg agriculture, hotel or sports management.
Curriculum GCSE, AS and A-levels. 16 subjects offered for GCSE, 8 AS- and 23 A-level (not A-level general studies). 24% take science A-levels; 40% arts/humanities; 36% both. *Vocational:* Work experience available. Also City & Guilds level 1 in IT. *Computing facilities:* 24 networked PCs in IT centre; languages network of 12 PCs; various others in departments. *Special provision:* Special needs unit with specialist part time staff. *Europe:* French (compulsory) and German offered to GCSE, AS and A-level; also Spanish AS- and A-level. Regular exchanges.
The arts *Music:* Up to 25% of pupils learn a musical instrument; instrumental exams can be taken. Some 13 musical groups including Baroque, brass, string and recorder ensembles, chamber group, choirs, jazz and wind orchestras, jazz singing, orchestra. Several recent prizewinners at Cornwall Music Festival. *Drama & dance*: Drama offered; LAMDA exams may be taken. Some pupils involved in school productions. *Art:* On average, 30 take GCSE, 16 A-level. Design and pottery also offered. Top national mark in CDT 1994.
Sport, community service and clubs *Sport and physical activities:* Compulsory sports: boys – rugby, soccer or hockey, cricket; girls – rounders tennis, hockey; for both boys and girls, at some stage – athletics, swimming, gymnastics, badminton, basketball, netball, rounders, tennis. Optional: trampolining, squash, volleyball, rifle-shooting, cross-country, aerobics, climbing. GCSE PE, RLSS, and RYA exams may be taken. County and regional honours every year in rugby, soccer, hockey, cricket, athletics, netball, swimming; 2 girls in national sailing squad (Optimist class). *Community service:* Pupils take bronze, silver and gold Duke of Edinburgh's Award (165 pupils involved). Community service optional. *Clubs and societies:* Over 30 clubs, eg Young Enterprise (county marketing cup 1994), chess (recent winner of Times competition), fly-fishing.
Uniform School uniform worn throughout.
Houses/prefects Competitive houses. Prefects, head of house and house prefects, appointed by Head after wide consultation including with sixth-form.
Religion Attendance at religious worship compulsory.
Social Trips abroad to France and Germany; Spanish exchange soon. Pupils may be allowed to bring own car/bike/motorbike. Meals self-service. School shop. No tobacco/alcohol allowed.
Discipline Pupils failing to produce homework once could expect to be kept in an lunchtime; continuation as a pupil if caught smoking cannabis on the premises might depend on willingness to submit to testing in future; counselling would be given.
Boarding 10% have own study bedrooms; 90% share (2–5). Single-sex houses of 22–75, divided by age. Resident qualified nurse. Sixth-form pupils can provide and cook own food. No limit to number of exeats. Visits to the local town allowed, increasing freedom with age.
Former pupils Roger Taylor (drummer in Queen), Robert Shaw (film actor), Nigel Terry (Shakespearean actor).

• TRURO HIGH

Truro High School, Falmouth Road, Truro, Cornwall TR1 2HU. Tel 01872 72830

• Pupils 425 • Boys 3–5 only (Day) • Girls 3–18 (Day/Board/Weekly) • Upper sixth 40 • Termly fees £1460 (Day) £2665 (Board) £2630 (Weekly) • GSA • Enquiries/application to the Head Master

What it's like

Founded in 1880 by Archbishop Benson, the first Bishop of Truro, it is a single-site school, with a fine view over the city and cathedral. The handsome and well-equipped buildings lie in most attractive gardens and grounds. The school prides itself on a happy, positive atmosphere and expertise in the special needs of girls. Regular prayers and services (including some in the cathedral) are held. A wide academic curriculum is available. The staff:pupil ratio is about 1:12. A well-qualified staff provides a sound general education with consistently good results in GCSE and A-level; almost all sixth-formers go on to university. There are many musical activities involving choirs and orchestra, and musical standards are high. Drama is also well supported. There is a wide range of games and sports and numerous clubs and societies for extra-curricular activities. There are many excursions, expeditions and cultural trips and the school also participates in the Duke of Edinburgh's Award Scheme with success.

School profile

Pupils Total age range 3–18; 425 pupils, 365 day, 60 boarding girls. Senior department 11–18, 319 girls. Main entry ages 3 (boys); up to 11 and into sixth (girls). 10% are children of former pupils. *State school entry:* 50% main intake, plus 8% to sixth.
Entrance Own entrance exam used. Ability to follow curriculum required; no special religious requirements. Parents not expected to buy textbooks. No compulsory extras. 33 pa assisted places. 14 pa scholarships/bursaries, up to half fees.
Parents 30+% live within 30 miles, 10% live overseas.
Head and staff *Head Master*: James Graham-Brown, 4 years in post. Educated at Sevenoaks and at Kent and Bristol universities (English literature). Previously Senior Master at Bournemouth and Head of English at Ratcliffe. Also Chief Examiner for Cambridge University's A-level, Plain Text English Literature paper. *Staff:* 32 full time, 16 part time. Annual turnover 5%. Average age 42.
Exam results In 1995, 40 pupils in fifth form, 40 in upper sixth. *GCSE:* In 1995, 29 pupils in fifth gained at least grade C in 8 subjects; 6 in 5–7 subjects. *A-levels:* 4 upper sixth passed in 4+ subjects; 26 in 3; 8 in 2; and 2 in 1 subject. Average UCAS points 20.4.
University and college entrance All 1995 sixth-form leavers went on to a degree course, 16% to Oxbridge; 10% took courses in medicine, dentistry and veterinary science, 30% in science and engineering, 30% in humanities and social sciences, 10% in art and design, 20% in other subjects eg drama and music.
Curriculum GCSE, AS and A-levels, RSA. 22 subjects offered (not A-level general studies). 18% take science A-levels; 43% arts/humanities; 40% both. *Vocational:* Work experience available. *Computing facilities:* Fully-equipped computer room and range of classroom computers in senior school. *Special provision:* Extra tuition arranged. *Europe:* French, German, Italian and Spanish offered to GCSE, AS and A-level; also Italian and Spanish as non-examined subject in the sixth. Regular exchanges to France, Germany and Italy.
The arts (Pupils aged 11 and over) *Music:* Over 30% of pupils learn a musical instrument; instrumental exams can be taken. Some 5 musical groups including choirs, orchestra, jazz band. Numerous winners of instrumental categories in county competitions. *Drama & dance*: Both offered. GCSE and A-level drama, Poetry Society and LAMDA exams may be taken. Majority of pupils are involved in school and house/other productions. *Art:* On average, 25 take GCSE, 12 A-level. Design, pottery, textiles and photography also offered. Art facilities open to non-examination pupils. St Ives Tate Painting Competition, winners and runners-up, U15, U16, U17.
Sport, community service and clubs (Pupils aged 11 and over) *Sport and physical activities:* Compulsory sports: netball, hockey, tennis, swimming, athletics. Optional: badminton, cricket, riding, archery, judo. BAGA and ASA swimming awards exams may be taken. Regular county representatives at netball, hockey, tennis and swimming at all levels. *Community service:* Pupils take bronze, silver and gold Duke of Edinburgh's Award. Community service optional. *Clubs and societies:* Up to 30 clubs, eg short tennis, ballet, speech & drama, photography, maths, sailing, debating.
Uniform School uniform worn, except in sixth.
Houses/prefects No competitive houses in senior school. All sixth-formers have responsibilities; some specific school officers. Head girl, heads of boarding houses, appointed by the Head, staff and sixth-form. School Council.
Religion Attendance at religious worship compulsory.
Social Social events, local music festivals, some trips abroad with other schools. Study

and recreational visits to France, Germany, Italy, Switzerland and Austria. Pupils allowed to bring own car/bike/motorbike. Meals self-service. School uniform shop. No tobacco/alcohol allowed.

Discipline Pupils failing to produce homework once could expect reprimand and extra work; those caught smoking cannabis on the premises could expect expulsion. Parents always informed of disciplinary action even if minor.

Boarding Most upper sixth have own study bedrooms; lower sixth and fifth forms in rooms of 2 or 3. Houses of 30–35, divided by age. Resident qualified nurse. Sixth-form pupils can provide and cook own food. Exeats by arrangement with parents. Daytime visits to the local town allowed from Year 8 (frequency increases with age: from once/ week to daily for sixth).

Alumni association is run by Mrs S Dowding, Secretary, Little Canaan, Truro.

• TUDOR HALL

Tudor Hall School, Wykham Park, Banbury, Oxfordshire OX16 9UR. Tel 01295 263434, Fax 01295 253264

• Pupils 260 • Boys None • Girls 11–18 (Day/Board) • Upper sixth 38 • Termly fees £2106 (Day) £3380 (Board) • GSA • Enquiries/application to the Headmistress

What it's like

Founded in 1850 at Forest Hill, the school moved twice before settling at Wykham Park. It is housed in a 17th-century manor house, and also in a fine 18th-century house next door, set in beautiful gardens and parkland. Boarding accommodation and general facilities are excellent. Some attention is given to religious education in the Anglican tradition, and on Sundays there is worship in one of the local parish churches. A large and well-qualified staff permits a favourable staff:pupil ratio of about 1:9. Academic standards are good and results very good. Most leavers go on to degree courses. There is much emphasis on music, with excellent facilities and an orchestra, choir and choral society. Facilities for sports and games are first class, and include new squash courts, open air pool and gym. Apart from the standard range of sports and games, fencing and riding are available. There is an impressive range of clubs and societies. The Duke of Edinburgh's Award Scheme is popular and quite a few girls are involved in local social and community services. There are resident staff for art, dance, CDT, cookery and drama.

School profile

Pupils Age range 11–18, 260 girls (30 day, 230 boarding). Main entry ages 11, 12, 13 and into sixth. *State school entry:* 2% main intake, plus 1% to sixth.

Entrance Common Entrance exam used. 4 pa scholarships: 1 music, 3 academic.

Head and staff *Headmistress:* Miss Nanette Godfrey, in post 12 years. Educated at Northampton School for Girls and London University (English). Previously Deputy Head at Ancaster House, Housemistress/Teacher at Abbots Bromley and English Teacher/ Housemistress at the Royal Ballet School. Also JP. *Staff:* 25 full time, 8 part time.

Exam results In 1995, 43 pupils in upper fifth, 36 in upper sixth. *GCSE:* In 1995, upper fifth gained grade C or above in an average of 9.2 subjects. *A-levels:* average upper sixth passed in 2.8 subjects. Average UCAS points 20.4.

University and college entrance 91% of 1995 sixth-form leavers went on to a degree course (41% after a gap year); others typically go on to cooking, secretarial courses. Of those going on to university, 3% went to Oxbridge; 6% took courses in medicine, dentistry and veterinary science, 23% in science and engineering, 6% in law, 42% in humanities and social sciences, 12% in art and design, 9% in other vocational subjects eg education, hospitality management, agriculture, physiotherapy, architecture.

Curriculum GCSE, AS and A-levels: 21 subjects offered, including AS- but not A-level general studies; classical Greek and Russian GCSE offered in sixth. *Vocational:* Work experience available. *Computing facilities:* IBM PC RM Net.LM network Cambridge Information Technology Certificate. *Europe:* French, German and Spanish offered to GCSE and A-level; Italian to Institute of Linguists; Russian to GCSE.

The arts *Music:* Over 50% of pupils learn a musical instrument; instrumental exams can be taken. Musical groups include orchestra, choir, choral society, wind band. *Drama &*

dance: Both offered. A-level drama and Guildhall exams may be taken. Majority of pupils are involved in school and house/other productions. *Art:* On average, 28 take GCSE, 2 AS-level, 10 A-level. Design, pottery, textiles, photography and CDT also offered.

Sport, community service and clubs *Sport and physical activities:* Compulsory sports: hockey, netball, lacrosse, rounders, tennis, athletics. Optional: fencing, squash, badminton, riding, polo. Sixth form only: sailing, golf, clay-pigeon shooting. National level fencing, cross-country; riding, frequent firsts at independent schools events. *Community service:* Pupils take bronze, silver and gold Duke of Edinburgh's Award. Community service compulsory at age 17. *Clubs and societies:* Various clubs, eg chemistry, needlework, art, CDT, bird-watching, photography.

Uniform School uniform worn except in fifth and sixth.

Houses/prefects Competitive houses. Prefects, head girl, head of house and house prefects appointed by the Headmistress. School Council.

Religion Attendance at religious worship compulsory until age 17.

Social Sports, choral society and guest lecturers jointly with other local schools. Trips abroad eg skiing, to Russia, art trip to Italy, history trip to Poland, recent expedition to Borneo. Upper sixth allowed to bring own car/bike to school. Meals self-service. School shop. No tobacco/alcohol allowed.

Discipline Pupils failing to produce homework once might expect to do it in their free time; those caught smoking cannabis on the premises would be expelled.

Boarding Upper sixth have own study bedrooms; lower sixth and fifth forms share with 2–3; 20% are in dormitories of 6+. Houses of 24–40, divided by age. Qualified resident nurse. Sixth form may cook own supper. 2 exeats per term, 2–4 days. Pupils over 14 may visit local town.

U

• UNIVERSITY COLLEGE SCHOOL

University College School, Frognal, Hampstead, London NW3 6XH. Tel 0171 435 2215
• Pupils 900 • Boys 7–18 (Day) • Girls None • Upper sixth 100 • Termly fees £2025-£2165 (Day)
• HMC • Enquiries/application to the Headmaster

What it's like

Founded in Gower Street in 1830 as part of University College London. A junior school was opened in Hampstead in 1891 and the main school moved to purpose-built accommodation in Hampstead in 1907. The school is set in pleasant grounds in a very agreeable residential area, 5 minutes' walk from Hampstead Heath; 27 acres of school's own playing field are within walking distance. There have been extensive additions to the original handsome buildings and the school has recently completed a major building and redevelopment programme. Facilities are first-rate. The main aims of the school's philosophy and policy are the pursuit of academic excellence, a respect for and encouragement of independent thought and individual judgement, a broad curriculum and the lack of any religious barriers. A large staff permits a staff:pupil ratio of about 1:11 in the senior department. Academic attainments are high and results very good. The vast majority of sixth-formers go on to degree courses each year, including many to Oxbridge. The school is very strong in music and drama and provides an excellent range of activities. It also has a distinguished record in games.

School profile

Pupils Total age range 7–18; 900 day boys. Senior department 11–18, 700 boys. Main entry ages 7, 8, 11, 13 and into sixth. Approx 5% are children of former pupils. *State school entry:* 100% intake at 11, 10% at 13.

Entrance Own exam used. No religious requirements; academic competence and an ability to contribute to the wider life of the school looked for. Parents are charged separately for textbooks. 10 pa assisted places at 11, plus 5 pa for sixth-form. No set number of scholarships; grants and bursaries available up to full fees.

Parents Most are professional people (doctors, lawyers, etc).

Head and staff *Headmaster:* Kenneth Durham, appointed in 1996. Educated at St John's, Leatherhead, and Oxford University (politics, philosophy and economics). Previously Director of Studies at King's (Wimbledon) and Head of Economics at St Albans. *Staff:* 66 full time (senior department), 10 part time (music). Annual turnover 2%. Average age mid-30s.

Exam results In 1995, 107 pupils in upper fifth, 101 in upper sixth. *GCSE:* In 1995, 104 upper fifth gained at least grade C in 8+ subjects; 3 in 5–7 subjects. *A-levels:* 6 upper sixth passed in 4+ subjects; 91 in 3; 4 in 2 subjects. Average UCAS points 23.5.

University and college entrance 96% of 1995 sixth-form leavers went on to a degree course (51% after a gap year); others typically go directly into employment or military service overseas. Of those going on to university, 18% went to Oxbridge; 9% took courses in medicine, dentistry and veterinary science, 23% in science and engineering, 5% in law, 55% in humanities and social sciences, 2% in art and design, 3% in other subjects eg architecture, comparative religion, Arabic, popular music and recording.

Curriculum GCSE and *A-levels:* 14 GCSE subjects offered; 17 at A-level (no A-level general studies). 25% took science A-levels; 56% arts/humanities; 20% both. *Vocational:* Work experience available. *Computing facilities:* New 30 station laboratory. *Europe:* French, Spanish and German offered to GCSE and A-level; Russian as non-examined subjects. Regular exchanges (to France, Germany and Netherlands).

The arts (Pupils aged 11 and over) *Music:* Over 50% of pupils learn a musical instrument; instrumental exams can be taken. Many musical groups including choral society, chamber choir, orchestras, wind band, numerous classical ensembles, several pop groups. *Drama & dance*: Drama offered and GCSE and A-level may be taken. Some pupils are involved in school and house/other productions. Recent productions include

Ibsen's An Enemy of the People (1994); The Vackees (1996). *Art:* On average, 20 take GCSE, 6 A-level. Design, pottery, photography also offered.
Sport, community service and clubs (Pupils aged 11 and over) *Sport and physical activities:* Compulsory sports: rugby, cricket (for school team players). Optional: hockey, football, cross-country, tennis, badminton, squash, fives, sailing, golf, volleyball, swimming, athletics. *Community service:* Community service optional. School 'Palm Courtet' provides old time entertainment for senior citizens in borough; annually some 300 elderly people attend concert and reception. *Clubs and societies:* Up to 30 clubs, eg art & design, chess, magic, film, fencing, computing, remote control, rock appreciation, debating, snooker and pool, role playing.
Uniform School uniform worn except the sixth.
Houses/prefects Competitive houses ('demes'). Head boy – appointed by the Headmaster. Heads of Demes but no prefects/monitors.
Religion No compulsory worship.
Social Plays, choral society etc in close co-operation with South Hampstead High School. Organised trips abroad including sporting exchange with the Lycèe Marcelin Berthelot (Paris). Pupils allowed to bring own bike/motorbike to school. Meals self-service. School tuck shop. No tobacco/alcohol allowed.
Discipline Pupils failing to produce homework once might expect a warning; those caught in possession of drugs on the premises must anticipate expulsion.
Former pupils Chris Bonnington; Roger Bannister; Stephen Spender; Julian Lloyd-Webber.

• UPPINGHAM

Uppingham School, Uppingham, Rutland LE15 9QE. Tel 01572 822216, Fax 01572 822332
Pupils 610 • Boys 11–18 (Day/Board) • Girls 16–18 (Day/Board) • Upper sixth 145 • Termly fees £2440 (Day) £4070 (Board) • HMC • Enquiries/application to the Headmaster

What it's like

Founded in 1584 by Robert Johnson, it lies in the centre of the small and attractive market town of Uppingham. The town itself is a conservation area and many of the school buildings are listed. The buildings and playing fields (of which there are 68 acres) are spread right across the town, providing a close town and gown relationship. There are many well-designed modern buildings and some from the period of the great 19th-century headmaster, Edward Thring, who provided a variety of musical, sporting and practical activities then virtually unknown in comparable schools. There is a fine theatre and a magnificent new art, design and technology centre (designed by Piers Gough). It is a C of E foundation and worship in the Anglican tradition is compulsory. A large staff allows a staff:pupil ratio of about 1:8. The standards of teaching are high and academic results are very good. Almost all sixth-form leavers go on to degree courses, including Oxbridge. The school's music is extremely strong; the drama is also well supported with many productions each year. The school has long had a high reputation for its achievements in sports and games, and there is a very active CCF. A wide range of extra-curricular activities is available. The community service unit is one of the largest in the country.

School profile

Pupils Age range 11–18; 610 pupils (510 boys, 100 girls); almost all boarding, very few day pupils. Main entry ages 11 (day boys), 13 (day and boarding boys) and into sixth (boys and girls). Approx 15% are children of former pupils. *State school entry:* 5% main intake, plus 20% to sixth.
Entrance Common Entrance used or internal interview and testing. No special skills required; C of E foundation, others accepted. Parents expected to buy some sixth-form textbooks; no compulsory extras. Some 30 pa scholarships/bursaries including all-rounder and up to 20 for music and art, design and technology, 10%–50% fees.
Parents 20+% are doctors, lawyers, etc; 30+% in industry or commerce; 25+% in agriculture and related activities. 10+% live within 30 miles; up to 10% live overseas.
Head and staff *Headmaster:* Dr Stephen Winkley, 6 years in post. Educated at St Edward's (Oxford) and Oxford University (classics and modern languages). Previously

Second Master and Housemaster of Scholars at Winchester and Housemaster of Sixth Form Centre at Cranleigh. *Staff:* 72 full time. Annual turnover 5%. Average age 37.

Exam results In 1995, 94 pupils in upper fifth, 144 in upper sixth. *GCSE:* In 1995, 64 upper fifth gained at least grade C in 8+ subjects; 26 in 5–7 subjects. *A-levels:* 6 upper sixth passed in 4+ subjects; 119 in 3; 15 in 2; and 2 in 1 subject. Average UCAS points 21.3.

University and college entrance 92% of 1995 sixth-form leavers went on to a degree course; others typically go on to HND courses (agriculture, physiotherapy) or straight into careers (eg army). Of those going on to university, 15% went to Oxbridge; 8% took courses in medicine, dentistry and veterinary science, 20% in science and engineering, 62% in humanities and social sciences, 8% in art and design, 3% in music.

Curriculum GCSE and A-levels. 19 GCSE subjects offered; 25 at A-level (including design and music; no A-level general studies). 34% take science A-levels; 46% arts/humanities; 20% both. *Vocational:* Work experience for all lower sixth year. *Computing facilities:* 45 Windows compatibles, Novell Ethernet LAN, 6 Archimedes, 5 Apple Macintosh; also computers in all departments and houses. *Special provision:* Limited assistance available. *Europe:* French, German and Spanish offered to GCSE and A-level; also AS-level French and German and non-examined Italian. Regular exchanges to France, Germany, Spain and Czech Republic. European students welcomed into sixth-form. A special booklet 'Uppingham and Europe' available from the Headmaster's office.

The arts *Music:* Over 50% of pupils learn a musical instrument; instrumental exams can be taken. Very large number of musical groups including full symphony orchestra, other orchestras, chamber groups, jazz, wind, swing, concert bands, choirs, choral society (220 voices), pop groups. Winners Schools Chamber Music Competition 3 years in succession; 3-week choir and swing band tour of Malaysia; concerts at St John's Smith Square, Snape Maltings Aldeburgh, Chapel Royal, Westminster Abbey, Southwell Minster, Lincoln Cathedral etc; recently issued CD; 55 music scholars in school; 15 Oxbridge choral awards in last 2 years. *Drama & dance*: Both offered; professional coach for theatrical events. A-level theatre studies exams may be taken. Many pupils are involved in school productions and some in house/other productions. *Art:* On average, 20 take GCSE, 30 A-level. Design and photography also offered. 4 out of 10 finalists in recent Bowater Design Competition. 1st prize in Kew Gardens/AGFA national competition.

Sport, community service and clubs *Sport and physical activities:* No compulsory sports, though most play rugby. Optional: rugby, hockey, cross-country, athletics, cricket, tennis, shooting, squash, Eton fives, swimming, golf, cycling, water polo, life saving, sailing, wind surfing, canoeing, sub aqua, badminton, volleyball, basketball, gymnastics, fencing, rock climbing available. 3 years Midlands rugby representation; national hockey finalists 1994/5. *Community service:* Pupils take bronze, silver and gold Duke of Edinburgh's Award. CCF or community service compulsory for 3 years at age 14/15. One of largest CCFs in UK – special invitation to join Commandos in Belize; own fire brigade; work with handicapped, old people etc – 400 pupils involved. *Clubs and societies:* Up to 30 clubs, eg musical, debating, discussion, sporting, chess, bridge, science, arts, field sports, climbing, live poets, creative writing, critical viewing.

Uniform School uniform worn throughout.

Houses/prefects Residential houses. Prefects, head boy/girl, head of house and house prefects – appointed by Headmaster or housemaster.

Religion Attendance at chapel compulsory.

Social Meals formal, in houses. Sixth-form centre, informal dances and disco for lower and upper sixth pupils and Summer Leavers' Ball. School shop. No tobacco allowed. New sixth-form centre with bar.

Discipline Firm line taken on major offences.

Boarding Single-sex houses of 50 for boys, 40 for girls, mixed ages. Dining rooms in houses. Resident qualified nurse. Limited exeats. Visits to local town allowed.

Alumni association is run by W M Bussey, c/o the school.

V

• VICTORIA (Belfast)

Victoria College Belfast, Cranmore Park, Belfast BT9 6JA. Tel 01232 661506, Fax 01232 666898 • Pupils 998 • Boys None • Girls 4–18 (Day/Board/Weekly) • Upper sixth 96 • Termly fees £75 (Day) £1265 (Board, EU national) £2155 (Board, non-EU nationals) • Enquiries/application to the Headmistress

What it's like

Founded in 1859, it is one of the longest established girls' schools in the British Isles. Since 1972 it has occupied its present site at Cranmore Park in beautiful grounds in a secluded and quiet residential area in south Belfast. The school operates on two campuses 4 minutes' walk apart. The purpose-built buildings are modern and compact and very well equipped. Drumglass House, an elegant Georgian building, is the boarding establishment. There are excellent sports and games facilities in the grounds. An inter-denominational school, it works a selective system and academic standards are high. Results are good and most sixth-formers go on to degree courses each year. Strong in music – an award-winning senior choir – and an active drama department. A very good range of sports and games (a large number of county and national representatives) and an equally good range of extra-curricular activities. There is a big commitment to local community services. The college has a phenomenal record in the Duke of Edinburgh's Award Scheme.

School profile

Pupils Total age range 4–18; 998 girls, 957 day, 41 boarding. Senior department 11–18; 853 girls. Main entry ages, 4, 11 and into the sixth. 30% are children of former pupils.
Entrance School looks for the academic ability to benefit from grammar school education. No tuition fee is payable for pupils who meet the school's admission criteria whose parents are EU nationals, and who are resident in Northern Ireland. 2 pa scholarships.
Parents 15+% are doctors, lawyers etc; 15+% in industry or commerce. 60+% live within 30 miles; up to 10% live overseas.
Head and staff *Headmistress:* Mrs M. Andrews, 3 years in post. *Staff:* 45 full time, 14 part time. Annual turnover 2%. Average age 36.
Exam results On average, 130 pupils in upper fifth, 96 in upper sixth. *GCSE:* On average, 72% upper fifth gain at least grade C in 8+ subjects; 24% in 5–7; and 4% in 1–4 subjects. *A-levels:* 84% upper sixth pass in 3+ subjects.
University and college entrance 90% of 1995 sixth-form leavers went on to a degree course; others typically go straight on to careers (eg armed services) or non-degree courses. Of those going on to university, 9% went to Oxbridge; 47% took courses in science and engineering, 53% in humanities and social sciences.
Curriculum GCSE, AS and A-levels. 23 subjects offered (including Latin, economics, politics, and computer science). 33% take science A-levels; 33% arts/humanities; 34% both. All lower sixth take additional non-A-level options either GCSE (eg business studies, child development) or other courses (eg Japanese, Young Enterprise). *Vocational:* RSA stage 1 and 2 word processing; RSA cetificate in business language competence (French, German, Italian, Japanese and Spanish). Work experience required of all lower sixth pupils. *Computing facilities:* 3 senior computer rooms; Nimbus network in library; Apple Macs in library, technology centre and most departments; Archimedes in art room; Nimbus in careers suite. *Special provision:* Private help available after school in maths and English. *Europe:* French, German, Italian and Spanish offered to GCSE and A-level. Regular exchanges to France and Germany. European studies offered to sixth-form pupils. Language, industry and trade programme (as part of NI Department of Education European Studies Project) which establishes e-mail communication with schools in a number of European countries.
The arts (Pupils aged 11 and over) *Music:* Over 15% of pupils learn a musical

instrument; instrumental exams can be taken. Some 12 musical groups including choirs, recorder ensembles, orchestras, band, string quartet, flute, guitar, Irish traditional, clarinet ensemble. Junior and senior choirs both 1st in Belfast Music Festival; flute quartet 1st in local festival; senior choir national winners McDonald's Music in the Community competition; many pupils member of City and Belfast Youth Orchestra. *Drama & dance*: Both offered. Some pupils are involved in school productions and all in house/other productions. Annual Shakespeare Competition (established 70+ years) high standard, all Year 9 pupils take part; joint annual musical with boys from RBAI (eg Oliver); annual cross-community (Protestant/Catholic) drama with professional actors, with both Belfast and Dublin pupils. *Art:* On average, 20 take GCSE, 8 A-level. Design, pottery, textiles, stage design, computer-aided design, calligraphy, creative embroidery and 3-dimensional construction also offered. A number of pupils accepted to art college each year.

Sport, community service and clubs (Pupils aged 11 and over) *Sport and physical activities:* Compulsory sports: hockey, netball, tennis. Optional: basketball, volleyball, squash, football, badminton, fencing, table tennis, water polo. GCSE exams may be taken. Irish hockey team U18, 2 pupils; Ulster tennis squads, several; Ulster table tennis, 2; GB-ranked athletics, 3 recent former pupils (1 Olympic & Commonwealth Games representative); Ulster representatives in athletics, hockey, fencing, tennis, swimming, cricket, golf, squash, badminton; school teams compete at Ulster and Irish levels in most sports. *Community service:* Pupils take bronze, silver and gold Duke of Edinburgh's Award. Community service optional. *Clubs and societies:* Over 30 clubs, eg Guides (est 1915), chess, BAYS, creative writing, technology, martial arts, Scripture Union, first aid, computer literacy, drama.

Uniform School uniform worn throughout.

Houses/prefects Competitive houses. No prefects. Head girl and deputies – elected by sixth-form, confirmed by staff. Junior, Middle and Senior School Councils.

Religion Compulsory non-denominational assembly unless parents request otherwise.

Social Sport, debates, conferences, quizzes, lectures, concerts, plays with other schools. Regular organised trips abroad (France, Germany, Spain, Italy); exchange visits with Irish Republic and other European countries. Meals formal in boarding house, self-service in school dining hall. Tuckshops on each campus. No tobacco/alcohol allowed.

Discipline A high standard of self-discipline is expected and insisted on. Pupils failing to produce homework once might expect a warning and a requirement to produce work next day; anyone guilty of conduct harmful to herself or to others would receive warning of dangers and counselling, and contact would be made with parents. In extreme cases, parents would be asked to remove the pupil from the school, at least until the problem was resolved.

Boarding 40% have own cubicle, 30% are in dormitories of 3+. 1 boarding house. Resident qualified medical staff. Central dining room. Some weekly boarders. Approved visits to local town allowed including theatre and cultural events; seniors indirectly supervised at weekends; juniors supervised.

Alumni association run by Hon Secretary, 1 Malone View Avenue, Belfast 9.

Former pupils Helen Waddell; local TV personalities; BBC producers, scientists, doctors and engineers.

• VICTORIA (Jersey)

Victoria College, St Helier, Jersey, Channel Islands. Tel 01534 37591

• Pupils 890 • Boys 7–19 (Day) • Girls None • Upper sixth 78 • Termly fees £594 (Day) • HMC
• Enquiries/application to the Headmaster

What it's like

Founded in 1852 it has an impressive site on a spur overlooking the town of St Helier with fine views over the bay to the south. There are parkland, gardens and playing fields. The original Victorian buildings (including the Great Hall) are still used, and there have been numerous modern additions. The prep school is sited at the south end of the college lawn. A well-run school, it has high academic standards and gets good results. Most sixth-formers go on to degree courses each year. Strong in drama and art. A wide variety of sports and games is available and high standards are achieved (representatives at county and national level). The college has a flourishing CCF and a large number of pupils take part in a wide range of activities.

School profile

Pupils Total age range 7–19; 890 day boys. Senior department 11–19, 615 boys. Main entry ages 7, 11, 13 and into sixth. Approx 25% are children of former pupils. Own prep provides more than 75% of senior intake. *State school entry:* 20% senior intake, plus 5% to sixth.

Entrance Common Entrance and own exam used. No special skills or religious requirements. Parents not expected to buy textbooks; £50 pa maximum extras, 4 pa scholarships/bursaries up to full fees.

Parents 15+% are doctors, lawyers etc; 15+% in industry or commerce; 15+% in finance. 90+% live within 10 miles; up to 10% live overseas.

Head and staff *Headmaster:* Jack Hydes, 4 years in post. Educated at Alsop High, Liverpool, and at universities of Sussex (philosophy), King's College, London (English literature) and Hull (education). Previously Deputy Head at Matthew Humberstone Comprehensive, Head of English at Great Cornard Upper, and Teacher at Ramsey Abbey Grammar. *Publications:* Techniques in Writing (Harrap), Touched with Fire (CUP). *Staff:* 45 full time, 8 part time. Annual turnover 7%. Average age 41.

Exam results In 1995, 97 pupils in upper fifth, 78 in upper sixth. *GCSE:* In 1995, 69% upper fifth gained at least grade C in 8+ subjects; 14% in 5–7 subjects. *A-levels:* 71% upper sixth passed in 4+ subjects; 21% in 3; 5% in 2; and 2% in 1 subject. Average UCAS points 17.7 (including general studies, 24.0).

University and college entrance 78% of 1995 sixth-form leavers went on to a degree course (10% after a gap year); others typically go in to employment locally. Of those going on to university, 5% went to Oxbridge; 5% took courses in medicine, dentistry and veterinary science, 26% in science and engineering, 14% in law, 35% in humanities and social sciences, 9% in art and design, 11% other subjects (eg education, environmental health, sport science, hotel management).

Curriculum GCSE and A-levels: 20 subjects offered (including theatre arts and A-level general studies). 33% take science A-levels; 54% arts/humanities; 13% both. *Vocational:* Work experience available; (compulsory for 16-year olds). *Computing facilities:* 20 computers in lab. Machines in most departments. *Europe:* French, German and Spanish offered to GCSE and A-level. Regular exchanges.

The arts *Music:* Over 15% of pupils learn a musical instrument; instrumental exams can be taken. Some 8+ musical groups including brass, woodwind, chamber ensembles, rock bands. Several members of Jersey Youth Orchestra. *Drama & dance*: Drama offered and GCSE and A-level may be taken. Some pupils are involved in school productions and majority in house/other productions. *Art:* On average, 16 take GCSE, 6 A-level. Design also offered.

Sport, community service and clubs *Sport and physical activities:* Compulsory sports: football, hockey, athletics, squash, swimming. Optional: tennis, cricket, rugby, cross-country, shooting, sailing, golf. GCSE and RYA exams may be taken. Hockey, regular Hampshire representatives; cross-country, 4 in English Schools; rugby, several Jersey representatives; very strong in swimming and shooting (7th at Bisley). Programme of sports tours to different European countries as boys progress through school (France, then Portugal, Holland, Germany, UK). *Community service:* Pupils take bronze, silver and gold Duke of Edinburgh's Award. CCF optional at age 13. Community service optional for 2 years at age 14. *Clubs and societies:* Up to 30 clubs, eg music, drama, sailing, flying, chess, photography, theatre, computer, DTP, Scouts, choir, bridge, sports, shooting.

Uniform School uniform worn throughout.

Houses/prefects Competitive houses. Prefects, head boy, head of house and house prefects – appointed by senior staff with pupils' advice. School Council.

Religion Daily Christian assembly; parents may request withdrawal.

Social Jersey Youth Orchestra and Theatre, local Eisteddfod; annual dramatic production with Girls' College. Regular French exchanges. Pupils allowed to bring own car/bike/motorbike to school. Meals self-service. School shops sell tuck, second-hand uniform. No tobacco/alcohol allowed.

Discipline Pupils failing to produce homework once might expect extra work; those caught smoking cannabis on the premises might expect suspension or expulsion.

Alumni association run by Dr Jonathan Osmont, Florence House, 39 Cleveland Road, St Helier, Jersey CI.

Former pupils Kenneth More; Air Chief Marshal Sir Michael Alcock; Ambassadors Sir Martin Le Quesne and Sir Arthur De La Mare; Sir William Haley (former Editor, The Times); Sir Peter Crill (Bailiff of Jersey); Dr A E Mourant FRS.

W

• WAKEFIELD HIGH

Wakefield Girls' High School, Wentworth Street, Wakefield, West Yorkshire WF1 2QS. Tel 01924 372490, Fax 01924 382080

• Pupils 745 • Boys None • Girls 11–18 (Day) • Upper sixth 90 • Termly fees £1374 • GSA
• Enquiries/application to the Headmistress

What it's like

Founded in 1878, the school occupies an extensive and agreeable site near the centre of Wakefield. The Georgian house in which it began has been adapted and extended over the years and now has excellent facilities. A few minutes' walk away are 15 acres of well-equipped playing fields. The junior school is nearby and enjoys fine grounds and buildings. Girls follow a broad curriculum which keeps a wide range of options open until A-level; co-operation with brother school, the Queen Elizabeth Grammar School, at sixth-form level has increased pupil choice and protected minority subjects. Academic standards are high and results are very good. Most leavers go on to higher education, including a number to Oxbridge. The staff:pupil ratio is about 1:13. Considerable strength in music and drama in which there are joint activities with the Queen Elizabeth Grammar School. A standard range of sports and games (including golf and orienteering) and a plentiful variety of clubs and societies. The community service unit is very active.

School profile

Pupils Age range 11–18; 745 day girls. Main entry ages 11, 13 and into sixth. Many pupilsl from own junior school, WGHS Junior School (tel 01924 374577). *State school entry:* 60% main senior intake, plus 60% to sixth.

Entrance Own exam used. Assisted places. Bursaries.

Head and staff *Headmistress:* Mrs Patricia Langham, in post for 9 years. Educated at Carlisle and County High School for Girls and Leeds University (English, Russian and education). Previously Deputy Head at Woodkirk High, Second in English Department at Brigshaw Comprehensive and English Teacher at Ilkley Grammar. Also Member of GSA Council and Education Committee. *Staff:* 56 full time, 8 part time. Annual turnover 4%.

Exam results In 1995, 128 pupils in upper fifth, 95 in upper sixth. *GCSE:* In 1995, 120 upper fifth gained at least grade C in 9+ subjects; and 8 in 5–8 subjects. *A-levels:* 86 upper sixth passed in 4+ subjects; 6 in 3; 3 in 2 subjects. Average UCAS points 21.9 (excluding general studies).

University and college entrance 96% of 1995 sixth-form leavers went on to a degree course (2% after a gap year); others typically go on to nursing, HND or art foundation courses. Of those going on to university, 10% went to Oxbridge; 6% took courses in medicine, dentistry and veterinary science, 26% in science and engineering, 12% in law, 38% in humanities and social sciences, 1% in art and design, 18% in vocational subjects eg hospitality management, architecture.

Curriculum GCSE and A-levels: 28 A-level subjects offered, including general studies. *Vocational:* Work experience available. *Computing facilities:* Wide range. Computing taught in first three years to all pupils. *Europe:* French, German and Spanish offered to GCSE and A-level; also French and German Institute of Linguists, French AS-level and Italian and Russian GCSE. Regular exchanges (France, Germany, Italy and Spain).

The arts *Music:* Over 30% of pupils learn a musical instrument; instrumental exams can be taken. Some 16 musical groups including swing band, choirs, concert band. *Drama & dance*: Both offered. Some pupils are involved in school and other productions. *Art:* On average, 25 take GCSE, 9 A-level. Design, pottery, textiles also offered.

Sport, community service and clubs *Sport and physical activities:* Compulsory sports: hockey, netball, tennis, athletics, basketball, volleyball, badminton, table tennis. Optional: lacrosse, swimming, squash, orienteering, cricket. Sixth form only: fencing, golf, outdoor activities, sailing, climbing, self defence. BAGA and fencing exams may be

taken. Regular county representatives, hockey 10, indoor hockey 1, netball 5, athletics 3; and regional reps in hockey and netball. *Community service:* Pupils take bronze, silver and gold Duke of Edinburgh's Award. Community service optional. *Clubs and societies:* Over 60 clubs, eg drama, literary & debating, geography, classics, chess, gym, dance.
Uniform School uniform worn throughout.
Houses/prefects No competitive houses. Prefects and head girl elected by the school.
Religion All girls are expected to attend morning assembly, whatever their religion.
Social Music and dramatic productions with Queen Elizabeth Grammar School; participation with local state schools. Adventure holidays and skiing trips; exchanges with Angouleme, Lille and Hanover, Gerona. Pupils allowed to bring own car/bike/motor/bike to school. School shop. No tobacco/alcohol allowed.
Discipline Pupils failing to produce homework once might expect a warning; those caught smoking cannabis on the premises, expulsion.

• WALTHAMSTOW HALL

Walthamstow Hall, Hollybush Lane, Sevenoaks, Kent TN13 3UL. Tel 01732 451334, Fax 01732 456156

• Pupils 500 • Boys None • Girls 3–18 (Day/Board/Weekly) • Upper sixth 56 • Termly fees £2115 (Day) £3925 (Board/Weekly) • GSA • Enquiries to the Registrar • Application to the Headmistress

What it's like

Founded in 1838 for the daughters of missionaries and sited in the village of Walthamstow. In 1882 the school moved to Sevenoaks where it has a most agreeable site on the outskirts of the town. The original Victorian house, in delightful grounds and gardens, is the heart of the school. Many modern buildings provide good all-round facilities including a theatre/music centre and a sixth-form centre. The school is inter-denominational. Formerly a direct grant school, it is still academically selective and offers a broad grammar school education. Academic results are very good and each year most girls go on to degree courses, including some to Oxbridge. The staff:pupil ratio is favourable, with 19 part-time teachers and 47 full-time. Music, drama and art are well supported. There is a good range of sports and games and girls play for Kent and England; plus a variety of extra-curricular activities. Local community service flourishes and the school has an impressive record in the Duke of Edinburgh's Award Scheme.

School profile

Pupils Total age range 3–18; 500 girls (447 day, 53 boarding). Senior department 11–18, 315 girls. Main entry ages 3, 4, 7, 11, 13 and into sixth. 2% are children of former pupils. Large intake from own junior department (Walthamstow Hall Junior School; tel 01732 451334). *State school entry:* 20% senior intake, plus 10% to sixth.
Entrance Own entrance exam used. No special skills or religious requirements but a Christian foundation. Parents not expected to buy textbooks. 9 pa assisted places. 6 pa scholarships (including one music £750); approx 35 pa bursaries; Wolfson Awards and scholarships in sixth-form.
Parents 15+% are doctors, lawyers etc; 15+% in industry. 60+% live within 30 miles; 10+% live overseas.
Head and staff *Headmistress:* Mrs Jacqueline Lang, in post for 12 years. Educated at Walthamstow Hall and Oxford (modern languages). Previously Head of Modern Languages at the Ursuline Convent High, Wimbledon (voluntary-aided comprehensive). Also GSA President-elect; Vice Chairman ISJC Assisted Places Committee. *Staff:* 47 full time, 19 part time. Annual turnover 4%.
Exam results In 1995, 72 pupils in upper fifth, 47 in upper sixth. *GCSE:* In 1995, 61 upper fifth gained at least grade C in 8+ subjects; 7 in 5–7 subjects. *A-levels:* 6 upper sixth passed in 4+ subjects; 31 in 3; 6 in 2; and 2 in 1 subject. Average UCAS points 20.8.
University and college entrance 94% of 1995 sixth-form leavers went on to a degree course (30% after a gap year); others typically go on to management training in eg retailing, banking. Of those going on to university, 11% went to Oxbridge; 13% took courses in medicine, dentistry and veterinary science, 17% in science and engineering, 35% in humanities and social sciences, 6% in art and design, 15% in vocational subjects

(eg nursing, ophthalmics, hotel managment), 13% in eg maths, business management, media, accounting.
Curriculum GCSE, AS and A-levels: 28 GCSE subjects offered; 26 at A-level (no A-level general studies). 13 take science A-levels; 19 arts/humanities; 15 both. *Vocational:* Work experience available; annual Challenge of Management Conference; RSA diploma in IT offered as an extra in sixth-form. *Computing facilities:* RML Nimbus. *Special provision:* Extra help from willing staff; occasional paid EFL tuition arranged. *Europe:* French (compulsory to GCSE) and German (compulsory for 1 year) both available at GCSE and A-level; also Spanish GCSE and Italian Institute of Linguists diploma in sixth. Regular exchanges.
The arts (Pupils aged 11 and over) *Music:* Over 40% of pupils learn a musical instrument; instrumental exams are taken. Some 10 musical groups including orchestras, wind band, flute choir, wind and string quartet, 3 choirs, chamber music ensembles. Pupils in county and regional youth orchestras. *Drama & dance*: Both offered. GCSE drama, A-level theatre studies and Guildhall exams may be taken. Majority of pupils are involved in school productions and all in house/other productions. Lloyds Bank Theatre Challenge shortlisted, regular drama workshops. *Art:* On average, 26 take GCSE, 10 A-level. Painting, drawing, design, creative textiles and photography offered.
Sport, community service and clubs (Pupils aged 11 and over) *Sport and physical activities:* Compulsory sports: lacrosse, netball, tennis, rounders, swimming, athletics, gym/dance, trampolining. Optional: squash, volleyball, badminton, table tennis, hockey, aerobics, fencing, dancing. Sixth form only: wind-surfing, self defence, rock climbing, dry-slope skiing, riding, carriage driving. GCSE, RLSS, Squash Assoc, ASA, AAA and fencing exams may be taken. *Community service:* Pupils take bronze, silver and gold Duke of Edinburgh's Award. Community service vigorous. Watch Club projects in conservation. *Clubs and societies:* Up to 16 clubs, eg electronics, drama, Watch Club, Christian Fellowship, art, debating, pottery, video, squash, Young Enterprise, Arts Society, chess.
Uniform School uniform worn except in sixth.
Houses/prefects Competitive houses. Prefects, head girl, head of house and house prefects – elected by school. School Council.
Religion Prayers each morning, and evening for boarders. Sunday evening service; local churches for Sunday morning.
Social Voluntary service unit involves all local schools. Links with Tonbridge School for music, drama and debating. Organised trips abroad to France and Germany; also skiing trips. Pupils allowed to bring own car/motorbike/bike to school on request. Meals formal. Second-hand uniform shop. No tobacco/alcohol allowed.
Discipline Pupils failing to produce homework once would be admonished; those caught smoking cannabis on the premises could expect expulsion.
Boarding All seniors have own study bedroom; juniors share double bedrooms. SRN cover 24 hours. Central dining room. Sixthformers are provided with and cook snacks. 2 weekend exeats each term. Visits to local town allowed; 8–13 weekly, escorted; 13+ in groups, on request.
Alumnae association is run by Mrs Carole Hills, c/o the school.

• WARMINSTER

Warminster School, Warminster, Wiltshire BA12 8PJ. Tel 01985 213038 Fax 01985 214129
• Pupils 432 • Boys 4–18 (Day/Board/Weekly) • Girls 4–18 (Day/Board/Weekly) • Upper sixth 40 • Termly fees £550–£1790 (Day) £2820–£3090 (Board/Weekly) • SHMIS, BSA • Enquiries/application to the Master

What it's like

Formed in 1973 by the amalgamation of two single-sex schools, the Lord Weymouth School (founded 1707) and the School of St Monica (founded 1874). Its handsome and well-equipped buildings lie in beautiful gardens and grounds, facing open country on the edge of the very attractive old town. The school has long-established and close links with the town and the locality where it enjoys strong support. The junior school is on a neighbouring site. Warminster is a small friendly school whose declared aim is to develop the potential and recognise the value of all pupils. A staff:pupil ratio of about 1:10; most sixth-formers go on to university. More than half the school is involved in music and about 120 pupils learn an instrument. A large number is engaged in dramatic activities and there is a strong design department. It has a high reputation in sport and games (a large number of representatives at county level); there is also a strong CCF contingent, a wide variety of extra-curricular activities, a substantial commitment to local community schemes and a well-established Duke of Edinburgh's Award Scheme.

School profile

Pupils Total age range 4–18; 432 pupils, 236 day (151 boys, 85 girls), 196 boarding (116 boys, 80 girls). Senior department 12–18, 298 pupils (182 boys, 116 girls). Main entry ages 5, 10, 11, 13 and into sixth. Approx 10% are children of former pupils. Own junior school provides more than 75% of senior intake. *State school entry:* 40% of intakes.

Entrance Common Entrance and own tests used. No special skills or religious requirements. Parents not expected to buy textbooks; other extras average £50. Scholarships/bursaries for 11+ and 16+ entrants; bursaries for other pupils.

Parents 25+% in armed services; 15+% in industry or commerce. 65+% live within 30 miles; 10+% live overseas.

Head and staff Master: Timothy Holgate, 6 years in post. Educated at Sydney Grammar School and Sydney University (chemistry). Previously Housemaster, Head of Chemistry and Administrative Assistant to the Headmaster at Marlborough. *Staff:* 46 full time, 3 part time. Annual turnover 5%. Average age 40.

Exam results On average, 64 pupils in upper fifth, 40 in upper sixth. *GCSE:* On average, 63% upper fifth gain at least grade C in 7+ subjects; 28% in 5–6; and 10% in 1–4 subjects. *A-levels:* 60% upper sixth pass in 3 subjects; 30% in 2; and 9% in 1 subject. Average UCAS points 13.

University and college entrance 75% of sixth-form leavers go on to a degree course (10% after a gap year); others typically go on to HND or art foundation courses. Of those going on to university, 2% went to Oxbridge; 5% took courses in medicine, dentistry and veterinary science, 40% in science and engineering, 1% in law, 40% in humanities and social sciences, 12% in art and design, 5% in other voctional subjects eg pharmacology, nursing, media studies.

Curriculum GCSE and A-levels: 19 subjects offered (including business studies, home economics, sports studies). 40% take science A-levels; 35% arts/humanities; 25% both. *Vocational:* Work experience available. *Computing facilities:* Recently updated computer centre and CAL for most departments. *Special provision:* Dyslexia unit and EFL teaching with qualified staff. *Europe:* French (from age 5), German (from 13) and Spanish to GCSE and A-level. Visits to France and Germany; pupils from Germany and Spain in school.

The arts (Pupils aged 11 and over) *Music:* Over 30% of pupils learn a musical instrument; instrumental exams can be taken. Some 6 musical groups including orchestra, concert band, stage band, clarinet choir, choir. Band at opening of new Safeway store, and receptions at Longleat and in Normandy; clarinet choir at Bembridge Music festival; choir tour to Denmark. *Drama & dance*: Drama offered. Some pupils are involved in school productions. *Art:* On average, 16 take GCSE, 6 A-level. Design and textiles also offered.

Sport, community service and clubs (Pupils aged 11 and over) *Sport and physical activities:* Main sports: soccer, cricket, hockey, athletics (boys), hockey, netball, athletics (girls). Optional: basketball, badminton, squash, cross-country, tennis, swimming, rounders, golf. County representation in hockey, athletics and cross-country. *Community service:* Pupils take bronze, silver and gold Duke of Edinburgh's Award; current expeditions to Iceland and Austria. CCF and community service optional. *Clubs and societies:* Over 30 clubs, eg computing, music and drama, aikido, various craft groups, school newspaper, shooting, electronics, cookery.

Uniform School uniform worn except the sixth.

Houses/prefects Competitive houses. Prefects, head boy and girl, head of house and house prefects – appointed by the Master or house staff. School Council.

Religion Daily assembly and Sunday morning chapel for boarders.

Social Drama, debates, social service, mini-enterprise. Regular skiing trips. Some meals formal, some self service. School shop. No tobacco/alcohol allowed.

Discipline Pupils failing to produce homework once might expect detention; those caught smoking cannabis on the premises can expect expulsion.
Boarding Fifth and sixth-forms have own study bedroom, 3% are in dormitories of 6+. Single-sex houses of 35–60. Central dining rooms. Senior pupils can provide and cook own food. Exeats at half-term and any weekend. Visits to local town allowed.
Alumni association is run by Miss Sarah Pearce, 344 Winchester Road, Upper Shirley, Southampton, SO1 2SJ.
Former pupils F Jaeger, C J Benjamin, E J Baddeley, F Bartholomew (actors); Ian Macdonald (racing driver); Thomas Arnold (headmaster); David Backhouse (sculptor); Lord Christopher Thynne; Major-General C E N Lomax; Major-General C H Foulkes; Admiral P H Hall-Thompson; E J Davies (world long jump record holder); Grosvenor Thomas (painter).

• WARWICK

Warwick School, Myton Road, Warwick CV34 6PP. Tel 01926 492484, Fax 01926 401259
• Pupils 1006 • Boys 7–19 (Day/Board/Weekly) • Girls None • Upper sixth 109 • Termly fees £1350–£1530 (Day) £3100–£3280 (Board) £2880–£3060 (Weekly) • HMC • Enquiries/application to the Headmaster

What it's like

Founded in c.914 in the reign of Edward the Confessor (the putative patron), it moved to its present site, on the banks of the Avon, in 1879. The main building is an arresting example of the rococo Tudor style and other buildings have developed round it in an E-shaped pattern. There are several impressive Victorian buildings and a variety of much more recent ones. Large playing fields lie alongside. A C of E foundation, in which attendance at chapel is compulsory with considerable emphasis on religious education. There are longstanding and very close associations between the school and the town and there is vigorous local support. Academic standards and achievements are of a high order: results are excellent and almost all leavers go on to degree courses each year, including very many to Oxbridge. The music, drama and art departments are very strong. The school boasts a number of clubs and societies which cater for almost every conceivable need. There is an excellent range of sports and games and high standards are attained (20 or more representatives at county level). Another notable feature is the substantial commitment to local community schemes and to the Duke of Edinburgh's Award Scheme.

School profile

Pupils Total age range 7–19; 1006 boys (948 day, 58 boarding). Senior department 11–19, 805 boys. Main entry ages 7, 11, 13 and into sixth. Approx 5% are children of former pupils. *State school entry:* 46% senior intake, plus 50% to sixth (4% total sixth-form).
Entrance Own entrance exam used. No special skills or religious requirements. Parents not expected to buy textbooks, paper/exercise books or pay exam fees; extras include lunch, instrumental tuition. 30 pa assisted places. 20 pa scholarships, bursaries for tuition or boarding fees.
Parents 15+% in industry or commerce. 60+% live within 30 miles; up to 5% live overseas.
Head and staff *Headmaster:* Dr Philip Cheshire, in post 9 years. Educated at Oakham and at King's College, London and St Batholomew's Hospital Medical College. Previously Head of Science at Rugby, Senior Research Officer at Huntingdon Research Centre and Lecturer in Physics Department at St Bartholomew's Hospital Medical College. Publications: various on cancer research. *Staff:* 64 full time, 8 part time. Annual turnover 5%. Average age 40.
Exam results In 1995, 145 pupils in upper fifth, 92 in upper sixth. *GCSE:* In 1995, 96% upper fifth gained at least grade C in 8+ subjects; 4% in 5–7 subjects. *A-levels:* 92% upper sixth passed in 4+ subjects; 5% in 3; 2% in 2; and 1% in 1 subject; many boys take AS-levels in addition. Average UCAS points 26.0 (including general studies 30.1).
University and college entrance 98% of 1995 sixth-form leavers went on to a degree course (9% after a gap year); others typically go on to non-degree courses eg HND. Of those going on to university, 19% went to Oxbridge; 2% took courses in medicine,

dentistry and veterinary science, 40% in science and engineering, 55% in humanities and social sciences, 2% in art and design.
Curriculum GCSE and A-levels. 25 subjects offered (including A-level general studies; GCSE Japanese in sixth-form; computing GCSE, AS and A-level). 28% take science A-levels; 24% arts/humanities; 48% both. *Computing facilities:* 70 Archimedes. *Europe:* French (from age 8) and German offered to GCSE, AS and A-level; also Russian GCSE and Spanish GCSE and AS-level. Regular exchanges to France and Germany.
The arts (Pupils aged 11 and over) *Music:* All pupils learn a musical instrument; instrumental exams can be taken. Some 8+ musical groups including wind band, orchestra, swing band, chamber group etc. Members of county youth orchestra, string orchestra. *Drama & dance*: Drama offered and GCSE and A-level may be taken. Many pupils involved in school and house/other productions. Regular performances in the community. Boys audition for and take part in RSC productions. *Art:* On average, 35 take GCSE, 9 A-level. Design, pottery, photography, sculpture, fashion, etching, silkscreen printing also offered. Pupils' work exhibited at ISADA exhibition.
Sport, community service and clubs (Pupils aged 11 and over) *Sport and physical activities:* Compulsory sports: rugby, cricket, athletics, swimming – up to 14. Optional: 14 upwards – rugby, cricket, swimming, hockey, cross-country, tennis, athletics. Sixth form only: badminton, squash, canoeing, soccer. Many county representatives in school's main games, occasionally national. *Community service:* Pupils take bronze, silver and gold Duke of Edinburgh's Award; currently 38 bronze, 15 silver, 25 gold participants. CCF or community service compulsory for 2 years at age 13. *Clubs and societies:* Some 20 clubs, eg archery, basketball, bridge, chess, clay-pigeon shooting, climbing, community service, geographical, golf, history & politics, photographic, Young Enterprise.
Uniform School uniform worn, modified in the sixth.
Houses/prefects 6 competitive houses. Prefects and boarding house prefects – elected; head boy appointed. School Council.
Religion Compulsory Chapel.
Social Joint concert, plays and society meetings with King's High School (Girls). Organised trips to Canada, USA, Germany, France. Pupils allowed to bring own car/bike/motorbike to school. Meals self-service. School shop. No tobacco/alcohol allowed.
Discipline Pupils failing to produce homework could expect detention; those caught smoking cannabis on the premises could expect expulsion.
Boarding Prefects and upper sixth have own study bedroom, most of the rest share with one other; junior and senior houses, divided by age. Central dining room. Sixth formers may prepare light snacks in own kitchen. Half-term and 2 weekend exeats each term. Visits to the local town allowed daily from the age of 13.
Alumni association is run by Mr P H E Bailey, Secretary, Old Warwickian Association, 24 Park Road, Leamington Spa, Warwickshire.

• WELBECK

Welbeck College, Worksop, Nottinghamshire S80 3LN. Tel 01909 476326

• Pupils 180 • Boys 16–19 (Board) • Girls 16–19 (Board) • Upper sixth 90 • Termly fees (means-tested) up to £850+ • BSA • Enquiries/application to the Principal

What it's like

Founded in 1953 to prepare young men for future professional service in the Army's technical corps; girls were admitted for the first time in 1992. It enjoys a superb site and magnificent amenities in a large park in the Dukeries. All students entering Welbeck have a common aim: to gain a commission in the technical corps of the Army. Two years' study at Welbeck for A-levels is followed by one year at the RMA Sandhurst or 3 years' degree study as officer cadets at the RMCS Shrivenham. Career officers have excellent opportunities to qualify, while serving, for membership of almost any of the professional bodies in the engineering field. Welbeck is a highly organised and highly motivated establishment. A large staff permits a staff:pupil ratio of about 1:9. Very good results are achieved and the vast majority of students proceed to degree courses. Music and drama are strong and an unusually wide variety of sports and games is available, many played on an inter-school basis. There is much emphasis on physical fitness and outdoor pursuits. As might be expected, the CCF is obligatory but Welbeck is not run as a military unit and in most respects is like any other boarding sixth-form college. However, those who successfully complete the two-year course are guaranteed a £9,500 salary when they move on to the next stage of training, either at university or at Sandhurst.

School profile

Pupils Age range 16–19; 180 boarding pupils (150 boys, 30 girls). Entry at 16, 90% from state schools.
Entrance Own 24-hour selection system, looking for leadership skills, aptitude for physical challenge and ability in mathematics and physics. No religious requirements. Parents not expected to buy textbooks or uniforms. Travel warrants provided at the beginning and end of each term.
Parents 10+% in the armed services. Up to 10% live overseas.
Head and staff *Principal:* J K Jones, 6 years in post. Previously Headmaster King's School, Gutersloh, Germany. *Staff:* 19 full time, 3 military, 2 part time. Annual turnover 5%.
Exam results In 1995, 90 pupils in upper sixth. *A-levels:* 90% passed in 4+ subjects; 6% in 3; 2% in 2; and 2% in 1 subject. Average UCAS points 26.3.
University and college entrance 90% students go on to a degree course (10% first taking a gap year); 55% go direct, 35% go to Sandhurst first. Of those going on to university, 7% go to Oxbridge; 95% take courses in science and engineering, 5% in other subjects eg management.
Curriculum A-levels (and AS-level contemporary French and German). 12 subjects offered including general studies. All students must study A-level mathematics and a compulsory core skills course. 80% take science/engineering A-levels; 20% take science with some arts/humanities. *Computing facilities:* Extensive Elonex, CI/LEO and Archimedes A5000 computing and word processing facilities; great deal of software. Currently over 60 machines available for class and individual student use.
The arts *Music:* Some pupils learn a musical instrument; instrumental exams can be taken. Some musical groups including band and choir. *Art:* Photography and pottery also offered.
Sport, community service and clubs *Sport and physical activities:* Sports: rugby, soccer, hockey, cross-country, cricket, athletics, tennis, swimming, sailing, rowing, canoeing, shooting, badminton, basketball, volleyball, fencing, judo, karate, climbing, table tennis, snooker, golf, squash, gymnastics. *Community service:* Pupils take Duke of Edinburgh's Award. CCF compulsory. *Clubs and societies:* Several clubs, eg chess, offshore sailing, film appreciation, bell-ringing, war games, popular music, classical music, debating, learning to drive.
Uniform Uniform worn.
Houses/prefects Competitive houses. Housemasters appoint house prefects and head of house, from whom Principal chooses Head of College.
Religion Compulsory worship.
Social Good social contacts with other boarding schools. Regular concert and theatre visits as well as extended cultural visit to London. Organised skiing trip to Germany; Mt Blanc expeditions, soccer tour to Germany; annual exchange visit to France; offshore sailing. All pupils attend a 2-week Outward Bound course in the first summer holidays as well as a 2-week college camp in the Lake District. Lunch and most evening meals formal, others self-service. School shop. Smoking not allowed: alcohol available in senior and junior social clubs.
Discipline A full self-explanatory set of college rules. Those caught smoking are gated; those with drugs expelled. Self discipline encouraged.
Boarding Boys are accommodated in study bedrooms for 1–6 pupils. Girls in study bedrooms of 2 or 3, housed in a separate lodge, under the care of a Housemother. Resident qualified nurse. Central dining room. Week-long half-terms plus some weekend exeats. Visits to local town allowed by arrangement with Housemaster or Housemother.
Alumni association is run by the Bursar, c/o the college.

• WELLINGBOROUGH

Wellingborough School, Wellingborough, Northamptonshire NN8 2BX. Tel 01933 222427, Fax 01933 271986

• Pupils 770 • Boys 3–18 (Day; Board/Weekly from 13) • Girls 3–18 (Day; Board/Weekly from 13) • Upper sixth 66 • Termly fees £1725 (Day) £2930 (Weekly) £3260 (Board) • HMC
• Enquiries/application to the Headmaster

What it's like

Founded in 1595 as a boys' school, it is now fully coeducational having first admitted girls in 1977. It has occupied its present site since 1881; this is an attractive, compact campus (on the south side of the town) with pleasant buildings, lovely gardens and ample playing fields (about 50 acres in all). There have been many developments in the last 20 years and the school has first-rate facilities. A pre-preparatory school provides the possibility of continuous education from 3–18. Chapel services and teaching are in accordance with the principles of the Church of England. A well-run school, it provides a sound general education with very good results. Almost all sixth-formers go on to degree courses each year, including many to Oxbridge. Music, drama, art and design technology are regarded as particularly important disciplines and activities; music is especially strong. An excellent range of sports and games in which high standards are achieved (a lot of representatives at county and national level). There is also a good variety of extra-curricular activities. Some commitment to local community services and a promising record in the Duke of Edinburgh's Award Scheme.

School profile

Pupils Total age range 3–18; 770 pupils. Senior department 13–18; 386 pupils, 339 day (231 boys, 108 girls), 47 boarding (31 boys, 16 girls). Main entry ages, 11, 13 and into the sixth. 9% are children of former pupils. Own junior school provides 70% senior intake. *State school entry:* 25% intakes over 11, plus 85% to sixth.

Entrance Common Entrance and own tests used. All skills welcomed; Christian environment (C of E chapel services). Parents expected to buy sixth-form textbooks. 20 pa assisted places. 22 pa scholarships (including sport), one-sixth to half fees; 5 pa Foundation scholarships at 11+, half fees; some bursaries.

Parents 15+% are doctors, lawyers etc; 15+% in industry or commerce. 60+% live within 30 miles; up to 10% live overseas.

Head and staff *Headmaster:* Ralph Ullmann, 4 years in post. Educated at Cambridge High School and Cambridge University (history, education). Previously Head of Ruthin School, Housemaster and Head of History at Bloxham, history master at Bishop's Stortford Senior School. *Staff:* 39 full time, 3 part time. Annual turnover 10%. Average age 40.

Exam results In 1995, 77 pupils in upper fifth, 66 in upper sixth. *GCSE:* In 1995, 65 upper fifth gained at least grade C in 8+ subjects; 9 in 5–7 subjects. *A-levels:* 18 upper sixth passed in 4+ subjects; 45 in 3; 2 in 2; and 1 in 1 subject. Average UCAS points 23.4.

University and college entrance 98% of 1995 sixth-form leavers went on to a degree course (14% after a gap year); others go on to eg equine managment course. Of those going on to university, 9% went to Oxbridge; 8% took courses in medicine, dentistry and veterinary science, 25% in science and engineering, 8% in law, 45% in humanities and social sciences, 10% in art and design, 3% in other vocational subjects eg nursing, medical technology.

Curriculum GCSE and A-levels: 18 subjects offered (including A-level general studies). 24% take science A-levels; 32% arts/humanities; 43% both. *Vocational:* Work experience available for 1 week after GCSE in fifth. *Computing facilities:* Network with 2 rooms, file server, 21 Sims PCs with CD-Rom and open integrated learning system; 12 BBC Masters; 10 networked Archimedes in design centre; PCs in boarding houses. *Special provision:* Extra help given to dyslexic pupils if needed (follow normal time-table). EFL arranged if needed. *Europe:* French (from age 11) and German offered at GCSE and A-level; also Russian GCSE and Spanish as a non-examined subject. Regular exchanges. European studies offered. Some European pupils board in school for 1–3 terms.

The arts (Pupils aged 11 and over) *Music:* Over 30% of pupils learn a musical instrument; instrumental exams can be taken. Several musical groups including orchestras, concert bands, flute ensemble, guitar, recorder groups. 1 pupil leader of county

youth orchestra. *Drama & dance*: Dance offered. Some pupils are involved in school productions and majority in house/other productions. *Art:* On average, 30 take GCSE, 8 A-level. Design, pottery, design and technology also offered.
Sport, community service and clubs (Pupils aged 11 and over) *Sport and physical activities:* Compulsory sports: football, cricket, athletics (boys); netball, hockey, athletics (girls). Optional: rugby, cross-country, tennis, shooting. County and regional hockey and county schools cricket representatives. *Community service:* Pupils take bronze, silver and gold Duke of Edinburgh's Award or CCF for 2 years at age 14. *Clubs and societies:* Extensive activities programme (60+ per week), including debating, music-making, history and politics, environment, public speaking, general knowledge.
Uniform School uniform worn throughout.
Houses/prefects Competitive houses (2 boarding, 7 day). Prefects, head boy/girl, head of house and house prefects – appointed by Headmaster after consultation.
Religion Compulsory morning chapel service (C of E) and 6 Sundays a term for boarders.
Social Sporting and cultural competitions with local schools. French exchange (Marseille). French visits (guardian scheme), exchange through Dragons International, German exchange (Anna-Schmidt Schule, Frankfurt), annual skiing party; musical production to USA. Lunch self-service. School shop. No tobacco/alcohol allowed.
Discipline Pupils failing to produce homework once might expect to do it for next morning, detention for repeated offence. Graded punishment dependent on nature of offence and circumstances of pupil.
Boarding Upper sixth have own study bedroom, 50% share with 1 other, 40% share in 3s or 4s. Single-sex boarding houses same as competitive houses. Qualified nurse resident when required; doctor visits 2 times/week. Central dining room. Pupils can provide and cook own food in limited facilities. Weekend exeats. (Boarders required to attend chapel 6 Sundays per term.) Visits to local town allowed.
Alumni association run by Mr M H Askham, c/o the school.
Former pupils David Wilson-Johnson (baritone); Ray Whitney MP; General Sir Peter Hudson; Major-General Richard Park.

• WELLINGTON (Ayr)

Wellington School, Carleton Turrets, Craigweil Road, Ayr KA7 2XH. Tel 01292 269321
• Pupils 423 • Boys 3–14 (Day) • Girls 3–18 (Day) • Higher year 55 • Termly fees £1595 (Day)
• GSA • Enquiries/application to the Headmistress

What it's like

Founded in 1836 to educate 'young ladies of quality' in French, history, music, art and embroidery. By 1900 it had a considerable reputation and had grown; in 1994 it started to progress to full co-education. In 1923 it moved to its present, semi-rural site, with all buildings within a few minutes' walk of each other. Ayr itself is a very attractive town, with two theatres and several museums, close to the sea. The school includes a junior department and a kindergarten. A well-run school, most pupils go on to higher education. It is strong in music and drama and there is a vigorous sporting tradition with a large number of representatives at national and county level (especially hockey). There are good sporting facilities on site. There is also a strong careers department and a work shadowing scheme for 17-year-olds. A wide range of extracurricular activities is available. An impressive record in the Duke of Edinburgh's Award Scheme.

School profile

Pupils Total age range 3–18; 423 pupils (boarding is being discontinued). Boys from age 3-14 admitted from 1995. Senior department 12–18, 325 girls and boys. Main entry ages 3, 10, 12 and into sixth. Approx 25% are children of former pupils. Own junior school, Sleaford House, provides more than 20% of intake.
Entrance Own entrance exam. Ability in English, maths, music and sport looked for; no religious requirements. Small hire charge for textbooks. 10% of pupils on assisted places. Some bursaries, variable value.
Parents 15+% in armed services; 15+% are doctors, lawyers etc; 15+% in industry or commerce; 15+% are teachers. 60+% live within 30 miles; 10+% live overseas.

Head and staff *Headmistress:* Mrs Dianne Gardner, 8 years in post. Educated at Ounsdale School and Liverpool University (medieval history). Previously Senior Mistress at Wellington (Ayr). Began career in the museum world and came to teaching through involvement with the Schools Museum Service. *Staff:* 47 full time, 17 part time. Annual turnover 5%. Average age 35.
Exam results On average 55 in S-grade year; 55 in Higher year; 35 in CSYS year. *S-grades*: On average, 2 pupils pass in 8+ subjects; 37 in 5–7; 16 in 4 subjects. *Highers:* 10 pass in 5+ subjects; 20 in 4; 11 in 3; 7 in 2; 6 in 1 subject.
University and college entrance 87% of 1995 sixth-form leavers went on to a degree course; others typically go on to non-degree courses eg orthoptics diploma, HND computing or to art college. Of those going on to university, 2% went to Oxbridge; 5% took courses in medicine, dentistry and veterinary science, 12% in science and engineering, 77% in humanities and social sciences, 5% in art and design, 1% in music.
Curriculum S-grades, Highers, CSYS (GCSE and A-level in special cases). Computing, Latin and Greek offered. *Vocational:* Work shadowing available. *Computing facilities:* 15 stand-alone systems in computer room, 12 in departments; pupils may use machines under supervision at lunch times. *Special provision:* can be made for dyslexia and EFL. *Europe:* French, German and Spanish offered at S-grade, Higher and CSYS; also non-examined Italian and Russian. Regular exchanges to France and Germany.
The arts (Pupils aged 11 and over) *Music:* Almost all pupils learn a musical instrument; instrumental exams can be taken. Some 5 musical groups including recorder, wind band, orchestras. *Drama & dance*: Both offered. Poetry Society, LAMDA, Scotvec drama exams may be taken. Some pupils are involved in school and house/other productions. *Art:* On average, 20 take S-grade, 10 Higher, 4 CSYS. Design, pottery, photography also offered. Successful entry to local and national competitions eg Edinburgh Festival poster competition.
Sport, community service and clubs (Pupils aged 11 and over) *Sport and physical activities:* Optional sports: hockey, netball, tennis, squash, swimming, rugby, gymnastics, fencing, badminton, aerobics. *Community service:* Pupils take bronze, silver and gold Duke of Edinburgh's Award. CCF and community service optional at age 15+. *Clubs and societies:* Up to 15 clubs, eg art, drama, sport, music, chess, debating.
Uniform School uniform worn throughout.
Houses/prefects Competitive houses. Prefects, head girl, head of house and house prefects – appointed by Headmistress with staff advice. School Council.
Religion Daily assembly (Jews excepted); boarders attend Sunday church of their choice (most attend Church of Scotland).
Social Debates, ESU, dances, trivial pursuit challenges, sport, music and drama festivals with other schools. Bi-annual French and German school exchange, trips to Germany, Russia, skiing. Pupils allowed to bring own car/bike/motorbike to school. Meals self-service. School shop. No tobacco/alcohol allowed.
Discipline School aims to praise for good and sensible behaviour as well as admonish for breaches of school rules (which are kept to a minimum). Any suggestion of involvement with drugs and the school would have no hesitation in bringing in the police.
Alumni association run by Mrs L Moore, c/o the school.
Former pupils Dr Elizabeth Hewat (theologian and historian); Miss Elizabeth Kyle (author); Miss Kirsty Wark (presenter, BBC TV).

• WELLINGTON (Berkshire)

Wellington College, Crowthorne, Berkshire RG45 7PU. Tel 01344 771588

• Pupils 788 • Boys 13–18 (Day/Board) • Girls 16–18 (Day/Board) • Upper sixth 158 • Termly fees £2985 (Day) £4090 (Board) • HMC • Enquiries/application to the Registrar

What it's like

Founded 1853, by public subscription in memory of the Duke and granted a Royal Charter the same year. The Monarch is the Visitor and Buckingham Palace still approves governors and changes in statutes. Its original grand buildings were designed by Shaw who, with remarkable foresight, provided each pupil with a bed-sitting room. The chapel was designed by Gilbert Scott. Many additional buildings now provide excellent accommodation and facilities. The college lies in an estate of over 400 acres and has fine gardens and superb playing fields. Its own prep school, Eagle House, has its grounds nearby. The spiritual and religious life of the college is of considerable importance and pupils are encouraged to commit themselves fully as Christians. High standards of teaching prevail and academic results are very good. Nearly all leavers go on to degree courses each year, including many to Oxbridge. The music department is immensely strong (there are orchestras, choirs, bands, and over 350 pupils learn an instrument) and the college is very strong, too, in drama and art. It has a reputation for excellence in games and sports of which a wide variety is provided. There are many clubs, societies and extra-curricular activities. The CCF has a large contingent and, while the college maintains its traditional links with the Army (many Wellingtonians have been distinguished soldiers), leavers now go into as wide a range of professions as any comparable school. There is a large commitment to local community schemes.

School profile

Pupils Age range 13–18; 788 pupils, 146 day (140 boys, 6 girls), 642 boarding (602 boys, 40 girls). Main entry ages 13 (boys) and into sixth (boys and girls). Approx 15% are children of former pupils. Eagle House Prep School provides significant proportion of intake. *State school entry:* A few (assisted places).

Entrance Common Entrance and own scholarship exam used; competitive exam and interview for sixth-form girls. No special skills or religious requirements. Parents expected to buy A-level textbooks; extras charged vary. 9 pa assisted places. 19 pa scholarships and exhibitions, up to half fees; two major music scholarships and a number of minor awards for candidates of sufficient ability; one art award, sometimes more.

Parents 10+% in the armed services; 40+% in industry or commerce. 50+% live within 30 miles; up to 10% live overseas.

Head and staff *Master*: C J ('Jonty') Driver, in post 7 years. Educated at St Andrew's College (Grahamstown) and at Cape Town and Oxford universities (English literature and education). Previously Headmaster at Berkhamsted, Principal at Island School, Hong Kong, Director of Sixth Form at Matthew Humberstone School, Research Fellow at York University, and Housemaster of the International Centre at Sevenoaks. Also FRSA; President of the National Union of South African Students (1964); Trustee of Lomans Trust; Governor of Benenden, Scaitcliffe, Eagle House. Publications: Four novels, four books of poetry, one biography. Editor of Conference and Common Room. *Staff:* 86 full time, 1 part time. Annual turnover 4%. Average age 39.

Exam results In 1995, 156 pupils in Block One (upper fifth), 186 in upper sixth. *GCSE:* In 1995, 153 Block One pupils gained at least grade C in 8+ subjects. *A-levels:* In 1995, 26 upper sixth passed in 4+subjects; 149 in 3; 8 in 2; and 2 in 1 subject. Average UCAS points 24.9.

University and college entrance 95% of 1995 sixth-form leavers went on to a degree course (66% after a gap year); others typically go on to tourism, armed services. Of those going on to university, 15% went to Oxbridge; 12% took courses in medicine, dentistry and veterinary science, 30% in science and engineering, 10% in law, 40% in humanities and social sciences, 5% in art and design, 3% in vocational subjects eg physiotherapy, sports science.

Curriculum GCSE, AS and A-levels: 21 GCSE subjects offered; 23 at A-level (including Arabic). 22% take science A-levels; 26% arts/humanities; 52% both. *Computing facilities:* Excellent facilities with IBM compatibles. *Europe:* French, German and Spanish offered to GCSE, AS and A-level. Regular exchanges.

The arts *Music:* Over 350 pupils learn a musical instrument; instrumental exams can be taken. Some 25+ musical groups including orchestras, string, wind and brass ensembles, 3 choirs, 3 bands, jazz orchestra, rock groups. Choir recently produced nationally reviewed CD. *Drama*: Extra-curricular drama offered. Large number of school and house/other productions every year. Drama thriving part of school life. *Art:* On average, 35 take GCSE, 23 A-level. Design, pottery, textiles, photography, craft, history of art also offered. On average 5 pupils go to art colleges each year.

Sport, community service and clubs *Sport and physical activities:* Major sports: rugby, hockey, cricket/athletics. Minor: tennis, swimming, cross-country, basketball, squash, soccer, fives, badminton, rackets, judo, climbing, fencing, golf, shooting, sailing, sub-aqua, karate. GCSE, RLSS, RYA, subaqua exams and judo awards may be taken. Sixth form only: aerobics. Regular county and divisional representation; some interna-

tional, particularly in rugby, hockey, cross-county, cricket, shooting. *Community service:* CCF compulsory in the second year. Community service compulsory in other non-CCF years eg estate work, looking after OAPs, helping in local schools and concert parties. *Clubs and societies:* Over 30 clubs, eg chess, debating, opera, bridge, poetry, Christian Forum, photographic, political, natural history, choral, classical.
Uniform School uniform worn, modified in sixth.
Houses/prefects The pastoral organisation is based in houses. Prefects, head boy and girl, heads of house and house prefects – appointed by Headmaster and housemasters.
Religion Some compulsory services and some voluntary.
Social Local events include choral/orchestral events, debates and occasional dances. French, Russian, Spanish, Indian and German exchanges; chamber choir to France/Germany; modern languages department to eg Bordeaux, Paris. Pupils allowed to bring own bike to school. Meals self-service. School shop. No tobacco allowed but a junior common room for the sixth-form.
Discipline Pupils failing to produce setwork might expect extra school; detentions used for serious disciplinary offences.
Boarding Most have own study bedroom after 1st year. 14 houses of approximately 55 for boys, one for the 46 girls. Sanatorium with two resident sisters; school doctor visits daily. Central dining hall. Half-term plus 2 weekend exeats in the winter terms, 1 in the summer term. Visits to local town allowed with Housemaster's permission.
Former pupils Sir Michael Palliser (ex-head of the Foreign Office); Sir David Scholey (S G Warburg); General Sir Roland Guy; Sebastian Faulks (novelist); Angus MacIntyre (historian); Jamie Salmon (International rugby player); Sir Robert Gatehouse (High Court Judge); Gavin Ewart (poet); the Right Revd Richard Harries (Bishop of Oxford); Robin McLaren (British Ambassador to China); Rory Bremner (comedian); Michael Heseltine (artist); Sir Michael Howard (historian), Robin Oakley (BBC political correspondent).

• WELLINGTON (Somerset)

Wellington School, Wellington, Somerset TA21 8NT. Tel 01823 668800, Fax 01823 668844
• Pupils 770 • Boys 10–18 (Day/Board) • Girls 10–18 (Day/Board) • Upper sixth 96. Termly fees £1466 (Day) £2680 (Board) • HMC, BSA • Enquiries/application to the Headmaster

What it's like

The school first came into existence on its present site, as a private boys' school, in 1837; girls were accepted in 1972. Lying on the southern side of Wellington, at the foot of the Blackdown Hills, it has pleasant well-equipped buildings in gardens with 13 hectares of playing fields. Results are very good and most sixth-formers go on to degree courses, including to Oxbridge. Music, art and drama are strong, with large numbers of pupils in many productions. A wide range of sports and games exist and high standards are achieved (a large number of representatives at county and national level). Considerable commitment to local community schemes. A flourishing CCF and much emphasis on Outward Bound activities (new climbing wall on site). An excellent record in the Duke of Edinburgh's Award Scheme.

School profile

Pupils Total age range 10–18; 770 pupils, 597 day (308 boys, 289 girls), 173 boarding (118 boys, 55 girls). Main entry ages 10, 11, 13 and into sixth. Approx 20% are children of former pupils. *State school entry:* 70% junior intake, plus 5% to sixth.
Entrance Common Entrance and own exam used. No special skills or religious requirements. Parents not expected to buy textbooks; £150 pa maximum extras. 40 pa assisted places (2 at sixth-form). Some scholarships.
Parents 20+% come from armed services; 30+% are in industry or commerce. 30+% live within 30 miles; up to 10% live overseas.
Head and staff *Headmaster:* A J Rogers, 6 years in post. Educated at Humphry Davy Grammar School, Penzance, and Oxford University (geography, PGCE). Previously Deputy Headmaster at Wellington (Somerset), Head of Geography at Wellington (Berkshire), Head of Geography and Geology at Arnold and geography master and master i/c Henley at Pangbourne. Publications: various in geographical education. *Staff:* 64 full time, 4 part time. Annual turnover 5%. Average age 35.

Exam results In 1995, 137 pupils in fifth, 80 in upper sixth. *GCSE:* In 1995, 77% fifth gained at least grade C in 8+ subjects; 16% in 5–7 subjects. *A-levels:* 12 upper sixth passed in 4+ subjects; 56 in 3; 6 in 2; and 6 in 1 subject. Average UCAS points 20.7.

University and college entrance 96% of sixth-form leavers go on to degree courses; others typically to eg catering, estate agency, RAF, nursing, farming, banking. Of those going on to university, 7% go to Oxbridge; 6% take courses in medicine, 26% in science and engineering, 60% in humanities and social sciences, 7% in art and design and 1% in music.

Curriculum GCSE and A-levels. 18 subjects offered (no A-level general studies). 27% take science A-levels; 33% arts/humanities; 40% both. *Vocational:* Work experience available. *Computing facilities:* Computer centre with Archimedes, open to all pupils; plus computers (Archimedes) in many departments. *Special provision:* Extra English tuition is provided by qualified EFL visiting teachers for overseas students. *Europe:* French and German offered to GCSE and A-level; also for business studies in lower sixth. Regular exchanges. French, German and Russian pupils in school for 1 term to 2 years.

The arts *Music:* Over 20% of pupils learn a musical instrument; instrumental exams can be taken. Some 8 musical groups: 2 orchestras, 2 choirs, male voice sextet, brass, woodwind, cello ensembles. Pupils selected for National Youth Orchestra, National Children's Orchestra. *Drama & dance*: Drama offered. Large number of pupils involved in school productions. *Art:* On average, 44 take GCSE, 8 A-level; design, pottery, textiles, photography also offered. Many carry on to foundation and degree courses.

Sport, community service and clubs *Sport and physical activities:* Compulsory sports: rugby, hockey, cricket (boys); netball, hockey, rounders (girls); athletics, swimming, tennis. Optional: badminton, ju-jitsu, aerobics, squash. County representatives in all sports; regional hockey reps and national in rugby, athletics. *Community service:* Pupils take bronze, silver and gold Duke of Edinburgh's Awards. CCF optional (including Corps of Drums), takes part in Ten Tors and the Nijmegen Marches. Community service optional. *Clubs and societies:* Over 30 clubs, eg chess, riding, bridge, yoga, satellite remote sensing, ju-jitsu, computer.

Uniform School uniform worn throughout; some concessions for sixth-form.

Houses/prefects Competitive houses. No prefects; school captains/vice-captains appointed by Headmaster; house captains/vice-captains by house staff.

Religion Daily chapel services; C of E worship encouraged; RE for all unless parents wish otherwise.

Social Public speaking competition with other schools. Exchanges with Lillebonne, France (town twinning) and Immenstadt, Bavaria; sixth-form visit to Berlin. Day pupils allowed to bring own car/bike/motorbike to school; boarders, bike only. Meals self-service. School tuckshop. No tobacco/alcohol allowed.

Discipline Pupils failing to produce homework once are expected to produce it within 24 hours; those caught smoking cannabis on the premises would expect immediate expulsion.

Boarding Single-sex houses, of approx 50, same as competitive houses. Resident qualified sister, doctor on call. Central dining room. Pupils can provide and cook own food. Exeats of 24 hours at discretion of house staff. Visits to local town allowed after school.

Former pupils David Suchet (actor); Jeffrey Archer (author); Keith Floyd (gourmet/broadcaster); Brigadier Shelford Bidwell (military historian); Michael Green (ITN correspondent); Prof Ellis Baker (pharmacologist); Judge John Baker; Kenneth Steele (former Chief Constable, Avon & Somerset); Frank Gillard (veteran broadcaster/war correspondent).

• WELLS CATHEDRAL

Wells Cathedral School, Wells, Somerset BA5 2ST. Tel 01749 672117, Fax 01749 670724

• Pupils 784 • Boys 3–18 (Day/Board) • Girls 3–18 (Day/Board) • Upper sixth 91 • Termly fees £902–£1889 (Day) £2811–£3217 (Board) • HMC, SHMIS, CSA • Enquiries/application to the Head Master

What it's like

Founded in the 12th century, the school has one of the finest sites in Europe, on the edge of Wells and a little to the north of the Cathedral. It occupies all but one of the medieval and 18th-century buildings of The Liberty in an important conservation area around the Cathedral. There are also lovely walled gardens and an area of parkland used for playing fields. The school is well equipped with modern facilities and accommodation, including well-equipped laboratories, libraries and a big Music School. Academic standards are high and results good. Most sixth-form leavers go on to degree courses each year, including to Oxbridge. Originally a boys' school, it is now fully co-educational, having accepted girls since 1965. An ancient church school, there are close links with the Cathedral and worship in the Anglican tradition is encouraged. One of the school's great strengths is music; it is one of the five music schools attracting government finance for its music pupils. Many pupils are involved in choirs, orchestras and bands and over 300 learn one or more instruments. The drama department is also strong. There is a broad range of games and sports available and a large and varied number of extra-curricular activities. The CCF has an active contingent and there is a sizeable community service group. There is a good record in the Duke of Edinburgh's Award Scheme and outdoor pursuits form an integral part of the school curriculum.

School profile

Pupils Total age range 3–18; 784 pupils 488 day (273 boys, 215 girls), 296 boarders (131 boys, 165 girls). Senior department 11–18; 610 pupils (301 boys, 309 girls). Main entry ages 11, 13 and into the sixth. Less than 1% are children of former pupils. Own junior school provides 80% senior intake. *State school entry:* 25% main intake, plus 10% to sixth.

Entrance Own exam used. No special skills or religious requirements. Maximum extras £70 plus lunch for day pupils. Aided pupils scheme for music specialists. 15 pa assisted places. A number of scholarships/bursaries per year.

Parents 20% in the armed services. 50+% live within 30 miles; 10+% live overseas.

Head and staff *Head Master*: John Baxter, in post for 10 years. Educated at Magdalen College School, and Durham and Oxford universities (modern history and education). Previously Housemaster and Head of History at Westminster. Also National Representative on HMC Committee and Chairman of HMC (SW Division); Chairman of Choir Schools Association. Publications: various in educational journals. *Staff:* 60 full time, 5 part time (plus 40 visiting music teachers). Annual turnover 5%. Average age 38.

Exam results In 1995, 85 pupils in upper fifth, 85 in upper sixth. *GCSE:* In 1995, 53 upper fifth gained at least grade C in 8+ subjects; 27 in 5–7 subjects. *A-levels:* 4 upper sixth passed in 4+ subjects; 50 in 3; 28 in 2; and 1 in 1 subject. Average UCAS points 18.6.

University and college entrance 88% of 1995 sixth-form leavers went on to a degree course (6% after a gap year); others typically go on to banking, retail management, art or music courses. Of the 88% going on to university, 10% went to Oxbridge; 6% took courses in medicine, dentistry and veterinary science, 45% in science and engineering, 2% in law, 41% in humanities and social sciences, 3% in art and design, 2% in other vocational subjects eg physiotherapy.

Curriculum GCSE and A-levels: 23 GCSE and A-level subjects offered (no A-level general studies). 50% take science/maths A-levels; 33% arts/humanities; 17% both. *Vocational:* Work experience available. *Computing facilities:* Dual-role computer centre for teaching and access by pupils. *Special provision:* EFL and pupils who are dyslexic or mildly visually handicapped. *Europe:* French, German and Spanish offered to GCSE and A-level; also French and German AS-level and French course in Foreign Language at Work in lower sixth. Regular exchanges. Some European pupils in sixth-form.

The arts *Music:* Over 50% of pupils learn a musical instrument; instrumental exams can be taken. Some 50 musical groups including chamber ensembles, choirs, orchestras, bands. 13 pupils in National Youth Orchestra, 6 members of National Children's Orchestra, 1 National Youth Chamber Orchestra; Taunton Festival cups and trophies; winner professional trumpet competition, choral scholarship to Cambridge, Wells Cathedral organ scholarship. *Drama & dance:* Both offered. GCSE and A-level theatre studies, LAMDA, Associated Guilds exams may be taken. Majority of pupils are involved in school and house/other productions. On average, 2 pupils to drama school each year. Annual musical (eg Oliver), annual Shakespeare. *Art:* On average, 18 take GCSE, 4 A-level. Pottery also offered. Recent successes: pupils direct entry to Slade and Ruskin, BP National Portrait Gallery Competition winner (£10,000) and commissioned to paint Harold Pinter.

Sport, community service and clubs *Sport and physical activities:* Compulsory sports: rugby, hockey, netball, cricket, tennis, rounders, swimming etc. Optional: golf, athletics, badminton, outdoor pursuits. Sixth form only: riding, squash, soccer, volleyball, basketball. GCSE may be taken. Various sporting successes, county representatives etc each year. *Community service:* Pupils take silver Duke of Edinburgh's Award. CCF optional; winners National Artillery Tremlett Trophy. Community service optional; annual weekend teaming up able-bodied child with handicapped one. *Clubs and societies:* Over 30 clubs, eg photography, calligraphy, literary, debating, tapestry.
Uniform School uniform worn throughout.
Houses/prefects Competitive houses. Prefects, head boy/girl, head of house and house prefects – appointed and elected by staff and school.
Religion Daily assemblies; the school worships in Cathedral weekly.
Social Debates, prefects' conferences, sport, sixth-form society. Organised trips abroad and exchange systems. Day pupils allowed to bring own car/bike to school. Meals self-service. School shop. No tobacco/alcohol allowed.
Discipline Pupils failing to produce homework once might expect to do it again; those caught smoking cannabis on the premises could expect expulsion.
Boarding 1% have own study bedroom, 70% share (with 1 or 2); 5% are in dormitories of 6+. Single-sex houses of 27–54, divided by age group (middle and senior). Resident qualified nurse. Central dining room. Pupils can provide and cook snacks. 2 exeats each term of 1½ days (11–14); flexible policy in upper school. Visits to local town allowed with permission.
Alumni association (Old Wellensians) run by Alwyn Gillen, c/o the school.

• WENTWORTH COLLEGE

Wentworth College, College Road, Bournemouth, Dorset BH5 2DY. Tel 01202 423266, Fax 01202 418030

• Pupils 240 • Boys None • Girls 11–18 (Day/Board/Weekly) • Upper sixth 28 • Termly fees £1847 (Day) £2945 (Board/Weekly) • GSA • Enquiries/application to the Headmistress

What it's like

A joint foundation in 1962 of Bournemouth Collegiate School for Girls and Milton Mount College, Crawley. The school has handsome buildings on the top of Boscombe Cliffs on the shores of Bournemouth Bay. The main and central buildings were formerly one of Lord Portman's mansions. Since 1970 there have been several additions, including a sixth-form complex, a design technology workshop, a swimming pool, and sports hall. Facilities are good and there are ample playing fields in the school grounds. The staff:pupil ratio is about 1:7 and results are good. Although inter-denominational, the ethos of the school's Christian foundation remains strong; the Milton Mount connection with the United Reformed Church is maintained through bursaries to daughters of lay and clerical members. The outdoor education department provides adventurous opportunities as well as the Duke of Edinburgh's Award Scheme.

School profile

Pupils Age range 11–18, 240 girls (144 day, 96 boarding). Main entry age 11, 12, 13 and into sixth-form. *State school entry:* 15% main intake.
Entrance Common Entrance and own exam used. Scholarships (academic, music and sports), up to 50% of fees; also bursaries available (including for daughters of ministers and lay members of URC).
Head and staff *Headmistress:* Miss Sandra Coe, 6 years in post. *Staff:* 34 full time; 14 part time.
Exam results In 1995, 52 pupils in fifth form, 35 in upper sixth. *GCSE:* On average, 58% fifth form gain at least grade C in 8+ subjects; 27% in 5–7; and 13% in 1–4 subjects. *A-levels:* 63% upper sixth pass in 3+ subjects; 11% in 2; and 15% in 1 subject. Average UCAS points 15.6.
University and college entrance 95% of 1995 sixth-form leavers went on to a degree course (5% after a gap year); others typically go on to art foundation courses. Of those going on to university, 2% went to Oxbridge; 33% took courses in medicine, dentistry and veterinary science, 6% in science and engineering, 6% in law, 6% in humanities and

social sciences, 12% in art and design, 37% in other subjects, eg English, languages, music, accountancy.

Curriculum GCSE and A-levels, 18 subjects offered. 34% take science A-levels; 48% arts/humanities; 17% both. *Vocational:* Work experience available; also RSA courses in CLAIT; community sports teaching award for sixth-form. *Computing facilities:* Technology suite with network of IBM compatibles plus BBC Bs and Masters for class use. *Special provision:* Individual tuition for dyslexics and those for whom English is a second language. *Europe:* French and German offered to GCSE and A-level; also Spanish GCSE and French for business studies in sixth-form. Regular exchanges. Lectures on European unity.

The arts *Music:* Over 30% of pupils learn a musical instrument; instrumental exams can be taken. Some 7 musical groups: 2 orchestras, 2 recorder groups, string, brass ensemble, choir. Several members of city youth orchestra. *Drama & dance*: Both offered. LAMDA exams may be taken. Some pupils are involved in school and house/other productions. Pupil's work published in national poetry competition. *Art:* On average, 30 take GCSE, 6 A-level. Pottery, textiles also offered. Pupil won first prize in national design competition.

Sport, community service and clubs *Sport and physical activities:* Compulsory sports: lacrosse, netball, tennis, rounders, swimming, athletics. Optional: aerobics, trampolining, riding, badminton. RLSS exams, community sports coaching awards may be taken. Lacrosse, 6 county senior team players; badminton, county players. *Community service:* Pupils take bronze, silver and gold Duke of Edinburgh's Award. Community service optional. School has its own outdoor education department. *Clubs and societies:* Up to 15 clubs, eg IT newsletter, science, cookery, pottery.

Uniform School uniform worn, except in sixth-form.

Houses/prefects Competitive houses. Prefects, head girl, heads of house – elected by the school. School council.

Religion Most pupils attend religious worship although not compulsory.

Social Public speaking, quiz evenings, sport with other local schools. Annual ski trip, French course, German exchange and choir trips abroad. Pupils allowed to bring own car/bike/motorbike to school. Most lunches formal; other meals self-service. School shop. No tobacco/alcohol allowed.

Discipline Pupils failing to produce homework once might expect a meeting with personal tutor and a session on time management if thought necessary by either party; those caught smoking cannabis on the premises might expect suspension and a meeting between the Head and parents. School has a clear discipline code, aiming to develop increasing self-discipline and maturity; integrated within tutorial and pastoral care.

• WEST BUCKLAND

West Buckland School, Barnstaple, Devon EX32 OSX. Tel 01598 760281

• Pupils 550 • Boys 4–18 (Day/Board/Weekly) • Girls 4–18 (Day/Board/Weekly) • Upper sixth 48 • Termly fees £790–£1710 (Day) £2468–£3150 (Board/Weekly) • HMC • Enquiries/application to the Head Master's Secretary

What it's like

Founded in 1858, it lies on the south-west edge of Exmoor, 10 miles from Barnstaple, on a 90-acre site. The school is contained in handsome 19th-century buildings with many modern additions, most recently an arts centre. It is an Anglican foundation and Christian teaching and principles underlie much of its life. Originally a boys' school, it accepted girls into the sixth-form in 1974 and became fully co-educational in 1980. It has developed a strong sense of community and there is much emphasis on everyone participating in the life of the school. The need for success is also emphasised. A sound general education is provided and results are good; most sixth-form leavers go on to degree courses each year. There are very active music, drama and art departments. A lot of emphasis on sports and games (standards are high; numerous county and some international representatives). The CCF contingent is flourishing and outdoor pursuits are popular. A most impressive record in the Duke of Edinburgh's Award Scheme.

School profile

Pupils Total age range 4–18; 550 pupils, 420 day (235 boys, 185 girls), 130 boarding (85 boys, 35 girls). Senior department 11–18, 460 pupils (280 boys, 180 girls). Main entry ages 4, 5, 7, 11, 13 and into sixth. Approx 10% are children of former pupils. *State school entry:* 50% senior intakes, plus 75% to sixth.

Entrance Common Entrance and own exam used. No special skills or religious requirements. Parents not expected to buy textbooks; lunches extra (£85 per term). 32 pa assisted places. 6 pa scholarships/bursaries, £342–£1575 per term.

Parents Parents come from broad mix of occupations. 80+% live within 30 miles; up to 10% live overseas.

Head and staff *Head Master*: Michael Downward, in post for 17 years. Educated at Epsom College and Cambridge (classics). Previously Housemaster and Head of Classics at Loughborough Grammar. *Staff:* 47 full time, 8 part time. Annual turnover under 5%. Average age 42.

Exam results On average, 79 pupils fifth, 43 in upper sixth. *GCSE:* On average, 60 upper fifth gain at least grade C in 8+ subjects; 12 in 5–7; and 7 in 1–4 subjects. *A-levels:* 25 upper sixth pass in 4+ subjects; 7 in 3; 6 in 2; and 4 in 1 subject. Average UCAS points 17.0.

University and college entrance 83% of 1995 sixth-form leavers went on to a degree course (35% after a gap year); others typically go on to employment with training eg estate agency. Of those going on to university, 5% went to Oxbridge; 5% took courses in medicine, dentistry and veterinary science, 40% in science and engineering, 8% in law, 37% in humanities and social sciences, 5% in art and design, 5% in vocational subjects.

Curriculum GCSE and A-levels. Approximately 16 subjects offered (including A-level general studies). 40% take science A-levels; 30% arts/humanities; 30% both. *Vocational:* Work experience available; also RSA course in CLAIT. *Computing facilities:* BBC Econet. 24 Archimedes in central lab; 12 elsewhere; all major departments connected. *Special provision:* 3 specialist ESL staff. *Europe:* French and German offered to GCSE and A-level; also GCSE Spanish. Regular exchanges to France, Germany and Spain. European pupils attend 3 weeks to 1 year.

The arts (Pupils aged 11 and over) *Music:* 40% of pupils learn a musical instrument; instrumental exams can be taken. 5 musical groups including orchestras, choir, chamber choir, string group. *Drama & dance*: Majority of pupils are involved in school productions. *Art:* On average, 35+ take GSCE, 6 A-level. Design, pottery, photography also offered.

Sport, community service and clubs (Pupils aged 11 and over) *Sport and physical activities:* Compulsory sports (to age 14): rugby, cricket, cross-country/hockey, netball, tennis. Optional: large choice for all pupils. BAGA exams may be taken. Regular county representatives (rugby, cricket, athletics). *Community service:* Pupils take bronze, silver and gold Duke of Edinburgh's Award; large numbers involved, often with emphasis on countryside, conservation etc. CCF compulsory for 2 years at age 13+, optional thereafter. Community service optional. *Clubs and societies:* Up to 30 clubs, eg art, bell-ringing, bridge, chess, Christian Union, computing, debating, drama etc.

Uniform School uniform worn, alternative suit for sixth-form.

Houses/prefects Competitive houses. Prefects, head boy and girl, head of house and house prefects – appointed.

Religion Morning assembly and Sunday service compulsory; lively voluntary Christian Union in lunch hour.

Social No regular events organised with local schools. Annual ski training and mountain expeditions. Annual exchanges with schools in France/Germany. Upper sixth allowed to bring own car/bike/motorbike to school. Meals self-service. School shops selling tuck, basic equipment and second-hand. Sixth form allowed tobacco/alcohol in restricted location.

Discipline Pupils failing to produce homework once might expect to have to complete it in extra work (Saturday detention for more serious offences); those caught smoking cannabis on the premises could expect to be withdrawn.

Boarding Sixth have own study bedroom; remainder in bedrooms for 2–6, according to age. Boarding accommodation is single-sex. Resident qualified nurse. Central dining room. Exeats to suit individual needs. Visits to local town (10 miles away) allowed weekly at 13+; special bus runs on Saturdays.

Former pupils R F Delderfield (playwright and novelist); Brian Aldiss (science fiction writer); John Ashworth (Director LSE); Victor Ubogu and Stephen Ojomoh (England and Bath rugby players); Jonathan Edwards (Olympic athlete).

• WEST HEATH

West Heath School, Ashgrove Road, Sevenoaks, Kent TN13 1SR. Tel 01732 452541

• Pupils 103 • Boys None • Girls 11–18 (Day/Board) • Upper sixth 14 • Termly fees £2585 (Day) £3680 (Board) • GSA, SHA, BSA • Enquiries/application to the School Secretary/Registrar

What it's like

Founded in 1865, it has pleasant, well-designed buildings and excellent facilities and accommodation (there is an indoor swimming pool and dance studio). It is situated in a rural site of 32 acres of woodland and grassland on the edge of town. A small school, providing a caring environment and a traditional education. Results are good and most sixth-formers go on to university. Strong in music, art and ceramics. Excellent sport, games and activities. A promising record in the Duke of Edinburgh's Award Scheme.

School profile

Pupils Age range 11–18; 103 girls (19 day, 84 boarding). Main entry ages 11, 13 and 16. Approx 25% are children of former pupils. *State school entry:* 5% main intake.
Entrance Common Entrance and own exam used. No special skills or religious requirements but school is wholly Christian. Extras variable. Scholarships at 11, 13 and 16; some bursaries available.
Parents 10+% live within 30 miles.
Head and staff *Principal:* Mrs Ann Williamson, appointed 1994. Educated at Talbot Heath and at universities of London (geography) and Cambridge (mathematics). Previously Head of Stratford House School and Head of Third Year at Highfield School, Letchworth. Also JP; FRSA; member of SHA Council and Executive and Chair of its International Committee; member of Employment Committee of Institute of Directors; ex-President of NW Kent Association of University Women. *Staff:* 20 full time, 6 part time. Annual turnover 5%. Average age 40.
Exam results In 1995, 18 pupils in upper fifth, 14 in upper sixth. *GCSE:* In 1995, 100% upper fifth gained grade C or above in at least 5 subjects. *A-levels:* 80% upper sixth pass in 3 subjects; 20% in 2 subjects. Average UCAS points 12.6.
University and college entrance 95% of sixth-form leavers go on to a degree course (50% after a gap year), others typically go on to nursing, secretarial courses. Of those going on to university, 5% took courses in medicine, dentistry and veterinary science, 10% in science and engineering, 5% in law, 50% in humanities and social sciences, 20% in art and design, 10% in other vocational subjects (eg pharmacy, physiotherapy).
Curriculum GCSE and A-levels: 20 subjects offered (including A-level general studies). 10% take science A-levels; 70 arts/humanities; 20% both. *Vocational:* Secretarial studies and work experience available. *Computing facilities:* Open-access computer room equipped with Acorn; also CD-Rom. Additional computers used for science, careers, etc. *Europe:* French, German and Spanish offered to GCSE and A-level; also Italian GCSE.
The arts *Music:* Over 50% of pupils learn a musical instrument; instrumental exams can be taken. Some 4 musical groups including flute ensemble, choirs, orchestra. *Drama & dance*: Drama offered and GCSE may be taken. Some pupils are involved in school productions and all in house/other productions. *Art:* On average, 18 take GCSE, 8 A-level. Pottery, textiles also offered.
Sport, community service and clubs *Sport and physical activities:* Compulsory sports: netball, lacrosse, rounders, tennis, swimming. Optional: fencing, badminton, volleyball. *Community service:* Pupils take bronze, silver and gold Duke of Edinburgh's Award. Community service optional for sixth-form. *Clubs and societies:* Up to 10 clubs, eg dance, gym, lacemaking, lifesaving, self-defence, scuba-diving.
Uniform School uniform worn except in the sixth.
Religion Compulsory attendance at services (either Church of England or Roman Catholic) for boarders.
Social Debates and conferences with local schools. Organised ski and cultural trips

abroad. Senior pupils allowed to bring own bike to school. Meals self-service. School shop. No tobacco/alcohol allowed.
Discipline Those caught smoking or drinking alcohol on the premises could expect expulsion after a warning and a fine.
Boarding Fifth and lower sixth have own study bedroom, upper sixth are in bungalows in the grounds; others in dormitories of between 2 and 7. Central dining rooms. Sixth form can provide and cook own suppers. Half-term and 2 fixed weekend exeats each term (other exeats by arrangement). Visits to the local town allowed for seniors.

• WESTFIELD

Westfield School, Oakfield Road, Gosforth, Newcastle upon Tyne NE3 4HS Tel 0191 285 1948, Fax 0191 213 0734

• Pupils 360 • Boys None • Girls 3–18 (Day) • Upper sixth 35 • Termly fees £444-£1380 (Day)
• GSA, Round Square • Enquiries/application to the Headmistress's Secretary

What it's like

Founded in 1959, it is suburban with senior and junior houses on a spacious 6-acre site. The school is an elected member of the Round Square – an international group of like-minded schools, sharing the same philosophy; students can spend a term on exchange at member schools. Gracious buildings and good modern facilities. A sound basic education is given and results are good; each year many sixth-formers go on to degree courses. Flourishing music, art and drama departments. A good standard in sports and games (county and national representatives) and an impressive range of activities. A very promising record in the Duke of Edinburgh's Award Scheme.

School profile

Pupils Total age range 3–18; 360 day girls. Senior department 11–18, 230 girls. Main entry at 9, 11 and into sixth. Approx 10% are children of former pupils. *State school entry:* 30+% senior intake.
Entrance Own entrance exam used. No special skills or religious requirements. Parents not expected to buy textbooks. Up to 10 pa scholarships/bursaries, 25%–90% of fees.
Parents 15+% in industry or commerce; 15+% are doctors lawyers, etc. 15+% farmers.
Head and staff *Headmistress:* Mrs Marion Farndale, 6 years in post. Educated at South Shields Grammar for Girls and at Westfield College, London and Oxford (English and education). Previously Housemistress at St Anne's (Windermere) and Sixth Form Tutor at Kenton School. *Staff:* 35 full time, 9 part time. Annual turnover 5%. Average age 36.
Exam results On average, 40 pupils in upper fifth, 35 in upper sixth. *GCSE:* 24 upper fifth gain at least grade C in 8+ subjects; 12 in 5–7; and 4 in 1–4 subjects. *A-levels:* 27 upper sixth pass in 3 subjects; 5 in 2; and 3 in 1 subject. Average UCAS points 15.2.
University and college entrance 79% of sixth-form leavers go on to a degree course (21% after a gap year), taking courses in eg civil engineering, maths, media, business studies, languages, English, geography, drama and music.
Curriculum GCSE and A-levels. 20 subjects offered, including GCSE general studies and a sixth-form business studies course. Typically 35% take science A-levels; 65% arts/humanities. *Vocational:* RSA courses. *Computing facilities:* Acorn, RM Windowbox, and network of RM Nimbus PCs; computer lab plus machines in some classrooms. *Special provision:* English specialist; visiting teacher from dyslexia unit (charged extra). *Europe:* French and German offered to GCSE, AS-level and A-level; also commercial Spanish (FLAW) and GCSE. Regular exchanges.
The arts (Pupils age 11 and over) *Music:* Some 25% of pupils learn a musical instrument. Musical groups include choir, wind band, folk band, string ensemble, orchestra. *Drama & dance*: Guildhall exams may be taken. Some pupils are involved in school productions; many workshops etc. Some pupils in local amateur/operatic societies.
Sport, community service and clubs (Pupils age 11 and over) *Sport and physical activities:* Sports: netball, hockey, lacrosse, swimming, tennis, trampolining, gymnastics, athletics, volleyball, rounders. 15 represent county at various sports. *Community service:* A large number of pupils take bronze, silver and gold Duke of Edinburgh's Award. *Clubs*

and societies: Some 20 clubs, eg computers, environmental committee, Amnesty International, tapestry, art, gardening, life drawing, debating.
Uniform School uniform worn; separate sixth-form uniform.
Houses/prefects Competitive houses. Prefects, head girl and head of house appointed jointly by the Head and school. School Council.
Religion Attendance at morning assembly compulsory, usually involves Christian worship.
Social Occasional social activities with various boys' schools. Organised trips to France, Germany, Russia from time to time. Exchanges with schools in Europe and elsewhere including Canada and Australia. Delegation of senior girls attends annual Round Square Conference (usually abroad); younger girls attend regional residential mini-conferences. Regular and well-attended skiing trips and tennis coaching holidays. Senior pupils allowed to bring own car/bike to school. Meals self-service. School shop. No tobacco/alcohol allowed.
Discipline Detentions given for failure to do homework. Great emphasis is placed on a high standard of behaviour and a respect for others.
Alumni association run by Mrs Kathleen Pears, c/o the school.

• WESTHOLME

Westholme School, Wilmar Lodge, Meins Road, Blackburn, Lancashire BB2 6QU. Tel 01254 53447

• Pupils 1009 • Boys 3–7 only (Day) • Girls 3–18 (Day) • Upper sixth 49 • Termly fees £875–£1230 (Day) • GSA • Enquiries/application to the Principal's secretary.

What it's like

Founded in 1923, the upper school is semi-rural and single-site. Its two prep departments are on two other sites. The well-designed and pleasant buildings stand in attractive gardens and grounds. Facilities are good and there has been continual development over the last 30 years. Its liberal and sound education is based on Christian principles and practice. Standards are good academically and very many sixth-formers go on to degree courses each year, including Oxbridge. Strong in music, drama and art. A good record in the Duke of Edinburgh's Award Scheme.

School profile

Pupils Total age range 3–18; 1009 day pupils (80 boys, 929 girls). Senior department 11–18, 660 girls. Main entry ages 3 (boys and girls), 7, 8, 11 and into sixth (girls). Approx 20% are children of former pupils. Own middle school provides 50% senior intake. *State school entry:* 50% senior intake plus 2% to sixth.
Entrance Own entrance exam used. No special skills or religious requirements; school is non-denominational Christian foundation. Parents not expected to buy textbooks; maximum extras £100. Assisted places. 20 pa scholarships/bursaries, £90 – £295 per term.
Parents 15+% in industry or commerce; 15+% are doctors, lawyers, etc.
Head and staff *Principal:* Mrs Lillian Croston, in post 8 years. Educated at Accrington High School and at Durham and Cambridge universities (geography, geology, mathematics and PGCE). Previously Deputy Headteacher at Sale Grammar, teacher of mathematics at Gorse Park Secondary, Stretford, Head of Geography at Stretford Grammar and Assistant Geography Mistress at Bolton Girls' School. Also Chief Examiner for JMB (1988); member of Lancaster University Court (1994); occasional GSA, HMC and Ofsted School Inspector (1994). *Staff:* 60 full time, 17 part time. Annual turnover 2%. Average age 40.
Exam results In 1995, 102 pupils in upper fifth, 49 in upper sixth. *GCSE:* In 1995, 97% upper fifth gained at least grade C in 8+ subjects; 2% in 5–7 subjects. *A-levels:* 82% passed in 4+ subjects; 6% in 3; 6% in 2; and 4% in 1 subject. Average UCAS points 20.0 (25.0 including general studies).
University and college entrance 86% of 1995 sixth-form leavers went on to a degree course (2% after a gap year); others typically went on to art foundation courses, HNDs, courses in beauty therapy or journalism. Of those going on to university, 8% went to Oxbridge; 6% took courses in medicine, dentistry and veterinary science, 25% in science and engineering, 4% in law, 55% in humanities and social sciences, 2% in art and design,

6% in eg physiotherapy, speech therapy.
Curriculum GCSE, AS, A-levels and S-levels. Subjects offered include A-level general studies. 23% take science A-levels; 53% arts/humanities; 24% both. *Vocational:* City and Guilds information technology offered, also NVQs level II general subjects connected with work experience scheme organised by local TEC. Work experience available. *Computing facilities:* 3 computer rooms; 1 room used largely for word processing; several departments have their own computers. *Special provision:* Physically handicapped children can cope well; all specialist facilities are at ground floor. *Europe:* French, German and Spanish offered to GCSE, AS and A-level, Institute of Linguists and as non-examined subjects. Regular exchanges. French (and occasionally German and Spanish) students often in school.
The arts (Pupils age 11 and over) *Music:* Over 30% of pupils learn a musical instrument; instrumental exams can be taken. Some 10 musical groups: senior orchestra, strings, woodwind, brass band, swing band, recorder groups, senior and junior choir, madrigal group, quartets. 1 pupil member of National Children's Orchestra; several county groups. *Drama & dance*: Both offered as extra-curricular activities; ESB exams may be taken. Some pupils are involved in school productions; all in house/other productions. Recent production of A Midsummer Night's Dream. *Art:* On average, 40 take GCSE, 16 A-level; design, textiles and photography also offered. 4–5 pupils a year accepted for art college.
Sport, community service and clubs (Pupils age 11 and over) *Sport and physical activities:* Compulsory sports: Hockey, netball, gymnastics, dance, athletics, tennis, rounders, swimming, badminton, volleyball, aerobics, water ballet (at some point in school career). Optional: ice skating, fitness centre, golf, squash, life saving, water polo, ballroom dancing. BAGA and ASA exams may be taken. Lancashire schools champions in badminton and netball; county/regional representatives in badminton, netball, swimming; 1 nationally ranked tennis player. *Community service:* Pupils take bronze, silver and gold Duke of Edinburgh's Award. Community service optional for all pupils, eg charity shops, conservation work, OAP homes, handicapped children; help with English Heritage and National Trust groups. *Clubs and societies:* Up to 20 clubs, eg chess, health and beauty, cookery, literary and debating, 3 environment groups, Young Enterprise, European literature, French, German, Spanish, Classics, geographical, history, textiles, recreational art.
Uniform School uniform worn; different in the sixth.
Houses/prefects Competitive houses. Prefects, head girl, head of house and house prefects – appointed by staff and pupils. School Council.
Religion Compulsory morning assembly.
Social Joint concerts and joint general studies lectures with local schools. Many trips abroad and exchanges (France, Germany, Spain, Kenya, Canada). Pupils allowed to bring own car/bike/motorbike/horse to school. Meals self-service. No tobacco/alcohol allowed.
Discipline Pupils failing to produce homework once might expect lunchtime detention; twilight detention for persistent offenders. Those caught smoking cannabis on the premises could expect expulsion after interview with parents.
Alumni association run by Mrs E Gibson, c/o the school.

• WESTMINSTER

Westminster School, 17 Dean's Yard, London SW1P 3PB. Tel 0171 963 1000, Fax 0171 963 1006
• Pupils 674 • Boys 13–18 (Day/Board/Weekly) • Girls 16–18 (Day/Board/Weekly) • Upper sixth 150 • Termly fees £2950 (Day) £4300 (Board/Weekly) • HMC • Enquiries/application to the Registrar.

What it's like

Founded by Elizabeth I in 1560. The Benedictine monks of Westminster Abbey had run a small school for boys before the Reformation but the monastery was dissolved in 1540 and Henry VIII included provision for 40 scholars in the Abbey's constitution. It has been well known since early in the 17th-century and remains one of the most distinguished in the country. It is renowned for its respect for learning, its individuality and nonconformity. It has a unique site beside the Abbey and Parliament and is blessed with many fine buildings, some of great architectural merit. The buildings are enhanced by pleasant gardens; the main playing field is at Vincent Square. It naturally has close links with the Abbey which is used regularly for worship. A large staff (plus a large part-time staff) allows a very favourable staff:pupil ratio. A very high-powered school academically, with a strong classical tradition. It achieves outstanding results and almost all its sixth-formers go to university, over a third to Oxbridge. The music, drama and art departments are well known for their excellence and there is a great deal of musical and dramatic activity. There is a wide range of sports and games (in which high standards are achieved) and a very wide variety of extra-curricular activities. Much use is made of the cultural facilities of London. Many distinguished speakers address clubs and societies. A flourishing Expeditions Society organises many events, both in the UK and abroad.

School profile

Pupils Age range 13–18; 674 pupils, 444 day (394 boys, 50 girls), 230 boarding (200 boys, 30 girls). Main entry ages 13 (boys) and into sixth (boys and girls). Approx 5% are children of former pupils. Westminster Under School (tel 0171 821 5788) provides approx 40% of intake. *State school entry:* None in main intake, 10 to sixth.

Entrance Common Entrance; own scholarship exam (The Challenge) and sixth-form entrance exam used. Skills in sport, music, art useful; no religious requirements. Parents expected to buy textbooks; maximum extras, £200 per term. Up to 8 pa assisted places for pupils from Under School. 8 pa scholarships, half boarding fee; some sixth-form bursaries.

Parents 15+% are doctors, lawyers etc. 60+% live within 30 miles; up to 10% live overseas.

Head and staff *Head Master*: David Summerscale, 11 years in post. Educated at Sherborne and Cambridge (English literature). Previously Master of Haileybury, Housemaster and Head of English at Charterhouse and Lecturer in English at University of Delhi. Also A-level Reviser in English; Vice-Chairman, ESU Scholarship Committee; has also been, at various times, a member of HMC Academic Policy Sub-Committee, Charing Cross and Westminster Medical School Council, Assam Valley Public School Council, Book Aid International Council, governor of seven schools; FRSA. Publications: articles on English and Indian literature; dramatisations of novels and verse. *Staff:* 65 full time, 30 part time. Annual turnover 4%. Average age 35.

Exam results In 1995, 125 pupils in upper fifth, 150 in upper sixth. *GCSE:* In 1995, all upper fifth gained at least grade C in 8+ subjects. *A-levels:* 44% upper sixth passed in 4+ subjects; 54% in 3 subjects; 2% in 2 subjects. Average UCAS points 31.4.

University and college entrance 98% of 1995 sixth-form leavers went on to a degree course, others typically go on to employment or tutorial college. Of those going on to university, 35% went to Oxbridge; 10% took courses in medicine, dentistry and veterinary science, 20% in science and engineering, 3% in law, 50% in humanities and social sciences, 2% in art and design, 10% in economics and management.

Curriculum GCSE, AS and A-levels: 18 subjects offered (no A-level general studies). 25% took science A-levels; 35% arts/humanities; 40% both. *Vocational:* Work experience available. *Computing facilities:* Open access to Apple Mac in computer rooms and laboratories. *Europe:* French, German, Russian and Spanish offered to GCSE, AS and A-level; French compulsory to GCSE and over 75% take one other language. Regular exchanges to Germany, Spain and Russia.

The arts *Music:* Over 30% of pupils learn a musical instrument; instrumental exams can be taken. Some 10 musical groups including choral society, madrigals, chamber choir, 3 jazz bands, several rock bands, orchestras. Winner of Young Soloist of the Year competition; lots of original compositions by pupils; annual opera and workshops (strong operatic tradition). *Drama & dance*: Drama offered and GCSE may be taken. Majority of pupils are involved in school and house/other productions. Recent productions have toured Paris & Delhi. Productions since 1995 include The Birds (Aristophanes), Un Simple Soldat (Dubé; in French) as well as plays by eg Albee, Schaffer, Shakespeare and Wilde. *Art:* On average, 30 take GCSE, 15 A-level. Design, etching, photography also offered. Art facilities open to non-examination pupils. Regular success in gaining places at the Slade, Ruskin and other art colleges.

Sport, community service and clubs *Sport and physical activities:* Compulsory sports: one of rowing, soccer, fencing, fives in first year. Optional: squash, tennis, martial arts,

swimming, rugby, netball. Fencing, winner of Independent Schools Championships 1994; rowing, finalists at Henley Regatta 2 years running, world junior sculls champion. *Community service:* Community service optional. *Clubs and societies:* Clubs include debating, chess, computers, bookbinding.
Uniform School uniform worn by boys throughout; girls have dress guidelines.
Houses/prefects Competitive houses. Prefects (monitors), head boy (captain of school), heads of house and house prefects (monitors) – appointed by Head Master.
Religion Compulsory morning service in Westminster Abbey 3 times/week. Weekly assembly in School Hall.
Social Joint events with other schools organised occasionally. Annual German exchange; group visits to Spain, Russia, Greece. Sixth form allowed to bring own bike to school. Lunch formal, others self-service. School shop. No tobacco/alcohol allowed.
Discipline Pupils failing to produce homework once might expect to produce it next lesson; threat of detention for future offence. Those caught smoking cannabis, whether on or off the premises, would expect expulsion.
Boarding 40% have own study bedroom, 40% share with 1 other, 20% are in dormitories of 6+. Single-sex houses of approx 70. Resident qualified nurse, visiting doctor. Central dining room for breakfast and supper. Most are weekly boarders, going home Saturday lunch-time to Monday am; full boarding available in one house. Visits to town allowed.
Alumni association c/o the school.
Former pupils Sir Peter Ustinov; Michael Flanders; Donald Swann; Lord Havers; Lord Carr; Lord Lawson of Blaby; Antony Howard; Dominic Harrod; Sir Andrew Lloyd Webber; Dan Topolski; Sir Henry Tizard; Sir Andrew Huxley; Sir John Gielgud; Sir Adrian Boult; Sir Angus Wilson; Tim Sebastian; Imogen Stubbs; Stephen Poliakoff; Helena Bonham-Carter.

• WESTONBIRT

Westonbirt School, Tetbury, Gloucestershire GL8 8QG. Tel 01666 880333, Fax 01666 880364
• Pupils 220 • Boys None • Girls 11–19 (Day/Board/Weekly) • Upper sixth 25 • Termly fees £2312 (Day) £3595 (Board/Weekly) • GSA, Allied • Enquiries to the Head • Applications to the Registrar

What it's like

Founded in 1928, it is centred on Westonbirt House, a magnificent Renaissance-style mansion in 500 acres of fine gardens and parkland. Over the years it has been adapted and new buildings added, most recently new science laboratories and a lecture theatre. Facilities and accommodation are first class. The ethos tends towards a good all-round education which develops individual talents, whatever they may be. Religious services (held in the village church) are Anglican and are compulsory. Academic standards are creditable and results good; most sixth-formers go on to degree courses each year. Very strong in music, art and drama. A good range of games, sports and activities. A promising record in the Duke of Edinburgh's Award Scheme and a thriving Young Enterprise Company.

School profile

Pupils Age range 11–19; 220 girls (40 day, 180 boarding). Main entry age 11; also 12, 13, 14 and into sixth. *State school entry:* 2% main intakes, plus 1% to sixth.
Entrance Common Entrance and own entrance papers used. Aptitude at music, drama, art, and sport helps; school is C of E and all are required to attend services. Parents not expected to buy textbooks; extras include music and sports coaching, excursions, public exam fees etc. 7 pa scholarships/bursaries, 10%–50% of fees.
Parents 10+% live within 30 miles; 10+% live overseas.
Head and staff *Head:* Mrs Gillian Hylson-Smith, 10 years in post. Educated at Wycombe Abbey and at Leicester and Hertfordshire universities (classics and careers education). Previously i/c Careers and Curriculum at Haberdashers' Aske's (Girls) and Head of RE at Marylebone Grammar School for Boys. Also Council Member of Independent Schools Careers Organization; ISIS. *Staff:* 32 full time, 11 part time. Annual turnover 5%. Average age 40+.

Exam results In 1995, 49 pupils in upper fifth, 25 in upper sixth. *GCSE:* In 1995, 41 upper fifth gained at least grade C in 7+ subjects; 4 in 5–6 subjects. *A-levels:* 70% upper sixth passed in 3 subjects; and 30% in 2 subjects. Average UCAS points 17.6.
University and college entrance 90% of 1995 sixth-form leavers went on to a degree course (30% after a gap year); others typically go on to secretarial college or nursery nurse training (NNEB). Of those going on to university, 3% went to Oxbridge; 5% took courses in medicine, dentistry and veterinary science, 5% in science and engineering, 5% in law, 50% in humanities and social sciences, 10% in art and design, 25% in other vocational subjects eg education, nursing, physiotherapy.
Curriculum GCSE and A-levels, including A-level theatre studies and business studies but not general studies. 22% take science A-levels; 55% arts/humanities; 22% both. *Vocational:* Work experience available; City and Guilds cookery and RSA word processing offered; Young Enterprise. *Computing facilities:* Room with 20 computers plus computers in other specialist departments. *Special provision:* EFL coaching; individual coaching paid for separately. *Europe:* French and Spanish offered to GCSE, AS and A-level. French compulsory from 11 to GCSE; Spanish optional from Year 10. Regular exchanges.
The arts *Music:* Over 60% of pupils learn a musical instrument; instrumental exams can be taken. Some 9 musical groups including 4 choirs and an orchestra. *Drama & dance*: Both offered; GCSE and A-level drama, ESB, LAMDA exams may be taken. Majority of pupils are involved in school and house/other productions. *Art:* Design, pottery, textiles and photography also offered.
Sport, community service and clubs *Sport and physical activities:* Compulsory sports: lacrosse, netball, tennis, rounders. Optional: golf, badminton. Sixth form only: squash. *Community service:* Pupils take bronze, silver and gold Duke of Edinburgh's Award. Community service optional at age 16. *Clubs and societies:* Up to 15 clubs, eg sugar flower making, film, guides.
Uniform School uniform worn except in the sixth.
Houses/prefects Competitive houses. All sixth-form have prefectorial duties. Head girl, head of house and house prefects – appointed by the Head after consultation with staff and girls.
Religion Compulsory daily prayers and Sunday service.
Social Music and discos with other independent schools. Organised French skiing trip, art history French trip. American lacrosse trips. Meals formal, except supper. School shop. No tobacco/alcohol allowed.
Discipline Pupils failing to produce homework once might expect detention; those caught smoking cannabis on the premises could expect expulsion.
Boarding 26% have own study bedroom, 2% share with one; very few are in dormitories of 6+. Houses of approximately 40, same as competitive houses. Resident qualified nurse and visiting doctor. Central dining room. Sixth-form pupils can provide and cook own food. 3 exeats each term, 1 or 2 nights. Visits to the local town allowed most weeks.
Alumni association c/o The Registrar, Westonbirt.

• WHITGIFT

Whitgift School, Haling Park, South Croydon, Surrey CR2 6YT. Tel 0181 688 9222
• Pupils 1100 • Boys 10–18 (Day) • Girls None • Upper sixth 127 • Termly fees £1832 (Day)
• HMC • Enquiries/application to the Headmaster

What it's like

Founded in 1596 by John Whitgift, Archbishop of Canterbury. In 1931 it moved to its present site in Haling Park: 45 acres of wooded parkland and exceptionally beautiful surroundings for an urban day school. The buildings are well designed and well equipped. One of the fundamental aims of the school is to balance an excellent academic record with a wide range of co-curricular activities. A friendly and happy school, it has an ecumenical approach to religious worship. Academically strong, it achieves very good results and almost all sixth-formers go on to degree courses including a high proportion to Oxbridge. Very strong in music, drama and art. Very high standards, too, in sports and games of which there is a wide variety; many representatives at regional and national level. A flourishing CCF and outdoor pursuits scheme. A plentiful range of extra-curricular activities, a substantial commitment to local community services and a good record in the Duke of Edinburgh's Award Scheme.

School profile

Pupils Total age range 10–18; 1100 day boys. Senior department 13–18, 740 boys. Main entry ages 10, 11, 13 and into sixth. Approx 5% are children of former pupils. *State school entry:* 43% at ages 10, 11.

Entrance Common Entrance and own exam used. No special skills or religious requirements. Parents not expected to buy textbooks. 13 pa assisted places. Whitgift Foundation provides scholarships/bursaries (over £1m).

Head and staff *Headmaster:* Dr Christopher Barnett, 6 years in post. Educated at Cedars School, Leighton Buzzard, and Oxford University (modern history). Previously Second Master and Deputy Head at Dauntsey's, Head of History at Bradfield and Lecturer, Economics Department, Brunel University. *Staff:* Annual turnover 5%.

Exam results In 1995, 150 pupils in fifth, 126 in upper sixth. *GCSE:* In 1995, all in fifth gained at least grade C in 5+ subjects. *A-levels:* Average pupil in upper sixth passed in 2.99 subjects. Average UCAS points 23.7.

University and college entrance 92% of 1995 sixth-form leavers went on to a degree course (18% after a gap year); others typically go on to art foundation courses or employment. Of those going on to university, 15% went to Oxbridge; 6% took courses in medicine, dentistry and veterinary science, 35% in science and engineering, 32% in humanities and social sciences, 9% in art, design, music and architecture, 18% in eg buiness, sports studies.

Curriculum GCSE and A-levels. 20 GCSE subjects offered; 19 at A-level (including business studies, Japanese and Greek; general studies course but not examined). *Vocational:* Work experience available. *Computing facilities:* Several computer laboratories and workshop; word-processing annexe to library; wide use of computers in departments. *Special provision:* Individual difficulties handled as appropriate. *Europe:* French and German offered to GCSE, AS and A-level; also GCSE Italian and Spanish, and Russian. Regular exchanges to Denmark, France, Germany and Italy. European Youth Parliament. Sixth-form study visits. Opportunity for senior pupils to spend up to 6 weeks in continental link schools.

The arts *Music:* Up to 25% of pupils learn a musical instrument; instrumental exams can be taken. Some 20 musical groups including orchestra, dance band, string quartet, choirs etc. *Drama & dance*: Drama offered. Some pupils are involved in school and house/other productions. Regular drama tours abroad. *Art:* On average, 20 take GCSE, 15 A-level. Design, pottery, photography also offered.

Sport, community service and clubs *Sport and physical activities:* Sports include: athletics, badminton, basketball, canoeing, climbing, cricket, cross-country, fives, golf, hockey, horse-riding, orienteering, judo, rugby, scuba diving, shooting, soccer, squash, swimming, table tennis, water polo. Numerous sporting achievements: several represent country each year at tennis, also area and region; many boys have represented England and Great Britain at rugby, hockey, fencing, shooting, table tennis, water polo etc. *Community service:* Pupils take bronze, silver and gold Duke of Edinburgh's Award. CCF and community service optional: many community projects such as special needs play scheme, fund-raising. *Clubs and societies:* Up to 30 clubs, eg chess, classical, cycling, debating, drama, history, Live Poets, science, model railway.

Uniform School uniform worn to 16; dress code in the sixth.

Houses/prefects Competitive houses. Prefects, head boy, head of house and house prefects – appointed by Headmaster or housemasters.

Religion Compulsory twice-weekly assembly for whole school; additional year-group assemblies.

Social Joint functions with local girls' schools; sailing and climbing journeys; strong on outdoor activities. School exchanges (France, Germany, Czech Republic, Russia, United States, Denmark, Italy) and other foreign links (strong East European links); skiing trips. Pupils allowed to bring own car/bike/motorbike to school. Meals self-service. No tobacco/alcohol allowed.

Former pupils Sir Reg Prentice; Martin Jarvis; Raman Subba Row; Ian Beer (former Headmaster of Harrow); Lord Bowness; Prof Sir Robert Boyd FRS (and 6 other FRS); Gp

Capt John Cunningham; Roger Freeman MP; Sir David Hancock (Permanent Sec DES); Lord Justice Mauer; Sir Bryan Roberts; Lord Wedderburn of Charlton; Sir Gordon Witteridge KCMG.

• WILLIAM HULME'S

William Hulme's Grammar School, Spring Bridge Road, Manchester M16 8PR. Tel 0161 226 2054, Fax 0161 226 8922

• Pupils 768 • Boys 11–18 (Day) • Girls 11–18 (Day) • Upper sixth 97 • Termly fees £1405 (Day) • HMC, SHA • Enquiries to the Headmaster • Application to Registrar

What it's like

Founded by the Hulme Trust and opened in 1887 as a boys' school, it admitted girls a hundred years later and is now co-educational. It has an urban site set in 16 acres of grounds 2 miles south of Manchester city centre. Steady expansion and development have taken place and it is now extremely well equipped. It is non-denominational. The academic standards are high and the results good; most pupils go on to degree courses each year, including to Oxbridge. There is an increasing amount of music and art, and drama is flourishing. A wide range of sports and games is available and high standards are attained (regular representation at county and national level). Extra-curricular activities are numerous and there is a voluntary and flourishing CCF and some commitment to the Duke of Edinburgh's Award Scheme. Extensive use is made of the school's own field study centre in Wensleydale and also of the cultural amenities of Manchester.

School profile

Pupils Age range 11–18; 768 day pupils (513 boys, 255 girls). Main entry ages 11 and some into sixth.

Entrance Own 11+ exam used. Oversubscribed. Range of aptitudes looked for; no special religious requirements. Parents not expected to buy textbooks; £234 for meals is only basic extra charge. 65 pa assisted places (50 at age 11, 5 at 13 and 10 in sixth-form). Scholarships/bursaries, value £1000–£2000.

Head and staff *Headmaster:* P D Briggs, in post for 9 years. Educated at Pocklington and Cambridge (English). Previously Senior Housemaster at Bedford. Publications: Parents' Guide to Independent Schools. *Staff:* 62 full time, 7 part time. Annual turnover 1%. Average age 39.

Exam results In 1995, 113 pupils in fifth, 112 in upper sixth. *GCSE:* In 1995, 80 fifth gained at least grade C in 8+ subjects; 27 in 5–7; and 6 in 1–4 subjects. *A-levels:* 73 upper sixth passed in 4+ subjects; 23 in 3; 12 in 2; and 4 in 1 subject. Average UCAS points 16.5.

University and college entrance 94% of 1995 sixth-form leavers went on to a degree course (5% after a gap year); others typically go straight in to careers eg forces, city. Of those going on to university, 4% went to Oxbridge; 6% took courses in medicine, dentistry and veterinary science, 36% in science and engineering, 6% in law, 51% in humanities and social sciences, 1% in art and design.

Curriculum GCSE and A-levels: 24 subjects offered (including A-level general studies). 29% took science A-levels; 48% arts/humanities; 23% both. *Vocational:* Work experience available. *Computing facilities:* New IT centre; computer lab (22 ICL PCs); design centre (5 Archimedes); various PCs in other departments. *Europe:* French, German and Spanish offered to GCSE and A-level; Greek (modern) to A-level. Regular exchanges.

The arts *Music:* About 15% of pupils learn a musical instrument; instrumental exams can be taken. Some 12 musical groups including orchestra, jazz group, clarinet group, recorder group, choir. *Drama & dance*: Some pupils are involved in school and in house/ other productions. 2 sixth-formers 1st and 2nd in regional final of Shakespeare from The Platform (winner in national final). *Art:* On average, 25 take GCSE, 7 A-level. Design, pottery and photography also offered as part of art and design course.

Sport, community service and clubs *Sport and physical activities:* Compulsory sports: rugby, lacrosse, cricket, athletics, gymnastics, basketball, swimming, tennis, netball, hockey. Optional: squash, dance, self-defence, cross-country. Sixth form only: badminton, aerobics. 2 pupils are junior international swimmers. *Community service:* Pupils take bronze, silver and gold Duke of Edinburgh's Award. CCF and community service optional. *Clubs and societies:* Up to 30 clubs, eg badminton, natural history, chess, photographic, mountaineering, stamp.

Uniform School uniform worn, modified in sixth.
Houses/prefects Competitive houses. Prefects, heads of school – appointed by Head; head of house and house prefects – appointed by housemaster. Elected committee runs sixth-form.
Religion Daily non-denominational Christian assembly; weekly Jewish religious assembly and opportunity for Muslim worship.
Social Debates, discussions, lectures, dances, industrial and European Conferences. Business experience visits to France, Germany and Spain. German and Russian exchanges; trips to France, Spain; sports tours to USA, Canada, West Indies. Pupils allowed to bring own car/bike/motorbike to school. Meals self-service. No tobacco/alcohol allowed.
Discipline Pupils failing to produce homework expect to do work next day and detention thereafter.
Alumni association Secretary: Mr P Marlton, 8 Stalmine Avenue, Heald Green, Cheshire SK8 3JG.
Former pupils Sir Robert Mark; Air Chief Marshal Sir Joseph Gilbert; Judge Michael Blackburn; John Lee; Michael Lord MP; Andrew Bennett MP; Sir C Stansfield Smith; J N Hopwood; John Midgley; Sir H J Seddon; DW Griffiths; Prof R Cocker; Sir P Rogers.

• WIMBLEDON HIGH

Wimbledon High School, Mansel Road, London SW19 4AB. Tel 0181 946 1756, Fax 0181 944 1989

• Pupils 827 • Boys None • Girls 4–18 (Day) • Upper sixth 75 • Termly fees £1192–£1548 (Day) • GSA, GPDST • Enquiries/application to the Headmistress

What it's like

Founded in 1880, it has occupied the same, conveniently situated campus ever since. The junior and senior departments are closely located and facilities are very good. The school is well reputed for its academic standards and pastoral care and draws its pupils from a wide social, cultural and ethnic background. The staff:pupil ratio is 1:13. Examination results are very good at all levels; most pupils go on to degree courses, including a large number to Oxbridge. Music, drama, sport and art are well-resourced and strongly supported; a new theatre has recently been opened. Some of the good sporting facilities, including a new 25-metre pool and sports hall, are on site; the playing fields, the original courts of the All England Lawn Tennis Club, are ten minutes' walk away. There is a thriving range of extra-curricular activities for all age groups and emphasis is laid on responsibilities to others by the girls' involvement in fund-raising for charities and by work in local community service.

School profile

Pupils Total age range 4–18; 827 day girls. Senior department 11–18, 568 girls. Main entry ages 4,5, 7, 11 and into sixth. Own junior provides some 50% senior intake.
Entrance Own entrance exam used. No special skills or religious requirements. Parents not expected to buy textbooks; music tuition (£120) and lunches extra. 10 pa assisted places at 11, 8 pa for sixth-form entry. 2 pa scholarships (including 1 sixth-form), half fees; bursaries.
Head and staff *Headmistress:* Dr Jill Clough, appointed 1995. Educated at Colson's (Girls) and London and Hull universities (English). Previously Headmistress of Royal Naval School (Haslemere), Deputy Head at Colston's (Girls) and Head of English and Drama at Moreton Hall. Also GSA representative on ISIS, GSA public relations officer. *Staff:* 47 full time, 39 part time (including 20 music). Annual turnover 10%. Average age 40.
Exam results In 1995, 80 pupils in upper fifth, 71 in upper sixth. *GCSE:* In 1995, 78 upper fifth gained at least grade C in 8+ subjects; 2 in 5–7 subjects. *A-levels:* 5 upper sixth passed in 4+ subjects; 58 in 3; 7 in 2; and 1 in 1 subject. Average UCAS points 23.9 .
University and college entrance 90% of 1995 sixth-form leavers went on to a degree course (12% after a gap year); others typically go on to art foundation courses. Of those going on to university, 14% went to Oxbridge; 9% took courses in medicine, dentistry and veterinary science, 20% in science and engineering, 2% in law, 55% in humanities and social sciences, 6% in art and design, 8% other vocational subjects (eg physiotherapy, accountancy).
Curriculum GCSE, AS and A-levels: 25 subjects offered (including A-level Latin and Greek, geology, economics; no A-level general studies). 30% take science A-levels; 36%

arts/humanities; 33% both. *Vocational:* Work experience available. *Computing facilities:* 15 Apple Macs networked. CD-Rom, 35 Apple Macs; 4 Archimedes; 5 BBC. *Special provision:* Some support for dyslexic and mildly handicapped pupils. *Europe:* French and German offered to GCSE, AS and A-level; also Spanish GCSE (80% take GCSE in more than 1 language). Regular exchanges.

The arts (Pupils aged 11 and over) *Music:* 80% of pupils learn a musical instrument; instrumental exams (including jazz) can be taken. Some 10 musical groups including orchestras, choirs, jazz, madrigal, windband, concert band, various chamber groups. Several in county orchestras and chamber choirs; a number attend London colleges of music on Saturdays; each year some go on to study music at university/college. *Drama & dance*: Both offered. GCSE theatre studies may be taken in sixth-form. Majority of pupils are involved in school and form/other productions. *Art:* On average, 30 take GCSE, 10 A-level, 10 history of art A-level; design, pottery, textiles, photography also offered.

Sport, community service and clubs (Pupils aged 11 and over) *Sport and physical activities:* Compulsory sports: hockey, netball, gymnastics, dance, swimming, tennis, athletics, rounders. Optional: trampolining, squash, volleyball, badminton, aerobics, rowing. Sixth form only: golf. Tennis and badminton England representatives. *Community service:* Pupils take bronze, silver and gold Duke of Edinburgh's Award. Community service optional in lower sixth (a third) – mostly working with elderly or young children. *Clubs and societies:* Up to 15 clubs, eg computer, drama, dance, book, gym, technology workshops.

Uniform School uniform worn except in the sixth.

Houses/prefects No competitive houses or prefects. Head girl, deputy head girls and sixth-form committee elected by staff and sixth-form.

Religion Daily non-denominational religious assembly.

Social Debating society, some drama, choir and orchestral participation and sixth-form non-exam courses with King's (Wimbledon). French and German exchanges; skiing, classical and art trips to Italy, Greece, France; activity courses. Meals self-service. No tobacco/alcohol allowed.

Discipline Pupils failing to produce homework once might expect verbal warning, and three times, a letter home.

Alumni association run by Mrs Jean Appleby, 1 Ridgeway Place, London SW19 4EW.

• WINCHESTER

Winchester College, College Street, Winchester, Hampshire SO23 9NA. Tel 01962 854328, Fax 01962 842972

• Pupils 674 • Boys 13–18 (Day/Board) • Girls None • Upper sixth 126 • Termly fees £3322 (Day) £4430 (Board) • HMC • Enquiries to Headmaster or Registrar • Application to Registrar

What it's like

Founded in 1382 by William of Wykeham, Bishop of Winchester and Chancellor to Richard II. It lies at the edge of the city and close to the water meadows. It has the longest unbroken history of any school in the country and has been in continuous occupation of its original buildings for 600 years. Most of them are still used for the purpose for which they were designed, and they are virtually without rival among school buildings for their venerability and beauty. The Scholars still live in the 14th-century 'College'; other buildings date from the 17th, 18th and 19th centuries, plus some recent structures. Accommodation and facilities are first rate; they include exceptionally good libraries, a theatre, a music school and an art school. Intellectually and academically, Winchester is one of the most distinguished schools in Britain and results are outstanding. A large staff permits a staff:pupil ratio of 1:8. Almost all pupils go on to university each year, and these include 40 plus to Oxbridge. A tremendously strong music department involves a majority of the school; two-thirds of the pupils learn a musical instrument and there are several choirs and orchestras. There are numerous school and house dramatic productions and the art department is also very strong. High standards prevail in sports and games, of which some 30 are available (including Winchester football which is peculiar to the College); there are many representatives at international and county level. A very large number of extra-curricular activities is available and an impressive commitment to local community schemes.

School profile

Pupils Age range 13–18; 674 boys (24 day, 650 boarding). Main entry ages 13 and a few into sixth. Approx 11% are children of former pupils.
Entrance Own entrance exam used. Oversubscribed (registration from age 8). Academic ability and other interests looked for; no religious requirements. Music tuition, books etc extra charge. 7 pa assisted places (5 at 13, 2 in sixth-form). 15 pa scholarships and up to 6 music awards, up to 50% of the full fee.
Head and staff *Headmaster:* J P Sabben-Clare, in post since 1985. Educated at Winchester and Oxford (classics). Previously Second Master and Head of Classics at Winchester, Visiting Fellow at All Souls College, Oxford and Assistant Master at Marlborough. Publications: Caesar and Roman Politics (1971); Fables from Aesop (1976); The Culture of Athens (1978); Winchester College (1981) and various articles in learned journals. *Staff:* 85 full time, 17 part time. Annual turnover 2%.
Exam results In 1995, 138 in upper fifth, 126 in upper sixth. *GCSE:* Typically, all pupils in upper fifth pass 8+ subjects. *A-levels:* All pass 3 or more A-levels. Average UCAS points 31.0.
University and college entrance 98% of 1995 sixth-form leavers went on to a degree course; others may improve A-level grades or direct into employment. Of those going on to university, 40% went to Oxbridge; 9% took courses in medicine, dentistry and veterinary science, 18% in science and engineering, 7% in law, 56% in humanities and social sciences, 5% in art and design, 5% other vocational subjects eg psychology, architecture, pharmacology.
Curriculum GCSE and A-levels. *Vocational:* Work experience available. *Computing facilities:* Two fully equipped computer rooms; many departments have own specialist facilities. *Europe:* French, German, Russian and Spanish offered to GCSE and A-level. Regular exchanges to France and Germany; visits to Russia and Spain.
The arts *Music:* 66% pupils learn a musical instrument; instrumental exams can be taken. Large number musical groups, including plainsong groups, large jazz/rock band, 2 symphony orchestras, chamber orchestra, symphonic band, brass groups, string quartets. Pupils in National Youth Choir, National Youth Wind Orchestra, Pro Corda, National Youth Orchestra; string final of Young Musician of the Year; winner of Rubenstein International Piano competition. Scholarships to music colleges and choral and instrumental awards to Oxbridge. *Drama*: About 50% pupils are involved in school productions; all in house/other productions. Some 12 productions per year, directed by both staff and pupils; some at Minack Theatre (Cornwall) and Edinburgh Festival. *Art:* On average, 27 take GCSE, 8 A-level; pottery and photography also offered (but not examined).
Sport, community service and clubs *Sport and physical activities:* No compulsory sports; 31 options, including athletics, badminton, basketball, canoeing, cricket, fencing, fishing, fives, gymnastics, hockey, judo, karate, rackets, rowing, sailing, shooting, soccer, squash, cross country, sub-aqua, swimming, tennis, trampoline, volleyball, water polo, weight and circuit training, Winchester football available. Water polo, pupils are county representatives, national semi-finals U16 and U19; basketball, occasional South of England representatives; cross-country, regular county representation; shooting, national team; rowing, national team. *Community service:* CCF compulsory for 1 year at age 14, optional thereafter. Community service optional for 3 years from age 15 (some 260 pupils involved). *Clubs and societies:* Up to 30 clubs eg archaeology, bellringing, bookbinding, bridge, chess, classical, clay-pigeon shooting, debating, drama, electronics, film, French poetry, green, natural history, photography, printing, railway, science, Spanish, stamps.
Uniform School uniform not worn, but dress regulations; scholars wear gowns.
Houses/prefects Competitive houses. Prefects, head of house and house prefects – chosen by Housemasters after consultation with prefects; approved by the Headmaster. Head boy chosen by Headmaster.
Religion Compulsory religious worship.
Social Debates, music, drama. Pupils allowed to bring own bike to school. Meals formal. School shop. No tobacco/alcohol allowed.
Discipline Pupils failing to produce homework once might expect a reprimand from teacher and work to be produced; those involved with drugs may expect to be expelled.
Boarding 15% have own study bedroom, 80% are in dormitories of 6+. Houses of 58–

60. The 75 scholars live together in College. Resident matron in each house. No central dining room. 5-day weekend exeats in summer and Easter terms; 10 days exeat in winter term. Visits to the local town allowed.
Alumni association run by P S W K Maclure, c/o the College.
Former pupils Viscount Whitelaw; Lord Howe; Douglas Jay; Peter Jay; Lord Penney; Sir Jeremy Morse; George Younger; Field Marshal Lord Carver; Professor Freeman Dyson; Howard Angus; William Mann; Tim Brooke-Taylor; Brian Trubshaw; Richard Noble; Lord Macleod.

• WITHINGTON

Withington Girls' School, Wellington Road, Fallowfield, Manchester M14 6BL Tel 0161 224 1077/8820

• Pupils 615 • Boys None • Girls 7–18 (Day) • Upper sixth 59 • Termly fees £1250 (Day) • GSA
• Enquiries/application to the Headmistress

What it's like

Founded in 1890, it is urban single-site, housed in a pleasant late 19th-century building with large adjoining playing fields. There have been many additions over the years and modern facilities are excellent. Academic standards are high and results excellent. All sixth-formers go on to higher education, including very many to Oxbridge. Extremely strong music and drama departments and a fine range of activities. The school has a high reputation for its achievements in sport and games – particularly tennis and lacrosse (there have been many representatives at county level). A promising record in the Duke of Edinburgh's Award Scheme. The school enjoys vigorous local support and has a strong commitment to local community services.

School profile

Pupils Total age range 7–18; 615 day girls. Senior department 11–18, 515 girls. Main entry ages 7, 11 and into sixth. Under 5% are children of former pupils. Own junior school provides more than 20% of intake. *State school entry:* 45% intake at 11, plus 80% to sixth.
Entrance Own entrance exam used. All-round ability and excellent potential looked for; no religious requirements. Parents not expected to buy textbooks; lunches (£210 pa) extra. 15 pa assisted places. Bursaries available in cases of need, assessed individually.
Parents 15+% in industry or commerce; 15+% are doctors, lawyers etc.
Head and staff *Headmistress:* Mrs Margaret Kenyon, in post for 11 years. Educated at Merchant Taylors' (Girls) and Oxford (modern languages). Previously Head of Languages at Withington. Also Member Granada Foundation; former President GSA. *Staff:* 40 full time, 8 part time. Annual turnover 5%. Average age 42.
Exam results In 1995, 70 pupils in upper fifth, 59 in upper sixth. *GCSE:* In 1995, all in upper fifth gained at least grade C in 9 subjects. *A-levels:* 50 upper sixth passed in 4+ subjects; 9 in 3 subjects. Average UCAS points 26.2 (including general studies 34.0.).
University and college entrance All sixth-form leavers go on to a degree course (12% after a gap year), 20% to Oxbridge; 18% take courses in medicine, dentistry and veterinary science, 12% in science and engineering, 11% in law, 40% in humanities and social sciences, 4% in art and design, 7% in vocational subjects.
Curriculum GCSE and A-levels. 18 subjects offered (including Greek and A-level general studies). 35% take science A-levels; 30% arts/humanities; 35% both. *Vocational:* Work experience available. *Computing facilities:* Nimbus network and stand-alone PCs (being extended throughout school). *Europe:* French and German offered to GCSE, AS and A-level; also GCSE Italian and Spanish. Regular exchanges to France and Germany. Reciprocal German sixth-formers exchange for 1 term.
The arts (Pupils aged 11 and over) *Music:* Over 30% of pupils learn a musical instrument; instrumental exams are taken by over 200 girls a year. Musical groups include 2 orchestras, large wind band, jazz band, 5 choirs. Occasional members of National Children's Wind and Chamber orchestras. Many girls compete successfully at local festivals. *Drama & dance*: Majority of pupils (in early years) are involved in school and house/other productions. *Art:* On average, 10 take GCSE, 2–3 A-level. Design, pottery, textiles also offered.
Sport, community service and clubs (Pupils aged 11 and over) *Sport and physical*

activities: Compulsory sports: hockey, netball, lacrosse, gymnastics (to 13), tennis, rounders, swimming, athletics. Optional: badminton, volleyball, basketball, aerobics. Sixth form only: squash, self-defence. GCSE, BAGA exams may be taken. 2 leading young British tennis players; frequent national and regional lacrosse squad players. *Community service:* Pupils take bronze and silver Duke of Edinburgh's Award. Community service optional: more than £10,000 raised by mid-1995 for local and national charities. *Clubs and societies:* Up to 25 clubs, eg scientific, bridge, Jewish Society, modern languages.
Uniform School uniform worn except in the sixth.
Houses/prefects Competitive houses. All upper sixth-form are prefects. Head girl, 2–3 deputies chosen by Headmistress after consulting sixth-form and staff. House captains and vice captains elected by houses. School Committee and School Council.
Religion All encouraged to take part. Assembly compulsory twice a week; separate Jewish assembly once weekly.
Social Girls are invited to lectures at Manchester Grammar School and audition for plays there. Organised skiing trips, adventure holidays in the Lake District and abroad for 12–13-year-olds; French/German trips for GCSE candidates and cultural visits abroad for sixth-form. Pupils allowed to bring own car to school. Meals self-service. No tobacco/alcohol allowed.
Discipline Pupils failing to produce homework once might expect a verbal reminder; those caught smoking cannabis on the premises would be expelled.
Alumni association run by Mrs Marjorie Rawsthorn, 20 Legh Road, Adlington, Macclesfield SK10 4NE.
Former pupils Judith and Sandra Chalmers.

• WOLDINGHAM

Woldingham School, Marden Park, Woldingham, Surrey CR3 7YA. Tel 01883 349431, Fax 01883 348653

• Pupils 536 • Boys None • Girls 11–18 (Day/Board) • Upper sixth 60 • Termly fees £2306 (Day) £3812 (Board) • GSA, BSA • Enquiries/application to Admissions Secretary

What it's like

Founded in 1842 by the Society of the Sacred Heart, the school moved from Roehampton to Woldingham in 1946. It is now under lay management, part of the international network of Sacred Heart Schools, and run according to its educational aims and philosophy. Set in magnificent grounds, surrounded by 600 acres of farmland, the buildings are a blend of styles from the 17th century to the present day. Recent developments include a sports centre and a design and technology workshop. A Roman Catholic school in the ecumenical tradition, its primary purpose is to provide a sound education which will help girls to become mature and committed Christians who can make independent decisions in their careers and personal lives. They are expected to play a full part in the running of the school and responsibilities and privileges are introduced at an early stage. A large staff allows a favourable staff:pupil ratio of about 1:9. Academic standards are high and results very good. Virtually all sixth-formers proceed to degree courses. A very big commitment to drama, music and art. A good range of sports and games and extra-curricular activities. Many participate in the Duke of Edinburgh's Award Scheme and there is a strong debating society.

School profile

Pupils Age range 11–18; 536 girls, 100 day, 436 boarding. Main entry age 11. *State school entry:* 1% main intake.
Entrance Common Entrance and own assessment day used. No special skills required; RC and other Christian denominations preferred.
Parents 35+% in industry or commerce. 10+% live within 30 miles; 20% overseas (half of whom are expats).
Head and staff *Headmistress:* Dr Philomena Dineen, in post for 12 years. Educated at St Joseph's, Newport, and at universities of Wales and London (English). Previously Headmistress at St Bede's, Redhill. *Staff:* 61 full time, 6 part time. Annual turnover 9%. Average age 38.

Exam results In 1995, 68 pupils in fifth, 52 in upper sixth. *GCSE:* In 1995, 60 upper fifth gained at least grade C in 8+ subjects; 5 in 5–7; and 3 in 1–4 subjects. *A-levels:* 4 upper sixth passed in 4 subjects; 40 in 3; and 8 in 2 subjects. Average of 23.7 UCAS points gained.
University and college entrance 98% of 1995 sixth-form leavers went on to a degree course (30% after a gap year); others typically go on to further training. Of those going on to university, 12% went to Oxbridge; 12% took courses in medicine, dentistry and veterinary science, 30% in science and engineering, 6% in law, 34% in humanities and social sciences, 12% in art and design, 6% in vocational subjects eg radiography, physiotherapy.
Curriculum GCSE and A-levels. 17 GCSE subjects offered; 18 at A-level (no A-level general studies, Japanese GCSE). 20% take science A-levels; 70% arts/humanities; 10% both. *Vocational:* Work experience available. *Computing facilities:* IT taught in all years via 125-station PC network in three IT rooms; work-stations in all departments, library and study areas. *Europe:* French, German and Spanish offered to GCSE, AS and A-level; also GCSE Italian. Regular exchanges to Germany, Austria, France and Spain (also staff exchanges in holidays). Associated with other Sacred Heart schools in Europe, principals of which hold regular meetings.
The arts *Music:* Almost all pupils learn a musical instrument; instrumental exams can be taken. Some 14 musical groups including senior choir (95), first orchestra (50), senior orchestra (55), concert band (30), junior chamber choir (40), saxophone quartet, 6 rock bands, flute choir. Some Saturday students at Royal Academy of Music. *Drama & dance:* Drama offered; GCSE, AS and A-level may be taken. Majority of pupils are involved in school productions, all in house/other productions. *Art:* On average, 35 take GCSE, 15 A-level. Design, pottery, textiles, photography and sculpture also offered. Pupils regularly accepted for art college.
Sport, community service and clubs *Sport and physical activities:* Netball, golf, hockey (winter), athletics, rounders, tennis (summer), competitive tennis and swimming (year round). Also available: badminton, trampolining, cross-country, gymnastics, football, volleyball, basketball, dance and squash. *Community service:* Pupils take bronze, silver and gold Duke of Edinburgh's Award. Community service optional. *Clubs and societies:* Up to 30 clubs, eg pottery, computer, judo, jazz, dancing, photography, riding, grooming, bridge, cookery, Amnesty International.
Uniform School uniform worn throughout.
Houses/prefects Competitive houses. Head girl, prefects, and heads of houses short-listed by sixth, selected by senior staff.
Religion Mass on Sunday. Retreats organised occasionally.
Social Regular debates and dances with local schools. Visits to France, Holland and Italy (history of art), France, Austria, Spain and Germany (languages), annual ski trip. Year 9 upwards allowed to bring own bike to school. School shop. No tobacco/alcohol allowed.
Discipline Pupils failing to produce homework once might expect tutorial direction; those caught smoking on the premises might expect a fine; involvement in drug-taking likely to incur exclusion from the school.
Boarding 42% have own study bedroom, 43% share (2+), 15% in dormitories of 5+. Not divided into houses. 2 resident qualified nurses; 2 doctors, dentist and physiotherapist in attendance. 2 central dining rooms. Exeats each weekend from Saturday noon. Visits to local town allowed (14+) and sixth to London on Saturday afternoons.
Alumnae association run by Mrs C Griffith c/o the school.

• WOLVERHAMPTON GRAMMAR

Wolverhampton Grammar School, Compton Road, Wolverhampton WV3 9RB. Tel 01902 21326, Fax 01902 21819

• Pupils 740 • Boys 11–18 (Day) • Girls 11–18 (Day) • Upper sixth 101 • Termly fees £1600 (Day) • HMC • Enquiries/application to the Headmaster

What it's like

Founded in 1512, it became a Voluntary Aided Grammar School in 1944, but reverted to independence in 1979. It was originally a boys' school but since 1992 has been fully co-educational (girls were first accepted to the sixth-form in 1984). Major recent building programmes have provided first-rate facilities. The curriculum combines specialist excellence with breadth and the school attracts bright boys and girls from all parts of the West Midlands, Staffordshire and Shropshire. An all-graduate staff (and staff:pupil ratio of about 1:12) ensures high academic standards and examination results. Nearly all the sixth-formers go on to higher education, with a good number proceeding to Oxbridge each year. Sport and the arts all thrive. Music has a strong reputation in the area and the school's choirs, orchestras, concert band, big band and choral society (number 200) regularly fill the town's Civic Hall, as well as making concert tours abroad. Drama is ambitious and well supported. A wide range of sports and games are provided and there is a fine new sports centre. Several representatives at county and regional levels in various sports each year. A great many extra-curricular activities are offered. Outdoor pursuits, including Outward Bound, sailing courses and the Duke of Edinburgh's Award Scheme, are very popular, as is the school's Scout Troop. Full use is made of the cultural amenities at Stratford, Birmingham and Wolverhampton.

School profile

Pupils Age range 11–18; 740 day pupils (570 boys, 170 girls). Main entry ages 11, 13 and into sixth. Small proportion are children of former pupils. *State school entry:* 80% main intake, plus 60% to sixth.

Entrance Own entrance exam used at 11 and 13. No special skills or religious requirements. Parents not expected to buy textbooks. 40 pa assisted places. 7 pa academic scholarships and music exhibition at 11 and 13.

Parents 15+% are doctors, lawyers etc; 15+% in industry.

Head and staff *Headmaster:* Bernard Trafford, 7 years in post. Educated at Downside and at universities of Oxford and Birmingham (music and education). Previously Head of Sixth Form and Director of Music at Wolverhampton Grammar, and Assistant Director of Music at the Royal Grammar School, High Wycombe. Also registered as PhD student at Birmingham University researching into power-sharing/democratic practice in schools. Vice-Chairman, British Federation of Young Choirs, and Advisory Board Member, The Citizenship Foundation. Publication: Sharing power in schools: raising standards (Education Now Books, 1993). *Staff:* 57 full time, 3 part time. Annual turnover 8%. Average age 35–40.

Exam results In 1995, 98 pupils in upper fifth, 101 in upper sixth. *GCSE:* In 1995, 98% upper fifth gained at least grade C in 8+ subjects; 1% in 5–7 subjects. *A-levels:* 93% upper sixth passed in 4+ subjects; 5% in 3; 1% in 2 subjects. Average UCAS points 23.8 (including general studies 30.8).

University and college entrance 98% of 1995 sixth-form leavers go on to a degree course (15% to Oxbridge). 15% take courses in medicine, dentistry and veterinary science, 36% in science and engineering, 43% in humanities and social sciences, 1% in art and design.

Curriculum GCSE and A-levels. 20 subjects offered (including A-level general studies). 36% took science A-levels; 34% arts/humanities; 30% both. *Vocational:* Work experience available. *Computing facilities:* A computer-aided learning centre, Computerised language laboratory, networked library and numerous departmental computers. *Europe:* French and German offered to GCSE and A-level (both compulsory to age 14); also Italian GCSE and business French and German courses in sixth. Regular exchanges. Regular talks from MEP to sixth, trips to European countries (including concert tours).

The arts *Music:* Over 30% of pupils learn a musical instrument; instrumental exams can be taken. Some 7 musical groups: orchestra, 2 concert bands, big band, string orchestra, choir, choral society plus occasional groups. *Drama & dance*: Drama offered. 3 major productions a year. *Art:* On average, 20 take GCSE 6 A-level; design and pottery also offered.

Sport, community service and clubs *Sport and physical activities:* Compulsory sports: soccer, netball, hockey, cricket, athletics, rounders. Optional: rugby, badminton, volleyball, table tennis, Eton fives, etc. GCSE sport available. Always several representatives in soccer, rugby, cricket, hockey, athletics. *Community service:* Pupils take bronze, silver and gold Duke of Edinburgh's Award. Community service compulsory for 1 year in fifth/sixth-form. Active charitable fund-raising. *Clubs and societies:* Clubs include aviation, stamps, scouts, religious groups.

Uniform School uniform worn throughout.
Houses/prefects No competitive houses. All upper sixth are prefects; head prefects – elected by their contemporaries.
Religion Compulsory daily assemblies.
Social Trips abroad organised annually. Pupils allowed to bring own car/motorbike to school. Meals self-service. School tuck shop. No tobacco/alcohol allowed.
Discipline Pupils failing to produce homework once would receive punishment only in aggravating circumstances; those caught with drugs on the premises could expect expulsion.
Alumni association The Old Wulfrunians Association c/o the school.
Former pupils Lord Normanbrook (Secretary to the War Cabinet); David Wright (HM Ambassador to Japan); John Hall (opera singer).

• WOODBRIDGE

Woodbridge School, Woodbridge, Suffolk IP12 4JH Tel 01394 385547, Fax 01394 380944
• Pupils 761 • Boys 4–18 (Day/Board/Weekly) • Girls 4–18 (Day/Board/Weekly) • Upper sixth 77 • Termly fees £863–£1699 (Day) £2792 (Board/Weekly) • HMC • Enquiries/application to the Headmaster's Secretary

What it's like

Founded in 1577, it fell into desuetude during the Civil War and was refounded in 1662. In 1864 it moved to its present fine site of 45 acres of wooded grounds and playing fields overlooking Woodbridge and the River Deben. Both the school and its own prep school, The Abbey, enjoy an unusually civilized environment. Many of the school's buildings are 16th and 19th century. Now fully co-educational, the school was founded as a boys' school and admitted girls in 1974. It is a C of E foundation; there is some emphasis on religious education and attendance at worship is compulsory. The staff:pupil ratio is about 1:13 and results are uniformly good. Nearly all leavers go on to degree courses, including Oxbridge. Music is especially flourishing (3 orchestras, 3 choirs, a band and sundry ensembles) and there is a purpose-built music school. Drama and art are also vigorously supported. Excellent facilities for sports and games (including a floodlit all-weather hockey pitch) and high standards are attained; the girls' hockey is outstanding. A wide range of clubs and societies caters for most needs. The CCF (Army and Air Force) is very popular, as is the Duke of Edinburgh's Award Scheme in which there has been much success. There is considerable involvement in local community services and an active Charity Committee. The school is highly thought of in the town and its neighbourhood.

School profile

Pupils Age range 4–18; 761 pupils, 724 day (360 boys, 364 girls), 37 boarding (14 boys, 23 girls). Senior department, 11–18, 506 pupils (240 boys, 266 girls). Main entry ages 4, 7, 11 and into sixth. Approx 5% are children of former pupils. 50% of senior intake from own prep school (The Abbey School; Tel 01394 382673). *State school entry:* 50% senior intake, plus 15% to sixth.
Entrance Common Entrance and own exam used. No special skills required, but sporting, artistic and other interests valued; no religious requirements. Parents not expected to buy textbooks; average extras, £100 a term. 16 pa assisted places at 11, 5 pa at sixth-form. Scholarships/bursaries at 11 and 16, £535 – £2676 pa.
Parents 15+% are in industry/commerce. 60+% live within 30 miles.
Head and staff *Headmaster:* S H Cole, in post since 1994. Educated at Dulwich and Oxford (physics). Previously Housemaster and Head of Science at Merchant Taylor's, Northwood, and Assistant Master at Wellington College. *Staff:* 68 full time, 14 part time. Annual turnover 5%. Average age 39.
Exam results In 1995, 83 pupils in Year 11, 77 in upper sixth. *GCSE:* In 1995, 68 Year 11 pupils gained at least grade C in 8+ subjects; 10 in 5–7; and 5 in 1–4 subjects. *A-levels:* 4 upper sixth passed in 4+ subjects; 57 in 3; 14 in 2; and 2 in 1 subject. Average UCAS points 18.7.
University and college entrance 92% of 1995 sixth-form leavers go on to a degree course (11% after a gap year); others typically go on to HND hotel management, art foundation courses, drama courses, employment or training. Of those going on to

university, 7% go to Oxbridge; 7% take courses in medicine, dentistry and veterinary science, 33% in science and engineering, 7% in law, 25% in humanities and social sciences, 8% in art and design, 9% other vocational subjects, 13% music, modern languages etc.

Curriculum GCSE and A-levels: 16 GCSE subjects offered, 19 A-level (including psychology but no general studies). 21% take science A-levels; 35% arts/humanities; 44% both. *Vocational:* Work experience available. *Computing facilities:* Two specialist rooms with PCs and Archimedes, plus other machines in departments and in prep school. *Special provision:* Special needs teaching for dyslexics outside school time. *Europe:* French, German and Spanish at GCSE and A-level; also Italian GCSE. All sixth-formers encouraged to continue with a language. Regular exchanges. Reciprocal scheme with school in Clermont-Ferand (A-level students work in partner school). East European students study in school for one year.

The arts *Music:* Over 30% pupils learn a musical instrument; instrumental exams can be taken. Some 20 musical groups, including 3 orchestras, 3 choirs, band, various ensembles of recorders, flutes, clarinets, saxophones, string quartets, percussion etc. Annual pop concert; biennial musical; biennial concert at Snape Maltings. 7 members of National Youth Choir. *Drama & dance*: Both offered. GCSE drama and LAMDA exams may be taken. Some pupils are involved in school and house/other productions. 1 pupil performing with National Youth Music Theatre at Edinburgh Festival in 1995. *Art:* On average, 20 take GCSE, 5 AS-level, 15 A-level. Design also offered.

Sport, community service and clubs *Sport and physical activities:* Compulsory sports: Rugby, hockey (boys and girls), cricket, athletics, cross-country, swimming. Optional: squash, volleyball, tennis, soccer, badminton, sailing, riding, golf, judo, indoor hockey, shooting. GCSE offered. Girls' hockey championships at all ages; 1 cross-country county champion. *Community service:* Pupils take bronze, silver and gold Duke of Edinburgh's Award. CCF optional (popular with girls and boys; shooting is successful at regional and national level). Community service optional. *Clubs and societies:* Up to 20 clubs eg chess, debating, Christian Union, literary, science, charity committee.

Uniform School uniform worn but dress guidelines in sixth.

Houses/prefects Competitive houses. Prefects, head boy/girl – appointed by the Headmaster; all sixth-formers in position of leadership. School council.

Religion Attendance at relgious worship compulsory.

Social Occasional joint lectures with local schools. Regular exchanges with French, German and Dutch schools. Adventurous activities in Norway and Iceland; numerous sports tours (eg Spain, Netherlands, USA, Italy). Pupils allowed to bring own car/bike/motorbike to school. Meals self-service. School shop. No tobacco/alcohol allowed.

Discipline Pupils failing to produce homework once may receive an extra study period after school; those caught smoking cannabis on the premises would be expelled.

Boarding Pupils share study bedrooms, 2–5. One mixed house. Resident matron. Pupils allowed to cook own food. Exeats any weekend if no school commitments (Friday evening to Monday morning). Visits to the local town allowed.

Alumni association is run by Mr David Houchell c/o the school.

• WOODHOUSE GROVE

Woodhouse Grove School, Apperley Bridge, West Yorkshire BD10 0NR. Tel 0113 250 2477, Fax 0113 250 5290

• Pupils 560 • Boys 11–18 (Day/Board) • Girls 11–18 (Day/Board) • Upper sixth 60 • Termly fees £1755 (Day) £2980 (Board) • HMC • Enquiries/application to the Headmaster

What it's like

Founded in 1812, the main school and the prep school, Bronte House, have fine buildings in spacious grounds in the Aire Valley between Leeds and Bradford. Excellent all-round facilities including a new business management school and comfortable boarding accommodation are provided. A Methodist foundation, it attempts to provide a caring community and each pupil is encouraged to develop individual talents to the full. Religious worship in the Methodist tradition is compulsory. Originally a boys' school, it first admitted girls to the sixth-form in 1979 and is now fully co-educational. Academic standards are high and results good. Most sixth-formers go on to degree courses each year. It is very strong in music and drama. Sporting facilities are first rate and the standards in sport and games are high (several county and national representatives). There is a genuine commitment to local community services, a strong fund-raising spirit and a good record in the Duke of Edinburgh's Award Scheme. Activities arranged for boarding pupils, including stays at outdoor centres.

School profile

Pupils Age range 11–18; 560 pupils, 420 day (275 boys, 145 girls), 140 boarding (95 boys, 45 girls). Main entry ages 11 and into sixth. Approx 5% are children of former pupils. 50% of intake from own prep school, Bronte House, (tel 0113 250 2811). *State school entry:* 33% main intake, plus 12% to sixth.

Entrance Mainly own exam; also Common Entrance. Aptitude in instrumental music, art and sport looked for; no religious requirements but school is Methodist. Textbooks provided by the school; extras include excursions, extra tuition eg music. 25 pa assisted places. About 20 pa academic and music scholarships, up to 50% of fees.

Parents 15+% are in the armed services. 60+% live within 30 miles; 10+% live overseas.

Head and staff *Headmaster:* David Humphreys, appointed in 1996. Educated at Southampton University (geography). Previously Deputy Head at Caterham and Head of Department at Wellingborough. *Staff:* 45 full time, 5 part time. Annual turnover 3%. Average age 43.

Exam results On average, 90 pupils in upper fifth, 65 in upper sixth. *GCSE:* on average, 70% upper fifth gain at least grade C in 8+ subjects; 20% in 5–7; and 10% in 1–4 subjects. *A-levels:* 10% upper sixth pass in 4+ subjects; 70% in 3; 20% in 2 subjects. Average UCAS points 19.6.

University and college entrance 85% of 1995 sixth-form leavers went on to a degree course; others typically go on to eg art college, other non-degree courses or straight into careers (eg industry, army). Of those going on to university, 5% went to Oxbridge; 3% took courses in medicine, dentistry and veterinary science, 47% in science and engineering, 41% in humanities and social sciences, 6% in art and design, 3% in music.

Curriculum GCSE and A-levels. 20 subjects offered (including A-level general studies). 40% take science A-levels; 40% arts/humanities; 20% both. *Vocational:* Advanced GNVQ in business. *Computing facilities:* Network of Viglen machines in business block and in other departments. *Special provision:* Dyslexia unit – extra tuition. EFL studies. *Europe:* French and German offered to GCSE and A-level; non-examined courses in both languages and in Spanish, also business language classes. Holiday courses often available (French, German, Russian and Spanish) and language classes for adults. Regular exchanges to France and Germany. Many Euro-boarders in school.

The arts *Music:* Over 50% pupils learn a musical instrument; instrumental exams can be taken. Some 8 musical groups, including 3 orchestras, concert band, string group, flute choir, brass ensemble. *Drama & dance*: Both offered. LAMDA, RAD and speech exams may be taken. Majority of pupils are involved in school and house/other productions. *Art:* On average, 10–15 take GCSE, 6 A-level. Pottery and photography also offered. 3 pupils went to art college in 1995.

Sport, community service and clubs *Sport and physical activities:* Compulsory sports: Rugby, cricket, netball, rounders. Optional: Athletics, hockey, cross-country, squash, volleyball, rowing, tennis. Sixth form only: Basketball, aerobics, mixed hockey. Many county players at rugby, several in cricket; national representatives in rugby, cricket, squash and swimming. *Community service:* Pupils take gold Duke of Edinburgh's Award. *Clubs and societies:* Up to 15 clubs eg photography, chess, pottery, films, technology, pets, choral singing.

Uniform School uniform worn until the fifth form. Sixth form has own uniform.

Houses/prefects Competitive houses. Prefects, head boy/girl, head of house and house prefects – appointed by the Head.

Religion Morning prayers compulsory.

Social Regular exchanges with France and Germany. Meals self-service. School shop. No tobacco/alcohol allowed.

Discipline School detentions held on a Saturday morning.

Boarding Upper sixth have own study bedroom, lower sixth share; about half in dormitories of 6+. Single-sex houses, in vertical groups. Resident qualified nurse(s).

Central dining room. At least two weekend exeats each term. Visits to the local town allowed with permission.
Alumni association is run by G H Knowles, Hon Secretary, Old Grovian Association, c/o the school.
Former pupils Lord Woolley (NFU); Sir Noel Stockdale (Chairman Asda); Alan Cuckston (harpsichord); Steven Burnhill (rugby international); Kenneth Hind MP; General Michael Walker; Sir Alistair Grant (Chairman Argyll Group plc).

• WORKSOP

Worksop College, Worksop, Nottinghamshire S80 3AP. Tel 01909 537127
• Pupils 350 • Boys 13–18 (Day/Board/Weekly) • Girls 13–18 (Day/Board/Weekly) • Upper sixth 70 • Termly fees £2480 (Day) £3595 (Board/Weekly) • HMC, Woodard, BSA • Enquiries/application to the Headmaster

What it's like

Founded in 1890, and the last of the Woodard Church of England schools to be founded personally by Canon Woodard. The college lies in a superb estate of 310 acres next to Sherwood Forest about a mile south of Worksop and overlooking the Clumber and Welbeck estates to which pupils of the college have free access. Its handsome if slightly austere brick buildings in the collegiate style form a compact group in a campus of gardens and lawns. Splendid playing fields lie alongside. There has been much recent modernisation. Originally a boys' school, it first admitted girls in 1978 and is now fully co-educational. Religious worship and instruction is central to the college's life and the chapel is a central feature of life. A large and well-qualified staff allows a staff:pupil ratio of about 1:9. Close attention is given to pupils at all levels. Most sixth-formers go on to degree courses. Music, drama and art are all strong: there are a number of choirs and instrumental ensembles and several plays are put on each year in one or other of the theatres. The art studios are very well equipped and work of a high standard is achieved. There is also a wide variety of sports and games and some 15 clubs and societies cater for most people's needs. The strong CCF contingent, comprising Army, Navy and Air Force sections, is very active for boys and girls who also participate in the Duke of Edinburgh's Award Scheme. The college has a big commitment to local community and social services in Worksop and Bassetlaw.

School profile

Pupils Age range 13–18, 350 pupils, 140 day (80 boys, 60 girls), 210 boarding (155 boys, 55 girls). Main entry age 13. Many pupils from Ranby House Preparatory School, Nr Retford (tel 01777 703138). *State school entry:* 10% main intake, plus some to sixth.
Entrance Common Entrance or entry test used. Assisted places. Scholarships (academic, art, sports, music and all-rounders).
Head and staff *Headmaster:* Roy A. Collard, in post from 1994. Educated at Chislehurst and Sidcup Grammar School and Cambridge University (geography). Previously Headmaster of Bristol Cathedral School, Director of Studies at Oundle, Head of Sixth Form Centre and i/c Community Service at Uppingham. Author of A-Level textbook The Physical Geography of Landscape. *Staff:* 36 full time, 7 part time.
Exam results In 1995, 60 pupils in upper fifth, 70 in upper sixth. *GCSE:* In 1995, 77% upper fifth gained at least grade C in 8+ subjects. *A-levels:* 53% upper sixth passed in 3 subjects; average pupil passes 2.6 subjects. Average UCAS points 15.1.
University and college entrance 96% of 1995 sixth-form leavers went on to a degree course (20% after a gap year); others typically go on to music college, family business or nursing. Of those going on to university, 5% went to Oxbridge; 10% took courses in medicine, dentistry and veterinary science, 20% in science and engineering, 10% in law, 40% in humanities and social sciences, 8% in art and design, 12% in vocational subjects eg agriculture, podiatry, physiotherapy.
Curriculum GCSE and A-levels. 18 subjects offered (including A-level general studies). 25% take science A-levels; 66% arts/humanities; 9% both. *Vocational:* Work experience available. *Computing facilities:* Fully equipped laboratory and in all departments. *Special provision:* Link with the Dyslexia Institute. *Europe:* French and Spanish offered to GCSE

and A-level. Regular exchanges to France and Spain. Talks from MEP. French students from a school in Bordeaux spend 3 weeks. Lower sixth have opportunity to attend a French school.
The arts *Music:* 40% of pupils learn a musical instruments; instrumental exams can be taken. Some 8 musical groups including orchestra, choirs, chamber, brass, rock band etc; distinction in singing exam; brass band player through to finals of national competition; 3 pupils in National Youth choir; 1 in National Youth Orchestra. *Drama & dance:* Drama offered. Majority of pupils are involved in school productions and all in house/other productions. *Art:* On average, 18 take A-level. Design, sculpture, textiles, photography also offered. Award winner Electricity Council illustrated calendar competition.
Sport, community service and clubs *Sport and physical activities:* Compulsory sports: rugby, cricket, hockey, netball, swimming. Optional: tennis, athletics, squash, clay-pigeon shooting, sailing, cross-country, golf, basketball, badminton, volleyball, archery. GCSE and RLSS exams may be taken. *Community service:* Pupils take bronze, silver and gold Duke of Edinburgh's Award. CCF and community service both optional for 4 years at age 14. *Clubs and societies:* Up to 15 clubs, eg advanced science, sailing, groundlings, Christian, chess, debating.
Uniform School uniform worn, modified in the sixth.
Houses/prefects Competitive houses. Prefects, head boy/girl, head of house and house prefects appointed by the Headmaster.
Religion Attendance at chapel services compulsory.
Social Exchanges with Acadis (Bordeaux) and a school in Tenerife. Pupils allowed to bring own car/bike/motorbike to school with specific permission. Meals self-service. School shop. No tobacco allowed; alcohol only in upper sixth bar.
Discipline Pupils failing to produce homework once may or may not be punished, depending on the circumstances; those caught smoking cannabis on the premises are likely to be requested to leave the school
Former pupils Chad Varah (founder, The Samaritans); Jack and Tom Buckner (international athletes); Sir David Naish (President NFU).

• WORTH

Worth School, Worth Abbey, Turners Hill, Crawley, West Sussex RH10 4SD. Tel 01342 715 911, Fax 01342 718298

• Pupils 370 • Boys 10–18 (Day/Board) • Girls None • Upper sixth 50 • Termly fees £2555 (Day) £3830 (Board) • HMC, BSA • Enquiries/application to the Headmaster

What it's like

Founded in 1933 as a prep school, in 1959 the upper school was opened for boys of 13+. In 1996 the two schools merged to form a single secondary school for boys of 10–18. Set in an estate of 500 acres of parkland, the Benedictine monastery and school are closely connected. Many of the lay staff live in houses on the estate so that, as far as possible, monks, lay staff and boys form one community. A well-equipped and energetic school, it offers five key features: work, play, love, morality, religion. All are first equal in importance. A Catholic school but Christians of other denominations are admitted. A staff:pupil ratio of about 1:7 – half a dozen or so staff are Benedictine monks. Academic standards are high and results good. Almost all students go on to degree courses, including some to Oxbridge. It is very strong in voluntary service, music, drama and art. There is a wide range of sports and games and an excellent variety of clubs and societies which cater for most extra-curricular activities.

School profile

Pupils Total age range 10–18; 370 boys (40 day, 330 boarding). Senior department 13–18, 300 boys. Main entry ages 10, 11, 13 and a few into sixth.
Entrance Common Entrance at 13, own assemssment at 10 or 11. Parents expected to buy A-level textbooks; £500 maximum extras. Scholarships 10–12 pa (at age 11, 13 and 16+), academic and music, 15%–50% of fees.
Parents 60+% live within 30 miles; 20+% live overseas.
Head and staff *Headmaster:* Father Christopher Jamison, 4 years in post. Educated at

Downside and at Oxford (modern languages) and Heythrop College (theology). Previously Housemaster at Worth. *Staff:* 41 full time, 11 part time. Annual turnover 2–4%. Average age 34.

Exam results In 1995, 75 pupils in fifth form, 44 in upper sixth. *GCSE:* In 1995, 88% fifth form gained at least grade C in 8+ subjects; 10% in 5–7 subjects. *A-levels:* 5 upper sixth passed in 4 subjects; 30 in 3; 7 in 2; and 2 in 1 subject. Average UCAS points 21.0.

University and college entrance Almost all sixth-form leavers go on to a degree course (10% go to Oxbridge); 28% take courses in science and engineering, 70% in humanities and social sciences, 2% in art and design.

Curriculum GCSE and A-levels. 16 GCSE subjects offered; 19 at A-level (no A-level general studies but all sixth-formers take a course on the individual in the community). 20% took science A-levels; 51% arts/humanities; 29% both. *Vocational:* Work experience available. *Computing facilities:* 100+ computers in classrooms and 2 network rooms; new technology centre. *Special provision:* Dyslexia and general special needs support. *Europe:* French, German, Italian and Spanish offered to GCSE and A-level; also French and Spanish AS-level. Regular exchanges (to Belgium, France and Spain).

The arts *Music:* Over 30% pupils learn a musical instrument; instrumental exams are taken. Some 12 musical groups, including string, brass and woodwind groups, orchestra, choral society and informal pop groups. *Drama*: All pupils are involved in school productions. *Art:* On average, 25 take GCSE, 1–2 AS-level, 6 A-level. Photography, pottery and sculpture also offered. Most art students accepted for art college each year, including the Slade.

Sport, community service and clubs *Sport and physical activities:* Main sports: Rugby, soccer, cross-country, cricket, tennis, gym, hockey, athletics. Optional: Golf, badminton, shooting, basketball, swimming, squash, volleyball, fencing, water polo. Over 20 boys each year represent the county in various sports. *Community service:* 100+ boys take part. Pupils take bronze, silver and gold Duke of Edinburgh's Award. *Clubs and societies:* Clubs include chess, classic film, cooking, debating, drama, justice and peace, shooting, technology, vintners.

Uniform School uniform worn throughout.

Houses/prefects Competitive houses. Prefects, head boy, head of house and house prefects – appointed by Headmaster and housemasters.

Religion Sunday Mass and evening prayers by houses. Chaplaincy offers many other outlets eg meditation, pilgrimages.

Social Plays with girls' schools, debates, choral society, sixth-form dances; special relationship developing with Woldingham. Language exchanges, skiing. Meals self-service. School shop. No tobacco allowed; limited alcohol for seniors at school functions and in sixth-form bar.

Boarding All sixth-formers have own study bedroom. Resident qualified nurse; doctor visits regularly. Central dining room. Saturday night exeats as families wish.

Alumni association run by K W Owers, c/o the school.

• WREKIN

Wrekin College, Wellington, Telford, Shropshire TF1 3BG. Tel 01952 240131, Fax 01952 240338 • Pupils 270 • Boys 11–18 (Day/Board 13+) • Girls 11–18 (Day/Board 13+) • Upper sixth 50 • Termly fees £1750–£2060 (Day) £3770 (Board) • HMC, Allied • Enquiries/application to the Headmaster

What it's like

Founded in 1880, it has a fine campus on an estate of about 100 acres stretching out to the Shropshire Plain and backed by the hills of the Wrekin and Ercall. The well-designed and attractive buildings are well dispersed among lawns and gardens with very fine playing fields close by on the edge of the market town. Modern facilities and accommodation are first rate. It was founded as a boys' schools, becoming co-educational in 1977. A C of E foundation, but interdenominational, there is a chapel service four mornings a week. The pastoral care system is of a high order. Academic standards are high and results are good and 90% of sixth-formers go on to degree courses. Music, art and drama departments are very vigorous. Sports and games (there is a wide variety) are an important feature and all take part in some compulsory sport. There have been many county and international representatives. An impressive range of extra-curricular activities. A strong commitment to local community services.

School profile

Pupils Age range 11–18; 270 pupils, 100 day (50 boys, 50 girls), 170 boarding (115 boys, 55 girls). Main entry ages 11 (day only), 13 and into sixth. Approx 10% are children of former pupils. *State school entry:* 7% main intake, plus 10% to sixth.
Entrance Common Entrance and own exam used. No special skills or religious requirements. Parents not expected to buy textbooks. 3 pa assisted places at 11+. 20 pa scholarships/bursaries, 10%–50% of fees.
Parents 15+% in industry or commerce. 10+%, live within 30 miles; up to 10% live overseas.
Head and staff *Headmaster:* P M Johnson, 5 years in post. Educated at Bec School and Oxford (geography). Previously Senior Housemaster at Radley. Also Oxford University representative on the Rugby Football Union Committee; Chairman of Trustees of the Rugby Football Union National Centre for Schools & Youth Rugby. *Staff:* 30 full time, 6 part time. Annual turnover 8%. Average age 35.
Exam results On average, 50+ pupils in upper fifth, 50 in upper sixth. *GCSE:* 80% upper fifth gain at least grade C in 8+ subjects. *A-levels:* Upper sixth pupils pass 2.7 subjects on average. Average UCAS points 18.0.
University and college entrance 90% of sixth-form leavers go on to a degree course (20% after a gap year); others typically go on to farming, local businesses (often family firms). Of those going on to university, 5% go to Oxbridge; 6% take courses in medicine, dentistry and veterinary science, 26% in science and engineering, 35% in humanities and social sciences, 5% in art and design, 5% to other vocational courses (optometry, nursing, accountancy), 23% to other subjects (journalism, acting, estate management, architecture).
Curriculum GCSE and A-levels: 18 A-level and 16 GCSE subjects offered. *Vocational:* Work experience available. RSA stage 1 typing and numeracy offered. *Computing facilities:* Archimedes and numerous IBM PC compatibles available at all times. *Special provision:* Dyslexic unit of three; individual lessons available. *Europe:* French and German offered to GCSE and A-level; Russian GCSE as an extra. Regular exchanges. 2–3 German pupils for 1 or 2 terms in fifth/sixth-form.
The arts *Music:* Over 40% pupils learn a musical instrument; instrumental exams can be taken. Some 10+ musical groups, including barbershop, string quartet, jazz bands, orchestra. *Drama & dance*: A-level theatre studies offered. Some pupils involved in school and in house/other productions. *Art:* On average, 40 take GCSE, 12 A-level; design, pottery, textiles and photography also offered.
Sport, community service and clubs *Sport and physical activities:* Majority take rugby, netball, hockey, athletics, swimming, cricket, rounders, tennis. Optional: Squash, fencing, basketball, fives, badminton, table tennis, gymnastics, horseriding, cycling, self-defence, croquet, etc. GCSE and A-level PE may be taken. National schools croquet champions; many representatives at county and regional level. *Community service:* Pupils take bronze, silver and gold Duke of Edinburgh's Award. CCF compulsory for 4 terms at age 13. Community service. *Clubs and societies:* Over 30 clubs eg car mechanics, conservation, fly fishing, Gilbert & Sullivan, jazz, political, wine and cheese.
Uniform School uniform worn.
Houses/prefects Competitive houses. Prefects, head boy and girl, head of house and house prefects – appointed by the Head and Housemasters.
Religion Daily chapel.
Social Choral works with several local schools. Various organised trips abroad each year (eg canoe trip up Moselle, cycling in Holland, skiing, sports tours). Meals self-service. School shop. No tobacco allowed; alcohol in supervised sixth-form bar.
Discipline High standards of behaviour and manners are expected. The ethos is one of self-discipline and respect for the community.
Boarding 20% have own study bedroom, 40% share (with one other); 20% are in dormitories of 6+. Single-sex houses of 50+. Resident qualified nurse and doctor. Central dining room. Pupils can provide and cook own food. 2 overnight exeats and half-term. Visits to the local town allowed.
Alumni association run by M J Joyner, c/o the college.

Former pupils Sir Peter Gadsden (Lord Mayor of London, 1980); Brian Epstein (Beatles managers); Cyril Holmes (Olympic athlete and rugby player); Harry Andrews (actor); Noel Murless (Keeper of Queen's Racehorses); Sir Peter Inge (Chief of the Defence Staff).

• WYCHWOOD

Wychwood School, 74 Banbury Road, Oxford OX2 6JR. Tel 01865 57976, Fax 01865 56806 • Pupils 160 • Boys None • Girls 11–18 (Day/Board) • Upper sixth 14 • Termly fees £1450 (Day), £2295 (Board) £2225 (Weekly) • GSA, SHA • Enquiries/application to the Headmistress

What it's like

Founded in 1897 it is urban and single-site on the Banbury Road half a mile from the middle of Oxford. It comprises four main houses and sundry other buildings; modern facilities are good. Worship is in the Anglican tradition. The school council plays a large part in the daily organisation. The atmosphere is friendly and relaxed. Academic standards are high and results are good; all sixth-former leavers go on to degree courses. A strong music department (virtually everyone is involved). Drama and art are also strong throughout the school. Full use is made of Oxford's cultural amenities. Adequate sports, games and activities. Some involvement in local community schemes including work experience.

School profile

Pupils Age range 11–18; 160 girls (80 day, 80 boarding). Main entry ages 11, 12, 14 and into sixth. Approx 20% are children of former pupils. Manor and Greycotes schools provide more than 20% of intake. *State school entry:* 20% main intakes.

Entrance Own entrance test used. Interesting children with any special talent encouraged; no religious requirements. Parents expected to buy textbooks for pupils in sixth-form; other extras variable. Sixth form bursaries and creative arts scholarships at 11.

Parents 30+% in industry or commerce; 30+% are doctors, lawyers etc. 30+% live within 30 miles; up to 10% live overseas.

Head and staff *Headmistress:* Mrs M L Duffill, 14 years in post. Educated at Neath Grammar and Westminster College, Oxford (biology). Wychwood is first and only teaching post. Previously ten years of genetic research at Medical Research Council (Harwell) and Atomic Energy of Canada Research Department. *Staff:* 14 full time, 12 part time. Annual turnover 1%. Average age 40.

Exam results In 1995, 33 pupils in upper fifth, 14 in upper sixth. *GCSE:* In 1995, 93% upper fifth gained at least grade C in 8+ subjects; 7% in 5–7 subjects. *A-levels:* 11 upper sixth passed in 3 subjects. Average UCAS points 20.0.

University and college entrance All sixth-form leavers go on to a degree course (20% after a gap year). 10% go to Oxbridge; 10% take courses in medicine, dentistry and veterinary science, 20% in science and engineering, 10% in law, 30% in humanities and social sciences, 20% in art and design, 10% other vocational subjects.

Curriculum GCSE and A-levels. 14 subjects offered (including GCSE and A-level photography). 45% take science A-levels; 45% arts/humanities; 10% both. *Vocational:* RSA level I-III typing offered. Work experience available for fifth year pupils. *Computing facilities:* Research machines; 1 girl to each computer. *Europe:* French, German and Italian offered to GCSE and A-level; also business studies French in sixth. Regular exchanges. Visits to Normandy (years 7 and 8), Grenoble (years 10–11) and Paris (sixth-form).

The arts *Music:* Over 75% pupils learn a musical instrument; instrumental exams can be taken. Musical groups include orchestra, choir, various chamber groups. Many pupils play in Thames Valley Youth Orchestra and county orchestra; one plays in youth big band. *Drama & dance*: Both offered. Majority of pupils are involved in school productions. One pupil has sung in 2 productions of English National Opera 1993. *Art:* On average, 15 take GCSE, 4 A-level. Textiles and photography also offered. 1 third year pupil has had pictures hung in local gallery.

Sport, community service and clubs *Sport and physical activities:* Compulsory sports: hockey, tennis, netball, rounders, swimming, cross country. Optional: squash, badminton, aerobics, keep fit, judo, fencing. BAGA exams may be taken. *Community service:*

Pupils take bronze, silver and gold Duke of Edinburgh's Award. Community service compulsory for 1 year at age 16. *Clubs and societies:* Some 10 clubs, eg gym, Caribbean dancing, drama, chess, pottery, debating, jewellery/hat making and others as requested.
Uniform School uniform worn except in the sixth.
Houses/prefects No competitive houses. No prefects but councillors elected by the school. Head girl appointed by Headmistress. School Council.
Religion Church attendance compulsory in first three years.
Social Theatre, operas, lectures etc organised. Use of the city and university facilities. First and fourth year have week's visit to Normandy. Field trips in UK. Pupils allowed to bring own bike to school in the third year. Meals informal. School tuckshop, opens twice a week. No tobacco/alcohol allowed.
Discipline The school has a well-tried and proven system of Majors which the girls promoted and therefore adhere to. A pupil caught drinking, smoking, or going out of school without permission could expect to be sent home immediately.
Boarding Upper sixth have own study bedroom, lower sixth share (2 or 3); all others in dormitories of up to 6. Central dining room. 2 weekend and 4 day exeats each term. Visits to city allowed for fourth form and above.

• WYCLIFFE

Wycliffe College, Stonehouse, Gloucestershire GL10 2JQ. Tel 01453 822432, Fax 01453 827634
• Pupils 350 • Boys 13–18 (Day/Board) • Girls 13–18 (Day/Board) • Upper sixth 85 • Termly fees £2730 (Day) £3995 (Board) • HMC • Enquiries/application to the Headmaster

What it's like

Founded in 1882 by G W Sibly, the first headmaster. It became a public school in 1931, by which time the Sibly family had given it a distinctive character which included a 'sturdy Protestant independence'. Originally a boys' school, it first admitted girls in 1971. It enjoys a very fine 60-acre, semi-rural site in the Gloucestershire countryside and is within easy range of Gloucester, Cheltenham, Bath and Bristol. The buildings – some dating from the sixteenth century, and some typically Cotswold – are loosely scattered over a campus which has magnificent grounds and playing fields. Many recent developments, including sixth-form houses (with ensuite facilities), a boarding house (with sauna and jacuzzi), a swimming pool and a science centre. The junior school is on an adjacent 27-acre site. It is interdenominational (the fine chapel was built by pupils and staff in the 1950s) and pupils from other religions are welcomed. An international flavour is provided by expatriate pupils and representatives of other nationalities. A well-organised school in which there is much enterprise and energy. Academic results are good and many pupils go on to degree courses, including to Oxbridge. The school originated a development sixth, a flexible one-year course before the 2-year A-level course. There is much strength in music, drama,art and design and technology. An excellent range of sports and games, including rowing, with a large number of representatives at county and national level. Over 90 extra-curricular activities, including CCF and the Duke of Edinburgh's Award Scheme.

School profile

Pupils Age range 13–18; 350 pupils, 142 day (94 boys, 48 girls), 208 boarding (147 boys, 61 girls). Main entry ages 13 and into sixth. Approx 5% are children of former pupils. Own junior school provides more than 40% of intake (transfer is automatic). *State school entry:* 5% main intake, plus 45% to sixth.
Entrance Common Entrance and own scholarship exams used. All skills welcomed; no religious requirements. 32 pa assisted places. 40 pa scholarships, 5%–50% of fees.
Parents 15+% are in industry or commerce. 30+% live within 30 miles; 15+% live overseas.
Head and staff *Headmaster:* David Prichard, in post from 1994. Educated at Radley and Oxford. Previously Headmaster at Port Regis and teacher at Monkton Combe and a lecturer. Also Governor of four schools; former chairman of Smallpiece Trust for Industrial Design; Co-chairman, Operation New World; Freeman of the City of London. *Staff:* 39 full time, 6 part time. Average age 38.
Exam results In 1995, 63 pupils in Year 11, 62 in upper sixth. *GCSE:* In 1995, 43 Year 11

gained at least grade C in 8+ subjects; 7 in 5–7 subjects. *A-levels:* 9 upper sixth passed in 4+ subjects; 35 in 3; 9 in 2; and 8 in 1 subject. Average UCAS points 19.6.

University and college entrance 95% of 1995 sixth-form leavers went on to a degree course (25% after a gap year); others typically go on to armed forces, family business. Of those going on to university, 10% went to Oxbridge; 7% took courses in medicine, dentistry and veterinary science, 20% in science and engineering, 3% in law, 28% in humanities and social sciences, 11% in art and design, 20% in vocational subjects eg business, landscape architecture, education, hotel managemnt, 11% in other subjects eg philosophy, computer visualisation.

Curriculum GCSE and A-levels: 18 GCSE subjects; 7 AS-level; 21 A-level (including theatre studies, sports studies, classical civilization and history of art). Lower sixth take Diploma of Achievement; also one year develpment course for sixth-form pupils wishing to spend further year preparing for A-levels and for pupils from overseas (comprises study for Certificate in Further Studies; information technology; foreign language skills; management and leadership training). 9% take science A-levels; 44% arts/humanities; 46% both. *Vocational:* Work experience available; also AEB Certificate in Further Studies in English/French for business. *Computing facilities:* Purpose-built computing department. *Special provision:* Individual EFL lessons; support English; specialist dyslexic provision. *Europe:* French, German and Spanish offered to GCSE and A-level; also French AS-level and A-Level French for Professional Use.

The arts *Music:* Over 30% of pupils learn a musical instrument and take instrumental exams. Some 8 musical groups including orchestra, strings, concert band, jazz orchestras, choirs, plus chamber groups. Several pupils in county youth orchestras, 1 National Youth Orchestra. *Drama & dance*: Drama and dance offered; GCSE and A-level theatre studies may be taken. School productions and plays popular. *Art:* On average, 25 take GCSE, 10 A-level. Design, pottery, photography, printmaking also offered.

Sport, community service and clubs *Sport and physical activities:* All optional: rugby, hockey, netball, squash, badminton, swimming, soccer, rowing, cricket, fencing, basketball, weights, athletics, canoeing, sub-aqua, climbing, cross-country. County representatives in athletics, cricket; county winners in hockey, netball and rugby (U16, U19); district/regional winners in hockey, netball (U16); also rugby England schools, England students; rowing, national regatta successes and national and international U21 representative. *Community service:* Pupils take bronze, silver and gold Duke of Edinburgh's Award. CCF and community service both optional. *Clubs and societies:* Numerous clubs, eg car mechanics, life drawing, business, French film, board games, bridge, music, pottery, rifle shooting.

Uniform School uniform worn throughout.

Houses/prefects Competitive houses. Prefects, head boy/girl, head of house and house prefects – appointed by Head.

Religion Worship encouraged. Compulsory daily chapel (certain faiths excused), Sunday service for boarders. Resident chaplain.

Social Sixth-form centre organised by pupils; discos, debates, quizzes with local schools; skiing, language, rugby, rowing trips abroad. Day pupils in upper sixth allowed to bring own car/bike/motorbike to school. Meals self-service. School shop (stationery, sports equipment, toiletries). No tobacco/alcohol allowed.

Discipline Detention to upgrade work; fines for smoking; help for drug experimenters; expulsion for pushing drugs.

Boarding 35% have own study bedroom, 35% share, 35% in dormitories of 4–6. Single sex houses of approximately 45. Three upper sixth houses with study bedrooms (ensuite bathrooms). Qualified nurse/doctor. Pupils can provide and cook own food. Frequent exeats possible. Visits to local town allowed.

Alumni association run by Frank Smith, c/o the college.

Former pupils Jeremy Nicholas and Mike Gwilym (actors); Simon Coombs MP; Air Chief Marshal Sir Michael Graydon; Jon Silkin (poet).

• WYCOMBE ABBEY

Wycombe Abbey School, High Wycombe, Buckinghamshire HP11 1PE. Tel 01494 520381, Fax 01494 473836

• Pupils 510 • Boys None • Girls 11–18 (Board/very few Day) • Upper sixth 85 • Termly fees £3060 (Day) £4080 (Board) • GSA • Enquiries to the Admissions Secretary • Application to the Head Mistress

What it's like

Founded in 1896, it is near the centre of High Wycombe. The main building is a very large mansion in 160 acres of fine grounds. Exceptionally good modern facilities and comfortable boarding accommodation are provided. Academic standards are extremely high and results excellent. Almost all girls go on to degree courses, including many to Oxbridge. It is a C of E school with its own chapel and all pupils are required to attend daily prayers and a Sunday service. Scripture lessons are also obligatory. A fine range of sports, games and activities is available and there are many representatives at county level. Strong in music, art and drama, with a very high level of participation. There is a strong commitment to local community schemes and the school has an excellent record in the Duke of Edinburgh's Award Scheme.

School profile

Pupils Age range 11–18; 510 girls (491 boarding, 19 day). Main entry ages 11, 12, 13 and the sixth. Approx 4% are children of former pupils. *State school entry:* 2% main intake.
Entrance Common Entrance exam used. Special skills are always of interest; no religious requirements. Parents expected to buy some textbooks; other extras variable. 10 pa junior, 3 pa sixth-form scholarships/bursaries, 10%–50% fees.
Parents Up to 20% live within 30 miles; 13% are overseas pupils.
Head and staff *Headmistress:* Mrs Judith Goodland, in post 7 years. Educated at Howell's (Denbigh), and Bristol University (modern languages) and Charlotte Mason College (education). Previously Headmistress at St George's (Ascot).
Exam results In 1995, 81 pupils in upper fifth, 85 in upper sixth. *GCSE:* In 1995, all upper fifth gained grade C or above in 8+ subjects. *A-levels:* 100% passed in 3+ subjects. Average UCAS points 27.0.
University and college entrance 98% of 1995 sixth-form leavers went on to a degree course, 25% went to Oxbridge; 12% took courses in medicine, dentistry and veterinary science, 30% in science and engineering, 56% in humanities and social sciences, 2% in art and design.
Curriculum GCSE and A-levels. 23 subjects at GCSE and A-level, including drama GCSE, Japanese A-level; no general studies. 25% take science A-levels; 50% arts/humanities; 25% both. *Vocational:* Work experience available. RSA exams offered. Weekly lectures for sixth-form from distinguished lecturers. *Computing facilities:* Two fully equipped computer rooms with Nimbus network, 36 terminals. *Europe:* French, German, Spanish, Italian and Russian offered to A-level. Regular exchanges Spain; for sixth-formers to France and Germany.
The arts *Music:* Over 70% pupils learn a musical instrument; instrumental exams can be taken. Some 14 musical groups, including 2 orchestras, choirs, wind band, clarinet groups, jazz group, chamber music (strings and flute), concert jazz band, choral society. Reached final of National Chamber competition recently; choir tours every 2 years (eg Hungary and Italy). Annual choral concert with Eton. *Drama & dance:* Both offered; GCSE drama, Poetry Society, LAMDA, RAD exams may be taken. Majority of pupils are involved in school and/or house/other productions. Winners of ESU Shakespeare-on-the-Platform competition; pupils regularly in National Youth Theatre. *Art:* On average, 20 take GCSE, 8 A-level, 12 A-level History of Art.
Sport, community service and clubs *Sport and physical activities:* Compulsory sports: lacrosse, tennis, netball, gymnastics, swimming, athletics, health-related fitness, trampolining, dance. Optional: fencing, extra tennis, karate, rowing, hockey, gym club, dance club, self defence, sailing, rock climbing, canoeing, hill walking, golf, rugby, squash. Sixth form and upper fifth only: volleyball, basketball, aerobics. RLSS exams may be taken. 10 county lacrosse players, 3 territorial; 1 black belt karate; 1 county cross country; 3 county athletics. *Community service:* Pupils take bronze, silver and gold Duke of Edinburgh's Award. Community service compulsory for 2 terms in sixth-form. *Clubs*

and societies: Up to 30 clubs eg philosophy, classical, chess, bridge, fine arts, wine, science.
Uniform School uniform worn except in the upper sixth.
Houses/prefects Competitive houses. Prefects, head girl, head of house and house prefects. School Council.
Religion Church of England worship compulsory.
Social Caledonian Society, choir, debating society, public speaking and dining clubs with boys' schools. Bi-annual organised choir trip to Europe, cultural visits. School shop. No tobacco allowed; alcohol only on certain occasions.
Boarding Pupils divided into different houses of approx 42, same as competitive houses.
Former pupils Lord Justice Butler-Sloss; Lady Elspeth Howe (Project 2000).

• WYNSTONES

Wynstones, Church Lane, Whaddon, Gloucester GL4 0UF. Tel 01452 22475, Fax 01452 525667
• Pupils 290 • Boys 4–18 (Day/Board/Weekly) • Girls 4–18 (Day/Board/Weekly) • Upper sixth 15 • Termly fees £860–£1250 (Day) £1695–£2085 (Board) £1456-£1846 (Weekly) • Steiner
• Enquiries/application to the College of Teachers

What it's like

Founded as a co-educational school, it has an agreeable semi-rural site with well-equipped buildings and gardens; the school farm is close by. Its programme is based on Rudolf Steiner principles, with the education following the inner developmental stages of the child. In the kindergarten, the main emphasis is on the development of the will, through play and group activities such as games, songs, verses, stories, artistic and practical work. In the lower school the emphasis is on the education of the heart – the life of feelings – to awaken imagination and a sound social sense. In the upper school the emphasis shifts to the development of clear thinking and the exercise of healthy critical judgement. A few pupils go on to degree courses each year, including Oxbridge. Music, drama and art are much emphasised. A full gym, sports and games programme is available and there are some extra-curricular activities.

School profile

Pupils Total age range 4–18; 290 pupils, 270 day (133 boys, 137 girls), 20 boarding (11 boys, 9 girls). Main entry ages, 6–7 and into the sixth. *State school entry:* 5% senior intake.
Entrance Entrance by interview. No special skills or religious requirements.
Parents 60+% live within 30 miles; up to 10% live overseas.
Head and staff Chairman of College of Teachers changes annually. *Staff:* 21 full time, 18 part time. Annual turnover 2%. Average age 40.
Exam results On average, 20+ pupils in upper fifth, 15 in upper sixth. *GCSE:* On average, 60% gain at least grade C in 5–7 subjects; and 35% in 1–4 subjects. *A-levels:* Some upper sixth pass in 2 subjects, some in 1. Average UCAS points 9.9.
University and college entrance 45% of 1995 sixth-form leavers go on to a degree course, 8% go to Oxbridge; 60% take courses in humanities and social sciences, 20% in art and design, 20% in drama/acting.
Curriculum GCSE and A-levels. 14 subjects offered (no A-level general studies). *Vocational:* Work experience available. *Special provision:* SEN provision; EFL course. *Europe:* French and German offered from age 7 up to A-level. Regular exchanges. Up to 5% pupils are European (French, German, Spanish). EFL programme included.
The arts (Pupils age 11 and over) *Music:* 70% pupils learn a musical instrument; instrumental exams can be taken. Musical groups include 3 orchestras, 2 choirs, wind ensemble, class groups, recorder groups. Recent productions include Les Miserables and the St Matthew Passion – all pupils age 14+ took part. *Drama & dance*: Drama and dance (eurythmy) offered; GCSE drama may be taken. All pupils are involved in school productions. *Art:* On average, 20 take GCSE, 5 A-level. Textiles, woodwork, basket-making, metalwork and bookbinding also offered. Each year a number of pupils go on to study art and music.
Sport, community service and clubs (Pupils age 11 and over) *Sport and physical activities:* Compulsory sports: hockey, basketball, gymnastics. Optional: tennis, swim-

ming. Basketball, county champions for past 2 years. *Clubs and societies:* Some 5 clubs eg basketball, drama, chamber orchestra.
Uniform Agreed dress code.
Houses/prefects No competitive houses or prefects.
Religion Non-denominational Christian assemblies/festivals.
Social Sporting functions with local schools. Organised trips abroad with other Rudolf Steiner schools. Pupils allowed to bring own car/bike/motorbike/horse to school. Meals self-service. No tobacco/alcohol allowed.
Discipline Pupils failing to produce homework would expect to stay in after school. Those caught smoking cannabis on the premises would be expelled.
Boarding In local, selected private family homes of school parents.
Alumni association run by Mrs Faith Hall, c/o the school.

Y

• YARM 

Yarm School, The Friarage, Yarm, Cleveland TS15 9EJ. Tel 01642 786023
• Pupils 780 • Boys 4–18 (Day) • Girls 16–18 (Day) • Upper sixth 90 • Termly fees £850–£1657 (Day) • HMC, SHMIS • Enquiries/application to the Registrar

What it's like

Yarm School is a boys' day grammar school, established in its present form in 1978; the sixth-form is co-educational. The major buildings are located at the Friarage, an 18th-century mansion in 14 acres of pleasant grounds alongside the River Tees. The prep school is adjacent. Excellent modern facilities are provided including a 400-seat theatre and a new science centre; a technology building is currently under construction. Academic standards are high and results good. Most leavers go on to degree courses. Music, drama and art are given considerable attention and a wide variety of sports and games are played. An extensive array of activities range from debating to rock climbing. The Duke of Edinburgh's Award Scheme attracts many participants and there is a CCF.

School profile

Pupils Total age range 4–18; 780 day pupils (745 boys, 35 girls). Senior department 11–18, 520 pupils (485 boys, 35 girls). Main entry ages 4, 5, 10, 11, 13 (boys), and into sixth (boys and girls). *State school entry:* 25% senior intake, plus several to sixth.

Entrance Common Entrance or own exam used. No religious requirements. Parents expected to buy some textbooks in sixth-form; lunches (£69) extra. 40 scholarships/bursaries at all age ranges, up to 33% of fees. 18 pa assisted places.

Parents 15+% in industry or commerce; 22+% are doctors, lawyers etc.

Head and staff *Headmaster:* Robin Neville Tate, in post for 18 years. Educated at Workshop and at universities of Southampton (engineering), Oxford (education) and Durham (history). Previously Head of Sixth Form House at Ardingley. *Staff:* 57 full time, 19 part time. Annual turnover 5% Average age 37.

Exam results In 1995, 72 pupils in fifth, 65 in upper sixth. *GCSE:* in 1995, 67 upper fifth gained at least grade C in 8+ subjects; and 3 in 5–7 subjects. *A-levels:* 49 upper sixth passed in 4+ subjects; 13 in 3; 3 in 2 subjects. Average UCAS points 20.7.

University and college entrance 96% of 1995 sixth-form leavers went on to a degree course (5% after a gap year); others typically go on to foundation courses. Of those going on to university, 7% went to Oxbridge; 19% took courses in medicine, dentistry and veterinary science, 39% in science and engineering, 31% in humanities and social sciences, 7% in art and design.

Curriculum GCSE, AS and A-levels. 21 subjects offered (including business studies, politics, A-level general studies for all sixth). 62% take science A-levels; 33% arts/humanities; 5% both. *Vocational:* Work experience available. *Computing facilities:* Two main computer rooms each have 20 486 PCs; other room has Acorn 500s; 37 other computers. *Special provision:* English as a foreign language. *Europe:* French and German offered from age 8 to GCSE, AS and A-level; also Italian and Spanish to GCSE and A-level. Regular exchanges to France and Germany. A few German pupils (age 16–17) spend 1 term in school.

The arts (Pupils age 11 and over) *Music:* 29% learn a musical instrument; instrumental exams can be taken. 12 musical groups including orchestras, jazz band, wind band, chamber group, madrigal singers, church choir. One pupil in National Youth Orchestra, one in quarter-final of Young Musician of the Year Competition. *Drama & dance*: Drama offered: GCSE drama and A-level theatre studies may be taken. Some pupils involved in school, majority in house/other productions. One pupil played lead in National Youth Music Theatre USA tour. *Art:* On average, 18 take GCSE, 4 A-level. Design and photography also offered.

Sport, community service and clubs (Pupils age 11 and over) *Sport and physical activities:* Compulsory sports: Rugby, hockey, cricket, athletics, tennis. Optional:

Squash, rowing, badminton, basketball, fencing. County rugby champions U13, U14, U15; U18 hockey (indoor), Northern champions. *Community service:* Pupils take bronze, silver and gold Duke of Edinburgh's Award. Community service optional for sixth-form. Active CCF. *Clubs and societies:* Up to 30 clubs eg debating, chess, photography, canoe, dry slope skiing, go-karting, creative writing, history, conservation, radio-controlled aircraft, drama groups, jazz club.
Uniform School uniform worn, modified in the sixth.
Houses/prefects Competitive houses. Prefects, head of school, head of house and house prefects – appointed by the Head.
Religion One compulsory chapel service per week.
Social Joint concerts and orchestral occasions with local musical societies. About 8 organised trips abroad each year plus regular exchanges with French and German schools. Sixth-form pupils allowed to bring own car to school. Meals self-service. Uniform shop; tuck shop. No tobacco/alcohol allowed.
Discipline In its approach to discipline, the school relies mainly on the pupils' own sense of personal responsibility. A system of 'discredits' is operated in addition to direct punishments such as detentions or extra work. A first offence of smoking a cigarette would attract 5 discredits, 10 for a second offence. If 40 discredits are acquired in a single school year the pupil must be withdrawn from the school.
Alumni association is run by C Daniels, c/o The Friarage, Yarm, Cleveland.

• YEHUDI MENUHIN

The Yehudi Menuhin School, Stoke d'Abernon, Cobham, Surrey KT11 3QQ. Tel 01932 864739, Fax 01932 864633

Pupils 50 • Boys 8–18 (Board) • Girls 8–18 (Board) • Upper sixth 9 • Termly fees £6481 (Board) • SHMIS, SHA, BSA • Enquiries/application to the Headmaster

What it's like

Founded in 1963 by Lord Menuhin, with the help of his colleague and friend Marcel Gazelle to provide the ideal conditions in which musically gifted boys and girls might develop their potential to the full. The buildings are sited in 18 acres of delightful gardens and grounds in a semi-rural area. The main building is a Gothic house dating from 1810. This houses the younger children and contains dining room, kitchen and elegant music rooms. The older boys are accommodated in the other main building, the White House, which contains the science laboratories and school offices. There are modern additions and the school is now very well equipped. It has an international reputation producing many distinguished musicians. Much of the teaching is done on a one-to-one basis. Apart from the music tuition which is provided for stringed instruments and piano, there is a broad general education to a high standard. About half of each day is devoted to musical studies. All pupils receive guidance in composition and take part in composers' workshops. To develop body suppleness and good posture, training in the Alexander technique is provided. As languages are an important asset for a travelling musician, French is compulsory for all students (except for the many overseas students where EFL is compulsory); German and Russian are also offered. In addition, all pupils are encouraged to work in a wide variety of media, including painting, ceramics, jewellery and textiles. The grounds are well equipped for leisure activities. Sports and games are regarded as important in a pupil's general development. Overall, the school has a highly civilized creative atmosphere and environment which fulfils the founder's intentions.

School profile

Pupils Total age range 8–18, 50 boarding pupils, boys and girls. Main entry age 8–13. Nearly 50% from overseas.
Entrance By stringent audition. Pupils must be musically gifted; no religious requirements. All EC students qualify for an Aided Place (overseas pupils qualify for the Scheme after three years' residence at the school). Provision for dyslexic pupils and those with special diets.
Head and staff *Headmaster:* Nicolas Chisholm, in post 8 years. Educated at Christ's Hospital and Cambridge (classics). Previously Head of Classics and Housemaster at Hurstpierpoint College, Classics and English Teacher at the Prebendal School, Chiche-

ster. Also Chairman of Sussex Association of Classics Teachers; Vice Chairman of SE Arts Performing Arts Advisory Panel. *Staff:* 17 full time staff. 22 part time. Annual turnover 10%. Average age 40.

Exam results In 1995, 4 in upper fifth, 7 in upper sixth. *GCSE:* 3 in upper fifth gained at least grade C in 5–7 subjects. *A-levels:* 2 upper sixth passed in 3 subjects; 2 in 2; 3 in 1 subject (pupils passed all the A-levels they took). As a specialist music school, the pupils take a more restricted range and number of subjects than at other schools.

University and college entrance All sixth-form leavers go on to degree courses to study music at national conservatoires.

The arts *Music:* All pupils learn at least two musical instruments. Some 14 musical groups including orchestra, 2 choirs, 10 chamber music groups. Winner of string section BBC Young Musician of the Year 1992; winner of Australia Prize Royal Overseas League 1993; Woking musician of the year; Audi Junior Musician 1993. *Drama & dance*: Drama offered. Some pupils involved in school productions. *Art:* Pottery, textiles, batik also offered.

Sport, community service and clubs *Sport and physical activities:* Compulsory sports: football, aerobics etc. Optional: badminton, tennis, swimming. *Clubs and societies:* Up to 5 clubs, eg debating, chess, badminton.

Uniform No school uniform worn.

Houses/prefects No competitive houses or prefects.

Religion No compulsory attendance at religious worship.

Social Concert tours to France, Switzerland, USA. Pupils allowed to bring own bike to school. Lunch formal, other meals self-service. No tobacco/alcohol allowed.

Discipline As the school is a small family, the aim is to keep sanctions to a minimum (extra work on a Saturday afternoon, gating or rustication with expulsion as the final resort for a serious offence like drugs or stealing).

• YORK COLLEGE FOR GIRLS

York College for Girls, 62 Low Petergate, York YO1 2HZ. Tel 01904 646421

• Pupils 170 • Boys 3–11 only (Day) • Girls 3–18 (Day) • Upper sixth 14 • Termly fees £350–£1790 (Day) • GSA, CSCL • Enquiries/application to the Head

What it's like

Founded in 1908, it is right in the city centre in the shadow of the Minster. Its very attractive buildings incorporate 15th-century, Georgian and Victorian architecture, plus a big modern wing and new sixth-form centre. The (co-educational) junior school is nearby and the playing fields are 7 minutes' walk away. It follows Anglican tradition and worship and keeps close links with the cathedral. A balanced all-round education is provided and pupils are taught by specialists throughout the school. Academic standards are high and results very good. All sixth-formers go on to degree courses. It is tremendously strong in music and drama. Very many pupils learn an instrument and most are involved at some time or another in dramatic productions. A good range of games and sports is available and there are plenty of activities. There is full commitment to local community schemes. There are regular exchanges with France, Germany and America.

School profile

Pupils Total age range 3–18; 170 day pupils (14 boys, 156 girls). Senior department 11–18, 120 girls. Main entry ages 3, 5, 8 (boys and girls), 11, 13 and into sixth (girls). Approx 2% are children of former pupils. *State school entry:* 50% senior intake, plus 3% to sixth.

Entrance Own entrance exam used (at 11 and 13). Anglican school but accepts pupils of all religious persuasions. Parents not expected to buy textbooks; extras include music, drama etc (£70 per term). 16 pa scholarships, 2–4 bursaries.

Head and staff *Headmistress:* Mrs Erica Taylor, appointed 1995. Educated at St Anne's Convent, Southampton, and the universities of East Anglia (mathematics and physics), Southampton and the Open University (education management). Previously founding Housemistress at Bootham and at Lancing, Head of Resources at King Edward VI School and Head of Physics at Atherley, both in Southampton. *Staff:* 10 full time, 21 part time. Annual turnover 5%. Average age between 40 and 50.

Exam results In 1995, 15 pupils in Year 11, 14 in upper sixth. *GCSE:* In 1995, 85% upper fifth gained at least grade C in 8+ subjects. *A-levels:* 2 upper sixth passed in 5+ subjects; 5 in 4; 2 in 3; and 2 in 1 subject. Average UCAS points 21.6 (including general studies 28.4).
University and college entrance All 1995 sixth-form leavers went on to a degree course (8% after a gap year), average of 12 % go to Oxbridge; 10% took courses in medicine, dentistry and veterinary science, 40% in science and engineering, 10% in law, 35% in humanities and social sciences, 5% in art and design.
Curriculum GCSE and A-levels. 19 subjects offered (including A-level general studies). 53% take arts/humanities A-levels; 47% both arts and sciences. *Vocational:* Work experience available. *Computing facilities:* Computer network to 2 resource areas; computers in most departments and in sixth-form centre. *Europe:* French and German offered at GCSE and A-level (French compulsory from age 5, German from 11); also Spanish GCSE in sixth-form. Regular exchanges. Satellite TV in sixth-form centre to increase language and European cultural awareness.
The arts (Pupils age 11 and over) *Music:* Over 50% pupils learn a musical instrument; instrumental exams can be taken. Musical groups: choir, concert band, chamber groups, orchestra. Three trophies at Harrogate Music Festival recently. *Drama & dance*: Drama offered. GCSE drama, A-level theatre studies, Guildhall and LAMDA exams may be taken. Majority of pupils are involved in school and other productions (Twelfth Night recently). *Art:* On average, 15 take GCSE, 3 A-level. Textiles also offered.
Sport, community service and clubs (Pupils age 11 and over) *Sport and physical activities:* Compulsory sports: tennis, rounders, swimming, hockey, athletics and cross-country. Optional: skiing. Sixth form only: fencing, badminton, squash. 4 recently selected for English Schools skiing training squad. *Community service:* Optional. *Clubs and societies:* Up to 10 clubs eg green, swimming, badminton, choir, fencing, crime prevention group.
Uniform School uniform worn except in the sixth.
Houses/prefects No houses or prefects. Head girl and deputy – elected by the staff and sixth-form.
Religion Daily assembly. Termly Eucharists and other services in the Minster. Saints Day communion in own chapel.
Social Organised trips abroad and exchange systems. Pupils allowed to bring own car/bike/motorbike to school. Meals self-service. No tobacco/alcohol allowed.
Discipline Pupils failing to produce homework once might expect a 'returned lesson' or a disorder mark; more serious offences could expect parental involvement and possible expulsion.
Alumni association run by Mrs G Sharper, Secretary OGA, Manor Garth, Church Lane, Skelton, York.
Former pupils Dame Janet Baker.

What's where

A geographical search index

This search index helps you find schools in a particular area which meet your requirements – for instance co-educational or single-sex, an assisted place or a scholarship.

UK SCHOOLS

These are presented under England, Northern Ireland, Scotland and Wales. In England, they are grouped by county, according to their postal address.

England

Europe and Hong Kong

Schools teaching the British curriculum are arranged under selected European countries and Hong Kong:

HOW TO READ THE TEN COLUMNS

Name of School	Boys/ Girls/ Co-ed	Day/ Board/ Weekly	Max termly fees	Financial help	Intake Age/ Prep	Special strengths	Special provisions	Religion	Affiliations

Name of School
This is the title under which you can look it up in the entry *School Reports*.

Asterisk (*)
Some schools in England and Wales are marked with *, which indicates that typically all sixth formers take three A-levels and pass all three with good grades – say, between 2 As and a B through to a B and 2 Cs. Schools marked with two asterisks (**) are schools with exceptional results – and therefore with exceptional pupils. This method of highlighting schools only applies in England and Wales; it is NOT used in Scotland, Northern Ireland, overseas or in any school offering the IB. They are crude indicators, not intended to imply that some schools are better than others; they are intended to highlight the relatively academic schools, which will best suit relatively academic children. Some bright children will, of course, get good grades in schools that accept a broader range of abilities.

Boys/Girls/Co-ed
This shows which pupils are accepted at secondary level in the school. A mixed sixth means only the sixth form is co-educational.

Day/Board/Weekly
This shows the type of attendance offered.

Max termly fees
These are the maximum fees for summer term 1996. Where full and weekly boarding fees are identical, only one figure is given.

Financial help
This outlines financial help on offer at the school (Asst places = Government assisted places; Schols = scholarships).

Intake age/Prep
This shows the main intake age(s) to the school and whether a secondary school has its own prep/junior.

Special strengths
This highlights the artistic, sporting and extra-curricular activities in which the school is strong. If the school is a specialist school, this is indicated explicitly.

Special provisions
This notes some specialist provision offered, mostly for dyslexic pupils or the teaching of English as a Foreign Language. It does not suggest that the school specialises in pupils with such difficulties.

Religion
The religion that predominates, not necessarily that from which pupils are exclusively drawn.

Affiliation
The affiliation of the school or the Head. It excludes bursars, governing bodies and prep/junior schools affiliations.

This geographical search index provides summary information only. Please read the full descriptions in the *School Reports*.

Name of School	Boys/ Girls/ Co-ed	Day/ Board/ Weekly	Max termly fees	Financial help	Intake Age/ Prep	Special strengths	Special provisions	Religion	Affiliations

England

AVON									
Badminton *	Girls	Day Board	£2075 £3750	Schols 20 pa	7, 11–13, 16	Music, Drama, Art		Inter-denom	GSA ECIS
Bath High *	Girls	Day	£1328	Asst places Schols	11, 16 Own junior	Pastoral system	Dyslexia	Non-denom	GSA GPDST
Bristol Cathedral *	Boys Mixed sixth	Day	£1398	Asst places 35 pa Schols	10, 11, 16	Music, Drama		C of E	CSA
Bristol Grammar *	Co-ed	Day	£1296	Asst places 50 pa Schols 7 pa	7, 11 13, 16	Drama, Sport		Inter-denom	HMC
Clifton *	Co-ed	Day Boarding	£2810 £4050	Asst places Schols 24 pa	13, 16 Own prep	Music, Art	Jewish House	Christian, Jewish	HMC
Clifton High *	Girls	Day Boarding Weekly	£1425 £2720 £2585	Asst places 23 pa Schols 20 pa	3, 7, 10, 11, 16	Music, Drama, Art, Sport		Christian	GSA
Colston's Collegiate	Co-ed	Day Boarding Weekly	£1915 £3530 £3380	Asst places 15 pa Schols 8 pa	11, 13, 16 Own junior	Sport, Drama	Dyslexia	C of E	HMC SHMIS
Colston's Girls	Girls	Day	£1195	Asst places 24 pa Schols 8 pa Bursaries	10	Music, Art, Languages		Non-denom	GSA
Downside	Boys	Day Boarding	£1980 £3710	Schols Bursaries	10, 13, 16	EC links, Music, Sport	EFL, Dyslexia, Physical and visual handicap	RC	HMC
King's Edward's (Bath) *	Boys Mixed sixth	Day	£1431	Asst places 18 pa Schols 5 pa Bursaries	11, 13, 16 Own junior	Music, Drama, Sport, Outdoor pursuits		Non-denom	HMC
Kingswood	Co-ed	Day Boarding Weekly	£2333 £3720	Asst places 6 pa Schols/ Bursaries	11, 13, 16 Own prep	Art, Sport	EFL, Some special needs help	Methodist	HMC
Monkton Combe	Co-ed	Day Boarding	£2695 £3895	Asst places 10 pa Schols 12 pa Bursaries 8 pa	11, 13, 16 Own junior	Sport, Art, Music, CCF	EFL, Dyslexia	Christian	HMC
MPW (Bristol)	Co-ed	Day Boarding	£2163	Schols 6 pa	15+				CIFE
Prior Park	Co-ed	Day Boarding	£1857 £3358	Asst places Schols	11, 13, 16 Own prep	Art, Music, Drama	EFL	RC	HMC

Name of School	Boys/ Girls/ Co-ed	Day/ Board/ Weekly	Max termly fees	Financial help	Intake Age/ Prep	Special strengths	Special provisions	Religion	Affiliations
Queen Elizabeth's Hospital *	Boys	Day Boarding	£1305 £2319	Asst places 25 pa Schols 6 pa Bursaries	11, 13	Music, Rugby, Cricket		Christian	HMC
Red Maids' *	Girls	Day Boarding	£1240 £2480	Asst places 25 pa Schols 8 pa	11, 16	Music, Sport, Creative design	EFL	Non-denom	GSA
Redland High *	Girls	Day	£1400	Asst places Schols Bursaries	11, 16	Art, Music		Christian	GSA SHA
Royal (Bath)	Girls	Day Boarding	£1962 £3560	Schols 20 pa Exhibitions	3, 5, 7, 9, 11, 13, 16	Music, Drama, Lacrosse	Special needs dept, EFL	C of E	GSA
Sidcot	Co-ed	Day Boarding Weekly	£1906 £3187	Schols/ Bursaries 40 pa	9, 11, 13, 16	Drama, Music	Dyslexia, EFL	Quaker	SHMIS
BEDFORDSHIRE									
Bedford *	Boys	Day Boarding	£2335 £3715	Asst places 14 pa Schols 32 pa Bursaries	7, 8, 11, 13, 16	Music, Sport, Drama, Techno-logy	EFL	Christian	HMC
Bedford High *	Girls	Day Boarding Weekly	£1583 £3014 £2980	Asst places 22pa Schols 6pa Bursaries	7, 8, 9, 11, 13, 16	Sport		Non-denom	GSA BSA
Bedford Modern *	Boys	Day Boarding	£1477 £2860	Asst places 25 pa Bursaries	7, 8, 9, 11, 13, 16	Sport, Music, Techno-logy		Non-specific	HMC
Dame Alice Harpur	Girls	Day	£1446	Bursaries Asst places	7, 9, 11, 13, 16	Music, Sport, Drama		Christian	GSA
BERKSHIRE									
Bearwood	Co-ed	Day Boarding Weekly	£1950 £3500	Schols Bursaries	11, 13, 16	Individual focus and development	Dyslexia, EFL	C of E	SHMIS
Bradfield *	Boys Mixed sixth	Day Boarding	£3058 £4075	Asst places 6 pa Schols/ Bursaries 18 pa	13, 16	Music, Drama, Sport, CDT		C of E	HMC
Claires Court	Co-ed	Day	£1700	Schols 10 pa	2½, 11, 16	Drama, Sport	Dyslexia, ESL	RC	ISAI
Douai	Co-ed	Day Boarding Weekly	£2175 £3375 £3275	Schols 10 pa Asst places 5 pa	10, 11, 13, 16	Music, Art, Sport	Dyslexia, EFL	RC Christian	HMC

Name of School	Boys/ Girls/ Co-ed	Day/ Board/ Weekly	Max termly fees	Financial help	Intake Age/ Prep	Special strengths	Special provisions	Religion	Affiliations
Downe House *	Girls	Day Boarding	£3000 £4140	Schols Asst places	11, 12, 13	Music, Lacrosse		C of E	GSA BSA
Eton *	Boys	Boarding	£4296	Schols 31 pa Bursaries 120 pa	13	Music, Sport, Art, Drama		C of E	HMC
Heathfield (Ascot) *	Girls	Boarding	£4175	Schols	11, 16	Music, Drama		C of E	GSA BSA SHA
Leighton Park *	Co-ed	Day Boarding	£2940 £3918	Schols/ Bursaries 10 pa	11, 13, 16	Music, Sport	Extra English, Dyslexia	Quaker	HMC
Licensed Victuallers' (Ascot)	Co-ed	Day Boarding Weekly	£1790 £3190 £3170	Schols/ Bursaries 12 pa	5, 7, 11, 13, 16	Art	Specialist unit for learning difficulties	C of E	ISAI
Oratory *	Boys	Day Boarding	£2740 £3920	Schols Bursaries	11, 13, 16	Music, Drama, Art	Mild dyslexia	RC	HMC
Padworth	Girls	Day Boarding Weekly	£1823 £3645 £3545	Schols 8 pa	14, 16+		EFL		BAC CIFE ARELS
Pangbourne	Co-ed	Day Boarding	£2640 £3770	Asst places 5 pa Schols 12 pa	11, 13, 16	CCF, Sport, Judo, Allrounders	Dyslexia, EFL	C of E	HMC
Queen Anne's (Caversham) *	Girls	Day Board	£2460 £3750	Schols 12 pa	11, 13, 16	Music, Debating Sport	EFL	C of E	GSA
Reading Blue Coat	Boys Mixed sixth	Day Boarding Weekly	£1838 £3350 £3245	Schols 6 pa	11, 13, 16	CCF, Music, Sport		C of E	HMC BSA
St George's (Ascot) *	Girls	Day Boarding	£2275 £3875	Schols Bursaries	11, 12, 13, 16	Lacrosse		Christian	GSA
St Mary's (Ascot) *	Girls	Day Boarding	£2367 £3945	Schols 2 pa Bursaries	11, 13, 16	Sport, Art, Drama Music		RC	GSA
Wellington (Berkshire) *	Boys Mixed sixth	Day Boarding	£2985 £4090	Asst places 9 pa Schols 19 pa	13, 16 Own prep	Drama, Music, Art, Sport		C of E	HMC
BUCKINGHAMSHIRE									
Pipers Corner	Girls	Day Boarding Weekly	£1936 £3234 £3194	Schols Bursaries	4–7, 11, 12, 16	Drama	EFL	C of E	GSA BSA AHIS
St Mary's (Gerrards Cross)	Girls	Day	£1695	Schols 12 pa Bursaries 2 pa	11, 12, 16 Own junior	Drama, Sport, Music	Remedial Mild handicap	Christian	GSA

Name of School	Boys/ Girls/ Co-ed	Day/ Board/ Weekly	Max termly fees	Financial help	Intake Age/ Prep	Special strengths	Special provisions	Religion	Affiliations
Stowe	Boys Mixed sixth	Day Boarding	£2990 £4260	Asst places 4 pa (sixth only) Schols 18 pa Exhibitions, Bursaries	13, 16	Sport, Art, Design, Drama, Music	Learning needs, EFL	C of E	HMC SHA Allied
Wycombe Abbey *	Girls	Boarding Day	£4080 £3060	Schols 13 pa	11, 12 13, 16	Sport, Music, Drama		C of E	GSA
CAMBRIDGESHIRE									
Cambridge Centre	Co-ed	Day Boarding	£2627 £4085	Schols 5 pa	14, 16		Individual teaching		CIFE
King's (Ely)	Co-ed	Day Boarding Weekly	£2442 £3829 £3739	Schols 50 pa	2, 4, 9, 11, 13, 16	Art, Drama, Games, Adventure training	Dyslexia, Learning problems	C of E	HMC BSA CSA SHA
Leys (The)	Co-ed	Day Boarding	£2900 £3980	Asst places 15 pa Schols 18 pa	13, 14, 16	Drama, Art	Dyslexia	Methodist	HMC GSA SHA
MPW (Cambridge)	Co-ed	Day Board	£2950 £4200	Schols 6 pa	14, 16				CIFE
Perse *	Boys Mixed sixth	Day	£1508	Asst places 11 pa Bursaries Schols	11, 13, 16 Own prep	Art, Sport, Music		Christian	HMC
Perse (Girls) *	Girls	Day	£1552	Asst places 20 pa Bursaries 15 pa	7–11, 16	Music, Art, Drama	Some available	Non-denom	GSA
St Mary's (Cambridge) *	Girls	Day Weekly	£1290 £2310	Asst places 25 pa	11–14, 16	Drama, Young Enterprise, Music		RC	GSA
CHANNEL ISLANDS									
Elizabeth College	Boys Mixed sixth	Day Boarding (boys only) Weekly	£820 £2045 £1830	Schols	7, 11, 13, 16	Music		C of E	HMC
Victoria (Jersey)	Boys	Day	£594	Schols 4 pa	7, 11, 13, 16	Sailing, Shooting, Sport CCF	EFL	Christian	HMC
CHESHIRE									
Cheadle Hulme	Co-ed	Day	£1362	Asst places 20 pa Schols/ Bursaries 4 pa	7, 8, 9, 11	Music, Art, Drama		Non-denom	HMC

Name of School	Boys/ Girls/ Co-ed	Day/ Board/ Weekly	Max termly fees	Financial help	Intake Age/ Prep	Special strengths	Special provisions	Religion	Affiliations
Grange *	Co-ed	Day	£1225	Asst places Schols	4, 11, 16	Drama		Christian	HMC
Hammond	Co-ed	Day Boarding	£1280 £3600	LEA Schols 2 pa	11	Classical ballet specialist Drama		C of E	ISAI
King's (Chester) *	Boys	Day	£1437	Asst places 16 pa Schols	7, 8, 9, 11, 16	Drama, Rowing		Co of E	HMC
King's (Macclesfield)	Boys Girls Mixed sixth	Day	£1465	Asst places 70 pa Schols 8 pa	7–11, 13, 16	Sport, Music Outdoor pursuits Drama	English	C of E	HMC
Mount Carmel	Girls	Day	£1196	Asst places Bursaries	11	Music		RC	ISAI
Queen's (Chester) *	Girls	Day	£1440	Asst places 11 pa Bursaries	5, 8, 11, 16		Some	Christian	GSA SHA
St Ambrose	Boys	Day	£1150	Asst places 14 pa Schols/ Bursaries 10 pa	4, 7, 11, 16	Sport, Choir		RC	HMC
St Hilary's (Alderley Edge)	Girls	Day	£1347	Schols Bursaries	3, 4, 7, 11, 16	Drama, Public Speaking		C of E	GSA Woodard
Stockport Grammar *	Co-ed	Day	£1299	Asst places 45 pa	4, 7, 11, 16	Music, Sport		Non-denom	HMC
CLEVELAND									
Teesside High	Girls	Day	£1312	Bursaries (sixth form) Asst places	3, 5, 7, 11, 16	Music, Sport	EFL, Dyslexia	Non-denom	GSA SHA
Yarm *	Boys Mixed sixth	Day	£1657	Schols 40 pa Asst places 18 pa	4, 5, 10, 11, 13	Hockey, D of E	EFL	Christian	HMC SHMIS
CORNWALL									
Duchy Grammar	Co-ed	Day Boarding Weekly	£1625 £2788 £2694	Schols 6 pa	11 Own Junior	Outdoor education	EFL Dyslexia	Christian	ISAI
Truro *	Coed	Day Boarding	£1536 £2860	Asst places 40 pa Schols 22 pa	11, 16	Music, Sport DoE		C of E	HMC
Truro High *	Girls	Day Boarding Weekly	£1460 £2665 £2630	Asst places 33 pa Schols 14 pa	3, 11, 16	Music, Drama, Sport		C of E	GSA

Name of School	Boys/ Girls/ Co-ed	Day/ Board/ Weekly	Max termly fees	Financial help	Intake Age/ Prep	Special strengths	Special provisions	Religion	Affiliations
CUMBRIA									
Austin Friars	Co-ed	Day Boarding (boys only)	£1578 £2652	Asst places Schols 8 pa	11–16	Sport,	EFL, Dyslexia	RC	SHMIS
Casterton *	Girls	Day Boarding	£2010 £3206	Asst places 9 pa Schols 7 pa	11 Own junior	Outdoor activities, Music	Mild dyslexia	C of E	GSA
St Anne's (Windermere)	Girls	Day Boarding	£2110 £3180	Schols Bursaries	3, 11, 13, 16	Music, Drama, Art Sport	EFL Dyslexia	Non-denom	GSA Round Square
St Bees	Co-ed	Day Boarding Weekly	£2406 £3497 £3331	Asst places 18 pa Schols Bursaries	11, 13, 16	Art, Drama, Outdoor education		C of E	HMC
Sedbergh	Boys	Day Boarding	£2715 £3880	Asst places 10 pa Schols Bursaries	11, 13, 16	Sport, Music		C of E	HMC
DERBYSHIRE									
Mount St Mary's (Spinkhill)	Co-ed	Day Boarding Weekly	£1964 £2906 £2689	Asst places 15 pa Schols 10 pa	13 Own prep	Music, Drama, Rugby	EFL, Dyslexia	RC	HMC
Repton *	Co-ed	Day Boarding	£2910 £3868	Asst places 12 pa Schols/ Exhibitions	13, 16 Own prep	Music, Tennis, Sport, Drama	Dyslexia	C of E	HMC
St Elphin's *	Girls	Day Boarding Weekly	£1886 £3237 £3075	Schols 7 pa	11 Own junior	Music	EFL, Dyslexia	C of E	GSA SHA BSA
DEVON									
Blundell's	Co-ed	Day Boarding	£2350 £3850	Schols 50+ pa	11, 13, 16	Music, Art, Sport	EFL, Dyslexia	Non-denom	HMC BSA
Edgehill	Co-ed	Day Boarding Weekly	£1755 £3190 £2885	Asst places 22 pa Schols	3, 5, 11, 13, 16	Music Sport	Remedial, Dyslexia, EFL	Methodist	GSA
Exeter *	Co-ed	Day Boarding (boys only) Weekly	£1400 £2650	Asst places 30 pa Schols/ Bursaries 4 pa	11, 12, 13, 16 Own prep	Music, Drama, Sport, CCF		C of E	HMC
Kelly College	Co-ed	Day Boarding Weekly	£2385 £3796 £3635	Schols 17 pa Exhibitions Bursaries	11, 13, 16	Music, Sport, Adventure training	Dyslexia	C of E	HMC

Name of School	Boys/ Girls/ Co-ed	Day/ Board/ Weekly	Max termly fees	Financial help	Intake Age/ Prep	Special strengths	Special provisions	Religion	Affiliations
Maynard *	Girls	Day	£1391	Asst places 31 pa Schols 6pa Bursaries 4 pa	7, 10, 11, 16	Sport, Music, Drama Pastoral care		Non-denom.	GSA SHA NAHT
St Dunstan's (Plymouth)	Girls	Day Boarding Weekly	£1500 £2670 £2370	Schols 7 pa	3, 4, 11, 16	Netball, Hockey, Drama	Some	Christian	GSA
Stover	Girls	Day Boarding Weekly	£1385 £2640 £2575	Schols 4 pa	11, 16	Sport		C of E	GSA BSA
Trinity (Teignmouth)	Co-ed	Day Boarding Weekly	£1370 £2780 £2710	Schols 5-10 pa Bursaries	3–18	Activities, Vocational courses	EFL, Dyslexia	RC Anglican	ISAI SHA
West Buckland	Co-ed	Day Boarding Weekly	£1710 £3150	Asst places 32 pa Schols 6 pa	4, 5, 7, 11, 13, 16	Sport	ESL	C of E	HMC
DORSET									
Bryanston *	Co-ed	Boarding	£4410	Schols 20 pa	13, 16	Music, Drama, Art, Sport		Christian	HMC
Canford *	Co-ed	Day Boarding	£3050 £4070	Asst places 20 pa Schols 35+ pa Bursaries	13, 16	Expeditions, Sport, Music, Art	Dyslexia	C of E	HMC SHA BSA
Clayesmore	Co-ed	Day Boarding	£2610 £3730	Schols 20 pa	13, 16 Own prep	Sport, Drama, Music Art	Dyslexia EFL	C of E	SHMIS
Croft House	Girls	Day Boarding Weekly	£2295 £3250	Schols 6 pa Bursaries	11, 12, 13, 16	Drama, Art, Riding, Sport	Individual tuition	C of E	GSA
Milton Abbey	Boys	Day Boarding	£2582 £3868	Schols 8 pa	13, 16	Art, CCF, Sport	Remedial, EFL	C of E	SHMIS
St Antony's-Leweston	Girls	Day Boarding	£2285 £3505	Asst places Schols Bursaries	11, 12, 13, 16 Own prep	Music, Drama, Art, Sport	EFL, Dyslexia	RC	GSA
St Mary's (Shaftesbury) *	Girls	Day Boarding	£2050 £3200	Asst places 7 pa Schols 7pa	9–13, 16	Music, Sport		RC	GSA BSA
Sherborne (Boys) *	Boys	Day Boarding	£3190 £4185	Schols 25 pa	13	Music, Drama, Sport		C of E	HMC
Sherborne (Girls) *	Girls	Day Boarding	£2650 £3850	Schols 11 pa	11, 12, 13, 16	Music, Drama, Sport	Mild dyslexia	C of E	GSA BSA

Name of School	Boys/ Girls/ Co-ed	Day/ Board/ Weekly	Max termly fees	Financial help	Intake Age/ Prep	Special strengths	Special provisions	Religion	Affiliations
Talbot Heath *	Girls	Day Boarding Weekly	£1750 £3050 £2970	Asst places 60 pa Schols/ Bursaries	3, 6, 7, 11–13, 16	Sport, Music, Drama	Language difficulties	C of E	GSA SHA
Wentworth College	Girls	Day Boarding Weekly	£1847 £2945	Schols Bursaries	11, 12, 13, 16	Music, Sport	Dyslexia, EFL	Inter-denom	GSA
DURHAM									
Barnard Castle	Co-ed	Day Boarding	£1649 £2786	Schols Asst places	4, 7, 11 13, 16	Sport, Music, Outdoor pursuits	Dyslexia, EFL	Christian	HMC
Durham	Boys Mixed sixth	Day Boarding	£2473 £3802	Schols 9 pa Asst places 8 pa	11, 13, 16	Sport	Dyslexia	C of E	HMC
Durham High	Girls	Day	£1495	Bursaries 3 pa Schols 5 pa	4, 10, 11, 16	Music, D of E		C of E	GSA
Polam Hall *	Girls	Day Boarding Weekly	£1422 £2903 £2888	Asst places 18 pa Schols	4, 9, 11, 13, 16	Music, Drama	Dyslexia, ESL	Christian	GSA
ESSEX									
Bancroft's *	Co-ed	Day	£1898	Asst places 25 pa Schols 10 pa Bursaries 5pa	7, 11, 13, 16	Sport, Drama, Music		Christian	HMC SHA
Brentwood *	Boys Girls Mixed sixth	Day Boarding	£1929 £3370	Asst places 23 pa Schols 16 pa Bursaries	11, 13, 16 Own prep (boys)	Sport, Music,	EFL Fencing	Anglican	HMC
Chigwell *	Boys Mixed sixth (Co-ed 1998)	Day Boarding Weekly	£2077 £3157 £2989	Asst places 15 pa Schols 6 pa	7, 11, 13, 16	Music, Sport	EFL	C of E	HMC
Felsted *	Co-ed	Day Boarding	£3010 £4120	Asst places 13 pa Schols 16 pa Bursaries	13, 16 Own prep	Music, Sport Art		C of E	HMC
Friends' (Saffron Walden)	Co-ed	Day Boarding Weekly	£2123 £3538	Asst places 15 pa Schols Bursaries	5, 7, 11, 16	Art, Drama, Hockey	Dyslexia EFL	Quaker	SHMIS
New Hall *	Girls	Day Boarding Weekly	£2201 £3438 £3370	Schols Bursaries	11, 16 Own prep	Drama	Educational needs, Handicaps	RC	GSA BSA

Name of School	Boys/ Girls/ Co-ed	Day/ Board/ Weekly	Max termly fees	Financial help	Intake Age/ Prep	Special strengths	Special provisions	Religion	Affiliations
GLOUCESTERSHIRE									
Cheltenham College *	Boys Mixed sixth (Co-ed 1998)	Day Boarding	£3075 £4070	Schols Bursaries 20 pa	13, 16 Own junior	Drama, Music, Technology Sport	Dyslexia	C of E	HMC
Cheltenham Ladies' *	Girls	Day Boarding	£2600 £4095	Asst places 10 pa Schols 12 pa	11, 12, 13, 16	Music, Drama, Sport	Dyslexia	Christian	GSA SHA BSA
Dean Close *	Co-ed	Day Boarding	£2845 £4075	Schols 12 pa Bursaries	12, 13, 16	Music, Sport	Dyslexia EFL	C of E	HMC
King's (Gloucester)	Co-ed	Day Boarding Weekly	£1700 £2900 £2800	Asst places Schols 15 pa Choristers free	4, 11, 13, 16	Music	Mild dyslexia, EFL	C of E	HMC SHMIS CSA
Rendcomb	Co-ed	Day Boarding Weekly	£2769 £3558	Asst places 5 pa Schols 12 pa Bursaries	11, 13, 16	Drama, Art, Music		Christian	HMC
St Edwards's (Cheltenham)	Co-ed	Day	£1795	Schols 18 pa Discretionary awards	4, 7, 11, 16	Sport, Creative arts	Special needs	RC	ISAI
Westonbirt	Girls	Day Boarding Weekly	£2312 £3595	Schols/ Bursaries 7 pa	11–13, 14, 16	Techno-logy, Art, Lacrosse, Music, Drama	EFL, Individual coaching	C of E	GSA Allied
Wycliffe	Co-ed	Day Boarding	£2730 £3995	Asst places 32 pa Schols 40 pa	13, 16 Own junior	Drama, Art, Music, Sport	EFL	Inter-denom	HMC
Wynstones	Co-ed	Day Boarding Weekly	£1250 £2085 £1846		6, 16	Music, Drama	SEN, EFL	Non-denom	Steiner
HAMPSHIRE									
Allington Manor	Co-ed	Day Boarding Weekly	Variable	Available	6-18	Children who do not fit into other schools	No expulsion		
Atherley	Girls	Day	£1424	Asst places Schols 5-6 pa	3, 11, 16			C of E	GSA SHA CSCL
Bedales *	Co-ed	Day Boarding	£2980 £4126	Asst places 5 pa Schols Bursaries	13 Own junior	Music, Drama, Pastoral care, Art	Dyslexia	Non-denom	HMC SHMIS SHA
Churcher's	Co-ed	Day	£1665	Asst places 24 pa Schols/ Bursaries	11, 12, 13 Own junior	Sport	Dyslexia	Non-denom	HMC
Embley Park	Co-ed	Day Boarding Weekly	£2020 £3315	Schols Bursaries	11, 13, 16 Own prep	Small groups,	Dyslexia, EFL Sport	C of E Ecumenical	SHMIS SHA BSA

Name of School	Boys/ Girls/ Co-ed	Day/ Board/ Weekly	Max termly fees	Financial help	Intake Age/ Prep	Special strengths	Special provisions	Religion	Affiliations
Farnborough Hill *	Girls	Day	£1476	Asst places 30 pa Bursaries 20 pa Schols 9 pa	11	Sport, Creative arts	Remedial help	RC	GSA SHA
King Edward (Southampton) *	Co-ed	Day	£1570	Asst places 40 pa Schols Bursaries	11, 13, 16	Sport Music		Non-denom	HMC
Lord Wandsworth	Boys Mixed sixth	Day Boarding Weekly	£2584 £3324	Asst places 27 pa Schols 25 pa	11, 13, 16			Non-denom	HMC
North Foreland Lodge	Girls	Day Boarding	£2200 £3600	Schols	11			C of E	GSA BSA
Portsmouth Grammar *	Co-ed	Day	£1495	Asst places Schols Bursaries	11 Own junior	Music, Art		Non-denom	HMC
Portsmouth High *	Girls	Day	£1326	Asst places 29 pa Schols 6 pa	11, 14, 16 Own junior	Music, Sport	Mild handicap	Non-denom	GSA GPDST
St Swithun's *	Girls	Day Boarding Weekly	£2240 £3710	Asst places 4 pa Schols 15 pa Bursaries	11, 12, 13, 16	Music, Drama, Sport	Dyslexia EFL	C of E	GSA BSA
Stanbridge Earls	Co-ed	Day Boarding Weekly	£2915 £3885	Schols 10 pa	11, 13, 16	Art, Drama	Remedial unit	Inter-denom	SHMIS BSA BDA
Winchester **	Boys	Day Boarding	£3322 £4430	Asst places 7 pa Schols 15 pa Music awards 6 pa	13	Music, Rowing Drama, Cross-country Swimming		C of E	HMC

HEREFORDSHIRE

Name of School	Boys/ Girls/ Co-ed	Day/ Board/ Weekly	Max termly fees	Financial help	Intake Age/ Prep	Special strengths	Special provisions	Religion	Affiliations
Hereford Cathedral *	Co-ed	Day Boarding	£1510 £2660	Asst places 70 pa Schols 7+ pa	3, 5, 7, 11, 13, 16	Music, Sport, Outdoor pursuits		C of E	HMC CSA

HERTFORDSHIRE

Name of School	Boys/ Girls/ Co-ed	Day/ Board/ Weekly	Max termly fees	Financial help	Intake Age/ Prep	Special strengths	Special provisions	Religion	Affiliations
Aldenham	Boys Mixed sixth	Day Boarding Weekly	£2620 £3820	Asst places 5 pa Schols	11, 13, 16	Sport, Pastoral care, Music	Dyslexia, EFL	C of E	HMC
Arts Educational (Tring)	Co-ed	Day Boarding	£2226 £3604	Aided places Schols Grants	8–14, 16	Dance, Drama, (specialist school)	English	Inter-denom	ISAI BSA SHA
Berkhamsted *	Boys Mixed sixth	Day Boarding Weekly	£2368 £3888	Asst places 5 pa Schols 10-12 pa	5, 10, 13, 16	Sport, Music, D of E, CCF	EFL, Extra English	C of E	HMC

Name of School	Boys/ Girls/ Co-ed	Day/ Board/ Weekly	Max termly fees	Financial help	Intake Age/ Prep	Special strengths	Special provisions	Religion	Affiliations
Bishop's Stortford *	Co-ed	Day Boarding	£2580 £3580	Asst places 10 pa Schols Awards Bursaries	13, 16 Own prep	Art, Music, Drama, Sport	Learning support department	Non-denom	HMC
Egerton-Rothesay	Co-ed	Day	£1830	Bursaries 15 pa	2–3, 11	Art, Drama	Special needs/ dyslexia	Christian	ISAI
Haberdashers' Aske's (Boys) *	Boys	Day	£1877	Asst places 35 pa Bursaries 12 pa Schols	7, 11 13, 16	Music, Drama, Art		Christian	HMC
Haberdashers' Aske's (Girls) *	Girls	Day	£1380	Asst places 26 pa Schols 6 pa	4, 5, 11, 16	Music, Sport		Christian	GSA
Haileybury *	Boys Mixed sixth	Day Boarding	£3075 £4240	Asst places Schols 15 pa	11, 13, 16	Music, Drama, Sport, Art	Mild dyslexia EFL	C of E	HMC
Northfield	Girls	Day	£1440	Schols Bursaries	3, 7, 11, 16	Art, Drama, Pastoral care	SLD	Inter-denom	AHIS SHA ISAI
Princess Helena	Girls	Day Boarding Weekly	£2320 £3330	Schols 4 pa Bursaries	11, 12 13, 16	Music	EFL, Dyslexia	C of E	GSA BSA
Queenswood *	Girls	Day Boarding	£2256 £3814	Schols 8 pa	11, 12, 13, 16	Music, Drama, Tennis Sport	Dyslexia	Christian	GSA BSA
Rickmans-worth Masonic	Girls	Day Boarding Weekly	£1787 £2937 £2912	Bursaries Schols 22 pa	7, 11, 16	Music, Design, Debating	Mild dyslexia	C of E	GSA
St Albans *	Boys Mixed sixth	Day	£1820	Asst places 25 pa Schols 12 pa	11, 13, 16	Music	Mild dyslexia	Christian	HMC
St Albans High *	Girls	Day	£1570	Asst places 15 pa Schols Bursaries	11, 16 Own prep	Music, Drama, Sport		C of E	GSA
St Christopher (Letchworth)	Co-ed	Day Boarding	£2062 £3640		2½, 9 11, 16	Family school, Drama, Art, Outdoor pursuits	Dyslexia EFL		SHMIS
Sherrards-wood	Co-ed	Day Boarding Weekly	£1479 £2795	Schols 2 pa	4, 11, 16		EFL	C of E	ISAI

Name of School	Boys/ Girls/ Co-ed	Day/ Board/ Weekly	Max termly fees	Financial help	Intake Age/ Prep	Special strengths	Special provisions	Religion	Affiliations
ISLE OF WIGHT									
Ryde	Co-ed	Day Boarding Weekly	£1450 £2959 £2780	Asst places 23 pa Schols 19 pa	9, 11, 13, 16	Sport		C of E	HMC SHMIS
KENT									
Ashford *	Girls	Day Boarding Weekly	£1950 £3493 £3448	Asst places 8 pa Schols 6 pa	3, 5, 7, 11, 13, 16	Music, D of E Young Enterprise	Some extra help	Non-denom	GSA
Baston	Girls	Day Boarding Weekly	£1485 £2900 £2850	Schols/ Bursaries 3 pa	3, 4, 5, 7, 11, 14, 16	Music, Art & crafts, Sport	EFL Dyslexia	Christian	ISAI
Bedgebury	Girls	Day Boarding Weekly	£2226 £3596	Schols 10 pa Bursaries	3–16	Art, Music, Riding, Outdoor pursuits	Dyslexia EFL	C of E	GSA BSA
Beechwood Sacred Heart *	Girls	Day Boarding Weekly	£2110 £3535	Schols 10 pa Bursaries	2, 5, 11 14, 16	Sport, Drama, Music	EFL Dyslexia	RC	GSA
Benenden *	Girls	Boarding	£4210	Schols	11, 12, 13, 16	Drama, Sport, Music	Short-term help	C of E	GSA
Bethany	Co-ed	Day Boarding Weekly	£2013 £3147	Schols 10 pa	11, 12, 13, 16	Small family school	Dyslexia	Christian	SHMIS
Bishop Challoner	Co-ed	Day	£1285	Schols/ Bursaries	4, 11, 16	Fencing	Dyslexia	RC	ISAI
Bromley High *	Girls	Day	£1548	Asst places 30 pa Schols	4, 11, 16	Performing arts		Christian Non-denom	GSA GPDST
Cobham Hall	Girls	Day Boarding Weekly	£2750 £4285	Asst places Schols 10 pa (sixth form)	11, 12, 13, 16	Art, Drama Music	Dyslexia, EFL	Inter-denom	GSA Round Square BSA
Combe Bank	Girls	Day	£1720	Schols 6 pa	3, 11-13, 16	Music	Dyslexia	RC Foundation	GSA SHA
Dover College	Co-ed	Day Boarding Weekly	£2050 £3840 £3625	Asst places 5 pa Schols/ Bursaries 12 pa	11, 13, 16 Own junior		EFL	C of E	HMC
Duke of York's	Co-ed	Boarding	£265	MoD	11, 13	CCF	Only children of service personnel admitted	C of E	SHMIS BSA

Name of School	Boys/ Girls/ Co-ed	Day/ Board/ Weekly	Max termly fees	Financial help	Intake Age/ Prep	Special strengths	Special provisions	Religion	Affiliations
Farringtons & Stratford House	Girls	Day Boarding Weekly	£1735 £3343 £3221	Bursaries 4 pa Organ schol 1 pa	2½, 5, 11, 16	Music, Art	EFL, Extra coaching	Methodist	GSA
Holy Trinity (Bromley)	Girls	Day	£1380	Schols 4 pa	3, 5, 11, 14			RC	GSA
Kent College (Canterbury)	Co-ed	Day Boarding	£2016 £3590	Asst places 17 pa Schols Bursaries	7, 11, 13, 16	Music, Sport	Dyslexia	Methodist	HMC
Kent College (Pembury)	Girls	Day Boarding Weekly	£2110 £3528 £3276	Schols 10 pa	Up to 11, 13, 16	Drama, Music, Extra-curricular	EFL, Dyslexia	Inter-denom	GSA BSA
King's (Canterbury) *	Co-ed	Day Boarding	£2945 £4265	Awards numerous	13, 16 Own junior	Drama, Music		C of E	HMC
King's (Rochester) *	Co-ed	Day Boarding Weekly	£2370 £3995	Asst places 12 pa Schols 17 pa	13, 16 Own prep	Music, Art, Drama, Sport		C of E	HMC CSA ESHA
St Edmund's (Canterbury)	Co-ed	Day Boarding Weekly	£2620 £4010	Asst places 23 pa Schols Bursaries	3, 7, 11, 13, 16	Music, CCF, Art, Sport		C of E	HMC CSA
St Lawrence *	Co-ed	Day Board Weekly	£2480 £3720	Asst places 5 pa Schols 20 pa	5, 7, 11, 13, 16	Hockey	EFL Mild dyslexia	C of E	HMC
Sevenoaks *	Co-ed	Day Boarding	£2358 £3873	Asst places 5 pa Schols 50+ pa	11, 13, 16	Music, Drama, Sport Art	Some	Inter-denom	HMC
Sutton Valence	Co-ed	Day Boarding Weekly	£2365 £3695	Asst places 10 pa Schols Bursaries	11, 13, 16 Own junior	Sport, Music, Drama	EFL, Dyslexia	C of E	HMC SHA BSA
Tonbridge *	Boys	Day Boarding	£3051 £4323	Asst places 3 pa Schols 35 pa Bursaries	13	Music, Art, Drama, Sport		C of E	HMC
Walthamstow Hall *	Girls	Day Boarding Weekly	£2115 £3925	Asst places 9 pa Schols 6 pa Bursaries 35 pa	3, 4, 7, 11, 13, 16	Music, Drama, D of E	EFL	Inter-denom	GSA
West Heath	Girls	Day Boarding	£2585 £3680	Bursaries Schols	11, 13, 16	Music, Sport, Art, Drama		C of E	GSA SHA BSA

Name of School	Boys/ Girls/ Co-ed	Day/ Board/ Weekly	Max termly fees	Financial help	Intake Age/ Prep	Special strengths	Special provisions	Religion	Affiliations
LANCASHIRE									
Arnold	Co-ed	Day	£1183	Asst places 15 pa Schols 10 pa	5, 7, 11, 16	Sport, CCF	Dyslexia	Christian	HMC
Bolton (Boys) *	Boys	Day	£1492	Asst places 38 pa	8, 11, 16	Music, Drama,Sport, Outdoor pursuits		Christian	HMC
Bolton (Girls) *	Girls	Day	£1492	Asst places 48 pa Music bursary 1 pa	4, 8, 11, 16	PE, Music, Art, Drama	Access for wheelchairs	Multi-denom	GSA
Bury Grammar (Boys)	Boys	Day	£1234	Asst places 40 pa Schols 5 pa	7–11, 16	Sport, Outdoor pursuits		Christian	HMC
Bury Grammar (Girls) *	Girls	Day	£1234	Asst places 35 pa Schols 5 pa	4, 11	Music, Sport		Christian	GSA
Hulme Grammar (Boys)	Boys	Day	£1183	Asst places 35 pa Bursaries 6 pa	7, 11, 16	Sport, Music			HMC
King Edward (Lytham)	Boys	Day	£1230	Asst places 32 pa Schols 3 pa Bursaries 5 pa	11, 13, 16 Own junior	Sport, Outdoor pursuits, Music		Non-denom	HMC
Kirkham Grammar	Co-ed	Day Boarding	£1225 £2325	Asst places 22 pa Schols 10 pa	4, 9, 11, 16	Drama, Sport, Music, Art	EFL	Non-denom	SHMIS BSA
Queen Elizabeth's (Blackburn)	Boys Mixed sixth	Day	£1314	Asst places 39 pa	7, 8, 9, 11, 16	Music		Inter-denom	HMC SHA
Rossall	Co-ed	Day Boarding	£1400 £3800	Asst places 7 pa Schols 15+ pa Bursaries	11, 13, 16 Own prep	CCF	Dyslexia, EFL	C of E	HMC
Scarisbrick Hall	Co-ed	Day	£894	Schols 5pa	3, 4, 7, 11, 16			Non-denom	ISAI
Stonyhurst *	Boys Mixed sixth	Day Boarding	£2375 £3824	Asst places 5 pa Schols 12 pa Bursaries	13, 16	Music, Games, Charitable work	Dyslexia ESL	RC	HMC
Westholme *	Girls	Day	£1230	Asst places Schols 20 pa	3, 7, 8, 11, 16	Sport, Art, Drama, Music	Physical handicap	Christian	GSA
LEICESTERSHIRE									
Dixie Grammar	Co-ed	Day	£1250	Schols 7 pa	10, 11, 13, 16 Own prep	Art, Music		Non-denom	SHA ISAI
Leicester Grammar *	Co-ed	Day	£1440	Asst places Schols	10, 11, 13, 16 Own junior	Music		C of E	HMC

Name of School	Boys/ Girls/ Co-ed	Day/ Board/ Weekly	Max termly fees	Financial help	Intake Age/ Prep	Special strengths	Special provisions	Religion	Affiliations
Lough-borough Grammar *	Boys	Day Boarding Weekly	£1497 £2772 £2439	Asst places 23 pa Schols Bursaries	10, 11, 13, 16	Sport, Art, Music, Drama		Non-denom	HMC
Lough-borough High *	Girls	Day	£1338	Asst places Schols Bursaries	11, 16 Own junior	Music, Drama, Young Enterprise, Sport		Non-denom	GSA
Oakham *	Co-ed	Day Boarding	£2150 £3890	Asst places Schols 35 pa	11, 13, 16	Music, Art, Sport, D of E	Some	Christian	HMC BSA SHA
Ratcliffe	Co-ed	Day Boarding Weekly	£2022 £3032	Asst places Schols Bursaries	10, 11, 12, 13, 16 Own prep	Drama, Music	EFL, Minor learning difficulties	RC	HMC
Uppingham *	Boys Mixed	Day Boarding	£2440 £4070	Schols 30 pa	11, 13, 16	Music, ADT	Dyslexia	C of E	HMC
LINCOLNSHIRE									
Lincoln School	Co-ed	Day Boarding Weekly	£1415 £2890 £2665	Schols	4, 11, 13, 16	Music	EFL, Dyslexia	Inter-denom	CSCL
Stamford *	Boys	Day Boarding	£1355 £2710	Asst places 15 pa Schols 15 pa	13 Own junior	Music, Sport, D of E, Young Enterprise	Dyslexia	C of E	HMC
Stamford High	Girls	Day Boarding Weekly	£1363 £2726 £2700	Asst places 30 pa Schols 6 pa LEA schols 25 pa	4, 8, 11, 16	Music, Drama, Art, Sport, D of E		Non-denom	GSA BSA
LONDON									
Alleyn's *	Co-ed	Day	£1880	Asst places 35 pa Schols 12 pa	11, 13, 16 Own junior	Music, Drama, Art, Sport		C of E	HMC
Arts Educational (London)	Co-ed	Day	£1854		8, 11	Dance and drama (specialist school)	Dyslexia	Non-denom	ISAI
Blackheath High	Girls	Day	£1548	Asst places 20 pa Schols 3 pa	4, 7, 11, 16	Art, Netball, Music	Dyslexia	Non-denom	GSA, GPDST
Channing *	Girls	Day	£1960	Asst places Schols 8 pa Bursaries	5, 11, 16	Music, Drama		Unitarian	GSA
City of London (Boys) *	Boys	Day	£1944	Asst places 25 pa Schols 25 pa	10, 11, 13, 16	Sport, Music	Wheelchair pupils	Non-denom	HMC

Name of School	Boys/ Girls/ Co-ed	Day/ Board/ Weekly	Max termly fees	Financial help	Intake Age/ Prep	Special strengths	Special provisions	Religion	Affiliations
City of London (Girls) *	Girls	Day	£1698	Asst places 20 pa Schols 6 pa Bursaries	7, 11, 16	Music, Drama, Art, Sport		Christian	GSA
Colfe's *	Boys Mixed sixth	Day	£1558	Asst places 36 pa Schols 30 pa	3–13, 16	Music, Rugby, Drama	Mild dyslexia	C of E	HMC
Davies Laing & Dick	Co-ed	Day	£2730	Schols/ Bursaries 10 pa	16				CIFE BAC
Dulwich *	Boys	Day Boarding Weekly	£2045 £4090 £3925	Asst places 57 pa Schols 30 pa	7, 11, 13, 16		Drama, Art, Music, Sport	C of E	HMC BSA SHA
Ealing College	Boys Mixed sixth	Day	£1360	Schols (sixth)	11, 12, 13, 16		EFL Dyslexia	Non-denom	ISAI
Eltham College *	Boys Mixed sixth	Day Boarding (boys only) Weekly	£1817 £3835 £3716	Asst places 25 pa Schols 30 pa	7, 8, 11, 16	Art, Music, Sport, Drama		Christian (non-denom)	HMC
Emanuel	Co-ed	Day	£1529	Asst places 46 pa Schols/ Bursaries 12 pa	10, 11, 13, 16	Rowing, Music		C of E	HMC
Forest School	Boys Girls Mixed sixth	Day Boarding (boys only) Weekly	£1828 £2870	Asst places Schols Bursaries	7, 11, 16	Music, Football		C of E	HMC
Francis Holland (Regent's Park) *	Girls	Day	£1765	Asst places 10 pa Schols 3 pa	11, 16	Drama, Art, Music		C of E	GSA
Francis Holland (Sloane Square)	Girls	Day	£1980	Schols 5 pa Bursaries	4, 5, 11, 16	Drama		C of E	GSA
Godolphin & Latymer *	Girls	Day	£1975	Asst places 28 pa Schols Bursaries	11, 16	Music		Non-denom	GSA
Highgate *	Boys	Day	£2375	Asst places 11 pa Schols 8+ pa Bursaries 30 pa	3, 7, 11, 13,	Sport, Music		C of E	HMC
Italia Conti	Co-ed	Day	£2375	Schol 1 pa	11, 16	Drama/ dance specialist		Inter-denom	ISAI CDET

Name of School	Boys/ Girls/ Co-ed	Day/ Board/ Weekly	Max termly fees	Financial help	Intake Age/ Prep	Special strengths	Special provisions	Religion	Affiliations
James Allen's (JAGS) *	Girls	Day	£1900	Asst places 30 pa Schols 20 pa	11, 16 Own prep	Music, Drama, Art, Sport, Extra-curricular activities		Non-denom	GSA
King Alfred (Hampstead)	Co-ed	Day	£2150		4, 7, 11 14, 16	All-round		Secular	
King's (Wimbledon) *	Boys	Day	£2090	Asst places 8 pa Schols 18 pa Bursaries	13, 16 Own junior	Sport, Music, Drama		C of E	HMC
Latymer Upper *	Boys Mixed sixth	Day	£1934	Asst places 10 pa Schols Bursaries	11, 13, 16 Own prep	Music, Sport, European links		Non-denom	HMC
Lycée	Co-ed	Day	£1118		4, 14, 16	Bi/tri-lingualism			
Mill Hill *	Co-ed	Day Boarding	£2510 £3880	Asst places 15 pa Schols 12 pa Bursaries	13, 16 Own junior	Sport, Drama, Music	Extra English, EFL	Non-denom	HMC
MPW (London)	Co-ed	Day	£3057	Schols 10 pa	14–18				CIFE
Notting Hill High *	Girls	Day	£1548	Asst places Schols 3 pa Bursaries	5, 7, 11, 16	Music, Drama		Non-denom	GSA GPDST
Putney High *	Girls	Day	£1548	Asst places 20 pa Schols Bursaries	4, 7, 11, 16	Music, Creative arts Tennis Netball		Non-denom	GSA GPDST
Queen's (London) *	Girls	Day	£1940	Asst places Schols	11, 13, 14, 16			C of E	GSA
Royal Ballet	Co-ed	Day Boarding	£3058 £5257	Aided pupils scheme	11, 16	Ballet (specialist school)			BSA
St Augustine's (London)	Girls	Day	£1265	Asst places 17 pa Schols 4 pa (sixth form)	4, 11, 16	Hockey, Music Drama		RC	
St Benedict's	Boys Mixed sixth	Day	£1620	Asst places 15 pa	11, 13, 16 Own junior		Some	RC	HMC
St Dunstan's (Catford) *	Co-ed	Day	£1790	Asst places 30 pa Schols 12 pa	4, 7, 11, 16	Music, Sport	Dyslexia	Christian	HMC
St Paul's (Boys) **	Boys	Day Boarding Weekly	£2694 £4119	Asst places 11 pa Schols 24 pa Bursaries	13 Own prep	Music, Art		C of E	HMC

Name of School	Boys/ Girls/ Co-ed	Day/ Board/ Weekly	Max termly fees	Financial help	Intake Age/ Prep	Special strengths	Special provisions	Religion	Affiliations
St Paul's (Girls) *	Girls	Day	£2094	Asst places Schols Foundation awards	11, 16	Music		C of E	GSA
South Hampstead High *	Girls	Day	£1548	Asst places 12 pa Schols 1–4 pa	4, 7, 11, 16	Music, Art, Drama		Non-denom	GSA GPDST
Southbank International	Co-ed	Day	£3160	Schols 15 pa	3, 11, 16	IB, Languages Drama	ESL	Inter-denom	ISAI ECIS
Streatham High	Girls	Day	£1548	Asst places 24 pa Schols 10 pa Bursaries	11 Own junior	Music		Non-denom	GSA GPDST
Sydenham High	Girls	Day	£1640	Asst places 23 pa Schols 8 pa	4, 5, 7, 11, 13, 16	Art, Gym, Fencing, Music, Drama		Non-denom	GSA GPDST
Sylvia Young	Co-ed	Day	£1175	LEA	9, 11, 14	Specialist stage school	Remedial	Non-denom	ISAI
University College School *	Boys	Day	£2165	Asst places 15 pa Schols Grants Bursaries	7, 8, 11, 13, 16	Music, Drama		Non-denom	HMC
Westminster **	Boys Mixed sixth	Day Boarding Weekly	£2950 £4300	Asst places 8 pa Schols 8 pa Bursaries (sixth)	13, 16 Own prep	Music, Art, Sport	Dyslexia	C of E	HMC
Wimbledon High *	Girls	Day	£1548	Asst places 18 pa Schols 2 pa Bursaries	4, 5, 7, 11, 16	Music, Drama, Sport, Art	Some	Non-denom	GSA GPDST

MANCHESTER

Name of School	Boys/ Girls/ Co-ed	Day/ Board/ Weekly	Max termly fees	Financial help	Intake Age/ Prep	Special strengths	Special provisions	Religion	Affiliations
Chetham's	Co-ed	Day Boarding	£4025 £5200	Aided places 240	8–17	Music specialist	Limited	Non-denom	HMC
Manchester Grammar *	Boys	Day	£1380	Asst places 45 pa Bursaries	11, 16	Art, Sport, Music, Drama		Multi-denom	HMC
Manchester High *	Girls	Day	£1305	Asst places 40 pa Schol 3 pa	4, 7, 8, 9, 11, 16			Un-denom	GSA
William Hulme's	Co-ed	Day	£1405	Asst places 65 pa Schols Bursaries	11, 16	Sport, Music		Non-denom	HMC SHA

Name of School	Boys/ Girls/ Co-ed	Day/ Board/ Weekly	Max termly fees	Financial help	Intake Age/ Prep	Special strengths	Special provisions	Religion	Affiliations
Withington *	Girls	Day	£1250	Asst places 15 pa Bursaries	7–11, 16	Music, Drama, Tennis, Lacrosse		Non-denom	GSA
MERSEYSIDE									
Belvedere	Girls	Day	£1380	Asst places 30 pa Schols Bursaries	3, 4, 7, 11	Drama, Music, PE		Non-denom	GSA GPDST
Birkenhead *	Boys	Day	£1221	Asst places 36 pa Schols 20 pa	3, 4, 11, 13, 16	Sport Music		Christian	HMC
Birkenhead High *	Girls	Day	£1200	Asst places 40 pa Schols	11, 16 Own junior	Drama, Music, Sport		Christian	GSA GPDST
Liverpool College	Co-ed	Day	£1360	Asst places 35 pa Schols 12+ pa	3–5 7, 11, 13, 16	Music, Sport, CCF		C of E	HMC
Merchant Taylors' (Crosby) *	Boys	Day	£1248	Asst places 30 pa Grants 10 pa	7, 11, 13, 16	Sport, Music, CCF	Dyslexia	Non-denom	HMC
Merchant Taylors' (Girls) *	Girls	Day	£1248	Asst places 38 pa Schols 7 pa	4, 11, 16	Music, Sport, Drama	Mild dyslexia	Non-denom	GSA
St Edwards (Liverpool)	Co-ed	Day	£1166	Asst places 55 pa Schols 18 pa	3, 5, 11, 16	Music, Athletics	Dyslexia EFL, Visual handicaps	RC	HMC
St Mary's (Crosby)	Co-ed	Day	£1248	Asst places 45 pa Bursaries 12 pa Schols	3, 7, 11, 13, 16	Art, Sport, Music		RC	HMC
MIDDLESEX									
Hampton *	Boys	Day	£1640	Asst places 15 pa Schols 12 pa	11, 13, 16	Music, Rowing	English	Non-denom	HMC
Harrow *	Boys	Boarding	£4475	Schols/ Bursaries 20 pa	13	Drama, Sport, Art, CCF, Music		C of E RC Jewish	HMC
Heathfield (Pinner) *	Girls	Day	£1548	Asst places 31 pa Schols Bursaries	3, 4, 7, 11, 16	Music, Lacrosse		Inter-denom	GSA GPDST
John Lyon *	Boys	Day	£1785	Asst places 15 pa Schols	11, 13	Music, Sport, Drama		Non-denom	HMC

Name of School	Boys/ Girls/ Co-ed	Day/ Board/ Weekly	Max termly fees	Financial help	Intake Age/ Prep	Special strengths	Special provisions	Religion	Affiliations
Lady Eleanor Holles *	Girls	Day	£1680	Asst places 15 pa Schols Bursaries	7, 11, 16	Drama, Sport, Music		C of E	GSA
Merchant Taylors' (Northwood) *	Boys	Day Boarding	£2217 £3680	Asst places 18 pa Schols 22 pa Bursaries	11, 13, 16	Pastoral care, range of activities	Special educational needs	C of E	HMC
North London Collegiate *	Girls	Day	£1616	Asst places 13 pa Schols 4 pa Bursaries 7 pa	4, 7, 11, 16	Music, Sport		Non-denom	GSA
Northwood *	Girls	Day	£1612	Asst places Schols 3 pa (sixth form)	4, 7, 11, 16	Music, Sport, Drama		Non-denom	GSA
Purcell *	Co-ed	Day Boarding	£2838 £4800	Aided pupils LEA Awards Schols	8, 11, 12, 13, 16	Music (specialist)	EFL	Non-denom	NAGC ISM SHA SHMIS
St David's (Ashford)	Girls Mixed sixth	Day Boarding Weekly	£1725 £2995 £2820	Asst places 14 pa Schols 7+ pa Bursaries	4, 11	D of E, Gymnastics, Drama Music	Dyslexia, EFL, Hearing impaired	C of E	GSA BSA
St Helen's *	Girls	Day Boarding Weekly	£1591 £2998 £2891	Asst places Schols 7 pa Bursaries	4, 7, 11, 12, 16	Art, Drama, Sport	Extra English, EFL	Christian foundation	GSA

NORFOLK

Name of School	Boys/ Girls/ Co-ed	Day/ Board/ Weekly	Max termly fees	Financial help	Intake Age/ Prep	Special strengths	Special provisions	Religion	Affiliations
Gresham's *	Co-ed	Day Boarding Weekly	£2750 £3930 £3535	Asst places 12 pa Schols 34 pa	13 Own prep	Sport, Music, D of E Shooting	Some remedial	C of E	HMC
Hethersett Old Hall	Girls	Day Boarding Weekly	£1450 £2850	Schols 7 pa	7, 8, 11, 16	Drama, Music Sport	Dyslexia, EFL	C of E	GSA
Langley	Co-ed	Day Boarding Weekly	£1820 £3500 £2840	Bursaries Schols	10, 11, 12, 13, 16 Own prep	Sport	EFL, Dyslexia	Inter-denom	SHMIS BSA
Norwich *	Boys Mixed sixth	Day	£1510	Asst places 18 pa Bursaries 8 pa	8, 9, 11, 12, 16	Music, Sport		Non-denom	HMC CSA
Norwich High *	Girls	Day	£1328	Asst places 50 pa Schols Bursaries	4, 7, 11, 16	Music, Drama, Art, Sport		Non-denom	GSA GPDST

Name of School	Boys/ Girls/ Co-ed	Day/ Board/ Weekly	Max termly fees	Financial help	Intake Age/ Prep	Special strengths	Special provisions	Religion	Affiliations
NORTHAMPTONSHIRE									
Bosworth	Co-ed	Day Boarding	£1947 £3567	Schol 1 pa Bursaries	14	Small classes	EFL, Dyslexia		BAC CIFE
Laxton	Co-ed	Day	£1588	Asst places 3 pa Bursaries Schols 4 pa	11, 13, 16	Music, Rugby, Cricket, Art	English	C of E	SHA
Northampton-shire Grammar	Boys	Day	£1660	Schols 7 pa Bursaries 10 pa	7–9, 11, 13	Rugby		Christian	
Oundle *	Co-ed	Boarding	£4285	Schols	11, 13	Music, Art, Technology, Drama	English	C of E	HMC
Welling-borough *	Co-ed	Day Boarding Weekly	£1725 £3260 £2930	Asst places 20 pa Schols 27 pa Bursaries	11, 13, 16 Own junior	Sport, Music, Drama	Dyslexia, EFL	C of E	HMC
NORTHUMBERLAND									
Longridge Towers	Co-ed	Day Boarding Weekly	£1350 £2700 £2550	Schols 6 pa Bursaries	4, 8, 11, 13, 16	Art, Sport	Dyslexia	Christian	SHA ISAI
NOTTINGHAMSHIRE									
Nottingham High (Boys) *	Boys	Day	£1548	Asst places 25 pa Schols 15 pa	11, 16	Music, Sport, Chess, Outdoor pursuits		Non-denom	HMC
Nottingham High (Girls) *	Girls	Day	£1328	Asst places 70 pa Schols Bursaries	4, 7, 11, 16	Art, Drama, Sport, Music, D of E		Non-denom	GSA GPDST SHA
Welbeck	Co-ed	Boarding	Up to £850	Fees means tested	16	Route to Army Technical Corps		C of E	BSA
Worksop	Co-ed	Day Boarding Weekly	£2480 £3595	Asst places Schols	13	Music, Art	Dyslexia	C of E	HMC Woodard BSA
OXFORDSHIRE									
Abingdon *	Boys	Day Boarding Weekly	£1754 £3283	Asst places 20 pa Schols 15 pa	11, 13, 16	Music, Rowing,	Dyslexia, EFL	C of E	HMC
Bloxham	Boys Mixed sixth	Day Boarding	£3085 £3950	Asst places 14 pa Schols	11, 13, 16		Dyslexia, EFL	C of E	HMC Woodard
Carmel College	Co-ed	Day Boarding	£2460 £4355 (UK) £5880 (Overseas)	Asst places 13 pa Schols 20 pa	11, 16	Art	EFL, Dyslexia	Jewish	SHMIS

Name of School	Boys/ Girls/ Co-ed	Day/ Board/ Weekly	Max termly fees	Financial help	Intake Age/ Prep	Special strengths	Special provisions	Religion	Affiliations
Cherwell Tutors	Co-ed	Day Boarding Weekly	£2800 £3750	Schols 5 pa	16		Dyslexia		BAC CIFE
d'Over-broeck's	Co-ed	Day Boarding	£3055 £4255	Schols	14, 16		Dyslexia	Non-denom	ISAI
Magdalen College School *	Boys	Day	£1603	Asst places 31 pa Schols 7 pa Bursaries	9, 11, 13, 16	Music (choir school)		C of E	HMC CSA
Our Lady's (Abingdon) *	Girls	Day	£1325	Schols Bursaries	11	Music		RC	ISAI SHA
Oxford High *	Girls	Day	£1268	Schols 8 pa Asst places 19 pa	9, 11, 16	Music, Art, Sport, D of E	Some available	Non-denom	GSA GPDST
Radley *	Boys	Boarding	£4100	Schols/ Exhibitions 20 pa	13	Sport, Music		C of E	HMC
Rye St Antony	Girls	Day Boarding Weekly	£1750 £2850 £2725	Schols	5, 7, 11, 13, 16	D of E Art	Small group tuition	RC	GSA
St Edward's (Oxford) *	Co-ed	Day Boarding	£3070 £4090	Asst places Schols 13 pa Bursaries	13, 16	Music, Drama, Sport	Mild dyslexia	Anglican	HMC
St Mary's (Wantage)	Girls	Day Boarding	£2400 £3620	Schols 4 pa	11–14, 16	Music, Drama, Art	Dyslexia, EFL	C of E	GSA
Shiplake	Boys	Day Boarding	£2510 £3725	Schols Bursaries	13	Sport, Art, Drama	Dyslexia, Remedial teaching	C of E	SHMIS
Sibford	Co-ed	Day Boarding Weekly	£1695 £3200 plus £690 (SLD)	Schols/ Bursaries	5–11, 13, 14, 16,	Drama, Music, Vocational courses	Dyslexia, Learning support	Quaker	SHMIS BSA
Tudor Hall *	Girls	Day Boarding	£2106 £3380	Schols 4 pa	11, 12, 13, 16	Music Art		C of E	GSA
Wychwood *	Girls	Day Boarding Weekly	£1450 £2295 £2225	Bursaries (sixth) Schols (arts)	11, 12, 14, 16	Music, Art		Non-denom	GSA SHA

SHROPSHIRE

Name of School	Boys/ Girls/ Co-ed	Day/ Board/ Weekly	Max termly fees	Financial help	Intake Age/ Prep	Special strengths	Special provisions	Religion	Affiliations
Adcote	Girls	Day Boarding Weekly	£1700 £3065 £2780	Schols Bursaries	5–14, 16		Dyslexia, EFL	C of E	GSA
Concord *	Co-ed	Day Boarding	£1450 £3950	Schols	12, 14 16	Languages	EFL		CIFE BAC
Moreton Hall *	Girls	Day Boarding	£2530 £3560	Asst places 14 pa Schols 14 pa Bursaries	11, 12, 13, 16	Lacrosse, Art, Drama, Business activities	Learning difficulties	C of E	GSA BSA SHA

Name of School	Boys/ Girls/ Co-ed	Day/ Board/ Weekly	Max termly fees	Financial help	Intake Age/ Prep	Special strengths	Special provisions	Religion	Affiliations
Oswestry	Co-ed	Day Boarding	£1772 £3030	Schols 10 pa	11, 13, 16	Sport Music	EFL, Dyslexia	Christian	SHMIS
Shrewsbury *	Boys	Day Boarding	£2900 £4125	Schols 22 pa	13, 16			C of E	HMC
Shrewsbury High *	Girls	Day	£1328	Asst places 25 pa	4–9, 11, 16			Non-denom	GSA GPDST
Wrekin	Co-ed	Day Boarding	£2060 £3770	Schols 20 pa Asst places 3 pa	11, 13, 16	Sport, Art, Gymnastics	Dyslexia	C of E	HMC Allied
SOMERSET									
Bruton (Sunny Hill) *	Girls	Day Boarding Weekly	£1262 £2330	Asst places 25 pa Schols 7 pa	8, 11, 13, 16	Hockey, Drama, Music	ESL, Dyslexia	Christian	GSA BSA
King's (Bruton) *	Boys Mixed sixth	Day Boarding	£2590 £3655	Asst places 2 pa Schols 10 pa	13, 16	Pastoral Sport Design	Mild dyslexia, EFL	C of E	HMC
King's (Taunton)	Co-ed	Day Boarding	£2520 £3830	Asst places 10 pa Schols 29 pa	13, 16 Own prep	Music, Drama, Art, Sport	EFL Dyslexia	C of E	HMC Woodard
Millfield	Co-ed	Day Boarding	£2940 £4595	Schols 50 pa	13, 16 Own junior	Sport, Music, Art	EFL, Dyslexia Unit	Multi-faith	HMC
Queen's (Taunton)	Co-ed	Day Boarding	£2118 £3231	Asst places 10 pa Schols	12, 13, 16. Own junior	D of E, Music, Drama	Dyslexia	Methodist	HMC
Wellington (Somerset) *	Co-ed	Day Boarding	£1466 £2680	Asst places 40 pa Schols	10, 11, 13, 16	Sport, Music, Art	EFL	C of E	HMC BSA
Wells Cathedral	Co-ed	Day Boarding	£1784 £3038	Aided places Asst places 15 pa Schols	11, 13, 16 Own junior	Music (specialist school), Drama	EFL Dyslexia	C of E	HMC SHMIS CSA
STAFFORDSHIRE									
Abbotsholme	Co-ed	Day Boarding Weekly	£2538 £3797	Schols 8 pa Bursaries	11, 12, 13, 16	Small family school, Art, Music	Dyslexia EFL	Inter-denom	HMC SHMIS Round Square
Denstone	Co-ed	Day Boarding Weekly	£2590 £3630	Asst places Schols Bursaries	11, 13, 16	Music, Sport, D of E, Drama	Dyslexia	C of E	HMC Woodard
Newcastle-under-Lyme *	Co-ed	Day	£1180	Asst places 82 pa Schols/ Bursaries 8 pa	8, 11, 13, 16	Music, Drama, Sport		Christian	HMC
St Dominic's (Brewood)	Girls	Day	£1300	Schols	2½, 11, 16	Drama, Music		RC	GSA

Name of School	Boys/ Girls/ Co-ed	Day/ Board/ Weekly	Max termly fees	Financial help	Intake Age/ Prep	Special strengths	Special provisions	Religion	Affiliations
St Dominic's (Stone)	Girls	Day	£1141	Asst places Bursaries	3, 11	Badminton, Music, Tennis, Netball,	Dyslexia	RC	ISAI CTF

SUFFOLK

Name of School	Boys/ Girls/ Co-ed	Day/ Board/ Weekly	Max termly fees	Financial help	Intake Age/ Prep	Special strengths	Special provisions	Religion	Affiliations
Culford	Co-ed	Day Boarding Weekly	£2257 £3467	Asst places 10 pa Schols 8 pa Bursaries	8, 11, 13	Music, Sport, Clubs	Dyslexia, EFL	Methodist	HMC
Framlingham	Co-ed	Day Boarding	£2072 £3229	Asst places Schols	13 Own junior	Sport, D of E CCF, Art, Music, Drama	Limited	C of E provision	HMC
Ipswich *	Co-ed	Day Boarding Weekly	£1684 £2884 £2802	Asst places 25 pa Schols 12–15 pa	11, 13, 16 Own prep	Music, Design, Drama, Sport		C of E	HMC
Ipswich High *	Girls	Day	£1328	Asst places 25 pa Bursaries Schols 3–4 pa	3, 4, 7, 9, 11, 16	Music, Drama, Sport		Non-denom	GSA GPDST
Royal Hospital	Co-ed	Day (sixth form only) Boarding	£1350 £2550	Schols Means tested fees for children or grandchildren of seafarers	11, 12, 13, 16	Sport, CCF, Music, Technology		Christian	SHMIS BSA
St Felix	Girls	Day Boarding Weekly	£2345 £3605	Asst places 9 pa Schols	11, 12, 16 Own junior	Music, Sport	Mild dyslexia, EFL, Gifted children	Non-denom	GSA
St Joseph's (Ipswich)	Co-ed	Day Boarding Weekly	£1610 £2812 £2531	Asst places 15 pa Schols 8 pa Bursaries	3, 5, 11, 16	Sport Music	EFL, Dyslexia	RC	BSA
Woodbridge	Co-ed	Day Board Weekly	£1699 £2792	Asst places 21 pa Schols Bursaries	4, 7, 11, 16	Music CCF Games	Dyslexia	C of E	HMC

SURREY

Name of School	Boys/ Girls/ Co-ed	Day/ Board/ Weekly	Max termly fees	Financial help	Intake Age/ Prep	Special strengths	Special provisions	Religion	Affiliations
Box Hill	Co-ed	Day Boarding Weekly	£2050 £3280 £3400	Schols 12 pa Bursaries	11, 12, 13, 16	Art, Music, Drama., Activities	Dsylexia, ESL	Non-denom	SHMIS Round Square
Caterham *	Co-ed	Day Boarding	£1932 £3532	Asst places 20 pa Schols 15 pa Bursaries	3–10, 11, 13, 16	Music, Games, Drama Art	Dyslexia	United Reformed Church	HMC SHA

Name of School	Boys/ Girls/ Co-ed	Day/ Board/ Weekly	Max termly fees	Financial help	Intake Age/ Prep	Special strengths	Special provisions	Religion	Affiliations
Charterhouse *	Boys Mixed sixth	Day Boarding	£3516 £4255	Asst places 5 pa (sixth form) Schols 32 pa Bursaries	13, 16	Music, Sport, Art		Christian	HMC
City of London Freemen's *	Co-ed	Day Boarding Weekly	£2046 £3189 £3092	Asst places 5 pa Schols 25 pa Bursaries 25 pa	7, 13, 16	Music, D of E Sport,	Art, Drama	C of E	HMC SHMIS
Commonweal Lodge	Girls	Day	£1505	Schols/ Bursaries 3 pa	3, 5, 8, 11	Small teaching groups, Music	EFL Dyslexia	Christian	GSA
Cranleigh *	Boys Mixed sixth	Day Boarding	£3110 £4140	Asst places Schols Exhibitions	13, 16 Own prep	Music, Drama Art, Sport	EFL Dyslexia	C of E	HMC
Croham Hurst	Girls	Day	£1530	Asst places Schols/bursaries 5 pa	4, 7, 11		Minor learning difficulties	Christian	GSA
Croydon High *	Girls	Day	£1548	Asst places 30 pa Schols 4 pa	4, 5, 7, 11, 16	Music, Sport, Drama		Non-denom	GSA GPDST
Dunottar	Girls	Day	£1510	Schols 7+ pa	4, 5, 7, 8, 11, 16	Music, Sport	Dyslexia	Christian (non-denom)	GSA SHA AHIS
Elmhurst	Co-ed	Day Boarding	£2340 £3190	Some LEAs	8	Dance specialist		C of E	SHMIS
Epsom College *	Co-ed	Day Boarding Weekly	£2872 £3865 £3812	Asst places 10 pa Schols 30 pa	13, 16	Art, Music, Sport Drama		C of E	HMC
Ewell Castle	Boys Mixed sixth	Day	£1475	Schols Bursaries	11, 13, 16	Sport Drama Music	Dyslexia EFL/ESL	Non-denom	SHMIS
Frensham Heights *	Co-ed	Day Boarding Weekly	£2490 £3890	Asst places Schols	11, 12, 13, 16 Own junior	Small classes, Arts	Dyslexia ESL	Non-denom	HMC BSA
Greenacre	Girls	Day	£1660	Schols Bursaries	3, 4, 11	Art, Drama	EFL	Christian	GSA
Guildford High *	Girls	Day	£1700	Asst places 5 pa Schols	4, 7, 11, 16	Music		C of E	GSA
King Edward's (Witley)	Co-ed	Day Boarding	£2080 £2990	Asst places 15 pa Schols/ Bursaries	11, 13, 16	Art, Music		C of E	HMC
Kingston Grammar	Co-ed	Day	£1795	Asst places Schols Bursaries	10, 11, 13, 16	Hockey, Music, Rowing, Art		Christian Non-denom	HMC

Name of School	Boys/ Girls/ Co-ed	Day/ Board/ Weekly	Max termly fees	Financial help	Intake Age/ Prep	Special strengths	Special provisions	Religion	Affiliations
Marymount	Girls	Day Boarding Weekly	£2567 £4450 £4383	Bursaries	11–16	International school	EFL	RC	GSA ECIS
Notre Dame (Cobham)	Girls	Day	£1575	Schols	11 Own junior	Art Drama		RC	GSA
Notre Dame (Lingfield)	Co-ed	Day	£1425	Ast places Schols	3–11, 13, 16	Music	Dyslexia,	Christian	ISAI
Old Palace *	Girls	Day	£1326	Asst places 35 pa Schols 12 pa Bursaries	11, 16 Own junior	Music		C of E	GSA
Parsons Mead *	Girls	Day Weekly	£1675 £2943	Schols 6 pa	3, 7, 11, 16		Extra coaching possible	C of E	GSA
Prior's Field	Girls	Day Boarding Weekly	£2185 £3270	Schols Bursaries	11, 12, 13, 16	Art, Music Drama Tennis	Dyslexia EFL	Christian	GSA
Reed's	Boys Mixed sixth	Day Boarding	£2580 £3413	Asst places 8 pa Schols Bursaries	11, 12, 13, 16	Music, Art	Dyslexia	C of E	HMC
Reigate Grammar *	Co-ed	Day	£1624	Asst places 30 pa Schols Bursaries	10, 11, 13, 16	Music, Games, Drama		Non-denom	HMC
Royal (Guildford) *	Boys	Day	£1985	Schols 20 pa Asst places 20 pa	11, 13	Music, Sport, Scouts		Non-denom	HMC
Royal (Haslemere)	Girls	Day Boarding Weekly	£1854 £3004	Schols 6 pa	11, 13, 14, 16	Music, D of E, Sport	Remedial, EFL	C of E	GSA
Royal Russell	Co-ed	Day Boarding Weekly	£1850 £3510	Schols Bursaries	11 Own junior	Model United Nations programme	Dyslexia, EFL	C of E	SHMIS
St Catherine's *	Girls	Day Boarding Weekly	£1960 £3210	Asst places 13 pa Schols 11 pa Bursaries	4, 7, 11	Music, Sport		C of E	GSA BSA
St George's (Weybridge)	Boys Mixed sixth	Day	£2085	Asst places 6 pa Schols 15 pa Bursaries	11, 13, 16 Own prep	Community service, Art, Music Sports	Mild dyslexia	RC	HMC SHMIS SHA
St John's (Leatherhead)	Boys Mixed sixth	Day Boarding Weekly	£2550 £3700	Asst places 6 pa Schols 15 pa Bursaries	13, 16		Dyslexia	C of E	HMC
St Maur's	Girls	Day	£1500	Asst places 15 pa Schols Bursaries	2, 4, 5, 11, 16	Music		RC	GSA

Name of School	Boys/ Girls/ Co-ed	Day/ Board/ Weekly	Max termly fees	Financial help	Intake Age/ Prep	Special strengths	Special provisions	Religion	Affiliations
St Teresa's	Girls	Day Boarding Weekly	£1690 £3595	Schols	11, 12, 13 Own prep	Art, Music, Sport, Public speaking	EFL	RC	GSA SHA CCSS BSA
Sir William Perkins's *	Girls	Day	£1365	Asst places 20 pa Schols	11	Music		Non-denom	GSA
Surbiton High *	Girls	Day	£1613	Asst places Bursaries Schols	4, 5, 7, 11, 16	Art, Music		C of E	GSA CSCL
Sutton High *	Girls	Day	£1548	Asst places 34 pa Schols 9 pa Bursaries	4, 6, 11, 16	Sport, Music, Drama Debating		Non-denom	GSA GPDST
Tormead *	Girls	Day	£1700	Asst places Schols Bursaries Exhibitions	4, 7, 11, 16	Drama, D of E, Music		Non-denom	GSA
Trinity (Croydon) *	Boys	Day	£1768	Asst places 25 pa Schols 30 pa Bursaries	10, 11, 13, 16	Music, Sport	Dyslexia	Non-denom	HMC
Whitgift *	Boys	Day	£1832	Asst places 13 pa Schols Bursaries	10, 11, 13, 16	Music, Drama, Sport		C of E	HMC
Woldingham *	Girls	Day Boarding	£2306 £3812		11	Sport, Drama, Music		RC	GSA BSA
Yehudi Menuhin	Co-ed	Boarding	£6481	Aided places (EU students)	8–16	Strings and piano (specialist music school)	Dyslexia	Non-denom	SHMIS SHA BSA

SUSSEX

Name of School	Boys/ Girls/ Co-ed	Day/ Board/ Weekly	Max termly fees	Financial help	Intake Age/ Prep	Special strengths	Special provisions	Religion	Affiliations
Ardingly	Co-ed	Day Boarding	£3065 £3880	Asst places 5 pa Schols 25 pa Clergy bursaries	3, 7, 11, 13, 16	Music, Drama, Art, Sports	EFL	C of E	HMC Woodard
Battle Abbey	Co-ed	Day Boarding Weekly	£1875 £3030	Forces bursaries	3-5, 7 11, 13 16	Design, Art	Dyslexia, Extra English, Learning difficulties	Christian	GSA
Brighton College *	Co-ed	Day Boarding Weekly	£2618 £3980 £3560	Asst places 15 pa Schols 30 pa	13, 16 Own prep	Art, Sport, Music, Drama	Dyslexia	C of E	HMC
Christ's Hospital *	Co-ed	Boarding	Means tested	Hospital endowments for all	11	Music, Drama, Art	Mild dyslexia	C of E	HMC SHA

Name of School	Boys/ Girls/ Co-ed	Day/ Board/ Weekly	Max termly fees	Financial help	Intake Age/ Prep	Special strengths	Special provisions	Religion	Affiliations
Eastbourne *	Co-ed	Day Boarding	£2673 £3621	Schols 18 pa Bursaries	13, 16	Music, Drama, Sport, Art		C of E	HMC
Farlington	Girls	Day Boarding	£1930 £3120	Schols 16 pa	11, 12, 13 Own junior	Music, Sport Riding	EFL Dyslexia	C of E	GSA BSA
Hamilton Lodge	Co-ed	Day Weekly	£4865 £6415	LEA	5, 7, 11		Specialist school for the deaf	Non-denom	
Hurstpier-point *	Co-ed	Day Boarding	£2920 £3660	Asst places 4 pa Schols 20 pa Bursaries	13, 16 Own junior	Sport, Music		C of E	HMC Woodard
Lancing *	Boys Mixed sixth	Day Boarding	£3015 £4010	Asst places 10 pa Schols and Exhibitions 30 pa	13, 16	Music		C of E	HMC Woodard
Lavant House Rosemead	Girls	Day Boarding Weekly	£1950 £3475	Schols 6 pa	3–14, 16	Lacrosse, Drama	Dyslexia EFL	C of E	GSA
Michael Hall	Co-ed	Day Boarding Weekly	£1225 £2675 £2525	Bursaries	3 up-wards	Arts	Remedial EFL	Non-denom	Steiner
Micklefield Wadhurst	Boys (ballet only) Girls	Day Boarding Weekly	£2140 £3370 £3340	Schols Bursaries	11, 12, 13, 16	Music, Ballet, Drama, Sport	Dyslexia EFL	Christian Inter-denom	
Moira House	Girls	Day Boarding Weekly	£2300 £3570	Schols 15 pa	3–10, 11, 12, 13, 16	Careers, Music, Drama	Dyslexia, EFL	Christian	GSA BSA
Roedean *	Girls	Day Boarding	£2455 £4325	Asst places 15 pa Schols 6 pa	10, 11, 12, 13, 16	Music, Drama, Art & design, D of E, Sport,		Christian	GSA
St Bede's (Hailsham)	Co-ed	Day Boarding	£2250 £3800	Schols/ Bursaries 12 pa	12, 13, 16	Tennis, Art, Drama, Music, Swimming	EFL, Dyslexia	Non-denom	SHMIS
St Leonards-Mayfield *	Girls	Day Boarding Weekly	£2300 £3450 £3425	Schols Bursaries	11, 13, 16	Art, Music, Sport	Dyslexia, EFL	RC	GSA ACSC
Seaford	Co-ed	Day Boarding (boys only)	£1975 £3210	Schols 20 pa	11, 13, 16	Art, Music, CDT	Dyslexia EFL	C of E	SHMIS
Worth	Boys	Day Boarding	£2555 £3830	Schols 10–12 pa	10, 11, 13, 16	Voluntary services, Music, D of E	Dyslexia	RC	HMC BSA

Name of School	Boys/ Girls/ Co-ed	Day/ Board/ Weekly	Max termly fees	Financial help	Intake Age/ Prep	Special strengths	Special provisions	Religion	Affiliations
TYNE & WEAR									
Central Newcastle High *	Girls	Day	£1328	Asst places 23 pa Bursaries Schols 4 pa	4, 7, 9, 11, 16	Sport, Music	Dyslexia	Non-denom	GSA GPDST
La Sagesse	Girls	Day	£1285	Asst places 28 pa Schols 6 pa Bursaries	11, 16 Own junior	Drama, Choir, Industrial/ business links		RC	GSA
Newcastle Church High	Girls	Day	£1245	Asst places 5 pa Exhibitions/ Schols 14 pa	3, 4, 7, 9, 11, 16		EFL	C of E	GSA
Royal (Newcastle) *	Boys	Day	£1203	Asst places 50 pa	11, 13, 16 Own, junior	Music, Drama, Art, Techno-logy, Sport		Non-denom	HMC
Sunderland High	Co-ed	Day	£1305	Asst places 16 pa Schols Bursaries	11, 13, 16 Own junior	Languages	Extra English	C of E	SHMIS CSCo
Westfield	Girls	Day	£1380	Schols 10 pa	3, 9, 11, 16	Sport, Drama, Music	Dyslexia	Christian	GSA Round Square
WARWICKSHIRE									
King's (Warwick) *	Girls	Day	£1365	Asst places 30 pa Schols 9 pa	11 Own prep	Sport, Music		Non-denom	GSA
Kingsley	Girls	Day	£1415	Asst places 30 pa Schols 6 pa	2½, 8, 11, 16	D of E, Performing arts	Dyslexia	C of E	GSA
Rugby *	Co-ed	Day Boarding	£3330 £4240	Schols 16 pa Foundationer-ships: 16 major, 28 minor	12 (day) 13, 16	Drama, Sport, Art, Music, Design, Media	Extra English, Dyslexia	C of E	HMC
Warwick *	Boys	Day Boarding Weekly	£1530 £3280 £3060	Asst places 30 pa Schols 20 pa Bursaries	7, 11, 13, 16	Sport		C of E	HMC
WEST MIDLANDS									
Bablake *	Coed	Day	£1250	Asst places 34 pa Schols 14 pa	7, 11, 16	Music, Drama, Sport		Non-denom	HMC
Edgbaston High	Girls	Day	£1405	Asst places Schols 8 pa	11 Own junior	Music, Art, Drama, D of E Sport		Non-denom	GSA

Name of School	Boys/ Girls/ Co-ed	Day/ Board/ Weekly	Max termly fees	Financial help	Intake Age/ Prep	Special strengths	Special provisions	Religion	Affiliations
Holy Child	Girls	Day	£1500	Asst places 30pa Schols	2, 11	Christian education with a European dimension	EFL Dyslexia	RC	GSA
King Edward's (Birmingham: Boys) *	Boys	Day	£1480	Asst places 40 pa Schols 20 pa	11, 13, 16	Music, Sport		Christian	HMC
King Edward (Birmingham: Girls) *	Girls	Day	£1410	Asst places 30 pa Schols 25 pa	11, 16	Music, Drama, Hockey		Non-denom	GSA
MPW Birmingham	Co-ed	Day	£2850	Schols 3 pa	13+				CIFE BAC
Old Swinford	Boys	Day Boarding Weekly	Nil £1400	Schols Bursaries	11, 13, 16	D of E, Music, Drama	Some special support	C of E	SHMIS BSA, STABIS
Royal (Wolver-hampton)	Co-ed	Day Boarding Weekly	£1725 £3015 £2900	Schols Bursaries	2½, 4, 11, 16	CCF, Sport	Some help available	C of E	SHMIS SHA
Solihull *	Boys Mixed sixth	Day	£1428	Asst places 30 pa, Schols 30 pa	7, 9, 10, 11, 13, 16	Music, Sport D of E		Anglican	HMC
Tettenhall	Co-ed	Day Boarding Weekly	£1880 £3049 £2537	Schols 7 pa	7, 11, 13, 16	Sport	EFL	Inter-denom	HMC SHMIS
Wolver-hampton Grammar *	Co-ed	Day	£1600	Asst places 40 pa Schols 7 pa	11, 13, 16	Music, Sport, Drama		Non-denom	HMC

WILTSHIRE

Name of School	Boys/ Girls/ Co-ed	Day/ Board/ Weekly	Max termly fees	Financial help	Intake Age/ Prep	Special strengths	Special provisions	Religion	Affiliations
Dauntsey's *	Co-ed	Day Boarding	£2164 £3514	Asst places 15 pa Schols Bursaries	11, 13, 16	Music, Art, Sport	EFL, Mild dyslexia	Christian	HMC
Godolphin	Girls	Day Boarding	£2152 £3593	Asst places 10 pa Schols Bursaries	11, 12, 13, 16 Own prep	Music, Art, Techno-logy	Dyslexia	C of E	GSA BSA
Marlborough *	Co-ed	Day Boarding	£2995 £4250	Schols 24 pa Bursaries	13, 16	Music, Art, Sport, Drama	Dyslexia, ESL	C of E	HMC SHA
St Mary's (Calne) *	Girls	Day Boarding	£2275 £3850	Schols 6 pa Bursaries	11, 12	Sport, Music, Drama, Art		C of E	GSA
Stonar	Girls	Day Boarding Weekly	£1763 £3182	Schols Bursaries	5, 11, 13, 16	Sport, Music, Riding	Dyslexia, EFL	C of E	GSA

Name of School	Boys/ Girls/ Co-ed	Day/ Board/ Weekly	Max termly fees	Financial help	Intake Age/ Prep	Special strengths	Special provisions	Religion	Affiliations
Warminster	Co-ed	Day Boarding Weekly	£1790 £3090	Schols Bursaries	4–16	Drama, Sport, CCF	Dyslexia	C of E	SHMIS BSA

WORCESTERSHIRE

Name of School	Boys/ Girls/ Co-ed	Day/ Board/ Weekly	Max termly fees	Financial help	Intake Age/ Prep	Special strengths	Special provisions	Religion	Affiliations
Alice Ottley *	Girls	Day	£1595	Asst places Schols	11 Own junior	Music, Sport	Extra coaching	C of E	GSA
Bromsgrove *	Co-ed	Day Boarding	£2050 £3275	Asst places 29 pa Schols Bursaries	7, 11, 13, 16	Outdoor activities	Some available	Christian	HMC
King's (Worcester) *	Co-ed	Day Boarding Weekly	£1697 £2931	Asst places 59 pa Schols/ bursaries 30 pa	7, 8, 11, 13, 16	Sport, Music, Drama	Mild visual handicaps	C of E	HMC
Malvern College *	Co-ed	Day Boarding	£2960 £4070	Asst places 20 pa Schols 20 pa	13, 16 Own junior	Music, Art, Drama Sport	SLD, EFL	C of E	HMC
Malvern (Girls) *	Girls	Day Boarding	£2600 £3900	Schols 10 pa	11, 12, 13, 16	Music, Sport, Art	Dyslexia, ESL	C of E	GSA
RNIB New College	Co-ed	Day Boarding	£5020 £7531	LEA/ FEFC pay fees	11+	Music, Sport	Specialist school for the visually impaired	Non-denom	HMC
Royal (Worcester) *	Boys	Day	£1446	Asst places Schols Bursaries	7-13, 16	Drama, Sport		Non-denom	HMC
St James's & the Abbey	Girls	Day Boarding Weekly	£2436 £3654	Schols Bursaries	11	Drama Art	Mild dyslexia, EFL	C of E	GSA

YORKSHIRE

Name of School	Boys/ Girls/ Co-ed	Day/ Board/ Weekly	Max termly fees	Financial help	Intake Age/ Prep	Special strengths	Special provisions	Religion	Affiliations
Ackworth	Co-ed	Day Boarding	£1772 £3111	Asst places Schols	7, 11, 13, 16	D of E, Activities, Music, Sport	EFL, Dyslexia	Quaker	HMC SHMIS
Ampleforth *	Boys	Day Boarding	£3245 £4005	Schols 12 pa Bursaries	13 Own junior	Music, Drama, Art, Sport	EFL, Learning difficulties Dyslexia	RC	HMC
Ashville *	Co-ed	Day Boarding Weekly	£1560 £2918	Asst places Schols 12 pa	4½, 7, 8, 11, 13, 16	Drama, Outdoor activities	Dyslexia, EFL	Methodist	HMC
Ayton	Co-ed	Day Boarding Weekly	£1475 £3165 £2785	Bursaries	4, 7, 11, 13, 16	Music, Drama, Art	EFL, Dyslexia	Quaker	BSA

Name of School	Boys/ Girls/ Co-ed	Day/ Board/ Weekly	Max termly fees	Financial help	Intake Age/ Prep	Special strengths	Special provisions	Religion	Affiliations
Batley	Co-ed	Day	£1209	Asst places 68 pa Schols 5–10 pa	11, 12, 13, 16	Music, D of E, Sport	Dyslexia	Christian	HMC
Birkdale *****	Boys Mixed Sixth	Day	£1533	Asst places Schols 10 pa	11, 16 Own prep	Sport, Music, Outdoor Pursuits	Dyslexia	Christian	SHA SHMIS
Bootham	Co-ed	Day Boarding	£2198 £3387	Asst places Schols 12 pa Bursaries	11, 13, 16	Art, Drama, Music	Dyslexia, EFL	Quaker	HMC
Bradford Grammar *****	Boys Mixed sixth	Day	£1411	Asst places 45 pa	8–11, 12, 13, 16	IT, Sport, Music		Christian	HMC
Bradford (Girls) *****	Girls	Day	£1332	Asst places 60 pa Bursaries	4, 9, 11	Art, Sport, CDT		Christian	GSA
Fulneck	Boys Girls Mixed sixth	Day Boarding Weekly	£1540 £2885 £2570	Schols 13 pa	3, 5, 7, 11, 13	Speech, Drama, Sport, Music	Dyslexia	Moravian (Protestant)	SHMIS GSA
Giggleswick	Co-ed	Day Boarding	£2552 £3848	Asst places Schols Bursaries	13, 16 Own prep	Sport, Art, Outdoor education, Drama	Dyslexia	C of E	HMC
Harrogate Ladies' *****	Girls	Day Boarding Weekly	£1995 £2995 £2920	Asst places 14 pa Schols	10, 11, 12, 13, 16	Music	Dyslexia, ESL	C of E	GSA
Hymers *****	Co-ed	Day	£1185	Asst places 25 pa Bursaries	8, 9, 11, 16	Music, Sport		Christian	HMC
Leeds Grammar *****	Boys	Day	£1615	Asst places 35 pa Schols 25 pa	7, 8, 10, 11, 13, 16	Drama, Music, Sport		Non-denom	HMC
Leeds High *****	Girls	Day	£1412	Asst places 21 pa Schols 7-10 pa	3, 4, 11	Sport, Music, Drama		Non-denom	GSA
Mount (York) *****	Girls	Day Boarding Weekly	£2085 £3390	Asst places 10 pa Bursaries/ Schols	11, 16	Music, Art	Dyslexia, EFL	Quaker	GSA BSA
Pocklington	Co-ed Boarding	Day £2896	£1614 26 pa	Asst places 16 Schols Bursaries	11, 13, CDT, Own junior	Sport, Dyslexia, Art	EFL, Cerebral Palsy	C of E BSA	HMC
Queen Elizabeth (Wakefield) *****	Boys	Day	£1374	Asst places 22 pa Schols 18 pa	7, 9, 11–13, 16	Art, Sport, Music, Drama		Non-denom	HMC
Queen Ethelburga's	Girls	Day Boarding Weekly	£2259 £3499	Schols Bursaries	5, 11, 13, 16	Music, Drama, Riding	Special needs, EFL	C of E	GSA

Name of School	Boys/ Girls/ Co-ed	Day/ Board/ Weekly	Max termly fees	Financial help	Intake Age/ Prep	Special strengths	Special provisions	Religion	Affiliations
Queen Margaret's (York) *	Girls	Day Boarding	£2158 £3406	Schols 10 pa Bursaries	11–13, 16	Art, Sport, Music	Slight academic difficulties	C of E	GSA BSA
Read	Co-ed	Day Boarding Weekly	£1205 £2485 £2325	Asst places Schols 8 pa	4, 8, 11, 13, 16	CCF, Games		C of E	ISAI BSA
Rishworth	Co-ed	Day Boarding Weekly	£1665 £3220	Schols 5 pa Bursaries	4, 7, 11	Music, Drama, Athletics	EFL, Dyslexia	C of E	SHMIS
St Hilda's (Whitby)	Co-ed	Day Boarding Weekly	£1600 £2950 £2600	Schols Bursaries	3–11, 13, 16	D of E, Music Art	Dyslexia, EFL	C of E	ISAI
St Peter's (York) *	Co-ed	Day Boarding	£2061 £3462	Asst places 29 pa Schols 7 pa	13, 16 Own junior	Sport, Music		C of E	HMC
Scarborough	Co-ed	Day Boarding	£1702 £3140	Asst places 45 pa Schols	11, 13 Own junior	Music, Drama, CCF, Sport	Dyslexia	Christian Inter-denom	SHMIS SHA
Sheffield High *	Girls	Day	£1328	Asst places 21 pa Schols Bursaries	4, 11, 16	Music, Sport		Non-denom	GSA GPDST
Wakefield High *	Girls	Day	£1374	Asst places Bursaries	11, 13, 16 Own junior	Music, Drama, Community service		Non-denom	GSA
Woodhouse Grove	Co-ed	Day Boarding	£1755 £2980	Asst places 25 pa Schols 20 pa	11, 16 Own junior	Music, Sport, Drama	Dyslexia, EFL	Methodist	HMC
York College for Girls *	Girls	Day	£1790	Schols 16 pa Bursaries 4 pa	3, 5, 8, 11, 13, 16	Music, Drama		C of E	GSA CSCL

Northern Ireland

Name of School	Boys/ Girls/ Co-ed	Day/ Board/ Weekly	Max termly fees	Financial help	Intake Age/ Prep	Special strengths	Special provisions	Religion	Affiliations
Belfast Royal Academy	Co-ed	Day	£80	LEA	4, 11	Music, Sport, Drama		Non-denom	HMC
Campbell College	Boys	Day Boarding Weekly	£331 £1765	Schols 4 pa LEA	11, 13, 16 Own prep	Music, Drama, Sport		Non-denom	HMC
Christian Brothers	Boys	Day	Nil		11	Sport		RC	
Coleraine	Boys	Day Boarding	£905 EU Res £1200 Non EU Res £2133	Bursaries	11, 16	Sport, Techno-logy	EFL	Christian	HMC

Name of School	Boys/ Girls/ Co-ed	Day/ Board/ Weekly	Max termly fees	Financial help	Intake Age/ Prep	Special strengths	Special provisions	Religion	Affiliations
Friends' (Lisburn)	Co-ed	Day Boarding Weekly	Nil £1085 £1043	LEA	4, 11, 16	Sport, D of E	EFL, Mild handicaps	Quaker	
Hunterhouse	Girls	Day Boarding	£65 £965 EU parents £833 (Day) £1798 (Boarding) Non-EU parents		11, 14, 16 Own junior	Music, Sport	EFL	Christian	Voluntary Grammar
Methodist College	Co-ed	Day Boarding	£55 £1886	Schols 10 pa	11, 16 Own junior	Music, Sport		Methodist	HMC
RBAI *	Boys	Day	£130	Schols	11 Own junior	Drama, Music, Sport, CCF		Non-denom	HMC SHA
Royal (Dungannon)	Co-ed	Day Boarding Weekly	£29 EU £931 Non-EU £2050	Schols 7 pa Bursaries 3 pa	11, 16 Own junior	Sport, Music Art	EFL	Protestant	SHMIS
Victoria (Belfast)	Girls	Day Boarding Weekly	£75 £1265 (EU) £2155 (Non-EU)	Schols 2 pa Free tuition for EU nationals resident in NI	4, 11, 16	Music, Sport, D of E		Inter-denom	

Scotland

Albyn	Girls	Day	£1308	Asst places 22 pa Schols	5, 10, 12	Sport, Art Music	Dyslexia	Non-denom	HAS
Belmont House	Boys	Day	£1270	Asst places 23 pa	3, 5, 12	Sport, Public speaking, Debating	Dyslexia	C of S Jewish Muslim	HAS SHA
Craigholme	Girls	Day	£1265	Asst places 5 pa Bursaries 4–6 pa	5, 12	Music, Sport, Public speaking	Dyslexia	Christian	SHA HAS
Daniel Stewart's & Melville	Boys	Day Boarding	£1470 £2760	Asst places Schols 6 pa	12 Own junior	Music, Sport Debating		Non-denom	HMC
Dundee High	Co-ed	Day	£1303	Asst places 25 pa Schols 30 pa	5, 9, 10, 11, 12	Sport, Music, Drama	Dyslexia	Christian	HMC SCIS
Edinburgh Academy	Boys Mixed sixth	Day Boarding Weekly	£1761 £3755	Asst places 7 pa Schols 9 pa	5, 10, 12, 16	Art, Music, Sports	Learning support	Christian	HMC

Name of School	Boys/ Girls/ Co-ed	Day/ Board/ Weekly	Max termly fees	Financial help	Intake Age/ Prep	Special strengths	Special provisions	Religion	Affiliations
Fernhill	Girls	Day	£1020	Asst places 6 pa	12 Own primary	Music, Chess		RC	
Fettes	Co-ed	Day Boarding	£2745 £4085	Asst places Awards Schols Bursaries	10–13, 16 Own junior	Music, Drama, Techno-logy	English and maths tuition	Christian	HMC SHA
George Heriot's	Co-ed	Day	£1250	Asst places 37 pa Schols 4 pa Foundation-ers 10 pa	5, 10, 12	Drama, Hockey, Debating, Rowing, Rugby	Dyslexia	Christian	HMC
George Watson's	Co-ed	Day Boarding	£1380 £2760	Asst places 35 pa Schols/ bursaries 11 pa	3, 5, 10, 11, 12	Drama, Sport, Music, D of E	Dyslexia, EFL	Christian	HMC
Glasgow Academy	Co-ed	Day	£1430	Asst places 10 pa Schols Bursaries	4, 8, 11	Sport		Christian	HMC
Glasgow High	Co-ed	Day	£1422	Asst places 6 pa Schols 2 pa Bursaries 5 pa	4, 10, 11	Sport, Music, Debating, Drama		Non-denom	HMC
Glenalmond	Co-ed	Boarding Day	£3850 £2550	Asst places Schols	12, 13, 16	Drama, Sport, Music, Adventurous activities		Episco-palian	HMC
Gordonstoun	Co-ed	Day Boarding	£2685 £4160	Asst places 26 pa Schols/ bursaries 30 pa	13, 16 Own prep	Outward Bound, Sailing, Art, Sport, Music, Drama	EFL Learning support	Inter-denom	HMC Round Square
Hutchesons'	Co-ed	Day	£1218	Asst places Schols/ bursaries 15 pa	4, 9, 12	Music, Sport		Non-denom	HMC
Keil	Co-ed	Day Boarding Weekly	£1600 £2900	Asst places 6 pa Schols 6 pa Bursaries 6 pa	10, 11, 12, 13, 16	Music, Drama, Art, Sport	EFL, Dyslexia	Church of Scotland	SHMIS
Kelvinside	Boys	Day	£1475	Asst places 10 pa Schols 7 pa	3, 7, 8, 11	Sport	Mild dyslexia	Christian	HMC
Kilgraston	Girls	Day Boarding Weekly	£1885 £3275	Asst places 7 pa Schols 2 pa	11, 13, 16 Own junior	Music, Drama, Art, Sport	EFL	RC	GSA SHA BSA HAS

Name of School	Boys/ Girls/ Co-ed	Day/ Board/ Weekly	Max termly fees	Financial help	Intake Age/ Prep	Special strengths	Special provisions	Religion	Affiliations
Laurel Park	Girls	Day	£1422	Asst places 7 pa	11, 12 Own junior	Music, Art, Public speaking, Sport	Learning support	Christian	GSA
Lomond	Co-ed	Day Boarding Weekly	£1515 £3310 £3205	Asst places 7 pa Schols 15 pa	12, 16	Sport, Traditional music	Specialised help available	Christian	SHMIS
Loretto	Co-ed	Day Boarding	£2580 £3870 Schols	Asst places 6 pa junior 10-12 pa	13, 16 Own D of E	Music, Sport, fibrosis	Dyslexia, Cystic	Ecumenical	HMC
Mary Erskine	Girls	Day Boarding Weekly	£1380 £2760	Asst places Schols 5 pa	12, 14 16 Own junior	Music, Sport		Non-denom	GSA
Merchiston Castle	Boys	Day Boarding	£2480 £3835	Asst places 5 pa Schols Bursaries	10–13, 16	Sport, Music, Art, Drama	Extra English	Inter-denom	HMC
Morrison's	Co-ed	Day Boarding	£1215 £3530	Asst places 24 pa Schols/ Bursaries 6 pa	5, 12, 16		ESL SLD	Non-denom	HMC GSA
Rannoch	Co-ed	Day Boarding	£1830 £3450	Asst places 6 pa Schols 10 pa	10–13, 16	Art, Sport, D of E, Music	Remedial	Christian	SHMIS Round Square
Robert Gordon's	Co-ed	Day	£1300	Asst places 15 pa Schols 35 pa	5, 9, 11, 16	Sport Music Debating	EFL	Non-denom	HMC
St Columba's (Kilmacolm)	Co-ed	Day	£1212	Asst places 6 pa	3, 11, 16	Music, Sport		Christian	SHA HAS
St Denis and Cranley	Girls	Day Boarding Weekly	£1495 £3050	Asst places 3 pa Schols 5 pa Bursaries	5, 9, 12	Music, Art	EFL, Dyslexia	Christian	GSA
St George's (Edinburgh)	Girls	Day Boarding	£1424 £2885	Asst places 31 pa Scholarships 2 pa (6th form)	3, 5, 9, 10, 11, 13, 16	Sport, Music, Art,	Drama	Christian Non-denom	GSA
St Leonards	Girls	Day Boarding	£2075 £3925	Asst places 38 pa Schols/ Bursaries 30 pa	12, 13, 14, 16	Drama, Art, Sport, Music	Dyslexia	Non-denom	GSA
St Margaret's (Aberdeen)	Girls	Day	£1234	Asst places 20 pa Schol 1 pa	3, 5, 11, 12	Music	Dyslexia, Mild visual handicap	Inter-denom	GSA HAS SHA
St Margaret's (Edinburgh)	Girls	Day Boarding	£1380 £2785	Asst places 15 pa Schols 5 pa	3, 5, 12, 16	Choir, D of E	EFL, Dyslexia	Christian	GSA
St Mary's Music	Co-ed	Day Boarding	Apply to school	Schols 16 pa Aided places 39	9–11, 16	Music (specialist school)		Christian	CSA

Name of School	Boys/ Girls/ Co-ed	Day/ Board/ Weekly	Max termly fees	Financial help	Intake Age/ Prep	Special strengths	Special provisions	Religion	Affiliations
Strathallan	Co-ed	Day Boarding	£2570 £3685	Asst places 6 pa Schols 6 pa	10, 11, 13, 16		Remedial English	Inter-denom	HMC
Wellington (Ayr)	Girls	Day	£1595	Asst places 5 pa Bursaries	3, 10, 12		Some for EFL, Dyslexia	Church of Scotland	GSA

Wales

Name of School	Boys/ Girls/ Co-ed	Day/ Board/ Weekly	Max termly fees	Financial help	Intake Age/ Prep	Special strengths	Special provisions	Religion	Affiliations
Atlantic College	Co-ed	Boarding	£4760 (only 2 terms pa)	Schols 170 pa	16	Inter-national environ-ment			United World Colleges
Christ College (Brecon)	Co-ed	Day Boarding	£2430 £3135	Asst places 26 pa Schols 20 pa	11, 13, 16	Music, Sport	Dyslexia, EFL	Anglican	HMC
Haberdashers' Monmouth *	Girls	Day Boarding	£1507 £2982	Asst places 13 pa Schols 6 pa	7, 11, 13, 16	Music, Rowing Lacrosse Athletics Photography		Non-denom	GSA
Howell's (Denbigh) *	Girls	Day Boarding	£2280 £3495	Asst places 15 pa Schols/ Bursaries 12 pa	11, 16 Own prep	Music, Art, Drama, Sport	Dyslexia	Anglican	GSA
Howell's (Llandaff) *	Girls	Day	£1328	Asst places 28 pa Schols	4, 11, 16	Music		Non-denom	GSA GPDST
Llandovery	Co-ed	Day Boarding Weekly	£2068 £3170	Asst places 12 pa Schols 10 pa	11, 13, 16	Sport	EFL, Dyslexia	C in W	HMC
Monmouth *	Boys	Day Boarding Weekly	£1636 £2725	Asst places 26 pa Schols	11, 13, 16 Own junior	Sport, Music	Mild dyslexia	C in W	HMC
Rougemont *	Co-ed	Day	£1478	Schols 9 pa	3, 4, 11, 16		EFL, Dyslexia	Christian	SHMIS
Rydal Penrhos (Co-ed)	Co-ed	Day Boarding	£2408 £3328	Asst places 16 pa Schols 12+ pa Bursaries	11, 13, 16 Own prep	Art, Drama, Sport	EFL, Dyslexia	Methodist	HMC
Rydal Penrhos (Girls)	Girls	Day Boarding Weekly	£2135 £3115	Asst places 13 pa Schols 5 pa	11-14, 16 Own prep	Music, Drama, Art, Outdoor activities	ESL, Dyslexia	Inter-denom	GSA
St Gerard's	Co-ed	Day	£890	Ast places Bursaries	3, 7, 11, 13, 16		Dyslexia	RC	ISAI

Europe and Hong Kong

Name of School	Boys/ Girls/ Co-ed	Day/ Board/ Weekly	Max termly fees	Financial help	Intake Age/ Prep	Special strengths	Special provisions	Religion	Affiliations
BELGIUM									
British School (Brussels)	Co-ed	Day	BF 181,000	Asst places	3–18	Drama, Music, Sport, Art	Learning support		HMC COBISEC ECIS
International (Antwerp)	Co-ed	Day	BF 261,000	Bursaries	3–18		EFL		ECIS
FRANCE									
International (Paris)	Co-ed	Day	F 28,000		4–18	Small classes			HMC ECIS NEASC
Mougins	Co-ed	Day	F 23,000	Schols Bursaries	3–17	Languages	ESL		COBISEC ECIS
GERMANY									
British High (Bonn)	Co-ed	Day	£2200		11, 13, 16	Music, Outdoor activities	Remedial EFL, ESL		COBISEC ECIS
HONG KONG									
Island School	Co-ed	Day	HK$ 21,000		11, 16	Extra curricular activities, Pastoral care	ESL	Multi-faith	HMC ESF
King George V	Co-ed	Day	£1750	Hardship allowance	11-16	Sport	Moderate learning difficulties	Multi-faith	HMC
ITALY									
International (Milan)	Co-ed	Day	Lit 4.5m		3–17	Drama, Art, Sport	ESL		ECIS RISA
St George's (Rome) *	Co-ed	Day	£2590	Bursaries	3, 5, 11 14, 16	Music	ESL,		HMC COBISEC ECIS
Sir James Henderson	Co-ed	Day	£1850		3–18	Music, Art	ESL		HMC COBISEC ECIS
MALTA									
St Edwards's	Boys Mixed sixth	Day	£M270	Schols 8 pa	5, 16	Young Enterprise	EFL	Catholic	HMC

Name of School	Boys/ Girls/ Co-ed	Day/ Board/ Weekly	Max termly fees	Financial help	Intake Age/ Prep	Special strengths	Special provisions	Religion	Affiliations
NETHERLANDS									
British School *	Co-ed	Day	Fl.6510	Asst places 10 pa Bursaries 2 pa	3–18	Sport, Public speaking, Music	ESL, Special needs		HMC COBISEC ECIS
International (Amsterdam)	Co-ed	Day	FL9133		Any age	IB International community	ESL, Special educational needs		ECIS
PORTUGAL									
St Julian's	Co-ed	Day	Esc 735,000	Schols 10 pa	3, 7, 11, 16		English	Christian Non-denom	COBISEC ECIS
SPAIN									
Baleares International	Co-ed	Day Boarding Weekly	£1335 £2860 £2775	Schols 4 pa	3, 16		ESL, Visually impaired, Dyslexia		COBISEC ECIS NABSS
Bellver International	Co-ed	Day	£1350	Bursaries 2 pa	Any age 3 upwards	Family-style school	ESL	Non-denom	COBISEC ECIS NABSS
International (Sotogrande)	Co-ed	Day Boarding	£1350 £2350	Bursaries 4 pa	3–18	Music Art Languages	ESL, Special needs	Non-denom	ECIS NABSS
King's (Madrid)	Co-ed	Day Boarding	Ptas 338,000 Ptas 637,000		2–17			Non-denom	HMC COBISEC ECIS NABSS
Runnymede	Co-ed	Day	£2240	Schols	3, 5, 11, 16		EFL		
Sierra Bernia	Co-ed	Day	Ptas 181,000		3–18				COBISEC NABSS
SWITZERLAND									
Aiglon	Co-ed	Day Boarding	Sfr 12,325 Sfr 17,618	Schols 6 pa	11, 14	Skiing, Community service, Outdoor activities	EFL	Non-denom	HMC Round Square COBISEC ECIS

Index